The Kanji Handbook

The
Kanji
Handbook

Vee David

TUTTLE PUBLISHING
Tokyo • Rutland, Vermont • Singapore

Published by Tuttle Publishing, an imprint of
Periplus Editions (HK) Ltd, with editorial offices at
364 Innovation Drive, North Clarendon, Vermont 05759 and
130 Joo Seng Road #06-01, Singapore 368357

Copyright © 2006 by Periplus Editions (HK) Ltd.

Library of Congress Cataloging-in-Publication Data
Library of Congress Control Number: 2006929281
ISBN 13: 978-0 8048 3779 8
ISBN 10: 0 8048 3779 1

Printed in Singapore

Distributed by:
North America, Latin America and Europe
Tuttle Publishing,
364 Innovation Drive,
North Clarendon, VT 05759, USA
Tel: (802) 773 8930
Fax: (802) 773 6993
info@tuttlepublishing.com
www.tuttlepublishing.com

Japan
Tuttle Publishing,
Yaekari Building, 3rd Floor
5-4-12 Osaki
Shinagawa-ku
Tokyo 141-0032
Tel: (813) 5437 0171
Fax: (813) 5437 0755
tuttle-sales@gol.com

Asia Pacific
Berkeley Books Pte Ltd,
130 Joo Seng Road #06-01
Singapore 368357
Tel: (65) 6280 1330
Fax: (65) 6280 6290
inquiries@periplus.com.sg
www.periplus.com

06 07 08 09 10   5 4 3 2 1

TUTTLE PUBLISHING® is a registered trademark of Tuttle Publishing,
a division of Periplus Editions (HK) Ltd.

想*magination is more* 要*mportant than* 知*nowledge...*
                                            — *Albert Einstein*

Preface

Linguistic scholars largely agree that Japanese is the most difficult second language to learn. With four different writing systems, those eager to learn Japanese have a long and demanding journey to undergo. Thus, the **Kanji Handbook** was conceived to map out learning strategies to systematically guide learners from beginner to advanced level in Kanji literacy. Unique learning tools were designed for this book to resolve the many aggravations commonly encountered by Kanji learners. All 1,945 **Jōyō** Kanji characters—the most commonly used Kanji characters as officially prescribed by the Japanese Ministry of Education since 1981—can be learned through this book. The **Kanji Handbook** was fashioned to offer an end to some of the most discouraging problems facing those who study Kanji characters. The biggest struggle in learning the 1,945 Kanji characters is the mission of memorizing them, their shades of meaning, myriad pronunciations and compounds. To encourage memory retention, all Kanji characters in this book appear as **KanjiHybrids**, or the combination of a Kanji character and its English meaning to form one, integral and indivisible unit. In addition, the pioneering concept of Veemuenics—where similar looking Kanji characters are placed as KanjiHybrids in a rhyming English sentence or phrase—will further help learners remember each Kanji character and the slight differences between them. For example:

> **KanjiHybrid**: 皇mperor, 星tar, 星lanet
> **Veemuenic**: *Roman* 皇*mperors shine like* 星*tars even from* 星*lanets afar...*

The concept of Veemuenics was created to help learners differentiate between the similar-looking Kanji characters nearly undistinguishable to beginners. Some Kanji characters may only differ because of a dash or a stroke, or a radical. In many cases, these slight differences only become visible after years of careful study and consistent use. How does one discern the difference between 皇 and 星? To manage this problem, each Kanji character presented in this book has a corresponding list of similar-looking Kanji characters

as not to confuse them. Diligent practice of writing the Veemuenics will serve the purpose of differentiating between similar-looking Kanji characters.

Another major hindrance for Kanji beginners is the lack of adequate learning tools. To find a Kanji character in the dictionary, one must know the Kanji character's stroke order, radical, ON-yomi or KUN-yomi readings. These prerequisites make it frustrating and utterly confusing for beginners. How does an *absolute* beginner search for 豊 and 農 without knowing anything? To that end, the Flip-It Index was created to allow absolute beginners to search for a Kanji character's meaning without knowing any basics whatsoever. To use the Flip-It Index, all one has to do is decide if a Kanji character is flippable, looking the same when inverted horizontally, non-flippable or partially-flippable to a certain degree. This simple, artistic way of finding the meaning of a Kanji character is a revolutionary learning tool designed to take the prerequisite guess work out of Kanji study. Finally, a new indexing system was created for this book to address some inadequacies. Usually, Kanji indices only list the page number in which to find each Kanji character, without the English core meaning. This process of first finding a Kanji character in the index, and then having to search for its corresponding page to know the core meaning, is time consuming and cumbersome. Additionally, sometimes learners confuse similar-looking Kanji characters and look up the wrong page, and have to begin all over again. These annoyances are quickly resolved in this book's indices of all 1,945 Kanji characters together with their English core meaning and corresponding page number.

These innovative problem-solving novelties make the **Kanji Handbook** radically different from other Kanji books. The study of Kanji characters has never been easier or enjoyable. With the publication of this book, learners will ideally find their journey to be a rewarding experience, thereby enriching Kanji characters as one of the most powerful mediums of world civilization.

To My Loving Mother...

In Collaboration
with

西浦勝男
Katsuo Nishiura
Juri Kathryn
Sara Marina
Yuko Hirota

Acknowledgement

First and foremost, I wish to express my sincerest thanks to the people at **Takahashi Educational Institution** for their overwhelming support towards the publication of this book. The Institution serves as a beacon of hope for striving researchers burning the candles of the night. Without their generosity, this book would not have seen the light of day. Let me also extend my gratitude to my superiors at the **Kyushu University of Health and Welfare**, Miyazaki, Japan; especially to Chancellor Miyako Kake for her guidance and leadership. Helpful advice from Dr. Norimasa Mori and Dr. Yōichi Minamijima kept me focused in times of missteps and disarray. Second, I wish to extend gratitude to the entire staff of **Tuttle Publishing** and **Periplus Editions**, for taking a decisive initiative in adopting this book project for world-wide distribution.

My deepest gratitude goes out to Katsuo Nishiura, a gentle soul whom I met in my second year living in Miyazaki, Japan. As a retired principal of six junior high schools, Mr. Nishiura's curriculum vitae reads like a page of a literature book. His expertise in the Japanese and English languages proved indispensable to the successful completion of this book. With painstaking efforts, he reviewed over 35,000 word compounds—word for word, letter by letter—including the Romaji spellings and word meanings on more than 2,000 draft pages. Sifting through the pages of this book, the **Kanji Handbook**, I can feel his reassuring presence. I cannot say enough to thank him for all the help he devoted to a helpless friend. I am indebted to him in ways he will never know, and a lot more than I can admit.

I also wish to thank my faithful wife, Yuko Hirota, and my lovely daughters, Jurisa and Sara, for their encouragement and inspiration. My wife's incessant questions as to whether I could still do better—page after page—could only have come from the famed Japanese spirit. Part of the draft was written on frequent flights to New York City to be home with my girls on extended visits. In their eyes, I see the glow of the future. To my student Nao Itō for dutifully checking the brush strokes of 1,945 Kanji characters that required microscopic focus: please accept my profound appreciation. To the following librarians Kiyomi Yamaguchi, Masako Tazume, and Hitomi Iwase: I wish to give overdue credit for their skilled compilation of previous drafts. I wish to extend my appreciation to Yūji Kumamaru of the Foreign Ministry of Japan; to Paul and Betty Muller of East Sussex, England; to Ricky Rondina, Marc Trombino, Mary Duzant, Jill Caruso and Daryl Duzant of Staten Island; to the memory of my friend, Jun'ichi Taniguchi, for transforming software programming into human form; to Nobuyo Hasegawa, Yuichi Kamimura,Takahiro Kamizaki,Tōru Moriyama, Mitsutaka Sasada and Dr. Kensuke Kiyomizu; and to my over-all English editor, Katie Berkedal of La Crosse, Wisconsin. Her meticulous attention to detail, combined with sophisticated writing skills, gave the book a new breath of life in the dying days until manuscript submission. I acknowledge my eternal debt to the Great Jack Halpern, whose piercing critique led to timely revisions. This book lives on the path of his previous works, particularly on Kanji core meanings. I wish to recognize the contribution of Wilfrido Villacorta, my college guru at the De La Salle University. On a visit to Miyazaki, Japan, in September 1993, I showed him the abstract concepts of what became this book. He immediately urged me to develop them into concrete form. Over the long years from conceptual framework to manuscript completion, there were times I nearly gave up; only to find myself back on my laptop. I was answering to an inner force that I could neither contend with, nor explain. I take full responsibility for both the form and contents. I apologize for imperfections, accepting the harshest blame which is mine alone. Finally, I wish to pay tribute to my loving parents, who gave so much to get so little; for putting their best years in the worst of times—never knowing the nights from the days of life in the tempest.

New York City
16 September 2006

Table of Contents

Theoretical Approach

Foreigners who study Japanese often question why all four writing systems must be learned to master the language. First, the four writing systems—Hiragana, Katakana, Kanji characters, and the Roman ABCs—each have unique roles. Hiragana is generally used for native words and grammatical values, while Katakana is reserved for foreign words. Here, the function of Katakana shows the cultural consciousness to draw a line between what is Japanese, and what is not. Roman alphabets are valued for initials, such as APEC, WHO, and EU, and for commercial advertisements. Kanji characters must be learned to differentiate between the large bodies of Japanese homophones; words that sound exactly alike though the meanings may differ. A separate Kanji character exists for all the homophones whose meanings would be unclear if written in a purely Hiragana or Katakana text. Second, and more obviously, one must learn all four writing systems to read Japanese text, which in one sentence can utilize Hiragana, Katakana, Kanji characters, and the Roman ABCs. In addition, as the usage of Japanese language is more defined by the regiments of Japanese culture than by conventional reason, one must gain a basic understanding of the Japanese way of life. As such, one cannot isolate the study of the language from the confines of Japanese culture itself.

The uniqueness of Japanese civilization was reinforced by its insularity as one of the few nations to never have been colonized, when colonization swept three-fourths of the globe. Predating Japanese society, the significance of Kanji characters can be understood as the oldest existing, and most widely-used writing system in the world. The earliest forms of Kanji characters were found on oracle bones made from tortoise shells dating back to 1,700 BC — 1,100 BC in Hénán, China. However, the evolution of modern-day recognizable Kanji characters was established in approximately 200 AD, reaching the shores of Japan two centuries later. Though other ancient writing systems, such as the Egyptian hieroglyphics and Sumerian scripts, have become nothing more than museum pieces, Kanji characters have flourished; surviving numerous tests of time. Moreover, attributable to the sheer population size of its users—China, Taiwan, Hong Kong, Japan, and the Koreas—Kanji is arguably the world's most widely-used writing system. Yet, in spite of these characteristics, Kanji characters remain a "black hole" to the rest of the world; a situation that need not continue.

Kanji characters and the Roman alphabets are separate and distinct writing systems. The Roman A-to-Z system is based on a combination of letters to form words expanding into sentences. Individually, English letters contain no inherent meaning. One could, therefore, create a new word, like common names or pronouns, without necessarily attaching any meaning. Kanji characters are the exact opposite. Each one already has assigned meanings *before* combining them to form word compounds. Consequently, one could not form a Kanji word compound stripped of meaning. For highly Kanji literate people, reading Kanji characters is somewhat like reading pictures. That's not entirely an exaggeration since each Kanji character represents an inherent meaning. Also, many Kanji characters resemble their meaning. For example, the characters for "person" and "river" actually look like a walking person, and a streaming river: 人 and 川.

Communication through symbols, like Kanji characters, takes place all over the world through universal ideograms. When we see the symbols ✚ and ✡, the immediate meanings conveyed are Christianity and Judaism. Quite recently, universal symbols such as: ♨ ℗ ♿ ♂ ♀ ☎ have become part of daily life— we see them everywhere in world airports and hotels —irrespective of the spoken version. Some advanced forms like the sentence "I ♥ NY" have found a niche in popular culture. Far more symbols exist today than a decade ago. Internet sophisticates have enlivened e-mail messages with "emoticons," which are nothing more than symbols. Nearly every corporation has its own logo, designed to instill its corporate image in seconds. Universal symbols, while widely accepted, are still elementary; unable to communicate complex messages or a philosophical discourse. Yet, imagine a time, decades in the making, when the universal symbols we know today will reach a stage of development that allows for higher coherence. Kanji characters preceded universal symbols, have been enriched through centuries, and are highly sophisticated in terms of communicative content and intellectual value.

Kanji characters are remarkably complex; the pronunciation of many characters sound alike, and even more numerous are the characters that look alike. The readings of each character can be split in two groups: ON-yomi, the Chinese reading, or KUN-yomi, the Japanese reading. A large number of Kanji characters may have the same ON-yomi reading. For example, the ON-yomi reading for the following characters can all be read as "kan," though their meanings are completely different: 間、官、感 and 漢. A quick count of the Jōyō (most common) Kanji characters pronounced as "kan" would reach the figure of 64, though their meanings are hardly related. Hence, the key to mastering Kanji characters is to aim for their core English meanings. When one contemplates an object in visual form, its pronunciation becomes secondary. When one sees David Beckham playing his game, whether it's to be called "football" or "soccer" becomes not so important. As a meaning-focused writing system—not pronunciation based—one major advantage is as follows: Though Chinese or Japanese people cannot necessarily converse in a common spoken medium, Kanji characters would enable the two vast cultures, nevertheless, to communicate.

Other Kanji books approach the teaching of Kanji the same way young children are taught Kanji in Japan; by means of the grade-level approach. The needs of children and adult language learners are much different, thus, this teaching method designed for children clearly cannot be the most effective way for adults to learn Kanji. While children learn languages with a symmetrical progression between simple ideas and simple linguistic skills, adult learners have to cope with an unbalanced equation between complex ideas and simple linguistic skills. For adults learning a second language, new linguistic skills must first catch up with his or her already complex thinking—a process that could be frustrating. The main theory behind this book is to simplify Kanji learning through the process of comparison. The study of Kanji through the grade-level approach would completely ignore a significant hindrance of learning Kanji: many Kanji characters look alike and are therefore difficult to differentiate.

In Kanji Handbook, the easily-confused Kanji characters are grouped together so the learner can notice the subtle differences between The similar-looking characters. The learning process navigates through visually distinguishing one from the other, to identify their unique differences, in order to get the core meaning. This book is a humble attempt toward the mastery of Kanji characters within a meaning-focused framework. The core meanings should be of central importance. The conventional presentation of Kanji characters in contemporary Kanji books has the Kanji characters and English words sitting side by side, such as: 水 = water, 山 = mountain, and 女 = woman. A better way to convey the meaning of each Kanji character, as in the case of universal symbols, needs to exist. Toward that objective, here is a ground-breaking alternative, whereby a Kanji character is combined with its English meaning to create one single and indivisible unit called *KanjiHybrids*. For example: 水ater, 山ountain, and 女oman. Next, to distinguish one Kanji character from another is a frustrating task, yet crucial. To that end, a second component, called *Veemuenics*, was created. The method is to identify similar-looking Kanji characters, and put them together as KanjiHybrids in a catchy English sentence or phrase. The following *Veemuenics* are examples of how visually-similar Kanji characters can be set apart within a meaning-focused methodology:

a) 今ow, the 念dea is to 含nclude 吟hants of
"Ave Maria..."

b) At the 寺emple's parade, a 侍amurai 持olding
a 詩oem of 特pecial 等rade...

c) 立tanding chorus 泣rying over their lost 位tatus...

d) 詐raudulent 酢inegar 作roduced by a beggar...

Finally, my theoretical approach runs along the following analogy: If one were to live in the same house with identical twin brothers, in two to three days, their overt dissimilarities would somehow come to be discerned. However, it would be difficult to tell them apart if they were to come to a sports club alternately. Dozens of Kanji characters are "identical twin brothers." How to know one from the other is the never-ending puzzle. By putting those "identical twins" side by side within the Veemuenics concept, the observer can clearly discern their differences.

This manner of comparison is where my theoretical approach to learning Kanji diverges from the current grade-level approach. Within this innovative perspective, I hope to highlight the uniqueness of each Kanji character; to look at each tree, in order to clearly see the larger forest.

With the realization of this book, I sincerely hope to contribute to a better understanding and appreciation of the Japanese language. Following the footsteps of other Kanji books, which provided much of the literature, I humbly offer this work, as a contribution to a yet unexplored path in the study of linguistics.

Miyazaki, Japan
26 December 2005

Diagram: Guide to Learners

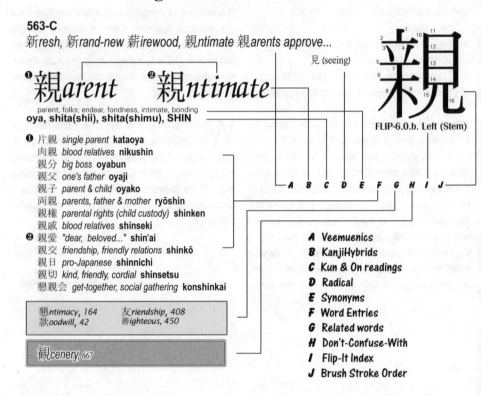

563-C

新resh, 新rand-new 薪irewood, 親ntimate 親arents approve...

❶親arent   ❷親ntimate

parent, folks; endear, fondness, intimate, bonding
oya, shita(shii), shita(shimu), SHIN

見 (seeing)

FLIP-6.0.b. Left (Stem)

A B C D E F G H I J

❶ 片親 *single parent* **kataoya**
肉親 *blood relatives* **nikushin**
親分 *big boss* **oyabun**
親父 *one's father* **oyaji**
親子 *parent & child* **oyako**
両親 *parents, father & mother* **ryōshin**
親権 *parental rights (child custody)* **shinken**
親戚 *blood relatives* **shinseki**
❷ 親愛 *"dear, beloved..."* **shin'ai**
親交 *friendship, friendly relations* **shinkō**
親日 *pro-Japanese* **shinnichi**
親切 *kind, friendly, cordial* **shinsetsu**
懇親会 *get-together, social gathering* **konshinkai**

懇ntimacy, 164   友riendship, 408
款oodwill, 42   善ighteous, 450

観cenery, 667

A Veemuenics
B KanjiHybrids
C Kun & On readings
D Radical
E Synonyms
F Word Entries
G Related words
H Don't-Confuse-With
I Flip-It Index
J Brush Stroke Order

The key components—A, B, C, D, E, F, G, H, I & J—outlined in the above diagram make up the very essence of The **Kanji Handbook**. Diligent learners must master the components and their relationship. The layout presentation was designed to appeal to the artistic sense. The subliminal approach of KanjiHybrids caters smoothly to one's subconscious mind. The result, therefore, is not just an understanding of Kanji characters, but well beyond that, a mental absorption. As a result, memory recall, at least in the passive stage, is immediately established. The idea is to convert Kanji characters into a form immediately recognizable to native English speakers. For learners to reach the active stage—where Kanji characters are written straight from memory—they must practice writing KanjiHybrids and Veemuenics on a daily basis. By writing them on a practice sheet, the lingua-motors in the brain will be stimulated in a way beneficial to memory recall. Just as one cannot learn to ride a bicycle by staying at home, no matter how imaginative, one cannot learn Kanji characters without writing practice. Once mastered through the attentive and consistent writing practice of Veemuenics, the Kanji characters will stay in the subconscious mind, just as one does not forget to ride a bike. The Kanji Handbook is full of unique concepts for learning Kanji, which will, if used according to suggestion, maximize memory retention and accelerate the learning process. The key components are briefly described, as follows:

A) **Veemuenics**: Links similar-looking or easily-confused Kanji characters, as KanjiHybrids, to form a coherent phrase or sentence, usually rhymed for ease of memory retention. The final objective is to distinguish one from another within a set of easily-confused Kanji characters, within a meaning-focused framework. Conscientious learners are encouraged to make their own Veemuenics. Take the initiative to "Veemuenize" as desired.

B) **KanjiHybrids:** The union of a Kanji character and its English core meaning to form one indivisible unit. Any attempt to entertain the equation form (山 = mountain, 川 = river) will negate the cardinal principle of this book. The equation form is somewhat limited in scope and effectiveness as a learning tool. This approach may be useful in learning a few dozen Kanji characters, but would prove inadequate as a tool used to master 1,945 Kanji characters. KanjiHybrids remain the viable alternative, in terms of learning quality and delivery of results. As such, KanjiHybrids must be taken as is, no variations.

C) **KUN-yomi & ON-yomi:** The presentation of the Kanji characters' readings in this book begins with the KUN-yomi, followed by the ON-yomi, for two distinct reasons. First, this book is about Japanese Kanji. Hence, the KUN-yomi, or the Japanese reading, must take precedence over the ON-yomi derived from Chinese readings. Second, the large amount of Kanji characters with the same ON-yomi reading can be overwhelming. KUN-yomi readings are not repeated nearly as much as ON-yomi readings, and are therefore, the better tool to identify or distinguish one Kanji character from another. Take note that when reading Kanji compounds, the foremost objective is comprehension of core meanings, followed by pronunciation. The meaning of Kanji characters will more or less stay, whereas the pronunciation may vary, or may be more than one.

D) **Radicals:** Radicals are usually sub-elements of Kanji characters that give a hint to the core meaning. For example the radical [扌] derived from the Kanji character [手] is associated with manual work or handiwork. Hence, all Kanji characters appearing with the radical [扌] have something to do with manual work, or labour. In a large number of Kanji

characters, the radical is found on the left side, or on top. A few examples include: 払ayment, 扱andling, 抽ulling and 投hrow with the radical [扌] appearing on the left side. Examples of radicals appearing on the top part of a Kanji character include: 雲loud, 電lectricity, 雪now, and 雷hunder. Their common radical [雨] on the top part immediately conveys that these Kanji characters are somewhat related to the weather or the natural climate. For that reason, Kanji characters can be grouped according to their radicals. Since the core meaning is related to its radical, it would be advantageous to master the radicals. Also, sometimes the whole Kanji character is the radical itself, especially those taught in the primary grade level. Common examples include: 人erson, 水ater, 山ountain, 竹amboo, 車heel, 金etal and 木ooden. Mastering the radicals will certainly allow for greater ease in using the Radical Index (p.1020). Exert effort to become familiarized with the Radical Index.

E) **Synonyms:** Appearing in smaller fonts in order to stimulate subliminal thinking, based on KanjiHybrids, the synonyms are more indicative than exhaustive, though the latter was clearly the objective. Because of the intrinsic differences between the English and Japanese languages, designating an exact English definition for each Kanji character is not always possible. Moreover, many Kanji characters carry shades of meanings that cannot squarely fit into the context of an English definition. For this reason, a set of synonyms—rather than simplistic definitions—will deliver better results. Learners must also explore the word entries with careful attention.

F) **Word Entries:** The word entries are a list of Kanji compounds, and their English meanings, related to the Kanji character in focus. Advanced learners should become familiar with the Kanji compounds. Each Kanji compound was carefully selected from classic Japanese literature, as well as from current newspapers. Though vigorous effort was made to weed out archaic Kanji compounds, that objective must be balanced with the mission to reach a wider audience, without excluding the greying population in Japan. While the English meaning is not always technical, in some cases, idiomatic expressions are necessary to deliver the core meaning. Learners who engage in pronunciation drills to distinguish double consonants and elongated sounds will find the quantity of word compounds sufficient for that purpose. Confusion arising from double consonants and elongated sounds is one of the most frustrating obstacles in the study of the Japanese language. Careful attention and sensitivity must be forthcoming. Word entries should be used more for pronunciation exercises than merely for lexicographic references.

G) **Related Words**: This key component is a listing of other Kanji characters with meanings similar to the Kanji character in focus. In a way, this key component is like a thesaurus. Diligent learners are strongly advised to study the related words to better understand the core meaning of each Kanji character, and to discern the differences between related words. One can attain a higher degree of knowledge by becoming familiar with synonyms, antonyms, and relative words of a certain Kanji character. Learners with an advanced vocabulary definitely have more leeway in expressing themselves.

H) **Don't-Confuse-With**: A fundamental problem confronting Kanji learners is the challenge of trying to make a distinction between the Kanji characters that look alike. For example, distinguishing [星] from [皇] can be confusing, yet of crucial importance. As KanjiHybrids, they look like this: 星tar and 皇mperor. The "Don't-Confuse-With" component serves to alert learners that other Kanji characters can be easily mistaken for the Kanji character in question.

I) **Flip-It Index**: Ideal for absolute beginners, the Flip-It Index is a new indexing system that allows Kanji characters to be searched and located without pre-existing knowledge. Flippable means the whole Kanji character, or sub-elements within, when inverted from left to right, or horizontally will remain *almost* the same—disregarding hooks, backlashes and "ink stops." Look for wholly-flippable or partially-flippable Kanji characters.

J) **Brush Strokes**: The brush strokes are sequentially numbered. Learners will find it convenient for writing practice. Brush strokes are symmetrically aligned and once basic familiarity is achieved, the rest is not difficult. Each Kanji character follows a brush stroke rhythm, and mastery of one Kanji character will lead to another. Familiarity with the brush strokes of [立] will enable a foothold on increasingly complex Kanji characters, where [立] appears as a radical, such as: [音], [部], [章], [童] and [競]. The brush strokes for [立] remain consistent even when it combines with other sub-elements to form more complex Kanji characters.

Learning Strategies

The study of Kanji for native Japanese speakers covers a time length extending to nine full-time years, employing a dozen textbooks. For non-native Japanese speakers to learn all 1,945 Kanji characters short of nine years, using a single volume textbook is definitely an immense challenge. For that reason, you must brace yourself for a commitment that would transform the course of your new life. Much will depend on the criteria of time availability, or the willingness to create it. Determination is one's ammunition. The will to succeed will be a constant weapon in the long and difficult struggle. The Learning Strategies from one to seven listed below follow a sequence. However, after familiarity has been established, feel free to design a different arrangement.

Strategy One: Take a general survey by going over all eleven chapters of this book from "Triple Treat" to "Zigzag." Your eyesight must be trained to read the KanjiHybrids, which are printed in large fonts draw immediate and lasting attention. Make a mental note of which KanjiHybrids you did not immediately recognize. Your list will be rather short—contrary to your initial fears—as the meaning of the majority of KanjiHybrids will already be morphed in your mind.

Strategy Two: Starting with the first chapter, make a persistent and repetitive effort to practice penmanship with the KanjiHybrids. Follow the brush stroke order determinedly. Then, write the remaining English letters of each KanjiHybrid. Each KanjiHybrid should be written a minimum of twenty-five times. Without the handwriting drill, your objective of mastering Kanji characters will definitely flounder. As a beginner, your penmanship is hardly expected to be smooth, much less refined like that of a native Japanese speaker. However, as the Kanji handwriting drill progresses over time, a distinctive pattern will emerge, which will be your Kanji handwriting style. The handwriting drill is not designed to make you a Kanji calligrapher

overnight. The consistent practice of writing each Kanji character, stroke-by-stroke, will definitely make them easier to remember. The nerves driving your writing hand are directly connected to your brain. Thus, the action of writing each Kanji character will reinforce memory retention. Take note that Japanese pupils do the same laborious task when learning to write Kanji flawlessly and straight from memory. You should be able to reach that level over time.

Strategy Three: For each KanjiHybrid, imagine other possible variations of core meanings. For example, the KanjiHybrid 動ovement can appear as: 動ove, 動oving, 動obile, or 動obility. The core meanings do not distinguish between nouns, verbs or adjectives. After mastering a KanjiHybrid, write a checkmark in the *Complete Listing of Jōyō Kanji Characters* found on page xlvi. Write the date so your learning progress can be monitored.

Strategy Four: After mastering a set of KanjiHybrids, you can move on to the next dimension: Veemuenics. Since KanjiHybrids are subsets of Veemuenics, the KanjiHybrids handwriting drill must be grouped within the context of a certain Veemuenic. Beyond KanjiHybrids, Veemuenics allow you to distinguish between similar-looking Kanji characters, while at the same time, ensuring memory retention of core meanings. Memorize as many Veemuenics as possible. The words usually rhyme for ease of memory retention.

Strategy Five: By this level, you must be ready for action, or practical applicability. I suggest keeping a separate notebook as a KanjiHybrid Diary, in which you will use your newly acquired knowledge. When writing in your KanjiHybrid Diary, use as many KanjiHybrids as you have mastered. You need not have completed all the chapters before you start keeping a KanjiHybrid diary. Even for yet to be learned KanjiHybrids, you must begin committing yourself to practice. Here's an example of a diary entry:

> 当his 朝orning, my 母other and I hosted a 特pecial 集athering. Her 友riends from 高igh 校chool came to 訪isit her. It was their 初irst 会eeting after so 多any, 多any 長ong 年ears. It brought back 貴herished 憶emories of their 若outhful 時imes. I have never 見een my 母other and the 全ntire 家amily so 喜appy...

Strategy Six: The reading drill is the next stage in learning Kanji characters. The handwriting drill and the reading drill are of equal importance in the process of learning Kanji characters. Get in the habit of reading news articles in Japanese newspapers. The Internet is a good place to find brief news articles in Japanese. The aim of this stage is to identify the meaning of some Kanji characters outside the comfort of this text. Neatly pronouncing every recognizable Kanji compound is not necessary. Reading Kanji characters means the ability to understand the core meaning. Concentrate on the meaning, meaning and meaning.

Strategy Seven: Welcome to the final stage: Kanji compounds. Go to the word entries section and pick out several Kanji compounds. This process will build your Kanji compound vocabulary. Break them apart into component Kanji characters. For example, the Kanji compound for seafood [海産物] can be broken down into three KanjiHybrids: 海cean, 産roduce, and 物hings. KanjiHybrids are not an end in itself, but a learning tool to further knowledge. The ultimate goal is familiarity with Kanji compounds, pure and simple.

You must set in motion a lifetime commitment for advancing your Kanji reading and writing skills through constant and continuous application. Devotion to these seven learning strategies will pave the way for you to penetrate one of the most restricted world languages yet devised by human ingenuity.

Flip-It Index: How to Search

SUMMARY: The new indexing system has two main components in which to categorize Kanji characters: Flippable and Non-flippable. Flippable means the whole Kanji character, or sub-elements within, when inverted horizontally will remain almost the same—disregarding hooks, backlashes and "ink stops." Examples include: 本,中 and 田. Most Kanji characters fit in the "Flippable" category, so many sub-categories were used to organize and make searching for them more time efficient. For example, some Kanji characters are only flippable on the top, the right side, the bottom, the top left side, etc. Nearly all sub-categories in the "Flippable" section are separated as having either a flat base or a stem base. A flat base means the baseline is all flat and touching the ground. Flat base flippable Kanji characters will look like the following: 山,田 or 西. Kanji characters with a stem base will look like it has legs sticking out or poles mounted on the ground: 本,川 or 卵. Non-flippable Kanji characters are those facing either the left or right side, or a combination of both. Examples include: 子 , 己 and 生 facing the left side (West), and 上 , 女 and 糸 facing the right side (East). Look for what appears to be a long, flat back with the front side protruding, or with an opening. Unlike other Kanji indexing systems, no pre-existing knowledge is required. Just look closely, flip it, then find its match in the correlating section. The Flip-In Index begins on page 1112.

EXERCISE: How does an absolute novice locate a Kanji character in the index? The examples below will illustrate the possibilities.

Example 1: Search for 舗
a) One can clearly see that the Kanji character 舗 is not wholly flippable; it would look very different when inverted horizontally.
b) However, one can conclude that its left side 舎 is flippable; it would look roughly the same when turned around.
c) In addition, the bottom part 口 of 舎 has a flat base —as distinguished from a stem base.

d) Hence, the Kanji character 舗 can be located in sub-section: 6.0.a. Left Whole (Flat Base) on page 1117.

Example 2: Search for 蚕

a) One can clearly see that the Kanji character 蚕 is not wholly flippable; it would look very different when inverted horizontally.

b) However, one can conclude that its top part 天 is flippable; it would look roughly the same when turned around.

c) Also, the bottom part of 天 has a stem base—two poles touching the ground.

d) Hence, the Kanji character 蚕 can be located in sub-section: 3.0.b. Top (Stem) on page 1115.

Example 3: Search for 態

a) One can clearly see that the Kanji character 態 is neither wholly nor partially flippable; none of its sub-elements would look the same when inverted from left to right, or vice versa.

b) The Kanji character 態 can be divided into two sub-elements, namely 能 and 心 on a horizontal split.

c) Looking for what appears to be the dominant protruding part, or an opening and a long-flat back, one clearly see that the sub-elements 能 and 心 are both facing to the right side or East.

d) Hence, the Kanji character 態 can be located in sub-section: 2.1. Facing East (Horizontal Split) on page 1123.

Example 4: Search for 張

a) One can clearly see that the Kanji character 張 is neither wholly nor partially flippable; none of its sub-elements would look the same when inverted from left to right or vice versa.

b) The Kanji character 張 can be divided into two sub-elements, namely 弓 and 長 on a vertical split.

c) Looking for what appears to be the dominant protruding side, or an opening and a long-flat back, one clearly see that the sub-element 弓 and 長 are both facing apart, or opposite each other.

d) Hence, the Kanji character 張 can be located in sub-section: 4.0. Facing Apart on page 1126.

The Flip-It Index: Origin

Over the years, the urge to devise a Kanji indexing system, accessible by absolute beginners, refused to subside. One extremely cold winter night, I was in a hot spring in Miyazaki, Japan contemplating semi-thoughts. Then, I noticed the glass wall in front of me had the letters "HOH" painted on it. I have seen and ignored these letters many times. I walked past the glass wall to the outer garden, and then took a hard look at the same inverted letters. I then realized something self-evident: Writing systems were meant to be symmetrical, which when inverted horizontally would look almost the same. That concept would later spring forth to life the Flip-It Index (see p. 1112), where Kanji characters are categorized according to their "flippability." Partially-flippable Kanji—meaning the bottom, top, left, or right side only, can be flipped—are grouped together. Non-flippable Kanji characters face either the West or East, based on what appears to be a long, flat back and something protruding. Thus, the Flip-It Index is categorized by whether a Kanji character is flippable, partially-flippable, or non-flippable. The end result is a new Kanji indexing system, where learners can navigate without any pre-existing knowledge. All one has to do is look carefully:

Flippable: 豊bundance, 奉dore, 同like, 堂ltar, 宣nnounce; or partially-flippable such as: 農arming (top), 盟lliance (bottom), 彰ward (left), and 細lender (right).

Non-Flippable: 子hildren (Facing West), 止top (Facing East), 約romise (Facing Across), and 私rivate (Facing Apart)

Short Versus Long Sounds

Sensivity with Kanji compounds consisting of double consonants and elongated sounds is of crucial importance. *Double consonants*: 作家 sakka (writer) and 活性 kassei (dynamism) should not confused with 坂 saka (hill) and 火星 kasei (Mars) respectively. Without the accent stressed on "kk" and "ss," another meaning will be conveyed. *Elongated vowels* are more difficult and need to be explained at length. Failure to distinguish between short vowels a, o, u from long vowels ā, ō, ū would surely court confusion and learning frustration. The meaning intended would entirely change, depending only on the elongated sounds. As an example, the words "kyodai," and "kyōdai," have entirely different meanings: The former 巨大 refers to "giant," and the latter 兄弟 means "brothers." Kanji researchers have spent much time and resources explaining this crucial matter. Transcription methods differ as to what the better way is. One method that attaches the letter "h" after the vowel was a trend in popular culture: **Satoh, Saitoh, Itoh, Katoh** and **Ohno**. The ease of typing the letter "h" with computers and cell phones may have led to the trend. However, for historical reasons, the overwhelming majority of English reference publications use the Hepburn style: ā, ū, ē, ō. This romanization system was pioneered by Dr. James Curtis Hepburn (1815–1911). The diacritic above the preceding letters represents the elongated sounds. To put it simply, one can think of the letter u as a mouth facing the sky and the *line above*, or ū, as depicting rising wavelengths of an elongated sound. Within the Hepburn style, the above common names should be spelt as: **Satō, Saitō, Itō, Katō** and **Ōno**. The Hepburn style is used by the Government of Japan in all official documents. Kanji dictionaries use the same approach. **The Kanji Handbook** is no exception. Concentrate on the subtle difference between the short and long syllables. A long accent is placed on elongated vowels, taking double the time to pronounce than short vowels. Success with this exercise will lead to greater confidence. Practice your pronunciation and listening skills, using the comparative list below:

Short	Long
a (aunt)	ā (grandmother)
叔母さん obasan	お婆さん obāsan
bo (fund raising)	bō (anti bacterial)
募金 bokin	防菌 bōkin
cho (savings)	chō (great service)
貯金 chokin	超勤 chōkin
do (Saturday)	dō (similar)
土曜 doyō	同様 dōyō
fu (guardians)	fū (scenery)
父兄 fukei	風景 fūkei
go (drink by mistake)	gō (coercion)
誤飲 goin	強引 gōin
gyo (seafood)	gyō (business world)
魚貝 gyokai	業界 gyōkai
ho (insurance)	hō (feudal)
保険 hoken	封建 hōken
jo (female)	jō (situation)
女性 josei	情勢 jōsei
ju (trees & bushes)	jū (working at home)
植樹 shokuju	職住 shokujū
ko (solid)	kō (take-turns)
固体 kotai	交替 kōtai
ku (haiku poetry)	kū (aerial defeat)
俳句 haiku	敗空 haikū
kyo (election)	kyō (war condition)
選挙 senkyo	戦況 senkyō
o (corruption)	ō (counter-attack)
汚染 osen	応戦 ōsen
ro (electric circuit)	rō (circular corridor)
回路 kairo	回廊 kairō
sho (household)	shō (invitation)
所帯 shotai	招待 shōtai
shu (odd specie)	shū (editing)
変種 henshu	編集 henshū
so (oxygen)	sō (mountain villa)
酸素 sanso	山荘 sansō
su (suitable)	sū (a few drops of)
素敵 suteki	数滴 sūteki
to (big city)	tō (melting)
都会 tokai	凍解 tōkai
yo (giving medicine)	yō (Oriental)
投与 toyo	東洋 toyō
yu (dissolving)	yū (priority)
湯煎 yusen	優先 yūsen

Bibliographical References

Campbell, Alan and Noble, David, editors, **Japan: An Illustrated Encyclopaedia,** Kodansha, Tokyo, Japan 1993

Foerster, Andreas and Tamura, Naoko **Kanji ABC, A Systematic Approach to Japanese Characters,** Charles Tuttle Publishing,Tokyo, Japan 1997

Habien, Yaeko, S. and Mathias, Gerald B. **The Complete Guide to Everyday Kanji**, Kodansha, Tokyo, Japan, 1991

Hadamitzky, Wolfgang and Spahn, Mark **Kanji & Kana,** Tuttle Publishing, Tokyo, Japan, 1996

Halpern, Jack **New Japanese-English Character Dictionary,** Kenkyusha, Tokyo, Japan 1991

Halpern, Jack **The Kodansha Kanji Learner's Dictionary,** Kodansha, Tokyo, Japan, 2001

Haig, John H., **The New Nelson: Japanese-English Character Dictionary (Andrew Nelson),** Charles Tuttle Publishing, Tokyo, Japan, 2002

Heisig, James W. **Remembering the Kanji I: A Complete Course on How Not to Forget the Meaning and Writing of Japanese Characters** (3rd ed.), Japan Publications Trading Co., Ltd, Tokyo, Japan 1986

Henshall, Kenneth **A Guide to Remembering Japanese Characters**, Charles Tuttle Publishing, Tokyo, Japan, 1998

Henshall, Kenneth; Seeley, Christopher and de Groot, Henke. **A Guide to Reading and Writing Japanese** (3rd ed.), Tuttle Publishing, US, 2003

Roget's New Millenium Thesaurus, First Edition, Copyright 2005, Lexico Publishing Group, LLC

Spahn, Mark and Hadamitzky, Wolfgang **The Kanji Dictionary,** Charles Tuttle Publishing, Tokyo, Japan, 2002

Takahashi, Genji et. al, **Obunsha's Comprehensive English-Japanese Dictionary,** Obunsha Publishing, Tokyo, Japan, 1992

Young, John and Nakajima-Okano, Kimiko, **Learn Japanese,** University of Hawaii Press, Honolulu, Hawaii, 1984

岡本恵年、「小学校自由自在」、受験研究社　日本国大阪市、　1990

佐伯梅友、森野宗明、小松英雄、「**例解古語辞典　第二版**」、三省堂　日本国東京都、1989

長澤規矩也、原田種成、戸川芳郎、「**新明解漢和辞典**」、三省堂　日本国東京都、1990

佐伯梅友、森野宗明、小松秀雄、「**例解古語辞典**」、三省堂　日本国東京都、1985

三省堂編集所編、「**広辞林・第六版**」、三省堂、日本国東京都、1993

貝塚茂樹、藤野岩友、「**角川・漢和中辞典**」、三省堂、日本国東京都、1993

小林信明「**新選・漢和辞典・第六版**」、小学館、日本国東京都、1997

国際交流基金・日本国際教育協会「日本語能力試験出題基準・改訂版」、凡人社、日本国東京都、2004*

宇野哲人、「**和洋併用新修・広辞典第六版**」、集英社、日本国東京都　昭和57年

守随憲治、今泉忠義、松村明、「**古語辞典・新訂版**」旺文社、日本国東京都　昭和53年

相賀徹夫、「**世界色百科事典 1~8**」旺文社、小学館、日本国東京都、昭和20年

Complete List of Veemuenics: Checklist I

Note: Diligent learners are strongly advised to master *Veemuenics*. The complete listing appears below. *Veemuenics* must be written exactly as is, without variations in your practice notebook. Writing each *Veemuenic* twenty-five times should be enough to achieve active memory recall. After that, check-mark the linked Kanji characters on the right side. Checklist II of the complete **Jōyō** Kanji characters on page xlvi will monitor your learning progress.

I. Triple Treat

☐ *001* No 人*erson* will 入*nter* a house on 火*ire*...　　人 0001　入 0035　火 0017

☐ *002* 六*ix* golfers in the North Pole aim for the 八*ighth* 穴*ole*...　　六 0008　八 0010　穴 0907

☐ *003* Hit with a 乙*econd* group of thorns, 己*elf-pride* 忌*ourns*...　　乙 1156　己 0838　忌 1802

☐ *004* 太*bese* 犬*ogs* with teeth 太*hick* & 大*arge* taking charge...　　太 0227　犬 0076　太 0227　大 0023

☐ *005* 士*entlemen* on the 土*round* at your 仕*ervice* all year round...　　士 0538　土 0021　仕 0313

☐ *006* 水*ater* 氷*roze* into 氷*ce* in the 永*ong* winter twice...　　水 0018　氷 0434　氷 0434　永 0806

☐ *007* My 主*aster's* 主*rincipal* 玉*ewel*, given by 王*ing* Emmanuel...　　主 0260　主 0260　玉 0078　王 0077

☐ *008* 末*ending* 末*atter-part*, about to be 抹*rossed-out*...　　末 0477　末 0476　抹 1915

☐ *009* One 日*unny* 日*ay* in 日*apan*, flew a 百*undred* 白*hite* swans...　　日 0005　日 0005　日 0005　百 0014　白 0067

☐ *010* 可*ossible* 拘*rrest* for libelous 句*erses*...　　可 0663　拘 1805　句 0656

☐ *011* 四*our* 匹*nimals* in the 西*estern* corall...　　四 0006　匹 1530　西 0105

☐ *012* Killed by 矢*rrow* puncture, not by 医*edicine* 失*ailure*...　　矢 0161　医 0278　失 0478

☐ *013* 冊*ooks* warned Pontius Pilate of a 血*loody* 皿*late*...　　冊 0948　血 0408　皿 0429

☐ *014* Grand 盟*lliance* in the 月*onth* of 明*rilliance*...　　盟 0878　月 0016　明 0082

☐ *015* 凸*rotrude* & 凹*oncave*, Japanese 円*en* in 円*ircles* were made...　　凸 1895　凹 1896　円 0013　円 0013

☐ *016* 金*etal* 栓*ork* made 全*ntirely* for New York...　　金 0020　栓 1847　全 0249

☐ *017* 廷*mperial* court men row a 艇*oat* by the 庭*arden*...　　廷 1242　艇 1678　庭 0431

☐ *018* Every 年*ear*, empty 缶*ans* left in the 岳*ummits* picked up by hermits...　　年 0033　缶 1663　岳 1409

☐ *019* 岩*ocks* & 炭*oal* on a 岸*oastal* 岸*hore* told in folklore...　　岩 0240　炭 0437　岸 0381　岸 0381

☐ *020* To 正*orrect* & 整*ectify*, 征*onquerors* live & die...　　正 0075　整 0363　征 1243

☐ *021* High 波*aves* didn't stop an 婆*ld-woman* from 渡*rossing* to Oman...　　波 0398　婆 1932　渡 1011

☐ *022* 忙*usily* we 忘*orget* 妄*elusions* of death...　　忙 1422　忘 0982　妄 1424

☐ *023* 画*aintings'* 価*alue* & 価*rice* depend on the 面*urface* size...　　画 0194　価 0671　価 0671　面 0295

☐ *024* 捜*earching*, 抽*ulling*, 押*ushing*, rock fans abusing...　　捜 1162　抽 1160　押 1159

☐ *025* 昆*nsects' thing*: 混*ixing* with 皆*verything*...　　昆 1879　混 0759　皆 1033

☐ 026 革eather 靴ootwear bloomed like 華lowers with 華hina's 革eformers...   革 0933　靴 1214　華 1213　華 1213　革 0933

☐ 027 No 殼usk no 穀rains, a farm's 款oodwill wanes...   殼 1737　穀 1002　款 1736

☐ 028 編diting 偏nclination 遍idespread on the Web...   編 0727　偏 1270　遍 1271

☐ 029 奴ellows' lack of 努ffort 怒ngered their cohorts...   奴 1934　努 0637　怒 1618

☐ 030 感eelings of 憾egret 減ecrease when guilt is the least...   感 0291　憾 1820　減 0735

☐ 031 図ketched in farmers' 脳rain, no 悩istress when it rains...   図 0192　脳 0967　悩 1351

☐ 032 漁ishing for long, not one 魚ish 無othing to relish...   漁 0566　魚 0186　無 0443

☐ 033 Battle 隻hips 集athered, 進dvance scattered...   隻 1374　集 0345　進 0346

☐ 034 Test 筒ube 菌acteria in few 箇laces sowed hysteria...   筒 1506　菌 1313　箇 1507

☐ 035 哲hilosophers 誓ledge to seek 哲isdom in 逝eath beyond...   誓 1439　哲 1441　逝 1440

☐ 036 Like 磁agnets, 慈ffection compliments soul 滋ourishment...   磁 0995　慈 1572　滋 1573

☐ 037 疑oubts on 擬mitation 凝tiffened irritation...   疑 0991　擬 1546　凝 1547

☐ 038 芽prouts for vaudeville, no 雅race no 邪vil...   芽 0633　雅 1491　邪 1492

☐ 039 勇ourage 通asses 通hrough 痛ainful 痛njury...   勇 0631　通 0138　通 0138　痛 0977　痛 0977

☐ 040 Her baby 振winging, 娠regnant mother 震rembling...   振 1138　娠 1140　震 1137

☐ 041 微light eye 徴ymptoms, 懲unished Peeping Toms...   微 1462　徴 1463　懲 1464

☐ 042 薄hin tiny 簿edger, 縛ound in thick leather...   薄 1485　簿 1486　縛 1484

☐ 043 避void 癖abit of climbing high 壁alls, lest you fall...   避 1521　癖 1520　壁 1519

☐ 044 While 僚olleagues 療ecuperate, their 寮ormitories wait...   僚 1384　療 1382　寮 1383

☐ 045 麗eautiful 薦ecommendations, 慶ejoice in 慶elebration...   麗 1646　薦 1647　慶 1648　慶 1648

☐ 046 膚kinny war 虜aptives, their 慮houghts depressive...   膚 1346　虜 1431　慮 1430

II. Imperfect Twins

☐ 047 七even dwarfs wept for Snow White's 亡eath...   七 0009　亡 0869

☐ 048 九ine 丸hips smoothly 丸ound running aground...   九 0011　丸 0229　丸 0229

☐ 049 Squid in the 千housands 干rying-up in Pusan...   千 0015　干 0857

☐ 050 刃word 刃lade with 勺[3.75 gm] of gold not to fade...   刃 1456　刃 1456　勺 1903

☐ 051 川ivers & 州andbanks in a 州rovince of Port-au-Prince...   川 0029　州 0272　州 0272

☐ 052 米merican 米ice 光hines with the sunrise...   米 0167　米 0167　光 0131

☐ 053 丹ed-faced demons quite 凡ommon...   丹 1229　凡 1236

☐ 054 Written 行extlines of 行rip dance for a 竹amboo 行erformance...   行 0101　行 0101　竹 0060　行 0101

☐ 055 Red-light 区istrict, moral 凶vils inflict...   区 0268　凶 1352

☐ 056 芋otatoes of yucky taste grown in 宇uter-space...   芋 1910　宇 0920

☐ *057* 託*ntrusted to cats, a* 宅*ouse of mouse...*   託 1652   宅 0827

☐ *058* 夫*usband unforgiven won't go to* 天*eaven...*   夫 0479   天 0064

☐ *059* 乏*overty forced Shawn to live on the* 芝*awn...*   乏 1059   芝 1007

☐ *060* *To* 史*istorians,* 中*hina was once the* 中*iddle Kingdom...*   史 0487   中 0025   中 0025

☐ *061* *For friends of* 五*ive,* 互*utuality abides...*   五 0007   互 1116

☐ *062* 右*ight-side of the* 后*mpress, a famous actress...*   右 0045   后 0939

☐ *063* 幼*hild of* 幻*antasy lives in ecstacy...*   幼 0956   幻 1318

☐ *064* *In their* 甲*eport,* 甲*irst group of nobles* 甲*peaking-humble...*   甲 1155   申 0304

☐ *065* 母*other on a* 舟*oat wearing a red coat...*   母 0119   舟 1230

☐ *066* 席*eating* 度*egree, many* 度*imes they disagree...*   席 0495   度 0329   度 0329

☐ *067* 国*ation's greatest* 宝*reasure, the people for sure...*   国 0088   宝 0832

☐ *068* 込*nwards this* 辺*icinity, no birds no bees...*   込 1065   辺 0582

☐ *069* 常*egular* 堂*ltar built in Gibraltar...*   常 0685   堂 0517

☐ *070* 述*ention "* 迅*peed," * 迅*uickly they heed...*   述 0788   迅 1803   迅 1803

☐ *071* *Severe* 代*ees* 伐*ut-down in haste, feudal* 代*poch* 代*eplaced...*   代 0289   伐 1539   代 0289   代 0289

☐ *072* 扶*amily-support in the* 渓*alley fell short...*   扶 1731   渓 1888

☐ *073* *Like* 汽*team,* 気*eelings can be mean...*   汽 0128   気 0062

☐ *074* 向*owards the suspect, no* 尚*urther* 尚*espect...*   向 0273   尚 1858   尚 1858

☐ *075* 弐*wo* 武*arriors battle gladiators...*   弐 1186   武 0795

☐ *076* 伺*nquiry on* 何*omething yielded nothing...*   伺 1767   何 0200

☐ *077* 弟*ounger brothers follow succession* 第*rder...*   弟 0203   第 0337

☐ *078* 知*nowledge in* 和*apanese:* 和*armony &* 和*eace...*   知 0162   和 0253   和 0253   和 0253

☐ *079* 抜*ull-out to* 披*pen the letter from Copenhagen...*   抜 1723   披 1722

☐ *080* 官*ublic officials in a* 宮*hrine pray for the* 宮*alace* 宮*rince to be fine...*   官 0483   宮 0402   宮 0402   宮 0402

☐ *081* *On the far* 丘*ills, an old* 匠*rtisan drills...*   丘 1408   匠 1410

☐ *082* *EU flags* 掛*anging in the* 街*istrict of Maastricht...*   掛 1499   街 0452

☐ *083* *Cops in* 追*ursuit,* 迫*ressing a thief on foot...*   追 0433   迫 1281

☐ *084* 卒*oldiers* 座*eated for* 卒*raduation, up for promotion...*   卒 0584   座 0890   卒 0584

☐ *085* 衡*alancing* 術*kills on bicycle wheels...*   衡 1608   術 0645

☐ *086* *Twilight* 歳*ears,* 茂*hicken with tears...*   歳 1020   茂 1502

☐ *087* 斉*niformity in* 斎*urification needs no altercation...*   斉 1510   斎 1511

☐ *088* *Roman* 皇*mperors shine like* 星*tars even from* 星*lanets afar...*   皇 0833   星 0234

☐ *089* 姉*lder-sister looks after the* 妹*ounger-sister...*   姉 0205   妹 0206

☐ *090* *Beaten black &* 青*lue,* 責*ondemned without a clue...*   青 0069   責 0720

☐ *091* *Tales* 書*ritten of* 事*ctions forbidden...*   書 0127   事 0245

☐ *092* 蒸*teamed bread* 承*pproved as the main food...*   蒸 0916   承 0784

☐ *093* *Swords to* 削*harpen* 前*efore battles happen...*   削 1628   前 0092

☐ *094* 衷*nner feelings* 喪*ourn death of the unborn...*   衷 1689   喪 1690

☐ *095* *Shoplifters* 奔*unning-away,* 茶*ea bags taken away...*   奔 1671   茶 0177

☐ *096* *The* 寒*hilling* 実*eality: No equality!*   寒 0355   実 0276

- [ ] 097 侯limate in Hebron wooed the 侯aron... 侯 0609 侯 1925
- [ ] 098 菓weets on the 巢est for little Agnes... 菓 1563 巢 0635
- [ ] 099 美eauty, the 業usiness of vanity... 美 0335 業 0296
- [ ] 100 Rare 島sland 鳥irds down to two-thirds... 島 0298 鳥 0184
- [ ] 101 Lethal syringe 揮randished, 挿nserted to punish... 揮 0999 挿 1665
- [ ] 102 楼ower of 桜herry blossoms look so awesome... 楼 1846 桜 0782
- [ ] 103 留ettlers 留tayed in barter 貿rade... 留 0749 留 0749 貿 0748
- [ ] 104 On the 階tairs of the dynasty rules Her 陛ajesty... 階 0382 陛 0858
- [ ] 105 Social 称itles & 株tocks, pride of aristocrats... 称 1151 株 0884
- [ ] 106 唱hanting and 晶rystals in the witches rituals... 唱 0638 晶 1660
- [ ] 107 陣ampsite of sedition sent a 陳etition... 陣 1448 陳 1449
- [ ] 108 隆rosperity ascends then somehow 降escends... 隆 1132 降 0917
- [ ] 109 Pay raise 項lause 頂eceived with applause... 項 1478 頂 0987
- [ ] 110 適ropriety in 商ommerce endear customers... 適 0668 商 0339
- [ ] 111 Like 雷hunder on 雪now rang Santa's, "Ho, ho!" 雷 1136 雪 0239
- [ ] 112 敗ailure in 販elling, mad boss yelling... 敗 0521 販 1193
- [ ] 113 組roup's shady 細etails sent them to jail... 組 0207 細 0233
- [ ] 114 惑emptations reign in 域egions with evil legions... 惑 1146 域 0919
- [ ] 115 陵ausoleum on the 陸round form a grave mound... 陵 1849 陸 0551
- [ ] 116 算alculate cash with a 筆riting-brush... 算 0236 筆 0254
- [ ] 117 Selling 率ate of 傘mbrellas enthused Cinderella... 率 0755 傘 1068
- [ ] 118 給upply of 絵rawings & 絵ketches for the art fest... 給 0489 絵 0195 絵 0195
- [ ] 119 短hort nautical 程egree set by Captain Smee... 短 0277 程 0670
- [ ] 120 賃alary 賃ayments below 貸ental increments... 賃 0885 賃 0885 貸 0743
- [ ] 121 Eiffel 塔ower 搭oads of steel power... 塔 1845 搭 1916
- [ ] 122 Fish 揚aised from the sea, 揚ried in 場lace for me... 揚 1038 揚 1038 場 0140
- [ ] 123 Take refuge in the 弧rc of 孤olitude... 弧 1514 孤 1513
- [ ] 124 壱ne by 壱ne, 老ld persons going, going, gone... 壱 1738 壱 1738 老 0533
- [ ] 125 Patient glows when donor of 腸ntestine 賜estows... 腸 0627 賜 1836
- [ ] 126 携articipate & 擁upport: No 携ortable phones in courts... 携 1698 擁 1725 携 1698
- [ ] 127 To 熟ipen & 熟ature, 塾utorial-schools assure... 熟 0871 熟 0871 塾 1686
- [ ] 128 熱everish 勢igour from youth's rigour... 熱 0550 勢 0716
- [ ] 129 曇oggy and 曇loudy, 雲louds make football fans rowdy... 曇 1039 曇 1039 雲 0228
- [ ] 130 銑ig iron indeed looks like 鉄ron... 銑 1906 鉄 0306
- [ ] 131 Even 数umbers for the same 類ype of lumbers... 数 0168 類 0459
- [ ] 132 僕asculine 僕ervant 撲eaten by a confidant... 僕 1892 僕 1892 撲 1893
- [ ] 133 絹ilk woven into 縄ope used to elope... 絹 0961 縄 1766
- [ ] 134 Fishermen's 網ets, 綱ord-of-life for foods we get... 網 1629 綱 1626
- [ ] 135 Tax 賦evy being lost to software 賊iracy... 賦 1813 賊 1812
- [ ] 136 寡ittle boy 寡lone met 賓uests in Bucharest... 寡 1856 寡 1856 賓 1857
- [ ] 137 Little girl 奪natched, 奮roused fury unmatched... 奪 1373 奮 0975

III. Family

☐ 168　巨iant 拒efused to walk the 距istance to Constance... 　　巨 1361　拒 1363　距 1362

☐ 169　White 布loth 布pread, 希esired for a 怖cary dead... 　　布 0724　布 0724　希 0560　怖 1819

☐ 170　Cow on 台latform 始tarted 治ealing his horns... 　　台 0223　始 0361　治 0516

☐ 171　On 堀anal 掘igging, town resistance 屈ielding... 　　堀 1809　掘 1808　屈 1807

☐ 172　丙hird group of 病ickness, due to 柄haracter stress... 　　丙 1157　病 0330　柄 1158

☐ 173　A 兆rillion 兆ymptoms, 挑hallenge to fathom... 　　兆 0636　兆 0636　挑 1587

☐ 174　眺azing deep, diver with a 桃each 跳eapt to 逃scape the heat... 　　眺 1588　桃 1590　跳 1586　逃 1589

☐ 175　英rilliant 映eflections, 央entral to 英ngland's dominions... 　　英 0490　映 0836　央 0316　英 0490

☐ 176　必bsolutely, not to 泌ecrete 密idden 秘ecrets of Uncle Pete... 　　必 0524　泌 1875　密 0893　秘 0894

☐ 177　東astern 棟oof-ridges near 凍rozen bridges... 　　東 0104　棟 1450　凍 1303

☐ 178　What is the sales 点oint of that 店tore? 　　点 0148　店 0147

☐ 179　... A 粘ersevering 占ortune-teller with 粘ticky make-up 占ccupying the first floor... 　　粘 1717　占 1716　占 1716

☐ 180　Tanning 彼heir 皮kin with no cream, 彼hey got 疲xhausted and thin... 　　彼 1150　皮 0420　彼 1150　疲 1381

☐ 181　再epeat the 講ecture on 溝itch structure! 　　再 0753　講 0754　溝 1177

☐ 182　吉ood luck 結onnects when 詰ompressed less... 　　吉 1259　結 0513　詰 1260

☐ 183　耳ars long 恥isgraced, 取aken to a far place... 　　耳 0039　恥 1702　取 0243

☐ 184　浄urity of 静ilence with 争onflict's absence... 　　浄 1042　静 0558　争 0475

☐ 185　拾ick-up a pen & paper, let's write a 合ombined 答nswer... 　　拾 0439　合 0142　答 0143

☐ 186　朱carlet 珠earls, 殊pecialty for the rich girl... 　　朱 1533　珠 1534　殊 1535

☐ 187　立tanding chorus 泣rying over their lost 位tatus... 　　立 0057　泣 0625　位 0447

☐ 188　舌ongue 話peaks of 活ctivities at peak... 　　舌 0810　話 0172　活 0171

☐ 189　The 翌ollowing day, an 翁ld man 習earned that birds of 異ifferent 翼ings and 羽eathers flock together... 　　翌 0859　翁 1931　習 0383　異 0930　翼 1204　羽 0226

☐ 190　梅lum cargo came by 海cean line 毎verytime... 　　梅 0640　海 0123　毎 0122

☐ 191　旨nstructions by 指inger: No 脂nimal-fat in my burger... 　　旨 1191　指 0426　脂 1192

☐ 192　城astle 成ecame 盛rosperous when the King got 誠eracious... 　　城 0881　成 0467　盛 0880　誠 0879

☐ 193　同imilar 洞averns lit with 銅opper lanterns... 　　同 0157　洞 1369　銅 0820

☐ 194　羊heeps by the 洋estern 洋cean, 祥ood-omen for Sebastian... 　　羊 0299　洋 0300　祥 1599

☐ 195　At the 寺emple parade, a 侍amurai 持olding a 詩oem of 特pecial 等rade... 　　寺 0089　寺 0089　持 0352　詩 0379　特 0471　等 0378

☐ 196　言ord of 誉onour earned 信aith for the Governor... 　　言 0099　誉 1070　信 0450

☐ 197　養aising a 良ood 娘aughter lest to 浪rift on 浪aves of disaster... 　　養 0500　良 0481　娘 1759　浪 1760　浪 1760

☐ 198　食ood & 飲rinks, no 飯eal on the rink..! 　　食 0191　飲 0309　飯 0482

☐ 199　求equests to 救escue the Earth's 球phere quickly grew... 　　求 0571　救 0572　球 0403

☐ 200 君ounger 君ulers in the 郡ounty shepherd the 群erds...

君 0409　郡 0454　群 0757

☐ 201 売elling 続ontinues to 読eaders looking for job news...

売 0173　続 0464　読 0175

☐ 202 On 赤ed 嚇hreat, let's 赦orgive & forget...

赤 0068　嚇 1919　赦 1593

☐ 203 系ineage to enlarge, 孫randchildren 係n charge...

系 0911　係 0417　孫 0603

☐ 204 By 宵arly evening, 硝alt-peter's fake 肖esemblance 消xtinguished at once...

宵 1859　硝 1860　肖 1086　消 0413

☐ 205 告eported news: 酷ruel drugs mass 造roduced...

告 0564　酷 1721　造 0729

☐ 206 達lural 幸appiness 執arried-out, 達eaches the highest bout...

達 0509　幸 0401　執 1046　達 0509

☐ 207 奇trange & 奇urious goat 寄pproaching Park 崎lope...

奇 1411　奇 1411　寄 0814　崎 1412

☐ 208 苗aplings & a black 猫at 描ketched on the doormat...

苗 1503　猫 1505　描 1504

☐ 209 Pedestrians 頻requently 歩alking, 頻requently 渉rossing...

頻 1852　歩 0210　頻 1852　渉 1014

☐ 210 Indian 長hief 張tretches to relax his 長ong and 脹wollen biceps...

長 0114　張 0800　長 0114　脹 1923

☐ 211 Policemen 奉ffered with large 棒tick & high 俸alary to fight burglary...

奉 1568　棒 0993　俸 1569

☐ 212 若oungsters' deal: Parental 諾onsent not to 匿onceal...

若 0850　諾 1775　匿 1776

☐ 213 Gilted 者erson's 煮oiling anger "too 著tark," 著riters remarked...

者 0264　煮 1800　著 0902　著 0902

☐ 214 週eekdays or not, 調heck the 調one & 周icinity 周aps...

週 0113　調 0314　周 0442　周 0442

☐ 215 昔ygones to 惜egret, 措easures to forget...

昔 0406　惜 1061　措 1299

☐ 216 What time will the Queen 聞isten to 閑eisure 問uestions & 問roblems?

聞 0098　閑 1561　問 0262　問 0262

☐ 217 ...Castle 関arrier 開pens or 閉loses based on 簡oncise orders, so be at the 門ate 間etween 7 & 8...

関 0498　開 0334　閉 0839　簡 0992　門 0144　間 0091

☐ 218 Chemistry 課ection gave 課esson on 果esults of 裸aked reactions...

課 0515　課 0515　果 0514　裸 1564

☐ 219 非egative 悲orrow for 罪uilty 輩ellow...

非 0686　悲 0425　罪 0776　輩 1189

☐ 220 On the 則egulation 側ide, strict 測imensions to abide...

則 0706　側 0545　測 0707

☐ 221 A 某ertain UN 媒ediator foiled a 謀onspirator...

某 1524　媒 1526　謀 1525

☐ 222 甚xtreme 勘ntuition allows 堪ndurance in affliction...

甚 1531　勘 1532　堪 1914

☐ 223 軍oldiers to 運ransport 輝parkling jewels to Frankfurt...

軍 0507　運 0347　輝 1666

☐ 224 納upply of body heat came from 内nside 肉lesh & 肉eat...

納 0887　内 0110　肉 0166　肉 0166

☐ 225 飛light with fuel of 升[1.8 litre] 昇scends in shivers...

飛 0530　升 1899　昇 1782

☐ 226 杯ine cups to 否efuse when 不egative of booze...

杯 1269　否 0958　不 0444

☐ 227 Convent 尼uns mad when roof is 漏eaking 泥ud...   尼 1636 漏 1811 泥 1637

☐ 228 共ogether, regents 供ook-after the 選hosen ruler...   共 0455 供 0828 選 0586

☐ 229 市ity 市arkets 遞radually 遞onvey healthy 肺ungs gone astray...   市 0153 市 0153 遞 1937 遞 1937 肺 0966

☐ 230 連lliance's 車ehicles & 車heels damaged, kept in a 庫torage...   連 0508 車 0061 車 0061 庫 0411

☐ 231 見ee & 覺erceive, 覺ecall what 寬eniency receives...   見 0043 覺 0544 覺 0544 寬 1194

☐ 232 Ghost 談alks by chimney 炎lame left me 淡ale & lame...   談 0384 炎 1393 淡 1394

☐ 233 佐ssistants on the 左eft, 惰dleness bereft...   佐 1751 左 0044 惰 1750

☐ 234 首ead with long 首eck quickly saw the 道oad 導uide to Quebec... 首 0136 首 0136 道 0137 導 0731

☐ 235 是orrect cement 提ubmitted for sea 堤mbankments...   是 1614 提 0713 堤 1615

☐ 236 Same 音ounds 韻hyme even in 暗ark times...   音 0079 韻 1010 暗 0315

☐ 237 既lready 慨eplored, 概pproximates we can't afford...   既 1493 慨 1495 概 1494

☐ 238 篤ordial 馬orses by the 駅rain-station take a vacation...   篤 1887 馬 0183 駅 0297

☐ 239 埋uried 厘ld coins, 黑lack as 墨nk in the 里ometown of 墨exico's crown...   埋 1831 厘 1901 黑 0159 墨 1715 墨 1715 里 0133

☐ 240 能bilities 罷ithdraw when 態onditions are raw...   能 0661 罷 1866 態 0662

☐ 241 般egular train 搬ransport of chess 盤oards, all aboard...   般 1232 搬 1732 盤 1233

☐ 242 章hapters of 彰itation for those 障njured in the liberation... 章 0414 彰 1832 障 0901

☐ 243 曹ergeant of 曹oble rank 遭ncounters 槽ater-tank...   曹 1930 曹 1930 遭 1658 槽 1659

☐ 244 祭estival on the 際erge of 察nspection 擦crapes for funding 際ccasion...   祭 0389 際 0709 察 0548 擦 1548 際 0709

☐ 245 Words of 敬espect in 警arnings quite 驚urprising...   敬 0876 警 0877 驚 1783

☐ 246 麻emp plants & lemons for 摩ubbing off 魔emons...   麻 1558 摩 1559 魔 1557

☐ 247 副ice mayor's 富ortune, for a very 福ucky baboon..   副 0569 富 0734 福 0438

☐ 248 替eplacement of net fibres, 贊pproved by scuba 潛ivers...   替 1058 贊 0742 潛 1128

☐ 249 錯ixed-up 借oan 籍egistry 散cattered in misery...   錯 1298 借 0578 籍 1297 散 0579

☐ 250 Revised 藩uedal 翻ranslation, after a 番umber of 審nspections... 藩 1428 翻 1035 番 0154 審 1429

☐ 251 憶emory caught a 億undred-million 意houghts...   憶 1012 億 0496 意 0255

☐ 252 義n-laws led 議iscussions on 儀ites of 義ighteous 犧acrifice... 義 0651 議 0472 儀 1053 義 0651 犧 1054

☐ 253 顧econsider 雇mployment on pay increments...   顧 1578 雇 1577

IV. Getting Less

☐ 254   *Noodle 汁oup or lemon 汁uice cost 十en cents to produce...*   汁 1799   汁 1799   十 0012

☐ 255   *French culinary 団roup 寸easured the soup...*   団 0684   寸 1005

☐ 256   *学tudy of 字etters made the 字istrict prosper...*   学 0053   字 0054   字 0054

☐ 257   *Tired 体ody takes a 休est in Buenos Aires...*   体 0096   休 0042

☐ 258   *When 引ulling in 弓rchery, don't you hurry...*   引 0163   弓 0160

☐ 259   *Machine for 写opying 与upplied with ink...*   写 0373   与 1025

☐ 260   *安afety is never 安heap for 女omen trailed by creeps...*   安 0251   安 0251   女 0051

☐ 261   *労abourers' 力trength go to extreme lengths...*   労 0462   力 0049

☐ 262   *Hands caught 窃tealing to be 切ut in the evening...*   窃 1727   切 0087

☐ 263   *初irst, sharpen the 刀nife's 刀lade then 初tart the raid...*   初 0562   初 0562   刀 0085   刀 0085

☐ 264   *In every 危anger, 厄isaster's no stranger...*   危 0847   厄 1398

☐ 265   *After 依equest for 衣lothes, donations flowed...*   依 1045   衣 0561

☐ 266   *To the 沼wamp was 召ummoned Monte Cristo's Edmond...*   沼 1166   召 1165

☐ 267   *Food 例amples in Khartoum, many wait in 列olumns...*   例 0546   列 0387

☐ 268   *Hear 弦tring-instruments' 玄rofound moments...*   弦 1317   玄 1316

☐ 269   *版ublished 片artiality breaches equality...*   版 0797   片 0928

☐ 270   *法udiciary for the Mafia Dons, not to 去bandon...*   法 0448   去 0340

☐ 271   *Old garden 囲nclosed, a wishing 井ell of ghosts...*   囲 0622   井 1294

☐ 272   *命estiny's highest prize: 令ommand of one's 命ife...*   命 0380   令 0591   命 0380

☐ 273   *拓learing-up 石tones, yielded dead bones...*   拓 1838   石 0046

☐ 274   *姻arriage 如quals a new heritage...*   姻 1755   如 1754

☐ 275   *Sea 界orld of 介hellfish, 介ediation in Atlantis...*   界 0354   介 1015   介 1015

☐ 276   *狩unters 守bide to 守rotect the wild...*   狩 1604   守 0360   守 0360

☐ 277   *荘olemn 荘illa for a 壮asculine gorilla...*   荘 1387   荘 1387   壮 1386

☐ 278   *Slavery 廃bolition 発tarted Southern sedition...*   廃 1142   発 0250

☐ 279   *独erman scientists have known that 虫nsects 独lone can live in a nuclear zone...*   独 0647   虫 0080   独 0647

☐ 280   *挙ttempt to raise your 手ands if police demands...*   挙 0587   手 0040

☐ 281   *遮ntercepted letters, all about 庶eneral-matters...*   遮 1772   庶 1771

☐ 282   *Cadaver's 背ack to face 北orth for luck...*   背 0962   北 0106

☐ 283   *草rass so curly to be cut 早arly...*   草 0073   早 0072

☐ 284   *When fortunes 衰ecline, 哀orrows incline...*   衰 1688   哀 1687

☐ 285   *索earch for 索ope found 糸hread instead...*   索 1202   索 1202   糸 0071

☐ 286   *With respectful 詞erses 司reside travel guides...*   詞 0899   司 0594

☐ 287   *Indian cooks 宰upervise blending of 辛pice...*   宰 1518   辛 1517

☐ 288   *Rice 俵acks on the 表hart, 表xpressions of the heart...*   俵 0824   表 0294   表 0294

☐ 289   *Stone 畝oof-ridge, 久ong-lasting indeed...*   畝 1902   久 0807

☐ 290　御onorables don't wail missing a 卸holesale...　　御 1052　卸 1051
☐ 291　致ring-about the 至tmost barbeque roast...　　致 1113　至 0909
☐ 292　The "B" in Kanji 附ttach, clearly 付ttached...　　附 1848　付 0453
☐ 293　透ransparency of cash reserves, accounting 秀uperb...　　透 1697　秀 1695
☐ 294　据et-in-place, 居esidential space...　　据 1837　居 0642
☐ 295　教eachings on 孝ilial-obedience take 教eligious precedence...　　教 0176　孝 0849
☐ 296　涼ool winds in the 京apital of Montreal...　　涼 1302　京 0155
☐ 297　For athletes' 脚egs, 却ithdraw ham & egg...　　脚 1789　却 1788
☐ 298　捨hrown in a jail 舍uarter, a well-known reporter...　　捨 0988　舍 0756
☐ 299　No 悪vils among 亜sian eels...　　悪 0302　亜 1633
☐ 300　Good 健ealth 建uilds vast wealth...　　健 0601　建 0600
☐ 301　Earth 圏phere 巻rapped, in Ozone trap...　　圏 1024　巻 0843
☐ 302　拷ortured 考hinking, after severe beating...　　拷 1730　考 0224
☐ 303　停top by the 亭estaurant for another croissant...　　停 0621　亭 1289
☐ 304　控efraining travel agency kept the 空kies 空mpty...　　控 1728　空 0063　空 0063
☐ 305　Berries so 紺ark-blue, how 甘weet to chew...　　紺 1523　甘 1522
☐ 306　惨iserable hobbit came for a 参emple-visit...　　惨 1734　参 0568
☐ 307　To 終inish by 冬inter, training of sprinters...　　終 0356　冬 0214
☐ 308　Garden 郭nclosed, 享njoy poetry & prose...　　郭 1685　享 1684
☐ 309　創reativity, 倉torage of infinity...　　創 0974　倉 0628
☐ 310　Drivers must 解omprehend 角orners' dead end...　　解 0678　角 0221
☐ 311　Motorbiking with no 帽eadgear, either 冒ourage or fear...　　帽 1239　冒 1238
☐ 312　Old shoulders of Mr. Magoo 硬ardening 更new...　　硬 1175　更 1174
☐ 313　Job of censors: 絶radicate 色rotic 色olours...　　絶 0741　色 0158　色 0158
☐ 314　郎asculine matador standing in the 廊orridor...　　郎 1153　廊 1154
☐ 315　露xposed to heavy 露ew, 露ussian 路oads will do...　　露 1135　露 1135　路 0258
☐ 316　勝ictory in cricket to earn new 券icket...　　勝 0364　券 0687
☐ 317　Blood 循irculation 盾hields cell mutation...　　循 1512　盾 1062
☐ 318　Keeping lockets of 髪air, 友riendship's loving care...　　髪 1264　友 0178
☐ 319　備repare for a 用urpose to 用tilize your utmost...　　備 0750　用 0117
☐ 320　損njured crew 員embers can't remember...　　損 0658　員 0263
☐ 321　Green 葉eaves fill the 世orld of Adam & Eve...　　葉 0287　世 0286
☐ 322　滑lippery 骨ones, old age bemoans...　　滑 1345　骨 0963
☐ 323　晩vening curfew 免xemption led to defection...　　晩 0882　免 1056
☐ 324　ODA 献onations go to 南outhern nations...　　献 1406　南 0107
☐ 325　愁rief in 秋utumn came brief for Tom...　　愁 1623　秋 0217
☐ 326　催ponsored summit drew only 仙ermits...　　催 1378　仙 1894
☐ 327　電lectricity in the 雨ain struck a walking cane...　　電 0118　雨 0026
☐ 328　New 式tyle 試ttempts to hire only temps...　　式 0370　試 0526
☐ 329　Weak 腰elvis 要ecessitates dialysis...　　腰 1366　要 0502
☐ 330　Clues 置eft-behind 直irectly point to Mr. Rhind...　　置 0503　直 0208
☐ 331　Cash 節onserved 即mmediately reserved...　　節 0510　即 1017
☐ 332　働abour 動ovement for job improvement...　　働 0461　動 0283

☐ 374　旧ormerly a 児hild, no longer wild...　　　　　　旧 0808　児 0623

☐ 375　万en-thousand audience 励ncourage 励iligence...　　　万 0081　励 1397　励 1397

☐ 376　比ompare before you 批riticize the 比hilippine price...　比 0758　批 0925　比 0758

☐ 377　父ather lost in 交rossing when streets are confusing...　父 0120　交 0121

☐ 378　毛kin-hair on trail points to a camel's 尾ail...　　　毛 0185　尾 1873

☐ 379　心eart 応esponds in seconds...　　　　　　　　　心 0115　応 0764

☐ 380　勺[18 ml] is 均qual to 勺[18 ml]...　　　　　　　勺 1904　均 0760　勺 1904

☐ 381　斤[600 gm] of socks wrongly 折olded got Fred badly scolded...　斤 1898　折 0632

☐ 382　以refixes 似imilar sound familiar...　　　　　　　以 0441　似 0817

☐ 383　Clients 処reatment 拠asis good at Macy's...　　　処 0943　拠 1257

☐ 384　The 性ature of 性ex 生auses 生aw 生ife complex...　生 0032　生 0032　生 0032　性 0641　性 0641

☐ 385　忠oyalty amidst 患ickness, charmed Her Highness...　忠 0980　患 1377

☐ 386　曲elody's fools, 曲ending of music 典ules...　　　曲 0325　曲 0325　典 0492

☐ 387　古ither in the cold, 苦uffer the 古ld...　　　　　古 0149　苦 0374　古 0149

☐ 388　先irst comes 洗ashing 先head of anything...　　　先 0034　洗 0873　先 0034

☐ 389　逐riven-out 逐ne-by-one, peace 遂inally 遂chieved by the gun...　逐 1254　逐 1254　遂 1253　遂 1253

☐ 390　使nvoys wrongly 使tilized, 便onvenience paid the price...　使 0312　使 0312　便 0486

☐ 391　足oot work & 足ufficient raw eggs 促rompt Rocky's 足egs...　足 0041　促 1581　足 0041

☐ 392　田ice-field 畑lantations feed Asian nations...　　田 0031　畑 0241

☐ 393　For every 帥ommander, an 師xpert 師eacher...　　帥 1013　師 0825　師 0825

☐ 394　半alf the 畔ice-paths had gold karats...　　　　半 0111　畔 1945

☐ 395　室oom with 窒itrogen 窒uffocates often...　　　室 0146　窒 1726　窒 1726

☐ 396　放eleased 倣mpostors thought to be doctors...　放 0366　倣 1781

☐ 397　Among 具ools, only the 真ruth rules...　　　　具 0341　真 0342

☐ 398　平lat house of 100 坪[3.3 sqm] built for beavers...　平 0275　坪 1897

☐ 399　氏urname on 紙aper, the serial raper...　　　　氏 0537　紙 0152

☐ 400　兵oldiers on the 浜each guarding a sea witch...　兵 0583　浜 1067

☐ 401　固ardened criminals are not plain 個ndividuals...　固 0611　個 0789

☐ 402　谷alleys' grain 容ontent, 容ppears affluent...　谷 0230　容 0719　容 0719

☐ 403　Workers 戒dmonished when 械achine was unpolished...　戒 1100　械 0529

☐ 404　In 旬en-days, 殉artyr to cast away...　　　　　旬 1009　殉 1804

☐ 405　民eople always 眠sleep, nothing to reap...　　民 0451　眠 1087

☐ 406　Rebels 到rriving to 倒verthrow the King...　　到 1114　倒 1115

☐ 407　徒isciples willingly 走un their master's errand...　徒 0504　走 0209

☐ 408　各very foetus, a possible 格tatus...　　　　　各 0549　格 0715

☐ 409　On the 卓able 悼rieves 卓rominent Steve...　　卓 1691　悼 1692

☐ 410　且urther 宜onvenience, a business sense...　　且 1927　宜 1224

☐ 411　When 余urplus 除xcluded, profits clouded...　　余 0799　除 0931

☐ 412　束undle of sticks burn 速uick...　　　　　　束 0519　速 0362

□ 451 戻eturned after 24 years, five with lots of 涙ears...   戻 1325　涙 1326

□ 452 臣ubjects & 臣etainers serve 姫rincess sisters...   臣 0593　臣 0593　姫 1763

□ 453 Kamikaze 隊quads to 墜escend at all odds...   隊 0585　墜 1252

□ 454 尊steemed audience showed 遵bedience ...   尊 0875　遵 1938

□ 455 恵lessed are the 穂rains when it rains...   恵 1310　穂 1312

□ 456 景cenic 影hadows, fantastic meadows...   景 0597　影 1089

□ 457 幾ow much 機hance would a 幾ew old 機achines run out of balance?   幾 1101　幾 1101　機 0528

□ 458 Heavy 需emands for virtues to please 儒onfucius...   需 1459　儒 1460

□ 459 Democratic voting with 票uffrage 標arkings...   票 0606　標 0607

□ 460 定scertain that all gates are blocked with 錠adlocks...   定 0318　錠 1823

□ 461 Captured troops 従omply fine on a 縦ertical-line...   従 0989　従 0989　縦 0990

□ 462 保reserve & 保bide, 褒xtolled far & wide...   保 0683　保 0683　褒 1071

□ 463 By one's 歯eeth, 齢ears-old can be told...   歯 0359　齢 1084

□ 464 Winner takes the 賞rize while the loser 償ndemnifies...   賞 0518　償 1147

□ 465 段teps of 鍛iscipline 鍛emper the soul clean...   段 0837　鍛 1822　鍛 1822

□ 466 優xcellent 優ctress in 憂istress over ripped dress...   憂 1187　優 0926

□ 467 帯ash of pigeons, keepsake of 滞tay in the 帯egion...   帯 0610　滞 1144　帯 0610

□ 468 In English 文iterature, the royal 紋rest endure...   文 0055　紋 1490

□ 469 客ustomers surprised at the bargain 額rice...   客 0396　額 0767

□ 470 禁rohibited for scholars, high 襟eck collars...   禁 0679　襟 1565

□ 471 Scandals once 暴xposed, 暴iolence 爆xplodes...   暴 0791　爆 1179

□ 472 頼equest to close the 瀬apids foiled a stampede...   頼 1542　瀬 1543

□ 473 Curtain 維ope & quilt made from a 羅hin-silk...   維 1321　羅 1865

□ 474 童hild with a silver 鐘ell playing well...   童 0338　鐘 1826

□ 475 蔵torage of pagans for 臓ody-organs...   蔵 0969　臓 0970

□ 476 県refecture 懸angs final 懸ffer to pro golfer..   県 0271　懸 1117　懸 1117

□ 477 両oth groom & bride happily 満atisfied...   両 0274　満 0456

□ 478 柔oft iceberg struck by a 矛alberd...   柔 1064　矛 1063

□ 479 Money 予dvanced, 預ntrust to chance...   予 0333　預 0665

VI. Look Up

□ 480 弁alve of 弁peech for a 怠azy leech...   弁 0732　弁 0732　怠 1365

□ 481 巡round the area of 災isaster, 巡atrols search faster...   巡 1066　災 0812　巡 1066

□ 482 省elf-reflection, not 劣nferior in the 省inistry of Interior...   省 0449　劣 1266　省 0449

□ 483 尿rine test at the 局ureau led to a 局ituation for Ichirō...   尿 1874　局 0266

□ 484 尺xhausted making 尺[30 cm] harpoon by high 昼oon...   尺 1735　尺 1006　昼 0219

VII. Look Down

☐ 519 肯ffirm soul 有xistence based on evidence...　　肯 1342　有 0292
☐ 520 聖acred 望esire, bishop's 呈ffer to retire...　　聖 0870　望 0559　呈 1613
☐ 521 What 芸rt 伝onveys, hearts obey...　　芸 0506　伝 0505
☐ 522 恭espect that 添ppends hardly ends...　　恭 1473　添 1472
☐ 523 盗tolen 塩alt mixed with malt...　　盗 1235　塩 0616
☐ 524 益rofit & 益enefit from sale of 温arm outfits...　　益 0736　益 0736　温 0394
☐ 525 看ook-after the 盲lind walking behind...　　看 0976　盲 1423
☐ 526 査nspection map for 畳atami-mats already
　　　 畳olded-up...　　査 0711　畳 1225
☐ 527 負wing 負efeat, 貢ributes paid complete...　　負 0365　負 0365　貢 1729
☐ 528 費pending on Earth's 資esources to protect
　　　 質ature's forces...　　費 0575　資 0744　質 0644
☐ 529 蛮arbarians steal 蚕ilkworm but 蛍ireflies
　　　 conform...　　蛮 1883　蚕 1004　蛍 1882
☐ 530 装earing rice 袋acks, 襲ttackers stole rice
　　　 crackers...　　装 0978　袋 1388　襲 1598
☐ 531 笛lute 笛histled with grace 届eliver 届otice to
　　　 宙uterspace...　　笛 0440　笛 0440　届 0922　届 0922　宙 0921

VIII. Look Left

☐ 532 Volcanic 圧ressure spews 灰shes to the
　　　 bushes...　　圧 0813　灰 0979
☐ 533 庁ublic-office 床loor with shiny colour...　　庁 0888　床 1081
☐ 534 在xistence of 存nowledge leads to courage...　　在 0649　存 0829
☐ 535 功erits to the police 攻ttack ended a hijack...　　功 0589　攻 1078
☐ 536 Better 拝ray before 打triking day...　　拝 0954　打 0423
☐ 537 好iking through old age, good for 婚arriage...　　好 0445　婚 1030
☐ 538 姓urname of 婿on-in-law that of Zorro...　　姓 1753　婿 1752
☐ 539 狂razy cardinal in 獄rison with 犯riminals...　　狂 1105　獄 1106　犯 0775
☐ 540 Boat 幅idth in 帳egistry 帆ailing to victory...　　幅 1427　帳 0430　帆 1237
☐ 541 吹lowing of horns brings 唯olitary scorns...　　吹 1338　唯 1323
☐ 542 In the 砂ands abandon an old war 砲anon...　　砂 0946　砲 1769
☐ 543 Billowing 煙moke from 炉urnaces choke...　　煙 1119　炉 1795
☐ 544 Noisy 郊uburbs 効ffectively disturb...　　郊 1077　効 0763
☐ 545 Follow the 峠ountain-trail to the 岬ape of
　　　 Whales...　　峠 1402　岬 1413
☐ 546 物bjects of 牧asture, old days to recapture...　　物 0244　牧 0573
☐ 547 Bullet 斜rajectory in 叙arration kept the
　　　 sensation...　　斜 1209　叙 1207
☐ 548 施estow 族amily 旅ravel to the 族ribe of Abel...　　施 1171　族 0279　旅 0280　族 0279
☐ 549 Children at 遊lay on 旋evolving rides they stay...　　遊 0422　旋 1172
☐ 550 腕rms, 胸hest & 胎terus saved from virus by
　　　 腕alents of Dr. Malthus...　　腕 1367　胸 0968　胎 1364　腕 1367
☐ 551 暇ree-time, too precious 時ime...　　暇 1205　時 0090
☐ 552 蚊osquito & 蛇nake frolic on the lake...　　蚊 1881　蛇 1880
☐ 553 耕ultivation to 耗essen when soil worsens...　　耕 0805　耗 1296
☐ 554 Rice 粒rains 粧dorn the wide plains...　　粒 1711　粧 1710
☐ 555 Beasts so 猛ierce, 猟unted by spears...　　猛 1602　猟 1603
☐ 556 期eriodic 欺raud stopped by Inspector Maude...　　期 0351　欺 1529

☐ 557 軸xle in 軟oft manuever, 軌ailroad 輸hipments 転oll-over...   軸 1161 軟 1793 軌 1792 輸 0692 転 0344

☐ 558 乾ried 幹ree-trunks from 朝ynasty Ming arrived this 朝orning...   乾 1293 幹 0803 朝 0218

☐ 559 趣urpose 超xceeds and 越vertakes in 越ietnam's wake...   趣 1170 越 1169 超 1168

☐ 560 飾ecorating at random leads to 飽oredom...   飾 1152 飽 1768

☐ 561 鎖hained to a food 鉢owl, prisoner cried foul...   鎖 1824 鉢 1825

☐ 562 Most 勧ecommended 歓leasure, 観iewing one's treasure...   勧 1195 歓 1196 観 0543

☐ 563 新resh, 新rand-new 薪irewood, 親ntimate 親arents approve...   新 0150 薪 1911 親 0151 親 0151

☐ 564 酵ermentation 酬eward offered at 酪airy barnyard...   酵 1871 酬 1869 酪 1870

☐ 565 践ctual 踊ance improves body balance...   践 1591 踊 1582

☐ 566 踏tepping on 跡elics convinced the skeptics...   踏 1583 跡 1592

☐ 567 験xamine a 騎orse-ride in the far & wide...   験 0531 騎 1885

☐ 568 Heavy 駄orseloads put horses in 駆alloping mode...   駄 1884 駆 1886

☐ 569 Feudal 縁elations govern 綿otton plantations...   縁 1251 綿 0804

☐ 570 所rovocation of special 房lusters for 啓nlightened masters...   所 0259 房 1324 啓 1442

☐ 571 扇olding-fan left by the 扉oor, my 肩houlders hot no more...   扇 1579 扉 1580 肩 1344

☐ 572 鮮ivid 鯨hales seen in 鮮resh Wales...   鮮 1049 鯨 1048 鮮 1049

☐ 573 疫pidemic of 痢peedy 痢iarrhoea—not a 痴oolish 疾isease, Mama Mia...   疫 1380 痢 1816 痴 1818 疾 1817

IX. Look Right

☐ 574 私rivate 払ayment to a 仏uddhist 仏rench, very urgent...   私 0826 払 1032 仏 0701 仏 0701

☐ 575 A ringing silver 鈴ell in the 冷hilly 冷old spell...   鈴 1827 冷 0592 冷 0592

☐ 576 孔onfucius kept 札oney-bills in the South Pole 札abeled in a 孔ole...   孔 1130 札 0619 札 0619 孔 1130

☐ 577 礼ituals without 礼espect, 乱haos to expect...   礼 0390 礼 0390 乱 0872

☐ 578 利rofits of hair 刈utting stylist to be 刊ublished...   利 0485 刈 1354 刊 0702

☐ 579 他nother 地and, 他nother 池ond...   他 0252 地 0124 他 0252 池 0125

☐ 580 Protein 泡ubble dwells in stem 胞ells...   泡 1770 胞 1355

☐ 581 村illagers 対gainst 討nvestigating 討ttack on Peking ducks...   村 0066 対 0324 討 0924 討 0924

☐ 582 Wrong 針eedle 計easure led to a tailor's closure...   針 0835 計 0193

☐ 583 糾wist & 叫hout in a dance bout...   糾 1713 叫 1336

☐ 584 A 都etropolitan 邦apanese loves the 邦ountry of Nice...   都 0270 邦 1072 邦 1072

☐ 585 仲olleagues 沖ffshore e-mail me no more...   仲 0630 沖 1399

☐ 586 的tyle of not 酌erving-wine 約romised until 釣ishing is finished...   的 0457 酌 1868 約 0458 釣 1867

☐ 587 培ultivators' annuity settled an 賠ndemnity...   培 1833 賠 1834

☐ 588　Sound 決ecision based on 快leasant conditions ...　　決 0319　快 0815

☐ 589　抵esistance to snow, a 低inimum 低ow...　　抵 1027　低 0535　低 0535

☐ 590　呼alling for 評ommentary on Bill & Hillary...　　呼 0959　評 0794

☐ 591　狀onditions for 伏ielding hideout in a building...　　狀 0712　伏 1407

☐ 592　社ompany boss of 社ociety wine 吐omitting at a 社hrine...　　社 0188　社 0188　社 0188　吐 1337

☐ 593　枝ree-branch on 岥orked-road fell on my abode...　　枝 0773　岥 1097

☐ 594　Crime 抑uppressed, 迎elcomed with 仰espect...　　抑 1201　迎 1199　仰 1200

☐ 595　赴roceeding-to-work, a 朴imple clerk...　　赴 1500　朴 1501

☐ 596　咲looming flowers 送ent with 朕mperial-consent...　　咲 1123　送 0348　朕 1922

☐ 597　妊regnancy 任ntrusts, parental 任uties a must...　　妊 1139　任 0655　任 0655

☐ 598　Summer 軒ouses by the river, dwellers 汗weat to their 肝ivers...　　軒 1291　汗 1292　肝 1347

☐ 599　侮espise or 悔egret but never forget...　　侮 1743　悔 1741

☐ 600　神od to 伸tretch, 紳entlemen to fetch...　　神 0305　伸 1240　紳 1241

☐ 601　On bargain 購urchase, buy 構osture in a haste...　　購 1176　構 0790

☐ 602　Wars 破estroy, 被ufferings annoy...　　破 0722　被 1149

☐ 603　Happy 況ituation calls for 祝elebration...　　況 1088　祝 0595

☐ 604　肥ertilizers in 把undles left to idle...　　肥 0822　把 1733

☐ 605　錬rill & 練rill, soldiers without meal...　　錬 1821　練 0405

☐ 606　就mployment 沈inks when job stinks...　　就 0914　沈 1127

☐ 607　珍are 診iagnosis shocked a pharmacist...　　珍 1308　診 1307

☐ 608　彫hiseled on a 杉edar-tree, crest of Robert Lee...　　彫 1265　杉 1877

☐ 609　Grapes 昨reviously 搾queezed made wine to please...　　昨 0491　搾 1527

☐ 610　詐raudulent 酢inegar 作roduced by a beggar...　　詐 1528　酢 1872　作 0197

☐ 611　枚heets of 政olitical 改eform created a firestorm...　　枚 0947　政 0680　改 0522

☐ 612　抄ummary so 妙uperb took 秒econds to be heard...　　抄 1267　妙 1268　秒 0432

☐ 613　Imperial 紀poch on 記ecord by the 妃rincess's word...　　紀 0493　記 0198　妃 1762

☐ 614　詠oetry about 泳wimming in Wyoming...　　詠 1304　泳 0435

☐ 615　秩ublic-order 迭lternates with people's faith...　　秩 1538　迭 1537

☐ 616　律egulation inside 津arbours, no wild boars...　　律 0868　津 1043

☐ 617　仮emporary bill 板oard on the 坂lopes had 報eports of smuggled 服lothes...　　仮 0798　板 0427　坂 0350　報 0728　服 0400

☐ 618　妨indrance to machine 紡pinning now thinning...　　妨 1287　紡 1864

☐ 619　肪bese 坊uddhist-monks 防rotect 訪isitors with valour...　　肪 1862　坊 1863　防 0688　訪 0952

☐ 620　汚irty 巧kills 朽ecay fair play...　　汚 1047　巧 1643　朽 1644

☐ 621　但rovided, patient's father 担ears a strong 胆all-bladder...　　但 1928　担 0965　胆 1348

☐ 622　垣ences around the maze confuse 恒lways...　　垣 1350　恒 1349

☐ 623　伯ount's 伯lder-uncle in a 舶hip 泊leeping-over to the 拍empo of a Harlem rapper...　　伯 1282　舶 1231　泊 1283　拍 1284

☐ 624　設et-up for 殺urder, 没unken cadaver...　　　　設 0700　殺 0539　没 1126

☐ 625　毆unch 投hrown by 役fficial facing dismissal...　　毆 1940　投 0424　役 0328

☐ 626　飢tarving in distress, 肌kinny writer at his 机esk...　飢 1371　肌 1372　机 0973

☐ 627　航avigation maps in a 坑haft placed by 抗esistance in Gdansk...　航 0590　坑 1630　抗 1080

☐ 628　往oming-&-going, clients 注ouring into the 住esidence with huge 柱illars & 駐arking fence...　往 0781　注 0320　住 0261　柱 0386　駐 1036

☐ 629　訳ranslation 釈xplains why the 沢wamp was 択hosen by Keynes...　訳 0860　釈 1034　沢 1164　択 1163

☐ 630　起wake to 配istribute The Times 配elivery route...　起 0327　配 0367

☐ 631　High 租evies so 粗ough 阻mpede our crops...　租 1221　粗 1222　阻 1223

☐ 632　沿long a 船hip decrepit, toxic 鉛ead creeps...　沿 0996　船 0199　鉛 1625

☐ 633　Material 裕ffluence can 溶issolve prudence...　裕 1436　溶 1437

☐ 634　劇rama script of "Crime & 罰unishment," 刷rinted for comments...　劇 0892　罰 1107　刷 0615

☐ 635　酔runkards 砕mashed a photo 枠rame, 粋urely as a game...　酔 1719　砕 1720　枠 1908　粋 1718

☐ 636　挟orked-road 狭arrows to the 峡avine of sparrows...　挟 1405　狭 1404　峡 1403

☐ 637　Rare 酸cid to 唆ntice 俊enius mice...　酸 0689　唆 1851　俊 1850

☐ 638　派actions of 衆eoples' 脈eins to 派ispatch Citizen Kane...　派 0912　衆 0891　脈 0604

☐ 639　Beneath the 桟lank-bridge, 銭oins of Nemo 残emain in a 浅hallow...　銭 0717　残 0553　浅 0552　桟 1907

☐ 640　寝leeping 侵nvader, 浸mmersed in cider...　寝 1217　侵 1215　浸 1216

☐ 641　退ithdrawal of age 限imits brightened the 眼yes of hermits...　退 0769　限 0770　眼 0771

☐ 642　根oots of 恨rudges: 銀ilver coins for judges...　根 0308　恨 1761　銀 0307

☐ 643　校roofreading of "校chool 較omparison" to end, deadline 絞ightened　校 0056　校 0056　較 1489　絞 1488

☐ 644　雄ourage of 離eparated 雄asculine 稚hildren praised so often...　雄 1432　離 1353　雄 1432　離 1353

☐ 645　雑arious friends 推ecommend the 准unior trend...　雑 0699　推 0957　准 1322

☐ 646　紛ixture of curry 粉owder, 紛istracted my clam chowder...　紛 1712　粉 0639　紛 1712

☐ 647　縫ewing kit left at the 峰ummit...　縫 1400　峰 1401

☐ 648　語alks that 悟nlighten, never forgotten...　語 0100　悟 1477

☐ 649　硫ulphur we don't know, poison to 流low...　硫 1861　流 0285

☐ 650　禅en-Buddhists 弾laying-music, as 弾ullets 弾ounce in the attic...　禅 1567　弾 1566　弾 1566　弾 1566

☐ 651　Napoleon's 植lants 値rice & 値alue 殖ncreased in Waterloo...　植 0343　値 0840　値 0840　殖 1536

☐ 652　帰eturning house 婦ife with a 掃weeping device...　帰 0189　婦 0653　掃 1218

☐ 653　論heory on 倫thics 論iscussed in the 輪ircles of the Olympics...　輪 0620　論 0831　倫 1274

☐ 654　探earching 深eep & 深ntense with Sherlock's lens...　　探 0848　深 0371　深 0371

☐ 655　症ickness needs 証vidence for school absence...　　症 1379　証 0681

☐ 656　With 酒lcohol, reflexes 猶elay whatever you say...　　酒 0368　猶 1606

☐ 657　Boxers 軽ightweight 経anage to 経ass-thru unknown fate...　　軽 0375　経 0693

☐ 658　請equest for 晴lear sky-wide, pilots' 精igourous 情eelings 清urified...　　請 1041　晴 0231　精 0721　情 0646　清 0557

☐ 659　諸arious seatbelt 緒traps buckle astronauts' lap...　　諸 0904　緒 1091

☐ 660　俳ctors dare not 排eject a Spielberg project....　　俳 0927　排 1188

☐ 661　違ifferent 衛roops on 緯orizontal cadence 衛uarding His 偉minence...　　違 1076　衛 0762　緯 1198　偉 1197

☐ 662　渦hirlpool of 過xcessive 禍alamity bred a tsunami...　　渦 1815　過 0667　禍 1814

☐ 663　Rubber 滴xtracts to be 摘lucked from tree cracks...　　滴 1482　摘 1483

☐ 664　No 潮urrent in the 湖ake, 朗ladness to a boating date...　　朗 1003　潮 0841　湖 0358

☐ 665　Tales of 裁ustices lavish 裁lothes, 載ublished in 載oads...　　裁 0940　裁 0940　載 1247　載 1247

☐ 666　Pineapple 栽aplings, lots of 繊bre strings...　　栽 1248　繊 1594

☐ 667　権uthority's might to 確nsure civil 権ights...　　権 0834　確 0704　権 0834

☐ 668　嫌espise being 謙umble, get into trouble...　　嫌 1700　謙 1699

☐ 669　Donor of 髄one-marrow to 賄urnish tomorrow...　　髄 1747　賄 1746

☐ 670　To ruin he went, 随ollowing his Dad's 堕escent...　　随 1748　堕 1749

☐ 671　喝colding without mercy got my boss so 渇hirsty...　　喝 1920　渇 1638

☐ 672　謁udience with the Crown after 掲oisting-a-flag that's 褐rown...　　謁 1921　褐 1639　掲 1640

☐ 673　謡oh-chantings kept 陶orcelains 揺haking...　　謡 1661　陶 1664　揺 1662

☐ 674　捕eizure of store 補upplements, owner vehement...　　捕 1109　補 0906

☐ 675　A 舗tore by the 浦eashore sells only liquor...　　舗 1481　浦 1480

☐ 676　現resent teaching 規tandards, 視bserved at Harvard...　　現 0652　規 0705　視 0862

☐ 677　Furious 偶pouse 偶ccasionally at the 隅orner of my house...　　偶 1654　隅 1655

☐ 678　紹ntroduced by King Federick, fair 詔mperial-edicts...　　紹 1016　詔 1889

☐ 679　焼oasted steak, served at 暁aybreak...　　焼 0605　暁 1670

☐ 680　旗anner of 棋hess hung in Budapest...　　旗 0613　棋 1840

☐ 681　換eplacing salmon got him police 喚ummons...　　換 1609　喚 1610

☐ 682　援upport once 暖arm, when 緩oosened may harm...　　援 1226　暖 0867　緩 1227

☐ 683　績chievement of 積umulative 債ebt, left only 漬ickles in my wallet...　　績 0801　積 0555　債 1244　漬 1798

☐ 684　嫁aughter-in-law found 稼aking-a-living by the 塚ound...　　嫁 1756　稼 1757　塚 1758

□ 685 略ummary of patients' 落ollapse, heart 絡onnexions perhaps... 略 0768　落 0412　絡 1085

□ 686 膜embranes X-ray 模atterns look too 漠bscure to configure... 膜 1468　模 0984　漠 1469

□ 687 護rotect thy 穫arvest & 獲cquired interest... 護 0811　穫 1376　獲 1375

□ 688 Size of 腹tomach 複ultiplies with large fries... 腹 0964　複 0779

□ 689 鎮alm & 慎iscreet, residents in Crete... 鎮 1791　慎 1790

□ 690 頭ead 煩nxiety for those fiesty... 頭 0180　煩 1854

□ 691 Smiling 顔ace 傾nclines to gaze... 顔 0181　傾 1479

□ 692 A 頑tubborn 題opic: 頒istribution of narcotics... 頑 1853　題 0317　頒 1855

□ 693 Sheep 飼reeding to soar for King's 嗣uccessor... 飼 0823　嗣 1918

□ 694 A 僧uddhist-monk once said: 増ncrease of 憎atred consumes the hater instead... 僧 1416　増 0733　憎 1415

□ 695 層ayers of 贈ifts to send by airlift... 層 0981　贈 1414

□ 696 Magic 鏡irror at the 境oundary in East Timor... 鏡 0598　境 0772

□ 697 隠idden 穏ranquillity in the islands of Tahiti... 隠 1095　穏 1096

□ 698 緑reen Peace laments 録ecord on 緑nvironment... 緑 0372　録 0532　緑 0372

□ 699 鳴owling 鶏hickens, when dawn thickens... 鳴 0238　鶏 1122

□ 700 Their defences 徹ierced, troops 撤ithdraw in tears... 徹 1465　撤 1466

□ 701 Be of good 徳irtue, 聴isten to your curfew... 徳 0796　聴 1190

□ 702 慢rrogant & 慢luggish officialdom at 漫andom... 慢 1453　漫 1454

□ 703 獣east so 黙ilent, turned out violent... 獣 1605　黙 1601

□ 704 壊estroyed encyclopaedia left only 懐ostalgia... 壊 1451　懐 1452

□ 705 墳ncient tombs 憤nraged, 噴pew-out plague... 墳 1674　憤 1673　噴 1672

□ 706 曜eekday of happy 躍umping, after dish 濯ashing... 曜 0083　躍 1584　濯 1585

□ 707 繰pinning to 操perate, need to concentrate... 繰 1667　操 1000

□ 708 藻ater-plants, 燥rying-up so fragrant... 藻 1669　燥 1668

□ 709 Farmer to 譲oncede, his 壌ertile cows breed... 譲 1178　　壌 1913

□ 710 醸rewer's 嬢aughter prefers tonic water... 醸 1842　嬢 1841

□ 711 職areer in 織nitting cottage, a skilled 識nowledge... 職 0660　織 0725　識 0726

□ 712 濫xcessive 鑑attern of 艦arships needs 鑑ppraisal for reversal... 濫 1944　艦 1677　鑑 1676　鑑 1676

X. Uncommon Commons

□ 713 三hree blind men in 一ne town climbing 上p & 下own... 三 0004　一 0002　上 0028　下 0027

□ 714 邸esidence 底ottom cool in autumn... 邸 1028　底 0536

□ 715 Fabulous 冠rown of 冗edundant clowns... 冠 1632　冗 1631

□ 716 A warden's 恩indness to all, 因ause of 囚risoner 困rouble... 恩 0696　因 0695　囚 1295　困 0853

□ 717 会eeting in 陰hadows, 陰idden John Does... 会 0141　陰 1094　陰 1094

□ 718 諮nquire how rice should be 炊ooked from a Chinese book... 諮 1774　炊 1796

□ 719 別pecial 号igns & 号umbers for 別eparated members... 別 0469　号 0293　別 0469

☐ 720 Pot-bellied 胴orso of an 興ntertaining virtuoso...   胴 1368 興 0659
☐ 721 尋nquiry so 急rgent on 当his detergent..!   尋 1220 急 0301 当 0108
☐ 722 印tamps of Ulysses Grant in the 潟agoon of   印 0614 潟 1642 虐 1597
        虐yrants...
☐ 723 来ome & 味aste wasabi paste...   来 0102 味 0303
☐ 724 理ogic in 裏everse, 理eason perversed...   理 0134 裏 0830 理 0134
☐ 725 Contour of 野ields & 野lains by 序rder of rains...   野 0170 野 0170 序 0751
☐ 726 In any 領erritory, no guts 零ero glory...   領 0766 零 1828
☐ 727 Sound 策olicies 刺ierce for many years...   策 0905 刺 1104
☐ 728 窮xtreme 謝pologies for being rude with no   窮 1111 謝 0777 謝 0777
        謝ratitude...
☐ 729 荷reight on the 河iver, 歌inging boatmen to   荷 0332 河 0664 歌 0201
        deliver...
☐ 730 示hown in all 宗eligions, 崇espect & devotion...   示 0708 宗 0863 崇 1467
☐ 731 逮rrested for hidden wealth, 隷ervants in good   逮 1110 隷 1935 康 0602
        康ealth...
☐ 732 徐lowly going, 塗ainting 途ngoing...   徐 1206 塗 1212 途 1211
☐ 733 In 産hildbirth, life is 産roduced the 牲ictim of   産 0470 産 0470 牲 1055
        pain cannot refuse...
☐ 734 充upply of 銃irearms won't 統ontrol 育pbringing   充 1082 銃 1083 統 0765 育 0284
        in trouble...
☐ 735 瓶ottles 併ombined near the 塀ence behind...   瓶 1272 併 1273 塀 1810
☐ 736 茎tems' 径iameter of a cactus, quite   茎 1508 径 0634 怪 1509
        怪uspicious...
☐ 737 虞hreat of one's 誤istake will never make...   虞 1941 誤 0910
☐ 738 No 涯uter-limits of 佳eauty in the 封eudal   封 1498 涯 1496 佳 1497
        scenery...
☐ 739 浴hower of 俗orldly 欲esire often inspire...   浴 0617 俗 1249 欲 0941
☐ 740 稲ice-plants may 陥all when no rain at all...   稲 1311 陥 1309
☐ 741 強trong 風inds in tornado 風tyle seen from a   強 0164 風 0084 風 0084
        mile...
☐ 742 Flower 香ragrance, 誘empts a romance...   香 1694 誘 1696
☐ 743 逆pposite 塑atterns used for Christmas   逆 0674 塑 1843
        lanterns...
☐ 744 Look 後fter your 後ack for 幽loom may hack...   後 0093 後 0093 幽 1319
☐ 745 修ultivate a balance of 悠eisure from a   修 0785 悠 1619 悠 1619
        悠istance...
☐ 746 宣nnouncement at the 壇odium after the   宣 0864 壇 1844
        symposium...
☐ 747 契ledge of chastity to 喫njoy one's 潔urity...   契 1029 喫 1327 潔 0809
☐ 748 Quality 品roducts & 器evices, 臨ttend to clients   品 0282 器 0527 臨 0897
        the highest...
☐ 749 奥nsiders' 迷onfusion at 菊hrysanthemum's   奥 1019 菊 1018 迷 0787
        evolution...
☐ 750 害njury to the 憲onstitution, not the solution...   害 0523 憲 0845
☐ 751 粛ilent officers to 粛urge 庸ediocres...   粛 1707 庸 1708
☐ 752 恐cared 築rchitect hiding in Czech...   恐 1624 築 0818
☐ 753 琴ither music 班quad playing a ballad...   琴 1335 班 0983
☐ 754 弱eak waves at the 湾ay near Bombay...   弱 0165 湾 1044

☐ 755 豪ustralian 家amily 家xpert built a 家ouse for 豚igs that's 豪plendid..!　　豪1683 家 0145 家 0145 豚 1069 豪 1683

☐ 756 寂onely 督ommander married a Hollander...　　寂 1681 督 1682

☐ 757 Cheap 棚abinets soon 崩ollapse like scraps...　　棚 1909 崩 1246

☐ 758 遣ispatch of 貴recious minds, 遺eaving nations in a bind...　　遣 1280 貴 0950 遺 0951

☐ 759 彩olourful 菜egetables, 採dopted in variables...　　彩 1125 菜 0608 採 0783

☐ 760 遠istant 園arden, in fact a 猿onkey's den...　　遠 0212 園 0213 猿 1607

☐ 761 Cremation 管ipes 管ontrol 棺offins in a 館ublic-hall...　　管 0484 管 0484 棺 1830 館 0311

☐ 762 準emi ghostly belief, 焦ocus on the 礁oral reef...　　焦 1167 準 0752 礁 1773

☐ 763 隣eighbours 瞬link at Sara's 傑xcellent mink...　　隣 1073 瞬 1740 傑 1739

☐ 764 諭dmonished for drinking 愉leasures, 癒ecuperating from heart seizure...　　諭 1621 愉 1620 癒 1622

☐ 765 触ouch a tortoise, hear a 濁urky 騒oise...　　触 1098 濁 1641 騒 1099

☐ 766 膨ulging corpus, like a 鼓rum in the 樹ush...　　膨 1261 鼓 1263 樹 0945

☐ 767 With 漢anjiHybrid no more 難ifficulties or grief, what a 嘆igh of relief...　　漢 0376 難 0852 嘆 1331

☐ 768 In a 暫hile, arriving 漸radual at the Nile...　　暫 1443 漸 1444

☐ 769 Light 紫urple, a 雌emale colour...　　紫 1434 雌 1433

☐ 770 Glamour 欄ulletin 潤mbellished for teens...　　欄 1300 潤 1301

☐ 771 湿oisture 顕pparent in summer tents...　　湿 1278 顕 1279

☐ 772 湯ot-water under the 陽un 易mply causes 傷njury to some...　　湯 0393 陽 0392 易 0747 傷 0866

☐ 773 薫ragrant 勲xploits don't 衝ollide in Detroit...　　薫 1779 勲 1778 衝 1777

☐ 774 鬼evils 卑espise 魂pirits that are nice...　　鬼 1552 卑 1550 魂 1554

☐ 775 Forgotten 碑ombstones, 塊umps of the Unknown...　　碑 1551 塊 1553

☐ 776 険teep 倹rugality to the core, a 剣word 検nspector...　　険 0691 倹 1102 剣 1103 検 0690

☐ 777 得dvantage to 待ait, fish to bait...　　得 0494 待 0353

☐ 778 Some 脱emove revenue before a 税ax 閲eview...　　脱 1419 税 0666 閲 1418

☐ 779 Too 悦leasant 説xplanations carry 鋭harp implications...　　悦 1417 説 0499 鋭 1420

☐ 780 様anner of 911 遅elay, 詳etails must convey....　　様 0336 遅 1050 詳 1600

☐ 781 閣abinet 閥liques in 闘ombat for power in Rabat...　　閣 0898 閥 1540 闘 1541

☐ 782 極xtreme 誇oast creates woes...　　極 0488 誇 1645

XI. Zigzag

☐ 783 郵ostal workers 睡sleep, when parcels missed the ship...　　郵 0846 睡 1210

☐ 784 Not to 伴ccompany 判udgements with money...　　伴 1185 判 0793

☐ 785 Either 倍ultiply or 剖ivide, stock markets ride...　　倍 0248 剖 1835

☐ 786 形hapes neatly 研olished look varnished...　　形 0202 研 0416

☐ 787 欧uropean tarots, Old World's 枢ivot...　　欧 1182 枢 1183

☐ 788 助ssistance from 祖ncestors made us victors...　　助 0391 祖 0710

☐ 789 辞uit 括undling forensics with 辞hetoric...　　辞 0563 括 1341 辞 0563

☐ 790 勅mperial-edics illuminate, not 疎lienate...   勅 1890 疎 1544 疎 1544
☐ 791 招nvited after a nap, a child 拐idnapped...   招 0676 拐 1917
☐ 792 部art of the 陪ury believed another theory...   部 0247 陪 1943
☐ 793 Friends' 継ontinuing 断efusal, highly unusual...   継 1184 断 0792
☐ 794 訓nstructions on word 順equence led to   訓 0581 順 0580
        coherence...
☐ 795 Unburied 故eceased 枯ithering with disease...   故 0643 枯 1148
☐ 796 Narcotic 剤rugs, 済ettled by thugs...   剤 1026 済 0851
☐ 797 謹espectful 勤mployees fired the least...   謹 1332 勤 0854
☐ 798 Distance 隔ntervals 融issolve with click &   隔 1612 融 1611
        portal...
☐ 799 厚hick writing of 願equests to the King...   厚 0714 願 0541
☐ 800 豊bundant harvest, farmers' 喜appiness...   豊 0786 喜 0618
☐ 801 Direct 嫡eirs of my 敵nemy, now after me..!   嫡 1933 敵 0669
☐ 802 貯tore-up savings net 寧ather-than be   貯 0577 寧 1455 寧 1455
        寧ourteous & 寧uiet...
☐ 803 割amaged steel 轄edge, 割ivided the bridge   割 0844 轄 1290 割 0844
        edge...
☐ 804 醜gly 魅harm does no harm...   醜 1556 魅 1555
☐ 805 乳ilk bottle that 浮loats thrown from a boat...   乳 0915 浮 1129
☐ 806 Golden 卵ggs for-free by the 柳illow-tree...   卵 0929 柳 1876
☐ 807 劾mpeached at a 刻oint-in-time, dictator turned   劾 1939 刻 0955
        刻culptor...
☐ 808 The 該[said] nations possess 核uclear   該 1306 核 1305
        weapons...
☐ 809 端xtreme 耐ndurance tests mind tolerance...   端 1461 耐 1458
☐ 810 鋼teel gong must be solid 剛trong...   鋼 0997 剛 1627
☐ 811 璽mperial-seal coming soon, for the movie,   璽 1891 繭 1912
        " 繭ocoon..."

1,945 Jōyō Kanji Characters: Checklist II

Note: Once you have mastered a Kanji character, place a check mark in the box. By "mastery", that would mean your ability to recognize its **core meaning** beyond the need of *KanjiHybrids*. Then, write the date on the underlined space like "01/01" in order to monitor your learning progress. The corresponding page number is on the right side.

First Grade

_____	☐ 0001 人	2
_____	☐ 0002 一	858
_____	☐ 0003 二	457
_____	☐ 0004 三	858
_____	☐ 0005 日	14
_____	☐ 0006 四	17
_____	☐ 0007 五	86
_____	☐ 0008 六	3
_____	☐ 0009 七	72
_____	☐ 0010 八	4
_____	☐ 0011 九	73
_____	☐ 0012 十	344
_____	☐ 0013 円	24
_____	☐ 0014 百	14
_____	☐ 0015 千	74
_____	☐ 0016 月	22
_____	☐ 0017 火	3
_____	☐ 0018 水	9
_____	☐ 0019 木	461
_____	☐ 0020 金	25
_____	☐ 0021 土	8
_____	☐ 0022 本	461
_____	☐ 0023 大	7
_____	☐ 0024 小	459
_____	☐ 0025 中	85
_____	☐ 0026 雨	417
_____	☐ 0027 下	859
_____	☐ 0028 上	859
_____	☐ 0029 川	76
_____	☐ 0030 山	172
_____	☐ 0031 田	482
_____	☐ 0032 生	474
_____	☐ 0033 年	27
_____	☐ 0034 先	478
_____	☐ 0035 入	2
_____	☐ 0036 出	173
_____	☐ 0037 口	458
_____	☐ 0038 目	462
_____	☐ 0039 耳	228
_____	☐ 0040 手	370
_____	☐ 0041 足	481
_____	☐ 0042 休	347

_____	☐ 0043 見	307
_____	☐ 0044 左	310
_____	☐ 0045 右	87
_____	☐ 0046 石	363
_____	☐ 0047 夕	187
_____	☐ 0048 名	425
_____	☐ 0049 力	351
_____	☐ 0050 男	597
_____	☐ 0051 女	350
_____	☐ 0052 子	456
_____	☐ 0053 学	346
_____	☐ 0054 字	346
_____	☐ 0055 文	558
_____	☐ 0056 校	773
_____	☐ 0057 立	234
_____	☐ 0058 林	526
_____	☐ 0059 森	526
_____	☐ 0060 竹	79
_____	☐ 0061 車	306
_____	☐ 0062 気	98
_____	☐ 0063 空	394
_____	☐ 0064 天	83
_____	☐ 0065 町	174
_____	☐ 0066 村	690
_____	☐ 0067 白	15
_____	☐ 0068 赤	261
_____	☐ 0069 青	115
_____	☐ 0070 貝	516
_____	☐ 0071 糸	375
_____	☐ 0072 早	373
_____	☐ 0073 草	373
_____	☐ 0074 花	191
_____	☐ 0075 正	30
_____	☐ 0076 犬	7
_____	☐ 0077 王	12
_____	☐ 0078 玉	11
_____	☐ 0079 音	314
_____	☐ 0080 虫	369

Second Grade

_____	☐ 0081 万	465
_____	☐ 0082 明	22
_____	☐ 0083 曜	849

_____	☐ 0084 風	894
_____	☐ 0085 刀	353
_____	☐ 0086 分	518
_____	☐ 0087 切	352
_____	☐ 0088 国	92
_____	☐ 0089 寺	248
_____	☐ 0090 時	653
_____	☐ 0091 間	286
_____	☐ 0092 前	118
_____	☐ 0093 後	897
_____	☐ 0094 午	178
_____	☐ 0095 今	182
_____	☐ 0096 体	347
_____	☐ 0097 自	462
_____	☐ 0098 聞	282
_____	☐ 0099 言	251
_____	☐ 0100 語	780
_____	☐ 0101 行	79
_____	☐ 0102 来	871
_____	☐ 0103 方	533
_____	☐ 0104 東	220
_____	☐ 0105 西	18
_____	☐ 0106 北	372
_____	☐ 0107 南	414
_____	☐ 0108 当	869
_____	☐ 0109 外	188
_____	☐ 0110 内	297
_____	☐ 0111 半	484
_____	☐ 0112 回	458
_____	☐ 0113 週	279
_____	☐ 0114 長	273
_____	☐ 0115 心	469
_____	☐ 0116 思	596
_____	☐ 0117 用	409
_____	☐ 0118 電	417
_____	☐ 0119 母	90
_____	☐ 0120 父	467
_____	☐ 0121 交	467
_____	☐ 0122 毎	241
_____	☐ 0123 海	241
_____	☐ 0124 地	688
_____	☐ 0125 池	689
_____	☐ 0126 公	180

☐ 0127 書 116	☐ 0174 買 516	☐ 0221 角 400
☐ 0128 汽 98	☐ 0175 読 260	☐ 0222 止 192
☐ 0129 原 431	☐ 0176 教 385	☐ 0223 台 209
☐ 0130 元 195	☐ 0177 茶 120	☐ 0224 考 392
☐ 0131 光 77	☐ 0178 友 408	☐ 0225 才 185
☐ 0132 工 176	☐ 0179 麦 606	☐ 0226 羽 240
☐ 0133 里 321	☐ 0180 頭 832	☐ 0227 太 6
☐ 0134 理 872	☐ 0181 顔 833	☐ 0228 雲 154
☐ 0135 少 459	☐ 0182 牛 179	☐ 0229 丸 73
☐ 0136 首 311	☐ 0183 馬 318	☐ 0230 谷 492
☐ 0137 道 312	☐ 0184 鳥 125	☐ 0231 晴 792
☐ 0138 通 59	☐ 0185 毛 468	☐ 0232 広 205
☐ 0139 戸 428	☐ 0186 魚 49	☐ 0233 細 138
☐ 0140 場 147	☐ 0187 線 531	☐ 0234 星 113
☐ 0141 会 864	☐ 0188 社 703	☐ 0235 声 428
☐ 0142 合 232	☐ 0189 帰 784	☐ 0236 算 141
☐ 0143 答 232	☐ 0190 科 194	☐ 0237 黄 197
☐ 0144 門 286	☐ 0191 食 255	☐ 0238 鳴 842
☐ 0145 家 909	☐ 0192 図 47	☐ 0239 雪 136
☐ 0146 室 485	☐ 0193 計 692	☐ 0240 岩 29
☐ 0147 店 222	☐ 0194 画 35	
☐ 0148 点 222	☐ 0195 絵 143	**Third Grade**
☐ 0149 古 477	☐ 0196 楽 447	☐ 0241 畑 482
☐ 0150 新 668	☐ 0197 作 724	☐ 0242 身 504
☐ 0151 親 69	☐ 0198 記 728	☐ 0243 取 229
☐ 0152 紙 489	☐ 0199 船 757	☐ 0244 物 647
☐ 0153 市 304	☐ 0200 何 101	☐ 0245 事 116
☐ 0154 番 338	☐ 0201 歌 878	☐ 0246 死 513
☐ 0155 京 386	☐ 0202 形 951	☐ 0247 部 957
☐ 0156 高 435	☐ 0203 弟 102	☐ 0248 倍 950
☐ 0157 同 245	☐ 0204 兄 203	☐ 0249 全 24
☐ 0158 色 403	☐ 0205 姉 114	☐ 0250 発 368
☐ 0159 黒 320	☐ 0206 妹 114	☐ 0251 安 350
☐ 0160 弓 348	☐ 0207 組 138	☐ 0252 他 688
☐ 0161 矢 18	☐ 0208 直 420	☐ 0253 和 103
☐ 0162 知 103	☐ 0209 走 497	☐ 0254 筆 141
☐ 0163 引 348	☐ 0210 歩 272	☐ 0255 意 340
☐ 0164 強 894	☐ 0211 近 184	☐ 0256 相 524
☐ 0165 弱 908	☐ 0212 遠 916	☐ 0257 想 524
☐ 0166 肉 297	☐ 0213 園 916	☐ 0258 路 405
☐ 0167 米 77	☐ 0214 冬 397	☐ 0259 所 676
☐ 0168 数 156	☐ 0215 春 579	☐ 0260 主 11
☐ 0169 多 187	☐ 0216 夏 606	☐ 0261 住 750
☐ 0170 野 873	☐ 0217 秋 415	☐ 0262 間 283
☐ 0171 活 237	☐ 0218 朝 662	☐ 0263 員 410
☐ 0172 話 236	☐ 0219 昼 575	☐ 0264 者 278
☐ 0173 売 259	☐ 0220 夜 508	☐ 0265 屋 427

_____ ☐ 0407 横 *197*	_____ ☐ 0452 街 *107*	_____ ☐ 0499 説 *943*
_____ ☐ 0408 血 *20*	_____ ☐ 0453 付 *382*	_____ ☐ 0500 養 *253*
_____ ☐ 0409 君 *258*	_____ ☐ 0454 郡 *258*	_____ ☐ 0501 量 *451*
_____ ☐ 0410 鼻 *169*	_____ ☐ 0455 共 *302*	_____ ☐ 0502 要 *419*
_____ ☐ 0411 庫 *306*	_____ ☐ 0456 満 *567*	_____ ☐ 0503 置 *420*
_____ ☐ 0412 落 *826*	_____ ☐ 0457 的 *696*	_____ ☐ 0504 徒 *497*
_____ ☐ 0413 消 *265*	_____ ☐ 0458 約 *697*	_____ ☐ 0505 伝 *619*
_____ ☐ 0414 章 *324*	_____ ☐ 0459 類 *156*	_____ ☐ 0506 芸 *619*
_____ ☐ 0415 究 *575*	_____ ☐ 0460 種 *430*	_____ ☐ 0507 軍 *295*
_____ ☐ 0416 研 *951*	_____ ☐ 0461 働 *422*	_____ ☐ 0508 連 *305*
_____ ☐ 0417 係 *263*	_____ ☐ 0462 労 *351*	_____ ☐ 0509 達 *267*
_____ ☐ 0418 豆 *519*	_____ ☐ 0463 協 *577*	_____ ☐ 0510 節 *421*
_____ ☐ 0419 登 *437*	_____ ☐ 0464 続 *260*	_____ ☐ 0511 季 *583*
_____ ☐ 0420 皮 *224*	_____ ☐ 0465 変 *581*	_____ ☐ 0512 歴 *595*
_____ ☐ 0421 昭 *529*	_____ ☐ 0466 愛 *593*	_____ ☐ 0513 結 *227*
_____ ☐ 0422 遊 *650*	_____ ☐ 0467 成 *244*	_____ ☐ 0514 果 *287*
_____ ☐ 0423 打 *636*	_____ ☐ 0468 最 *423*	_____ ☐ 0515 課 *287*
_____ ☐ 0424 投 *745*	_____ ☐ 0469 別 *866*	_____ ☐ 0516 治 *210*
_____ ☐ 0425 悲 *289*	_____ ☐ 0470 産 *883*	_____ ☐ 0517 堂 *94*
_____ ☐ 0426 指 *242*	_____ ☐ 0471 特 *250*	_____ ☐ 0518 賞 *554*
_____ ☐ 0427 板 *732*	_____ ☐ 0472 議 *341*	_____ ☐ 0519 束 *502*
_____ ☐ 0428 箱 *616*	_____ ☐ 0473 単 *517*	_____ ☐ 0520 府 *429*
_____ ☐ 0429 皿 *21*	_____ ☐ 0474 戦 *517*	_____ ☐ 0521 敗 *137*
_____ ☐ 0430 帳 *641*	_____ ☐ 0475 争 *231*	_____ ☐ 0522 改 *725*
_____ ☐ 0431 庭 *27*	_____ ☐ 0476 末 *13*	_____ ☐ 0523 害 *904*
_____ ☐ 0432 秒 *727*	_____ ☐ 0477 未 *12*	_____ ☐ 0524 必 *218*
_____ ☐ 0433 追 *108*	_____ ☐ 0478 失 *19*	_____ ☐ 0525 毒 *578*
_____ ☐ 0434 氷 *10*	_____ ☐ 0479 夫 *83*	_____ ☐ 0526 試 *418*
_____ ☐ 0435 泳 *729*	_____ ☐ 0480 料 *194*	_____ ☐ 0527 器 *902*
_____ ☐ 0436 息 *586*	_____ ☐ 0481 良 *253*	_____ ☐ 0528 機 *547*
_____ ☐ 0437 炭 *29*	_____ ☐ 0482 飯 *256*	_____ ☐ 0529 械 *493*
_____ ☐ 0438 福 *333*	_____ ☐ 0483 官 *105*	_____ ☐ 0530 飛 *298*
_____ ☐ 0439 拾 *231*	_____ ☐ 0484 管 *917*	_____ ☐ 0531 験 *673*
_____ ☐ 0440 笛 *630*	_____ ☐ 0485 利 *686*	_____ ☐ 0532 録 *841*
	_____ ☐ 0486 便 *480*	_____ ☐ 0533 老 *149*
Fourth Grade	_____ ☐ 0487 史 *85*	_____ ☐ 0534 材 *186*
_____ ☐ 0441 以 *472*	_____ ☐ 0488 極 *947*	_____ ☐ 0535 低 *700*
_____ ☐ 0442 周 *280*	_____ ☐ 0489 給 *143*	_____ ☐ 0536 底 *860*
_____ ☐ 0443 無 *49*	_____ ☐ 0490 英 *217*	_____ ☐ 0537 氏 *489*
_____ ☐ 0444 不 *300*	_____ ☐ 0491 昨 *722*	_____ ☐ 0538 士 *8*
_____ ☐ 0445 好 *637*	_____ ☐ 0492 典 *476*	_____ ☐ 0539 殺 *744*
_____ ☐ 0446 案 *609*	_____ ☐ 0493 紀 *727*	_____ ☐ 0540 念 *182*
_____ ☐ 0447 位 *235*	_____ ☐ 0494 得 *940*	_____ ☐ 0541 願 *964*
_____ ☐ 0448 法 *360*	_____ ☐ 0495 席 *91*	_____ ☐ 0542 博 *514*
_____ ☐ 0449 省 *572*	_____ ☐ 0496 億 *340*	_____ ☐ 0543 観 *667*
_____ ☐ 0450 信 *252*	_____ ☐ 0497 欠 *460*	_____ ☐ 0544 覚 *307*
_____ ☐ 0451 民 *495*	_____ ☐ 0498 関 *284*	_____ ☐ 0545 側 *291*

_____	☐ 0685 常	94	_____	☐ 0732 弁	570	_____	☐ 0779 複	830
_____	☐ 0686 非	288	_____	☐ 0733 増	837	_____	☐ 0780 復	442
_____	☐ 0687 券	406	_____	☐ 0734 富	333	_____	☐ 0781 往	749
_____	☐ 0688 防	736	_____	☐ 0735 減	46	_____	☐ 0782 桜	127
_____	☐ 0689 酸	764	_____	☐ 0736 益	622	_____	☐ 0783 採	915
_____	☐ 0690 検	939	_____	☐ 0737 営	580	_____	☐ 0784 承	117
_____	☐ 0691 険	938	_____	☐ 0738 件	179	_____	☐ 0785 修	898
_____	☐ 0692 輸	660	_____	☐ 0739 許	180	_____	☐ 0786 豊	965
_____	☐ 0693 経	791	_____	☐ 0740 像	530	_____	☐ 0787 迷	904
_____	☐ 0694 財	186	_____	☐ 0741 絶	403	_____	☐ 0788 述	95
_____	☐ 0695 因	862	_____	☐ 0742 賛	334	_____	☐ 0789 個	491
_____	☐ 0696 恩	862	_____	☐ 0743 貸	145	_____	☐ 0790 構	714
_____	☐ 0697 条	607	_____	☐ 0744 資	626	_____	☐ 0791 暴	561
_____	☐ 0698 志	426	_____	☐ 0745 貧	594	_____	☐ 0792 断	958
_____	☐ 0699 雑	776	_____	☐ 0746 賀	202	_____	☐ 0793 判	949
_____	☐ 0700 設	743	_____	☐ 0747 易	933	_____	☐ 0794 評	701
_____	☐ 0701 仏	683	_____	☐ 0748 貿	128	_____	☐ 0795 武	100
_____	☐ 0702 刊	687	_____	☐ 0749 留	128	_____	☐ 0796 徳	844
_____	☐ 0703 授	539	_____	☐ 0750 備	409	_____	☐ 0797 版	359
_____	☐ 0704 確	804	_____	☐ 0751 序	873	_____	☐ 0798 仮	732
_____	☐ 0705 規	814	_____	☐ 0752 準	919	_____	☐ 0799 余	501
_____	☐ 0706 則	290	_____	☐ 0753 再	225	_____	☐ 0800 張	274
_____	☐ 0707 測	291	_____	☐ 0754 講	226	_____	☐ 0801 績	822
_____	☐ 0708 示	878	_____	☐ 0755 率	142	_____	☐ 0802 移	188
_____	☐ 0709 際	328	_____	☐ 0756 舎	388	_____	☐ 0803 幹	662
_____	☐ 0710 祖	953	_____	☐ 0757 群	259	_____	☐ 0804 綿	675
_____	☐ 0711 査	624	_____	☐ 0758 比	466	_____	☐ 0805 耕	655
_____	☐ 0712 状	702	_____	☐ 0759 混	38	_____	☐ 0806 永	10
_____	☐ 0713 提	313	_____	☐ 0760 均	470	_____	☐ 0807 久	379
_____	☐ 0714 厚	964	_____	☐ 0761 夢	167	_____	☐ 0808 旧	464
_____	☐ 0715 格	498	_____	☐ 0762 衛	796	_____	☐ 0809 潔	901
_____	☐ 0716 勢	153	_____	☐ 0763 効	645	_____	☐ 0810 舌	236
_____	☐ 0717 銭	767	_____	☐ 0764 応	469	_____	☐ 0811 護	828
_____	☐ 0718 燃	445	_____	☐ 0765 統	885	_____	☐ 0812 災	571
_____	☐ 0719 容	492	_____	☐ 0766 領	874	_____	☐ 0813 圧	632
_____	☐ 0720 責	115	_____	☐ 0767 額	559	_____	☐ 0814 寄	269
_____	☐ 0721 精	792	_____	☐ 0768 略	825	_____	☐ 0815 快	699
_____	☐ 0722 破	715	_____	☐ 0769 退	770	_____	☐ 0816 墓	602
_____	☐ 0723 妻	611	_____	☐ 0770 限	771	_____	☐ 0817 似	472
_____	☐ 0724 布	208	_____	☐ 0771 眼	771	_____	☐ 0818 築	907
_____	☐ 0725 織	855	_____	☐ 0772 境	839	_____	☐ 0819 鉱	206
_____	☐ 0726 識	856	_____	☐ 0773 枝	704	_____	☐ 0820 銅	246
_____	☐ 0727 編	42	_____	☐ 0774 技	200	_____	☐ 0821 属	441
_____	☐ 0728 報	733	_____	☐ 0775 犯	640	_____	☐ 0822 肥	717
_____	☐ 0729 造	267	_____	☐ 0776 罪	289	_____	☐ 0823 飼	835
_____	☐ 0730 総	433	_____	☐ 0777 謝	876	_____	☐ 0824 俵	378
_____	☐ 0731 導	312	_____	☐ 0778 慣	532	_____	☐ 0825 師	483

Sixth Grade

☐ 0966 肺 305		☐ 1011 渡 33		☐ 1058 替 334
☐ 0967 脳 47		☐ 1012 憶 339		☐ 1059 乏 84
☐ 0968 胸 652		☐ 1013 帥 483		☐ 1060 架 202
☐ 0969 蔵 565		☐ 1014 渉 273		☐ 1061 惜 281
☐ 0970 臓 565		☐ 1015 介 365		☐ 1062 盾 407
☐ 0971 覧 592		☐ 1016 紹 816		☐ 1063 矛 568
☐ 0972 我 443		☐ 1017 即 421		☐ 1064 柔 568
☐ 0973 机 747		☐ 1018 菊 903		☐ 1065 込 93
☐ 0974 創 399		☐ 1019 奥 903		☐ 1066 巡 571
☐ 0975 奮 162		☐ 1020 歳 111		☐ 1067 浜 490
☐ 0976 看 623		☐ 1021 企 193		☐ 1068 傘 142
☐ 0977 痛 60		☐ 1022 掌 614		☐ 1069 豚 910
☐ 0978 装 629		☐ 1023 符 582		☐ 1070 誉 252
☐ 0979 灰 632		☐ 1024 圏 391		☐ 1071 褒 552
☐ 0980 忠 475		☐ 1025 与 349		☐ 1072 邦 694
☐ 0981 層 838		☐ 1026 剤 961		☐ 1073 隣 920
☐ 0982 忘 34		☐ 1027 抵 700		☐ 1074 舞 167
☐ 0983 班 908		☐ 1028 邸 860		☐ 1075 葬 513
☐ 0984 模 827		☐ 1029 契 900		☐ 1076 違 796
☐ 0985 暮 601		☐ 1030 婚 637		☐ 1077 郊 645
☐ 0986 幕 601		☐ 1031 侍 249		☐ 1078 攻 635
☐ 0987 頂 134		☐ 1032 払 682		☐ 1079 江 176
☐ 0988 捨 388		☐ 1033 皆 39		☐ 1080 抗 749
☐ 0989 従 551		☐ 1034 釈 752		☐ 1081 床 633
☐ 0990 縦 551		☐ 1035 翻 338		☐ 1082 充 884
☐ 0991 疑 56		☐ 1036 駐 751		☐ 1083 銃 884
☐ 0992 簡 285		☐ 1037 祈 184		☐ 1084 齢 553
☐ 0993 棒 275		☐ 1038 揚 147		☐ 1085 絡 826
☐ 0994 奏 579		☐ 1039 曇 154		☐ 1086 肖 265
☐ 0995 磁 54		☐ 1040 宴 610		☐ 1087 眠 495
☐ 0996 沿 756		☐ 1041 請 791		☐ 1088 況 716
☐ 0997 鋼 975		☐ 1042 浄 230		☐ 1089 影 546
☐ 0998 仁 457		☐ 1043 津 731		☐ 1090 響 452
☐ 0999 揮 126		☐ 1044 湾 909		☐ 1091 緒 794
☐ 1000 操 851		☐ 1045 依 355		☐ 1092 環 165
☐ 1001 糖 439		☐ 1046 執 268		☐ 1093 還 165
☐ 1002 穀 41		☐ 1047 汚 737		☐ 1094 陰 864
☐ 1003 朗 800		☐ 1048 鯨 679		☐ 1095 隠 840
☐ 1004 蚕 628		☐ 1049 鮮 679		☐ 1096 穏 840
☐ 1005 寸 345		☐ 1050 遅 944		☐ 1097 岐 704
☐ 1006 尺 574		☐ 1051 卸 380		☐ 1098 触 923
		☐ 1052 御 380		☐ 1099 騒 924
Middle School		☐ 1053 儀 342		☐ 1100 戒 493
☐ 1007 芝 84		☐ 1054 犠 342		☐ 1101 幾 547
☐ 1008 恋 581		☐ 1055 牲 883		☐ 1102 倹 938
☐ 1009 旬 494		☐ 1056 免 413		☐ 1103 剣 939
☐ 1010 韻 315		☐ 1057 逸 527		☐ 1104 刺 875

☐ 1246 崩 912	☐ 1293 乾 661	☐ 1340 扱 189
☐ 1247 載 802	☐ 1294 井 361	☐ 1341 括 954
☐ 1248 栽 803	☐ 1295 囚 863	☐ 1342 肯 616
☐ 1249 俗 892	☐ 1296 耗 655	☐ 1343 脅 577
☐ 1250 殿 522	☐ 1297 籍 336	☐ 1344 肩 678
☐ 1251 縁 675	☐ 1298 錯 335	☐ 1345 滑 412
☐ 1252 墜 543	☐ 1299 措 282	☐ 1346 膚 69
☐ 1253 遂 479	☐ 1300 欄 930	☐ 1347 肝 711
☐ 1254 逐 479	☐ 1301 潤 930	☐ 1348 胆 740
☐ 1255 懇 164	☐ 1302 涼 386	☐ 1349 恒 741
☐ 1256 墾 164	☐ 1303 凍 221	☐ 1350 垣 740
☐ 1257 拠 473	☐ 1304 詠 729	☐ 1351 悩 48
☐ 1258 繕 450	☐ 1305 核 973	☐ 1352 凶 80
☐ 1259 吉 227	☐ 1306 該 973	☐ 1353 離 775
☐ 1260 詰 228	☐ 1307 診 720	☐ 1354 刈 687
☐ 1261 膨 925	☐ 1308 珍 720	☐ 1355 胞 690
☐ 1262 肢 200	☐ 1309 陥 893	☐ 1356 抱 503
☐ 1263 鼓 925	☐ 1310 恵 545	☐ 1357 賢 598
☐ 1264 髪 408	☐ 1311 稲 893	☐ 1358 堅 599
☐ 1265 彫 721	☐ 1312 穂 545	☐ 1359 緊 599
☐ 1266 劣 572	☐ 1313 菌 52	☐ 1360 繁 434
☐ 1267 抄 726	☐ 1314 畜 528	☐ 1361 巨 206
☐ 1268 妙 726	☐ 1315 蓄 528	☐ 1362 距 207
☐ 1269 杯 299	☐ 1316 玄 358	☐ 1363 拒 207
☐ 1270 偏 43	☐ 1317 弦 358	☐ 1364 胎 652
☐ 1271 遍 43	☐ 1318 幻 88	☐ 1365 怠 570
☐ 1272 瓶 886	☐ 1319 幽 897	☐ 1366 腰 419
☐ 1273 併 886	☐ 1320 稚 776	☐ 1367 腕 651
☐ 1274 倫 787	☐ 1321 維 563	☐ 1368 胴 867
☐ 1275 普 455	☐ 1322 准 777	☐ 1369 洞 246
☐ 1276 譜 455	☐ 1323 唯 642	☐ 1370 餓 443
☐ 1277 霊 444	☐ 1324 房 676	☐ 1371 飢 746
☐ 1278 湿 931	☐ 1325 戻 541	☐ 1372 肌 747
☐ 1279 顕 931	☐ 1326 涙 541	☐ 1373 奪 162
☐ 1280 遣 913	☐ 1327 喫 900	☐ 1374 隻 50
☐ 1281 迫 108	☐ 1328 憩 169	☐ 1375 獲 829
☐ 1282 伯 741	☐ 1329 臭 586	☐ 1376 穫 829
☐ 1283 泊 742	☐ 1330 腐 429	☐ 1377 患 475
☐ 1284 拍 743	☐ 1331 嘆 927	☐ 1378 催 416
☐ 1285 帝 432	☐ 1332 謹 962	☐ 1379 症 788
☐ 1286 締 432	☐ 1333 含 183	☐ 1380 疫 680
☐ 1287 妨 734	☐ 1334 吟 183	☐ 1381 疲 225
☐ 1288 傍 587	☐ 1335 琴 907	☐ 1382 療 67
☐ 1289 亭 393	☐ 1336 叫 693	☐ 1383 寮 67
☐ 1290 轄 968	☐ 1337 吐 703	☐ 1384 僚 66
☐ 1291 軒 710	☐ 1338 吹 642	☐ 1385 丈 463
☐ 1292 汗 710	☐ 1339 及 190	☐ 1386 壮 367

1810 塀 887	1857 賓 161	1904 勺 470
1811 漏 301	1858 尚 99	1905 錘 505
1812 賊 160	1859 宵 264	1906 銑 155
1813 賦 160	1860 硝 264	1907 桟 768
1814 禍 799	1861 硫 781	1908 枠 761
1815 渦 798	1862 肪 735	1909 棚 912
1816 痢 680	1863 坊 736	1910 芋 81
1817 疾 681	1864 紡 735	1911 薪 668
1818 痴 681	1865 羅 563	1912 繭 976
1819 怖 209	1866 罷 322	1913 壊 853
1820 憾 46	1867 釣 697	1914 堪 294
1821 錬 718	1868 酌 696	1915 抹 13
1822 鍛 555	1869 酬 670	1916 搭 146
1823 錠 550	1870 酪 670	1917 拐 956
1824 鎖 665	1871 酵 669	1918 嗣 836
1825 鉢 666	1872 酢 723	1919 嚇 261
1826 鐘 564	1873 尾 468	1920 喝 808
1827 鈴 683	1874 尿 573	1921 謁 809
1828 零 874	1875 泌 219	1922 朕 708
1829 霧 518	1876 柳 971	1923 脹 274
1830 棺 918	1877 杉 721	1924 爵 593
1831 埋 319	1878 桑 608	1925 侯 122
1832 彰 325	1879 昆 38	1926 矯 163
1833 培 698	1880 蛇 654	1927 且 500
1834 賠 698	1881 蚊 654	1928 但 739
1835 剖 950	1882 蛍 628	1929 偵 506
1836 賜 150	1883 蛮 627	1930 曹 326
1837 据 384	1884 駄 674	1931 翁 238
1838 拓 363	1885 騎 673	1932 婆 32
1839 碁 590	1886 駆 674	1933 嫡 966
1840 棋 819	1887 篤 317	1934 奴 44
1841 嬢 854	1888 渓 97	1935 隷 880
1842 醸 854	1889 詔 817	1936 屯 198
1843 塑 896	1890 勅 955	1937 逓 304
1844 壇 899	1891 璽 976	1938 遵 544
1845 塔 146	1892 僕 157	1939 劾 972
1846 楼 127	1893 撲 157	1940 殴 745
1847 栓 25	1894 仙 416	1941 虞 889
1848 附 382	1895 凸 23	1942 痘 519
1849 陵 140	1896 凹 23	1943 陪 957
1850 俊 765	1897 坪 488	1944 濫 856
1851 唆 764	1898 斤 471	1945 畔 484
1852 頻 272	1899 升 298	
1853 頑 834	1900 斗 195	
1854 煩 832	1901 厘 319	
1855 頒 835	1902 畝 379	
1856 寡 161	1903 匁 75	

001-A

No 人erson will 入nter a house on 火ire...

人⇔亻 (person)

人uman 人erson

hito, JIN, NIN

human, person, people, individual, somebody, someone

FLIP: 1.0.b. Whole (stem)

人嫌い *unsociable, extremely shy* **hitogirai**
人殺し *murder, manslaughter* **hitogoroshi**
美人 *pretty woman* **bijin**
婦人 *lady, young woman* **fujin**
夫人 *wife, married woman, Mrs.* **fujin**
人々 *people, crowd* **hitobito**
人柄 *character, personality* **hitogara** *213 - character*
人質 *hostage, kidnap victim* **hitojichi** *528 - hostage*
一人 *one individual* **hitori, ichinin**
法人 *legal entity, incorporated* **hōjin**
人事 *personnel; human affairs* **jinji**
人権 *human rights* **jinken**
人工 *artificial, man-made* **jinkō**
人口 *population* **jinkō**
人民 *citizens, people* **jinmin**
人類 *mankind, humanity* **jinrui**
人生 *human life* **jinsei**
恋人 *boyfriend, girlfriend* **koibito**
仲人 *matchmaker, nakōdo* **695**

人間 *human, person* **ningen**
人魚 *mermaid* **ningyo**
人形 *doll, mannequin* **ningyō**
人気① *popularity, public acclaim* **ninki**
人気② *sign of life* **hitoke**
人数 *number of people* **ninzū**
大人 *adult, grown-up* **otona**
素人 *amateur, novice, greenhorn* **shirōto**
他人 *stranger, another fellow* **tanin**
人道的 *humane, humanitarian* **jindōteki**
見物人 *spectator, audience* **kenbutsunin**
日本人 *Japanese person* **nihonjin, nipponjin**
外国人 *non-Japanese, foreigner* **gaikokujin**

者erson, 278	紳entleman, 713
子hildren, 456	男asculine, 597
家xpert, 909	女emale, 350
士entleman, 8	

001-B

No 人erson will 入nter a house on 火ire...

入 (enter)

入nter 入ut-inside

hai(ru), i(ru), i(reru), NYŪ

enter, get inside, put-inside

FLIP: 2.0.b. Sort Of (stem)
Facing: 1.0. 🦀 West (W)

編入 *change course (university)* **hennyū**
入口 *opening, door* **iriguchi**
介入 *intervention, intercession* **kainyū**
加入 *enter, join* **kanyū**
記入 *write down, record* **kinyū**
購入 *buy, purchase* **kōnyū**
密入 *smuggling* **mitsunyū**
入学 *school admissions* **nyūgaku**
入費 *entrance-, admission fee* **nyūhi**
入院 *hospital confinement* **nyūin**
入場 *admission, entrance* **nyūjō**
入金 *payment, deposit* **nyūkin**
入国 *arrival in a foreign country* **nyūkoku**
入門 *introductory, primer* **nyūmon**
入札 *auction, bidding* **nyūsatsu**
入社 *joining a company* **nyūsha**
入賞 *winning an award* **nyūshō**
侵入 *invade, attack* **shinnyū**
収入 *income, salary* **shūnyū**

挿入 *insert* **sō'nyū**
出入り *coming & going, in & out* **deiri**
入れ歯 *false teeth, dentures* **ireba**
入り用 *need, necessary, necessity* **iriyō**
札入れ *wallet, purse* **satsuire**
嫁入り *marriage, taking a bride* **yomeiri**
入り込む *get in, steal into* **hairikomu**
恥じ入る *be ashamed of* **hajiiru**
一括購入 *bulk purchase* **ikkatsu kōnyū**
入り浸る *overstay one's welcome* **iribitaru** *170 S*
刈り入れ *crop harvest* **kariire** *687 co*
受け入れ *acceptance, treatment* **ukeire**

置eave-behind, 420	内nside, 297
据et-in-place, 384	出epart, 173
奥nside, 903	

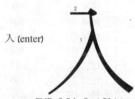

人uman, 2

扴 - katsu - bundle
714 購 -koo - purchase

001-C

No 人erson will 入nter a house on 火ire...

火⇔灬 (fire)

火ire　　火lame

hi, ho, KA

fire, flame, torch, burning

防火 *fire prevention* **bōka**
小火 *small fire, fire-prevented* **boya**
中火 *medium heat, moderate fire* **chūbi**
発火 *catching fire, igniting* **hakka**
花火 *fireworks* **hanabi**
火花 *sparks* **hibana**
火色 *flame colour* **hiiro**
火元 *fire source* **himoto**
放火 *arson, setting in flames* **hōka**
火影 *flickering light* **hokage**
情火 *fire of passion* **jōka**
火炎 *flame, blaze* **kaen**
火片 *sparks* **kahen**
火事 *fire outbreak* **kaji**
⇒山火事 *forest fire* **yamakaji**
火気 *fire, spark* **kaki**
火の気 *fire, spark* **hinoke**
火口 *crater* **kakō**
火急 *urgency, emergency* **kakyū**

FLIP: 2.0.b. Sort Of (stem)

火熱 *flame heat* **kanetsu**
火災 *fire disaster* **kasai**
火星 *Planet Mars* **kasei**
火線 *line of fire (battle)* **kasen**
火葬 *cremation* **kasō**
火山 *volcano* **kazan**
口火 *pilot light* **kuchibi**
急火 *sudden outbreak of fire* **kyūka**
烈火 *raging fire* **rekka**
戦火 *flames of war* **senka**
消火 *fire fighting, ~extinguishing* **shōka**
出火 *fire outbreak* **shukka**
大火 *conflagration* **taika**
点火 *igniting* **tenka**
不審火 *fire of unknown origin* **fushinbi**

災*isaster, 571*
熱*eat, 153*

犬*anine, 7*

002-A

六ix golfers in the North Pole aim for the 八ighth 穴ole...

八 (eight, divisible)

六ix

mut(tsu), mu(tsu), mu, mui, ROKU

six

FLIP: 1.0.b. Whole (stem)

甚六 *simpleton* **jinroku**
六日 *sixth day of the month* **muika**
六書 *Kanji six classics* **rikusho**
六角 *hexagon* **rokkaku**
六角形 *hexagon shape* **rokkakukei, rokkakkei**
六感 *the six senses* **rokkan**
六月 *June* **rokugatsu**
六尺 *palanquin bearer; 6 feet tall, ~long* **rokushaku**
六法 *six statutory legal codes* **roppō**
六法全書 *compendium of laws* **roppō zensho**
双六 *Japanese backgammon* **sugoroku**
宿六 *my old man; my husband* **yadoroku**
第六感 *hunch, sixth sense, intuition* **dairokkan**
十六夜 *the 16th night of a lunar calendar* **izayoi**
六文儀 *sextant* **rokubungi**
六大州 *the six continents* **rokudaishū**
六三三制 *pre-university school years* **rokusansansei**
二二六事件 *26 February 1936 incident* **niniroku jiken**
六十の手習い *starting anew in one's sixtyish* **rokujū no tenarai**

一*ne, 858*	十*en, 344*
二*econd, 457*	数*umber, 156*
三*hree, 858*	百*undred, 14*
四*our, 17*	千*housand, 74*
五*ive, 86*	万*en thousand, 465*
七*even, 72*	億*undred-million, 340*
八*ight, 4*	零*ero, 874*
九*ine, 73*	

八*ight, 4*　　穴*ole, 4*

002-B
六*ix golfers in the North Pole aim for the* 八*ighth* 穴*ole...*

八 (eight, divisible)

八*ight*

yat(tsu), ya(tsu), ya, yō, HACHI
eight

FLIP: 1.0.b. Whole (stem)

八丁	skillfullness **hacchō**	八重桜	double cherry blossoms **yaezakura**
八月	August **hachigatsu**	八百長	rigged contest, fixed game **yaochō**
尺八	bamboo flute **shakuhachi**	八百屋	fruit & vegetable shop **yaoya**
八幡	god of war **hachiman**	八十路	eighty years old **yasoji**
八面	all sides; eight faces **hachimen**	八つ手	Japanese fatsia **yatsude**
八戸市	Hachinohe City, Aomori Pref. **hachinohe**	八ヶ岳	Mt. Yatsugatake **yatsugatake**
間八	amberjack **kanpachi**	八方美人	everybody's friend **happō bijin**
八方	far & wide, high & low **happō**	百八十度	about face **hyakuhachijūdo**
八日	eight day of the month **yōka**	一か八か	all-or-nothing **ichika bachika**
八字髭	long-pointed moustache **hachijihige**	十中八九	in all likelihood, in 9-to-10 **jicchūhakku**
八角形	octagon **hakkakukei, hakkakkei**	四苦八苦	struggle, strive **shikuhakku**
八宝菜	chopsuey, mixed veggies dish **happōsai**		
八頭身	well-shaped woman **hattōshin**		
十八金	18 karat gold **jūhachikin**		
口八丁	quick tongue, sweet talker **kuchihacchō**		
村八分	ostracism, disowning **murahachibu**		
十八番	favourite **jūhachiban, ohako**		
嘘八百	nothing but lies, rubbish talk **usohappyaku**		
八重歯	double tooth **yaeba**		

一*ne, 858*	四*our, 17*	七*even, 72*
二*econd, 457*	五*ive, 86*	九*ine, 73*
三*hree, 858*	六*ix, 3*	十*en, 344*

穴*ole, 4*

002-C
六*ix golfers in the North Pole aim for the* 八*ighth* 穴*ole...*

穴 (hole, cave)

穴*ole* 穴*avity*

ana, KETSU
hole, cavity, cranny, pore, puncture, opening

FLIP: 1.0.b. Whole (stem)

穴凹	pothole **anaboko**	横穴	tunnel, cave **yokoana**
穴熊	badger **anaguma**	穴開け	punching, piercing, drilling **anaake**
穴蔵	cellar **anagura**	穴塞ぎ	stopgap **anafusagi**
穴子	conger eel **anago**	穴掘り	hole digging **anahori**
欠隙	crevice, cleft, crack, cranny **ketsugeki**	穴探し	fault-finder, complainer **anasagashi**
穴馬	dark horse **anauma**	穴埋め	making up, covering **anaume**
穴場	good find, little-known place **anaba**	穴釣り	ice fishing **anazuri**
墓穴	grave, tomb **boketsu**	穴居人	caveman **kekkyojin**
洞穴	cave, cavern **dōketsu, horaana**	抜け穴	loophole, secret path **nukeana**
岩穴	cave, cavern **iwaana**	焼け穴	burnt hole **yakeana**
鍵穴	keyhole **kagiana**	落とし穴	pitfall, trap, catch **otoshiana**
風穴	air hole, air ventilation **kazaana**		
毛穴	hair pore **keana**		
経穴	acupuncture points **keiketsu**		
節穴	knothole, loophole **fushiana**		
大穴	large hole **ooana**		
穴居	living in a cave **kekkyo**		
縦穴	pit, shaft **tateana**		
虎穴	tiger's lair, tigers den **koketsu**		

孔*ole, 684*	
口*pening, 458*	

八*ight, 4*

003-A

Hit with a 乙econd group of thorns, 己elf-pride 忌ourns...

乙⇔乚 (fish hook)

乙art B   乙econd group

OTSU
  Part B, second group

Facing: 1.0. 🕊️ West (W)

甲乙 *former & latter, A & B* **kōotsu**
乙姫 *younger princess* **otohime**
乙女 *virgin, maiden* **otome**
乙女心 *girlish thinking* **otomegokoro**
乙女座 *Virgo* **otomeza**
乙種 *second grade, grade B* **otsushu**

二econd, 457
次ext, 460
副eputy, 332

己elf, 5

003-B

Hit with a 乙econd group of thorns, 己elf-pride 忌ourns...

己 (self)

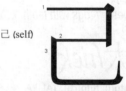

己elf   己ne's own

onore, KO, KI
  self, one's own, oneself

Facing: 1.0. 🕊️ West (W)

知己 *acquaintance, casual friendship* **chiki**
一己 *oneself, one's person* **ikko**
自己 *oneself, one's person* **jiko**
自己紹介 *self-introduction* **jiko shōkai**
自己主義 *egoism, narcissism* **jiko shugi**
克己 *self-restraint, self-denial* **kokki**
克己心 *sense of self-denial* **kokkishin**
利己 *self-interest, selfishness* **riko**
利己的 *selfish, self-centred* **rikoteki**
利己主義 *egotism, narcissism* **riko shugi**
己惚れ *self-conceited, narcissistic* **unubore**

我elf, 443
自elf, 462
身elf, 504
私rivate, 682

乙econd class, 5   忌bhor, 6

003-C

Hit with a 乙econd group of thorns, 己elf-pride 忌ourns...

心⇔忄⇔杰 (feelings)

忌*ourning*　　忌*bhor*

i(mu), i(mawashii), KI
mourning, abhor, loathe, bereavement

忌明け *end of mourning* **imiake**
忌み日 *abstinence day; unlucky day* **imibi**
忌み嫌う *hate, detest, abhor* **imikirau**
忌み言葉 *taboo words* **imikotoba**
忌むべき *detestable, abhorrible* **imubeki**
忌忌しい *disgusting, sickening* **imaimashii**
回忌 *death anniversary* **kaiki**
嫌忌 *dislike, aversion* **kenki**
忌引き *mourning leave days* **kibiki**
忌中 *mourning, grieving, wailing* **kichū**
忌服 *mourning attire, funeral clothes* **kifuku**
忌避 *evasion, skirting, ducking* **kihi**
⇒徴兵忌避 *draft dodging* **chōhei kihi**
⇒徴兵忌避者 *draft dodger* **chōhei kihisha**
忌諱 *displeasure of a person* **kii**
忌日 *death anniversary to the day* **kinichi**
禁忌 *taboo, contra-indication* **kinki**
年忌 *death anniversary* **nenki**
猜忌 *hate, avoid* **saiki**

Facing: 3.0. ☞☜ Across

周忌 *death anniversary* **shūki**
一周忌 *first death anniversary* **isshūki**
物忌み *purification by abstinence* **mono imi**
三回忌 *second death anniversary* **sankaiki**
忌憚なく *candidly, honestly* **kitannaku**

弔*ourning, 538*		死*eath, 513*
喪*ourning, 119*		逝*eath, 54*
愁*orrows, 415*		亡*eath, 72*
悲*orrows, 289*		

志*ntention, 426*	忘*orget, 34*

004-A

太bese 犬ogs with teeth 太hick & 大arge taking charge...

大 (grand)

太*hick*　　太*bese*

futo(i), futo(ru), TAI, TA
thick, fat, obese, plump, burly, corpulent

太字 *bold-faced type* **futoji**
太目 *thick, fat* **futome**
太股 *thigh* **futomomo**
骨太 *thick-boned person* **honebuto**
丸太 *log* **maruta**
肉太 *thick strokes* **nikubuto**
太陰 *moon* **taiin**
太陰暦 *lunar calendar* **taiinreki**
太古 *ancient times, pre-history* **taiko**
太鼓 *drum* **taiko**
太鼓判 *large seal* **taikoban**
太鼓腹 *potbelly, beer belly* **taikobara**
太虚 *solar energy* **taikyo**
太子 *crown prince* **taishi**
⇒聖徳太子 *prince shohtoku* **shōtoku taishi**
太初 *Genesis* **taisho**
太守 *governor-general, viceroy* **taishu**
太祖 *dynasty founder* **taiso**
太陽 *the sun* **taiyō**

FLIP: 2.0.b. Sort Of (stem)

太陽系 *solar system* **taiyōkei**
皇太后 *empress dowager* **kōtaigō**
皇太子 *crown prince* **kōtaishi**
皇太子妃 *crown princess* **kōtaishihi**
太書き *thick writing strokes* **futogaki**
太公望 *angler* **taikōbō**
与太者 *hooligan, hoodlum, thug, bully* **yotamono**
図太い *audacious, impudent* **zubutoi**
太刀打ち *cross sword with* **tachiuchi**
太平洋 *Pacific Ocean* **taiheiyō**
太平洋戦争 *Pacific War* **taiheiyō sensō**

肪*bese, 735*	濃*hick, 446*
厚*hick, 964*	

大*arge, 7*	犬*anine, 7*

004-B

太*bese* 犬*ogs with teeth* 太*hick &* 大*arge taking charge...*

犬⇔犭 (dog; beast)

犬*og*   犬*anine*

inu, KEN
dog, canine

愛犬 *favourite dog, pet dog* **aiken**
愛犬家 *dog lover, dog breeder* **aikenka**
番犬 *watchdog* **banken**
畜犬 *pet dog* **chikuken**
忠犬 *one's faithful dog* **chūken**
軍犬 *military dog* **gunken**
犬釘 *spikes* **inukugi**
犬侍 *disgraced-, coward samurai* **inuzamurai**
犬猿 *mortal enemies (dog & monkey)* **ken'en**
犬儒 *cynical, eccentric, obstinate* **kenju**
犬歯 *canine tooth* **kenshi**
子犬 *puppy, little dog* **koinu**
狂犬 *mad dog, hound dog* **kyōken**
猛犬 *fierce dog* **mōken**
雄犬 *male dog* **osuinu**
猟犬 *hunting dog, hound dog* **ryōken**
柴犬 *small dog, midget dog* **shibaken**
闘犬 *dogfight, rumble, free-for-all* **tōken**

FLIP: 2.0.b. Sort Of (stem)

野犬 *stray-, homeless dog* **yaken**
山犬 *wild dog, mad dog* **yamainu**
犬狩り *wild dog, mad dog* **inugari**
犬小屋 *kennel, dog house* **inugoya**
犬食い *eating like a dog* **inugui**
犬死に *senseless-, useless death* **inuji(ni)**
犬掻き *dog paddle* **inukaki**
犬泳ぎ *dog paddle* **inuoyogi**
飼い犬 *pet dog, house dog* **kaiinu**
警察犬 *police dog* **keisatsuken**
負け犬 *loser, defeated* **makeinu**
盲導犬 *eye-seeing dog* **mōdōken**

愛*ove*, 593	飼*aising*, 835	激*ierce*, 170
親*ntimate*, 669	烈*ierce*, 585	猛*ierce*, 657

大*arge*, 7	太*hick*, 6

004-C

太*bese* 犬*ogs with teeth* 太*hick &* 大*arge taking charge...*

大 (grand)

大*arge*   大*rand*   大*ig*

ō(kii), ōi(ni), DAI, TAI
large, grand, big, *abbreviative suffix for universities*

大学 *university* **daigaku**
大臣 *cabinet minister* **daijin**
大名 *feudal lord* **daimyō**
拡大 *expand, enlarge* **kakudai**
寛大 *magnanimous, generous* **kandai**
誇大 *exaggeration, boasting* **kodai**
大雨 *heavy rain, rainpour* **ōame**
大型 *large-scale* **ōgata**
大手 *large, major* **ōte**
大家 *landlord, owner* **ōya**
大人 *adult, grown up* **otona**
盛大 *splendour, grandeur* **seidai**
大変 *hard, difficult* **taihen**
大会 *large gathering, ~assembly* **taikai**
大金 *vast amount of money* **taikin, ōgon**
大国 *Great Powers, colonial powers* **taikoku**
大乱 *large-scale rioting* **tairan**
大陸 *continent* **tairiku**
大使 *ambassador, envoy, emissary* **taishi**

FLIP: 1.0.b. Whole (stem)

大和 *ancient name of Japan* **yamato**
超大国 *superpower* **chōtaikoku**
大部分 *majority, greater part* **daibubun**
大丈夫 *OK, fine, "no problem..."* **daijōbu**
大音響 *loud noise* **daionkyō**
大統領 *The President* **daitōryō**
大いに *very much, extremely* **ōi(ni)**
大き目 *large, big* **ōkime**
大文字 *capitalized letters, large caps* **ōmoji**
大して *"not very much..."* **taishite**
大安売り *bargain sale* **ōyasuuri**
文化大革命 *cultural revolution* **bunka daikakumei**
東大 *Tōkyō University* **tōdai**

拡*nlarge*, 205	巨*iant*, 206
広*arge*, 205	

丈*obust*, 463	太*hick*, 6

7

005-A

土entlemen on the 土round at your 仕ervice all year round...

土 (samurai, warrior)

土entleman 土ighter

samurai, SHI
gentleman, fighter, masculine, samurai

FLIP: 1.0.a. Whole (flat)

❶ 学士 university graduate **gakushi**
技士 technician, skilled expert **gishi**
博士 doctorate, doctoral **hakase**, **hakushi**
土女 male & female **shijo**
紳士 gentleman **shinshi**
紳士協定 gentlemen's agreement **shinshi kyōtei**
紳士録 "Who's Who..." **shinshiroku**
修士 master of arts, ~of science **shūshi**
弁護士 lawyer, barrister **bengoshi**
弁理士 patent lawyer **benrishi**
代議士 Diet member, lawmaker **daigishi**
栄養士 dietician, nutritionist **eiyōshi**
看護士 male nurse **kangoshi**
計理士 accountant **keirishi**
操縦士 airline pilot **sōjūshi**
闘牛士 bullfighter, matador, picador **tōgyūshi**

❷ 武士 samurai, warrior **bushi**
武士道 samurai spirit, warrior spirit **bushidō**

同士 fellow~, colleague, comrade **dōshi**
兵士 soldier, private **heishi**
騎士 knight **kishi**
烈士 hero, patriot **resshi**
力士 sumo wrestler **rikishi**
戦士 soldier, fighter **senshi**
士族 samurai family **shizoku**
策士 tactician, strategist **sakushi**
士官 military officer **shikan**
士気 fighting spirit, espirit-de-corps **shiki**
闘士 fighter, activist, champion **tōshi**
勇士 brave man, hero **yūshi**

紳entleman, 713		僕asculine, 157	
壮asculine, 367		雄asculine, 775	
男asculine, 597		郎asculine, 404	

土round, 8

005-B

土entlemen on the 土round at your 仕ervice all year round...

土 (ground, soil)

土round 土oil

tsuchi, DO, TO
ground, soil, earth

FLIP: 1.0.a. Whole (flat)

土壌 earth, soil **dojō**
土管 earthen pipe **dokan**
土建 building, structure **doken**
土器 earthenware **doki**
土間 soil-, dirt floor **doma**
土日 weekend, Saturday & Sunday **donichi**
土星 planet Saturn **dosei**
土質 soil nature **doshitsu**
土手 embankment, riverbank **dote**
土俵 sumo wrestling arena; sandbag **dohyō**
⇒初土俵 sumo wrestler's debut **hatsudohyō**
土俵際 brink of, critical moment **dohyōgiwa**
土俵入り sumo opening rituals **dohyōiri**
風土 natural resources **fūdo**
本土 mainland **hondo**
浄土 Buddhist paradise **jōdo**
壁土 plaster **kabetsuchi**
国土 territory, country **kokudo**
郷土 hometown, birthplace **kyōdo**

郷土愛 love of hometown **kyōdoai**
粘土 clay, earthen **nendo**
黄土 ochre **ōdo**
領土 territory, domain **ryōdo**
焦土 burnt ground, scorched land **shōdo**
土地 land, property **tochi**
土煙 cloud of dust **tsuchikemuri**
土塊 lump of earth, clod **tsuchikure**
沖積土 alluvial soil **chūsekido**
泥土層 soil-, dirt bed **deidosō**
土壇場 place of execution, critical moment **dotanba**
土曜日 Saturday **doyōbi**
土足厳禁 "take off your shoes..." **dosoku genkin**
土産物店 souvenir shop **miyagemonoten**

地and, 688	
陸and, 140	

土entleman, 8

005-C

土*entlemen on the* 土*round at your* 仕*ervice all year round...*

仕*ervice*　　仕*ction*

人⇔亻 (person)

tsuka(eru), SHI, JI
service, action, serve, do

FLIP: 7.0.a. Right (flat)

奉仕 *service, serving* **hōshi**	
給仕 *waiter, waitress, meal servant* **kyūji**	仕入れ *putting in stock* **shiire**
仲仕 *heaver, stevedore, longshoreman* **nakashi**	仕返し *revenge, retaliation, get back at* **shikaeshi**
仕儀 *course of events* **shigi**	仕切り *dividing line, demarcation* **shikiri**
仕事 *work, job, task, labour* **shigoto**	仕込み *education, training, preparation* **shikomi**
仕事場 *workplace, worksite* **shigotoba**	仕組み *clever plan & execution* **shikumi**
仕事量 *work load* **shigotoryō**	仕置き *punishment, execution, sentence* **shioki**
仕官 *entering civil service* **shikan**	仕打ち *treatment, disposition* **shiuchi**
仕方 *way of doing things* **shikata**	仕訳帳 *journal, bulletin* **shiwakechō**
仕舞 *Noh dance* **shimai**	仕掛ける *set up, fixed* **shikakeru**
仕度 *arrangements, preparation* **shitaku**	仕向ける *urge, force, agitate* **shimukeru**
仕業 *act, deed* **shiwaza**	仕分ける *sort out, segregate* **shiwakeru**
仕様 *ways & means; specifications* **shiyō**	

仕出し *catering, meals delivery* **shidashi**
仕出し屋 *caterer, caterers shop* **shidashiya**
荒仕事 *hard work, hard labour* **arashigoto**
泥仕合 *mudslinging* **dorojiai**
針仕事 *needlework* **harishigoto**
仕上げ *finishing touches* **shiage**

勤*ervice, 962*	奉*ffer, 275*
務*ervice, 454*	呈*ffer, 618*
努*fforts, 44*	催*ponsor, 416*

付*ttach, 382*　　代*poch, 96*

006-A

水*ater* 氷*roze into* 氷*ce in the* 永*ong winter twice...*

水*ater*　　水*qua*

水⇔氵 (water)

mizu, SUI
water, aqua

FLIP: 2.0.b. Sort Of (stem)

減水 *receding of water level* **gensui**	
排水 *drainage, sewerage canal* **haisui**	水揚げ *unloading from the sea; watering* **mizuage**
湖水 *lake* **kosui**	水引き *ceremonial paper strings* **mizuhiki**
給水 *water supply* **kyūsui**	水溜り *pool, puddle* **mizutamari**
吸水 *pumping out water* **kyūsui**	飲み水 *potable-, drinking water* **nomimizu**
水飴 *malt syrup* **mizuame**	水曜日 *Wednesday* **suiyōbi**
水腹 *survive on water* **mizubara, mizuppara**	治水工事 *embankment works* **chisui kōji**
汚水 *slops, sewage water* **osui**	寒中水泳 *mid-winter swimming* **kanchū suiei**
利水 *irrigation water* **risui**	警戒水位 *dangerous level* **keikaisuii**
節水 *saving water, water conservation* **sessui**	水っぽい *watery, washy, thin* **mizuppoi**
清水 *fresh water* **shimizu**	水しぶき *water spray* **mizushibuki**
水圧 *water pressure* **suiatsu**	温水プール *heated swimming pool* **onsui pūru**

水圧計 *hydraulic gauge* **suiatsukei**
水防 *flood control* **suibō**
水泳 *swimming* **suiei**
水運 *water transportation* **suiun**
貯水池 *water reservoir* **chosuichi**
浄水場 *water purification plant* **jōsuijō**
給水管 *water pipes* **kyūsuikan**

海*cean, 241*	液*iquid, 508*
洋*cean, 247*	泳*wimming, 729*
河*iver, 877*	氷*ce, 10*
川*iver, 76*	

氷*ce, 10*　　永*ternal, 10*

006-B

水ater 氷roze into 氷ce in the 永ong winter twice...

水 ⇔ 氵 (water)

氷reeze　　氷ce

kōri, hi, kō(ru), HYŌ
freeze, ice, glaciate

FLIP: 2.0.b. Sort Of (stem)

着氷 *ice coating* **chakuhyō**
浮氷 *floating ice* **fuhyō**
薄氷 *thin ice* **hakuhyō, usugōri**
初氷 *the year's first freezing (river)* **hatsugōri**
氷室 *icehouse, cold room* **himuro**
氷雨 *cold autumn rain* **hisame**
氷柱 *icicle, ice pillar* **hyōchū**
氷河 *glacier* **hyōga**
氷原 *ice field* **hyōgen**
氷壁 *wall of ice* **hyōheki**
氷解 *melting away, thawing* **hyōkai**
氷塊 *block of ice* **hyōkai**
氷海 *frozen sea* **hyōkai**
氷結 *freezing, icebound* **hyōketsu**
氷嚢 *ice bag* **hyōnō**
氷雪 *ice & snow* **hyōsetsu**
氷晶 *ice crystals* **hyōshō**
氷炭 *irreconcilable differences* **hyōtan**
氷点 *freezing point* **hyōten**

氷山 *iceberg* **hyōzan**
樹氷 *ice-covered trees* **juhyō**
解氷 *thawing, de-icing* **kaihyō**
氷枕 *ice pillow (fever)* **kōrimakura**
氷水 *ice water* **kōrimizu**
氷屋 *iceman, ice shop* **kōriya**
霧氷 *frost, rime* **muhyō**
流氷 *floating-, drifting ice* **ryūhyō**
製氷 *ice-making* **seihyō**
氷菓子 *frozen sweets* **kōrigashi**
氷砂糖 *rock-, sugar candy* **kōrizatō**

凍*reeze, 221*		寒*hills, 121*	
冬*inter, 397*		冷*hilly, 684*	

水*ater, 9*	永*ternal, 10*

006-C

水ater 氷roze into 氷ce in the 永ong winter twice...

水 ⇔ 氵 (water)

永ong-lasting　　永ternal

naga(i), EI
long-lasting, endless, eternal, immortal

Facing: 1.0. 🠐 West (W)

永別 *long separation* **eibetsu**
永遠 *eternity, immortality* **eien**
永劫 *eternity, everlasting* **eigō**
永住 *permanent residence* **eijū**
永住権 *right of permanent stay* **eijūken**
永訣 *final farewell, death* **eiketsu**
永久 *permanent, eternal* **eikyū**
永久歯 *permanent tooth* **eikyūshi**
永眠 *eternal rest, death* **eimin**
永年 *many long years* **einen**
永生 *eternal life, immortality* **eisei**
永世 *permanence, eternity* **eisei**
永代 *perpetual, eternal* **eitai**
永続 *permanence, perpetuity* **eizoku**
永続性 *permanence, perpetuity* **eizokusei**
半永久的 *semi-permanent* **han'eikyūteki**

長*ong, 273*	久*ternal, 379*
寿*ongevity, 440*	時*ime, 653*

水*ater, 9*	氷*reeze, 10*

007-A

My 主aster's 主rincipal 玉ewel, given by 王ing Emmanuel...

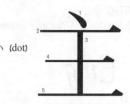

ヽ (dot)

主aster   主rincipal

nushi, omo(ni), SHU
master, principal

FLIP: 2.0.a. Sort Of (flat)

地主	*landlord, landed gentry* **jinushi**	
自主	*autonomy, self-governing* **jishu**	
株主	*stock-, shareholder* **kabunushi**	
君主	*monarch, sovereign, ruler* **kunshu**	
荷主	*shipper, consignor* **ninushi**	
領主	*feudal lord* **ryōshu**	
船主	*shipowner* **senshu**	
主調	*keynote, main point* **shuchō**	
主張	*principal object* **shuchō**	
主演	*starring, leading role* **shuen**	
主婦	*housewife, lady of the house* **shufu**	
主義	*ideology, doctrine* **shugi**	
⇒独裁主義	*dictatorship* **dokusai shugi**	
⇒社会主義	*socialism* **shakai shugi**	
主語	*sentence subject* **shugo**	
主筆	*chief editor, head writer* **shuhitsu**	
主因	*primary cause, leading factor* **shuin**	
主人	*husband, owner* **shujin**	

主幹	*head, chief* **shukan**
主権	*sovereignty, suzerainty* **shuken**
主任	*officer-in-charge* **shunin**
主力	*lord, master* **shuryoku**
主流	*main current* **shuryū**
主催	*sponsorship, auspices* **shusai**
主要	*main point, gist* **shuyō**
亭主	*proprietor; one's husband* **teishu**
店主	*shop-, storekeeper* **tenshu**
家主	*landlord, house owner* **yanushi**
買い主	*buyer, purchaser* **kainushi**
主観性	*subjectivity* **shukansei**

頭*hief, 832*	本*ain, 461*	筋*uscle, 584*
導*uidance, 312*	旨*ain point, 242*	要*ssential, 419*

玉*phere, 11*	生*ife, 474*

007-B

My 主aster's 主rincipal 玉ewel, given by 王ing Emmanuel...

王⇔玉 (jewel)

❶玉phere   ❷玉ewel

tama, GYOKU
sphere; jewel, gem

FLIP: 2.0.a. Sort Of (flat)

❶悪玉	*villain, bad guy* **akudama**	
飴玉	*candy balls* **amedama**	
円玉	*Japanese yen coins* **endama**	
火玉	*fireball* **hidama**	
蟹玉	*crabmeat omelette* **kanitama**	
剣球	*cup & ball game* **kendama**	
薬玉	*scented balls* **kusudama**	
目玉	*eyeball* **medama**	
親玉	*ringleader, chief, boss* **oyadama**	
玉子	*mini balls* **tamago**	
玉虫	*scarab beetle* **tamamushi**	
玉葱	*onion* **tamanegi**	
年玉	*New Year gift for children* **toshidama**	
矢玉	*arrows & bullets* **yadama**	
槍玉	*given example* **yaridama**	
湯玉	*boiling water bubbles* **yudama**	
善玉	*good thing, good deed* **zendama**	
替え玉	*substitute, replacement* **kaedama**	
肝っ玉	*guts, nerve, mettle, courage* **kimottama**	

算盤玉	*abacus beads* **sorobandama**
玉突き	*billiards, pool* **tamatsuki**

❷玉杯	*jade cup* **gyokuhai**
玉砕	*glorious-, honourable death* **gyokusai**
玉石	*gems & stone's* **gyokuseki**
玉将	*king, monarch, ruler* **gyokushō**
玉座	*throne, seat of power* **gyokuza**
宝玉	*precious stones, jewel* **hōgyoku**
上玉	*precious stones* **jōdama**
珠玉	*jewel, gem; the greatest* **shugyoku**
玉手箱	*Pandora's box; treasure chest* **tamatebako**

石*tone, 363*	
貴*recious, 913*	

主*aster, 11*	生*ife, 474*

007-C

M/王aster's 主rincipal 玉ewel, given by 王ing Emmanuel...

王⇔玉 (jewel)

王*ing*   王*onarch*

Ō
king, monarch, sovereign

FLIP: 1.0.a. Whole (flat)

藩王 *rajah, sultan* **han'ō**
女王 *queen* **joō**
勤王 *loyalty to the monarch* **kinnō**
国王 *king, monarch, ruler* **kokuō**
魔王 *Satan, Lucifer* **maō**
王朝 *dynasty, dynastic rule* **ōchō**
王位 *throne, crown* **ōi**
王者 *king, champion* **ōja**
王子 *prince* **ōji**
王事 *monarchical cause* **ōji**
王冠 *crown, bottle cap* **ōkan**
王権 *royalty, sovereign power* **ōken**
王侯 *nobility & royalty* **ōkō**
王国 *kingdom* **ōkoku**
王宮 *royal palace* **ōkyū**
王様 *king, monarch, ruler* **ōsama**
王政 *royal government, monarchy* **ōsei**
王室 *royal family* **ōshitsu**
王手 *check, checkmate* **ōte**

王党 *royalist, loyalist* **ōtō**
王座 *throne, premier place* **ōza**
王族 *royalty, royal family* **ōzoku**
竜王 *dragon king* **ryūō**
親王 *imperial prince* **shinnō**
尊王 *reverence to the king* **sonnō**
帝王 *emperor, monarch* **teiō**
帝王切開 *Caesarean delivery, C-section*
  teiō sekkai
海王星 *Planet Neptune* **kaiōsei**
天王星 *Planet Uranus* **tennōsei**
ローマ法王 *Roman Catholic Pope, Pontiff*
  rōma hōō

皇*mperor*, 113	国*ation*, 92
帝*mpire*, 432	

生*ife*. 474

008-A

未ending 未atter-part, about to be 抹rossed-out...

木 (wooden)

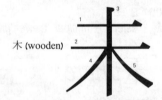

未*ending*   未*ot yet*

MI, imada(ni)
pending, not yet

FLIP: 1.0.b. Whole (stem)

未着 *yet to arrive* **michaku**
未熟 *unripe, immature* **mijuku**
未開地 *underdeveloped-, virgin land* **mikaichi**
未開人 *primitive man, savage* **mikaijin**
未開社会 *primitive society* **mikai shakai**
未確認 *unconfirmed, unverified* **mikakunin**
未確定 *pending, unsettled, unclear* **mikakutei**
未刊 *unpublished novel* **mikan**
未完 *unfinished, uncompleted* **mikan**
未見 *unseen, yet-to-be-seen* **miken**
未婚 *unmarried, single* **mikon**
未満 *under-, below* **miman**
未納 *unpaid, unsettled account* **minō**
未来 *future* **mirai**
未了 *unfinished, uncompleted* **miryō**
未済 *unpaid, unsettled account* **misai**
未設 *yet-to-install, uninstalled* **misetsu**
未収 *accrued, outstanding balance* **mishū**
未定 *undecided, "decision pending"* **mitei**

未到 *yet-to-reach, unachieved* **mitō**
未然に *"before something happens..."* **mizen(ni)**
未曾有 *unprecedented, unheard-of* **mizōu**
未成年 *minor, under-aged, below 18* **miseinen**
未決囚 *unconvicted prisoner* **miketsushū**
未亡人 *widow* **mibōjin**
未知語 *unknown word* **michigo**
未知数 *unknown quantity, ~amount* **michisū**
未払い *unpaid account* **miharai, mibarai**
未実施 *undone, unexecuted* **mijisshi**
未経験者 *inexperienced, amateur* **mikeikensha**
未遂 *attempted action* **misui**
自殺未遂 *attempted suicide* **jisatsu misui**
殺害未遂 *attempted murder* **satsugai misui**

不*[negative]*, 300	無*othing*, 49
非*[negative]*, 288	零*ero*, 874

夫*usband*, 83	扶*amily-support*, 97

008-B

未*ending* 末*atter-part, about to be* 抹*rossed-out...*

木 (wooden)

末*atter-part* 末*nding*

sue, MATSU, BATSU
latter-part, ending, closing

FLIP: 1.0.b. Whole (stem)

幕末 *Shogunate last days* **bakumatsu**
場末 *poor suburbs, ~outskirts* **basue**
粉末 *powder* **funmatsu**
月末 *end of the month* **getsumatsu**
巻末 *near the books end* **kanmatsu**
結末 *conclusion, closing* **ketsumatsu**
期末 *end of term* **kimatsu**
季末 *season end* **kimatsu**
末期 *end, close, last stage* **makki**
末筆 *"with best regards..."* **mappitsu**
末尾 *end, close* **matsubi**
末代 *succeeding generations* **matsudai**
末日 *last day* **matsujitsu**
末路 *end, last days, fate* **matsuro**
末端 *end, closing, closure* **mattan**
年末 *year-end* **nenmatsu**
歳末 *year-end* **saimatsu**
瑣末 *frivolous, trivial, petty* **samatsu**

始末 *matter to take care* **shimatsu**
週末 *weekend, Saturdays & Sundays* **shūmatsu**
終末 *conclusion* **shūmatsu**
粗末 *miserable, careless* **somatsu**
末娘 *youngest daughter* **suemusume**
端末 *terminal, endpoint* **tanmatsu**
①行末 *the future* **yukusue**
②行く末 *end of line (text)* **ikusue**
末っ子 *youngest child* **suekko**
世紀末 *end of a century* **seikimatsu**
末長く *forever & ever* **suenagaku**
末広がり *fan, spread* **suehirogari**

端*ndpoint, 974*　了*inish, 456*　未*ot yet, 12*
終*inish, 397*　遂*inally, 479*

未*ot yet, 12*　示*howing, 878*

008-C

未*ending* 末*atter-part, about to be* 抹*rossed-out...*

手 ⇔ 扌 (hand, manual)

抹*ross-out* 抹*ipe-out*

MATSU
cross-out, wipe-out

FLIP: 7.0.b1. Right (stem)

一抹 *somewhat, "a touch of..."* **ichimatsu**
抹茶 *green tea powder* **maccha**
抹香 *incense stick* **makkō**
抹香鯨 *sperm whale* **makkō kujira**
抹香臭い *smack of religion* **makkōkusai**
抹殺 *wiping out, denial, killing* **massatsu**
抹消 *erasure, crossing off* **masshō**
塗抹 *painting over* **tomatsu**

絶*radicate, 403*　脱*emove, 941*
消*elete, 265*　止*erminate, 192*
廃*bolish, 368*　停*top, 393*
外*emove, 188*

末*atter-part, 13*　示*howing, 878*

009-A

One 日 *unny* 日 *ay in* 日 *apan, flew a* 百 *undred* 白 *hite swans...*

日 (sunlight, daytime)

 ay   *un*   日 *apan*

hi, ka, JITSU, NICHI
day, sun, Japan

FLIP: 1.0.a. Whole (flat)

❶朝日 *morning sun* **asahi**
元日 *New Year's day* **ganjitsu**
半日 *half day* **hannichi**
期日 *fixed date, fixed term* **kijitsu**
昨日 *yesterday, day before today* **kinō**
毎日 *every day* **mainichi**
命日 *death anniversary* **meinichi**
日録 *daily journal* **nichiroku**
祭日 *holiday* **saijitsu**
週日 *weekday* **shūjitsu**
祝日 *national holiday* **shukujitsu**
短日 *a few days* **tanjitsu**
定日 *appointed date* **teijitsu**
曜日 *day of the week* **yōbi**
給料日 *payday, salary day* **kūryōbi**
面会日 *visiting days (hospital)* **menkaibi**
年月日 *date, month & year (exact date)* **nengappi**
参観日 *parental visiting day (school)* **sankanbi**
出勤日 *regular workday* **shukkinbi**

誕生日 *birthday* **tanjōbi**
日延べ *postponement, deferment* **hinobe**
❷入り日 *setting sun* **irihi**
日焼け *sun-burned, sun-tanned* **hiyake**
西日 *setting sun, sunset* **nishibi**
日食 *solar eclipse* **nisshoku**
日英 *Japan & England* **nichiei**
❸日本 *Japan* **nihon, nippon**
来日 *visit to Japan* **rainichi**
日の丸 *Japanese flag, rising-sun flag* **hinomaru**
駐日大使 *ambassador to Japan* **chūnichi taishi**

曜 *eekday, 849*	昼 *aytime, 575* 和 *apanese, 103*
暁 *aybreak, 818*	邦 *apan, 694* 陽 *un, 932*

旧 *ormerly, 464*	担 *esponsible, 739*

009-B

One 日 *unny* 日 *ay in* 日 *apan, flew a* 百 *undred* 白 *hite swans...*

白 (white)

百 *undred*

HYAKU, BYAKU, PYAKU, momo
hundred

FLIP: 1.0.a. Whole (flat)

凡百 *all varieties, many kinds* **bonpyaku**
百計 *by all means, at all cost* **hyakkei**
百倍 *100% times, a hundred fold* **hyakubai**
百害 *nothing-but-harm, no good* **hyakugai**
百芸 *Jack-of-all-trades* **hyakugei**
百獣 *all animals, animal kingdom* **hyakujū**
百万 *one million* **hyakuman**
百難 *all sorts of difficulties* **hyakunan**
百人 *multitude, one hundred persons* **hyakunin**
百雷 *one hundred thunderclaps* **hyakurai**
百錬 *well-tempered, well-trained* **hyakuren**
百姓 *peasant, farmer* **hyakushō**
百出 *arising in great numbers* **hyakushutsu**
百態 *various situations* **hyakutai**
百点 *full marks, 100 score* **hyakuten**
百薬 *all kinds of medicines* **hyakuyaku**
百般 *all sort of things* **hyappan**
百方 *by all means, in every way* **hyappō**
百舌 *shrike* **mozu**

百足 *centipede* **mukade**
百貨店 *department store* **hyakkaten**
百分率 *percentage* **hyakubunritsu**
百面相 *comic faces* **hyakumensō**
百年祭 *centenary, centennial* **hyakunensai**
百人力 *tremendous strength* **hyakuninriki**
百日紅 *crape myrtle* **sarusuberi**
白百合 *white lily flower* **shirayuri**
嘘八百 *"nothing but lies..."* **usohappyaku**
百科事典 *encyclopaedia* **hyakka jiten**
一罰百戒 *punish-one-for-all* **ichibatsu hyakkai**

一 *ne, 858*	億 *undred-million, 340*
十 *en, 344*	零 *ero, 874*
千 *housand, 74*	数 *umber, 156*
万 *en thousand, 465*	

白 *hite, 15*	再 *epeat, 225*

009-C
One 日unny 日ay in 日apan, flew a 百undred 白hite swans...

白 (white)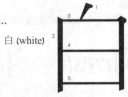

白hite

shiro(i), shira, HAKU, BYAKU
white

FLIP: 1.0.a. Whole (flat)

白バイ *police motorcycle* **shirobai**
独白 *monologue, siloloquy* **dokuhaku**
白金 *platinum* **hakkin**
白亜 *chalky white* **hakua**
白墨 *blackboard chalk* **hakuboku**
白鳥 *white swan* **hakuchō**
白衣 *white uniform (medical worker)* **hakui, byakui**
白人 *Caucasian, white race* **hakujin**
白魔 *heavy snowfall* **hakuma**
白米 *polished rice* **hakumai**
白面 *fair complexion* **hakumen**
白熱 *incandescence, luminescence* **hakunetsu**
白紙 *blank sheet* **hakushi**
白書 *white paper, official policy* **hakusho**
白票 *spoiled ballot* **hakūyō**
漂白 *bleaching, whitening* **hyōhaku**
自白 *confession, guilt admission* **jihaku**
建白 *petition, appeal* **kenpaku**
潔白 *purity, innocence* **keppaku**

紅白 *red & white* **kōhaku**
告白 *confession, recantation* **kokuhaku**
空白 *blank, empty space* **kūhaku**
明白 *clear, apparent, unmistakable* **meihaku**
精白 *refined, smooth* **seihaku**
白浜 *white beach* **shirahama**
白黒 *black & white* **shirokuro, byakkoku**
白眼視 *indifference, callousness* **hakuganshi**
鼻白む *lose all interest* **hanajiromu**
真っ白 *snow-, pure white* **masshiro**
腕白坊主 *prankish-, naughty boy* **wanpaku bōzu**

明*lear, 22*
朗*lear, 800*
黒*lack, 320*

百*undred, 14*   日*un, 14*

010-A
可ossible 拘rrest for libelous 句erses...

口 (mouth)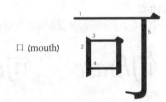

可Jossible   可Jpproval

KA
possible, approval, concur, consent, ~able

FLIP: 8.0.a. Inner (flat)

可分 *divisible, separable* **kabun**
可聴 *audible, can be heard* **kachō**
可動 *movable, mobility* **kadō**
可読 *readable, legible* **kadoku**
可逆 *reversible, changeable* **kagyaku**
可否 *right-or-wrong, pros & cons* **kahi**
可決 *approval, adoption, passage* **kaketsu**
可成 *"fairly, rather, pretty..."* **kanari**
可燃 *combustible, flammable* **kanen**
可憐 *cute, adorable* **karen**
可惜 *deep regrets* **kashaku**
可視 *visible, apparent, obvious* **kashi**
可塑 *plastic, vinyl* **kaso**
可鍛 *malleable* **katan**
可算 *countable, counting* **kazan, kasan**
許可 *permit, license, authorization* **kyoka**
許可証 *license certificate, permit* **kyokashō**
認可 *approval, permission, license* **ninka**
裁可 *sanction, approval, consent* **saika**

不可知 *unknown, x-factor* **fukachi**
不可解 *incomprehensible, mysterious* **fukakai**
不可欠 *indispensable, essential* **fukaketsu**
不可能 *impossible, improbable* **fukanō**
不可侵 *inviolable; non-aggression* **fukashin**
可変性 *variability, adjustability* **kahensei**
可能性 *possibility, likelihood, probability* **kanōsei**
可愛い *tiny, cute, charming, dainty* **kawaii**
可哀想 *pitiful, miserable* **kawaisō**
可溶性 *solubility, dissolvability* **kayōsei**
可笑しい *funny, "something's wrong..."* **okashii**

承*pproval, 117*   許*ermit, 180*
賛*pproval, 334*   免*xempt, 413*
諾*onsent, 277*

句*erse, 16*   旬*[10 days], 494*

010-B

可*ossible* 拘*rrest for libelous* 句*erses...*

❶拘*rrest*　　**❷拘***dherence*

手⇔扌 (hand, manual)

KŌ

arrest, apprehend, accost; adhere, abide

❶拘置 *confinement, detention* **kōchi**
拘置所 *prison, jail, gaol* **kōchisho**
拘引 *arrest, detain, confine* **kōin**
拘引状 *arrest warrant, summons* **kōinjō**
拘禁 *detention, custody* **kōkin**
拘留 *custody, detention* **kōryū**
拘留状 *warrant of arrest* **kōryūjō**
拘留所 *detention cell, lockup* **kōryūsho**
拘束 *restraint, custody* **kōsoku**
拘束力 *binding force* **kōsokuryoku**
拘束時間 *entire time spent* **kōsoku jikan**

❷拘泥 *adherence, abiding* **kōdei**

FLIP: 8.0.a. Inner (flat)

虜*aptive, 70*	守*bide, 366*
逮*apture, 880*	応*omply, 469*
捕*eize, 812*	従*omply, 551*
獄*rison, 639*	尊*bedience, 544*
囚*rison, 863*	

句*[10 days], 494*　　殉*artyr, 494*

010-C

可*ossible* 拘*rrest for libelous* 句*erses...*

句*hrase*　　句*erse*

口 (mouth)

KU

phrase, verse, *Haiku*

題句 *epigraph* **daiku**
語句 *words & phrases* **goku**
俳句 *17-syllabled Japanese poem* **haiku**
字句 *words & phrases* **jiku**
冗句 *redundant phrase* **jōku**
警句 *witty remark, wisecrack* **keiku**
句法 *phrasing, diction* **kuhō**
禁句 *taboo words* **kinku**
句心 *poetic instinct* **kugokoro**
句意 *phrase meaning, phrase context* **kui**
句会 *Haiku association* **kukai**
句境 *poetic state-of-mind* **kukyō**
句作 *Haiku composition* **kusaku**
句点 *period* **kuten**
句読 *punctuation* **kutō**
句読点 *punctuation marks* **kutōten**
名句 *famous phrase, noted verse* **meiku**
文句 *complaint; phrase* **monku**
⇒殺し文句 *death threat* **koroshi monku**

FLIP: 8.0.a. Inner (flat)

⇒脅し文句 *intimidating phrase* **odoshi monku**
成句 *idiomatic expression* **seiku**
節句 *season festival* **sekku**
詩句 *verse, stanza* **shiku**
対句 *anti-thesis, couplet* **tsuiku**
絶句 *dying words; "find no words..."* **zekku**
副詞句 *adverbial phrase* **fukushiku**
慣用句 *idiom, way-of-saying* **kanyōku**
挿入句 *parenthesis* **sōnyūku**
一言半句 *dumbfounded, "left speechless..."*
　ichigon-, ichigen hanku

言*ord, 251*	弁*peech, 570*
語*ord, 780*	詞*hrase, 376*
文*iteracy, 558*	

可*ossible, 15*　　句*[10 days], 494*

011-A

四our 匹nimals in the 西estern corall...

四our

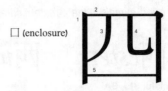

☐ (enclosure)

FLIP: 1.0.a. Whole (flat)

yot(tsu), yo(tsu), yo, yon, SHI
four, quarter

四月	*April*	**shigatsu**
四囲	*situation, circumstances*	**shii**
四海	*all the worlds oceans*	**shikai**
四角	*square, rectangle*	**shikaku**
四季	*four seasons, all-year round*	**shiki**
四股	*sumo leg posture*	**shiko**
四国	*Shikoku Islands*	**shikoku**
四面	*all four sides*	**shimen**
四隣	*whole neighbourhood*	**shirin**
四散	*scatter, scramble, disperse*	**shisan**
四声	*four tone's in the Chinese language*	**shisei**
四聖	*Buddha, Christ, Confucius & Socrates*	**shisei**
四肢	*four limbs, extremities*	**shishi**
四書	*four Chinese classics*	**shisho**
四則	*basic math (+, -, x, ÷)*	**shisoku**
四日	*fourth day of the month*	**yokka**
四桁	*four-digit number*	**yonketa**
四隅	*four corners, all sides*	**yosumi**
四半期	*quarter of a year*	**shihanki**

四重唱	*singing-, vocal quartet*	**shijūshō**
四次元	*four dimensions*	**yojigen**
四人組	*gang of four*	**yoningumi**
四十代	*40~49 years old, one's fortyish*	**yonjūdai**
四つ足	*four-legged animal*	**yotsuashi**
四十路	*forty years of age*	**yosoji**
四つ子	*quadruplets*	**yotsugo**
四つ角	*crossroads*	**yotsukado**
真四角	*rectangle*	**masshikaku**
四苦八苦	*struggle, strive*	**shiku hakku**
四捨五入	*rounding off numbers*	**shisha gonyū**
四つ切り	*quarter, one-fourth*	**yotsugiri**

一*ne, 858*	五*ive, 86*	八*ight, 4*
二*econd, 457*	六*ix, 3*	九*ine, 73*
三*hree, 858*	七*even, 72*	十*en, 344*

匹*[animal], 17*   西*estern, 18*

011-B

四our 匹nimals in the 西estern corall...

匹 *[animal]*

∟ (side box)

FLIP: 2.0.a. Sort Of (flat)

hiki, HITSU
[counter for animals]

馬匹	*several horses*	**bahitsu**
匹夫	*uncultivated-, ill-bred man*	**hippu**
匹婦	*uncultivated-, ill-bred woman*	**hippu**
匹敵	*good match, equal, tantamount*	**hitteki**
数匹	*several animals*	**sūhiki**
一匹狼	*lone wolf*	**ippiki ōkami**
猫一匹	*one cat*	**neko ippiki**
男一匹	*full-grown man*	**otoko ippiki**

飼*reeding, 835*	養*reeding, 253*
畜*reeding, 528*	牧*reeding, 647*

四*our, 17*   西*estern, 18*

011-C

四our 匹nimals in the 西estern corall...

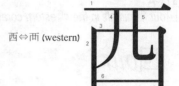

西⇔両 (western)

西estern 西uropean

nishi, SEI, SAI
Western, European, Occident

FLIP: 1.0.a. Whole (flat)

西蔵 *Tibet* **chibetto**
以西 *west of ~* **isei**
関西 *Kansai region (Ōsaka-Kōbe)* **kansai**
江西 *Jianxi province, China* **kōsei**
真西 *directly facing west* **manishi**
西日 *setting sun, afternoon sun* **nishibi**
西側 *westside* **nishigawa**
西風 *Western winds* **nishikaze**
西宮 *Nishinomiya City, Hyōgo Pref.* **nishinomiya**
西下 *travel to Kansai from Tōkyō* **saika**
最西 *Westernmost part* **saisei**
西土 *Western lands* **seido**
西方 *westward* **seihō**
西北 *northwest* **seihoku**
西人 *Westerner* **seijin**
西経 *west longitude* **seikei**
西南 *southwest* **seinan**
西欧 *Western Europe* **seiō**
西欧化 *Westernisation, internationalisation* **seiōka**

西暦 *Anno Domini, A.D., Christian year* **seireki**
西瓜 *watermelon* **suika**
泰西 *West, Occident* **taisei**
東西 *East & West* **tōzai**
西半球 *Western hemisphere* **nishihankyū**
西進中 *advancing westward* **seishinchū**
西洋風 *European style* **seiyōfū**
西洋人 *Westerner, Caucasian* **seiytjin**
大西洋 *Atlantic ocean* **taiseiyō**
西明かり *Western twilight* **nishiakari**
西洋文明 *European civilization* **seiyō bunmei**
西洋野菜 *Western vegetables* **seiyō yasai**

東*astern, 220*
北*orthern, 372*
南*outhern, 414*

両*oth, 567*   丙*hird class, 212*

012-A

Killed by 矢rrow puncture, not by 医edicine 失ailure...

矢 (archery arrow)

矢rrow 矢art

ya, SHI
arrow, dart, spike

FLIP: 2.0.b. Sort Of (stem)

毒矢 *poisoned arrow* **dokuya**
火矢 *flaming arrow* **hiya**
遠矢 *long-distance archery* **tōya**
矢羽 *arrow feathers* **yabane**
矢場 *archery field* **yaba**
矢文 *letter attached to an arrow* **yabumi**
矢玉 *arrow & bullet* **yadama**
矢種 *remaining arrow* **yadane**
矢柄 *arrow shaft* **yagara**
矢尻 *arrowhead, arrowbarb* **yajiri**
矢印 *arrow* **yajirushi**
矢面 *target, "brunt of···"* **yaomote**
矢来 *palisade, stockade* **yarai**
矢先 *arrowhead* **yasaki**
矢師 *arrow craftman* **yashi**
矢立 *portable brush & ink case* **yatate**
矢筒 *quiver* **yazutsu**
弓矢 *bow & arrow* **yumiya**
弓矢八幡 *god of war* **yumiya hachiman**

矢庭に *immediately, suddenly* **yaniwani**
吹き矢 *blow pipe* **fukiya**
石火矢 *ancient canon* **ishibiya**
流れ矢 *stray arrow* **nagareya**
竹矢来 *bamboo palisade* **takeyarai**
矢飛白 *arrow-feather pattern* **yagasuri**
矢車草 *cornflower* **yagurumasō**
矢の根 *arrowhead* **yanone**
矢鱈漬 *mixed-vegetable pickles* **yatarazuke**
無理矢理 *by force, under compulsion* **muriyari**
白羽の矢 ① *one's lucky arrow* **shirahanoya**
白羽の矢 ② *"being singled out..."* **shirahanoya**

弓*rchery, 348*
射*hoot, 504*

失*ailure, 19*   天*eaven, 83*   医*edicine, 19*

012-B
Killed by 矢rrow puncture, not by 医edicine 失ailure...

匚 (side box)

医*edicine*　　　医*octor*

I

medicine, doctor, physician

Facing: 3.0. ☞☜ Across

軍医 *military doctor* **gun'i**
医学 *medical science, medicine* **igaku**
医学博士 *doctor of medicine*, **igaku hakushi**, **hakase**
医学実習生 *medical intern* **igaku jisshūsei**
医学界 *medical profession* **igakukai**
医学生 *medical student* **igakusei**
医院 *medical clinic, doctor's office* **iin**
医術 *medicine, medical technology* **ijutsu**
医官 *government doctor* **ikan**
医局 *medical office* **ikyoku**
医者 *medical doctor, physician* **isha**
医師 *medical doctor, physician* **ishi**
医薬 *medical treatment, ~cure* **iyaku**
女医 *female physician, lady doctor* **joi**
獣医 *veterinarian, vet, animal doctor* **jūi**
校医 *school doctor* **kōi**
名医 *famous doctor, skilled physician* **meii**
眼科医 *eye doctor, opthamologist* **gankai**
外科医 *surgeon* **gekai**

歯医者 *dentist, dental doctor* **haisha**
保健医 *healthcare physician* **hoken'i**
漢方医 *Chinese herbal doctor* **kanpōi**
産科医 *obstetrician* **sankai**
接骨医 *bone doctor, bone-setter* **sekkotsui**
藪医者 *quack doctor, poor doctor* **yabuisha**
婦人科医 *gynaecologist* **fujinkai**
皮膚科医 *dermatologist, skin doctor* **hifukai**
医科大学 *college of medicine* **ika daigaku**
脳外科医 *brain surgeon* **nōgekai**
精神医学 *psychiatry* **seishin igaku**

薬*rugs, 447*	病*ickness, 213*
剤*rugs, 961*	治*ecuperate, 210*
患*ickness, 475*	癒*ecuperate, 923*
症*ickness, 788*	療*ecuperate, 67*

失*issing, 19*	矢*rrow, 18*

012-C
Killed by 矢rrow puncture, not by 医edicine 失ailure...

大 (grand)

失*ailure*　　　失*issing*

ushina(u), SHITSU

failure, missing, unsuccessful, blunder, slip

FLIP: 2.0.b. Sort Of (stem)

凡失 *stupid error* **bonshitsu**
紛失 *lost-, missing-, unfound item* **funshitsu**
遺失 *lost, missing, misplaced, unfound* **ishitsu**
過失 *fault, mistake, error* **kashitsu**
失地 *lost domain* **shicchi**
失火 *accidental fire* **shikka**
失格 *disqualification, disenfranchisement* **shikkaku**
失敬 *apology, atonement* **shikkei**
失権 *forfeiture of rights, disenfranchisement* **shikken**
失禁 *incontinence, loss of control* **shikkin**
失効 *invalidation, non-validity, expiry* **shikkō**
失脚 *loss of position, downfall* **shikkyaku**
失敗 *failure, mistake, error* **shippai**
失費 *expenses, spendings* **shippi**
失策 *blunder, fiasco, boo-boo* **shissaku**
失跡 *disappearance* **shisseki**
失笑 *roaring laughter* **shisshō**
失速 *stalling, sudden stop* **shissoku**
失望 *disappointment, disheartening* **shitsubō**

失言 *slip of the tongue, blurting out* **shitsugen**
失業 *unemployment* **shitsugyō**
失意 *disappointment, despair* **shitsui**
失念 *forgotten idea* **shitsunen**
失礼 ① *impolite, discourteous* **shitsurei**
失礼 ② *"excuse me, pardon..."* **shitsurei**
失点 *points deducted* **shitten**
失投 *clumsy pitch (baseball)* **shittō**
失当 *improper, wrongful* **shittō**
損失 *loss, unfound, misplaced* **sonshitsu**
喪失 *loss, losing, forfeiture* **sōshitsu**
得失 *gains & losses* **tokushitsu**

敗*ailure, 137*	落*ollapse, 826*
欠*bsence, 460*	陥*ollapse, 893*
崩*ollapse, 912*	

先*efore, 478*	矢*rrow, 18*

013-A

卌ooks warned Pontius Pilate of a 血loody 灬late...

☐ (inverted box) 5

冊 *[books]*

SATSU, SAKU
[counter for books]

FLIP: 1.0.b. Whole (stem)

別冊 *separate book* **bessatsu**
別冊付録 *supplement volumes* **bessatsu furoku**
分冊 *separate volume* **bunsatsu**
冊子 *booklet, pamphlet* **sasshi**
冊数 *number of books* **sassū**
書冊 *books, reading materials* **shosatsu**
大冊 *humongous-, bulky volume* **taisatsu**
短冊 *long strip of haiku paper* **tanzaku**
小冊子 *pamphlet, booklet* **shōsasshi**

本*ook, 461*	書*ritings, 116*
文*iteracy, 558*	館*ibrary, 918*
読*eading, 260*	

血*lood, 20*　　　　灬*late, 21*

013-B

卌ooks warned Pontius Pilate of a 血loody 灬late...

血 (blood)

血*lood*　　　血*leeding*

chi, KETSU
blood, bleeding, corpuscle

FLIP: 1.0.a. Whole (flat)

血豆 *blood blisters* **chimame**
血迷う *"lose one's sanity..."* **chimayō**
血眼 *frenzy, bloodshot* **chimanako**
血肉 *flesh & blood* **chiniku**
血糊 *blood clot* **chinori**
血筋 *blood, stock* **chisuji**
鼻血 *nosebleed, bleeding nose* **hanaji**
貧血 *anaemia* **hinketsu**
充血 *congestion, clogging* **jūketsu**
血管 *blood vessel, vein, artery* **kekkan**
血気 *vigour-of-youth* **kekki**
血行 *blood circulation* **kekkō**
血痕 *bloodstain* **kekkon**
血球 *blood corpuscle* **kekkyū**
献血 *blood donation* **kenketsu**
血色 *complexion* **kesshoku**
血圧 *blood pressure* **ketsuatsu**
血液 *blood* **ketsueki**
血液型 *blood type* **ketsuekigata**

血縁 *blood relation, ~relationship* **ketsuen**
血族 *blood relative* **ketsuzoku**
混血 *mixed parentage* **konketsu**
混血児 *child of mixed race* **konketsuji**
吸血 *blood sucking, vampire* **kyūketsu**
吸血鬼 *vampire, bloodsucker* **kyūketsuki**
熱血 *hot blood, ardour* **nekketsu**
採血 *collecting-, drawing blood* **saiketsu**
鮮血 *fresh blood* **senketsu**
心血 *heart & soul* **shinketsu**
出血 *bleeding, haemorrhage* **shukketsu**
輸血 *blood transfusion* **yuketsu**
脳溢血 *brain haemorrhage, apoplexy* **nōikketsu**

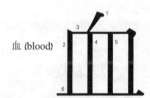

係*elative, 263*	縁*elationship, 675*
系*ineage, 262*	祖*ncestor, 953*

冊*[books], 20*　　　　灬*late, 21*

013-C

卌ooks warned Pontius Pilate of a 血loody 皿late...

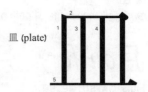

皿 (plate)

皿late   皿ish

sara
plate, dish

灰皿 *ashtray, smoking stand* **haizara**
平皿 *flat plate* **hirazara**
一皿 *a dish of (cuisine)* **hitosara**
火皿 *dish served on fire* **hizara**
木皿 *wooden plate* **kizara**
小皿 *small plate* **kozara**
中皿 *medium-sized plate* **chūzara**
蒸発皿 *evaporating dish* **jōhatsuzara**
菓子皿 *cake dish, sweets plate* **kashizara**
銘々皿 *small plate* **meimeizara**
皿洗い *dish washing, dishwasher* **saraarai**
皿洗い機 *dish washing machine* **saraaraiki**
皿立て *dish rack* **saratate**
皿回し *dish-spinning trick* **saramawashi**
製氷皿 *ice-making dish* **seihyōzara**
手塩皿 *small dish, saucer* **teshiozara**
取り皿 *small plate* **torizara**
受け皿 *saucer* **ukezara**

FLIP: 1.0.a. Whole (flat)

盤*isk, 324*
盆*ray, 594*

卌*[books], 20*   血*lood, 20*

014-A

Grand 盟lliance in the 月onth of 明rilliance...

皿 (plate)

盟

FLIP: 4.0.a. Bottom (flat)

盟lliance   盟onfederacy

aka(rui), aki(raka), akira, MEI, MYŌ
alliance, confederacy, federation, league, coalition

同盟 *alliance, confederacy* **dōmei**
⇒非買同盟 *boycott strike* **hibai dōmei**
⇒不払い同盟 *non-payment strike* **fubarai dōmei**
同盟軍 *allied military, allied armed forces* **dōmeigun**
同盟国 *allied nation, ally* **dōmeikoku**
非同盟 *non-aligned, neutral* **hidōmei**
加盟 *joining, affiliation, membership* **kamei**
加盟国 *member state* **kameikoku**
血盟 *blood compact* **ketsumei**
盟邦 *allied nation, ally* **meihō**
盟主 *leading power* **meishu**
盟約 *alliance pact* **meiyaku**
盟友 *sworn friends, allies* **meiyū**
連盟 *league, federation, alliance* **renmei**
⇒国際連盟 *League of Nations (1924-1946)* **kokusai renmei**
締盟 *enter into a treaty* **teimei**
締盟国 *treaty signatory nation* **teimeikoku**

連*lliance, 305*   団*roup, 345*
同*imilar, 245*   閥*lique, 946*
組*roup, 138*

盤*oard, 324*   盛*rosperity, 244*

014-B

Grand 盟lliance in the 月onth of 明rilliance...

月 (moon; body part)

⓵月onth ⓶月oon

tsuki, GATSU, GETSU
month, moon, lunar

FLIP: 2.0.b. Sort Of (stem)

❶風月 *natures beauty* **fūgetsu**
月経 *menstruation period* **gekkei**
月給 *monthly salary* **gekkyū**
月謝 *monthly tuition* **gessha**
月額 *monthly sum* **getsugaku**
半月 ① *half a month* **hantsuki**
葉月 *August* **hazuki**
如月 *February* **kisaragi**
今月 *this month* **kongetsu**
毎月 *every month* **maitsuki**
何月 *what month* **nangatsu**
来月 *next month* **raigetsu**
歳月 *time, years* **saigetsu**
先月 *last month* **sengetsu**
正月 *New Year day* **shōgatsu**
祥月 *month of death* **shōtsuki**
月々 *each month, every month* **tsukizuki**
月刊誌 *monthly magazine* **gekkanshi**
月桂樹 *laurel* **gekkeiju**

月末 *end of the month* **getsumatsu**
月掛け *monthly instalment* **tsukigake**
月日 *time, year* **tsukihi**
月割り *monthly instalment* **tsukiwari**
星月夜 *starlit night, starry night* **hoshizukiyo**
❷月光 *moonlight* **gekkō**
半月 ② *half moon* **hangetsu**
満月 *full moon* **mangetsu**
月影 *moonlight, moonshine* **tsukikage**
月見 *moon viewing* **tsukimi**
残月 *moon in the morning* **zangetsu**
月曜日 *Monday* **getsuyōbi**
皆既月食 *total lunar eclipse* **kaiki gesshoku**
月ロケット *moon rocket* **tsukiroketto**
月並み *ordinary, common* **tsukinami**

曜eekday, 849	
週eekly, 279	月ed colour, 78

014-C

Grand 盟lliance in the 月onth of 明rilliance...

日 (sunlight, daytime)

明right 明lear

akari, aka(rui), aki(raka), a(keru), aka(rumu), aka(ramu), a(ku), a(kasu),
a(kuru), MEI, MYŌ
bright, brilliance, clear, radiant

FLIP: 6.0.a. Left (flat)

明日 *clarification, elucidation* **asu, myōnichi**
文明 *civilization* **bunmei**
不明 *unclear, unknown* **fumei**
⇒行方不明 *missing person* **yukue fumei**
発明 *discovery, invention* **hatsumei**
表明 *express, announce* **hyōmei**
公明 *fair & just* **kōmei**
明暗 *contrast, sharpness, clarity* **meian**
明度 *brightness* **meido**
明示 *clearly displayed, ~stated* **meiji**
明解 *clear explanation* **meikai**
明快 *lucid, explicit* **meikai**
明確 *clear, definite* **meikaku**
明記 *clearly stated, ~written* **meiki**
明朗 *clear, cheerful* **meirō**
明細 *details, specifics* **meisai**
明察 *insight, discernment* **meisatsu**
明色 *bright colours* **meishoku**
明哲 *wisdom, intelligence* **meitetsu**

明答 *definite reply* **meitō**
明星 *Planet Venus* **myōjō**
鮮明 *clear, distinch* **senmei**
説明 *explanation, elucidation* **setsumei**
釈明 *explanation, apology* **shakumei**
神明 *divine, deity, god* **shinmei**
証明 *proof, evidence* **shōmei**
松明 *torch, torchlight* **taimatsu**
明石市 *Akashi City, Hyōgo Pref.* **akashi-shi**
明らか *clear, distinct, stark* **akiraka**
雪明り *light from the snow* **yukiakari**
明治維新 *Meiji Restoration* **meiji ishin**

照hine, 529	昭right, 529
光hining, 77	英rilliance, 217
澄ake clear, 437	

盟lliance, 21

015-A

凸rotrude & 凹oncave, Japanese 円en in 円ircles were made...

凵 (open box)

凸rotrude   凸onvex

TOTSU
  protrude, convex

FLIP: 1.0.a. Whole (flat)

凸レンズ *convex lens* **totsu renzu**
凸凹 *jagged, uneven* **dekoboko**
凸型 *convexity* **dekokata**
凸溜り *pond formed on a hollow* **kubotamari**
お凸 *brow, forehead* **odeko**
凹凸 *jaggedness, concave & convex* **ōtotsu**
凹凸レンズ *concave-convex lens* **ōtotsu renzu**
凸角 *salient angle* **tokkaku**
凸起 *projection* **tokki**
凸鏡 *convex lens* **tokkyō**
凸面 *convex* **totsumen**
凸面鏡 *convex mirror* **totsumenkyō**
凸版印刷 *relief printing* **toppan insatsu**

凹*oncave, 23*   凸*ome-out, 173*
形*hape, 951*

凹*oncave, 23*

015-B

凹rotrude & 凹oncave, Japanese 円en in 円ircles were made...

凵 (open box)

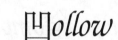

凹oncave   凹ollow

Ō
  concave, hollow

FLIP: 1.0.a. Whole (flat)

凹み *hollow, depression, bowl* **hekomi**
凹レンズ *concave lens* **ōrenzu**
穴凹 *hole, hollow* **anaboko**
凸凹 *jagged, uneven* **dekoboko**
凹版 *intaglio printing* **ōban**
凹部 *concavity* **ōbu**
凹地 *low spot, hollow* **ōchi**
凹形 *concavity* **ōkei**
凹所 *hollow, depression, bowl* **ōsho**
凹凸 *unevenness, concave & convex* **ōtotsu**
凹凸レンズ *concave-convex lens* **ōtotsu renzu**
凹眼鏡 *concave lens (eyeglasses)* **ōgankyō**
凹面鏡 *concave mirror* **ōmenkyō**
凸凹紙 *embossed printing* **totsuōshi**
凹版印刷 *intaglio printing* **ōban insatsu**

凸*ortrude, 23*   入*ut-inside, 2*
形*hape, 951*

凸*ortrude, 23*

015-C

凸rotrude & 凹oncave, Japanese 円en in 円ircles were made...

冂 (inverted box)

¹円en   ²円ircle

maru(i), EN
yen; circle, round

FLIP: 1.0.b. Whole (stem)

❶円高 *strong yen* **endaka**
円玉 *Japanese yen coins* **endama**
円価 *yen purchase price* **enka**
円安 *cheap yen, weak yen* **enyasu**
円建て *price in yen* **endate**
円借款 *yen-denominated loan* **enshakkan**
円相場 *yen exchange rate* **ensōba**
円切り上げ *yen appreciation* **enkiriage**
円切り下げ *yen devaluation* **enkirisage**

❷長円 *oval, oblong* **chōen**
円舞 *waltz, circular dance* **enbu**
円陣 *circle* **enjin**
円熟 *mature, mellow* **enjuku**
円環 *circle* **enkan**
円滑 *smooth, fine* **enkatsu**
円形 *circle* **enkei**
円弧 *circular arc* **enko**
円満 *smooth & well-rounded* **enman**

円周 *perimetre, circular constant* **enshū**
円周率 *pi* **enshūritsu**
円錐 *cone, circular cone* **ensui**
円卓 *round table* **entaku**
円座 *circular seat* **enza**
半円 *semi-circle* **han'en**
方円 *certain shape* **hōen**
楕円形 *ellipse, oval* **daenkei**
円やか *smooth shape object* **maroyaka**
高円宮 *Prince Takamado (1955-2002)* **takamado-no-miya**
円形劇場 *amphitheatre* **enkei gekijō**
前方後円墳 *circular tomb* **zenpōkōenfun**

丸*ound, 73*	幣*oney, 171*
金*oney, 25*	札*oney-bills, 685*

丹*ed colour, 78*

016-A

金etal 栓ork made 全ntirely for New York...

人⇔亻 (person)

全ntire   全hole   全omplete

matta(ku), sube(te), ZEN
entire, whole, complete, total

FLIP: 1.0.a. Whole (flat)

万全 *full-proof, assured* **banzen**
完全 *perfection, completion* **kanzen**
健全 *healthy, wholesome* **kenzen**
全部 *the whole, all parts* **zenbu**
全治 *heal completely* **zenchi**
全額 *full amount, total price* **zengaku**
全域 *whole area* **zen'iki**
全員 *all members, everyone in the group* **zen'in**
全壊 *complete destruction, annihilation* **zenkai**
全快 *complete recovery* **zenkai**
全開 *opening all the way* **zenkai**
全巻 *whole volume, reel* **zenkan**
全国 *whole nation, all-Japan* **zenkoku**
全面 *all sides, entirety* **zenmen**
全納 *full payment* **zennō**
全廃 *total abolition* **zenpai**
全般 *the whole, entire* **zenpan**
全裸 *fully-naked* **zenra**
全身 *whole body* **zenshin**

全書 *compendium* **zensho**
⇒六法全書 *laws compendium* **roppō zensho**
全集 *complete works* **zenshū**
全損 *complete wreckage* **zenson**
全体 *entire, whole* **zentai**
全然 *entirely, totally* **zenzen**
全音符 *whole musical note* **zen'onpu**
全世界 *entire world, all countries* **zensekai**
交通安全 *safe driving* **kōtsū anzen**
全会一致 *unanimity, consensus* **zenkai icchi**
全快祝い *feast of full recovery* **zenkai iwai**

皆*verything, 39*
総*otality, 433*

余*xtra, 501*

016-B

金etal 栓ork made 全ntirely for New York...

❶ 金oney ❷ 金etal ❸ 金old

金 (metal)

kane, kana, KIN, KON
money, currency, denomination, legal tender; metal, alloy; gold

FLIP: 1.0.a. Whole (flat)

❶頭金 down payment **atamakin**
罰金 fine, penalty **bakkin**
募金 fund raising **bokin**
賃金 wages, pay **chingin**
貯金 savings **chokin**
官金 government funds **kankin**
献金 cash gift, cash donation **kenkin**
金庫 cash box, safe **kinko**
金納 cash payment **kinnō**
金力 power of money **kinryoku**
金策 ways of raising money **kinsaku**
金融 finance, banking system **kinyū**
拠金 contribution, donation **kyokin**
涙金 consolation money **namidakin**
納金 payment, account settlement **nōkin**
料金 fee, rate, charge **ryōkin**
借金 debt, loan **shakkin**
集金 collecting money **shūkin**
即金 ready cash, cash deal **sokkin**

税金 tax **zeikin**
剰余金 surplus money **jōyokin**
滞納金 arrears **tainōkin**
金曜日 Friday **kinyōbi**
❷合金 metal alloys **gōkin**
白金 platinum **hakkin**
純金 pure, solid gold **junkin**
金物 metalware **kanamono**
貴金属 precious metal **kikinzoku**
❸金魚 gold fish **kingyo**
金髪 blonde **kinpatsu**
黄金 gold **ōgon**
砂金 gold dust~, powder **sakin**

円en, 24   札oney-bills, 685   鋳asting, 440
幣oney, 171   鉄ron, 155

余urplus, 501   全ntire, 24

016-C

金etal 栓ork made 全ntirely for New York...

栓ork 栓topper

木 (wooden)

SEN
cork, stopper

FLIP: 5.0.a. Left & Right

血栓 thrombus **kessen**
血栓症 thrombosis, blood clotting **kessenshō**
耳栓 earplug **mimisen**
木栓 wooden cork **mokusen**
元栓 main tap **motosen**
音栓 organ stopper **onsen**
塞栓 clogged blood vessel **sokusen**
水栓 water tap, water hydrant **suisen**
防火栓 fire hydrant, ~extinguisher **bōkasen**
ガス栓 gas tap, spigot **gasusen**
給水栓 water tap, hydrant **kyūsuisen**
脳血栓 cerebral thrombosis **nōkessen**
栓抜き corkscrew, bottle opener **sennuki**
消火栓 fire hydrant, ~extinguisher **shōkasen**
水道栓 water hydrant, tap **suidōsen**

瓶ottle, 886

検nspection, 939

017-A

廷*mperial court men row a* 艇*oat by the* 庭*arden...*

廴 (stretch)

廷*mperial court*

TEI
imperial court

朝廷 *imperial court* **chōtei**
閉廷 *court suit dismissal* **heitei**
法廷 *court of law* **hōtei**
⇒模擬法廷 *moot court* **mogi hōtei**
開廷 *opening of a court hearing* **kaitei**
公廷 *public court* **kōtei**
宮廷 *imperial court* **kyūtei**
休廷 *court adjournment, ~recess* **kyūtei**
内廷 *inner court* **naitei**
入廷 *entering a court* **nyūtei**
出廷 *court attendance, subpoena* **shuttei**
退廷 *court expulsion* **taitei**
廷内 *court grounds* **teinai**
廷吏 *court clerk* **teiri**
廷臣 *official retainer* **teishin**
廷丁 *court clerk* **teitei**
公判廷 *public court* **kōhantei**
宮廷文学 *court of literary world* **kyūtei bungaku**

FLIP: 7.1. Right (Sort Of)
Facing: 1.1. West (H)

宮廷画家 *court painter* **kyūtei gaka**
宮廷詩人 *court poet* **kyūtei shijin**

殿*alace, 522*	妃*rincess, 728*
城*astle, 243*	姫*rincess, 542*
皇*mperor, 113*	裁*udgement, 802*
后*mpress, 87*	判*udgement, 949*
王*onarch, 12*	

延*rolong, 515*   庭*arden, 27*

017-B

廷*mperial court men row a* 艇*oat by the* 庭*arden...*

舟 (vessel)

艇*oat*   艇*essel*

TEI
boat, *small boat,* vessel

艦艇 *naval vessel* **kantei**
汽艇 *steam boat* **kitei**
競艇 *boat race* **kyōtei**
小艇 *small boat* **shōtei**
舟艇 *boat, small vessel* **shūtei**
漕艇 *boat rowing* **sōtei**
漕艇者 *boat rowman* **sōteisha**
短艇 *small boat* **tantei**
端艇 *small boat* **tantei**
艇長 *boat skipper* **teichō**
艇員 *boat crew, sailor* **teiin**
艇身 *length of a boat* **teishin**
艇首 *bow of a boat* **teishu**
艇隊 *flotilla, convoy* **teitai**
駆潜艇 *submarine chaser* **kusentei**
魚雷艇 *torpedo boat, seaplane* **gyoraitei**
飛行艇 *seaplane* **hikōtei**
巡視艇 *patrol boat* **junshitei**
警備艇 *coast guard boat* **keibitei**

Facing: 1.2. West (V)

救助艇 *rescue boat* **kyūjotei**
救命艇 *lifeboat, liferaft* **kyūmeitei**
潜航艇 *submarine* **senkōtei**
消防艇 *fire-fighting boat* **shōbōtei**
掃海艇 *minesweeper* **sōkaitei**
水雷艇 *torpedo boat* **suiraitei**

航*avigation, 748*	舶*hip, 742*
舟*hip, 90*	丸*[ships], 73*
船*hip, 757*	隻*[ships], 50*

般*eneral, 323*

017-C

廷mperial court men row a 艇oat by the 庭arden...

广 (rooftop)

庭arden

niwa, TEI
garden; courtyard (original meaning)

Facing: 3.0. ☞☜ Across

茶庭 *tea ceremony garden* **chatei**
営庭 *parade grounds* **eitei**
箱庭 *miniature garden* **hakoniwa**
平庭 *flat garden, plain garden* **hiraniwa**
石庭 *sand & rock garden* **ishiniwa**
家庭 *family, household* **katei**
⇒父子家庭 *single-father family* **fushi katei**
⇒母子家庭 *single-mother family* **boshi katei**
家庭的 *domestic affairs, within the family* **kateiteki**
家庭教師 *private tutor* **katei kyōshi**
径庭 *great difference* **keitei**
校庭 *school garden* **kōtei**
後庭 *backyard, rear garden* **kōtei**
庭番 *garden watchman* **niwaban**
庭石 *garden stone* **niwaishi**
庭木 *garden tree* **niwaki**
庭師 *gardener* **niwashi**
奥庭 *backyard, rear garden* **okuniwa**
庭園 *garden* **teien**

⇒屋上庭園 *rooftop garden* **okujō teien**
庭球 *lawn tennis* **teikyū**
庭前 *garden* **teizen**
内庭 *quadrangle, inner court* **uchiniwa, naitei**
裏庭 *backyard* **uraniwa**
矢庭に *all of a sudden, immediately* **yaniwa(ni)**
前庭 *front garden* **zentei, maeniwa**
庭下駄 *garden sandals* **niwageta**
家庭裁判所 *family court* **katei saibansho**

園*arden*, 916
芝*awn*, 84
草*rass*, 373

延*rolong*, 515　廷*mperial court*, 26

018-A

Every 年ear, empty 缶ans left in the 岳ummits picked up by hermits...

干 (drying)

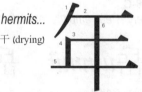

年nnual　年ear

toshi, NEN
annual, year

Facing: 1.0. ☜ West (W)

晩年 *later years* **bannen**
没年 *age at death* **botsunen**
元年 *first year of an imperial reign* **gannen**
半年 *half year, six months* **hantoshi, hannen**
今年 *this year, present year* **kotoshi, konnen**
去年 *last year, the year past* **kyonen**
毎年 *every year* **maitoshi, mainen**
年長 *seniority* **nenchō**
年度 *fiscal-, academic year (April-to-March)* **nendo**
年額 *annual sum, yearly amount* **nengaku**
年鑑 *yearbook* **nenkan**
年間 *number of years* **nenkan**
年忌 *death anniversary* **nenki**
年金 *pension money, pension income* **nenkin**
年齢 *death age, age at death* **nenrei**
年数 *number of years* **nensū**
来年 *next year, coming year* **rainen**
例年 *average-, every year* **reinen**
昨年 *last year, the year past* **sakunen**

新年 *New Year* **shinnen**
少年 *juvenile, minor, under-aged* **shōnen**
周年 *anniversary* **shūnen**
年下 *younger, one's juniour* **toshishita**
未成年 *under-aged, minor, below 18* **miseinen**
年賀状 *New Year greeting card* **nengajō**
暦年齢 *chronological age* **rekinenrei**
年の功 *hard experience* **toshi no kō**
年格好 *look, appearance* **toshikakkō**
年越し *New Year's eve* **toshikoshi**
年寄り *senior citizens, old people* **toshiyori**

日*ay*, 14　　週*eekly*, 279
曜*eekday*, 849　月*onth*, 22

岳*ountain peak*, 28　　缶*an*, 28

018-B

Every 年ear, empty 缶ans left in the 岳ummits picked up by hermits...

缶 (earthen jar)

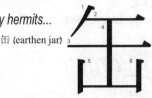

缶*an* 缶*anister*

KAN
can, canister

FLIP: 2.0.a. Sort Of (flat)

茶缶 *tea canister* **chakan**
茶筒 *tea canister* **chazutsu**
牛缶 *canned beef* **gyūkan**
蟹缶 *canned crab meat* **kanikan**
缶詰 *canned food* **kanzume**
汽缶 *boiler* **kikan**
汽缶室 *boiler room* **kikanshitsu**
鮭缶 *canned salmon* **sakekan**
薬缶 *kettle, boiling pot* **yakkan**
空き缶 *empty can* **akikan**
缶ビール *canned beer* **kan bi-ru**
缶ジューズ *canned juice* **kan jūzu**
缶切り *can-, tin opener* **kankiri**
缶焚き *stoking, stirring up* **kantaki**
製缶工場 *canning factory, cannery* **seikan kōjō**

栓*topper, 25*	倉*torage, 399*
容*ontent, 492*	蔵*torage, 565*
庫*torage, 306*	貯*torage, 967*

岳*ountain peak, 28*	年*ear, 27*

018-C

Every 年ear, empty 缶ans left in the 岳ummits picked up by hermits...

山 (mountain)

岳*ummit* 岳*ountain peak*

take, GAKU
summit, mountain peak

FLIP: 4.0.a. Bottom (flat)

富岳 *Mt. Fuji* **fugaku**
岳父 *one's father-in-law* **gakufu**
岳麓 *foot of Mt. Fuji* **gakuroku**
山岳 *mountain ranges* **sangaku**
山岳部 *mountaineering club* **sangakubu**
山岳病 *acrophobia, fear of heights* **sangakubyō**
朝日岳 *Mt. Asahi* **asahidake**
岳友会 *mountaineering club* **gakuyūkai**
穂高岳 *Mt. Hodakatake* **hodakadake**
    (border of Gifu and Nagano Prefectures)
雲仙岳 *Mt. Unzen (Nagasaki Prefecture)* **unzendake**
槍ヶ岳 *Mt. Yarigatake (Nagano Prefecture)* **yarigatake**
八ヶ岳 *Mt. Yatsugatake* **yatsugatake**

峠*ountain trail, 646*	山*ountain, 172*
岬*ape, 646*	

缶*an, 28*	年*ear, 27*

019-A
岩ocks & 炭oal on a 岸oastal 岸hore told in folklore...

山 (mountain)

岩ock

iwa, GAN
rock

岩盤	bedrock, stronghold **ganban**
岩塩	rock salt **gan'en**
岩脈	dike, dyke **ganmyaku**
岩石	rock **ganseki**
岩床	rock bottom **ganshō**
岩礁	shore, reef **ganshō**
岩穴	cave, cavern **iwaana**
岩場	rocky area **iwaba**
岩壁	rock wall, cliff **iwakabe**
岩魚	char **iwana**
岩戸	rock cover to a cave **iwato**
岩山	rocky mountains **iwayama**
奇岩	strange-looking rocks **kigan**
砂岩	sandstone **sagan**
溶岩	volcano lava **yōgan**
溶岩流	volcano lava stream, ~flow **yōganryū**
玄武岩	basalt **genbugan**
凝灰岩	tuff **gyōkaigan**
変成岩	metamorphic rock **henseigan**

FLIP: 3.0.a. Top (flat)

岩田帯	pregnancy-, maternity belt **iwataobi**
花崗岩	granite **kakōgan**
火成岩	igneous rock **kaseigan**
削岩機	rock drill **sakuganki**
石灰岩	limestone **sekkaigan**
水成岩	aqueous rock **suiseigan**

砂ands, 643	浦eashore, 813
石tone, 363	浜eashore, 490
涯eashore, 890	

炭oal, 29	岸hore, 30

019-B
岩ocks &炭oal on a 岸oastal 岸hore told in folklore...

火 ⇔ 灬 (fire)

炭oal   炭ignite

sumi, TAN
coal, charcoal, lignite

亜炭	lignite **atan**
貯炭	coal supply **chotan**
貯炭庫	bunker, underground safeplace **chotanko**
泥炭	peat **deitan**
氷炭	irreconcilable differences **hyōtan**
堅炭	hard charcoal **katazumi**
褐炭	lignite, brown coal **kattan**
黒炭	black charcoal **kokutan**
豆炭	oval briquette **mametan**
木炭	charcoal **mokutan**
練炭	briquettes **rentan**
採炭	coal mining **saitan**
石炭	mineral coal **sekitan**
出炭	coal production **shuttan**
炭火	charcoal fire **sumibi, tanka**
炭団	charcoal briquettes **tandan**
炭田	coalfield **tanden**
炭肺	black lungs, anthracosis **tanhai**
炭塵	coal dust **tanjin**

FLIP: 3.0.a. Top (flat)

炭化	carbonisation **tanka**
炭化水素	hydrocarbon **tanka suiso**
炭坑	coal mine shaft **tankō**
炭鉱	coal mine, colliery **tankō**
炭酸	carbohydrates **tansan**
炭酸水	carbonated water **tansansui**
炭素	carbon **tanso**
炭層	coal-bed deposits **tansō**
塗炭	misery, anxiety, distress **totan**
消し炭	burned-out charcoals, cinders **keshizumi**
炭焼き	charcoal making **sumiyaki**

燃urning, 445	火ire, 3
熱eat, 153	煙moke, 644

岩ock, 29	岸hore, 30

019-C

岩ocks & 炭oal on a 岸oastal 岸hore told in folklore...

山 (mountain)

岸oastal　　岸eashore

kishi, GAN
coastal, seashore, seaside

FLIP: 3.0.a. Top (flat)
FLIP: 8.0.b. Inner (stem)

着岸 *reaching shore from the sea* **chakugan**
沿岸 *coast, shore* **engan**
沿岸漁業 *coastal-, inshore fishery* **engan gyogyō**
岸壁 *quay, wharf, shorewall* **ganpeki**
岸頭 *standing on the shore* **gantō**
傲岸 *arrogance, snub-nosed, haughty* **gōgan**
彼岸 *equinoctial week* **higan**
彼岸桜 *early-blooming cherry blossoms* **higanzakura**
北岸 *northern coast* **hokugan**
河岸 *riverbank, fish market* **kagan, kashi**
海岸 *beach, seashore, coast, shoreline* **kaigan**
海岸線 *coastline* **kaigansen**
海岸沿い *along the seashore* **kaiganzoi**
海岸通り *coastal road* **kaigandoori**
川岸 *riverside, riveredge* **kawagishi**
岸辺 *along the beach* **kishibe**
南岸 *southern shore* **nangan**
離岸 *set sail, leaving a shore* **rigan**
両岸 *both sides of the shore* **ryōgan, ryōgishi**

左岸 *left riverbank* **sagan**
西岸 *western coast* **seigan**
接岸 *coming alongside* **setsugan**
対岸 *opposite side, ~bank* **taigan**
東岸 *eastern coast* **tōgan**
右岸 *right riverbank* **ugan**
魚河岸 *coastal fish market* **uogashi**
河岸端 *riverside, riveredge* **kashibata**
岸和田 *Kishiwada City, Ōsaka* **kishiwada**
護岸工事 *shore protection works* **gogan kōji**
太平洋岸 *US west coast* **taiheiyōgan**
湾岸戦争 *Gulf War (1991)* **wangan sensō**

涯*eashore, 890*	海*cean, 241*
浦*eashore, 813*	洋*cean, 247*
浜*eashore, 490*	

岩*ock, 29*	炭*oal, 29*

020-A

To 正orrect & 整ectify, 征onquerors live & die...

止 (stopping)

正orrect　　正ccurate　　正recise

tada(shii), tada(su) masa(ni), SEI, SHŌ
correct, accurate, precise, proper, right

Facing: 2.0. East ☞ (W)

賀正 *Happy New Year* **gashō**　*202 - celebration*
厳正 *strictness, discipline* **gensei**　*359 - severe*
改正 *revision, rewriting* **kaisei**　*725 - reform*
規正 *improvement, betterment* **kisei**
校正 *proof-reading* **kōsei**
矯正 *correction, remedy, cure* **kyōsei**　*163 - rectify*
正副 *chief & deputy* **seifuku**　*247 332 deputy*
正義 *justice, right* **seigi**
正業 *noble profession* **seigyō**
正常 *normal person, ~physique* **seijō**
正価 *net price, regular price* **seika**
正課 *regular curriculum, ~subject* **seika**
正解 *the correct answer* **seikai**
正確 *accurate, precise, unmistakable* **seikaku**　*804*
正規 *normal procedure* **seiki**　*814*
正論 *sound argument, good reasoning* **seiron**
正式 *formal, formality, decorum* **seishiki**
正賞 *highest prize, top award* **seishō**
正答 *correct answer* **seitō**

a mmend

正月 *New Year's day* **shōgatsu**
正午 *high noon, 12 o'clock noon* **shōgo**
正絹 *pure silk, 100% silk* **shōken**
正気 *sanity, consciousness* **shōki**
粛正 *cleanup, cleansing* **shukusei**　*905*
修正 *modification, correction* **shūsei**　*878 mast*
僧正 *bishop, archbishop, cardinal* **sōjō**　*836 mo*
訂正 *correction, editing* **teisei**　*174 edit*
適正 *proper, reasonable, fair* **tekisei**　*135 suit*
是正 *correction, redress* **zesei**　*313 fair*
正誤表 *list of errata* **seigohyō**　*889 Erro*

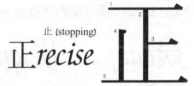

是*orrect, 313*	肯*ffirmative, 616*
義*ighteous, 341*	整*ectify, 31*
善*ighteous, 450*	

止*top, 192*

020-B
To 正orrect & 整ectify, 征onquerors live & die...

父 (action)

整ectify   整ut in order

totono(eru), totono(u), SEI
rectify, put in order, adjust

FLIP: 6.1. Left Top

調整 *adjustment, modification* **chōsei**
不整 *irregularity, inconsistency* **fusei**
補整 *manipulation, adjustment* **hosei** *812-Supplement*
均整 *balance, symmetry* **kinsei** *470-equal*
均整美 *proportional beauty* **kinseibi**
整備 *repair, check-up, maintenance* **seibi** *409-Prepare*
整地 *levelling of land, soil preparation* **seichi**
整風 *rectification, correction* **seifū**
整合 *coordination, integration* **seigō**
製版 *block printing* **seihan** *359-printing*
整髪 *haircut, hairdressing* **seihatsu** *408 hair*
整髪剤 *hairdressing solution* **seihatsuzai**
整除 *divisibility, divisible number* **seijo** *501-div evelude*
整形 *orthopaedics* **seikei**
整形外科 *orthopaedics* **seikei geka**
整骨 *bone-setting, osteopathy* **seikotsu**
整列 *stand in line, queue* **seiretsu**
整理箱 *filing cabinet* **seiribako**
整理整頓 *neat & tidy* **seiri seiton**

整流 *rectification, correction* **seiryū**
整枝 *pruning* **seishi**
整数 *integer, integral number* **seisū**
整頓 *neatness, proper order* **seiton**
整然 *systematic, well-organized* **seizen**
修整 *retouch, touch up* **shūsei**
端整 *neat & orderly* **tansei** *974 utmost*
整腸剤 *intestinal medicine* **seichōzai**
人員整理 *labour cut, staff reduction* **jin'in seiri**
場内整理 *area maintenance* **jōnai seiri**
区画整理 *land re-adjustment* **kukaku seiri**

扱andling, 189		正orrect, 30
掌dminister, 614		直irect, 420

製anufacture, 534	聖acred, 617

020-C
To 正orrect & 整ectify, 征onquerors live & die...

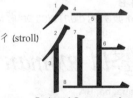

彳 (stroll)

征onquest   征onquer

SEI
conquest, conquer

Facing: 4.0. ⫸ Apart

長征 *Long March (China, 1934-1935)* **chōsei**
遠征 *military expedition* **ensei**
外征 *overseas deployment* **gaisei**
征伐 *conquest, subjugation* **seibatsu** *96-attack*
征服 *conquest, subjugation* **seifuku**
征服者 *conqueror, subjugator* **seifukusha**
征服欲 *desire to subjugate* **seifukuyoku**
征夷 *subjugating (barbarians)* **seii**
征衣 *military uniform; travel clothes* **seii**
征戦 *military expedition* **seisen**
征途 *military expedition; journey* **seito**
征討 *conquest, subjugation* **seitō**
親征 *military expedition led by the emperor* **shinsei**
出征 *going to the battlefield* **shussei**

克onquer, 204	有ossess, 617
抑uppress, 705	勝ictory, 406
覇egemony, 603	

祉elfare, 193	正orrect, 30

021-A

High 波aves didn't stop an 婆ld-woman from 渡rossing to Oman...

水 ⇔ 氵 (water)

波aves 波urrent

nami, HA
waves, current, stream

FLIP: 4.0.b. Bottom (stem)

荒波 violent waves, rough seas **aranami** *419 507*
波長 wavelength **hachō**
波動 wave motion, undulation **hadō**
波状 wavy, choppy waters **hajō**
波及 spread, extension, influence **hakyū**
波紋 ripple, water ring, sensation **hamon**
波乱 rise & fall, vicissitudes **haran**
波浪 waves, current **harō**
波線 wavy line **hasen**
波涛 waves, rough seas **hatō**
波頭 crest of waves **hatō, namigashira**
穂波 waves of rice plants **honami**
寒波 cold wave **kanpa**
波路 sea route, sea lanes **namiji**
波風 wind & waves, storm, trouble **namikaze**
波間 waves, current **namima**
波音 sound of ocean waves **namioto**
難波 shipwreck, cast away **nanpa**
脳波 brain waves **nōha**

音波 sound waves **onpa**
逆波 choppy waters **sakanami** 逆 *gyaku- opp 743*
周波 cycle **shūha** *280- lap*
短波 shortwaves **tanpa**
年波 getting old, greying, ageing **toshinami**
津波 tidal wave **tsunami**
波立つ choppy, run high **namidatsu**
波打つ wave, ripple **namiutsu**
電磁波 electromagnetic waves **denjiha**
波止場 wharf, pier, quay **hatoba**
衝撃波 shock wave **shōgekiha**

流current, 781	海cean, 241
漂rift-about, 604	洋cean, 247
浪rifting, 254	

彼[3rd person], 224	被uffer, 715

021-B

High 波aves didn't stop an 婆ld-woman from 渡rossing to Oman...

女 (woman)

婆ld woman 婆randma

baba, bā, BA
old woman, grandma, granny, matriarch, old matron

FLIP: 7.2.b. Right Top (stem)
Facing: 2.1. East ☞ (H)

婆屋 old housekeeper; midwife **bāya**
鬼婆 hag, witch **onibaba**
老婆 old lady, old woman, hag **rōba**
⇒冷酷老婆 nasty old woman **reikoku rōba**
老婆心 grandmotherly worries **rōbashin**
産婆 midwife **sanba**
娑婆 outside world; this world **shaba**
狸婆 cunning old hag **tanuki baba**
塔婆 wooden grave tablet **tōba**
妖婆 hag, witch **yōba**
婆抜き exclusion of old persons **babānuki**
婆羅門 Brahman **baramon**
お転婆 bubbling, high-spirited; tomboy **otenba**
卒塔婆 wooden grave tablet **sotoba**
阿婆擦れ hussy, bitch; extra cargo **abazure**
お婆さん grandmother, elderly woman **obāsan**
遣り手婆 brothel-, whorehouse madamme **yarite babā**

老lderly, 149	翁ld man, 238
古ld, 477	仙ermit, 416

波aves, 32

021-C

High 波aves didn't stop an 婆ld-woman from 渡rossing to Oman...

水⇔氵 (water)

渡ross-over   渡and-over

wata(ru), wata(su), TO
cross-over, hand-over, traverse

譲渡 *transfer, negotiation* **jōto**   853 – assign rights

譲渡抵当 *mortgage, collateral* **jōto teitō**

渡米 *go to America* **tobei**

渡英 *going to England, UK-bound* **toei**

渡河 *crossing a river* **toka**

渡航 *voyaging, going abroad, ~overseas* **tokō**

渡航者 *passenger* **tokōsha**

渡欧 *visit to Europe* **toō**

渡来 *coming from a foreign country* **torai**

渡世 *making a livelihood, getting by* **tosei**

渡船 *ferry, ferry boat* **tosen**

明け渡し *evacuation, surrender* **akewatashi**

不渡り *dishonouring a cheque* **fuwatari**

橋渡し *mediation, intercession* **hashiwatashi**

刃渡り *blade length* **hawatari**

火渡り *walk on fire* **hiwatari**

過渡期 *transition period* **katoki**

倉渡し *extra warehouse* **kurawatashi**

先渡し *future delivery* **sakiwatashi**

FLIP: 4.0.b. Bottom (stem)
Facing: 2.2. East ☞ (V)

綱渡り *ropewalking (circus)* **tsunawatari**

内渡し *partial delivery* **uchiwatashi**

渡り者 *migrant workers* **watarimono**

世渡り *livelihood, subsistence* **yowatari**

申し渡す *tell, say, inform* **mōshiwatasu**

鳴り渡る *resound, ring, echo* **nariwataru**

利権譲渡 *transfer of rights* **riken jōto**

知れ渡る *be widely known* **shirewataru**

澄み渡る *be perfectly clear* **sumiwataru**

受け渡し *delivery, handing over* **ukewatashi**

行き渡る *spread, go around* **yukiwataru**

交*rossing, 467*	渉*ross-over, 273*
往*ome & go, 749*	搬*and-over, 323*
出*epart, 173*	輪*and-over, 660*

度*egree, 91*

022-A

忙usily we 忘orget 妄elusions of death...

心⇔忄 (heart, feelings)

忙usy   忙ectic

isoga(shii), BŌ
busy, hectic, occupied

忙しい *hard, busy* **isogashii**

忙しない *busy, restless* **sewashinai**

忙中 *busy, "do not disturb..."* **bōchū**

忙殺 *crushed to death* **bōsatsu**

繁忙 *extremely busy* **hanbō**

煩忙 *extremely busy* **hanbō**

忽忙 *busy, in a hurry* **sōbō**

多忙 *extremely busy* **tabō**

Facing: 2.2. East ☞ (V)

働*abour, 422*	閑*eisure, 283*
労*abour, 351*	悠*eisure, 898*
暇*ree time, 653*	

忘*orget, 34*	亡*eath, 72*

022-B

忙*usily we* 忘*orget* 妄*elusions of death...*

心⇔忄⇔㣺 (feelings)

忘*orget* 忘*blivion*

wasu(reru), BŌ
forget, oblivion, amnesia

Facing: 2.1. East ☞ (H)

備忘 *reminder, cue, hint* **bibō**
備忘録 *memorandum, notice* **bibōroku**
忘我 *self-oblivion; trance* **bōga**
忘却 *forgetfulness, memory lapse* **bōkyaku**
忘恩 *ingratitude, ungratefulness* **bōon**
健忘 *forgetfulness, short memory* **kenbō**
健忘症 *dementia, amnesia* **kenbōshō**
初忘 *naïvety, gullible* **shoshin**
忘年会 *year-end party* **bōnenkai**
度忘れ *memory lapse* **dowasure**
胴忘れ *forgetfulness, memory lapse* **dōwasure**
物忘れ *forgetfulness, memory lapse* **monowasure**
寝忘れ *forget to sleep* **newasure**
面忘れ *fail to recognize* **omowasure**
年忘れ *year-end party* **toshiwasure**
忘れ物 *forgotten belongings* **wasuremono**
勿忘草 *"forget-me-not plant..."* **wasurenagusa**
聞き忘れ *forget to hear* **kikiwasure**

見忘れる *forget to recognize* **miwasureru**
忘れ形見 *memento, keepsake* **wasuregatami**
置き忘れる *forget to leave on* **okiwasureru**
忘れっぽい *forgetful, short memory* **wasureppoi**

妄*houghtless, 34*	失*ailure, 19*
疎*eglect, 955*	敗*ailure, 137*
慢*egligence, 845*	覚*ecall, 307*

亡*eath, 72*	志*ntention, 426*

022-C

忙*usily we* 忘*orget* 妄*elusions of death...*

女 (woman)

妄*elusion* 妄*houghtless*

MŌ, BŌ
delusion, thoughtless, rash

Facing: 2.1. East ☞ (H)

妄言 *thoughtless-, careless remarks* **bōgen**
虚妄 *falsehood, untrue* **kyomō**
狂妄 *crazy, mad* **kyomō, kyōbō**
迷妄 *illusion, delusion* **meimō**
妄動 *rush action* **mōdō**
⇒軽挙妄動 *rash action* **keikyo mōdō**
妄語 *falsehood, untrue* **mōgo**
妄評 *unfair criticism* **mōhyō, bōhyō**
妄念 *distracting thoughts* **mōnen**
妄説 *fallacious report, fallacy* **mōsetsu, bōsetsu**
妄信 *blind belief* **mōshin, bōshin**
妄執 *delusion, illusion* **mōshū, bōshū**
妄想 *delusion, wild fancy* **mōsō, bōsō**
⇒被害妄想 *persecuted complex, paranoia* **higai mōsō**
⇒誇大妄想 *megalomania, illusion of grandeur* **kodai mōsō**

疎*eglect, 955*	失*ailure, 19*
慢*egligence, 845*	敗*ailure, 137*
忘*orget, 34*	

安*afety, 350*	妥*ontentment, 610*

023-A

画*aintings'* 価*alue &* 価*rice depend on the* 面*urface size...*

田 (cultivated field)

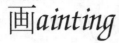

画*icture*　画*ainting*

GA, KAKU
picture, painting, draw a plan

FLIP: 1.0.a. Whole (flat)

描画 *drawing, sketch* **byōga**
映画 *movie, film* **eiga**
画家 *artist, painter* **gaka**
画面 *screen* **gamen**
画廊 *art gallery* **garō**
画才 *artistic talent* **gasai**
画商 *art dealer, picture dealer* **gashō**
画集 *book of paintings, ~pictures* **gashū**
画素 *picture pixel, dot* **gaso**
画像 *image, picture* **gazō**
劇画 *story comic, comic strip* **gekiga**
版画 *handblock print* **hanga**
壁画 *mural* **hekiga**
邦画 *Japanese film, ~movie* **hōga**
陰画 *film negative* **inga**
絵画 *picture, painting* **kaiga**
画策 *scheme, plan, programme* **kakusaku**
画然 *clear distinction* **kakuzen**
計画 *project, planning* **keikaku**

企画 *programme-of-action* **kikaku**
漫画 *comics, caricature, cartoon* **manga**
名画 *famous film* **meiga**
録画 *videotaping, ~recording* **rokuga**
略画 *sketch, drawing* **ryakuga**
陽画 *positive picture (film)* **yōga**
洋画 *Western film, ~movie* **yōga**
自画像 *self-portrait* **jigazō**
画期的 *epoch-making* **kakkiteki**
画一化 *standardization* **kakuitsuka**
写生画 *sketch, drawing* **shaseiga**

図*rawing, 47*	描*ketch, 271*
絵*rawing, 143*	撮*hotograph, 423*

面*urface, 36*	再*epeat, 225*

023-B

画*aintings'* 価*alue &* 価*rice depend on the* 面*urface size...*

人⇔イ (person)

価*alue*　価*rice*

atai, KA
value, price, worth

FLIP: 7.0.a. Right (flat)

安価 *cheap, low-priced* **anka**
買価 *purchase price* **baika**
米価 *price of rice* **beika**
物価 *commodity prices* **bukka**
代価 *price, cost* **daika**
同価 *equivalent price* **dōka**
円価 *price in Japanese yen* **enka**
原価 *cost, price* **genka**
減価 *price reduction* **genka**
平価 *par, parity, par value* **heika**
評価 *evaluation, appraisal* **hyōka**
時価 *market price* **jika**
株価 *stock prices* **kabuka**
価値 *value, worth* **kachi**
価格 *price, value* **kakaku**
高価 *expensive, costly* **kōka**
無価 *priceless* **muka**
無価値 *priceless* **mukachi**
廉価 *cheap price* **renka**

声価 *reputation, name value* **seika**
正価 *net price, regular price* **seika**
市価 *market price* **shika**
真価 *true value, real worth* **shinka**
対価 *compensation, payment* **taika**
単価 *unit price, unit cost* **tanka**
定価 *list price, fixed price* **teika**
等価 *equivalent, equal, parity* **tōka**
特価 *reduced price* **tokka**
予価 *price estimate, quoted price* **yoka**
栄養価 *nutritive value* **eiyōka**

値*rice, 783*	幣*oney, 171*
貴*recious, 913*	札*oney-bills, 685*
金*oney, 25*	

面*urface, 36*	西*estern, 18*	両*oth, 567*

023-C

画*aintings'* 価*alue* & 価*rice depend on the* 面*urface size...*

面 (surface, front)

面*ace*　　　　面*urface*

FLIP: 1.0.a. Whole (flat)

omote, omo, tsura, MEN
face, surface, dimension, sector

部面	*phase, section* **bumen**
帳面	*notebook, books* **chōmen** *641*
覆面	*face mask* **fukumen**
額面	*face value, par value* **gakumen**
画面	*scene, screen, window* **gamen**
顔面	*face surface* **ganmen**
画廊	*art gallery, art exhibit* **garō**
背面	*backside, rear surface* **haimen**
白面	*face without cosmetics* **hakumen**
表面	*surface, outward look* **hyōmen**
渋面	*grimace, wince, sneer* **jūmen, shibuttsura**
球面	*spherical shape* **kyūmen**
面会	*interview, interpellation* **menkai**
面積	*land size, floor area* **menseki**
面接	*interview, interpellation* **mensetsu**
面識	*acquaintance* **menshiki**
面子	*honour, face, name* **mentsu**
面前	*"in the presence of..."* **menzen**
能面	*Noh mask* **nōmen**

面影	*image, face, shadow* **omokage**
斜面	*slope, slant* **shamen**
側面	*side, lateral* **sokumen**
底面	*bottom, depth* **teimen**
横面	*cheek* **yokkotsura**
全面	*entirety, wholly* **zenmen**
仏頂面	*sullen look, sour face* **bucchōzura**
面食い	*liking good looks* **menkui**
面持ち	*look, face* **omomochi**
面構え	*one's face* **tsuragamae**
面汚し	*disgrace, humiliation* **tsurayogoshi**

前*rontal, 118*	後*osterior, 897*
表*utlook, 378*	裏*osterior, 872*

画*ainting, 35*	雨*aining, 417*

024-A

捜*earching,* 抽*ulling,* 押*ushing, rock fans abusing...*

手⇔扌 (hand, manual)

捜*earch*　　　捜*ook for*

FLIP: 7.0.b2. Right (stem)

saga(su), SŌ
search, finding, look-for

博捜	*thorough & extensive search* **hakusō**
捜査	*investigation, search* **sōsa**
捜査員	*detective, investigator* **sōsain**
捜査令状	*search warrant* **sōsa reijō**
捜索	*search, manhunt* **sōsaku**
⇒家宅捜索	*search in a house* **kataku sōsaku**
捜索状	*search warrant* **sōsakujō**
捜索隊	*search & rescue mission* **sōsakutai**
捜査網	*"long arm of the law...", police dragnet* **sōsamō**
捜し絵	*picture puzzle* **sagashie**
捜し物	*something to look for, missing item* **sagashimono**
捜し回る	*hunting around* **sagashimawaru**
捜し出す	*find out, discover* **sagashidasu**
捜し当てる	*find out, locate, ferret out* **sagashiateru**
捜し求める	*seek* **sagashimotomeru**
絵捜し	*picture puzzle* **esagashi**

索*earch, 375*	
探*earch, 787*	
覧*ook at, 592*	

理*eason, 872*	埋*ury, 319*

024-B

捜earching, 抽ulling, 押ushing, rock fans abusing...

手⇔扌 (hand, manual)

押ushing 押ressing

o(su), o(saeru), Ō
press, pushing

FLIP: 7.0.b1. Right (stem)

押さえ *presser foot, weight* **osae**
花押 *written seal, signature* **kaō**
押印 *personal seal* **ōin**
押下 *pressing down* **ōka**
押捺 *affixing seal* **ōnatsu**
押収 *confiscation, sequestration, forfeiture* **ōshū**
押送 *escorting a convict* **ōsō**
後押し *pushing-, shoving behind* **atooshi**
一押し *push, endeavour, undertake* **hitooshi**
糸押え *thread presser* **itoosae**
空押し *emboss, impress* **karaoshi**
中押し *wide margin, big edge* **nakaoshi**
押え腕 *presser arm* **osaeude**
押え不良 *defective clamping* **osaefuryō**
押し圧 *operation pressure* **oshiatsu**
押し葉 *pressed leaf* **oshiba**
押し花 *pressed flower* **oshibana**
押しボタン *push button* **oshibotan**
押し目 *relapse, retrogression* **oshime**

押し麦 *rolled barley* **oshimugi**
押し屋 *passenger train pusher* **oshiya**
押し鮨 *Ōsaka-style sushi* **oshizushi**
押し切る *break down* **oshikiru**
押し問答 *heated argument* **oshimondō**
押し売り *pushy selling* **oshiuri**
尻押し *passenger train pusher* **shirioshi**
下押し *decline, fall, sag* **shitaoshi**
手押し車 *handcart, pushcart* **teoshiguruma**
念を押す *remind-, alert someone* **nen o osu**
仮差押え *sequestration* **karisashiosae**

迫*ress for, 108*
尽*ursue, 574*
追*ursue, 108*

抽*xtract, 37*　　軸*xle, 659*

024-C

捜earching, 抽ulling, 押ushing, rock fans abusing...

手⇔扌 (hand, manual)

抽ulling 抽xtract

hi(ku), CHŪ
extract, pulling, draw out

FLIP: 7.0.a. Right (flat)

抽選 *lottery, lotto, drawing* **chūsen**
抽選券 *lotto ticket* **chūsenken**
抽象 *abstraction, conceptual* **chūshō**
抽象物 *abstraction, conceptual* **chūshōbutsu**
抽象画 *abstract painting* **chūshōga**
抽象派 *abstractionism, conceptualism* **chūshōha**
抽象論 *abstract thought, ~concept* **chūshōron**
抽象的 *abstract, ~conceptual* **chūshōteki**
抽象概念 *abstraction, conceptual* **chūshō gainen**
抽出 *extraction, pulling out* **chūshutsu**
抽出し *cabinet drawer* **hikidashi**
抽斗 *cabinet drawer* **hikidashi**
抽んでる *be outstanding, excel* **nukinderu**

引*xtract, 348*　　退*ithdraw, 770*
滴*xtract, 799*　　撤*ithdraw, 843*
拾*ick-up, 231*　　罷*ithdraw, 322*
却*ithdraw, 387*　　外*emove, 188*

油*etroleum, 540*　　押*ushing, 37*

025-A

昆nsects' thing: 混ixing with 皆verything...

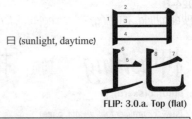

日 (sunlight, daytime)

昆nsect

KON
insect

昆布 *sea tangle, kelp* **konbu, kobu**
昆布茶 *Tang-flavoured tea* **kobucha**
昆虫 *insect* **konchū**
昆虫学 *entomology* **konchūgaku**
昆虫採集 *collecting insects* **konchū saishū**
朧昆布 *sliced tangle* **oborokonbu**

FLIP: 3.0.a. Top (flat)

虫nsect, 369	蚊osquito, 654
蛍irefly, 628	

鬼evil, 935	恵lessing, 545

025-B

昆nsects' thing: 混ixing with 皆verything...

混ixture   混lending

水⇔氵 (water)

ma(zeru), ma(zaru), ma(jiru), KON
mixture, blending, mingling, scrambling

FLIP: 7.2.a. Right Top (flat)

混紡 *mixed spinning* **konbō**   735
混濁 *muddled, clouded, murky* **kondaku**   924
混同 *confusion, mixing, blending* **kondō**
混合 *mixture, blending, mixing* **kongō**
混合物 *mixture, blend* **kongōbutsu**
混合肥料 *compound fertilizer* **kongō hiryō**
混血 *mixed parentage* **konketsu**
混血児 *child of mixed parentage* **konketsuji**
混交 *mixture, blending* **konkō**
混迷 *confusion, disorder, chaos* **konmei**
混入 *mix, dissolve with* **konnyū**
混乱 *confusion, disorder, chaos* **konran**
混載 *consolidated, merged* **konsai**   662
混作 *mixed cultivation, ~crops* **konsaku**
混声 *assorted voices, crowd noise* **konsei**
混成 *mixture, compound* **konsei**
混線 *entanglement, confusion* **konsen**
混戦 *free-for-all, scuffle, rumble* **konsen**
混信 *interference, intervention* **konshin**

混色 *mixed colour* **konshoku**
混沌 *chaos, confusion* **konton**
混和 *mixing, mingling* **konwa**
混浴 *mixed bathing (gender)* **konyoku**   891-b面
混用 *mix, dissolve together* **konyō**
混在 *mixture, blending* **konzai**
混雑 *congestion, jam, crowding* **konzatsu**
混然 *whole, entire, harmonious* **konzen**
混ぜ物 *mixture, assortment* **mazemono**
混ぜ返す *interrupt, make fun of; stir up* **mazekaesu**

紛ixture, 778	雑arious, 776
錯ixed-up, 335	諸arious, 794
争onflict, 231	

湯ot-water, 932	浪aves, 254

025-C

昆nsects' thing: 混ixing with 皆verything...

白 (white)

皆veryone　　皆verything

mina, KAI
everyone, everything, total

FLIP: 4.0.a. Bottom (flat)

皆伝① *expertise, proficiency* **kaiden**
皆伝② *initiation to all mysteries (Buddhism)* **kaiden**
⇒免許皆伝 *proficiency license* **menkyo kaiden**
皆伐 *land clearing* **kaibatsu**
皆伐地 *cleared site* **kaibatsuchi**
皆兵 *compulsory military conscription* **kaihei**
皆既 *total eclipse* **kaiki**
皆既月食 *total lunar eclipse* **kaiki gesshoku**
皆既日食 *total solar eclipse* **kaiki nisshoku**
皆勤 *perfect work attendance* **kaikin**
皆勤賞 *perfect attendance award* **kaikinshō**
皆既食 *totality, universality* **kaikishoku**
皆目 *wholly, totally, entirety* **kaimoku**
皆無 *completely nil, impossible* **kaimu**
皆納 *tax payment in full* **kainō**
皆済 *full payment, fully-paid* **kaisai**
皆様 *"to everyone present..."* **minasama**
皆殺し *extermination, genocide* **minagoroshi**
皆々様 *"to everyone present..."* **minaminasama**

全*ntire, 24*
各*very, 498*
毎*very, 241*

習*earning, 238*　　比*ompare, 466*

026-A

革eather 靴ootwear bloomed like 華lowers with 雛hina's 革eformers...

革 (leather)

❶革eform　❷革eather

kawa, KAKU
reform, modernize, renewal, improve, ugrade; leather, hide

FLIP: 1.0.b. Whole (stem)

❶沿革 *history, development* **enkaku** 756
行革 *administrative reform* **gyōkaku** 725
保革 *reformists & conversatives* **hokaku**
改革 *reform, reformation* **kaikaku** 725
⇒業務改革 *business reform* **gyōmu kaikaku**
⇒宗教改革 *Reformation Age* **shūkyō kaikaku**
⇒税制改革 *tax reform* **zeisei kaikaku**
改革案 *reform bill* **kaikakuan**
革命 *revolution* **kakumei**
⇒産業革命 *Industrial Revolution* **sangyō kakumei**
⇒文化大革命 *Cultural Revolution* **bunka daikakumei**
革命家 *revolutionary, reformist* **kakumeika**
革命政府 *revolutionary government* **kakumei seifu**
革命運動 *revolutionary movement* **kakumei undō**
革新 *innovation, reform* **kakushin**
⇒技術革新 *technological revolution* **gijutsu kakushin**
革新的 *progressive, reformist* **kakushinteki**
変革 *reform, change* **henkaku**
❷牛革 *cowhide, leather* **gyukawa, gyugawa**

皮革 *leather, hide* **hikaku** 1075
紐革 *strap, string* **himokawa**
革質 *leathery* **kakushitsu**
革具 *leathercraft, leather goods* **kawagu**
革靴 *leather shoes* **kawagutsu**
革装 *leather-bound* **kawasō**
背革 *leather back* **segawa**
製革 *tanning* **seikaku**
革表紙 *leather-covered* **kawabyōshi**
革製品 *leather goods, ~products* **kawaseihin**
革細工 *leather goods, ~products* **kawazaiku**

改*eform, 725*　　措*easures, 282*
変*hange, 581*　　略*ummary, 825*
新*ew, 668*　　牛*attle, 179*
策*olicy, 875*

帯*egion, 557*　　帝*mpire, 432*

026-B

革*eather* 靴*ootwear bloomed like* 華*lowers with* 華*hina's* 革*eformers...*

革 (leather)

靴*ootwear*   靴*hoes*

kutsu, KA
footwear, shoes

FLIP: 6.0.b. Left (stem)

靴べら *shoehorn* **kutsu bera**
靴ブラシ *shoebrush* **kutsu burashi**
靴ずれ *sore from wearing shoes* **kutsuzure**
雨靴 *rain boots, galoshes* **amagutsu**
泥靴 *muddy shoes* **dorogutsu**
深靴 *long boots* **fukagutsu**
軍靴 *combat boots* **gunka**
革靴 *leather shoes* **kawagutsu**
靴紐 *shoestring, shoelace* **kutsu himo**
靴音 *sound of footsteps* **kutsuoto**
靴下 *socks, stockings* **kutsushita**
靴下止め *garters, suspenders* **kutsushitadome**
靴屋 *shoe store, shoemaker* **kutsuya**
靴底 *shoe sole* **kutsuzoko**
靴墨 *shoe polish* **kutsuzumi**
長靴 *boots, galoshes, rainshoes* **nagagutsu**
製靴 *shoemaking* **seika**
短靴 *low shoes* **tangutsu**
上靴 *footwear worn inside one's house* **uwagutsu**

藁靴 *straw shoes* **waragutsu**
雪靴 *snowshoes* **yukigutsu**
乗馬靴 *horseriding shoes* **jōbagutsu**
靴拭き *doormat* **kutsufuki**
靴磨き *shoeshine* **kutsumigaki**
靴直し *shoe repair* **kutsunaoshi**
靴脱ぎ *removing one's shoes* **kutsunugi**
戦闘靴 *combat boots* **sentōgutsu**
紳士靴 *men's shoes* **shinshigutsu**
登山靴 *mountaineering boots* **tozangutsu**
運動靴 *sports shoes, rubber shoes* **undōgutsu**

足*oot, 481*	脚*egs, 387*
歩*alk, 272*	

革*eather, 39*	戦*attle, 517*

026-C

革*eather* 靴*ootwear bloomed like* 華*lowers with* 華*hina's* 革*eformers...*

艹 (grass)

❶華*lower*   ❷華*hina*

hana, KA, KE
blossom, flower, magnificent; China

FLIP: 1.0.b. Whole (stem)

❶華やか *bright, brilliant* **hanayaka**
華やぐ *merry & cheerful* **hanayagu**
栄華 *luxury, opulence, ostentation* **eiga**   フ2³
豪華 *luxurious, gorgeous* **gōka**
華美 *pomp & pageantry, splendour* **kabi**
華道 *flower arrangement* **kadō**
華言 *flowery language* **kagen**
華実 *flowers & fruits* **kajitsu**
華麗 *splendid, gorgeous, brilliant* **karei**
華氏 *fahrenheit* **kashi**
華族 *peer, noble* **kazoku**
香華 *flowers & incense* **kōge**
散華 *die gloriously* **sange**
精華 *flower, quintessence* **seika**
昇華 *sublimation* **shōka**
万華鏡 *kaleidoscope* **mangekyō**
豪華版 *deluxe edition* **gōkaban**
華華しい *brilliant & splendid* **hanabanashii**
繁華街 *downtown, commercial district* **hankagai**

詞華集 *anthology, compilation* **shikashū**
豪華絢爛 *gorgeous, dazzling* **gōka kenran**
華燭の典 *wedding ceremony* **kashōku no ten**
❷中華 *China, Chinese* **chūka**
中華料理 *Chinese food, ~cuisine* **chūka ryōri**
中華民国 *Republic of China (Taiwan)*
    chūka minkoku
中華人民共和国 *People's Republic of China*
    chūka jinmin kyōwakoku
華中 *central China* **kachū**
華北 *northern China* **kahoku**
華僑 *overseas Chinese trader* **kakyō**
華商 *overseas Chinese trader* **kashō**
日華 *Japanese-Chinese* **nikka**

花*lower, 191*	香*ragrance, 895*	中*hina, 85*
薫*ragrance, 934*	芳*ragrance, 533*	唐*hinese, 439*

革*eather, 39*	草*rass, 373*

027-A

No 殻usk no 穀rains, a farm's 款oodwill wanes...

殻usk   殻hell

夂 (pike)

殻

1 2 9
3 8
5
4 7 10
6 11

kara, KAKU
husk, shell

FLIP: 5.0.b. Left & Right

紅殻 *red ochre* **benigara**
茶殻 *consumed tea leaves* **chagara**
血殻 *specks of blood* **chigara**
地殻 *earth crust* **chikaku**
外殻 *shell, crust, husk* **gaikaku**
灰殻 *ashes* **haigara**
耳殻 *external ear, auricle* **jikaku**
貝殻 *shell, seashell* **kaigara**
貝殻骨 *shoulder blade* **kaigarabone**
貝殻追放 *ostracism, exclusion* **kaigara tsuihō**
貝殻細工 *shellworks* **kaigara zaiku**
殻長 *shell apex* **kakuchō**
殻竿 *flail* **karazao**
豆殻 *bean husk* **mamegara**
籾殻 *rice hull* **momigara**
卵殻 *egg shell* **rankaku, tamagokara**
空き殻 *empty shell* **akigara**
出し殻 *spent tea leaves* **dashigara**
甲殻類 *crustacean, shell fishes* **kōkakurui**

燃え殻 *cinder, ashes* **moegara**
抜け殻 *cast-off skin (snake)* **nukegara**
石炭殻 *coal cinders* **sekitangara**
吸い殻 *cigarette butt* **suigara**

穀rains, 41
穂rains, 545
粒rains, 656

款oodwill, 42   穀ereal, 41

放 –hō – 486 –release (hanasu)

027-B

No 殻usk no 穀rains, a farm's 款oodwill wanes...

穀ereal   穀rain

禾 (tree branch)

穀

1 2 12
3 11
4 6 13
7 14
9 10

KOKU
cereal, grain, granule

FLIP: 7.0.b2. Right (stem)

米穀 *rice, cereal, grain* **beikoku**
脱穀 *threshing* **dakkoku**
脱穀機 *thresher, threshing machine* **dakkokuki**
五穀 *the five staple grains* **gokoku**
穀粉 *grain flour* **kokufun**
穀物 *grains & cereals (staple food)* **kokumotsu**
穀類 *cereals* **kokurui**
穀粒 *grain* **kokuryū, kokutsubu**
穀商 *rice dealer, ~merchant* **kokushō**
穀食 *cereal diet* **kokushoku**
穀倉 *granary* **kokusō**
穀倉地帯 *granary region* **kokusō chitai**
新穀 *fresh grains* **shinkoku**
雑穀 *cereals, grain* **zakkoku**
雑穀商 *grains merchant* **zakkokushō**
穀潰し *"good-for-nothing..."* **gokutsubushi**
穀断ち *grains abstinence* **kokudachi**
穀象虫 *rice weevil* **kokuzōmushi**

麦arley, 606   粒rain, 656
殻usk, 41   稲ice plant, 893
穂rain, 545

款oodwill, 42   殻usk, 41

027-C

No 殻usk no 穀rains, a farm's 款oodwill wanes...

❶款rticle　　❷款oodwill

欠 (lacking)

款

KAN

article, clause, goodwill

❶ 条款　*article, stipulation, proviso, caveat* **jōkan**
落款　*signature & seal* **rakkan**
定款　*articles of incorporation* **teikan**
約款　*contract stipulations* **yakkan**
⇒担保約款　*mortgage clause* **tanpo yakkan**

❷ 款待　*cordial reception, warm welcome* **kantai**
交款　*goodwill exchange* **kōkan**
満款　*highest score* **mankan**
借款　*borrowings, debt, loan* **shakkan**
⇒円借款　*yen-denominated loan* **enshakkan**

FLIP: 6.0.b. Left (stem)

懇*ntimacy, 164*	善*ighteous, 450*
親*ntimate, 669*	但*roviso, 739*
友*riendship, 408*	条*rticle, 607*

殻*hell, 41*	穀*ereal, 41*

028-A

編diting 偏nclination 遍idespread on the Web...

❶編diting　　❷編nitting

糸 (thread, continuity)

編

a(mu), HEN

editing, compilation, revision; knitting

❶ 編著　*writer & editor* **hencho**
編曲　*arrangement, adjustment* **henkyoku**
編入　*entry, incorporate* **hennyū**
編纂　*compilation, editing* **hensan**
⇒史料編纂　*historiography* **shiryō hensan**
編成　*putting together, composition* **hensei**
編制　*organize, form* **hensei**
編者　*editor, compiler* **hensha**
編集　*editing, compilation* **henshū**
上編　*first volume* **jōhen**
改編　*reorganization, restructuring* **kaihen**
後編　*latter part (story)* **kōhen**
巨編　*great literary work* **kyohen**
正編　*main-, principal story* **seihen**
掌編　*short story* **shōhen**
小編　*short story* **shōhen**
前編　*first sequel, first volume* **zenpen**
続編　*sequel, second volume* **zokuhen**
番外編　*additional version, extra* **bangaihen**

FLIP: 7.3.b. Right Bottom (stem)

姉妹編　*companion piece* **shimaihen**
予告編　*preview, preliminary view* **yokokuhen**
❷編み針　*knitting needle, crochet hook* **amibari**
編み棒　*knitting needle, ~pin* **amibō**
編み機　*knitting machine* **amiki**
編み目　*stitching, sewing* **amime**
編み物　*knitting, crochet* **amimono**
編み出す　*work out, think out, devise* **amidasu**
編み込む　*knit* **amikomu**
飛行編隊　*squadron, flight formation* **hikō hentai**

訂*diting, 174*	紡*pinning, 735*
校*roof-reading, 773*	糸*hread, 375*
縫*ewing, 779*	衣*lothes, 355*

偏*ncline, 43*	遍*idespread, 43*

028-B

編*diting* 偏*nclination* 遍*idespread on the Web...*

偏*ncline*   偏*artial*

人⇔亻 (person)

katayo(ru), HEN
incline, partial, predilection, proclivity, propensity, trending

FLIP: 7.3.b. Right Bottom (stem)

不偏 *impartiality, disinterested, fairness* **fuhen,**
不偏不党 *non-partisan* **fuhen futō** *203 - political parts*
偏愛 *favouritism, partiality, bias* **hen'ai**
偏旁 *left & right radicals* **henbō**
偏重 *overimportance, overemphasis* **henchō**
偏土 *remote region* **hendo**
偏人 *eccentric* **henjin**
偏見 *bias, prejudice* **henken**
偏向 *deviation, inclination* **henkō**
偏光 *polarized light* **henkō**
偏屈 *stubborn, eccentric* **henkutsu**
偏狂 *monomaniac* **henkyō**
偏狭 *narrow-minded* **henkyō** *639 - crazy*
偏頗 *partiality, bias, discrimination* **henpa**
偏平 *flat* **henpei**
偏平足 *flat-footed person* **henpeisoku**
偏流 *drifting, diversion* **henryū**
偏差 *deviation, inclination* **hensa**
偏差値 *deviation standard* **hensachi** *値 - 783 - value*

⇒標準偏差 *standard deviation*
　　　hyōjun hensa *標 - hyō - cat - symbol*
偏心 *eccentricity, idiosyncracy* **henshin**
偏食 *unbalanced diet* **henshoku**
偏執 *paranoid, phobia, bigotry* **henshū** *執 - 208 - group*
偏桃 *almond* **hentō** *桃 - 215 peach*
偏在 *mal-distribution, unequal* **henzai**
無偏 *unbiased, impartial* **muhen**
偏頭痛 *migraine, headache*
　　　henzutsū, hentōtsu

斜*iagonal*, 648	片*artial*, 359
方*irection*, 533	側*art*, 291

備*urnish*, 409	倫*thics*, 787

028-C

編*diting* 偏*nclination* 遍*idespread on the Web...*

遍*idespread*   遍*ervasive*

辶 (transport)

amane, HEN
widespread, pervasive, rampant, sweeping, all over

FLIP: 7.3.b. Right Bottom (stem)
FLIP: 8.0.b. Inner (stem)

五遍 *five times* **gohen**
遍歴 *travel experience* **henreki**
遍路 *pilgrimage, pilgrim* **henro**
遍在 *omnipresence, everywhere* **henzai**
一遍 *once, altogether* **ippen**
⇒通り一遍 *passing, causal, perfunctory* **toori ippen**
何遍 *how many times* **nanben**
二遍 *twice, three times* **nihen**
三遍 *twice, three times* **sanben**
普遍性 *universality* **fuhensei**
普遍的 *universal, generic* **fuhenteki**
百万遍 *a million times* **hyakumanben**
万遍なく *evenly, equally* **manbennaku**

普*ommon*, 455	拡*nlarge*, 205
常*egular*, 94	広*arge*, 205
般*egular*, 323	豊*bundance*, 965
平*lain*, 488	

偏*ncline*, 43	編*diting*, 42

029-A

奴ellows' lack of 努ffort 怒ngered their cohorts...

女 (woman)

奴ellow   奴olleague

yatsu, yakko, DO
colleague, fellow

FLIP: 7.0.b2. Right (stem)

彼奴 *that guy, that fellow* **aitsu**
奴輩 *servant, slave* **dohai**   *290-fellow*
奴隷 *slave, slavery* **dorei**   *隷 - 880 - slave*
奴隷解放 *slave emancipation* **dorei kaihō**
奴隷制度 *slavery system* **dorei seido**
黒奴 *black-, African slave* **kokudo**
此奴 *"you little rascal..."* **koyatsu**
匈奴 *Huns* **kyōdo**
何奴 *"what-the-heck..."* **naniyatsu**
農奴 *serf* **nōdo**
奴婢 *helpers, servants* **nuhi**
奴凧 *ancient kite* **yakkodako**
奴等 *"those fellows..."* **yatsura**
奴さん *fellow, chap* **yakkosan**
奴豆腐 *chilled tofu cubes* **yakkodōfu**
売国奴 *traitor, renegade, quisling* **baikokudo**
冷や奴 *chilled tofu* **hiyayakko**

黒い奴 *racist term for blacks* **kuroiyatsu**
守銭奴 *miser, niggard, cheapshot* **shusendo**

仲ellow, 695	僚ellow, 66
輩ellow, 290	相ellow, 524

好iking, 637	妊regnancy, 709

029-B

奴ellows' lack of 努ffort 怒ngered their cohorts...

力 (strength, force)

努ffort   努xert

tsuto(meru), DO
effort, exert, diligence, endeavour, forbearance

FLIP: 7.2.b. Right Top (stem)

努努 *"never, never..."* **yumeyume**
努力 *effort, toil* **doryoku**
努力型 *hard-working* **doryokugata**   *型) - kata 536 pattern*
努力家 *hard worker, workaholic* **doryokuka**
努力賞 *consolation prize* **doryokushō**

働abour, 422	勉fforts, 527
労abour, 351	力trength, 351
伸tretch, 713	勢igour, 153
張tretch, 274	精igour, 792

始tart, 210	妨indrance, 734

029-C

奴ellows' lack of 努ffort 怒ngered their cohorts...

心⇔忄 (heart, feelings)

怒*ngry*　　　怒*esent*

oko(ru), ika(ru), DO

angry, resent, fuming, furious, incense, indignant, infuriate, outrage, enrage

FLIP: 7.2.b. Right Top (stem)

怒り	anger, rage, fury, wrath **ikari**
怒り肩	square shoulder **ikarigata**
怒り上戸	angry when drunk **okorijōgo**
怒りっぽい	quick-tempered, mercurial **okorippoi**
怒張	blood over swelling **dochō**
怒号	roar, bellowing, bluster **dogō**
怒気	anger, rage, fury, wrath **doki**
怒声	angry-, furious voice **dosei**
怒濤	violent waves, choppy waters **dotō**
憤怒	anger, rage, fury, wrath **fundo, funnu**
激怒	rage, fury, ire, wrath **gekido**
怒鳴り	shouting, yelling, screaming **donari**
怒鳴る	shout, yell, scream **donaru**
嚇怒	fury, rage **kakudo**
喜怒	joy & anger **kido**
喜怒哀楽	feelings, emotions **kido airaku**
怒髪天	flushed with anger, outraged **dohatsuten**

嫌*espise*, 805　　侮*espise*, 711
卑*espise*, 936　　憎*atred*, 837

悠*istant*, 898　　急*udden*, 868

030-A

感eelings of 憾egret 減ecrease when guilt is the least...

心⇔忄 (heart, feelings)

感*eelings*　　　感*motions*

KAN

feelings, emotions, sentiments

FLIP: 8.0.a. Inner (flat)

敏感	sensitive, delicate **binkan**
同感	sympathy, empathy, commiseration **dōkan**
五感	five senses **gokan**
反感	antipathy, animosity, hostility **hankan**
快感	pleasure, sensation **kaikan**
感激	deep emotion, strong passions **kangeki**
感情	feelings, emotions **kanjō**
感状	letter of commendation **kanjō**
感覚	sense, awareness **kankaku**
感謝	gratitude, thanks **kansha**
感心	admiration, praise **kanshin**
感想	impressions, thoughts **kansō**
好感	favourable impression **kōkan**
音感	sense of pitch **onkan**
霊感	inspiration, spiritual sentiments **reikan**
量感	massiveness, enormity, largesse **ryōkan**
性感	sexual arousal, ~passions **seikan**
予感	premonition, foreboding **yokan**
直感力	intuition, hunch, perception **chokkanryoku**

第六感	hunch, sixth sense, intuition **dairokkan**
義務感	sense of duty, dutifulness **gimukan**
劣等感	inferiority complex **rettōkan**
正義感	sense of justice **seigikan**
責任感	sense of responsibility **sekininkan**
疎外感	sense of alienation **sogaikan**
体感的	sensible, sensual **taikanteki**
優越感	superiority complex **yūetsukan**
罪悪感	guilty conscience **zaiakukan**
感慨深い	deeply-touched **kangaibukai**
感極まる	deeply-touched **kankiwamaru**

気*eelings*, 98　　　心*eart*, 469
情*eelings*, 793

感*emptation*, 139　　減*ecrease*, 46

030-B

感*eelings of* 憾*egret* 減*ecrease when guilt is the least...*

心⇔忄⇔忝 (feelings)

憾*egret*　　　憾*explore*

ura(mu), KAN
regret, deplore, denounce, condemn

憾み *regret, grudge, bad blood* **urami**
憾み言 *whining, words of regret* **uramigoto**
遺憾 *regret, regrettable* **ikan**
遺憾なく *"fully, to the fullest..."* **ikan naku**

FLIP: 8.0.a. Inner (flat)

悔*egret, 712*	惜*egret, 281*
慨*egret, 316*	

憶*emory, 339*

030-C

感*eelings of* 憾*egret* 減*ecrease when guilt is the least...*

水⇔氵 (water)

減

減*ecrease*　　減*educe*　　減*inus*

he(ru), he(rasu), GEN
decrease, reduce, minus, lessen, minimize

激減 *sudden decrease, ~fall* **gekigen**
減額 *reduction, decrease* **gengaku**
減員 *reduced staff* **gen'in**
減刑 *commutation, reduced punishment* **genkei** 576 *punish*
減配 *reduced distribution* **genpai**
減俸 *pay cut, salary reduction* **genpō** 俸-hō *salary* 276
減法 *subtraction, minus* **genpō**
減作 *poor crop* **gensaku**
減産 *reduced production* **gensan**
減資 *capital decrease, ~reduction* **genshi**
減少 *decrease, decline* **genshō**
減食 *diet, dieting, eating less* **genshoku**
減収 *reduced income, salary cut* **genshū** 収-shū *collect* 178
減速 *speed reduction* **gensoku**
減衰 *decline, warning* **gensui** 衰-374-*decline*
減反 *reduced cultivation* **gentan**
減税 *tax cut, tax decrease* **genzei**
半減 *reducing by half* **hangen**
加減 *high & low, plus or minus, give or take* **kagen**

軽減 *mitigation, commutation* **keigen**
削減 *reduction, curtailment* **sakugen** 削-421-*sak shar*
節減 *reduction, curtailment* **setsugen**
逓減 *gradual diminution* **teigen** 逓-304-*teé gra*
漸減 *gradual decrease, ~reduction* **zengen**
意加減 *haphazard, random, unreliable* **ikagen**
好い加減 *"take it easy..."* **iikagen**
目減り *weight loss* **meberi**
塩加減 *food saltiness* **shiokagen**
手加減 *exercise one's discretion* **tekagen**
減らず口 *retort, rejoinder, rebuttal* **herazuguchi**
減り込む *sink, submerge* **herikomu**

耗*essen, 655*	落*all-down, 826*
陥*all-down, 893*	衰*ecline, 374*
堕*all-down, 807*	少*ew, 459*

滅*erish, 520*	激*ierce, 170*

FLIP: 8.0.a. Inner (flat)

031-A

図*ketched in farmers'* 脳*rain, no* 悩*istress when it rains...*

□ (enclosure)

図*ketch*   図*rawing*

haka(ru), ZU, TO
sketch, drawing, illustration

FLIP: 2.0.a. Sort Of (flat)

地図 *map* **chizu**
意図 *intention, volition, will* **ito**
異図 *ulterior-, hidden motive* **ito**
系図 *genealogy, family tree* **keizu**
⇒家系図 *family tree, ancestral roots* **kakeizu**
企図 *plan, strategy* **kito**
構図 *art composition* **kōzu**
略図 *sketch, rough map* **ryakuzu**
縮図 *miniaturized scale (sketch)* **shukuzu**
図書 *collection of books* **tosho**
図書館 *library* **toshokan**
要図 *outline, drawing* **yōzu**
雄図 *ambitious plan* **yūto**
図案 *design, plan, chest* **zuan**
図画 *drawing, painting* **zuga**
図解 *diagram, illustration* **zukai**
図鑑 *illustrated-, picture book* **zukan**
図形 *figure, drawing* **zukei**
図工 *drawing & manual arts* **zukō**

図面 *architectural blueprint* **zumen**
図示 *illustration, drawing, sketch* **zushi**
図式 *diagram, chart, graph* **zushiki**
案内図 *guide map, travel map* **annaizu**
鳥瞰図 *bird's-eye view* **chōkanzu**
掛け図 *wall map, wall chart* **kakezu**
航海図 *navigational map* **kōkaizu**
設計図 *draft, plan* **sekkeizu**
側面図 *side view* **sokumenzu**
天気図 *weather map* **tenkizu**
投影図 *projection chart* **tōeizu**

描*ketch, 271*
絵*rawing, 143*
画*icture, 35*
撮*hotograph, 423*
写*-ortray, 349*

団*roup, 345*   囲*nclose, 361*

031-B

図*ketched in farmers'* 脳*rain, no* 悩*istress when it rains...*

肉⇔月 (flesh, body part)

脳*rain*   脳*erebral*

NŌ
brain, cerebral, cranium, intellect, mind

FLIP: 7.1. Right (Sort Of)

中脳 *midbrain, mesencephalon* **chūnō**
大脳 *cerebrum* **dainō**
後脳 *hindbrain, posterior brain* **kōnō**
脳炎 *brain inflammation, encephalitis* **nōen**
脳波 *brain waves* **nōha**
脳膜 *brain membrane* **nōmaku**
脳乱 *anguish, anxiety, distress* **nōran**
脳裏 *one's inner-mind* **nōri**
脳死 *brain dead* **nōshi**
脳天 *head crown* **nōten**
脳髄 *brain organ* **nōzui**
洗脳 *brainwashing* **sennō**
小脳 *cerebellum* **shōnō**
首脳 *head, leader* **shunō**
主脳 *head, leader* **shunō**
頭脳 *brain, intelligence* **zunō**
脳外科 *brain surgery, ~operation* **nōgeka**
脳貧血 *cerebral anaemia* **nōhinketsu**
脳溢血 *cerebral haemorrhage, apoplexy* **nōikketsu**

脳血栓 *cerebral thrombosis* **nōkessen**
脳細胞 *brain cells* **nōsaibō**
脳神経 *cranial nerves* **nōshinkei**
脳震盪 *brain concussion* **nōshintō**
脳出血 *cerebral haemorrhage,* **nōshukketsu**
脳腫瘍 *brain tumour* **nōshuyō**
脳卒中 *cerebral apoplexy* **nōsocchū**
脳下垂体 *pituitary gland* **nōka suitai**
脳軟化症 *softening of the brain* **nōnan kashō**
脳性麻痺 *cerebral palsy* **nōsei mahi**
脳死判定 *deemed brain dead* **nōshi hantei**
脳死移植 *organ transplant from a brain dead*
    nōshi ishoku
首脳会談 *summit talks* **shunō kaidan**

意*dea, 340*
想*dea, 524*
念*dea, 182*
慮*hought, 70*

胸*hest, 652*   眺*aze at, 215*

031-C

図ketched in farmers' 脳rain, no 悩istress when it rains...

心⇔忄⇔忝 (feelings)

悩istress 悩nguish

naya(mu), naya(masu), NŌ
distress, anguish, suffer, misery, torment, agony

FLIP: 7.1. Right (Sort Of)

言い悩む	unwilling to speak up **iinayamu**
伸び悩む	make littler progress **nobinayamu**
思い悩む	agonize, be tormented **omoinayamu**
立ち悩む	be anxious, ~distressed **tachinayamu**
行き悩む	come to an impasse, ~standstill **yukinayamu**
悩み	worry, distress, anguish **nayami**
⇒恋の悩み	torments-of-love **koi no nayami**
煩悩	worldly passions, ~desires **bonnō**
苦悩	suffering, anguish **kunō**
苦痛	pain, agony **kutsū**
脳乱	anguish, anxiety **nōran**
悩殺	enchantment, fascination **nōsatsu**
懊悩	anguish, anxiety, distress **ōnō**
子煩悩	fond, doting **kobonnō**

哀orrows, 374	苦nguish, 477
愁orrows, 415	難ifficulty, 927
悲orrows, 289	悔egret, 712

図rawing, 47	脳rain, 47

032-A

漁ishing for long, not one 魚ish 無othing to relish...

水⇔氵 (water)

漁ishing

GYO, RYŌ
fishing

Facing: 1.2. West (V)

不漁	poor fish catch **furyō**
漁業	fishery, fishing industry **gyogyō**
⇒沿岸漁業	coastal fishery **engan gyogyō**
⇒沿海漁業	coastal fishery **enkai gyogyō**
漁業権	fishing rights **gyogyōken**
漁法	fishing method **gyohō**
漁場	fishing grounds **gyojō**
漁期	fishing season **gyoki**
漁港	fishing port **gyokō**
漁区	fishing area, ~ground **gyoku**
漁民	fishermen, fisher folks **gyomin**
漁労	fishing, fishery **gyorō**
漁船	fishing boat, ~vessel **gyosen**
漁礁	fish-inhabited reef **gyoshō**
漁食	fish meal **gyoshoku, ryōshoku**
漁色	womanising, philandering **gyoshoku**
漁村	fishing village **gyoson**
漁族	fishes **gyozoku**
豊漁	good fish catch **hōryō**

漁火	fish-luring fire at night **isaribi**
禁漁	fishing ban, ~prohibition **kinryō**
休漁	cease fishing **kyūryō**
密漁	illegal fishing, fish poaching **mitsuryō**
漁師	fisherman **ryōshi**
大漁	large fishing catch **tairyō**
漁獲高	fishing catch volume **gyokakudaka**
入漁権	fishing rights **nyūgyoken**
買い漁る	buy one after another **kaiasaru**

魚ishes, 49	洋cean, 247
釣ishing, 697	河iver, 877
海cean, 241	川iver, 76

魚ishes, 49	無othing, 49

032-B

漁*ishing for long, no* 魚*ish,* 無*othing to relish...*

魚 (fishes)

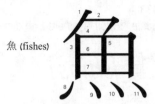

Facing: 1.0. 🐟 West (W)

魚*ishes*   魚*eafoods*

sakana, uo, GYO, RYŌ
fishes, seafoods, sea animals

稚魚	small fry, baby fish	**chigyo**
魚群	shoal-, school of fishes	**gyogun**
魚介	fish & shells, seafood	**gyokai**
魚肉	fish meat	**gyoniku**
魚雷	torpedo	**gyorai**
魚類	kinds of fishes	**gyorui**
魚灯	fishing lamp	**gyotō**
川魚	river fish	**kawauo, kawazakana**
金魚	gold fish	**kingyo**
木魚	wooden drum	**mokugyo**
人魚	mermaid	**ningyo**
魚屋	fish store, fish dealer	**sakanaya**
鮮魚	fresh raw fish	**sengyo**
衣魚	clothes moth, bookworm	**shimi**
塩魚	salted fish	**shiozakana**
章魚	octopus	**tako**
魚心	mutuality, reciprocity	**uogokoro**
養魚	fish farming, fish breeding	**yōgyo**
雑魚	small fry, unimportant fellow	**zako**

干し魚	dried fish	**hoshiuo**
近海魚	coastal fish	**kinkaigyo**
魚釣り	fishing	**sakanatsuri, uotsuri**
深海魚	deep-sea fish	**shinkaigyo**
淡水魚	fresh-water fish	**tansuigyo**
飛び魚	flying fish	**tobiuo**
魚の目	foot corn, foot fungus	**uonome**
魚市場	fish market	**uoichiba**
焼き魚	grilled fish	**yakizakana**

漁*ishing,* 48	海*cean,* 241
釣*ishing,* 697	洋*cean,* 247

角*orner,* 400	無*othing,* 49

032-C

漁*ishing for long, no* 魚*ish,* 無*othing to relish...*

火 ⇔ 灬 (fire)

無*othing* 無*ithout* 無*bsence*

na(i), MU, BU
nothing, without, absence, empty, non-existence

FLIP: 2.0.b. Sort Of (stem)

虚無	nihility, nothingness	**kyomu**
無駄	waste, futility, in vain	**muda**
無断	without permission	**mudan**
無益	useless, inutile, futile	**mueki**
無縁	unknown, x-factor	**muen**
無害	harmless, weak	**mugai**
無学	illiterate, unschooled	**mugaku**
無限	limitless, infinite	**mugen**
無為	idleness, inactivity	**mui**
無形	intangible, shapeless	**mukei**
無給	free-of-charge, pro bono, gratis	**mukyū**
無理	unreasonable, impossible	**muri**
無慮	as many as, no fewer than	**muryo**
無職	unemployed, out-of-work	**mushoku**
無敵	unrivalled, undefeated	**muteki**
無闇	thoughtless, clumsy	**muyami**
無残	merciless, cruel	**muzan**
無遠慮	lack of manners, ~restraint	**buenryo**
台無し	spoiled child, brat	**dainashi**

無意味	meaningless, senseless	**muimi**
無意識	unconscious, lethargic	**muishiki**
無医村	village without a doctor	**muison**
無感覚	insensibility, callousness	**mukankaku**
無関係	unrelated, irrelevant	**mukankei**
無記名	unnamed, the bearer	**mukimei**
無差別	indiscriminate, sporadic	**musabetsu**
無思慮	indiscretion, misconduct	**mushiryo**
無投票	without vote, by acclamation	**mutōhyō**
難無く	without difficulty, "a cakewalk..."	**nannaku**
心許無い	uneasy, uncertain	**kokoromotonai**

不*[negative],* 300	零*ero,* 874
非*[negative],* 288	

焦*ocus,* 919	魚*ishes,* 49

033-A

Battle 隻*hips* 集*athered,* 進*dvance scattered...*

隹 (long-tailed birds)

°隻*[ships]*　　**°隻***ne of a set*

SEKI
[counter for ships]; one of a set

FLIP: 4.0.b. Bottom (stem)

❶一隻 *one ship* **isseki**
一隻眼 *discerning-, critical eye* **issekigan**
二隻 *two ships* **niseki**
数隻 *several ships* **sūseki**

❷隻影 *speck of clouds, disperse clouds* **sekiei**
隻眼 *one-eyed person* **sekigan**
隻語 *few words* **sekigo**
⇒片言隻語 *a few words, phrase* **hengen sekigo**
隻手 *one-armed person* **sekishu**
隻句 *a few words, phrase* **sekku**
⇒片言隻句 *a few words, phrase* **hengen sekku**

丸*[ships]*, 73	船*hip*, 757
航*avigation*, 748	舶*hip*, 742
艇*oat*, 26	帆*ailing*, 641
舟*essel*, 90	

焦*ocus*, 919	集*ollect*, 50

033-B

Battle 隻*hips* 集*athered,* 進*dvance scattered...*

隹 (long-tailed birds)

集*ather*　　**集***ollect*

atsu(maru), atsu(meru), tsudo(u), SHŪ
gather, collect, put together

FLIP: 4.0.b. Bottom (stem)

募集 *recruitment, hiring* **boshū**
文集 *anthology, collection of-* **bunshū**
徴集 *levy, duty, tax* **chōshū**
画集 *book of paintings, ~photos* **gashū**
群集 *crowd, mass, multitude* **gunshū**
編集 *editing, revising, rewriting* **henshū**
歌集 *anthology of poetry, ~songs* **kashū**
結集 *concentrate, focus* **kesshū**
密集 *crowding, swarming* **misshū**
採集 *collecting, gathering* **saishū**
詩集 *collection of poems* **shishū**
招集 *summons, convocation* **shōshū**
集中 *concentration, focus* **shūchū**
集団 *group, squad* **shūdan**
集合 *gathering, collection, assembly* **shūgō**
集配 *collection & delivery* **shūhai**
集荷 *cargo retrieval, ~claim* **shūka**
集会 *assembly, gathering, rally* **shūkai**
集計 *total, totalling, summing up* **shūkei**

集結 *concentration, gathering* **shūketsu**
集金 *money-, bill collecting* **shūkin**
集光 *lights condensation* **shūkō**
集録 *compilation, collection* **shūroku**
集散 *collect & distribute* **shūsan**
集札 *ticket collection, ~inspection* **shūsatsu**
収集 *collecting, gathering* **shūshū**
特集 *special edition* **tokushū**
雲集 *gathering clouds* **unshū**
全集 *complete works, compendium* **zenshū**
聖歌集 *hymnal, gospel music* **seikashū**
随筆集 *collection of essays* **zuihitsushū**

収*ollect*, 178	括*undle*, 954
共*ogether*, 302	束*undle*, 502
合*ogether*, 232	会*eeting*, 864

業*usiness*, 124	葉*eaf*, 411

033-C

Battle 隻*hips* 集*athered,* 進*dvance scattered...*

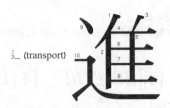

辶 (transport)

進*dvance*　進*rogress*

susu(mu), susu(meru), SHIN
advance, progress, forward, momentum, upgrade

Facing: 4.0. 🚢 Apart

栄進	*promotion, advance, improvement* **eishin**	進級	*promotion, advance, improvement* **shinkyū**
逆進	*regression, relapse, retrogression* **gyakushin**	進路	*course, route* **shinro**
発進	*off to a start, upstart* **hasshin**	新進	*up & coming, upstart, budding* **shinshin**
高進	*speed acceleration* **kōshin**	進出	*advance, progress* **shinshutsu**
行進	*march, advance* **kōshin**	進水	*launching, starting off* **shinsui**
後進	*younger person* **kōshin**	昇進	*promotion, advance, improvement* **shōshin**
邁進	*pushing forward* **maishin**	促進	*promotion, encouragement* **sokushin**
盲進	*blind advance* **mōshin**	推進	*promotion, propulsion* **suishin**
猛進	*furious advance* **mōshin**	特進	*accelerated promotion* **tokushin**
累進	*successive promotions* **ruishin**	躍進	*remarkable progress* **yakushin**
進学	*academic progress* **shingaku**	前進	*advance, stride* **zenshin**
進撃	*attack, advance* **shingeki**	漸進	*gradual progress* **zenshin**
進言	*advice, counsel, suggestion* **shingen**	突き進む	*advance, thrust thru* **tsukisusumu**
進軍	*advancing soldiers* **shingun**		
進化	*evolution, progress* **shinka**		
進化論	*theory of evolution, Darwinism* **shinkaron**		
進攻	*attack, advance* **shinkō**		
進行	*advance, progress, march* **shinkō**		
進境	*remarkable progress* **shinkyō**		

展*rogress, 522*	動*ovement, 422*
歩*rogress, 272*	続*ontinue, 260*

焦*ocus, 919*	集*ollect, 50*

034-A

Test 筒*ube* 菌*acteria in few* 箇*laces sowed hysteria...*

竹 (bamboo)

筒*ipe*　筒*ube*

tsutsu, TŌ
pipe, tube

FLIP: 4.0.b. Bottom (stem)

茶筒	*tea caddy* **chazutsu**	矢筒	*quiver, shudder* **yazutsu**
円筒	*circular cylinder* **entō**	発煙筒	*smoke pot* **hatsuentō**
煙筒	*chimney* **entō**	筒切り	*cut round slices* **tsutsugiri**
筆筒	*brush case* **fudezutsu**	筒状花	*tube flower* **tsutsujōbana**
封筒	*envelope, paper case* **fūtō**	筒抜け	*news leakage* **tsutsunuke**
花筒	*flower vase* **hanazutsu**		
火筒	*gunfire* **hozutsu**		
井筒	*well curb* **izutsu**		
気筒	*cylinder* **kitō**		
大筒	*cannon* **oozutsu**		
水筒	*water bottle, ~cylinder* **suitō**		
竹筒	*bamboo pipe* **takezutsu**		
短筒	*revolver, pistol* **tanzutsu**		
筒鳥	*himalayan cuckoo* **tsutsudori**		
筒形	*cylinder* **tsutsugata**		
筒井	*round well* **tsutsui**		
筒音	*sound of gunfire* **tsutsuoto**		
筒先	*muzzle, nozzle* **tsutsusaki**		
筒袖	*tight sleeves* **tsutsusode**		

轄*ontrol, 968*	導*uidance, 312*
操*perate, 851*	管*ontrol, 917*

箇*[objects], 52*	答*nswer, 232*

034-B

Test 筒ube 菌acteria in few 箇laces sowed hysteria...

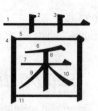

艾 (grass)

菌acteria 菌isease

KIN
bacteria, disease, infection, virus, contamination

FLIP: 2.0.a. Sort Of (flat)

黴菌 *bacteria, germ, microbe* **baikin**
病菌 *germ, virus* **byōkin**
桿菌 *bacillus* **kankin**
菌毒 *poison mushroom* **kindoku**
菌類 *fungus* **kinrui**
菌類学 *mycology* **kinruigaku**
菌糸 *mycelium* **kinshi**
抗菌 *anti-bacterial* **kōkin**
球菌 *micrococcus* **kyūkin**
滅菌 *sterilization, pasteurisation* **mekkin**
無菌 *germ-free, aseptic, sterilized* **mukin**
細菌 *bacteria, germ, microbe* **saikin**
細菌学 *bacteriology, microbiology* **saikingaku**
細菌培養 *bacterial cultivating* **saikin baiyō**
殺菌 *sterilization, pasteurisation* **sakkin**
⇒低温殺菌 *pasteurisation* **teion sakkin**
殺菌剤 *germicide, bactericide* **sakkinzai**
雑菌 *miscellaneous germs* **zakkin**
培養菌 *cultured bacteria* **baiyōkin**

保菌者 *virus carrier* **hokinsha**
結核菌 *tubercle bacillus* **kekkakukin**
乳酸菌 *lactic ferments, lactic bacilli* **nyūsankin**
赤痢菌 *dysentery bacillus* **sekirikin**
真菌症 *mycosis* **shinkinshō**

毒*oison, 578*	病*ickness, 213*
患*ickness, 475*	汚*irty, 737*
症*ickness, 788*	

箇*[objects], 52*	夢*ream, 167*

034-C

Test 筒ube 菌acteria in few 箇laces sowed hysteria...

竹 (bamboo)

❶箇[objects] ❷箇[places]

KA, KO
[counter for objects]; [counter for places]

FLIP: 4.0.a. Bottom (flat)

❶箇条 *article, clause, item* **kajō**
箇条書き *written clause, ~article* **kajōgaki**
一箇年 *one year* **ikkanen**
何箇月 *how many months* **nankagetsu**
三箇日 *first three days of the year* **sanganichi**

❷箇所 *location, site, point* **kasho**
三箇所 *three locations, three sites* **sankasho**

物*hings, 647*	所*ocation, 676*
荷*reight, 877*	場*ocation, 147*
何*omething, 101*	

答*nswer, 232*	筒*ipe, 51*

035-A

哲hilosophers 誓ledge to seek 哲isdom in 逝eath beyond...

言 (speaking)

誓ledge   誓wear   誓vow

chika(u), SEI
pledge, swear, avow, attest, commitment, compact, covenant

FLIP: 4.0.a. Bottom (flat)

誓い vow, oath, pledge **chikai**
祈誓 vow, oath, pledge **kisei**
誓願 vow, oath, pledge **seigan**
誓言 vow, oath, pledge **seigon**
誓文 written oath, promissory note **seimon**
誓文払い Kimono bargain sale **seimonbarai**
誓詞 vow, oath, pledge **seishi**
誓紙 written oath **seishi**
誓約 vow, oath, pledge **seiyaku**
誓約者 oath-taker, pledger **seiyakusha**
誓約書 written oath, ~pledge **seiyakusho**
宣誓 oath-taking, swearing in **sensei**
宣誓式 oath-taking ceremony **senseishiki**
宣誓書 written oath **senseisho**
宣誓供述書 affidavit, sworn statement
　　sensei kyōjutsusho

約romise, 697　　嘱ntrust, 441
契ledge, 900　　託ntrust, 82
信aith, 252　　任ntrust, 709
委ntrust, 583　　預ntrust, 569

逝eath, 54　　哲isdom, 53

035-B

哲hilosophers 誓ledge to seek 哲isdom in 逝eath beyond...

口 (mouth)

哲isdom   哲hilosophy

TETSU
wisdom, philosophy, sagacity

FLIP: 4.0.a. Bottom (flat)

中哲 Chinese philosophy **chūtetsu**
変哲 common, ordinary, mediocre **hentetsu**
十哲 ten sages of Buddhism **jittetsu**
賢哲 wise person, sage **kentetsu**
明哲 wisdom, intelligence **meitetsu**
西哲 Western philosophy **seitetsu**
先哲 old wise man **sentetsu**
哲学 study of philosophy **tetsugaku**
⇒宗教哲学 theological philosophy
　　shūkyō tetsugaku
哲学者 philosopher **tetsugakusha**
哲学史 history of philosophy **tetsugakushi**
哲人 philosopher, wise person **tetsujin**
哲理 philosophical principles **tetsuri**
聖哲 old wise man, wizard **seitetsu**

啓nlightenment, 677　　由eason, 540
悟nlightenment, 780　　理eason, 872
賢ntelligent, 598　　故eason, 960
寛agnanimity, 308　　脳rain, 47

誓ledge, 53　　逝eath, 54

035-C

哲hilosophers 誓ledge to seek 哲isdom in 逝eath beyond...

辶 (transport)

逝eath　　逝emise

yu(ku), SEI

death, demise, dead, dying, passing away

長逝 *dying, passing away* **chōsei**
急逝 *sudden death, untimely demise* **kyūsei**
逝去 *death, demise, passing away* **seikyo**
早逝 *early death, short life* **sōsei**
夭逝 *premature death* **yōsei**
逝く春 *the departing spring* **yuku haru**
逝く年 *the departing year* **yuku toshi**

Facing: 4.0. 🐭☞ Apart

死*eath, 513*	墓*ravesite, 602*
亡*eath, 72*	碑*ombstone, 937*
葬*urial, 513*	

逆*everse, 896*	誓*ledge, 53*

036-A

Like 磁agnets, 慈ffection compliments soul 滋ourishment...

石 (stone)

❶磁agnet　　❷磁orcelain

JI

magnet; porcelain

❶電磁 *electromagnet* **denji**
電磁波 *electromagnet wave* **denjiha**
電磁気 *electromagnetism* **denjiki**
電磁石 *electromagnet* **denjishaku**
磁場 *magnetic field* **jiba, jijō**
磁化 *magnetization* **jika**
磁界 *magnetic field* **jikai**
磁気 *magnetism* **jiki**
磁気学 *magnetics science* **jikigaku**
磁気圏 *magnetic sphere* **jikiken**
磁気性 *magnetism* **jikisei**
磁極 *magnetic pole* **jikyoku**
磁力 *magnetic force* **jiryoku**
磁力計 *magnetometer* **jiryokukei**
磁力線 *line of magnetic force* **jiryokusen**
磁性 *magnetism* **jisei**
磁石 *magnet* **jishaku, jiseki**
磁針 *compass needle* **jishin**
磁束 *magnet flux* **jisoku**

FLIP: 7.2.a. Right Top (flat)
Facing: 2.2. East ☞ (V)

磁鉄 *iron bearing* **jitetsu**
消磁 *demagnetisation* **shōji**
地磁気 *Earth's magnetic force* **chijiki**
磁方位 *magnetic bearing* **jihōi**
磁鉄鉱 *loadstone, magnetite* **jitekkō**
透磁率 *magnetic permeability* **tōjiritsu**
❷青磁 *celadon porcelain* **aoji, seiji**
白磁 *white porcelain* **hakuji**
磁土 *china clay, kaolin* **jido**
磁器 *porcelain, chinaware* **jiki**
陶磁器 *pottery, chinaware* **tōjiki**

石*tone, 363*	陶*orcelain, 811*
引*ulling, 348*	陶*ottery, 811*
抽*ulling, 37*	窯*eramics, 576*

滋*uxuriant, 55*	慈*ffection, 55*

036-B

Like 磁agnets, 慈ffection compliments soul 滋ourishment...

心 ⇔ 忄 ⇔ 柰 (feelings)

慈ffection 慈enevolence

itsuku(shimu), JI
affection, benevolence, endearment

FLIP: 3.0.b. Top (stem)
Facing: 2.1. East ☞ (H)

慈しみ *love & affection* **itsukushimi**
慈愛 *affection, benevolence* **jiai**
慈母 *motherly love* **jibo**
慈父 *fatherly love* **jifu**
慈眼 *deep eyes of Buddha* **jigan, jigen**
慈悲 *mercy, pity* **jihi**
慈悲深い *deeply merciful* **jihibukai**
慈方位 *magnetic bearing* **jihōi**
慈兄 *brotherly love* **jikei**
慈恵 *charity, philanthropy* **jikei**
仁慈 *benevolence, magnanimity* **jinji**
慈鉄 *iron magnet* **jitetsu**
慈雨 *blessed rain, welcome rain* **jiu**
慈善 *charity, benevolence* **jizen**
慈善家 *philanthropist* **jizenka**
慈善事業 *charity work, philanthropy* **jizen jigyō**
慈姑① *waterplant* **kuwai**
慈姑② *merciful mother-in-law* **jiko**

慕*ffectionate, 600*
懇*ntimacy, 164*
親*ntimatcy, 669*

恋*omance, 581*   窓*indow, 433*

036-C

Like 磁agnets, 慈ffection compliments soul 滋ourishment...

水 ⇔ 氵 (water)

滋ourishment 滋uxuriant

JI
nourishment, luxuriant

FLIP: 7.2.a. Right Top (flat)
Facing: 2.2. East ☞ (V)

滋味 *deliciousness, good taste* **jimi**
滋殖 *deliciousness, good taste* **jishoku**
滋養 *nourishment, nutrition* **jiyō**
滋養分 *nutritious element* **jiyōbun**
滋養物 *nourishing food* **jiyōbutsu**
滋賀県 *Shiga Prefecture* **shiga-ken**
滋強飲料 *tonic drink* **jikyō inryō**
滋養過多 *hypertrophy, profusion* **jiyō kata**

剰*urplus, 511*   愛*ove, 593*
余*urplus, 501*   恵*lessing, 545*
富*ortune, 333*

慈*ffection, 55*   落*ollapse, 826*

037-A

疑oubts on 擬mitation 凝tiffened irritation...

疑oubt　　疑uspicion

GI, utaga(u)
doubt, suspicion, questionable, scepticism, distrust

遅疑 *reluctance, hesitance, dilly dally* **chigi**
疑義 *doubts, scepticism* **gigi**
疑獄 *scandal, disgrace, shameful act* **gigoku**
疑問 *doubt, question, query* **gimon**
疑問文 *interrogative sentence* **gimonbun**
疑問符 *question mark* **gimonfu**
疑念 *doubt, suspicion, distrust* **ginen**
疑心 *doubt, suspicion* **gishin**
疑心暗鬼 *"suspicion creates itself..."* **gishin anki**
疑点 *suspicious point* **giten**
疑雲 *cloud of doubt* **giun**
疑惑 *doubt, suspicion* **giwaku**
被疑者 *crime suspect* **higisha**
懐疑 *scepticism, doubt, disbelief* **kaigi**
懐疑論 *scepticism* **kaigiron**
懐疑説 *scepticism, disbelief* **kaigisetsu**
嫌疑 *doubt, suspicion* **kengi**
孤疑 *doubt, indecisive* **kogi**
猜疑 *under suspicion* **saigi**

疋 (animal counter)

Facing: 3.0. 　Across
Facing: 4.0. 　Apart

猜疑心 *doubt, suspicion* **saigishin**
信疑 *credibility, belief-or-doubt* **shingi**
質疑 *inquiry, interpellation* **shitsugi**
質疑応答 *question & answer session* **shitsugi ōtō**
容疑 *doubt, suspicion* **yōgi**
容疑者 *crime suspect* **yōgisha**
半信半疑 *dubious, untrustworthy* **hanshin hangi**
疑い深い *highly-untrustworthy* **utagaibukai**

怪*ubious*, 888
奇*trange*, 269

凝*arden*, 57　　　擬*mitate*, 56

037-B

疑oubts on 擬mitation 凝tiffened irritation...

擬mitation　　擬imulation

GI
imitation, simulation, counterfeit, disguise, mimicry

擬爆弾 *decoy bomb* **gibakudan**
擬似 *psuedo, imitation* **giji**
擬似軍事 *para-military* **giji gunji**
擬古 *fake classical goods* **giko**
擬古文 *psuedo-classical text* **gikobun**
擬古典的 *pseudo classic* **gikotenteki**
擬薬 *placebo, fake drugs* **giyaku**
擬毛 *imitation-, synthetic wool* **gimō**
擬音 *sound imitation, ~mimicry* **gion**
擬音語 *onomatopoeia, repetitive words* **giongo**
擬音効果 *sound effects* **gion kōka**
擬制 *fiction, fictitious* **gisei**
擬勢 *sham show-of-force, empty posturing* **gisei**
擬戦 *mock battle* **gisen**
擬死 *feigning death* **gishi**
擬装 *camouflage, disguise* **gisō**
擬態 *mimicry, imitation* **gitai**
擬態語 *mimesis* **gitaigo**
模擬 *imitation* **mogi**

手⇔扌 (hand, manual)

Facing: 3.0. 　Across
Facing: 4.0. 　Apart

模擬店 *booth, stand, stall* **mogiten**
模擬法廷 *moot court* **mogi hōtei**
模擬裁判 *moot court* **mogi saiban**
模擬試験 *drill examination* **mogi shiken**
擬人化 *personification, embodiment* **gijinka**
擬似的 *suspected, imitative* **gijiteki**
擬革紙 *fake leather* **gikakushi**
擬声語 *onomatopoeic words* **giseigo**

倣*mitate*, 486　　　同*imilar*, 245
似*imilar*, 472　　　装*retend*, 629

撤*ithdraw*, 843　　　凝*arden*, 57

037-C

疑oubts on 擬mitation 凝tiffened irritation...

凝tiffen 凝arden

冫 (freezing, ice)

ko(ru), ko(rasu), GYŌ
stiffen, harden, congeal, coagulate

凝着 *adhesion, fastening* **gyōchaku**
凝議 *thorough-, exhaustive deliberation* **gyōgi**
凝塊 *clot* **gyōkai**
凝結 *condensation, freezing* **gyōketsu**
凝血 *blood cut, ~wound* **gyōketsu**
凝固 *congelation, coagulation* **gyōko**
凝乳 *curdled milk* **gyōnyū**
凝立 *totally still* **gyōritsu**
凝視 *stare, gaze, watch* **gyōshi**
凝脂 *lard, frozen oil* **gyōshi**
凝縮 *condensation* **gyōshuku**
凝集 *be coherent* **gyōshū**
凝滞 *delay* **gyōtai**
凝結点 *freezing point, congeal point* **gyōketsuten**
凝り性 *perfectionistic, single-minded* **korishō**
凝り屋 *perfectionist* **koriya**
凝り固まる *fanatical, bigot, zealot* **korikatamaru**
肩凝り *stiff shoulders* **katakori**

Facing: 3.0. ☞☜ Across
Facing: 4.0. ☜☞ Apart

緊*ard, 599*
固*arden, 491*
硬*ardness, 402*

擬*mitate, 56*   撤*ithdraw, 843*

038-A

芽prouts in Brazzaville, no 雅race no 邪vil...

芽prout 芽aplings

艹 (grass)

me, me(gumu), GA
sprout, saplings, budding

麦芽 *malt, wheat germ* **bakuga**
麦芽糖 *malt sugar, maltose* **bakugatō**
芽胞 *spore* **gahō**
胚芽 *embryo; germ* **haiga**
胚芽米 *unpolished rice* **haigamai**
花芽 *sprout, bud* **haname**
発芽 *germination, budding* **hatsuga**
萌芽 *signs, makings of* **hōga**
芽接 *in-lay grafting* **metsugi**
肉芽 *granulation, grating, pulverizing* **nikuga**
新芽 *sprout, shoot* **shinme**
出芽 *budding, sprouting, germinating* **shutsuga**
胎芽 *propagule* **taiga**
摘芽 *thinning out of buds* **tekiga**
若芽 *young bud, shoot, sprout* **wakame**
幼芽 *grain germs* **yōga**
葉芽 *leaf bud* **yōga**
木の芽 *bud, sprout* **kinome**
芽生え *sprout, shoot, awakening* **mebae**

FLIP: 3.0.b. Top (stem)
Facing: 1.1. ☜ West (H)

芽出度い *happy, celebrative* **medetai**

植*lant, 783*   藻*ater plants, 852*
畑*lantation, 482*   栽*aplings, 803*
稲*ice plant, 893*   苗*aplings, 270*

草*rass, 373*   苦*nguish, 477*

038-B

芽*prouts for vaudeville, no* 雅*race no* 邪*vil...*

隹 (long-tailed birds)

雅*raceful*　　雅*legant*

GA, miyabi
graceful, elegant

Facing: 4.0. ⟵⟶ Apart

風雅 *elegant, refined, graceful* **fūga**
雅文 *elegant prose* **gabun**
雅致 *elegance, sophisticated* **gachi**
雅談 *graceful conversations* **gadan**
雅楽 *imperial court music* **gagaku**
雅言 *elegant expression* **gagen**
雅語 *graceful-, elegant words* **gago**
雅号 *pen name, pseudonym* **gagō**
雅人 *person with exquisite taste* **gajin**
雅歌 *graceful-, elegant words* **gaka**
雅壊 *aesthetic mood* **gakai**
雅客 *sophisticate, writer* **gakaku**
雅兄 *honorific for writing a friend* **gakei**
雅名 *pen name, pseudonym* **gamei**
雅味 *sophisticated taste* **gami**
雅量 *generosity, magnanimity* **garyō**
雅称 *pen name, pseudonym* **gashō**
雅趣 *elegance, good taste* **gashu**
雅俗 *refined-or-unrefined style* **gazoku**

博雅 *erudition, broad knowledge* **hakuga**
閑雅 *grace, elegance* **kanga**
古雅 *classical grace* **koga**
高雅 *elegant, refined, graceful* **kōga**
温雅 *refined, mild-mannered* **onga**
典雅 *elegant, graceful woman* **tenga**
都雅 *urbane-, socialite taste* **toga**
優雅 *elegant, graceful, exquisite* **yūga**
雅か *graceful, exquisite* **miyabika**

淑*raceful, 510*
韻*raceful, 315*

雌*emale-animal, 929*　　雄*ourage, 775*

038-C

芽*prouts for vaudeville, no* 雅*race no* 邪*vil...*

阝⟷阜 (village), (right)

邪*vil*　　邪*ad*

yokoshi(ma), JA, ZE
evil, bad

Facing: 4.0. ⟵⟶ Apart

破邪 *defeating evil* **haja**
邪悪 *wicked, evil, malicious* **jaaku**
邪道 *wicked ways, evil ways* **jadō**
邪飛 *baseball foul fly* **jahi**
邪淫 *wicked lustfulness* **jain**
邪見 *wrong view* **jaken**
邪険 *harsh, cruel* **jaken**
邪気 *malice, evil intent, ill will* **jaki**
⇒無邪気 *innocence, simplicity* **mujaki**
邪教 *blasphemy, heresy, sacreligious* **jakyō**
邪教徒 *heretic, infidel* **jakyōto**
邪魔 *hindrance, bothersome* **jama**
邪魔っ気 *troublesome, bothersome* **jamakke**
邪魔者 *nuisance, irksome, annoyance* **jamamono**
邪念 *evil thoughts, malice, ill will* **janen**
邪恋 *illicit love, forbidden love* **jaren**
邪論 *heteroxy, iconoclastic* **jaron**
邪正 *right & wrong* **jasei**
邪説 *heresy, heretical doctrine* **jasetsu**

邪心 *evil mind, evil heart* **jashin**
邪神 *devil, evil gods* **jashin**
邪宗 *heretical sect* **jashū**
邪推 *baseless suspicion* **jasui**
邪欲 *lust, lewd desire* **jayoku**
風邪 *cold in the nose, ~head* **kaze**
⇒鼻風邪 *cold in the nose, ~head* **hanakaze**
⇒夏風邪 *summer cold, summer chill* **natsukaze**
風邪声 *hoarse, nasal voice* **kazegoe**
正邪 *right-or-wrong, propriety* **seija**
天の邪鬼 *pervert, lewd, gross* **ama no jaku**

悪*vil, 389*　　鬼*evil, 935*
凶*vil, 80*　　魔*evil, 332*

雅*raceful, 58*　　芽*prout, 57*

039-A

勇*ourage* 通*asses* 通*hrough* 痛*ainful* 痛*njury...*

力 (strength, force)

勇*ourage* 勇*ravery*

isa(mu), isa(mushii), isa(mashii), YŪ
courage, bravery, embolden, valour

FLIP: 8.0.a. Inner (flat)
Facing: 3.0. ☞☜ Across

蛮勇	*reckless valour*	**banyū**
武勇	*fearless warrior, ~soldier*	**buyū**
沈勇	*calm courage*	**chinyū**
知勇	*wisdom & courage*	**chiyū**
忠勇	*loyalty & courage*	**chūyū**
義勇	*loyalty & courage*	**giyū**
剛勇	*brave, valiant, intrepid*	**gōyū**
豪勇	*courage, valour, daring*	**gōyū**
真勇	*genuine courage*	**shinyū**
大勇	*courage, valour, daring*	**taiyū**
勇断	*firm-, resolute decision*	**yūdan**
勇敢	*bravery, courage, valour*	**yūkan**
勇健	*stout-hearted, strong-willed*	**yūken**
勇気	*courage, valour, daring*	**yūki**
勇侠	*chivalrous, gallant*	**yūkyō**
勇名	*fame, celebrity, famous*	**yūmei**
勇猛	*bold, valiant*	**yūmō**
勇猛心	*dauntless, daring, bold*	**yūmōshin**
勇猛果敢	*dauntless, daring*	**yūmō kakan**

勇烈	*brave, valiant, intrepid*	**yūretsu**
勇者	*brave, courageous person*	**yūsha**
勇戦	*courageous-, desperate battle*	**yūsen**
勇士	*brave man, hero*	**yūshi**
勇姿	*valiant person*	**yūshi**
勇将	*valiant general*	**yūshō**
勇壮	*courage, valour, daring*	**yūsō**
勇退	*voluntary resignation*	**yūtai**
勇躍	*high spirits*	**yūyaku**
勇み足	*overeagerness*	**isamiashi**
勇み立つ	*strong, brave*	**isamitatsu**
勇み肌	*strong-skinned*	**isamihada**
喜び勇む	*high spirits*	**yorokobi isamu**

敢*ourage,* 449	冒*ourage,* 401
胆*ourage,* 740	雄*ourage,* 775

男*asculine,* 597	虜*aptive,* 70

039-B

勇*ourage* 通*asses* 通*hrough* 痛*ainful* 痛*njury...*

辶 (transport)

❶通*assing* ❷通*ommunicate*

too(ru), too(su), ka(you), too(shi), doo(shi), TSŪ, TSU
passing, through; communicate

Facing: 1.1. ☜ West (H)

❶便通	*bowel movement*	**bentsū**
直通	*direct line (telephone)*	**chokutsū**
普通	*usually, common, normally, regularly*	**futsū**
貫通	*penetration, piercing*	**kantsū**
交通	*traffic, transportation*	**kōtsū**
通学	*attending school, way to school*	**tsūgaku**
通貨	*currency, denomination*	**tsūka**
通過	*passage, crossing*	**tsūka**
通勤	*commuting to work*	**tsūkin**
通行	*passage, traffic*	**tsūkō**
通路	*pathway, alley, aisle*	**tsūro**
面通し	*line up*	**mendooshi**
通り雨	*passing thru rainfall*	**tooriame**
裏通り	*back street, alley*	**uradoori**
歩き通す	*walk thru*	**arukitoosu**
走り通す	*run thru*	**hashiritoosu**
一方通行	*one-way traffic*	**ippō tsūkō**
交通安全	*safe driving*	**kōtsū anzen**
最後通牒	*ultimatum*	**saigo tsūchō**

その通り	*"just like that..."*	**sono toori**
透き通る	*become transparent*	**sukitooru**
❷疎通	*understanding, comprehension*	**sotsū**
通知	*notice, notification*	**tsūchi**
通帳	*notebook, bankbook*	**tsūchō**
通信	*correspondence, communication*	**tsūshin**
通訳	*translation, interpretation*	**tsūyaku**
通告	*notification, announcement*	**tsūkoku**
隠し通す	*prevent from leakage*	**kakushitoosu**

路*oad,* 405	来*oming,* 871	往*ome & go,* 749
交*rossing,* 467	出*eave,* 173	径*ath,* 888
行*rip,* 79	道*ath,* 312	旅*ravel,* 650

角*orner,* 400	進*dvance,* 51

039-C

勇*ourage* 通*asses* 通*hrough* 痛*ainful* 痛*njury...*

痛*ainful*   痛*njury*

疒 (sickness)

ita(mu); ita(meru); ita(i), TSŪ
painful, injury, agonizing, hurting, harm

FLIP: 7.0.b2. Right (stem)
Facing: 3.0. ☞☜ Across

苦痛	*ache, pain*	**kutsū**
劇痛	*acute pain, severe pain*	**gekitsū**
激痛	*acute pain, severe pain*	**gekitsū**
心痛	*anguish, anxiety, distress*	**shintsū**
痛言	*brutal criticism*	**tsūgen**
胸痛	*chest pains*	**kyōtsū**
陣痛	*childbirth-, labour pains*	**jintsū**
産痛	*childbirth-, labour pains*	**santsū**
痛恨	*deep regret, deep remorse*	**tsūkon**
鈍痛	*dull pain*	**dontsū**
沈痛	*grave-, acute-, sharp pain*	**chintsū**
痛飲	*heavy drinking*	**tsūin**
腰痛	*lower back pain*	**yōtsū**
頭痛	*migraine, headache*	**zutsū**
痛痒	*pain & itch*	**tsūyō**
痛撃	*painful blow*	**tsūgeki**
痛感	*painful realization, "baptism of fire..."*	**tsūkan**
痛点	*painful spot*	**tsūten**

痛手	*painful wound*	**itade**
無痛	*painless, harmless*	**mutsū**
悲痛	*sadness, grief, sorrow*	**hitsū**
痛覚	*sense of pain*	**tsūkaku**
腹痛	*stomach ache, colic*	**fukutsū**
胃痛	*stomach pain, ~pain*	**itsū**
痛憤	*strong indignation, resentment*	**tsūfun**
歯痛	*toothache*	**shitsū**
鎮痛剤	*anodyne, lenitive, analgesic*	**chintsūzai**
偏頭痛	*migraine, headache*	**henzutsū**
筋肉痛	*muscle pains*	**kinnikutsū**
神経痛	*neuralgia, nerve pains*	**shinkeitsū**

害*njury, 904*	障*njury, 325*
傷*njury, 933*	損*njury, 410*

番*umber, 338*	雷*hunder, 136*

040-A

Her baby 振*winging,* 娠*regnant mother* 震*rembling...*

振*wing*   振*remble*

手⇔扌 (hand, manual)

fu(ruu), fu(ru), SHIN
swing, shake, tremble, vibrate

Facing: 4.0.. ☜☞ Apart

防振	*anti-vibration, vibration resistance*	**bōshin**
振替	*transfer*	**furikae**
不振	*dullness, depression, slack*	**fushin**
⇒営業不振	*business slack*	**eigyō fushin**
発振	*oscillation, fluctuation*	**hasshin**
共振	*resonance, reverberation*	**kyōshin**
強振	*forceful swing*	**kyōshin**
三振	*strike out*	**sanshin**
振動	*vibration, quiver, shake*	**shindō**
振興	*promotion, rousing*	**shinkō**
振幅	*vibration amplitude*	**shinpuku**
羽振り	*influential & powerful*	**haburi**
空振り	*swing & miss*	**karaburi**
身振り	*gesture, body language*	**miburi**
女振り	*pretty woman*	**onnaburi**
男振り	*male reputation*	**otokoburi**
素振り	*behaviour, demeanour, manner*	**suburi**
手振り	*hand gesture, hand mannerism*	**teburi**
振り子	*pendulum*	**furiko**

振り込み	*payment by wire transfer*	**furikomi**
振り回す	*abuse, show off, brandish*	**furimawasu**
振り向く	*turn around, about-face*	**furimuku**
振り絞る	*exert, make efforts*	**furishiboru**
振り出し	*starting point, drawing out*	**furidashi**
振り出す	*draw, shake out*	**furidasu**
振り仮名	*kana reading, ~pronunciation*	**furigana**
割り振り	*allotment, allocation*	**warifuri**
揺さ振る	*shake, quiver*	**yusaburu**
久し振り	*"long time, no see..."*	**hisashiburi**
振る舞う	*behave, act; entertain, treat*	**furumau**

揺*remble, 811*
震*remble, 61*

握*rasp, 427*	掲*oist(flag), 810*

040-B

Her baby 振*winging,* 娠*regnant mother* 震*rembling...*

女 (woman)

娠*regnancy*   娠*onception*

SHIN
pregnancy, conception, child bearing

Facing: 2.2. East ☞ (V)

妊娠 *pregnancy, conceiving a child* **ninshin**
⇒想像妊娠 *imagined pregnancy* **sōzō ninshin**
妊娠中毒 *illness during pregnancy (vomitting...)*
　ninshin chūdoku
妊娠中絶 *artificial abortion, pregnancy termination*
　ninshin chūzetsu

妊*regnancy, 709*	生*ife, 474*
女*emale, 350*	命*ife, 362*
児*hildren, 464*	童*hildren, 564*
稚*hildren, 776*	誕*hildbirth, 515*
子*hildren, 456*	産*hildbirth, 883*

嬢*aughter, 854*	妊*regnancy, 709*

040-C

Her baby 振*winging,* 娠*regnant mother* 震*rembling...*

雨 (weather)

震*remble*   震*arthquake*

furu(eru), furu(u), SHIN
tremble, earthquake, tremors, jitters, seismic

FLIP: 3.0.b. Top (stem)

微震 *slight earthquake, ~tremors* **bishin**
中震 *mild earthquake* **chūshin**
激震 *severe earthquake, ~shock* **gekishin**
弱震 *slight earthquake shock* **jakushin**
地震 *earthquake* **jishin**
軽震 *light earthquake, tremor* **keishin**
強震 *violent-, severe earthquake* **kyōshin**
烈震 *violent-, severe earthquake* **resshin**
震度 *seismic intensity, ~magnitude* **shindo**
震動 *shock, quake, tremor* **shindō**
震駭 *terror, horror, shock* **shingai**
震害 *earthquake damage* **shingai**
震撼 *shaking, reverberating* **shinkan**
震央 *epicentre, ground zero* **shin'ō**
震幅 *seismic intensity, ~magnitude* **shinpuku**
震災 *earthquake calamity* **shinsai**
震盪 *cerebral concussion* **shintō**
耐震 *earthquake resistance* **taishin**
耐震ビル *earthquake-resistant building* **taishin biru**

耐震性 *resistance to earthquake* **taishinsei**
余震 *earthquake aftershocks* **yoshin**
予震 *earthquake foreshocks* **yoshin**
前震 *foreshocks* **zenshin**
震え声 *trembling voice* **furuegoe**
震え上がる *swing, shudder, tremble*
　furueagaru
身震い *shiver, shaking, shudder* **miburui**
脳震盪 *brain concussion* **nōshintō**
震源地 *epicentre, ground zero* **shingenchi**
震天動地 *"heaven & earth trembling..."*
　shinten dōchi
震るい付く *affectionate embrace* **furuitsuku**

揺*remble, 811*
振*winging, 60*

霊*pirit, 444*	霜*rost, 615*

041-A

微*light* eye 徴*ymptoms*, 懲*unished Peeping Toms...*

彳 (stroll)

微*light* 微*inute*

BI

slight, minute, insignificant, minuscule, negligible

FLIP: 8.0.b. Inner (stem)

微微 slight, tiny, little **bibi**
微分 differential calculus **bibun**
微動 tremor, slight quiver **bidō**
微粉 fine powder **bifun**
微弱 faint, weak **bijaku**
微光 faint light **bikō**
微行 travelling incognito, secret trip **bikō**
微熱 slight fever **binetsu**
微温 lukewarm, slightly hot **bion**
微量 sight amount **biryō**
微力 limited ability **biryoku**
微細 minute, delicate, fine **bisai**
微震 weak-, mild earthquake **bishin**
微少 slight, minute **bishō**
微罪 minor-, petty offence **bizai**
極微 infinitesimal, microscopic **gokubi**
隠微 subtle, obscure **inbi**
軽微 slight, mild **keibi**
機微 niceties, courtesy **kibi**

微塵 particle, fragments **mijin**
衰微 decline, wane, fade-out **suibi**
微調整 slight fine-tuning **bichōsei**
微粒子 particle, corpuscle **biryūshi**
微生物 micro-organism, microbe **biseibutsu**
微生物学 microbiology **bisei butsugaku**
微積分 differential & integral calculus **bisekibun**
微視的 microscopic, minuscule **bishiteki**
顕微鏡 microscope **kenbikyō**
微笑み smile, smiling face **hohoemi**
微笑ましい heart-warming, **hohoemashii**

寡*ittle*, 161	少*ew*, 459
若*ittle*, 276	小*mall*, 459
幾*ew*, 547	子*ittle*, 456

徹*ierce-thru*, 843	撤*ithdraw*, 843

041-B

微*light* eye 徴*ymptoms*, 懲*unished Peeping Toms...*

彳 (stroll)

❶徴*emand* ❷徴*ymptoms*

CHŌ

demand, levy; symptoms

FLIP: 8.0.a. Inner (flat)

❶徴募 enlistment, recruitment **chōbo**
徴発 commandeering, seizure **chōhatsu**
徴発令 requisition orders **chōhatsurei**
徴兵 military conscription **chōhei**
徴兵忌避 draft evasion, ~dodging **chōhei kihi**
徴収 levy, tribute **chōshū**
⇒源泉徴収 main income tax **gensen chōshū**
徴集 levy, tribute **chōshū**
徴用 commandeering, seizure **chōyō**
徴税 tax collection **chōzei**
徴税吏 tax collector **chōzeiri**
性徴 sexual character **seichō**
追徴 additional tax collection **tsuichō**
追徴金 additional collection, surcharge **tsuichōkin**
増徴 additional tax, surtax **zōchō**
課徴金 surcharge, extra fee **kachōkin**
徴収令 calling up draftees **chōshūrei**
徴兵免除 draft exemption **chōhei menjo**

❷徴候 sign, symptom **chōkō**
標徴 uniqueness, distinguishing feature **hyōchō**
吉徴 lucky charm, good omen **kicchō**
明徴 clarification, elucidation **meichō**
象徴 symbol, emblem **shōchō**
象徴的 symbolic, tokenism **shōchōteki**
象徴主義 symbolism **shōchō shugi**
特徴 characteristic, unique **tokuchō**

威*uthority*, 520	響*ffect*, 452
権*uthority*, 804	果*esult*, 287
政*dministration*, 725	因*ause*, 862
兆*ymptoms*, 214	根*oot*, 772

徹*ierce-thru*, 843	撤*ithdraw*, 843

041-C

微light eye 徴ymptoms, 懲unished Peeping Toms...

心⇔忄⇔忝 (feelings)

懲*enalty*　　懲*unitive*

FLIP: 8.0.a. Inner (flat)

ko(rasu), ko(rashimeru), ko(riru), CHŌ
penalty, punishment, punitive

懲悪 *punishment, penalty* **chōaku**
⇒勧善懲悪 *reward good & punish evil*
　kanzen chōaku
懲罰 *punishment, discipline* **chōbatsu**
懲役 *penal servitude* **chōeki**
⇒無期懲役 *life imprisonment* **muki chōeki**
懲戒 *reprimand, censure* **chōkai**
懲戒免職 *disciplinary dismissal* **chōkai menshoku**
懲戒処分 *disciplinary punishment* **chōkai shobun**
性懲り *"learn the hard way..."* **shōkori**
性懲りもない *incorrigible, persistent* **shōkorimonai**
懲り懲り *learning from experience* **korigori**

獄*rison, 639*	罪*riminal, 289*
囚*risoner, 863*	犯*riminal, 640*
刑*unishment, 536*	禁*rohibit, 560*
罰*unishment, 759*	

徳*irtue. 844*	癒*ecuperate. 923*

042-A

薄hin tiny 簿edger, 縛ound in thick leather...

艾 (grass)

❶薄*hin*　　❷薄*ight*

FLIP: 8.0.a. Inner (flat)

usu(i), usu(maru), usu(ragu), usu(reru), usu(meru), HAKU
thin; light

❶浮薄 *flippant behaviour* **fuhaku**
薄幸 *unfortunate, unhappy* **hakkō**
薄光 *faint light, flicker of light* **hakkō**
薄給 *low salary, small pay* **hakkyū**
薄暮 *evening, dusk, nightfall* **hakubo**
薄情 *heartless, cruel, cold-hearted* **hakujō**
薄命 *short life, early death* **hakumei**
薄利 *small profit, token earnings* **hakuri**
薄謝 *token of gratitude* **hakusha**
薄志 *weak-willed, weak-kneaded* **hakushi**
軽薄 *insincere, frivolous, dishonest* **keihaku**
希薄 *thin, weak* **kihaku**
厚薄 *relative thickness* **kōhaku**
酷薄 *heartless, cruel, cold-hearted* **kokuhaku**
肉薄 *coming close, nearing* **nikuhaku**
浅薄 *flimsy, shallow, frivolous* **senpaku**
品薄 *stock shortage, low stock* **shinausu**
薄味 *weak taste, bland flavour* **usuaji**
薄刃 *thin blade* **usuba**

❷薄手 *thin, eggshell* **usude**
薄紅 *pinkish* **usubeni**
薄日 *little sunlight* **usubi**
薄紙 *thin paper* **usugami**
薄着 *thin-, light clothing* **usugi**
薄絹 *light silk* **usuginu**
薄目 *half-closed eyes* **usume**
薄緑 *pale green* **usumidori**
薄汚い *dirty, unclean* **usugitanai**
薄暗い *dim, dusky, dull* **usugurai**
薄笑い *faint smile, feigned smile* **usuwarai**
薄汚れる *dirty, sullied, stained* **usuyogoreru**
薄気味悪い *spooky, creepy* **usukimi warui**

淡*aint, 309*	透*ransparency, 383*
漠*bscure, 828*	

籍*egistry. 336*	

042-B

薄*hin tiny* 簿*edger,* 縛*ound in thick leather...*

簿*edger*　簿*ecord*

竹 (bamboo)

FLIP: 8.0.a. Inner (flat)

BO
ledger, record, roster, registry

簿外 *unlisted, off-the-books, concealed* **bogai**
簿外負債 *hidden debts* **bogai fusai**
簿外資産 *hidden wealth* **bogai shisan**
簿記 *bookkeeping, accounting record* **boki**
簿記帳 *account book* **bokichō**
帳簿 *account book, ledger* **chōbo**
名簿 *name list, roster* **meibo**
登簿 *registration* **tōbo**
学籍簿 *school attendance record* **gakusekibo**
人名簿 *name list, roster* **jinmeibo**
家計簿 *family expenses book* **kakeibo**
計算簿 *account book* **keisanbo**
戸籍簿 *family register* **kosekibo**
出勤簿 *work attendance record* **shukkinbo**
出席簿 *attendance record* **shussekibo**
出納簿 *account book* **suitōbo**
登記簿 *registry, registration list* **tōkibo**
登録簿 *register, journal* **tōrokubo**

通知簿 *report card* **tsūchibo**
通信簿 *correspondence card* **tsūshinbo**

記*ecord, 728*	歴*istory, 595*
録*ecord, 841*	暦*alendar, 595*
紀*arration, 727*	

籍*egistry, 336*	薄*ight, 63*

042-C

薄*hin tiny* 簿*edger,* 縛*ound in thick leather...*

縛*inding*　縛*ie-up*

糸 (thread, continuity)

FLIP: 7.2.a. Right Top (flat)

shiba(ru), imashime, BAKU
binding, tie-up

縛り首 *hanging criminals* **shibarikubi**
縛り上げる *tie up, bind up* **shibariageru**
縛り付ける *tie up, bind up* **shibaritsukeru**
捕縛 *arrest, capture* **hobaku**
呪縛 *spellbinding, awesome* **jubaku**
緊縛 *tight binding, tightening* **kinbaku**
就縛 *be arrested, taken into custody* **shūbaku**
収縛 *arrest & tie-up* **shūbaku**
束縛 *restraint, restriction* **sokubaku**
金縛り *bound hands & feet* **kanashibari**
自縄自縛 *"caught in one's trap..."* **jijō jibaku**

括*undle, 954*	拘*rrest, 16*
束*undle, 502*	逮*rrest, 880*
把*undle, 717*	

籍*egistry, 336*	薄*ight, 63*

043-A
避*void* 癖*abit of climbing high* 壁*alls, lest you fall...*

避*void*　　避*lude*　　避*vade*

辶 (transport)

sa(keru), HI
avoid, avert, evade, elude, desist, duck

FLIP: 7.0.b1. Right (stem)

避寒 *spending the winter, wintering* **hikan**
避寒地 *winter resort* **hikanchi**
避難 *taking refuge* **hinan**
⇒緊急避難 *emergency evacuation* **kinkyū hinan**
避難所 *refuge, shelter* **hinanjo**
避難民 *refugee, evacuee* **hinanmin**
避妊 *contraception, anti-pregnancy* **hinin**
避妊法 *anti-pregnancy method* **hininhō**
避妊薬 *contraceptive, birth control drug* **hininyaku**
避暑 *spending the summer* **hisho**
避暑客 *summer visitors* **hisho kyaku**
避暑地 *summer resort* **hishochi**
回避 *evasion, avoidance* **kaihi**
忌避 *evasion, challenge* **kihi**
⇒徴兵忌避 *draft evasion, ~dodging* **chōhei kihi**
退避 *taking refuge, ~shelter* **taihi**
待避 *shunting, sidetracking* **taihi**
待避線 *sidetrack, sidepath* **taihisen**
逃避 *escape, evasion, refuge* **tōhi**

逃避行 *escape journey, exit route* **tōhikō**
雨避け *rain shelter* **amayoke**
不可避 *unavoidable, inevitable* **fukahi**
避病院 *quarantine hospital* **hibyōin**
避雷針 *lightning rod, lightning bolt* **hiraishin**

却*ithdraw*, 387　　撤*ithdraw*, 843
退*ithdraw*, 770　　罷*ithdraw*, 322

癖*abitual*, 65　　壁*arrier* 66

043-B
避*void* 癖*abit of climbing high* 壁*alls, lest you fall...*

癖*abitual*　　癖*annerism*

疒 (sickness)

kuse, HEKI
habitual, mannerism, penchant, queerness, repetitious

FLIP: 7.0.b1. Right (stem)

悪癖 *bad habit* **akuheki**
足癖 *peculiar walking style* **ashikuse**
病癖 *getting a bad habit* **byōheki**
一癖 *quirk, peculiarity* **hitokuse**
髪癖 *peculiar hairstyle* **kamikuse, kamiguse**
癇癖 *quick-tempered, mercurial* **kanpeki**
肩癖 *stiff shoulders* **kenpeki**
潔癖 *cleanly, tidy, punctilious* **keppeki**
奇癖 *eccentricity, odd habit* **kiheki**
口癖 *favourite phrase, ~expression* **kuchiguse**
癖毛 *dishevelled-, untidy hairstyle* **kusege**
難癖 *fault-finder, complainer* **nankuse**
寝癖 *sleeping peculiarity* **neguse**
女癖 *womaniser, philanderer* **onnaguse**
男癖 *promiscuous woman* **otokoguse**
酒癖 *drunken behaviour* **sakeguse**
性癖 *natural inclination* **seiheki**
尻癖 *promiscuous, lewdness* **shirikuse**
習癖 *habit, peculiarity* **shūheki**

手癖 *sticky hands* **tekuse**
盗癖 *thievish, kleptomaniac* **tōheki**
放浪癖 *vagrant-, vagabond habit* **hōrōheki**
飲酒癖 *drinking habit* **inshuheki**
書き癖 *handwriting style* **kakikuse**
怠け癖 *laziness habit, idleness* **namakekuse**
寝る癖 *peculiar way of sleeping* **nerukuse**
飲み癖 *peculiar way of drinking* **nomikuse**
浪費癖 *squandering-, wasteful habit* **rōhikuse**
其の癖 *nevertheless, and yet* **sonokuse**
読み癖 *peculiar way of reading* **yomikuse**

慣*abit*, 532
事*ction*, 116
習*earning*, 238

避*void*, 65　　壁*all*, 66

043-C

避*void* 癖*abit of climbing high* 壁*alls, lest you fall...*

土 (ground, soil)

壁*all*　　壁*arrier*

kabe, HEKI
wall, barrier

FLIP: 4.0.a. Bottom (flat)
FLIP: 7.2.b. Right Top (stem)

粗壁 *rough surface wall* **arakabe**
防壁 *protective wall* **bōheki**
腹壁 *abdominal wall* **fukuheki**
外壁 *exterior-, outer wall* **gaiheki**
岸壁 *quay, wharf* **ganpeki**
岩壁 *rock wall, cliff* **ganpeki**
壁画 *art mural* **hekiga**
壁面 *wall surface* **hekimen**
氷壁 *wall of ice* **hyōheki**
胃壁 *stomach walls* **iheki**
城壁 *castle wall* **jōheki**
壁紙 *wallpaper* **kabegami**
壁際 *near the wall* **kabegiwa**
壁土 *wall plaster* **kabetsuchi**
隔壁 *partition, divider wall* **kakuheki**
胸壁 *chest walls* **kyōheki**
内壁 *inner wall* **naiheki**
生壁 *wet-paint wall* **namakabe**

塁壁 *rampart, barricade* **ruiheki**
白壁 *white wall* **shirakabe**
障壁 *barrier, wall* **shōheki**
鉄壁 *iron wall, iron curtain* **teppeki**
絶壁 *precipice, cliff* **zeppeki**
防火壁 *fire-resistant wall* **bōkaheki**
壁掛け *wall decoration* **kabekake**
壁塗り *wall plastering* **kabenuri**
壁新聞 *wall newspaper* **kabeshinbun**
火口壁 *crater wall* **kakōheki**
断崖絶壁 *overhanging cliff* **dangai zeppeki**
言葉の壁 *language barrier* **kotoba no kabe**

関*arrier, 284*	境*oundary, 839*
限*imit, 771*	

避*void.* 65	癖*abitual.* 65

044-A

While 僚*olleagues* 療*ecuperate, their* 寮*ormitories wait...*

人⇔イ (person)

僚*ellow*　　僚*olleague*

RYŌ
fellow, colleague, associate

FLIP: 7.1. Right (Sort Of)

幕僚 *staff officers, executive* **bakuryō**
同僚 *colleague, fellow* **dōryō**
閣僚 *cabinet ministers* **kakuryō**
官僚 *bureaucracy, bureaucrat* **kanryō**
官僚制 *bureaucracy, bureaucratic* **kanryōsei**
官僚的 *bureaucratic* **kanryōteki**
官僚主義 *bureaucratism* **kanryō shugi**
下僚 *petty official* **karyō**
僚艦 *escort-, consort ship* **ryōkan**
僚官 *fellow official* **ryōkan**
僚機 *escort-, consort airplane* **ryōki**
僚船 *escort-, consort ship* **ryōsen**
僚友 *co-worker, officemate* **ryōyū**

仲*ellow, 695*	奴*ellow, 44*
輩*ellow, 290*	相*ellow, 524*

億*undred-million.* 340	境*oundary.* 839

044-B

While 僚olleagues 療ecuperate, their 寮ormitories wait...

疒 (sickness)

療ecuperate 療reatment

RYŌ
recuperate, treatment, convalesce, getting well

FLIP: 7.1. Right (Sort Of)

物療 *physiotherapy, physical therapy* **butsuryō**
治療 *treatment, therapy, care* **chiryō**
⇒揉み治療 *massage therapy* **momichiryō**
⇒内科治療 *internal medicine cure* **naika chiryō**
⇒早期治療 *early treatment* **sōki chiryō**
治療代 *doctor's fee* **chiryōdai**
治療学 *therapy science* **chiryōgaku**
治療法 *cure, remedy* **chiryōhō**
治療師 *therapist* **chiryōshi**
治療所 *clinic, dispensary, infirmary* **chiryōsho**
医療 *medical treatment* **iryō**
加療 *patient treatment, ~care* **karyō**
療法 *cure, treatment, therapy* **ryōhō**
⇒熱療法 *medical therapy by heat* **netsuryōhō**
⇒断食療法 *fasting cure* **danjiki ryōhō**
⇒民間療法 *traditional cure* **minkan ryōhō**
⇒催眠療法 *hypnotic treatment* **saimin ryōhō**
⇒指圧療法 *finger-massage* **shiatsu ryōhō**
⇒素人療法 *amateur cure* **shirōto ryōhō**

⇒薬物療法 *drug therapy* **yakubutsu ryōhō**
療治 *medical treatment* **ryōji**
療養 *treatment, care* **ryōyō**
療養中 *recuperating* **ryōyōchū**
療養所 *sanitarium, infirmary* **ryōyōjo**
施療 *free-medical treatment* **seryō**
診療 *medical treatment, ~care* **shinryō**
診療所 *clinic, dispensary* **shinryōsho**
診療時間 *consultation hours* **shinryō jikan**
手療治 *home treatment* **teryōji**
荒療治 *hit-or-miss treatment* **araryōji**

診*iagnosis,* 720	症*ickness,* 788
医*edicine,* 19	病*ickness,* 213
剤*edicine,* 961	治*ecuperate,* 210
患*ickness,* 475	癒*ecuperate,* 923

僚*olleague,* 66	寮*ormitory,* 67

044-C

While 僚olleagues 療ecuperate, their 寮ormitories wait...

宀 (cover, lid)

寮ormitory 寮uarters

RYŌ
dormitory, quarters, hostel

FLIP: 2.0.b. Sort Of (stem)

茶寮 *cottage for tea-ceremony* **charyō**
学寮 *school dormitory* **gakuryō**
寮母 *dormitory matron, dorm landlady* **ryōbo**
寮長 *dormitory superintendent* **ryōchō**
寮費 *room & board charge* **ryōhi**
寮歌 *dormitory song* **ryōka**
寮監 *dormitory superintendent* **ryōkan**
寮生 *boarder, boarding student* **ryōsei**
寮舎 *dormitory, boarding house* **ryōsha**
独身寮 *dormitory for bachelor staff* **dokushinryō**
学生寮 *student dormitory* **gakuryō**

舎*uarters,* 388	宅*esidence,* 82
居*esidence,* 384	邸*esidence,* 860
住*esidence,* 750	

僚*olleague,* 66	療*ecuperate,* 67

045-A

麗eautiful 薦ecommendations, 慶ejoice in 慶elebration...

鹿 (deer)

麗eautiful　麗retty

uruwa(shii), ura(raka), REI
beautiful, pretty, aesthetic

FLIP: 3.0.b. Top (stem)

美麗 *beautiful, lovely* **birei**
艶麗 *fascinating, alluring* **enrei**
豊麗 *voluptuous, sensual* **hōrei**
華麗 *splendour, magnificent* **karei**
奇麗 *clean, neat; beautiful, lovely* **kirei**
綺麗 *clean, neat; beautiful, lovely* **kirei**
高麗 *ancient Korea* **kōrai**
麗筆 *beautiful brushwork* **reihitsu**
麗人 *beauty, belle* **reijin**
麗句 *beautiful phrase* **reiku**
⇒美辞麗句 *flowery words, highfalutin* **bijireiku**
麗姿 *beautiful shape* **reishi**
麗質 *charm, beauty* **reishitsu**
麗容 *beautiful form* **reiyō**
流麗 *flowing & elegant* **ryūrei**
⇒行文流麗 *beautiful handwriting* **kōbun ryūrei**
鮮麗 *bright paintings* **senrei**
秀麗 *beautiful, dazzling* **shūrei**

壮麗 *splendour, lustre, brilliance* **sōrei**
端麗 *fine looking* **tanrei**
典麗 *elegant, graceful* **tenrei**
奇麗好き *fond of cleanliness* **kireizuki**
麗麗しい *ostentatious, showing off* **reireishii**
見目麗しい *good-looking* **mime uruwashii**
御機嫌麗しい *good humour* **gokigen uruwashii**
麗らかな気分 *cheerfulness* **uraraka na kibun**

美*eautiful, 124*	雅*raceful, 58*
佳*eauty, 891*	淑*raceful, 510*
韻*raceful, 315*	

薦*recommend, 68*	慶*ejoice, 69*

045-B

麗eautiful 薦ecommendations, 慶ejoice in 慶elebration...

艹 (grass)

薦ecommend　薦ndorse

susu(meru), SEN
recommend, endorse, advice, counsel, stump for, vouch for, enjoin

FLIP: 3.0.b. Top (stem)
Facing: 2.1. East ☞ (H)

自薦 *self-recommendation* **jisen**
薦骨 *sacrum, rump* **senkotsu**
薦挙 *recommendation, endorsement* **senkyo**
推薦 *recommendation, endorsement* **suisen**
推薦状 *letter of recommendation* **suisenjō**
推薦者 *nominator, recommender* **suisensha**
特薦 *special recommendation* **tokusen**
被推薦者 *nominated candidate* **hisuisensha**

勧*ecommend, 666*	賛*pproval, 334*
推*ecommend, 777*	肯*ffirmative, 616*
可*pproval, 15*	援*upport, 820*
承*pproval, 117*	助*upport, 953*

薫*ragrance, 934*	覆*onceal, 602*

045-C

麗*eautiful* 薦*ecommendations,* 慶*ejoice in* 慶*elebration...*

❶ 慶*elebration*

❷ 慶*ejoice*

心⇔忄⇔恭 (feelings)

KEI

celebraion, felicitation; rejoice

❶ 同慶 *mutual congratulations* **dōkei**
御慶 *greetings, congratulations* **gyokei**
慶弔 *congratulation-or-condolence* **keichō**
慶兆 *lucky omen* **keichō**
慶大 *Keiō University* **keidai**
慶賀 *congratulation, celebration* **keiga**
慶事 *happy occasion, joyful event* **keiji**
慶祝 *congratulation, celebration* **keishuku**

❷ 吉慶 *rejoice, congratulatory* **kikkei**
大慶 *great happiness* **taikei**
弁慶草 *orpine* **benkeisō**
陰弁慶 *"tough at home, meek outside..."* **kagebenkei**
内弁慶 *"strict at home, weak outside..."* **uchibenkei**
延慶時代 *Enkei Era (1308-1311)* **enkei jidai**
元慶時代 *Gangyō Era (877-885)* **gangyō jidai**
慶長時代 *Keichō Era (1596-1615)* **keichō jidai**
慶応時代 *Keiō Era (1865-68)* **keiō jidai**

Facing: 3.0. ☞☜ Across

正慶時代 *Shōkei Era (1332-1338)* **shōkei jidai**
天慶時代 *Tengyō Era (938-947)* **tengyō jidai**

賀*elebration*, 202	勝*ictory*, 406
祝*elebration*, 716	果*esult*, 287
功*uccess*, 635	

麗*eautiful*, 68	薦*ecommend*, 68

046-A

膚*kinny war* 虜*aptives, their* 慮*houghts depressive...*

膚*kin*   膚*erma*

肉⇔月 (flesh, body part)

hada, FU

skin, derma, epidermis

赤膚 *abraded skin* **akahada**
膚着 *underwear, undergarments* **hadagi**
膚色 *flesh colour* **hadairo**
膚身 *nude, naked body* **hadami**
膚身離さず *keep to oneself* **hadami hanasazu**
皮膚 *skin* **hifu**
皮膚病 *skin disease* **hifubyō**
皮膚科 *dermatology* **hifuka**
皮膚科医 *dermatologist, skin doctor* **hifukai**
人膚 *warmth of the skin* **hitohada**
完膚 *smooth skin* **kanpu**
餅膚 *smooth white skin* **mochihada**
諸膚 *half-naked, bare chest* **morohada**
鮫膚 *fishskin, scaly skin* **samehada**
素膚 *bare skin* **suhada**
鳥膚 *goose bumps* **torihada**
山膚 *mountain surface* **yamahada**
雪膚 *"skin white as snow..."* **yukihada**
膚襦袢 *kimono undergarments* **hadajuban**

FLIP: 8.0.a. Inner (flat)

膚脱ぎ *half-naked, bare chest* **hadanugi**
膚寒い *"chilled to the skin..."* **hadasamui**
膚触り *the feel, the touch* **hadazawari**

肌*kin*, 747	毛*kin hair*, 468
皮*kin*, 224	

虜*hreat*, 889	層*ayer*, 838

046-B

膚kinny war 虜aptives, their 慮houghts depressive...

虜aptive   虜risoner

虍 (tiger)

FLIP: 8.0.a. Inner (flat)

toriko, RYO
captive, prisoner, inmate, detainee

俘虜 *captive, prisoner-of-war* **furyo**
捕虜 *prisoner, captive, POW* **horyo**
捕虜収容所 *prisoner-of-war camp* **horyo shūyōjo**
虜囚 *prisoner-of-war, captive soldier* **ryoshū**

逮apture, 880	捕eize, 812
拘rrest, 16	獄rison, 639
逮rrest, 880	囚risoner, 863

男asculine, 597	慮houghts, 70

046-C

膚kinny war 虜aptives, their 慮houghts depressive...

慮hought   慮dea

心⇔忄⇔忝 (feelings)

FLIP: 8.0.a. Inner (flat)

omonbaka(ru), RYO
thought, idea, concept, conjecture, notion, thinking

凡慮 *ordinary-, common thinking* **bonryo**
知慮 *wisdom, sagacity, foresight* **chiryo**
智慮 *wisdom, sagacity, foresight* **chiryo**
遠慮 *reserve manner, modest* **enryo**
⇒無遠慮 *lack of manners* **buenryo**
⇒深謀遠慮 *far-sighted thinking* **shinbō enryo**
遠慮深い *diffident, modest, reserve* **enryobukai**
不慮 *unexpected, sudden* **furyo**
不慮の死 *unexpected death* **furyonoshi**
配慮 *consideration, trouble* **hairyo**
熟慮 *careful deliberation, ~consideration* **jukuryo**
賢慮 *clever idea, brilliant plot* **kenryo**
顧慮 *consideration, thinking* **koryo**
考慮 *consideration, thoughtfulness* **kōryo**
苦慮 *thorough thinking, pondering* **kuryo**
無慮 *infinite, countless* **muryo**
念慮 *thoughtful, consideration* **nenryo**
慮外 *unexpected; rude* **ryogai**
聖慮 *divine will, imperial wishes* **seiryo**

浅慮 *imprudence, shallow-minded* **senryo**
千慮 *careful, prudent, discreet* **senryo**
深慮 *thoughtfulness, considerateness* **shinryo**
神慮 *divine will* **shinryo**
思慮 *consideration, thoughtfulness* **shiryo**
⇒無思慮 *indiscretion, imprudence* **mushiryo**
思慮深い *deeply considerate* **shiryobukai**
焦慮 *worry, anxiety, angst* **shōryo**
短慮 *impulsive, rashness, haste* **tanryo**
憂慮 *anxiety, worry, apprehension* **yūryo**

意hought, 340	妄houghtless, 34
想hought, 524	癖annerism, 65
念hought, 182	慣abit, 532

思hink, 596	膚kin, 69

List of Kanji Characters with Multiple Meanings

Important Kanji characters—exactly alike—but with two or three different meanings. *Continued on page 977.*

047-A

七even dwarfs wept for Snow White's 亡eath...

七*even*

nana(tsu), nana, nano, SHICHI
  seven

七重 *seventh fold* **nanae**
七色 *colours of rainbow* **nanairo**
七十 *seventy* **nanajū, shichijū**
七草 *seven autumn flowers* **nanakusa**
七草がゆ *rice porridge with 7 herbs* **nanakusagayu**
七曲 *winding, tormentous* **nanamagari**
七月 *July* **shichigatsu**
七輪 *earthen charcoal holder* **shichirin**
七生 *seven lives* **shichishō**
七生報国 *absolute patriotism* **shichishō hōkoku**
七光り *influence, "thanks to..."* **nanahikari**
御七夜 *seventh day of one's birth* **oshichiya**
七福神 *seven gods of fortune* **shichi fukujin**
七五三 *children ages of 3, 5 & 7* **shichigosan**
七回忌 *seventh death anniversary* **shichikaiki**
七面鳥 *turkey* **shichimenchō**
七面倒 *troublesome, great burden* **shichimendō**
七宝焼 *cloisonne ware* **shippōyaki**
初七日 *7th day after death* **shonanoka**

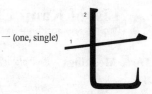

一 (one, single)

Facing: 2.0. East ☞ (W)

七夕祭 *Star Festival (7 July)* **tanabata matsuri**
北斗七星 *Big Dipper* **hokuto shichisei**
七不思議 *Seven World Wonders* **nanafushigi**
七つ道具 *complete set of tools* **nanatsu dōgu**
七分三分 *70-30 split* **shichibu sanbu**
七転び八起き *failures before triumph*
    nanakorobi yaoki

一*ne, 858*	九*ine, 73*
二*wo, 457*	十*en, 344*
三*hree, 858*	数*umber, 156*
四*our, 17*	百*undred, 14*
五*ive, 86*	千*housand, 74*
六*ix, 3*	万*en thousand, 465*
八*ight, 4*	億*undred-million, 340*

亡*emise, 72*

047-B

七even dwarfs wept for Snow White's 亡eath...

亡*eath*   亡*emise*

na(i), BŌ, MŌ
  death, demise, dead, dying, passing away

亡母 *one's late mother* **bōbo**
亡夫 *one's late husband* **bōfu**
亡父 *one's late father* **bōfu**
亡兄 *one's late elder brother* **bōkei**
亡国 *high treason, traitor, quisling* **bōkoku**
亡魂 *dead spirits* **bōkon**
亡命 *exile, asylum, defection* **bōmei**
亡命者 *exile, refugee, asylee* **bōmeisha**
亡霊 *spirit, ghost, soul* **bōrei**
亡妻 *one's deceased wife* **bōsai**
亡失 *lost-, missing-, unfound item* **bōshitsu**
亡友 *deceased friend* **bōyū**
敗亡 *defeat* **haibō**
興亡 *rise & fall, fate* **kōbō**
滅亡 *downfall, extinction* **metsubō**
亡者 *"the deceased, the late..."* **mōja**
亡骸 *remains, corpse, cadaver* **nakigara**
流亡 *wandering far from home* **ryūbō**
死亡 *death, dead, deceased* **shibō**

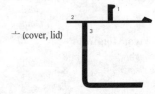

亠 (cover, lid)

Facing: 2.0. East ☞ (W)

死亡数 *number of fatalities* **shibōsū**
死亡率 *death rate* **shibōritsu**
存亡 *matter of life-or-death, fate* **sonbō**
損亡 *loss, be defeated* **sonmō**
衰亡 *decline, ruin* **suibō**
逃亡 *escape, flight, getaway* **tōbō**
逃亡者 *fugitive, runaway, stowaway* **tōbōsha**
残亡 *defeat & death* **zanbō**
未亡人 *widow* **mibōjin**
亡祖父 *one's late grandfather* **bōsofu**
亡き人 *deceased, dead* **nakihito**
我利我利亡者 *greedy-, selfish* **garigari mōja**

墓*ravesite, 602*	葬*urial, 513*
碑*ombstone, 937*	死*eath, 513*
陵*ausoleum, 140*	逝*eath, 54*

忙*usy, 33*   忘*orget, 34*

048-A

九ine 丸hips smoothly 丸Lound running aground...

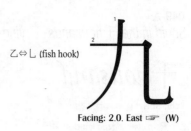

乙⇔し (fish hook)

九ine

kokono(tsu), kokono, KYŪ, KU
nine

Facing: 2.0. East ☞ (W)

九月 September **kugatsu**
九九 Japanese rhymed-multiplication **kuku**
九州 Kyūshū islands (southern Japan) **kyūshū**
九星術 astrology **kyūseijutsu**
九死に near death, escaping sure death **kyūshi(ni)**
十中八九 in all likelihood, in 9-to-10 **jicchūhakku**
九分九厘 in a scale of ten-to-one **kubukurin**
三々九度 sake-sipping in Shintō wedding **sansankudo**

一ne, 858	八ight, 4
二wo, 457	十en, 344
三hree, 858	数umber, 156
四our, 17	百undred, 14
五ive, 86	千housand, 74
六ix, 3	万en thousand, 465
七even, 72	億undred-million, 340

 力trength, 351

048-B

九ine 丸hips smoothly 丸Lound running aground...

丶 (dot)

❶丸Lound   ❷丸[ships]

maru(i), maru(meru), maru, GAN
round; [counter for ships]

Facing: 2.0. East ☞ (W)

❶弾丸 bullet, shell **dangan**
丸薬 pill, drug **ganyaku**
砲丸 cannon fire **hōgan**
銃丸 bullet, shell **jūgan**
睾丸 testicles, scrotum **kōgan**
丸顔 round face, moon face **marugao**
丸形 circular-shaped **marugata**
丸腰 unarmed, harmless **marugoshi**
丸裸 full nudity, stark naked **maruhadaka**
丸印 circle **marujirushi**
丸首 round neck **marukubi**
丸窓 round window **marumado**
丸丸 completely, entirely, totally **marumaru**
丸み roundness **marumi**
丸材 log, timber, woods, lumber **maruzai**
丸損 total loss **maruzon**
日の丸 Japanese flag **hinomaru**
真ん丸 perfect circle **manmaru**
丸暗記 rote memorization **maruanki**

丸干し dried whole (fish) **maruboshi**
丸出し exposed, obvious, apparent **marudashi**
丸取り all taken, nothing left out **marudori**
丸二日 two full days **marufutsuka**
丸勝ち total victory **marugachi**
丸刈り close-cropped hair, crew cut **marugari**
丸儲け killing profits, price gorging **marumōke**
丸飲み gulping down, swallowing **marunomi**
丸焼き roasted whole (chicken) **maruyaki**
丸め込む cajole, coax, win over **marumekomu**

❷氷川丸 Hikawa ship (Yokohama) **hikawa-maru**

輪ircle, 786	回otate, 458	航avigation, 748
周ap, 280	隻[ships], 50	船essel, 757

九ine, 73

049-A
Squid in the 千housands 干rying-up in Pusan...

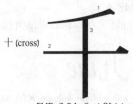

十 (cross)

千 *housand*

chi, SEN
thousand

FLIP: 2.0.b. Sort Of (stem)

千鳥 *plover; zigzag* **chidori**
千鳥足 *unsteady, reeling steps* **chidoriashi**
千草 *flora & fauna* **chigusa**
千尋 *bottomless* **chihiro**
千歳 *a thousand years* **chitose**
千分 *thousandth* **senbun**
千金 *priceless, invaluable* **senkin**
千古 *eternity, all ages* **senko**
千慮 *wise, careful* **senryo**
千載 *a thousand years* **senzai**
数千 *several thousands* **sūsen**
高千穂 *Takachiho (Miyazaki Pref.)* **takachiho**
千葉県 *Chiba Prefecture* **chiba-ken**
千切る *pluck, tear away* **chigiru**
針千本 *porcupine fish* **harisenbon**
千羽鶴 *chain of paper cranes* **senbazuru**
千切り *shredding,* **sengiri**
千年祭 *millennium* **sennensai**
千里眼 *clairvoyance, visionary* **senrigan**

千秋楽 *last day, last night* **senshūraku**
千切れ雲 *scattered clouds* **chigiregumo**
千代田区 *Chiyoda ward, Tōkyō* **chiyoda-ku**
一攫千金 *rich quick scheme* **ikkaku senkin**
食い千切る *bite off* **kuichigiru**
千言万語 *flowery words* **sengen bango**
千枚張り *multi-layered* **senmaibari**
千枚通し *eyeleteer* **senmaidooshi**
千変万化 *infinite variety* **senpen banka**
千両役者 *leading role* **senryō yakusha**
千差万別 *multifarious, various* **sensa banbetsu**
千姿万態 *multifarious, various* **senshi bantai**

一 *ne, 858*	万 *en thousand, 465*
十 *en, 344*	億 *undred-million, 340*
百 *undred, 14*	零 *ero, 874*

干 *rying-up, 74*	午 *fternoon, 178*

049-B
Squid in the 千housands 干rying-up in Pusan...

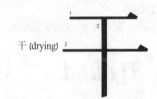

干 (drying)

干 *rying*   干 *esiccate*

hi(ru), ho(su), KAN
drying, desiccate

FLIP: 1.0.b. Whole (stem)

干支 *Zodiac signs* **eto, kanshi**
干潟 *tideland* **higata**
干物 *dried fish* **himono**
干す *dry, drying* **hosu**
若干 *"a little, rather..."* **jakkan**
干潮 *low tide, ebb tide* **kanchō**
干害 *drought calamity* **kangai**
干城 *bulwark, rampart* **kanjō**
干満 *ebb & flow, tide* **kanman**
干犯 *infringement, violation, breach* **kanpan**
干渉 *interference, intervention* **kanshō**
干拓 *reclamation by draining* **kantaku**
干天 *drought, dry weather* **kanten**
欄干 *railing, rail, balustrade* **rankan**
日干し *drying under the sun* **hiboshi**
干葡萄 *raisin, currant* **hoshibudō**
干し柿 *dried persimmon* **hoshigaki**
干し草 *hay, dried grass* **hoshikusa**
干し物 *laundry clothes for drying* **hoshimono**

陰干し *drying under the shade* **kageboshi**
物干し *frame for drying clothes* **mono hoshi**
虫干し *airing, letting air in* **mushiboshi**
潮干狩 *shellfish gathering, ~collecting* **shiohigari**
梅干し *pickled plum* **umeboshi**
干上がる *dry up* **hiagaru**
刈り干す *cut & dry* **karihosu**
満ち干き *ebb & flow* **michihiki**
飲み干す *gulp down* **nomihosu**
干からびる *dry up* **hikarabiru**

乾 *rying, 661*	日 *un, 14*
燥 *rying-up, 852*	陽 *un, 932*

午 *fternoon, 178*	千 *housand, 74*

050-A

刃*word* 刃*lade* with 匁*[3.75 gm] of gold not to fade...*

刃*word*　　刃*lade*

刀⇔刂 (blade, cutting)

ha, JIN
sword, blade

Facing: 1.0. West (W)

出刃 *pointed kitchen knife* **deba**
出刃包丁 *pointed kitchen knife* **deba bōchō**
毒刃 *assassin's dagger* **dokujin**
白刃 *drawn blade, ~sword* **hakujin, shiraha**
刃物 *blunt-, sharp weapon* **hamono**
刃先 *blade edge* **hasaki**
兵刃 *soldiers sword* **heijin**
氷刃 *perpetually sharp sword* **hyōjin**
自刃 *suicide by sword* **jijin**
片刃 *single blade sword* **kataha**
切刃 *cutting edge* **kiriha**
凶刃 *assassin's dagger* **kyōjin**
兇刃 *assassin's dagger* **kyōjin**
諸刃 *double-bladed sword* **moroha**
寝刃 *dull blade* **netaba**
刃傷 *bloodshed, bloodletting, carnage* **ninjō**
刃傷沙汰 *bloodshed, carnage* **ninjō zata**
利刃 *sharp sword* **rijin**
両刃 *double-bladed sword* **ryōba**

刀刃 *sword blade* **tōjin**
薄刃 *thin blade* **usuba**
焼刃 *tempered sword* **yakiba**
刃渡り *blade length* **hawatari**
刃向かう *resist, stand against* **hamukau**
付け焼刃 *affection, pretension* **tsukeyakiba**

侍*amurai*, 249	武*arrior*, 100	切*utting*, 352
士*amurai*, 8	戦*ighting*, 517	削*harpen*, 118
刀*lade*, 353	鋭*harp*, 943	戦*ombat*, 517

丸*ound*, 73

050-B

刃*word* 刃*lade* with 匁*[3.75 gm] of gold not to fade...*

匁*[3.75gm]*

monme
[3.75 gram]

勹 (wrapping)

壱匁 *3.75 grams (pearls)* **ichimonme**

Facing: 1.0. West (W)

升*[1.8 ltr]*, 298	寸*[3 cm]*, 345
旬*[10 day]*, 494	坪*[3.3 sqm]*, 488
斗*[18 ltr]*, 195	尺*[30 cm]*, 574
勺*[18 ml]*, 470	斤*[600 gm]*, 471

及*s well as*, 190

051-A

川 *ivers* & 州 *andbanks in a* 州 *rovince of Port-au-Prince...*

川 (river)

川 *iver*

kawa, SEN
river

河川	*river*	**kasen**
川端	*riverbank*	**kawabata**
川床	*riverbed*	**kawadoko**
川岸	*riverside, riveredge*	**kawagishi**
川越し	*crossing a river*	**kawagoshi**
川幅	*river width*	**kawahaba**
川尻	*tail of a river*	**kawajiri**
川上	*upper level of a river*	**kawakami**
川風	*river breeze*	**kawakaze**
川面	*river surface*	**kawamo**
川原	*river shore*	**kawara**
川瀬	*rapids, shallows*	**kawase**
川下	*riverbed, river bottom*	**kawashimo**
川筋	*river*	**kawasuji**
川魚	*riverfish*	**kawauo, kawazakana**
川獺	*otter*	**kawauso**
川底	*river bottom, riverbed*	**kawazoko**
溝川	*ditch, canal*	**mizokawa**
小川	*brook, stream*	**ogawa**

FLIP: 2.0.b. Sort Of (stem)

谷川	*mountain stream*	**tanigawa**
徳川	*Tokugawa Shogunate*	**tokugawa**
天の川	*milky way, galaxy*	**amanogawa**
川下り	*going down the river*	**kawakudari**
川向こう	*across the river*	**kawamukō**
川流れ	*riverflow, ~current*	**kawanagare**
川沿い	*along the river, river edge*	**kawazoi**
川伝い	*follow the riverflow*	**kawazutai**
品川区	*Shinagawa Ward, Tōkyō*	**shinagawa-ku**
神奈川県	*Kanagawa Prefecture*	**kanagawa-ken**
川明かり	*shining river surface*	**kawaakari**

河 *iver, 877*	潟 *agoon, 870*	浜 *each, 490*
海 *cean, 241*	泳 *wimming, 729*	沖 *ffshore, 695*
洋 *cean, 247*	江 *ay, 176*	浦 *eashore, 813*
湖 *ake, 801*	湾 *ay, 909*	浜 *eashore, 490*

州 *rovince, 76*

051-B

川 *ivers* & 州 *andbanks in a* 州 *rovince of Port-au-Prince...*

川 (river)

❶ 州 *rovince* ❷ 州 *andbank*

su, SHŪ
province; sandbank

❶
米州	*America*	**beishū**
豪州	*Australia*	**gōshū**
九州	*Kyūshū Islands*	**kyūshū**
満州	*Manchuria, Manchukuo*	**manshū**
満州国	*Manchuria, Manchukuo*	**manshūkoku**
欧州	*Europe*	**ōshū**
欧州共同体	*European Union*	**ōshū kyōdōtai**
神州	*land of deities*	**shinshū**
座州	*running aground*	**zashū**
州都	*state capital*	**shūto**
州内	*intra-province*	**shūnai**
州際	*inter-province*	**shūsai**
州議会	*state legislature*	**shūgikai**
州政府	*state government*	**shūseifu**
大洋州	*oceania*	**taiyōshū**
州立大学	*state university*	**shūritsu daigaku**
温州蜜柑	*Mandarin orange*	**unshū mikan**

FLIP: 2.0.b. Sort Of (stem)

九州保健福祉大学
Kyūshū University of Health & Welfare
kyūshū hoken fukushi daigaku

❷ 砂州 *sandbank* **sasu**

県 *refecture, 566*
堤 *mbankment, 314*
溝 *itch, 226*

川 *iver, 76*

052-A

米merican 米ice 光hines with the sunrise...

❶米ice   ❷米merica

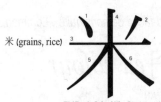

米 (grains, rice)

FLIP: 1.0.b. Whole (stem)

kome, BEI, MAI
rice; America

❶
米価	*price of rice*	**beika**
米穀	*rice, cereals, grain*	**beikoku**
米作	*rice crop, ~harvest*	**beisaku**
米食	*rice-based dish*	**beishoku**
外米	*non-Japanese rice*	**gaimai**
白米	*white-, polished rice*	**hakumai**
玄米	*unpolished rice*	**genmai**
米俵	*straw rice bag*	**komedawara**
米粒	*grain of rice*	**kometsubu**
米屋	*rice shop, ~dealer*	**komeya**
精米	*polished white rice*	**seimai**
米産地	*rice-producing region*	**beisanchi**
貯蔵米	*stored rice*	**chozōmai**

❷
米ドル	*US dollar, greenbuck*	**beidoru**
米語	*American English*	**beigo**
米軍	*US armed forces*	**beigun**
米寿	*one's eighty-eighth birthday*	**beiju**
米貨	*US money, green buck*	**beika**

米国	*United States of America*	**beikoku**
米産	*Made-in-USA, US products*	**beisan**
米州	*America*	**beishū**
米ソ	*US-Soviet union*	**beiso**
訪米	*visit to America*	**hōbei**
南米	*South America*	**nanbei**
日米	*US Japan*	**nichibei**
欧米	*The West, Europe & America*	**ōbei**
親米	*pro-American*	**shinbei**
滞米	*staying in America*	**taibei**
渡米	*visit to America*	**tobei**
在米	*living in America*	**zaibei**

田*ice field, 482*	畔*ice-field path, 484*
稲*ice plant, 893*	飯*ooked rice, 256*

光*hining, 77*

052-B

米merican 米ice 光hines with the sunrise...

光hining 光lluminate

儿 (human legs)

FLIP: 1.0.b. Whole (stem)

hikari, hika(ru), KŌ
shining, illuminate, glowing

栄光	*glory, fame, prestige*	**eikō**
眼光	*light penetration*	**gankō**
月光	*moonlight*	**gekkō**
逆光	*backlights*	**gyakkō**
発光	*luminous, emitting light*	**hakkō**
偏光	*optical- lights polarization*	**henkō**
威光	*authority, power*	**ikō**
稲光	*lightning*	**inabikari**
観光	*sight-seeing, tourism*	**kankō**
蛍光	*fluorescence, luminescence*	**keikō**
金光	*glittering, shining*	**kinpika**
光度	*light intensity, brightness*	**kōdo**
光栄	*honour, glory, privilege*	**kōei**
光学	*optics, light science*	**kōgaku**
光源	*light source, illuminant*	**kōgen**
光景	*view, scenery, sight*	**kōkei**
光輝	*glory, brilliance*	**kōki**
光年	*light year*	**kōnen**
光熱	*light & heat*	**kōnetsu**

光彩	*lustre, brilliance, glow*	**kōsai**
光線	*ray, beam, light*	**kōsen**
光沢	*lustre, glossy, shine*	**kōtaku**
脚光	*footlights, spotlight, limelight*	**kyakkō**
日光	*sunlight, sunshine*	**nikkō**
露光	*light exposure*	**rokō**
採光	*lighting*	**saikō**
陽光	*sunlight, sunshine*	**yōkō**
残光	*afterglow, evening glow*	**zankō**
光合成	*photosynthesis*	**kōgōsei**
黒光り	*shining black*	**kurobikari**

照*hine, 529*	昭*right, 529*
輝*parkling, 296*	明*right, 22*

米*ice, 77*

053-A

丹*ed-faced demons quite* 凡*ommon...*

丹*ed colour*   丹*innabar*

丶 (dot) 4

ni, TAN
red colour, cinnabar

牡丹 *peony, shrub* **botan**
牡丹杏 *plum* **botankyō**
牡丹雪 *snowflakes* **botanyuki**
牡丹餅 *bean jam & rice cake* **botamochi**
鉛丹 *reddish lead* **entan**
丹波 *ancient Kyoto & Hyogo* **tanba**
丹毒 *rose, erysipelas* **tandoku**
丹花 *red flower* **tanka**
丹念 *diligence, perseverance, painstaking* **tannen**
丹精 *exertion, diligence, tenacity* **tansei**
丹誠 *sincerity, efforts, diligence* **tansei**
丹心 *sincerity, genuine* **tanshin**
丹朱 *red, vermilion* **tanshu**
丹前 *men's padded kimono* **tanzen**
雲丹 *sea urchin* **uni**
丹塗り *red-painted* **ninuri**
丹頂鶴 *red-crested white crane* **tanchōzuru**

FLIP: 2.0.b. Sort Of (stem)

赤*ed colour, 261*	
紅*carlet, 175*	
朱*carlet, 233*	

舟*oat, 90*	母*other, 90*

053-B

丹*ed-faced demons quite* 凡*ommon...*

凡*rdinary*   凡*ommon*

凡 (table; windy)

BON, HAN
ordinary, common, plain, average

凡打 *eased out (baseball)* **bonda**
凡眼 *layman's eyes* **bongan**
凡愚 *common person* **bongu**
凡人 *ordinary person* **bonjin**
凡骨 *ordinary person* **bonkotsu**
凡夫 *ordinary person* **bonpu**
凡百 *many kinds, varied* **bonpyaku**
凡慮 *ordinary minds* **bonryo**
凡才 *mediocre-, inferior person* **bonsai**
凡作 *mediocre work* **bonsaku**
凡策 *mediocre policy* **bonsaku**
凡戦 *mediocre-, boring game* **bonsen**
凡失 *foolish-, stupid mistake* **bonshitsu**
凡書 *ordinary book* **bonsho**
凡手 *mediocre skill, ordinary talent* **bonshu**
凡退 *be put out easily* **bontai**
凡庸 *mediocrity, inferiority, weakness* **bonyō**
凡庸な人 *mediocre-, inferior person* **bonyō na hito**
凡俗 *vulgarity; mediocrity* **bonzoku**

FLIP: 2.0.b. Sort Of (stem)

超凡 *uncommon, extraordinary* **chōbon**
凡例 *explanatory notes* **hanrei**
平凡 *common, ordinary* **heibon**
平々凡々 *boring day, nothing new* **heihei bonbon**
非凡 *rare, unique, uncommon* **hibon**
大凡 *approximately, roughly* **ooyoso**
凡試合 *boring match, dull contest* **bonshiai**

普*rdinary, 455*	庸*rdinary, 906*
劣*nferior, 572*	平*lain, 488*

丹*ed colour, 78*	舟*oat, 90*

054-A

Written 行extlines of 行rip dance for a 竹amboo 行erformance...

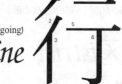

行 (going)

⓿行*oing* ❷行*erform* ❸行*extline*

i(ku), yu(ku), okona(u), KŌ, AN, GYŌ
going, trip; carry out, execute, perform; textline

Facing: 1.2. 🢰 West (V)

❶代行 *in place of, acting capacity* **daikō**
現行 *present times, nowadays* **genkō**
銀行 *bank* **ginkō**
行政 *public documentation* **gyōsei**
発行 *publication, publishing* **hakkō**
犯行 *crime, felony, serious offence* **hankō**
歩行 *take a walk, going on foot* **hokō**
行楽 *excursion, going out, outing* **kōraku**
急行 *express, rush* **kyūkō**
旅行 *travel, trip, journey* **ryokō**
流行 *fashion, popular* **ryūkō**
走行 *running, moving, in service* **sōkō**
運行 *transportation, trucking* **unkō**
続行 *continuation, resumption* **zokkō**
通行 *path, traffic* **tsūkō**
一方通行 *one-way traffic* **ippō tsūkō**
行き先 *destination* **yukisaki, ikisaki**
行き違い *misunderstanding* **ikichigai**

成り行き *course, process, outcome* **nariyuki**
東京行き *Tōkyō-bound* **tōkyō yuki**
行き渡る *go around, spread out* **yukiwataru, ikiwataru**
行き止まり *dead end, blind alley* **ikidomari**
行き当たりばったり *happy-go-lucky, unplanned* **iki'atari battari**
❷品行 *conduct, behaviour, demeanour* **hinkō**
実行 *execute, put into action* **jikkō**
行動 *action, behaviour* **kōdō**
興行 *performance, entertainment, show* **kōgyō**
行為 *offence, misdeed, crime* **kōi**
執行 *execution, enforcement* **shikkō**
素行 *conduct, behaviour, demeanour* **sokō**
❸一行目 *first line of a text* **ichigyōme**

竹*amboo*, 79

054-B

Written 行extlines of 行rip dance for a 竹amboo 行erformance...

竹 (bamboo)

竹*amboo*

take, CHIKU
bamboo

Facing: 1.2. 🢰 West (V)

青竹 *green bamboo* **aodake**
爆竹 *firecracker* **bakuchiku**
竹林 *bamboo grove* **chikurin, takebayashi**
破竹 *splitting bamboo* **hachiku**
糸竹 *koto strings & bamboo flute* **itotake**
寒竹 *solid bamboo* **kanchiku**
漢竹 *solid bamboo* **kanchiku**
黒竹 *black bamboo* **kurochiku**
真竹 *regular bamboo* **madake**
群竹 *bamboo stand* **muratake**
石竹 *china pink* **sekichiku**
竹刀 *bamboo sword* **shinai**
竹篦 *bamboo paddle* **takebera**
竹箒 *bamboo broom* **takebōki**
竹緣 *bamboo flooring* **takeen**
竹垣 *bamboo fence* **takegaki**
竹箸 *bamboo chopsticks* **takehashi**
竹籠 *bamboo basket* **takekago**
竹光 *bamboo sword* **takemitsu**

竹馬 *bamboo stilts* **takeuma, chikuba**
竹馬の友 *childhood playmate* **chikuba no tomo**
竹藪 *bamboo clump* **takeyabu**
竹槍 *bamboo spear* **takeyari**
竹竿 *bamboo pole* **takezao**
竹筒 *bamboo fube* **takezutsu**
筮竹 *divination bamboo stick* **zeichiku**
竹の皮 *bamboo sheath* **takenokawa**
竹の子 *bamboo shoots* **takenoko**
竹矢来 *bamboo palisade* **takeyarai**
竹細工 *bamboo works* **takezaiku**

| 木*ood*, 461 | 林*oods*, 526 | 棒*tick*, 275 |
| 材*oods*, 186 | 草*rass*, 373 | 植*lant*, 783 |

行*rip*, 79

055-A
Red-light ⊠istrict, social ⊠vils inflict...

⊠istrict ⊠rea

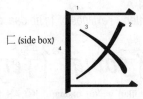

匸 (side box)

FLIP: 2.0.a. Sort Of (flat)

KU
district, area, locality, zone

地区 *area, district* **chiku**
学区 *school zone* **gakku**
漁区 *fishing area, ~grounds* **gyoku**
管区 *jurisdiction, administration* **kanku**
鉱区 *mining area* **kōku**
区別 *distinction, sorting out* **kubetsu**
区分 *classification, division* **kubun**
区長 *ward chief* **kuchō**
区域 *zone, area, district* **kuiki**
⇒住宅区域 *residential area* **jūtaku kuiki**
⇒管轄区域 *jurisdiction* **kankatsu kuiki**
⇒危険区域 *danger zone* **kiken kuiki**
区会 *ward assembly* **kukai**
区画 *demarcation, block* **kukaku**
区画整理 *land zoning* **kukaku seiri**
区間 *section, segment* **kukan**
区区 *various, diverse; petty* **kuku**
区民 *ward residents* **kumin**

区内 *inside the ward* **kunai**
教区 *parish* **kyōku**
教区民 *parishoners* **kyōkumin**
線区 *railroad district* **senku**
市区 *municipal district; streets* **shiku**
解放区 *liberated areas* **kaihōku**
禁漁区 *marine preserve* **kinryōku**
禁猟区 *"no hunting area..."* **kinryōku**
区議会 *ward assembly* **kugikai**
区切る *divide, partition* **kugiru**
区役所 *ward office, district hall* **kuyakusho**
選挙区 *voting district* **senkyoku**

街*istrict,* 107	郷*ometown,* 452
市*ity,* 304	里*ometown,* 321

⊠*vil,* 80

055-B
Red-light ⊠istrict, social ⊠vils inflict...

⊠vil ⊠trocity

凵 (open box)

FLIP: 1.0.a. Whole (flat)

KYŌ
evil, bad, atrocity

大凶 *bad omen* **daikyō**
元凶 *ringleader, gang boss* **genkyō**
豊凶 *good-or-bad harvest* **hōkyō**
吉凶 *fortune, good-or-bad* **kikkyō**
凶悪 *heinous, atrocious, brutal* **kyōaku**
凶悪犯人 *heinous criminal* **kyōaku hannin**
凶悪犯罪 *heinous crime* **kyōaku hanzai**
凶暴 *violent, atrocious, brutal* **kyōbō**
凶聞 *bad news, disappointing news* **kyōbun**
凶兆 *bad omen* **kyōchō**
凶弾 *gunshot, gunfire* **kyōdan**
凶変 *calamity, disaster* **kyōhen**
凶報 *bad news, disappointing news* **kyōhō**
凶事 *tragedy, mishap, disaster* **kyōji**
凶刃 *assassin's sword, ~dagger* **kyōjin**
凶日 *unlucky day, bad day* **kyōjitsu**
凶状 *crime, felony* **kyōjō**
凶漢 *ruffian, assassin* **kyōkan**
凶器 *lethal weapon* **kyōki**

凶行 *violence, felony, crime* **kyōkō**
凶荒 *famine, food shortage* **kyōkō**
凶猛 *fierce, ferocious* **kyōmō**
凶年 *year of poor harvest* **kyōnen**
凶作 *poor harvest* **kyōsaku**
凶手 *assassin, gun-for-hire* **kyōshu**
凶徒 *thug, mob, hooligan* **kyōto**

悪*vil,* 389	罪*riminal,* 289
邪*vil,* 58	犯*riminal,* 640
鬼*evil,* 935	魔*evil,* 332

⊠*istrict,* 80

056-A

芋otatoes of yucky taste grown in 宇uter-space...

宇 (cover, lid)

宇uterspace   宇elestial

U

outer space, celestial, cosmos, deep space, extra-terrestrial, universe, galaxy

FLIP: 1.0.b. Whole (stem)

眉宇 eyebrows **biu**
堂宇 temple hall **dōu**
御宇 imperial rule, ~reign **gyo**
行宇 imperial rule, ~reign **gyōu**
胸宇 in one's heart **kyōu**
羅宇 bamboo stem **rau**
宇部 Ube city, Yamaguchi Prefecture **ube**
宇都宮 Utsunomiya City, Tochigi Pref.
　　 utsunomiya
宇宙 outer space, celestial bodies **uchū**
⇒大宇宙 the universe, celestial body **daiuchū**
⇒小宇宙 microcosm, infinitesimal **shōuchū**
宇宙学 astronomy, cosmology **uchūgaku**
宇宙人 extra-terrestrial aliens **uchūjin**
宇宙線 cosmic rays **uchūsen**
宇宙船 spaceship **uchūsen**
宇宙中継 satellite broadcast **uchū chūkei**
宇宙衛星 space satellite **uchū eisei**
宇宙飛行 space flight **uchū hikō**

宇宙ロケット space rocket **uchū roketto**
宇宙飛行士 astronaut, cosmonaut
　　 uchū hikōshi
宇宙科学 space science, astronomy
　　 uchū kagaku
宇宙空間 outer space, celestial bodies
　　 uchū kūkan
宇宙遊泳 space walk **uchū yūei**
宇内 the whole world, the universe **udai**
八紘一宇 universal brotherhood **hakkō ichiu**
気宇広大 magnanimous, generous **kiu kōdai**
宇多時代 Uda Era (887-897) **uda jidai**

宙uterspace, 631　　天eaven, 83
星tars, 113　　空ky, 394

宅esidence, 82

056-B

芋otatoes of yucky taste grown in 宇uter-space...

艸 (grass)

芋otato

imo, U

potato

FLIP: 1.0.b. Whole (stem)

じゃが芋 sweet potato **jagaimo**
芋版 printing with potato **imoban**
芋虫 caterpillar **imomushi**
芋侍 idle-, declining samurai **imozamurai**
芋蔓 sweet potato vines **imozuru**
菊芋 artichoke yam **kikuimo**
長芋 Chinese yam **nagaimo**
里芋 taro **satoimo**
種芋 potato seeds **taneimo**
海芋 calla **umiimo**
山芋 yam **yamaimo**
芋茎 taro stem **zuiki**
焼き芋 roasted sweet potato **yakiimo**
薩摩芋 sweet potato **satsumaimo**

畑lantation, 482
植lant, 783
食oods, 255

宇uterspace, 81

057-A

託*ntrusted to cats, a* 宅*ouse of mouse...*

託*ntrust*   託*onsign*

言 (speaking)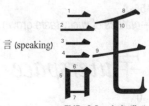

TAKU

entrust, consign, authorize

FLIP: 6.0.a. Left (flat)
Facing: 2.2. ☞ East (V)

付託 *submit to a committee* **futaku**
負託 *trust, mandate* **futaku**
御託 *repetitive speech* **gotaku**
依託 *entrust, request* **itaku**
委託 *trust, consignment* **itaku**
委託品 *consignment goods* **itakuhin**
委託金 *money in trust, deposited money* **itakukin**
委託販売 *consignment sale* **itaku hanbai**
受託 *be entrusted with* **jutaku**
仮託 *excuse, pretext, alibi* **kataku**
結託 *conspiracy, collusion* **kettaku**
寄託 *deposition, bailment* **kitaku**
屈託 *worry, anxiety, perplexity* **kuttaku**
供託 *depositing, entrusting* **kyōtaku**
供託金 *deposit money* **kyōtakukin**
請託 *solicitation* **seitaku**
信託 *trust, confidence* **shintaku**
神託 *oracle, divine message* **shintaku**

嘱託 *part-time employment* **shokutaku**
託言 *excuse, pretext, alibi* **takugen**
託宣 *oracle, divine message* **takusen**
託送 *consignment, shipment* **takusō**
預託 *money-in-trust, deposited amount* **yotaku**
託児所 *nursery, day-care centre* **takujisho**
信託統治 *board-of-trustees* **shintaku tōchi**

| 委*ntrust, 583* | 任*ntrust, 709* |
| 嘱*ntrust, 441* | 預*ntrust, 569* |

| 詐*raudulent, 723* |

057-B

託*ntrusted to cats, a* 宅*ouse of mouse...*

宅*esidence* 宅*omicile*

宀 (cover, lid)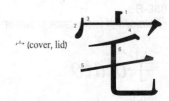

TAKU

residence, domicile, shelter, abode, dwelling, housing

FLIP: 3.0.b. Top (stem)
Facing: 2.1. ☞ East (H)

別宅 *second residence, summer house* **bettaku**
弊宅 *"my humble house..."* **heitaku**
本宅 *principal residence* **hontaku**
自宅 *one's home* **jitaku**
住宅 *residence* **jūtaku**
住宅難 *housing shortage* **jūtakunan**
住宅区域 *residential area* **jūtaku kuiki**
住宅ローン *home mortgage* **jūtaku rōn**
家宅 *house, residence* **kataku**
火宅 *house on fire; this tormenting world* **kataku**
帰宅 *return home* **kitaku**
お宅 *you, your (honorific)* **otaku**
社宅 *company dormitory* **shataku**
舎宅 *small house* **shataku**
私宅 *private residence* **shitaku**
妾宅 *house of one's mistress* **shōtaku**
宅地 *residential land, residential lot* **takuchi**
宅配 *home delivery* **takuhai**
宅配便 *home parcel delivery* **takuhaibin**

宅診 *medical consultation in a clinic* **takushin**
宅送 *home delivery* **takusō**
邸宅 *mansion, residence* **teitaku**
在宅 *staying home, at home* **zaitaku**
宅急便 *express mail* **takkyūbin**
宅扱い *home delivery* **takuatsukai**
簡易住宅 *simple frame house* **kan'i jūtaku**
県営住宅 *prefectural housing* **ken'ei jūtaku**
公営住宅 *public housing* **kōei jūtaku**
市営住宅 *city housing* **shiei jūtaku**
建て売り住宅 *brand-new house for sale* **tateuri jūtaku**

| 住*esidence, 750* | 邸*esidence, 860* |
| 家*ouse, 909* | 屋*ouse, 427* |

| 宇*uterspace, 81* |

058-A

夫*usband unforgiven won't go to* 天*eaven...*

大 (grand)

❶夫*usband*   ❷夫*ale labourer*

otto
husband, hubby, mister; male labourer

FLIP: 1.0.b. Whole (stem)

❶ 夫々 *respectively, each, every* **sorezore**
亡夫 *one's late husband* **bōfu**
凡夫 *mediocre, inferior, weakling* **bonpu**
田夫 *rustic, bumpkin* **denpu**
夫婦 *married couple* **fūfu**
夫婦喧嘩 *marital bickering, marital spats* **fūfu genka**
夫婦愛 *marital love* **fūfuai**
夫婦仲 *marital relationship* **fūfunaka**
夫人 *Mrs., lady, wife* **fujin**
⇒男爵夫人 *viscountess, baroness* **danshaku fujin**
⇒子爵夫人 *viscountess, baroness* **shishaku fujin**
夫君 *husband* **fukun**
夫妻 *husband & wife, mr.& mrs.* **fusai**
匹夫 *person of humble birth* **hippu**
丈夫 *tough, stout, firm, robust* **jōbu**
⇒大丈夫 *all right, fine, OK* **daijōbu**
姦夫 *adulterer, philanderer* **kanpu**
先夫 *ex-husband* **senpu**
有夫 *married woman* **yūfu**

前夫 *ex-husband* **zenpu**
❷ 駅夫 *station porter, baggage boy* **ekifu**
漁夫 *fisherman, fisher folks* **gyofu**
鉱夫 *mine worker, ~labourer* **kōfu**
坑夫 *miner, mine worker* **kōfu**
工夫 *labourer, worker* **kōfu, kofū**
人夫 *labourer, worker* **ninpu**
農夫 *farmer, peasant* **nōfu**
車夫 *rickshaw puller* **shafu**
潜水夫 *sea diver* **sensuifu**
炭鉱夫 *collier, coal miner* **tankōfu**

妻*ife, 611*	家*amily, 909*
婦*ife, 785*	族*amily, 649*
姻*arriage, 364*	扶*amily-support, 97*
婚*arriage, 637*	稼*ake-a-living, 824*

未*ot yet, 12*

058-B

夫*usband unforgiven won't go to* 天*eaven...*

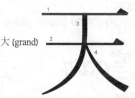

大 (grand)

天*eaven*   天*elestial*

ame, ama, TEN
heaven, celestial

FLIP: 1.0.b. Whole (stem)

曇天 *cloudy weather, cloudy sky* **donten**
寒天 *cold weather* **kanten**
荒天 *stormy-, rough weather* **kōten**
脳天 *crown of the head* **nōten**
晴天 *fair-, fine weather, clear sky* **seiten**
昇天 *passing away, going to heaven* **shōten**
天罰 *divine punishment, wrath of God* **tenbatsu**
天国 *heaven* **tengoku**
天狗 *long-nosed goblin, boastful* **tengu**
天井 *ceiling* **tenjō**
天下 *world, earth* **tenka**
天気 *weather, climate* **tenki**
天候 *weather, climate* **tenkō**
天工 *work of god, work of nature* **tenkō**
天空 *sky, heavens* **tenkū**
天然 *nature, natural resources* **tennen**
天皇 *Emperor of Japan* **tennō**
天火 *oven* **tenpi**
天災 *natural calamity, disaster* **tensai**

天才 *genius, brilliant, intelligent* **tensai**
天成 *natural-born, born (artist)* **tensei**
天使 *angel* **tenshi**
天水 *rain water* **tensui, amamizu**
天体 *heavenly body, celestial body* **tentai**
天の川 *milky way, galaxy* **amanogawa**
摩天楼 *skyscraper, skyline* **matenrō**
天文学 *astronomy, cosmology* **tenmongaku**
天王星 *Planet Uranus* **tennōsei**
天麩羅 *deep-fried battered shrimp* **tenpura**
露天風呂 *open-air bath, hot springs* **rotenburo**

空*ky, 394*
雲*loud, 154*
無*othing, 49*

元*rigin, 195*

059-A

乏overty forced Shawn to live on the 芝awn...

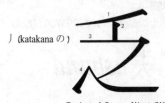

丿 (katakana の)

乏overty 乏estitute

tobo(shii), BŌ
poverty, destitute, scanty, impoverished, indigent, pauper

Facing: 1.0. ☜ West (W)

貧乏 *poverty, penury, destitution* **binbō**
⇒器用貧乏 *"all trades, master of none..."* **kiyō binbō**
貧乏くじ *blank, unlucky number* **binbōkuji**
貧乏人 *poor, pauper, destitute* **binbōnin**
貧乏性 *poverty, penury, destitution* **binbōshō**
貧乏神 *god of poverty* **binbōgami**
貧乏生活 *living in poverty* **binbō seikatsu**
貧乏暮らし *living in poverty* **binbōgurashi**
貧乏揺すり *absent-mindedness* **binbōyusuri**
欠乏 *scarcity, insufficiency, shortage* **ketsubō**
窮乏 *indigence, poverty, impoverishment* **kyūbō**
耐乏 *austerity, frugality, thrift* **taibō**

貧overty, 594	低inimum, 700
少carce, 459	餓unger, 443

芝awn, 84	欠bsence, 460

059-B

乏overty forced Shawn to live on the 芝awn...

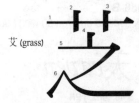

艾 (grass)

芝awn 芝urf

shiba
lawn; turf

FLIP: 3.0.b. Top (stem)
Facing: 1.0. ☜ West (W)

芝地 *grass field, meadows* **shibachi**
芝生 *lawn, grass* **shibafu**
芝居 *stage play* **shibai**
⇒安芝居 *cheap theatre* **yasushibai**
⇒紙芝居 *picture card show* **kamishibai**
⇒猿芝居 *monkey tricks* **sarushibai**
⇒一人芝居 *solo performance show* **hitori shibai**
⇒人形芝居 *puppet theatre* **ningyō shibai**
⇒お伽芝居 *children's theatre* **otogi shibai**
芝居小屋 *playhouse, theatre* **shibai goya**
芝居見物 *theatre-watching* **shibai kenbutsu**
芝居気 *striving for stage effect* **shibaigi**
芝草 *lawn, grass* **shibakusa**
芝刈機 *lawn mower* **shibakariki**

草rass, 373
竹amboo, 79

乏overty, 84	欠bsence, 460

060-A

To 史istorians, 中hina was once the 中iddle Kingdom...

口 (mouth)

史istory

SHI
history

FLIP: 2.0.b. Sort Of (stem)

哀史 *tragic history* **aishi**
外史 *unofficial history* **gaishi**
秘史 *hidden history* **hishi**
女史 *Ms., Mrs., madame, lady* **joshi**
情史 *love story* **jōshi**
国史 *national history, Japanese history* **kokushi**
歴史 *history* **rekishi**
歴史学 *study of history* **rekishigaku**
歴史家 *historian* **rekishika**
略史 *brief history* **ryakushi**
精史 *annals, history* **seishi**
戦史 *war history* **senshi**
先史 *pre-history, ancient times* **senshi**
史伝 *historical legend* **shiden**
史学 *study of history* **shigaku**
史劇 *historical play, ~drama* **shigeki**
史実 *historical fact* **shijitsu**
史上 *based on history* **shijō**
史家 *historian, history scholar* **shika**

史観 *historical view* **shikan**
史論 *historical theory* **shiron**
史料 *historical artifacts, memorabilia* **shiryō**
史跡 *historic spot, historic relics* **shiseki**
史詩 *historical poem* **shishi**
史書 *history books* **shisho**
有史 *recorded in history* **yūshi**
前史 *previous history* **zenshi**
文化史 *cultural history* **bunkashi**
郷土史 *local history, folk history* **kyōdoshi**
世界史 *world history* **sekaishi**

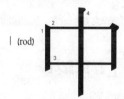

歴*istory, 595*	簿*ecord, 64*
暦*alendar, 595*	録*ecord, 841*
記*ecord, 728*	紀*arration, 727*

吏*fficial, 463*

060-B

To 史istorians, 中hina was once the 中iddle Kingdom...

| (rod)

❶中iddle ❷中hina

naka, CHŪ
middle, inside, interior; China

FLIP: 1.0.b. Whole (stem)

❶中火 *moderate heat, ~fire* **chūbi**
中尉 *first-, lieutenant* **chūi**
中継 *broadcast, relay* **chūkei**
中央 *centre, core* **chūō**
中立 *neutral & objective* **chūritsu**
中世 *Middle Ages* **chūsei**
中正 *fair & square, impartial, just* **chūsei**
中止 *termination, discontinuation* **chūshi**
中心 *centre, midpoint, concentration* **chūshin**
中退 *leaving, quitting (school)* **chūtai**
中天 *mid-air* **chūten**
中東 *Middle East, Arab countries* **chūtō**
中庸 *moderation, temperance* **chūyō**
忌中 *mourning, grieving* **kichū**
真ん中 *right in the middle* **mannaka**
喪中 *mourning, wailing, grieving* **mochū**
仲間 *friend, colleague, mate* **nakama**
集中 *concentration, self-immersion* **shūchū**
的中 *hit, being hit* **tekichū**

途中 *on the way, in the middle of~* **tochū**
中学校 *junior high-, middle scho* **chūgakkō**
営業中 *"open for business..."* **eigyōchū**
午前中 *in the morning, a.m.* **gozenchū**
一日中 *within one day* **ichinichijū**
お中元 *summer gift to one's superior* **ochūgen**
作業中 *while working, in operation* **sagyōchū**
車中談 *informal talks* **shachūdan**
仕事中 *on the job, busy-at-work* **shigotochū**
世の中 *the public, society-at-large* **yononaka**

❷中国 *People's Republic of China* **chūgoku**
日中 *Japan & China* **nicchū**

央*entral, 218*	唐*hinese, 439*
核*uclear, 973*	漢*anji, 926*
奥*nside, 903*	呉*[Wu dynasty], 453*
内*nside, 297*	唐*athay, 439*

061-A
For friends of 五.ive, 互.utuality abides...

二 (two, second)

五*ive*

itsu(tsu), GO
five

Facing: 2.0. East ☞ (W)

五月 *May* **gogatsu**
五官 *five organs* **gokan**
五感 *the five senses* **gokan**
五桁 *five-digit number* **goketa**
五経 *Confucian five classics* **gokyō**
五指 *human hands, five fingers* **goshi**
五色 *five basic colours* **goshiki, goshoku**
五体 *whole body* **gotai**
⇒五体満足 *non-handicapped* **gotai manzoku**
五臓 *five internal human organs* **gozō**
源五郎 *Japanese water beetle* **gengorō**
五十肩 *frozen shoulder, one's fiftyish* **gojūkata**
五十音 *Japanese syllabary* **gojūon**
五重奏 *quintet* **gojūsō**
五目飯 *Japanese pilaf* **gomokumeshi**
五輪旗 *Olympic flag (five rings)* **gorinki**
五線紙 *music sheet, music notebook* **gosenshi**
五寸釘 *long nail, uncut nail* **gosunkugi**
五つ子 *quintuplets* **itsutsugo**

十五夜 *night of a full moon* **jūgoya**
五月雨 *early summer rain* **samidare**
七五三 *children ages of 3, 5 & 7* **shichigosan**
五月人形 *boys festival dolls* **gogatsu ningyō**
五絃楽器 *five-stringed instrument* **gogen gakki**
五重の塔 *five-storied pagoda* **gojū no tō**
五目並べ *ancient Japanese chess* **gomokunarabe**
五里霧中 *at a complete loss* **gorimuchū**
五種競技 *pentathlon* **goshu kyōgi**
四分五裂 *splitting apart* **shibu goretsu**
四捨五入 *rounding up (numbers)* **shisha go'nyū**

一*ne, 858*	四*our, 17*	八*ight, 4*
二*econd, 457*	六*ix, 3*	九*ine, 73*
三*hree, 858*	七*even, 72*	十*en, 344*

互*utual, 86*

061-B
For friends of 五.ive, 互.utuality abides...

二 (two, second)

互*utual*   互*eciprocal*

taga(i), GO
mutual, reciprocal, sharing, commonality, compatible, equal

FLIP: 2.0.a. Sort Of (flat)

互助 *mutual assistance, reciprocal help* **gojo**
互譲 *mutual concessions* **gojō**
互角 *equality, parity, reciprocity* **gokaku**
互換 *interchange, convertible, reversible* **gokan**
互換性 *interchangeability* **gokansei**
互恵 *reciprocity, mutual* **gokei**
互恵的 *reciprocal, mutual* **gokeiteki**
互生 *alternate, rotation, taking turns* **gosei**
互選 *mutual vote* **gosen**
交互 *alternate, rotation, taking turns* **kōgo**
相互 *mutuality, reciprocity* **sōgo**
相互性 *mutuality, reciprocity* **sōgosei**
互助会 *mutual aid group, cooperative* **gojokai**
相見互い *mutuality, reciprocity* **aimitagai**
互い違い *alternate, taking turns* **tagai chigai**
相互扶助 *mutual assistance* **sōgo fujo**
相互依存 *interdependence* **sōgo izon**
相互関係 *mutual relationship* **sōgo kankei**

相互契約 *mutual agreement* **sōgo keiyaku**
相互作用 *reciprocal action* **sōgo sayō**

共*ogether, 302*	似*imilar, 472*
合*ogether, 232*	同*imilar, 245*

五*ive, 86*

062-A

右ight-side of the 后mpress, a famous actress...

右ight-side

口 (mouth)

migi, U, YŪ

right-side

極右	ultra-rightist **kyokuu**
右足	right foot, right leg **migiashi**
右側	right side, right flank **migigawa**
右端	right end **migihashi, utan**
右下	bottom right **migishita**
右手	right hand **migite**
右腕	right arm **migiude, uwan**
右上	upper right **migiue**
左右	control, manipulate **sayū**
右岸	right embankment **ugan**
右舷	starboard **ugen**
右派	right wing, rightist **uha**
右辺	right side, right flank **uhen**
右傾	leaning on the right side **ukei**
右折	right turn **usetsu**
右折禁止	"no right turn..." **usetsu kinshi**
右端	right edge **utan**
右翼	right wing, rightist **uyoku**
右翼手	right-handed athlete **uyokushu**

FLIP: 4.0.a. Bottom (flat)
Facing: 2.0. ☞ East (W)

右筆	literary genius; one's right hand **yūhitsu**
座右	one's favourite **zayū**
右回転	turning clockwise **migikaiten**
右書き	writing from right to left side **migikaki**
右利き	right-handed person **migikiki**
右巻き	clockwise **migimaki**
右回り	clockwise **migimawari**
右打ち	right-handed punch **migiuchi**
右寄り	leaning to the right side **migiyori**
右心房	right auricle **ushinbō**
右心室	right ventricle **ushinshitsu**

左eft-side, 310   下own, 859
上pper, 859

石ock, 363

062-B

右ight-side of the 后mpress, a famous actress...

后mpress

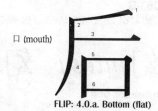

口 (mouth)

KŌ

empress

母后	empress dowager **bokō**
皇后	empress **kōgō**
皇后陛下	her majesty, the empress **kōgō heika**
后妃	empress, queen, princess **kōhi**
后宮	inner palace **kōkyū**
太后	empress dowager **taigō, taikō**
皇太后	empress dowager **kōtaigō, kōtaikō**

FLIP: 4.0.a. Bottom (flat)

皇mperor, 113	妃rincess, 728
王onarch, 12	姫rincess, 542
宮rince, 105	

石ock, 363

063-A

幼hild of 幻antasy lives in ecstacy...

幺 (short thread)

幼hildhood 幼nfancy

osana(i), YŌ
childhood, infancy

Facing: 2.2. East ☞ (V)

長幼 young & old **chōyō**
幼宮 young lord **itomiya**
幼顔 baby face, chubby face **osanagao**
幼子 little child, baby **osanago**
幼心 childish mind, child-at-heart **osanagokoro**
老幼 old & young **rōyō**
幼木 young tree **yōboku**
幼鳥 young bird **yōchō**
幼虫 larva **yōchū**
幼童 small child **yōdō**
幼魚 young fish **yōgyo**
幼弱 young & weak **yōjaku**
幼児 infant, little child **yōji**
幼時 childhood memories, ~years **yōji**
幼児期 infancy, childhood **yōjiki**
幼児食 baby food **yōjishoku**
幼児教育 infant education **yōji kyōiku**
幼女 little girl **yōjo**
幼樹 young tree **yōju**

幼気 young & cute **yōki**
幼君 young lord **yōkun**
幼名 childhood name, pet name **yōmyō**
幼年 childhood, infancy years **yōnen**
幼年時代 childhood, infancy years **yōnen jidai**
幼齢 young age **yōrei**
幼少 childhood, infancy **yōshō**
乳幼児 infant, baby **nyūyōji**
幼馴染 childhood-, bosom buddy **osananajimi**
幼稚園 kindergarten school **yōchien**
幼年労働 child labour **yōnen rōdō**

児hildren, 464	子hildren, 456
稚hildren, 776	童hildren, 564

幻antasy, 88	玄rofound, 358

063-B

幼hild of 幻antasy lives in ecstacy...

幺 (short thread)

幻antasy 幻llusion

maboroshi, GEN
fantasy, illusion, phantom, mirage

Facing: 3.0. ☞☜ Across

幻聴 hearing hallucination **genchō**
幻影 illusion, hallucination **gen'ei**
幻術 wizardry, sorcery, witchcraft **genjutsu**
幻怪 strange, eerie **genkai**
幻覚 hallucination, illusion **genkaku**
幻覚剤 hallucinogen **genkakuzai**
幻滅 disillusionment, delusion **genmetsu**
幻夢 dreams & visions **genmu**
幻出 ghost-like appearance **genshutsu**
幻世 this fleeting world **gense**
幻視 visual hallucination, illusion **genshi**
幻想 fantasy, illusion **gensō**
幻想曲 fantasia, fantasy **gensōkyoku**
幻想的 fantastic, fanciful **gensōteki**
幻灯 photo slides **gentō**
幻灯機 slide projector **gentōki**
幻惑 dazzle, dazzling **genwaku**
幻惑的 dazzling, fantasy-like **genwakuteki**
幻像 phantom, illusion, hallucination **genzō**

変幻 constant transformation **hengen**
変幻自在 constantly changing **hengen jizai**
夢幻 dreams, illusions, fantasy **mugen**

玄rofound, 358	夢ream, 167
著tark, 279	象mage, 530

玄rofound, 358	幼hildhood, 88

064-A

In their 申*eport,* 甲*irst group of nobles* 申*peaking-humble...*

田 (cultivated field)

甲*art A*   甲*irst group*

kabuto, KŌ, KAN
Part A, first group

FLIP: 1.0.b. Whole (stem)

鼈甲 *tortoise shell* **bekkō**
鼈甲色 *amber colour* **bekkōiro**
甲蟹 *horseshoe crab* **kabutogani**
甲冑 *armour & helmet* **kacchū**
甲板 *ship deck* **kanpan**
亀甲 *tortoise shell* **kikkō**
機甲 *mechanized unit* **kikō**
甲虫 *beetle* **kōchū**
①甲高 *high insteps, shrill* **kōdaka**
②甲高い *high insteps, shrill* **kandakai**
甲殻 *shell* **kōkaku**
甲殻類 *crustacean specie* **kōkakurui**
甲乙 *former & latter, a & b* **kōotsu**
甲羅 *shell, husk (turtle)* **kōra**
甲種 *first grade, grade a* **kōshu**
甲鉄 *armour plate* **kōtetsu**
装甲 *armoured* **sōkō**
装甲車 *armoured car* **sōkōsha**
鉄甲 *iron armour* **tekkō**

足の甲 *instep* **ashi no kō**
甲斐性 *resourcefulness* **kaishō**
肩甲骨 *shoulder blade, scapula* **kenkōkotsu**
甲府市 *Kōfu City, Yamanashi Prefecture* **kōfu-shi**
甲状腺 *thyroid gland* **kōjōsen**
正甲板 *main deck* **seikanpan**
手の甲 *back of the hand* **tenokō**
言い甲斐 *worth saying* **iigai**
生き甲斐 *"something to live for..."* **ikigai**
甲論乙駁 *pros & con* **kōron otsubaku**
甲斐甲斐しい *diligently, briskly* **kaigaishii**

始*tart, 210*		発*tart, 368*	
初*tart, 353*		先*head, 478*	

甲*peak humble, 89*

064-B

In their 申*eport,* 甲*irst group of nobles* 申*peaking-humble...*

田 (cultivated field)

❶申*peak humbly*   ❷申*eport*

mō(su), SHIN
speak humbly; report

FLIP: 1.0.b. Whole (stem)

❶申し分 *something to retort* **mōshibun**
申し出 *proposal, overtures, offer* **mōshide**
申し子 *heaven-sent child* **mōshigo**
申し上げる *tell, say, inform* **mōshiageru**
申し合わせ *mutual consent* **mōshiawase**
申し開き *justification, explanation* **mōshihiraki**
申し入れ *offer, proposal, overtures* **mōshiire**
申し兼ねる *"pardon me, but..."* **mōshikaneru**
申し込み *application, offer* **mōshikomi**
申し込み順 *by order it was received* **mōshikomijun**
申し越し *request, appeal* **mōshikoshi**
申し遅れる *"pardon to say it late..."* **mōshiokureru**
申し送り *send message* **mōshiokuri**
申し立て *declaration, statement* **mōshitate**
申し付ける *tell, instruct* **mōshitsukeru**
申し受ける *ask to pay, ~receive* **mōshiukeru**
申し渡す *tell, sentence* **mōshiwatasu**
物申す *speak up, protest, object* **monomōsu**
申し訳 *excuse, apology* **mōshiwake**

❷復申 *response; retort* **fukushin**
上申 *reporting to one's superior* **jōshin**
内申 *confidential report, top secret* **naishin**
申告 *report, statement* **shinkoku**
申告書 *application form* **shinkokusho**
申請 *written application, ~request* **shinsei**
答申 *submitting a report* **tōshin**
答申案 *draft report* **tōshin'an**
答申書 *written report* **tōshinsho**
追伸 *postscript, P.S.* **tsuishin**
具申書 *written report* **gushinsho**

恭*espect, 620*		尚*espect, 99*	
仰*espect, 706*		崇*espect, 879*	
謹*espect, 962*		礼*espect, 685*	
敬*espect, 329*			

甲*irst-class, 89*

065-A

母other on a 舟oat wearing a red coat...

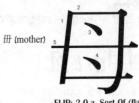

母other   母ommy

丹 (mother)

FLIP: 2.0.a. Sort Of (flat)

haha, BO
mother, mommy, maternal, mama

母音 *vowel* **boin, boon**
母艦 *depot ship* **bokan**
⇒航空母艦 *aircraft carrier ship* **kōkū bokan**
母系 *maternal side* **bokei**
母権 *maternal rights* **boken**
母校 *alma mater, one's old school* **bokō**
母港 *home port* **bokō**
母国 *mother country* **bokoku**
母国語 *mother tongue* **bokokugo**
母乳 *mother's milk* **bo'nyū**
母性 *maternity, motherhood* **bosei**
母子 *mother & child* **boshi**
母子家庭 *fatherless family* **boshi katei**
母胎 *womb, uterus* **botai**
分母 *denominator* **bunbo**
父母 *parents, father & mother* **fubo, chichihaha**
義母 *mother-in-law* **gibo**
母親 *mother* **haha'oya**
保母 *guardian, nurse* **hobo**

酵母 *yeast, leaven* **kōbo**
空母 *aircraft carrier ship* **kūbo**
継母 *stepmother* **mamahaha, keibo**
叔母 *aunt* **oba**
聖母 *Holy Mother, Virgin Mary* **seibo**
祖母 *grandmother* **sobo**
乳母 *nurse, midwife* **uba**
雲母 *mica* **unmo**
お母さん *one's own mother* **okāsan**
母の日 *Mother's Day* **haha no hi**
祖父母 *grandparents* **sofubo**

父 *ather, 467*	誕 *hildbirth, 515*
子 *hildren, 456*	産 *hildbirth, 883*
家 *amily, 909*	

舟 *oat, 90*	丹 *ed colour, 78*

065-B

母other on a 舟oat wearing a red coat...

舟oat

舟 (vessel)

FLIP: 2.0.b. Sort Of (stem)

fune, funa, SHŪ
boat, small boat

舟人 *sailor, seaman* **funabito**
舟歌 *boatman's song* **funauta**
箱舟 *Noah's ark* **hakobune**
扁舟 *small boat* **henshū**
軽舟 *lightweight speedboat* **keishū**
小舟 *small boat* **kobune**
孤舟 *lone boat* **koshū**
笹舟 *bamboo-leaf toy boat* **sasabune**
舟行 *navigation, sailing* **shūkō**
舟航 *navigation, sailing* **shūkō**
舟艇 *boat, craft* **shūtei**
⇒上陸用舟艇 *landing boat* **jōrikuyō shūtei**
舟運 *water transportation* **shūun**
助け舟 *lifeboat, liferaft* **tasukebune**
鉄舟 *steel boat* **tesshū**
釣り舟 *fishing boat* **tsuribune**
渡し舟 *ferry boat* **watashibune**
舟遊び *rowing, boating* **funaasobi**
貸し舟 *rental boat* **kashibune**

丸木舟 *canoe log boat* **marukibune**
舫い舟 *moored ship, shipwreck* **moyaibune**
高瀬舟 *riverboat* **takasebune**

航 *avigation, 748*	帆 *ailing, 641*
船 *hip, 757*	海 *cean, 241*
舶 *hip, 742*	洋 *cean, 247*

丹 *ed colour, 78*	母 *other, 90*

066-A

席eating 度egree, many 度imes they disagree...

巾 (cloth, fabric)

FLIP: 8.O.b. Inner (stem)

席eating   席hair

SEKI
seating, chair, attendance

相席	table sharing, seated together	**aiseki**
別席	separate seating	**besseki**
着席	seated, sitting down	**chakuseki**
同席	seated along, "rubbing elbows with..."	**dōseki**
宴席	banquet, feast	**enseki**
議席	rental meeting room	**giseki**
昼席	matinee, afternoon show	**hiruseki**
次席	next seat, second in rank	**jiseki**
定席	assigned seat	**jōseki**
会席	meeting room	**kaiseki**
欠席	absence, non-attendance	**kesseki**
空席	empty seat, vacant seat	**kūseki**
客席	guest seat, "reserved seats..."	**kyakuseki**
満席	"no seats available..."	**manseki**
末席	lower seat	**masseki**
升席	box seat	**masuseki**
列席	attendance (formal occasion)	**resseki**
隣席	next seat	**rinseki**
席次	seating order, ~list	**sekiji**

席上	time, occasion, seat	**sekijō**
席順	seating order, ~list	**sekijun**
席巻	overrunning enemy lines	**sekken**
主席	party chairman	**shuseki**
出席	attendance, presence	**shusseki**
退席	leaving one's seat	**taiseki**
座席	seat	**zaseki**
判事席	judge bench, magistrate seat	**hanjiseki**
観客席	seat, stands, bleachers	**kankyakuseki**
証人席	witness stand, ~box	**shōninseki**
立ち見席	standing room only, SRO	**tachimiseki**

座eating, 109		賓uest, 161
宴anquet, 610		宴arty, 610
客uest, 559		

度egree, 91

066-B

席eating 度egree, many 度imes they disagree...

广 (rooftop)

FLIP: 4.O.b. Bottom (stem)

度egree   度ime

tabi, DO, TAKU, TO
degree, extent, time(s)

度合	degree, condition	**doai**
度胸	nerve, guts, mettle, courage	**dokyō**
度量	capacity, measure	**doryō**
度数	frequency, number of times	**dosū**
限度	limit, boundary	**gendo**
純度	purity, essence, innocence	**jundo**
角度	angle	**kakudo**
輝度	brightness, clarity	**kido**
硬度	hardness, solidness	**kōdo**
年度	fiscal year (April-thru-March)	**nendo**
濃度	concentration, density, thickness	**nōdo**
再度	another time, second time	**saido**
精度	accuracy, precision	**seido**
制度	system, organization	**seido**
鮮度	freshness (fish)	**sendo**
節度	moderation, sobriety, temperation	**setsudo**
震度	seismic intensity, magnitude	**shindo**
湿度	humidity, moisture, damp	**shitsudo**
速度	speed, swiftness	**sokudo**

態度	attitude, behaviour, conduct	**taido**
程度	degree, extent, standard	**teido**
知名度	name-recognition, ~recognition	**chimeido**
度外れ	excessive, unbelievable	**dohazure**
度外視	ignoring, disregard	**dogaishi**
度忘れ	lapse of-, slip of memory	**dowasure**
加速度	speed acceleration	**kasokudo**
傾斜度	gradient, slope	**keishado**
落ち度	fault, blame, slip	**ochido**
透明度	degree of clarity, ~contrast	**tōmeido**
度し難い	depressed, disheartened	**doshigatai**

程egree, 144		回otate, 458
倍ultiply, 950		周ap, 280
複ultiply, 830		

席eating, 91

067-A

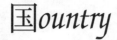ation's greatest reasure, the people for sure...

口 (enclosure)

国ation   国ountry

FLIP: 2.0.a. Sort Of (flat)

kuni, KOKU
nation, country

建国 *founding of a nation* **kenkoku**
帰国 *returning to one's country* **kikoku**
国歌 *national anthem* **kokka**
国家 *state, nation, country* **kokka**
国会 *national assembly, diet* **kokkai**
国権 *sovereignity* **kokken**
国旗 *national flag, country's flag* **kokki**
国境 *national boundary* **kokkyō**
国道 *national government-built road* **kokudō**
国営 *government-managed* **kokuei**
国営化 *nationalization* **kokueika**
国益 *national interest* **kokueki**
国語 *national language* **kokugo**
国威 *national prestige, ~dignity* **kokui**
国民 *people, citizen* **kokumin**
国運 *national destiny* **kokuun**
国王 *king, ruler, monarch* **kokuō**
国連 *United Nations* **kokuren**
国立 *national government-owned* **kokuritsu**

鎖国 *national isolation* **sakoku**
島国 *island nation* **shimaguni**
帝国 *empire* **teikoku**
帝国主義 *imperialism* **teikoku shugi**
全国 *nation-wide, all-Japan* **zenkoku**
属国 *dependent nation, protectorate* **zokkoku**
母国語 *native language, mother tongue* **bokokugo**
国造り *nation-building* **kunizukuri**
君主国 *monarchy, monarchist nation* **kunshukoku**
隷属国 *subject nation, dependency* **reizokukoku**
債務国 *debtor nation* **saimukoku**
侵略国 *aggressor nation* **shinryakukoku**

邦*ountry, 694*	府*overnment, 429*
政*olitics, 725*	民*eople, 495*

同*imilar, 245*	向*owards, 99*

067-B

国ation's greatest 宝reasure, the people for sure...

宀 (cover, lid)

宝reasure   宝ewel

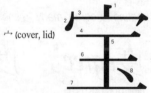

FLIP: 2.0.a. Sort Of (flat)

takara, HŌ
treasure, jewel

秘宝 *hidden wealth, secret treasure* **hihō**
宝玉 *precious stone, gem* **hōgyoku**
宝冠 *bejewelled crown* **hōkan**
宝鑑 *precious book* **hōkan**
宝器 *treasured article, precious item* **hōki**
宝庫 *treasure house, treasury* **hōko**
宝石 *jewel, gem, precious stone* **hōseki**
宝石商 *jeweller, gemmologist* **hōsekishō**
宝飾 *jewelry & ornaments* **hōshoku**
宝珠 *precious pearl, jewel* **hōju**
宝典 *thesaurus; precious books* **hōten**
宝刀 *treasure sword* **hōtō**
宝蔵 *treasure house, treasury* **hōzō**
重宝 *priceless treasure* **jūhō, chōhō**
家宝 *family treasure* **kahō**
子宝 *one's own children* **kodakara**
国宝 *national treasure, ~heritage* **kokuhō**
至宝 *the greatest treasure* **shihō**
宝箱 *treasure box, treasure chest* **takarabako**

宝船 *treasure ship* **takarabune**
宝貝 *cowry, porcelain shell* **takaragai**
宝島 *treasure island* **takarajima**
宝籤 *lottery, lotto, sweepstake* **takarakuji**
宝物 *treasure, heirloom* **takaramono, hōmotsu**
財宝 *treasures, riches* **zaihō**
⇒金銀財宝 *money & valuables* **kingin zaihō**
七宝焼 *cloisonne ware* **shippōyaki**
宝探し *treasure hunting* **takarasagashi**
宝永時代 *Hōei Era (1704-1711)* **hōei jidai**
宝治時代 *Hōji Era (1247-1249)* **hōji jidai**

貴*recious, 913*	輝*parkling, 296*
金*oney, 25*	石*tone, 363*
幣*oney, 171*	玉*ewel, 11*

害*amage, 904*	実*eality, 121*

068-A

込nwards this 辺icinity, no birds no bees...

込nward

辶 (transport)

Facing: 1.1. 🖙 West (H)

ko(mu), ko(meru)
inward; emphatic verb suffix

尻込み	*flinch, shrink, hesitate*	**shirigomi**
吹き込む	*blow in, bring, inspire, record*	**fukikomu**
振り込み	*payment by wire transfer*	**furikomi**
降り込む	*come into, fall into*	**furikomu**
振り込む	*pay, deposit, transfer*	**furikomu**
払い込む	*pay up, settle the account*	**haraikomu**
張り込む	*keep a watch, treat oneself*	**harikomu**
冷え込む	*get cold extremely*	**hiekomu**
刻み込む	*cut, remember, engrave*	**kizamikomu**
込み合う	*get crowded, ~congested*	**komiau**
込み入る	*complicated, be intricate*	**komiiru**
舞い込む	*come, drop by, stop by*	**maikomu**
迷い込む	*stray, wander about*	**mayoikomu**
持ち込む	*bring in, carry into*	**mochikomu**
潜り込む	*creep, get in*	**mogurikomu**
申し込む	*propose, file, apply*	**mōshikomu**
投げ込む	*throw in*	**nagekomu**
寝込む	*fall asleep*	**nekomu**
飲み込む	*drink up, finish drinking*	**nomikomu**

乗り込む	*board, get on*	**norikomu**
落ち込み	*fall, decline, disappointment*	**ochikomi**
追い込む	*drive away, repel*	**oikomu**
絞り込み	*tightening, focusing*	**shiborikomi**
染み込む	*imbue, soak, immerse*	**shimikomu**
座り込む	*sit down*	**suwarikomu**
詰め込む	*stuff, cram, overfill*	**tsumekomu**
撃ち込む	*shoot, open fire*	**uchikomu**
打ち込む	*devote oneself, input, drive*	**uchikomu**
読み込み	*serious reading*	**yomikomi**

入*ut-inside,* 2	内*nside,* 297
奥*nside,* 903	済*ettle,* 961

辺*icinity,* 93

068-B

込nwards this 辺icinity, no birds no bees...

辺icinity   辺urroundings

辶 (transport)

Facing: 1.1. 🖙 West (H)

ata(ri), HEN
vicinity, surroundings, adjacent, neighbouring, proximity

長辺	*rectangular length*	**chōhen**
縁辺	*border, edge, boundary*	**enpen**
浜辺	*seashore, beach, coast*	**hamabe**
辺地	*environs, surroundings*	**henchi**
辺土	*remote-, distant region*	**hendo**
辺境	*frontier, border area*	**henkyō**
一辺	*one side of a triangle*	**ippen**
官辺	*government source*	**kanpen**
近辺	*neighbourhood, nearby*	**kinpen**
岸辺	*shore, riverbank, riveredge*	**kishibe**
口辺	*around the lips*	**kōhen**
窓辺	*near the window*	**madobe**
道辺	*roadside, wayside*	**michibe**
水辺	*waterside, near the waters*	**mizube**
無辺	*infinite, limitless*	**muhen**
左辺	*left side (math equation)*	**sahen**
斜辺	*oblique side*	**shahen**
四辺	*all sides, whole, entire*	**shihen**
身辺	*one's surroundings*	**shinpen**

周辺	*circumference*	**shūhen**
対辺	*opposite side*	**taihen**
底辺	*triangle base*	**teihen**
等辺	*equilateral, symmetrical*	**tōhen**
右辺	*right side (math equation)*	**uhen**
海辺	*coast, beach, seashore*	**umibe**
上辺	*outward appearance*	**uwabe**
不等辺	*inequilateral, uneven*	**futōhen**
多辺形	*polygon*	**tahenkei**

周*icinity,* 280	
近*earby,* 184	
巡*round,* 571	

込*nward,* 93

069-A

常egular 堂ltar built in Gibraltar...

巾 (cloth, fabric)

常egular　常ormal

tsune, toko, JŌ
regular, normal, routine, general

FLIP: 1.0.b. Whole (stem)

平常 *usual, normal* **heijō**
非常に *very much, extremely* **hijō(ni)**
非常勤 *part-time employment* **hijōkin**
異常 *abnormal, unusual* **ijō**
⇒精神異常 *mental disorder* **seishin ijō**
尋常 *ordinary, average, common* **jinjō**
常備 *regular reserve* **jōbi**
常駐 *permanent deployment* **jōchū**
常道 *common practice* **jōdō**
常時 *always, at all times* **jōji**
常軌 *common sense, track* **jōki**
常勤 *full time-, regular staff* **jōkin**
常務 *managing director, executive* **jōmu**
常任 *permanent, regular staff* **jōnin**
常温 *normal temperature* **jōon**
常連 *regular client* **jōren**
常設 *permanently- constructed* **jōsetsu**
常識 *common manners* **jōshiki**
常食 *staple diet, daily food* **jōshoku**

常習 *habit, mannerism* **jōshū**
常習犯 *habitual offender, recidivist* **jōshūhan**
常数 *constant number* **jōsū**
常態 *normal condition* **jōtai**
常用 *regular-, common use* **jōyō**
綱常 *public morals, morality* **kōjō**
日常 *daily, everyday* **nichijō**
正常 *normalcy, normal life* **seijō**
常春 *eternal spring* **tokoharu**
常夏 *eternal summer* **tokonatsu**
恒常的 *constant, steady* **kōjōteki**

般egular, 323	平lain, 488
普ommon, 455	正orrect, 30

党olitical party, 203　　堂ltar, 94

069-B

常egular 堂ltar built in Gibraltar...

土 (ground, soil)

❶堂ltar　❷堂all

DŌ
altar, pedestal; hall

FLIP: 1.0.a. Whole (flat)

❶堂々と *stately, openly, boldly* **dōdōto**
堂々巡り *going round nowhere* **dōdō meguri**
母堂 *mother (polite)* **bodō**
仏堂 *Buddha hall* **butsudō**
殿堂 *palace, sanctuary* **dendō**
堂上 *court nobility, aristocracy* **dōjō**
学堂 *academy* **gakudō**
本堂 *temple main hall* **hondō**
一堂 *faction leaders meeting* **ichidō**
会堂 *assembly hall, plenary hall* **kaidō**
講堂 *lecture hall* **kōdō**
金堂 *golden hall (Buddhist temple)* **kondō**
経堂 *Sutra library* **kyōdō**
満堂 *general assembly, whole audience* **mandō**
参堂 *temple visit* **sandō**
聖堂 *sacred hall* **seidō**
僧堂 *meditation hall* **sōdō**
草堂 *monks' quarters* **sōdō**
天堂 *heaven, paradise* **tendō**

辻堂 *shrine on wayside* **tsujidō**
禅堂 *Zen meditation hall* **zendō**
大会堂 *cathedral, basilica* **daikaidō**
礼拝堂 *chapel, prayer hall* **reihaidō, raihaidō**

❷ 堂守り *building guard* **dōmori**
公会堂 *public hall, community centre* **kōkaidō**
能楽堂 *Noh hall, noh theatre* **nōgakudō**
納骨堂 *charnel house* **nōkotsudō**
音楽堂 *concert hall* **ongakudō**
食堂 *dining hall, mess hall* **shokudō**
国会議事堂 *National Diet* **kokkaigijidō**

聖acred, 617	祈rayer, 184
神ivine, 712	拝rayer, 636

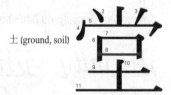

党olitical party, 203　　常ormal, 94

070-A

述*ention "* 迅*peed," * 迅*uickly they heed...*

辶 (transport)

述*ention*   述*tatement*

FLIP: 3.0.b. Top (stem)

no(beru), JUTSU
mention, statement, quote

陳述 *statement, representation* **chinjutsu**
⇒冒頭陳述 *opening statement* **bōtō chinjutsu**
陳述書 *statement, declaration* **chinjutsusho**
著述 *writings, book, literary work* **chojutsu**
著述業 *the literary profession* **chojutsugyō**
著述家 *writer, author* **chojutsuka**
伝述 *pass on, relay* **denjutsu**
叙述 *narration, depiction, portrayal* **jojutsu**
上述 *above-mentioned* **jōjutsu**
述懐 *reminiscence, recollection, nostalgia* **jukkai**
述作 *literary work* **jussaku**
述部 *sentence predicate* **jutsubu**
述語 *sentence predicate* **jutsugo**
既述 *previously-mentioned* **kijutsu**
記述 *narration, depiction, portrayal* **kijutsu**
後述 *afterwards, the following* **kōjutsu**
口述 *oral statement* **kōjutsu**
公述 *sworn statement, affidavit* **kōjutsu**
供述 *statement, deposition* **kyōjutsu**

論述 *statement, declaration* **ronjutsu**
略述 *outline, framework* **ryakujutsu**
撰述 *writer, author, compile* **senjutsu**
説述 *explanation, exposition* **setsujutsu**
詳述 *detailed explanation* **shōjutsu**
主述 *subject & predicate* **shujutsu**
祖述 *extolling one's predecessor* **sojutsu**
訳述 *translation, interpretation* **yakujutsu**
前述 *above-mentioned* **zenjutsu**

叙*arrate*, 648		談*alks*, 308	
言*alking*, 251		告*nnounce*, 266	
語*alking*, 780		宣*nnounce*, 899	

迅*uick*, 95

070-B

述*ention "* 迅*peed," * 迅*uickly they heed...*

辶 (transport)

迅*peedy*   迅*uick*

JIN
speedy, quick, haste, rapid, swift, fast, brisk

奮迅 *strong provocations* **funjin**
⇒獅子奮迅 *strong & speedy* **shishifunjin**
迅雷 *thunderclap, thunderbolt* **jinrai**
⇒疾風迅雷 *lightning quick* **shippū jinrai**
迅速 *swift, prompt, quick* **jinsoku**

FLIP: 8.0.b. Inner (stem)
Facing: 1.1. ☜ West (H)

疾*peedy*, 681		徐*lowly*, 881
速*peedy*, 502		鈍*luggish*, 199

述*ention*, 95

071-A

Severe 代ees 伐ut-down in haste, feudal 代poch 代eplaced...

人⇔亻 (person)

❶代eplace ❷代poch ❸代ee

ka(waru), ka(eru), yo, shiro, DAI, TAI
replace, in place of, in lieu of, substitute, supplant, switch with; epoch, period, era; fee, charge

Facing: 4.0. Apart

❶代読 *reading on behalf of another* **daidoku**
代印 *proxy affixing of personal seal* **daiin**
代講 *substitute teaching* **daikō**
代任 *acting on behalf of* **dainin**
代理 *substituting, on behalf of~* **dairi**
代作 *ghost-writing* **daisaku**
代数 *algebra* **daisū**
代用 *replacement, substitution* **daiyō**
代議員 *representative, delegate* **daigiin**
代議士 *Diet member, lawmaker* **daigishi**
代表者 *representative, delegate* **daihyōsha**
代行者 *agent, proxy* **daikōsha**
縫い代 *margin to sew up* **nuishiro**
肩代わり *take-over* **katagawari**
身の代金 *ransom money* **minoshirokin**
成り代わる *turn, manuever* **narikawaru**
取って代わる *replace, in place of* **tottekawaru**
❷現代 *modern times, present age* **gendai**
時代 *era, period* **jidai**

次代 *next-, coming generation* **jidai**
十代 *adolescence, teen years* **jūdai**
末代 *succeeding generations* **matsudai**
年代 *decade, period of ten years* **nendai**
世代 *generation* **sedai**

❸代価 *price, cost* **daika**
代金 *price, cost* **daikin**
代休 *substitute leave* **daikyū**
部屋代 *rental room fee* **heyadai**
飲み代 *money for drinking* **nomidai**

| 換eplace, 819 | 時ime, 653 |
| 替eplace, 334 | 金oney, 25 |

| 付ttach, 382 | 仕ervice, 9 |

071-B

Severe 代ees 伐ut-down in haste, feudal 代poch 代eplaced...

人⇔亻 (person)

❶伐ttack ❷伐ut down

BATSU
attack, offence; cut down

Facing: 4.0. Apart

❶攻伐 *subjugation* **kōbatsu**
殺伐 *bloody, fierce, savage* **satsubatsu**
征伐 *conquest, subjugation* **seibatsu**
討伐 *suppression, subjugation* **tōbatsu**
討伐軍 *punitive force* **tōbatsugun**

❷伐採 *cutting down trees, lumbering* **bassai**
伐木 *lumbering, cutting trees* **batsuboku**
間伐 *deforestation, denudation* **kanbatsu**
乱伐 *excessive tree-cutting* **ranbatsu**
輪伐 *area lumbering* **rinbatsu**
採伐 *timbering, felling trees* **saibatsu**
盗伐 *illegal logging, ~lumbering* **tōbatsu**

責ondemn, 115	襲ttack, 630
撃ttack, 613	討ttack, 691
攻ttack, 635	批riticize, 466

| 代poch, 96 | 伏end down, 702 |

072-A

扶amily-support in the 渓alley fell short...

扶amily-support

FU
family-support, sustain
扶持 *stipend, allowance* **fuchi, fuji**
⇒宛行扶持 *discretionary stipend* **ategaibuchi**
⇒食い扶持 *food & board expenses* **kuibuchi**
扶持米 *rice allowance* **fuchimai**
扶育 *raising one's children* **fuiku**
扶助 *family support, ~sustenance* **fujo**
⇒相互扶助 *mutual aid, ~assistance* **sōgo fujo**
扶助料 *family support money* **fujoryō**
扶植 *plant, establish* **fushoku**
扶桑 *Japan* **fusō**
扶翼 *aid, support* **fuyoku**
扶養 *family support* **fuyō**
扶養料 *family support money* **fuyōryō**
扶養者 *breadwinner, head of the family* **fuyōsha**
扶養義務 *obligation of family support* **fuyō gimu**
扶養家族 *dependants* **fuyō kazoku**
扶養手当 *family support stipend* **fuyō teate**
家扶 *steward* **kafu**
里扶持 *child adoption expenses* **satobuchi**

手⇔扌 (hand, manual)

FLIP: 7.0.b2. Right (stem)

夫*usband, 83*	族*amily, 649*
妻*ife, 611*	援*upport, 820*
婦*ife, 785*	支*upport, 201*
姻*arriage, 364*	助*upport, 953*
婚*arriage, 637*	任*bligation, 709*
家*amily, 909*	稼*ake-a-living, 824*

夫*usband, 83*

072-B

扶amily-support in the 渓alley fell short...

渓alley   渓avine

KEI
valley, ravine, gorge
渓間 *ravine, valley* **keikan**
渓谷 *valley, glen, gorge, ravine* **keikoku**
渓流 *mountain stream* **keiryū**
渓声 *sound of valley stream* **keisei**
渓泉 *valley spring* **keisen**
渓水 *mountain stream* **keisui**
雪渓 *snowy valley, ~gorge* **sekkei**

水⇔氵 (water)

FLIP: 7.0.b2. Right (stem)
FLIP: 7.3.b. Right Bottom (stem)

坂*lope, 733*	峡*avine, 763*
丘*lope, 106*	谷*avine, 492*
崎*lope, 270*	

採*dopt, 915*

073-A

Like 汽team, 気eelings can be mean...

汽team   汽apour

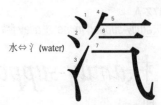

水⇔氵 (water)

Facing: 1.2. 🐦 West (V)

KI
steam, vapour

汽圧 *steam pressure* **kiatsu**
汽缶 *boiler* **kikan**
汽罐 *boiler* **kikan**
汽管 *steam pipe* **kikan**
汽関 *boiler, steam generator* **kikan**
汽船 *steamship, steamer, liner* **kisen**
汽車 *steam train* **kisha**
汽車便 *mail sent by train* **kishabin**
汽車賃 *train fare* **kishachin**
汽車ぽっぽ *choo-choo, puff-puff* **kishapoppo**
汽艇 *warship-borne steamboat* **kitei**
汽笛 *steam whistle, ~siren* **kiteki**
夜汽車 *night train* **yogisha**

蒸team, 117	
煙moke, 644	
燃urning, 445	

気eelings, 98	沈inking, 719

073-B

Like 汽team, 気eelings can be mean...

気eelings   気pirit

气 (steam)

Facing: 1.0. 🐦 West (W)
FLIP: 8.0.b. Inner (stem)

KI, KE
feelings, spirit, sentiments, gas

病気 *illness, disease, sickness* **byōki**
元気 *vigour, cheerful, feeling good* **genki**
平気 *coolness, calmness* **heiki**
本気 *serious, bent on, mind-set* **honki**
色気 *sex appeal, amorousness* **iroke**
活気 *vigour, life, spirit, elan vita* **kakki**
景気 *robust, ~brisk economy* **keiki**
気圧 *air, atmospheric pressure* **kiatsu**
気心 *disposition, emotional outlook* **kigokoro**
気温 *temperature* **kion**
気流 *air stream, air current* **kiryū**
気運 *good fortune, luck* **kiun**
根気 *perseverance, endurance* **konki**
空気 *air, open space* **kūki**
殺気 *threat, menace, intimidation* **sakki**
寒気 *cold, chills* **samuke**
精気 *spirit, vigour, energy* **seiki**
士気 *fighting spirit, espirit-de-corps* **shiki**
酒気 *alcohol smell* **shuki**

短気 *short, quick temper, mercurial* **tanki**
天気 *weather, climate* **tenki**
強気 *assertiveness, aggressiveness* **tsuyoki**
悪気 *malice, ill will, evil intent* **warugi**
弱気 *timidity, docility, meekness* **yowaki**
勇気 *courage, bravery, daring* **yūki**
血の気 *blood* **chinoke**
雰囲気 *ambiance, atmosphere* **fun'iki**
川蒸気 *river steamboat* **kawajōki**
陸蒸気 *steam train* **okajōki**
気安い *friendly, relaxed, familiar* **kiyasui**
乗り気 *enthusiasm, eagerness* **noriki**
やる気 *work vigour, willingness to work* **yaruki**

情eelings, 793	浮igh spirits, 970
感eelings, 45	心eart, 469

汽team, 98

074-A

向owards the suspect, no 尚urther 尚espect...

向owards   向acing

mu(kau), mu(ku), mu(keru), mu(kō), KŌ
towards, facing

口 (mouth)

FLIP: 1.0.b. Whole (stem)

動向 *trend, tendency* **dōkō**
外向 *outward-looking, extrovert* **gaikō**
偏向 *deviation, inclination* **henkō**
方向 *direction, destination* **hōkō**
意向 *intention, opinion* **ikō**
傾向 *tendency, inclination* **keikō**
内向 *inward-focused, introvert* **naikō**
性向 *character, personality* **seikō**
志向 *aim, intention* **shikō**
指向 *point out, indicate* **shikō**
趣向 *idea, device, plan* **shukō**
仰向け *upside-down* **aomuke**
向学心 *intellectual thirst* **kōgakushin**
向上心 *desire to advance* **kōjōshin**
双方向 *both directions* **sōhōkō**
前向き *vigorously, positively* **maemuki**
表向き *formality, protocol, decorum* **omotemuki**
縦向き *lengthwise, "this side up..."* **tatemuki**
横向き *sideways, lateral* **yokomuki**

用向き *business, affair, case* **yōmuki**
後ろ向き *back side, posterior* **ushiromuki**
刃向かう *oppose, stand against* **hamukau**
向き合う *counterpoise, facing across* **mukiau**
向き直る *turn around, ~toward* **mukinaoru**
仕向ける *urge, force, compell* **shimukeru**
筋向かい *across the street* **sujimukai**
振り向く *turnaround, about face* **furimuku**
暮らし向き *making a living* **kurashimuki**
真っ向から *flatly, head-on* **makkōkara**
立ち向かう *stand up to, confront* **tachimukau**

対*gainst, 691*   前*rontal, 118*
面*ace, 36*   方*irection, 533*

同*imilar, 245*

074-B

向owards the suspect, no 尚urther 尚espect...

❶尚urther   ❷尚espect

nao, SHŌ
further, still; courtesy, respect

小 (little)

FLIP: 1.0.b. Whole (stem)

❶尚の事 *"all the more..."* **nao no koto**
尚且つ *"besides, and yet..."* **naokatsu**
尚以って *"all the more..."* **naomotte**
今尚 *"still, even now..."* **imanao**
尚又 *"besides, furthermore..."* **naomata**
尚更 *"all the more, so much so..."* **naosara**
尚早 *premature, ahead of time* **shōsō**
⇒時機尚早 *ahead of proper time* **jiki shōsō**

❷好尚 *favourite, liking* **kōshō**
高尚 *advanced, sophisticated* **kōshō**
和尚 *Buddhist priest* **oshō**
尚武 *martial, militaristic* **shōbu**
尚古 *ancient worship; longing for the past* **shōko**
尚友 *reading ancient books* **shōyū**

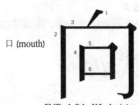

恭*espect, 620*   敬*espect, 329*
仰*espect, 706*   崇*espect, 879*
謹*espect, 962*   礼*espect, 685*

向*owards, 99*

075-A
弐wo 武arriors battle gladiators...

弐*wo*

NI
two
弐月 *February* **nigatsu**
弐万円 *twenty thousand Japanese yen* **niman'en**
弐万年 *twenty thousand years* **nimannen**

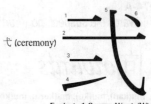

弋 (ceremony)

Facing: 1.0. ☜ West (W)
FLIP: 8.0.a. Inner (flat)

二*wo, 457*	両*oth, 567*

武*arrior, 100*

075-B
弐wo 武arriors battle gladiators...

武*arrior*　　武*artial*

止 (stopping)

take, BU, MU
fighter, martial, warrior, combatant
武備 *armaments, defences* **bubi**
武道 *martial arts* **budō**
武芸 *military arts* **bugei**
武具 *weapon, arms* **bugu**
武人 *warrior, soldier* **bujin**
武術 *martial arts, fighting skills* **bujutsu**
武官 *military officer* **bukan**
武家 *warrior-, samurai clan* **buke**
武器 *weapon, arms* **buki**
武功 *military exploits, combat success* **bukō**
武勲 *brilliant military exploits* **bukun**
武門 *samurai family* **bumon**
武運 *war fortune, spoils of war* **buun**
文武 *"the pen & the sword…"* **bunbu**
武力 *armed might, firepower* **buryoku**
武士 *samurai, warrior, bushido* **bushi**
武士道 *chivalry, way of the samurai* **bushidō**
武将 *general, samurai* **bushō**
武装 *armament, bearing of arms* **busō**

Facing: 3.0. ☞☜ Across

⇒非核武装 *non-nuclear armament* **hikaku busō**
武勇 *fearless warrior, ~soldier* **buyū**
武者 *warrior, soldier* **musha**
尚武 *martial spirit* **shōbu**
核武装 *nuclear armament* **kakubusō**
玄武岩 *basalt* **genbugan**
神武天皇 *Emperor Jinmu (660-585 BC)*
　　 jinmu tennō
桓武天皇 *Emperor Kanmu (781-806)* **kanmu tennō**
建武時代 *Kenmu Era (1334-1336)* **kenmu jidai**
聖武天皇 *Emperor Shōmu (724-749)*
　　 shōmu tennō
天武天皇 *Emperor Tenmu (673-686)* **tenmu tennō**

戦*ighting, 517*	兵*oldier, 490*	衛*oldier, 796*
軍*ilitary, 295*	隊*oldier, 543*	

域*egion, 139*	栽*aplings, 803*

076-A

伺nquiry on 何omething yielded nothing...

伺nquire　伺equest

ukaga(u), SHI
inquire, request, question, solicit

伺い　visit, request **ukagai**
⇒進退伺い　resignation request **shintai ukagai**
⇒暑中伺い　summer greetings **shochū ukagai**
伺い書　written request **ukagaisho**
伺い知る　tell, guess, infer **ukagaishiru**
奉伺　attend, serve, mind **hōshi**
伺候　courtesy call, formal visit **shikō**

人⇔亻 (person)

FLIP: 8.0.a. Inner (flat)

諮nquire, 865	依equest, 355
尋nquire, 868	願equest, 964
聞nquire, 282	求equest, 256
応omply, 469	請equest, 791
答nswer, 232	頼equest, 562

何omething, 101

076-B

伺nquiry on 何omething yielded nothing...

何omething　何hat

nani, nan, KA
something, what

何処　where, whereabouts **doko**
如何　how are you, how is it **ikaga**
如何に　in what way **ikani**
何時　what time, when **itsu, nandoki, nanji**
何時か　someday, one of these days **itsuka**
幾何　geometry **kika**
何番　what number **nanban**
何で　why, by what means **nande**
何事　something, everything **nanigoto**
何程　about how much **nanihodo**
何者　who the heck **nanimono**
何様　"really..." **nanisama**
何人　how many people **nannin, nanibito**
何等　whatsoever, nonetheless **nanra**
何等かの　some, a few **nanrakano**
何歳　how old, what age **nansai**
何て　"what the heck..." **nante**
何故　why, how come, for what reason **naze, naniyue**
誰何　challenge, dare **suika**

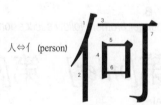

人⇔亻 (person)

FLIP: 8.0.a. Inner (flat)

何だかんだ　somehow **nanda kanda**
何か　something, somehow **nanika**
何かしら　somewhat, somehow **nanikashira**
何彼と　one thing & another **nanikato**
何くそ　"damn it, what the hell..." **nanikuso**
何もかも　completely, entirely **nanimokamo**
何十もの　several, various **nanjūmono**
何回も　many times **nankaimo**
何億もの　hundreds of millions **nan'okumono**
何とか　somehow **nantoka**
何となく　"for some reasons..." **nantonaku**

某omething, 292	事ction, 116
物hings, 647	活ctivity, 237

伺nquire, 101

077-A

弟ounger brothers follow succession 第rder...

弓 (archery bow)

弟ounger brother

otōto, TEI, DAI, DE
younger brother

Facing: 1.0. ☜ West (W)

弟子 *disciple, follower, protégé* **deshi**
義弟 *brother-in-law* **gitei**
愚弟 *"my foolish brother..." (humble)* **gutei**
実弟 *younger brother* **jittei**
賢弟 *wise younger brother* **kentei**
高弟 *masters leading pupil* **kōtei**
兄弟 *brothers, male siblings* **kyōdai**
兄弟愛 *brotherhood, fraternal love* **kyōdaiai**
兄弟喧嘩 *sibling quarrel ~rivalry* **kyōdaigenka**
末弟 *one's youngest brother* **mattei**
門弟 *disciple, pupil* **montei**
従弟 *younger male cousin* **itoko, jūtei**
弟分 *treated as younger brother* **otōtobun**
弟嫁 *one's younger brothers wife* **otōtoyome**
舎弟 *one's younger brother* **shatei**
師弟 *teacher-&-student* **shitei**
子弟 *one's children* **shitei**
弟妹 *younger brother or sister* **teimai**
徒弟 *apprentice, instructee, acolyte* **totei**

相弟子 *fellow pupils* **aideshi**
兄弟子 *seniour disciple* **anideshi**
乳兄弟 *foster brother, ~sister* **chikyōdai**
義兄弟 *brother-in-law* **gikyōdai**
直弟子 *immediate pupil* **jikideshi**
孫弟子 *disciples of one's disciples* **magodeshi**
愛弟子 *favourite student* **manadeshi**
又弟子 *student of a masters student* **matadeshi**
弟弟子 *younger disciple, ~pupil* **otōtodeshi**
内弟子 *live-in apprentice, ~instructee* **uchideshi**
又従兄弟 *second cousin* **mataitoko**

兄*lder-brother, 203*
姉*lder sister, 114*
妹*ounger sister, 114*

第*[order], 102*   売*erchandise, 259*

077-B

弟ounger brothers follow succession 第rder...

竹 (bamboo)

第[order] 第[sequence]

DAI
[order], [sequence]

Facing: 1.1. ☜ West (H)

次第 *contingent on, conditional* **shidai**
登第 *passing an exam* **tōdai**
及第 *passing an exam* **kyūdai**
及第点 *passing mark, ~score, ~point* **kyūdaiten**
落第 *failing an exam, flunking* **rakudai**
落第点 *failing mark, ~score, ~point* **rakudaiten**
第六感 *sixth sense, hunch, intuition* **dairokkan**
第五列 *fifth column* **daigoretsu**
第一次 *first* **daiichiji**
第一流 *first-class* **daiichiryū**
第一歩 *first step, one big leap* **daiippo**
第一線 *forefront, frontline* **daiissen**
第一人者 *authority, leading expert* **daiichininsha**
第一次世界大戦 *First World War*
　　daiichiji sekai taisen
第二次世界大戦 *Second World War*
　　dainiji sekai taisen
第一印象 *first impression* **daiichi inshō**
第三の火 *nuclear energy* **daisan no hi**

第三世界 *Third World nations* **daisan sekai**
第三国 *third country, neutral country* **daisangoku**
第三紀 *geological tertiary* **daisanki**
第三者 *third person, external-, neutral party*
　　daisansha
努力次第 *"depending on one's efforts..."*
　　doryoku shidai
安全第一 *"safety above-all..."* **anzen daiichi**

順*equence, 959*
番*umber, 338*
号*umber, 866*

筆*riting-brush, 141*

078-A

知nowledge in 和apanese: 和armony & 和eace...

矢 (archery arrow)

知nowledge 知wareness

shi(ru), CHI
knowledge, awareness, cognizance, consciousness

FLIP: 7.0.a. Right (flat)

知米	pro-American **chibei**		承知	agreement, approval, consent **shōchi**
知恵	wisdom, intelligence, wit **chie**		周知	common knowledge **shūchi**
知遇	favour, blessings **chigū**		衆知	popular wisdom, common knowledge **shūchi**
知人	acquaintance, casual friend **chijin**		探知	detection, looking out **tanchi**
知覚	perception, sensation **chikaku**		通知	notice, notification **tsūchi**
知能	intelligence, wisdom **chinō**		府知事	metropolitan governor **kenchiji**
知略	innovative, resourceful **chiryaku**		県知事	prefectural governor **kenchiji**
知慮	wisdom, sagacity, foresight **chiryo**		都知事	metropolitan governor **tochiji**
知識	knowledge, intelligence **chishiki**		未知語	unknown word **michigo**
知将	resourceful general **chishō**		知らん顔	feigning ignorance **shirankao**
知勇	wisdom & courage **chiyū**		知り合い	acquaintance **shiriai**
英知	intelligence, wisdom **eichi**		顔見知り	acquaintance, casual friend **kaomishiri**
報知	information, report **hōchi**		計り知れない	unknown amount **hakarishirenai**
人知	human understanding **jinchi**			
熟知	familiarity, familiar knowledge **jukuchi**			
既知	well-known, noted, famous **kichi**			
認知	recognition, acknowledgement **ninchi**			
察知	guess, surmise, judgement **sacchi**			
才知	wit, intelligence **saichi**			

識wareness, 856   念hought, 182
存nowledge, 634   想hought, 524
意dea, 340   思hinking, 596

和armony, 103

078-B

知nowledge in 和apanese: 和armony & 和eace...

口 (mouth)

❶和armony ❷和apanese

yawa(rageru), yawa(ragu), nago(mu), nago(yaka), WA, O
harmony; Japanese

FLIP: 7.0.a. Right (flat)

❶調和	harmony, peaceful **chōwa**			
同和	sympathy, commiseration **dōwa**		和親	amity, goodwill **washin**
平和	peace **heiwa**		融和	harmony, reconciliation **yūwa**
飽和	saturation, congestion **hōwa**		宥和	appeasement, conciliatory **yūwa**
緩和	relaxation, detente **kanwa**		違和感	sense of incongruity **iwakan**
混和	mix, mingle, blend **konwa**			
講和	reconciliation, rapproachment **kōwa**		❷和裁	Japanese dressmaking **wasai**
穏和	moderate **onwa**		和算	Japanese math **wasan**
唱和	chorale, choir singing **shōwa**		和式	Japanese style **washiki**
昭和	1924~1989 (Emperor Hirohito's reign) **shōwa**		和室	tatami room **washitsu**
和英	Japanese & English **waei**		和食	Japanese cuisine **washoku**
和風	Japanese-style **wafū**		和訳	Japanese translation **wayaku**
和学	Japanese literature **wagaku**		大和魂	Japanese fighting spirit **yamatodamashii**
和議	peace talks, ~negotiations **wagi**			
和合	harmony, concord, agreement **wagō**			
和歌	31-syllable Japanese poem **waka**			
和解	compromise, settlement **wakai**			
和音	chord, melody **waon**			
和戦	war & peace **wasen**			

泰erenity, 612   日apan, 14
穏ranquillity, 840   邦apan, 694
康ranquillity, 881

知wareness, 103

079-A

抜ull-out to 披pen the letter from Copenhagen...

手⇔扌 (hand, manual)

抜ull-out   抜xtract

nu(ku), nu(keru), nu(karu), nu(kasu), BATSU
pull-out, extract, pluck out, take out

FLIP: 7.3.b. Right Bottom (stem)

抜け穴	loophole, escape route **nukeana**
抜け殻	cast-off skin, slough **nukegara**
抜き荷	goods pilferage **nukini**
抜き出す	pick out, select, single out **nukidasu**
抜き書き	extract, selection, excerpt **nukigaki**
抜き差し	plugging in & out **nukisashi**
抜き取り	picking out, selection **nukitori**
抜き刷り	offprint, offset printing **nukizuri**
抜剣	drawn sword **bakken**
抜歯	tooth extraction **basshi**
抜刀	drawn sword **battō**
海抜	above sea level **kaibatsu**
選抜	select, choose, single out **senbatsu**
秀抜	excellent, pre-eminent **shūbatsu**
卓抜	excellent, pre-eminent **takubatsu**
婆抜き	old maid card game **babā nuki**
抜本的	drastic, radical **bapponteki**
骨抜き	fish deboning **hone nuki**
息抜き	breathing space **ikinuki**

腰抜け	coward, timid, sissy **koshinuke**
釘抜き	nail puller **kuginuki**
栓抜き	corkscrew, bottle opener **sennuki**
出し抜く	forestall, get the better of **dashinuku**
選び抜く	select, choose **erabinuku**
吹き抜け	well, stairwell **fukinuke**
踏み抜く	step, tread thru **fuminuku**
生え抜き	native-born **haenuki**
掘り抜く	dig thru **horinuku**
勝ち抜く	step up to the next round **kachinuku**
知り抜く	know thoroughly **shirinuku**

引|xtract, 348	退ithdraw, 770
抽xtract, 37	撤ithdraw, 843
滴xtract, 799	罷ithdraw, 322
却ithdraw, 387	

技echnique, 200	坂lope, 733

079-B

抜ull-out to 披pen the letter from Copenhagen...

手⇔扌 (hand, manual)

披pen

HI
open, pry open, unseal

FLIP: 7.3.b. Right Bottom (stem)

直披	confidential letter **chokuhi**
披見	opening & reading a letter **hiken**
披講	introduction in a poetry party **hikō**
披瀝	revelation, disclosure **hireki**
披露	announcement, notification **hirō**
披露宴	wedding party **hirōen**
⇒結婚披露宴	wedding party **kekkon hirōen**
お披露目	debut, first presentation **ohirome**

開pen, 284	拓evelop, 363
口pening, 458	空mpty, 394

彼[third person], 224	抜ull-out, 104

080-A

官 *ublic officials in a* 宮 *hrine pray for the* 宮 *alace* 宮 *rince to be fine...*

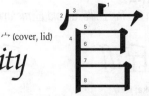

宀 (cover, lid)

官 *ublic official* 官 *uthority*

KAN
public official, authority, bureaucrat

FLIP: 2.0.b. Sort Of (stem)

武官 *military-, naval officer* **bukan**
長官 *high-ranking officials, VIP* **chōkan**
⇒内閣官房長官 *chief cabinet secretary* **naikaku kanbō chōkan**
五官 *the five organs* **gokan**
次官 *vice-minister, undersecretary* **jikan**
官房 *secretariat, executive staff* **kanbō**
官庁 *government office* **kanchō**
官権 *government authority* **kanken**
官紀 *public official discipline* **kanki**
官金 *government funds, public money* **kankin**
官命 *government orders* **kanmei**
官民 *government & the people* **kanmin**
官能 *sensual, sensuous* **kannō**
官費 *government expenses* **kanpi**
官報 *official gazette* **kanpō**
官吏 *civil servant, public employee* **kanri**
官舎 *official residence* **kansha**
官職 *government post* **kanshoku**

官邸 *official residence* **kantei**
⇒首相官邸 *premier's residence* **shushō kantei**
警官 *police officer* **keikan**
高官 *government dignitary, vip* **kōkan**
教官 *professor in a state university* **kyōkan**
任官 *appointment to a public post* **ninkan**
神官 *Shintō priest* **shinkan**
官公庁 *government offices* **kankōchō**
監察官 *inspector, auditor* **kansatsukan**
監督官 *supervisor* **kantokukan**
裁判官 *judge, magistrate* **saibankan**
司令官 *commander* **shireikan**

庁 *ublic office, 633*	国 *ation, 92*
役 *fficial, 746*	政 *dministration, 725*
公 *ublic, 180*	吏 *fficial, 463*

宮 *alace, 105*

080-B

官 *ublic officials in a* 宮 *hrine pray for the* 宮 *alace* 宮 *rince to be fine...*

宀 (cover, lid)

❶宮 *hrine* ❷宮 *alace* ❸宮 *rince*

miya, KYŪ, GŪ, KU
shrine; palace, chateau; prince

FLIP: 1.0.a. Whole (flat)

❶宮司 *chief Shintō priest* **gūji**
神宮 *Shintō shrine* **jingū**
宮城県 *Miyagi Prefecture* **miyagi-ken**
宮参り *infant's first shrine visit* **miyamairi**
宮崎県 *Miyazaki Prefecture* **miyazaki-ken**
遷宮式 *new shrine dedication* **sengūshiki**
宵宮 *festival eve* **yoimiya**
❷箱宮 *miniature palace* **hakomiya**
幼宮 *child prince* **itomiya**
皇宮 *imperial palace* **kōgū**
後宮 *inner palace* **kōkyū**
宮中 *imperial court* **kyūchū**
宮殿 *palace, court* **kyūden**
宮城 *imperial palace* **kyūjō**
宮門 *palace gates* **kyūmon**
宮室 *imperial family* **kyūshitsu**
宮廷 *imperial court* **kyūtei**
迷宮 *maze, labyrinth, snarl* **meikyū**
迷宮入り *remaining unsolved* **meikyūiri**

宮居 *imperial palace; shrine compound* **miyai**
宮家 *imperial prince house* **miyake**
宮様 *prince, princess* **miyasama**
王宮 *royal palace* **ōkyū**
離宮 *imperial villa* **rikyū**
竜宮 *dragon palace* **ryūgū**
子宮 *womb, uterus* **shikyu**
若宮 *young prince* **wakamiya**
宮内庁 *Imperial Household Agency* **kunaichō**
宮仕え *palace service* **miyatsukae**
❸高円宮 *Prince Takamado (1955-2002)* **takamado-no-miya**

殿 *alace, 522*	寺 *emple, 248*
城 *astle, 243*	妃 *rincess, 728*
社 *hrine, 703*	姫 *rincess, 542*

営 *anagement, 580*

081-A

On the far 丘ills, an old 匠rtisan drills...

丘*ill*　　　丘*lope*

oka, KYŪ
hill, slope

比丘 *Buddhist monk* **biku**
比丘尼 *Buddhist female monk* **bikuni**
段丘 *terrace* **dankyū**
円丘 *knoll* **enkyū**
墳丘 *grave mound, tumulus* **funkyū**
片丘 *steeper hill* **kataoka**
丘陵 *hill* **kyūryō**
丘辺 *hilly area* **okabe**
砂丘 *sand hill, dune* **sakyū**
火口丘 *volcano cone* **kakōkyū**

一 (one, single)

Facing: 2.0. East ☞ (W)

坂*lope, 733*	登*limb, 437*
崎*lope, 270*	高*igh, 435*

近*earby, 184*

081-B

On the far 丘ills, an old 匠rtisan drills...

匠*rtisan*　　匠*raftsman*

SHŌ, JŌ
artisan, craftsman

意匠 *idea, plan* **ishō**
工匠 *craftsman* **kōshō**
巨匠 *great master, ~artist* **kyoshō**
名匠 *master craftsman* **meishō**
船匠 *ship artisan* **senshō**
師匠 *great-, master teacher* **shishō**
匠気 *showmanship* **shōki**
宗匠 *master teacher* **sōshō**
鷹匠 *falconer, hawker* **takajō**
刀匠 *swordsmith* **tōshō**
鵜匠 *cormorant fisherman* **ujō**

匸 (side box)

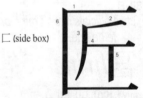

Facing: 2.0. East ☞ (W)

工*raft, 176*	術*kills, 110*
匠*rtisan, 106*	芸*rts, 619*
巧*killful, 738*	

兵*oldier, 490*

082-A

EU flags 掛anging in the 街istrict of Maastricht...

❶ 掛*ang up* ❷ 掛*xpense*

手⇔扌 (hand, manual)

ka(karu), ka(keru), kakari
hang up, suspending; expenditure, expense

FLIP: 8.0.a. Inner (flat)

❶ 掛け声 *shout, call, shriek* **kakegoe**
掛け橋 *go-between, pipeline* **kakehashi**
掛け算 *multiplication* **kakezan**
掛け布団 *quilt, padded* **kakebuton**
掛け離れる *far, quite different* **kakehanareru**
掛け替える *replace, substitute* **kakekaeru**
願掛け *pray, say a prayer* **gankake**
壁掛け *wall decoration, ~display* **kabekake**
心掛け *mental attitude, ~posture* **kokorogake**
見掛け *appearance, outward looks* **mikake**
仕掛け *device, mechanism* **shikake**
水掛け論 *futile argument* **mizukakeron**
足掛かり *foothold, footing* **ashigakari**
衣紋掛け *coat-, dress hanger* **emonkake**
呼び掛け *appeal, hail, call* **yobikake**
帆掛け船 *sailboat, sailing ship* **hokakebune**
振り掛ける *sprinkle, scatter* **furikakeru**
話し掛ける *initiate a conversation* **hanashikakeru**
乗り掛かる *set about, embark upon* **norikakaru**

襲い掛かる *jump on, pounce on* **osoikakaru**
飛び掛かる *spring, leap, pounce* **tobikakaru**
問い掛ける *ask, inquire* **toikakeru**
詰め掛ける *crowd, besiege* **tsumekakeru**
寄り掛かる *rely on, lean, depend* **yorikakaru**
掛け合い *negotiations, conference* **kakeai**
掛け売り *credit sale, sell on credit* **kakeuri**
掛け引き *bargaining, maneuvering* **kakehiki**

❷ 掛け金 *instalment payment* **kakekin**
日掛け *daily instalments* **higake**
月掛け *monthly instalment* **tsukigake**

垂*ang down, 505*	縣*anging, 566*	賃*ayment, 145*
架*anging, 202*	費*xpense 626*	払*ayment, 682*

街*istrict, 107*

082-B

EU flags 掛anging in the 街istrict of Maastricht...

街*istrict* 街*owntown*

行 (going)

machi, GAI
district, downtown

FLIP: 8.0.a. Inner (flat)

街路 *street, avenue* **gairo**
街路樹 *street trees* **gairoju**
街娼 *street walker* **gaishō**
街灯 *street lamp, lamppost* **gaitō**
花街 *red-light district* **hanamachi, kagai**
街道 *road, highway* **kaidō**
街角 *street corner* **machikado**
街頭 *on the street* **gaitō**
街頭募金 *street fund-raising* **gaitō bokin**
街頭演説 *street speech* **gaitō enzetsu**
街頭録音 *street interview* **gaitō rokuon**
暗黒街 *underworld, gangster turf* **ankokugai**
地下街 *underground shopping mall* **chikagai**
繁華街 *downtown, commercial district* **hankagai**
貧民街 *slum area, squatter district* **hinmingai**
住宅街 *residential district* **jūtakugai**
官庁街 *government offices district* **kanchōgai**
歓楽街 *amusement area* **kanrakugai**
露店街 *open-air booth* **rotengai**

市街 *street, city* **shigai**
市街地 *urban area* **shigaichi**
市街戦 *urban warfare* **shigaisen**
娯楽街 *amusement area* **gorakugai**
商業街 *commercial area* **shōgyōgai**
商店街 *commercial area* **shōtengai**
問屋街 *wholesale district* **tonyagai**
裏街道 *back-, side road* **urakaidō**
中国人街 *chinatown* **chūgokujingai**

市*ity, 304*	業*usiness, 124*	
区*istrict, 80*	商*ommerce, 135*	
丁*lock-of-houses, 173*	営*anagement, 580*	

衛*rotect, 796*

083-A

Cops in 追ursuit, 追ressing a thief on foot...

辶 (transport)

追ursue　　追rive away

o(u), TSUI
pursue, drive away, run after, dove-tail, back-trail, chase

Facing: 4.0. ☜☞ Apart

急追	hot pursuit, hot trail **kyūtsui**	追送	sending, dispatch **tsuisō**
猛追	hot pursuit, hot trail **mōtsui**	追想	remembrance, recollection **tsuisō**
追手	pursuer **otte**	追悼	mourning, grieving **tsuitō**
追尾	following, going after **tsuibi**	追突	coming from behind, side entry **tsuitotsu**
追慕	cherishing a dead's memory **tsuibo**	追善	funeral mass, necrological mass **tsuizen**
追徴	additional collection **tsuichō**	長追い	long pursuit **nagaoi**
追撃	running after, hot chase **tsuigeki**	追試験	make-up exam **tsuishiken**
追放	banishment, exile, expulsion **tsuihō**	追い出す	expel, throw out **oidasu**
追加	addition, supplement **tsuika**	追い返す	turn back **oikaesu**
追記	postscript, P.S. **tsuiki**	追い越し	overtaking, overpassing **oikoshi**
追及	thorough investigation **tsuikyū**	追い着く	catch up, overtake **oitsuku**
追究	investigation, inquiry **tsuikyū**	追い打ち	attacking a retreating enemy **oiuchi**
追求	pursue, follow, seek after **tsuikyū**		

追認 ratification, confirmation **tsuinin**
追納 additional payment **tsuinō**
追録 addendum **tsuiroku**
追跡 chase, pursuit, running after **tsuiseki**
追伸 postscript, P.S. **tsuishin**
追訴 additional indictment **tsuiso**

走unning, 497
奔un-away, 120
逃scape, 216

尺ursue, 574
逐rive-out, 479
迫ress for, 108

追ress for, 108

083-B

Cops in 追ursuit, 追ressing a thief on foot...

辶 (transport)

迫ress for

sema(ru), HAKU
press for

FLIP: 3.0.a. Top (flat)

圧迫 pressure, oppression **appaku**
迫害 persecution, oppression **hakugai**
迫害者 despot, oppressor, tyrant **hakugaisha**
迫撃 close attack **hakugeki**
迫撃砲 mortar **hakugekihō**
迫力 powerful, compelling **hakuryoku**
迫真 realistic, true-to-life **hakushin**
迫真性 true-to-life, realistic **hakushinsei**
逼迫 impending, pressing **hippaku**
気迫 spirit, determination, drive **kihaku**
緊迫 tension, strain **kinpaku**
脅迫 threat, intimidation **kyōhaku**
強迫 forcing, compulsion, coercion **kyōhaku**
急迫 urgency, pressing **kyūhaku**
窮迫 difficult-, vexing situation **kyūhaku**
切迫 tense situation **seppaku**
脅迫状 threatening letter **kyōhakujō**
脅迫電話 phone threat **kyōhaku denwa**
強迫観念 obsession, infatuation **kyōhaku kannen**

迫り出す protrude, stick-, push out **semaridasu**
押し迫る press hard **oshisemaru**
差し迫る imminent, impending **sashisemaru**

尺ursue, 574
逐rive-out, 479
追ursue, 108

追ursue, 108

084-A

卒oldiers 座eated for 卒raduation, up for promotion...

十 (cross)

❶ 卒raduate ❷ 卒oldier

SOTSU
graduate; soldier

FLIP: 1.0.b. Whole (stem)

❶ 番卒 sentry, guard **bansotsu**
中卒 middle school graduate **chūsotsu**
大卒 college grad, university graduate **daisotsu**
何卒 "please, kindly..." **dōzo, nanitozo**
学卒 school graduation **gakusotsu**
高卒 high school graduate **kōsotsu**
新卒 fresh graduate **shinsotsu**
卒中 apoplexy, stroke **socchū**
卒業 graduation, completing school **sotsugyō**
卒業生 graduate **sotsugyōsei**
卒業式 graduation ceremony **sotsugyōshiki**
卒業論文 graduation thesis **sotsugyō ronbun**
卒業試験 graduation examination **sotsugyō shiken**
卒業証書 diploma, graduation certificate
　　sotsugyō shōsho
卒寿 one's ninetieth birthday **sotsuju**
卒倒 fainting, passing out, collapse **sottō**
倉卒 rash, hurried, sudden **sōsotsu**
忽卒 rash, hurried, sudden **sōsotsu**

卒然 suddenly, abruptly **sotsuzen**
輸卒 delivery soldier **yusotsu**
既卒者 college graduate **kisotsusha**
脳卒中 cerebral apoplexy **nōsocchū**
卒園式 kindergarten graduation **sotsuenshiki**
❷ 獄卒 prison warden, jailer, gaoler **gokusotsu**
兵卒 soldier, private **heisotsu**
弱卒 coward soldiers **jakusotsu**
従卒 officers' servant, orderly **jūsotsu**
士卒 private, soldier **shisotsu**
将卒 officers & soldiers **shōsotsu**

教ducate, 385	完omplete, 196
習earning, 238	了omplete, 456
修aster, 898	軍oldier, 295

座eating, 109

084-B

卒oldiers 座eated for 卒raduation, up for promotion...

广 (rooftop)

座eating　座hair

suwa(ru), ZA
seating, chair

FLIP: 8.0.a. Inner (flat)

便座 toilet seat, ~cover **benza**
台座 pedestal, base **daiza**
銀座 Ginza, Tōkyō **ginza**
講座 university chair, ~lecture **kōza**
口座 bank account **kōza**
王座 seat of power **ōza**
星座 constellation; horoscope **seiza**
単座 single-seater (plane) **tanza**
座長 presiding chairperson **zachō**
座員 troupe member **zain**
座高 seated height **zakō**
座骨 hipbone **zakotsu**
座興 amusement, entertainment **zakyō**
座礼 bowing seated **zarei**
座席 seat, chair **zaseki**
座視 doing nothing, fence-sitting **zashi**
座敷 drawing room; Japanese-style room **zashiki**
座礁 running aground, being stranded **zashō**
座卓 low table **zataku**

座禅 Zen meditation **zazen**
座像 seated figure **zazō**
居座る stay, settle down **isuwaru**
座蒲団 seat cushion **zabuton**
座右の銘 motto, precepts **zayū no mei**
牡羊座 Aries **ohitsujiza**
牡牛座 Taurus **oushiza**
双子座 Gemini, twins **futagoza**
蟹座 Cancer **kaniza**
獅子座 Leo **shishiza**
乙女座 Virgo, the Virgin **otomeza**
天秤座 Libra **tenbinza**
蠍座 Scorpio **sasoriza**
射手座 Sagittarius, archer **iteza**
山羊座 Capricorn **yagiza**
水瓶座 Aquarius **mizugameza**
魚座 Pisces, Fishes **uoza**

席eating, 91　　傘mbrella, 142

085-A
衡alancing 術kills on bicycle wheels...

行 (going)

衡alance   衡quilibrium

KŌ
balance, equilibrium

平衡 *balance, equilibrium* **heikō**
権衡 *equilibrium* **kenkō**
均衡 *balance, proportionate* **kinkō**
⇒不均衡 *disproportionate, unbalance* **fukinkō**
⇒貿易不均衡 *trade imbalance* **bōeki fukinkō**
衡平 *equitable, balanced* **kōhei**
衡器 *balance, scales* **kōki**
選衡 *choosing, selection* **senkō**
度量衡 *weights & measures* **doryōkō**
斉衡時代 *Saikō Era (854-857)* **saikō jidai**

FLIP: 8.0.a. Inner (flat)
FLIP: 8.0.b. Inner (stem)

均*qual, 470*	似*imilar, 472*
斉*qual, 112*	同*imilar, 245*
如*qual, 364*	平*-lain, 488*

衝*ollision, 935*   衛*rotect, 796*

085-B
衡alancing 術kills on bicycle wheels...

行 (going)

術kills   術echnique

JUTSU
skills, technique, knack for, aptitude, know-how

馬術 *equestrian, horsemanship* **bajutsu**
美術 *fine arts* **bijutsu**
学術 *academics* **gakujutsu**
芸術 *fine arts* **geijutsu**
技術 *skill, technique* **gijutsu**
医術 *medicine, medical technology* **ijutsu**
柔術 *jujitsu martial arts* **jūjutsu**
術語 *technical term, terminology* **jutsugo**
術策 *trick, fraud, deceit, shenanigan* **jutsusaku**
剣術 *fencing, swordsmanship* **kenjutsu**
奇術 *magic, jugglery, wizardry* **kijutsu**
魔術 *magic, spell* **majutsu**
忍術 *ninja martial arts* **ninjutsu**
算術 *arithmetic, mathematics* **sanjutsu**
戦術 *war strategy, combat tactics* **senjutsu**
手術 *surgery, operation, incision* **shujutsu**
話術 *articulation, story-telling arts* **wajutsu**
腹話術 *ventriloquism* **fukuwajutsu**
護身術 *art of self-defence* **goshinjutsu**

FLIP: 8.0.b. Inner (stem)

記憶術 *mnemonics, art of memorizing* **kiokujutsu**
航海術 *navigation, sailing skills* **kōkaijutsu**
航空術 *aeronautics* **kōkūjutsu**
錬金術 *alchemy* **renkinjutsu**
催眠術 *hypnotism, mesmerism* **saiminjutsu**
処世術 *street smart wisdom* **shoseijutsu**
速記術 *shorthand, stenography* **sokkijutsu**
測量術 *surveying, measuring* **sokuryōjutsu**
雄弁術 *articulation, elocution, oratory* **yūbenjutsu**
権謀術数 *trickery, deceit, fraud* **kenbō jutsusū**
占星術師 *astrologer, fortune-teller*
　　　sensei jutsushi

巧*killful, 738*	匠*rtisan, 106*
技*echnique, 200*	芸*rts, 619*
工*raft, 176*	

街*istrict, 107*

086-A

Twilight 歳*ears,* 茂*hicken with tears...*

歳*ears old*

止 (stopping)

Facing: 2.1. East ☞ (H)
FLIP: 8.0.b. Inner (stem)

SAI, SEI
  years old, age, *age suffix*
万歳 *"hurray, long live..."* **banzai**
千歳 *a thousand years* **chitose**
一歳 *one year old* **issai**
何歳 *how old, what age* **nansai**
歳晩 *year end* **saiban**
歳月 *time, years* **saigetsu**
歳費 *annual expenditure* **saihi**
歳事 *year's activities* **saiji**
祭事 *year's activities* **saiji**
歳計 *annual account* **saikei**
歳末 *end of the year, year-end* **saimatsu**
歳入 *annual revenue* **sainyū**
歳歳 *annual, yearly* **saisai**
歳星 *Planet Jupiter* **saisei**
歳首 *start of the year* **saishu**
歳出 *annual expenditure* **saishutsu**
歳旦 *New Year day* **saitan**
歳余 *longer than a year* **saiyo**
当歳 *this year* **tōsai**

零歳 *infant less than a year old* **zerosai**
二十歳 *20 years old* **hatachi**
歳の市 *year-end market* **toshi no ichi**
歳の瀬 *year end* **toshi no se**
お歳暮 *year-end gift to one's superior* **oseibo**
歳時記 *almanac, yearbook* **saijiki**

才*ears old, 185*	永*ong-lasting, 10*
齢*ears old, 553*	久*ong-lasting, 379*
寿*ongevity, 440*	

歯*eeth, 553*

086-B

Twilight 歳*ears,* 茂*hicken with tears...*

茂*row thick*

⺾ (grass)

FLIP: 3.0.b. Top (stem)
Facing: 2.1. East ☞ (H)

shige(ru), MO
  grow thick, thicken
茂み *thicket, bush, copse, shrubbery* **shigemi**
繁茂 *growing thick, luxuriance* **hanmo**
茂林 *dense forest, thick forest* **morin**
逆茂木 *abatis* **sakamogi**
茂り合い *growing luxuriant* **shigeriai**
生い茂る *grow thickly, luxuriant* **oishigeru**

厚*hick, 964*
太*hick, 6*
濃*hick, 446*

若*oung, 276*

087-A

斉niformity in 斎urification needs no altercation...

文 (literacy)

斉qual 斉niform

SEI
equal, uniform

FLIP: 1.0.b. Whole (stem)

不斉 *uneven, not uniform* **fusei**
均斉 *symmetry, well balanced* **kinsei**
斉一 *uniformity, standardization* **seiitsu**
斉家 *household management* **seika**
整斉 *symmetrical, proportional* **seisei**
斉射 *fusillade, hail of gunfire* **seisha**
斉唱 *unison, wholesome* **seishō**
一斉に *all together, all at once* **issei(ni)**
一斉射撃 *volley, fusillade* **issei shageki**
斉衡時代 *Saikō Era (854-857)* **saikō jidai**
斉明天皇 *Lady Emperor Saimei (655-661)* **saimei tennō**

均qual, 470	同imilar, 245
如qual, 364	平lain, 488
似imilar, 472	

斎urification, *112*

087-B

斉niformity in 斎urification needs no altercation...

文 (literacy)

斎urification 斎leansing

SAI
purification, cleansing, *religious abstinence*

FLIP: 1.0.b. Whole (stem)

潔斎 *purification by food abstinence* **kessai**
斎服 *ritual vestments* **saifuku**
斎日 *fasting day* **saijitsu**
斎場 *place of religious service* **saijō**
斎戒 *purification, spiritual cleansing* **saikai**
書斎 *study room, private library* **shosai**
小斎 *abstinence, self-denial* **shōsai**

清urify, 793	浄urity, 230
潔urity, 901	粋urity, 762
純urity, 199	

斉niform, *112*

088-A

Roman 皇mperors shine like 星tars even from 星lanets afar...

白 (white)

皇*mperor*　　皇*onarch*

KŌ, Ō
emperor, monarch

FLIP: 1.0.a. Whole (flat)

去皇 *abdicated emperor* **hōō**
上皇 *retired emperor* **jōkō**
皇后 *empress* **kōgō**
皇后陛下 *her majesty, the empress* **kōgō heika**
皇宮 *imperial palace* **kōgū**
皇軍 *Imperial Japanese Army* **kōgun**
皇妃 *empress* **kōhi**
皇位 *throne* **kōi**
皇女 *imperial princess* **kōjo**
皇国 *empire of Japan* **kōkoku**
皇居 *imperial palace* **kōkyo**
皇室 *imperial family, ~household* **kōshitsu**
皇太后 *empress dowager* **kōtaigō**
皇太孫 *eldest imperial grandson* **kōtaison**
皇太子 *crown prince* **kōtaishi**
皇太子妃 *crown princess* **kōtaishihi**
皇妃 *empress, queen* **kōhi**
皇紀 *Emperor Jinmu ascension (660 BC)* **kōki**
皇旗 *imperial standard* **kōki**

皇恩 *imperial favour* **kōon**
皇霊 *spirits of imperial ancestors* **kōrei**
皇祖 *imperial founder, first emperor* **kōso**
皇宗 *imperial ancestors* **kōsō**
皇帝 *emperor* **kōtei**
皇統 *imperial line* **kōtō**
皇族 *imperial family* **kōzoku**
教皇 *Roman Catholic Pope* **kyōkō**
天皇 *Emperor of Japan* **tennō**
天皇制 *emperor system* **tennōsei**
天皇家 *imperial family* **tennōke**

王*onarch, 12*	日*apan, 14*
帝*mpire, 432*	邦*apan, 694*
国*ation, 92*	和*apanese, 103*

皇*ffer, 618*	星*tars, 113*

088-B

Roman 皇mperors shine like 星tars even from 星lanets afar...

日 (sunlight, daytime)

星*tar*　　星*lanet*

hoshi, SEI, SHŌ
star, planet

FLIP: 2.0.b. Sort Of (stem)
FLIP: 3.0.a. Top (flat)

土星 *Planet Saturn* **dosei**
衛星 *satellite* **eisei**
銀星 *upset defeat of a sumo wrestler* **ginsei**
彦星 *altair* **hikoboshi**
海星 *starfish* **hitode**
星影 *starlight* **hoshikage**
星屑 *star dust* **hoshikuzu**
星空 *starry sky* **hoshizora**
火星 *Planet Mars* **kasei**
金星 *Planet Venus* **kinsei**
黒星 *bull's eye; lost star* **kuroboshi**
目星 *aim, mark, target* **meboshi**
木星 *Planet Jupiter* **mokusei**
流星 *shooting star* **ryūsei**
星学 *astronomy, cosmology* **seigaku**
星雲 *nebula* **seiun**
星座 *constellation, cluster of stars* **seiza**
星図 *star chart, constellation map* **seizu**
白星 *winning star, white star* **shiroboshi**

水星 *Planet Mercury* **suisei**
惑星 *planet* **wakusei**
超新星 *supernova* **chōshinsei**
星回り *one's lucky star* **hoshimawari**
星占い *astrology, horoscope* **hoshiuranai**
星月夜 *starlight-, starry night* **hoshizukiyo**
勝ち星 *winning star* **kachiboshi**
海王星 *Planet Neptune* **kaiōsei**
綺羅星 *glittering stars* **kiraboshi**
冥王星 *Planet Pluto* **meiōsei**
天王星 *Planet Uranus* **tennōsei**
星明かり *starlight* **hoshiakari**

宇*elestial, 81*	
宙*elestial, 631*	

皇*mperor, 113*

089-A

姉lder-sister looks after the 妹ounger-sister...

女 (woman) 姉

姉 *lder sister*

ane, SHI
elder sister

FLIP: 7.0.b1. Right (stem)

姉君	elder sister (honorific)	**anegimi**
姉御	one's elder sister (honorific)	**anego**
姉貴	husband of one's elder sister	**aneki**
姉婿	brother-in-law	**anemuko**
姉娘	elder daughter	**anemusume**
姉様	elder sister (honorific)	**anesama**
姉上	elder sister	**aneue**
義姉	elder sister-in-law, elder stepsister	**gishi**
義姉妹	elder sister-in-law, elder stepsister	**gishimai**
従姉	elder female cousin	**itoko, jūshi**
実姉	blood elder sister	**jisshi**
姉様	elder sister	**anesama**
令姉	one's elder sister (honorific)	**reishi**
姉妹	sisters, female siblings	**shimai**
姉妹都市	sister city	**shimai toshi**
姉妹編	companion books	**shimaihen**
姉妹校	sister school	**shimaikō**

諸姉 *"dear friends, ladies..."* **shoshi**
十姉妹 *lovebirds; society flinch* **jūshimatsu, jūshimai**
又従姉 *elder female cousin* **mataitoko**
諸兄姉 *"dear all, ladies & gentlemen..."* **shokeishi**

> 妹*ounger sister, 114*
> 弟*ounger brother, 102*
> 兄*lder-brother, 203*

妹*ounger sister, 114*

089-B

姉lder-sister looks after the 妹ounger-sister...

女 (woman) 妹

妹 *ounger sister*

imōto, MAI
younger sister

FLIP: 7.0.b1. Right (stem)

義妹	younger sister-in-law; younger stepsister	**gimai**
義姉妹	younger sister-in-law; ~stepsister	**gishimai**
愚妹	*"my foolish younger sister..."* (humble)	**gumai**
妹背	man & wife; brother & sister	**imose**
妹婿	husband of a younger sister	**imōtomuko**
妹娘	younger daughter	**imōto musume**
妹御	*"your younger sister..."* (honorific)	**imōtogo**
従妹	younger female cousin	**itoko**
実妹	blood younger sister	**jitsumai**
姉妹	sisters, female siblings	**shimai**
姉妹都市	sister city	**shimai toshi**
姉妹編	companion piece	**shimaihen**
姉妹校	sister school	**shimaikō**
弟妹	younger brother or sister	**teimai**
十姉妹	lovebirds	**jūshimatsu**
充姉妹	younger female cousin	**jūshimai**
又従妹	second female cousin	**mataitoko**

> 姉*lder sister, 114*
> 弟*ounger brother, 102*
> 兄*lder-brother, 203*

姉*lder sister, 114*

090-A

Beaten black & 青lue, 責ondemned without a clue...

青⇔青 (blue)

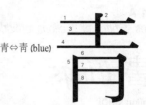

❶青*lue colour*　❷青*nripe*

ao(i), ao, SEI, SHŌ
blue colour; unripe, *green*

FLIP: 1.0.b. Whole (stem)

❶青っぽい *bluish* **aoppoi**
青青 *deep blue, navy blue* **aoao**
青畳 *fresh-, new tatami mat* **aodatami**
青蛙 *green frog* **aogaeru**
青息 *panting, grasping air* **aoiki**
青豆 *green peas* **aomame**
青物 *greens, vegetables* **aomono**
青色 *blue colour* **aoiro, seishoku**
青筋 *blue veins, arteries* **aosuji**
青田 *green paddy field* **aota**
青空 *blue sky, sapphire sky* **aozora**
群青 *ultramarine* **gunjō**
紺青 *deep blue, navy blue* **konjō**
青銅 *bronze* **seidō**
青磁 *celadon* **seiji**
青果 *fruits & vegetables* **seika**
青果物 *cyanide* **seikabutsu**
青酸 *cyanic acid* **seisan**
青天 *blue sky, sapphire sky* **seiten**

青雲 *blue sky, sapphire sky* **seiun**
青雲の志 *lofty ambitions* **seiun no kokorozashi**
青黒い *black & blue, dark-green* **aoguroi**
青写真 *blueprint* **aojashin**
青海原 *blue sea* **aounabara**
真っ青 *deep blue, navy blue* **massao**

❷青春 *youth, minority age* **seishun**
青年 *youth, minority age* **seinen**
青臭い *inexperienced, greenhorn* **aokusai**
青少年 *minor, under-aged* **seishōnen**

赤*ed colour, 261*	若*outhful, 276*
熟*aturity, 152*	君*[younger], 258*

責*ondemn, 115*

090-B

Beaten black & 青lue, 責ondemned without a clue...

貝 (shell, old money)

責*ondemn*　責*esponsible*

se(meru), SEKI
condemn, responsible, liability, accountable, denounce, duty-bound

FLIP: 1.0.b. Whole (stem)

文責 *literary responsibility* **bunseki**
言責 *responsibility for one's utterance* **genseki**
引責 *taking responsibility for subordinates* **inseki**
自責 *self-reproach, censure oneself* **jiseki**
自責点 *earned innings (baseball)* **jisekiten**
重責 *heavy responsibility* **jūseki**
譴責 *reprimand, censure* **kenseki**
免責 *immunity, exemption* **menseki**
面責 *personal responsibility* **menseki**
問責 *censure, rebuke* **monseki**
責務 *duty, obligation, responsibility* **sekimu**
責任 *responsibility* **sekinin**
責任感 *sense of responsibility* **sekininkan**
責任者 *officer-in-charge* **sekininsha**
責苦 *torture, torment* **semeku**
叱責 *dressing-down, scolding, reprimand* **shisseki**
職責 *work duties, job description* **shokuseki**
罪責 *criminal liability* **zaiseki**
火責め *fire torture* **hizeme**

自賠責 *automobile insurance* **jibaiseki**
水責め *water torture* **mizuzeme**
無責任 *lirresponsible* **musekinin**
無答責 *non-liability* **mutōseki**
湯責め *boiling water torture* **yuzeme**
刑事責任 *criminal liability* **keiji sekinin**
責め道具 *torture devices* **seme dōgu**
担保責任 *mortgage obligations* **tanpo sekinin**
責め立てる *torture, torment; urging* **semetateru**
責め付ける *unsparing critique* **semetsukeru**

撃*ttack, 613*	討*ttack, 691*
攻*ttack, 635*	伐*ttack, 96*
襲*ttack, 630*	批*riticize, 466*

青*lue colour, 115*

091-A
Tales 書ritten of 事ctions forbidden...

日 (sunlight, daytime)

書*ritings*　　書*ook*

ka(ku), SHO
writings, write, book

FLIP: 2.0.a. Sort Of (flat)
FLIP: 4.0.a. Bottom (flat)

愛書 *favourite book* **aisho**
悪書 *poor handwriting, illegible* **akusho**
文書 *writing, document* **bunsho**
読書 *book reading* **dokusho**
白書 *official policy; white paper* **hakusho**
秘書 *private secretary* **hisho**
辞書 *dictionary* **jisho**
聖書 *Holy Bible* **seisho**
信書 *letter, correspondence* **shinsho**
親書 *handwritten-, autographed letter* **shinsho**
書道 *Kanji calligraphy* **shodō**
書風 *calligraphy style* **shofū**
書記 *general-secretary* **shoki**
書類 *papers, documents* **shorui**
書店 *bookstore, bookshop* **shoten**
草書 *cursive, running style* **sōsho**
投書 *newspaper contribution* **tōsho**
全書 *complete selection, compendium* **zensho**
供述書 *deposition, sworn statement* **kyōjutsusho**

履歴書 *resume, curriculum vitae* **rirekisho**
品書き *menu, catalogue* **shinagaki**
証明書 *certificate, proof* **shōmeisho**
図書館 *library* **toshokan**
裏書き *endorsement* **uragaki**
書き込む *write in, take down notes* **kakikomu**
書き言葉 *written language* **kakikotoba**
書き残す *leave behind a writing* **kakinokosu**
書き取り *dictation* **kakitori**
書き写す *copy by handwriting* **kakiutsusu**
読み書き *reading & writing* **yomikaki**

筆*riting-brush, 141*　文*iteracy, 558*
冊*[books], 20*　字*etter, 346*
本*ook, 461*　記*ecord, 728*

量*uantity, 451*

091-B
Tales 書ritten of 事ctions forbidden...

亅 (hook, barb)

事*ction*　　事*ctivity*

koto, JI, ZU
action, activity, things, *something*

FLIP: 2.0.b. Sort Of (stem)

万事 *everything, all things* **banji**
判事 *presiding judge, magistrate* **hanji**
返事 *answer, reply, response* **henji**
事実 *fact, fait accompli* **jijitsu**
事件 *incident, case, affair* **jiken**
事故 *accident, incident, mishap* **jiko**
事項 *items for discussion, agenda* **jikō**
人事 *personnel affairs, human resources* **jinji**
事態 *situation, condition* **jitai**
従事 *being engaged* **jūji**
火事 *fire outbreak* **kaji**
家事 *domestic work, chores, errands* **kaji**
刑事 *detective, prosecutor* **keiji**
記事 *news article, news item* **kiji**
工事 *construction works* **kōji**
事柄 *matter, affair, business* **kotogara**
難事 *difficult thing, hard task* **nanji**
領事 *consul* **ryōji**
仕事 *work, job, occupation* **shigoto**

食事 *meal, dinner, supper* **shokuji**
徒事 *petty thing, trivial matter* **tadagoto**
俗事 *daily grind, routine* **zokuji**
出来事 *occurrence, happenstance* **dekigoto**
不祥事 *scandal, disgrace* **fushōji**
祝い事 *fortunate occasion* **iwaigoto**
事務所 *small office* **jimusho**
考え事 *something to think about* **kangaegoto**
府知事 *metropolitan governor (Ōsaka)* **fuchiji**
道知事 *metropolitan governor (Hokkaidō)* **dōchiji**
県知事 *prefectural governor* **kenchiji**
都知事 *metropolitan governor (Tōkyō)* **tochiji**
願い事 *wish, something to ask* **negaigoto**
笑い事 *laughing stock, joke* **waraigoto**

活*ctivity, 237*　　動*ovement, 422*

妻*arried lady, 611*

092-A
蒸*teamed bread* 承*pproved as the main food...*

⺾ (grass)

蒸*team*　　蒸*apour*

mu(su), mu(reru), mu(rasu), JŌ, SEI
steam, vapour, evaporate

FLIP: 3.0.b. Top (stem)
Facing: 1.1. ☞ West (H)

蒸発	*evaporation, vaporization*	**jōhatsu**
蒸発熱	*vapour heat*	**jōhatsunetsu**
蒸発皿	*evaporating dish*	**jōhatsuzara**
蒸気	*steam, vapour heat*	**jōki**
蒸気タービン	*steam turbine*	**jōki tābin**
蒸気圧	*steam pressure*	**jōkiatsu**
蒸気船	*steamboat, ~ship*	**jōkisen**
蒸気機関	*steam engine*	**jōki kikan**
蒸民	*the people, masses*	**jōmin**
蒸留	*distillation, condensation*	**jōryū**
蒸留酒	*distilled liquor, ~alcohol*	**jōryūshu**
蒸散	*transpiration, occurrence*	**jōsan**
勲蒸	*fumigating*	**kunjō**
蒸釜	*steam kettle*	**mushigama**
蒸鍋	*steamer, casserole*	**mushinabe**
蒸籠	*steam basket*	**seirō**
蒸し器	*food steamer*	**mushiki**
蒸し物	*steamed food*	**mushimono**
蒸し暑い	*sultry, humid, skodgy*	**mushiatsui**

蒸し風呂	*steam bath, turkish bath*	**mushiburo**
蒸し菓子	*steamed cake*	**mushigashi**
蒸し返す	*re-steam, rehash*	**mushikaesu**
空蒸し	*steamed food*	**karamushi**
御飯蒸	*rice steamer*	**gohanmushi**
蒸気力	*steam power*	**jōkiryoku**
蒸留水	*distilled water*	**jōryūsui**
川蒸汽	*river steamboat*	**kawajōki**
陸蒸気	*steam train*	**okajōki**
水蒸気	*water vapour*	**suijōki**
茶碗蒸し	*steamed egg dish*	**chawanmushi**

食*uisine*, 255	火*ire, 3*
汽*team, 98*	水*ater, 9*
燃*urning, 445*	

承*pproval, 117*

092-B
蒸*teamed bread* 承*pproved as the main food...*

手⇔扌 (hand, manual)

承*pproval*　　承*onsent*

uketamawa(ru), SHŌ
approval, consent, concur, agreement

Facing: 1.0. ☞ West (W)

伝承	*tradition, transmission*	**denshō**
⇒民間伝承	*folklore, folktale*	**minkan denshō**
拝承	*"I was informed that..."*	**haishō**
継承	*succession to the throne*	**keishō**
⇒王位継承	*succession to the throne*	**ōikeishō**
継承者	*successor, heir, replacement*	**keishōsha**
口承	*oral tradition, oral history*	**kōshō**
了承	*acknowledgement, consent*	**ryōshō**
諒承	*acknowledge, take note*	**ryōshō**
承知	*agreement, approval, consent*	**shōchi**
承諾	*consent, assent, approval*	**shōdaku**
⇒事後承諾	*ex-post facto consent*	**jigo shōdaku**
承服	*consent, assent, approval*	**shōfuku**
承引	*consent, approval*	**shōin**
承継	*succession, inheritance, continuity*	**shōkei**
承認	*approval, agreeing, consent*	**shōnin**
承前	*continued from the previous text*	**shōzen**
相承	*inherited, acquired*	**sōshō**
不承知	*disapproval, refusal, denial*	**fushōchi**

不承諾	*refusal, non-consent*	**fushōdaku**
不承不承	*grudging, reluctant*	**fushō bushō**
永承時代	*Eijō Era (1046-1053)*	**eijō jidai**
承安時代	*Jōan Era (1171-1175)*	**jōan jidai**
承元時代	*Jōgen Era (1207-1211)*	**jōgen jidai**
承久時代	*Jōkyū Era (1219-1222)*	**jōkyū jidai**
承応時代	*Jōō Era (1652-1655)*	**jōō jidai**
承暦時代	*Jōryaku Era (1077-1081)*	**jōryaku jidai**
嘉承時代	*Kajō Era (1106-1108)*	**kajō jidai**
承平時代	*Shōhei Era (931-938)*	**shōhei jidai**
承和時代	*Shōwa Era (834-848)*	**shōwa jidai**

可*pproval, 15*	可*onsent, 15*
賛*pproval, 334*	諾*oncur, 277*
肯*ffirmative, 616*	

蒸*team, 117*

093-A
Swords to 削*harpen* 前*efore battles happen...*

刀⇔刂 (blade, cutting)

削*harpen*　　削*rind*

kezu(ru), so(gu), SAKU
sharpen, grind, chippings

FLIP: 6.0.b. Left (stem)

削り節　*dried fish shavings*　**kezuribushi**
削りくず　*shavings, chips*　**kezurikuzu**
削り取る　*scrape, rub*　**kezuritoru**
筆削　*writing erasure*　**hissaku**
開削　*excavation, diggings*　**kaisaku**
研削　*grinding*　**kensaku**
研削盤　*grinding plate*　**kensakuban**
掘削　*excavation, diggings*　**kussaku**
掘削機　*excavator, steam shovel*　**kussakuki**
削減　*reduction, curtailment*　**sakugen**
削片　*splinter, chip, shard*　**sakuhen**
削除　*elimination, deletion*　**sakujo**
旋削　*turning on a lathe*　**sensaku**
切削　*mining cut, machining*　**sessaku**
添削　*correction, marking test papers*　**tensaku**
荒削り　*roughing, sharpening*　**arakezuri**
削岩機　*rock drilling machine*　**sakuganki**
一字削り　*delete a letter, ~a character*　**ichijikezuri**

兵員削減　*troop reduction*　**heiin sakugen**
鉛筆削り　*pencil sharpening*　**enpitsu kezuri**
鉛筆削り器　*pencil sharpener*　**enpitsu kezuriki**

鋭*harp*, 943	擦*riction*, 329
研*olish*, 951	摩*crape*, 331
錬*olish*, 718	

消*xtinguish*, 265

093B
Swords to 削*harpen* 前*efore battles happen...*

刀⇔刂 (blade, cutting)

❶前*efore*　　❷前*rontal*

mae, ZEN
before, erstwhile, previous; anterior, frontal

FLIP: 3.0.a. Top (flat)
Facing: 1.2. 🠒 West (V)

❶前金　*advance payment, deposit*　**maekin**
前払い　*advance payment, deposit*　**maebarai**
前もって　*in advance, beforehand*　**maemotte**
午前　*in the morning*　**gozen**
前半　*first half*　**zenhan, zenpan**
前科　*criminal record*　**zenka**
前回　*last time*　**zenkai**
前期　*first semester, first term*　**zenki**
前記　*previous item*　**zenki**
前奏　*prelude, overture music*　**zensō**
前提　*premise, assumption*　**zentei**
紀元前　*B.C. (before Jesus Christ)*　**kigenzen**
前科者　*ex-convict, released felon*　**zenkamono**
前々日　*day before yesterday*　**zenzenjitsu**
婚前性交　*pre-marital sex, fornication*　**konzen seikō**
霊前　*dead spirits, departed spirits*　**reizen**
前言　*previous remarks*　**zengen**

❷人前　*in public, in front of others*　**hitomae**

腕前　*skill, ability, agility*　**udemae**
前衛　*avant guard, vanguard*　**zen'ei**
前後　*approximately, front & back*　**zengo**
前景　*foreground scene, horizon*　**zenkei**
前面　*front, façade*　**zenmen**
前線　*frontline*　**zensen**
真ん前　*right in front*　**manmae**
目の前　*"in the presence of..."*　**menomae**
門前町　*cathedral-, temple town*　**monzenmachi**
建て前　*pretext; ridgepole raising*　**tatemae**
割り前　*share, cut*　**warimae**
当たり前　*natural, proper, the right thing*　**atarimae**

先*head*, 478
面*urface*, 36

削*rind*, 118

094-A
衷 nner feelings 喪 ourn death of the unborn...

衣⇔衤 (clothing)

衷 nner feelings

CHŪ
inner feelings, real emotions

FLIP: 3.0.a. Top (flat)
Facing: 2.0. East ☞ (W)

微衷 real intention, innermost feelings **bichū**
衷情 deepest feelings **chūjō**
衷心 innermost-, bottom of the heart **chūshin**
苦衷 dilemma, predicament **kuchū**
折衷 compromise, concession **secchū**
⇒和洋折衷 blending of Japanese & Western styles
　　wayō secchū
折衷主義 eclecticism **secchū shugi**
和衷 harmony **wachū**

感 eelings, 45	隠 onceal, 840
気 eelings, 98	匿 onceal, 277
情 eelings, 793	忍 onceal, 535
陰 idden, 864	覆 onceal, 602
隠 idden, 840	内 nside, 297
秘 idden, 219	奥 nside, 903

衰 ecline, 374

094-B
衷 nner feelings 喪 ourn death of the unborn...

口 (mouth)

喪 ourning　喪 ereavement

mo, SŌ
mourning, grief, bereavement, funeral

FLIP: 3.0.a. Top (flat)
Facing: 2.0. East ☞ (W)

服喪 mourning, grieving, wailing **fukumo**
発喪 death notices, ~bulletin **hatsumo**
国喪 state mourning **kokusō**
喪中 mourning, grieving, wailing **mochū**
喪服 mourning attire **mofuku**
喪章 mourning badge **moshō**
喪主 chief mourner, bereaved family **moshu**
喪具 funeral ornaments (Buddhism) **sōgu**
喪家 bereaved family **sōka**
喪心 stupor, absent-minded **sōshin**
喪神 stupor, absent-minded **sōshin**
喪失 loss, missing, unfound **sōshitsu**
⇒記憶喪失 amnesia, memory lapse **kioku sōshitsu**
⇒心神喪失 lunatic, whacko **shinshin sōshitsu**
⇒書類喪失 loss of documents **shorui sōshitsu**
阻喪 discouragement, depression **sosō**
沮喪 dejection **sosō**
大喪 imperial mourning **taisō**

弔 ourning, 538	死 eath, 513
忌 ourning, 6	逝 eath, 54
愁 orrows, 415	亡 eath, 72
悲 orrows, 289	

衷 nner feelings, 119

095-A

Shoplifters 奔unning-away, 茶ea bags taken away...

奔*un-away*   奔*ush*

大 (grand)

FLIP: 2.0.b. Sort Of (stem)

HON
run-away, rush

奔馬	*wild galloping horse*	**honba**
奔放	*unrestrained, wild*	**honpō**
奔流	*torrent, rapid stream*	**honryū**
奔出	*gushing out, spouting*	**honshutsu**
奔走	*good offices, mediation*	**honsō**
奔騰	*soaring, skyrocketing*	**hontō**
淫奔	*wantonness, lewdness*	**inpon**
狂奔	*busy, full, occupied*	**kyōhon**
出奔	*running away, galloping*	**shuppon**
東奔西走	*get busy*	**tōhon seisō**

走*unning, 497*　　尽*ursue, 574*
逃*scape, 216*　　逐*rive-out, 479*
追*ursue, 108*

茶*ea, 120*

095-B

Shoplifters 奔unning-away, 茶ea bags taken away...

茶*ea*

⧾⧾ (grass)

FLIP: 1.0.b. Whole (stem)

CHA, SA
tea

番茶	*coarse tea, unrefined tea*	**bancha**
茶腹	*overdrinking tea*	**chabara**
茶瓶	*teapot, tea kettle*	**chabin**
茶道	*tea ceremony*	**chadō, sadō**
茶園	*tea plantation, ~garden*	**chaen**
茶釜	*tea kettle, teapot*	**chagama**
茶殻	*consumed tea leaves*	**chagara**
茶色	*brown*	**chairo**
茶菓	*tea refreshments, ~sweets*	**chaka, saka**
茶会	*tea party, ~ceremony*	**chakai**
茶缶	*tea canister*	**chakan**
茶器	*tea set*	**chaki**
茶目	*pranks, mischief*	**chame**
茶室	*tea ceremony room*	**chashitsu**
茶碗	*tea cup*	**chawan**
茶屋	*tea dealer, ~shop*	**chaya**
紅茶	*tea, black tea*	**kōcha**
抹茶	*green tea powder*	**maccha**
銘茶	*well-known tea brand*	**meicha**

麦茶	*barley tea*	**mugicha**
緑茶	*green tea*	**ryokucha**
茶の間	*living room, parlour*	**chanoma**
茶飲み	*tea drinking*	**chanomi**
茶の湯	*tea ceremony*	**chanoyu**
茶断ち	*tea abstinence*	**chadachi**
茶こし	*tea strainer*	**chakoshi**
茶さじ	*teaspoon*	**chasaji**
喫茶店	*tea shop, coffee shop*	**kissaten**
焦げ茶	*dark brown*	**kogecha**
茶飯事	*everyday happenstance*	**sahanji**

飲*rink, 255*
渇*hirsty, 808*
憩*elaxation, 169*

奔*un-away, 120*

096-A

The 寒hilling 実eality: No equality!

ウ (cover, lid)

FLIP: 2.0.b. Sort Of (stem)

寒old　　寒hills

samu(i), KAN
cold, chills, chilling

朝寒 *morning chill, morning cold* **asasamu**
大寒 *coldest season* **daikan**
寒地 *cold region* **kanchi**
寒中 *midwinter* **kanchū**
寒暖 *temperature reading* **kandan**
寒暖計 *thermometer* **kandankei**
寒害 *winter damage* **kangai**
寒極 *extreme cold in Artic & Antarctica* **kankyoku**
寒波 *cold wave* **kanpa**
寒貧 *extremely poor* **kanpin**
寒風 *cold wind, icy wind* **kanpū**
寒流 *cold current* **kanryū**
寒心 *lamentable, deplorable, regrettable* **kanshin**
寒色 *cold colours* **kanshoku**
寒村 *deserted village* **kanson**
寒帯 *frigid zone's* **kantai**
寒天 *wintry sky; jelly* **kanten**
向寒 *getting colder* **kōkan**
悪寒 *chills* **okan**

寒気 *cold, chills* **samuke, kanki**
寒寒 *cold, chilly* **samuzamu**
寒空 *cold weather, wintry sky* **samuzora**
小寒 *period of lesser cold, lukewarm* **shōkan**
耐寒 *cold-proofing, cold resistance* **taikan**
余寒 *residual-, lingering cold* **yokan**
亜寒帯 *sub-arctic-, sub-antarctic zone* **akantai**
肌寒い *chilly, cold* **hadasamui, hadazamui**
避寒地 *winter resort* **hikanchi**
寒の入り *beginning of winter* **kan no iri**
薄ら寒い *chilly* **usurasamui, usurazamui**

冷 *hilly, 684*		氷 *reeze, 10*	
氷 *ce, 10*		冬 *inter, 397*	
凍 *reeze, 221*			

実 *eality, 121*

096-B

The 寒hilling 実eality: No equality!

ウ (cover, lid)

FLIP: 1.0.b. Whole (stem)

実eality　　実ruth

mi, mino(ru), JITSU
reality, truth, genuine, authentic, veracity

着実 *steady, stable, constant* **chakujitsu**
忠実 *loyal, faithful* **chūjitsu**
事実 *fact, truth* **jijitsu**
⇒既成事実 *given fact, established fact* **kisei jijitsu**
実家 *parents' house* **jikka**
実感 *genuine feelings* **jikkan**
実刑 *penal sentence, punishment* **jikkei**
実験 *experiment, trial, "test balloon"* **jikken**
実行 *execution, putting into action* **jikkō**
実況 *real condition* **jikkyō**
実費 *actual expenses incurred* **jippi**
実際 *fact, truth, reality* **jissai**
実績 *actual results, ~outcome* **jisseki**
実践 *puting into practice* **jissen**
実施 *enforcing, carrying out* **jisshi**
実現 *realization, materialization* **jitsugen**
実技 *performance, real ability* **jitsugi**
実業 *business, industry* **jitsugyō**
実印 *registered-, official seal* **jitsuin**

実力 *real ability, actual capability* **jitsuryoku**
実用 *practice use* **jitsuyō**
情実 *personal consideration* **jōjitsu**
充実 *fulfilment, attainment* **jūjitsu**
果実 *fruit* **kajitsu**
確実 *sure, certain, unmistakable* **kakujitsu**
堅実 *steadiness, stability* **kenjitsu**
誠実 *sincere, genuine* **seijitsu**
史実 *historical fact* **shijitsu**
真実 *truth, reality* **shinjitsu**
実習生 *intern, trainee* **jisshūsei**

真 *incere, 487*		廉 *onest, 525*
誠 *incere, 245*		

宝 *reasure, 92*

097-A
候limate in Hebron wooed the 候aron...

候*limate*   候*eather*

人 ⇔ 亻 (person)

Facing: 1.2. ⟿ West (V)

sōrō, KŌ
climate, weather, temperature

兆候 *sign, symptoms* **chōkō**
徴候 *sign, symptoms* **chōkō**
潮候 *tide season* **chōkō**
居候 *parasite, freeloader, free rider* **isōrō**
時候 *season, weather* **jikō**
気候 *climate, weather* **kikō**
気候学 *study of weather, climatology* **kikōgaku**
気候帯 *climate zone* **kikōtai**
候鳥 *migratory birds* **kōchō**
候補 *candidate, nominee* **kōho**
候補地 *proposed site* **kōhochi**
候補者 *candidate, nominee* **kōhosha**
斥候 *scout, patrol, reconnoitring* **sekkō**
伺候 *waiting for someone* **shikō**
症候 *symptoms, signs of illness* **shōkō**
症候群 *syndrome, symptoms* **shōkōgun**
候文 *Japanese literary classics* **sōrōbun**
天候 *weather, climate* **tenkō**

悪天候 *inclement weather* **akutenkō**
測候所 *weather observatory* **sokkōjo**
立候補者 *election candidate* **rikkō hosha**
士官候補生 *military cadet* **shikan kōhosei**

季*eason,* 583
節*eason,* 421
空*ky,* 394

候*aron,* 122

097-B
候limate in Hebron wooed the 侯aron...

侯*aron*   侯*obility*

人 ⇔ 亻 (person)

Facing: 1.2. ⟿ West (V)

KŌ
baron, nobility, feudal lord, aristocrat

侯爵 *marquis, marquess* **kōshaku**
侯爵夫人 *marchioness* **kōshaku fujin**
王侯 *nobility, royalty, aristocracy* **ōkō**
諸侯 *feudal lord, Daimyo* **shokō**
列侯 *a line of feudal lords* **rekkō**
藩侯 *feudal lord, Daimyo* **hankō**
小村寿太郎侯 *Baron Jutarō Komura (1855-1911)*
   komura jutarō-kō

宮*rince,* 105   爵*ristocrat,* 593
妃*rincess,* 728   姫*rincess,* 542

候*limate,* 122

098-A

菓weets on the 巣est for little Agnes...

.⁺⁺ (grass)

菓*onfectionery*   菓*weets*

KA
confectionery, sweets, candies, snacks

FLIP: 1.0.b. Whole (stem)

米菓 *rice crackers* **beika**
茶菓 *tea & cakes, refreshments* **chaka**
氷菓 *ice cream, ice candy* **hyōka**
菓子 *sweets, confectionery* **kashi**
菓子器 *candy tray* **kashiki**
菓子屋 *candy-, sweet shop* **kashiya**
菓子皿 *cake dish, sweets plate* **kashizara**
菓子折り *box of sweets* **kashiori**
銘菓 *brand-name sweets* **meika**
冷菓 *chilled sweets, ~candies* **reika**
製菓 *confectionery, sweets* **seika**
製菓業 *confectionery industry* **seikagyō**
粗菓 *cakes, sweets* **soka**
糖菓 *confectionery, sweets* **tōka**
茶菓子 *tea cake, refreshments* **chagashi**
駄菓子 *cheap sweets* **dagashi**
干菓子 *dried sweets* **higashi**
水菓子 *water-based sweets* **mizugashi**
生菓子 *fresh sweets* **namagashi**

和菓子 *Japanese sweets* **wagashi**
洋菓子 *cake, confection* **yōgashi**
盛り菓子 *sweets-filled basket* **morigashi**
蒸し菓子 *steamed cake* **mushigashi**
練り菓子 *bean cake* **nerigashi**
打ち菓子 *figurine cakes* **uchigashi**

甘*weet, 395*
糖*ugar, 439*
味*aste, 871*

巣*est, 123*

098-B

菓weets on the 巣est for little Agnes...

木 (wooden)

巣*est*   巣*radle*

su, SŌ
nest, cradle

FLIP: 1.0.b. Whole (stem)

病巣 *foci* **byōsō**
病巣感染 *focal infection* **byōsō kansen**
営巣 *nest building* **eisō**
古巣 *old nest* **furusu**
蜂の巣 *beehive, honeycomb* **hachi no su**
蜂巣 *beehive, hive* **hōsō**
卵巣 *ovary* **ransō**
精巣 *spermary, testis* **seisō**
巣窟 *den, lair, haunt, hide-out* **sōkutsu**
巣箱 *bird house, hive* **subako**
空き巣 *sneak thief, burglar* **akisu**
空き巣ねらい *target of a sneak thief* **akisunerai**
帰巣性 *homing instinct* **kisōsei**
帰巣本能 *homing instinct* **kisō honnō**
蜘蛛の巣 *spider web* **kumo no su**
巣立つ *go out to the world* **sudatsu**
巣篭もる *nestle, nest-making* **sugomoru**

若*oung, 276*
寡*ittle, 161*
小*ittle, 459*

果*esult, 287*

099-A

美eauty, the 業usiness of vanity...

羊 (sheep)

美eautiful   美retty

utsuku(shii), BI
beautiful, pretty, good-looking, aesthetic

FLIP: 1.0.b. Whole (stem)

美談 *impressive tale* **bidan**
美風 *virtue, ethics, manners* **bifū**
美学 *aesthetics, sense of beauty* **bigaku**
美技 *fine performance* **bigi**
美人 *pretty woman* **bijin**
美女 *beautiful girl* **bijo**
美術 *fine arts* **bijutsu**
美化 *beautification* **bika**
美感 *sense of beauty* **bikan**
美観 *beautiful view, scenery* **bikan**
美挙 *commendable act, good deed* **bikyo**
美名 *good reputation* **bimei**
美身 *beautiful body* **bimi, bishin**
美質 *good quality, virtue* **bishitsu**
美称 *euphemism* **bishō**
美食 *rich food* **bishoku**
美点 *merit, virtue* **biten**
美徳 *virtue, deed, righteousness* **bitoku**
褒美 *reward, prize* **hōbi**

甘美 *sweet* **kanbi**
賛美 *praise, admiration* **sanbi**
審美 *aesthetic appreciation* **shinbi**
唯美 *aesthetics* **yuibi**
善美 *gorgeous, voluptuous* **zenbi**
均整美 *beauty proportion* **kinseibi**
曲線美 *beauty of curves* **kyokusenbi**
肉体美 *physical beauty* **nikutaibi**
裸体美 *naked beauty* **rataibi**
美辞麗句 *flowery expressions, highfalutin* **bijireiku**

麗eautiful, 68	雅raceful, 58
佳eauty, 891	淑raceful, 510
韻raceful, 315	

業usiness, 124

099-B

美eauty, the 業usiness of vanity...

木 (wooden)

業usiness   業ndustry

waza, GYŌ, GŌ
business, industry, enterprise, occupation, commerce, trade

FLIP: 1.0.b. Whole (stem)

営業 *management, business* **eigyō**
副業 *sideline, second job* **fukugyō**
業病 *incurable disease, terminal illness* **gōbyō**
業界 *business world* **gyōkai**
業務 *business, service* **gyōmu**
業績 *achievement, attainment* **gyōseki**
業者 *dealer, manufacturer* **gyōsha**
業種 *business category* **gyōshu**
廃業 *going-out-of-business, bankruptcy* **haigyō**
偉業 *exploits, feat* **igyō**
事業 *business, enterprise* **jigyō**
授業 *class, lesson* **jugyō**
神業 *miracle, act-of-God, divine intervention* **kamiwaza**
軽業 *acrobatics* **karuwaza**
企業 *enterprise, big business* **kigyō**
工業 *industry* **kōgyō**
農業 *agriculture, farming* **nōgyō**
作業 *manual work, blue-collar labour* **sagyō**

産業 *industry* **sangyō**
失業 *unemployment* **shitsugyō**
仕業 *act, deed* **shiwaza**
商業 *commerce, business* **shōgyō**
職業 *occupation, profession* **shokugyō**
修業 *coursework completion* **shūgyō**
就業 *employment* **shūgyō**
終業 *closing of work, ~of school* **shūgyō**
卒業 *graduation, completing school* **sotsugyō**
残業 *overtime work* **zangyō**
営業中 *"open for business..."* **eigyōchū**
接客業 *service industry* **sekkyakugyō**

工raft, 176	金oney, 25
商ommerce, 135	富ortune, 333
株orporation, 130	

美eautiful, 124

100-A
Rare 島sland 鳥irds down to two-thirds...

島*sland*

山 (mountain)

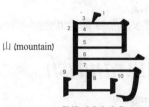

shima, TŌ
island

遠島 *distant islands* **entō**
群島 *archipelago, group of islands* **guntō**
半島 *peninsula* **hantō**
本島 *main island, the largest island* **hontō**
小島 *islet* **kojima**
孤島 *solitary island* **kotō**
中島 *island within a river* **nakajima**
列島 *islands, archipelago* **rettō**
敷島 *Shikishima (ancient Japan)* **shikishima**
島国 *island country* **shimaguni**
島国根性 *reclusive-, insularity culture*
　　　 shimaguni konjō
島影 *island's shadows* **shimakage**
諸島 *various islands* **shotō**
宝島 *treasure island* **takarajima**
島人 *island inhabitants* **tōjin**
島民 *islander, island inhabitants* **tōmin**
全島 *the archipelago, entire islands* **zentō**
絶島 *isolated island* **zettō**

FLIP: 6.2. Left Bottom
Facing: 2.0. East ☞ (W)

広島県 *Hiroshima Prefecture* **hiroshima-ken**
択捉島 *Etorofu islands, Hokkaidō* **etorofūtō**
八丈島 *Hachijohjima Island, Tōkyō* **hachijōjima**
離れ島 *solitary island* **hanarejima**
鹿児島県 *Kagoshima Pref.* **kagoshima-ken**
無人島 *uninhabited island* **mujintō**
女護島 *Isle of Amazons* **nyogoshima**
佐渡島 *Sadogashima, Niigata Pref.* **sadogashima**
珊瑚島 *coral islands* **sangotō**
島巡り *tour of the islands* **shima meguri**
島流し *banishment, exile* **shima nagashi**
島破り *escape from island exile* **shima yaburi**

海*cean, 241*	地*and, 688*
洋*cean, 247*	陸*and, 140*

鳥*irds, 125*

100-B
Rare 島sland 鳥irds down to two-thirds...

鳥*ird*　　　鳥*owl*

鳥 (birds)

tori, CHŌ
bird, fowl

愛鳥 *pet bird* **aichō**
千鳥 *plover* **chidori**
鳥人 *ace pilot, top gun* **chōjin**
鳥獣 *birds & beasts* **chōjū**
鳥銃 *bird-hunting rifle* **chōjū**
鳥類 *birds, fowls* **chōrui**
鳥葬 *leaving corpse to vultures* **chōsō**
益鳥 *one's lucky bird* **ekichō**
漁鳥 *birds & fishes* **gyochō**
蜂鳥 *humming bird* **hachidori**
白鳥 *white swan* **hakuchō**
禁鳥 *"hunting prohibited..."* **kinchō**
駒鳥 *robin* **komadori**
雌鳥 *hen* **mendori**
猛鳥 *bird of prey* **mōchō**
雄鳥 *henhouse, hencoop* **ondori**
親鳥 *mother bird* **oyadori**
雷鳥 *snow grouse* **raichō**
探鳥 *bird watching* **tanchō**

Facing: 2.0. East ☞ (W)

鳥肌 *goose flesh, ~bumps* **torihada**
鳥目 *night blindness* **torime**
海鳥 *sea bird, coastal bird* **umidori**
若鳥 *tender chicken meat* **wakadori**
野鳥 *wild bird* **yachō**
山鳥 *mountain bird* **yamadori**
極楽鳥 *birds of paradise* **gokurakuchō**
七面鳥 *turkey* **shichimenchō**
渡り鳥 *migratory bird* **wataridori**
焼き鳥 *marinated chicken barbeque* **yakitori**
一石二鳥 *"killing two birds with one stone..."*
　　　 isseki nichō

飛*light, 298*	鳴*owling, 842*
鶏*hicken, 842*	翼*ings, 239*

島*sland, 125*

101-A

Lethal syringe 揮randished, 挿nserted to punish...

手⇔扌 (hand, manual)

揮*randish*   揮*onductor*

furu(u), KI
brandish, flaunt, wield, conductor

FLIP: 7.0.b1. Right (stem)

発揮 *exhibit, display* **hakki**
揮毫 *write, sketch, paint* **kigō**
揮発 *volatilisation* **kihatsu**
揮発物 *petrol, flammable substance* **kihatsubutsu**
揮発性 *volatility, buoyancy* **kihatsusei**
揮発油 *volatile oil* **kihatsuyu**
指揮 *command, direction* **shiki**
指揮棒 *baton* **shikibō**
指揮下 *"under the command..."* **shikika**
指揮官 *commander* **shikikan**
指揮者 *orchestra conductor* **shikisha**
指揮刀 *sabre, sword* **shikitō**
総指揮 *overall command* **sōshiki**
総指揮官 *supreme commander* **sōshikikan**

揺*remble, 811*	譜*usical note, 455*
震*remble, 61*	奏*usic play, 579*
振*winging, 60*	

軍*ilitary, 295*

101-B

Lethal syringe 揮randished, 挿nserted to punish...

手⇔扌 (hand, manual)

挿*nsert*   挿*ierce*

sa(su), SŌ
insert, pierce, put inside, stabbing

FLIP: 7.1. Right (Sort Of)

挿し木 *tree-cutting* **sashiki**
挿絵 *illustration, sketch, drawing* **sashie**
挿絵画家 *illustrator, sketch artist* **sashie gaka**
外挿 *extrapolation* **gaisō**
内挿 *interpolation* **naisō**
挿画 *book illustration* **sōga**
挿花 *flower arrangement* **sōka**
挿入 *insertion, inject* **sōnyū**
挿入句 *parenthesis* **sōnyūku**
挿話 *episode, anecdote* **sōwa**
挿図 *figure, illustration* **sōzu**
一輪挿し *flower vase with one stem* **ichirinzashi**

突*hrust, 576*	徹*ierce-thru, 843*
刺*ierce, 875*	刺*ierce, 875*

揮*randish, 126*

102-A

楼ower of 桜herry blossoms look so awesome...

楼ower 楼urret

RŌ
tower, turret, tall building

木 (wooden)

FLIP: 7.2.b. Right Top (stem)

望楼 *watchtower, viewing tower* **bōrō**
妓楼 *whorehouse, brothel* **girō**
高楼 *tall building* **kōrō**
楼上 *balcony, upstairs* **rōjō**
楼閣 *main castle* **rōkaku**
楼門 *two-story building* **rōmon**
青楼 *whorehouse, brothel* **seirō**
鐘楼 *bell tower, belfry* **shōrō**
白玉楼 *"world of the dead..."* **hakugyokurō**
摩天楼 *skyscraper, skyline* **matenrō**
蜃気楼 *mirage* **shinkirō**

閣ower, 945
塔ower, 146
城astle, 243

桜herry blossom, 127

102-B

楼ower of 桜herry blossoms look so awesome...

桜herry blossom

sakura, Ō
cherry blossom, sakura, cherry

木 (wooden)

Facing: 2.2. East ☞ (V)

徒桜 *short-lived cherry blossoms* **adazakura**
葉桜 *cherry blossom leaf* **hazakura**
糸桜 *droopy cherry blossoms* **itozakura**
観桜 *cherry blossom viewing* **kan'ō**
観桜会 *cherry blossom viewing party* **kan'ōkai**
桜花 *cherry blossoms* **ōka, sakurabana**
桜桃 *cherry blossom tree* **ōtō**
桜色 *pink colour* **sakurairo**
桜時 *cherry-blossom season* **sakuradoki**
桜貝 *tellinacean, cherry shell* **sakuragai**
桜肉 *horse meat* **sakuraniku**
桜草 *primrose* **sakurasō**
山桜 *wild cherry tree* **yamazakura**
夜桜 *cherry-blossom tree at night* **yozakura**
美女桜 *verbena* **bijozakura**
彼岸桜 *early cherry blossoms* **higanzakura**
桜ん坊 *cherry* **sakuranbō**
桜漬け *pickled cherry blossom leaves* **sakurazuke**

桜前線 *cherry-blossom lined road*
  sakura zensen
八重桜 *double cherry blossoms* **yaezakura**
枝垂れ桜 *weeping cherry* **shidare zakura**

咲looming, 707	華lower, 40
花lower, 191	桃each, 215

楼ower, 127

103-A

留ettlers 留tayed in barter 貿rade...

田 (cultivated field)

留

FLIP: 4.0.a. Bottom (flat)

留taying 留ettle

to(meru), to(maru), RYŪ, RU
staying, settle, keeping

分留	fractional distillation	**bunryū**
駐留	troop deployment	**chūryū**
慰留	persuade not to resign	**iryū**
蒸留	distillation, carbonisation	**jōryū**
書留	registered mail	**kakitome**
乾留	distillation, carbonisation	**kanryū**
繋留	mooring, berthing	**keiryū**
係留	mooring, berthing	**keiryū**
寄留	temporary stay	**kiryū**
勾留	detention, internment, confinement	**kōryū**
拘留	custody, detention	**kōryū**
帯留	sash clip	**obidome**
留守	absence, non-attendance	**rusu**
留守番	remaining in place as caretaker	**rusuban**
留守番電話	voice mail	**rusuban denwa**
留置	custody, detention	**ryūchi**
留学	overseas studies	**ryūgaku**
留学生	foreign student	**ryūgakusei**
留保	reserving one's rights	**ryūho**

留意	paying attention	**ryūi**
留年	flunking an academic year	**ryūnen**
留任	staying in office	**ryūnin**
逗留	stay, sojourn	**tōryū**
抑留	detention, internment, imprisonment	**yokuryū**
在留	residing, living	**zairyū**
残留	staying behind	**zanryū**
保留所	concentration camp	**horyūjo**
停留所	bus stop	**teiryūjo**
局留め	general delivery, poster	**kyokudome**
取り留める	ascertain, establish	**toritomeru**

滞taying, 557	宅esidence, 82
居esidence, 384	邸esidence, 860
住esidence, 750	

貿rading, 128

103-B

留ettlers 留tayed in barter 貿rade...

貝 (shell, old money)

貿

FLIP: 4.0.b. Bottom (stem)

貿rading 貿arter

BŌ
trading, trade, barter

貿易	trade, trading, import & export	**bōeki**
⇒保護貿易	trade protectionism	**hogo bōeki**
⇒自由貿易	free trade	**jiyū bōeki**
⇒海外貿易	foreign-, overseas trade	**kaigai bōeki**
⇒輸出入貿易	export-import trade	**yushutsunyū bōeki**
貿易国	trading country	**bōekikoku**
貿易商	trader, merchant	**bōekishō**
貿易品	import-, export goods	**bōekihin**
貿易場	overseas market	**bōekijō**
片貿易	one-sided trade (import or export)	**katabōeki**
密貿易	smuggling, black-market trading	**mitsubōeki**
貿易赤字	trade deficit, ~in the red	**bōeki akaji**
貿易会社	trading company	**bōeki gaisha**
貿易業者	trader, merchant	**bōeki gyōsha**
貿易黒字	trade surplus, in the black	**bōeki kuroji**
貿易摩擦	trade friction	**bōeki masatsu**
貿易収支	balance of trade	**bōeki shūshi**

貿易相手国	trading partner	**bōeki aitekoku**
貿易不均衡	trade imbalance	**bōeki fukinkō**

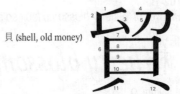

交rossing, 467	販elling, 137
購urchase, 714	益rofit, 622
買urchase, 516	得rofit, 940
売elling, 259	

留ettle, 128

104-A

On the 階tairs of the dynasty rules Her 陛ajesty...

ß ⇔ 阜 (village, right)

階tairs　　階evel

KAI
stairs, storeys, level

地階 *basement, underground-level* **chikai**
段階 *stage, rank* **dankai**
位階 *imperial rank* **ikai**
一階 *ground floor* **ikkai**
階段 *stairs, staircase, ladder* **kaidan**
⇒非常階段 *emergency staircase* **hijō kaidan**
階位 *grade, rank, status* **kaii**
階乗 *factorial* **kaijō**
階上 *upper floor* **kaijō**
階下 *lower floor* **kaika**
階級 *class, rank, grade* **kaikyū**
⇒中層階級 *middle class* **chūsō kaikyū**
⇒無産階級 *classless society* **musan kaikyū**
⇒有閑階級 *leisure class, elite* **yūkan kaikyū**
階級意識 *class consciousness* **kaikyū ishiki**
階級闘争 *class struggle* **kaikyū tōsō**
階層 *class, stratum, floor level* **kaisō**
階層的 *stratification, hierarchical* **kaisōteki**
階梯 *stairs, staircase, ladder* **kaitei**

FLIP: 7.3.a. Right Bottom (flat)

各階 *each floor, all floors* **kakukai**
音階 *musical notes* **onkai**
⇒長音階 *music major scale* **chōonkai**
⇒半音階 *chromatic scale* **han'onkai**
三階 *third floor* **sankai, sangai**
職階 *civil service rank* **shokkai**
職階制 *job ranking system* **shokkaisei**
二階家 *two-story house* **nikaiya**
二階建て *two-story house* **nikaidate**
短音階 *music minor scale* **tan'onkai**

等*rade, 251*	級*evel, 189*
格*tatus, 498*	準*evel, 919*

陛*ajesty, 129*

104-B

On the 階tairs of the dynasty rules Her 陛ajesty...

ß ⇔ 阜 (village, right)

陛ajesty

HEI
imperial highness, majesty, royal highness

陛下 *His Majesty, Her Majesty* **heika**
女王陛下 *Her Majesty, the Queen* **joō heika**
皇后陛下 *Her Majesty, the Empress* **kōgō heika**
天皇陛下 *His Majesty, the Emperor* **tennō heika**

FLIP: 7.3.a. Right Bottom (flat)

王*onarch, 12*	帝*mpire, 432*
皇*mperor, 113*	后*mpress, 87*

階*tairs, 129*

105-A
Social 称itles & 株tocks, pride of aristocrats...

禾 (tree branch)

称itular 称itle

tata(eru), SHŌ
titular, title, appelation

FLIP: 7.1. Right (Sort Of)
Facing: 1.2. 🢀 West (V)

愛称 *nickname* **aishō**
蔑称 *insult, slur, derogatory term* **besshō**
遠称 *non-proximal terms* **enshō**
偽称 *stolen identity, impostor* **gishō**
併称 *ranking with* **heishō**
異称 *another name* **ishō**
自称 *self-professed, ~avowed* **jishō**
仮称 *tentative name* **kashō**
過称 *undeserved praise* **kashō**
敬称 *honorary title* **keishō**
近称 *proximal terms* **kinshō**
誇称 *exaggeration, boasting* **koshō**
呼称 *name to call* **koshō**
公称 *official, nominal* **kōshō**
旧称 *former title, ex-rank* **kyūshō**
名称 *name, title* **meishō**
人称 *personal pronoun* **ninshō**
略称 *abbreviation, short name, acronym* **ryakushō**
詐称 *misrepresentation, fraud, deceit* **sashō**

称美 *praise, admiration, adulation* **shōbi**
称号 *title, degree* **shōgō**
称賛 *praise, admiration, adulation* **shōsan**
尊称 *honorific title* **sonshō**
総称 *generic name* **sōshō**
相称 *symmetry, proportion* **sōshō**
対称 *symmetry, proportion* **taishō**
他称 *third person, third party* **tashō**
通称 *nickname, popular name* **tsūshō**
俗称 *popular name, nickname* **zokushō**

氏*urname, 489*	記*ecord, 728*
姓*urname, 638*	号*umber, 866*
名*urname, 425*	呼*alling, 701*

秩*ublic order, 730*	株*orporation, 130*

105-B
Social 称itles & 株tocks, pride of aristocrats...

木 (wooden)

株tocks 株orporation

kabu
stocks, corporation

FLIP: 7.1. Right (Sort Of)

頭株 *leader, leading power* **atamakabu**
頭株 *boss, chief, leader* **atamakabu**
古株 *old-timer, ~stump* **furukabu**
端株 *old stocks* **hakabu**
実株 *actual shares being traded* **jitsukabu**
株価 *stock prices* **kabuka**
株券 *stock certificate* **kabuken**
株金 *money invested in stocks* **kabukin**
株主 *stockholder, shareholder* **kabunushi**
株主総会 *stockholders' meeting* **kabunushi sōkai**
株式 *stock, shares* **kabushiki**
株式配当 *stock dividend* **kabushiki haitō**
株式会社 *corporation, incorporated* **kabushiki kaisha**
株式市場 *stock market* **kabushiki shijō**
株式取引所 *stock exchange* **kabushiki torihikijo**
株屋 *stockbroker* **kabuya**
切り株 *stump, stubble* **kirikabu**
満株 *fully-subscribed shares* **mankabu**
実株 *spot, stocks, shares* **mikabu**

持ち株 *shares, stock holdings* **mochikabu**
持ち株会社 *holding company* **mochikabu gaisha**
御株 *one's forte, expertise* **okabu**
親株 *parent root (plant); old stock* **oyakabu**
新株 *new stocks, ~shares* **shinkabu**
株分け *branching out of roots (plant)* **kabuwake**
刈り株 *stubble* **karikabu**
景品株 *bonus stock* **keihinkabu**
大株主 *large shareholder* **ookabunushi**
債務株 *debenture stock* **saimukabu**
優先株 *preferred shares, ~stocks* **yūsenkabu**

社*ompany, 703*	営*anagement, 580*
業*usiness, 124*	商*ommerce, 135*

珠*earl, 233*

106-A

唱*hanting and* 晶*rystals in the witches rituals...*

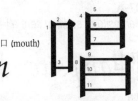

口 (mouth)

唱*hanting*　　唱*ncantation*

tona(eru), SHŌ
chanting, incantation, singing

FLIP: 5.0.a Left & Right

唱える　*chant, advocate, advance* **tonaeru**
愛唱　*lover of songs* **aishō**
暗唱　*reciting from memory* **anshō**
伝唱　*advocate, propose, espouse* **denshō**
独唱　*vocal solo, vocalist* **dokushō**
詠唱　*chanting, aria* **eishō**
復唱　*repeating an order* **fukushō**
合唱　*chorus, chorale* **gasshō**
合唱曲　*chorus, chorale* **gasshōkyoku**
吟唱　*oral recitation* **ginshō**
歌唱　*singing* **kashō**
歌唱力　*singing ability, ~talent* **kashōryoku**
高唱　*singing aloud* **kōshō**
熱唱　*singing heartily* **nesshō**
輪唱　*troll, round* **rinshō**
三唱　*three cheers* **sanshō**
斉唱　*chorus, chorale* **seishō**
唱道　*advocating a cause* **shōdō**
唱導　*advocating a cause* **shōdō**

唱導者　*advocate, proponent* **shōdōsha**
唱歌　*song, singing* **shōka**
唱名　*Buddhist chanting* **shōmyō**
唱和　*joining a chorus* **shōwa**
主唱　*advocacy, propagation* **shushō**
低唱　*low-pitch singing* **teishō**
提唱　*propose, advocate, expound* **teishō**
唱値　*asking price* **tonaene**
絶唱　*excellent-, superb poetry* **zesshō**
二重唱　*vocal duet* **nijūshō**

| 吟*hant, 183* | 祈*rayer, 184* | 声*oice, 428* |
| 謡*hant, 810* | 拝*rayer, 636* | 音*one, 314* |

喝*colding, 808*

106-B

唱*hanting and* 晶*rystals in the witches rituals...*

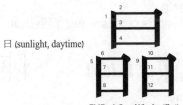

日 (sunlight, daytime)

晶*rystal*

SHŌ
crystal

FLIP: 1.0.a. Whole (flat)

液晶　*liquid crystal* **ekishō**
液晶テレビ　*LCD television* **ekishōterebi**
氷晶　*ice crystals* **hyōshō**
結晶　*crystallization* **kesshō**
⇒愛の結晶　*"crystal of love..."* **ai no kesshō**
⇒氷の結晶　*ice crystals* **kōri no kesshō**
結晶学　*science of crystals* **kesshōgaku**
結晶核　*crystal nucleus* **kesshōkaku**
晶化　*crystallization* **shōka**
晶光　*brilliant lights, illumination* **shōkō**
水晶　*crystal, quartz* **suishō**
⇒煙水晶　*smoke of quartz* **kemuri zuishō**
⇒紫水晶　*amethyst* **murasaki zuishō**
水晶体　*lens of one's eyes* **suishōtai**
非晶体　*shapeless, formless* **hishōtai**
草入り水晶　*crystal impurities* **kusairizuishō**

輝*parkling, 296*	英*rilliance, 217*
昭*right, 529*	光*hining, 77*
明*right, 22*	貴*recious, 913*

晶*roducts, 901*

107-A

陣*ampsite of sedition sent a* 陳*etition...*

阝⇔阜 (village, right)

陣*ampsite*　陣*attle formation*

JIN

campsite, encampment, battle formation

FLIP: 7.0.b1. Right (stem)

円陣　*circle* **enjin**
布陣　*battle ready position* **fujin**
軍陣　*military camp, barracks* **gunjin**
方陣　*square formation* **hōjin**
本陣　*headquarters, GHQ* **honjin**
陣地　*battle position* **jinchi**
陣中　*encamped, in the field* **jinchū**
陣営　*camp, encampment* **jin'ei**
陣形　*battle formation* **jinkei**
陣門　*capitulation, surrender* **jinmon**
陣頭　*battle leader* **jintō**
陣痛　*childbirth pains* **jintsū**
陣容　*battle formation* **jinyō**
従陣　*column of soldiers* **jūjin**
堅陣　*stronghold, bedrock* **kenjin**
後陣　*reservists corps* **kōjin**
内陣　*inner camp* **naijin**
論陣　*firm stand; argument* **ronjin**
戦陣　*battle formation* **senjin**

先陣　*vanguard, advance troops* **senjin**
出陣　*going to the frontlines* **shutsujin**
対陣　*contraposition, facing each other* **taijin**
退陣　*retreat, resignation* **taijin**
殺陣　*sword fighting* **tate, satsujin**
敵陣　*enemy line* **tekijin**
初陣　*first campaign* **uijin**
陣立て　*battle formation* **jindate**
陣取る　*place oneself* **jindoru**
経営陣　*management team* **keieijin**
教授陣　*faculty, professors* **kyōjujin**

側*ide, 291*
盟*lliance, 21*
連*lliance, 305*

陳*etition, 132*

107-B

陣*ampsite of sedition sent a* 陳*etition...*

阝⇔阜 (village, right)

陳*etition*　陳*et forth*

CHIN

petition, entreaty, set forth

FLIP: 7.0.b1. Right (stem)

陳弁　*explanation, statement* **chinben**
陳情　*petition, representation* **chinjō**
陳情団　*lobby group* **chinjōdan**
陳情者　*petitioner, lobbyist* **chinjōsha**
陳情書　*written petition, ~appeal* **chinjōsho**
陳述　*statement, declaration* **chinjutsu**
⇒冒頭陳述　*opening statement* **bōtō chinjutsu**
陳述書　*written statement* **chinjutsusho**
陳皮　*dried orange skin* **chinpi**
陳腐　*orthodox, stereotype, outdated* **chinpu**
陳列　*display, exhibition* **chinretsu**
陳列棚　*display case, exhibition rack* **chinretsudana**
陳列室　*showroom* **chinretsushitsu**
陳謝　*apology, atonement* **chinsha**
具陳　*formal statement, deposition* **guchin**
開陳　*holding on one's views* **kaichin**
出陳　*submitting to an exhibition* **shucchin**
前陳　*the above-mentioned* **zenchin**
新陳代謝　*metabolism* **shinchin taisha**

側*ide, 291*　　　組*roup, 138*
盟*lliance, 21*　　団*roup, 345*
連*lliance, 305*

陣*ampsite, 132*

108-A

隆*rosperity ascends then somehow* 降*escends...*

阝⇔阜 *(village, right)*

隆*rosperity*　　隆*hriving*

RYŪ

prosperity, thriving, bountiful, plenitude

Facing: 3.0. ☞ ☜ Across

興隆　*prosperity, good times* **kōryū**
隆起　*upheaval, sharp rise, upsurge* **ryūki**
隆肉　*hunchback, camel's hump* **ryūniku**
隆々　*thriving, prosperous* **ryūryū**
隆盛　*well & prosperous* **ryūsei**
隆昌　*prosperity, good times* **ryūshō**
隆運　*good fortune, prosperity* **ryūun**
隆鼻術　*nasal-, rhino surgery* **ryūbijutsu**

富*ortune, 333*	繁*rosperity, 434*
豊*bundance, 965*	盛*rosperity, 244*
裕*ffluence, 758*	益*rofit, 622*

陶*orcelain, 811*

108-B

隆*rosperity ascends then somehow* 降*escends...*

降*escend*　　降*ownward*

阝⇔阜 *(village, right)*

o(riru), o(rosu), fu(ru), KŌ

descend, downward

Facing: 3.0. ☞ ☜ Across

沈降　*subsiding, precipitation* **chinkō**
以降　*"since then, thereafter..."* **ikō**
乗降　*boarding & alighting (vehicle)* **jōkō**
滑降　*downhill descent* **kakkō**
降板　*getting knocked out* **kōban**
降伏　*surrender, capitulation* **kōfuku**
降下　*descent, fall, landing* **kōka**
降格　*demotion, downgrading* **kōkaku**
降給　*pay reduction, salary cut* **kōkyū**
降任　*demotion, downgrading* **kōnin**
降臨　*advent & descent, fluctuation* **kōrin**
降参　*surrender, submission, capitulation* **kōsan**
降雪　*snowfall, snow* **kōsetsu**
降車　*boarding & alighting (vehicle)* **kōsha**
降神　*spiritism* **kōshin**
降誕　*birth of jesus christ* **kōtan**
降等　*demolition, destruction* **kōtō**
降雨　*rainfall* **kōu**
降雨量　*rainfall, raindrops* **kōuryō**

昇降　*ascent & descent, fluctuation* **shōkō**
降り込む　*come into, fall into* **furikomu**
降り頻る　*fall steadily* **furishikiru**
降り注ぐ　*rainpour, rain down* **furisosogu**
乗り降り　*getting on & off* **noriori**
雨降り　*rainfall, raindrops* **amefuri**
急降下　*nose dive, sudden drop* **kyūkōka**
直滑降　*straight descent, nosedive* **chokkakkō**
吹き降り　*driving rain* **fukiburi**
飛び降り　*jump-down, plunge, dive* **tobiori**
駆け降りる　*run down* **kakeoriru**

下*escend, 859*	落*all-down, 826*
陥*all-down, 893*	衰*ecline, 374*
堕*all-down, 807*	

隆*rosperity, 133*

109-A

Pay raise 項lause 頂eceived with applause...

頁 (large shell, page)

項*lause*   項*hapter*

KŌ
clause, chapter, section

FLIP: 7.0.b2. Right (stem)

別項 *another chapter* **bekkō**
一項 *an item for discussion; paragraph* **ikkō**
移項 *transposition* **ikō**
事項 *item, agenda* **jikō**
⇒注意事項 *"caution...," nota bene* **chūi jikō**
⇒議決事項 *agreed matters* **giketsu jikō**
⇒決議事項 *agenda, deliberation matter*
   ketsugi jikō
⇒記載事項 *mentioned items* **kisai jikō**
⇒協議事項 *meeting agenda* **kyōgi jikō**
⇒了解事項 *agreed items, decided matters*
   ryōkai jikō
条項 *provisions, stipulations* **jōkō**
各項 *each clause, ~item* **kakukō**
後項 *following paragraph* **kōkō**
項目 *heading, chapter* **kōmoku**
内項 *internal items* **naikō**
二項 *binomial co-efficient* **nikō**

多項 *polynomial* **takō**
多項式 *polynomial* **takōshiki**
要項 *essentials, gist* **yōkō**
前項 *preceding clause* **zenkō**
同類項 *similar terms* **dōruikō**
項垂れる *hanging down one's head* **unadareru**

条*lause*, 607
款*rticle*, 42
但*roviso*, 739

頂*eceive*, 134

109-B

Pay raise 項lause 頂eceived with applause...

頁 (large shell, page)

❶頂*eceive*   ❷頂*ummit*

itadaki, itada(ku), CHŌ
receive, accept, obtain, ~humbly; summit

FLIP: 7.0.b2. Right (stem)

❶頂ける *able to receive, ~accept* **itadakeru**
頂きます *receive, accept (polite)* **itadakimasu**
頂戴 *"please give it to me..."* **chōdai**
頂物 *something to receive* **itadakimono**
骨頂 *height, elevation* **kocchō**
仏頂面 *sullen-, sour face* **bucchōzura**
頂戴物 *something to receive* **chōdaimono**

押し頂く *raising to one's head* **oshiitadaku**
丹頂鶴 *red-crested white crane* **tanchōzuru**
有頂天 *ecstasy, exaltation* **uchōten**
頂門の一針 *intense reproach, censure*
   chōmon no isshin

請*equest*, 791
受*eceive*, 539

項*lause*, 134

❷頂上 *top, summit, peak* **chōjō**
頂角 *vertical angle* **chōkaku**
頂点 *apex, peak, climax, vertex* **chōten**
頂度 *exact, precise, accurate* **chōdo**
円頂 *circular peak, mound* **enchō**
山頂 *mountain summit* **sanchō**
天頂 *zenith, summit peak* **tenchō**
天頂点 *zenith, summit peak* **tenchōten**
頭頂 *top, tip, vertex* **tōchō**
登頂 *reaching the mountain peak* **tōchō, tochō**
絶頂 *top, summit, peak* **zecchō**

110-A

適ropriety in 商ommerce endear customers...

辶 (transport)

適*ropriety* 適*uitable*

TEKI
propriety, suitable, appropriate

FLIP: 3.0.a. Top (flat)

自適 *comfort, serenity* **jiteki**
快適 *cosy, comfortable* **kaiteki**
好適 *ideal, suitable, fitting, proper* **kōteki**
最適 *the most appropriate* **saiteki**
適度 *moderation, toleration* **tekido**
適宜 *properly, suitably* **tekigi**
適合 *adaptation, adjustment* **tekigō**
適否 *unsuitable, inappropriate* **tekihi**
適法 *legally permissible* **tekihō**
適評 *suitable criticism* **tekihyō**
適時 *timely, opportune* **tekiji**
適格 *suitable qualifications* **tekikaku**
適任 *right person for the job* **tekinin**
適温 *suitable temperature* **tekion**
適応 *adaptation, suitability* **tekiō**
適齢 *proper age, reasonable age* **tekirei**
適例 *appropriate example* **tekirei**
適量 *suitable amount* **tekiryō**
適作 *suitable crop* **tekisaku**

適性 *fitness, aptitude, suitability* **tekisei**
適正 *suitable, reasonable, fair* **tekisei**
適切 *appropriate, proper, suitable* **tekisetsu**
適者 *suitable person* **tekisha**
適者生存 *survival of the fittest* **tekisha seizon**
適職 *suitable job* **tekishoku**
適当 *appropriate, proper, suitable* **tekitō**
適役 *proper role* **tekiyaku**
適訳 *suitable translation* **tekiyaku**
適用 *application, practicality* **tekiyō**
適材適所 *"right person in the right place..."*
　　tekizai tekisho

善*ighteous, 450*　　正*orrect, 30*
是*orrect, 313*

週*eekly, 279*

110-B

適ropriety in 商ommerce endear customers...

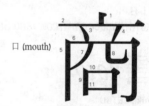

口 (mouth)

商*ommerce* 商*usiness*

akina(u), SHŌ
commerce, business, industry, mercantile, trade

FLIP: 1.0.b. Whole (stem)

画商 *art dealer, painting dealer* **gashō**
豪商 *wealthy businessman, ~woman* **gōshō**
協商 *commercial agreement* **kyōshō**
年商 *business year* **nenshō**
政商 *politician's financial stake* **seishō**
商売 *business, trade, profession* **shōbai**
商談 *business talks* **shōdan**
商道 *business ethics* **shōdō**
商議 *business meeting* **shōgi**
商号 *tradename, trademark* **shōgō**
商業 *commerce, trade, business* **shōgyō**
商品 *merchandise goods, sales item* **shōhin**
商法 *commercial laws* **shōhō**
商事 *business activities* **shōji**
商科 *business course* **shōka**
商会 *company, firm* **shōkai**
商館 *trading house* **shōkan**
商権 *commercial rights* **shōken**
商機 *business opportunity, ~chance* **shōki**

協商 *entente, agreement* **kyōshō**
商工 *commerce & industry* **shōkō**
商魂 *business talent, knack-for-money* **shōkon**
商況 *market situation, the market* **shōkyō**
商務 *business affairs* **shōmu**
商人 *businessman, ~woman, merchant* **shōnin**
商才 *business talent, knack-for-money* **shōsai**
商船 *commercial ship* **shōsen**
商社 *large trading conglomerate* **shōsha**
商都 *commercial centre* **shōto**
商運 *business fortunes* **shōun**
隊商 *roving merchants* **taishō**

業*usiness, 124*　　盛*rosperity, 244*
株*orporation, 130*　　益*rofit, 622*
営*anagement, 580*　　富*ortune, 333*
得*rofit, 940*　　任*bligation, 709*

産*roduce, 883*

111-A

Like 雷*hunder on* 雪*now rang Santa's," Ho, ho!"*

雨 (weather)

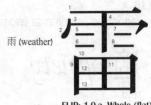

FLIP: 1.0.a. Whole (flat)

雷*hunder*

kaminari, RAI
thunder, thunderbolt

雷おやじ *hot-tempered old man* **kaminari oyaji**
爆雷 *depth charge* **bakurai**
万雷 *thunderous-, roaring applause* **banrai**
遠雷 *distant thunder* **enrai**
魚雷 *torpedo* **gyorai**
魚雷艇 *torpedo boat* **gyoraitei**
百雷 *thunderous, roaring* **hyakurai**
人雷 *human torpedo (WWII)* **jinrai**
地雷 *land mine* **jirai**
機雷 *underwater mine, sea mine* **kirai**
機雷源 *minefield* **kiraigen**
空雷 *aerial torpedo* **kūrai**
熱雷 *heat thunderstorm* **netsurai**
雷鳥 *ptarmigan, snow grouse* **raichō**
雷電 *thunder & lightning* **raiden**
雷撃 *torpedo attack* **raigeki**
雷撃機 *aircraft-borne torpedo* **raigekiki**
雷神 *god of thunder* **raijin**
雷火 *thunder-induced fire* **raika**

雷管 *detonator, ignition device* **raikan**
雷公 *god of thunder* **raikō**
雷鳴 *thunderous-, roaring applause* **raimei**
雷名 *fame, renown, noted, popular* **raimei**
雷雨 *thunderstorm* **raiu**
雷雲 *thunderclouds* **raiun**
落雷 *thunder-hit* **rakurai**
春雷 *spring thunder* **shunrai**
水雷 *torpedo* **suirai**
水雷艇 *torpedo boat* **suiraitei**
避雷針 *lightning rod* **hiraishin**

雨*aining*, 417	電*lectricity*, 417	爆*xplosion*, 561
叫*cream*, 693	熱*eat*, 153	騒*oise*, 924

電*lectricity*, 417

111-B

Like 雷*hunder on* 雪*now rang Santa's," Ho, ho!"*

雨 (weather)

FLIP: 3.0.b. Top (stem)

雪*now*

yuki, SETSU
snow

淡雪 *light snow* **awayuki**
豪雪 *heavy snowing, ~snowfall* **gōsetsu**
氷雪 *ice & snow* **hyōsetsu**
除雪 *removing-, snow clearing* **josetsu**
粉雪 *powdery snow, fine snow* **konayuki**
降雪 *snowfall, snowing* **kōsetsu**
雪崩 *avalanche, snowslide* **nadare**
根雪 *incessant snow blanket* **neyuki**
雪渓 *snowy valley, snowy gorge* **sekkei**
雪白 *snow white, immaculate white* **seppaku**
雪害 *snow damage* **setsugai**
雪原 *snowfield* **setsugen***snowfield* **setsugen**
雪冤 *vindication, exoneration* **setsuen**
雪辱 *vindication, exoneration* **setsujoku**
耐雪 *snow-resistant* **taisetsu**
綿雪 *large snowflakes* **watayuki**
雪嵐 *snow storm* **yukiarashi**
雪雲 *snow clouds* **yukigumo**
雪煙 *snow spray* **yukikemuri**

雪見 *snow-viewing* **yukimi**
雪美 *picturesque snow* **yukimi**
雪見酒 *drinking sake on snowfall* **yukimizake**
雪女 *snow fairy* **yukionna**
雪空 *snowy sky* **yukizora**
残雪 *lingering snow, specks of snow* **zansetsu**
花吹雪 *shower of cherry blossoms* **hanafubuki**
雪上車 *snowmobile, snowbike* **setsujōsha**
雪達磨 *snowman* **yukidaruma**
雪解け *thaw, defreeze, dissolve* **yukidoke**
雪合戦 *snowball fight* **yukigassen**
雪景色 *snow landscape, snow view* **yukigeshiki**
雪除け *shelter from snow, snowshed* **yukiyoke**

寒*hills*, 121	雨*aining*, 417
冷*hilly*, 684	白*hite*, 15

雷*hunder*, 136

112-A
敗ailure in 販elling, mad boss yelling...

攵 (action)

敗efeat 敗ailure

yabu(reru), HAI
defeat, failure, blunder, unsuccessful

FLIP: 6.0.a. Left (flat)

腐敗 *rot, decay, spoiling* **fuhai**
不敗 *unbeatable, undefeated* **fuhai**
敗亡 *loss, defeat* **haibō**
敗北 *defeat, reverses, vanquished* **haiboku**
敗軍 *defeated troops* **haigun**
敗兵 *defeated troops* **haihei**
敗報 *news of defeat* **haihō**
敗因 *cause of defeat* **haiin**
敗滅 *crushing defeat, shutout* **haimetsu**
敗戦 *defeat, loss* **haisen**
敗戦国 *defeated-, vanquished nation* **haisenkoku**
敗者 *defeated, loser* **haisha**
敗将 *beaten general* **haishō**
敗色 *signs of defeat* **haishoku**
敗訴 *losing a suit* **haiso**
敗走 *rout, flight* **haisō**
敗退 *defeat, retreat, losing a game* **haitai**
敗残 *lose & survive* **haizan**
敗残兵 *remnant soldiers* **haizanhei**

完敗 *complete defeat, ~failure* **kanpai**
連敗 *consecutive defeats* **renpai**
酸敗 *acidify* **sanpai**
成敗 *bring to justice* **seibai**
惜敗 *narrow defeat* **sekihai**
失敗 *failure, fiasco, blunder, boo-boo* **shippai**
勝敗 *outcome, victory-or-defeat* **shōhai**
惨敗 *crushing defeat, shutout* **zanpai**
全敗 *complete defeat* **zenpai**
零敗 *losing with a zero score* **zerohai, reihai**
敗血症 *septicaemia, blood poisoning* **haiketsushō**

負*efeat, 625*	非*[negative], 288*
失*ailure, 19*	起*waken, 754*
不*[negative], 300*	習*earning, 238*

財*inance, 186*

112-B
敗ailure in 販elling, mad boss yelling...

貝 (shell, old money)

販elling 販erchandise

HAN
selling, merchandise, marketing, exchange for money, peddle

FLIP: 6.0.b. Left (stem)

販売 *sales, selling, marketing* **hanbai**
⇒委託販売 *consignment sale* **itaku hanbai**
⇒一手販売 *exclusive agency* **itte hanbai**
⇒特価販売 *bargain-, clearance sale* **tokka hanbai**
販売員 *salesman, saleslady* **hanbaiin**
販売網 *sales network* **hanbaimō**
販売元 *seller, selling side* **hanbaimoto**
販売人 *seller, salesman, saleslady* **hanbainin**
販売所 *shop, store, stall* **hanbaisho**
販売店 *store, shop* **hanbaiten**
販売価格 *selling price* **hanbai kakaku**
販売合戦 *sales war* **hanbai kassen, ~gassen**
販売促進 *sales promotion, marketing*
　　　　hanbai sokushin
販路 *marketing route* **hanro**
販促 *sales promotion, marketing* **hansoku**
自販 *automobile selling, car for sale* **jihan**
自販機 *vending machine* **jihanki**
量販 *sales volume* **ryōhan**

再販 *resale, reselling* **saihan**
市販 *marketing, selling* **shihan**
信販 *credit sale, sell on credit* **shinpan**
酒販 *liquor selling* **shūhan**
通販 *mail order marketing* **tsūhan**

売*erchandise, 259*	払*ayment, 682*
賃*ayment, 145*	料*ayment, 194*
納*ayment, 296*	財*inance, 186*

敗*ailure, 137*

113-A

組*roup's shady* 細*etails sent them to jail...*

糸 (thread, continuity)

組*roup*   組*rganize*

kumi, ku(mu), SO
group, organize, syndicate, assemblage, union

FLIP: 7.0.a. Right (flat)

改組 *organization, composition, structure* **kaiso**
組合 *labour union, workers' co-operative* **kumiai**
組版 *typesetting pattern* **kumiban, kumihan**
組員 *gangster member* **kumiin**
労組 *labour union, staff union* **rōso**
職組 *labour union, staff union* **shokuso**
組閣 *forming a Cabinet* **sokaku**
組成 *composition, make-up* **sosei**
組織 *organization, composition* **soshiki**
縁組み *wedding engagement, betrothal* **engumi**
骨組み *skeleton, framework* **honegumi**
石組み *garden stone arrangement* **ishigumi**
気組み *preparedness, readiness* **kigumi**
心組み *character, demeanour* **kokorogumi**
組み替え *rearrangement, readjustment* **kumikae**
組み立て *assembling, putting together* **kumitate**
組み付く *grapple, close, grip & hold on* **kumitsuku**
組み打ち *grapple, hold, grasp* **kumiuchi**
組み分け *grouping, sorting out* **kumiwake**

乗組員 *crew* **norikumiin**
仕組み *contrive, devise, innovate* **shikumi**
腕組み *folded arms* **udegumi**
枠組み *outline, frame, structure* **wakugumi**
横組み *horizontal typesetting* **yokogumi**
二人組み *two-some, duo, pair* **futarigumi**
入り組む *complicate, make complex* **irikumu**
組み合わせ *combination, matching* **kumiawase**
組み入れる *insert, work, incorporate* **kumiireru**
取り組む *grapple, deal with* **torikumu**

団*roup, 345*	員*ember, 410*
盟*lliance, 21*	班*eam, 908*
連*lliance, 305*	協*ooperate, 577*

祖*ncestor, 953*

113-B

組*roup's shady* 細*etails sent them to jail...*

糸 (thread, continuity)

❶細*etails*   ❷細*lender*

hoso(i), komaka(i), SAI
details, slender, specifics, minute

FLIP: 7.0.a. Right (flat)

❶微細 *minute, delicate, detailed* **bisai**
骨細 *delicate, thin-boned* **honeboso**
細筆 *fine handwriting* **hosofude**
委細 *details, particulars* **isai**
明細 *details, particulars* **meisai**
明細書 *list of particulars* **meisaisho**
零細 *frivolous, petty, trifle* **reisai**
細別 *subdivision* **saibetsu**
細胞 *cell* **saibō**
⇒脳細胞 *brain cells* **nōsaibō**
⇒単細胞 *single cell; simple-minded* **tansaibō**
細大 *smallest detail* **saidai**
細片 *chips, splinters, fragments* **saihen**
細事 *minor details* **saiji**
細菌 *bacteria, germ, microbe* **saikin**
細工 *workmanship, craftsmanship* **saiku**
⇒革細工 *leather products, ~goods* **kawazaiku**
⇒竹細工 *bamboo products* **takezaiku**
⇒漆細工 *lacquer ware, ~ work* **urushizaiku**

細君 *wife, Madame, lady of the house* **saikun**
細民 *the poor masses* **saimin**
細密 *closely, minutely* **saimitsu**
細論 *detailed discussion* **sairon**
細説 *detailed explanation* **saisetsu**
細心 *close-, great care* **saishin**
繊細 *sensitive, delicate, fine, exquisite* **sensai**
子細 *details, reason, circumstances* **shisai**
詳細 *details, particulars* **shōsai**

❷細引き *cord* **hosobiki**
細身 *slender body* **hosomi**
細切れ *small pieces, minced, chopped* **komagire**

繊*lender, 803*	薄*hin, 63*
長*ong, 273*	

畑*lantation, 482*

114-A

惑emptations reign in 域egions with evil legions...

心⇔忄 (heart, feelings)

惑*emptation*　　惑*nticement*

mado(u), WAKU
temptation, enticement, inducement, bewilder

FLIP: 8.0.a. Inner (flat)
Facing: 2.1. East ☞ (H)

惑わす *mislead, puzzle* **madowasu**
不惑 *one's fortyish, 40-49 years old* **fuwaku**
眩惑 *bewilderment, baffling, puzzling* **genwaku**
疑惑 *doubt, suspicion* **giwaku**
困惑 *perplexity, puzzlement* **konwaku**
迷惑 *troublesome, annoying, nuisance* **meiwaku**
⇒有難迷惑 *unwelcome favour* **arigata meiwaku**
魅惑 *fascination, charm* **miwaku**
魅惑的 *charming, fascinating* **miwakuteki**
思惑 *intention, expectation* **omowaku**
思惑師 *speculator* **omowakushi**
思惑違い *erroneous thinking* **omowakuchigai**
戸惑う *bewilderment, baffling* **tomadō**
戸惑い *confusion, perplexity* **tomadoi**
当惑 *confusion, perplexity* **tōwaku**
惑溺 *infatuation, addiction* **wakudeki**
惑乱 *troublesome, annoying, nuisance* **wakuran**
惑星 *planet* **wakusei**
惑星間 *interplanetary* **wakuseikan**

誘惑 *temptation, luring, enticement* **yūwaku**
誘惑者 *seducer, tempter* **yūwakusha**
逃げ惑う *perplexed about escaping* **nigemadō**
思い惑う *unable to decide* **omoimadō**

| 誘*emptation*, 895 | 唆*nticement*, 764 |
| 釣*llure*, 697 | 幻*antasy*, 88 |

感*motion*, 45

114-B

惑emptations reign in 域egions with evil legions...

土 (ground, soil)

域*egion*　　域*erritory*

IKI
region, territory, locality

FLIP: 8.0.a. Inner (flat)
Facing: 2.2. East ☞ (V)

雨域 *rainy area* **ameiki**
地域 *area, region* **chiiki**
芸域 *range of skills* **geiiki**
異域 *strange land* **iiki**
域外 *outside the premises* **ikigai**
域内 *within the premises* **ikinai**
海域 *ocean zone* **kaiiki**
広域 *wide area* **kōiki**
区域 *zone, area, district* **kuiki**
空域 *territorial airspace* **kūiki**
境域 *border, boundary* **kyōiki**
音域 *range, reach, span* **on'iki**
霊域 *sacred-, holy ground* **reiiki**
領域 *territory, domain, sphere* **ryōiki**
流域 *basin, valley* **ryūiki**
聖域 *sacred-, holy ground* **seiiki**
声域 *voice range, hearing distance* **seiiki**
戦域 *war zone, war theatre, battlefield* **sen'iki**
識域 *consciousness, awareness* **shikiiki**

職域 *occupation, responsibility* **shokuiki**
水域 *water area, river basin* **suiiki**
帯域 *range, reach, span* **taiiki**
全域 *entire area, expanse* **zen'iki**
暴風域 *storm-affected area* **bōfūiki**
峡帯域 *narrow-band* **kyōtaiiki**

| 帯*egion*, 557 | 環*nvirons*, 165 |
| 緑*nvironment*, 841 | 地*arth*, 688 |

減*ecrease*, 46

115-A

陵*ausoleum on the* 陸*round form a grave mound...*

阝⇔阜 (village, right)

陵*ausoleum*

misasagi, RYŌ
mausoleum

御陵 *imperial mausoleum* **goryō**
皇陵 *imperial mausoleum* **kōryō**
丘陵 *hill* **kyūryō**
丘陵地帯 *hilly areas* **kyūryō chitai**
陵墓 *imperial mausoleum* **ryōbo**
陵辱 *insult, humiliation* **ryōjoku**
帝陵 *imperial mausoleum* **teiryō**
高陵土 *porcelain clay* **kōryōdo**

FLIP: 7.2.a. Right Top (flat)
Facing: 3.0. ☞☜ **Across**

墓*ravesite, 602*	死*eath, 513*
碑*ombstone, 937*	逝*eath, 54*
葬*urial, 513*	亡*eath, 72*

陸*round, 140*

115-B

陵*ausoleum on the* 陸*round form a grave mound...*

阝⇔阜 (village, right)

陸*round*　陸*and*

RIKU
ground, land

着陸 *aircraft landing* **chakuriku**
上陸 *aircraft landing* **jōriku**
空陸 *army & air force* **kūriku**
内陸 *in-land* **nairiku**
陸稲 *upland rice plant, dryland* **okabo, rikutō**
陸橋 *overpass, flyover, crossover* **rikkyō**
陸運 *land transportation, ~vehicle* **rikuun**
陸地 *land area* **rikuchi**
陸棚 *continental shelf* **rikudana**
陸風 *land-to-sea breeze* **rikufū**
陸岸 *shore, land* **rikugan**
陸軍 *army* **rikugun**
陸上 *land, ground, shore* **rikujō**
陸海 *land & the sea* **rikukai**
陸海軍 *army & navy* **rikukaigun**
陸離 *brilliant, dazzling* **rikuri**
陸路 *route, path* **rikuro**
陸産 *land-based products, farm produce* **rikusan**
陸産物 *land-based products* **rikusanbutsu**

FLIP: 7.0.a. Right (flat)

陸生 *earthly, mundane; living on land* **rikusei**
陸棲 *living on land* **rikusei**
陸戦 *land war, ground war* **rikusen**
離陸 *aircraft take-off* **ririku**
水陸 *land & water, amphibious* **suiriku** ·
大陸 *continent* **tairiku**
⇒南極大陸 *Antarctic Continent* **nankyoku tairiku**
揚陸 *unloading, landing* **yōriku**
軟着陸 *soft & smooth landing* **nanchakuriku**
陸揚げ *discharge, unloading, landing* **rikuage**
陸揚港 *port-of-discharge, ~arrival* **rikuagekō**

土*round, 8*	平*lains, 488*
野*lains, 873*	原*lains, 431*

陵*ausoleum, 140*

116-A

算alculate cash with a 筆riting-brush...

竹 (bamboo)

算alculate   算ompute

soro, SAN
calculate, compute, summing-up

FLIP: 8.0.a. Inner (flat)

暗算	mental calculation, ~computation	**anzan**
概算	rough estimate, approximate	**gaisan**
逆算	counting backwards	**gyakusan**
換算	conversion, exchange	**kansan**
換算率	conversion rate	**kansanritsu**
加算	addition, inclusion	**kasan**
計算	calculation, computation	**keisan**
⇒原価計算	cost accounting	**genka keisan**
計算機	calculation, computation	**keisanki**
起算	reckoning	**kisan**
採算	profit, gain, yield	**saisan**
算術	arithmetic, mathematics	**sanjutsu**
算出	computation, calculation	**sanshutsu**
算数	arithmetic, mathematics	**sansū**
算定	calculation, computation	**santei**
清算	liquidation, settlement	**seisan**
精算	settlement, calculation	**seisan**
試算	trial calculation, ~computation	**shisan**
勝算	winning chances, odds for	**shōsan**

珠算	abacus calculation	**shuzan**
速算	rapid-, quick calculation	**sokusan**
算盤	abacus	**soroban**
予算	budget, estimate	**yosan**
電算機	calculator	**densanki**
引き算	subtract, subtraction	**hikizan**
掛け算	multiplication, multiplying	**kakezan**
胸算用	mental calculation	**munazanyō**
足し算	addition, adding	**tashizan**
割り算	division, dividing	**warizan**
算用数字	Arabic numerals	**sanyō sūji**

数umber, 156	済ettle, 961
経ime-lapse, 791	計ompute, 692

筆riting-brush, 141

116-B

算alculate cash with a 筆riting-brush...

竹 (bamboo)

筆riting-brush   筆andwriting

fude, HITSU
writing-brush, handwriting, calligraphy, penmanship, scribble, script

Facing: 1.1. 🢀 West (H)

遅筆	slow writing, ~style	**chihitsu**
絵筆	paint brush	**efude**
鉛筆	pencil	**enpitsu**
筆箱	pen case, pencil box	**fudebako**
筆削	correction, erasure	**fudekezuri**
筆まめ	good handwriting	**fudemane**
画筆	paintbrush	**gahitsu**
筆致	touch, style	**hicchi**
筆記	writing down, taking notes	**hikki**
筆法	penmanship style	**hippō**
筆跡	handwriting	**hisseki**
筆者	writer, author	**hissha**
一筆	"a stroke of the pen..."	**hitofude, ippitsu**
筆談	written communication	**hitsudan**
筆意	writing	**hitsui**
筆力	power of the pen, literary power	**hitsuryoku**
筆頭	first on the list	**hittō**
自筆	one's own handwriting	**jihitsu**
健筆	prolific writer	**kenpitsu**

名筆	master calligrapher	**meihitsu**
毛筆	writing brush	**mōhitsu**
乱筆	hasty scribbling, illegible writing	**ranpitsu**
才筆	literary genius	**saihitsu**
紙筆	paper & pen, in writing	**shihitsu, kamifude**
執筆	handwriting, penmanship	**shippitsu**
主筆	editor-in-chief, chief editor	**shuhitsu**
速筆	quick writing	**sokuhitsu**
随筆	essay, composition	**zuihitsu**
筆不精	not good at writing often	**fudebushō**
筆立て	pen stand	**fudetate**
色鉛筆	coloured pencil	**iroenpitsu**
万年筆	fountain pen	**mannenhitsu**

書ritings, 116	掲ublish, 810
刊ublication, 687	載ublish, 802

津arbour, 731	律egulation, 731

117-A

Selling 率ate of 傘mbrellas enthused Cinderella...

玄 (darkness)

❶ 率roportion **❷ 率eadership**

hiki(iru); RITSU, SOTSU
proportion, percentage, rate, ratio

FLIP: 2.0.b. Sort Of (stem)
Facing: 2.1. East ☞ (H)

❶ 倍率 *magnification, enlargement* **bairitsu**
同率 *same percentage* **dōritsu**
比率 *ratio, percentage* **hiritsu**
効率 *efficiency, efficacious, effectiveness* **kōritsu**
高率 *high rate, ~interest* **kōritsu**
能率 *efficiency, efficacious* **nōritsu**
能率給 *efficiency wages* **nōritsukyū**
利率 *interest rate* **riritsu**
勝率 *winning percentage* **shōritsu**
率直 *frank, candid, straightforward* **socchoku**
定率 *fixed rate* **teiritsu**
税率 *tax rate, tariff rate* **zeiritsu**
膨張率 *expansion rate* **bōchōritsu**
円周率 *pi, circular constant* **enshūritsu**
百分率 *percentage* **hyakubunritsu**
稼動率 *operating rate* **kadōritsu**
拡大率 *magnifying power* **kakudairitsu**
換算率 *exchange rate* **kansanritsu**
効率的 *efficient, efficacious* **kōritsuteki**

屈折率 *refractive index* **kussetsuritsu**
占有率 *share, percentage* **senyūritsu**
視聴率 *audience rating, attendance* **shichōritsu**
失業率 *unemployment rate* **shitsugyōritsu** ~
収益率 *earning rate* **shūekiritsu**
就学率 *school attendance rate* **shūgakuritsu**
増加率 *rate of increase* **zōkaritsu**

❷ 率先 *taking the lead, ~initiative* **sossen**
統率 *leadership, command* **tōsotsu**

度*egree, 91*	複*ultiply, 830*
程*egree, 144*	数*umber, 156*
倍*ultiply, 950*	

傘*mbrella, 142*

117-B

Selling 率ate of 傘mbrellas enthused Cinderella...

人⇔亻 (person)

傘mbrella

kasa, SAN
umbrella, parasol

FLIP: 1.0.b. Whole (stem)

雨傘 *umbrella* **amagasa**
番傘 *coarse umbrella* **bangasa**
日傘 *parasol* **higasa**
唐傘 *paper umbrella* **karagasa**
傘屋 *umbrella maker, umbrella shop* **kasaya**
傘寿 *one's eightieth birthday* **sanju**
傘下 *affiliate company, subsidiary* **sanka**
鉄傘 *iron dome* **tessan**
洋傘 *umbrella* **yōgasa**
相々傘 *"under the same umbrella..."* **aiaigasa**
傘立て *umbrella stand* **kasadate**
蝙蝠傘 *umbrella* **kōmorigasa**
置き傘 *spare umbrella* **okigasa**
落下傘 *parachute* **rakkasan**
落下傘兵 *paratrooper* **rakkasanhei**
蛇の目傘 *target design umbrella* **janomegasa**

雨*aining, 417*	雲*loud, 154*
候*eather, 122*	空*ky, 394*
水*ater, 9*	雷*hunder, 136*
候*eather, 122*	

座*eating, 109*

118-A

給upply of 絵rawings & 絵ketches for the art fest...

糸 (thread, continuity)

給upply　給rovision

KYŪ

supply, provision, pay, dispense

FLIP: 7.0.a. Right (flat)

月給	monthly pay, ~salary **gekkyū**
配給	supply, rationing **haikyū**
発給	issuance, provision **hakkyū**
薄給	cheap salary, low pay **hakkyū**
補給	supply, provisions, materiel **hokyū**
俸給	salary, wage **hōkyū**
本給	basic-, regular pay **honkyū**
自給	self-supply, self-sufficiency **jikkyū**
時給	hourly pay **jikyū**
需給	supply & demand **jukyū**
受給	receiving payment, being paid **jukyū**
供給	supply, service **kyōkyū**
給付	benefit, payment, provisions **kyūfu**
給費	paid-up expenses **kyūhi**
給仕	waiter, waitress **kyūji**
給血	blood donation **kyūketsu**
給料	salary, wage **kyūryō**
給紙	loading paper, paper supply **kyūshi**
給食	school lunch, lunch service **kyūshoku**

給水	water supply **kyūsui**
給与	pay, salary, wages **kyūyo**
給油	lubrication, oiling, greasing **kyūyu**
恩給	pension money **onkyū**
支給	supply, allowance, payment **shikyū**
昇給	raise, pay rise **shōkyū**
週給	weekly pay, ~wages **shūkyū**
定給	fixed income, regular salary **teikyū**
有給	gainfully employed **yūkyū**
基本給	base salary, ~wage **kihonkyū**

充upply, 884	与upply, 349
納upply, 296	品oodies, 901

絵rawing, 143

118-B

給upply of 絵rawings & 絵ketches for the art fest...

糸 (thread, continuity)

絵ketch　絵rawing

KAI, E

sketch, drawing, illustration

FLIP: 7.2.a. Right Top (flat)
Facing: 2.2. East ☞ (V)

油絵	oil painting **aburae**
絵札	picture card **efuda**
絵筆	paintbrush **efude**
絵柄	painting pattern, ~design **egara**
絵心	artistically-oriented **egokoro**
絵詞	caption, picture description **ekotoba**
絵本	picture-, illustrated book **ehon**
絵馬	votive picture **ema**
絵師	painter, artist **eshi**
絵姿	portrait, likeness **esugata**
絵図	drawing, illustration, plan **ezu**
色絵	coloured painting **iroe**
影絵	shadow picture **kagee**
絵画	picture, painting **kaiga**
口絵	frontispiece **kuchie**
錦絵	woodblock printing **nishikie**
挿絵	illustration, sketch, drawing **sashie**
姿絵	portrait **sugatae**
墨絵	Indian-ink drawing **sumie**

砂絵	sand illustration **sunae**
漆絵	lacquer drawing **urushie**
絵葉書	postcard **ehagaki**
絵入り	pictorial, illustrated **eiri**
絵描き	painter, artist **ekaki**
絵巻物	picture scroll **emakimono**
絵日記	picture diary, sketch diary **enikki**
絵の具	colours, paints **enogu**
隠し絵	picture puzzle **kakushie**
塗り絵	colouring lines **nurie**
笑い絵	comic illustration **waraie**

図rawing, 47	彩olour, 914
描ketch, 271	色olour, 403
画ainting, 35	芸rts, 619

給upply, 143

119-A

短*hort nautical* 程*egree set by Captain Smee...*

矢 (archery arrow)

短*hort*　短*rief*

mijika(i), TAN
short, brief

FLIP: 7.0.a. Right (flat)

最短 *the shortest~* **saitan**
短文 *short sentence* **tanbun**
短調 *minor key* **tanchō**
短大 *junior college (two-years)* **tandai**
短銃 *pistol, handgun* **tanjū**
短歌 *tanka, Japanese poem (17-syllable)* **tanka**
短剣 *dagger, short sword* **tanken**
短見 *short-sighted, near-sighted* **tanken**
短期 *short term, ~period* **tanki**
短気 *short-, quick temper* **tanki**
短命 *short life, early death* **tanmei**
短音 *short sound* **tan'on**
短波 *shortwave* **tanpa**
短髪 *short hair* **tanpatsu**
短編 *selected writings, short story* **tanpen**
短評 *short remarks, brief comment* **tanpyō**
短絡 *simplistic thinking* **tanraku**
短慮 *imprudence, rashness* **tanryo**
短詩 *short poem* **tanshi**

短資 *short-term loan* **tanshi**
短信 *brief letter, short news* **tanshin**
短針 *clock short hand* **tanshin**
短所 *shortcomings, weak points* **tansho**
短縮 *reduction, downsizing* **tanshuku**
短足 *short-legged person* **tansoku**
短冊 *paper strips* **tanzaku**
手短 *short, quick* **temijika**
超短波 *ultrashort waves* **chōtanpa**
短時日 *short time, temporary* **tanjijitsu**
短距離 *short distance* **tankyori**

小*mall, 459*	細*lender, 138*
少*ew, 459*	長*ong, 273*

程*egree, 144*

119-B

短*hort nautical* 程*egree set by Captain Smee...*

禾 (tree branch)

程*egree*　程*xtent*

hodo, TEI
degree, extent, established form

FLIP: 7.0.a. Right (flat)

道程 *distance, gap, interval* **dōtei**
程程 *moderate, temperate* **hodohodo**
上程 *submitting a bill for passage* **jōtei**
課程 *course, curriculum* **katei**
⇒博士課程 *Ph.D., doctoral course* **hakashi katei**
⇒修士課程 *MA, MS, master's course* **shūshi katei**
過程 *process, procedure* **katei**
規程 *rules & regulations* **kitei**
航程 *flight, cruise* **kōtei**
工程 *work progress* **kōtei**
教程 *course, curriculum* **kyōtei**
中程 *half-way, mid-way* **nakahodo**
何程 *about how much* **nanihodo**
成程 *"no wonder..." (colloquial)* **naruhodo**
日程 *daily schedule* **nittei**
後程 *later, afterwards* **nochihodo**
音程 *musical interval* **ontei**
里程 *distance, gap, interval* **ritei**
路程 *itinerary, travel schedule* **rotei**

旅程 *travel distance, mileage* **ryotei**
先程 *a little while ago* **sakihodo**
射程 *shooting range* **shatei**
程度 *degree, level, extent, standard* **teido**
程度問題 *question of degree* **teido mondai**
山程 *voluminous, numerous* **yamahodo**
余程 *extremely, very much* **yohodo**
程合い *moderation, temperance* **hodoai**
程近い *nearby, adjacent* **hodochikai**
方程式 *mathematical equation* **hōteishiki**

度*egree, 91*	回*otate, 458*
倍*ultiply, 950*	周*ap, 280*
複*ultiply, 830*	

税*axes, 941*

120-A

賃*alary* 賃*ayments below* 貸*ental increments...*

貝 (shell, old money)

賃*ayment* 賃*alary*

CHIN
payment, salary, charge

FLIP: 4.0.b. Bottom (stem)

賃上げ *wage increase, ~hike* **chin'age**
賃金 *wage, salary* **chingin**
賃金カット *pay cut, salary reduction* **chinginkatto**
賃金格差 *wage differential* **chingin kakusa**
賃銭 *wages, salary* **chinsen**
賃借 *lease, rent out* **chinshaku**
賃借権 *tenancy rights* **chinshakuken**
賃借人 *lessee, tenant* **chinshakunin**
賃借料 *rental fee* **chinshakuryō**
賃仕事 *piecemeal work* **chinshigoto**
賃貸 *rental, lease* **chintai**
賃貸人 *lessor, landowner* **chintainin**
賃貸料 *rent, rental fee* **chintairyō**
賃貸借 *lease, rent out* **chintaishaku**
賃貸契約 *lease contract* **chintai keiyaku**
駄賃 *tip, reward* **dachin**
船賃 *freight fare, cargo fee* **funachin**
工賃 *wage, salary* **kōchin**
無賃 *gratis, free-of-charge* **muchin**

労賃 *wages, salary* **rōchin**
店賃 *store rent* **tanachin**
運賃 *freight fare, ~charges* **unchin**
⇒往復運賃 *round-trip fare* **ōfuku unchin**
⇒旅客運賃 *passenger fares* **ryokyaku unchin**
家賃 *house rent* **yachin**
宿賃 *lodging-, hotel bill* **yadochin**
借り賃 *rent, hire* **karichin**
最賃法 *minimum wage law* **saichinhō**
手間賃 *wage, salary* **temachin**
泊まり賃 *hotel charges, ~bill* **tomarichin**

納*ayment, 296*		金*oney, 25*	
払*ayment, 682*		幣*oney, 171*	
料*ayment, 194*		財*inance, 186*	

債*ebts, 823*

120-B

賃*alary* 賃*ayments below* 貸*ental increments...*

貝 (shell, old money)

貸*ental* 貸*ease*

ka(su), TAI
rental, lease, loan-out, rent-out

FLIP: 4.0.b. Bottom (stem)

賃貸 *rental, "for rent..."* **chintai**
賃貸人 *lessor, tenant* **chintainin**
賃貸料 *rent, lease* **chintairyō**
金貸し *money lending* **kanekashi**
賃貸契約 *lease contract* **chintai keiyaku**
貸間 *rental room* **kashima**
貸与 *lending out, loaning* **taiyo**
貸し本 *loan bookkeeping; rental books* **kashihon**
貸し方 *creditor, lender* **kashikata**
貸し金 *loan, debt, borrowings* **kashikin**
貸し元 *financier, lender; boss* **kashimoto**
貸し主 *lender, creditor, landlord* **kashinushi**
貸し席 *meeting room for rent* **kashiseki**
貸し家 *house-for-rent* **kashiya**
貸しビル *building for rent* **kashibiru**
貸し金庫 *rental safety-deposit box* **kashikinko**
貸し切る *charter, reserve* **kashikiru**
貸し別荘 *summer house for rent* **kashi bessō**
貸し倒れ *non-performing loan* **kashidaore**

貸し出し *loan-, lending business* **kashidashi**
貸し衣装 *rental costume* **kashiishō**
貸し付け *loan, debt, borrowings* **kashitsuke**
前貸し *advance payment, ~deposit* **maegashi**
間貸し *rental room* **magashi**
又貸し *sublease, subletting* **matagashi**
貸借 *debts & credits, loan* **taishaku**
貸借関係 *financial relationship* **taishaku kankei**
貸借期限 *life of a loan* **taishaku kigen**
担保貸し *secured-, collateral loan* **tanpogashi**
転貸 *sub-lease, subletting* **tentai**

借*orrow, 336*		払*ayment, 682*	
賃*ayment, 145*		料*ayment, 194*	
納*ayment, 296*		財*inance, 186*	

貨*reight, 191*

121-A
Eiffel 塔ower 搭oads of steel power...

土 (ground, soil)

塔*ower*　　塔*urret*

TŌ
tower, turret

仏塔　*Buddhist pagoda* **buttō**
堂塔　*temple tower* **dōtō**
砲塔　*gun turret* **hōtō**
石塔　*stone pagoda, tombstone* **sekitō**
尖塔　*steeple pinnacle* **sentō**
斜塔　*leaning tower* **shatō**
鉄塔　*steel tower* **tettō**
塔婆　*magnificent building* **tōba**
蟻の塔　*anthill* **ari no tō**
貯水塔　*water tower* **chosuitō**
慰霊塔　*memorial tower for the dead* **ireitō**
管制塔　*pagoda, tower* **kanseitō**
⇒航空管制塔　*flight control tower* **kōkū kanseitō**
金字塔　*monumental landmark* **kinjitō**
広告塔　*ivory tower; column advertising* **kōkokutō**
給水塔　*water control tower* **kyūsuitō**
信号塔　*signal tower* **shingōtō**
司令塔　*command-, control tower* **shireitō**
卒塔婆　*grave wooden tablet* **sotoba**

FLIP: 7.0.a. Right (flat)

五重の塔　*five-storied pagoda* **gojūnotō**
象牙の塔　*memorial tower* **zōgenotō**
エッフェル塔　*Eiffel Tower* **efferutō**

閣*ower, 945*
楼*ower, 127*
城*astle, 243*

搭*reight, 146*

121-B
Eiffel 塔ower 搭oads of steel power...

手⇔扌 (hand, manual)

搭*oading*　搭*reight*

TŌ
loading, freight, boarding

搭乗　*boarding, going on board* **tōjō**
搭乗橋　*boarding bridge* **tōjōbashi**
搭乗口　*boarding gate* **tōjōguchi**
搭乗員　*transportation crew, ~staff* **tōjōin**
搭乗券　*boarding pass, ~ticket* **tōjōken**
搭乗者　*passenger* **tōjōsha**
搭乗手続き　*boarding procedures* **tōjō tetsuzuki**
搭載　*loading, equipping* **tōsai**

FLIP: 7.0.a. Right (flat)

運*ransport, 295*	届*eliver, 631*
搬*ransport, 323*	荷*reight, 877*
輸*hipment, 660*	貨*reight, 191*
送*ending, 708*	乗*ide on, 511*

塔*ower, 146*

122-A

Fish 揚aised from the sea, 揚ried in 場lace for me...

手⇔扌 (hand, manual)

°揚*aise*   °揚*rying*

a(geru), a(garu), YŌ
raise, rise high, exalt; frying

FLIP: 7.2.a. Right Top (flat)

❶浮揚 *floating, drifting* **fuyō**
発揚 *enhance, boost* **hatsuyō**
飛揚 *flight, flying* **hiyō**
掲揚 *hoisting a flag, flag carrier* **keiyō**
高揚 *elevation, raising to a height* **kōyō**
昂揚 *raise, heighten, uplift* **kōyō**
止揚 *sublation* **shiyō**
称揚 *extol, praise, admire* **shōyō**
揚言 *boasting, bragging, self-conceit* **yōgen**
抑揚 *intonation, modulation* **yokuyō**
揚陸 *unloading, landing* **yōriku**
揚陸料 *landing fee* **yōrikuryō**
揚力 *lifting power* **yōryoku**
悠揚 *serene composure* **yūyō**
揚げ戸 *push-up door, shutter* **agedo**
揚羽蝶 *swallowtail butterfly* **agehachō**
揚げ句 *in the end, ultimately* **ageku**
胴揚げ *hoist (someone) shoulder-high* **dōage**
旗揚げ *flag-raising* **hataage**

水揚げ *raising fish catch from water* **mizuage**
荷揚げ *unloading, discharging* **niage**
帯揚げ *obi bustle* **obiage**
陸揚げ *landing, unloading* **rikuage**
意気揚々 *exultant, triumphant* **ikiyōyō**
揚げ足取り *faultfinding, complainer* **ageashidori**
引き揚げる *withdraw, pull back* **hikiageru**
❷油揚げ *fried tofu* **aburaage**
揚げ物 *fries, fried food* **agemono**
空揚げ *deep-fried chicken* **karaage**
精進揚げ *vegetable tempura* **shōjin'age**

炊*ooking, 865*
飯*ooked rice, 256*
拾*ick-up, 231*
昇*scend, 299*
上*scend, 859*
登*limb, 437*

場*ocation, 147*

122-B

Fish 揚aised from the sea, 揚ried in 場lace for me...

土 (ground, soil)

場*ocation*   場*lace*

ba, JŌ
location, place, locality, venue

FLIP: 7.2.a. Right Top (flat)

場合 *case, occasion* **baai**
場面 *scene, sight, view* **bamen**
場所 *place, room* **basho**
議場 *assembly hall, chamber* **gijō**
広場 *open space* **hiroba**
市場 *market* **ichiba, shijō**
場外 *outside* **jōgai**
場内 *place, grounds, hall* **jōnai**
会場 *meeting place* **kaijō**
欠場 *absence, non-attendance* **ketsujō**
球場 *baseball field* **kyūjō**
満場 *whole house, ~audience* **manjō**
農場 *farm, plantation, ranch* **nōjō**
入場 *entrance, admission* **nyūjō**
酒場 *bar, pub, night club* **sakaba**
戦場 *battlefield, theatre-of-war* **senjō**
式場 *ceremonial hall* **shikijō**
職場 *worksite, workplace* **shokuba**
宿場 *stage* **shukuba**

相場 *market price* **sōba**
為替相場 *currency market* **kawase sōba**
立場 *point of view, viewpoint* **tachiba**
山場 *turning point, main event* **yamaba**
場違い *out of place, wrong place* **bachigai**
場所柄 *uniqueness of a place* **bashogara**
宴会場 *banquet hall* **enkaijō**
飛行場 *airport, airfield* **hikōjō**
歌劇場 *opera house* **kagekijō**
置き場 *place, place to put something* **okiba**
仕事場 *workplace, ~shop* **shigotoba**
売り場 *selling counter* **uriba**

所*ocation, 676*
箇*[places], 52*

湯*ot-water, 932*

123-A
Take refuge in the 弧rc of 孤olitude...

弧rc

弓 (archery bow)

KO
arc

電弧	electric arc **denko**
円弧	circular arc **enko**
括弧	parenthesis **kakko**
弧度	radian, circular **kodo**
弧状	arc-shaped **kojō**
弧形	arc curve **kokei**
弧光	arc lamp **kokō**
弧線	arc of a circle **kosen**
弧愁	solitary contemplation **koshū**
劣弧	minor arc **rekko**

Facing: 4.0. 🐦🐦 Apart

弓 *rchery, 348*
矢 *rrow, 18*

孤 *lone, 148*

123-B
Take refuge in the 弧rc of 孤olitude...

孤olitary   孤lone

子 (child)

KO
solitary, alone, insularity, isolated

孤独	solitude, solitary, isolated **kodoku**
孤影	lone image (solitary island) **koei**
孤軍	isolated army **kogun**
孤児	orphan, parentless child **koji**
孤城	isolated castle **kojō**
孤客	lone traveller, solo guest **kokyaku**
孤高	proud loneliness **kokō**
孤立	isolation, helplessness **koritsu**
孤立政策	isolationist-, autarky policy **koritsu seisaku**
孤立主義	national isolationism **koritsu shugi**
孤塁	isolated position **korui**
孤島	solitary island **kotō**
戦災孤児	war orphan **sensai koji**
天涯孤独	completely isolated, ~alone **tengai kodoku**
絶海の孤島	distant solitary island **zekkai no kotō**

Facing: 4.0. 🐦🐦 Apart

自 *elf, 462*	寡 *lone, 161*
己 *elf, 5*	唯 *olitary, 642*
独 *lone, 369*	一 *ne, 858*

弧 *rc, 148*

124-A

壱ne by 壱ne, 老ld persons going, going, gone...

士 (samurai, warrior)

壱ne

ICHI
one

壱月　January **ichigatsu**
壱万円　ten thousand Japanese yen **ichiman'en**
壱岐島　Ikijima island, Nagasaki Prefecture **ikijima**

FLIP: 3.0.a. Top (flat)

一ne, 858		百undred, 14	
逐ne-by-one, 479		千housand, 74	
半ne-half, 484		万en thousand, 465	
片ne-sided, 359		億undred-million, 340	
十en, 344			

売elling, 259

124-B

壱ne by 壱ne, 老ld-persons going, going, gone...

老 (old person)

老lderly　老ld person

o(iru), fu(keru), RŌ
elderly, old person, aged

中老　elderly, senior citizen **chūrō**
元老　elder statesman, grand old man **genrō**
古老　old persons focus on the past **korō**
老婆　old woman **rōba**
老婆心　grandmotherly concern **rōbashin**
老害　troubles done by old people **rōgai**
老眼　old age farsightedness **rōgan**
老眼鏡　glasses for the elderly **rōgankyō**
老後　old age, remaining years **rōgo**
老廃　wasted, spent, useless **rōhai**
老兵　old soldier **rōhei**
老舗　very old shop **rōhō**, **shinise**
老人　old person, elderly **rōjin**
老化　ageing, greying society **rōka**
老化現象　ageing phenomena **rōka genshō**
老巧　experienced old hand **rōkō**
老骨　working past old age **rōkotsu**
老境　old age, senior citizen **rōkyō**
老朽　superannuation **rōkyū**

Facing: 2.0. East ☞ (W)

老年　old age, senior citizen **rōnen**
老齢　old age, senior citizen **rōrei**
老成　experienced hand, professional **rōsei**
老子　Lao-Tse, Lao-Tzu **rōshi**
老死　death by old age **rōshi**
老醜　senility ugliness **rōshū**
老体　old body **rōtai**
老残　feeble old body **rōzan**
早老　premature ageing **sōrō**
老い先　twilight, remaining years **oisaki**
敬老の日　respect-for-the-aged day **keirō no hi**

古ld, 477	
翁ld man, 238	
婆ld woman, 32	

考hinking, 392

125-A
Patient glows when donor of 腸ntestine 賜estows...

肉⇔月 (flesh, body part)

腸*ntestine*

CHŌ
intestine

FLIP: 7.2.a. Right Top (flat)

腸炎 *intestinal inflammation* **chōen**
直腸 *rectum* **chokuchō**
腸満 *abdominal dropsy* **chōman**
脱腸 *hernia* **dacchō**
大腸 *large intestine* **daichō**
大腸炎 *intestinal colitis* **daichōen**
断腸 *heartbreak, heartache* **danchō**
胃腸 *digestion, stomach & intestines* **ichō**
胃腸病 *gastronomic illness* **ichōbyō**
胃腸薬 *indigestion drug* **ichōyaku**
灌腸 *enema* **kanchō**
結腸 *colon* **kecchō**
鼓腸 *tympanites* **kochō**
盲腸 *appendix, cecum* **mōchō**
盲腸炎 *appendicitis* **mōchōen**
小腸 *small intestines* **shōchō**
羊腸たる *zigzag road* **yōchōtaru**
腸閉塞 *intestinal clogging* **chōheisoku**
腸潰瘍 *ulcer in the intestines* **chōkaiyō**

腸捻転 *volvulus, twisted intestines* **chōnenten**
腸詰め *sausage* **chōzume**
整腸剤 *intestinal medicine* **seichōzai**
十二指腸 *duodenum* **jūni shichō**

胃 *tomach, 598*
腹 *tomach, 830*

腹 *tomach, 830*

125-B
Patient glows when donor of 腸ntestine 賜estows...

貝 (shell, old money)

賜

賜*estow*　賜*equeath*

tamawa(ru), SHI
bestow, bequeath, endow

FLIP: 6.0.b. Left (stem)
FLIP: 7.2.a. Right Top (flat)

下賜 *imperial grant* **kashi**
恩賜 *imperial gift* **onshi**
賜宴 *court banquet* **shien**
賜杯 *emperor's cup, ~trophy* **shihai**
賜暇 *leave of absence, furlough* **shika**
賜金 *cash grant, cash reward* **shikin**
賞賜 *reward* **shōshi**
賜物 *gift, boon* **tamamono**

施 *estow, 649*　　贈 *onation, 838*
催 *ponsor, 416*　　頂 *eceive, 134*
献 *onation, 414*　　謝 *ratitude, 876*

腸 *ntestine, 150*

126-A

携articipate & 擁upport: No 携ortable phones in courts...

手⇔扌 (hand, manual)

❶携articipate ❷携andcarry

tazusa(eru), tazusa(waru), KEI
participate, partake; handcarry

Facing: 4.0. ～ Apart

❶ 連携 coalition, tie up **renkei**
提携 coalition, tie up **teikei**
⇒技術提携 technical tie-up **gijutsu teikei**
相携えて together-, along with **aitazusaete**

❷ 必携 indispensable book **hikkei**
携行 carrying, portable **keikō**
携帯 carrying, portable **keitai**
携帯品 personal effects carry-ons **keitaihin**
携帯電話 cell phone, mobile phone **keitai denwa**

加articipate, 201	協ooperate, 577
共ogether, 302	合ogether, 232

擁upport, 151

126-B

携articipate & 擁upport: No 携ortable phones in courts...

手⇔扌 (hand, manual)

❶擁upport ❷擁mbrace

YŌ
support, backing, help; hugging, embrace

FLIP: 7.2.b. Right Top (stem)
Facing: 4.0. ～ Apart

❶ 擁立 assistance, support **yōritsu**
擁護 protection, support, defence **yōgo**
擁護者 protector, supporter, defender **yōgosha**

❷ 抱擁 embrace, hug **hōyō**

援upport, 820	助upport, 953
貢upport, 625	協ooperate, 577
支upport, 201	採dopt, 915

推ecommend, 777

127-A

To 熟ipen & 熟ature, 塾utorial-schools assure...

火⇔灬 (fire)

FLIP: 6.1. Left Top

熟ipen   熟aturity

u(reru), JUKU
ripen, maturity

円熟	*maturity, mellowness* **enjuku**
半熟	*half-boiled; half ripe* **hanjuku**
豊熟	*abundant harvest, ripening* **hōjuku**
熟考	*careful deliberation, ~consideration* **jukkō**
熟知	*familiarity, full knowledge* **jukuchi**
熟談	*mature-, careful discussion* **jukudan**
熟読	*intensive reading, perusal* **jukudoku**
熟議	*careful deliberation, ~consideration* **jukugi**
熟語	*idiom, figurative speech* **jukugo**
熟眠	*deep-, good-, sound sleep* **jukumin**
熟年	*middle age, one's fortyish* **jukunen**
熟覧	*scrutiny, minute inspection* **jukuran**
熟練	*skill, mastery, expertise* **jukuren**
熟慮	*deliberation, careful thinking* **jukuryo**
熟成	*maturation, ripening* **jukusei**
熟視	*intent stare, ~gaze, ~stare* **jukushi**
熟思	*careful consideration* **jukushi**
熟柿	*ripe persimmon* **jukushi**
熟睡	*deep-, good-, sound sleep* **jukusui**

熟達	*mastery, proficiency, expertise* **jukutatsu**
完熟	*full matured, fully-ripened* **kanjuku**
黄熟	*turning yellow (ripening)* **kōjuku**
未熟	*unripe, inexperienced, greenhorn* **mijuku**
未熟児	*premature baby* **mijukuji**
未熟者	*greenhorn, inexperienced* **mijukumono**
老熟	*maturity, mellowness* **rōjuku**
成熟	*maturity, ripening* **seijuku**
習熟	*mastery, proficiency, expertise* **shūjuku**
修熟	*mastery, proficiency, expertise* **shūjuku**
早熟	*precocity, genius* **sōjuku**

> 満*aturate, 567*
> 完*omplete, 196*

> 熱*eat, 153*

127-B

To 熟ipen & 熟ature, 塾utorial-schools assure...

土 (ground, soil)

FLIP: 4.0.a. Bottom (flat)
FLIP: 6.1. Left Top

塾utorial school

JUKU
tutorial school, cram school

義塾	*private school* **gijuku**
塾長	*cram school director* **jukuchō**
塾生	*cram school student* **jukusei**
家塾	*private school* **kajuku**
入塾	*entering a cram school* **nyūjuku**
私塾	*private lessons after school* **shijuku**
学習塾	*private cram school* **gakushūjuku**

> 学*tudy, 346*　　修*aster, 898*
> 校*chool, 773*　　考*hinking, 392*
> 教*ducate, 385*　　勉*fforts, 527*
> 習*earning, 238*

> 熟*ipen, 152*

128-A

熱everish 勢igour from youth's rigour...

熱*hermal*   熱*eat*

火⇔灬 (fire)

熱

FLIP: 6.1. Left Top

atsu(i), NETSU
thermal, heat, fever

熱っぽい	passionate, feverish	**netsuppoi**
微熱	slight fever	**binetsu**
防熱	heat resistance	**bōnetsu**
白熱	incandescence, radiance, lustre	**hakunetsu**
発熱	heat emission	**hatsunetsu**
比熱	specific heat	**hinetsu**
情熱	passion, enthusiasm	**jōnetsu**
加熱	heating	**kanetsu**
光熱	light & heating	**kōnetsu**
高熱	intense heat	**kōnetsu**
熱血	hot blood, ardour, passion	**nekketsu**
熱気	heat, hot air, enthusiasm	**nekki**
熱狂	enthusiasm, excitement	**nekkyō**
熱発	having a fever	**neppatsu**
熱賛	overpraising, overextolling	**nessan**
熱誠	earnestness, eagerness	**nessei**
熱心	eager, enthusiastic	**nesshin**
熱愛	ardent-, passionate love	**netsuai**
熱病	fever, temperature	**netsubyō**

熱度	heat temperature	**netsudo**
熱演	enthusiastic performance	**netsuen**
熱願	ardent wish, burning desire	**netsugan**
熱意	zeal, zest, enthusiasm	**netsui**
熱情	passion, ardour, fervour	**netsujō**
熱感	feverish, passion, bullish	**netsukan**
熱帯	tropics, tropical regions	**nettai**
亜熱帯	subtropical-, semitropical zone	**anettai**
蒸発熱	evaporation heat	**jōhatsunetsu**
熱射病	heatstroke, sunstroke	**nesshabyō**
熱処理	heat treatment, heat therapy	**netsushori**

温*ot temperature, 622*	夏*ummer, 606*
暑*ot weather, 615*	汗*erspire, 710*

勢*igour, 153*

128-B

熱everish 勢igour from youth's rigour...

勢*igour*   勢*itality*

力 (strength, force)

勢

FLIP: 6.1. Left Top

ikio(i), SEI
vigour, vitality, enthusiasm, audacity, drive, vibrant, power

病勢	patient's condition	**byōsei**
現勢	present state-of-affairs, status quo	**gensei**
語勢	emphasis, stress	**gosei**
豪勢	luxurious, sumptuous, elegant	**gōsei**
強勢	emphasis, stress	**gōsei**
筆勢	Kanji writing strokes	**hissei**
威勢	spirits, power, strength	**isei**
時勢	spirit of times	**jisei**
情勢	state-of-affairs, circumstances	**jōsei**
加勢	help, support, assistance	**kasei**
火勢	flames, blaze	**kasei**
形勢	state-of-affairs, circumstances	**keisei**
権勢	power & influence	**kensei**
気勢	spirit, ardour, elan vita	**kisei**
国勢	state of the nation	**kokusei**
攻勢	offensive, attack, assault, strike	**kōsei**
虚勢	bluff, bluster, ruse	**kyosei**
去勢	castration, emasculation, gelding	**kyosei**
劣勢	inferiority, mediocrity, weakness	**ressei**

勢力	power, force, strength	**seiryoku**
勢力家	influential family	**seiryokuka**
勢揃い	array, muster	**seizoroi**
姿勢	posture, attitude, demeanour	**shisei**
守勢	defensive posture	**shusei**
衰勢	decline, waning	**suisei**
態勢	attitude, condition	**taisei**
退勢	decline, waning	**taisei**
運勢	fortune, luck	**unsei**
余勢	reserve strength, remaining vigour	**yosei**
勢力範囲	sphere-of-influence	**seiryoku han'i**

精*igour, 792*	張*tretch, 274*
力*trength, 351*	構*osture, 714*
伸*tretch, 713*	努*fforts, 44*

熱*ipen, 152*

129-A

曇*oggy and* 曇*loudy,* 雲*louds make football fans rowdy...*

日 (sunlight, daytime)

 曇*oggy*　　　曇*loudy*

FLIP: 3.0.a. Top (flat)

kumo(ru), DON
foggy, cloudy, fuzzy

曇天　*overcast, cloudy skies* **donten**
花曇　*springtime cloudy weather* **hanagumori**
晴曇　*fine & cloudy weather* **seidon**
雪曇り　*looks of snowfall* **yukigumori**
雨曇り　*overcast-, cloudy weather* **amagumori**
朝曇り　*overcast-, cloudy morning* **asagumori**
本曇り　*overcast skies* **hongumori**
高曇り　*high clouds* **takagumori**
薄曇り　*slightly cloudy* **usugumori**
掻き曇り　*overcast skies* **kakikumori**
曇りがち　*cloudy weather* **kumorigachi**

雲*loud, 154*	霧*oggy, 454*
空*ky, 394*	雰*oggy, 518*
晴*lear-up, 792*	

鼻*ose, 169*

129-B

曇*oggy and* 曇*loudy,* 雲*louds make football fans rowdy...*

雨 (weather)

雲*louds*

kumo, UN
clouds

FLIP: 3.0.b. Top (stem)

雨雲　*rain clouds* **amagumo**
暗雲　*dark clouds* **an'un**
風雲　*windy clouds* **fūun**
片雲　*speck of clouds* **hen'un**
雲雀　*Japanese skylark* **hibari**
巻雲　*cirrus* **ken'un**
絹雲　*cirrus* **ken'un**
雲脚　*cloud movement* **kumoashi**
雲助　*palanquin bearer thugs* **kumosuke**
黒雲　*dark clouds* **kurokumo, kokuun**
密雲　*dense clouds* **mitsuun**
群雲　*gathering clouds* **murakumo**
夏雲　*summer clouds* **natsugumo**
雷雲　*thunderclouds* **raiun**
彩雲　*shining clouds* **saiun**
星雲　*Nebula* **seiun**
戦雲　*war clouds, signs of war* **sen'un**
雲丹　*sea urchin* **uni**
雲海　*sea of clouds* **unkai**

雲母　*Mica* **unmo**
雲霧　*foggy clouds* **unmu**
雲水　*wandering Buddhist monk* **unsui**
闇雲　*recklessly, at random, stray* **yamikumo**
夕雲　*evening sky, night sky* **yūgumo**
雪雲　*snow clouds* **yukigumo**
雲行きが怪しい　*"not looking good..."*
　　kumoyuki ga ayashii
浮き雲　*floating clouds* **ukigumo**
夕立雲　*shower clouds* **yūdachigumo**
青雲の志　*lofty ambitions* **seiun no kokorozashi**
雲泥の差　*heaven & earth gap* **undei no sa**

曇*oggy, 154*	高*igh, 435*
空*ky, 394*	白*hite, 15*

雲*loudy, 154*

130-A

銑*ig iron indeed looks like* 鉄*ron...*

銑*ig iron*

SEN
  pig iron
白銑 *white pig iron* **hakusen**
銑鉄 *pig iron* **sentetsu**
溶銑 *molten iron* **yōsen**

金 (metal)

FLIP: 6.0.b. Left (stem)
FLIP: 7.1. Right (Sort Of)

金*etal, 25*	鉄*ron, 155*
鋳*asting, 440*	鋼*teel, 975*

鉄*ron, 155*	鋭*harp, 943*

130-B

銑*ig iron indeed looks like* 鉄*ron...*

鉄*ron*

kurogane, TETSU
  iron
鋳鉄 *cast iron, forged steel* **chūtetsu**
金鉄 *ironware, steel products* **kintetsu**
鋼鉄 *steel, iron* **kōtetsu**
錬鉄 *wrought iron* **rentetsu**
砂鉄 *iron sand* **satetsu**
銑鉄 *pig iron* **sentetsu**
寸鉄 *bare-handed, unarmed* **suntetsu**
蹄鉄 *blacksmith, horseshoe* **teitetsu**
鉄管 *iron pipe* **tekkan**
鉄拳 *iron fist, strong blow* **tekken**
鉄器 *ironware, steel products* **tekki**
鉄筋 *reinforcing bars* **tekkin**
鉄甲 *iron armour* **tekkō**
鉄鉱 *iron ore, iron deposits* **tekkō**
鉄鋼 *steel, iron* **tekkō**
鉄鉱石 *ironstone* **tekkōseki**
鉄骨 *steel frame* **tekkotsu**
鉄橋 *iron-, railroad bridge* **tekkyō**
鉄板 *steel plate* **teppan**

金 (metal)

FLIP: 6.0.a. Left (flat)
FLIP: 7.1. Right (Sort Of)

鉄砲 *gun, firearm* **teppō**
鉄則 *spartan rule* **tessoku**
鉄道 *railway, railroad* **tetsudō**
鉄人 *man of steel* **tetsujin**
鉄兜 *steel helmet* **tetsukabuto**
鉄材 *iron material* **tetsuzai**
地下鉄 *subway* **chikatetsu**
鉄工所 *ironworks, ironsmith* **tekkōsho**
鉄格子 *iron bars* **tetsugōshi**
鉄条網 *wire obstacles* **tetsujōmō**

銑*ig iron, 155*	鋳*asting, 440*
金*etal, 25*	鋼*teel, 975*

131-A

Even 数umbers for the same 類ype of lumbers...

攵 (action)

数umber 数ount

kazu, kazo(eru), SŪ, SU

number, numeral, count, mathematics

FLIP: 6.1. Left Top

頭数 *number of persons* **atamakazu**	品数 *inventory, in-stock* **shinakazu**
度数 *frequency, number of times; volume* **dosū**	指数 *exponent* **shisū**
複数 *plural* **fukusū**	素数 *prime number* **sosū**
負数 *negative number* **fusū**	数学 *mathematics, arithmetic* **sūgaku**
偶数 *even number* **gūsū**	数字 *number, numeral* **sūji**
因数 *factor, multiple* **insū**	数量 *volume, quantity* **sūryō**
除数 *divisor* **josū**	数詞 *numeral* **sūshi**
常数 *constant* **jōsū**	数式 *formula, numerical equation* **sūshiki**
数珠 *rosary beads* **juzu**	対数 *logarithm* **taisū**
回数 *frequency, number of times* **kaisū**	数え年 *one's age at the year's end* **kazoedoshi**
関数 *math function* **kansū**	得票数 *number of votes* **tokūhyōsū**
係数 *co-efficient* **keisū**	数え切れない *countless* **kazoekirenai**
基数 *cardinal number* **kisū**	
奇数 *odd number* **kisū**	
級数 *progression, series* **kyūsū**	
年数 *number of years* **nensū**	
乱数 *random numbers* **ransū**	
算数 *mathematics, arithmetic* **sansū**	
整数 *integer* **seisū**	

番*umber, 338*	第*[order], 102*
号*umber, 866*	順*equence, 959*

類*ype, 156*

131-B

Even 数umbers for the same 類ype of lumbers...

頁 (large shell, page)

類ype 類ategory

RUI

type, category, classification, genre

FLIP: 5.0.b. Left & Right

分類 *classification, category* **bunrui**	類型 *type, prototype, pattern* **ruikei**
部類 *category, grouping* **burui**	類例 *parallel case, similar instance* **ruirei**
鳥類 *birds* **chōrui**	類書 *similar books* **ruisho**
同類 *same class, ~kind* **dōrui**	類焼 *enveloping fire* **ruishō**
魚類 *kinds of fishes* **gyorui**	類推 *analogy, guess, conjecture* **ruisui**
比類 *parallel case, equal* **hirui**	親類 *immediate relatives* **shinrui**
衣類 *clothes, garments* **irui**	書類 *documents, papers* **shorui**
人類 *mankind, humanity* **jinrui**	生類 *living things* **shōrui**
菌類 *fungi, fungus* **kinrui**	種類 *kind, type* **shurui**
着類 *clothes, clothing* **kirui**	残類 *similar remnants* **zanrui**
穀類 *cereals, grains* **kokurui**	霊長類 *primates* **reichōrui**
無類 *"one of a kind...," the best* **munrui**	
連類 *same class; accomplice* **renrui**	
類別 *classification, category* **ruibetsu**	
類題 *similar themes* **ruidai**	
類語 *synonym, words with same meaning* **ruigo**	
類本 *similar books* **ruihon**	
類似 *resemblance, similarity* **ruiji**	
類化 *assimilate, incorporate* **ruika**	

種*ariety, 430*
雑*arious, 776*
諸*arious, 794*

数*umber, 156*

132-A

僕*asculine-servant* 撲*eaten by a confidant...*

人⇔亻 (person)

僕*asculine-servant*

BOKU
masculine-servant

FLIP: 7.0.b2. Right (stem)

僕夫 *hostler, horse keeper* **bokufu**
僕従 *male servant* **bokujū**
僕等 *we (masculine)* **bokura**
僕達 *we (masculine)* **bokutachi**
忠僕 *loyal servant* **chūboku**
学僕 *student servant* **gakuboku**
下僕 *male servant* **geboku**
義僕 *loyal servant* **giboku**
婢僕 *servant, attendant* **hiboku**
従僕 *servant, attendant* **jūboku**
家僕 *male servant, houseboy* **kaboku**
公僕 *civil servant* **kōboku**
校僕 *school servant* **kōboku**

士*entleman,* 8	壮*asculine,* 367
紳*entleman,* 713	男*asculine,* 597
父*ather,* 467	雄*asculine,* 775
兄*lder-brother,* 203	郎*asculine,* 404

美*eautiful,* 124	業*usiness,* 124

132-B

僕*asculine* 僕*ervant* 撲*eaten by a confidant...*

手⇔扌 (hand, manual)

撲*trike*   撲*auling*

BOKU, MŌ
strike, mauling, storming, assault, charging, hitting

FLIP: 7.0.b2. Right (stem)

撲滅 *eradication, extermination* **bokumetsu**
撲殺 *death by beating* **bokusatsu**
打撲 *blow, strike* **daboku**
打撲傷 *bruise, contusion* **dabokushō**
相撲 *sumo wrestling* **sumō**
相撲取り *sumo wrestler* **sumōtori**
力相撲 *sumo bout of strength* **chikarazumō**
花相撲 *off-season sumo wrestling* **hanazumō**
草相撲 *amateur sumo wrestling* **kusazumō**
前相撲 *amateur sumo bouts* **maezumō**
大相撲 *grand sumo wrestling* **oozumō**
腕相撲 *arm wrestling* **udezumō**
指相撲 *thumb wrestling* **yubizumō**
独り相撲 *"shadow wrestling..."* **hitorizumō**

打*trike,* 636	伐*ttack,* 96
撃*ttack,* 613	痛*ainful,* 60
攻*ttack,* 635	障*njury,* 325
襲*ttack,* 630	損*njury,* 410

美*eautiful,* 124	業*usiness,* 124

133-A

絹*ilk woven into* 縄*ope used to elope...*

糸 (thread, continuity)

FLIP: 7.0.b2. Right (stem)

絹*ilk*

kinu, KEN
silk

絵絹	silk canvas	**eginu**
本絹	pure silk, 100% silk	**honken**
人絹	synthetic silk, rayon	**jinken**
純絹	pure silk, 100% silk	**junken**
絹紡	spun silk	**kenbō**
絹本	painting canvas	**kenpon**
絹布	silk cloth	**kenpu**
絹雲	cirrus	**ken'un**
絹針	silk needle	**kinubari**
絹絵	painting on silk fabric	**kinue**
絹糸	silk thread	**kinuito, kenshi**
絹地	silk fabrics	**kinuji**
絹物	silk goods	**kinumono**
絹莢	silk peas	**kinusaya**
絹綿	silk floss	**kinuwata**
紅絹	red silk	**kōken**
正絹	pure silk, 100% silk	**shōken**
素絹	coarse silk	**soken**
薄絹	thin silk	**usuginu**

富士絹	Fuji silk fabrics	**fujiginu**
絹張り	covered with silk	**kinubari**
絹織物	silk fabrics	**kinuorimono**
練り絹	glossy silk fabric	**neriginu**

蚕	ilkworm, 628
羅	hin silk, 563

編diting, 42

133-B

絹*ilk woven into* 縄*ope used to elope...*

糸 (thread, continuity)

FLIP: 7.1. Right (Sort Of)

縄*ope*　　　縄*ord*

nawa, JŌ
rope, cord

荒縄	coarse straw rope	**aranawa**
粗縄	straw rope	**aranawa**
麻縄	hempen rope	**asanawa**
泥縄	"too late an expediency..."	**doronawa**
泥縄式	11th hour, last minute rush	**doronawashiki**
延縄	trawl line	**haenawa**
火縄	fuse cord	**hinawa**
火縄銃	matchlock, gunlock	**hinawajū**
捕縄	rope to tie-up criminals	**hojō**
縄墨	inked straw rope	**jōboku**
縄文	straw rope	**jōmon**
縄文時代	Jōmon Era (10,000~300 BC)	**jōmon jidai**
準縄	rule, standard	**junjō**
鉤縄	grapnel rope	**kaginawa**
腰縄	waistcord	**koshinawa**
縄目	dragnet	**nawame**
荷縄	packing rope	**ninawa**
墨縄	string for inking	**suminawa**
一筋縄	a rope, a means	**hitosujinawa**

糞縄え	bottlegreen fly	**kusobae**
投げ縄	lariat, lasso	**nagenawa**
縄梯子	rope ladder	**nawabashigo**
縄跳び	jumping-, skipping rope	**nawatobi**
沖縄県	Okinawa Prefecture	**okinawa-ken**
注連縄	New Year decorative rope	**shimenawa**
捕り縄	rope for arresting criminals	**torinawa**
縄張り	sphere-of-influence	**nawabari**
縄張り争い	turf battle	**nawabari arasoi**
縄のれん	rope curtain	**nawanoren**
自縄自縛	"caught in one's trap..."	**jijō jibaku**

維	ope, 563	結	onnect, 227
綱	ope, 159	絡	onnect, 826
綱	ord, 159		

細etails, 138

134-A

Fishermen's 網ets, 網ord-of-life for foods we get...

糸 (thread, continuity)

網*et*　　　網*ragnet*

ami, MŌ
　net, dragnet

FLIP: 7.1. Right (Sort Of)

網代 *wickerwork, basketwork* **ajiro**	警戒網 *police cordon* **keikaimō**
網版 *halftone* **amihan**	巻き網 *round hauling net* **makiami**
網棚 *rack, shelf* **amidana**	流し網 *drift net* **nagashiami**
網戸 *screen door, window screen* **amido**	連絡網 *correspondence chain* **renrakumō**
魚網 *fishing net* **gyomō**	刺し網 *barbeque grill net* **sashiami**
法網 *"long arm of the law..."* **hōmō**	捜査網 *"long arm of the law..."* **sōsamō**
金網 *wire screen (door)* **kanaami**	鉄道網 *railroad network* **tetsudōmō**
網状 *rectangular, net-like* **mōjō**	鉄条網 *barbed wires* **tetsujōmō**
網状組織 *network, recticulum* **mōjō soshiki**	通信網 *communications network* **tsūshinmō**
網膜 *eye retina* **mōmaku**	焼き網 *roasting grill* **yakiami**
網羅 *inclusion, containing* **mōra**	地引き網 *dragnet* **jibikiami**
天網 *Heaven's reach* **tenmō**	
投網 *fishing by net* **toami**	
鳥網 *net for fowls* **toriami**	
網の目 *net meshes* **aminome**	
網杓子 *skimmer, ladle strainer* **amishakushi**	
網焼き *grilling, roasting* **amiyaki**	
販売網 *sales network* **hanbaimō**	
捕虫網 *insect net* **hochūami**	

捕*eize, 812*	把*undle, 717*
括*undle, 954*	漁*ishing, 48*
束*undle, 502*	釣*ishing, 697*

網*ope, 159*

134-B

Fishermen's 網ets, 綱ord-of-life for foods we get...

糸 (thread, continuity)

❶綱*ope*　　　❷綱*ssentials*

tsuna, KŌ
　rope, cord, essentials

FLIP: 7.0.b2. Right (stem)

❶
亜綱 *sub-class* **akō**
太綱 *cable, wide rope* **futotsuna**
鼻綱 *halter, strap, bridle* **hanazuna**
端綱 *halter, strap, bridle* **hazuna**
帆綱 *halyard, cordage* **hozuna**
命綱 *life line* **inochizuna**
髪綱 *hair braiding* **kamitsuna**
綱鉄 *steel, metal* **kōtetsu**
綱手 *rope for towing* **tsunade**
綱具 *rigging equipment* **tsunagu**
横綱 *grand sumo champion* **yokozuna**
引き綱 *towline (fishing)* **hikizuna**
甲殻綱 *crustacean* **kōkakukō**
舫い綱 *rope for towing* **moyaitsuna**
綱梯子 *rope ladder* **tsunabashigo**
綱引き *tug-of-war* **tsunahiki**
綱渡り *ropewalking (circus)* **tsunawatari**
頼みの綱 *last resort, no choice* **tanomi no tsuna**
物干し綱 *clothesline* **monohoshi tsuna**

❷
綱常 *morality, public morals* **kōjō**
綱紀 *"law of the land..."* **kōki**
綱目 *details, particulars, items* **kōmoku**
綱領 *summary, outline* **kōryō**
綱要 *elements; summary* **kōyō**
政綱 *political platform, ~agenda* **seikō**
大綱 *fundamental principles* **taikō**
手綱 *reins, bridle* **tazuna**
要綱 *elements; summary* **yōkō**

縄*ord, 158*	絡*onnect, 826*
維*ope, 563*	糸*hread, 375*
結*onnect, 227*	

網*et, 159*

135-A

Tax 賦evy being lost to software 賊iracy...

貝 (shell, old money)

FLIP: 6.0.b. Left (stem)

❶賦*evy*　　**❷賦***nstalment*

FU

levy, tariff, tribute; instalment

❶賦役 *forced-, compulsory labour* **fueki**
賦課 *levy, assessment* **fuka**
賦存 *existence of resources* **fuson**
賦与 *endowment, grant* **fuyo**
賦税 *taxation* **fuzei**
貢賦 *taxes & tributes* **kōfu**
天賦 *inborn, inherent* **tenpu**
⇒運否天賦 *"leaving it to chance..."* **unpu tenpu**

❷月賦 *monthly instalment* **geppu**
割賦 *instalment payment* **kappu, warifu**
年賦 *annual instalment* **nenpu**
賦払い *instalment payment* **fubarai**

税*axes, 941*	賃*ayment, 145*
金*oney, 25*	納*ayment, 296*
庁*ubic office, 633*	払*ayment, 682*
財*reasury, 186*	料*ayment, 194*

賊*iracy, 160*

135-B

Tax 賦evy being lost to software 賊iracy...

貝 (shell, old money)

FLIP: 6.0.b. Left (stem)

賊*iracy*　　**賊***anditry*

ZOKU

piracy, banditry, mobster, gangster, outlaw, thugs, hooligans

馬賊 *horseriding bandit* **bazoku**
土賊 *bandit, gangster, outlaw* **dozoku**
義賊 *Robin Hood banditry* **gizoku**
逆賊 *traitor, rebel, quisling* **gyakuzoku**
匪賊 *bandit, gangster* **hizoku**
烏賊 *squid, cuttlefish* **ika**
海賊 *pirate* **kaizoku**
国賊 *traitor to one's country* **kokuzoku**
兇賊 *rowdy gang, bandit* **kyōzoku**
山賊 *mountain bandits* **sanzoku**
木賊 *scouring rush* **tokusa, mokuzoku**
盗賊 *robber, burglar, thief* **tōzoku**
賊害 *damage caused by piracy* **zokugai**
賊軍 *bandit army* **zokugun**
賊虐 *ill-treatment, abuse* **zokugyaku**
賊名 *branded as traitor* **zokumei**
賊子 *rebellious child; rebel, renegade* **zokushi**
賊臣 *rebel, traitor, quisling* **zokushin**
賊将 *rebel general* **zokushō**

賊徒 *bandit, gangster, outlaw* **zokuto**
甲烏賊 *cuttlefish* **kōika**

窃*tealing, 352*	障*njury, 325*
盗*tealing, 621*	痛*njury, 60*
侵*iolate, 769*	罪*riminal, 289*
害*njury, 904*	犯*riminal, 640*
傷*njury, 933*	悪*vil, 389*

賦*ribute, 160*

136-A

寡*ittle boy* 寡*lone met* 賓*uests in Bucharest...*

宀 (cover, lid)

FLIP: 8.0.a. Inner (flat)

❶寡*ittle*   ❷寡*lone*

KA
little, few; alone, lonesome

❶ 寡聞 *little knowledge, ill-informed* **kabun**
寡言 *"a person of few words..."* **kagen**
寡兵 *small army* **kahei**
寡黙 *reticent, taciturn, silent, quiet* **kamoku**
寡作 *unprolific, inarticulate* **kasaku**
寡少 *little, few* **kashō**
寡欲 *"a person of few wants..."* **kayoku**
寡慾 *"a person of few wants..."* **kayoku**
寡勢 *small force* **kazei**
衆寡 *outnumbered* **shūka**
多寡 *amount, number, quantity* **taka**

❷ 寡婦 *widow* **kafu, yamome**
寡夫 *widower* **kafu**
寡人 *"my humble self..."* **kajin**
寡居 *widowhood* **kakyo**
寡占 *oligopoly, oligopsony* **kasen**
寡頭政治 *oligarchical regime* **katō seiji**

小*ittle, 459*   少*ew, 459*
若*ittle, 276*   小*mall, 459*
幾*ew, 547*   微*light, 62*

募*ecruit, 600*

136-B

寡*ittle boy* 寡*lone met* 賓*uests in Bucharest...*

貝 (shell, old money)

FLIP: 4.0.b. Bottom (stem)

賓*uest*   賓*isitor*

HIN
guest, visitor

迎賓 *welcoming guests* **geihin**
迎賓館 *guest house* **geihinkan**
賓辞 *object of a verb* **hinji**
賓客 *honoured guest* **hinkyaku, hinkaku**
貴賓 *distinguished guests* **kihin**
貴賓席 *royal box* **kihinseki**
貴賓室 *royal suite, vip room* **kihinshitsu**
公賓 *public guest* **kōhin**
国賓 *state guest* **kokuhin**
来賓 *visitor, guest* **raihin**
正賓 *guest-of-honour* **seihin**
社賓 *corporate guest* **shahin**
主賓 *guest-of-honour* **shuhin**

訪*isit, 737*   暖*armth, 821*
呼*nvite, 701*   懇*ntimacy, 164*
招*nvite, 956*   親*ntimacy, 669*
客*uest, 559*   友*riendship, 408*
宴*anquet, 610*   迎*elcome, 705*

貫*arry out, 532*

137-A
Little girl 奪natched, 奮roused fury unmatched...

奪*natch*   奪*surp*

大 (grand)

Facing: 3.0. ⟨🖼️⟩ Across

uba(u), DATSU
snatching, grabbing, robbery, usurpation

奪い合い *scramble, rumble, scuffle* **ubaiai**
奪い返す *recover, recapture, retake* **ubaikaesu**
奪い取る *plunder, loot, abscond* **ubaitoru**
褫奪 *deprive, strip* **chidatsu**
奪回 *regaining, winning back* **dakkai**
奪還 *recapturing, retaking* **dakkan**
奪取 *capture, seizure* **dasshu**
奪掠 *pillage, plunder* **datsuryaku**
奪略 *pillage, plunder* **datsuryaku**
強奪 *abduction, seizure* **gōdatsu**
強奪物 *plunder, spoil, loot, booty* **gōdatsubutsu**
剥奪 *forfeiture, divesting* **hakudatsu**
⇒権利剥奪 *divestiture, disenfranchisement*
    kenri hakudatsu
横奪 *usurp, steal* **ōdatsu**
略奪 *plunder, pillage, loot* **ryakudatsu**
略奪物 *plunder, spoil, loot, booty* **ryakudatsubutsu**
略奪品 *plunder, spoil, loot, booty* **ryakudatsuhin**
略奪者 *plunderer, looter, con artist* **ryakudatsusha**

掠奪 *plunder, pillage, loot* **ryakudatsu**
簒奪 *usurpation* **sandatsu**
侵奪 *usurpation* **shindatsu**
争奪 *scramble, struggle* **sōdatsu**
争奪戦 *struggle, strife, combat* **sōdatsusen**
与奪 *give-or-take away (power)* **yodatsu**
⇒生殺与奪 *"power to kill or let-live..."*
    seisatsu yodatsu
奪胎 *adaptation* **dattai**
⇒換骨奪胎 *recasting, adapting* **kankotsu dattai**

窃*tealing*, 352
盗*tealing*, 621
賊*iracy*, 160

奮*gitate*, *162*

137-B
Little girl 奪natched, 奮roused fury unmatched...

奮*rouse*   奮*xcite*

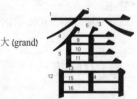

大 (grand)

FLIP: 4.0.a. Bottom (flat)

furu(u), FUN
arouse, excite, stimulate, agitate, animate, enliven

奮い立つ *enliven, arouse* **furuitatsu**
奮い起こす *arouse, stir up, agitate* **furuiokosu**
奮撃 *fierce attack* **fungeki**
奮迅 *dashing fiercely* **funjin**
奮起 *rousing, stirring agitated* **funki**
奮発 *exerting effort, bring to bear* **funpatsu**
奮飛 *flying away, spirited away* **funpi**
奮励 *strenuous efforts* **funrei**
奮戦 *fierce battle* **funsen**
奮闘 *laborious-, strenuous battle* **funtō**
奮然 *vigour, courage* **funzen**
奮進 *rigorous push* **funshin**
発奮 *inspiring, stirring into action* **happun**
感奮 *inspiring, stirring* **kanpun**
興奮 *excitement, arousal, stimulation* **kōfun**
興奮剤 *drug stimulant* **kōfunzai**

感*eelings*, 45
気*eelings*, 98
情*eelings*, 793

奪*natch*, *162*

138-A

Old 橋ridge to 矯ectify or many cars will fly...

橋*ridge*

木 (wooden)

FLIP: 7.1. Right (Sort Of)

hashi, KYŌ
bridge

土橋	*wooden bridge*	**dobashi**
橋台	*bridge platform*	**hashidai**
橋桁	*bridge girder*	**hashigeta**
石橋	*stone bridge*	**ishibashi**
開橋	*bridge opening*	**kaikyō**
架橋	*bridge construction*	**kakyō**
艦橋	*bridge of a warship*	**kankyō**
橋脚	*pier, wharf, port*	**kyōkyaku**
橋梁	*bridge*	**kyōryō**
橋頭	*area of a bridge*	**kyōtō**
橋頭堡	*bridge-, beachhead*	**kyōtōho**
陸橋	*overpass, crossover, skyway*	**rikkyō**
桟橋	*pier, quay, wharf*	**sanbashi**
神橋	*holy bridge*	**shinkyō**
鉄橋	*iron-, railroad bridge*	**tekkyō**
船橋市	*Funabashi city, Chiba Pref.*	**funabashi-shi**
跳ね橋	*drawbridge*	**hanebashi**
橋普請	*bridge construction*	**hashibushin**
橋渡し	*mediation, serving as liaison*	**hashiwatashi**

歩道橋	*pedestrian overpass*	**hodōkyō**
一本橋	*log bridge*	**ipponbashi**
開閉橋	*drawbridge*	**kaiheikyō**
掛け橋	*go-between, mediator*	**kakehashi**
懸け橋	*suspension bridge*	**kakehashi**
前橋市	*Maebashi City, Gunma Pref.*	**maebashi-shi**
丸木橋	*log bridge*	**marukibashi**
眼鏡橋	*arch bridge*	**meganebashi**
渡橋式	*bridge inauguration rites*	**tokyōshiki**
豊橋市	*Toyohashi City, Aichi Pref.*	**toyohashi-shi**
釣り橋	*hanging bridge*	**tsuribashi**

懸*anging, 566*	川*iver, 76*
掛*ang up, 107*	峡*avine, 763*
架*anging, 202*	渓*avine, 97*
河*iver, 877*	谷*avine, 492*

矯*eformatory, 163*

138-B

Old 橋ridge to 矯ectify or many cars will fly...

矯*ectify*   矯*eformatory*

矢 (archery arrow)

FLIP: 7.1. Right (Sort Of)

ta(meru), KYŌ
rectify, reformatory, corrective

矯め直す	*correct, straighten out*	**tamenaosu**
奇矯	*eccentric, bizarre, odd*	**kikyō**
矯風	*moral reform*	**kyōfū**
矯激	*extreme, radical*	**kyōgeki**
矯幣	*reforming evil habits*	**kyōhei**
矯正	*correction, remedy, cure*	**kyōsei**
矯正院	*reformatory institution*	**kyōseiin**
矯正保護	*correction & rehabilitation*	**kyōsei hogo**
矯正歯列	*corrected teeth*	**kyōsei shiretsu**
矯正教育	*reformatory education*	**kyōsei kyōiku**
矯正視力	*corrected sight*	**kyōsei shiryoku**
矯飾	*pretext, pretending*	**kyōshoku**
矯めつ眇めつ	*meticulous scrutiny*	
	tametsu sugametsu	

正*orrect, 30*	倫*thics, 787*
是*orrect, 313*	善*ighteous, 450*
改*eform, 725*	義*ighteous, 341*
訂*diting, 174*	徳*irtue, 844*

橋*ridge, 163*

139-A

墾eclaimed lands by 懇ntimate hands...

墾*eclaim land*　墾*ultivate*

土 (ground, soil)

KON

reclaim land, cultivate

開墾 *land reclamation* **kaikon**
開墾地 *reclaimed area* **kaikonchi**
未墾 *uncultivated land* **mikon**
墾田 *newly-cultivated rice field* **konden**

FLIP: 4.0.a. Bottom (flat)

耕*ultivate, 655*　　稲*ice plant, 893*
培*ultivate, 698*　　畑*lantation, 482*
植*lant, 783*

懇*ntimacy, 164*

139--B

墾eclaimed lands by 懇ntimate hands...

懇*ntimacy*　懇*riendship*

心⇔忄 (heart, feelings)

nengo(ro), KON

intimacy, friendship, cordial, earnest, goodwill, bonding

別懇 *intimate feelings* **bekkon**
昵懇 *close friendship* **jikkon**
懇談 *friendly talks, chattering* **kondan**
懇談会 *social gathering, get-together* **kondankai**
懇願 *entreaty, solicitation* **kongan**
懇願者 *petitioner* **kongansha**
懇意 *friendship, cordiality* **kon'i**
懇情 *kind feelings, cordiality* **konjō**
懇命 *kind words* **konmei**
懇望 *entreaty, solicitation* **konmō, konbō**
懇請 *entreaty, solicitation* **konsei**
懇切 *cordial, exhaustive, detailed* **konsetsu**
懇親 *friendship, cordiality, intimacy* **konshin**
懇親会 *get-together, social gathering* **konshinkai**
懇篤 *cordiality, kindness, warmth* **kontoku**
懇話 *friendly talks, chattering* **konwa**
懇話会 *friendly get-together* **konwakai**
懇懇と *earnest, eager, anxious* **konkonto**

Facing: 4.0. 🌫☞ Apart

親*ntimate, 669*
款*oodwill, 42*
友*riendship, 408*

墾*ultivate, 164*

140-A

還*eturn the lions to jungle* 環*nvirons...*

還*eturn*   還*epatriate*

辶 (transport)

KAN
return, repatriate, revert, sending back

奪還	*recapture, winning back* **dakkan** └·
還俗	*return to secular life* **genzoku**
返還	*return, repayment* **henkan**
還元	*reduction, deoxidisation* **kangen**
還御	*emperor's return to the capital* **kangyo**
還啓	*empress's return to the capital* **kankei**
還行	*emperor's return to the capital* **kankō**
還付	*return, refund* **kanpu**
還暦	*one's sixtieth birthday* **kanreki**
還流	*return current* **kanryū**
帰還	*return, repatriation* **kikan**
帰還兵	*repatriated soldiers* **kikanhei**
帰還者	*repatriated soldier* **kikansha**
往還	*coming and going, traffic; road* **ōkan**
生還	*return home safe* **seikan**
生還者	*survivor, returnee* **seikansha**
召還	*recall, summons* **shōkan**
償還	*repayment, refund* **shōkan**

- redsem a bond

FLIP: 3.0.a. Top (flat)
FLIP: 7.1. Right (Sort Of)

召還状	*letter of recall* **shōkanjō**
送還	*repatriation, deportation* **sōkan**
償還期限	*term of repayment* **shōkan kigen**

帰*eturn, 784*	戻*eturn, 541*
返*eturn, 537*	復*estoration, 442*

環*nvirons, 165*

140-B

還*eturn the lions to jungle* 環*nvirons...*

環*nvirons*   環*urroundings*

王⇔玉 (jewel)

KAN
environs, surroundings

円環	*circle, ring* **enkan**
花輪	*garland, wreath* **hanawa**
一環	*link, part* **ikkan**
循環	*circulation, patrol, making rounds* **junkan**
⇒悪循環	*vicious cycle* **akujunkan**
循環系	*circulatory system* **junkankei**
循環器	*circulatory organ* **junkanki**
循環論法	*round-about argument* **junkan ronpō**
環状	*circle* **kanjō**
環状道路	*beltway, elliptical road* **kanjō dōro**
環海	*adjacent seas, neighbouring seas* **kankai**
環境	*environment, surroundings* **kankyō**
環境破壊	*environmental disruption* **kankyō hakai**
環境保護	*environmental protection* **kankyō hogo**
環境汚染	*environmental pollution* **kankyō osen**
環節	*worm segment* **kansetsu**
環視	*concentrated attention of others* **kanshi**
環礁	*atoll, reef* **kanshō**
金環	*gold ring* **kinkan**

FLIP: 3.0.a. Top (flat)
FLIP: 7.1. Right (Sort Of)

金環食	*annular eclipse* **kinkanshoku**
光観	*corona* **kōkan**
耳環	*earrings* **mimiwa**
連環	*chain link* **renkan**
指環	*ring* **yubiwa**
子午環	*meridian circle* **shigokan**

近*earby, 184*	周*icinity, 280*
囲*nclose, 361*	辺*icinity, 93*

還*eturn, 165*

141-A

磨rushing the 礎ornerstone, honour the Unknown...

石 (stone)

磨rush   磨olish

miga(ku), su(ru), MA
brush, polish, burnish

FLIP: 8.0.b. Inner (stem)

磨き *polishing* **migaki**
磨き粉 *polishing powder* **migakiko**
磨き砂 *polishing sand* **migakizuna**
磨き上げる *polish up* **migakiageru**
消磨 *abrasion, bruise* **shōma**
練磨 *practice, drill, training* **renma**
⇒百戦錬磨 *battle-tested* **hyakusen renma**
磨損 *friction loss* **mason**
磨耗 *abrasion, wearing away* **mamō**
磨滅 *wear & tear, defacement* **mametsu**
研磨 *polishing, grinding* **kenma**
減磨 *lubrication, friction decrease* **genma**
達磨 *Dharma doll* **daruma**
鈍磨 *dullness* **donma**
血達磨 *filled with blood* **chidaruma**
火達磨 *enveloped in flames* **hidaruma**
歯磨き *tooth brushing* **hamigaki**
研磨紙 *sandpaper* **kenmashi**
球磨川 *Kumagawa River, Kumamoto Pref.* **kumagawa**

靴磨き *shoeshine boy, bootblack* **kutsumigaki**
雪達磨 *snowman* **yukidaruma**
切磋琢磨 *workaholic* **sessa takuma**
磨り潰す *mash, grind down, crush* **suritsubusu**
磨り減らす *rub down, wear & tear* **suriherasu**
練り歯磨き *toothpaste* **nerihamigaki**

摩*crape, 331*	研*olish, 951*
擦*riction, 329*	錬*olish, 718*

麻*emp-plant, 331*

141-B

磨rushing the 礎ornerstone, honour the Unknown...

石 (stone)

礎onerstone   礎oundation

ishizue, SO
cornerstone, foundation, underpinning

FLIP: 7.2.b. Right Top (stem)

基礎 *foundation, basics* **kiso**
基礎的 *fundamental, basic* **kisoteki**
基礎知識 *fundamental knowledge* **kiso chishiki**
基礎工事 *foundation construction* **kiso kōji**
基礎体温 *basal temperature* **kiso taion**
国疎 *pillar of the nation* **kokuso**
礎石 *bedrock, cornerstone* **soseki**
礎材 *foundation materials* **sozai**
定礎 *laying a cornerstone* **teiso**
定礎式 *cornerstone laying* **teisoshiki**

根*oot, 772*	本*ain, 461*
基*oundation, 590*	旨*ain point, 242*
拠*asis, 473*	

襟*eck collar, 560*

142-A

夢*reams of* 舞*ancing, acrobats prancing...*

夕 (evening, night)

夢*ream*　夢*antasy*

yume, MU
dream, fantasy, vision

FLIP: 3.0.a. Top (flat)

徒夢 *idle dreaming* **adayume**
悪夢 *nightmare, bad dream* **akumu**
初夢 *first dream in the new year* **hatsuyume**
正夢 *prophetic dream* **masayume**
迷夢 *illusion, delusion* **meimu**
夢寐 *asleep, while sleeping* **mubi**
夢中 *completely absorbed, ~engrossed* **muchū**
夢幻 *fantasy, flight of fancy* **mugen**
夢魔 *nightmare, bad dream* **muma**
夢精 *wet dream, dreaming sweats* **musei**
夢想 *dream, fancy, fantasy* **musō**
夢想家 *dreamer, visionary* **musōka**
霊夢 *revelation, vision, apparition* **reimu**
逆夢 *dreaming the opposite* **sakayume**
空夢 *fabricated dream* **sorayume**
夢路 *dreamland, fantasy land* **yumeji**
夢枕 *in a dream* **yumemakura**
夢見 *dreaming, seeing a dream* **yumemi**
夢現 *half-asleep, trance* **yumeutsutsu**

瑞夢 *auspicious dream* **zuimu**
白昼夢 *awaking dream* **hakuchūmu**
白日夢 *daydreaming* **hakujitsumu**
夢遊病 *sleepwalking, somnambulism* **muyūbyō**
夢語り *account of one's dream* **yumegatari**
夢心地 *trance, dreamland* **yumegokochi**
夢物語 *fantastic tale* **yumemonogatari**
夢解き *dream interpretation* **yumetoki**
夢占い *dream fortune-telling* **yumeuranai**
夢合わせ *dream interpretation* **yumeawase**

寝*leeping, 769*	観*iew, 667*
眠*leeping, 495*	覚*emember, 307*
睡*leeping, 948*	

舞*ance, 167*

142-B

夢*reams of* 舞*ancing, acrobats prancing...*

舛 (dancing)

舞*ancing*

mai, ma(u), BU
dancing

Facing: 1.1. 🔚 West (H)

舞楽 *dance music* **bugaku**
舞曲 *dance melody* **bukyoku**
舞台 *stage, scene* **butai**
舞台劇 *stage play, dramatic* **butaigeki**
舞台裏 *backstage* **butaiura**
舞台道具 *stage scenery, props* **butai dōgu**
舞台負け *stage fears, stage fright* **butaimake**
舞踏 *dance, dancing* **butō**
舞踏場 *dance hall* **butōjō**
舞踊 *dance, dancing* **buyō**
円舞 *waltz, circular dancing* **enbu**
群舞 *group dancing* **gunbu**
剣舞 *sword dance* **kenbu**
鼓舞 *encouraging, cheering up, rooting* **kobu**
木舞 *lath* **komai**
舞姫 *female dancer* **maihime**
舞子 *dancing girl* **maiko**
舞手 *dancing girl* **maite**
乱舞 *wild dancing (butterfly)* **ranbu**

輪舞 *circular dancing* **rinbu**
仕舞 *Noh dance* **shimai**
洋舞 *Western dance* **yōbu**
歌舞伎 *Kabuki play* **kabuki**
歌舞伎役者 *Kabuki actor* **kabuki yakusha**
見舞い *affection, greetings, sympathy* **mimai**
⇒暑中見舞い *summer greetings* **shochū mimai**
二の舞 *same, similar* **ninomai**
回り舞台 *revolving stage* **mawari butai**
立ち居振る舞い *behaviour, demeanour* **tachii furumai**

踊*ancing, 671*	祝*elebration, 716*
興*ntertainment, 867*	足*egs, 481*
慶*ejoice, 69*	足*oot, 481*
賀*elebration, 202*	脚*egs, 387*

夢*ream, 167*

143-A

騰xpansion sloppy in the 謄fficial-registry...

馬 (horse)

騰xpand　　　騰psurge

TŌ

expand, upsurge, bloated, bulge, rise, gorging

FLIP: 7.2.b. Right Top (stem)
Facing: 4.0. ◁▷ Apart

暴騰 *sudden rise* **bōtō**
噴騰 *sudden rise, upsurge* **funtō**
沸騰 *seething, boiling, scalding* **futtō**
沸騰点 *boiling point* **futtōten**
反騰 *stock rally, reactionary rise* **hantō**
奔騰 *soaring, jumping* **hontō**
上騰 *rise, upsurge, advance* **jōtō**
高騰 *sudden price increases* **kōtō**
昂騰 *sudden price increases* **kōtō**
狂騰 *sudden price increases* **kyōtō**
急騰 *sudden rise, upsurge* **kyūtō**
昇騰 *rise, upsurge, soar* **shōtō**
騰貴 *sudden rise, jumping* **tōki** *tō'ki*
⇒物価騰貴 *commodity price increase* **bukka tōki**
騰落 *rise & fall, fluctuation* **tōraku**
騰勢 *rising trend, upward move* **tōsei**
続騰 *continuing increase* **zokutō**

展*xpand, 522*	殖*ncrease, 784*
漢*xpanse, 828*	増*ncrease, 837*
拡*nlarge, 205*	昇*scend, 299*
複*ultiply, 830*	上*scend, 859*
倍*ultiply, 950*	

謄fficial copy, *168*

143-B

謄xpansion sloppy in the 謄fficial-registry...

言 (speaking)

謄fficial registry　　謄ranscript

TŌ

official registry, certified copy, transcript

FLIP: 7.0.a. Right (flat)

謄本 *official register* **tōhon**
⇒戸籍謄本 *family register* **koseki tōhon**
謄写 *making an official copy* **tōsha**
謄写版 *mimeograph* **tōshaban**
謄写機 *mimeograph machine* **tōshaki**
謄写料 *mimeographing fee* **tōsharyō**

記*ecord, 728*	録*ecord, 841*	撮*hotograph, 423*
簿*ecord, 64*	公*ublic, 180*	写*opy, 349*

騰xpand, *168*

144-A

憩*elax your* 鼻*ose by smelling a rose...*

憩*elaxation*　　　憩*espite*

心⇔忄 (heart, feelings)

iko(i); iko(u), KEI
relaxation, respite

憩室 *relaxation room* **ikoi shitsu**
休憩 *rest, relaxation* **kyūkei**
休憩所 *rest & relaxation area* **kyūkeijo**
休憩室 *rest & relaxation room* **kyūkeishitsu**
少憩 *brief rest* **shōkei**

FLIP: 7.2.a. Right Top (flat)

休*ecess, 347*	娯*musement, 453*
閑*eisure, 283*	宴*anquet, 610*
悠*eisure, 898*	

息*reathe, 586*

144-B

憩*elax your* 鼻*ose by smelling a rose...*

鼻*asal*　　　鼻*ose*

鼻 (nose)

hana, BI
nasal, nose

鼻つまみ *disgusting, sickening* **hanatsumami**
鼻薬 *bribe, hush money* **hanagusuri**
鼻緒 *clog thong, geta straps* **hanao**
目鼻 *eyes & nose; taking shape* **mehana**
鉤鼻 *hook nose* **kagibana**
鼻歌 *hum, humming* **hanauta**
鼻面 *muzzle* **hanazura**
鼻音 *nasal* **bion**
鼻骨 *nasal bone* **bikotsu**
鼻炎 *nasal inflammation* **bien**
鼻声 *nasal voice* **hanagoe**
鼻翼 *nasal wings* **biyoku**
鼻筋 *nose* **hanasuji**
鼻柱 *nose bridge* **hanabashira**
鼻糞 *nose dirt* **hanakuso**
小鼻 *nose wings* **kobana**
鼻血 *nosebleed, bleeding nose* **hanaji**
鼻毛 *nostril hairs* **hanage**
鼻孔 *nostrils* **bikō**

FLIP: 2.0.b. Sort Of (stem)

赤鼻 *reddened nose* **akabana**
鼻水 *running nose* **hanamizu**
鼻息 *snort, nose breathing* **hanaiki**
鼻先 *tip of the nose* **hanasaki**
鼻白 *total lost of interest* **hanashiro**
鼻白む *total lost of interest* **hanajiramu**
鼻濁音 *nasal sound* **bidakuon**
団子鼻 *snob nose, snobbish*
　　　dangobana, dangoppana
鼻風邪 *cold in the nose, ~head* **hanakaze**
耳鼻科 *ear & nose* **jibika**
鼻が高い *self-conceited, aloof* **hana ga takai**

臭*mell, 586*	芳*ragrance, 533*
薫*ragrance, 934*	花*lower, 191*
香*ragrance, 895*	華*lower, 40*

息*reathe, 586*

145-A

Fire 敷cattered when 激ntense heat gathered...

女 (action)

敷catter　敷pread-out

shi(ku), FU
scatter, spread out, lay-out, disperse

FLIP: 6.1. Left Top
Facing: 3.0. ☞☜ Across

敷き砂 *paving sand for gardening* **shikisuna**
敷き板 *wooden stand* **shikiita**
敷き写し *tracing* **shikiutsushi**
跡敷き *head of the family* **atojiki**
板敷き *wooden floor* **itajiki**
釜敷き *kettle pad* **kamashiki**
中敷き *shoe insole* **nakashiki, nakajiki**
下敷き *paving sand for gardening* **shitajiki**
上敷き *carpet, rug* **uwashiki, uwajiki**
敷衍 *amplification, elaboration* **fuen**
敷設 *construction, laying* **fusetsu**
金敷 *iron anvil* **kanashiki**
桟敷 *upper box, upper stand* **sajiki**
敷地 *site, lot, land* **shikichi**
敷布 *mattress sheet* **shikifu**
敷皮 *fur rug, inner sole* **shikigawa**
敷居 *threshold, door sill* **shikii**
敷石 *paving stone, flagstone* **shikiishi**
敷金 *initial deposit, key money (rent)* **shikikin**

敷物 *rug, carpet, mat* **shikimono**
屋敷 *manor house, estate* **yashiki**
座敷 *drawing room* **zashiki**
家屋敷 *house & lot, estate* **ieyashiki**
河川敷 *flooded plain* **kasenshiki**
倉敷市 *Kurashiki City, Okayama Pref.* **kurashiki-shi**
敷蒲団 *mattress, futon beddings* **shikibuton**
敷き紙 *paper mat* **shikigami**
土瓶敷き *tea mat* **dobinshiki**
組み敷く *being pinned down* **kumishiku**
敷島の道 *famous Japanese poem*
　　shikishima no michi
敷きレンガ *paving bricks* **shikirenga**

散*catter, 337*	漠*xpanse, 828*
漫*andom, 845*	遍*idespread, 43*

激*ntense, 170*

145-B

Fire 敷cattered when 激ntense heat gathered...

水⇔氵 (water)

激ntense　激ierce

hage(shii), GEKI
intense, fierce, stinging, aggressive, violent

FLIP: 8.0.a. Inner (flat)
Facing: 3.0. ☞☜ Across

憤激 *indignation, rage, fury* **fungeki**
奮激 *arouse, inspire* **fungeki**
激怒 *rage, fury, ferocity* **gekido**
激動 *turbulence, agitation* **gekidō**
激越 *vehement, emphatic* **gekietsu**
激減 *sharp fall, plummet* **gekigen**
激発 *outrage, outburst* **gekihatsu**
激変 *sudden change, upset* **gekihen**
激情 *emotion-filled, passionate* **gekijō**
激化 *intensification, aggravation* **gekika**
激務 *strenuous, laborious, meticulous* **gekimu**
激励 *encouragement, inspiration* **gekirei**
激烈 *violent, use-of-force* **gekiretsu**
激浪 *roaring-, raging waves* **gekirō**
激論 *heated argument, verbal war* **gekiron**
激流 *raging-, erratic current* **gekiryū**
激戦 *fierce battle* **gekisen**
激震 *violent earthquake* **gekishin**
激賞 *high praise, extolling, accolade* **gekishō**

激闘 *fierce battle* **gekitō**
激突 *crashing, slamming* **gekitotsu**
激痛 *sharp pain, intense pain* **gekitsū**
激増 *sudden increase, upsurge* **gekizō**
激高 *flying into rage, infuriated* **gekkō**
激昂 *exasperation, indignation* **gekkō, gekikō**
過激 *radical, extreme* **kageki**
過激派 *radical, extremist group* **kagekiha**
感激 *stirring emotions* **kangeki**
急激 *rapid, sudden, drastic* **kyūgeki**
刺激 *stimulus, impetus* **shigeki**

猛*ierce, 657*	深*ntense, 788*
烈*ierce, 585*	厳*evere, 449*

敷*catter, 170*

146-A

弊*umble* 幣*hrine-paper can't be used with* 幣*oney to* 弊*buse...*

巾 (cloth, fabric)

①幣*oney*　　**②**幣*hinto paper*

HEI

money, currency, denomination, legal tender; Shinto paper

❶ 幣貢 *tribute, offering* **heikō** ✓
幣制 *monetary system* **heisei**
法幣 *legal tender in china* **hōhei** ✓
貨幣 *coin, money, currency* **kahei**　*ka¹hei*
貨幣学 *numismatics* **kaheigaku**
貨幣価値 *value of money* **kahei kachi**
貨幣制度 *monetary-, currency system* **kahei seido**
貨幣単位 *monetary unit* **kahei tan'i**
国幣社 *national shrine* **kokuheisha**
紙幣 *bill, paper money, note* **shihei**
⇒小額紙幣 *small note, small bill* **shōgaku shihei**
造幣 *mintage, coinage* **zōhei**

❷ 御幣 *Shintō white paper strips* **gohei**
幣物 *Shintō offering* **heibutsu**
幣殿 *Shintō inner sanctuary* **heiden**
幣帛 *Shintō cloth offering* **heihaku**
幣束 *Shintō offerings (cloth, rope & cut paper)* **heisoku**
奉幣 *Shintō wand & paper streamers* **hōhei**

FLIP: 6.1. Left Top
FLIP: 4.0.b. Bottom (stem)

金*oney, 25*	神*ivine, 712*	
札*oney-bills, 685*	祈*rayer, 184*	
財*reasury, 186*	拝*rayer, 636*	
貴*recious, 913*	聖*acred, 617*	

弊*umble, 171*

146-B

弊*umble* 幣*hrine-paper can't be used with* 幣*oney to* 弊*buse...*

廾 (clasped hands)

①弊*buse*　　**②**弊*umble*

HEI

abuse; humble

それは語弊があ反

❶ 悪弊 *evil practices, sinful behaviour* **akuhei**
病弊 *ills, evil practices* **byōhei**
語弊 *evil expressions* **gohei**　*go¹hei*
弊風 *evil practices, sinful behaviour* **heifū** (L.)
弊害 *ill-effect, evil, abuse* **heigai**　*heígaí*
弊衣 *shabby clothes* **heii** (L.)
弊政 *misrule, maladministration* **heisei** (L.)
⚐ 弊習 *evil customs* **heishū**
疲弊 *impoverished, wretched* **hihei** (suru) (L.)
⚐ 時弊 *evils of times* **jihei**
⚐ 情弊 *favouritism* **jōhei**
旧弊 *past abuses, old sins* **kyūhei**
積弊 *deep-rooted evils* **sekihei**
宿弊 *deeply-rooted evils* **shukuhei**
党弊 *evils of partisan politics* **tōhei**
通弊 *common evil* **tsūhei**
余弊 *lasting evil* **yōhei**

❷ 弊舗 *"our shop..."* **heiho**

FLIP: 6.1. Left Top

弊社 *"our humble company..."* **heisha**
弊村 *"our humble village..."* **heison**
弊宅 *"my humble house..."* **heitaku**
弊店 *"our shop..."* **heiten**

倹*rugal, 938*	卑*peak humble, 89*	
慎*odest, 831*	謙*umility, 805*	
謙*odesty, 805*		

幣*oney, 171*

147-A

⛰ountain climbers without a chart 拙lumsily 凸epart...

山 (mountain)

⛰ountain

yama, SAN
mountain, alpine, cordillera, sierra

FLIP: 1.0.a. Whole (flat)

冬山 *mountain in the winter* **fuyuyama**
氷山 *iceberg* **hyōzan**
鉱山 *mining* **kōzan**
山河 *mountains & rivers* **sanga**
山岳 *mountains & hills* **sangaku**
山海 *all lands & seas* **sankai**
山門 *main temple gate* **sanmon**
深山 *mountain depths* **shinzan, miyama**
沢山 *a lot, plenty, numerous* **takusan**
⇒盛り沢山 *numerous, plentiful* **moridakusan**
登山 *mountain climbing* **tozan**
裏山 *mountain behind* **urayama**
山彦 *echo, reverberating sound* **yamabiko**
山寺 *mountain temple* **yamadera**
山国 *mountainous area* **yamaguni**
山芋 *yam potato* **yamaimo**
山気 *speculative, ambitious* **yamake**
山奥 *mountain depths* **yamaoku**
山々 *mountain ranges* **yamayama**

富士山 *Mount Fuji* **fujisan**
案山子 *scarecrow* **kakashi**
活火山 *active volcano* **kakkazan**
休火山 *dormant volcano* **kyūkazan**
山の幸 *land-, farm products* **yamanosachi**
山開き *start of mountaineering season* **yamabiraki**
山越え *crossing a mountain* **yamagoe**
山ほど *countless, numerous* **yamahodo**
山火事 *forest fire* **yamakaji**
山の手 *top-notch, high society* **yamanote**

岳*ountain peak, 28*	崎*lope, 270*
峠*ountain trail, 646*	峡*avine, 763*
岬*ape, 646*	渓*avine, 97*
丘*lope, 106*	峰*ummit, 779*

凸*ortrude, 23*

147-B

⛰ountain climbers without a chart 拙lumsily 凸epart...

手⇔扌 (hand, manual)

拙lumsy   拙actless

tsutana(i), SETSU
clumsy, tactless

FLIP: 7.0.a. Right (flat)

拙い文章 *illegible handwriting* **tsutanai bunshō**
稚拙 *poorly-done, amateurish* **chisetsu**
古拙 *rough beauty* **kosetsu**
巧拙 *skill, workmanship* **kōsetsu**
拙著 *"my humble work..."* **seccho**
拙攻 *weak offensive* **sekkō**
拙工 *poor artisan* **sekkō**
拙稿 *"my poor manuscript..."* **sekkō**
拙筆 *poor handwriting* **seppitsu**
拙策 *imprudent measure* **sessaku**
拙作 *"my clumsy manuscript..."* **sessaku**
拙者 *i (archaic humble)* **sessha**
拙守 *weak defence* **sesshu**
拙速 *rough, coarse* **sessoku**
拙悪 *clumsy, fumbling* **setsuaku**
拙文 *"my clumsy writing..."* **setsubun**
拙技 *"my clumsy efforts..."* **setsugi**
拙劣 *bungling, clumsiness* **setsuretsu**
拙宅 *"my humble house..."* **settaku**

妄*houghtless, 34*	慢*eglect, 845*
忘*orget, 34*	失*ailure, 19*
愚*tupid, 591*	敗*ailure, 137*
疎*eglect, 955*	

仙*ermit, 416*

147-C

山ountain climbers without a chart 拙lumsily 出epart...

凵 (open box)

出epart　　　出ut out

FLIP: 1.0.a. Whole (flat)

da(su), de(ru), SHUTSU, SUI
depart, emerge, leave, exit, come-out, put-out; *emphatic verb suffix*

案出 *devise, invent, innovate* **anshutsu**
出口 *exit door* **deguchi**
外出 *outside one's house or office* **gaishutsu**
家出 *running away from home, stowaway* **iede**
出張 *official travel, business trip* **shucchō**
出火 *fire outbreak* **shukka**
出荷 *goods shipment, delivery* **shukka**
出血 *blood-letting* **shukketsu**
出国 *leaving a country* **shukkoku**
出版 *publication, publishing* **shuppan**
出発 *departure, leaving* **shuppatsu**
出産 *childbirth, baby delivery* **shussan**
出席 *attendance, presence* **shusseki**
出願 *application, petition* **shutsugan**
出現 *appearance, emergence* **shutsugen**
提出 *propose, suggest; submit, hand in* **teishutsu**
輸出 *export, sell overseas* **yushutsu**
続出 *succession, continuity* **zokushutsu**
出稼ぎ *migrant worker* **dekasegi**

出来事 *occurrence, event* **dekigoto**
思い出 *reminiscences, recollections* **omoide**
出し抜く *pre-empt, forestall* **dashinuku**
出し渋り *grudge, bad blood* **dashishiburi**
言い出す *blurt out, utter carelessly* **iidasu**
聞き出す *hear out the truth* **kikidasu**
流れ出す *pour out, start to flow* **nagaredasu**
東京出身 *Tōkyō-born* **tōkyō shusshin**
売り出す *put on sale, start selling* **uridasu**
頭脳流出 *brain drain* **zunō ryūshutsu**
出し惜しみ *grudging, bad blood* **dashioshimi**
追い出される *be expelled* **oidasareru**

外utside, 188	入nter, 2
野lains, 873	往ome & go, 749

山ountain, 172

148-A

丁lock-of-houses in 町own, 訂diting with 灯amplights by sundown...

一 (one, single)

丁lock-of-houses

FLIP: 2.0.b. Sort Of (stem)

CHŌ, TEI
block-of-houses, *miscellaneous counter*

馬丁 *groom* **batei**
丁度 *exactly, precisely* **chōdo**
丁半 *gambling dice* **chōhan**
丁子 *clove* **chōji**
丁目 *street block address* **chōme**
丁髷 *topknot* **chonmage**
丁数 *number of pages; even numbers* **chōsū**
丁稚 *apprentice* **decchi**
園丁 *gardener, garden caretaker* **entei**
延丁 *court attendant* **entei**
符丁 *code, password* **fuchō**
八丁 *skillful, clever* **hacchō**
⇒口八丁 *eloquent, articulate* **kuchihacchō**
包丁 *kitchen knife* **hōchō**
一丁 *one residential block* **icchō**
一丁字 *"cannot read even one letter..."* **itteiji**
落丁 *missing-, torn pages* **rakuchō**
乱丁 *out-of-sequence, incoherent* **ranchō**
拉丁 *Latin* **ratei**

使丁 *aide, servant* **shitei**
装丁 *cover design, book-binding* **sōtei**
丁重 *courteous, polite, respectful* **teichō**
丁寧 *careful, polite, respectful* **teinei**
丁年 *legal age, age-of-maturity* **teinen**
丁付け *pagination, collation* **chōzuke**
沈丁花 *Daphne* **jinchōge**
長丁場 *long horizon, panorama* **nagachōba**
丁字形 *T-shape* **teijikei**
丁字路 *T-shaped intersection* **teijiro**
丁稚奉公 *apprenticeship* **decchi bōkō**

住esidence, 750	軒[houses], 710
街istrict, 107	居esidence, 384
邸esidence, 860	宅esidence, 82

打trike, 636

148-B

丁 *lock-of-houses in* 町 *own,* 訂 *diting with* 灯 *amplights by sundown...*

田 (cultivated field)

町*own*

machi, CHŌ
town

FLIP: 6.0.a. Left (flat)

町長 *mayor, town head* **chōchō**
町営 *town-managed* **chōei**
町家 *town houses* **chōka**
町会 *town council* **chōkai**
町名 *town name* **chōmei**
町民 *townspeople, townfolks* **chōmin**
町内 *street, city* **chōnai**
町人 *townfolks, town resident* **chōnin**
町立 *town-owned* **chōritsu**
町制 *town organizations* **chōsei**
町政 *town government* **chōsei**
町村 *towns & villages* **chōson**
花町 *downtown* **hanamachi**
色町 *red-light district* **iromachi**
町筋 *town streets* **machisuji**
港町 *harbour-, port town* **minatomachi**
裏町 *back-alley district* **uramachi**
横町 *alley, lane, narrow street* **yokochō**
田舎町 *rural town, countryside* **inakamachi**

城下町 *town around a castle* **jōkamachi**
町外れ *town outskirts* **machihazure**
町医者 *town doctor* **machiisha**
町並み *rows of houses* **machinami**
町役場 *town hall* **machiyakuba, chōyakuba**
門前町 *cathedral-, temple town* **monzenmachi**
市町村 *cities, towns & villages* **shichōson**
宿場町 *town around the stage* **shukubamachi**
町住まい *town living* **machizumai**
室町時代 *Muromachi Era (1336-1573)*
　　muromachi jidai

街*owntown, 107*	里*ometown, 321*
郷*ometown, 452*	市*ity, 304*
民*nhabitant, 495*	

畔*ice-field path, 484*

148-C

丁 *lock-of-houses in* 町 *own,* 訂 *diting with* 灯 *amplights by sundown...*

言 (speaking)

訂*diting*　　訂*orrection*

TEI
editing, revision, correction

FLIP: 6.0.a. Left (flat)
FLIP: 7.1. Right (Sort Of)

補訂 *revision & expansion* **hotei**
改訂 *revision, rewriting* **kaitei**
改訂版 *revised edition* **kaiteiban**
改訂増補 *revised & enlarged version* **kaitei zōho**
校訂 *revision, proof reading* **kōtei**
校訂本 *revised edition* **kōteihon**
校訂者 *revising editor* **kōteisha**
再訂 *new revision, second review* **saitei**
新訂 *new revision, updating* **shintei**
新訂版 *newly-revised edition* **shinteiban**
訂正 *correction, revisions, changes* **teisei**
全訂 *complete revision* **zentei**
増訂 *revised & enlarged version* **zōtei**

編*diting, 42*	文*iteracy, 558*
校*roof-reading, 773*	書*ritings, 116*

訂*nvestigate, 691*　　計*easurement, 692*

148-D

丁 *lock-of-houses in* 町 *own,* 訂 *diting with* 灯 *amplights by sundown...*

火⇔灬 (fire)

灯 *amplight*　灯 *antern*

hi, TŌ
lamplight, lantern

FLIP: 7.1. Right (Sort Of)
Facing: 3.0. ☞☜ Across

尾灯　*tail light, tail lamp* **bitō**
電灯　*electric light* **dentō**
⇒懐中電灯　*flash light* **kaichū dentō**
街灯　*street light, lamppost* **gaitō**
外灯　*outdoor lamp* **gaitō**
舷灯　*side lights* **gentō**
幻灯　*photo slides* **gentō**
魚灯　*fishing lamp* **gyotō**
角灯　*square lantern* **kakutō**
孤灯　*arc lamp* **kotō**
紅灯　*red light* **kōtō**
門灯　*gate lamp* **montō**
神灯　*sacred festival lantern* **shintō**
消灯　*turning off lights* **shōtō**
灯台　*lighthouse* **tōdai**
灯影　*flicker of light* **tōei**
灯火　*lamplight* **tōka**
灯下　*"by the light of..."* **tōka**
灯光　*lamplight, flashlight* **tōkō**

灯火　*lamplight, lamppost* **tomoshibi**
灯明　*sacred light* **tōmyō**
灯籠　*garden lantern* **tōrō**
灯心　*wick, small lamp* **tōshin**
灯油　*kerosene, paraffin oil* **tōyu**
洋灯　*lamp* **yōtō**
探照灯　*search, flood light* **tanshōtō**
点灯中　*lights on, lighted* **tentōchū**
釣り灯　*hanging lantern* **tsuritō**

昭 *right, 529*	光 *hining, 77*
明 *right, 22*	照 *hining, 529*
英 *rilliance, 217*	輝 *parkling, 296*

打 *trike, 636*

149-A

紅 *carlet* 工 *rafts at the* 江 *ay float on a raft...*

糸 (thread, continuity)

❶ 紅 *carlet*　❷ 紅 *ipstick*

beni, kurenai, KŌ, KU
scarlet, crimson; lipstick

FLIP: 7.0.a. Right (flat)

❶ 紅生姜　*red pickled ginger* **beni shōga**
紅花　*safflower* **benibana**
紅柄　*red-ochre rouge* **benigara**
紅色　*deep red; crimson* **beniiro**
紅染め　*red dyed fabric* **benizome**
紅蓮　*shocking red* **guren**
紅梅　*plum with red blossoms* **kōbai**
紅茶　*black tea* **kōcha**
紅茶茶碗　*teacup* **kōcha jawan**
紅潮　*flush, blushing, reddening* **kōchō**
紅衛兵　*red guards* **kōeihei**
紅顔　*rosy face, young & energetic* **kōgan**
紅玉　*ruby* **kōgyoku**
紅白　*red & white* **kōhaku**
紅白試合　*game between two teams* **kōhaku ji'ai**
紅一点　*"the only female..."* **kōitten**
紅海　*red sea* **kōkai**
紅旗　*red flag* **kōki**
紅毛　*red hair* **kōmō**

紅涙　*feminine tears* **kōrui**
紅唇　*red lips* **kōshin**
紅色　*colour red* **kōshoku**
紅葉　*autumn colours, red leaves* **kōyō, momiji**
紅葉狩り　*autumn excursion* **momijigari**
百日紅　*crape myrtle* **sarusuberi**
鮮紅　*bright red* **senkō**
深紅　*deep scarlet; crimson* **shinku**

❷ 棒紅　*red lipstick* **bōbeni**
口紅　*lipstick, rouge* **kuchibeni**

朱 *carlet, 233*
赤 *ed colour, 261*
丹 *ed colour, 78*

江 *ay, 176*

149-B

紅*carlet* 工*rafts at the* 江*ay float on a raft...*

工*raft*　　　工*onstruct*

工 (craftmanship)

KŌ, KU
craft, construct, artisan

FLIP: 1.0.a. Whole (flat)

着工	*start of construction*	**chakkō**
大工	*carpenter*	**daiku**
男工	*male worker*	**dankō**
電工	*electrician*	**denkō**
人工	*man-made, artificial*	**jinkō**
加工	*processing, manufacturing*	**kakō**
完工	*completion of construction works*	**kankō**
工学	*engineering*	**kōgaku**
工芸	*craft, industrial arts*	**kōgei**
工具	*tool, implement*	**kōgu**
工業	*industry*	**kōgyō**
工員	*factory worker*	**kōin**
工事	*construction*	**kōji**
工人	*industrial worker, factory worker*	**kōjin**
工女	*female factory worker*	**kōjo**
工場	*factory, assembly plant*	**kōjō**
工科	*engineering course*	**kōka**
工期	*construction period*	**kōki**
工務	*engineering works*	**kōmu**

工作	*fabrication, assembly*	**kōsaku**
工匠	*craftsman, artisan*	**kōshō**
木工	*woodwork, carpentry*	**mokkō**
理工	*science & engineering*	**rikō**
細工	*work-, craftsmanship*	**saiku**
施工	*execution, operation*	**sekō**
職工	*worker, labourer*	**shokkō**
商工	*commerce & industry*	**shōkō**
鉄工	*ironworks, ironsmith*	**tekkō**
図工	*art drawing, ~sketching*	**zukō**
起工式	*ground-breaking rite*	**kikōshiki**

匠*rtisan, 106*	作*roduce, 724*
芸*rts, 619*	産*roduce, 883*
巧*killful, 738*	造*roduce, 267*
術*kills, 110*	建*onstruct, 390*

土*oil, 8*	土*entleman, 8*

149-C

紅*carlet* 工*rafts at the* 江*ay float on a raft...*

江*arrows*　　　江*ay*

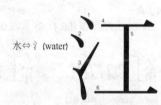

水⇔氵 (water)

e, KŌ
narrows, bay, anchorage, inlet-water

FLIP: 7.0.a. Right (flat)

長江	*Yangtze River (China)*	**chōkō**
堀江	*canal*	**horie**
江湖	*the public, society-at-large*	**kōko**
江口	*estuary*	**kōkō**
江村	*river village*	**kōson**
江戸前	*edo-style (cooking)*	**edomae**
入り江	*inlet waters, bay*	**irie**
濁り江	*muddy inlet, creek*	**nigorie**
江戸っ子	*Tōkyō-born (third generation)*	**edokko**
江戸時代	*Edo Era (1600-1868)*	**edo jidai**

湾*ay, 909*	涯*eashore, 890*
浜*each, 490*	岸*eashore, 30*
沖*ffshore, 695*	湖*ake, 801*
浦*eashore, 813*	潟*agoon, 870*
浜*eashore, 490*	

工*raft, 176*

150-A

又*gain* 収*ollecting*, 双*win beggars panhandling...*

又*gain* 又*lso*

又 (again)

mata
again, also, besides

FLIP: 1.0.b. Whole (stem)

将又 *"and also..."* **hatamata**
又々 *"again & again..."* **matamata**
又隣 *next-next door neighbour* **matadonari**
又の日 *some other day* **matanohi**
又の名 *pen name, alias* **matanona**
又頼み *requesting on behalf of another* **matadanomi**
又弟子 *student of a masters student* **matadeshi**
又借り *borrowing from a borrower, sublease* **matagari**
又貸し *sublease, subletting (landlord)* **matagashi**
又聞き *hearsay, rumour* **matagiki**
又と無い *one-of-a-kind, unique* **matatonai**
又従兄弟 *second cousin* **mataitoko**
尚又 *"besides, furthermore..."* **naomata**
且つ又 *"furthermore, moreover..."* **katsumata**
三つ又 *three-pronged fork* **mitsumata**

再*epeat*, 225	換*eplace*, 819
二*econd*, 457	替*eplace*, 334
冗*edundant*, 861	代*eplace*, 96

反*gainst*, 537

150-B

又*gain* 収*ollecting*, 双*win beggars panhandling...*

双*air* 双*win*

又 (again)

futa, SŌ
pair, both, twin, set-of-two

FLIP: 2.0.b. Sort Of (stem)

双葉 *cotyledons, bud, sprout* **futaba**
双子 *twins* **futago**
双子座 *gemini, twins* **futagoza**
一双 *pair, couple* **issō**
無双 *matchless, peerless* **musō**
双眸 *both eyes* **sōbō**
双眼 *both eyes* **sōgan**
双眼鏡 *binoculars, field glasses* **sōgankyō**
双璧 *"the best two..."* **sōheki**
双方 *both, both sides* **sōhō**
双方向 *both directions* **sōhōkō**
双肩 *both shoulders* **sōken**
双務 *bilateral, reciprocal, mutual* **sōmu**
双務条約 *bilateral treaty* **sōmu jōyaku**
双生 *growing in pairs* **sōsei**
双生児 *twins* **sōseiji**
双書 *simultaneous writing* **sōsho**
双手 *both hands* **sōshu**
双頭 *two-headed* **sōtō**

双頭政治 *diarchy* **sōtō seiji**
双翼 *both wings* **sōyoku**
双六 *backgammon chess* **sugoroku**
絵双紙 *picture book* **ezōshi**
草双紙 *picture storybook* **kusazōshi**
双の手 *both hands* **sōnote**
双胴機 *twin-fuselage plane* **sōdōki**
双発機 *twin-engine plane* **sōhatsuki**
双曲線 *hyperbola* **sōkyokusen**
双球菌 *diplococcus* **sōkyūkin**

両*oth*, 567	弐*wo*, 100
二*wo*, 457	

収*ollect*, 178

150-C

又gain 収ollecting, 双win beggars panhandling...

又 (again)

收

收ollect   收ather

osa(meru), osa(maru), SHŪ
collect, gather, take in, accrue

FLIP: 7.0.b2. Right (stem)

買収 purchase, buying up **baishū**
没収 confiscation, seizure **bosshū**
減収 decreased income **genshū**
月収 monthly income, ~salary **gesshū**
実収 net income, ~proceeds **jisshū**
回収 collection, gathering **kaishū**
検収 income verification, ~check **kenshū**
吸収 absorption, suction **kyūshū**
未収 accrued, outstanding balance **mishū**
押収 confiscation, seizure **ōshū**
査収 checking & receiving **sashū**
接収 requisition, written request **sesshū**
収益 profit, earnings, yields **shūeki**
収受 receive, receipt, acceptance **shūju**
収穫 crop harvest **shūkaku**
収監 confinement, imprisonment, detention **shūkan**
収納 receipt of payment; harvest **shūnō**
収入 income, earnings **shūnyū**
収支 revenue & expenditure **shūshi**

収拾 control, management **shūshū**
収集 collection, gathering **shūshū**
収縮 contraction, shrinkage **shūshuku**
収賄 bribe taking, "on the take..." **shūwai**
収用 expropriation, confiscation **shūyō**
収容 prison, detention **shūyō**
収容所 prison, detention **shūyōjo**
収税 tax collection **shūzei**
収蔵 storing up, loading up **shūzō**
撤収 dismantling, withdrawal **tesshū**
増収 increased income **zōshū**
領収書 official receipt **ryōshūsho**

集ollect, 50
請eceipt, 791
受eceive, 539
頂eceive, 134
納ayment, 296
払ayment, 682
料ayment, 194

双win, 177

151-A

午fternoon talks on 牛attle 件atters, 許ermitted by headquarters...

十 (cross)

午

午fternoon   午oontime

GO
afternoon, noontime

FLIP: 2.0.b. Sort Of (stem)

午後 in the afternoon, p.m. **gogo**
午後零時 twelve high noon **gogo reiji**
午砲 signal gun for 12 o'clock **gohō**
午餐 luncheon **gosan**
午餐会 lunch meeting, luncheon **gosankai**
午睡 take a nap, ~siesta **gosui**
午前 morning, a.m. **gozen**
午前中 in the morning **gozenchū**
午前零時 12 o'clock midnight **gozen reiji**
正午 twelve high noon **shōgo**
子午線 acupuncture line, meridian line **shigosen**
端午の節句 Boy's festival (5th May) **tango no sekku**

秒econds, 727
日ay, 14
曜eekday, 849
週eekly, 279
月onth, 22
年ear, 27

牛attle, 179

151-B

午fternoon talks on 牛attle 件atters, 許ermitted by headquarters...

牛⇔牛 (cattle)

牛attle　　牛eef

ushi, GYŪ
cattle, cow, beef

FLIP: 2.0.b. Sort Of (stem)

牛蒡 *bullock* **gobō**
牛丼 *beef rice bowl* **gyūdon**
牛歩 *snail walking* **gyūho**
牛革 *cowhide, leatherware* **gyūkaku**
牛缶 *canned beef* **gyūkan**
牛鍋 *sukiyaki pan* **gyūnabe**
牛肉 *beef, cattle meat* **gyūniku**
牛乳 *cow milk, dairy milk* **gyūnyū**
牛乳瓶 *milk bottle* **gyūnyūbin**
牛乳屋 *milk shop, dairy* **gyūnyūya**
牛舎 *cowshed, cattle barn* **gyūsha**
牛脂 *beef tallow* **gyūshi**
牛刀 *butcher's knife* **gyūtō**
子牛 *calf, young cow* **koushi**
肉牛 *beef cattle* **nikugyū**
乳牛 *dairy milk, cattle milk* **nyūgyū**
雄牛 *bull, ox* **ōshi**
酪牛 *dairy cattle, milk cow* **rakugyū**
水牛 *water buffalo* **suigyū**

種牛 *stud bull* **taneushi**
闘牛 *bullfight* **tōgyū**
闘牛場 *bull ring, ~arena* **tōgyūjō**
闘牛士 *bullfighter, matador, picador* **tōgyūshi**
海牛 *sea slug* **umiushi**
牛方 *oxcart pusher; teamster* **ushikata**
野牛 *wild ox, buffalo* **yagyū**
牛耳る *domineering, dominate* **gyūjiru**
去勢牛 *bullock* **kyoseigyū**
牛小屋 *cow shed* **ushigoya**
牛飼い *cowboy, cowherd* **ushikai**

乳*ilk, 970*	畜*aising, 528*
牧*asture, 647*	肉*eat, 297*
飼*aising, 835*	養*aising, 253*

午*fternoon, 178*

151-C

午fternoon talks on 牛attle 件atters, 許ermitted by headquarters...

人⇔亻 (person)

件atter　　件ubject

KEN
matter, subject, affair, case

FLIP: 7.1. Right (Sort Of)

案件 *issue, case, matter* **anken**
別件 *another matter, ~crime* **bekken**
別件逮捕 *arrest for another crime* **bekken taiho**
物件 *property; material object* **bukken**
本件 *this case, ~affair* **honken**
一件 *affair, matter, business* **ikken**
事件 *incident, case, affair* **jiken**
⇒汚職事件 *corruption case* **oshoku jiken**
⇒殺害事件 *murder case* **satsugai jiken**
⇒殺人事件 *murder case* **satsujin jiken**
⇒傷害事件 *injury case* **shōgai jiken**
⇒証拠物件 *evidence, exhibit* **shōko bukken**
⇒訴訟事件 *court case, lawsuit* **soshō jiken**
⇒盗難事件 *theft, robbery, burglary* **tōnan jiken**
⇒贈賄事件 *bribery case* **zōwai jiken**
事件目録 *list of causes* **jiken mokuroku**
条件 *condition, term* **jōken**
⇒無条件 *unconditional* **mujōken**
⇒妥結条件 *terms of agreement* **daketsu jōken**

⇒必須条件 *non-negotiable condition*
　hissu jōken
⇒必要条件 *requirement, prerequisite*
　hitsuyō jōken
⇒希望条件 *conditions desired* **kibō jōken**
⇒勤務条件 *working conditions* **kinmu jōken**
⇒交換条件 *bargaining point* **kōkan jōken**
⇒雇用条件 *terms of employment* **koyō jōken**
条件反射 *conditioned response* **jōken hansha**
難件 *difficult case* **nanken**
用件 *business, matter* **yōken**
要件 *necessary condition* **yōken**
雑件 *miscellaneous affairs* **zakken**

問*atter, 283*	物*hings, 647*
何*omething, 101*	

任*uty, 709*

151-D

午*fternoon talks on* 牛*attle* 件*atters,* 許*ermitted by headquarters...*

言 (speaking)

許*ermit* 許*orgive*

yuru(su), KYO
permit, forgive, acquiescence, allow, authorize, leave, sanction

FLIP: 6.0.a. Left (flat)
FLIP: 7.1. Right (Sort Of)

勅許 *imperial sanction, ~consent* **chokkyo**
許嫁 *fiance, fiancee* **iinazuke**
允許 *permit, license* **inkyo**
官許 *government permission* **kankyo**
形許 *"for formality's sake..."* **katachimoto, keikkyo**
公許 *official permit, license* **kōkyo**
許諾 *assent, consent, approval* **kyodaku**
許否 *approval-or-disapproval* **kyohi**
許可 *permission, license* **kyoka**
⇒再入国許可 *re-entry permit to a country*
　　sai'nyūkoku kyoka
許可制 *licensure* **kyokasei**
許可証 *permit, license* **kyokashō**
⇒輸出許可証 *export license*
　　yushutsu kyokashō
許容 *allowance, permission, authorization* **kyoyō**
許容量 *authorized limit* **kyoyōryō**
免許 *license, permit* **menkyo**
免許料 *license fees* **menkyoryō**

免許証 *license certificate* **menkyoshō**
黙許 *tacit approval, acquiescence* **mokkyo**
認許 *consent, approval, recognition* **ninkyo**
親許 *parent's home* **oyamoto**
手許 *at one's hand, readily-available* **temoto**
特許 *patent, license* **tokkyo**
⇒新案特許 *provisional patent* **shin'an tokkyo**
特許品 *patented goods* **tokkyohin**
特許法 *patent law* **tokkyohō**
特許権 *patent rights* **tokkyoken**
無免許 *unlicensed, without permit* **mumenkyo**
心許無い *uneasy, uncertain* **kokoromotonai**
不許複製 *"copy prohibited..."* **fukyo fukusei**

可*pproval, 15*	賛*pproval, 334*
承*pproval, 117*	肯*ffirmative, 616*

許*ntrust, 82*

152-A

On 公*ublic cutting of* 松*ine-trees, the* 訟*ccused gave no excuse...*

八 (eight, divisible)

公*ublic* 公*ommunity*

ōyake, KŌ
public, community, official

Facing: 2.0. East ☞ (W)

奉公 *apprenticeship* **hōkō**
公安 *public peace, safety* **kōan**
公売 *public auction, ~bidding* **kōbai**
公募 *invite public participation* **kōbo**
公営 *public-, government managed* **kōei**
公益 *common good, public welfare* **kōeki**
公園 *public park* **kōen**
公演 *public performance, ~lecture* **kōen**
公害 *public harm* **kōgai**
公平 *fairness, impartial, objectivity* **kōhei**
公法 *public law* **kōhō**
公表 *official announcement, public notice* **kōhyō**
公海 *high seas, open seas* **kōkai**
公開 *public exhibition, open-to-the-public* **kōkai**
公告 *public announcement, ~notice* **kōkoku**
公立 *government-owned* **kōritsu**
公算 *"in all probability..."* **kōsan**
公設 *government-built* **kōsetsu**
公式 *public, official* **kōshiki**

公訴 *indictment, prosecution* **kōso**
公邸 *official residence* **kōtei**
公廷 *public court* **kōtei**
公約 *public vow, official oath* **kōyaku**
公用 *official use, official business* **kōyō**
公家 *court noble* **kuge**
公論 *public opinion* **kōron**
官公吏 *government officials* **kankōri**
公会堂 *public hall, community centre* **kōkaidō**
公務員 *civil servant, government employee* **kōmuin**
聖公会 *Anglican, Episcopal* **seikōkai**

衆*opulace, 766*	京*apital, 386*
衆*eople, 766*	都*etropolis, 694*

分*ivide, 518*

152-B

On 公ublic cutting of 松ine-trees, the 訟ccused gave no excuse...

木 (wooden)

松ine-tree

matsu, SHŌ
pine tree

松の木	*pine trees* **matsunoki**
松の内	*new year's first week* **matsunouchi**
赤松	*red pine tree* **akamatsu**
姫松	*small pine tree* **himematsu**
市松	*checkered design* **ichimatsu**
門松	*new year's pine ornaments* **kadomatsu**
唐松	*larch tree* **karamatsu**
黒松	*black pine* **kuromatsu**
松葉	*pine needle* **matsuba**
松葉杖	*crutches* **matsubazue**
松林	*pine grove* **matsubayashi**
松虫	*grasshopper* **matsumushi**
松茸	*special kind of mushroom* **matsutake**
松竹	*New Year pine & bamboo ornaments* **matsutake**
老松	*old pine tree* **rōshō**
青松	*green pine* **seishō**
松柏	*pines & oaks* **shōhaku**
松露	*mushroom* **shōro**
松明	*torchlight* **taimatsu**

Facing: 2.2. East ☞ (V)
FLIP: 6.0.b. Left (stem)

松明行列	*torchlight parade* **taimatsu gyōretsu**
杜松	*juniper tree* **toshō**
海松	*pine trees along seashore* **umimatsu**
這い松	*creeping pine tree* **haimatsu**
浜松市	*Hamamatsu City, Shizuoka* **hamamatsu-shi**
松江市	*Matsue City, Shimane Pref.* **matsue-shi**
松本市	*Matsumoto City, Nagano* **matsumoto-shi**
松並木	*rows of pine trees* **matsunamiki**
松山市	*Matsuyama City, Ehime* **matsuyama-shi**
松阪市	*Matsuzaka City, Mie Pref.* **matsuzaka-shi**
高松市	*Takamatsu City, Kagawa* **takamatsu-shi**

植*lant, 783*
材*oods, 186*
木*ree, 461*

枚*[sheets],724*

152-C

On 公ublic cutting of 松ine-trees, the 訟ccused gave no excuse...

言 (speaking)

訟ccusation   訟ndictment

SHŌ
accusation, indictment, allegation, court suit, lawsuit, litigation, charges

訴訟	*lawsuit, court suit* **soshō**
⇒刑事訴訟	*criminal complaint* **keiji soshō**
⇒民事訴訟	*civil case, civil suit* **minji soshō**
⇒離婚訴訟	*divorce suit* **rikon soshō**
⇒集団訴訟	*class action suit* **shūdan soshō**
訴訟人	*plaintiff, complainant, accuser* **soshōnin**
訴訟法	*courtsuit procedure* **soshōhō**
訴訟事件	*court case* **soshō jiken**
訴訟手続	*legal proceedings* **soshō tetsuzuki**
争訟	*court-, legal dispute* **sōshō**

FLIP: 6.0.a. Left (flat)
Facing: 2.2. ☞ East (V)

訴*ppeal, 424*	決*udgement, 699*
廷*oyal-Court, 26*	裁*udgement, 802*
法*egal, 360*	判*udgement. 949*

公*ublic, 180*

153-A

今ow, the 念dea 含ncludes 吟hants of Ave Maria...

人⇔亻 (person)

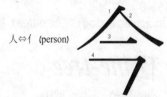

 今ow   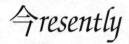 今resently

ima, KON, KIN
now, presently, this

FLIP: 2.0.b. Sort Of (stem)
Facing: 1.2. ☞ West (V)

現今 present days, nowadays **genkon**
今時 nowadays, these few days **imadoki**
今際 hour of death **imagiwa**
今頃 nowadays, these days **imagoro**
今尚 still, even now **imanao**
今に before long, soon **ima(ni)**
今にも at any moment **ima(ni)mo**
今更 all the more **imasara**
今や now, at this time **imaya**
今朝 this morning **kesa**
古今 ancient & modern ages **kokon**
今度 this time; next time **kondo**
今月 this month **kongetsu**
今次 this time, present life **konji**
今生 this life **konjō**
今回 this time **konkai**
今期 this term, ~session **konki**
今般 this time, nowadays **konpan**
今週 this week **konshū**

今春 this spring season **konshun**
今年 this year **kotoshi**
今日 today **kyō, konnichi**
昨今 lately, recently **sakkon**
只今 just now; "I'm home...." **tadaima**
当今 at present, nowadays **tōkon**
今一つ somehow, a little **imahitotsu**
今一度 once again, once more **imaichido**
今すぐ "right now, right after this..." **imasugu**
今後とも "as always..." **kongotomo**
今までにない unprecedented, a first **imadeninai**

現resent, 814
途n-going, 882
既lready, 316

分ivide, 518   介ediate, 365

153-B

今ow, the 念dea 含ncludes 吟hants of Ave Maria...

心⇔忄 (heart, feelings)

 念dea   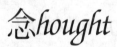 念hought

NEN
idea, thought, abstraction, concept

Facing: 3.0. ☞☞ Across

悪念 evil thoughts, ~intention **akunen**
断念 giving up an idea **dannen**
概念 general idea, concept, notion **gainen**
疑念 doubt, suspicion, distrust **ginen**
一念 wholehearted desire **ichinen**
⇒初一念 original idea **shoichinen**
邪念 evil thoughts, ~intention **janen**
情念 innermost feelings **jōnen**
観念 idea, conception, thought **kannen**
懸念 fear, anxiety, concern **kenen**
祈念 prayer, earnest wish **kinen**
記念 anniversary-, memorial **kinen**
念仏 Buddhist invocation **nenbutsu**
念願 heart's desire **nengan**
念珠 rosary, prayer beads **nenju**
念力 will power, determination **nenriki**
念写 psychic photography **nensha**
念頭 bearing in mind **nentō**
怨念 deep-seated grudge, bad blood **onnen**

専念 devotion, concentration **sennen**
信念 faith, conviction, belief **shinnen**
執念 persistence, diligence, tenacity **shūnen**
想念 thought, notion, idea **sōnen**
諦念 spiritual awakening **tainen, teinen**
余念 total immersion in one's work **yonen**
残念 deplorable, regrettable, lamentable **zannen**
雑念 stray ideas, random thoughts **zatsunen**
俗念 secular-, earthly desires **zokunen**
朴念仁 dunce, dullard, moron **bokunenjin**
記念日 anniversary-, memorial date **kinenbi**
念のため "to leave no doubt..." **nen no tame**

意dea, 340   慮hought, 70
想dea, 524   志ntention, 426
提roposal, 313

怠azyness, 570

153-C

今*ow, the* 念*dea* 含*ncludes* 吟*hants of Ave Maria...*

口 (mouth)

含*nclude*   含*ontain*

fuku(mu); fuku(meru), GAN
include, contain

含み声 *muffled voice* **fukumigoe**
含み笑い *suppressed laughter, chuckle* **fukumiwarai**
含蓄 *significance, suggestion* **ganchiku**
含意 *hidden meaning, implication, hint* **gan'i**
含味 *taste, relish* **ganmi**
含侵 *impregnation* **ganshin**
含有 *containing, including* **ganyū**
含有量 *amount of content, volume* **ganyūryō**
包含 *inclusion, implication* **hōgan**
含水化 *hydration* **gansuika**
含水炭素 *carbohydrate* **gansui tanso**
言い含める *explain, elaborate, amplify* **iifukumeru**

FLIP: 4.0.a. Bottom (flat)
FLIP: 2.0.a. Sort Of (flat)

括*undle, 954*	郭*nclose, 398*
束*undle, 502*	奥*nside, 903*
把*undle, 717*	内*nside, 297*
囲*nclose, 361*	

合*ogether, 232*

153-D

今*ow, the* 念*dea* 含*ncludes* 吟*hants of Ave Maria...*

口 (mouth)

吟*hanting*   吟*ncantation*

GIN
chanting, incantation, mantra

愛吟 *poet, favourite poem* **aigin**
沈吟 *bitter groaning, ~whining* **chingin**
独吟 *solo recitation* **dokugin**
吟詠 *Chinese poem recitation* **gin'ei**
吟醸 *first rate sake wine* **ginjō**
吟味 *careful-, meticulous selection* **ginmi**
⇒再吟味 *review, re-examine* **saiginmi**
吟唱 *reciting a poem* **ginshō**
感吟 *passionate recitation* **kangin**
高吟 *loud poem recitation* **kōgin**
苦吟 *poem-writing difficulties* **kugin**
名吟 *Haiku masterpiece* **meigin**
連吟 *poem duet* **rengin**
朗吟 *poem recitation* **rōgin**
詩吟 *Chinese poem recitation* **shigin**
呻吟 *groaning, moaning* **shingin**
秀吟 *excellent poem* **shūgin**
即吟 *impromptu poem recitation* **sokugin**
低吟 *low-pitch recitation, ~singing* **teigin**

FLIP: 6.0.a. Left (flat)
FLIP: 7.1. Right (Sort Of)

唱*hant, 131*	祈*rayer, 184*
謡*hant, 810*	拝*rayer, 636*

含*nclude, 183*

154-A

近*earby scientists* 祈*raying for correct* 析*nalysis...*

辶 (transport)

Facing: 4.0.　　Apart

近*earby*　　　近*ecent*

chika(i), KIN
nearby, recent, close, neighbouring, proximity, adjacent

近頃	*recently, lately, nowadays* **chikagoro**
近々	*very soon* **chikajika, kinkin**
近間	*nearby, neighbouring, adjacent* **chikama**
近道	*shortcut, secret road* **chikamichi**
卑近	*familiar, common* **hikin**
近著	*recent writings* **kincho**
近影	*recent photo* **kin'ei**
近眼	*near-, short-sightedness* **kingan**
近因	*immediate cause, primary factor* **kin'in**
近似	*approximation, approach* **kinji**
近日	*in a few days* **kinjitsu**
近所	*neighbour, neighbourhood* **kinjo**
近火	*neighbourhood fire* **kinka**
近海	*nearby seas* **kinkai**
近刊	*newly-published* **kinkan**
近景	*foreground, forefront* **kinkei**
近郊	*suburbs, outskirts* **kinkō**
近況	*present condition, status quo* **kinkyō**
近来	*recently, lately* **kinrai**

近視	*near-, short-sightedness* **kinshi**
近親	*immediate relatives* **kinshin**
間近	*near, at hand, close* **majika**
身近	*familiar, common* **mijika**
最近	*recently, lately* **saikin**
接近	*approach, access* **sekkin**
親近感	*sense of closeness* **shinkinkan**
側近	*closest associates* **sokkin**
隣近所	*neighbour, neighbourhood* **tonarikinjo**
近寄る	*approach, come near* **chikayoru**

囲 *nclose, 361*	辺 *icinity, 93*
周 *icinity, 280*	環 *nvirons, 165*

辺 *icinity, 93*	迎 *elcome, 705*

154-B

近*earby scientists* 祈*raying for correct* 析*nalysis...*

示 ⇔ ネ (display, show)

祈*rayer*

Facing: 2.2. East ☞ (V)

ino(ru), KI
prayer, pray

祈願	*prayer, wish* **kigan**
祈求	*prayer, wish* **kikyū**
祈念	*prayer* **kinen**
祈誓	*sacred vow* **kisei**
祈請	*sacred vow* **kisei**
祈祷	*prayer, grace* **kitō**
祈祷書	*prayer book* **kitōsho**
主の祈り	*"Our Father, who art in heaven..."*
	shu no inori

信 *aith, 252*	依 *equest, 355*
聖 *acred, 617*	願 *equest, 964*
神 *ivine, 712*	求 *equest, 256*
拝 *rayer, 636*	請 *equest, 791*
宗 *eligion, 879*	頼 *equest, 562*

所 *ocation, 676*

154-C

近earby scientists 祈raying for correct 析nalysis...

木 (wooden)

析nalysis　　　析issection

SEKI
analysis, dissection

Facing: 2.2. East ☞ (V)

分析 analysis, dissection **bunseki**
⇒市場分析 market analysis **shijō bunseki**
⇒定量分析 quantitative analysis **teiryō bunseki**
⇒定性分析 qualitative analysis **teisei bunseki**
解析 analysis, thorough thinking **kaiseki**
析出 separation, deposition **sekishutsu**
透析 dialysis, blood sterilization **tōseki**
⇒人工透析 dialysis, blood sterilization **jinkō tōseki**

割ivide, 968	解nderstand, 400
分ivide, 518	締onclude, 432
剖ivide, 950	

折reak, 471

155-A

才ge 才enius on 財inance sold 材oods & 材aterials at once...

手⇔扌 (hand, manual)

❶才enius　　❷才ears old

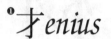

SAI
genius, smart, talent; years old, age suffix

Facing: 1.0. ⬅ West (W)

❶悪才 evil genius **akusai**
凡才 mediocre-, inferior person **bonsai**
文才 literary genius **bunsai**
鈍才 dull-witted, stupid **donsai**
英才 brilliant, gifted, genius **eisai**
学才 scholarly, studious, academic **gakusai**
画才 artistic, creative **gasai**
非才 incapacity, inability **hisai**
偉才 genius, wise **isai**
奇才 outstanding-, exceptional talent **kisai**
鬼才 genius, wise **kisai**
漫才 stage comedy **manzai**
才物 talented & intelligent **saibutsu**
才知 wit, intelligence **saichi**
才媛 talented woman **saien**
才人 talented-, clever **saijin**
才女 talented-, intelligent woman **saijo**
才覚 wit, management **saikaku**
才幹 able, gifted **saikan**

才能 talent, ability, capacity **sainō**
才略 clever scheme, wise plan **sairyaku**
才色 beauty & brains **saishoku**
才徳 talent & virtue **saitoku**
才腕 ability, skill, talent **saiwan**
詩才 poetic genius **shisai**
商才 business talent, knack-for-money **shōsai**
俊才 talented-, clever **shunsai**
秀才 brilliant, gifted, talented **shūsai**
天才 genius, wise **tensai**

❷何才 what age **nansai**
十才 ten years old **jūsai, jussai**

俊enius, 765	年ear, 27
齢ears old, 553	

寸 [3 cm], 345

155-B

才*ge* 才*enius on* 財*inance sold* 材*oods &* 材*aterials at once...*

貝 (shell, old money)

財*inance*　財*reasury*

ZAI, SAI
finance, treasury, bursary

FLIP: 6.0.b. Left (stem)

蓄財 *thrift, frugality, saving money* **chikuzai**
浄財 *donation, subscription* **jōzai**
家財 *household effects, ~belongings* **kazai**
巨財 *enormous wealth* **kyozai**
理財 *finance, economy* **rizai**
財布 *wallet, pocketbook, purse* **saifu**
散財 *squandering money* **sanzai**
借財 *debts, borrowings* **shakuzai**
私財 *private property, personal wealth* **shizai**
殖財 *money-making, income earning* **shokuzai**
余財 *extra cash, spare money* **yozai**
財閥 *moneyed elite, ruling class* **zaibatsu**
財団 *foundation* **zaidan**
財源 *source of revenue* **zaigen**
財宝 *treasures, riches, wealth* **zaihō**
財貨 *commodity, property* **zaika**
財界 *financial world, banking circles* **zaikai**
財形 *assets, holdings* **zaikei**
財務 *financial affairs* **zaimu**

財力 *financial strength* **zairyoku**
財産 *property, estate* **zaisan**
⇒隠し財産 *hidden wealth* **kakushi zaisan**
財産税 *property tax, estate tax* **zaisanzei**
財政 *public finance* **zaisei**
財政難 *financial insolvency* **zaiseinan**
財用 *uses of money* **zaiyō**
文化財 *cultural heritage* **bunkazai**
管財人 *administrator, receivership* **kanzainin**
消費財 *consumer goods* **shōhizai**

金*oney, 25*	札*oney-bills, 685*	富*ortune, 333*
幣*oney, 171*	宝*reasure, 92*	盛*rosperity, 244*

敗*efeat, 137*

155-C

才*ge* 才*enius on* 財*inance sold* 材*oods &* 材*aterials at once...*

木 (wooden)

❶材*oods*　❷材*aterials*

ZAI
woods, timber, lumber; materials

Facing: 3.0. ☞☜ Across

❶丸材 *log, timber* **maruzai**
木材 *lumber, wood, timber* **mokuzai**
製材 *lumber, sawing, timber* **seizai**
製材所 *sawmill, lumber mill* **seizaisho**
用材 *material, lumber, timber* **yōzai**
材木 *lumber, wood, timber* **zaimoku**
材木屋 *lumber-, timber dealer* **zaimokuya**

❷部材 *parts, components* **buzai**
題材 *theme, topic, subject* **daizai**
外材 *foreign-, imported timber* **gaizai**
逸材 *talented, gifted* **itsuzai**
偉材 *extraordinary talent* **izai**
人材 *staff member, work force* **jinzai**
角材 *square lumber, ~timber* **kakuzai**
建材 *construction-, building materials* **kenzai**
器材 *equipment parts* **kizai**
鋼材 *steel materials* **kōzai**
教材 *teaching materials* **kyōzai**

良材 *materials, goods* **ryōzai**
石材 *building stone* **sekizai**
線材 *wire rod* **senzai**
資材 *materials, ingredients* **shizai**
取材 *media theme, ~coverage* **shuzai**
素材 *material, subject matter* **sozai**
鉄材 *iron materials* **tetsuzai**
材料 *materials, cooking ingredients* **zairyō**
材質 *quality of materials* **zaishitsu**
耐火材 *fireproof materials* **taikazai**
塗装材 *coating-, paint materials* **tosōzai**
適材適所 *"right person in the right place..."*
　　tekizai tekisho

料*aterials, 194*
量*mount, 451*

村*illage, 690*

156-A

One 夕vening 多lenty 移ransferred 外utside the suburbs...

夕 (evening, night)

 夕vening   夕ight time

yū, SEKI
evening, nightfall, night time

Facing: 1.0. ☜ West (W)

朝夕 *mornings & evenings* **asayū**
一夕 *one night* **isseki**
毎夕 *every night* **maiyū**
日夕 *day & night* **nisseki**
旦夕 *day & night* **tanseki**
⇒命旦夕 *brink of death* **meitanseki**
夕べ *evening, night* **yūbe**
夕立 *rainshower* **yūdachi**
夕顔 *bottle gourd; moonflower* **yūgao**
夕方 *evening, night* **yūgata**
夕霧 *evening mist* **yūgiri**
夕雲 *evening cloud* **yūgumo**
夕日 *setting sun* **yūhi**
夕刊 *evening newspaper* **yūkan**
夕風 *evening breeze* **yūkaze**
夕刻 *evening, night* **yūkoku**
夕靄 *evening haze* **yūmoya**
夕波 *waves at night* **yūnami**

夕食 *dinner, supper, evening meal* **yūshoku**
夕菅 *yellow lily* **yūsuge**
夕月 *evening moon* **yūzuki**
夕闇 *dusk, twilight* **yūyami**
夕空 *evening sky* **yūzora**
七夕祭 *Star Festival (7 July)* **tanabata matsuri**
夕映え *sunset glow, night glow* **yūbae**
夕暮れ *evening, night* **yūgure**
夕涼み *evening cool* **yūsuzumi**
夕焼け *sunset glow* **yūyake**
夕明かり *evening afterglow* **yūakari**

晩 *vening, 413*	眠 *leeping, 495*
夜 *vening, 508*	寝 *leeping, 769*

勹 *[18ml], 470*   多 *lenty, 187*

156-B

One 夕vening 多lenty 移ransferred 外utside the suburbs...

夕 (evening, night)

 多lenty   多umerous

ō(i), TA
plenty, numerous, plural

Facing: 1.1. ☜ West (H)

過多 *excess of~* **kata**
多目 *large portion* **oome**
最多 *the most number of~* **saita**
多忙 *extremely busy, ~full* **tabō**
多分 *maybe, perhaps...* **tabun**
多病 *sickly person* **tabyō**
多読 *voracious reading, devour reading* **tadoku**
多額 *large amount* **tagaku**
多言 *speaking at length, long speech* **tagen**
多情 *full of emotion, passion* **tajō**
多感 *varied emotions* **takan**
多血 *hot-tempered, mercurial* **taketsu**
多幸 *happiness, joy* **takō**
多項 *polynomial, multinomial* **takō**
多国 *multinational* **takoku**
多極 *multi-polar* **takyoku**
多面 *polygonal, multi-sided* **tamen**
多難 *lots of difficulties* **tanan**
多才 *versatility, multi-talented* **tasai**

多作 *prolific writing, literacy genius* **tasaku**
多産 *bearing many children* **tasan**
多謝 *many thanks, deep gratitude* **tasha**
多生 *transmigration* **tashō**
多色 *multi-coloured, colourful* **tashoku**
多数 *plurality, large number* **tasū**
多党 *multi-party* **tatō**
雑多 *miscellaneous, various* **zatta**
幾多の *many, various* **ikuta no**
滅多に *seldom, rarely, not often* **metta(ni)**
多角的 *diversified, varied* **takakuteki**

豊 *lenty, 965*
裕 *ffluence, 758*
少 *ew, 459*

夕 *vening, 187*

156-C

One 夕vening 多lenty 移ransferred 外utside the suburbs...

禾 (tree branch)

移ransfer 移elocate

utsu(ru), utsu(su), I
transfer, relocate, shift, moving

Facing: 1.2. ➣ West (V)

変移 *change, transition* **hen'i**
移築 *reconstruction in a new site* **ichiku**
移調 *transposition* **ichō**
移駐 *transfer to another post* **ichū**
移動 *movement, moving* **idō**
移譲 *transfer of rights (new ownership)* **ijō**
移住 *emigration, immigration* **ijū**
移管 *transfer of jurisdiction* **ikan**
移行 *switchover, shift* **ikō**
移項 *transposition* **ikō**
移民 *immigration, emigration* **imin**
移入 *bringing in, introduction* **inyū**
移籍 *registration transfer of residence* **iseki**
移植 *transplant, transplantation* **ishoku**
⇒角膜移植 *corneal transplantation*
　kakumaku ishoku
⇒臓器移植 *organ transplant* **zōki ishoku**
移出 *sending out, shipment* **ishutsu**
移送 *transfer, move location* **isō**

移転 *transfer, removal* **iten**
遷移 *transition, change* **sen'i**
推移 *change, transition, progress* **suii**
転移 *transfer, metastasis, spread* **ten'i**
心移り *change-of-heart* **kokoro utsuri**
口移し *mouth-to-mouth feeding* **kuchi utsushi**
目移り *being puzzled, ~baffled* **meutsuri**
移り気 *capricious, whimsical, fickle* **utsurigi**
乗り移る *be possessed, transfer* **noriutsuru**
燃え移る *spread of fire* **moeutsuru**
飛び移る *jump, flutter, spring* **tobiutsuru**
移り変わり *change, transition* **utsurikawari**

譲ransfer, 853　　所ocation, 676
遷hange, 603　　場ocation, 147
変hange, 581

多lenty, 187

156-D

One 夕vening 多lenty 移ransferred 外utside the suburbs...

夕 (evening, night)

外utside 外emove

soto, hoka, hazu(reru), hazu(su), GAI, GE
outside, remove, take off, external

Facing: 4.0. ➣➣ Apart

案外 *beyond one's expectation* **angai**
番外 *extra, extraneous* **bangai**
外圧 *outside pressure* **gaiatsu**
外部 *external, outer* **gaibu**
外聞 *reputation, social status* **gaibun**
外人 *foreigner, non-Japanese person* **gaijin**
外貨 *foreign currency* **gaika**
外海 *high seas, ocean* **gaikai**
外界 *outside world* **gaikai**
外角 *exterior angle, outside corner* **gaikaku**
外観 *outward appearance* **gaikan**
外形 *contours* **gaikei**
外気 *the air, open air* **gaiki**
外勤 *outside duty* **gaikin**
外交 *diplomacy, international relations* **gaikō**
外出 *outside one's house or office* **gaishutsu**
外科 *surgery, incission* **geka**
法外 *excessive, ridiculous* **hōgai**
除外 *exclusion, exemption* **jogai**

場外 *outside, outer premises* **jōgai**
海外 *foreign countries, overseas* **kaigai**
郊外 *suburbs, suburbia* **kōgai**
内外 *inside & outside* **naigai, uchisoto**
例外 *exception, exclusion* **reigai**
論外 *out of question, irrelevant* **rongai**
渉外 *public relations, publicity* **shōgai**
疎外 *alienation, neglect* **sogai**
部外者 *outsider, outcast* **bugaisha**
意外性 *unexpected, surprise* **igaisei**
外回り *circumstance, outside work* **sotomawari**

出epart, 173
野lains, 873
内nside, 297

死eath, 513

157-A

扱andling 級evels due to skills 吸bsorption 及s well...

手⇔扌 (hand, manual)

扱andling 扱reatment

atsuka(u), ko(ku)
handling, treatment

Facing: 4.0. ☜☞ Apart

扱い方 *way of handling, -dealing* **atsukaikata**
扱い人 *person in-charge* **atsukainin**
取扱 *handling, treatmen t* **toriatsukai**
⇒事務取扱 *managing director* **jimu toriatsukai**
取扱所 *room, chamber, cluster* **toriatsukaijo**
⇒荷物取扱所 *baggage room* **nimotsu toriatsukaijo**
⇒貨物取扱所 *freight office* **kamotsu toriatsukaijo**
稲扱き *threshing* **inekoki**
客扱い *expert, skilled person* **kyakuatsukai**
根扱ぎ *uprooting* **nekogi**
荷扱い *freight handling* **niatsukai**
宅扱い *home-delivery* **takuatsukai**
取り扱う *deal with, handle, accept* **toriatsukau**
腕扱き *expert, skilled, savvy* **udekoki**
扱き使う *boss around someone* **kokitsukau**
子供扱い *treating one as a child* **kodomo atsukai**
取り扱い店 *dealership store* **toriatsukaiten**
取り扱い時間 *service hours* **toriatsukai jikan**
扱き下ろす *excoriate, criticize severely* **kokiorosu**

扱き落とす *thresh, strip off* **kokiotosu**

処reatment, 473	受ccept, 539
療reatment, 67	偶ccasional, 815
宰anage, 377	
営anagement, 580	

及s well as, 190

157-B

扱andling 級evels due to skills 吸bsorption 及s well...

糸 (thread, continuity)

級evel 級rade

KYŪ
level, grade, ranking

Facing: 2.2. East ☞ (V)

分級 *classification, grouping by level* **bunkyū**
中級 *middle class* **chūkyū**
同級 *same class* **dōkyū**
同級生 *classmate, grademate* **dōkyūsei**
学級 *class, grade* **gakkyū**
⇒養護学級 *disabled children class* **yōgo gakkyū**
学級委員 *class president* **gakkyū iin**
原級 *original class* **genkyū**
比較級 *comparative degree* **hikakukyū**
一級 *first-class, highest quality* **ikkyū**
上級 *upper level* **jōkyū**
上級生 *upperclass person* **jōkyūsei**
階級 *class, rank, grade* **kaikyū**
⇒有閑階級 *leisure class* **yūkan kaikyū**
階級闘争 *class struggle* **kaikyū tōsō**
下級生 *underclass person* **kakyūsei**
高級 *high class* **kōkyū**
級数 *mathematical progression* **kyūsū**
⇒等比級数 *geometric series* **tōhi kyūsū**

⇒等差級数 *arithmetic series* **tōsa kyūsū**
級友 *classmate, school friend* **kyūyū**
船級 *ships classification* **senkyū**
進級 *promotion, advancement* **shinkyū**
初級 *beginner's class, entry-level* **shokyū**
昇級 *promotion, advancement* **shōkyū**
低級 *lower grade, low class* **teikyū**
特級 *best quality, highest grade* **tokkyū**
特級酒 *the highest grade sake* **tokkyūshu**
等級 *grade, class, rank* **tōkyū**
全級 *entire class* **zenkyū**
学級委員 *class president* **gakkyūlin**

等rade, 251	段evel, 555
準evel, 919	階evel, 129
格tatus, 498	

紛istract, 778

157-C

扱andling 級evels due to skills 吸bsorption 及s well...

口 (mouth)

吸

1 2 5 4 6 3

吸uction   吸bsorption

su(u), KYŪ
suction, absorption, breathe in

FLIP: 6.0.a. Left (flat)
Facing: 2.2. East ☞ (V)

呼吸 *breathing, respiration* **kokyū**
⇒腹式呼吸 *abdominal breathing*
    fukushiki kokyū
吸盤 *sucking disk* **kyūban**
吸着 *adhesion, absorption* **kyūchaku**
吸引 *absorption, attraction* **kyūin**
吸引力 *suction force* **kyūinryoku**
吸管 *suction pipe, siphon* **kyūkan**
吸血 *blood sucking, vampire* **kyūketsu**
吸血鬼 *vampire, bloodsucker* **kyūketsuki**
吸気 *breathing, respiration* **kyūki**
吸入 *inhaling, breathing* **kyūnyū**
⇒酸素吸入 *oxygen inhalation* **sanso kyūnyū**
吸音 *sound absorption, ~proofing* **kyūon**
吸湿 *absorbing moisture* **kyūshitsu**
吸収 *absorption, suction* **kyūshū**
吸収合併 *corporate take-over* **kyūshū gappei**
吸水 *sucking water, siphon off* **kyūsui**
深呼吸 *deep breathing* **shinkokyū**

吸い殻 *cigarette butt* **suigara**
吸い物 *soup, broth* **suimono**
吸い出す *draw out, suck out* **suidasu**
吸い込む *inhale, breath-, suck in* **suikomu**
吸い付く *stick, adhere, cling to* **suitsuku**
吸い取る *absorb, soak-, sponge up* **suitoru**
吸い飲み *feeding cup* **suinomi**
吸い上げる *pump up, suck up* **suiageru**
吸い殻入れ *ashtray, cigarette tray* **suigaraire**
吸い取り紙 *blotting paper, blotter* **suitorigami**
吸い付ける *attract, draw, pull* **suitsukeru**
吸い寄せる *attract, draw, pull* **suiyoseru**

圧ressure, 632	引xtract, 348
力orce, 351	滴xtract, 799
抽xtract, 37	拾ick-up, 231

及s well as, 190

157-D

扱andling 級evels due to skills 吸bsorption 及s well...

丿 (katakana の)

及

2 1 3

及each   及s well

腰 koshi-waist 419

oyo(bu), oyo(bosu); oyo(bi), KYŪ
reach, as well

Facing: 2.0. East ☞ (W)

及ぼす *exert, bring to bear* **oyobosu**
及び腰 *no self-confidence; slanted back* **oyobigoshi**
普及 *diffusion, dispersion, spread* **fukyū**
普及版 *popular edition* **fukyūban** 扱 printing
言及 *mention, reference* **genkyū**
波及 *spread, influence* **hakyū**
企及 *aiming to achieve* **kikyū**
及第 *passing an exam* **kyūdai**
及第点 *passing mark, ~score, ~point* **kyūdaiten**
及落 *pass-or-fail* **kyūraku**
論及 *reference* **ronkyū**
遡及 *ex-post-facto, retroactive* **sokyū**
遡及的 *ex-post-facto, retroactive* **sokyūteki**
追及 *thorough investigation* **tsuikyū**
過不及 *lacking-or-excess* **kafukyū**
可及的 *as (far) as possible* **kakyūteki**
聞き及ぶ *learn about, overhear* **kikioyobu**
思い及ぶ *think of, ponder* **omoioyobu**
説き及ぶ *mention, reference* **tokioyobu**

達each, 267	両oth, 567
等uch as, 251	遍idespread, 43

扱andling, 189

158-A

Arrival of 花lowers' 貨reight so late, owners 化ecame irate...

⁺⁺ (grass)

花*lower* 花*lossom*

hana, KA
flower, blossom

FLIP: 3.0.b. Top (stem)
Facing: 4.0. ⬅➡ Apart

弔花	condolence-, funeral flowers **chōka**	草花	flower, flowering plant **kusabana**
花火	fireworks, firecrackers **hanabi**	綿花	raw cotton **menka**
花札	flower cards **hanafuda**	雄花	masculine flower **obana**
花曇	cloudy skies in spring **hanagumori**	花魁	courtesan, red zone woman **oiran**
花見	flower viewing (cherry blossoms) **hanami**	落花	falling sakura petals **rakka**
花道	the golden way, path of glory **hanamichi**	総花	across-the-board **sōbana**
花婿	bridegroom **hanamuko**	造花	artificial flower; tip for geisha **zōka**
花束	floral bouquet **hanataba**	花びら	flower petal **hanabira**
花屋	flower shop, florist **hanaya**	花吹雪	storm of sakura petals **hanafubuki**
花嫁	bride **hanayome**	花入れ	flower vase **hanaire**
花園	flower garden **hanazono**	花言葉	flowery language, highfalutin **hanakotoba**
生花	flower arrangement **ikebana, seika**	死に花	glorious death **shinibana**
花弁	petal **kaben**		
花瓶	flower vase **kabin**		
花壇	bed of flowers, ~of roses **kadan**		
花粉	pollen **kafun**		
開花	flowering, blooming, blossoming **kaika**		
献花	floral offering **kenka**		
国花	national flower **kokka**		

華*lower*, 40	植*egetation*, 783
植*lant*, 783	畑*lantation*, 482

化*ecome*, 192

158-B

Arrival of 花lowers' 貨reight so late, owners 化ecame irate...

貝 (shell, old money)

❶貨*oods* ❷貨*reight*

KA
goods, commodity, money, currency; freight, loads

FLIP: 4.0.b. Bottom (stem)

❶悪貨	blood money, dirty money **akka**		
米貨	US dollar, green buck **beika**	雑貨商	general merchandize store **zakkashō**
鋳貨	coinage, mintage **chūka**	雑貨店	general shop, grocery **zakkaten**
銅貨	copper coins **dōka**	白銅貨	nickel coins **hakudōka**
円貨	yen currency **enka**	百貨店	department store **hyakkaten**
外貨	foreign currency **gaika**		
銀貨	silver coins **ginka**	❷貨物	freight, load, goods **kamotsu**
邦貨	Japanese money **hōka**	貨物駅	freight depot, goods station **kamotsueki**
貨幣	coin, money, currency **kahei**	貨物船	cargo ship, freighter **kamotsusen**
貨幣単位	monetary unit **kahei tan'i**	貨車	freight car, goods wagon **kasha**
貨殖	money-making, profit-earning **kashoku**	⇒無蓋貨車	open-freight car **mugai kasha**
金貨	gold coin, gold currency **kinka**	⇒有蓋貨車	boxcar, van **yūgai kasha**
硬貨	coins **kōka**	集貨	freight collection **shūka**
良貨	good money **ryōka**		
銭貨	coins **senka**		
滞貨	accumulation of goods **taika**		
通貨	currency, money **tsūka**		
財貨	property, wealth, fortune **zaika**		
雑貨	miscellaneous goods **zakka**		

箇*[objects]*, 52	運*ransport*, 295
荷*argo*, 877	輸*elivery*, 660

賃*ayment*, 145

158-C

Arrival of 花lowers' 貨reight so late, owners 化ecame irate...

ヒ (spoon)

化ecome   化ransform

ba(keru), ba(kasu), KA, KE
become, transform, change into

Facing: 4.0. ☜☞ Apart

悪化 *worsening, deterioration* **akka**	緑化 *reforestation, tree-planting* **ryokuka**
化け物 *beast, monster* **bakemono**	酸化 *oxidization, oxidation* **sanka**
化けの皮 *hidding, secret* **bakenokawa**	進化 *evolution, progress* **shinka**
美化 *beautification* **bika**	消化 *digestion, consumption* **shōka**
文化 *culture* **bunka**	転化 *change, transformation* **tenka**
同化 *assimilation, mingling* **dōka**	暗号化 *encryption, cryptograph, encoding* **angōka**
鈍化 *getting dull, decadence* **donka**	複雑化 *complication, aggravation* **fukuzatsuka**
液化 *liquefaction, liquidization* **ekika**	具体化 *materialization, actualisation* **gutaika**
権化 *embodiment, materialization* **gonge**	標準化 *standardization* **hyōjunka**
純化 *purification* **junka**	機械化 *mechanization* **kikaika**
化学 *chemistry, science* **kagaku**	高齢化 *ageing, greying society* **kōreika**
化合 *chemical mixture* **kagō**	深刻化 *aggravation, deterioration* **shinkokuka**
開化 *enlightenment; civilization* **kaika**	単一化 *unification, simplification* **tan'itsuka**
化成 *transformation, regeneration* **kasei**	統一化 *unification, union, merger* **tōitsuka**
化石 *fossil, fossilization* **kaseki**	
化生 *metamorphosis* **keshō**	成*ecome, 244* 式*tyle, 418* 的*tyle, 696*
帰化 *naturalization, new citizenship* **kika**	
硬化 *hardening, stiffening* **kōka**	代*poch, 96*
乳化 *emulsification* **nyūka**	

159-A

"止top 祉elfare 企lan," says a selfish clan...

止 (stopping)

止top   止erminate

to(maru), to(meru), ya(meru), SHI
stop, terminate, cease, discontinue, freeze, put an end

Facing: 2.0. East ☞ (W)

防止 *preventing, precluding, forestalling* **bōshi**	射止める *shoot, win* **itomeru**
中止 *discontinuance, termination, stoppage* **chūshi**	臭気止め *deodorizer, deodorant* **shūkidome**
廃止 *abolishing, cancellation* **haishi**	滑り止め *skid, tire chain, stopper* **suberidome**
禁止 *prohibition, forbidden* **kinshi**	止まり木 *perch* **tomarigi**
休止 *standstill, dormancy* **kyūshi**	踏み止まる *restrain, hold back* **fumitodomaru**
黙止 *keeping quiet, ignoring* **mokushi**	消し止める *put out, extinguish* **keshitomeru**
静止 *standstill, rest, stillness* **seishi**	食い止める *prevent, arrest, stem, stop* **kuitomeru**
制止 *restraint, control* **seishi**	思い止まる *relinquish, renounce* **omoitodomaru**
止血 *stanching, stop bleeding* **shiketsu**	突き止める *locate, track down, trace* **tsukitomeru**
止揚 *sublation* **shiyō**	受け止める *react, catch* **uketomeru**
終止 *end, stop, termination* **shūshi**	呼び止める *call to stop, challenge* **yobitomeru**
阻止 *obstruction, prevention* **soshi**	
停止 *stoppage, suspension* **teishi**	停*top, 393* 廃*bolish, 368*
抑止 *restraint, suppression* **yokushi**	終*inish, 397* 棄*bolish, 608*
足止め *prevent, preclude, forestall* **ashidome**	了*inish, 456* 絶*radicate, 403*
歯止め *brake, drag, stop* **hadome**	
波止場 *wharf, pier* **hatoba**	企*lan, 193* 正*orrect, 30*
色止め *colour preservative, colour fixing* **irodome**	
口止め *buying one's silence* **kuchidome**	

159-B

"止top 祉elfare 企lan," says a selfish clan...

示⇔ネ (display, show)

祉*elfare*   祉*lessed*

SHI

welfare, well-being, blessed

福祉 *welfare, well-being* **fukushi**
⇒社会福祉 *social welfare* **shakai fukushi**
福祉国家 *welfare state* **fukushi kokka**
福祉政策 *welfarism, welfare policy* **fukushi seisaku**

Facing: 2.2. East ☞ (V)

福*ucky, 333*	賜*estow, 150*
義*ighteous, 341*	催*ponsor, 416*
善*ighteous, 450*	贈*onation, 838*
施*estow, 649*	献*onation, 414*

社*ociety, 703*

159-C

"止top 祉elfare 企lan," says a selfish clan...

人⇔イ (person)

企*lan*   企*roject*

kuwada(teru), KI

plan, project, scheme, programme

企希 *looking forward to, yearning for* **kibō**
企業 *enterprise, business* **kigyō**
大企業 *large enterprise, big business* **daikigyō**
大手企業 *conglomerate, big business* **ōtekigyō**
⇒私企業 *private company* **shikigyō**
⇒中小企業 *small-to-medium size companies*
    chūshō kigyō
⇒複合企業 *conglomerate, big business*
    fukugō kigyō
⇒公営企業 *government corporation* **kōei kigyō**
⇒民間企業 *private business* **minkan kigyō**
⇒零細企業 *small enterprise, small business*
    reisai kigyō
企及 *attempt, undertaking* **kikyū**
企図 *plan, draft* **kito**
企業家 *entrepreneur, industrialist* **kigyōka**
企業機密 *company secrets* **kigyō kimitsu**
企画 *project, planning, programme* **kikaku**
企画力 *planning ability, sense of planning* **kikakuryoku**

FLIP: 2.0.a. Sort Of (flat)
Facing: 2.1. ☞ East (H)

策*olicy, 875*
略*ummary, 825*
段*tep, 555*

止*top, 192*

零 - rei - 873 - zero

160-A

科aculty 料ayments in Saudi riyals include 斗[18 ltr] of fuel 料aterials...

禾 (tree branch)

①科aculty ②科enalty

shina, toga, KA

faculty, course of study; penalty, retribution

Facing: 1.2. ☞ West (V)

❶ 分科 section, department, branch **bunka**
文科 liberal arts **bunka**
学科 subject, department **gakka**
眼科 ophthalmology, optometric **ganka**
外科 surgery, surgical operation **geka**
外科医 surgeon, operating physician **gekai**
皮膚科 dermatology **hifuka**
本科 regular course **honka**
実科 practical course **jikka**
科学 science, natural science **kagaku**
科学者 scientist **kagakusha**
科目 academic course **kamoku**
⇒必修科目 prerequisite subject **hisshū kamoku**
教科 academic subject **kyōka**
内科 internal medicine **naika**
理科 science **rika**
選科 elective-, optional course **senka**
専科 special course **senka**
歯科 dentistry, dental medicine **shika**

商科 business course **shōka**
転科 change of studies **tenka**
薬科 pharmacology course **yakka**
普通科 general course **futsūka**
医科大 college of medicine **ikadai**
研究科 graduate course **kenkyūka**
❷ 厳科 severe punishment **genka**
科料 fine, penalty fee **karyō**
罪科 punishment **zaika**
前科 criminal past, crime record **zenka**
前科者 ex-convict **zenkamono**

授eaching, 539		校chool, 773	
訓eachings, 959		教ducate, 385	
習earning, 238		修aster, 898	
学tudy, 346		罪riminal, 289	

料aterials, 194

160-B

科aculty 料ayments in Saudi riyals include 斗[18 ltr] of fuel 料aterials...

斗 (amount)

①料ayment ②料aterials

RYŌ

payment; materials

FLIP: 6.0.b. Left (stem)

❶ 科料 fine, penalty fee **karyō**
給料 salary, wage **kyūryō**
無料 gratis, free-of-charge **muryō**
料金 charge, fee **ryōkin**
席料 room-, cover charge **sekiryō**
損料 rental fee **sonryō**
送料 postage fee **sōryō**
有料 fee, payment **yūryō**
扶養料 family-support expenses **fuyōryō**
保管料 holding-, storage fee **hokanryō**
授業料 school fees, tuition **jugyōryō**
講演料 lecturer's fee **kōenryō**
入場料 entrance fee **nyūjōryō**
手数料 commission, fees **tesūryō**
速達料 express delivery charge **sokutatsuryō**
郵送料 postage, mailing cost **yūsōryō**
❷ 顔料 colour pigment **ganryō**
原料 raw materials **genryō**
肥料 fertilizer, animal feed **hiryō**

衣料 clothes, garments **iryō**
燃料 fuel **nenryō**
⇒核燃料 nuclear fuel **kakunenryō**
料理 cooking, cuisine, food **ryōri**
料亭 Japanese high-class restaurant **ryōtei**
史料 historical materials, memorabilia **shiryō**
資料 materials, data **shiryō**
食料 cooking ingredients **shokuryō**
塗料 paints, coating material **toryō**
材料 materials used, raw materials **zairyō**
香辛料 spices & flavouring **kōshinryō**

材aterials, 186		作roduce, 724	
資esources, 626		賃ayment, 145	
源ource, 431		払ayment, 682	

科aculty, 194

160-C

科*aculty* 料*ayments in Saudi riyals include* 斗*[18 ltr] of fuel* 料*aterials...*

斗 (amount)

❶ `斗[18 litre]` **❷** `斗ipper`

TO
[18 litre]; Dipper

Facing: 1.0. 🢀 West (W)

❶ 抽斗 *cabinet drawer* **hikidashi**
壱斗 *1.8 litre* **itto**
熨斗 *gift wrapping paper-strip* **noshi**
漏斗 *funnel* **rōto**
漏斗状 *funnel-shaped* **rōtojō**
星斗 *stars* **seito**
泰斗 *great authority* **taito**
斗酒 *kegs of sake wine* **toshu**

❷ 北斗 *big Dipper* **hokuto**
北斗星 *big Dipper* **hokutosei**
斗南 *Sagittarius constellation* **tonan**

升*[1.8 ltr]*, 298	坪*[3.3 sqm]*, 488
旬*[10 day]*, 494	匁*[3.75 gm]*, 75
勺*[18 ml]*, 470	尺*[30 cm]*, 574
寸*[3 cm]*, 345	斤*[600 gm]*, 471

161-A

Study on Earth's 元*rigins by an* 院*nstitution nearing* 完*ompletion...*

儿 (human legs)

元

元*rigin*   元*eginning*

moto, GEN, GAN
origin, original, first-hand, beginning, square one

FLIP: 2.0.b. Sort Of (stem)

復元 *restoration, rehabilitation* **fukugen**
元日 *New Year's day* **ganjitsu**
元金 *principal, capital* **gankin**
元年 *first year of an imperial reign* **gannen**
元来 *by nature, essentially* **ganrai**
元利 *principal plus interest* **ganri**
元祖 *originator, founder* **ganso**
元気 *healthy, fine, in good spirits* **genki**
元老 *elder statesman, grand old man* **genrō**
元首 *sovereign, head of state* **genshu**
元素 *element, chemical element* **genso**
元帥 *general, marshal, fleet admiral* **gensui**
一元 *unitary* **ichigen**
家元 *head of school, school master* **iemoto**
次元 *dimension, level* **jigen**
地元 *native, local* **jimoto**
改元 *change of era* **kaigen**
還元 *reduction, resolution; deoxidisation* **kangen**
紀元 *era, epoch, period, age* **kigen**

紀元前 *B.C. (Before Christ)* **kigenzen**
根元 *root, base* **kongen**
身元 *one's person, personal identity* **mimoto**
元手 *capital, funds* **motode**
元々 *"by nature, originally..."* **motomoto**
元値 *cost, price* **motone**
親元 *parent's home* **oyamoto**
単元 *unit, academic unit* **tangen**
手元 *at hand, in one's hand* **temoto**
火の元 *fire origin* **hinomoto**
お中元 *summer gift to one's superior* **ochūgen**
多元論 *pluralism theory* **tagenron**

源*rigin*, 431	始*egin*, 210
原*riginal*, 431	初*tart*, 353
先*efore*, 478	発*tart*, 368
前*efore*, 118	

161-B

Study on Earth's 元rigins by an 院nstitution nearing 完ompletion...

阝 ⇔ 阜 (village=left)

院nstitution 院nstitute

IN
institution, institute

FLIP: 7.0.b2. Right (stem)

病院 *hospital* **byōin**
⇒救急病院 *emergency hospital* **kyūkyū byōin**
議院 *Diet, parliament* **giin**
⇒衆議院 *house of representatives* **shūgiin**
医院 *medical clinic, doctor's office* **iin**
⇒外科医院 *surgery clinic* **gekaiin**
院長 *hospital chief physician* **inchō**
院外活動 *political lobbying* **ingai katsudō**
院外勢力 *outside influence, ~pressure*
　　　ingai seiryoku
院外団 *political lobbyist, lobby group* **ingaidan**
院内 *within the institution* **innai**
院生 *graduate student* **insei**
寺院 *temple, mosque* **jiin**
⇒回教寺院 *mosque* **kaikyō jiin**
開院 *"Diet, library, hospital open..."* **kaiin**
下院 *lower house* **kain**
門院 *Empress Dowager* **mon'in**
入院 *hospital confinement, ~admission* **nyūin**

両院 *both chambers (bicameral)* **ryōin**
産院 *maternity-, baby-delivery hospital* **san'in**
僧院 *monastery, cloister, convent* **sōin**
⇒尼僧院 *convent, nunnery* **nisōin**
退院 *hospital discharge* **taiin**
登院 *attending a diet session* **tōin**
通院 *seeing a doctor regularly* **tsūin**
大学院 *graduate school* **daigakuin**
一院制 *unicameral* **ichiinsei**
感化院 *reformatory school* **kankain**
孤児院 *orphanage, orphan asylum* **kojiin**
二院制 *bi-cameral* **niinsei**
少年院 *juvenile asylum* **shōnen'in**

建*uilding, 390*	施*acilities, 649*
堂*all, 94*	賜*estow, 150*

完*omplete, 196*

161-C

Study on Earth's 元rigins by an 院nstitution nearing 完ompletion...

宀 (cover, lid)

完omplete 完erfect

KAN
complete, perfect, culminate, fulfil, accomplish

FLIP: 1.0.b. Whole (stem)

補完 *complement, supplement* **hokan**
補完税 *surtax, additional tax* **hokanzei**
完備 *fully-furnished (apartment)* **kanbi**
完治 *complete recuperation, ~recovery* **kanchi**
完熟 *fully-ripened* **kanjuku**
完結 *conclusion, completion* **kanketsu**
完工 *completion of construction* **kankō**
完納 *full payment, full delivery* **kannō**
完敗 *overwhelming defeat* **kanpai**
完璧 *perfect, impeccable* **kanpeki**
完本 *complete set of~* **kanpon**
完膚 *overwhelming defeat* **kanpu**
完封 *absolute blockade, shutting out* **kanpū**
完了 *completion, finishing* **kanryō**
⇒過去完了 *past perfect tense* **kako kanryō**
⇒未来完了 *future perfect tense* **mirai kanryō**
完了形 *perfect tense* **kanryōkei**
完済 *full payment, fully-paid* **kansai**
完成 *completion, perfection* **kansei**

完成品 *finished goods, ~products* **kanseihin**
完勝 *complete victory* **kanshō**
完遂 *fulfilling one's dream* **kansui**
完投 *pitch in a whole baseball game* **kantō**
完訳 *complete translation* **kanyaku**
完全 *perfection, completion* **kanzen**
⇒不完全 *incomplete, imperfect* **fukanzen**
完全犯罪 *perfect crime* **kanzen hanzai**
完全雇用 *full employment* **kanzen koyō**
完全無欠 *absolutely perfect* **kanzen muketsu**
未完 *unfinished, uncompleted* **mikan**

終*inish, 397*	満*ulfill, 567*
了*inish, 456*	

宗*eligion, 879*

162-A

"The 黄ellow Romance," played as a 横ide 演erformance...

黄 (yellow)

黄ellow-colour

FLIP: 1.0.b. Whole (stem)

ki, ko, KŌ, Ō
yellow-colour

浅黄	*pale yellow*	**asagi**
硫黄	*sulphur*	**iō**
黄色	*yellow*	**kiiro, ōshoku, kōshoku**
黄身	*yoke*	**kimi**
黄緑	*yellow-green*	**kimidori**
黄萱	*yellow day lily*	**kisuge**
黄道	*ecliptic, circular road*	**kōdō**
黄河	*yellow river*	**kōga**
黄禍	*yellow peril*	**kōka**
黄海	*yellow sea*	**kōkai**
黄口	*inexperienced, greenhorn*	**kōkō**
黄砂	*yellow sand*	**kōsa**
黄色	*yellow*	**kōshoku**
黄葉	*yellow leaves*	**kōyō**
黄疸	*jaundice*	**ōdan**
黄土	*yellow ochre*	**ōdo, kōdo**
黄金	*gold*	**ōgon**
黄金色	*gold colour, golden*	**koganeiro**
黄金虫	*gold beetle, goldbug*	**koganemushi**

黄金時代	*golden age*	**ōgon jidai**
黄玉	*topaz*	**ōgyoku**
黄変	*turning yellow*	**ōhen**
黄桃	*yellow peach*	**ōtō**
卵黄	*egg yolk*	**ran'ō**
緑黄	*yellow green*	**ryokuō**
黄昏	*twilight, dusk*	**tasogare**
黄な粉	*soybean flour*	**kinako**
黄褐色	*yellowish brown*	**ōkasshoku**
黄色人種	*yellow race, mongoloid*	**ōshoku jinshu**

彩 *olour*, 914
色 *olour*, 403

横 *idewards*, 197

162-B

"The 黄ellow Romance," played as a 横ide 演erformance...

木 (wooden)

横ideward   横ateral

FLIP: 7.0.b2. Right (stem)

yoko, Ō
sideward, sideway, lateral

縦横	*length & breadth*	**jūō, tateyoko**
真横	*side, lateral*	**mayoko**
横暴	*arbitrariness, perversity*	**ōbō**
横断	*crossing, pedestrian*	**ōdan**
横断歩道	*crosswalk, pedestrian lane*	**ōdan hodō**
横臥	*lying, reposing*	**ōga**
横柄	*arrogant, overbearing, haughty*	**ōhei**
横行	*infestation, swarming*	**ōkō**
横領	*embezzlement, absconding*	**ōryō**
専横	*arbitrariness, despotism*	**sen'ō**
横穴	*tunnel, cave*	**yokoana**
横顔	*profile, face in profile*	**yokogao**
横車	*unreasonable ideas*	**yokoguruma**
横糸	*weft, woof*	**yokoito**
横槍	*interruption, obstruction, hiatus*	**yokoyari**
横綱	*grand sumo champion*	**yokozuna**
横隔膜	*diaphragm*	**ōkakumaku**
横歩き	*walking side wards*	**yokoaruki**
横太り	*fat & short*	**yokobutori**

横倒し	*falling on the side*	**yokodaoshi**
横取り	*snatching, stealing*	**yokodori**
横組み	*horizontal typesetting*	**yokogumi**
横浜市	*Yokohama City*	**yokohama-shi**
横向き	*side profile*	**yokomuki**
横流し	*dubious side*	**yokonagashi**
横殴り	*side punch*	**yokonaguri**
横滑り	*side slip*	**yokosuberi**
横っ面	*cheek*	**yokottsura**
横割り	*horizontal connexion*	**yokowari**

並 *arallel*, 444
沿 *longside*, 756

構 *osture*, 714   黄 *ellow*, 197

162-C

"The 黄ellow Romance," played as a 横ide 演erformance...

演*how*   演*erformance*

水⇔氵 (water)

EN
show, performance, presentation, recital

FLIP: 7.0.b2. Right (stem)

演じる *perform, play, act, enact* **enjiru**
独演 *solo performance, ~recital* **dokuen**
演題 *lecture theme, topic of discussion* **endai**
演壇 *rostrum, platform* **endan**
演芸 *entertainment, performance* **engei**
演劇 *drama, play* **engeki**
演劇界 *theatrical profession* **engekikai**
演技 *performance, acting* **engi**
演技者 *performer* **engisha**
演習 *practice, drill, maneuvers* **enshū**
演出 *performance, show* **enshutsu**
演奏 *musical performance* **ensō**
演算 *operation, calculation* **enzan**
演説 *speech, address, lecture* **enzetsu**
⇒質問演説 *interpellation, question & answer*
　　shitsumon enzetsu
実演 *performance* **jitsuen**
助演 *supporting role* **joen**
開演 *opening, curtain rising* **kaien**

口演 *narration, storytelling* **kōen**
講演 *lecture* **kōen**
公演 *performance, show* **kōen**
好演 *good performance, ~acting* **kōen**
共演 *co-star, co-starring, joint appearance* **kyōen**
休演 *absence from stage performance* **kyūen**
熱演 *enthusiastic performance* **netsuen**
再演 *repeat performance, rerun* **saien**
初演 *premiere, first screening* **shoen**
主演 *starring, leading role* **shuen**
出演 *performance, acting* **shutsuen**
演繹法 *deductive reasoning* **en'ekihō**

劇*rama,* 759	集*ather,* 50
講*ecture,* 226	聴*isten,* 844
宴*anquet,* 610	娯*musement,* 453

宙*uterspace,* 631

163-A

屯eployed war strategists, 純urely 鈍luggish...

屯*eployment*   屯*tationing*

屮 (sprout)

tamuro, TON
deployment, stationing

Facing: 2.0. East ☞ (W)

駐屯 *stationing, deployment* **chūton**
駐屯地 *garrison town, post* **chūtonchi**
駐屯軍 *stationed troops, garrison* **chūtongun**
一屯 *single deployment* **ichiton**
屯田 *troop stationing in the countryside* **tonden**
屯田兵 *peasant soldier, farmer conscript* **tondenhei**
屯営 *barracks, military station* **ton'ei**
屯所 *army quarters, police detachment* **tonsho**

隊*quad,* 543	送*ispatch,* 708
軍*oldier,* 295	搬*ransport,* 323
衛*rotect,* 796	輸*hipment,* 660

市*ity,* 304

163-B

屯*eployed war strategists,* 純*urely* 鈍*luggish...*

糸 (thread, continuity)

純*urity*   純*bsolute*

JUN
purity, absolute, pristine, undiluted, wholesome

Facing: 2.2. East ☞ (V)

不純	*impurity, adulteration*	**fujun**
純愛	*pure love, platonic love*	**jun'ai**
純朴	*simple-minded*	**junboku**
純度	*purity grade*	**jundo**
純益	*net profit, net earnings*	**jun'eki**
純銀	*pure silver*	**jungin**
純一	*purity*	**jun'itsu, jun'ichi**
純情	*pure heart, pure mind*	**junjō**
純化	*purification*	**junka**
純潔	*purity, chastity*	**junketsu**
純血	*pure blooded*	**junketsu**
純血種	*thoroughbred*	**junketsushu**
純金	*pure gold*	**junkin**
純綿	*pure cotton*	**junmen**
純毛	*pure wool*	**junmō**
純白	*pure white, snow white*	**junpaku**
純理	*pure logic & reason*	**junri**
純利	*net profit, net earnings*	**junri**
純良	*pure, genuine*	**junryō**

純正	*pure, genuine*	**junsei**
純真	*purity, innocence*	**junshin**
純粋	*genuine, pure, unmixed*	**junsui**
純水	*pure water*	**junsui**
純然	*pure, absolute*	**junzen**
純増	*net increase*	**junzō**
清純	*pure & innocent*	**seijun**
至純	*absolute purity*	**shijun**
単純	*plain & simple*	**tanjun**
純文学	*pure literature*	**junbungaku**
純収入	*take-home pay, net income*	**junshū'nyū**

清*urify,* 793	浄*urity,* 230
潔*urity,* 901	粋*urity,* 762

鈍*luggish, 199*

163-C

屯*eployed war strategists,* 純*urely* 鈍*luggish...*

金 (metal)

鈍*luggish*   鈍*tagnate*

nibu(i), nibu(ru), noro, DON
sluggish, stagnate, dull

FLIP: 6.0.a. Left (flat)
Facing: 2.2. East ☞ (V)

遅鈍	*dull-witted, sluggish*	**chidon**
鈍物	*dumb-head*	**donbutsu**
鈍調	*slack market*	**donchō**
鈍重	*dull-witted, sluggish*	**donjū**
鈍化	*getting dull, stagnating*	**donka**
鈍角	*obtuse angle*	**donkaku**
鈍角三角形	*obtuse-angled triangle*	
		donkaku sankakkei
鈍感	*insensitivity, apathy, callousness*	**donkan**
鈍器	*blunt weapon*	**donki**
鈍行	*slow-moving*	**donkō**
鈍行列車	*local train*	**donkō ressha**
鈍根	*dull-witted, slow brain*	**donkon**
鈍麻	*dullness*	**donma**
鈍才	*dull-witted, slow brain*	**donsai**
鈍足	*slow runner*	**donsoku**
鈍刀	*dull sword*	**dontō**
鈍痛	*dull pain, acute pain*	**dontsū**
愚鈍	*stupidity, imbecility*	**gudon**

鈍色	*dark grey*	**nibuiro**
鈍間	*dull-minded*	**noroma**
利鈍	*sharpness-or-dullness*	**ridon**
魯鈍	*stupid, dumb*	**rodon**
運鈍根	*luck, tenacity, & patience (3 keys to success)*	**undonkon**
鈍臭い	*clumsy, sluggish*	**norokusai**
焼鈍し	*annealing*	**yakinamashi**
鈍百姓	*dumb peasant*	**donbyakushō**

庸*ediocre,* 906	鋭*harp,* 943
普*rdinary,* 455	削*harpen,* 118
凡*rdinary,* 78	

純*urity, 199*

164-A

技*echnique for* 肢*imb* 支*upport to serve as life-support...*

手⇔扌 (hand, manual)

技*echnique*　　技*kills*

waza, GI
technique, skills, knack, aptitude, know-how

FLIP: 7.0.b2. Right (stem)

荒技　*rough-, rugged training* **arawaza**
美技　*splendid-, artistic performance* **bigi**
演技　*performance, show* **engi**
技法　*technique, skill* **gihō**
技術　*skill, technique, know-how* **gijutsu**
技監　*chief engineer, ~technician* **gikan**
技巧　*art, technique, skill* **gikō**
技工　*craftsman, artisan* **gikō**
技能　*skill, technique, know-how* **ginō**
技量　*skill, ability, capacity* **giryō**
技師　*engineer, technical expert* **gishi**
早技　*slight of hand* **hayawaza**
秘技　*secret technique* **hiwaza**
実技　*practical skills* **jitsugi**
神技　*act-of-god* **kamiwaza, shingi**
国技　*national sport, popular game* **kokugi**
競技　*contest, competition* **kyōgi**
球技　*ballgame* **kyūgi**
妙技　*outstanding performance* **myōgi**

寝技　*groundwork techniques* **newaza**
手技　*skill, technique* **shugi**
体技　*physical match* **taigi**
闘技　*competition, contest* **tōgi**
特技　*special talent, extra-ordinary skills* **tokugi**
余技　*hobby, past time* **yogi**
遊技　*amusement, past time* **yūgi**
技巧的　*technical, artificial* **gikōteki**
放れ技　*feat, stunt, exploits* **hanarewaza**
技術援助　*technical assistance* **gijutsu enjo**
至難の技　*utmost difficulty* **shinan no waza**

術*echnique, 110*	工*raft, 176*
巧*killful, 738*	匠*rtisan, 106*

枝*ree-branch, 704*

164-B

技*echnique for* 肢*imb* 支*upport to serve as life-support...*

肉⇔月 (flesh, body part)

肢*imbs*　　肢*ppendage*

SHI
limbs, appendage

FLIP: 7.0.b2. Right (stem)

義肢　*artificial limb* **gishi**
上肢　*upper limbs* **jōshi**
下肢　*lower limbs* **kashi**
後肢　*hind legs* **kōshi**
四肢　*limbs, legs & arms* **shishi**
肢体　*limbs, legs & arms* **shitai**
前肢　*forelegs, forelimbs* **zenshi**

身*ody, 504*	足*oot, 481*
体*ody, 347*	胴*orso, 867*
手*and, 370*	

肺*ungs, 305*

164-C

技*echnique for* 肢*imb* 支*upport to serve as life-support...*

❶支*upport*   **❷支*ranch***

支 (branch)

sasa(eru), SHI

support, backing, help, aide; branch, subsidiary

FLIP: 1.0.b. Whole (stem)

干支 *Zodiac signs* **eto, kanshi**
支弁 *defray, pay* **shiben**
支柱 *supporting pillar* **shichū**
支援 *support, backup* **shien**
支援者 *supporter, backer* **shiensha**
支配 *rule, control* **shihai**
支配階級 *ruling class, ruling elite* **shihai kaikyū**
支配民族 *master race* **shihai minzoku**
支払い *payment, compensation* **shiharai**
支持 *support, help, assistance* **shiji**
支給 *provision, allowance* **shikyū**
支流 *tributary* **shiryū**
支障 *hindrance, hitch, obstacle* **shishō**
支出 *expenditures, expenses, spendings* **shishutsu**
支度 *prepare, make arrangements* **shitaku**
⇒嫁入り支度 *bridal outfit* **yomeiri shitaku**
支点 *fulcrum, supporting point* **shiten**
収支 *revenues & expenditures* **shūshi**
⇒貿易外収支 *invisible trade balance* **bōekigaishūshi**

冬支度 *winter preparations* **fuyujitaku**
臨時支出 *special disbursement* **rinjishi shutsu**
❷支部 *branch, local chapter* **shibu**
支局 *branch office, ~agency* **shikyoku**
支脈 *feeder, branch* **shimyaku**
支線 *branch line* **shisen**
支社 *branch office* **shisha**
支署 *branch office* **shisho**
支所 *branch office* **shisho**
支店 *branch office* **shiten**
海外支店 *overseas office, ~branch* **kaigai shiten**
支族 *branch family* **shizoku**

助*upport*, 953   扶*amily-support*, 97
擁*upport*, 151

技*echnique*, 200

165-A

加*ddition of* 架*anging bridge in* 加*anada, to* 賀*elebrate in Granada...*

❶加*ddition*   **❷加*anada***

力 (strength, force)

kuwa(eru), kuwa(waru), KA

addition, increasing, join-in, partake, participate; Canada

FLIP: 7.0.a. Right (flat)

❶倍加 *doubling, geometric increase* **baika**
奉加 *donation, offerings* **hōga**
加圧 *put pressure* **kaatsu**
加減 *allowance, plus & minus* **kagen**
加護 *divine protection* **kago**
加俸 *additional allowance* **kahō**
加法 *addition, summing up* **kahō**
加重 *aggravation, deterioration* **kajū**
加工 *processing, manufacture* **kakō**
加給 *salary increase, pay raise* **kakyū**
加味 *add seasoning, ~flavouring* **kami**
加熱 *heating, calefaction* **kanetsu**
加入 *admission, subscription* **kanyū**
加療 *patient treatment* **karyō**
加算 *addition, inclusion* **kasan**
加勢 *help, support, assistance* **kasei**
加速 *speed acceleration* **kasoku**
加速度 *acceleration rate, ~degree* **kasokudo**
加点 *adding points* **katen**

累加 *acceleration, progression* **ruika**
添加 *addition, annexing* **tenka**
参加 *participate, take part, joining* **sanka**
参加者 *participant* **sankasha**
不参加 *non-participation* **fusanka**
添加物 *additive, flavouring* **tenkabutsu**
添加品 *additive, flavouring* **tenkahin**
追加 *add, supplement* **tsuika**
増加 *increase, addition, increment* **zōka**
増加率 *rate of increase, addition* **zōkaritsu**
加害者 *assailant, murderer, killer* **kagaisha**
加盟国 *member state* **kameikoku**
好い加減 *haphazard, unreliable* **iikagen**
❷日加 *Japan-Canada* **nikka**

増*ncrease*, 837   合*ogether*, 232   携*articipate*, 151
足*ddition*, 481   併*erge*, 886   共*ogether*, 302

如*qual*, 364

165-B

加ddition of 架anging bridge in 加anada, to 賀elebrate in Granada...

木 (wooden)

架anging   架uspension

ka(keru), ka(karu), KA
hanging, suspension, lay across

FLIP: 4.0.b. Bottom (stem)

画架 *easel* **gaka**
筆架 *pen rack* **hikka**
銃架 *rifle stand, arms rack* **jūka**
架電 *sending by telegram* **kaden**
開架 *open stack* **kaika**
架空 *overpass, overhead; not real, virtual* **kakū**
架橋 *bridge construction* **kakyō**
架線 *wire, wiring* **kasen**
架設 *construction, installation* **kasetsu**
高架 *elevated, hanging, suspended* **kōka**
後架 *toilet, restroom* **kōka**
橋架 *bridge girder* **kyōka**
書架 *book shelf, book case* **shoka**
担架 *stretcher* **tanka**
十字架 *Holy Cross, Crucifix* **jūjika**
高架橋 *hanging high bridge* **kōkakyō**
三脚架 *tripod* **sankyakuka**

懸*anging, 566*
垂*ang down, 505*
掛*ang up, 107*

加*ddition, 201*

165-C

加ddition of 架anging bridge in 加anada, to 賀elebrate in Granada...

貝 (shell, old money)

賀elebration   賀ongratulate

GA
celebration, congratulate, jubilation

FLIP: 4.0.b. Bottom (stem)

朝賀 *New Year's greetings (imperial)* **chōga**
賀宴 *feast, banquet* **gaen**
賀意 *congratulatory mood* **gai**
賀状 *greeting card* **gajō**
賀詞 *congratulatory speech* **gashi**
賀正 *Happy New Year* **gashō**
拝賀 *congratulations, greetings* **haiga**
慶賀 *congratulation, celebration* **keiga**
恭賀 *congratulatory respects* **kyōga**
年賀 *New Year's greetings* **nenga**
年賀状 *New Year's card* **nengajō**
年賀葉書 *New Year's card* **nenga hagaki**
参賀 *congratulatory visit* **sanga**
祝賀 *celebration, congratulations, thanksgiving* **shukuga**
祝賀状 *congratulatory letter, ~card* **shukugajō**
祝賀会 *celebration party, thanksgiving party* **shukugakai**
謹賀新年 *Happy New Year* **kinga shinnen**
横須賀市 *Yokosuka City, Kanagawa Pref.* **yokosuka-shi**

祝*elebration, 716*
慶*ejoice, 69*

賀*rading, 128*

166-A

兄*lder-brother's* 党*arty in* 克*onquest of* 競*ivalry...*

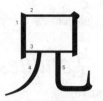

儿 (human legs)

兄*lder-brother*

ani, KEI, KYŌ
older brother

FLIP: 1.0.b. Whole (stem)

兄貴 *one's elder brother* **aniki**
兄上 *elder brother* **aniue**
兄嫁 *older brother's wife* **aniyome**
亡兄 *one's late elder brother* **bōkei**
長兄 *eldest brother* **chōkei**
父兄 *parents, guardians* **fukei**
父兄会 *parents-teachers association* **fukeikai**
義兄 *brother-in-law* **gikei**
義兄弟 *brother-in-law* **gikyōdai**
愚兄 *"my foolish brother..."* **gukei**
伯兄 *eldest brother* **hakkei**
従兄弟 *cousin* **itoko**
次兄 *second eldest brother* **jikei**
実兄 *one's real brother, blood brothers* **jikkei**
仁兄 *"buddy, chum, pal..."* **jinkei**
従兄 *elder male cousin* **jūkei**
家兄 *elder brother* **kakei**
兄事 *regard as one's elder brother* **keiji**
賢兄 *wise elder brother* **kenkei**

兄弟 *brothers, male siblings* **kyōdai**
兄弟愛 *brotherly-, fraternal love* **kyōdaiai**
兄弟分 *sharing like siblings* **kyōdaibun**
兄弟喧嘩 *sibling quarrel, ~bickering* **kyōdai genka**
諸兄 *"friends, gentlemen..."* **shokei**
諸兄姉 *"ladies & gentlemen..."* **shokeishi**
親兄弟 *parents & siblings* **oyakyōdai**
兄弟子 *senior disciple* **anideshi**
乳兄弟 *step siblings* **chichikyōdai**
又従兄弟 *second cousin* **mataitoko**

弟*ounger brother, 102* 家*amily, 909*
姉*lder sister, 114* 族*amily, 649*
妹*ounger sister, 114*

況*ituation, 716*

166-B

兄*lder-brother's* 党*arty in* 克*onquest of* 競*ivalry...*

儿 (human legs)

党*olitical party*

TŌ
political party

FLIP: 1.0.b. Whole (stem)

悪党 *rogue, scalawag, scamp* **akutō**
甘党 *non-drinker, teetotaller, abstemious* **amatō**
脱党 *quitting one's political party* **dattō**
復党 *rejoining one's party* **fukutō**
解党 *party disbanding, ~dissolution* **kaitō**
辛党 *drinker* **karatō**
結党 *forming a new party* **kettō**
公党 *political party* **kōtō**
入党 *joining a political party* **nyūtō**
離党 *party withdrawal, ~resignation* **ritō**
立党 *forming a new party* **rittō**
政党 *political party* **seitō**
党派 *party faction* **tōha**
党員 *party member* **tōin**
党人 *party member* **tōjin**
党規 *party rules* **tōki**
党紀 *party discipline* **tōki**
党務 *party affairs* **tōmu**
党内 *within the party* **tōnai**

党利 *party interests* **tōri**
党論 *party platform* **tōron**
党略 *party strategy, policy* **tōryaku**
党籍 *party register, ~registry* **tōseki**
党首 *party leader* **tōshu**
党則 *party rules* **tōsoku**
野党 *opposition party* **yatō**
与党 *ruling party, party in power* **yotō**
友党 *allied party, coalition party* **yūtō**
残党 *party remnants* **zantō**
党大会 *party caucus* **tōtaikai**

政*olitics, 725* 公*ublic, 180*
府*overnment, 429* 官*ublic official, 105*
庁*ubic office, 633* 票*uffrage, 549*

営*anagement, 580*

166-C
兄*lder-brother's* 党*arty in* 克*onquest of* 競*ivalry...*

儿 (human legs)

克*onquest*

KOKU
conquest, conquer

超克 surmounting, overcoming **chōkoku**
克己 self-denial, self-restraint **kokki**
克己心 spirit of self-denial **kokkishin**
克復 restoration, rehabilitation **kokufuku**
克服 conquest, colonization **kokufuku**
克明 diligence, perseverance, tenacity **kokumei**
相克 conflict, rivalry, strife **sōkoku**
下克上 lower dominating the higher **gekokujō**

FLIP: 3.0.b. Top (stem)
FLIP: 2.0.b. Sort Of (stem)

征*onquer, 31* 　有*ossess, 617*
抑*uppress, 705* 　勝*ictory, 406*

売*elling, 259*

166-D
兄*lder-brother's* 党*arty in* 克*onquest of* 競*ivalry...*

立 (standing)

競*ivalry* 　競*ompetition*

kiso(u), se(ru), KYŌ, KEI
rivalry, competition

FLIP: 5.0.b. Left & Right

競馬 horse race **keiba**
競輪 bicycle race **keirin**
競売 public auction, ~bidding **kyōbai**
競映 film festival, ~competition **kyōei**
競泳 swimming race **kyōei**
競泳大会 swimming contest **kyōei taikai**
競演 performance contest **kyōen**
競技 game, match, contest **kyōgi**
⇒団体競技 team sports **dantai kyōgi**
⇒陸上競技 track & field **rikujō kyōgi**
競技場 field, stadium, ground **kyōgijō**
競技種目 sports event **kyōgi shumoku**
競技大会 athletic meet, ~match **kyōgi taikai**
競合 rivalry, competition, contest **kyōgō**
競歩 walking race **kyōho**
競作 artistic-, literary competition **kyōsaku**
競争 competition, contest, game **kyōsō**
競走 running race, ~contest **kyōsō**

⇒障害物競走 obstacle race
　 shōgaibutsu kyōsō
競艇 race boat, motor boat **kyōtei**
競漕 boat rowing race **kyōsō**
競い肌 gallantry **kioihada**
草競馬 amateur horse race **kusa keiba**
競売人 auctioneer **kyōbainin**
競り市 auction-, bidding market **seriichi**
競争意識 sense of rivalry **kyōsō ishiki**
競り合い rivalry, competition, contest **seriai**
競り落とす auction winning **seriotosu**

敵*nemy, 966* 　失*ailure, 19*
勝*ictory, 406* 　敗*ailure, 137*
功*uccess, 635* 　克*onquest, 204*

韻*hyme, 315*

167-A

広*arge* 拡*xpansion of* 鉱*ineral-ore all the more...*

广 (rooftop)

広*arge* 広*ide*

hiro(i), hiro(geru), hiro(meru), hiro(garu), hiro(maru), KŌ
large, wide

Facing: 2.0. East ☞ (W)

広場 *wide open area, square ground* **hiroba**
広広 *extensive, wide* **hirobiro**
広幅 *wide width* **hirohaba**
広口 *wide mouth (bottle)* **hiroguchi**
広間 *hall, lobby* **hiroma**
広島 *Hiroshima Prefecture* **hiroshima**
広漠 *vast, extensive* **kōbaku**
広大 *broad, extensive* **kōdai**
広遠 *broad, far-reaching* **kōen**
広言 *big talk, boast, exaggeration* **kōgen**
広原 *wide open field* **kōgen**
広義 *broad-, wide sense* **kōgi**
広汎 *extensive, wide-ranging* **kōhan**
広範 *wide range* **kōhan**
広報 *public information* **kōhō**
広域 *wide area* **kōiki**
広角 *wide angle* **kōkaku**
広闊 *spacious, vast, roomy* **kōkatsu**
広軌 *broad gauge* **kōki**

広告 *advertisement, classified ads* **kōkoku**
広狭 *wideness-or-narrowness, width* **kōkyō**
広量 *generosity; broadminded* **kōryō**
広野 *wide plain, open field* **kōya**
背広 *business suit* **sebiro**
長広舌 *loquacious, talking long* **chōkōzetsu**
幅広い *extensive, wide* **habahiroi**
広東省 *Guangdong, China (Canton)* **kantonshō**
広葉樹 *broad leaf* **kōyōju**
手広い *extensive, wide, spacious* **tebiroi**

膨*welling, 925*	巨*iant, 206*
脹*welling, 274*	超*xceed, 664*
大*arge, 7*	遍*idespread, 43*
拡*nlarge, 205*	大*rand, 7*

去*eave-out, 360*

167-B

広*arge* 拡*xpansion of* 鉱*ineral-ore all the more...*

手⇔扌 (hand, manual)

拡*nlarge* 拡*xpand*

hiro(garu), KAKU
enlarge, expand, broaden, propagate

Facing: 4.0. ☜☞ Apart

拡がり *stretch, expanse* **hirogari**
軍拡 *re-armament, arms build-up* **gunkaku**
拡張 *expansion, extension* **kakuchō**
拡大 *expansion, extension* **kakudai**
拡大鏡 *magnifying glass* **kakudaikyō**
拡大率 *rate of magnification* **kakudairitsu**
拡大解釈 *broad interpretation* **kakudai kaishaku**
拡充 *expansion, extension* **kakujū**
拡散 *diffusion, proliferation* **kakusan**
不拡大 *non-expansion* **fukakudai**
胃拡張 *gastric dilatation* **ikakuchō**
拡声器 *loudspeaker, megaphone* **kakuseiki**

膨*welling, 925*	巨*iant, 206*
脹*welling, 274*	超*xceed, 664*
大*arge, 7*	遍*idespread, 43*
広*arge, 205*	幅*idth, 640*

披*pen, 104*

167-C

広*arge* 拡*xpansion of* 鉱*ineral-ore all the more...*

金 (metal)

鉱*ineral-ore*　　鉱*re-deposits*

KŌ

mineral ore, ore deposits

鉛鉱	*lead ore* **enkō**
富鉱	*high-grade ore* **fukō**
原鉱	*unprocessed-, crude ore* **genkō**
銀鉱	*silver mine* **ginkō**
貧鉱	*low-grade ore* **hinkō**
金鉱	*gold mine* **kinkō**
鉱物	*mineral, ore deposits* **kōbutsu**
鉱毒	*mining pollutants* **kōdoku**
鉱夫	*mine worker, miner* **kōfu**
鉱害	*mining pollution* **kōgai**
鉱業	*mining exploration* **kōgyō**
鉱区	*mining diggings, ~excavation* **kōku**
鉱脈	*vein of ore, lode* **kōmyaku**
鉱滓	*slag, cinders, recrement* **kōsai**
鉱石	*mineral, ore* **kōseki**
鉱泉	*mineral water* **kōsen**
鉱床	*ore deposits* **kōshō**
鉱層	*ore bed* **kōsō**
鉱水	*mineral water* **kōsui**

FLIP: 6.0.a. Left (flat)
Facing: 2.2. East ☞ (V)

鉱油	*mineral oil* **kōyu**
鉱山	*mine, mine field* **kōzan**
燐鉱	*mineral phosphate* **rinkō**
選鉱	*ore sorting* **senkō**
探鉱	*ore deposits exploration* **tankō**
炭鉱	*coal mine, colliery* **tankō**
鉄鉱	*iron ore* **tekkō**
⇒磁鉄鉱	*lodestone, magnetite* **jitekkō**
⇒黄鉄鉱	*fool's gold, iron pyrites* **ōtekkō**
⇒白鉄鉱	*marcasite* **shirotekkō**

銅*opper, 246*	鉄*ron, 155*
鉛*ead, 757*	鋼*teel, 975*

鈍*luggish, 199*

168-A

巨*iant* 拒*efused to walk the* 距*istance to Constance...*

二 (two, second)

巨*iant*　　巨*olossal*

KYO

giant, colossal, enormous, gargantuan, mammoth

巨悪	*heinous, unspeakable crime* **kyoaku**
巨大	*colossal, monstrous* **kyodai**
巨大都市	*megalopolis* **kyodai toshi**
巨弾	*heavy shell, bombshell* **kyodan**
巨編	*voluminous works* **kyohen**
巨富	*vast fortune* **kyofu**
巨額	*large amount of money* **kyogaku**
巨岩	*giant rock* **kyogan**
巨費	*great cost* **kyohi**
巨歩	*giant strides* **kyoho**
巨砲	*big gun* **kyohō**
巨人	*giant, great figure* **kyojin**
巨魁	*ringleader, chief, boss* **kyokai**
巨漢	*big man, the boss* **kyokan**
巨艦	*large warship* **kyokan**
巨躯	*massive built* **kyoku**
巨万	*millions; immense sum* **kyoman**
巨利	*big profit, great yields* **kyori**
巨細	*large & small matters; details* **kyosai**

Facing: 2.0. East ☞ (W)

巨星	*giant star, great person* **kyosei**
巨石	*huge stone* **kyoseki**
巨船	*colossal ship* **kyosen**
巨資	*huge-, enormous capital* **kyoshi**
巨匠	*great master* **kyoshō**
巨体	*massive physique, muscular built* **kyotai**
巨頭	*prominent-, eminent figure* **kyotō**
巨財	*great fortune* **kyozai**
巨材	*giant timber; great man* **kyozai**
巨像	*huge statue* **kyozō**
巨視的	*macro, broad spectrum* **kyoshiteki**

大*arge, 7*	広*arge, 205*
拡*nlarge, 205*	超*xceed, 664*

巨*etainer, 542*

168-B

巨*iant* 拒*efused to walk the* 距*istance to Constance...*

手⇔扌 (hand, manual)

拒*efusal*　　　　拒*ejection*

koba(mu), KYO
refusal, rejection, repudiation, denial, disapproval, turn-down
抗拒　*resist, reject* **kōkyo**
拒否　*denial, refusal, veto* **kyohi**
⇒登校拒否　*school drop-out* **tōkō kyohi**
拒否権　*veto right, veto power* **kyohiken**
拒止　*refusal, rejection* **kyoshi**
拒絶　*refusal, rejection* **kyozetsu**
拒絶反応　*dealing with rejection* **kyozetsu hannō**

Facing: 4.0. ⇦⇨ Apart

非*[negative]*, 288	断*efusal*, 958
不*[negative]*, 300	否*efusal*, 300

巨*iant*, 206

168-C

巨*iant* 拒*efused to walk the* 距*istance to Constance...*

足 (feet, legs)

距*istance*

KYO
distance, range
角距　*angular distance* **kakkyo**
高距　*altitude, sea-level elevation* **kōkyo**
距骨　*ankle bone* **kyokotsu**
距離　*distance, mileage* **kyori**
⇒射距離　*firearm's range* **shakyori**
⇒長距離　*long distance* **chōkyori**
⇒中距離　*middle distance* **chūkyori**
⇒遠距離　*long distance* **enkyori**
⇒近距離　*short distance* **kinkyori**
⇒測距儀　*range finder* **sokkyogi**
⇒短距離　*short distance* **tankyori**
⇒等距離　*equal distance* **tōkyori**
⇒着弾距離　*range of a firearm* **chakudan kyori**
⇒弾着距離　*range of a firearm* **danchaku kyori**
⇒航続距離　*range of a flight* **kōzoku kyori**
⇒至近距離　*point-blank range* **shikin kyori**
⇒焦点距離　*focal distance, ~length* **shōten kyori**
⇒走行距離　*distance, mileage* **sōkō kyori**
距離感　*sense of distance* **kyorikan**

Facing: 2.2. East ☞ (V)

距離計　*range finder* **kyorikei**
距爪　*cockspur* **kyosō**
輪距　*wheel track* **rinkyo**

隔*istance*, 963	疎*istant*, 955
遠*istant*, 916	悠*istant*, 898

拒*efusal*, 207

169-A

White 布loth 布pread, 希esired for a 怖cary dead...

 布loth   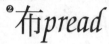 *布pread*

巾 (cloth, fabric)

nuno, FU
cloth; spread

Facing: 2.0. East ☞ (W)

❶布巾 *dish towel* **fukin**
布団 *mattress, bedclothes, quilt* **futon**
⇒羽根布団 *feather quilt* **hane buton**
画布 *painting canvas* **gafu**
綿布 *cotton cloth* **menpu**
毛布 *blanket* **mōfu**
布引 *cloth stretching* **nunobiki**
布地 *cloth material, fabric* **nunoji**
布子 *padded clothes* **nunoko**
布目 *fabric texture* **nunome**
財布 *wallet, purse, pocketbook* **saifu**
布切れ *piece of cloth* **nunogire**
❷瀑布 *waterfalls* **bakufu**
布陣 *battle ready position* **fujin**
布告 *proclamation, declaration* **fukoku**
⇒宣戦布告 *declaration of war* **sensen fukoku**
布教 *missionary work, vocation, calling* **fukyō**
布令 *official proclamation* **furei**
布石 *strategy, tactic* **fuseki**

配布 *distribution, delivery, allocation* **haifu**
頒布 *distribution, circulation* **hanpu**
発布 *promulgation, declaration, issuance* **happu**
昆布 *sea tangle, kelp* **konbu**
散布 *spraying, sprinkling* **sanpu**
宣布 *declaration of war, war proclamation* **senpu**
敷布 *cloth sheet, piece of cloth* **shikifu**
湿布 *poultice* **shippu**
塗布 *pasting, applying (ointment)* **tofu**
塗布剤 *ointment* **tofuzai**
若布 *wakame seaweeds* **wakame**

縫*ewing, 779*	衣*lothes, 355*	織*nitting, 855*
繰*pinning, 851*	裁*lothes, 802*	編*nitting, 42*
紡*pinning, 735*	服*lothes, 734*	糸*hread, 375*

存*xist, 634*

169-B

White 布loth 布pread, 希esired for a 怖cary dead...

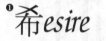 *希esire*   *希are*

巾 (cloth, fabric)

KI
desire, aspire, wish, preference, penchant, liking; rare

FLIP: 4.0.b. Bottom (stem)

❶希有 *highly-unusual, extra-ordinary* **keu**
希望 *hope, wish, desire* **kibō**
希望者 *candidate, applicant* **kibōsha**
希望的 *wishful, hopeful, desirable* **kibōteki**
希望的観測 *wishful thinking* **kibōteki kansoku**
希望条件 *conditions desired* **kibō jōken**
希薄 *thin, weak, weakling* **kihaku**
希薄化 *weakening, thinning, diluting* **kihakuka**
希求 *longing for, yearning for* **kikyū**
希釈 *dilution, dissolution* **kishaku**

❷希書 *rare book, old book* **kisho**
希少 *rare, scarce, uncommon* **kishō**
希少価値 *scarcity-, rarity value* **kishō kachi**
古希 *one's seventieth birthday* **koki**
希土 *rare soil* **kido**
希世 *rare, scarce* **kisei**
希代 *rare, scarce* **kidai**
希元素 *rare element* **kigenso**

望*esire, 618*	求*equest, 256*
欲*esire, 892*	請*equest, 791*
依*esire, 355*	頼*equest 562*
願*equest, 964*	珍*are, 720*

布*loth, 208*

169-C

White 布 loth 布 pread, 希 esired for a 怖 cary dead...

心⇔忄 (heart, feelings)

怖cary　　怖earsome

kowa(i), FU
scary, fearsome, horrendous, horror, shocking, spooky, terrifying, unnerving

FLIP: 7.3.b. Right Bottom (stem)

怖がる *afraid, get frightened, ~scared* **kowagaru**
怖怖 *timidly, hesitantly, reluctantly* **kowagowa**
怖い顔 *grim face, angry-looking* **kowaikao**
怖いものなし *fearless, unafraid* **kowaimononashi**
畏怖 *awe, dread, fear* **ifu**
恐怖 *fear, terror, horror* **kyōfu**
恐怖心 *fear, scare, frightening* **kyōfushin**
恐怖症 *morbid fear, phobia* **kyōfushō**
高所恐怖症 *fear of heights* **kyōsho kyōfushō**
閉所恐怖症 *claustrophobia* **heisho kyōfushō**
人怖じ *person-shy, unsociable* **hitooji**
物怖じ *timidity, shyness* **monooji**
恐怖感 *morbid fear, phobia* **kyōfukan**
恐怖政治 *reign of terror* **kyōfu seiji**
怖ず怖ず *timidly, hesitantly, reluctantly* **ozuozu**
怖じ気づく *get scared, ~frightened* **ojikezuku**

恐 *cary, 906*	驚 *care, 330*
威 *hreat, 520*	威 *uthority, 520*
嚇 *hreat, 261*	権 *uthority, 804*
虞 *hreat, 889*	戒 *dmonish, 493*
脅 *hreaten, 577*	諭 *dmonish, 922*

依 *equest, 355*

170-A

Cow on 台 latform 始 tarted 治 ealing his horns...

口 (mouth)

台latform　　台[vehicle]

DAI, TAI
platform, elevated stand; [counter for vehicles]

FLIP: 4.0.a. Bottom (flat)

舞台 *stage, scene, field* **butai**
鎮台 *garrison* **chindai**
台秤 *platform scale* **daibakari**
台地 *terrace, heights, plateau* **daichi**
台帳 *ledger, register* **daichō**
台所 *kitchen* **daidokoro**
台本 *script, scenario* **daihon**
台形 *trapezoid, trapezium* **daikei**
台紙 *mount, pasteboard* **daishi**
台数 *number* **daisū**
砲台 *artillery-, canon platform* **hōdai**
鏡台 *dressing table; vanity* **kyōdai**
露台 *balcony* **rodai**
台詞 *one's line, one's part* **serifu**
台風 *typhoon, storm* **taifū**
台北 *Taipei City, Taiwan* **taipei**
台頭 *rise, gaining power* **taitō**
高台 *elevated ground, upland* **takadai**
灯台 *lighthouse, watch tower* **tōdai**

屋台 *stand, stall, booth* **yatai**
卓袱台 *dining table* **chabudai**
跳躍台 *springboard* **chōyakudai**
台無し *spoil* **dainashi**
踏み台 *footstool, stepping stone* **fumidai**
楽譜台 *music sheet stand* **gakufudai**
交換台 *switchboard* **kōkandai**
絞首台 *gallows, hanging platform* **kōshudai**
聖火台 *Olympic torch* **seikadai**
滑り台 *playground slide* **suberidai**
展望台 *observatory, viewing deck* **tenbōdai**
車二台 *two cars, two vehicles* **kuruma nidai**

卓 *able, 499*	高 *levated, 435*	車 *ehicle, 306*
級 *evel, 189*	上 *scend, 859*	

各 *very, 498*

170-B

Cow on 台latform 始tarted 治ealing his horns...

始*tart*　始*egin*

女 (woman)

FLIP: 7.3.a. Right Bottom (flat)

haji(meru), haji(maru), SHI
start, begin, commence, initiate

原始 *origin, inception; primitive, ancient* **genshi**
原始人 *primitive person, aborigine* **genshijin**
原始的 *primitive, primordial* **genshiteki**
開始 *start, begin, commence* **kaishi**
無始 *infinite past, eternal past* **mushi**
年始 *beginning of the year* **nenshi**
始動 *start, first, starting (machine)* **shidō**
始原 *origin, conception, inception* **shigen**
始業 *opening, start of work* **shigyō**
始業式 *opening ceremony* **shigyōshiki**
始発 *first train, first bus, first flight* **shihatsu**
始発駅 *starting station of a train* **shihatsueki**
始終 *always, often, all the time* **shijū**
始期 *initial period, first term* **shiki**
始球 *first pitch in a baseball game* **shikyū**
始末 *management, disposition* **shimatsu**
⇒後始末 *settle, bring to an end* **atoshimatsu**
⇒不始末 *wasteful; spendthrift* **fushimatsu**
始末書 *written explanation, ~apology* **shimatsusho**

始末屋 *frugal-, thrifty person* **shimatsuya**
始祖 *founder, originator* **shiso**
終始 *from beginning to end* **shūshi**
終始一貫 *unwavering, consistent* **shūshi ikkan**
創始 *origination, creation, foundation* **sōshi**
創始者 *founder, originator* **sōshisha**
月始め *start of a month* **tsukihajime**
御用始め *first day of public offices in the year* **goyōhajime**
仕始める *starting, beginning* **shihajimeru**
手始めに *"first of all..."* **tehajime(ni)**

初*tart, 353*	先*efore, 478*
発*tart, 368*	前*efore, 118*

治*ecuperate, 210*

170-C

Cow on 台latform 始tarted 治ealing his horns...

治*ecuperate*　治*reatment*

水⇔氵 (water)

FLIP: 7.3.a. Right Bottom (flat)

osa(meru), osa(maru), nao(ru), nao(su), JI, CHI
recuperate, treatment, convalesce, getting well, abate, administer, govern

文治 *civil administration* **bunchi**
治安 *public order, peace & order* **chian**
治平 *peace & tranquillity* **chihei**
治下 *under the rule of~* **chika**
治国 *government* **chikoku**
治乱 *war & peace* **chiran**
治療 *treatment, therapy, cure* **chiryō**
治療代 *doctor's fee* **chiryōdai**
治療法 *cure, remedy* **chiryōhō**
治産 *property management* **chisan**
治世 *reign, rule* **chisei**
治績 *administration record* **chiseki**
治水 *flood control* **chisui**
治癒 *healing, recuperation, recovery* **chiyu**
法治 *constitutional government* **hōchi**
法治国 *constitutional state* **hōchikoku**
自治 *autonomy, self-government, self-rule* **jichi**
完治 *complete recuperation* **kanchi**
根治 *complete recuperation* **konji**

難治 *healing difficulties* **nanji**
政治 *government, administration* **seiji**
退治 *extermination, eradication, extinction* **taiji**
統治 *reign, rule* **tōchi**
⇒委任統治 *mandate, fiat* **inin tōchi**
湯治 *hot spring treatment* **tōji**
湯治場 *spa* **tōjiba**
全治 *complete recuperation* **zenchi**
荒療治 *hit-or-miss medical cure* **araryōji**
鍛治屋 *blacksmith, ~shop* **kajiya**
禁治産 *legally incompetent* **kinchisan**

癒*ecuperate, 923*	健*ealthy, 390*
療*ecuperate, 67*	病*ickness, 213*
患*ickness, 475*	医*edicine, 19*
症*ickness, 788*	剤*rugs, 961*

沿*longside, 756*

171-A

On 堀*anal* 掘*igging, town resistance* 屈*ielding...*

土 (ground, soil)

堀*anal*　　堀*aterway*

hori, ho(ru)
canal, dike, waterway

FLIP: 7.3.a. Right Bottom (flat)

堀端	*moat embankment*	**horibata**
堀江	*canal, waterway*	**horie**
堀川	*canal, waterway*	**horikawa**
空堀	*dry moat, ditch*	**karabori**
外堀	*outer moat*	**sotobori**
内堀	*inner moat*	**uchibori**
釣り堀	*fishing pond*	**tsuribori**

井*ater well, 361*
溝*aterway, 226*
槽*ater-tank, 327*

掘*igging, 211*

171-B

On 堀*anal* 掘*igging, town resistance* 屈*ielding...*

手⇔扌 (hand, manual)

掘*igging*　　掘*xcavation*

ho(ru), KUTSU
digging, excavation

FLIP: 7.3.a. Right Bottom (flat)

掘り池	*artificial pond*	**horiike**
掘り開く	*dig open*	**horihiraku**
掘り割り	*canal, ditch*	**horiwari**
掘り抜く	*dig thru*	**horinuku**
掘り出す	*dig out*	**horidasu**
掘り井戸	*water well*	**horiido**
掘り炬燵	*floor hole to stretch one's legs*	**horigotatsu**
掘り返す	*dig up*	**horikaesu**
掘り込む	*dig in (to)*	**horikomu**
掘り崩す	*demolish*	**horikuzusu**
掘り起こす	*dig into, dig up, dig out*	**horiokosu**
掘り下げる	*dig into, look into*	**horisageru**
掘り当てる	*strike*	**horiateru**
掘り出し物	*good buy, bargain*	**horidashimono**
掘り抜き井戸	*water well*	**horinukiido**
発掘	*excavation, exhumation*	**hakkutsu**
掘削	*diggings, excavation*	**kussaku**
掘削機	*excavator, steam shovel*	**kussakuki**
掘進	*excavation, digging out*	**kusshin**

乱掘	*indiscriminate mining*	**rankutsu**
採掘	*mining, digging*	**saikutsu**
採掘権	*mining rights, ~concessions*	**saikutsuken**
試掘	*prospecting, speculating*	**shikutsu**
盗掘	*illegal mining*	**tōkutsu**
内掘	*inner moat (within a castle)*	**uchibori**
穴掘り	*diggings, excavation*	**anahori**
墓掘り	*grave digging*	**hakahori**
金掘り	*miner*	**kanehori**
露天掘り	*open-air mining*	**rotenbori**
用水掘り	*irrigation ditch, ~dike*	**yōsuibori**
根掘り葉掘り	*nosy details*	**nehori hahori**

埋*ury, 319*　　　土*oil, 8*
溝*itch, 226*

堀*anal, 211*

171-C

On 堀anal 掘igging, town resistance 屈ielding...

❶屈*ielding*   **❷屈***ending*

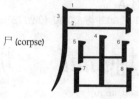

尸 (corpse)

kaga(mu), KUTSU
bending, twisting; capitulate, give-up, succumb, yielding

FLIP: 4.0.a. Bottom (flat)

❶不屈 *indomitable, unrelenting, unyielding* **fukutsu**
⇒不撓不屈 *indomitable, unrelenting, unyielding* **futō fukutsu**
偏屈 *stubborn, eccentric, obstinate* **henkutsu**
卑屈 *obsequious, servile, docile* **hikutsu**
屈伏 *submission, yielding* **kuppuku**
屈服 *submission, yielding* **kuppuku**
屈辱 *humiliation, insult, indignity* **kutsujoku**
屈辱的 *humiliating, shameful* **kutsujokuteki**
屈従 *submission, yielding, capitulation* **kutsujū**
屈託 *worry, anxiety, perplexity* **kuttaku**
窮屈 *tight, cramped* **kyūkutsu**
理屈 *reason, theory, argument* **rikutsu**
理屈屋 *argumentative person* **rikutsuya**
退屈 *boring, dull, monotonous* **taikutsu**
退屈凌ぎ *killing time, whiling away time* **taikutsu shinogi**
屈光性 *phototropism* **kukkōsei**

❷後屈 *bending backwards, retroflexion* **kōkutsu**
屈強 *robust, sturdy, brisk* **kukkyō**
屈曲 *bending, winding, refraction* **kukkyoku**
屈折 *refraction, bending* **kussetsu**
屈折率 *refraction index* **kussetsuritsu**
屈指 *leading, foremost, pre-eminent* **kusshi**
屈伸 *expansion & contraction* **kusshin**
屈肉 *flexor muscle* **kutsuniku**
前屈 *bending forward* **zenkutsu**

伏*ield, 702*
辞*uitting, 954*
曲*ending, 476*

尿*rine, 573*

172-A

丙hird group of 病ickness, due to 柄haracter stress...

丙*art C*   **丙***hird group*

― (one, single)

HEI
Part C, third group

FLIP: 1.0.b. Whole (stem)

丙種 *third grade, part C* **heishu**
丙夜 *12:00 am to 2:00 am* **heiya**
甲乙丙 *a, b, c; 1, 2, 3* **kōotsuhei**

三*hree, 858*

両*oth, 567*

172-B

丙hird group of 病ickness, due to 柄haracter stress...

广 (sickness)

FLIP: 8.0.b. Inner (stem)

病ickness 病llness

ya(mu), yamai, BYŌ, HEI
sickness, illness, disease, infection, virus

病臥	bedridden, confined to bed	**byōga**
病原	cause of an illness	**byōgen**
病因	cause of a disease	**byōin**
病院	hospital	**byōin**
病弱	invalid, sickly, weak	**byōjaku**
病状	patient's condition, illness condition	**byōjō**
病気	illness, disease, sickness	**byōki**
病菌	germ, virus	**byōkin**
病根	disease, evil	**byōkon**
病苦	illness pain	**byōku**
病人	sick person, invalid	**byōnin**
病死	death by illness	**byōshi**
病身	illness, sickness	**byōshin**
病室	sickroom, ward	**byōshitsu**
病床	sickbed	**byōshō**
業病	incurable disease, terminal illness	**gōbyō**
胃病	stomach trouble, ~disorder	**ibyō**
仮病	fake illness, malingering	**kebyō**
罹病	disease infected	**ribyō**

闘病	one's battle with illness	**tōbyō**
伝染病	epidemic, contagious disease	**densenbyō**
皮膚病	skin disease	**hifubyō**
肝臓病	liver illness, ~disease	**kanzōbyō**
狂犬病	rabies, hydrophobia	**kyōkenbyō**
夢遊病	sleepwalking, somnambulism	**muyūbyō**
熱射病	heatstroke, sunstroke	**nesshabyō**
精神病	mental illness, insanity	**seishinbyō**
潜水病	bends, caisson disease	**sensuibyō**
傷病兵	invalid soldiers	**shōbyōhei**
職業病	occupational disease	**shokugyōbyō**

治ecuperate, 210	症ickness, 788
癒ecuperate, 923	医edicine, 19
療ecuperate, 67	剤edicine, 961
患ickness, 475	菌acteria, 52

渡ross-over, 33

172-C

丙hird group of 病ickness, due to 柄haracter stress...

木 (wooden)

FLIP: 7.0.b2. Right (stem)

❶柄haracter ❷柄attern

gara, HEI
character, personality; pattern, template, handle

❶
人柄	personality, character	**hitogara**
家柄	family reputation, ~character	**iegara**
国柄	national character	**kunigara**
銘柄	brandname, trademark	**meigara**
身柄	one's person, body	**migara**
仕事柄	one's way of working, job attitude	**shigotogara**
続き柄	family, lineage relations	**tsuzukigara**

❷
間柄	connexion, relationship	**aidagara**
絵柄	pattern, design	**egara**
花柄	flower pattern	**hanagara**
日柄	suitable day	**higara**
柄杓	scoop, ladle	**hishaku**
辞柄	pretext, excuse	**jihei**
権柄	power, authority	**kenpei**
小柄	small nature	**kogara**
心柄	mood, frame of mind	**kokorogara**
事柄	matter, affair, business	**kotogara**
長柄	long handle	**nagae**

中柄	medium-sized	**nakae**
横柄	haughty, overbearing, arrogant	**ōhei**
大柄	large-built (body)	**oogara**
作柄	crop, harvest	**sakugara**
新柄	new pattern, fresh design	**shingara**
手柄	exploit, deed, feat	**tegara**
話柄	conversation theme, ~subject	**wahei**
矢柄	arrow shaft	**yagara**
野柄	field-, farming conditions	**yagara**
役柄	part, position, duty	**yakugara**
葉柄	leafstalk, petiole	**yōhei**
図柄	pattern, design	**zugara**

格tatus, 498	型attern, 536
模attern, 827	塑attern, 896
鑑attern, 857	

丙hird class, 212

173-A

A 兆rillion 兆ymptoms, 挑hallenge to fathom...

儿 (human legs)

°兆rillion °兆ymptoms

kiza(shi), kiza(su), CHŌ
trillion; symptoms

FLIP: 1.0.b. Whole (stem)

❶ 一兆円 *one trillion Japanese yen* **icchōen**
億兆 *multitude, throng, crowd* **okuchō**

❷ 兆候 *sign, symptom, indication* **chōkō**
慶兆 *good omen* **keichō**
吉兆 *good sign, ~omen* **kicchō**
兆し *sign, indication, symptom* **kizashi**
凶兆 *bad omen* **kyōchō**
前兆 *omen, portent, foreboding* **zenchō**
瑞兆 *good omen* **zuichō**

一 *ne, 858*	徴 *ymptoms, 62*
十 *en, 344*	響 *ffect, 452*
百 *undred, 14*	果 *esult, 287*
千 *housand, 74*	因 *ause, 862*
万 *en thousand, 465*	根 *oot, 772*
億 *undred-million, 340*	姿 *ppearance, 609*
零 *ero, 874*	

非 *[negative], 288*

173-B

A 兆rillion 兆ymptoms, 挑hallenge to fathom...

手 ⇔ 扌 (hand, manual)

挑hallenge 挑aring

ido(mu), CHŌ
challenge, daring, venture, provoke

FLIP: 7.0.b2. Right (stem)

挑発 *provocation, incitement* **chōhatsu**
挑発的 *provocative, inciteful* **chōhatsuteki**
挑戦 *challenge, provoke* **chōsen**
挑戦状 *written challenge* **chōsenjō**
挑戦者 *challenger* **chōsensha**
挑戦的 *challenging, provocative* **chōsenteki**

試 *rial, 418*	勝 *ictory, 406*
貫 *arry out, 532*	失 *ailure, 19*
敢 *aring, 449*	敗 *ailure, 137*
功 *uccess, 635*	

桃 *each, 215*

174-A

眺azing deep, diver with a 桃each 跳eapt to 逃scape the heat...

目 (eyesight, visual)

眺cenery   眺aze at

naga(meru), CHŌ
scenery, gaze at, spectacle, vista, look out over
眺め *view, scenery* **nagame**
眺める *look, watch, stare, gaze* **nagameru**
眺望 *view, prospect* **chōbō**

FLIP: 5.0.b. Left & Right

目*ye, 462*	観*iew, 667*
眼*yesight, 771*	視*bserve, 815*
見*eeing, 307*	

跳*ounce, 216*

174-B

眺azing deep, diver with a 桃each 跳eapt to 逃scape the heat...

木 (wooden)

桃each

momo, TŌ
peach
白桃 *white peace* **hakutō**
扁桃 *almond nuts* **hentō**
扁桃腺 *tonsils* **hentōsen**
扁桃腺炎 *tonsillitis, tonsils inflammation* **hentōsen'en**
苔桃 *cowberry* **kokemomo**
胡桃 *walnut* **kurumi**
胡桃割り *walnut cracker, nutcracker* **kurumiwari**
桃色 *pink, rosy* **momoiro**
桃色遊戯 *sex scene* **momoiro yūgi**
桃園 *peach orchard* **momozono**
黄桃 *yellow peach* **ōtō**
桜桃 *cherry tree* **ōtō**
桃源 *Shangri-la, paradise* **tōgen**
桃源郷 *paradise (Shangri-la)* **tōgenkyō**
桃源境 *paradise (Shangri-la)* **tōgenkyō**
桃花 *peach blossom* **tōka**
桃李 *peach & plum* **tōri**
梅桃 *nanking cherry* **umemomo**
山桃 *bayberry* **yamamomo**

桃割れ *coiffure* **momoware**
桃の節句 *Doll Festival (3 March)* **momo no sekku**
桃山時代 *Momoyama Era (1573-1615)*
   momoyama jidai

FLIP: 7.0.b2. Right (stem)

赤*ed colour, 261*	朱*carlet, 233*
丹*ed colour, 78*	梅*lum, 240*
紅*carlet, 175*	果*ruit, 287*

挑*hallenge, 214*

174-C

跳azing deep, diver with a 桃each 跳eapt to 逃scape the heat...

足 (feet, legs)

跳eap　　跳ounce

tobu, ha(neru), CHŌ
leap, bounce

FLIP: 7.0.b2. Right (stem)

跳び箱 *vaulting horse* **tobibako**
飛び下り *jumping off* **tobiori**
跳び上がる *jumping up* **tobiagaru**
飛び跳ねる *jumping about* **tobihaneru**
跳馬 *long vaulting horse* **chōba**
跳梁 *widespread, rampancy* **chōryō**
跳躍 *jump, leaping* **chōyaku**
跳躍台 *springboard, launching pad* **chōyakudai**
跳躍運動 *jumping exercise* **chōyaku undō**
跳ね橋 *drawbridge* **hanebashi**
跳ね板 *springboard, launching pad* **haneita**
跳ね返り *rebound, bouncing back* **hanekaeri**
跳ね出す *spring out* **hanedasu**
跳ね返る *rebound, bounce back* **hanekaeru**
跳ね返す *reject, repulse, bounce* **hanekaesu**
跳ね回る *jump-, skip-, bounce around* **hanemawaru**
跳ね除ける *push-, brush aside* **hanenokeru**
跳ね起きる *jump-, leap-, spring up* **haneokiru**
跳ね上がる *jump-, leap-, spring up* **haneagaru**

跳開橋 *drawbridge* **chōkaikyō**
泥跳ね *splash of mud* **dorohane**
幅跳び *broad-, long jump* **habatobi**
蛙跳び *leapfrog* **kaerutobi**
縄跳び *jump rope* **nawatobi**
馬跳び *leapfrog* **umatobi**
棒高跳び *pole jump, -vault* **bōtakatobi**
背面跳び *backward jumping* **haimentobi**
三段跳び *"hop, step & jump..."* **sandantobi**
走り幅跳び *long jump running* **hashiri habatobi**
走り高跳び *running high jump* **hashiri takatobi**

踊*ancing, 671*	慶*ejoice, 69*
舞*ancing, 167*	賀*elebration, 202*
興*ntertainment, 867*	祝*elebration, 716*

跳*elics, 672*

174-D

跳azing deep, diver with a 桃each 跳eapt to 逃scape the heat...

辶 (transport)

逃scape　　逃vade

ni(geru), noga(reru), ni(gasu), noga(su), TŌ
escape, evade, elude, get away-with

FLIP: 3.0.b. Top (stem)

逃がす *set free, miss* **nigasu**
逃げる *break loose, run away* **nigeru**
逃げ足 *flight; preparation to escape* **nigeashi**
逃げ場 *refuge, shelter, sanctuary* **nigeba**
逃げ腰 *posture to escape; evasive* **nigegoshi**
逃げ口 *escape route, loophole* **nigeguchi**
逃げ口上 *excuse, pretext, alibi* **nigekōjō**
逃げ出す *run away, escape* **nigedasu**
逃げ道 *escape path, exit route* **nigemichi**
逃げ路 *escape route, loophole* **nigemichi**
逃げ水 *mirage of water* **nigemizu**
逃げ去る *run off, flee, escape* **nigesaru**
逃げ惑う *running in confusion* **nigemadō**
逃げ回る *run about* **nigemawaru**
逃げ延びる *successful escape* **nigenobiru**
逃げ遅れる *fail to escape* **nigeokureru**
見逃す *escape notice of* **minogasu**
引き逃げ *hit & run* **hikinige**
言い逃れ *evasion, excuse* **iinogare**

勝ち逃げ *quitting at one's prime* **kachinige**
食い逃げ *running off in a restaurant* **kuinige**
持ち逃げ *make off with, abscond with* **mochinige**
その場逃れ *makeshift, stopgap* **sonoba nogare**
取り逃がす *fail to catch, miss* **torinigasu**
逃亡 *escape, fleeing, getaway* **tōbō**
逃亡者 *fugitive, runaway* **tōbōsha**
逃避 *escape, flight, evasion* **tōhi**
逃避行 *escape journey* **tōhikō**
逃走 *escape, fleeing, getaway* **tōsō**
夜逃げ *flee at night* **yonige**

走*unning, 497*	尺*ursue, 574*
奔*un-away, 120*	逮*rive-out 479*
追*ursue, 108*	

逃*onfusion, 904*

175-A

英*rilliant* 映*eflections,* 央*entral to* 英*ngland's dominions...*

-++- (grass)

❶英*ngland*　❷英*rilliance*

hanabusa, EI
England; brilliance, radiant, distinguished

FLIP: 1.0.b. Whole (stem)

❶駐英　*posted in England* **chūei**
英米　*US-British, America & England* **eibei**
英文　*English writing, ~sentence* **eibun**
英仏　*British-French* **eifutsu**
英語　*English language* **eigo**
英語圏　*English-speaking countries* **eigoken**
英字　*English letters, Roman letters* **eiji**
英貨　*British pound & sterling* **eika**
英国　*England, United Kingdom* **eikoku**
英日　*British-Japan* **einichi**
英書　*English books* **eisho**
英和　*English-Japanese* **eiwa**
英訳　*English translation* **eiyaku**
日英　*Japan & England* **nichiei**
渡英　*visit to England* **toei**
和英　*Japanese-English* **waei**
英会話　*English conversation* **eikaiwa**
英作文　*English composition* **eisakubun**
英単語　*English word* **eitango**

❷英知　*intelligence, wisdom* **eichi**
英断　*smart decision, wise judgement* **eidan**
英気　*brilliance, radiance, luminescence* **eiki**
英魂　*departed spirits* **eikon**
英明　*great intelligence, ~wisdom* **eimei**
英霊　*heroes spirits* **eirei**
英才　*brilliant, gifted, genius* **eisai**
英雄　*hero, martyr* **eiyū**
育英　*elite special education* **ikuei**
石英　*quartz* **sekiei**
俊英　*noted mathematician* **shun'ei**

昭*right*, 529	朗*lear*, 800
明*rilliance*, 22	光*hining*, 77
輝*parkling*, 296	欧*urope*, 952

央*entral*, 218

175-B

英*rilliant* 映*eflections,* 央*entral to* 英*ngland's dominions...*

日 (sunlight, daytime)

映*eflect*　映*lluminate*

utsu(su), utsu(ru), ha(eru), EI
reflect, illuminate, project

FLIP: 5.0.b. Left & Right

映画　*movie, film, motion picture* **eiga**
映画評論　*film criticism, movie review* **eiga hyōron**
映画監督　*movie-, film director* **eiga kantoku**
映画界　*the movies, movie industry* **eigakai**
映画館　*movie theatre, cinema* **eigakan**
映画祭　*film festival* **eigasai**
映倫　*movie ethics* **eirin**
映写　*film projection* **eisha**
映写機　*screen projector* **eishaki**
映写巻く　*movie reel* **eishamaku**
映像　*image, reflection* **eizō**
反映　*reflection, illumination* **han'ei**
放映　*broadcasting, televising* **hōei**
上映　*film showing, ~screening* **jōei**
競映　*film competition, film fest* **kyōei**
再映　*return screening* **saiei**
終映　*movie ending, "the end..."* **shūei**
投影　*image projection* **tōei**
続映　*screening hours* **zokuei**

劇映画　*dramatic movie* **gekieiga**
着映え　*suitable, fitting, proper* **kibae**
目映い　*dazzling beauty* **mabayui**
見映え　*awkward appearance* **mibae**
夕映え　*evening-, sunset glow* **yūbae**
出来映え　*effect, result, outcome* **dekibae**
面映ゆい　*feel embarrassed* **omohayui**
代わり映え　*"change for the better..."* **kawaribae**
照り映える　*glowing, shining* **terihaeru**

劇*rama*, 759	眺*aze at*, 215
射*hoot*, 504	興*ntertainment*, 867
観*iew*, 667	娯*musement*, 453

央*entral*, 218

175-C

英*rilliant* 映*eflections,* 央*entral to* 英*ngland's dominions...*

大 (grand)

央*entral* 央*iddle*

ō

central, middle

中央 *centre, hypocentre, core* **chūō**
中央部 *midsection* **chūōbu**
中央値 *median* **chūōchi**
中央銀行 *central bank* **chūō ginkō**
中央市場 *entrepot, central market* **chūō shijō**
道央 *central Hokkaidō* **dōō**
月央 *middle of a month, mid-month* **getsuō**
震央 *earthquake epicentre, ground zero* **shin'ō**

FLIP: 1.0.b. Whole (stem)

中*iddle, 85*	奥*nside, 903*
核*uclear, 973*	衡*quilibrium, 110*

史*istory, 85*

176-A

必*bsolutely, not to* 泌*ecrete* 密*idden* 秘*ecrets of Uncle Pete...*

心⇔忄 (heart, feelings)

必*bsolutely* 必*ithout fail*

kanara(zu), HITSU

absolutely, precisely, without fail

必着 *"must arrive without fail..."* **hicchaku**
必中 *hit on target* **hicchū**
必携 *indispensable, essential* **hikkei**
必見 *must see (movie)* **hikken**
必殺 *deadly blow, fatal blow* **hissatsu**
必死 *desperate, despondent, last-ditch* **hisshi**
必至 *inevitable, unpreventable, unavoidable* **hisshi**
必勝 *certain victory, sure win* **hisshō**
必修 *necessary expenses* **hisshū**
必修科目 *prerequisite subject* **hisshū kamoku**
必須 *indispensable, essential* **hissu**
必読 *required reading* **hitsudoku**
必定 *inevitable, unpreventable, unavoidable* **hitsujō**
必需 *necessary, needful* **hitsuju**
必需品 *necessity, necessary* **hitsujuhin**
必要 *necessity, necessary, requirement* **hitsuyō**
必要条件 *requirement, necessary condition*
       hitsuyō jōken
必要悪 *necessary evil* **hitsuyōaku**

Facing: 2.0. East ☞ (W)

必要品 *necessities, essentials* **hitsuyōhin**
必然 *necessary, inevitable* **hitsuzen**
不必要 *not necessary* **fuhitsuyō**
必ずしも *necessarily* **kanarazushimo**
信賞必罰 *sure reward & sure punishment*
       shinshō hitsubatsu

確*onfirm, 804*	真*ruth, 487*
本*rue, 461*	肯*ffirmative, 616*
実*ruth, 121*	有*xist, 617*

心*eart, 469*

176-B

必bsolutely, not to 泌ecrete 密idden 秘ecrets of Uncle Pete...

水⇔氵 (water)

泌ecrete

HITSU, HI
secrete, leakage

Facing: 2.2. East ☞ (V)

分泌 *secretion* **bunpi, bunpitsu**
分泌物 *secreted thing* **bunpibutsu**
泌尿器 *urinary organs* **hinyōki**
泌尿器病 *urinary disease* **hinyōkibyō**
泌尿器科 *urology* **hinyōkika**
泌泌 *keenly, deeply, thoroughly* **shimijimi**
外分泌 *external secretion* **gaibunpi**
内分泌 *internal secretion* **naibunpi**
内分泌腺 *endocrine gland* **naibunpisen**

密*ecret, 220*	忍*onceal, 535*
秘*ecret, 219*	覆*onceal, 602*
隠*onceal, 840*	尿*rine, 573*
匿*onceal, 277*	

必*bsolutely, 218*

176-C

必bsolutely, not to 泌ecrete 密idden 秘ecrets of Uncle Pete...

禾 (tree branch)

秘idden   秘ecret

hi(meru), HI
hidden, secret, confidential, covert

Facing: 4.0. ☜☞ Apart

便秘 *constipation* **benpi**
極秘 *top secret* **gokuhi**
秘本 *secret book* **hibon**
秘伝 *secret, mysteries* **hiden**
秘儀 *secret ritual* **higi**
秘宝 *hidden treasure* **hihō**
秘法 *secret method* **hihō**
秘方 *secret method* **hihō**
秘術 *hidden skills* **hijutsu**
秘計 *covert plan* **hikei**
秘訣 *secret, "the key..."* **hiketsu**
秘境 *virgin-, unexplored regions* **hikyō**
秘密 *secret, confidential, covert* **himitsu**
秘文 *magic formula* **himon**
秘奥 *secrets, mysteries* **hiō**
秘策 *hidden measures* **hisaku**
秘跡 *sacrament, liturgy* **hiseki**
秘史 *untold history, inside story* **hishi**
秘書 *private secretary* **hisho**

秘匿 *hidden, secret, cover* **hitoku**
秘話 *untold story, inside story* **hiwa**
秘技 *secret technique* **hiwaza**
秘薬 *secret medicine, wonder drug* **hiyaku**
黙秘 *silence, quietness, stillness* **mokuhi**
神秘 *mystery, enigma, riddle* **shinpi**
秘め事 *secret, confidential, covert* **himegoto**
秘蔵っ子 *favourite pupil, favourite son* **hizōkko**
秘中の秘 *confidential, top secret* **hichūnohi**

密*ecret, 220*	匿*onceal, 277*	漏*eakage, 301*
泌*ecrete, 219*	忍*onceal, 535*	
守*bide, 366*	覆*onceal, 602*	

秒*econds, 727*

176-D

必bsolutely, not to 泌ecrete 密idden 秘ecrets of Uncle Pete...

宀 (cover, lid)

密lose   密idden

MITSU
close, confidential, covert, hidden, secret

FLIP: 4.0.a. Bottom (flat)

厳密 closeness, exactness **genmitsu**
秘密 secret, confidential, covert **himitsu**
過密 overcrowding, congestion **kamitsu**
気密 airtight, airproof **kimitsu**
緊密 closeness, tightly-packed **kinmitsu**
綿密 minute, exact, scrupulous **menmitsu**
密会 secret-, closed-door meeting **mikkai**
密計 secret plan **mikkei**
密航 unknown passage, hidden route **mikkō**
密行 incognito travelling, secret trip **mikkō**
密告 betrayal, secret disclosure **mikkoku**
密生 growing thick, ~in clusters **missei**
密接 close, intimate **missetsu**
密使 secret emissary, secret envoy **misshi**
密室 locked room **misshitsu**
密書 secret letter, coded message **missho**
密集 crowding, swarming **misshū**
密葬 private funeral **missō**
密売 smuggling, black-market **mitsubai**

密度 density, thickness **mitsudo**
密議 secret meeting **mitsugi**
密事 secret, confidential, covert **mitsuji**
密雲 dense clouds **mitsuun**
密林 thick-, dense forest **mitsurin**
密猟 poaching, illegal hunting **mitsuryō**
密約 secret agreement **mitsuyaku**
濃密 thick fog **nōmitsu**
細密 close, minute, detailed **saimitsu**
精密 precision, accuracy, exactness **seimitsu**

秘ecret, 219	忍onceal, 535
泌ecrete, 219	覆onceal, 602
隠onceal, 840	逆everse, 896
匿onceal, 277	裏everse, 872

窓indow, 433

177-A

東astern 棟oof-ridges near 凍rozen bridges...

木 (wooden)

東astern   東riental

azuma, higashi, TŌ
eastern, Oriental

FLIP: 1.0.b. Whole (stem)

東男 eastern Japanese man **azuma otoko**
東屋 arbour, bower **azumaya**
中東 Middle East, Arab countries **chūtō**
以東 eastward **itō**
広東 Canton region (Guandong), China **kanton**
近東 near east **kintō**
極東 far east, the orient **kyokutō**
真東 right in the mid-east **mahigashi**
最東 easternmost **saitō**
東雲 daybreak, dawn **shinonome**
東岸 eastern coast **tōgan**
東上 go east to Tōkyō **tōjō**
東経 east longitude **tōkei**
東京 Tōkyō City **tōkyō**
東欧 Eastern Europe **tōō**
東洋 Orient **tōyō**
東漸 spread to the Asian region **tōzen**
毛沢東 Mao Zedong (1893-1976) **mōtakutō**
東海道 Tōkaidō highway from Kyōto to Edo **tōkaidō**

東進中 proceeding east **tōshinchū**
東洋人 oriental person **tōyōjin**
古今東西 all times & places **kokontōzai**
東宮殿下 His Imperial Highness, the Crown Prince
　　tōgū denka
東京大学 Tōkyō University **tōkyō daigaku**
東京都庁 Tōkyō Metropolitan Gov't **tōkyō tochō**
東洋美術 Oriental Arts **tōyō bijutsu**
東洋介護 Oriental Healthcare **tōyō kaigo**
東向きの家 house facing sunrise
　　higashimuki no ie
関東大地震 Great Tōkyō Earthquake (1923)
　　kantō daijishin
東南アジア Southeast Asia **tōnan ajia**

西estern, 18	南outhern, 414
北orthern, 372	

恵lessing, 545

177-B

東*astern* 棟*oof-ridges near* 凍*rozen bridges...*

棟*oof-ridge*　　棟*lock*

木 (wooden)

mune, muna, TŌ
roof ridge, block

FLIP: 7.0.b1. Right (stem)

別棟　*separate building, annex* **betsumune**
病棟　*hospital ward* **byōtō**
棟瓦　*ridge tiles* **munagawara**
棟木　*ridgepole* **munagi**
棟上　*ridgepole raising* **muneage**
棟上式　*ridgepole raising rites* **muneageshiki**
棟梁　*lead carpenter* **tōryō**
翼棟　*wing of a building* **yokutō**
上棟式　*roof-laying ceremony* **jōtōshiki**

畝*oof-ridge, 379*　　築*rchitect, 907*
建*uilding, 390*

東*astern, 220*

177-C

東*astern* 棟*oof-ridges near* 凍*rozen bridges...*

凍*reeze*　　　凍*cing*

冫 (freezing, ice)

kō(ru), kogo(eru), TŌ
freeze, icing, glaciate

FLIP: 7.0.b1. Right (stem)

不凍　*anti-freeze, freeze resistant* **futō**
不凍港　*ice-free harbour* **futōkō**
不凍剤　*anti-freeze agent* **futōzai**
解凍　*thawing, defrosting* **kaitō**
凍り付く　*be frozen* **kooritsuku**
凍え死　*frozen to death* **kogoeji**
冷凍　*freezing, refrigeration* **reitō**
冷凍魚　*frozen seafoods* **reitōgyo**
冷凍器　*freezer, refrigerator* **reitōki**
冷凍船　*refrigerator ship* **reitōsen**
冷凍車　*refrigerator vehicle* **reitōsha**
冷凍剤　*coolant, refrigerant* **reitōzai**
冷凍食品　*frozen food* **reitō shokuhin**
凍土　*frozen soil* **tōdo**
凍害　*freezing damage* **tōgai**
凍原　*frozen field* **tōgen**
凍結　*freezing, icing* **tōketsu**
凍肉　*frozen meat* **tōniku**
凍死　*freezing to death* **tōshi**

凍死者　*frozen dead* **tōshisha**
凍傷　*frostbite, chilblain* **tōshō**
凍瘡　*freezing damage* **tōsō**

冬*inter, 397*　　　寒*hills, 121*
氷*ce, 10*　　　冷*hilly. 684*

東*astern, 220*

178-A
What is the sales 点*oint of that* 店*tore?*

点*oint*   点*core*

火 ⇔ 灬 (fire)

FLIP: 2.0.b. Sort Of (stem)

tsu(keru), tsu(ku), tomo(su), TEN
point, score, tally, dot

罰点	*incorrect marks (exam)*	**batten**
頂点	*apex, summit, zenith*	**chōten**
氷点	*freezing point*	**hyōten**
基点	*basic-, cardinal point*	**kiten**
交点	*point of intersection*	**kōten**
拠点	*position, point, base*	**kyoten**
満点	*perfect score, 100%*	**manten**
盲点	*blind spot, loophole*	**mōten**
難点	*weakness, difficult point*	**nanten**
零点	*zero point, "love" (game)*	**reiten**
論点	*point of argument*	**ronten**
採点	*grading, marking*	**saiten**
視点	*point of view, view point*	**shiten**
焦点	*focus, focal point*	**shōten**
争点	*point in dispute, ~in question*	**sōten**
点眼	*applying eye lotion*	**tengan**
点字	*braille codes*	**tenji**
点火	*ignition, sparking*	**tenka**
点検	*checking, inspection*	**tenken**

点呼	*roll call*	**tenko**
点差	*difference in points*	**tensa**
点睛	*finishing touches*	**tensei**
点線	*dotted lines*	**tensen**
点滴	*dripping liquid, dextrose*	**tenteki**
点在	*being dotted, scattering*	**tenzai**
得点	*score, scoring*	**tokuten**
点点と	*"here & there..."*	**tentento**
着眼点	*point of view, viewpoint*	**chakuganten**
妥協点	*point of compromise*	**dakyōten**
合格点	*passing score*	**gōkakuten**
交差点	*railroad crossing, interchange*	**kōsaten**
句読点	*punctuation marks*	**kutōten**
類似点	*similarity, similar point*	**ruijiten**

目 *oint, 462*
焦 *ocus, 919*

点 *ccupy, 223*

178-B
What is the sales 点*oint of that* 店*tore?*

店*hop*   店*tore*

广 (rooftop)

FLIP: 4.0.a. Bottom (flat)
Facing: 2.1. East ☞ (H)

mise, TEN
shop, store, outlet

売店	*kiosk, booth, stall*	**baiten**
角店	*corner store*	**kadomise**
名店	*well-known store*	**meiten**
店番	*tending, tender*	**miseban**
店台	*store counter*	**misedai**
店先	*shop front*	**misesaki**
来店	*coming to the store*	**raiten**
露店	*street stall*	**roten**
質店	*pawn shop*	**shichiten**
支店	*branch store, ~office*	**shiten**
書店	*bookstore*	**shoten**
商店	*store, shop*	**shōten**
店子	*store tenant, ~lessee*	**tanako**
店長	*store manager*	**tenchō**
店員	*salesclerk*	**ten'in**
店内	*inside a store*	**tennai**
店舗	*store, shop, stall, booth*	**tenpo**
店主	*store-, shopkeeper*	**tenshu**
店頭	*front store, show window*	**tentō**

夜店	*night stall*	**yomise**
代理店	*dealership store*	**dairiten**
販売店	*store, shop*	**hanbaiten**
百貨店	*department store*	**hyakkaten**
家具店	*furniture store*	**kaguten**
喫茶店	*coffee-, tea room*	**kissaten**
免税店	*duty-free shop*	**menzeiten**
店卸し	*inventory counting*	**tanaoroshi**
店屋物	*order food from restaurant*	**tenyamono**
洋品店	*boutique, clothes shop*	**yōhinten**
雑貨店	*grocery, general store*	**zakkaten**

舗 *tore, 813*
屋 *tore, 427*

点 *ccupy, 223*

179-A

*A 粘ersevering 占ortune-teller with 粘ticky make-up
占ccupying the first floor...*

卜 (divine, sacred)

❶ 占*ccupy* **❷ 占***ortune-telling*

shi(meru), urana(u), SEN
occupy; fortune-telling, horoscope, palmistry, divine

FLIP: 4.0.a. Bottom (flat)
Facing: 2.1. East ☞ (H)

❶ 独占 *monopoly, cartel* **dokusen**
寡占 *oligopoly, oligopsony* **kasen**
占拠 *occupation, holding* **senkyo**
占領 *occupation, capture* **senryō**
占領軍 *occupation forces* **senryōgun**
占領地 *occupied territory* **senryōchi**
占星術師 *astrologer, fortune-teller* **sensei jutsushi**
占守 *occupying, taking possession* **senshu**
占取 *pre-occupation* **senshu**
占用 *personal use* **senyō**
占有 *possession, occupancy* **senyū**
占有権 *right of possession, ~ownership* **senyūken**
占有率 *share, percentage* **senyūritsu**
占有者 *occupant, possessor* **senyūsha**
独り占め *monopoly, cartel* **hitorijime**
買い占め *corner a market* **kaishime**

星占い *astrology, horoscope* **hoshiuranai**
夢占い *dream interpretation* **yumeuranai**

克*onquest,* 204	領*overn,* 874
征*onquer,* 31	将*uture,* 521
覇*egemony,* 603	生*ife,* 474
統*overn,* 885	命*ife,* 362

古*ld,* 477

❷ 辻占 *fortune-telling paper* **tsujiura**
占師 *fortune-teller* **uranaishi**

179-B

*A 粘ersevering 占ortune-teller with 粘ticky make-up
占ccupying the first floor...*

米 (grains, rice)

粘*ticky* **粘***ersevere*

neba(ru), NEN
sticky, persevere, persisting, steadfast, tenacity, holding fast

FLIP: 6.0.b. Left (stem)
FLIP: 7.3.a. Right Bottom (flat)

粘り *stickiness, patience* **nebari**
粘り気 *viscosity, stickiness* **nebarike**
粘付く *tacky, dowdy, vulgar* **nebatsuku**
粘り強い *tenacious, persevering* **nebarizuyoi**
粘着 *adhesion, stickiness* **nenchaku**
粘着力 *adhesive power* **nenchakuryoku**
粘着テープ *adhesive tape* **nenchaku tēpu**
粘度 *viscosity, adhesiveness* **nendo**
粘土 *clay, mud, earth* **nendo**
⇒紙粘土 *paper-mache* **kaminendo**
粘土細工 *clay works, clay modelling* **nendo zaiku**
粘粘 *sticky* **nebaneba**
粘液 *viscous-, sticky liquid* **nen'eki**
粘膜 *mucous membrane* **nenmaku**
粘力 *tenacity, viscosity* **nenryoku**
粘性 *viscosity, stickiness* **nensei**
粘質 *viscosity, stickiness* **nenshitsu**
粘体 *viscous-, sticky body* **nentai**

粘板岩 *clay rock* **nenbangan**

忍*ersevere,* 535	労*abour,* 351
励*iligence,* 465	勉*fforts,* 527
張*xert,* 274	

粋*urity,* 762

180-A

Tanning彼heir 皮kin with no cream, 彼hey got 疲xhausted and thin...

彼[third person]

彳 (stroll)

kare, kano, HI
[third person]

FLIP: 7.3.b. Right Bottom (stem)

彼方① "over there..." **achira**
彼方② far distance **anata**, **kanata**
彼是 this or that **arekore**
彼処 that place, over there **asoko**
誰彼 they **darekare**
彼我 he & I; they & we **higa**
彼岸 equinoctial week **higan**
彼女 she, girl friend **kanojo**
彼女等 they (feminine) **kanojora**
彼此 "this & that..." **karekore**
彼等 they (masculine) **karera**
彼氏 male; one's boyfriend **kareshi**
彼処 "over there..." **kashiko**
彼れ程 "that much, that little..." **arehodo**
彼れ位 "that much..." **arekurai**
彼れ迄 until then, up to that time **aremade**
彼れ式 such a trivial thing **areshiki**
何彼と "one way or another, somehow..."
　　nanikato

壮asculine, 367	雄asculine, 775
男asculine, 597	郎asculine, 404
僕asculine, 157	女emale, 350

波urrent, 32	皮kin, 224

180-B

Tanning彼heir 皮kin with no cream, 彼hey got 疲xhausted and thin...

皮kin　　皮erma

皮 (skin)

kawa, HI
skin, derma, epidermis

FLIP: 4.0.b. Bottom (stem)

脱皮 casting off, outgrowing **dappi**
外皮 outer skin **gaihi**
牛皮 cowhide **gyūhi**
皮膚 skin **hifu**
皮下 underneath the skin **hika**
皮革 leather, hide **hikaku**
皮膜 membrane, skin layer **himaku**
皮肉 irony, sarcasm, satire **hiniku**
一皮 underneath the skin **hitokawa**
包皮 foreskin **hōhi**
表皮 epidermis, cuticle **hyōhi**
上皮 outer skin, epidermis **jōhi**
獣皮 animal skin **jūhi**
樹皮 tree bark, tree hide **juhi**
果皮 pericarp, shell **kahi**
皮衣 fur **kawagoromo**
毛皮 fur **kegawa**
桂皮 cinnamon, cassia **keihi**
木皮 tree bark **mokuhi**

内皮 endodermis **naihi**
生皮 raw hide **namakawa**
渋皮 polished & good-looking **shibukawa**
敷皮 fur rug, inner sole **shikigawa**
杉皮 cryptomeria bark **sugikawa**
靭皮 bast **utsubokawa**
鰐皮 crocodile skin **wanigawa**
皮鞣し tanning **kawanameshi**
皮相的 superficial, flimsy, frivolous **hisōteki**
皮切り start, beginning **kawakiri**
皮剥き器 parer, peeler **kawamukiki**

肌kin, 747	髪air, 408
膚kin, 69	毛kin hair, 468

被uffer, 715

180-C

*Tanning*彼*heir* 皮*kin with no cream,* 彼*hey got* 疲*xhausted and thin...*

疒 (sickness)

疲*iredness*   疲*xhaustion*

tsuka(reru); tsuka(rasu), HI

FLIP: 8.0.b. Inner (stem)

お疲れさま *"a job well done..."* **otsukaresama**
疲れ切る *tire out, wear out* **tsukarekiru**
疲れ果てる *"tired to the bone's..."* **tsukarehateru**
疲弊 *exhaustion, fatigue* **hihei**
疲労 *fatigue, exhaustion* **hirō**
人疲れ *crowd phobia* **hitozukare**
気疲れ *mental fatigue* **kizukare**
旅疲れ *travel fatigue* **tabitsukare**
湯疲れ *tiredness after a long hotbath* **yuzukare**

努*fforts, 44*	労*abour, 351*
勉*fforts, 527*	休*est 347*
働*abour, 422*	張*tretch, 274*

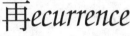
疫*pidemic, 680*

181-A

再*epeated* 講*ecture on* 溝*itch structure...*

冂 (inverted box)

再*epeat*   再*ecurrence*

futata(bi), SAI, SA
repeat, recurrence, repetition

FLIP: 1.0.b. Whole (stem)

再度 *another time, second time* **saido**
再読 *reading again, re-reading* **saidoku**
再演 *repeat performance, rerun* **saien**
再現 *reappearance, re-emergence* **saigen**
再拝 *bowing repeatedly* **saihai**
再版 *second edition* **saihan**
再犯 *repeat offence, recidivist* **saihan**
再訪 *revisit, come again* **saihō**
再会 *meeting again, reunion* **saikai**
再開 *reopening, resumption* **saikai**
再刊 *reprinting, republishing* **saikan**
再建 *reconstruction, rebuilding* **saiken**
再起 *return engagement* **saiki**
再興 *revival, restoration* **saikō**
再婚 *re-marriage* **saikon**
再挙 *new attempt, second try* **saikyo**
再燃 *recurrence, relapse* **sainen**
再任 *reappointment* **sainin**
再認 *permit renewal* **sainin**

再来 *second coming, second advent (Christ)* **sairai**
再生 *regeneration; playback (VCR)* **saisei**
再選 *re-election* **saisen**
再軍備 *rearmament, arms build up* **saigunbi**
再発見 *re-discovery* **saihakken**
再発行 *re-issuance (lost card)* **saihakkō**
再確認 *reconfirmation, reaffirmation* **saikakunin**
再帰的 *reflexive* **saikiteki**
再入国 *re-entry to a country* **sainyūkoku**
再生紙 *recycled paper* **saiseishi**

又*gain, 177*	替*eplace, 334*
二*econd, 457*	代*eplace, 96*
換*eplace, 819*	

用*tilize, 409*   百*undred, 14*

181-B

再*epeated* 講*ecture on* 溝*itch structure...*

講*ecture*   講*esson*

KŌ

lecture, lesson, speech

FLIP: 5.0.b. Left & Right

聴講 *sitting in a lecture; audition* **chōkō**
代講 *substitute lecturing* **daikō**
補講 *make-up lecture* **hokō**
受講 *sitting in a lecture* **jukō**
開講 *opening of a lecture* **kaikō**
欠講 *cancelled lecture, "no classes..."* **kekkō**
講武 *military training, ~exercise* **kōbu**
講談 *story, storytelling, narration* **kōdan**
講壇 *lecture platform* **kōdan**
講堂 *lecture hall* **kōdō**
講読 *reading & explaining* **kōdoku**
講演 *lecture, speech* **kōen**
講演会 *lecture meeting* **kōenkai**
講演料 *lecturer's fee* **kōenryō**
講演者 *lecturer, speaker* **kōensha**
講義 *lecture, lesson* **kōgi**
講義録 *transcript of lectures* **kōgiroku**
講究 *specialized research, ~study* **kōkyū**
講釈 *lecture, explanation* **kōshaku**

講釈師 *storyteller, narrator* **kōshakushi**
講師 *assistant professor, lecturer* **kōshi**
講習 *class, instruction, lesson* **kōshū**
講習生 *student, learner* **kōshūsei**
講話 *lecture, talk* **kōwa**
講和 *treaty conclusion* **kōwa**
講座 *university chair* **kōza**
休講 *cancelled lecture* **kyūkō**
進講 *lecture in the imperial presence* **shinkō**
講談師 *storyteller, narrator* **kōdanshi**

言*alking, 251*		叙*arrate, 648*	
談*alks, 308*		紀*arration, 727*	
語*alking, 780*		記*ecord, 728*	
聞*isten, 282*		録*ecord, 841*	

溝*itch, 226*

181-C

再*epeated* 講*ecture on* 溝*itch structure...*

溝*itch*   溝*anal*

mizo, KŌ

ditch, canal, dike, waterway

FLIP: 7.0.b2. Right (stem)

地溝 *rift valley* **chikō**
溝板 *ditches coverboard* **dobuita**
溝水 *ditch water* **dobumizu**
海溝 *sea trench, ocean deep* **kaikō**
⇒日本海溝 *Japan Deep* **nihon kaikō**
溝渠 *ditch, sewer, canal* **kōkyo**
溝川 *ditch with running water* **mizogawa**
側溝 *side ditch* **sokkō**
下水溝 *sewerage canal* **gesuikō**
排水溝 *drainage, canal* **haisuikō**

堤*mbankment, 314*		礁*unken, 920*	
州*andbank, 76*		潜*ubmerge, 335*	
沼*wamp, 356*		没*inking, 744*	
沢*wamp, 753*		掘*igging, 211*	

講*ecture, 226*

182-A

吉*ood luck* 結*onnects when* 詰*ompressed less...*

口 (mouth)

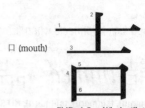

FLIP: 1.0.a. Whole (flat)

吉*ortunate*   吉*ucky*

KICHI, KITSU
fortunate, lucky, good luck, opportune, fortuitous

大吉 *special good luck* **daikichi**
不吉 *bad omen* **fukitsu**
吉兆 *lucky omen* **kicchō**
吉徴 *lucky omen* **kicchō**
吉事 *auspicious event* **kichiji**
吉日 *lucky day* **kichijitsu, kitsujitsu**
吉例 *festive custom* **kichirei**
吉慶 *congratulatory, celebrative* **kikkei**
吉凶 *fortune, good-or-bad* **kikkyō**
吉報 *good news, glad tidings* **kippō**
吉相 *good omen* **kissō**
小吉 *a bit of good luck* **daikichi**
吉原町 *old red-light district in Tōkyō* **yoshiwara-chō**
石部金吉 *person of strict morals* **ishibe kinkichi**
嘉吉時代 *Kakitsu Era (1441-1444)* **kakitsu jidai**

富*ortune, 333*	隆*rosperity, 133*
豊*bundance, 965*	盛*rosperity, 244*
裕*ffluence, 758*	多*lenty, 187*
繁*rosperity, 434*	命*estiny, 362*

古*ld, 477*

182-B

吉*ood luck* 結*onnects when* 詰*ompressed less...*

糸 (thread, continuity)

FLIP: 7.0.a. Right (flat)

結*onnect*   結*inkage*

musu(bu), yu(waeru), yu(u), KETSU
connect, linkage

直結 *direct connexion* **chokketsu**
妥結 *agreement, settlement* **daketsu**
団結 *union, solidarity, unity* **danketsu**
凝結 *coagulation, condensation* **gyōketsu**
氷結 *freezing, frosty, frigid* **hyōketsu**
完結 *conclusion, completion, closure* **kanketsu**
結果 *result, outcome, end result* **kekka**
結核 *tuberculosis, lung disease* **kekkaku**
結構 *very much, pretty much, rather* **kekkō**
結婚 *marriage, matrimony, wedding* **kekkon**
結局 *"after all, in the end..."* **kekkyoku**
結髪 *hair-dressing, hairstyle* **keppatsu**
結氷 *freezing over* **keppyō**
結社 *association, affiliation* **kessha**
結審 *conclusion of a trial* **kesshin**
結束 *uniting, banding together* **kessoku**
結団 *forming a new group* **ketsudan**
結合 *merging, fusion, union* **ketsugō**
結実 *fruition, realization* **ketsujitsu**

結論 *conclusion* **ketsuron**
結託 *conclusion, collusion* **kettaku**
結党 *forming a new party* **kettō**
帰結 *conclusion, result, outcome* **kiketsu**
連結 *connection, coupling, joint* **renketsu**
論結 *conclusion* **ronketsu**
集結 *gathering, get-together* **shūketsu**
終結 *termination, conclusion* **shūketsu**
凍結 *freezing, freeze* **tōketsu**
結納 *betrothal gift, dowry* **yuinō**
増結 *addition, increase* **zōketsu**

絡*onnect, 826*	縁*elationship, 675*
盟*lliance, 21*	網*etwork, 159*
連*lliance, 305*	

続*ontinue, 260*

182-C

吉ood luck 結onnects when 詰ompressed less...

詰ammed 詰ompressed

言 (speaking)

tsu(mu), tsu(meru), tsu(maru), KITSU
jammed, compressed, stuff, reprimand

FLIP: 5.0.a Left & Right

缶詰 *canned food, ~goods* **kanzume**
詰責 *reprimand, censure* **kisseki**
詰問 *cross-examination* **kitsumon**
面詰 *reprimand in person* **menkitsu**
難詰 *blame, censure, reproach* **nankitsu**
理詰 *reason, cogent logic* **rizume**
瓶詰め *bottling* **binzume**
大詰め *finale, final scene* **ōzume**
鮨詰め *"packed like sardines..."* **sushizume**
詰め物 *packing, stuffing* **tsumemono**
詰め所 *station, office* **tsumesho**
詰め寄る *end in a draw* **tsumeyoru**
詰め替える *repack, rebottle* **tsumekaeru**
詰め掛ける *crowd, besiege* **tsumekakeru**
息詰まる *oppressive, repressive* **ikizumaru**
金詰まり *financial distress, money problem* **kanezumari**
気詰まり *uneasiness, unsettling* **kizumari**
見詰める *gazing, staring at* **mitsumeru**

煮詰まる *boil down* **nitsumaru**
折り詰め *food packed in a box* **orizume**
張り詰める *tense, strain, intensify* **haritsumeru**
切り詰める *reduce, cut down* **kiritsumeru**
食い詰める *fall into poverty* **kuitsumeru**
追い詰める *drive to a corner* **oitsumeru**
思い詰める *think hard, ponder* **omoitsumeru**
立ち詰める *keep standing* **tachizumeru**
問い詰める *grill, question closely* **toitsumeru**
突き詰める *investigate thoroughly* **tsukitsumeru**
行き詰まる *end in a stalemate* **yukizumaru**
詰め合わせる *assort, sort out* **tsumeawaseru**

満aturate, 567
抑uppress, 705

詰hronicle, 426

183-A

耳ars long 恥isgraced, 取aken to a far place...

耳ars

耳 (ears)

mimi, JI
ears, audio

FLIP: 2.0.b. Sort Of (stem)

福耳 *plump ears (said to be money luck)* **fukumimi**
初耳 *brand-new news* **hatsumimi**
早耳 *quick ears, good listener* **hayamimi**
耳順 *one's sixtieth birthday, 60 years old* **jijun**
耳目 *eyes & ears* **jimoku**
耳痛 *painful ears* **jitsū**
片耳 *one ear* **katamimi**
耳垢 *earwax* **mimiaka**
耳孔 *earhole* **mimiana**
耳元 *close to one's ears* **mimimoto**
耳栓 *earplug* **mimisen**
耳輪 *earrings* **mimiwa**
空耳 *playing deaf* **soramimi**
遠耳 *hearing difficulties* **toomimi**
牛耳る *domineering, dominate* **gyūjiru**
耳垂れ *running ears* **mimidare**
耳学問 *learning by ear* **mimigakumon**
耳掻き *earcleaning, earpick* **mimikaki**
耳鳴り *ringing in the ears* **miminari**

耳覆い *earmuffs* **mimiooi**
耳たぶ *earlobe* **mimitabu**
耳打ち *whispering* **mimiuchi**
耳寄り *welcome, tempting, inviting* **mimiyori**
耳鼻咽喉 *ear, nose & throat* **jibiinkō**
耳新しい *unfamiliar, "never heard..."* **mimiatarashii**
耳慣れる *become familiar with* **miminareru**
耳を傾ける *listen intently* **mimi o katamukeru**
耳障りな音 *jarring, harsh & grating noise* **mimizawari na oto**
耳に残っている *reverberating in the ears* **mimi(ni) nokkotteiru**

音ound, 314   諮nquire, 865
声oice, 428   尋nquire, 868
聞isten, 282   聞nquire, 282
聴isten, 844

且urther, 500

183-B

耳ars long 恥isgraced, 取aken to a far place...

心 ⇔ 忄 ⇔ 小 (feelings)

恥*hame*   恥*isgrace*

haji, ha(jiru), ha(jirasu), ha(zukashii), CHI
shame, disgrace, disrepute, ignominy, infamy

Facing: 4.0. ⇦⇨ Apart

恥じ入る *be ashamed, ~embarrassed* **hajiiru**
恥じらい *blushing, flushing, reddening* **hajirai**
恥ずべき *must be shameful, ~disgraceful* **hazubeki**
恥ずかしい *shameful, embarrassing* **hazukashii**
恥曝し *disgrace, shame* **hajisarashi**
破廉恥 *shameless, disgraceful* **harenchi**
生き恥 *living in disgrace, ~shame* **ikihaji**
廉恥心 *sense of shame (honour)* **renchishin**
死に恥 *shameful death* **shi(ni)haji**
恥知らず *shameless, disgraceful* **hajishirazu**
物恥ずかしい *shy, ashamed, embarrassing*
　　　monohazukashii
空恥ずかしい *being shy for no reason*
　　　sorahazukashii
赤恥 *shame, humiliation* **akahaji**
恥部 *genitals, private parts* **chibu**
恥辱 *shame, disgrace* **chijoku**
恥骨 *pubic bone* **chikotsu**
恥丘 *mons pubis* **chikyū**

恥毛 *genital hair* **chimō**
国恥 *national humiliation* **kokuhaji**
無恥 *shameless, disgraceful* **muchi**
羞恥 *shyness, bashful* **shūchi**
羞恥心 *sense of shame* **shūchishin**

辱*umiliate, 588*

取*ake, 229*

183-C

耳ars long 恥isgraced, 取aken to a far place...

又 (again)

取*aking*   取*etting*

to(ru), SHU
taking, getting

FLIP: 7.0.b2. Right (stem)

略取 *capture, seize, catch* **ryakushu**
採取 *withdraw, call off, drop* **saishu**
詐取 *swindle, defraud, dupe* **sashu**
取得 *acquire, gain, obtain* **shutoku**
取材 *media coverage* **shuzai**
段取り *plan, course-of-action* **dandori**
草取り *weeding, picking (edible plants)* **kusatori**
面取り *chamfering* **mentori**
寝取り *stealing somebody's spouse* **netori**
取り皿 *small dish plate* **torizara**
勝ち取る *gain, obtain, win* **kachitoru**
買い取る *buy, purchase* **kaitoru**
書き取り *dictation, taking down notes* **kakitori**
巻き取る *reel, rewind* **makitoru**
乗っ取り *hijacking, commandeering* **nottori**
取り扱い *handling, treatment* **toriatsukai**
取り引き *dealings, transactions* **torihiki**
取り囲む *surround, encircle* **torikakomu**
取り壊す *break apart, isassemble* **torikowasu**

取り付け *install, attach* **toritsuke**
受け取る *receive, take, accept* **uketoru**
読み取り *reading* **yomitori**
揚げ足取り *fault-finding, complainer* **ageashidori**
現金取引 *cash deal, cash payment* **genkin**
　　　torihiki
取り違える *wrong comprehension* **torichigaeru**
取って返す *retrace one's steps, ~past* **tottekaesu**
取って置く *save, hold, have in store* **totteoku**
取り押さえる *capture, arrest* **toriosaeru**
取締役社長 *company president (formal title)*
　　　torishimariyaku shachō

持*olding, 249*　　　得*ains, 940*
握*rasp, 427*　　　獲*ains, 829*

恥*isgrace, 229*

184-A

浄*urity* of 静*ilence* with 争*onflict's absence*...

浄*urity*　　　浄*lean*

水 ⇔ 氵 (water)

JŌ

purity, clean, pristine, undiluted, sterilize, wholesome

Facing: 1.2. West (V)

不浄 *uncleanliness, dirty, untidy* **fujō**
自浄 *self-purification, ~cleansing* **jijō**
浄地 *sacred grounds* **jōchi**
浄土 *paradise, "land of the pure..."* **jōdo**
⇒極楽浄土 *Buddhist paradise* **gokuraku jōdo**
浄土宗 *jōdo Buddhism sect* **jōdoshū**
浄衣 *"robe of purity..."* **jōi**
浄域 *sacred precincts* **jōiki**
浄化 *purification, cleansing* **jōka**
浄火 *sacred fire* **jōka**
浄界 *Buddhist paradise* **jōkai**
浄戒 *precepts, commandments* **jōkai**
浄写 *clean copy* **jōsha**
浄書 *clean copy* **jōsho**
浄水 *fresh-, clean water* **jōsui**
浄水場 *water treatment plant* **jōsuijō**
浄財 *giving without expecting in return* **jōzai**
浄罪 *purgation from sins* **jōzai**
洗浄 *washing, laundry* **senjō**

洗浄薬 *laundry-, washing detergent* **senjōgusuri**
清浄 *purity, cleanliness* **shōjō**
浄瑠璃 *Japanese ballad drama* **jōruri**
御不浄 *lavatory* **gofujō**

清*urify*, 793	粋*urity*, 762
潔*urity*, 901	斎*urification*, 112
純*urity*, 199	

泡*ubbles*, 689

184-B

浄*urity* of 静*ilence* with 争*onflict's absence*...

静*uiet*　　　静*tillness*

青 (blue)

shizu, shizu(ka), shizu(meru), shizu(maru), SEI, JŌ

quiet, stillness, hush-hush

FLIP: 6.0.b. Left (stem)

安静 *peace & quiet* **ansei**
鎮静 *subsiding, getting calm* **chinsei**
鎮静剤 *sedative, tranquilliser* **chinseizai**
動静 *movements, state of things* **dōsei**
平静 *calmness, serenity* **heisei**
静脈 *vein, artery* **jōmyaku**
閑静 *quietness, silence* **kansei**
冷静 *self-possessed, calm* **reisei**
静物 *still life, quiet life* **seibutsu**
静聴 *"your kind attention..."* **seichō**
静謐 *peace & tranquillity, serenity* **seihitsu**
静寂 *stillness, silence, tranquillity* **seijaku**
静観 *wait-and-see* **seikan**
静穏 *calmness, tranquillity, serenity* **seion**
静止 *standstill, rest, stillness* **seishi**
静思 *meditation, contemplation* **seishi**
静粛 *silence, quietness* **seishuku**
静水 *still water (not running)* **seisui**
静態 *static, stationary* **seitai**

静的 *static* **seiteki**
静夜 *silent night, quiet evening* **seiya**
静養 *rest, recover, recuperate* **seiyō**
静座 *meditation, contemplation* **seiza**
大静脈 *main vein, ~artery, vena cava* **daijōmyaku**
心静か *calm, serene, tranquil* **kokoroshizuka**
物静か *still, calm, quiet* **monoshizuka**
静電気 *static electricity* **seidenki**
静電学 *electrostatics* **seidengaku**
静力学 *static science* **seirikigaku**
静止衛星 *stationary satellite* **seishi eisei**

寧*uiet*, 967	穏*ranquillity*, 840
黙*uiet*, 846	康*ranquillity*, 881
幽*uiet*, 897	康*olace*, 881

青*lue colour*, 115

184-C

浄*urity of* 静*ilence with* 争*onflict's absence...*

」 (hook, barb)

争*ispute*　　争*onflict*

araso(u), SŌ
dispute, conflict, strife, struggle, quarrel, contend

Facing: 1.0. 🖙 West (W)

紛争 *dispute, strife, conflict* **funsō**
係争 *conflict, controversy, dispute* **keisō**
繋争 *dispute, struggle* **keisō**
抗争 *dispute, struggle* **kōsō**
競争 *competition, contest* **kyōsō**
内争 *internal strife, infighting* **naisō**
論争 *argument, dispute* **ronsō**
政争 *political strife* **seisō**
戦争 *war, battle* **sensō**
⇒核戦争 *nuclear war* **kakusensō**
⇒侵略戦争 *war of aggression* **shinryaku sensō**
争奪 *struggle, strife* **sōdatsu**
争奪戦 *struggle, strife* **sōdatsusen**
争議 *labour dispute, strike* **sōgi**
⇒山猫争議 *wildcat strike* **yamaneko sōgi**
争覇 *struggle for domination* **sōha**
争乱 *conflict, controversy* **sōran**
争論 *dispute, contention, struggle* **sōron**
争端 *start of a quarrel* **sōtan**

争点 *point of dispute* **sōten**
闘争 *strife, struggle, dispute* **tōsō**
⇒階級闘争 *class struggle* **kaikyū tōsō**
党争 *intra-party dispute* **tōsō**
権力争い *power struggle* **kenryoku arasoi**
縄張り争い *turf war* **nawabari arasoi**
勢力争い *power struggle* **seiryoku arasoi**
相続争い *inheritance dispute* **sōzoku arasoi**

戦*ighting, 517*	武*arrior, 100*
迷*onfusion, 904*	闘*ombat, 946*
乱*onfusion, 686*	敵*nemy, 966*

色*olour, 403*

185-A

拾*ick-up a pen & paper, let's write a* 合*ombined* 答*nswer...*

手⇔扌 (hand, manual)

拾*ick-up*

hiro(u), JŪ, SHŪ
pick-up

FLIP: 7.0.a. Right (flat)

拾い物 *found article, recovered item* **hiroimono**
拾い主 *finder* **hiroinushi**
拾い出し *pick-out, picking out* **hiroidashi**
拾い読み *skim reading* **hiroiyomi**
拾い上げる *pick up* **hiroiageru**
拾い集める *gather, collect pick up* **hiroiatsumeru**
拾遺 *gleaning, compiling* **shūi**
収拾 *adoption-or-rejection* **shūshū**
拾得 *picking up, finding* **shūtoku**
拾得物 *acquired property* **shūtokubutsu**
拾得者 *finder* **shūtokusha**
球拾い *picking up balls; caddy* **tamahiroi**
命拾い *escape from death* **inochibiroi**
拾万円 *ten thousand Japanese yen* **jūman'en**
骨拾い *gathering the dead's ashes* **kotsuhiroi**
屑拾い *ragpicking, ragpicker* **kuzuhiroi**
落ち穂拾い *gleaning, gleaner* **ochibohiroi**

抽*xtract, 37*	
引*xtract, 348*	
滴*xtract, 799*	

拾*hrow-away, 388*　　合*ogether, 232*

185-B

拾ick-up a pen & paper, let's write a 合ombined 答nswer...

口 (mouth)

FLIP: 1.0.a. Whole (flat)

合nify   合ogether

a(u), a(waseru), a(wasu), GŌ, GA, KAI
unify, together, unison, combine, fit, converge

合印	correct marks (exam) **aiin**
合間	interval, pause **aima**
暗合	coincidence, happenstance **angō**
調合	mixing, compounding **chōgō**
合併	merger, consolidation, union **gappei**
合唱	chorus, chorale **gasshō**
合宿	staying in the same dormitory **gasshuku**
合弁	joint management **gōben**
合議	consultation, conference **gōgi**
合法	legitimacy, lawful **gōhō**
合意	agreement, consent **gōi**
合一	unification, union **gōitsu**
合格	exam passing **gōkaku**
合格点	passing mark **gōkakuten**
合計	grand total, sum total **gōkei**
合憲	constitutional **gōken**
合金	alloy, alloyed metals **gōkin**
合理	rationalization, streamlining **gōri**
合流	pooling, combining **gōryū**

合戦	battle, combat **kassen**
組合	association, grouping **kumiai**
都合	convenience, situation **tsugō**
合わせ目	joint, seam **awaseme**
話し合い	talks, negotiations **hanashiai**
顔合わせ	getting-to-know-you meeting **kaoawase**
知り合い	acquaintance, casual friend **shiriai**
付き合い	acquaintance, relationship **tsukiai**
寄り合い	businessmen's gathering **yoriai**
申し合わせ	mutual consent **mōshiawase**
問い合わせ	inquiry, reference **toiawase**

共ogether, 302	併erge, 886
併ombine, 886	

含nclude, 183

185-C

拾ick-up a pen & paper, let's write a 合ombined 答nswer...

竹 (bamboo)

FLIP: 4.0.a. Bottom (flat)

答nswer   答esponse

kota(eru), kota(e), TŌ
answer, response, reply

珍答	absurd reply, stupid answer **chintō**
直答	prompt response **chokutō**
返答	reply, answer **hentō**
筆答	written answer **hittō**
直答	straight answer **jikitō**
回答	answer **kaitō**
解答	solution, correct answer **kaitō**
確答	clear-, definite answer **kakutō**
決答	definite response **kettō**
口答	verbal-, oral answer **kōtō**
迷答	absurd reply, stupid answer **meitō**
名答	correct answer **meitō**
明答	definite-, precise answer **meitō**
問答	question & answer **mondō**
応答	reply, response **ōtō**
正答	correct answer **seitō**
即答	immediate reply **sokutō**
答案	question & answer **tōan**
答弁	reply, explanation **tōben**

答電	reply telegram **tōden**
答訪	return visit **tōhō**
答辞	valedictory speech **tōji**
答礼	return salute, ~call **tōrei**
答謝	acknowledgement **tōsha**
答申	report, submitting a report **tōshin**
答申案	draft report **tōshin'an**
答申書	written report **tōshinsho**
贈答	exchange of gifts **zōtō**
無答責	non-liable **mutōseki**
受け答え	reply, answer, response **ukekotae**

応esponse, 469	尋nquire, 868
伺nquire, 101	聞nquire, 282
諮nquire, 865	応omply, 469

溶ilute, 758

186-A
朱carlet 珠earls, 殊pecialty for the rich girl...

木 (wooden)

朱carlet 朱ermilion

ake, SHU
scarlet, vermilion

FLIP: 2.0.b. Sort Of (stem)

朱顔 *flushed face, reddened face* **shugan**
朱筆 *cinnabar brush* **shuhitsu**
朱印 *red seal* **shuin**
⇒御朱印 *Shogun-sealed letter* **goshuin**
朱印状 *red-sealed official document* **shuinjō**
朱色 *vermilion, cinnabar* **shuiro**
朱門 *red-painted gate* **shumon**
朱肉 *vermilion inkpad* **shuniku**
朱書 *writing in red* **shusho**
朱墨 *cinnabar stick* **shusumi**
丹朱 *vermilion, cinnabar* **tanshu**
堆朱 *red lacquerware* **tsuiake**
朱塗り *red-painted* **shunuri**
朱子学 *Neo-Confucianism* **shushigaku**
朱鳥時代 *Shuchō Era (686-701)* **shuchō jidai**

紅*carlet, 175*
赤*ed colour, 261*
丹*ed colour, 78*

先*head, 478*

186-B
朱carlet 珠earls, 殊pecialty for the rich girl...

王⇔玉 (jewel)

珠earl

SHU, JU
pearl

FLIP: 7.1. Right (Sort Of)
FLIP: 6.0.a. Left (flat)

胚珠 *ovule* **haishu**
数珠 *rosary beads* **juzu**
念珠 *rosary beads* **nenju**
連珠 *five-in-a-row game* **renju**
真珠 *pearl* **shinju**
⇒模造真珠 *imitation-, artificial pearl* **mozō shinju**
珠玉 *jewel, gem* **shugyoku**
珠印 *red seal* **shuin**
珠算 *abacus calculation* **shuzan**
珠暖簾 *bead curtain* **tamanoren**
珊瑚珠 *coral beads* **sangoju**
真珠貝 *pearl oyster* **shinjugai**
真珠色 *pearlish, pearl colour* **shinjuiro**
真珠層 *mother-of-pearl* **shinjusō**
真珠湾 *Pearl Harbor, Hawaii* **shinjuwan**
真珠取り *pearl diving* **shinjutori**

宝*reasure, 92*　白*hite, 15*
財*reasury, 186*　王*ewel, 11*
貴*recious, 913*　宝*ewel, 92*

株*tocks, 130*

186-C

朱carlet 珠earls, 殊pecialty for the rich girl...

歹 (dried bones)

殊pecialty　殊nique

koto(ni), SHU
specialty, unique, distinct, extraordinary

FLIP: 7.1. Right (Sort Of)
Facing: 1.2. ☜ West (V)

文殊 wise proverb **monju**
文殊の知恵 superb wisdom **monju no chie**
殊遇 special favour, ~request **shugū**
殊功 meritorius deed **shukō**
殊勲 distinguished service **shukun**
殊勲賞 excellent service award **shukunshō**
殊恩 special favour, ~request **shuon**
殊勝 praiseworthy, admirable **shushō**
特殊 special, unique, novel **tokushu**
殊更 unintentional, by chance **kotosara**
殊の外 exceedingly, exceptionally **koto no hoka**

特pecial, 250	異ifferent, 239
違ifference, 796	別eparate, 866
差ifference, 589	栄istinction, 580

株tocks, 130

187-A

立tanding chorus 泣rying over their lost 位tatus...

立 (standing)

立tand-up　立uild

ta(tsu), ta(teru), RITSU, RYŪ
stand-up, erect, build, establish

FLIP: 1.0.a. Whole (flat)

直立 rising up, standing up **chokuritsu**
町立 town-running **chōritsu**
中立 neutral, objective, impartial **chūritsu**
独立 independence, self-governing **dokuritsu**
自立 self-governing, autonomous **jiritsu**
県立 prefecture-owned **kenritsu**
木立 grove, thicket **kodachi**
国立 state-owned **kokuritsu**
孤立 isolation, helplessness **koritsu**
立案 devise, make a plan, innovate **ritsuan**
成立 origin, founding, establishment **seiritsu**
設立 establishment, foundation **setsuritsu**
存立 existence, present & existing **sonritsu**
創立 establishment, foundation **sōritsu**
立場 standpoint, point-of-view **tachiba**
筆立て pen stand **fudetate**
顔立ち features, looks **kaodachi**
立ち見 stand & watch **tachimi**
取立て newly-caught (fish) **toritate**

役立つ useful, meritorious **yakudatsu**
道具立て preparation, arrangement **dōgudate**
独り立ち self-sustaining **hitoridachi**
組み立て assembling, structure **kumitate**
降り立つ get off (a vehicle) **oritatsu**
立ち会い in the presence of **tachiai**
立ち回り scuffle, rough-and-tumble **tachimawari**
立ち退き evacuation, eviction **tachinoki**
立ち去る leave out, omit **tachisaru**
立ち寄る drop in, drop by **tachiyoru**
焼き立て "fresh from the oven..." **yakitate**

起rise, 754
建onstruct 390

豆eans, 519

187-B

立*tanding chorus* 泣*rying over their lost* 位*tatus...*

泣*rying* 泣*eeping*

水 ⇔ 氵 (water)

FLIP: 7.0.a. Right (flat)

na(ku), KYŪ
crying, weeping, wailing, sobbing

号泣 *crying bitterly, wailing* **gōkyū**
感泣 *move to tears* **kankyū**
泣訴 *tearful pleading* **kyūso**
空泣 *fake-, crocodile tears* **soranaki**
泣き所 *weak point, weakness* **nakidokoro**
泣き顔 *weeping-, crying face* **nakigao**
泣き声 *tearful voice, sobbing* **nakigoe**
泣き言 *complaint, whimper* **nakigoto**
泣き虫 *cry baby, blubberer* **nakimushi**
泣き上戸 *sentimental drunkard* **nakijōgo**
泣き真似 *fake-, crocodile tears* **nakimane**
泣き味噌 *cry-baby* **nakimiso**
泣き叫ぶ *cry out, break into tears* **nakisakebu**
泣きっ面 *weeping-, crying face* **nakittsura**
泣き喚く *scream, cry out* **nakiwameku**
泣き笑い *tearful smile* **nakiwarai**
泣き暮らす *live in sorrow* **nakikurasu**
泣き崩れる *burst into tears* **nakikuzureru**
泣き寝入り *cry oneself to sleep* **nakineiri**

泣き濡れる *be tear-stained* **nakinureru**
泣き落とし *tearful entreaty* **nakiotoshi**
男泣き *crying male* **otokonaki**
夜泣き *baby crying at night* **yonaki**
人泣かせ *annoyance, irksome* **hitonakase**
貰い泣き *weeping in sympathy* **morainaki**
咽び泣く *sob, blubber* **musebinaku**
啜り泣く *sob, blubber* **susurinaku**
嬉し泣き *tears-of-joy* **ureshinaki**
忍び泣き *sobbing, crying* **shinobinaki**
泣き明かす *weep thru the night* **nakiakasu**

涙*rying, 541*	愁*orrows, 415*
哀*orrows, 374*	悲*orrows, 289*

沿*longside, 756*

187-C

立*tanding chorus* 泣*rying over their lost* 位*tatus...*

位*tatus* 位*anking*

人 ⇔ 亻 (person)

FLIP: 7.0.a. Right (flat)

kurai, I
status, ranking, position

地位 *rank, status* **chii**
電位 *electric potential* **den'i**
風位 *wind direction* **fūi**
学位 *university degree* **gakui**
廃位 *dethronement, deposition* **haii**
品位 *character, dignity; goods quality* **hin'i**
方位 *direction* **hōi**
本位 *principle, fundamentals* **hon'i**
位置 *position, location* **ichi**
位牌 *grave tablet* **ihai**
位相 *phase, topology* **isō**
譲位 *abdication, relinquishing* **jōi**
順位 *order, ranking* **jun'i**
各位 *everyone, each person, all* **kakui**
高位 *high status, high rank* **kōi**
皇位 *imperial throne* **kōi**
勲位 *order of merit* **kun'i**
無位 *without rank, without status* **mui**
爵位 *title of nobility* **shakui**

首位 *top, first place* **shui**
即位 *enthronement, coronation* **sokui**
水位 *water level* **suii**
体位 *physique, posture, build* **taii**
退位 *abdication, relinquishing* **taii**
単位 *academic unit, credit* **tan'i**
帝位 *imperial throne* **teii**
転位 *transposition* **ten'i**
優位 *predominance, superiority* **yūi**
在位 *reign, rule* **zaii**
位取り *place of decimal point* **kuraidori**

格*tatus, 498*	階*tairs, 129*
級*evel, 189*	段*tep, 555*
等*rade, 251*	

泣*rying, 235*

188-A

舌ongue 話peaks of 活ctivities at peak...

舌ongue

shita, ZETSU
tongue

悪舌 *spiteful tongue, foul-mouthed* **akuzetsu**
弁舌 *eloquent, articulate, oratorical* **benzetsu**
毒舌 *spiteful tongue, foul-mouthed* **dokuzetsu**
筆舌 *beyond description, ~words* **hitsuzetsu**
饒舌 *loquacious, articulate* **jōzetsu**
口舌 *empty words, false promises* **kōzetsu**
百舌 *shrike* **mozu**
猫舌 *used to cold food* **nekojita**
両舌 *double-dealing, duplicitous* **ryōzetsu**
舌長 *talkative, noisy person* **shitanaga**
舌先 *tip of the tongue* **shitasaki**
舌鼓 *smacking one's lips* **shitatsuzumi**
舌禍 *slip of tongue* **zekka**
舌根 *tongue root, back of the tongue* **zekkon**
舌鋒 *sharp tongue* **zeppō**
舌戦 *verbal warfare, word war* **zessen**
舌代 *notice, circular* **zetsudai, shitadai**
舌癌 *tongue cancer* **zetsugan**
舌状 *tongue-shaped* **zetsujō**

舌 (tongue)

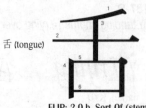

FLIP: 2.0.b. Sort Of (stem)

舌音 *lingual-, labial sound* **zetsu'on**
舌端 *tip of the tongue* **zettan**
舌頭 *tip of the tongue* **zettō**
長広舌 *loquacious, lengthy talker* **chōkōzetsu**
巻き舌 *rolling one's tongue* **makijita**
二枚舌 *double-dealing, duplicitous* **nimaijita**
舌利き *food taster* **shitakiki**
舌打ち *clicking one's tongue* **shitauchi**
舌触り *pleasant taste* **shitazawari**
三寸の舌 *loquacious, articulate* **sanzun no shita**
舌足らず *"speak like a child..."* **shitatarazu**

弁*peech, 570*	言*alking, 251*	伝*onvey, 619*
味*aste, 871*	語*alking, 780*	声*oice, 428*

告*eport, 266*

188-B

舌ongue 話peaks of 活ctivities at peak...

話peak　話erbal

hanashi, hana(su), WA
speak, speech, verbal

談話 *informal talk, conversations* **danwa**
電話 *telephone* **denwa**
童話 *fable, fairy tale, nursery story* **dōwa**
原話 *original story* **genwa**
話中 *busy talking (on the phone)* **hanashichū**
逸話 *anecdote* **itsuwa**
実話 *true story, real life story* **jitsuwa**
会話 *conversation, dialogue* **kaiwa**
懇話 *friendly talk* **konwa**
訓話 *moral story, moral lesson* **kunwa**
民話 *folk tale, folklore* **minwa**
昔話 *reminiscences, old tales* **mukashi banashi**
説話 *narration, old tale, legend* **setsuwa**
世話 *care, help, aid* **sewa**
神話 *myth, mythology* **shinwa**
手話 *sign language* **shuwa**
対話 *dialogue, one-on-one talks* **taiwa**
裏話 *inside story, untold story* **urabanashi**
話題 *topic, subject, theme* **wadai**

言 (speaking)

FLIP: 7.1. Right (Sort Of)
FLIP: 6.0.a. Left (flat)

話法 *narration, storytelling* **wahō**
話術 *conversation skills, elocution* **wajutsu**
話し上手 *sweet talker, good talker* **hanashi jōzu**
話し掛ける *tell, speak* **hanashi kakeru**
話し言葉 *spoken language, colloquial*
　hanashi kotoba
話し合い *consultation, negotiations* **hanashiai**
話し相手 *conversation partner* **hanashi aite**
例え話 *allegory, parable, fable* **tatoe banashi**
作り話 *made-up story, fabrication* **tsukuri banashi**
別れ話 *divorce-, separation talks* **wakare banashi**
笑い話 *funny story, joke, gag, jest* **warai banashi**

申*peak humble, 89*	語*alking, 780*	伝*onvey, 619*
言*alking, 251*	談*alks, 308*	声*oice, 428*

舌*ongue, 236*

188-C

舌*ongue* 話*peaks of* 活*ctivities at peak...*

水 ⟺ 氵 (water)

活*ctivity* 活*ively*

KATSU
activity, action, lively

FLIP: 7.1. Right (Sort Of)
Facing: 1.2. ☜ West (V)

敏活 *quick, prompt* **binkatsu**
部活 *school club activities, ~circles* **bukatsu**
復活 *restoration, revival* **fukkatsu**
自活 *self-supporting, independent* **jikatsu**
快活 *cheerfulness, liveliness* **kaikatsu**
活気 *vigour, spirited, elan vita* **kakki**
活況 *lively, prosperity, good times* **kakkyō**
活版 *letterpress, typography* **kappan**
活発 *brisk, lively, animated, dynamic* **kappatsu**
活殺 *life-or-be killed* **kassatsu**
活性 *active, animated, dynamic* **kassei**
活線 *live electric wire* **kassen**
活写 *graphical description* **kassha**
活動 *activities, projects* **katsudō**
活眼 *piercing look* **katsugan**
活劇 *action drama* **katsugeki**
活魚 *live fish* **katsugyo**
活人 *active person* **katsujin**
活気 *zestful, energetic* **kakki**

活路 *way out, exit route* **katsuro**
活力 *vitality, zest, vigour* **katsuryoku**
活躍 *activity, action* **katsuyaku**
活用 *practical application* **katsuyō**
生活 *living, lifestyle, livelihood* **seikatsu**
生活費 *living expenses, cost of living* **seikatsuhi**
死活 *life-or-death* **shikatsu**
活け花 *flower arranging* **ikebana**
活火山 *active volcano* **kakkazan**
活字体 *block letters, large caps* **katsujitai**
私生活 *private life, one's lifestyle* **shiseikatsu**

事*ction, 116*
動*ovement, 422*

浜*each, 490*

189-A

The 翌*ollowing day, an* 翁*ld man* 習*earned that birds of*
翼*ifferent* 翼*ings and* 羽*eathers flock together...*

羽 (feathers, wings)

翌*ollowing* 翌*ubsequent*

YOKU
following, subsequent, next, ensuing, succeeding

FLIP: 4.0.a. Bottom (flat)

翌朝 *next-, the following day* **yokuasa, yokuchō**
翌晩 *the following night* **yokuban**
翌月 *next-, the following month* **yokugetsu**
翌暁 *tomorrows day* **yokugyō**
翌日 *next-, the following day* **yokujitsu**
翌年 *next-, the following year* **yokunen, yokutoshi**
翌週 *next-, the following week* **yokushū**
翌翌日 *day after tomorrow* **yokuyokujitsu**
翌翌年 *the year after next year* **yokuyokunen**

随*ollowing, 807*
次*ext, 460*
亜*ext to, 389*

順*equence, 959*
第*[order], 102*
働*abour, 422*

羽*ings, 240*

189-B

*The 翌ollowing day, an 翁ld man 習earned that birds of
異ifferent 翼ings and 羽eathers flock together...*

翁ld man

羽 (feathers, wings)

okina, Ō
old man, patriarch, old fogey

玄翁 *bush hammer* **gennō**
漁翁 *old fisherman* **gyoō**
翁貝 *lantern* **okinagai**
老翁 *old man* **rōō**
塞翁 *mysterious, inscrutable* **saiō**
村翁 *village elder, ~wiseman* **son'ō**
翁の面 *old mans mask* **okina no men**
白頭翁 *grey haired old man* **hakutōō**
信天翁 *albatross* **shinten'ō**

Facing: 4.0. ☜☞ Apart

老lderly, 149	婆ld woman, 32
古ld, 477	仙ermit, 416
齢geing, 553	

念dea, 182

189-C

*The 翌ollowing day, an 翁ld man 習earned that birds of
異ifferent 翼ings and 羽eathers flock together...*

習earning   習ustom

羽 (feathers, wings)

nara(u), SHŪ
learning, gaining knowledge, erudition, custom

FLIP: 4.0.a. Bottom (flat)

悪習 *evil manners* **akushū**
独習 *self-study, self-learning* **dokushū**
演習 *practice, exercise* **enshū**
復習 *review, going over* **fukushū**
学習 *study, learning* **gakushū**
弊習 *evil custom* **heishū**
補習 *supplementary lesson* **hoshū**
自習 *self-learning, self-study* **jishū**
実習 *internship, apprenticeship* **jisshū**
実習生 *intern, trainee apprentice* **jisshūsei**
常習 *habit, penchant* **jōshū**
慣習 *custom, convention* **kanshū**
既習 *mastered matter* **kishū**
奇習 *strange custom* **kishū**
講習 *short course, lesson* **kōshū**
習わし *custom, practice, tradition* **narawashi**
温習 *review, rehearse* **onshū**
練習 *practice, training* **renshū**
習字 *penmanship, handwriting* **shūji**

習熟 *skill, expertise* **shūjuku**
習慣 *habit, custom, way-of-doing-things* **shūkan**
習練 *practice, drill, training* **shūren**
習作 *study, etude* **shūsaku**
習性 *habit, behaviour, attitude* **shūsei**
習得 *learning, master* **shūtoku**
習俗 *manners & customs, usage* **shūzoku**
予習 *lesson preparation, advanced study* **yoshū**
俗習 *street-smart, ways-of-the-world* **zokushū**
因習的 *conventional* **inshūteki**
習い事 *something to learn, ~master* **naraigoto**

教ducate, 385	徒isciple, 497
読eading, 260	師eacher, 483
書ritings, 116	授eaching, 539
修aster, 898	

皆veryone, 39

189-D

The 翌ollowing day, an 翁ld man 習earned that birds of 異ifferent 翼ings and 羽eathers flock together...

異*ifferent* 異*ther*

田 (cultivated field)

FLIP: 1.0.b. Whole (stem)

koto, I
different, other, else

異 variation, mutation **hen'i**
異物 alien substance **ibutsu**
異同 similarity-or-difference **idō**
異議 objection, protest **igi**
異人 different person; foreigner **ijin**
異常 unusual, extraordinary **ijō**
異状 malfunction, dysfunction **ijō**
異見 different view, ~opinion **iken**
異国 foreign country **ikoku**
異教 paganism, heathenism **ikyō**
異名 another name, nom-de-guerre **imyō**
異例 exceptional case **irei**
異論 objection, protest **iron**
異彩 conspicuousness, stark **isai**
異才 genius, prodigy **isai**
異性 opposite sex **isei**
異説 different view, another opinion **isetsu**
異心 grudge, bad blood **ishin**
異質 heterogeneous **ishitsu**

異色 unique, novel, innovative **ishoku**
異種 different kind, variety **ishu**
異臭 nasty odour, funny smell **ishū**
異端 paganism, heathenism **itan**
異存 "no objection..." **izon**
奇異 strange, weird **kii**
驚異 marvellous, surprising **kyōi**
特異 peculiar, unique **tokui**
異文化 foreign, non-Japanese culture **ibunka**
異母兄弟 half-siblings (different mothers)
　ibo kyōdai
異父兄弟 half-siblings (different fathers)
　ifu kyōdai

違*ifference, 796*　似*imilar, 472*　他*nother, 688*
差*ifference, 589*　同*imilar, 245*

塁*ampart, 597*

189-E

The 翌ollowing day, an 翁ld man 習earned that birds of 異ifferent 翼ings and 羽eathers flock together...

翼*ings*

羽 (feathers, wings)

FLIP: 4.0.b. Bottom (stem)

tsubasa, YOKU
wings

尾翼 tail of planes **biyoku**
⇒垂直尾翼 vertical stabilizer **suichoku biyoku**
鼻翼 nose wings **biyoku**
扶翼 aid, support **fuyoku**
銀翼 silver wings **ginyoku**
比翼 wings abreast **hiyoku**
比翼塚 lovers' common grave **hiyokuzuka**
補翼 assist, aid, help **hoyoku**
一翼 one wing **ichiyoku**
機翼 aircraft wing **kiyoku**
両翼 both wings **ryōyoku**
左翼 leftist; left field (baseball) **sayoku**
左翼手 leftist; left-handed **sayokushu**
左翼分子 left-wing elements **sayoku bunshi**
左翼団体 left-wing organization **sayoku dantai**
主翼 main wing (airplane) **shuyoku**
双翼 both wings/ flanks **sōyoku**
右翼 right wing, rightist **uyoku**
右翼手 right fielder (baseball) **uyokushu**

羽翼 wings; assistance **uyoku**
右翼分子 right-wing elements **uyoku bunshi**
右翼団体 right-wing organization **uyoku dantai**
翼状 wing shape **yokujō**
翼桁 spar **yokuketa**
翼賛 support, approval **yokusan**
翼翼 prudent, discreet **yokuyoku**
⇒小心翼翼 timid, cautious **shōshin yokuyoku**
有翼 with wings **yūyoku**
最左翼 ultra-leftist **saisayoku**
水平欲 horizontal shape **suiheiyoku**

羽*ings, 240*
鳥*irds, 125*
飛*light, 298*

異*ifferent, 239*

189-F

The 翌ollowing day, an 翁ld man 習earned that birds of 異ifferent 翼ings and 羽eathers flock together...

羽ings 羽eather

羽 (feathers, wings)

ha, hane, U
wings, feather

Facing: 1.2. West (V)

羽箒 feather duster **habōki, hanebōki**
羽衣 robe of feathers **hagoromo**
羽目 position **hame**
羽目板 wainscot, panel **hameita**
羽虫 leave beetle **hamushi**
羽田 haneda airport **haneda**
羽織 half-length Japanese kimono **haori**
羽音 sound of flapping wings **haoto**
羽浦 rearside of wings **haura**
合羽 raincoat **kappa**
毛羽 nap, fluff **keba**
木羽 shingles **koba**
手羽 chicken wings **teba**
羽化 grow wings **uka**
羽毛 feather, plume **umō**
羽翼 wings **uyoku**
矢羽 feathers on the arrow **yabane**
揚羽蝶 swallowtail butterfly **agehachō**
羽振り influence, sway, spell **haburi**

羽二重 habutae (italic) silk **habutae**
羽子板 battledore **hagoita**
羽飾り feather on the lapel **hanekazari**
羽撃つ fluttering wings **haneutsu**
羽抜け moulting **hanuke**
羽織る put on, wear **haoru**
星羽白 pochard **hoshibaneshiro**
三羽烏 trio, triumvirate **sanbagarasu**
千羽鶴 a thousand paper cranes **senbazuru**
羽根布団 feather quilt **hane buton**
白羽の矢 one's lucky arrow **shiraha no ya**

翼eather, 239
飛light, 298
鳥irds, 125

兆rillion, 214

190-A

梅lum cargo came by 海cean line 毎very time...

梅lum

木 (wooden)

ume, BAI
plum

Facing: 1.2. West (V)

塩梅 seasoning; "this situation..." **anbai**
青梅 unripe plum **aoume**
梅毒 syphilis **baidoku**
梅園 plum orchard **baien**
梅花 plum flower **baika**
梅林 plum grove **bairin**
梅雨 rainy season **baiu, tsuyu**
⇒菜種梅雨 early rainy season **natane tsuyu**
梅雨前線 seasonal rain front **baiu zensen**
寒梅 early rainy season **kanbai**
観梅 plum viewing **kanbai**
紅梅 plum with red blossoms **kōbai**
生梅 fresh plums **namaume**
入梅 start of rainy season **nyūbai**
白梅 white plums **shiraume**
梅畑 plum orchard **umebatake**
梅暦 plum blossoms (good luck) **umegoyomi**
梅見 plum viewing **umemi**
梅酒 plum wine **umeshu**

梅酢 plum vinegar **umezu**
梅干し pickled plum **umeboshi**
寒紅梅 winter red plum **kankōbai**
空梅雨 dry rainy season **karatsuyu**
漬け梅 pickled plum **tsukeume**

果ruit, 287   甘weet, 395
桃each, 215   酒iquor, 789
酢inegar, 723

侮espise, 711

190-B

梅*lum cargo came by* 海*cean line* 毎*very time...*

海*cean*　　海*aritime*

水⇔氵 (water)

umi, KAI
ocean, sea, marine, maritime

Facing: 1.2. ☞ West (V)

荒海　rough sea, violent waves **araumi**
沿海　coast, seashore **enkai**
氷海　frozen sea **hyōkai**
樹海　sea of trees **jukai**
海没　sinking into the sea **kaibotsu**
海外　foreign countries, overseas **kaigai**
海岸　beach, seashore, coast **kaigan**
海軍　navy, naval forces **kaigun**
海員　sailor, seaman **kaiin**
海国　island nation **kaikoku**
海況　sea-faring conditions **kaikyō**
海嶺　sunken ridge **kairei**
海運　maritime shipping **kaiun**
海洋　ocean, sea **kaiyō**
海図　navigational map **kaizu**
近海　nearby seas, coastal seas **kinkai**
公海　high seas, open seas **kōkai**
航海　navigation, sailing **kōkai**
⇒処女航海　maiden voyage **shojo kōkai**

臨海　seaside, seashore, shoreline **rinkai**
領海　territorial waters **ryōkai**
深海　deep sea **shinkai**
海亀　turtle **umigame**
青海原　blue sea **aounabara**
北海道　Hokkaido **hokkaidō**
海王星　Planet Neptune **kaiōsei**
制海権　command of the seas **seikaiken**
海の幸　sea produce, seafoods **umi no sachi**
海開き　start of ocean swim season **umibiraki**
絶海の孤島　solitary island **zekkai no kotō**

洋cean, 247	隻[ships], 50
魚ishes, 49	舟oat, 90
丸[ships], 73	漁ishing, 48

毎very, 241

190-C

梅*lum cargo came by* 海*cean line* 毎*very time...*

毎*very*

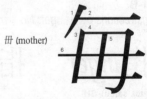

毌 (mother)

MAI
every, each

Facing: 1.0. ☞ West (W)

毎朝　every morning **maiasa**
毎晩　every evening **maiban**
毎秒　every second **maibyō**
毎度　every time, always **maido**
毎分　every minute **maifun**
毎号　every issue **maigō**
毎時　every time **maiji**
毎回　every time **maikai**
毎期　every term **maiki**
毎戸　every house **maiko**
毎日　every day, daily **mainichi**
毎日曜日　every sunday **mainichiyōbi**
毎週　every week **maishū**
毎年　every year **maitoshi, mainen**
毎月　every month **maitsuki, maigetsu**
毎夜　every night **maiyo, maiya**
毎夕　every night **maiyū**
日毎に　"every day that comes..." **higoto(ni)**
家毎に　door-to-door, house-to-house **iegoto(ni)**

門毎に　door-to-door, house-to-house
　　kadogoto(ni)
戸毎に　door-to-door, house-to-house **kogoto(ni)**
事毎に　at all times, in everything **kotogoto(ni)**
月毎に　every month **tsukigoto(ni)**
夜毎に　every night **yogoto(ni)**
毎月曜日　every Monday **maigetsuyōbi**

各very, 498	完omplete, 196
全ntire, 24	総otality, 433

海cean, 241

191-A

旨nstructions by 指inger: No 脂nimal-fat in my burger...

❶旨nstruct ❷旨ighlight ❸旨killful

日 (sunlight, daytime)

mune, uma(i), SHI
instruct; highlight, main point, purport; skillful

FLIP: 4.0.a. Bottom (flat)

❶ 勅旨 imperial instructions **chokushi**
教旨 doctrine, tenet, canons **kyōshi**
密旨 secret orders **misshi**
内旨 secret imperial orders **naishi**
聖旨 sacred-, imperial instruction **seishi**
宣旨 imperial command **senji**
旨趣 good purple **shishu**
趣旨 purpose, aim; meaning **shushi**
宗旨 religion, sect, denomination **shūshi**
宗旨変え faith-, religion conversion **shūshigae**
特旨 special considerations **tokushi**
諭旨 official suggestion **yushi**
諭旨免職 officially-hinted resignation
yushi menshoku
❷ 本旨 main point, principal objective **honshi**
論旨 point-of-contention **ronshi**
主旨 main gist, main point **shushi**
旨い汁 lion's share, the cream **umaishiru**
要旨 the point, gist **yōshi**

❸ 旨い good, skillful; delicious **honshi**
旨く point-of-contention **ronshi**
旨み attractive point **ronshi**

要ssential, 419	焦ocus, 919
導uidance, 312	訓nstruction, 959

指inger, 242

191-B

旨nstructions by 指inger: No 脂nimal-fat in my burger...

指inger 指oint

手⇔扌 (hand, manual)

yubi, sa(su), SHI
finger, point

FLIP: 7.3.a. Right Bottom (flat)

指し手 a shogi move **sashite**
五指 human five fingers **goshi**
小指 the little finger **koyubi**
屈指 foremost, outstanding **kusshi**
薬指 fourth finger, ring finger **kusuriyubi**
親指 thumb, big toe **oyayubi**
指圧 finger-pressure massage **shiatsu**
指弾 rejection, refusal, denial **shidan**
指導 leadership, guidance **shidō**
指標 index finger **shihyō**
指示 pointing out, instruction **shiji**
指揮 command, lead, direct **shiki**
指向 pointing to, alluding **shikō**
指名 designation, nomination **shimei**
指紋 fingerprint, thumbprint **shimon**
指南 instruction, teaching **shinan**
指令 order, command **shirei**
指針 compass needle **shishin**
指数 exponent; index finger **shisū**

指定 designation, specification **shitei**
指摘 pointing out, indicating **shiteki**
食指 strong appetite, deep craving **shokushi**
指笛 finger whistling **yubibue**
指先 fingertip **yubisaki**
指輪 ring, wedding ring **yubiwa**
目指す aim at, make as objective **mezasu**
名指し criticizing by name **nazashi**
突き指 sprained finger **tsukiyubi**
指相撲 finger wrestling **yubizumō**

旨ain point, 242	導uidance, 312
手and, 370	訓nstruction, 959

措easures, 282

191-C

旨*nstructions by* 指*inger: No* 脂*nimal-fat in my burger...*

肉⇔月 (flesh, body part)

脂*nimal fat*

abura, SHI
animal fat

FLIP: 7.3.a. Right Bottom (flat)

脂ぎる *become greasy, ~oily* **aburagiru**
脂ぎった *greasy, oily* **aburagitta**
脂汗 *greasy sweat* **aburaase**
脂足 *greasy feet* **aburaashi**
脂気 *greasy, oily* **aburake**
脂身 *fatty meat* **aburami**
脂性 *lardiness, greasiness* **aburashō**
脱脂 *de-greasing, grease removal* **dasshi**
脱脂乳 *low fat-, skimmed milk* **dasshi'nyū**
臙脂 *rouge* **enji**
臙脂色 *scarlet red* **enjiiro**
牛脂 *beef suet* **gyūshi**
樹脂 *plastic, resins* **jushi**
獣脂 *animal fat* **jūshi**
鯨脂 *whale oil* **kujira abura**
脂肪 *fat, grease* **shibō**
⇒皮下脂肪 *subcutaneous fat* **hika shibō**
脂肪分 *fatty-, oily content* **shibōbun**
脂肪酸 *fatty acid* **shibōsan**

脂肪油 *oil from fat* **shibōyu**
脂肪太り *obese, fat, hefty* **shibōbutori**
脂肪過多 *excessive fat* **shibō kata**
脂粉 *cosmetics, makeup* **shifun**
脂質 *fat lipids* **shishitsu**
豚脂 *lard, pork fat* **tonshi**
油脂 *oils & fats* **yushi**
脂染み *stains from oil fat* **aburajimi**
脂っ濃い *fatty-, greasy food* **aburakkoi**
脂取り紙 *cleansing paper* **aburatorigami**
樹脂加工 *plasticization* **jushi kakō**

太*bese*, 6	油*il*, 540
肪*bese*, 735	

指*inger*, 242

192-A

城*astle* 成*ecame* 盛*rosperous when the King got* 誠*eracious...*

土 (ground, soil)

城*astle*   城*ortress*

shiro, JŌ
castle, fortress, chateau, citadel

Facing: 2.2. East ☞ (V)

築城 *castle construction* **chikujō**
出城 *branch castle* **dejiro**
牙城 *fortress, inner citadel* **gajō**
城代 *castle warden* **jōdai**
城外 *outside a castle* **jōgai**
城壁 *castle walls* **jōheki**
城郭 *castle walls* **jōkaku**
城門 *castle gate* **jōmon**
城内 *within a castle* **jōnai**
城塁 *fort, fortress* **jōrui**
城塞 *fortress, citadel* **jōsai**
城市 *castle town, walled town* **jōshi**
城址 *castle ruins* **jōshi**
城主 *lord of a castle* **jōshu**
開城 *surrender of a castle* **kaijō**
金城 *impregnable castle* **kinjō**
孤城 *isolated castle* **kojō**
古城 *old fortress* **kojō**
名城 *famous castle* **meijō**

根城 *stronghold, base* **nejiro**
入城 *castle entrance* **nyūjō**
王城 *royal castle* **ōjō**
落城 *fall of a castle* **rakujō**
籠城 *siege, hole up, encamp* **rōjō**
城跡 *castle ruins* **shiroato**
登城 *go to the castle* **tojō**
山城 *mountain castle* **yamajiro**
不夜城 *"a city that doesn't sleep..."* **fuyajō**
城下町 *castle town* **jōkamachi**
大阪城 *Ōsaka castle* **ōsakajō**

殿*alace*, 522	妃*rincess*, 728
王*onarch*, 12	姫*rincess*, 542
帝*mpire*, 432	

域*egion*, 139

192-B

城astle 成ecame 盛rosperous when the King got 誠eracious...

戈 (spear)

成chieve　成ecome

na(ru), na(su), SEI, JŌ
achieve, become, forming

Facing: 2.0. East ☞ (W)

晩成 *late bloomer* **bansei**
合成 *synthesis, composite* **gōsei**
育成 *rearing, training, upbringing* **ikusei**
助成 *aid, help, subsidy* **josei**
醸成 *brewing, distilling* **jōsei**
完成 *completion, perfection* **kansei**
形成 *formation, composition* **keisei**
既成 *already existing* **kisei**
混成 *mixed, compounded* **konsei**
構成 *composition, configuration* **kōsei**
成金 *upstart, new rich* **narikin**
賛成 *approval, agreeing* **sansei**
成分 *ingredient, component* **seibun**
成長 *growth, growing years* **seichō**
成育 *growth, growing up* **seiiku**
成人 *grown up, adult* **seijin**
成果 *result, outcome, performance* **seika**
成型 *formation, pressing* **seikei**
成形 *moulding* **seikei**

成功 *success, attainment* **seikō**
成句 *idiomatic expression, figurative speech* **seiku**
成年 *adult, legal age* **seinen**
成立 *founding, establishment* **seiritsu**
成算 *prospects of success, promising* **seisan**
生成 *cremation, formation* **seisei**
成績 *achievement, accomplishment* **seiseki**
組成 *composition, structure* **sosei**
創成 *creation, Genesis* **sōsei**
大成 *complete, accomplish* **taisei**
達成 *achievement, accomplishment* **tassei**

化ecome, 192	風tyle, 894
的tyle, 696	

威uthority, 520

192-C

城astle 成ecame 盛rosperous when the King got 誠eracious...

皿 (plate)

盛rosperity　盛ffluence

saka(n), saka(ru), mo(ru), SEI, JŌ
prosperity, affluence, plenitude, largesse

FLIP: 4.0.a. Bottom (flat)

繁盛 *prosperity, flourishing* **hanjō**
旺盛 *full of energy, ~vitality, ~vigour* **ōsei**
隆盛 *well & prosperous* **ryūsei**
盛大 *enthusiastic, splendid, grandeur* **seidai**
盛代 *the good times, prosperity era* **seidai**
盛儀 *grand ceremony* **seigi**
盛業 *brisk-, bullish-, robust business* **seigyō**
盛夏 *midsummer* **seika**
盛会 *successful meeting, ~conference* **seikai**
盛観 *splendid view, ~scene* **seikan**
盛況 *successful, flourishing* **seikyō**
盛装 *gala dress, best clothes* **seisō**
盛衰 *rise & fall, vicissitudes* **seisui**
盛運 *fortune, wealth, estate* **seiun**
全盛 *"all the glory..."* **zensei**
日盛り *days primetime* **hizakari**
目盛り *gradation, scale* **memori**
娘盛り *prime of girlhood* **musumezakari**
大盛り *large food serving* **oomori**

男盛り *prime of manhood* **otokozakari**
酒盛り *drinking party, ~banquet* **sakamori**
若盛り *prime of youth* **wakazakari**
山盛り *bountiful, abundant, plentiful* **yamamori**
働き盛り *prime of working life* **hataraki zakari**
真っ盛り *at one's best* **massakari**
燃え盛る *blaze, burn brightly* **moesakaru**
盛り返す *recover, reacquire, repossess* **morikaesu**
盛り沢山 *various, diverse, assorted* **moridakusan**
御手盛り *one's advantage, benefit* **otemori**
盛り上げる *animate, enliven, energize* **moriageru**

繁rosperity, 434	豊bundance, 965
隆rosperity, 133	富ortune, 333
裕ffluence, 758	

盗obbery, 621

192-D

城*astle* 成*ecame* 盛*rosperous when the King got* 誠*eracious...*

言 (speaking)

誠*incere*   誠*eracity*   誠*ruth*

makoto, SEI
sincere, veracity, truth, authentic, genuine

FLIP: 6.0.a. Left (flat)
Facing: 2.2. ☞ East (V)

誠に *"really, honestly, frankly..."* **makoto(ni)**
忠誠 *loyalty, allegiance, fidelity* **chūsei**
忠誠心 *sense of loyalty, ~allegiance* **chūseishin**
熱誠 *earnest, diligent* **nessei**
誠忠 *loyalty, allegiance, fidelity* **seichū**
誠意 *good faith, sincerity* **seii**
⇒不誠意 *insincerity, dishonesty* **fuseii**
⇒誠心誠意 *sincere intentions* **seishin seii**
誠実 *sincere, honest, faithful* **seijitsu**
⇒不誠実 *insincerity, dishonesty* **fuseijitsu**
誠心 *sincerity, honesty* **seishin**
赤誠 *sincerity, honesty* **sekisei**
至誠 *sincerity, honesty* **shisei**
丹誠 *sincerity, honesty* **tansei**

真*incere, 487*	潔*urity, 901*
実*ruth, 121*	純*urity, 199*
廉*onest, 525*	

試*ttempt, 418*

193-A

同*imilar* 洞*averns lit with* 銅*opper lanterns...*

口 (mouth)

同*imilar*   同*like*

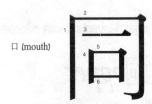

ona(ji), DŌ
similar, alike

FLIP: 1.0.b. Whole (stem)

同断 *"same as..."* **dōdan**
同封 *enclosed in a letter* **dōfu**
同意 *agreement, consent, approval* **dōi**
同意語 *synonym, same meaning* **dōigo**
同一 *same, similar, alike* **dōitsu**
同上 *same as above...* **dōjō**
同情 *sympathy, compassion* **dōjō**
同乗 *riding together* **dōjō**
同化 *assimilation, adaptation* **dōka**
同格 *same rank, ~status* **dōkaku**
同感 *sympathy, commiseration* **dōkan**
同系 *similar, relative* **dōkei**
同慶 *heartful congratulations* **dōkei**
同好 *same interests & liking* **dōkō**
同行 *accompanying, going together* **dōkō**
同姓 *same surname* **dōsei**
同士 *fellow~, colleague, comrade* **dōshi**
同定 *categorize with* **dōtei**
同点 *tie score in a game* **dōten**

同罪 *equal culpability, conspiracy* **dōzai**
合同 *combined, combination* **gōdō**
協同 *cooperation, collaboration* **kyōdō**
賛同 *agreement, consent, approval* **sandō**
同様に *"similarly, in the same context..."*
  dōyō(ni)
同国人 *compatriot, fellow citizen* **dōkokujin**
同性愛 *homosexuality, lesbianism* **dōseiai**
同窓会 *alumni association* **dōsōkai**
隣同士 *neighbours* **tonaridōshi**
男女同権 *gender-, sexual equality*
  danjo dōken
同音異義 *homonym* **dōon'igi**

似*imilar, 472*	較*ompare, 774*
違*ifference, 796*	比*ompare, 466*
異*ifferent, 239*	

向*owards, 99*

193-B
同imilar 洞averns lit with 銅opper lanterns...

水⇔氵 (water)

洞avern   洞ave

hora, DŌ
cavern, cave

FLIP: 7.0.b2. Right (stem)

雪洞 *paper lantern* **bonbori**
洞観 *insight, intuition* **dōkan**
洞見 *insight, intuition* **dōken**
洞穴 *cave, cavern, hollow* **dōketsu, horaana**
洞窟 *cave, cavern, hollow* **dōkutsu**
洞門 *cave entrance* **dōmon**
洞察 *penetration, insight* **dōsatsu**
洞察力 *sense of insight* **dōsatsuryoku**
洞視 *insight, intuition* **dōshi**
風洞 *wind tunnel* **fūdō**
空洞 *cave, cavern, hollow* **kūdō**
空洞化 *hollowing out* **kūdōka**
洞ヶ峠 *take a wait-and-see attitude* **horagatōge**
石灰洞 *limestone cave* **sekkaidō**
鐘乳洞 *limestone cave, ~cavern* **shōnyūdō**

穴ole, 4	坂lope, 733
孔ole, 684	崎lope, 270
丘lope, 106	山ountain, 172

同imilar, 245

193-C
同imilar 洞averns lit with 銅opper lanterns...

金 (metal)

銅opper

DŌ
copper

FLIP: 5.0.b. Left & Right

銅メダル *bronze medal* **dōmedaru**
銅版 *copper plate* **dōban**
銅板 *copper sheet* **dōban**
銅色 *bronze colour* **dōiro, dōshoku**
銅貨 *copper coin* **dōka**
銅器 *copper-, bronze utensil* **dōki**
銅鉱 *copper ore* **dōkō**
銅鏡 *copper mirror* **dōkyō**
銅鑼 *gong, cymbal* **dora**
銅製 *copper-made* **dōsei**
銅線 *copper wire* **dōsen**
銅銭 *copper coin* **dōsen**
銅臭 *mercenary spirit* **dōshū**
銅鐸 *bronze bell* **dōtaku**
銅山 *copper mine* **dōzan**
銅像 *bronze statue* **dōzō**
分銅 *copper weight, ~content* **fundō**
白銅 *nickel & copper alloy* **hakudō**
黄銅 *brass* **ōdō**

青銅 *bronze* **seidō**
精銅 *refined copper* **seidō**
粗銅 *black copper* **sodō**
銅婚式 *bronze wedding anniversary* **dōkonshiki**
銅相場 *copper market price* **dōsōba**
銅細工 *copperware* **dōzaiku**
黄銅鉱 *copper pyrites, chalcopyrites* **ōdōkō**
硫酸銅 *copper sulphate* **ryūsandō**
赤銅色 *brown colour* **shakudōiro**
和銅時代 *Wadō Era (708-715)* **wadō jidai**

鉛ead, 757	鉱ineral-ore, 206
鉄ron, 155	鋼teel, 975

銘recepts, 425

194-A

羊heeps by the 洋estern 洋cean, 祥ood-omen for Sebastian...

羊 (sheep)

羊heep　　羊amb

hitsuji, YŌ
sheep, lamb

FLIP: 1.0.b. Whole (stem)

牧羊 sheep raising **bokuyō**
牧羊地 sheep meadow **bokuyōchi**
郡羊 sheep flock **gunyō**
子羊 lamb **kohitsuji**
小羊 lamb **kohitsuji**
牝羊 female sheep, ewe **mehitsuji**
綿羊 sheep **menyō**
緬羊 sheep **menyō**
羊歯 fern **shida, yōshi**
山羊 mountain goat, goat **yagi**
山羊髯 goatee beard **yagihige**
羊腸 meandering, zigzag **yōchō**
羊郡 sheep flock **yōgun**
羊皮 sheep skin **yōhi**
羊皮紙 parchment **yōhishi**
羊羹 sweet jelly beans **yōkan**
羊毛 wool **yōmō**
羊毛製品 woollen goods **yōmō seihin**
羊肉 mutton **yōniku**

羊水 amniotic solution **yōsui**
羊頭 sheep's head **yōtō**
羊小屋 sheep barn **hitsujigoya**
羊飼い shepherd **hitsujikai**
子山羊 baby goat, young goat **koyagi**

飼aising, 835
畜aising, 528
養aising, 253

洋cean, 247

194-B

羊heeps by the 洋estern 洋cean, 祥ood-omen for Sebastian...

水⇔氵 (water)

❶洋estern　❷洋cean

YŌ
Western; ocean

FLIP: 7.0.b1. Right (stem)

❶西洋 Western, Occident **seiyō**
東洋 East Asia, Orient **tōyō**
洋舞 Western-style dancing **yōbu**
洋風 Western style **yōfū**
洋服 Western suit, foreign clothes **yōfuku**
洋画 foreign film, ~painting **yōga**
洋楽 Western-, European music **yōgaku**
洋銀 silver nickel **yōgin**
洋品 clothes, accessories **yōhin**
洋館 Western-style building **yōkan**
洋犬 Western dogs **yōken**
洋行 travel to Western countries **yōkō**
洋弓 Western bow **yōkyū**
洋間 Western-style room **yōma**
洋菜 Western vegetables **yōna**
洋蘭 Western orchids **yōran**
洋裁 dressmaking **yōsai**
洋式 Western style **yōshiki**
洋室 Western-style room **yōshitsu**

洋書 Western books **yōsho**
洋食 Western cuisine, continental food **yōshoku**
洋酒 Western liquors **yōshu**
洋装 Western-style clothes, foreign attire **yōsō**
洋菓子 cake, cookies, confectionery **yōgashi**

❷遠洋 open seas, high seas **enyō**
海洋 ocean, seas **kaiyō**
大洋 ocean, seas **taiyō**
洋上 at the sea, maritime **yōjō**
太平洋 Pacific Ocean, Pacific **taiheiyō**
大西洋 Atlantic Ocean, Atlantic **taiseiyō**

海cean, 241　　欧urope, 952
西estern, 18　　米merica, 77

祥ood-omen, 248

194-C

羊*heeps by the* 洋*estern* 洋*cean,* 祥*ood-omen for Sebastian...*

示⇔ネ (display, show)

❶祥*appiness* ❷祥*ood-omen*

SHŌ

happiness, felicity, joviality; foreboding, good-omen, harbinger, auspicious

FLIP: 7.0.b1. Right (stem)

❶ 発祥 *origins, beginnings* **hasshō**
発祥地 *birthplace, cradle* **hasshōchi**
清祥 *well & prosperous* **seishō**
祥月 *month of death* **shōtsuki**
祥月命日 *death anniversary* **shōtsuki meinichi**
不祥事 *scandal, shameful act* **fushōji**

喜*appiness, 965*	賀*elebration, 202*
幸*appiness, 268*	祝*elebration, 716*
慶*ejoice, 69*	

❷ 吉祥 *good omen, good signs* **kichijō, kisshō**
瑞祥 *good omen, good signs* **zuishō**
嘉祥時代 *Kashō Era (848-851)* **kashō jidai**

洋*cean, 247*

195-A

At the 寺*emple parade, a* 侍*amurai* 持*olding a* 詩*oem of*
特*pecial* 等*rade...*

寸 (measurement)

寺*emple*

tera, JI
temple

FLIP: 3.0.a. Top (flat)

尼寺 *convent, nunnery* **amadera**
仏寺 *Buddhist temple* **butsuji**
寺院 *temple, mosque* **jiin**
寺社 *temples & shrines* **jisha**
古寺 *old temple* **koji, furudera**
末寺 *branch temple* **matsuji**
社寺 *shrines & temples* **shaji**
寺守 *temple sexton* **teramori**
寺男 *temple male attendant* **teraotoko**
寺銭 *gambling fee* **terasen**
氏寺 *clan temple* **ujidera**
山寺 *mountain temple* **yamadera**
禅寺 *Zen Buddhism temple* **zendera**
菩提寺 *one's family temple* **bodaiji**
勅願寺 *temple built at imperial behest* **chokuganji**
銀閣寺 *temple in Kyōto City* **ginkakuji**
本能寺 *Honnoji temple* **honnōji**
金閣寺 *golden pavilion temple* **kinkakuji**
寺子屋 *private primary school (Edo Era)* **terakoya**

縁切り寺 *temple sanctuary for runaway wives*
  enkiridera
お寺参り *temple visit* **oteramairi**
お寺巡り *pilgrimage to famous temples*
  oterameguri

神*ivine, 712*	坊*uddhist monk, 736*
幣*hinto paper, 171*	禅*en Buddhism, 782*
仏*uddha, 683*	祈*rayer, 184*
盆*uddhist Feast, 594*	拝*rayer, 636*
僧*uddhist monk, 836*	

侍*amurai, 249*

195-B

At the 寺*emple parade, a* 侍*amurai* 持*olding a* 詩*oem of*
          特*pecial* 等*rade...*

人⇔亻 (person)

侍*amurai*　　侍*wordsman*

samurai, JI
  samurai, swordsman, attend upon

FLIP: 7.2.a. Right Top (flat)

犬侍 *disgraced samurai* **inuzamurai**
侍中 *imperial adviser* **jichū**
侍医 *palace-, court physician* **jii**
侍女 *lady-in-waiting, lady's maid* **jijo**
侍従 *chamberlain* **jijū**
侍従長 *grand chamberlain* **jijūchō**
寺講 *imperial tutor* **jikō**
寺者 *court attendant; altar boy* **jisha**
侍史 *respectfully yours; private secretary* **jishi**
近侍 *palace-, court attendant* **kinji**
内侍 *lady-in-waiting, lady's maid* **naishi**
典侍 *lady-in-waiting, lady's maid* **tenji**
若侍 *young samurai* **wakazamurai**
田舎侍 *countryside samurai* **inakazamurai**
侍堅気 *samurai spirit* **samurai katagi**

刃*lade, 75*	武*arrior, 100*
刀*lade, 353*	戦*ighting, 517*

佳*eauty, 891*

195-C

At the 寺*emple parade, a* 侍*amurai* 持*olding a* 詩*oem of*
          特*pecial* 等*rade...*

手⇔扌 (hand, manual)

持*olding*　　持*arrying*

mo(tsu), JI
  holding, carrying

FLIP: 7.2.a. Right Top (flat)

護持 *defend, uphold, preserve* **goji**
保持 *preserve, maintain* **hoji**
維持 *maintenance, restoration* **iji**
持病 *chronic illness* **jibyō**
持久 *tenacity, perseverance* **jikyū**
持久走 *long distance run* **jikyūsō**
持論 *personal theory, private hypothesis* **jiron**
持薬 *habitual medicine* **jiyaku**
持続 *lasting, continuous* **jizoku**
堅持 *holding fast, sticking* **kenji**
固持 *persistence, insistence, tenacity* **koji**
支持 *support, aid, help* **shiji**
所持 *possession, belongings* **shoji**
力持ち *strong & influential* **chikaramochi**
金持ち *rich fellow, wealthy person* **kanemochi**
気持ち *feeling, mood* **kimochi**
面持ち *look, face* **omomochi**
手持ち *at hand, holding* **temochi**
身持ち *behaviour, conduct, attitude* **mimochi**

持ち札 *"the card in the hand..."* **mochifuda**
持ち歌 *repertoire song* **mochiuta**
癇癪持ち *mercurial temper* **kanshakumochi**
持ち腐れ *useless possession* **mochigusare**
持ち運び *portable, carry-on* **mochihakobi**
持ち帰り *take-out, take home* **mochikaeri**
持ち込み *bringing over* **mochikomi**
持ち越す *carry over* **mochikosu**
持ち去る *run away with, abscond* **mochisaru**
持ち寄り *bringing together* **mochiyori**
受け持ち *taking charge* **ukemochi**
持ち合わせ *things on hand* **mochiawase**

運*ransport, 295*	蔵*torage, 565*
庫*torage, 306*	貯*torage, 967*
倉*torage, 399*	保*reserve, 552*

待*aiting, 940*

195-D

At the 寺emple parade, a 侍amurai 持olding a 詩oem of 特pecial 等rade...

言 (speaking)

詩*oetry*

SHI
poetry, poem

FLIP: 6.0.a. Left (flat)
FLIP: 7.2.a. Right Top (flat)

劇詩 *dramatic poem* **gekishi**
漢詩 *Chinese poetry* **kanshi**
詩劇 *verse-, poetic drama* **shigeki**
詩吟 *Chinese poem-reading* **shigin**
詩篇 *book of psalms* **shihen**
詩碑 *poem-inscribed monument* **shihi**
詩歌 *poetry* **shiika**
詩人 *poet* **shijin**
⇒宮廷詩人 *palace poet* **kyūtei shijin**
詩情 *poetic sentiments* **shijō**
詩句 *verse, stanza* **shiku**
詩興 *poetic inspiration* **shikyō**
詩論 *poetry theory* **shiron**
詩才 *poetic genius* **shisai**
詩作 *poem writing, ~composition* **shisaku**
詩聖 *genius poet* **shisei**
詩選 *selected poem* **shisen**
詩仙 *master poet* **shisen**
史詩 *historical poem* **shishi**

詩心 *poetic inspiration* **shishin**
詩趣 *poetry-, poetic interest* **shishu**
詩集 *collection of poems, anthology* **shishū**
詩想 *poetic thoughts, ~sentiments* **shisō**
詩的 *poetic, romantic* **shiteki**
短詩 *short poem* **tanshi**
訳詩 *translated poem* **yakushi**
田園詩 *countryside poetry* **den'enshi**
叙事詩 *epic poetry* **jojishi**
叙情詩 *lyric poetry, lyric* **jojōshi**
即興詩 *extemporaneous poem* **sokkyōshi**

歌*oem, 878*
詠*oetry, 729*
能*/Noh], 321*

詰*ompressed, 228*

195-E

At the 寺emple parade, a 侍amurai 持olding a 詩oem of 特pecial 等rade...

牛⇔牛 (cattle)

特*pecial*   特*xtra*

TOKU
special, extra, extraordinary, peculiar, unique, distinct, exceptional

FLIP: 7.2.a. Right Top (flat)
Facing: 1.2. 🡒 West (V)

特価 *bargain price, discounted price* **tokka**
特恵 *special treatment* **tokkei**
特権 *prerogative, privilege* **tokken**
特記 *special mention* **tokki**
特攻隊 *special attack forces, Kamikaze* **tokkōtai**
特訓 *special-, intensive training* **tokkun**
特許 *patent, license* **tokkyo**
特急 *express train* **tokkyū**
特級 *superior quality* **tokkyū**
特売 *special sale, bargain* **tokubai**
特別 *special, distinct, unique* **tokubetsu**
特長 *strongest point, specialty, forte* **tokuchō**
特徴 *characteristic, peculiarity* **tokuchō**
特注 *specially-ordered, customs-made* **tokuchū**
特種 *scoop, exclusive* **tokudane**
特技 *special talent, specialty, forte* **tokugi**
特配 *extra ration, ~delivery* **tokuhai**
特発 *special train* **tokuhatsu**
特報 *flash bulletin, news flash* **tokuhō**

特命 *special mission, assignment* **tokumei**
特産 *special product, delicacy* **tokusan**
特撮 *camera effects* **tokusatsu**
特製 *specially-made* **tokusei**
特選 *specially-chosen* **tokusen**
特赦 *amnesty, special pardon* **tokusha**
特待生 *student on scholarship* **tokutaisei**
特典 *advantage, edge* **tokuten**
特有 *peculiar* **tokuyū**

殊*pecialty, 234*
別*eparate, 866*

待*aiting, 940*

195-F

At the 寺*emple parade, a* 侍*amurai* 持*olding a* 詩*oem of* 特*pecial* 等*rade...*

竹 (bamboo)

rade   uch as

hito(shii), nado,TŌ
grade, level, classification, ranking; such as, as follows

FLIP: 8.0.a. Inner (flat)
Facing: 1.1. 🖝 West (H)

❶ 平等 *equality, fairness* **byōdō**
⇒ 男女平等 *gender-, sexual equality* **danjo byōdō**
中等 *middle grade* **chūtō**
減等 *down-grade* **gentō**
品等 *product grade, ~quality* **hintō**
上等 *first-class* **jōtō**
官等 *official rank* **kantō**
均等割り *per capita rate* **kintōwari**
勲等 *order of merit* **kuntō**
親等 *degree of kinship* **shintō**
等級 *grade, class, rank* **tōkyū**
一等賞 *first prize winner, top prize* **ittōshō**
劣等感 *inferiority complex* **rettōkan**
高等学校 *high school* **kōtō gakkō**
均等 *equality, parity* **kintō**
等分 *equal division* **tōbun**
等号 *equal mark* **tōgō**
等辺 *equilateral* **tōhen**
等比 *geometric* **tōhi**

等価 *equivalent* **tōka**
等量 *equal amount* **tōryō**
等式 *equality, parity* **tōshiki**
等親 *immediate relatives* **tōshin**
等質 *homogeneous* **tōshitsu**
等圧線 *isobar* **tōatsusen**
等高線 *contours* **tōkōsen**
等温線 *isotherm* **tōonsen**
❷ 彼等 *they (masculine)* **karera**
我等 *we (informal)* **warera**
彼女等 *they (feminine)* **kanojora**
それら等 *"such as those..."* **soreranado**

級*evel, 189*	階*evel, 129*
準*evel, 919*	段*tep, 555*

策*easure, 875*

196-A

言*ord of* 誉*onour earned* 信*aith for the Governor...*

言 (speaking)

言*ord*   言*alking*

koto, i(u), GEN, GON
word, talking, speak, verbal

FLIP: 1.0.a. Whole (flat)

断言 *declaration, affirmation* **dangen**
伝言 *leave a message (phone call)* **dengon**
言語 *language, speech* **gengo**
発言 *utterance, outburst* **hatsugen**
方言 *dialect, local language* **hōgen**
放言 *careless, improper remark* **hōgen**
過言 *exaggeration, overstatement* **kagon**
苦言 *candid, frank, outspoken* **kugen**
極言 *say frankly* **kyokugen**
名言 *wise proverb, famous saying* **meigen**
無言 *silence, mute (phone call)* **mugon**
宣言 *declaration, proclamation* **sengen**
進言 *advice, suggestion, proposal* **shingen**
証言 *testimony, witness* **shōgen**
多言 *speaking at length, long speech* **tagen**
他言 *revelation, leakage* **tagon**
提言 *proposal, suggestion* **teigen**
予言 *predict, foretell, foresee* **yogen**
遺言 *last will, dying wish* **yuigon**

前言 *previous remarks* **zengen**
花言葉 *flowery language, ~words* **hanakotoba**
独り言 *mutter, murmur, thinking loud* **hitorigoto**
話し言葉 *spoken language, colloquial*
  hanashikotoba
言い残す *tell, leave word* **iinokosu**
言い出す *say out, blurt out* **iidasu**
言い回し *expression, way of saying* **iimawashi**
言い渋る *hesitate to say* **iishiburu**
書き言葉 *written language, literary* **kakikotoba**
言い捨てる *say with anger, spit out* **iisuteru**
言い尽くす *say all, "empty one's chest..."*
  iitsukusu

口*outh, 458*	談*alks, 308*	弁*peech, 570*
語*alking, 780*	声*oice, 428*	

信*aith, 252*

196-B

言ord of 誉onour earned 信aith for the Governor...

言 (speaking)

誉onour   **誉**ignity

homa(re), YO
honour, dignity, acclaim

FLIP: 2.0.b. Sort Of (stem)

栄誉 honour, glory **eiyo**
毀誉 fame-or-criticism **kiyo**
毀誉褒貶 famous-or-unknown **kiyo hōhen**
名誉 honour, glory **meiyo**
名誉心 sense of honour, desiring fame **meiyoshin**
名誉職 honorary post **meiyoshoku**
名誉欲 desiring fame, vanity **meiyoyoku**
名誉教授 professor emeritus **meiyo kyōju**
名誉市民 honorary citizen **meiyo shimin**
声誉 fame, reputation **seiyo**
誉望 honour & glory **yobō**
不名誉 dishonourable, disgrace **fumeiyo**
誉め殺し praise in order to damage **hometataeru**
誉め称える admire, praise **homegoroshi**

| 栄lory, 580 | 勲xploits, 934 |
| 名ame, 425 | 誇ride, 947 |

| 賞ward, 554 |

196-C

言ord of 誉onour earned 信aith for the Governor...

人⇔亻 (person)

❶信elief   **❷信**essage

SHIN
belief, conviction, faith; message

FLIP: 7.0.a. Right (flat)

❶ 不信 distrust, non-confidence **fushin**
誤信 mistaken-, wrong belief **goshin**
背信 breach of faith, betrayal **haishin**
威信 prestige, dignity **ishin**
自信 self-confidence **jishin**
確信 conviction, firm belief **kakushin**
過信 overrate, overestimate **kashin**
軽信 gullibility, credulity **keishin**
狂信 fanaticism **kyōshin**
迷信 superstition **meishin**
盲信 blind belief, blind faith **mōshin**
信義 faith, fidelity **shingi**
信者 believer, follower, faithful **shinja**
信心 faith, devotion, piety **shinjin**
信条 principle, creed, credo **shinjō**
信金 credit union, trust fund **shinkin**
信仰 faith, belief **shinkō**
信教 religion, faith **shinkyō**
信頼 faith, belief, confidence **shinrai**

信託 trust, confidence **shintaku**
信用 faith, belief **shinyō**
半信半疑 skepticism, doubt **hanshin hangi**
返信 reply, answer by e-mail **henshin**
❷ 外信 foreign news **gaishin**
貴信 your letter (honorific) **kishin**
急信 urgent message **kyūshin**
信号 traffic signal **shingō**
信書 letter, correspondence **shinsho**
私信 private letter, ~message **shishin**
送信 sending e-mail **sōshin**

慮hought, 70	意dea, 340
考hinking, 392	想dea, 524
志ntention, 426	念dea, 182

| 言alking, 251 |

197-A

養*aising a* 良*ood* 娘*aughter lest to* 浪*rift on* 浪*aves of disaster...*

食 (food)

養*aising* 養*reeding*

yashina(u), YŌ
raising, breeding, hatchery, foster

FLIP: 3.0.a. Top (flat)

培養 *cultivation, culture* **baiyō**
栄養 *nutrition, nutrients, nourishment* **eiyō**
扶養 *family support, ~sustenance* **fuyō**
保養 *recreation, amusement* **hoyō**
孝養 *filial obligations, duties to parents* **kōyō**
休養 *recuperation, rest* **kyūyō**
給養 *supplies, provisions* **kyūyō**
療養 *getting medical care* **ryōyō**
静養 *recuperation, rest* **seiyō**
飼養 *breeding, raising* **shiyō**
修養 *self-discipline* **shūyō**
素養 *well-grounded* **soyō**
養分 *nourishment, nutrition* **yōbun**
養護 *nursing, nurse care* **yōgo**
養魚 *fish farming, fish breeding* **yōgyo**
養蜂 *raising bees* **yōhō**
養育 *upbringing, rearing, raising* **yōiku**
養女 *adopted daughter, foster child* **yōjo**
養生 *taking care of oneself* **yōjō**

養家 *foster family* **yōka**
養鶏 *poultry raising, chicken farm* **yōkei**
養毛 *hair tonic* **yōmō**
養老 *old age, senility, twilight years* **yōrō**
養蚕 *silkworm raising* **yōsan**
養成 *upbringing, rearing, raising* **yōsei**
養子 *foster-, adopted child* **yōshi**
養殖 *cultivation, raising, breeding* **yōshoku**
養豚 *piggery, hog raising* **yōton**
養父母 *foster parents, adoptive parents* **yōfubo**
目の保養 *feast for the eyes* **menohoyō**

畜*aising, 528*		教*ducate, 385*
飼*aising, 835*		授*eaching, 539*
育*pbringing, 885*		訓*nstruction, 959*

美*eautiful, 124*

197-B

養*aising a* 良*ood* 娘*aughter lest to* 浪*rift on* 浪*aves of disaster...*

艮⇔良 (good)

良*ood* 良*avourable*

yo(i), RYŌ
good, favourable, better

Facing: 2.0. East ☞ (W)

純良 *pure grade, high grade* **junryō**
改良 *improvement, reform* **kairyō**
良案 *good proposal* **ryōan**
良縁 *good match, suitable partners* **ryōen**
良否 *quality, good-or-bad* **ryōhi**
良貨 *clean & honest money* **ryōka**
良家 *good & reputable family* **ryōke**
良好 *good, OK, satisfactory* **ryōkō**
良民 *law-abiding people* **ryōmin**
良妻 *good wife* **ryōsai**
良策 *good idea, good measure* **ryōsaku**
良性 *benign, gentle* **ryōsei**
良識 *good sense* **ryōshiki**
良心 *conscience* **ryōshin**
良質 *good quality* **ryōshitsu**
良書 *good book* **ryōsho**
良種 *good quality* **ryōshu**
良薬 *good medicine* **ryōyaku**
良材 *good material* **ryōzai**

良俗 *ethics, decency standards* **ryōzoku**
優良 *superior, excellent* **yūryō**
仲良し *close friendship, in good terms* **nakayoshi**
不良品 *defective-, inferior goods* **furyōhin**
良導体 *good conductor (electricity)* **ryōdōtai**
古き良き *good old stuff* **furukiyoki**
栄養不良 *undernourishment* **eiyō furyō**
不良債権 *uncollectible debts* **furyō saiken**
品種改良 *breed improvement* **hinshu kairyō**
送り不良 *defective feeding* **okuri furyō**
消化不良 *indigestion, dyspepsia* **shōka furyō**

悦*leasant, 942*		喫*leasure, 900*
快*leasant, 699*		娯*leasure, 453*
楽*leasure, 447*		愉*leasure, 922*
歓*leasure, 667*		

食*uisine, 255*

197-C

養aising a 良ood 娘aughter lest to 浪rift on 浪aves of disaster...

女 (woman)

娘aughter　娘oung girl

musume
daughter, young girl

Facing: 2.2. East ☞ (V)

姉娘　*elder daughter* **anemusume**
妹娘　*younger daughter* **imōto musume**
生娘　*virgin, maiden* **kimusume**
小娘　*young girl, teen girl* **komusume**
孫娘　*granddaughter* **mago musume**
愛娘　*one's favourite daughter* **mana musume**
娘婿　*son-in-law* **musume muko**
娘心　*girlish innocence* **musumegokoro**
末娘　*youngest daughter* **suemusume**
一人娘　*only daughter* **hitori musume**
田舎娘　*country-, rural girl* **inaka musume**
看板娘　*show girl* **kanban musume**
小町娘　*town lass, beauty queen* **komachi musume**
娘時代　*girlhood years* **musume jidai**
娘盛り　*prime of girlhood* **musume zakari**
娘気質　*nature of a young girl* **musumekatagi**
総領娘　*eldest daughter* **sōryō musume**
箱入り娘　*overprotected girl* **hakoiri musume**
花売り娘　*flower-selling girl* **hanauri musume**

婿取り娘　*acceptance of daughter's husband*
mukotori musume

> 嬢*aughter,* 854
> 嬢*oung girl,* 854
> 嫁*aughter-in-law,* 824

> 媒*ediator,* 292

197-D

養aising a 良ood 娘aughter lest to 浪rift on 浪aves of disaster...

水⇔氵 (water)

❶浪aves　❷浪rifting

RŌ
waves, current, stream; drifting, billow, wander

Facing: 2.2. East ☞ (V)

❶風浪　*wind & waves, high seas* **fūrō**
激浪　*roaring-, raging waves* **gekirō**
波浪　*waves, high seas* **harō**
波浪注意報　*high tide warning*
　　harō chūihō
放浪癖　*wanderlust* **hōrō heki**
漂浪　*wandering* **hyōrō**
逆浪　*choppy seas* **sakanami**
津浪　*tidal wave* **tsunami**
山津浪　*landslide, mudslide* **yamatsunami**

❷浮浪　*vagrancy, vagabond* **furō**
浮浪児　*street children* **furōji**
浮浪者　*street bum, tramp, homeless* **furōsha**
放浪　*wandering, roaming* **hōrō**
浪費　*waste, extravagance* **rōhi**
浪費家　*squanderer, spendthrift* **rōhika**
浪費癖　*wasteful habit, squanderer* **rōhiguse**
浪曲　*Niniwabushi chanting* **rōkyoku**

浪人　*entrance exam flunker* **rōnin**
浪人生　*entrance exam flunker* **rōninsei**
浪浪　*unemployed, wandering* **rōrō**
流浪　*wandering, roaming* **rurō**
浪花節　*wanderer, tramp* **naniwabushi**
素浪人　*retainer with a lord* **surōnin**
浪漫主義　*romanticism, idealism* **rōman shugi**

> 嬢*aughter,* 854
> 嬢*oung girl,* 854
> 嫁*aughter-in-law,* 824

> 湯*ot-water,* 932

198-A
食ood & 飲rinks, no 飯eal on the rink..!

食oods 食uisine 食ating

食 (food)

ta(beru), ku(u), ku(rau), SHOKU, JIKI
foods, meal, cuisine, culinary, eating, refreshment

Facing: 2.0. East ☞ (W)

甘食 *sweet foodstuff* **amashoku**
米食 *rice-based meal* **beishoku**
朝食 *breakfast, morning meal* **chōshoku**
昼食 *lunch, luncheon* **chūshoku**
断食 *fasting, abstinence* **danjiki**
副食 *side dish* **fukushoku**
減食 *diet, dieting, eating less* **genshoku**
飲食 *eating & drinking* **inshoku**
常食 *staple diet, daily food* **jōshoku**
過食 *over-eating, gluttony* **kashoku**
欠食 *undernourished, malnourished* **kesshoku**
乞食 *beggar, panhandler* **kojiki**
給食 *meal service, school lunch* **kyūshoku**
日食 *solar eclipse* **nisshoku**
節食 *eating moderately* **sesshoku**
寝食 *living together* **shinshoku**
食間 *in between meals* **shokkan**
食堂 *eating hall, cafeteria* **shokudō**
食言 *breaking one's promise* **shokugen**

食事 *meal, dinner* **shokuji**
食卓 *dining table* **shokutaku**
食用 *edible* **shokuyō**
少食 *light meals* **shōshoku**
主食 *staple diet, daily food* **shushoku**
和食 *Japanese cuisine* **washoku**
洋食 *Western cuisine* **yōshoku**
衣食住 *food, clothing & shelter* **ishokujū**
固形食 *solid food* **kokeishoku**
面食い *good looks* **menkui**
食い荒らす *eating like a beast* **kuiarasu**
食べ物 *food, cuisine, meal* **tabemono**
夕食 *supper, diner* **yūshoku**

糧oodstuff, 451   炊ooking, 865
飯ooked rice, 256

食avourable, 253

198-B
食ood & 飲rinks, no 飯eal on the rink..!

飲rinking   飲everage

食 (food)

no(mu), IN
drinking, beverage

Facing: 3.0. ☞☜ Across

愛飲 *habitual drinker* **aiin**
暴飲 *excessive drinking* **bōin**
暴飲暴食 *heavy drinking & eating* **bōin bōshoku**
茶飲み *tea-drinking* **chanomi**
茶飲み友達 *bosom friend, buddy, pal*
   chanomi tomodachi
鯨飲 *drink like a fish* **geiin**
強飲 *heavy drinking* **gōin**
飲酒 *alcohol drinking, intoxicated* **inshu**
飲酒運転 *drunk driving* **inshu unten**
飲用 *drinkable-, potable water* **inyō**
丸飲み *gulping down* **marunomi**
飲み頃 *urge to drink* **nomigoro**
飲み薬 *oral medicine* **nomigusuri**
飲み干す *gulp down* **nomihosu**
飲み込み *drink-up; full comprehension* **nomikomi**
飲み口 *water tap* **nomikuchi**
飲み食い *eating & drinking* **nomikui**
飲み水 *drinkable-, potable water* **nomimizu**

飲み物 *drink, beverage, liquor* **nomimono**
飲みニケーション *pleasant talks while drinking*
   nominike-shon
飲み残り *liquor leftovers* **nominokori**
飲み代 *drinking money* **nomishiro**
飲み友達 *drinking buddy* **nomitomodachi**
飲み屋 *bar, pub, nightclub* **nomiya**
溜飲 *drinking satisfaction* **ryūin**
酒飲み *drinker, drunkard, boozer* **sakenomi**
試飲 *wine-tasting, connoisseur* **shiin**
痛飲 *heavy drinking* **tsūin**
湯飲み *teacup, cup* **yunomi**
乳飲み子 *breast-feeding* **chinomigo**

水ater, 9   酒lcohol, 789
乳ilk, 970   酔runk, 760

飽oredom, 665

198-C

食ood & 飲rinks, no 飯eal on the rink..!

❶飯eal　　❷飯ooked rice

食 (food)

meshi, HAN
meal, refreshment; cooked rice

FLIP: 7.3.b. Right Bottom (stem)

❶朝飯　breakfast, morning meal **asameshi**
晩飯　dinner, supper **banmeshi**
噴飯　utterly absurd, purely baseless **funpan**
飯場　worker's temporary eatery **hanba**
飯台　Japanese-style dining **handai**
飯盒　mess kit, utensils **hangō**
早飯　quick meal **hayameshi**
飯時　meal time **meshidoki**
飯屋　cheap eatery **meshiya**
大飯　large serving (food) **ōmeshi**
粗飯　frugal meal, cheap food **sohan**
夕飯　dinner, supper **yūhan**
残飯　food left-overs **zanpan**
冷や飯　chilled food **hiyameshi**
飯盛り　hotel maidservant **meshimori**

❷飯米　rice grown for oneself **hanmai**
飯粒　cooked rice grains **meshitsubu**
米飯　cooked rice; us rice **beihan**

御飯　boiled rice, meal **gohan**
御飯蒸　rice steamer, ~cooker **gohanmushi**
牛飯　beef & rice **gyūmeshi**
釜飯　rice cuisine on a small pot **kamameshi**
強飯　rice & red beans **kowameshi**
飯櫃　container for cooked rice **meshibitsu**
麦飯　boiled rice & barley **mugimeshi**
握り飯　rice-ball **nigirimeshi**
赤飯　steamed rice & red beans **sekihan**
炊飯器　rice cooker **suihanki**
焼き飯　fried rice **yakimeshi**

炊ooking, 865
糧oodstuff, 451
食uisine, 255

飲rink, 255

199-A

求equests to 救escue the Earth's 球phere quickly grew...

求equest　　求emand

水 ⇔ 氵 (water)

moto(meru), KYŪ
request, solicit, demand, pleading

FLIP: 2.0.b. Sort Of (stem)

希求　longing for, yearning **kikyū**
購求　purchase, buy **kōkyū**
求愛　courting, courtship **kyūai**
求道　seeking the truth, fact-finding **kyūdō**
求人　job recruitment **kyūjin**
求人難　labour shortage **kyūjinnan**
求刑　prosecution, accuser, plaintiff **kyūkei**
求婚　marriage proposal **kyūkon**
求心　centripetal **kyūshin**
求職　job hunting, looking for a job **kyūshoku**
求職者　job seeker, ~applicant **kyūshokusha**
請求　request, claim **seikyū**
請求額　amount claimed **seikyūgaku**
請求権　right of claim **seikyūken**
請求人　claimant, requesting person **seikyūnin**
請求書　bill, invoice **seikyūsho**
探求　quest, search for **tankyū**
追求　pursuit, demand **tsuikyū**
欲求　desire, wants, will **yokkyū**

欲求不満　frustration, disappointment **yokkyū fuman**
要求　requirement, demand **yōkyū**
買い求める　purchase, buy **kaimotomeru**

依equest, 355　　請equest, 791
願equest, 964　　頼equest, 562

水ater, 9

199-B

求*equests to* 救*escue the Earth's* 球*phere quickly grew...*

文 (action)

救*escue*　　救*ife-saving*

suku(u), KYŪ
rescue, life-saving, redemption, salvage

FLIP: 6.0.b. Left (stem)
FLIP: 7.1. Right (Sort Of)

救援 *relief, rescue, life-saving* **kyūen**
救援隊 *search & rescue party* **kyūentai**
救援物資 *relief supplies* **kyūen busshi**
救援活動 *search & rescue mission* **kyūen katsudō**
救護 *relief, aid, help* **kyūgo**
救護班 *search & rescue squad* **kyūgohan**
救護米 *rice for disaster victims* **kyūgomai**
救護所 *first-aid station* **kyūgosho**
救助 *rescue, relief, life-saving* **kyūjo**
⇒災害救助 *disaster assistance* **saigai kyūjo**
救助艇 *rescue boat, life boat* **kyūjotei**
救急 *emergency, crisis, life-threatening* **kyūkyū**
救急箱 *first-aid kit* **kyūkyūbako**
救急車 *ambulance, hospital van* **kyūkyūsha**
救急病院 *emergency hospital* **kyūkyū byōin**
救命 *life-saving, rescue* **kyūmei**
救命台 *lifeboat, liferaft* **kyūmeidai**
救難 *rescue, assist in an emergency* **kyūnan**

救済 *relief, aid* **kyūsai**
救済策 *relief measures, remedy* **kyūsaisaku**
救出 *rescue, relief delivery* **kyūshutsu**
救貧 *poverty alleviation* **kyūhin**
球治 *cure, remedy* **kyūji**
救国 *national salvation* **kyūkoku**
救急法 *first aid* **kyūkyūhō**
救急薬 *first aid medicine* **kyūkyūyaku**
救民 *rescued disaster victims* **kyūmin**
救助法 *life-saving, rescue* **kyūjohō**
救助船 *rescue boat, life boat* **kyūjosen**
救い米 *rice for disaster victims* **sukuimai**

援*upport, 820*	助*upport, 953*
頁*upport, 625*	擁*upport, 151*
支*upport, 201*	

枚*[sheets], 724*

199-C

求*equests to* 救*escue the Earth's* 球*phere quickly grew...*

王⇔玉 (jewel)

球*phere*　　球*lobe*

tama, KYŪ, SHU
sphere, ball, globe

FLIP: 7.1. Right (Sort Of)

地球 *earth, globe* **chikyū**
直球 *straight pitch* **chokkyū**
電球 *electric bulb* **denkyū**
眼球 *eyeball* **gankyū**
半球 *hemisphere* **hankyū**
飛球 *fly ball (baseball)* **hikyū**
血球 *corpuscle* **kekkyū**
剣球 *cup & ball game* **kendama**
好球 *good pitch* **kōkyū**
硬球 *hard ball* **kōkyū**
球団 *baseball team* **kyūdan**
球技 *ball game* **kyūgi**
球児 *baseball for children, minor league* **kyūji**
球場 *baseball stadium* **kyūjō**
球界 *baseball world* **kyūkai**
球形 *spherical shape, ~object* **kyūkei**
球菌 *coccus* **kyukin**
球根 *bulb, tuber* **kyūkon**
球面 *spherical surface* **kyūmen**

球審 *chief umpire* **kyūshin**
球体 *sphere, globe* **kyūtai**
軟球 *soft ball* **nankyū**
死球 *dead ball* **shikyū**
初球 *first pitch* **shokyū**
卓球 *table tennis, ping-pong* **takkyū**
球算 *abacus calculation* **tamazan, shuzan**
庭球 *lawn tennis* **teikyū**
野球 *baseball* **yakyū**
変化球 *curve, screwball* **henkakyū**
白血球 *white blood cells* **hakkekyu**
制球力 *ball control (baseball)* **seikyūryoku**
赤血球 *red corpuscle* **sekkekkyū**
選球眼 *batting eye* **senkyūgan**

玉*phere, 11*	円*ircle, 24*
丸*ound, 73*	輪*ircle, 786*

求*equest, 256*

200-A

君ounger 君ulers in the 郡ounty shepherd the 群erds...

口 (mouth)

FLIP: 4.0.a. Bottom (flat)

❶君[younger]　❷君uler

kimi, KUN
[younger]; ruler

❶尼君　nun (polite) **amagimi**
姉君　elder sister (polite) **anegimi**
細君　one's wife **saikun**
諸君　"ladies & gentlemen, my friends..." **shokun**
幼君　child lord **yōkun**
❷主君　lord, master **shukun**
若君　young lord **wakagimi**
遊君　courtesan **yūkun**
君が代　Japanese national anthem **kimigayo**
暴君　tyrant, despot **bōkun**
亡君　one's late lord **bōkun**
忠君　loyalty to the ruler **chūkun**
夫君　husband **fukun**
厳君　"your esteemed father..." **genkun**
母君　mother (honourific) **hahagimi**
姫君　princess **himegimi**
人君　sovereign ruler **jinkun**
仁君　benevolent ruler **jinkun**
国君　sovereign ruler **kokkun**

君臨　reigning, ruling **kunrin**
君子　honorable-, virtuous person **kunshi**
君臣　sovereign & subject **kunshin**
君主　monarch, sovereign, ruler **kunshu**
⇒専制君主　despot, tyrant **sensei kunshu**
君主国　monarchism **kunshukoku**
君主政体　monarchist government **kunshu seitai**
名君　enlightened ruler **meikun**
明君　brilliant ruler **meikun**
大君　His Majesty **ōkimi**

若ittle, 276	姉lder sister, 114
親ntimate, 669	妹ounger sister, 114
愛ove, 593	嬢oung girl, 854
弟ounger brother, 102	懇ordial, 164

若oung, 276

200-B

君ounger 君ulers in the 郡ounty shepherd the 群erds...

阝⇔阜 (village-right)

郡ounty

GUN
county

郡部　rural districts **gunbu**
郡長　district chief **gunchō**
郡県　counties & prefectures **gunken**
郡内　within the county **gunnai**
郡役所　county hall, county office **gunyakusho**

FLIP: 6.2. Left Bottom
Facing: 2.2. East ☞ (V)

邦ountry, 694	字istrict, 346
村illage, 690	里ometown, 321
郷ometown, 452	

群lock, 259

200-C

君*ounger* 君*ulers in the* 郡*ounty shepherd the* 群*erds...*

羊 (sheep)

群*lock*　　　群*erd*

mu(re), mura, mu(reru), GUN
flock, herd

FLIP: 7.0.b1. Right (stem)

抜群 *outstanding, prominent* **batsugun**	群雄 *group of warlords* **gunyū**
群星 *constellation, cluster of stars* **gunboshi**	群像 *flock, herd, column* **gunzō**
群青 *sea blue, navy blue* **gunjō**	魚群 *school of fishes* **gyogun**
群起 *occurring together* **gunki**	群雲 *gathering clouds* **murakumo**
群居 *gregarious, sociable, amiable* **gunkyo**	群竹 *bamboo trees* **muratake**
群盲 *blind masses* **gunmō**	群れ *group, flock, herd* **mure**
群発 *cluster of explosion (earthquake)* **gunpatsu**	大群 *large herd* **taigun**
群発地震 *series of earthquakes* **gunpatsu jishin**	群馬県 *Gunma Prefecture* **gunma-ken**
群落 *community, colony* **gunraku**	群千鳥 *flock of ply over birds* **murachidori**
群生 *growing crowds* **gunsei**	流星群 *cluster of stars* **ryūseigun**
群臣 *bunch of officials, VIP delegation* **gunshin**	症候群 *syndrome, symptoms* **shōkōgun**
群小 *minor, insignificant* **gunshō**	
群小国家 *lesser powers* **gunshō kokka**	
群衆 *crowd, throng* **gunshū**	衆*ultitude, 766*　　団*roup, 345*
群集 *crowd, mass* **gunshū**	集*ather, 50*　　　組*roup, 138*
群集心理 *mass-, mob psychology* **gunshū shinri**	
群体 *coral colony* **guntai**	詳*etails, 945*
群島 *archipelago, cluster of islands* **guntō**	
群盗 *bunch of thieves* **guntō**	

201-A

売*elling* 続*ontinues to* 読*eaders looking for job news...*

士 (samurai, warrior)

売*elling*　　売*erchandise*

u(ru), u(reru), BAI
selling, exchange for money, marketing, merchandise, peddle

FLIP: 1.0.b. Whole (stem)

売買 *sale, selling* **baibai**	発売中 *"now on sale..."* **hatsubaichū**
売文 *literary hacking, pliagriasm* **baibun**	前売り *advance sales* **maeuri**
売国 *treason, betrayal of one's country* **baikoku**	身売り *selling oneself to bondage* **miuri**
売却 *panic-, underselling, fire sale* **baikyaku**	売り場 *counter, sales office* **uriba**
売名 *self-advertisement* **baimei**	売り子 *salesman, marketing agent* **uriko**
売春 *prostitution* **baishun**	量り売り *selling by measurement* **hakariuri**
売店 *kiosk, booth, stall* **baiten**	卸し売り *wholesale, bulk sale* **oroshiuri**
売約 *"sold already..."* **baiyaku**	捨て売り *sacrifice-, fire sale* **suteuri**
分売 *selling separately* **bunbai**	売り上げ *sales volume* **uriage**
直売 *direct sale (no middleman)* **chokubai**	売り出し *bargain-, clearance sale* **uridashi**
販売 *selling, sale* **hanbai**	
公売 *public auction, ~bidding* **kōbai**	販*elling, 137*　　買*urchase, 516*
競売 *auction, bidding* **kyōbai**	市*arket, 304*　　金*oney, 25*
密売 *blackmarketting* **mitsubai**	購*urchase, 714*　　財*inance, 186*
廉売 *bargain sale, selling cheap* **renbai**	
商売 *trade, business* **shōbai**	赤*ed colour, 261*
即売 *on the spot selling* **sokubai**	
特売 *bargain sale* **tokubai**	
売地 *"lot for sale..."* **urichi**	

201-B

売elling 続ontinues to 読eaders looking for job news...

続ontinue　　　　　続ollow

糸 (thread, continuity)

続 FLIP: 7.0.b2. Right (stem)

tsuzu(ku), tsuzu(keru), ZOKU
continue, follow, lasting, on-going

断続	intermittent, on & off **danzoku**
永続	permanence, perpetuity, eternity **eizoku**
持続	continuing, serial **jizoku**
継続	continuation, renewal **keizoku**
勤続	continuous service **kinzoku**
連続	consecutive, continuing, serial **renzoku**
接続	direct connexion, continuity **setsuzoku**
存続	continuity, lasting **sonzoku**
続き	resumption, continuation **tsuzuki**
続き柄	personal relationship **tsuzukigara**
続き物	serial story, sequel **tsuzukimono**
続開	resumption, continuation **zokkai**
続刊	serial publication **zokkan**
続行	continuation, resumption **zokkō**
続映	serial film showing **zokuei**
続演	serial performance **zokuen**
続編	sequel, continuation **zokuhen**
続発	rapid occurrence, succession **zokuhatsu**
続報	follow-up report **zokuhō**

続落	continued decline **zokuraku**
続出	succession, continuity **zokushutsu**
続騰	continued price increase **zokutō**
続続	successive, repeated **zokuzoku**
血続き	blood relationship **chitsuzuki**
陸続き	one after another **rikutsuzuki**
手続き	procedures, preparation **tetsuzuki**
航続時間	airborne time, air mileage **kōzoku jikan**
引き続く	continuous, continuing **hikitsuzuku**
遺産相続	property inheritance **isan sōzoku**
勝ち続ける	continuous winnings **kachitsuzukeru**

継ontinuity, 958	翌ollowing, 237
連onfederacy, 305	結onnect, 227
随ollowing, 807	絡onnect, 826

統overn, 885

201-C

売elling 続ontinues to 読eaders looking for job news...

読eading

言 (speaking)

読 FLIP: 5.0.b. Left & Right

yo(mu), DOKU, TOKU, TŌ
reading

愛読	love to read, voracious reading **aidoku**
代読	reading on behalf of another **daidoku**
読了	finish reading **dokuryō**
読者	reader, subscriber **dokusha**
読書	book reading **dokusho**
閲読	book perusal, skimming thru **etsudoku**
拝読	solemn reading **haidoku**
判読	deciphering, making-out **handoku**
熟読	intensive reading, perusal **jukudoku**
回読	taking turns in reading **kaidoku**
購読	subscription, circulation **kōdoku**
句読	punctuation **kutō**
味読	devour-, voracious reading **midoku**
輪読	reading alternately **rindoku**
訳読	reading & translation **yakudoku**
棒読み	monotonous reading **bōyomi**
秒読み	countdown **byōyomi**
読解力	reading comprehension **dokkairyoku**
票読み	vote counting, ~tabulation **hyōyomi**

訓読み	Japanese Kanji pronunciation **kunyomi**
読み物	reading materials **yomimono**
走り読み	quick reading **hashiriyomi**
盗み読み	opening someone's letter **nusumiyomi**
読み返す	read again, re-read **yomikaesu**
読み書き	reading & writing **yomikaki**
読み込み	reading **yomikomi**
読み取り	reading comprehension **yomitori**
読み落とす	miss, overlook **yomiotosu**

本ook, 461	文iteracy, 558
冊[books], 20	字etter, 346
書ritings, 116	刊ublication, 687

説xplanation, 943

202-A

On 赤ed 嚇hreat, let's 赦orgive & forget...

赤ed colour

赤 (red)

aka(i), aka(rameru), SEKI, SHAKU
red-colour

FLIP: 2.0.b. Sort Of (stem)

赤ちゃん	baby, infant, toddler	**akachan**
赤っぽい	reddish	**akappoi**
赤らめる	blush	**akarameru**
赤鼻	red nose	**akabana**
赤札	clearance goods; sold goods	**akafuda**
赤貝	ark shell	**akagai**
赤恥	humiliation, disgrace, shame	**akahaji**
赤旗	red flag	**akahata**
赤字	loss, deficit	**akaji**
⇒貿易赤字	trade deficit	**bōeki akaji**
⇒累積赤字	running deficit	**ruiseki akaji**
赤目	blood-shot eyes	**akame**
赤錆	metal rust	**akasabi**
赤線	red-light district	**akasen**
赤卵	red egg, brown egg	**akatamago**
赤土	red soil	**akatsuchi**
赤道	earth's equator	**sekidō**
赤軍	Japanese Red Army	**sekigun**
赤飯	red beans rice	**sekkekkyū**

赤貧	extreme poverty	**sekihin**
赤面	blushing with shame	**sekimen**
赤痢	dysentery	**sekiri**
赤黒い	dark-red	**akaguroi**
赤ん坊	baby, infant, toddler	**akanbō**
赤蜻蛉	red dragonfly	**akatonbo**
真っ赤	deep-red, crimson	**makka**
赤外線	infra-red rays	**sekigaisen**
赤十字	Red Cross	**sekijūji**
赤裸々	stark, naked reality	**sekirara**
赤血球	red corpuscles	**sekkekkyū**
赤坂宮殿	Akasaka Imperial Palace	
	akasaka kyūden	

青lue colour, 115	朱carlet, 233
紅carlet, 175	

売elling, 259

202-B

On 赤ed 嚇hreat, let's 赦orgive & forget...

嚇enace   嚇hreat

口 (mouth)

odo(su), odo(kasu), KAKU
menace, threat, intimidate, terror

FLIP: 7.0.b2. Right (stem)

威嚇	threat, intimidation, bluff	**ikaku**
威嚇的	threatening, menacing	**ikakuteki**
威嚇射撃	warning shot	**ikaku shageki**
嚇怒	fury, rage, indignation	**kakudo**
赫赫	glorious, bright	**kakukaku**
脅嚇	threat, intimidation	**kyōkaku**
恐嚇	threat, intimidation	**kyōkaku**

脅hreaten, 577	驚care, 330
威hreat, 520	怖cary, 209
虞hreat, 889	恐cary, 906
恐enace, 906	

隷ervant, 880

202-C

On 赤ed 嚇hreat, let's 赦orgive & forget...

赤 (red)

赦orgive   赦ardon

SHA
forgive, pardon, absolution, amnesty

FLIP: 6.0.b. Left (stem)
Facing: 3.0. ☞ ☜ Across

恩赦 amnesty, pardon, parole **onsha**
赦免 pardon, remission **shamen**
赦免状 letter of pardon **shamenjō**
大赦 general amnesty, ~pardon **taisha**
特赦 special pardon, amnesty **tokusha**
容赦 pardon, tolerance, overlooking **yōsha**
容赦ない merciless, unsparing, heartless **yōshanai**

寛eniency, 308	恩indness, 862
許ermit, 180	謝pology, 876
忘orget, 34	

教ducate, 385

203-A

系ineage to enlarge when 孫randchildren are 係n-charge...

糸 (thread, continuity)

系

系ineage   系ystem

KEI
lineage, system

Facing: 2.0. East ☞ (W)

母系 maternal side, maternity **bokei**
傍系 collateral, subsidiary **bōkei**
直系 direct descendant **chokkei**
男系 male lineage **dankei**
同系 affiliated, associated **dōkei**
父系 paternal side, paternity **fukei**
一系 single-family kinship **ikkei**
女系 female lineage **jokei**
純系 pure lineage **junkei**
家系 family line, lineage, kinship **kakei**
家系図 family tree, family roots **kakeizu**
系譜 genealogy **keifu**
系列 affiliation **keiretsu**
系列会社 subsidiary, affiliated company
　　　　 keiretsu gaisha
系統 system **keitō**
⇒神経系統 nervous system **shinkei keitō**
系統樹 family tree **keitōju**
系統的 systematic, methodical **keitōteki**

系図 genealogy, lineage, family tree **keizu**
系図学 genealogy **keizugaku**
山系 mountain ranges **sankei**
庶系 illegitimate lineage **shokei**
体系 system **taikei**
大系 compendium of ~ **taikei**
銀河系 galactic system, galaxy **gingakei**
日系人 Japanese born & raised overseas **nikkeijin**
消化系 digestive system **shōkakei**
体系化 systematisation **taikeika**
太陽系 solar system **taiyōkei**
二成文系 binary system **nisei bunkei**

将uture, 521	血lood, 20
祖ncestor, 953	縁inship, 675
係elative, 263	

糸hread, 375

203-B

系*ineage to enlarge when* 孫*randchildren are* 係*n-charge...*

人⇔亻 (person)

❶係*elative* ❷係*n charge*

kaka(ru), kaka(ri), KEI
relative, connect; in-charge, clerk

Facing: 4.0. ⇆ **Apart**

❶関係 *relationship, connexion* **kankei**
⇒無関係 *unrelated, no connexion* **mukankei**
⇒力関係 *power relationship* **chikara kankei**
⇒需給関係 *supply & demand relation* **jukyū kankei**
⇒雇用関係 *employment relationship* **koyō kankei**
⇒肉体関係 *sexual relations* **nikutai kankei**
⇒相互関係 *mutual relationship* **sōgo kankei**
⇒相関関係 *correlation, interrelation* **sōkan kankei**
⇒友好関係 *friendly relations (nations)* **yūkō kankei**
係累 *family ties, kinship* **keirui**
係留 *anchoring, mooring, berthing* **keiryū**
係船 *moored ship* **keisen**
係争 *dispute, law suit, court case* **keisō**
係数 *math co-efficient* **keisū**
係属 *relationship, connexion* **keizoku**
連係 *connexion, affiliation* **renkei**
係り *person in-charge* **kakari**
❷⇒教育係り *teacher, faculty* **kyōiku gakari**
⇒飼育係 *animal keeper, breeder* **shiiku gakari**

⇒操車係 *train dispatcher* **sōsha gakari**
⇒校正係 *proof-reader* **kōsei gakari**
⇒会計係 *accountant, treasurer* **kaikei gakari**
⇒案内係 *usher, usherette, escort* **annai gakari**
⇒帳簿係 *accountant, bookkeeper* **chōbogakari**
⇒道具係 *stagehand* **dōgu gakari**
⇒風紀係 *vice squad* **fūkigakari**
係長 *chief clerk, head clerk* **kakarichō**
係員 *attendant, clerk, person in-charge* **kakariin**
係官 *officer in-charge* **kakarikan**

系*ineage, 262*	縁*elationship, 675*
祖*ncestor, 953*	血*lood, 20*

孫*randchild, 263*

203-C

系*ineage to enlarge when* 孫*randchildren are* 係*n-charge...*

子 (child)

孫*randchild* 孫*escendant*

mago, SON
grandchild, descendant

Facing: 4.0. ⇆ **Apart**

愛孫 *beloved grandchild* **aison**
嫡孫 *eldest son of one's eldest son* **chakuson**
外孫 *grandchild of one's daughter* **gaison, sotomago**
玄孫 *great-great grandchild* **genson, yashago**
初孫 *first grandchild* **hatsumago**
曾孫 *great-great grandchild* **himago, sōson**
児孫 *descendants, children & grandchildren* **jison**
皇孫 *imperial grandchild* **kōson**
孫子 *descendants, children & grandchildren* **magoko**
孫娘 *granddaughter* **magomusume**
末孫 *posterity, progeny, legacy* **masson**
王孫 *royal grandchild* **ōson**
子孫 *descendant, offspring, scion* **shison**
天孫 *divine descendants* **tenson**
内孫 *child of one's heir* **uchimago, naison**
皇太孫 *emperor's eldest grandson* **kōtaison**
孫引き *quoting second-hand, hearsay* **magobiki**
孫弟子 *disciples of one's disciples* **magodeshi**
孫息子 *grandson* **magomusuko**

孫の手 *back scratcher* **magonote**
子子孫孫 *distant relatives* **shishi sonson**

係*elative, 263*	稚*hildren, 776*
系*ineage, 262*	子*hildren, 456*
祖*ncestor, 953*	児*hildren, 464*
将*uture, 521*	童*hildren, 564*

係*lerk, 263*

204-A

By 宵arly evening, 硝alt-peter's fake 肖esemblance
消xtinguished at once...

宀 (cover, lid)

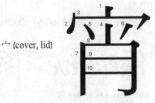

宵arly evening

yoi, SHŌ
early evening

今宵	tonight, this evening **koyoi**
春宵	spring evening **shunshō**
終宵	all night long **shūshō**
徹宵	all night long **tesshō**
宵宮	festival eve **yoimiya**
宵寝	sleeping early **yoine**
宵月	evening moon **yoitsuki**
宵闇	evening dusk, twilight **yoiyami**
宵の口	early evening **yoi no kuchi**
宵越し	leftovers from last night **yoigoshi**
宵祭り	festival eve **yoimatsuri**
宵っ張り	night owl, staying up all night **yoippari**
宵の明星	evening star, venus **yoi no myōjō**

FLIP: 1.0.b. Whole (stem)

早arly, 373	晩ightfall, 413
遅ardy, 944	夜ightfall, 508
夕ightfall, 187	

消xtinguish, 265

204-B

By 宵arly evening, 硝alt-peter's fake 肖esemblance
消xtinguished at once...

石 (stone)

硝alt-peter   硝iter

SHŌ
salt-peter, niter

煙硝	powder smoke **enshō**
硝子	glass **garasu**
⇒色硝子	coloured glass **irogarasu**
⇒磨り硝子	frosted glass **surigarasu**
硝安	ammonium nitrate **shōan**
硝煙	gunpowder smoke **shōen**
硝化	nitrification **shōka**
硝酸	nitric acid **shōsan**
⇒希硝酸	dilute nitric acid **kishōsan**
硝酸塩	nitrate **shōsan'en**
硝酸銀	silver nitrate **shōsangin**
硝石	nitre, saltpetre **shōseki**
硝薬	gunpowder **shōyaku**

FLIP: 7.0.b2. Right (stem)

塩alt, 621	
酸cid, 764	

確onfirm, 804

204-C

By 宵*arly evening,* 硝*alt-peter's fake* 肖*esemblance*
　　消*xtinguished at once...*

肉⇔月 (flesh, body part)

肖*esemble*　　肖*odel*

ayaka(ru), SHŌ
　resemble, replica, model, look-alike

FLIP: 1.0.b. Whole (stem)

不肖 *ungrateful-, unfilial child* **fushō**
肖像 *portrait* **shōzō**
肖像権 *portrait rights* **shōzōken**
肖像画家 *portrait artist* **shōzō gaka**
肖り者 *lucky guy, lucky duck* **ayakarimono**
肖像画 *portrait* **shōzōga**

似*imilar, 472*	異*ifferent, 239*
同*imilar, 245*	較*ompare, 774*
違*ifference, 796*	比*ompare, 466*

尚*espect, 99*

204-D

By 宵*arly evening,* 硝*alt-peter's fake* 肖*esemblance*
　　消*xtinguished at once...*

水⇔氵 (water)

消

消*elete*　　　消*xtinguish*

ke(su); ki(eru), SHŌ
　delete, extinguish, consume, spending, disappear, erasure, cross-out, cancel

FLIP: 7.0.b2. Right (stem)

解消 *cancellation, invalidation* **kaishō**
消印 *postmark, post-dated* **keshiin**
抹消 *erasure, crossing off* **masshō**
消防 *fire fighting, ~extinguishing* **shōbō**
消防士 *fireman, fire fighter* **shōbōshi**
消長 *rise & fall, vicissitudes* **shōchō**
消毒 *anti-septic, disinfectant* **shōdoku**
消費 *consumption, using, availing* **shōhi**
消費者 *consumer, end-user* **shōhisha**
消費財 *consumer goods* **shōhizai**
消費税 *consumption tax, sales tax* **shōhizei**
消化 *digestion, consumption* **shōka**
消火 *fire extinguishing, ~fighting* **shōka**
消却 *erasure, crossing off, deletion* **shōkyaku**
消滅 *becoming extinct, disappearing* **shōmetsu**
消耗 *consumption, using, availing* **shōmō**
消耗品 *expendable items* **shōmōhin**
消音 *silencer, muffler* **shōon**
消散 *evaporation, vanishing* **shōsan**

消息 *news, information, whereabouts* **shōsoku**
消灯 *turning off lights* **shōtō**
消然 *dispirited, dejected, withdrawn* **shōzen**
帳消し *cancellation, writing off (debts)* **chōkeshi**
毒消し *antidote, counter-actant* **dokukeshi**
不消化 *indigestion, dyspepsia* **fushōka**
消しゴム *rubber eraser* **keshigomu**
消し炭 *burned-out charcoals* **keshizumi**
消極的 *negative, passive* **shōkyokuteki**
打ち消し *denial, negation* **uchikeshi**
吹き消す *blow out* **fukikesu**
消え去る *disappear, vanish* **kiesaru**
取り消す *cancellation, call-off* **torikesu**

絶*radicate, 403*	外*emove, 188*	停*top, 393*
廃*bolish, 368*	脱*emove, 941*	
抹*ross-out, 13*	止*erminate, 192*	

泊*leep-over, 742*

205-A

告*eported news:* 酷*ruel drugs mass* 造*roduced...*

口 (mouth)

告*eport* 告*nnounce*

tsu(geru), KOKU
report, announce, convey, disclose, make known, notify

FLIP: 2.0.b. Sort Of (stem)

忠告 *advice, counsel* **chūkoku**
布告 *proclamation, declaration* **fukoku**
⇒宣戦布告 *declaration of war* **sensen fukoku**
原告 *plaintiff, accuser, complainant* **genkoku**
被告 *defendant, accused* **hikoku**
報告 *report, notice* **hōkoku**
⇒調査報告 *inquiry report* **chōsa hōkoku**
上告 *court appeal* **jōkoku**
戒告 *warning, reprimand, censure* **kaikoku**
勧告 *advice, recommendation* **kankoku**
警告 *warning, caution* **keikoku**
謹告 *"respectfully submitted..."* **kinkoku**
抗告 *protest, complaint* **kōkoku**
広告 *advertisement, classified ads* **kōkoku**
⇒募集広告 *subscription advertisement*
　　boshū kōkoku
公告 *official notice, public announcement* **kōkoku**
告知 *notification, announcement* **kokuchi**
告白 *confession, admission of guilt* **kokuhaku**

告発 *complaint, grievance* **kokuhatsu**
告辞 *message, speech, address* **kokuji**
告訴 *indictment, accusation* **kokuso**
訓告 *reprimand, censure, rebuke* **kunkoku**
急告 *urgent report, flash news* **kyūkoku**
密告 *betrayal, secret report* **mikkoku**
論告 *conclusive-, final argument* **ronkoku**
催告 *notification, notice* **saikoku**
宣告 *sentence, judgement* **senkoku**
申告 *report, declaration, deposition* **shinkoku**
通告 *notification, announcement* **tsūkoku**
予告 *previous announcement* **yokoku**

伝*onvey, 619*	報*eport, 733*
告*eport, 266*	逓*onvey, 304*

舌*ongue, 236*

205-B

告*eported news:* 酷*ruel drugs mass* 造*roduced...*

酉 (liquor)

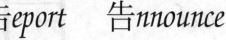

酷*ruelty* 酷*rutality*

hido(i), KOKU
brutality, cruelty, ruthless, savagery, inhuman, severe, atrocity

FLIP: 6.0.a. Left (flat)

酷い *severe, cruel, harsh* **hidoi**
⇒手酷い *harsh, cruel, severe* **tehidoi**
酷い目 *bitter experience, cruel episode* **hidoime**
過酷 *oppressive, severe, cruel* **kakoku**
苛酷 *severe, cruel, stern* **kakoku**
酷寒 *severe winter* **kokkan**
酷刑 *severe punishment* **kokkei**
酷遇 *mistreatment, abuse* **kokugū**
酷薄 *cruel, brutal, cold-hearted* **kokuhaku**
酷評 *brutal-, harsh criticism* **kokuhyō**
酷似 *close resemblance* **kokuji**
酷熱 *intense heat, torrid heat* **kokunetsu**
酷烈 *vigorous, intense* **kokuretsu**
酷吏 *exacting court official* **kokuri**
酷使 *rough handling, ~usage* **kokushi**
酷暑 *intense heat, torrid heat* **kokusho**
酷税 *excessive taxation* **kokuzei**
冷酷 *cruelty, barbaric, cold-blooded* **reikoku**
残酷 *cruel, brutal, heartless* **zankoku**

虐*yranny, 870*	烈*ierce, 585*
激*ierce, 170*	拷*orture, 392*
猛*ierce, 657*	

酪*airy, 670*

205-C

告*eported news:* 酷*ruel drugs mass* 造*roduced...*

辶 (transport)

造*roduce*　　造*anufacture*

FLIP: 7.1. Right (Sort Of)

tsuku(ru), ZŌ
produce, manufacture

築造 *building, construction* **chikuzō**
鋳造 *metal casting, founding* **chūzō**
偽造 *fake, forgery, fabrication, phoney* **gizō**
変造 *alteration, changing* **henzō**
人造 *artificial, man-made* **jinzō**
醸造 *brewing, distillation* **jōzō**
改造 *remodelling, reorganization* **kaizō**
⇒内閣改造 *Cabinet re-shuffle* **naikaku kaizō**
構造 *structure, composition, organization* **kōzō**
模造 *imitation, fake, phoney, fabrication* **mozō**
乱造 *shoddy manufacture* **ranzō**
製造 *manufacture, production* **seizō**
新造 *newly-built* **shinzō**
創造 *Genesis, creation* **sōzō**
⇒天地創造 *Genesis, creation* **tenchi sōzō**
造営 *building, construction* **zōei**
造園 *landscape gardening* **zōen**
造語 *coined word, word contraction* **zōgo**
造反 *rebellion, resistance, opposition* **zōhan**

造幣 *coin minting* **zōhei**
造花 *artificial flower, plastic flower* **zōka**
造形 *moulding, casting* **zōkei**
造血 *blood-making, haematosis* **zōketsu**
造作 *fixtures, fittings, furnishings* **zōsa**
⇒無造作 *with ease; simplistic, artless* **muzōsa**
造成 *land & housing development* **zōsei**
造成地 *land-cleared for housing* **zōseichi**
造船 *shipbuilding, ship construction* **zōsen**
荷造り *packing, packaging* **nizukuri**
造り酒屋 *sake brewery* **tsukurizakaya**

材*aterials*, 186	品*roducts*, 901
作*roduce*, 724	匠*rtisan*, 106
産*roduce*, 883	工*raft*, 176

速*uick*, 502

206-A

達*lural* 幸*appiness* 執*arried-out,* 達*eaches the highest bout...*

辶 (transport)

❶達*each*　　❷達*[plural]*

FLIP: 3.0.a. Top (flat)

TATSU, TACHI
reach, attain; [plural]

❶ 調達 *procurement, supplies* **chōtatsu**
達磨 *Dharma doll* **daruma**
伝達 *transmittal, relaying (message)* **dentatsu**
栄達 *successful life* **eitatsu**
配達 *delivery, shipment* **haitatsu**
発達 *development, growth* **hattatsu**
示達 *instructions, directions* **jitatsu**
上達 *achieving progress* **jōtatsu**
熟達 *mastery, proficiency* **jukutatsu**
闊達 *magnanimous, generous* **kattatsu**
先達 *master, leader* **sendatsu**
速達 *special-, express delivery* **sokutatsu**
送達 *delivery, shipment* **sōtatsu**
達観 *philosophical view* **takkan**
達見 *foresight, far-sightedness* **takken**
達筆 *clear handwriting* **tappitsu**
達成 *achievement, accomplishment* **tassei**
達者 *proficient, in good health* **tassha**
達文 *clear sentences* **tatsubun**

達眼 *eclectic, broad-minded; foresight* **tatsugan**
達意 *lucid, clear, obvious* **tatsui**
達人 *master, expert* **tatsujin**
友達 *friend, buddy* **tomodachi**
到達 *arrival, reaching, landing, delivery* **tōtatsu**
通達 *official notice, ~bulletin* **tsūtatsu**
御用達 *purveyor to the government* **goyōtashi**
飲み友達 *drinking buddy* **nomitomodachi**
練達の士 *expert, professional* **rentatsu no shi**
❷ 人達 *persons, people* **hitotachi**
私達 *"we" (formal)* **watashitachi**

及*each*, 190
両*oth*, 567
普*ommon*, 455

幸*appiness*, 268

206-B

達lural 幸appiness 執arried-out, 達eaches the highest bout...

干 (drying)

FLIP: 1.0.b. Whole (stem)

幸appiness　幸lissful

saiwa(i), shiawa(se), sachi, KŌ
happiness, blissful, felicity, fortune, joviality

不幸 *misfortune, tragedy* **fukō**
⇒幸不幸 *happiness-or-misery* **kōfukō**
⇒最高の不幸 *tragedy of tragedies* **saikō no fukō**
行幸 *imperial visit* **gyōkō**
薄幸 *ill fortune, unhappiness* **hakkō**
巡幸 *imperial tour* **junkō**
還幸 *return of the emperor* **kankō**
幸便 *favourable opportunity* **kōbin**
幸福 *happiness, fortune* **kōfuku**
幸甚 *"be happily obliged..."* **kōjin**
幸運 *good fortune, ~luck* **kōun**
幸運児 *child of fortune* **kōunji**
御幸 *royalty attendance* **miyuki**
臨幸 *visit by the emperor* **rinkō**
幸先 *omen, foreboding, premonition* **saisaki**
遷幸 *emperor's leaving the capital* **senkō**
潜幸 *emperor's secret visit* **senkō**
至幸 *supreme bliss* **shikō**
多幸 *happiness, blessings* **takō**

射幸心 *spirit of speculation* **shakōshin**
海の幸 *sea products, seafoods* **uminosachi**
山の幸 *land products, farm produce* **yamanosachi**
勿怪の幸い *stroke of good luck* **mokke no saiwai**

喜*appiness, 965*	賀*elebration, 202*
祥*appiness, 248*	祝*elebration, 716*
慶*ejoice, 69*	

辛*picy, 377*	南*outhern, 414*

206-C

達lural 幸appiness 執arried-out, 達eaches the highest bout...

土 (ground, soil)

FLIP: 6.0.b. Left (stem)

❶執arry-out　❷執rasp

to(ru), SHITSU, SHŪ
carry-out, execute; seize, clinch, clutches, grasp, glutches

❶執行 *execution, enforcement* **shikkō**
執行部 *executive branch* **shikkōbu**
執行権 *executive authority* **shikkōken**
執行吏 *bailiff, court official* **shikkōri**
執行命令 *execution order* **shikkō meirei**
執行猶予 *stay of execution* **shikkō yūyo**
執務 *job performance* **shitsumu**
執り成し *intercession, interjection* **torinashi**
執り成す *intercede, mediate, interject* **torinasu**
執り行う *hold* **toriokonau**
死刑執行 *death execution* **shikei shikkō**
遺言執行者 *last will executor* **yuigon shikkōsha**

❷愛執 *attachment, fondness* **aishū**
我執 *egocentrism, egoistic* **gashū**
偏執 *bigotry, obstinacy* **henshū**
確執 *discord, rift* **kakushitsu**
固執 *adherence, persistence* **koshū, koshitsu**
妄執 *infatuation, obsession* **mōshū**

執権 *regent, executor* **shikken**
執筆 *handwriting, penmanship* **shippitsu**
執筆者 *writer, contributor* **shippitsusha**
執政 *administration, administrator* **shissei**
執事 *steward, butler* **shitsuji**
執拗 *obstinate, persistent, pushy* **shitsuyō**
執刀 *performance of an operation* **shittō**
執着 *persistence, tenacity, diligence* **shūchaku**
執着心 *sense of belonging* **shūchakushin**
執念 *persistence, tenacity, diligence* **shūnen**
執念深い *tenacious; vindictive* **shūnenbukai**
執心 *devotion, attachment, infatuation* **shūshin**

貫*arry out, 532*	握*rasp, 427*
行*erform, 79*	掌*rasp, 614*
致*arry-out, 381*	

報*eport, 733*

207-A

奇*trange* & 奇*urious goat* 寄*pproaching Park* 崎*lope...*

大 (grand)

奇*urious*   奇*trange*

mezura(shii), KI
curious, strange, unusual

FLIP: 3.0.b. Top (stem)

珍奇	*novel & curious*	**chinki**
偏奇	*eccentricity, idiosyncrasy*	**henki**
怪奇	*mystery, enigma*	**kaiki**
奇病	*rare disease*	**kibyō**
奇知	*extraordinary wisdom*	**kichi**
奇談	*strange curiosity*	**kidan**
奇縁	*strange coincidence*	**kien**
奇遇	*unexpected-, chance meeting*	**kigū**
奇癖	*eccentricity, odd habit*	**kiheki**
奇異	*queer, strange, odd, weird*	**kii**
奇人	*eccentric, obstinate*	**kijin**
奇術	*magic, jugglery*	**kijutsu**
奇遇	*odd-or-even numbers*	**kijū**
奇怪	*mysterious, bizarre, eerie*	**kikai**
奇行	*eccentricity, idiosyncrasy*	**kikō**
奇妙	*strange, odd, queer*	**kimyō**
奇麗	*beautiful, pretty; clean*	**kirei**
奇才	*exceptional ability*	**kisai**
奇策	*clever scheme, brilliant plan*	**kisaku**

奇声	*queer voice*	**kisei**
奇跡	*miracle, wonder*	**kiseki**
奇勝	*beautiful scenery*	**kishō**
奇手	*surprise move*	**kishu**
奇襲	*surprise-, sudden attack*	**kishū**
奇数	*odd numbers*	**kisū**
奇態	*strange, odd, curious*	**kitai**
奇天烈	*strange, funny*	**kiteretsu**
好奇心	*curiosity, inquisiteness*	**kōkishin**
猟奇心	*strange-, bizarre curiosity*	**ryōkishin**
難問奇問	*tricky question*	**nanmon kimon**

珍*are*, 720
少*carce*, 459

寄*pproach*, 269

207-B

奇*trange* & 奇*urious goat* 寄*pproaching Park* 崎*lope...*

宀 (cover, lid)

寄*pproach*   寄*ontribution*

yo(ru), yo(seru), KI
approach, contribution, proximity, draw near

FLIP: 3.0.b. Top (stem)

寄付	*contribution, donation*	**kifu**
寄金	*cash donation*	**kikin**
寄留	*temporary stay*	**kiryū**
寄生	*parasitism, dependency*	**kisei**
寄信	*sending a letter*	**kishin**
奇書	*published contribution*	**kisho**
寄食	*parasitic lifestyle*	**kishoku**
寄宿	*lodging, boarding*	**kishuku**
寄託	*deposition, bailment*	**kitaku**
寄与	*academic-, university bulletin*	**kiyo**
寄贈	*donation, contribution, offering*	**kizō**
近寄る	*approach, come near*	**chikayoru**
幅寄せ	*loop guide*	**habayose**
片寄る	*concentrate on one side*	**katayoru**
耳寄り	*good news, glad tidings*	**mimiyori**
身寄り	*relatives; reliable person*	**miyori**
最寄り	*nearby, nearest, closely*	**moyori**
年寄り	*old person, senior citizen*	**toshiyori**
寄り道	*dropping in, dropping by*	**yorimichi**

寄り合い	*businessmen's gathering*	**yoriai**
寄り集まる	*gather, assemble*	**yoriatsumaru**
寄り掛かる	*rely on, lean*	**yorikakaru**
歩み寄り	*compromise, concession*	**ayumiyori**
言い寄る	*court, woo, win over*	**iiyoru**
駆け寄る	*run up*	**kakeyoru**
持ち寄り	*bringing food together*	**mochiyori**
忍び寄る	*creep up, draw near*	**shinobiyoru**
擦り寄る	*draw close, edge up*	**suriyoru**
立ち寄る	*drop by, drop in*	**tachiyoru**
呼び寄せる	*campaign call*	**yobiyoseru**
思いも寄らない	*"not even in my dream..."*	
	omoi mo yoranai	
寄席	*vaudeville theater*	**yose**
寄せ集め	*odds & ends*	**yoseatsume**

近*earby*, 184   接*ontact* 587

奇*urious*, 269

207-C

奇 *trange* & 奇 *urious goat* 寄 *pproaching Park* 崎 *lope...*

山 (mountain)

崎 *lope*　　　崎 *ills*

saki, KI
slope, hills, promontory

州崎　*sand spit* **suzaki**
尼崎市　*Amagasaki City, Hyōgo Pref.* **amagasaki-shi**
川崎市　*Kawasaki City, Kanagawa Pref.* **kawasaki-shi**
宮崎県　*Miyazaki Prefecture* **miyazaki-ken**
宮崎市　*Miyazaki city, Miyazaki Pref.* **miyazaki-shi**
長崎県　*Nagasaki Prefecture* **nagasaki-ken**
長崎市　*Nagasaki City, Nagasaki Pref.* **nagasaki-shi**
岡崎市　*Okazaki City, Aichi Prefecture* **okazaki-shi**
高崎市　*Takazaki City, Gunma Prefecture* **takazaki-shi**

FLIP: 6.0.a. Left (flat)

丘 *lope, 106*	登 *limb, 437*
坂 *lope, 733*	滑 *lide, 412*
山 *ountain, 172*	

奇 *urious, 269*

208-A

苗 *aplings* & *a black* 猫 *at* 描 *ketched on the doormat*

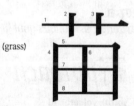

⺾ (grass)

苗 *aplings*　　　苗 *prout*

nae, nawa, BYŌ
saplings, sprout

苗圃　*seedbed* **byōho**
育苗　*seedling culture* **ikubyō**
苗字　*last-, family name, surname* **myōji**
苗床　*nursery, seedbed* **naedoko**
苗木　*sapling, seedlings* **naegi**
苗水　*water irrigation for rice saplings* **nawamizu**
苗代　*rice nursery* **nawashiro**
早苗　*rice sprouts* **sanae**
種苗　*seeds & saplings* **shubyō**
痘苗　*vaccine, anti-bacterial, anti-septic* **tōbyō**
苗畔作　*lucky seedlings* **naehansaku**
杉の苗　*cedar saplings* **sugi no nae**

FLIP: 1.0.a. Whole (flat)

栽 *aplings, 803*	種 *eedling, 430*
芽 *prout, 57*	耕 *ultivate, 655*

笛 *lute, 630*

208-B

苗*aplings & a black* 猫*at* 描*ketched on the doormat...*

犬⇔犭 (dog; beast)

猫*at* 猫*eline*

FLIP: 7.0.a. Right (flat)

neko, BYŌ
cat, feline

愛猫 *pet cat* **aibyō**
秒猫 *very small* **byōneko**
子猫 *kitten, little cat* **koneko**
斑猫 *tiger beetle* **madaraneko**
猫足 *carved leg* **nekoashi**
猫車 *wheelbarrow* **nekoguruma**
猫舌 *used to cold food* **nekojita**
猫耳 *stinky ears, foul odour ears* **nekomimi**
猫柳 *pussy willow* **nekoyanagi**
猫背 *round shoulders* **nekoze**
牡猫 *tomcat* **osuneko**
虎猫 *tiger cat, tabby cat* **toraneko**
海猫 *black-tailed gull* **umineko**
山猫 *wild cat, lynx* **yamaneko**
化け猫 *goblin cat* **bakeneko**
どら猫 *stray cat, homeless cat* **doraneko**
飼い猫 *pet cat* **kaineko**
猫被り *fake modesty, hypocrisy* **nekokaburi**
猫目石 *cats eyes* **nekomeishi**

野良猫 *stray cat, homeless cat* **noraneko**
大山猫 *lynx, wild cat* **ooyamaneko**
捨て猫 *stray cat, homeless cat* **suteneko**
猫なで声 *cat voice, coaxing voice* **nekonadegoe**
猫いらず *rat poison* **nekoirazu**

犬*og, 7*
飼*aising, 835*
家*ouse, 909*

猟*unting, 657*

208-C

苗*aplings & a black* 猫*at* 描*ketched on the doormat...*

手⇔扌 (hand, manual)

描*ketch* 描*rawing*

FLIP: 7.0.a. Right (flat)

ega(ku), BYŌ
sketch, drawing, illustration, depict

描画 *drawing, sketching* **byōga**
描法 *painting skills* **byōhō**
描写 *depiction, drawing* **byōsha**
描出 *depiction, portrayal* **byōshutsu**
白描 *plain sketch* **hakubyō**
線描 *line drawing* **senbyō**
素描 *rough sketch* **sobyō**
寸描 *short sketch* **sunbyō**
点描 *drawing, sketching* **tenbyō**
絵描き *painter, artist* **ekaki**
手描き *hand painting skills* **tegaki**
描き眉 *painted eyebrows* **kakimayu**
描き出す *portray, depict* **egakidasu**
実物描写 *model drawing* **jitsubutsu byōsha**
思い描く *mental image* **omoiegaku**
性格描写 *character portrayal* **seikakubyōsha**

絵*rawing, 143* 撮*hotograph, 423*
図*rawing, 47* 複*opy, 830*
芸*rts, 619* 写*opy, 349*

猫*at, 271*

209-A

Pedestrians 頻requently 歩alking, 頻requently 渉rossing...

頻requent　　頻ften

頁 (large shell, page)

sukobu(ru), HIN
frequent, often, always, constant, incessant

FLIP: 7.0.b2. Right (stem)

頻度 *frequency* **hindo**
頻度数 *frequency* **hindosū**
頻尿 *frequent urination* **hinnyō**
頻繁 *frequent, incessant* **hinpan**
頻発 *frequent occurrence* **hinpatsu**
頻頻 *frequently, often* **hinpin**
頻死 *one's dying moments* **hinshi**
頻出 *occurring frequently* **hinshutsu**
頻数 *frequency, number of times* **hinsū**
降り頻る *fall steadily* **furishikiru**

恒lways, 741	度imes, 91
珍are, 720	回otate, 458

傾ncline, 833

209-B

Pedestrians 頻requently 歩alking, 頻requently 渉rossing...

❶歩alking　❷歩rogress

止 (stopping)

aru(ku), ayu(mu), HO, BU, FU
walking, strolling; progress, stride

Facing: 4.0. 〓〓 Apart

❶牛歩 *snail-paced walking* **gyūho**
歩調 *step, pace* **hochō**
歩道 *sidewalk, pavement* **hodō**
歩幅 *step, pace* **hohaba**
歩兵 *infantry, foot soldier* **hohei**
歩行 *walk, going on foot* **hokō**
放浪 *roaming, pacing* **hōrō**
歩哨 *sentry, sentinel* **hoshō**
歩測 *pacing* **hosoku**
歩数 *number of footsteps* **hosū**
巨歩 *leap, giant step* **kyoho**
競歩 *walking contest* **kyōho**
漫歩 *park strolling* **manpo**
散歩 *taking a walk, going for a stroll* **sanpo**
速歩 *fast-, brisk walking* **sokuho**
徒歩 *walking, strolling* **toho**
第一歩 *first step, one big leap* **daiippo**
横歩き *walking sideways* **yokoaruki**
練り歩く *parade, march* **neriaruku**

渡り歩く *change, move, wander* **watariaruku**
歩き回る *walk about, walk around* **arukimawaru**
歩き通す *walk thru* **arukitoosu**

❷歩合 *rate, percentage, commission* **buai**
歩合給 *percentage pay* **buaikyū**
日歩 *daily loan interest* **hibu**
譲歩 *concession, compromise* **jōho**
進歩 *progress, advance* **shinpo**
初歩 *rudiments, elements* **shoho**
退歩 *retrogression, deterioration* **taiho**
歩み寄り *compromise, concession* **ayumiyori**

脚egs, 387	踏tep on, 672
展rogress, 522	進rogress, 51
段tep, 555	往ome & go, 749

渉ross-over, 273

209-C

Pedestrians 頻*requently* 歩*alking,* 頻*requently* 渉*rossing...*

水⇔氵 (water)

渉*ross-over*　　渉*raverse*

SHŌ
cross-over, traverse, have relations

Facing: 4.0. 〰️〰️ Apart

跋渉 *going thru extensively* **basshō**
干渉 *interference, intervention* **kanshō**
交渉 *negotiation, bargaining* **kōshō**
⇒婚前交渉 *pre-marital sex, fornication*
　　konzen kōshō
渉外 *public relations, publicity* **shōgai**
渉猟 *extensive reading, ~searching* **shōryō**
渡渉 *wading ashore* **toshō**
没交渉 *unrelated, no bearing* **botsu kōshō**
不干渉 *non-intervention, neutrality* **fukanshō**
無干渉 *non-intervention* **mukanshō**
渉禽類 *wading birds* **shōkin rui**

渡*ross-over, 33*	訪*isit, 737*
談*onverse, 308*	旅*ravel, 650*

歩*alk, 272*

210-A

Indian 長*hief* 張*tretches to relax his* 長*ong and* 脹*wollen biceps...*

長 (long)

❶長*ong*　　❷長*hief*

naga(i), CHŌ
long; chief, boss, leader

Facing: 2.0. East ☞ (W)

❶長円 *oval, oblong* **chōen**
長寿 *long life, longevity* **chōju**
長欠 *lengthy absence* **chōketsu**
長期 *long-term* **chōki**
長音 *prolonged sound* **chōon**
延長 *extension, postponement* **enchō**
波長 *wavelength* **hachō**
冗長 *wordy, verbose, redundant* **jōchō**
長雨 *long spell of rain, continuous rainfall* **nagaame**
長尻 *overstaying one's welcome* **nagajiri**
長屋 *tenement houses* **nagaya**
最長 *the longest* **saichō**
身長 *height, body length* **shinchō**
伸長 *expansion, extension* **shinchō**
縦長 *oblong, oval* **tatenaga**
長引く *be prolonged, drag on* **nagabiku**
長い間 *long time, many years* **nagaiaida**
八百長 *rigged contest, fixed game* **yaochō**
秋の夜長 *long nights of autumn* **aki no yonaga**

❷部長 *director, division chief* **buchō**
長官 *chief, director-general* **chōkan**
学長 *university president* **gakuchō**
議長 *presiding chairperson* **gichō**
院長 *chief physician, head doctor* **inchō**
課長 *section chief* **kachō**
校長 *school principal, school master* **kōchō**
局長 *bureau director, postmaster* **kyokuchō**
霊長 *spiritual lord* **reichō**
首長 *head, chief* **shuchō**
理事長 *university chancellor* **rijichō**
億万長者 *billionaire, very rich* **okumanchōja**
長野県 *Nagano Prefecture* **nagano-ken**

永*ternal, 10*	首*ead, 311*
久*ternal, 379*	頭*ead, 832*
細*lender, 138*	統*overn, 885*

表*hart, 378*

210-B

Indian 長*hief* 張*tretches to relax his* 長*ong and* 脹*wollen biceps...*

弓 (archery bow)

張*tretch* 張*xert*

ha(ru), CHŌ
stretch, exert, spread, strain

Facing: 4.0. 🠔🠖 Apart

膨張 *swelling, bulging* **bōchō** *925 - bulge*
張力 *tension, stress* **chōryoku**
怒張 *over swelling, overbulging* **dochō**
拡張 *expansion, extension* **kakuchō** *拡 - 205 - expand*
緊張 *strain, tension, stress* **kinchō** *緊 - 595 - tight*
誇張 *exaggeration, overstatement* **kochō** *947 - boastful*
伸張 *expansion, elongation* **shinchō** *伸 713*
出張 *official travel, business trip* **shucchō**
主張 *stress, emphasize* **shuchō**
張本人 *ringleader, gang boss* **chōhonnin**
頑張る *exert best efforts* **ganbaru**
骨張る *obstinacy, hard-headed* **honebaru**
威張る *arrogant, haughty, boastful* **ibaru**
息張る *panting, grasping for air* **ikibaru**
気張る *exert oneself* **kibaru**
見張り *lookout, watchman* **mihari**
縄張り *territory, sphere-of-influence* **nawabari**
筋張る *serious, sinewy* **sujibaru**
矢張り *"just as I thought..."* **yahari, yappari**

欲張り *greedy, avaricious, covetous* **yokubari**
出っ張る *protrude, project* **depparu**
張り合い *competition, contest* **hariai**
張り出す *put up, project* **haridasu**
張り切る *full of energy, vigorous* **harikiru**
張り込み *stakeout, outstretch* **harikomi**
上っ張り *smock, overalls* **uwappari**
張り替える *paper over, re-upholster* **harikaeru**
張り巡らす *stretch around* **harimegurasu**
張り付ける *stick, attach, paste on* **haritsukeru**
張り詰める *tense, strain* **haritsumeru**

伸*tretch, 713*	力*trength, 351*
努*fforts, 44*	勢*igour, 153*
勉*fforts, 527*	精*igour, 792*

帳*egistry, 641*

210-C

Indian 長*hief* 張*tretches to relax his* 長*ong and* 脹*wollen biceps...*

肉⇔月 (flesh, body part)

脹*welling* 脹*ulge*

fuku(ramu), fuku(reru), CHŌ
swelling, bulge, bloated

Facing: 4.0. 🠔🠖 Apart

膨脹 *swelling, expansion, bloating* **bōchō**
脹面 *sullen look, pouty face* **fukutsura**
火脹れ *burn blisters* **hibukure**
下脹れ *swelling on the lower part* **shimobukure**
水脹れ *blisters* **mizubukure**
腫脹 *swelling, boil* **shuchō**

膨*welling, 925*	巨*iant, 206*
大*arge, 7*	超*xceed, 664*
広*arge, 205*	

帳*egistry, 641*

211-A

Policemen 奉ffered with large 棒tick & high 俸alary to fight burglary...

dore   ffering

大 (grand)

tatematsu(ru), HŌ, BU
adore, esteem; offering, dedicate, oblation

FLIP: 1.0.b. Whole (stem)

❶奉行 *feudal judge, ~magistrate* **bugyō**
供奉 *accompanying the emperor* **gubu**
奉加 *shrine donation, ~offering* **hōga**
奉加帳 *list of subscription* **hōgachō**
奉迎 *"welcome to the imperial family..."* **hōgei**
奉拝 *worship, praying* **hōhai**
奉幣 *white paper strips in a Shintō shrine* **hōhei**
捧持 *holding up, bearing with, enduring* **hōji**
奉還 *imperial restoration* **hōkan**
⇒大政奉還 *restoration of emperor rule* **taisei bōkan**
奉祝 *celebration to the imperial family* **hōshuku**
奉呈 *presenting a scroll to the emperor* **hōtei**
奉答 *reply to the emperor* **hōtō**
❷奉献 *offering, dedication* **hōken**
奉公 *public duty, ~obligation* **hōkō**
⇒只奉公 *working for free* **tadabōkō**
⇒丁稚奉公 *apprehenticeship* **decchi bōkō**
⇒滅私奉公 *unselfish patriotism* **messhi bōkō**
⇒年期奉公 *apprehenticeship* **nenki bōkō**

奉公人 *servant, attendant, minder* **hōkōnin**
奉納 *dedication, offering* **hōnō**
奉納額 *Shintō offering tablet* **hōnōgaku**
奉仕 *service, volunteer work* **hōshi**
奉仕事業 *public welfare work* **hōshi jigyō**
奉仕価格 *bargain price* **hōshi kakaku**
奉書 *thick Japanese paper* **hōsho**
奉職 *government service* **hōshoku**
奉灯 *dedicated lantern* **hōtō**
遵奉 *observance, commemoration* **junpō**
信奉 *keeping faith* **shinpō**

仕*ervice, 9*	呈*ffer, 618*
勤*ervice, 962*	催*ponsor, 416*
務*ervice, 454*	聖*acred, 617*

奏*usic play, 579*

211-B

Policemen 奉ffered with large 棒tick & high 俸alary to fight burglary...

棒tick   棒ole

木 (wooden)

sasage, BŌ
stick, pole, rod

FLIP: 7.0.b1. Right (stem)

棒グラフ *bar graph* **bōgurafu**
相棒 *partner, accomplice* **aibō**
筬棒 *absurd, preposterous* **berabō**
棒紅 *lipstick* **bōbeni**
棒縞 *vertical stripes* **bōjima**
棒状 *cylindrical shape* **bōjō**
棒術 *stick fighting* **bōjutsu**
棒線 *straight line* **bōsen**
棒球 *easy pitch* **bōtama**
泥棒 *burglar, thief, robber* **dorobō**
金棒 *metal rod* **kanabō**
片棒 *involvement, participation* **katabō**
警棒 *night stick* **keibō**
棍棒 *cudgel, club* **konbō**
綿棒 *cotton swab* **menbō**
麺棒 *rolling pin for making noodles* **menbō**
乳棒 *pestle* **nyūbō**
先棒 *front palanquin bearer* **sakibō**
心棒 *axle, shaft* **shinbō**

鉄棒 *iron rod* **tetsubō**
痛棒 *heavy censure, ~reprimand* **tsūbō**
飴ん棒 *candy stick* **amenbō**
編み棒 *knitting needle, ~pin* **amibō**
棒暗記 *rote memorization* **bōanki**
棒立ち *standing erect, ~upright* **bōdachi**
棒読み *monotonous reading* **bōyomi**
延べ棒 *bar, ingot* **nobebō**
用心棒 *bodyguard, escort* **yōjinbō**
棒高跳び *pole jump, pole vault* **bōtakatobi**
玉突き棒 *cue* **tamatsukibō**

木*ood, 461*	林*oods, 526*
材*oods, 186*	細*lender, 138*

俸*alary, 276*

211-C

Policemen 俸ffered with large 棒tick & high 俸alary to fight burglary...

人⇔亻 (person)

俸*alary* 　俸*emuneration*

HŌ
salary, remuneration, pay check

罰俸 *salary suspension (punishment)* **bappō**
減俸 *salary deduction, pay cut* **genpō**
現俸 *present salary* **genpō**
号俸 *pay-, salary level* **gōhō**
俸給 *salary, wage* **hōkyū**
俸給日 *payday, salary day* **hōkyūbi**
奉米 *rice payment in lieu of salary* **hōmai**
本俸 *basic salary* **honpō**
俸禄 *retainer's salary* **hōroku**
加俸 *additional allowance, extra stipend* **kahō**
⇒年功加俸 *long service pay* **nenkō kahō**
年俸 *annual income, ~salary* **nenpō**
増俸 *salary increase* **zōhō**

FLIP: 7.0.b1. Right (stem)

賃*alary, 145*	務*ervice, 454*
納*ayment, 296*	勤*ervice, 962*
払*ayment, 682*	仕*ervice, 9*
料*ayment 194*	働*abour, 422*

棒*tick, 275*

212-A

若oungsters' deal: parental 諾onsent not to 匿onceal...

艹 (grass)

❶若*oung* 　❷若*ittle*

waka(i); mo(shikuwa), JAKU, NYAKU
young, youthful; little

FLIP: 4.0.a. Bottom (flat)
Facing: 2.1. East ☞ (H)

❶若ぶる *act young* **wakaburu**
瞠若 *astonished, ~flabbergasted, ~baffled* **dōjaku**
若輩 *young fellow* **jakuhai**
若年 *younger years* **jakunen**
自若 *self-possessed, self-absorbed* **jijaku**
老若 *young & old* **rōnyaku**
若葉 *young leaves* **wakaba**
若鳥 *young bird, ~chicken* **wakadori**
若気 *youthful enthusiasm* **wakage**
若木 *sapling, young tree* **wakagi**
若君 *young prince, ~lord* **wakagimi**
若草 *young grass* **wakakusa**
若芽 *young bud, shoot, sprout* **wakame**
若布 *seaweeds* **wakame**
若緑 *fresh greens* **wakamidori**
若者 *youth, youngster* **wakamono**
若菜 *young greens* **wakana**
若鷺 *pond smelt* **wakasagi**
若手 *young member* **wakate**

若湯 *one's first hot bath in the new year* **wakayu**
若僧 *youngster, stripling, brat* **wakazō**
若人 *youth, young person* **wakōdo**
若返る *rejuvenate, reinvigorate* **wakagaeru**
若禿げ *premature balding* **wakahage**
若い衆 *young men* **wakaishū**
若死に *early death, die young* **wakaji(ni)**
若向き *youth-oriented* **wakamuki**
若白髪 *premature grey hair* **wakashiraga**
若作り *youthfully-dressed* **wakazukuri**

❷若干 *"a little, rather..."* **jakkan**

児*hild, 464*	子*hild, 456*
稚*hild, 776*	童*hild, 564*
幼*hildhood, 88*	

苦*nguish, 477*

212--B

若*oungsters' deal: parental* 諾*onsent not to* 匿*onceal...*

言 (speaking)

諾*onsent*　諾*pproval*

DAKU
consent, approval, concur

FLIP: 6.0.a. Left (flat)
FLIP: 7.2.b. Right Top (stem)

諾諾 *"yes, yes..."* **dakudaku**
諾否 *accepted-or-not* **dakuhi**
受諾 *acceptance, consent* **judaku**
快諾 *immediate-, ready consent* **kaidaku**
許諾 *consent, assent* **kyodaku**
黙諾 *tacit consent, acquiescence* **mokudaku**
内諾 *informal consent* **naidaku**
日諾 *Japan & Norway* **nichidaku**
認諾 *consent, assent, approval* **nindaku**
応諾 *consent, assent, approval* **ōdaku**
承諾 *consent, assent, approval* **shōdaku**
⇒不承諾 *refusal, no consent* **fushōdaku**
⇒事後承諾 *ex-post facto approval* **jigo shōdaku**
約諾 *promise, commitment* **yakudaku**
諾成契約 *consensual contract* **dakusei keiyaku**
唯唯諾諾 *readily, obligedly* **iidakudaku**

可*pproval, 15*	賛*pproval, 334*
承*pproval, 117*	肯*ffirmative, 616*

若*oung, 276*

212-C

若*oungsters' deal: parental* 諾*onsent not to* 匿*onceal...*

匚 (side box)

匿*onceal*　匿*idden*

kakuma(u), TOKU
conceal, hidden, confidential, covert, secret

FLIP: 8.0.a. Inner (flat)
Facing: 2.0. East ☞ (W)

秘匿 *concealment, keeping secret* **hitoku**
隠匿 *concealment, covert, camouflage* **intoku**
⇒犯罪隠匿 *wrongful imprisonment* **hanzai intoku**
匿名 *anonymity, pen name* **tokumei**
匿名批評 *anonymous criticism* **tokumei hihyō**
蔵匿 *concealed, hidden* **zōtoku**

裏*everse, 872*	隠*onceal, 840*
陰*idden, 864*	忍*onceal, 535*
隠*idden, 840*	覆*onceal, 602*
秘*idden, 219*	

唇*ips, 588*

213-A

Gilted 者erson's 煮oiling anger "too 著tark," 著riters remarked...

扌 (person)

者*erson*

mono, SHA
person, individual, somebody, someone

FLIP: 4.0.a. Bottom (flat)

著者	*writer, author*	**chosha**
医者	*medical doctor, physician*	**isha**
従者	*follower, acolyte*	**jūsha**
患者	*medical patient, sick person*	**kanja**
記者	*journalist, newspaper staff*	**kisha**
後者	*the latter*	**kōsha**
者共	*way master calls a servant*	**monodomo**
忍者	*spy samurai*	**ninja**
死者	*dead person*	**shisha**
只者	*ordinary, mediocre, inferior*	**tadamono**
前者	*the former*	**zensha**
慌て者	*careless-, hasty, impulsive*	**awatemono**
忠義者	*loyal person*	**chūgimono**
仲介者	*intermediary, mediator*	**chūkaisha**
被爆者	*atomic bomb survivor*	**hibakusha**
被害者	*aggrieved party, victim*	**higaisha**
邪魔者	*nuisance, bothersome*	**jamamono**
加害者	*offending party*	**kagaisha**
婚約者	*engaged couple*	**konyakusha**

盲唖者	*blind & dumb person*	**mōasha**
怠け者	*lazy fellow, lazybone*	**namakemono**
責任者	*in-charge, responsible officer*	**sekininsha**
志望者	*applicant, hopeful*	**shibōsha**
創立者	*originator, founder*	**sōritsusha**
崇拝者	*admirer, fan*	**sūhaisha**
推薦者	*nominator, recommender*	**suisensha**
担当者	*person-in-charge*	**tantōsha**
笑い者	*laughingstock, ~matter*	**waraimono**
藪医者	*quack doctor, poor doctor*	**yabuisha**
厄介者	*nuisance-, annoying person*	**yakkaimono**
贈呈者	*presenter, donor*	**zōteisha**

人*erson, 2*		士*entleman, 8*
家*xpert, 909*		紳*entleman, 713*

煮*oiling, 278*

213-B

Gilted 者erson's 煮oiling anger "too 著tark," 著riters remarked...

火⇔灬 (fire)

煮*oiling*

ni(eru), ni(ru), SHA
boiling, seething

FLIP: 8.0.a. Inner (flat)

煮え湯	*boiling water*	**nieyu**
煮え返る	*boil, seethe*	**niekaeru**
煮え立つ	*boil up*	**nietatsu**
煮えたぎる	*boil, seethe*	**nietagiru**
煮え切らない	*half-hearted, noncommittal*	**niekiranai**
飴煮	*soy sauce & sugar-boiled dish*	**ameni**
粗煮	*boiling in water*	**arani**
水煮	*boil in water*	**mizuni**
煮豆	*boiled beans*	**nimame**
煮物	*cooked food, cuisine, meal*	**nimono**
煮魚	*boiled fish*	**nizakana**
煮沸	*boil, seethe*	**shafutsu**
煮沸消毒	*sterilization by boiling*	**shafutsu shōdoku**
佃煮	*preserved food boiled in soysauce*	**tsukudani**
甘煮	*sugar-boiled dish*	**umani**
雑煮	*rice cakes & veggies soup*	**zōni**
半煮え	*half-boiled, underboiled*	**hannie**
甘露煮	*sweet-boiled*	**kanroni**
蒸し煮	*steamed food*	**mushini**

生煮え	*half-boiled dish*	**namanie**
煮込む	*boil well, seethe*	**nikomu**
煮干し	*dried small sardines*	**niboshi**
煮凝り	*meat broth, meal soup*	**nigokori**
煮炊き	*cooking*	**nitaki**
煮立つ	*begin to boil*	**nitatsu**
煮付け	*hard-boiled food*	**nitsuke**
煮染める	*boil hard in soy sauce*	**nishimeru**
煮過ぎる	*overboil*	**nisugiru**
煮詰める	*boil down*	**nitsumeru**
煮売り屋	*cheap eatery*	**niuriya**

沸*oiling, 538*		熱*eat, 153*
燃*urning, 445*		暑*ot weather, 615*
湯*ot-water, 932*		

者*erson, 278*

213-C

Gilted 者erson's 煮oiling anger "too 著tark," 著riters remarked...

ː (grass)

FLIP: 4.0.a. Bottom (flat)

❶著uthor **❷著tark**

arawa(su), ichijiru(shii), CHO
author, writer; stark, conspicuous

❶ 著述 *book writing, literary work* **chojutsu**
著述業 *literary profession* **chojutsugyō**
著述家 *writer, author* **chojutsuka**
著名 *famous, well-known, popular* **chomei**
著作 *book, writing* **chosaku**
著作家 *writer, author* **chosakuka, chosakka**
著作権 *copyrights* **chosakuken**
著者 *writer, author* **chosha**
著書 *literary work* **chosho**
原著 *original work* **gencho**
合著 *joint authorship, co-authorship* **gocho**
遺著 *posthumous works* **icho**
自著 *one's own book* **jicho**
顕著 *conspicuous, striking* **kencho**
高著 *your writings (honorific)* **kōcho**
近著 *recent works* **kincho**
共著 *joint authorship, co-authorship* **kyōcho**
名著 *masterpiece work* **meicho**
拙著 *one's writings, published works* **seccho**

新著 *new writings* **shincho**
大著 *voluminous work* **taicho**
前著 *above-cited, ibid* **zencho**

❷ 著しい *remarkable, marked, striking* **ichijirushii**

窮*xtreme, 876*	掲*ublish, 810*
極*xtreme, 947*	載*ublish, 802*
甚*xtreme, 293*	刷*rinting, 760*
最*aximum, 423*	版*rinting, 359*
刊*ublication, 687*	

者*erson, 278*

214-A

週eekdays or not, 調heck the 調one & 周icinity 周aps...

辶 (transport)

FLIP: 3.0.b. Top (stem)

週eekly **週eekday**

SHŪ
weekly, weekday

次週 *next week* **jishū**
隔週 *bi-weekly, every other week* **kakushū**
今週 *this week* **konshū**
毎週 *every week* **maishū**
来週 *next week* **raishū**
先週 *last week* **senshū**
週番 *weekly on duty* **shūban**
週報 *weekly bulletin* **shūhō**
週評 *weekly review* **shūhyō**
週日 *weekday* **shūjitsu**
週間 *week, weeks* **shūkan**
週休 *weekly holiday* **shūkyū**
週給 *weekly pay* **shūkyū**
週末 *weekend* **shūmatsu**
翌週 *next week* **yokushū**
前週 *last week* **zenshū**
一週間 *one week* **isshūkan**
受難週 *Passion Week* **junanshū**
再来週 *the week after next* **saraishū**

週明け *early next week* **shūake**
週刊誌 *weekly magazine* **shūkanshi**

日*ay, 14*	月*onth, 22*
曜*eekday, 849*	暁*aybreak, 818*
旬*[10 days], 494*	昼*aytime, 575*

過*xcessive, 798*

214-B

週*eekdays or not,* 調*heck the* 調*one &* 周*icinity* 周*aps...*

言 (speaking)

❶調*heck*   **❷調***one*

shira(beru), totono(eru), totono(u), CHŌ
check, auditing, inspection, review, scrutiny, probe; tone

FLIP: 5.0.b. Left & Right

❶ 復調 *detection, demodulation* **fukuchō**
破調 *broken metre* **hachō**
調査 *investigation, research, inquiry* **chōsa**
論調 *commentary, critique, analysis* **ronchō**
調べ物 *something to check* **shirabemono**
証拠調べ *evidence verification* **shōkoshirabe**
❷ 哀調 *sentimental melody* **aichō**
調合 *mixing, compounding* **chōgō**
調印 *signing, signature* **chōin**
調教 *training, instruction* **chōkyō**
調理 *food processing, ~preparation* **chōri**
調整 *adjusting, regulating, control* **chōsei**
調節 *control, adjust, modulate* **chōsetsu**
調子 *physical condition, tune, tone* **chōshi**
調色 *colour blending* **chōshoku**
調剤 *mixed-, compound medicine* **chōzai**
歩調 *step, pace* **hochō**
移調 *transposition* **ichō**
順調 *favourable, satisfactory* **junchō**

格調 *tone, style, pitch* **kakuchō**
堅調 *steady, firm, certain* **kenchō**
基調 *base, basis, foundation* **kichō**
口調 *tone, expression* **kuchō**
空調 *air conditioning, ventilation* **kūchō**
協調 *cooperation, harmony* **kyōchō**
強調 *stress, emphasis* **kyōchō**
軟調 *weak point, weakness* **nanchō**
主調 *main point, gist, "the beef..."* **shuchō**
体調 *physical condition* **taichō**
単調 *monotonous, one-kind* **tanchō**

察*nspection, 328*	閲*nspection, 942*
審*nspection, 339*	確*erify, 804*
検*nspection, 939*	定*ertain, 550*
査*nspection, 624*	

周*icinity, 280*

214-C

週*eekdays or not,* 調*heck the* 調*one &* 周*icinity* 周*aps...*

口 (mouth)

❶周*icinity*   **❷周***ap*

mawa(ri), SHŪ, SHU
vicinity, proximity; lap, periphery

FLIP: 1.0.b. Whole (stem)

❶ 円周 *perimeter, outer line* **enshū**
円周率 *circumference-to-diameter ratio* **enshūritsu**
外周 *outskirts, environs* **gaishū**
半周 *semi circle* **hanshū**
一周 *one lap, one turn* **isshū**
内周 *internal circumference* **naishū**
周知 *common knowledge* **shūchi**
周波 *cycle* **shūha**
周波数 *frequency, number of times* **shūhasū**
周辺 *surroundings; circumference* **shūhen**
周囲 *circumference, periphery* **shūi**
周回 *circumference, surroundings* **shūkai**
周忌 *death anniversary* **shūki**
周期 *period, cycle* **shūki**
⇒公転周期 *solar revolution* **kōten shūki**
周期性 *periodic, cyclical* **shūkisei**
周航 *circumnavigation* **shūkō**
周密 *exhaustive, thorough* **shūmitsu**
周年 *anniversary* **shūnen**

❷ 周旋 *good offices, mediation* **shūsen**
周旋業 *brokerage, commission* **shūsengyō**
周旋料 *brokerage, commission* **shūsenryō**
周旋屋 *broker, employment agency* **shūsenya**
周到 *meticulous, laborious* **shūtō**
⇒用意周到 *extreme care* **yōi shūtō**
周遊 *field trip, excursion* **shūyū**
周遊券 *excursion ticket* **shūyūken**
高周波 *high-frequency* **kōshūha**
低周波 *low-frequency* **teishūha**
周章狼狽 *consternation, dismay* **shūshō rōbai**

察*nspection, 328*	閲*nspection, 942*
審*nspection, 339*	確*erify, 804*
検*nspection, 939*	定*ertain, 550*
査*nspection, 624*	

固*olid, 491*

215-A
昔*ygones* to 惜*egret*, 措*easures* to forget...

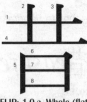

日 (sunlight, daytime)

昔*ast*　　昔*ygones*

mukashi, SEKI, SHAKU
past, by-gones, olden-times

FLIP: 1.0.a. Whole (flat)

昔ながら *time-honoured* **mukashi nagara**
一昔 *about a decade ago* **hitomukashi**
幾昔 *how ancient* **ikumukashi**
今昔 *past & present* **konjaku**
昔話 *legend, reminiscences* **mukashi banashi**
昔語り *reminiscences, nostalgic talks* **mukashigatari**
昔昔 *"once upon a time..."* **mukashi mukashi**
昔風 *old-fashioned, conservative* **mukashifū**
昔者 *old folks, old persons, oldies* **mukashimono**
大昔 *time immemorial, many years ago* **ōmukashi**
昔時 *olden times, bygone years* **sekiji**
昔日 *olden times, the past* **sekijitsu**
昔年 *olden times, the past* **sekinen**
昔の事 *thing of the past* **mukashi no koto**
昔気質 *conservative ideas, ~thinking* **mukashi katagi**
昔馴染み *old friend, ~acquaintance* **mukashi najimi**

時*ime, 653*	枯*ither, 960*
去*eave-out, 360*	朽*ecay, 738*

借*orrow, 336*

215-B
昔*ygones* to 惜*egret*, 措*easures* to forget...

心⇔忄 (heart, feelings)

惜*egret*　　惜*isgiving*

o(shii), o(shimu), SEKI
regret, misgiving, irksome, denounce, condemn, deplore, disappointment, fretful

FLIP: 7.0.a. Right (flat)

惜しむ *grudge, regret, misgivings* **oshimu**
愛惜 *deep regret, misgivings* **aiseki**
哀惜 *mourning pains, death sorrows* **aiseki**
惜し気 *regret, misgiving* **oshige**
惜し気なく *without regret* **oshigenaku**
悋惜 *with grudges, poor loser* **rinseki**
惜別 *reluctance to part, ~leave* **sekibetsu**
惜敗 *narrow defeat* **sekihai**
惜春 *regret of one's lost youth* **sekishun**
通惜 *deep sorrows* **tsūseki**
物惜しみ *stingy* **mono oshimi**
一文惜しみ *stingy* **ichimon oshimi**
負け惜しみ *sour graping* **makeoshimi**
名残惜しい *unwillingness to part* **nagorioshii**
残り惜しい *regret, reluctance* **nokorioshii**
売り惜しみ *regrets on selling out* **urioshimi**

悔*egret, 712*
慨*egret, 316*
憾*egret, 46*

借*orrow, 336*

215-C

昔ygones to 惜egret, 措easures to forget...

措easures 措onduct

手⇔扌 (hand, manual)

FLIP: 7.0.a. Right (flat)

oku, SO
measures, step, conduct, dispose

挙措 *manner, behaviour, attitude* **kyoso**
措置 *measure, step, action* **sochi**
⇒移行措置 *provisional measures* **ikō sochi**
⇒緊急措置 *emergency measures* **kinkyū sochi**
措辞 *words & phrases* **soji**
措辞法 *syntax* **sojihō**
措止 *demeanour, behaviour, conduct* **soshi**
措定 *supposition, assumption, premise* **sotei**

策*olicy, 875*	応*omply, 469*
略*ummary, 825*	従*omply, 551*

惜*egret, 281*

216-A

What time will the Queen 聞isten on 閑eisure 問uestions & 問roblem?

聞nquire 聞isten

耳 (ears)

FLIP: 2.0.b. Sort Of (stem)

ki(ku), ki(koeru), BUN, MON
inquire, listen, hearing, harken, question, audio

伝聞 *rumor, hearsay* **denbun**
外聞 *reputation, esteem* **gaibun**
上聞 *imperial audience* **jōbun**
怪聞 *scandal, disgrace* **kaibun**
奇聞 *strange news* **kibun**
旧聞 *old news* **kyūbun**
内聞 *secret, confidential, covert* **naibun**
漏聞 *leakage, overheard* **rōbun**
新聞 *newspapers, dailies* **shinbun**
醜聞 *scandal, disgrace* **shūbun**
余聞 *gossip, rumour* **yobun**
聴聞会 *public hearing* **chōmonkai**
空聞き *absent-minded* **karakiki**
又聞き *hearsay, rumour* **matagiki**
生聞き *half-truths, superficial knowledge* **namagiki**
聞かせる *tell, say, state* **kikaseru**
聞き違う *hear wrong* **kikichigau**
聞き書き *exact dictation, verbatim* **kikigaki**
聞き入る *listen intently* **kikiiru**

聞き上手 *good listener* **kikijōzu**
聞き嚙り *smattering* **kikikajiri**
聞き込み *picking up information* **kikikomi**
聞き取り *hearing, listening* **kikitori**
盗み聞き *eavesdropping* **nusumigiki**
立ち聞き *overhear, eavesdrop* **tachigiki**
伝え聞く *hear from others* **tsutaekiku**
聞き古す *"sick & tired of hearing..."* **kikifurusu**
聞き惚れる *be enraptured* **kikihoreru**
聞き慣れる *familiar-sounding* **kikinareru**
聞き損なう *hear wrong* **kikisokonau**
聞き届ける *grant, comply with* **kikitodokeru**

耳*ars, 228*	尋*nquire, 868*
聴*isten, 844*	諮*onsult, 865*
諮*nquire, 865*	

閑*pen, 284*

216-B

What time will the Queen 聞*isten on* 閑*eisure* 問*uestions*
*& * 問*roblem?*

門 (gate, entrance)

閑*eisure*   閑*elaxation*

KAN
leisure, relaxation, quiet

FLIP: 1.0.b. Whole (stem)

安閑 *peace & quiet* **ankan**
閑地 *quiet place* **kanchi**
閑談 *casual talk, chat* **kandan**
閑雅 *refined & graceful* **kanga**
閑寂 *quiet, tranquil* **kanjaku**
閑人 *leisure person* **kanjin, himajin**
閑中 *during a recess* **kanjū**
閑暇 *spare-, leisure time* **kanka**
閑却 *negligence, carelessness* **kankyaku**
閑居 *quiet life, retired life* **kankyo**
閑散 *nearly deserted, ~abandoned* **kansan**
閑静 *silence, quietness* **kansei**
閑職 *sinecure, leisurely post* **kanshoku**
閑話 *idle talk, leisure conversation* **kanwa**
閑話休題 *return to the subject matter* **kanwa kyūdai**
休閑 *inactive, inert, fallowing* **kyūkan**
等閑 *negligence, overlooking* **naozari, tōkan**
長閑 *calm & peaceful* **nodoka**
清閑 *quiet & secluded* **seikan**

深閑 *still, quiet* **shinkan**
森閑 *nice & quiet* **shinkan**
小閑 *short break, brief recess* **shōkan**
少閑 *short break, brief recess* **shōkan**
消閑 *whiling away, killing time* **shōkan**
有閑 *leisureliness, idleness* **yūkan**
有閑階級 *leisure class* **yūkan kaikyū**
閑日月 *freetime, leisure time* **kanjitsugetsu**
閑古鳥 *cuckoo* **kankodori**
農閑期 *farming slack season* **nōkanki**

悠*eisure*, 898	喫*njoy*, 900
暇*ree time*, 653	享*njoy*, 398
楽*njoy*, 447	遊*njoy*, 650

閑*lose*, 285

216-C

What time will the Queen 聞*isten on* 閑*eisure* 問*uestions*
*& * 問*roblem?*

口 (mouth)

問*uestion*   問*atter*

to(i), ton, to(u), MON
question, matter

FLIP: 1.0.b. Whole (stem)

珍問 *strange question* **chinmon**
弔問 *condolence visit* **chōmon**
聴問 *public hearing* **chōmon**
不問 *overlooking, ignoring* **fumon**
疑問 *doubt, question* **gimon**
拷問 *torture* **gōmon**
愚問 *silly-, foolish question* **gumon**
反問 *retort, return question* **hanmon**
訪問 *visit, courtesy call* **hōmon**
自問 *soul-searching, question oneself* **jimon**
尋問 *questioning, interrogation* **jinmon**
下問 *consulting subordinates* **kamon**
喚問 *summons, sub-poena* **kanmon**
検問 *examination, inspection* **kenmon**
詰問 *interrogation, grilling* **kitsumon**
顧問 *advisor, consultant, counsellor* **komon**
糾問 *cross-examine, grill* **kyūmon**
問題 *question, problem* **mondai**

⇒死活問題 *matter of life-or-death*
　　　shikatsu mondai
問答 *question & answer* **mondō**
問責 *rebuke, censure, reprimand* **monseki**
問診 *detailed questions* **monshin**
問罪 *accusation, indictment, charge* **monzai**
査問 *inquire, interrogate* **samon**
設問 *question, inquiry, query* **setsumon**
諮問 *inquiry, consulting* **shimon**
質問 *question, inquiry, query* **shitsumon**
問屋 *wholesale store, ~dealer* **tonya**
耳学問 *learning by ear* **mimigakumon**

件*atter*, 179
題*ubject*, 834
課*esson*, 287

閂*ate*, 286

217-A

...Castle 関*arrier* 開*pens or* 閉*losesbased on* 簡*oncise orders, so be at the* 門*ate* 間*etween 7 & 8...*

門 (gate, entrance)

関*arrier*　　関*entry*

seki, KAN
barrier, sentry, concern

FLIP: 1.0.b. Whole (stem)

玄関 *front door, main entrance* **genkan**
関知 *concern, interest* **kanchi**
関係 *background, relation* **kankei**
関門 *gateway, checkpoint* **kanmon**
関白 *domineering hubby; emperor's advisor* **kanpaku**
関連 *relation, association* **kanren**
関西 *Kansai region (Ōsaka & Kōbe)* **kansai**
関節 *joint, connexion* **kansetsu**
関心 *concern, interest, admiration* **kanshin**
関心事 *matter of concern* **kanshinji, kanshingoto**
関数 *mathematical function* **kansū**
関東 *Kantō region (East Honshu & Tōkyō)* **kantō**
関頭 *critical-, crucial point* **kantō**
関与 *participation, involvement* **kanyo**
関税 *customs, duty, levy* **kanzei**
機関 *facilities, institution* **kikan**
汽関 *steam generator, boiler* **kikan**
難関 *difficulty, deadlock, stalemate, impasse* **nankan**
大関 *second-rank sumo wrestler* **oozeki**

関守 *barrier sentry, ~guard* **sekimori**
関所 *gateway, checkpoint, barrier* **sekisho**
関取 *ranking sumo wrestler* **sekitori**
関脇 *third rank sumo wrestler* **sekiwake**
相関 *correlation, interrelation* **sōkan**
通関 *customs clearing* **tsūkan**
税関 *customs, duty, taxes* **zeikan**
無関係 *unrelated, no bearing* **mukankei**
関の山 *"exerting one's best efforts..."* **seki no yama**
下関市 *Shimonoseki City, Yamaguchi Prefecture* **shimonoseki-shi**

錠*adlock, 550*	限*oundary, 771*
鎖*hain, 665*	締*onclude, 432*
境*oundary, 839*	視*bserve, 815*

閉*lose, 285*

217-B

...Castle 関*arrier* 開*pens or* 閉*losesbased on* 簡*oncise orders, so be at the* 門*ate* 間*etween 7 & 8...*

門 (gate, entrance)

❶開*pen*　　❷開*evelop*

a(ku), a(keru), hira(keru), hira(ku), KAI
open; develop

FLIP: 2.0.b. Sort Of (stem)

❶開け放す *throw open* **akehanasu**
打開 *break, opening, turn* **dakai**
開演 *opening, curtain rising* **kaien**
開園 *garden opening* **kaien**
開眼 ① *opening of one's eyes* **kaigan**
開眼 ② *enlightenment (Buddhism)* **kaigen**
開票 *vote counting, opening the ballots* **kaihyō**
開院 *opening of the diet; "library, hospital open..."* **kaiin**
開化 *enlightenment; civilization* **kaika**
開会 *opening of a meeting* **kaikai**
開館 *"library, hall open..."* **kaikan**
開局 *station, office opening* **kaikyoku**
開幕 *curtain rising* **kaimaku**
開廷 *court opening* **kaitei**
開通 *road opening, new road* **kaitsū**
公開 *opening to the public* **kōkai**
満開 *full blossom, at one's best* **mankai**
再開 *reopening, resumption* **saikai**
疎開 *evacuation, withdrawal* **sokai**

全開 *opening completely* **zenkai**
幕開け *opening, inaugural, premiere* **makuake**
海開き *start of swimming season* **umibiraki**
山開き *start of mountaineering season* **yamabiraki**
❷開発 *development, progress* **kaihatsu**
開花 *flowering, blooming, blossoming* **kaika**
開拓 *reclamation, clearing of land* **kaitaku**
開運 *improvement of fortune* **kaiun**
未開 *primitive, undeveloped, virgin* **mikai**
展開 *development, evolution* **tenkai**
新開地 *newly-developed land* **shinkaichi**

披*pen, 104*	拓*evelop, 363*
口*pening, 458*	幕*nveil, 601*

聞*isten, 282*

217-C

...Castle 関arrier 開pens or 閉losesbased on 簡oncise orders,
so be at the 門ate 間etween 7 & 8...

門 (gate, entrance)

閉*lose* 閉*hut*

shi(meru), to(jiru), shi(maru), HEI
close, shut

FLIP: 2.0.b. Sort Of (stem)

開け閉て *opening & closing, on & off* **aketate**
腸閉塞 *intestine disruption* **chōheisoku**
閉園 *garden closing* **heien**
閉業 *going-out-of-business* **heigyō**
閉院 *"building closed..."* **heiin**
閉場 *area closing* **heijō**
閉会 *meeting closing* **heikai**
閉会式 *closing ceremony* **heikaishiki**
閉館 *"library, hall closed..."* **heikan**
閉経 *menopause* **heikei**
閉校 *"school closed..."* **heikō**
閉口 *"speechless, dumb-founded..."* **heikō**
閉居 *staying indoors, encamped* **heikyo**
閉幕 *curtain closing* **heimaku**
閉門 *gate closing* **heimon**
閉鎖 *shutting down, locking out* **heisa**
閉止 *closing, stoppage, off-limits* **heishi**
閉所 *place closing* **heisho**
閉塞① *blockade, siege, interception* **heisoku**

閉塞② *closing of the tomb* **heisoku**
閉廷 *case dismissal (law suit)* **heitei**
閉店 *"shop closed..."* **heiten**
閉山 *mountain off limits* **heizan**
開閉 *opening & closing* **kaihei**
開閉器 *on-off switch, make-or-break* **kaiheiki**
開閉橋 *drawbridge* **kaiheikyō**
密閉 *shut tight* **mippei**
幽閉 *confinement, imprisonment, detention* **yūhei**
閉じ込める *shut in, lock in* **tojikomeru**
閉じ篭る *staying indoors, encamped* **tojikomoru**

錠*adlock, 550*	奥*nside, 903*
鎖*hain, 665*	内*nside, 297*

関*arrier, 284*

217-D

...Castle 関arrier 開pens or 閉losesbased on 簡oncise orders,
so be at the 門ate 間etween 7 & 8...

竹 (bamboo)

簡*oncise* 簡*imple*

KAN
concise, simple, basic, compact

FLIP: 4.0.a. Bottom (flat)

竹簡 *bamboo strip for writing* **chikukan**
繁簡 *complexity & simplicity* **hankan**
簡抜 *selection, choosing* **kanbatsu**
簡便 *handy, simple & easy* **kanben**
簡易 *easy, plain, simplified* **kan'i**
簡易保険 *postal insurance* **kan'i hoken**
簡易住宅 *simple frame house* **kan'i jūtaku**
簡易食堂 *cafeteria, eatery* **kan'i shokudō**
簡易宿泊所 *flophouse* **kan'i shukuhakujo**
簡潔 *concise, brief* **kanketsu**
簡明 *concise, brief, terse* **kanmei**
簡略 *simple, brief, concise* **kanryaku**
簡略化 *simplification* **kanryakuka**
簡裁 *summary court* **kansai**
簡札 *wooden tag* **kansatsu**
簡素 *simple, frugal, thrifty* **kanso**
簡素化 *simplification* **kansoka**
簡単 *easy, simple, brief* **kantan**
簡単服 *simple clothes* **kantanfuku**

簡約 *brief, concise* **kanyaku**
了簡 *idea; decision, discretion* **ryōken**
了簡違い *wrong idea; indiscretion* **ryōkenchigai**
書簡 *letter, correspondence* **shokan**
⇒航空書簡 *aerogramme, airmail* **kōkū shokan**
手簡 *letter* **shukan**
簡体字 *simplified Kanji character* **kantaiji**
書簡紙 *stationery* **shokanshi**

易*imple, 933*	朴*imple, 707*
素*imple, 578*	

間*etween, 286*	節*eason, 421*

217-E

...Castle 関*arrier* 開*pens or* 閉*losesbased on* 箇*oncise orders, so be at the* 門*ate* 間*etween 7 & 8...*

門 (gate, entrance)

門*ate*   門*ntrance*

kado, MON
gate, entrance

FLIP: 1.0.b. Whole (stem)

部門 *classification; department* **bumon**
武門 *military family, family of soldiers* **bumon**
獄門 *prison gate, jail, gaol* **gokumon**
軍門 *surrender, capitulation* **gunmon**
閉門 *"gate closed..."* **heimon**
陣門 *capitulate, giving up* **jinmon**
門出 *"from the gates to a fresh start..."* **kadode**
門口 *front entrance, main gate* **kadoguchi**
門松 *New Year pine ornaments* **kadomatsu**
権門 *influential family* **kenmon**
校門 *school main gate* **kōmon**
門番 *gatekeeper, porter* **monban**
門閥 *birth lineage, family roots* **monbatsu**
門地 *family roots, ancestral line* **monchi**
門柱 *gatepost* **monchū**
門外 *outside the gate* **mongai**
門限 *curfew, prohibition hours* **mongen**
門戸 *door, opening; possibility* **monko**
門札 *nameplate* **monsatsu**

門弟 *disciple, pupil* **montei**
門徒 *disciple, follower* **monto**
門灯 *gate lamp* **montō**
入門 *primer, introductory* **nyūmon**
正門 *main entrance* **seimon**
専門 *expertise, specialty, forte* **senmon**
宗門 *sect, denomination* **shūmon**
僧門 *becoming a Buddhist monk* **sōmon**
総門 *main gate* **sōmon**
裏門 *rear-, back entrance* **uramon**
禅門 *Zen Buddhism sect* **zenmon**
門司市 *Mōji City, Fukuoka Prefecture* **mōji-shi**
門下生 *pupil, student, disciple* **monkasei**
門前町 *cathedral-, temple town* **monzenmachi**

扉*oor, 678*	戸*oor, 428*

問*atter, 283*

217-F

...Castle 関*arrier* 開*pens or* 閉*losesbased on* 箇*oncise orders, so be at the* 門*ate* 間*etween 7 & 8...*

門 (gate, entrance)

間*etween* 間*nterval*

aida, ma, KAN, KEN
between, interval, duration, interlude, spacing

FLIP: 1.0.b. Whole (stem)

合間 *interval, pause* **aima**
昼間 *daytime, noon* **hiruma**
居間 *living room* **ima**
時間 *time, hour* **jikan**
間隔 *interval, space* **kankaku**
間接 *indirect* **kansetsu**
期間 *term, period, season* **kikan**
区間 *section, part* **kukan**
間借り *rental room, room-for-rent* **magari**
間借り人 *lodger, boarder* **magarinin**
間際 *last moment* **magiwa**
間口 *frontage, scope; width* **maguchi**
間近 *near at hand, very soon* **majika**
民間 *civilian, folks, people* **minkan**
仲間 *colleague, friend, buddy* **nakama**
年間 *number of years* **nenkan**
人間 *human being* **ningen**
世間 *world, society, public* **seken**
週間 *week, weeks* **shūkan**

隙間 *crevice, crack, cranny* **sukima**
茶の間 *living room (Japanese house)* **chanoma**
間引く *thinning out* **mabiku**
間違い *error, mistake* **machigai**
長い間 *for a long time* **nagaiaida**
間もなく *before long, shortly* **mamonaku**
間に合う *be in time, enough, sufficient* **maniau**
林間学校 *open-air school* **rinkan gakkō**
間違いない *certain, unmistakable* **machigainai**
間違い電話 *"dialed wrong..."* **machigai denwa**
他国間条約 *multilateral treaty* **takokukan jōyaku**

隔*nterval, 963*	差*ifference, 589*
違*ifference, 796*	距*istance, 207*

問*atter, 283*

218-A

Chemistry 課*ection gave* 課*esson on* 果*esults of* 裸*aked reactions...*

言 (speaking)

❶課*ection*　**❷**課*esson*

KA
section; lesson

FLIP: 5.0.b. Left & Right

❶ 分課　*office section*　**bunka**
賦課　*levy, tax imposition*　**fuka**
課長　*section chief, ~head*　**kachō**
課員　*section staff member*　**kain**
課金　*billing, charge, invoice*　**kakin**
課税　*taxation, tax*　**kazei**
⇒源泉課税　*principal income tax*　**gensen kazei**
課税品　*taxable-, dutiable goods*　**kazeihin**
課税率　*tax rate*　**kazeiritsu**
考課　*efficiency report*　**kōka**
日課　*daily work, ~routine, ~schedule*　**nikka**
総務課　*general-affairs section*　**sōmuka**
非課税　*tax exemption*　**hikazei**
秘書課　*secretarial pool*　**hishoka**
人事課　*human resources section*　**jinjika**
課徴金　*surcharge*　**kachōkin**
会計課　*finance-, accounting section*　**kaikeika**
鬼課長　*abusive-, cruel boss*　**onikachō**
庶務課　*general-affairs section*　**shomuka**

❷ 学課　*lesson, studies*　**gakka**
課題　*subject, theme, topic*　**kadai**
課題曲　*set piece*　**kadaikyoku**
課業　*lesson, studies*　**kagyō**
課外　*extra-curricular*　**kagai**
課外活動　*extra-curricular activities*　**kagai katsudō**
課程　*course, curriculum*　**katei**
⇒博士課程　*Ph.D., doctoral course*　**hakushi katei**
⇒修士課程　*MA, MS, masteral course*
　　　shūshi katei
放課後　*after school*　**hōkago**
正課　*regular curriculum*　**seika**

度*egree, 91*	回*otate, 458*
倍*ultiply, 950*	周*ap. 280*
複*ultiply, 830*	

課*onspiracy, 293*

218-B

Chemistry 課*ection gave* 課*esson on* 果*esults of* 裸*aked reactions...*

木 (wooden)

❶果*esult*　**❷**果*ruit*

ha(tasu), ha(teru), ha(te), KA
result, effect, outcome; fruit

FLIP: 1.0.b. Whole (stem)

❶ 美果　*beautiful results*　**bika**
釣果　*fish catch*　**chōka**
因果　*causality, cause & effect*　**inga**
因果者　*unlucky fellow*　**ingamono**
果断　*decisive, resolute, prompt*　**kadan**
果皮　*pericarp*　**kahi**
果敢に　*fearless, daring*　**kakan(ni)**
果然　*as expected*　**kazen**
結果　*result, outcome*　**kekka**
効果　*effect, result, outcome*　**kōka**
⇒逆効果　*opposite-, counter-result*　**gyakukōka**
⇒演出効果　*stage effects*　**enshutsu kōka**
成果　*result, success, performance*　**seika**
戦果　*military achievements, war exploits*　**senka**
善果　*favourable results*　**zenka**
弱り果てる　*be exhausted, wear thin*　**yowarihateru**
朽ち果てる　*decay completely*　**kuchihateru**
使い果たす　*exhaust, deplete, drain*　**tsukaihatasu**
変わり果てる　*revamp, change entirely*　**kawarihateru**

❷ 果報　*luck, fortune*　**kahō**
果実　*fruit*　**kajitsu**
果樹　*fruit tree*　**kaju**
果汁　*fruit juice*　**kajū**
果樹園　*orchard*　**kajuen**
核果　*drupe*　**kakuka**
果肉　*fruit pulp, juice pulp*　**kaniku**
果糖　*fructose*　**katō**
堅果　*nut*　**kenka**
果物　*fruit*　**kudamono**
青果　*vegetables & fruits*　**seika**

化*ecome, 192*
成*ecome, 244*

界*orld, 365*

218-C

Chemistry 課ection gave 課esson on 果esults of 裸aked reactions...

衣⇔ネ (clothing)

裸udity　　裸aked

hadaka, RA
nudity, naked, stripped, bare-skinned, threadbare, unclothed

FLIP: 7.0.b1. Right (stem)

赤裸 *fully-naked, total nudity* **akahadaka, sekira**
裸麦 *rye* **hadakamugi**
裸虫 *scantily-dressed person* **hadakamushi**
裸値 *break-even price* **hadakane**
裸線 *bare wire* **hadakasen**
裸馬 *naked-, unsaddled horse* **hadakauma**
裸山 *bare mountains* **hadakayama**
裸足 *bare foot* **hadashi**
半裸 *semi nude* **hanra**
半裸体 *semi-naked* **hanratai**
丸裸 *fully naked* **maruhadaka**
裸婦 *nude-, naked woman* **rafu**
裸眼 *naked eye, unaided eye* **ragan**
裸女 *naked woman* **rajo**
裸身 *nude-, naked body* **rashin**
裸出 *uncovered, unprotected* **rashutsu**
裸体 *nude, naked body* **ratai**
裸体美 *physical beauty* **rataibi**
裸体画 *nude painting* **rataiga**

裸像 *nude sculpture* **razō**
全裸 *fully-naked, total nudity* **zenra**
裸一貫 *"no property but one's body..."*　**hadaka ikkan**
裸電球 *unshaded electric bulb* **hadakadenkyū**
裸ん房 *naked child* **hadakanbō**
真っ裸 *stark naked* **mappadaka**
赤裸々 *frank, outspoken* **sekirara**
素っ裸 *stark, naked, bare* **suppadaka**

質*ature, 627*	皮*kin, 224*
性*ature, 474*	膚*kin, 69*
然*ature, 445*	性*ex, 474*

禅*en Buddhism, 782*

219-A

非egative 悲orrow for 罪uilty 輩ellow...

非 (negaltive)

非 [negative]

HI
[negative]

FLIP: 2.0.b. Sort Of (stem)

非番 *off-duty, on leave* **hiban**
非凡 *extraordinary, unusual* **hibon**
非望 *improper desire* **hibō**
非道 *unjust, arbitrary* **hidō**
非情 *cold heartedness* **hijō**
非常 *emergency, non-regular* **hijō**
非常に *"very much, remarkably..."* **hijō (ni)**
非常階段 *emergency staircase* **hijō kaidan**
非核 *non-nuclear, conventional (weapons)* **hikaku**
非行 *delinquency, dereliction* **hikō**
非難 *criticism, critique* **hinan**
非礼 *disrespect, impoliteness* **hirei**
非力 *helpless, unfit, good-for-nothing* **hiriki**
非才 *poor ability, ineptitude* **hisai**
非運 *misfortune, bad luck* **hiun**
理非 *right-or-wrong, propriety* **rihi**
是非 *"by all means, all the more..."* **zehi**
前非 *past excesses, past misdeeds* **zenpi**
非暴力 *non-violence, peaceful* **hibōryoku**

非同盟 *non-aligned, neutral* **hidōmei**
非合法 *unlawfulness, illegality* **higōhō**
非常勤 *part-time employment* **hijōkin**
非課税 *tax exemption* **hikazei**
非金属 *non-metallic* **hikinzoku**
非国民 *unpatriotic citizen* **hikokumin**
非公式 *unofficial, informal* **hikōshiki**
非人情 *callousness, indifference* **hininjō**
非晶体 *formless, shapeless* **hishōtai**
非行少年 *juvenile delinquent* **hikō shōnen**
非科学的 *unscientific, non-scientific* **hikagakuteki**

不*[negative], 300*	断*efusal, 958*
拒*efusal, 207*	否*efusal, 300*

俳*cting, 795*

219-B

非*egative* 悲*orrow for* 罪*uilty* 輩*ellow...*

心⇔忄 (heart, feelings)

悲*orrows*   悲*ragedy*

FLIP: 3.0.b. Top (stem)

kana(shii), kana(shimu), HI
sorrows, tragedy, wretchedness, melancholy, misfortune, sadness

悲しげ *sad-looking* **kanashige**
悲しみ *sorrow, grief, sadness* **kanashimi**
悲しがる *feel sorry* **kanashigaru**
悲哀 *sorrow, grief, sadness, misery* **hiai**
悲調 *plaintive atmosphere* **hichō**
悲憤 *indignation, resentment, fury* **hifun**
悲願 *earnest wish, fervent hope* **higan**
悲劇 *tragedy, disaster, calamity* **higeki**
悲業 *misfortune, tragedy* **higō**
悲報 *death notice, obituary* **hihō**
悲歌 *elegy, sad tune* **hika**
悲観 *pessimism, gloomy view* **hikan**
悲喜 *joy & sorrow* **hiki**
悲喜劇 *tragicomedy* **hikigeki**
悲境 *adverse situation* **hikyō**
悲況 *sorrowful, lamentable* **hikyō**
悲曲 *elegy, sad tune* **hikyoku**
悲鳴 *scream, shriek, yell* **himei**
悲恋 *tragic love* **hiren**

悲惨 *misery, agony* **hisan**
悲愁 *sorrows, pathos* **hishū**
悲壮 *pathetic, tragic* **hisō**
悲愴 *overcoming grief* **hisō**
悲嘆 *grief, sorrows* **hitan**
悲痛 *grief, sorrows* **hitsū**
悲運 *tragic fortune* **hiun**
悲話 *tragic story* **hiwa**
慈悲 *mercy, pity* **jihi**
慈悲心 *mercy & compassion* **jihishin**
慈悲深い *merciful, pitiful* **jihibukai**

惜*orrow, 336*	禍*ragedy, 799*
哀*orrows, 374*	惨*ragedy, 396*
愁*orrows, 415*	厄*ragedy, 354*

罪*riminal, 289*

219-C

非*egative* 悲*orrow for* 罪*uilty* 輩*ellow...*

罒 (net, eye crown)

罪*uilty*   罪*riminal*

FLIP: 2.0.b. Sort Of (stem)

tsumi, ZAI
guilty, criminal, culpable, fault, felony, hoodlum, mobster, villain, culprit

微罪 *petty offence, misdemeanour* **bizai**
大罪 *heavy crime, mortal sin* **daizai**
断罪 *conviction, "guilty..."; decapitation* **danzai**
原罪 *original sin* **genzai**
犯罪 *crime, offence* **hanzai**
⇒凶悪犯罪 *heinous crime, atrocity* **kyōaku hanzai**
功罪 *merits & demerits* **kōzai**
免罪 *acquittal, not guilty verdict* **menzai**
問罪 *indictment, charges* **monzai**
無罪 *innocent, "not guilty..."* **muzai**
流罪 *banishment, exile* **ruzai**
謝罪 *apology, atonement* **shazai**
死罪 *death penalty, capital punishment* **shizai**
宿罪 *sins from previous life* **shukuzai**
余罪 *other crimes* **yozai**
有罪 *conviction, "guilty..."* **yūzai**
罪悪 *crime, offence* **zaiaku**
罪状 *offence, charge, violation* **zaijō**
罪名 *name of offence* **zaimei**

罪人 *sinner, criminal, offender* **zainin**
斬罪 *beheading-, decapitation sentence* **zanzai**
罪作り *sinful, vicious* **tsumitsukuri**
偽証罪 *falsification of documents* **gishōzai**
偽造罪 *forgery, fabrication* **gizōzai**
放火罪 *arson, arson crime* **hōkazai**
詐欺罪 *fraud, con artist* **sagizai**
殺人罪 *murder crime* **satsujinzai**
性犯罪 *sexual crime* **seihanzai**
罪深い *sinful, wicked person* **tsumibukai**
贈賄罪 *bribery, pay-off, hush money* **zōwaizai**
罪滅ぼし *atonement, amends* **tsumihoroboshi**

犯*riminal, 640*	懲*unishment, 63*
囚*risoner, 863*	罰*unishment, 759*
刑*unishment, 536*	科*enalty, 194*

悲*orrows, 289*

219-D

非egative 悲orrow for 罪uilty 輩ellow...

車 (vehicle, wheel)

輩ellow   輩olleague

yakara, HAI
fellow, associate, colleague

FLIP: 1.0.b. Whole (stem)
FLIP: 4.0.b. Bottom (stem)

同輩 colleague, fellow, mate **dōhai**	
輩出 outpouring, outflowing **haishutsu**	
朋輩 comrade, fellow **hōbai**	
傍輩 companion, mate, colleague **hōbai**	
若輩 young fellow, ~colleague **jakuhai**	
弱輩 young fellow, inexperience **jakuhai**	
軽輩 underling, orderly **keihai**	
後輩 younger-, junior colleague **kōhai**	
末輩 underling, orderly **mappai**	
年輩 older-, senior colleague **nenpai**	
老輩 elderly, senior citizens **rōhai**	
先輩 senior fellow, ~colleague **senpai**	
党輩 partymates, ~colleagues **tōhai**	
我輩 I (first person) **wagahai**	
吾輩 I, me **wagahai**	
雑輩 rank & file **zappai**	
俗輩 throng, crowd **zokuhai**	
同年輩 one's contemporary, same-age group **dōnenpai**	
青年輩 young fellow, ~colleague **seinenhai**	

相ellow, 524   奴ellow, 44
仲ellow, 695   僚ellow. 66

非[negative], 288

220-A

On the 則egulation 側ide, strict 測imensions to abide...

刀⇔刂 (blade, cutting)

則

則egulation   則ule

SOKU
regulation, rule, policy

FLIP: 6.0.b. Left (stem)

罰則 penal-, prison regulations **bassoku**	正則 regular, normal **seisoku**
附則 additional rule **fusoku**	社則 company rules **shasoku**
付則 additional rule **fusoku**	四則 add-subtract-multiply&divide **shisoku**
概則 general rules & regulations **gaisoku**	総則 general rules **sōsoku**
学則 university rules & regulations **gakusoku**	定則 law, rule **teisoku**
原則 principle, fundamental, basics **gensoku**	天則 natural law, natures way **tensoku**
獄則 prison rules **gokusoku**	典則 rules & regulations **tensoku**
反則 breach of regulations **hansoku**	鉄則 iron rules, inviolable **tessoku**
変則 anomaly, irregularity, abnormality **hensoku**	党則 party rules **tōsoku**
補則 supplementary rules **hosoku**	通則 common rule **tsūsoku**
法則 law, rule, statutes **hōsoku**	雑則 miscellaneous rules **zassoku**
準則 rule, criterion **junsoku**	
会則 group, club rules **kaisoku**	
館則 library rules & regulations **kansoku**	典ules, 476 規tandard, 814
禁則 prohibition, forbidden **kinsoku**	法aw, 360 律egulation, 731
規則 rule, regulation **kisoku**	
校則 school rules & regulations **kōsoku**	貝hellfish, 516
教則 teacher's rules **kyōsoku**	
細則 detailed rules **saisoku**	

220-B

On the 則*egulation* 側*ide, strict* 測*imensions to abide...*

人⇔亻 (person)

側*ide*　　側*ehalf*

kawa, soba(mu), SOKU
side, behalf, part

FLIP: 8.0.b. Inner (stem)

縁側	*veranda, porch*	**engawa**
舷側	*side of a ship*	**gensoku**
銀側	*silver casing*	**gingawa**
片側	*one side*	**katagawa**
金側	*gold casing*	**kingawa**
窓側	*window side*	**madogawa**
右側	*right-hand side*	**migigawa**
両側	*both sides*	**ryōgawa**
船側	*side of a ship*	**sensoku**
側役	*personal attendant, ~servant*	**sobayaku**
側近	*close friends, buddy, chum*	**sokkin**
側溝	*side ditch*	**sokkō**
側圧	*lateral pressure*	**sokuatsu**
側女	*concubine, mistress*	**sokume**
側聞	*heard by chance, overheard*	**sokubun**
側壁	*sidewall, side embankment*	**sokuheki**
側面	*side-, lateral view*	**sokumen**
側目	*intense-, attentive watching*	**sokumoku**
側線	*sidetrack*	**sokusen**

側室	*concubine, mistress*	**sokushitsu**
外側	*outerside, exterior*	**sotogawa**
敵側	*enemy's side, ~viewpoint*	**tekigawa**
内側	*innerside, interior*	**uchigawa**
裏側	*back, rear*	**uragawa**
遮光側	*covered side*	**shakōgawa**
中央側	*offside*	**chūōgawa**
反対側	*opposite-, reverse side*	**hantaigawa**
権力側	*the powerful side*	**kenryokugawa**
攻撃側	*offensive side*	**kōgekigawa**
労働者側	*workers' side*	**rōdōshagawa**

陣*ampsite, 132*	傾*ncline, 833*
盟*lliance, 21*	偏*ncline, 43*
連*lliance, 305*	

測*imension, 291*

220-C

On the 則*egulation* 側*ide, strict* 測*imensions to abide...*

水⇔氵 (water)

測*easurement*　　測*imension*

haka(ru), SOKU
measurement, dimension, length, calibration, conjecture

FLIP: 8.0.b. Inner (stem)

不測	*unforeseen, unexpected*	**fusoku**
歩測	*pacing, strolling*	**hosoku**
実測	*actual measurement, ~dimension*	**jissoku**
観測	*observation, watching*	**kansoku**
計測	*measurements, dimensions*	**keisoku**
目測	*eyesight measurement*	**mokusoku**
憶測	*guess, conjecture*	**okusoku**
臆測	*speculation, conjecture*	**okusoku**
測地	*land surveying*	**sokuchi**
測度	*measurement, gauging*	**sokudo**
測鉛	*plumb bob, sounding lead*	**sokuen**
測量	*measurement, surveying*	**sokuryō**
測量術	*surveying technique*	**sokuryōjutsu**
測量図	*survey map*	**sokuryōzu**
測線	*measuring line*	**sokusen**
測深	*sounding out*	**sokushin**
測定	*measurement, surveying*	**sokutei**
測定法	*measurement method*	**sokuteihō**
推測	*guess, conjecture, surmise*	**suisoku**

探測	*sounding out*	**tansoku**
天測	*astronomical observation*	**tensoku**
予測	*prediction, forecasting*	**yosoku**
測り難い	*unfathomable*	**hakarigatai**
測り知る	*understand, fathom*	**hakarishiru**
測候所	*weather observatory*	**sokkōjo**
測微計	*micrometer*	**sokubikei**
測音器	*sonometer, phonometer*	**sokuonki**

寸*easurement, 345*
幅*easurement, 640*
計*easurement, 692*

側*ide, 291*

221-A

A 某ertain UN 媒ediator foiled a 謀onspirator...

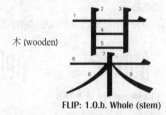

木 (wooden)

某ertain 某omething

nanigashi, BŌ
certain, something

某か *something* **soregashika**
某某 *so-&-so* **bōbō**
某月 *a certain month* **bōgetsu**
某日 *a certain day* **bōjitsu**
某女 *a certain woman* **bōjo**
某国 *a certain country* **bōkoku**
某年 *a certain year* **bōnen**
某氏 *a certain person* **bōshi**
某所 *a certain place* **bōsho**
何某 *a certain person* **nanigashi**
誰其れ *Mr. So and So* **daresore**
某博士 *Doctor X* **bōhakase**

FLIP: 1.0.b. Whole (stem)

何omething, 101
物hings, 647
事ction, 116
活ctivity, 237

謀onspiracy, 293

221-B

A 某ertain UN 媒ediator foiled a 謀onspirator...

女 (woman)

媒ediator 媒ntermediary

BAI
mediator, intermediary, go-between

媒介 *mediation, medium* **baikai**
媒介物 *medium, carrier* **baikaibutsu**
媒染 *colouring, colour fixing* **baisen**
媒酌 *matchmaking, go-between* **baishaku**
媒酌人 *matchmaker, go-between* **baishakunin**
媒質 *medium, carrier (physics)* **baishitsu**
媒体 *medium, conductor* **baitai**
霊媒 *medium, carrier* **reibai**
触媒 *catalyst, hastening agent* **shokubai**
触媒作用 *catalytic action* **shokubai sayō**
溶媒 *solvent* **yōbai**
媒汚剤 *mordant* **baiozai**
媒染剤 *colour fixative* **baisenzai**
鳥媒花 *ornithophilous flower* **chōbaika**
虫媒花 *entomophilous flower* **chūbaika**
風媒花 *wind pollination* **fūbaika**

FLIP: 7.0.b1. Right (stem)

介ediate, 365
渉ross-over, 273
談alks, 308
隔nterval, 963
仲ellow, 695
奴ellow, 44
輩ellow, 290
僚ellow, 66

嫌espise, 805

221-C

A 某ertain UN 媒ediator foiled a 謀onspirator...

言 (speaking)

謀cheme   謀onspiracy

haka(ru), BŌ, MU
scheme, conspiracy, plot, collusion, connivance

FLIP: 5.0.b. Left & Right

謀議 *plot, conspiracy* **bōgi**
謀略 *plot, trick, secret plan* **bōryaku**
謀殺 *premeditated murder* **bōsatsu**
謀臣 *strategist, tactician* **bōshin**
謀計 *plot, strategy, modus operandi* **bōkei**
知謀 *ingenuity, resourcefulness* **chibō**
智謀 *ingenuity, resourcefulness* **chibō**
遠謀 *foresight* **enbō**
陰謀 *conspiracy, plot* **inbō**
陰謀家 *plotter, conspirator* **inbōka**
権謀 *scheme, strategy, plot* **kenbō**
権謀家 *schemer, plotter* **kenbōka**
権謀術数 *trickery, fraud, deceit, shenanigan*
  kenbō jutsusū
共謀 *conspiracy, plot* **kyōbō**
密謀 *covert plan, secret plot* **mitsubō**
無謀 *reckless, irresponsible* **mubō**
謀反 *treason, rebellion, revolt* **muhon**
謀反人 *traitor, rebel, quisling* **muhonnin**

謀叛 *treason, rebellion, revolt* **muhon**
謀叛人 *traitor, rebel, quisling* **muhonnin**
策謀 *scheme, intrigue* **sakubō**
参謀 *staff officer* **sanbō**
参謀長 *chief of staff* **sanbōchō**
深謀 *careful, deliberate* **shinbō**
首謀者 *ringleader, mastermind* **shubōsha**
深謀遠慮 *long-term plan, vision* **shinbō enryo**
宿謀 *premeditated, planned* **shukubō**

罪 *riminal, 289*
犯 *riminal, 640*
共 *ogether, 302*
合 *ogether, 232*

課 *ection, 287*

222-A

甚xtreme 勘ntuition allows 堪ndurance in affliction...

甘 (sweet)

甚xtreme   甚tmost

hanaha(da), hanaha(dashii), JIN
extreme, utmost, ultra, ultimate

FLIP: 3.0.a. Top (flat)

甚だしい *serious, severe, gross* **hanahadashii**
激甚 *intense, grave, severe* **gekijin**
劇甚 *intense, grave, severe* **gekijin**
甚大 *immense, serious, grave* **jindai**
甚六 *simpleton, blockhead* **jinroku**
幸甚 *"very glad, much obliged..."* **kōjin**
深甚 *deep, serious, grave* **shinjin**
蝕甚 *maximum eclipse* **shokujin**
甚振る *torment, harass, annoy, badger* **itaburu**
勘違い *misunderstand, miscomprehend* **kanchigai**

極 *xtreme, 947*   端 *ndpoint, 974*
窮 *xtreme, 876*   最 *aximum, 423*
極 *xtreme, 947*

基 *oundation, 590*

222-B

甚*xtreme* 勘*ntuition allows* 堪*ndurance in affliction...*

力 (strength, force)

勘*ntuition*　　勘*remonition*

KAN
intuition, premonition, hunch, foreboding, sixth sense

FLIP: 6.1. Left Top

勅勘 *imperial imputation* **chokkan**
勘案 *consideration, idea* **kan'an**
勘弁 *pardon, excuse, forgiveness* **kanben**
勘違い *mistaken guess* **kanchigai**
勘所 *vital point, critical point* **kandokoro**
勘当 *disinheritance, disown* **kandō**
勘繰り *suspicion, suspecting* **kanguri**
勘定 *accounts, calculation, bill* **kanjō**
⇒別勘定 *separate account* **betsukanjō**
⇒相殺勘定 *offset account* **sōsai kanjō**
勘定書 *bill, invoice* **kanjōsho**
勘定違い *miscalculation* **kanjōchigai**
勘気 *displeasure, disgrace* **kanki**
勘考 *consideration, deliberation* **kankō**
勘校 *examine & correct* **kankō**
勘付く *foreboding of dangers* **kanzuku**
総勘定 *final settlement of accounts* **sōkanjō**
山勘 *guess, guesswork* **yamakan**
割り勘 *Dutch treat, paying for oneself* **warikan**

意*dea, 340*	感*eeling, 45*
想*dea, 524*	気*eelings, 98*
念*dea, 182*	情*eelings, 793*
衷*nner feelings, 119*	

堪*ndure, 294*

222-C

甚*xtreme* 勘*ntuition allows* 堪*ndurance in affliction...*

土 (ground, soil)

堪*ndure*　　堪*ear-with*

ta(eru), ta(maru), KAN, TAN
endure, bear-with, cope-with

FLIP: 7.2.a. Right Top (flat)

堪え難い *intolerable, unbearable* **taegatai**
堪え忍ぶ *bear, stand, put up with* **taeshinobu**
堪らない *unbearable, intolerable* **tamaranai**
堪り兼ねる *unbearable, intolerable* **tamarikaneru**
堪能 *satisfaction, proficiency* **tannō**
不堪 *incompetent, unskilful* **fukan**
堪忍 *patience, forgiveness* **kannin**
堪忍袋 *patience, forbearance* **kanninbukuro**
堪え性 *endurance, perseverance* **koraeshō**
踏み堪える *bear with, put up with* **fumikotaeru**
持ち堪える *hold on, stand, endure* **mochikotaeru**

耐*ndure, 974*
励*iligence, 465*
寿*ongevity, 440*

媒*ediator, 292*

223-A

軍*oldiers to* 運*ransport* 輝*parkling jewels to Frankfurt...*

車 (vehicle, wheel)

軍*ilitary*　軍*oldier*

ikusa, GUN
military, soldier, uniformed service, armed forces

FLIP: 1.0.b. Whole (stem)

援軍　reinforcement troops **engun**
軍閥　military clique **gunbatsu**
軍団　army corps **gundan**
軍医　military doctor **gun'i**
軍人　soldier, conscript **gunjin**
軍歌　war song, battle song **gunka**
軍艦　warship **gunkan**
軍紀　military discipline **gunki**
軍機　military secrets; war planes **gunki**
軍略　military strategy **gunryaku**
軍政　military government **gunsei**
軍籍　military profession, ~service **gunseki**
軍帥　supreme commander **gunshi**
軍職　military service **gunshoku**
軍縮　disarmament, arms reduction **gunshuku**
軍葬　military funeral **gunsō**
軍隊　military, army, soldiers **guntai**
敗軍　defeated army **haigun**
国軍　armed forces of a nation **kokugun**

陸軍　army **rikugun**
将軍　Shōgun **shōgun**
駐屯軍　stationed troops **chūtongun**
軍事力　military power **gunjiryoku**
軍資金　war chest, ~funds **gunshikin**
派遣軍　expeditionary army **hakengun**
十字軍　crusade **jūjigun**
再軍備　rearmament **saigunbi**
占領軍　occupation forces **senryōgun**
侵略軍　invading army **shinryakugun**
軍国主義　militarism **gunkoku shugi**

武*arrior, 100*	兵*oldier, 490*
戦*ighting, 517*	隊*oldier, 543*
闘*ombat, 946*	

車*heel, 306*

223-B

軍*oldiers to* 運*ransport* 輝*parkling jewels to Frankfurt...*

辶 (transport)

運*ransport*　運*ortune*

hako(bu), UN
transport, fortune, deliver, bring-over, carry-over, driving

FLIP: 3.0.b. Top (stem)

悪運　ill fortune, bad luck **akuun**
武運　fortunes of war **buun**
非運　ill fortune, bad luck **hiun**
悲運　sad fortune, miserable fate **hiun**
海運　commercial shipping **kaiun**
金運　money luck **kin'un**
機運　opportunity, chance **kiun**
国運　national destiny **kokuun**
幸運　good fortune, ~luck **kōun**
社運　company fortunes **shaun**
勝運　fortune, luck **shōun**
衰運　declining-, falling fortune **suiun**
運賃　transport fare **unchin**
運動　movement; sports **undō**
⇒革命運動　revolutionary movement **kakumei undō**
運営　management, administration **un'ei**
運河　canal, waterway **unga**
運航　navigation, plying, running **unkō**
運行　service, movement **unkō**

運休　suspension of transport service **unkyū**
運命　fate, destiny **unmei**
運搬　delivery, shipment, trucking **unpan**
運筆　brush stroke **unpitsu**
運針　acupuncture skills **unshin**
運送　transportation, trucking **unsō**
運転　motor-vehicle driving **unten**
⇒試運転　trial run, test drive **shiunten**
運輸　transportation, trucking **unyu**
運試し　trial of luck **undameshi**
運動会　sports festival **undōkai**
持ち運び　portable, mobile **mochihakobi**

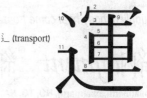

搬*ransport, 323*	荷*reight, 877*
輸*hipment, 660*	貨*reight, 191*
送*ending, 708*	搭*reight, 146*
届*eliver, 631*	命*estiny, 362*

軍*ilitary, 295*

223-C

軍*oldiers to* 運*ransport* 輝*parkling jewels to Frankfurt...*

車 (vehicle, wheel)

輝*parkling*　　輝*ustre*

kagaya(ku), KI
sparkling, shining, lustre

FLIP: 5.0.b. Left & Right

輝き brilliance, radiance **kagayaki**	
輝度 degree of brightness **kido**	
輝輝 brightness, luminescence **kiki**	
輝石 pyroxene **kiseki**	
輝線 luminous line **kisen**	
輝点 dots-, blips on radar screen **kiten**	
光輝 glory, brilliance **kōki**	
光り輝く glory, brilliance **hikarikagayaku**	

晶*rystal*, 131	英*rilliance*, 217
昭*right*, 529	光*hining*, 77
明*right*, 22	

揮*randish*, 126

224-A

納*upply of body heat come from* 内*nside* 肉*lesh &* 肉*eat...*

糸 (thread, continuity)

❶納*ayment*　❷納*upply*

osa(meru), osa(maru), NŌ, TŌ, NA, NAN
payment, settle account, put away; supply, dispense

FLIP: 7.0.b2. Right (stem)

❶
分納 instalment payment **bunnō**	
物納 payment-in-kind **butsunō**	
代納 payment on behalf of, "paid for by..." **dainō**	
延納 deferred payment **ennō**	
不納 default, non-payment **funō**	
返納 refund, repayment, buy back **hennō**	
受納 payment receipt **junō**	
完納 full payment, ~delivery **kannō**	
未納 unpaid, unsettled account **minō**	
納付 payment, delivery **nōfu**	
納金 payment, money due **nōkin**	
納入 delivery, payment, supply **nōnyū**	
納税 tax payment, ~settlement **nōzei**	
即納 prompt payment **sokunō**	
出納 expenses & revenues **suitō**	
滞納 non-payment, arrears **tainō**	
追納 additional-, extra payment **tsuinō**	
前納 advance payment, ~deposit **zennō**	
全納 full payment, ~delivery **zennō**	

❷
奉納 dedication, offering **hōnō**	
直納 direct supply **jikinō**	
献納 contributions, donations **kennō**	
納戸 storehouse, storage **nando**	
納豆 fermented soybeans **nattō**	
納得 consent, understanding **nattoku**	
納屋 barn, shed **naya**	
納品 delivery, supplying **nōhin**	
納本 delivered books **nōhon**	
納会 last meeting of the year **nōkai**	
納期 delivery time-limit **nōki**	
結納 gift, present, engagement **yuinō**	

払*ayment*, 682	済*onsummate*, 961
料*ayment*, 194	備*urnish*, 409
収*ollect*, 178	賄*urnish*, 806

級*rade*, 189

224-B

納*upply of body heat come from* 内*nside* 肉*lesh* & 肉*eat*...

冂 (inverted box)

内*nside* 内*nternal*

uchi, NAI, DAI
inside, internal, interior, intra-

FLIP: 1.0.b. Whole (stem)

案内	guidance, information	**annai**
場内	place, grounds, hall	**jōnai**
家内	household, one's wife	**kanai**
県内	within the prefecture	**kennai**
国内	nationwide, domestic	**kokunai**
坑内	shaft, pit	**kōnai**
内圧	internal pressure	**naiatsu**
内談	private talks, secret conversation	**naidan**
内縁	common-law marriage	**naien**
内外	inside & outside	**naigai, uchisoto**
内意	intention, private thinking	**naii**
内科	internal medicine	**naika**
内海	in-land sea	**naikai, uchiumi**
内角	interior angle, inside	**naikaku**
内閣	cabinet government	**naikaku**
内見	"for your eyes only..."	**naiken**
内妻	common-law wife	**naisai**
内債	domestic loans, borrowings	**naisai**
内済	out-of-court settlement	**naisai**

内政	domestic administration	**naisei**
内戦	civil war	**naisen**
内緒	secret, confidential, covert	**naisho**
内職	sideline job, moonlighting	**naishoku**
内定	informal decision	**naitei**
内気	shy, introvert	**uchiki**
内幕	inside story	**uchimaku**
内面	in good humour at home	**uchitsura**
内訳	itemized accounting	**uchiwake**
内税	tax-included price	**uchizei**
枠内	within limits	**wakunai**
内々に	secretly, privately, covertly	**nainai(ni)**
宮内庁	imperial household agency	**kunaichō**
内渡し	partial delivery	**uchiwatashi**

奥*nside*, 903	外*utside*, 188
入*ut-inside*, 2	出*ome-out* 173

囚*risoner*, 863

224-C

納*upply of body heat come from* 内*nside* 肉*lesh* & 肉*eat*...

肉⇔月 (flesh, body part)

肉*eat* 肉*lesh*

NIKU
meat, flesh

FLIP: 1.0.b. Whole (stem)

肋肉	spare ribs	**abaraniku**
豚肉	pork	**butaniku**
鯨肉	whale meat	**geiniku**
魚肉	fish meat	**gyoniku**
牛肉	beef	**gyūniku**
皮肉	irony, sarcasm	**hiniku**
印肉	seal inkpad	**inniku**
果肉	flesh, pulp	**kaniku**
筋肉	muscle	**kinniku**
骨肉	blood relationship	**kotsuniku**
苦肉	desperate, despondent	**kuniku**
肉弾	human shield, human torpedo	**nikudan**
肉眼	naked eye, unaided eye	**nikugan**
肉牛	beef cattle	**nikugyū**
肉筆	bare handwriting	**nikuhitsu**
肉汁	meat juice	**nikujū**
肉増し	flesh thickening	**nikumashi**
肉声	voice without a microphone	**nikusei**
肉親	blood relative	**nikushin**

肉食	carnivorousness, meat-eating	**nikushoku**
肉体	body, flesh, sexual	**nikutai**
肉体美	physical beauty	**nikutaibi**
肉体関係	blood relationship	**nikutai kankei**
肉体労働	physical labour	**nikutai rōdō**
肉屋	meat shop, butcher	**nikuya**
生肉	fresh meat	**seiniku, namaniku**
死肉	dead flesh, carcass	**shiniku**
朱肉	vermilion inkpad	**shuniku**
鶏肉	chicken meat	**toriniku, keiniku**
肉感的	erotic, sensual, sensous	**nikkanteki**
謝肉祭	carnival	**shanikusai**

牛*attle*, 179	菜*egetable*, 915
豚*ig*, 910	食*oods*, 255
鶏*hicken*, 842	

内*nside*, 297

225-A

飛*light with fuel of* 升*[1.8 litre]* 昇*-scends in shivers...*

飛*light*　飛*irborne*　飛*erial*

飛 (flying)

to(bu), to(basu), HI
aerial, airborne, flight

Facing: 4.0. 〰️☞ Apart

飛び魚 *flying fish* **tobiuo**
飛び散る *fly about, splash, scatter* **tobichiru**
飛び火 *jumping fire, leap of fire* **tobihi**
飛び入り *rushing in the spur of the moment* **tobiiri**
飛び掛かる *spring, leap* **tobikakaru**
飛び込み *plunge, dive* **tobikomi**
飛び越す *jump, leap over* **tobikosu**
飛び回る *flutter, busy, romp about* **tobimawaru**
飛び降り *jump-down* **tobiori**
飛び去る *fly away* **tobisaru**
飛び移る *jump, flutter, spring, fly* **tobiutsuru**
吹き飛ぶ *be blown away* **fukitobu**
消し飛ぶ *vanish, blast, disappear* **keshitobu**
飛瀑 *waterfalls* **hibaku**
飛鳥 *bird in flight* **hichō**
飛行 *flight* **hikō**
⇒計器飛行 *instrument-, blind flying* **keiki hikō**
⇒旋回飛行 *circular flight* **senkai hikō**
⇒処女飛行 *maiden flight, ~voyage* **shojo hikō**

⇒宇宙飛行 *space flight* **uchū hikō**
飛行機 *aircraft, airplane* **hikōki**
飛行艇 *seaplane* **hikōtei**
飛球 *fly ball (baseball)* **hikyū**
飛沫 *sea wave splash* **himatsu**
飛来 *come flying* **hirai**
飛散 *scatter out, scramble* **hisan**
飛躍 *jump, leap, spring* **hiyaku**
突飛 *weird, eerie, ghastly* **toppi**
雄飛 *ambitious, aiming high* **yūhi**
流言飛語 *wild-, groundless rumour* **ryūgen higo**

鳥*irds, 125*	羽*eather, 240*	軽*ightweight, 790*
空*ky, 394*	翼*eather, 239*	

算*alculate, 141*

225-B

飛*light with fuel of* 升*[1.8 litre]* 昇*-scends in shivers...*

升*[1.8 litre]*

十 (cross)

masu, SHŌ
[1.8 litre]

Facing: 1.0. 〰️ West (W)

一升 *1.8 litre* **isshō**
一升瓶 *1.8 litre bottle* **isshōbin**
升形 *square-shaped* **masugata**
升目 *square measure* **masume**
升席 *box seat* **masuseki**
升酒 *sake in a wooden cup* **masuzake**

旬*[10 day], 494*	坪*[3.3 sqm], 488*
斗*[18 ltr], 195*	匁*[3.75 gm], 75*
勺*[18 ml], 470*	尺*[30 cm], 574*
寸*[3 cm], 345*	斤*[600 gm], 471*

井*ater well, 361*

225-C

飛*light with fuel of* 升*[1.8 litre]* 昇*-scends in shivers...*

日 (sunlight, daytime)

昇*scend*　　昇*levate*

nobo(ru), SHŌ
　ascend, elevate, upward

FLIP: 3.0.a. Top (flat)

上昇　*ascending, going-up* **jōshō**
⇒物価上昇　*commodities price hike* **bukka jōshō**
上昇気流　*rising current* **jōshō kiryū**
昇段　*job promotion* **shōdan**
昇殿　*entry into inner sanctum* **shōden**
昇叙　*promotion, advancement* **shōjo**
昇順　*ascending order* **shōjun**
昇華　*sublimation* **shōka**
昇格　*promotion, raising of status* **shōkaku**
昇降　*ascent & descent, fluctuation* **shōkō**
昇降機　*elevator, lift* **shōkōki**
昇級　*promotion, advancement* **shōkyū**
昇給　*salary raise, pay increase* **shōkyū**
昇任　*be promoted, career advance* **shōnin**
昇進　*job promotion* **shōshin**
昇天　*ascension to heaven, death* **shōten**
昇騰　*rise, soar, upsurge* **shōtō**
昇り藤　*lumpine* **noborifuji**
昇り竜　*rising dragon* **nobiriryū**

上*scend, 859*	起*rise, 754*
登*limb, 437*	立*tand up, 234*

最*aximum, 423*

226A

杯*ine cups to* 否*efuse when* 不*egative of booze...*

木 (wooden)

杯*ine cup*

sakazuki, HAI
　wine cup, glass of drink, cup

FLIP: 7.1. Right (Sort Of)

罰杯　*"loser must drink..."* **bappai**
別杯　*farewell drink* **beppai**
銀杯　*silver cup* **ginpai**
玉杯　*jade cup* **gyokuhai**
杯盤　*plates & glasses* **haiban**
杯洗　*cleaning basin for cups* **haisen**
返杯　*offering a toast in return* **henpai**
一杯　*a cup of drink* **ippai**
⇒力一杯　*lots of strength* **chikaraippai**
⇒精一杯　*with all one's strength* **seiippai**
⇒手一杯　*have one's hands full* **teippai**
乾杯　*toast of drink, "cheers..."* **kanpai**
献杯　*offering a cup of sake* **kenpai**
金杯　*golden cup* **kinpai**
苦杯　*bitter ordeal* **kuhai**
満杯　*fill up, full to capacity* **manpai**
水杯　*farewell drinks of water* **mizusakazuki**
木杯　*wooden cup* **mokuhai**
賜杯　*trophy awarded by the emperor* **shihai**

賞杯　*trophy, prize cup* **shōhai**
酒杯　*cup of wine* **shuhai**
祝杯　*congratulatory toast* **shukuhai**
大杯　*large cup* **taihai**
優勝杯　*championship trophy* **yūshōhai**
茶二杯　*two cups of tea* **cha nihai**
砂糖三杯　*three spoonful of sugar* **satō sanbai**

飲*rink, 255*	酒*lcohol, 789*
宴*anquet, 610*	酔*runk, 760*
興*ntertainment, 867*	慶*ejoice, 69*

枚*[sheets], 724*

226-B

杯*ine cups to* 否*efuse when* 不*egative of booze...*

口 (mouth)

否*efusal* 否*ejection*

ina(mu), HI

refusal, rejection, repudiation, disapproval

FLIP: 2.0.a. Sort Of (flat)
FLIP: 4.0.a. Bottom (flat)

安否 *well-being, safe-or-unsafe* **anpi**
諾否 *accept-or-reject* **dakuhi**
合否 *pass-or-fail, yes-or-no* **gōhi**
否決 *rejection, voting down* **hiketsu**
否認 *denial, disapproval, rejection* **hinin**
否定 *denial, refusal, rejection* **hitei**
⇒二重否定 *double negative* **nijū hitei**
否定文 *negative sentence* **hiteibun**
否定的 *negative* **hiteiteki**
否運 *misfortune, tragic* **hiun**
実否 *true-or-false* **jippi**
可否 *propriety, right-or-wrong* **kahi**
拒否 *denial, refusal, veto, turn down* **kyohi**
⇒登校拒否 *refusal to attend school* **tōkō kyohi**
拒否権 *veto right, veto power* **kyohiken**
認否 *approval-or-disapproval* **ninpi**
⇒罪状認否 *arraignment, court plea* **zaijō ninpi**
良否 *quality, good-or-bad* **ryōhi**
採否 *adoption-or-rejection* **saihi**

賛否 *approval-or-disapproval* **sanpi**
正否 *right-or-wrong* **seihi**
成否 *success-or-failure* **seihi**
真否 *true-or-false* **shinpi**
存否 *existence, dead-or-alive* **sonpi**
適否 *propriety, aptness, suitability* **tekihi**
当否 *right-or-wrong* **tōhi**
運否天賦 *leaving to chance* **unpi tenpu**

非*[negative]*, 288	拒*efusal*, 207
不*[negative]*, 300	断*efusal*, 958

苦*uffer*, 477

226-C

杯*ine cups to* 否*efuse when* 不*egative of booze...*

一 (one, single)

不*[negative]*

FU, BU

[negative]

FLIP: 2.0.b. Sort Of (stem)

不安 *insecurity, unrest, anxiety* **fuan**
不安定 *unstable, precarious* **fuantei**
不遇 *obscure, unfortunate* **fugū**
不敗 *invincible, powerful* **fuhai**
不意 *abruptness, suddenness* **fui**
不実 *insincere, dishonest* **fujitsu**
不可 *impossible, not allowed* **fuka**
不可欠 *indispensable, essential* **fukaketsu**
不況 *economic recession* **fukyō**
不満 *unsatisfactory, lacking, insufficient* **fuman**
不明 *unknown, unclear, vague* **fumei**
不納 *non-payment* **funō**
不良 *defective, inferior, substandard* **furyō**
不信 *unfaithfulness, infidelity* **fushin**
不足 *insufficiency, lacking* **fusoku**
不運 *misfortune, ill luck* **fuun**
不動産 *real estate, realty* **fudōsan**
不払い *non-payment* **fubarai**
不合格 *exam failure, flunking* **fugōkaku**

不一致 *inconsistency, disagreement* **fuicchi**
不十分 *insufficient, lacking, not enough* **fujūbun**
不可侵 *non-aggression* **fukashin**
不均衡 *disproportionate, unequal* **fukinkō**
不公平 *unjust, impartial, bias* **fukōhei**
不明確 *indefinite, uncertain* **fumeikaku**
不思議 *mysterious, incomprehensible* **fushigi**
不祥事 *disdainful, scandal* **fushōji**
親不孝 *ungrateful-, unfilial child* **oyafukō**
不身持ち *immoral, promiscuous* **fumimochi**
不眠不休 *lacking sleep or rest* **fumin fukyū**
不慮の死 *unexpected death* **furyo no shi**

無*othing*, 49
非*[negative]*, 288

斤*[600 gms]*, 471

227-A

Convent 尼uns mad when roof is 漏eaking 泥ud...

尸 (corpse)

尼*un*　　　尼*riestess*

ama, NI
nun, priestess

Facing: 2.1. East ☞ (H)

尼寺　*convent, nunnery* **amadera**
尼君　*nun (polite)* **amagimi**
尼僧　*nun, sister* **nisō**
尼僧院　*convent, nunnery* **nisōin**
尼僧院長　*mother superior* **nisōinchō**
僧尼　*monks & nuns* **sōni**
禅尼　*Zen Buddhist nun* **zenni**
尼っ子　*broad skirt* **amakko**
尼崎市　*Amagasaki City, Hyōgo Pref.* **amagasaki-shi**
尼奉師　*Buddhist nun* **amahōshi**
尼将軍　*female general, lady warrior* **amashōgun**
連月尼　*name of a famous Buddhist nun* **rengetsuni**
修道尼　*nun, prioress* **shūdōni**

堂*ltar, 94*	仏*uddha, 683*
聖*acred, 617*	盆*uddhist Feast, 594*
神*ivine, 712*	僧*uddhist monk, 836*
祈*rayer, 184*	坊*uddhist monk, 736*
拝*rayer, 636*	女*emale, 350*

民*eople, 495*

227-B

Convent 尼uns mad when roof is 漏eaking 泥ud...

水⇔氵 (water)

漏*eakage*　漏*ripping*

mo(ru), mo(reru), mo(rasu), RŌ
leakage, dripping, discharge, disclosure, draining

FLIP: 7.3.b. Right Bottom (stem)

脱漏　*omission, leaving out* **datsurō**
遺漏　*oversight, omission* **irō**
耳漏　*ear discharge, earwax* **jirō**
欠漏　*omission* **ketsurō**
膿漏　*pyorrhoea* **nōrō**
⇒歯槽膿漏　*pyorrhoea* **shisō nōrō**
漏電　*electric short circuit* **rōden**
漏洩　*leakage, leak* **rōei**
⇒秘密漏洩　*secret leakage* **himitsu rōei**
漏口　*leak, vent* **rōkō**
漏刻　*water clock* **rōkoku**
漏出　*leakage, leak* **rōshutsu**
漏水　*water leakage* **rōsui**
漏斗　*funnel* **rōto**
疎漏　*carelessness, negligence* **sorō**
粗漏　*carelessness, oversight* **sorō**
早漏　*uncontrolled ejaculation* **sōrō**
杜漏　*careless, negligent* **zurō**
雨漏り　*leaking rain, dripping rain* **amamori**

水漏れ　*leaking water* **mizumore**
ガス漏れ　*gas leak* **gasumore**
漏れ聞く　*hear by chance, overhear* **morekiku**
漏れ無く　*without exception* **morenaku**
税金漏れ　*tax cheating* **zeikinmore**
言い漏らす　*forget to say* **iimorasu**
書き漏らす　*omit, leave out* **kakimorasu**
聞き漏らす　*miss hearing* **kikimorasu**
討ち漏らす　*let escape, fail to kill* **uchimorasu**

出*ome-out, 173*	流*lowing, 781*
泉*prings, 531*	雨*aining, 417*
破*estroy, 715*	泌*ecrete, 219*

涙*rying, 541*

227-C

Convent 尼uns mad when roof is 漏eaking 泥ud...

泥uddy   泥lay

水 ⇔ 氵 (water)

doro, DEI
muddy, clay, dirt, marshy

Facing: 2.2. East ☞ (V)

沈泥 silt **chindei**
泥中 soiled, mudded **deichū**
泥土 mud, dirt **deido, dorotsuchi**
泥土層 dirt bed **deidosō**
泥状 muddy, murky **deijō**
泥濘 quagmire, marsh **deinei**
泥流 mud flow **deiryū**
泥酔 dead drunk **deisui**
泥炭 peat, sod **deitan**
泥棒 thief, robber, burglar **dorobō**
泥棒猫 stealing cat **dorobōneko**
泥亀 soft shell crab **dorogame**
泥道 muddy road **doromichi**
泥水 muddy water **doromizu**
泥縄 "too late an expediency..." **doronawa**
泥沼 bog, marsh, swamp **doronuma**
銀泥 silver paint **gindei**
拘泥 adherence, adhesion **kōdei**
金泥 gold plant **kondei, kindei**

軟泥 ooze, shime, mire **nandei**
汚泥 sludge, waste, refuse **odei**
障泥 saddle flap **shōdei**
雲泥 "a world of difference..." **undei**
雲泥の差 great difference **undei no sa**
泥跳ね splash of mud **dorohane**
泥試合 mudslinging **dorojiai**
泥仕合 mudslinging **dorojiai**
泥火山 mud volcano **dorokazan**
泥臭い unrefined, crude **dorokusai**
泥除け fender, mudguard **doroyoke**
泥塗れ covered with mud **doromamire**
自動車泥 carnapper, car thief **jidōshadoro**

濁uddy, 924	沢wamp, 753
汚irty, 737	排ejection, 795
沼wamp, 356	土oil, 8

尼un, 301

228-A

共ogether, regents 供ook-after the 選hosen ruler...

共ogether   共ommon

八 (eight, divisible)

tomo, KYŌ
together, common, joint, shared, combined, unison

FLIP: 1.0.b. Whole (stem)

防共 anti-communist **bōkyō**
反共 anti-communist **hankyō**
公共 common, public **kōkyō**
共謀 conspiracy, plot **kyōbō**
共著 joint authorship, co-writer **kyōcho**
共同 co-operation, collaboration **kyōdō**
共益 public interest, common good **kyōeki**
共演 co-star, co-starring **kyōen**
共学 co-education **kyōgaku**
⇒男女共学 co-education **danjo kyōgaku**
共犯 conspiracy crime, complicity **kyōhan**
共編 joint editing **kyōhen**
共感 sympathy, empathy **kyōkan**
共起 association **kyōki**
共催 joint auspices, co-sponsorship **kyōsai**
共済 mutual aid, ~assistance **kyōsai**
共済組合 co-operative, mutual aid **kyōsai kumiai**
共産圏 communist bloc **kyōsanken**
共産党 communist party **kyōsantō**

共産主義 communism **kyōsan shugi**
共生 symbiosis **kyōsei**
共振 resonate with **kyōshin**
共闘 joint struggle **kyōtō**
共通 in common, sameness **kyōtsū**
共存 co-existence, "live & let live..." **kyōzon**
容共 pro-communist **yōkyō**
共和国 republic, Republic of~ **kyōwakoku**
共和制 republican system **kyōwasei**
共稼ぎ dual-income family **tomokasegi**

合ogether, 232	伴ccompany, 949
随ccompany, 807	般ommon, 323
添ccompany, 620	普ommon, 455

井ater well, 361

228-B

共*ogether, regents* 供*ook-after the* 選*hosen ruler...*

供*ttend to*   供*ook-after*

人⇔亻 (person)

sona(eru), KYŌ, KU
attend to, look-after, offer

FLIP: 7.0.b2. Right (stem)

自供 *confession, guilt admission* **jikyō**
子供 *child, children* **kodomo**
子供扱い *look after a child* **kodomo atsukai**
子供部屋 *children's room* **kodomobeya**
子供心 *childish, child-like* **kodomogokoro**
口供 *oral statement* **kōkyō**
口供書 *written deposition, affidavit* **kōkyōsho**
供物 *offering, contribution* **kumotsu**
供述 *statement, deposition* **kyōjutsu**
供述書 *deposition, sworn statement* **kyōjutsusho**
⇒宣誓供述書 *affidavit, sworn statement, deposition*
      sensei kyōjutsusho
供給 *supply, service* **kyōkyū**
供給不足 *short supply, "running low on..."*
      kyōkyū busoku
供給源 *source of supply* **kyōkyūgen**
供給者 *supplier, provider* **kyōkyūsha**
供米 *rice for the government* **kyōmai, kumai**
供応 *entertainment, entreatment* **kyōō**

供覧 *display, exhibit* **kyōran**
供託 *depositing, entrusting* **kyōtaku**
供託物 *deposited articles* **kyōtakubutsu**
供託金 *money on deposit* **kyōtakukin**
供託者 *depositor* **kyōtakusha**
供与 *grant, supply* **kyōyo**
供用 *open to the public* **kyōyō**
大供 *adult, grown up* **ōdomo**
節供 *season festival* **sekku**
試供 *offer as a sample* **shikyō**
提供 *offer, providing, sponsorship* **teikyō**
御供え *offering, contribution* **osonae**

看*ook after, 623*	臨*ttend, 902*	臨*aring, 902*
構*ook after, 714*	護*aring, 828*	

共*ogether, 302*

228-C

共*ogether, regents* 供*ook-after the* 選*hosen ruler...*

辶 (transport)

選*hoice*   選*election*

era(bu), SEN
choice, selection, elective, option, pick out

FLIP: 7.3.b. Right Bottom (stem)

抽選 *lottery, lotto, drawing* **chūsen**
厳選 *careful selection* **gensen**
互選 *mutual vote* **gosen**
本選 *final selection* **honsen**
人選 *selecting a candidate* **jinsen**
自選 *personal choice* **jisen**
改選 *re-election* **kaisen**
官選 *government-appointed* **kansen**
国選 *national election, state-appointed* **kokusen**
公選 *mass-, popular election* **kōsen**
入選 *running in an election* **nyūsen**
選抜 *choice, selection* **senbatsu**
選別 *sorting out* **senbetsu**
選外 *not chosen, rejected* **sengai**
選者 *judge, selector* **senja**
選歌 *selected poems, ~songs* **senka**
選考 *selection, choosing* **senkō**
選挙 *suffrage, election, voting* **senkyo**
選曲 *selected music* **senkyoku**

選局 *tuning in (radio)* **senkyoku**
選民 *"the chosen people..."* **senmin**
選良 *duly-elected* **senryō**
選書 *selected works, anthology, collection* **sensho**
選手 *athlete, player, sportsman, ~woman* **senshu**
選択 *choice, alternative* **sentaku**
詩選 *selected poems* **shisen**
特選 *specially-chosen* **tokusen**
当選 *winning an election, ~ a prize* **tōsen**
選球眼 *batting eye* **senkyūgan**

択*hoice, 753*	判*udgement, 949*
決*ecide, 699*	志*ntention, 426*

港*arbour, 512*

229-A

市*ity* 市*arkets* 逓*radually* 逓*onvey healthy* 肺*ungs gone astray...*

❶ 市*ity* ❷ 市*arket*

巾 (cloth, fabric)

ichi, SHI
city, municipal; market

FLIP: 1.0.b. Whole (stem)

❶ 市長 *city mayor* **shichō**
市道 *city-built road* **shidō**
市営 *city-managed* **shiei**
市街 *street, city* **shigai**
市外 *suburb, outskirts* **shigai**
市外局番 *phone area code* **shigai kyokuban**
市会 *city assembly* **shikai**
市況 *market conditions, the market* **shikyō**
市民 *citizen, people* **shimin**
市内 *within the city, inner-city* **shinai**
市政 *entrepot* **shisei**
市有 *city-owned* **shiyū**
都市 *city administration* **toshi**
⇒学園都市 *university town, ~village* **gakuen toshi**
⇒巨大都市 *megalopolis, mega city* **kyodai toshi**
⇒姉妹都市 *sister cities* **shimai toshi**
市庁舎 *townhall office* **shichōsha**
市町村 *cities, tows & counties* **shichōson**
市街戦 *urban warfare, street fighting* **shigaisen**

市議会 *city assembly, ~council* **shigikai**
市役所 *city hall, municipal hall* **shiyakusho**
市街地 *city area* **shigaichi**
❷市販 *market selling, marketing* **shihan**
市場 *market* **shijō, ichiba**
⇒為替市場 *currency markets* **kawase shijō**
⇒海外市場 *overseas markets* **kaigai shijō**
⇒証券市場 *securities market* **shōken shijō**
市価 *market price, price* **shika**
馬市 *horse fair* **umaichi**
闇市 *blackmarket* **yamiichi**
競り市 *auction-, bidding market* **seriichi**

京 *apital, 386*	区 *istrict, 80*
都 *etropolis, 694*	商 *ommerce, 135*
街 *owntown, 107*	業 *usiness, 124*

屯 *eployment, 198*

229-B

市*ity* 市*arkets* 逓*radually* 逓*onvey healthy* 肺*ungs gone astray...*

❶ 逓*radual* ❷ 逓*onvey*

辶 (transport)

TEI
gradual, regulated; convey, relay

FLIP: 8.0.b. Inner (stem)

❶ 逓減 *diminution, degrading* **teigen**
逓次 *successively, consecutively* **teiji**
逓増 *gradual increase* **teizō**

❷ 逓伝 *conveying a message* **teiden**
駅逓 *mail transport (Meiji Era)* **ekitei**
逓信 *communication, correspondence* **teishin**
逓送 *forwarding* **teisō**

伝 *onvey, 619*	報 *eport, 733*
告 *eport, 266*	

透 *ransparency, 383*

229-C

市ity 市arkets 逓radually 逓onvey healthy 肺ungs gone astray...

肉⇔月 (flesh, body part)

肺*ung*

HAI
lung

肺病	lung disease, tuberculosis **haibyō**
肺炎	pneumonia **haien**
肺腑	innermost mind; lungs **haifu**
肺癌	lung cancer **haigan**
肺魚	lung fish, dipnoan **haigyo**
肺胞	pulmonary alveoli **haihō**
肺肝	innermost heart, liver & gall **haikan**
肺患	lung illness **haikan**
肺門	hilum of lungs **haimon**
肺尖	pulmonary apex **haisen**
肺葉	lobe of lungs **haiyō**
肺臓	lungs organ **haizō**
心肺	heart & lungs **shinpai**
炭肺	black lungs, anthracosis **tanhai**
肺活量	breathing capacity **haikatsuryō**
肺結核	tuberculosis, lung disease **haikekkaku**
肺浸潤	pulmonary tuberculosis **haishinjun**
肺出血	blood vomiting from lungs **haishukketsu**
鉄の肺	iron lungs **tetsu no hai**

FLIP: 7.0.b1. Right (stem)

息*reathe*, 586
吹*lowing*, 642

肪*bese*, 735

230-A

連lliance's 車ehicles & 車heels damaged, kept in a 庫torage...

辶 (transport)

連lliance 連onfederacy

tsu(reru), tsura(naru), tsura(neru), REN
alliance, confederacy, coalition, federation, league, linkage, succession

FLIP: 3.0.b. Top (stem)

常連	frequent, regular **jōren**
関連	association, connexion, relation **kanren**
国連	United Nations **kokuren**
連番	consecutive numbers **renban**
連中	linked with, allied with **renchū**
連弾	playing piano together **rendan**
連動	linking with, in association **rendō**
連合	alliance, aggrupation **rengō**
連日	consecutive days **renjitsu**
連係	connection, contact **renkei**
連携	linking, collaboration **renkei**
連結	connection, coupling **renketsu**
連休	consecutive holidays **renkyū**
連盟	alliance, allies, confederacy **renmei**
連名	joint signature, co-signatory **renmei**
連破	successive winnings **renpa**
連覇	successive winnings **renpa**
連敗	successive defeats **renpai**
連発	continuous firing **renpatsu**

連峰	mountain ranges **renpō**
連絡	communication, correspondence **renraku**
連立	coalition, confederacy, alliance **renritsu**
連鎖	chain **rensa**
連載	serial publishing **rensai**
連作	same crop farming **rensaku**
連戦	successive battles **rensen**
連署	joint signature petition **rensho**
連帯	aggrupation, solidarity **rentai**
ソ連	Soviet Union, USSR **soren**
脇連	Noh supporting actor **wakiren**
道連れ	travelling companion **michizure**

盟*lliance*, 21	団*roup*, 345	同*imilar*, 245
敵*nemy*, 966	組*roup*, 138	共*ommon*, 302

車*ehicle*, 306

230-B

連*lliance's* 車*ehicles* & 車*heels damaged, kept in a* 庫*torage...*

車 (vehicle, wheel)

車*ehicle* 車*heel*

kuruma, SHA
vehicle, automobile, car, transportation, wheel, locomotive

FLIP: 1.0.b. Whole (stem)

愛車 *one's favourite car* **aisha**
馬車 *carriage, coach* **basha**
駐車 *parking, car park* **chūsha**
電車 *electric train* **densha**
風車 *windmill* **fūsha**
外車 *foreign-made cars* **gaisha**
配車 *dispatch transport service* **haisha**
糸車 *spinning wheel* **itoguruma**
貨車 *freight car* **kasha**
汽車 *steam train* **kisha**
降車 *get off a vehicle* **kōsha**
車蝦 *prawn, jumbo shrimp* **kurumaebi**
空車 *"for hire..." (taxi)* **kūsha**
荷車 *cart, wagon* **niguruma**
列車 *train* **ressha**
洗車 *car wash* **sensha**
車道 *roadway, driveway* **shadō**
車軸 *axle* **shajiku**
車検 *vehicle-safety inspection* **shaken**

車輪 *wheel* **sharin**
車両 *motor vehicle* **sharyō**
車線 *road lane* **shasen**
車掌 *conductor, guard* **shashō**
車窓 *train window, car window* **shasō**
横車 *selfishness; side wheel* **yokoguruma**
自動車 *car, automobile* **jidōsha**
車椅子 *wheelchair* **kurumaisu**
車酔い *road sickness* **kurumayoi**
給水車 *water-supply truck* **kyūsuisha**
矢車草 *cornflower* **yagurumasō**

運*ransport, 295*	速*peedy, 502*
旅*ravel, 650*	迅*peedy, 95*
乗*ide on, 511*	運*riving, 295*

東*astern, 220*

230-C

連*lliance's* 車*ehicles* & 車*heels damaged, kept in a* 庫*torage...*

广 (rooftop)

庫*torage* 庫*torehouse*

KO, KU
storage, storehouse, storeroom, depository

FLIP: 8.0.b. Inner (stem)

武庫 *armoury, arsenal* **buko**
文庫 *private library* **bunko**
宝庫 *treasure house, treasury* **hōko**
官庫 *government warehouse* **kanko**
金庫 *safe, cash box* **kinko**
⇒貸し金庫 *safety-deposit box* **kashikinko**
⇒手提げ金庫 *small cash box* **tesagekinko**
国庫 *national treasury* **kokko**
公庫 *government treasury* **kōko**
庫裏 *Buddhist temple kitchen* **kuri**
入庫 *stock pile, stockpiling* **nyūko**
車庫 *garage, car port* **shako**
書庫 *collection of written materials* **shoko**
出庫 *shipping out, delivery shipment* **shukko**
倉庫 *warehouse, storage* **sōko**
炭庫 *coal storehouse* **tanko**
艇庫 *boathouse* **teiko**
在庫 *in stock, inventory* **zaiko**
在庫品 *in stock, available goods* **zaikohin**

武器庫 *armoury, arsenal* **bukiko**
貯炭庫 *bunker, underground safeplace* **chotanko**
貯蔵庫 *storehouse, storage* **chozōko**
兵器庫 *armoury, arsenal* **heikiko**
兵庫県 *Hyōgo Prefecture* **hyōgo-ken**
格納庫 *hangar* **kakunōko**
火薬庫 *gunpowder storehouse* **kayakuko**
機関庫 *locomotive shed* **kikanko**
手文庫 *box of papers* **tebunko**

倉*torage, 399*
蔵*torage, 565*
貯*torage, 967*

車*ehicle, 306*

231-A

見ee & 覚erceive, 覚ecall what 寛eniency receives...

見 (seeing)

見*eeing*　　見*ooking*

FLIP: 2.0.b. Sort Of (stem)

mi(ru), mi(seru), KEN

seeing, looking, visual

味見 *food tasting* **ajimi**
外見 *outward appearance* **gaiken, sotomi**
発見 *discovery* **hakken**
花見 *cherry-blossom viewing* **hanami**
意見 *opinion, idea, comment* **iken**
会見 *press conference* **kaiken**
形見 *souvenir, memento* **katami**
見物 *sight-seeing, tour* **kenbutsu**
見学 *observation, inspection* **kengaku**
見解 *opinion, viewpoint* **kenkai**
見当 *guess, estimate* **kentō**
見事 *something to watch* **migoto**
見本 *sample, specimen* **mihon**
了見 *intention, idea, judgement* **ryōken**
散見 *appear, emerge* **sanken**
政見 *political view, opinion* **seiken**
私見 *personal opinion* **shiken**
所見 *opinion, impressions, comment* **shoken**
予見 *foresight, anticipation* **yoken**

夢見 *dreaming, seeing a dream* **yumemi**
見舞い *arranged engagement* **mimai**
見せ場 *highlight, climax* **miseba**
見せ物 *something to show* **misemono**
見通し *prospect, outlook* **mitooshi**
立ち見 *stand & watch* **tachimi**
見え透く *obvious, transparent* **miesuku**
見定める *verify by sight* **misadameru**
見せ合う *show each other* **miseau**
見積もり *price estimate, quotation* **mitsumori**
重く見る *consider seriously* **omokumiru**

目 *ye, 462*	眺 *aze at, 215*
眼 *yesight, 771*	観 *iew, 667*

目 *ye, 462*

231-B

見ee & 覚erceive, 覚ecall what 寛eniency receives...

見 (seeing)

❶覚*erception*　　❷覚*emember*

FLIP: 2.0.b. Sort Of (stem)

obo(eru); sa(meru), sa(masu), KAKU

perception, sense, sensation; remember, memory, memorize, recall, recollection

❶圧覚 *pressure derived from sensation* **akkaku**
知覚 *perception, sensation* **chikaku**
聴覚 *sense of hearing* **chōkaku**
直覚 *intuition, hunch, sixth sense* **chokkaku**
幻覚 *hallucination, illusion, fantasy* **genkaku**
発覚 *detection, discovery, disclosure* **hakkaku**
自覚 *consciousness, awareness* **jikaku**
覚悟 *resolution, preparedness* **kakugo**
感覚 *senses* **kankaku**
⇒無感覚 *insensibility, callousness* **mukankaku**
⇒方向感覚 *sense of direction* **hōkō kankaku**
⇒色彩感覚 *sense of colour* **shikisai kankaku**
味覚 *taste, palate* **mikaku**
温覚 *sense of heat* **onkaku**
才覚 *resourceful, witty* **saikaku**
錯覚 *illusion, fantasy* **sakkaku**
視覚 *sense of sight, vision* **shikaku**
触覚 *sense of touch* **shokkaku**
統覚 *control of one's consciousness* **tōkaku**

痛覚 *sense of pain* **tsūkaku**
寝覚め *wake up, get up from bed* **nezame**
目覚める *wake up, get up from bed* **mezameru**
覚め際 *"just about to wake up..."* **samegiwa**
予覚 *foreboding, premonition* **yokaku**
覚醒剤 *stimulant, pep pill* **kakuseizai**

❷心覚え *memory, reminder* **kokoro oboe**
物覚え *memory ability, memorizing* **monooboe**
覚書き *notice, memo, reminder* **oboegaki**
先覚者 *pioneer, forerunner, explorer* **enkakusha**
空覚え *rote memorization* **sora oboe**

起 *waken, 754*	知 *wareness, 103*
憶 *emory, 339*	識 *wareness, 856*

見 *eeing, 307*

231-C

見ee & 覚erceive, 覚ecall what 寛eniency receives...

宀 (cover, lid)

寛eniency 寛agnanimity

hiro(i), KAN
leniency, magnanimity, forgiving

FLIP: 2.0.b. Sort Of (stem)

寛大 *generous, lenient, kind-hearted* **kandai**
寛厳 *leniency-or-severity* **kangen**
寛恕 *tolerance, magnanimity* **kanjo**
寛仮 *tolerant, magnanimous* **kanka**
寛厚 *kindness & open-mindedness* **kankō**
寛典 *leniency, magnanimity* **kanten**
寛容 *tolerance, generosity* **kanyō**
寛裕 *generosity, magnanimity* **kanyū**
長寛時代 *Chōkan Era (1163-1165)* **chōkan jidai**
寛文時代 *Kanbun Era (1661-1672)* **kanbun jidai**
寛永時代 *Kan'ei Era (1624-1643)* **kan'ei jidai**
寛延時代 *Kan'en Era (1748-1750)* **kan'en jidai**
寛元時代 *Kangen Era (1242-1246)* **kangen jidai**
寛治時代 *Kanji Era (1087-1093)* **kanji jidai**
寛弘時代 *Kankō Era (1004-1011)* **kankō jidai**
寛仁時代 *Kannin Era (1017-1020)* **kannin jidai**
寛保時代 *Kanpō Era (1741-1743)* **kanpō jidai**
寛平時代 *Kanpyō Era (889-897)* **kanpyō jidai**
寛政時代 *Kansei Era (1789-1800)* **kansei jidai**

寛正時代 *Kanshō Era (1460-1465)* **kanshō jidai**
寛徳時代 *Kantōku Era (1044-1045)* **kantoku jidai**
寛和時代 *Kawa Era (985-986)* **kanwa jidai**

義*ighteous, 341*	許*ermit, 180*
懇*ntimacy, 164*	赦*orgive, 262*
親*ntimacy, 669*	忘*orget, 34*
迎*ordial, 705*	徳*ighteous, 844*
暖*ordial, 821*	善*ighteous, 450*

覚*emember, 307*

232-A

Ghost 談alks by chimney 炎lame left me 淡ale & lame...

言 (speaking)

談onverse 談alks

DAN
converse, talks, discussion, discourse

FLIP: 6.0.a. Left (flat)
FLIP: 7.1. Right (Sort Of)

談合 *talks, consultation* **dangō**
談判 *negotiations, bargaining* **danpan**
談笑 *friendly talks, chattering* **danshō**
談話 *informal talk, conversation* **danwa**
縁談 *marriage proposal* **endan**
雅談 *elegant conversation* **gadan**
芸談 *arts conversation* **geidan**
破談 *broken-, cancelled talks* **hadan**
筆談 *written correspondence* **hitsudan**
放談 *free-wheeling talk* **hōdan**
示談 *amicable, out-of-court settlement* **jidan**
示談金 *money paid as compromise* **jidankin**
冗談 *joke, jocular, jest* **jōdan**
会談 *conference, dialogue* **kaidan**
怪談 *ghost story* **kaidan**
歓談 *pleasant talk, ~chat* **kandan**
閑談 *casual talk, leisure chat* **kandan**
綺談 *embellished story* **kidan**
講談 *story, storytelling* **kōdan**

講談師 *storyteller, narrator* **kōdanshi**
懇談 *friendly talk, chat* **kondan**
懇談会 *friendship get-together* **kondankai**
空談 *idle talk, gossip* **kūdan**
漫談 *comic chat, idle talk* **mandan**
政談 *political talk, ~discourse* **seidan**
相談 *consultation, counselling* **sōdan**
用談 *subject matter, theme* **yōdan**
冒険談 *adventure story* **bōkendan**
懐旧談 *reminiscences, recollection* **kaikyūdan**
車中談 *informal talks* **shachūdan**

言*alking, 251*
語*alking, 780*
懇*ntimacy, 164*

淡*aint, 309*

232-B

Ghost 談alks by chimney 炎lame left me 淡ale & lame...

炎*lame* 炎*urning*

火 ⇔ 灬 (fire)

hono'o, EN
flame, burning, combustion, inflammation, torch

FLIP: 2.0.b. Sort Of (stem)

鼻炎 *nasal catarrh* **bien**
防炎 *fire prevention* **bōen**
炎炎 *flames, blaze* **en'en**
炎上 *going up in the blaze* **enjō**
炎暑 *intense-, severe heat* **ensho**
炎症 *inflammation* **enshō**
炎天 *scorching-, blazing sun* **enten**
炎天下 *scorching-, blazing sun* **entenka**
肺炎 *pneumonia* **haien**
胃炎 *gastritis* **ien**
耳炎 *ear inflammation* **jien**
腎炎 *kidney inflammation* **jin'en**
情炎 *burning desire* **jōen**
火炎 *flame, blaze* **kaen**
火炎瓶 *molotov cocktail* **kaenbin**
火炎放射器 *flame thrower* **kaen hōshaki**
陽炎 *heat haze* **kagerō**
肝炎 *hepatitis, liver inflammation* **kan'en**

⇒血清肝炎 *serum hepatitis* **kessei kan'en**
気炎 *lively, enthusiastic, spirited* **kien**
骨炎 *bone inflammation, osteitis* **kotsuen**
紅炎 *prominence, eminence* **kōen**
脳炎 *brain inflammation, encephalitis* **nōen**
消炎 *inflammation treatment* **shōen**
虫垂炎 *appendicitis* **chūsuien**
腹膜炎 *peritonitis* **fukumakuen**
腎盂炎 *pyelitis* **jinuen**
角膜炎 *cornea inflammation* **kakumakuen**
骨髄炎 *osteomyelitis* **kotsuzuien**
盲腸炎 *appendicitis* **mōchōen**

火*lame, 3*	煙*moke, 644*
熱*eat, 153*	燃*urning, 445*

淡*aint, 309*

232-C

Ghost 談alks by chimney 炎lame left me 淡ale & lame...

淡*aint* 淡*ale*

水 ⇔ 氵 (water)

awa(i), TAN
faint, pale, faded, whiten

FLIP: 7.0.b2. Right (stem)

淡い *light, faint, pale* **awai**
淡雪 *light snowfall* **awayuki**
平淡 *plain & dispassionate manner* **heitan**
枯淡 *refined simplicity* **kotan**
濃淡 *shade, light & shade* **nōtan**
冷淡 *cold-heartedness* **reitan**
淡影 *adumbration, hinting* **tan'ei**
淡湖 *fresh-water lake* **tanko**
淡味 *bland-, plain taste* **tanmi**
淡泊 *weak taste, bland flavour* **tanpaku**
淡彩 *light-, pale colouring* **tansai**
淡色 *light-, pale colouring* **tanshoku**
淡水 *fresh water* **tansui**
淡淡 *calm, dispassionate* **tantan**
淡淡と *dispassionately, serenely* **tantanto**
淡褐色 *light brown* **tankasshoku**
淡黄色 *light yellow, straw colour* **tan'ōshoku**
淡緑色 *light green* **tanryokushoku**
淡赤色 *rose colour* **tansekishoku**

淡紫色 *light purple* **tanshishoku**
淡紅色 *pink, rose pink* **tankōshoku**
淡水魚 *fresh-water fish* **tansuigyo**
淡水湖 *fresh-water lake* **tansuiko**

漠*bscure, 828*	劣*nferior, 572*
弱*eakling, 908*	柔*oft, 568*
薄*hin, 63*	軟*oft, 659*

炎*lames, 309*

233-A

佐*ssistants on the* 左*eft,* 惰*dleness bereft...*

人⇔亻 (person)

佐*ssistant* 佐*ield officer*

SA
assistant, field officer, one's right-hand

FLIP: 7.3.a. Right Bottom (flat)
Facing: 4.0. ⟊ Apart

中佐 *army lieut. colonel, naval cmdr.* **chūsa**
補佐 *aid, help, support* **hosa**
輔佐 *aid, help, support* **hosa**
佐幕 *pro-Shōgunate* **sabaku**
佐幕派 *pro-Shōgun clique* **sabakuha**
佐官 *field officer* **sakan**
少佐 *army major, lieutenant cmdr.* **shōsa**
大佐 *army colonel, naval captain* **taisa**
補佐役 *mentor, supporter* **hosayaku**
佐渡島 *Sadogashima Island, Niigata Pref.*
 sadogashima
佐賀県 *Saga Prefecture* **saga-ken**
佐保姫 *god of spring* **sahohime**
佐世保 *Sasebo City, Nagasaki Prefecture* **sasebo**

補*upplement, 812*	貢*upport, 625*
副*eputy, 332*	支*upport, 201*
援*ssist, 820*	擁*upport, 151*
助*ssist, 953*	

左*eft-side, 310*

233-B

佐*ssistants on the* 左*eft,* 惰*dleness bereft...*

工 (craftmanship)

左*eft-side*

hidari, SA
left-side

左隣 *leftside neighbour* **hidaridonari**
左前 *"left-side first..."* **hidarimae**
左下 *bottom left* **hidarishita**
左手 *left hand* **hidarite**
左上 *upper left* **hidariue**
左岸 *left embankment* **sagan**
左舷 *port, harbour* **sagen**
左派 *leftist party, left-leaning* **saha**
左方 *left side, left flank* **sahō**
左官 *plasterer* **sakan**
左傾 *leftist ideology* **sakei**
左記 *as shown on the leftside* **saki**
左遷 *demotion, relegation* **sasen**
左折 *turning left* **sasetsu**
左折禁止 *"no left turn..."* **sasetsu kinshi**
左党 *leftist party, leftist* **satō**
左腕 *left-handed* **sawan**
左右 *right & left, control* **sayū**
左図 *left figure* **sazu**

FLIP: 4.0.a. Bottom (flat)

証左 *evidence, proof* **shōsa**
左回転 *counter-clockwise* **hidari kaiten**
左利き *left handed* **hidarikiki**
左巻き *counter clockwise* **hidarimaki**
左回り *counter clockwise* **hidarimawari**
左打ち *left handed blow* **hidariuchi**
最左翼 *ultra-left, extremists* **saisayoku**
左翼主 *leftist ideology* **sayokushu**
左様なら *farewell, goodbye* **sayōnara**
左右対称 *symmetrical, proportional*
 sayū taishō
左右運動 *left-right movement* **sayū undō**

右*ight-side, 87*	下*own, 859*
上*pper, 859*	

在*xist, 634*

233-C

佐ssistants on the 左eft, 惰dleness bereft...

惰*aziness* 惰*dleness*

心⇔忄 (heart, feelings)

FLIP: 7.3.b. Right Bottom (stem)

DA

laziness, idleness, indolence, lackadaisical

惰弱 *impoverished, weak* **dajaku**
惰気 *inactivity, dullness* **daki**
惰眠 *idle slumber, lethargy* **damin**
惰力 *indolence, passivity, pathetic* **daryoku**
惰性 *inertia, momentum* **dasei**
惰性的 *inertial, momentary* **daseiteki**
勤惰 *diligence-or-laziness* **kinda**
怠惰 *laziness, idleness* **taida**
遊惰 *indolence, passivity, pathetic* **yūda**

怠*aziness, 570*	閑*eisure, 283*
暇*ree time, 653*	悠*eisure, 898*
飽*oredom, 665*	

情*eelings, 793*

234-A

首ead with long 首eck quickly saw the 道oad 導uide to Quebec...

首eck　　首ead

首 (head, neck)

kubi, SHU

neck, head

FLIP: 1.0.a. Whole (flat)

足首 *ankle* **ashikubi**
乳首 *breast nipple* **chikubi**
襟首 *nape of the neck* **erikubi**
元首 *sovereign, head of state* **genshu**
首筋 *scruff of the neck* **kubisuji**
首輪 *necklace* **kubiwa**
丸首 *round neck* **marukubi**
船首 *ships bow, stem* **senshu**
首尾 *first-to-last, head-to-tail* **shubi**
首長 *head, chief* **shuchō**
首題 *main theme* **shudai**
首位 *top, first place* **shui**
首脳会談 *summit meeting* **shunō kaidan**
首脳 *head, leader, chief* **shunō**
首領 *ringleader, mastermind* **shuryō**
首席 *top seat, presidential table* **shuseki**
首相 *prime minister, premier* **shushō**
首相官邸 *prime minister's residence* **shushō kantei**
首足 *head & feet* **shusoku**

首都 *capital, metropolis* **shuto**
首座 *seat of honour* **shuza**
手首 *hand wrist* **tekubi**
党首 *party leader* **tōshu**
斬首 *beheading, decapitation* **zanshu**
絞首台 *gallows, gibbet, noose* **kōshudai**
絞首刑 *death by hanging* **kōshukei**
首実検 *identification, identity* **kubijikken**
首巻き *scarf* **kubimaki**
首飾り *necklace* **kubikazari**
首切り *decapitation; job dismissal, ~firing* **kubikiri**
首吊り *suicide by hanging* **kubitsuri**
百人一首 *old playing cards* **hyakunin isshu**

頭*ead, 832*	督*eader, 911*
長*hief, 273*	統*overn, 885*
高*igh, 435*	脳*rain, 47*

道*oad, 312*

234-B

首*ead with long* 首*eck quickly saw the* 道*oad* 導*uide to Quebec...*

辶 (transport)

道*ath*　　　道*oad*

michi, DŌ, TŌ
path, road, course, highway, passage

FLIP: 3.0.a. Top (flat)

茶道 *tea ceremony* **chadō, sadō**
道義 *public morals, morality* **dōgi**
道義心 *moral sense* **dōgishin**
道具 *tool, instrument, implement* **dōgu**
道場 *gym, gymnasium* **dōjō**
道楽 *hobby, amusement, past time* **dōraku**
道路 *road, street* **dōro**
道徳 *buffoonery* **dōtoku**
枝道 *branch road* **edamichi**
花道 *the golden way, path of glory* **hanamichi**
歩道 *ecliptic, circular road* **hodō**
報道 *report, news, coverage* **hōdō**
柔道 *judo martial arts* **jūdō**
歌道 *art of tanka poetry* **kadō**
街道 *road, highway* **kaidō**
県道 *prefectural road, ~highway* **kendō**
剣道 *Japanese fencing* **kendō**
弓道 *Japanese archery* **kyūdō**
求道 *seeking the truth, fact-finding* **kyūdō**

道順 *route, way* **michijun**
道草 *loitering* **michikusa**
道筋 *route, course* **michisuji**
坂道 *slope, hill* **sakamichi**
鉄道 *railway, rairoad* **tetsudō**
武士道 *bushido, samurai spirit* **bushidō**
帰り道 *one's way home, return trip* **kaerimichi**
道案内 *road map, road guide* **michiannai**
通り道 *passage, way, path* **toorimichi**
登山道 *mountain trail* **tozandō**
裏街道 *side-, back road* **urakaidō**

路*oad*, 405	軌*ailroad*, 660
畔*ice-field path*, 484	通*assing*, 59
岐*orked-road*, 704	

首*eck*, 311

234-C

首*ead with long* 首*eck quickly saw the* 道*oad* 導*uide to Quebec...*

寸 (measurement)

導*uidance*　　　導*upervision*

michibi(ku), DŌ
guidance, supervision, leadership, overseeing

FLIP: 7.2.a. Right Top (flat)

伝導 *conduct, transmit* **dendō**
導因 *inducement, incentive* **dōin**
導管 *conduit, pipe, tube* **dōkan**
導尿 *urinate, catherize* **dōnyō**
導入 *introduction, induction* **dōnyū**
導線 *lead wire, conducting wire* **dōsen**
導者 *guide* **dōsha**
導師 *celebrating priest* **dōshi**
導水 *route water into* **dōsui**
導体 *conductor* **dōtai**
補導 *guidance, direction* **hodō**
訓導 *teach, instruct* **kundō**
教導 *teach, instruct* **kyōdō**
先導 *guidance, leadership* **sendō**
指導 *guidance, direction* **shidō**
⇒職業指導 *job counselling* **shokugyō shidō**
指導者 *leader, coach, instructor* **shidōsha**
唱導 *advocacy, propagation* **shōdō**
唱導者 *advocate, mover, proponent* **shōdōsha**

主導 *take leadership* **shudō**
誘導 *guidance, induction, derivation* **yūdō**
誘導体 *derivative* **yūdōtai**
誘導尋問 *leading question* **yūdō jinmon**
誘導ミサイル *guided missile* **yūdō misairu**
善導 *proper guidance* **zendō**
超電導 *superconductor* **chōdendō**
導火線 *fuse, primer, cause* **dōkasen**
半導体 *semi-conductor* **handōtai**
盲導犬 *seeing-eye dog* **mōdōken**
良導体 *good conductor* **ryōdōtai**

令*ommand*, 362	監*upervise*, 592
帥*ommander*, 483	訓*uidance*, 959
督*ommander*, 911	領*overn*, 874
指*inger*, 242	

道*oad*, 312

235-A

是*orrect cement* 提*ubmitted for sea* 堤*mbankments...*

日 (sunlight, daytime)

是*airness*　是*orrect*

kore, ZE
fairness, correct, right

FLIP: 3.0.a. Top (flat)

彼是 *this & that* **arekore**
国是 *national policy* **kokuze**
校是 *school policy* **kōze**
社是 *company policy* **shaze**
党是 *party platform* **tōze**
是非 *"go ahead..."; right & wrong* **zehi**
是認 *approval, approbation* **zenin**
是正 *correction, redress* **zesei**
頑是無い *innocuous, harmless* **ganzenai**
昨非今是 *change of heart, ~thinking* **sakuhi konze**
是是非非 *fair & square, fair & just* **zeze hihi**

適*uitable, 135*	肯*ffirmative, 616*
善*ighteous, 450*	正*orrect, 30*

堤*mbankment, 314*

235-B

是*orrect cement* 提*ubmitted for sea* 堤*mbankments...*

手⇔扌 (hand, manual)

提*roposal*　提*ubmit*

sa(geru), TEI, CHŌ, DAI
proposal, proposition, submit, present

FLIP: 7.2.a. Right Top (flat)

菩提 *repose of one's soul* **bodai**
菩提寺 *one's family's temple* **bodaiji**
菩提樹 *Bo tree; linden tree; lime tree* **bodaiju**
提灯 *paper lantern* **chōchin**
提灯持ち *lantern bearer; hype* **chōchinmochi**
提案 *suggestion, proposition* **teian**
提案者 *proposer, initiator* **teiansha**
提言 *verbal suggestion* **teigen**
提議 *proposal, suggestion* **teigi**
提示 *presentation, display* **teiji**
提携 *tie-up, coalition* **teikei**
⇒技術提携 *technical agreement* **gijutsu teikei**
提起 *raising an issue* **teiki**
提琴 *violin* **teikin**
提供 *offer, providing, sponsorship* **teikyō**
提唱 *proposal, advocacy, espousal* **teishō**
提出 *presentation, submission, handing-in* **teishutsu**
提出物 *documents to submit* **teishutsubutsu**
提出期限 *submission deadline* **teishutsu kigen**

提訴 *filing court suit, taking to court* **teiso**
提督 *rear admiral, fleet admiral* **teitoku**
提要 *compendium, summary* **teiyō**
手提げ *handbag* **tesage**
手提げ袋 *handbag* **tesage bukuro**
手提げ鞄 *briefcase, grip* **tesage kaban**
手提げ金庫 *cash box, portable safe* **tesage kinko**
前提 *premise, supposition, assumption* **zentei**
⇒大前提 *major premise* **daizentei**
⇒小前提 *minor premise* **shōzentei**

意*dea, 340*	念*dea, 182*
想*dea, 524*	志*ntention, 426*

堤*mbankment, 314*

235-C

是orrect cement 提ubmitted for sea 堤mbankments...

土 (ground, soil)

堤mbankment   堤reakwater

tsutsumi, TEI
embankment, breakwater

FLIP: 7.2.a. Right Top (flat)

築堤 embankment **chikutei**
堰堤 dam, weir **entei**
堤防 levee, embankment **teibō**
突堤 breakwater, sea wall **tottei**
防諜堤 embankment, sea wall **bōchōtei**
防波堤 breakwater **bōhatei**

州andbank, 76
砂ands, 643
洪looding, 512

提roposal, 313

236-A

Same 音ounds 韻hyme even in 暗ark times...

音 (sound)

音ound   音oise

oto, ne, ON, IN
sound, noise, tone, blare, sonance

FLIP: 1.0.a. Whole (flat)

雨音 rain sound **amaoto**
足音 footstep, steps **ashioto**
爆音 explosion, blast, roar **bakuon**
鼻音 nasal sound **bion**
母音 word vowel **boin, boon**
防音 soundproofing **bōon**
聴音 hearing, listening **chōon**
濁音 sonant, voiced sound **dakuon**
福音 glad tidings, good news **fukuin**
擬音 imitation sound, sound effects **gion**
半音 half tone **han'on**
羽音 flapping wings **haoto**
発音 pronunciation **hatsuon**
本音 true-, real intention, "in reality..." **honne**
物音 sound, noise **monooto**
波音 sound of ocean waves **namioto**
音色 tone, rhythm **neiro**
音楽 music **ongaku**
音源 sound source **ongen**

音階 musical note **onkai**
音感 sense of pitch **onkan**
音響 sound, echo **onkyō**
音声 voice, sound **onsei**
音節 syllable **onsetsu**
音信 letter, correspondence **onshin**
音質 sound quality **onshitsu**
録音 recording, taping **rokuon**
子音 word consonant **shiin, shion**
騒音 noise **sōon**
低音 low tone, bass **teion**
雑音 street noise, chattering **zatsuon**

声oice, 428   聴isten, 844
曲elody, 476   聞isten, 282
騒oise, 924   耳ars, 228

竜ragon, 523

236-B

Same 音*ounds* 韻*hyme even in* 暗*ark times...*

音 (sound)

FLIP: 5.0.b. Left & Right

❶韻*hyme*　❷韻*raceful*

IN
rhyme, sound-alike; graceful, elegant

❶韻文 *verse, poetry* **inbun**
韻語 *word rhyming* **ingo**
韻字 *word rhyming* **inji**
韻脚 *metrical foot* **inkyaku**
韻律 *rhythm, meter* **inritsu**
韻律学 *prosody* **inritsugaku**
脚韻 *rhyme, rhyming* **kyakuin**
押韻 *rhyme, rhyming* **ōin**
頭韻 *alliteration* **tōin**
余韻 *reverberation, after-taste* **yoin**
無韻詩 *unrhymed poem* **muinshi**
押韻詩 *poetry rhyming* **ōinshi**
音韻学 *phonology* **on'ingaku**
音韻論 *phonology* **on'inron**

❷風韻 *grace, elegance* **fūin**
韻致 *elegance, excellent taste* **inchi**
韻事 *artistic pursuit* **inji**

気韻 *grace, elegance* **kiin**
神韻 *heavenly elegance* **shin'in**

雅*raceful, 58*		詩*oetry, 250*	
淑*raceful, 510*		詠*oetry, 729*	
音*ound, 314*		声*oice, 428*	

音*oise, 314*

236-C

Same 音*ounds* 韻*hyme even in* 暗*ark times...*

日 (sunlight, daytime)

暗*ark*　　暗*loomy*

kura(i), AN
dark, gloomy, dimmed, dismal, dusky

暗影 *shadow, gloom* **an'ei**
暗号 *code, cipher* **angō**
暗合 *coincidence, chance* **angō**
暗愚 *stupid, absurd, imbecile* **angu**
暗弱 *feeble mind* **anjaku**
暗示 *hint, suggestion* **anji**
暗記 *memorizing* **anki**
暗黒 *darkness* **ankoku**
暗幕 *blackout curtain* **anmaku**
暗黙 *dark & silent, silence* **anmoku**
暗譜 *memorizing a song* **anpu**
暗涙 *silent tears* **anrui**
暗流 *undercurrent* **anryū**
暗殺 *assassination, ambush* **ansatsu**
暗礁 *reef; deadlock, stalemate, stand-off* **anshō**
暗証 *code, cipher, cryptograph, encryption* **anshō**
暗色 *dark colours* **anshoku**
暗転 *changing of stage scenes* **anten**
暗闘 *secret strife, war-of-nerves* **antō**

FLIP: 5.0.a Left & Right

暗夜 *dark night* **anya**
暗躍 *shady manuevers* **anyaku**
暗算 *mental calculation* **anzan**
暗然 *gloom, grief* **anzen**
暗闇 *darkness, dark* **kurayami**
明暗 *light & shade* **meian**
真っ暗 *dark, pitch-dark, hopeless* **makkura**
丸暗記 *rote memorization* **maruanki**
薄暗い *dim, dusky, dull* **usugurai**
後ろ暗い *shady, suspicious* **ushirogurai**

憂*loomy, 556*		愁*orrows, 415*	
黒*lack, 320*		悲*orrows, 289*	
哀*orrows, 374*			

音*ound, 314*

237-A

既*lready* 慨*eplored*, 概*pproximates we can't afford...*

旡⇔无 (without)

既*lready* 既*oregone*

sude(ni), KI
already, done-with, foregone

Facing: 3.0. ☞☜ Across

既に "already, by this time..." **sude(ni)**
既知 already known, the given factor **kichi**
既電 previous message **kiden**
既報 known beforehand **kihō**
既述 above-mentioned **kijutsu**
既刊 published beforehand **kikan**
既決 settled-, decided matter **kiketsu**
既決囚 convict, felon, criminal **kiketsushū**
既婚 already married **kikon**
既往 the past, bygones **kiō**
既往症 medical case history **kiōshō**
既成 existing, established **kisei**
既製 ready-made **kisei**
既設 already established, ~built **kisetsu**
既習 matter already learned **kishū**
既存 existing, present **kison**
既遂 consummated, perpetrated **kisui**
既定 pre-arrangement, agreed beforehand **kitei**
既得 vested, already acquired **kitoku**

既得権 vested rights **kitokuken**
既得権益 vested interests **kitoku ken'eki**
皆既食 total eclipse **kaikishoku**
既発表 already published **kihappyō**
既製服 ready-made clothes, rtw **kiseifuku**
既製品 ready-made articles **kiseihin**
既卒者 graduate **kisotsusha**
皆既月食 total lunar eclipse **kaiki gesshoku**
皆既日食 total solar eclipse **kaiki nisshoku**
既成概念 profiling-, stereotype mind **kisei gainen**
既成事実 given fact, established fact **kisei jijitsu**

即*mmediate, 421*	今*ow, 182*
終*inish, 397*	現*resent, 814*

即*lready,421*

237-B

既*lready* 慨*eplored*, 概*pproximates we can't afford...*

心⇔忄 (heart, feelings)

慨*eplore* 慨*egret*

GAI
deplore, regret, condemn, denounce, disappointment, fretful, misgiving, irksome

Facing: 3.0. ☞☜ Across

憤慨 indignation, resentment, rage **fungai**
概世 public welfare-oriented **gaisei**
慨嘆 deploring, lamentation **gaitan**
慨然 deploring, lamentation **gaizen**
感慨 deep emotions, passions **kangai**
感慨無量 filled with emotions **kangai muryō**
感慨深い deeply-moved, touching **kangaibukai**
慷慨 patriotic regrets **kōgai**

悔*egret, 712*	嘆*eplore, 927*
憾*egret, 46*	惜*egret, 281*

既*lready, 316*

237-C

既lready 慨eplored, 概pproximates we can't afford...

木 (wooden)

概

2 5 10
1 8 11 13
3 6 12
9 14

槪pproximate   概ummary

GAI

approximate, summary, estimate, general, overview, digest

Facing: 3.0. ☞☜ Across

概して *"generally speaking, on the whole..."* **gaishite**
概貌 *general appearance* **gaibō**
概言 *summary, overview, outline* **gaigen**
概評 *general commentary* **gaihyō**
概観 *surveying, approximating* **gaikan**
概括 *summary, outline* **gaikatsu**
概計 *rough estimate, ~quotation* **gaikei**
概見 *summary, overview, outline* **gaiken**
概況 *general outlook* **gaikyō**
⇒天気概況 *general weather conditions* **tenki gaikyō**
概念 *general concept* **gainen**
⇒類概念 *general idea* **ruigainen**
⇒抽象概念 *abstract concept* **chūshō gainen**
⇒既成概念 *profiling-, stereotyping* **kisei gainen**
概念論 *conceptualism* **gainenron**
概念的 *conceptual* **gainenteki**
概論 *outline, introduction* **gairon**
概略 *outline, summary* **gairyaku**

概算 *rough estimate, ~quotation* **gaisan**
概説 *summary, overview, outline* **gaisetsu**
概則 *general rules, governing principles* **gaisoku**
概数 *round numbers, approximate figure* **gaisū**
概要 *outline, summary* **gaiyō**
気概 *mettle, guts, unyielding spirit* **kigai**
梗概 *summary, overview, outline* **kōgai**
大概 *"in general, mostly..."* **taigai**
一概に *"generally, necessarily..."* **ichigai(ni)**

約bout, 697	限oundary, 771
囲nclose, 361	涯imit, 890
奥nside, 903	限imit, 771
内nside, 297	最aximum, 423
境oundary, 839	

既lready, 316

238-A

篤ordial 馬orses by the 駅rain-station take a vacation...

竹 (bamboo)

篤

5
8 9
10
11
12
14 15 16
13

❶篤erious   ❷篤ordial

atsu(i), TOKU

serious; cordial, amicable, righteous, goodness, devoted

Facing: 2.1. East ☞ (H)
Facing: 3.0. ☞☜ Across

❶篤い信仰 *deep faith* **atsui shinkō**
重篤 *critically-ill* **jūtoku**
危篤 *critically-ill* **kitoku**
篤学 *love of learning, studious* **tokugaku**
篤実 *sincere, honest, truthful* **tokujitsu**
篤信 *devoutness, loyalty, faithfulness* **tokushin**
篤農家 *exemplary farmer* **tokunōka**

❷篤い友情 *cordial friendship* **atsui yūjō**
篤い持てなし *cordial reception, warm welcome*
    atsui motenashi
懇篤 *cordial, kind, friendly* **kontoku**
篤行 *good deeds, charitable acts* **tokkō**
篤志 *charity, benevolence* **tokushi**
篤志家 *philanthropist, charitable person*
    tokushika

迎elcome, 705	暖armth, 821
呼nvite, 701	懇ntimacy, 164
招nvite, 956	親ntimate, 669
客uest, 559	友riendship, 408
宴anquet, 610	

焦ocus, 919

238-B

篤ordial 馬orses by the 駅rain-station take a vacation...

馬 (horse)

馬orse

uma, ma, BA
horse

Facing: 2.0. East ☞ (W)

穴馬 *dark horse* **anauma**
馬場 *riding grounds, race track* **baba**
馬具 *harness* **bagu**
馬術 *horsemanship, equestrian* **bajutsu**
馬鹿 *fool, idiot, nonsense* **baka**
馬券 *betting ticket* **baken**
馬齢 *waste of time, squandered years* **barei**
馬車 *carriage, coach, wagon* **basha**
跳馬 *vaulting horse* **chōba**
調馬 *horse training* **chōba**
絵馬 *votive picture* **ema**
裸馬 *barebacked-, unsaddled horse* **hadakauma**
早馬 *steed, pacer, stallion* **hayauma**
乗馬 *horse riding, equestrian* **jōba**
競馬 *horse race* **keiba**
曲馬 *circus horse* **kyokuba**
縞馬 *zebra* **shimauma**
竹馬 *bamboo stilts* **takeuma, chikuba**

種馬 *stallion, studhorse* **taneuma**
頓馬 *fool, idiot, nonsense* **tonma**
馬市 *horse fair* **umaichi**
馬面 *horse-looking face* **umazura**
駅馬車 *stagecoach* **ekibasha**
去勢馬 *castrated horse* **kyoseiba**
荷馬車 *wagon, cart* **nibasha**
走馬灯 *revolving lantern* **sōmatō**
馬小屋 *horse stable, horse barn* **umagoya**
馬跳び *leapfrog, leap & bounds* **umatobi**
野次馬 *nosy person* **yajiuma**

騎orse ride, 673
駄orseload, 674
駆alloping, 674

焦ocus, 919

238-C

篤ordial 馬orses by the 駅rain-station take a vacation...

馬 (horse)

駅rain station

EKI
train station

Facing: 2.2. East ☞ (V)

着駅 *arrival station* **chakueki**
駅路 *post road* **ekiro**
駅弁 *boxed lunch sold at station* **ekiben**
駅ビル *station building* **ekibiru**
駅長 *train stationmaster* **ekichō**
駅伝 *long-distance relay race* **ekiden**
駅夫 *station clerk* **ekifu**
駅員 *train station clerk* **ekiin**
駅前 *in front of the train station* **ekimae**
駅舎 *station building* **ekisha**
駅手 *station clerk* **ekishu**
駅逓 *postal service* **ekitei**
駅頭 *near the station* **ekitō**
発駅 *originating station* **hatsueki**
各駅 *every station* **kakueki**
宿駅 *relay station* **shukueki**
中間駅 *intermediate stations* **chūkan'eki**
駅馬車 *stagecoach* **ekibasha**
駅留め *delivered to the station* **ekidome**

駅売り *station vendors* **ekiuri**
貨物駅 *freight depot* **kamotsueki**
始発駅 *starting station* **shihatsueki**
終着駅 *terminal station, last stop* **shūchakueki**
出発駅 *starting station* **shuppatsueki**
到着駅 *arrival station* **tōchakueki**
通過駅 *skipped stations* **tsūkaeki**
乗り換え駅 *train junction, concourse* **norikaeeki**

軌ailroad, 660   旅ravel, 650
車ehicle, 306   乗ide on, 511
運ransport, 295

駆alloping, 674

239-A

埋uried 厘ld coins, 黒lack as 墨nk in the 里ometown of
墨exico's crown...   土 (ground, soil)

埋ury   埋ntomb

u(maru), u(meru), u(moreru), ike(ru), MAI
bury, entomb, inter

FLIP: 5.0.a Left & Right
FLIP: 7.0.a. Right (flat)

埋ける *bury, inter* **ikeru**
埋まる *get buried, ~filled up* **umaru**
埋め地 *reclaimed land* **umechi**
埋め草 *covering an empty space* **umekusa**
埋め湯 *hot water cooled by adding water* **umeyu**
埋め立て *reclamation, reclaimed land* **umetate**
埋め立て地 *reclaimed land* **umetatechi**
埋め合わせ *compensation* **umeawase**
埋め替える *rebury, reinter* **umekaeru**
埋没 *buried under landslide, caved in* **maibotsu**
埋伏 *bury to hide; impacted (tooth)* **maifuku**
埋骨 *burial of ashes* **maikotsu**
埋線 *underground wirings* **maisen**
埋設 *laying underground* **maisetsu**
埋葬 *burial, interment* **maisō**
埋葬許可証 *burial permit* **maisō kyokashō**
埋蔵 *deposits, buried things* **maizō**
埋蔵物 *something buried* **maizōbutsu**

埋蔵金 *buried gold* **maizōkin**
埋蔵量 *reserves* **maizōryō**
穴埋め *making up for, compensating* **anaume**
埋み火 *banked fire* **uzumibi**
生き埋め *buried alive* **ikiume**
埋もれ木 *bogwood* **umoregi**

陰idden, 864	匿onceal, 277
隠idden, 840	忍onceal, 535
秘idden, 219	覆onceal. 602

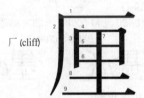
理eason, 872

239-B

埋uried 厘ld coins, 黒lack as 墨nk in the 里ometown of
墨exico's crown...   厂 (cliff)

厘ld coin

RIN
old coin, ancient coin

FLIP: 8.0.a. Inner (flat)

一厘 *one rin (old money)* **ichirin**
⇒一分一厘 *"some little, some light..."* **ichibu ichirin**
厘毛 *trifle, petty, frivolous* **rinmō**
九分九厘 *"in 9 out of 10, ~all likelihood..."* **kubun kurin**
八分五厘 *interest of 8.5%* **hachibun gorin**

昔lden-times, 281	幣oney, 171
金oney, 25	札oney-bills. 685

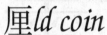
埋ury, 319

239-C

埋uried 厘ld coins, 黒lack as 墨nk in the 里ometown of 墨exico's crown...

黒 (black, charred)

FLIP: 1.0.b. Whole (stem)

黒lack

kuro(i), KOKU
black

暗黒 *darkness* **ankoku**
黒子① *mole* **hokuro**
黒子② *stage pupeteer in black clothes* **kuroko**
黒海 *black sea* **kokkai**
黒板 *blackboard chalkboard* **kokuban**
黒鳥 *black swan* **kokuchō**
黒鉛 *black lead, graphite* **kokuen**
黒煙 *black smoke* **kokuen**
黒人 *black person, African-American* **kokujin**
黒雲 *black clouds* **kokuun**
黒炭 *black coal* **kokutan**
黒点 *sunspot, blackspot* **kokuten**
黒星 *black star, failure* **kuroboshi**
黒船 *Perry's Black Ships (1853)* **kurofune**
黒黒 *dark, black* **kuroguro**
黒字 *surplus, in the black* **kuroji**
黒髪 *black hair* **kurokami**
黒豆 *black soybean* **kuromame**
黒目 *eye pupil* **kurome**

黒帯 *blackbelt, blackbelter* **kuroobi**
黒潮 *The Japan current* **kuroshio**
黒白 *black & white* **kuroshiro**
黒枠 *black frame for the dead* **kurowaku**
黒山 *large crowd, multitude* **kuroyama**
白黒 *black or white* **shirokuro**
青黒い *black & blue, dark-green* **aoguroi**
浅黒い *dark* **asaguroi**
腹黒い *malicious, evil intent* **haraguroi**
黒光り *shining black* **kurobikari**
黒焼き *charred* **kuroyaki**
真っ黒 *completely black* **makkuro**

白hite, 15	暗loomy, 315
暗ark, 315	憂loomy, 556

里ometown, 321

239-D

埋uried 厘ld coins, 黒lack as 墨nk in the 里ometown of 墨exico's crown...

土 (ground, soil)

FLIP: 1.0.b. Whole (stem)

❶墨nk ❷墨exico

sumi, BOKU
ink; Mexico

❶墨刑 *tattooing punishment* **bokkei**
墨痕 *calligraphy brush strokes* **bokkon**
墨客 *calligraphy expert* **bokkyaku**
墨池 *stone ink well* **bokuchi**
墨画 *India-ink drawing* **bokuga**
墨汁 *Indian ink, China ink* **bokujū**
墨守 *adherence to old traditions* **bokushu**
白墨 *blackboard, chalkboard* **hakuboku**
筆墨 *pen & ink* **hitsuboku**
芳墨 *scented ink; your esteemed letter* **hōboku**
遺墨 *dead person's autograph* **iboku**
靴墨 *shoe polish* **kutsuzumi**
眉墨 *eyebrow marker, ~eye liner* **mayuzumi**
鍋墨 *kettle soot* **nabezumi**
石墨 *graphite* **sekiboku**
墨絵 *Indian-ink drawing* **sumie**
墨江 *India-ink drawing* **sumie**
墨色 *India ink* **sumiiro**
墨糸 *ink-marked string* **sumiito**

墨縄 *ink-marked string* **suminawa**
墨壺 *carpenter's inking device* **sumitsubo**
薄墨 *pale ink* **usuzumi**
墨書き *India ink drawings* **sumigaki**
墨付き *handwriting, signed* **sumitsuki**
墨染め *dyeing black; Buddhist monk robe* **sumizome**
入れ墨 *tattooing, tattoo* **irezumi**
水墨画 *India-ink painting* **suibokuga**
お墨付き① *official authorization* **ōsumitsuki**
お墨付き② *endorsement from a VIP* **ōsumitsuki**
❷日墨 *Japan & Mexico* **nichiboku**

黒lack, 320	図rawing, 47
泥irt, 302	描rawing, 271
絵rawing, 143	芸rts, 619

黒lack, 320

239-E

埋uried 厘ld coins, 黒lack as 墨nk in the 里ometown of
墨exico's crown...

里 (hometown)

里ometown   里irthplace

sato, RI
hometown, birthplace, homeland, league

FLIP: 1.0.a. Whole (flat)

万里 *great distance* **banri**
故里 *hometown, birthplace* **furusato**
人里 *village, hometown* **hitozato**
色里 *red-light district* **irozato**
海里 *nautical miles* **kairi**
片里 *far remote village* **katazato**
郷里 *native-, hometown* **kyōri**
親里 *one's ancestral village* **oyazato**
里標 *milestone, epoch, landmark* **rihyō**
里人 *villagers, village residents* **rijin, satobito**
里数 *mileage, distance* **risū**
里程 *distance, mileage* **ritei**
里子 *adopted child, foster child* **satogo**
里心 *homesickness, nostalgia* **satogokoro**
里芋 *taro, potato* **satoimo**
里方 *one's wife family* **satokata**
里親 *foster parents* **satooya**
千里 *a thousand leagues* **senri**
千里眼 *clairvoyance, intuition* **senrigan**

山里 *mountain village* **yamazato**
遊里 *amusement area* **yūri**
一里塚 *milestone, epoch, landmark* **ichirizuka**
片山里 *remote mountain village* **katayamazato**
里言葉 *rural dialect* **sato kotoba**
里帰り *re-visit one's hometown* **satogaeri**
里神楽 *Shintō sacred dance* **satokagura**
遠山里 *far remote mountain village* **tooyamazato**
万里の長城 *Great Wall of China*
　　　banri no chōjō

郷ometown, 452	帰eturn, 784
村illage, 690	戻eturn, 541

黒lack, 320

240-A

能bilities 罷ithdraw when 態onditions are raw...

肉⇔月 (flesh, body part)

❶能bility   ❷能[Noh]

NŌ
ability, adeptness, capability, talent; [Noh]

Facing: 2.2. East ☞ (V)

❶万能 *all-powerful, almighty, omnipotent* **bannō**
知能 *wisdom, intelligence, knowledge* **chinō**
不能 *impossible; incompetent* **funō**
芸能 *show business, entertainment* **geinō**
技能 *skill, technique, forte, expertise* **ginō**
十能 *charcoal utensils* **jūnō**
官能 *sense, sensual; voluptuous* **kannō**
権能 *authority, power* **kennō**
機能 *function, role* **kinō**
効能 *effect, function* **kōnō**
無能 *inefficient, incompetent* **munō**
能弁 *eloquent, articulate, oratorical* **nōben**
能動 *active, dynamic, lively* **nōdō**
能筆 *skilful hand, professional, expert* **nōhitsu**
能事 *work, duty* **nōji**
能吏 *able officer* **nōri**
能率 *efficiency, efficacy* **nōritsu**
能力 *ability, faculty, competence* **nōryoku**
才能 *talent, ability, gift* **sainō**

性能 *performance, efficiency* **seinō**
職能 *professional efficiency* **shokunō**
堪能 *satisfaction, proficiency* **tannō**
多能 *versatile, multiple skills* **tanō**
低能 *low-level skills, inefficient* **teinō**
全能 *omnipotence, all-powerful, almighty* **zennō**
可能性 *possibility, likelihood* **kanōsei**
能書き *statement of virtues* **nōgaki**

❷能楽 *Noh play, Noh drama* **nōgaku**
能面 *Noh mask* **nōmen**
能役者 *Noh actor* **nōyakusha**

巧killful, 738	腕alent, 651	博xpertise, 514	
術kills, 110	力trength 351	興ntertainment, 867	

態ppearance, 322

240-B

能*bilities* 罷*ithdraw when* 態*onditions are raw...*

ㅁ (net, eye crown)

罷*ithdraw* 罷*etreat*

maka(ri), ya(meru), HI
withdraw, retreat, job dismissal

FLIP: 3.0.a. Top (flat)

罷り出る *leave, withdraw* **makarideru**
罷り越す *go to, visit, call on* **makarikosu**
罷り通る *remain unpunished* **makaritooru**
罷り間違えば *"if worse comes to worst..."*
    makari machigaeba
罷業 *labour strike, walk-out* **higyō**
罷官 *removal from a government job* **hikan**
罷免 *dismissal, discharge, firing* **himen**
身罷る *die, pass away* **mimakaru**
総罷業 *general labour strike* **sōhigyō**

引*xtract,* 348	却*ithdraw,* 387
抽*xtract,* 37	退*ithdraw,* 770
棄*bandon,* 608	撤*ithdraw,* 843

能*bility,* 321

240-C

能*bilities* 罷*ithdraw when* 態*onditions are raw...*

態

心⇔忄 (heart, feelings)

態*ondition* 態*ppearance*

TAI
condition, appearance, situation, state

Facing: 2.1. East ☞ (H)

態と *deliberately, intently, willed* **waza(to)**
悪態 *bad condition, sorry plight* **akutai**
病態 *illness condition* **byōtai**
痴態 *foolish behaviour* **chitai**
動態 *dynamic, energetic, vigorous* **dōtai**
変態 *pervert, sex maniac* **hentai**
百態 *various situations* **hyakutai**
事態 *situation, circumstances* **jitai**
実態 *real-, actual situation* **jittai**
常態 *normal condition* **jōtai**
状態 *condition, state* **jōtai**
重態 *critically ill, terminally sick* **jūtai**
形態 *form, shape, configuration* **keitai**
奇態 *strange, odd, curious* **kitai**
狂態 *crazy behaviour* **kyōtai**
嬌態 *flirtatiousness, lustfulness* **kyōtai**
旧態 *former conditions, status-quo-ante* **kyūtai**
生態 *way of life, lifestyle* **seitai**
静態 *static, stationary, stillness* **seitai**

姿態 *figure, form, shape* **shitai**
失態 *blunder, fiasco, bungling, boo-boo* **shittai**
醜態 *shameful misconduct* **shūtai**
酔態 *intoxication, drunkness* **suitai**
態度 *attitude, behaviour, conduct* **taido**
態勢 *attitude, condition* **taisei**
態態 *deliberately, intently, willed* **wazawaza**
様態 *aspect, phase, condition* **yōtai**
擬態語 *mimesis* **gitaigo**
受動態 *passive voice* **judōtai**
能動態 *active, dynamic condition* **nōdōtai**

姿*ppearance,* 609	形*hape,* 951
容*ppearance,* 492	況*ituation,* 716
構*osture,* 714	状*ondition,* 702

能*bility,* 321

241-A

般*egular train* 搬*ransport of chess* 盤*oards, all aboard...*

舟 (vessel)

般*eneral*　般*egular*

HAN
general, regular, common, sort of, standard

FLIP: 7.0.b2. Right (stem)

万般　*all sort of things*　**banpan**
百般　*all sort of things*　**hyappan**
一般　*general, regular*　**ippan**
一般人　*common person*　**ippannin**
一般性　*generality, commonality*　**ippansei**
一般的　*general, regular*　**ippanteki**
一般車　*private vehicle*　**ippansha**
過般　*recently, sometime ago*　**kahan**
過般来　*sometime*　**kahanrai**
各般　*all, each, every*　**kakuhan**
今般　*this time, nowadays*　**konpan**
先般　*the other time*　**senpan**
諸般　*various things*　**shohan**
全般　*whole, entire, general*　**zenpan**
全般的　*on the whole, entirety*　**zenpanteki**

常*egular, 94*	庸*ediocre, 906*
普*ommon, 455*	平*lain, 488*
凡*ommon, 78*	

航*avigation, 748*

241-B

般*egular train* 搬*ransport of chess* 盤*oards, all aboard...*

手⇔扌 (hand, manual)

搬*ransport*　搬*elivery*

HAN
transport, delivery, bring-over, hand-over, carry

FLIP: 7.0.b2. Right (stem)

搬入　*carrying in, bringing in*　**hannyū**
搬出　*carrying out, bringing out*　**hanshutsu**
搬送　*carriage, conveyance*　**hansō**
搬送波　*carrier wave*　**hansōha**
運搬　*transportation, conveyance*　**unpan**
運搬費　*shipment charges, haulage*　**unpanhi**
運搬人　*porter, carrier*　**unpannin**
可搬式　*portable, carry-on*　**kahanshiki**

運*ransport, 295*	荷*reight, 877*
輸*hipment, 660*	貨*reight, 191*
送*ending, 708*	搭*reight, 146*
届*eliver, 631*	

般*egular, 323*

241-C

般*egular train* 搬*ransport of chess* 盤*oards, all aboard...*

皿 (plate)

盤*oard*　　　盤*isk*

BAN
board, disk

FLIP: 4.0.a. Bottom (flat)

盤台 *oblong basin; fish catch tub* **bandai**
盤石 *huge rock* **banjaku**
⇒大盤石 *"solid as rock..."* **daibanjaku**
盤面 *surface* **banmen**
中盤 *middle stage* **chūban**
銅盤 *bronze plate* **dōban**
円盤 *disk, discus* **enban**
岩盤 *bedrock* **ganban**
原盤 *original record* **genban**
銀盤 *silver plate, skating rink* **ginban**
碁盤 *Go playing board* **goban**
地盤 *ground, foundation* **jiban**
序盤 *early stage* **joban**
鍵盤 *piano keyboard* **kenban**
基盤 *base, foundation* **kiban**
骨盤 *pelvis* **kotsuban**
吸盤 *sucking disk* **kyūban**
音盤 *disk, record* **onban**
落盤 *caving in* **rakuban**

路盤 *road bed* **roban**
旋盤 *lathe* **senban**
旋盤工 *turner, lathe worker* **senbankō**
算盤 *abacus* **soroban**
算盤玉 *abacus beads* **sorobandama**
水盤 *water basin* **suiban**
胎盤 *placenta* **taiban**
羅針盤 *mariner's compass* **rashinban**
制御盤 *control panel* **seigyoban**
将棋盤 *shogi chessboard* **shōgiban**
終盤戦 *endgame* **shūbansen**

> 盆*ray, 594*
> 皿*ish, 21*
> 鉢*owl, 666*

般*egular, 323*

242-A

章*hapters of* 彰*itation for those* 障*njured in the liberation...*

立 (standing)

❶章*hapter*　❷章*adge*

SHŌ
chapter, section, clause; badge, emblem, insignia

FLIP: 1.0.b. Whole (stem)

❶憲章 *charter, constitution* **kenshō**
⇒児童憲章 *children's rights charter*
　　jidō kenshō
章句 *verse, passage* **shōku**
章節 *chapters & sections* **shōsetsu**
前章 *preceding chapter* **zenshō**
文章 *writing, sentence* **bunshō**
断章 *fragmented chapters* **danshō**
楽章 *musical movement* **gakushō**
玉章 *precious composition* **gyokushō**
序章 *foreword, preface, prologue* **joshō**
❷帽章 *badge on a cap* **bōshō**
襟章 *badge, emblem* **erishō**
褒章 *medal of honour* **hōshō**
印章 *seal, stamp* **inshō**
受章 *receiving a medal, ~an award* **jushō**
家章 *family crest (aristocrat)* **kashō**
肩章 *shoulder strap, epaulet* **kenshō**
記章 *badge, emblem* **kishō**

国章 *national emblem* **kokushō**
校章 *school badge* **kōshō**
勲章 *decoration, order, medal* **kunshō**
⇒文化勲章 *culture award* **bunka kunshō**
紋章 *coat of arms, crest* **monshō**
喪章 *mourning ribbon* **moshō**
略章 *miniature decoration* **ryakushō**
社章 *company pin, ~badge* **shashō**
章魚 *octopus* **tako**
腕章 *arm band* **wanshō**
会員章 *membership badge* **kaiinshō**
日章旗 *Japanese rising flag* **nisshōki**

> 紋*rest, 558*　　款*rticle, 42*
> 但*roviso, 739*　条*rticle, 607*

意*dea, 340*　　草*rass, 373*

242-B

章*hapters of* 彰*itation for those* 障*njured in the liberation...*

彡 (hair ornament)

彰*itation*　彰*ward*

SHŌ
citation, award, conferment, accolade

FLIP: 6.0.b. Left (stem)

表彰 *award, citation, plaque* **hyōshō**
表彰状 *plaque of citation* **hyōshōjō**
顕彰 *manifestation, display* **kenshō**
彰明 *manifestation, display* **shōmei**
彰徳 *praising in public* **shōtoku**

勲 *xploits, 934*	祝 *ongratulate, 716*
賞 *ward, 554*	慶 *ejoice, 69*

影 *hadows, 546*

242-C

章*hapters of* 彰*itation for those* 障*njured in the liberation...*

阝 ↔ 阜 (village=left)

障*njury*　障*andicapped*

sawa(ru), SHŌ
injury, handicapped, impaired, paralyzed, invalid, crippled, disabled, harm

FLIP: 7.0.b1. Right (stem)

障泥 *saddle flap* **aori**
万障 *numerous obstacles* **banshō**
保障 *guarantee, security, warranty* **hoshō**
⇒安全保障 *peace & order* **anzen hoshō**
重障 *serious handicap* **jūshō**
故障 *broken, "out-of-order..."* **koshō**
⇒車両故障 *vehicular breakdown* **sharyō koshō**
故障中 *broken, "out-of-order..."* **koshōchū**
高障害 *great obstacles* **kōshōgai**
故障車 *car break down* **koshōsha**
支障 *hindrance, hitch, trouble* **shishō**
障害 *obstacle, handicap* **shōgai**
障害物 *obstacle, hindrance* **shōgaibutsu**
障害者 *handicapped, disabled person* **shōgaisha**
⇒身体障害者 *physically-disabled* **shintai shōgaisha**
障壁 *barrier, wall* **shōheki**
障子 *sliding paper door* **shōji**
⇒腰高障子 *hip-level paper sliding door*
　　koshidaka shōji

障子紙 *sliding door paper* **shōjigami**
罪障 *sins, offence* **zaishō**
油障子 *Japanese door paper* **aburashōji**
襖障子 *blurry paper sliding door* **fusuma shōji**
白内障 *eye cataract* **hakunaishō, shirosokohi**
黒内障 *black cataract* **kokunaishō, kurosokohi**
目障り *blocking one's view* **mezawari**
耳障り *grating noise* **mimizawari**
緑内障 *glaucoma* **ryokunaishō**
差し障り *hindrance, obstacle* **sashisawari**
気に障る *hurt one's feelings* **ki(ni)sawaru**

害 *njury, 904*	損 *njury, 410*
傷 *njury, 933*	痛 *njury, 60*

章 *hapter, 324*

243-A

曹ergeant of 曹oble rank 遭ncounters 槽ater-tank...

日 (sunlight, daytime)

¹曹obility ²曹ergeant

SŌ, ZŌ

nobility, aristocrat; sergeant

❶ 法曹　barrister, lawyer, attorney **hōsō**
法曹界　legal luminaries **hōsōkai**
重曹　baking soda **jūsō**
海曹　petty naval officer **kaisō**
曹達　soda **sōda**
曹司　scion of a noble family **zōshi**
曹子　heir to a vast wealth **zōshi**
御曹司　scion of a noble family **onzōshi**

❷ 軍曹　army sergeant **gunsō**
兵曹　warrant officer **heisō**
陸曹　non-commissioned officer **rikusō**
曹長　master sergeant **sōchō**

FLIP: 1.0.a. Whole (flat)

尉ieutenant, 438	爵obility, 593
軍oldier, 295	侯obility, 122
兵oldier, 490	

著uthor, 279

243-B

曹ergeant of 曹oble rank 遭ncounters 槽ater-tank...

辶 (transport)

遭ncounter　遭hance upon

a(u), SŌ

encounter, chance upon, coincidental, stumble, accidental

遭遇　encounter, coming across **sōgū**
遭難　shipwreck, disaster, accident **sōnan**
遭難船　wrecked ship, decrepit ship **sōnansen**
遭難者　victim, survivor **sōnansha**
遭難信号　distress signal, SOS code
　　　sōnan shingō
遭難現場　scene of disaster, tragic scene
　　　sōnan genba
遭難救助隊　search & rescue party
　　　sōnan kyūjotai

FLIP: 3.0.a. Top (flat)

遇ncounter, 591
会eeting, 864
合ogether, 232

曹ergeant, 326

243-C

曹ergeant of 曹oble rank 遭ncounters 槽ater-tank...

槽ater-tank 槽eservoir

木 (wooden)

fune, SŌ
water-tank, reservoir

FLIP: 7.0.a. Right (flat)

水槽 water reservoir, ~tank **suisō**
⇒貯水槽 water reservoir, ~tank **chosuisō**
浴槽 bathtub, bath tank **yokusō**
湯槽 bathtub, bath tank **yubune**
油槽 oil tank **yusō**
湯槽 bathtub **yusō**
沈殿槽 settling tank **chindensō**
浄化槽 purification-, septic tank **jōkasō**
養魚槽 fish-breeding tank **yōgyosō**
油槽船 oil tanker ship **yusōsen**
歯槽膿漏 pyorrhoea **shisō nōrō**

井ater well, 361	蔵torage, 565
容ontent, 492	貯torage, 967
庫torage, 306	缶an, 28
倉torage, 399	水ater, 9

横idewards, 197

244-A

祭estival on the 際erge of 察nspection 擦crapes for funding
際ccasion...

示⇔ネ (display, show)

祭estival 祭iesta

matsu(ru), matsu(ri), SAI
festival, fiesta, festivity, frolic

FLIP: 2.0.b. Sort Of (stem)

助祭 Catholic deacon **josai**
例祭 annual festival, ~fair **reisai**
祭壇 altar **saidan**
祭殿 sanctuary, shrine **saiden**
祭事 religious rituals, rites **saiji**
祭神 enshrined deity **saijin**
祭日 national holiday, public holiday **saijitsu**
⇒祝祭日 public-, national holiday **shukusaijitsu**
祭器 ritual implements, ~ornaments **saiki**
祭礼 festival, rituals **sairei**
祭神 enshrined deity **saishin**
祭主 celebrating-, officiating priest **saishu**
祭典 festival, fete **saiten**
司祭 priest **shisai**
文化祭 university fair, school festival **bunkasai**
映画祭 film festival **eigasai**
復活祭 Easter **fukkatsusai**
学園祭 school festival **gakuensai**
芸術祭 art festival **geijutsusai**

百年祭 centenary, centennial **hyakunensai**
慰霊祭 prayer for the dead **ireisai**
夏祭り summer festival **natsumatsuri**
謝肉祭 carnival, circus **shanikusai**
植樹祭 Arbour Day **shokujusai**
体育祭 athletic festival, field day **taiikusai**
七夕祭 Star Festival (7 July) **tanabata matsuri**
宵祭り eve of a festival **yoimatsuri**
前夜祭 eve of a festival **zenyasai**
冠婚葬祭 ceremonial occasions **kankon sōsai**

盆uddhist Feast, 594	祝elebration, 716
公ublic, 180	幸appiness, 268
宴arty, 610	祥appiness, 248
慶ejoice, 69	喜appiness, 965
賀elebration, 202	

桑ulberry, 608

244-B

祭estival on the 際erge of 察nspection 擦crapes for funding 際ccasion...

β⇔阜 (village=left)

際ccasion 際erge

kiwa, SAI
occasion, verge, event, instance

FLIP: 7.1. Right (Sort Of)

に際して *"amidst, in the face of..."* **(ni)saishite**
分際 *one's reputation, ~social standing* **bunzai**
出際 *setting out time* **degiwa**
土俵際 *crucial moment* **dōhyōgiwa**
不手際 *poor, clumsy, unskilled* **futegiwa**
学際 *inter-disciplinary studies* **gakusai**
生え際 *hairline, hairstretch* **haegiwa**
一際 *conspicuous, remarkable, stark* **hitokiwa**
今際 *one's dying moment* **imawa**
実際 *actual practice, application* **jissai**
国際 *international, cosmopolitan* **kokusai**
国際化 *internationalisation* **kokusaika**
交際 *association, exchange, intercourse* **kōsai**
窓際 *by the window; fence-sitter* **madogiwa**
間際 *just as, right in the middle of* **magiwa**
水際 *waterside, waterway* **mizugiwa**
根際 *"just about to sleep..."* **negiwa**
際涯 *limits, extremity* **saigai**
際限 *limit, end* **saigen**

際会 *meet, face, confront* **saikai**
手際 *skill, technique* **tegiwa**
海際 *seashore, beach, shoreline* **umigiwa**
山際 *mountain village* **yamagiwa**
際どい *risky, close, narrow* **kiwadoi**
覚め際 *on the verge of awakening* **samegiwa**
瀬戸際 *brink, verge* **setogiwa**
死に際 *deathbed, dying moments* **shinigiwa**
無辺際 *limitless, infinite, boundless* **muhensai**
際立つ *remarkable, stand out* **kiwadatsu**
波打ち際 *seashore, shoreline* **namiuchigiwa**

時 *ime, 653*
経 *ime-lapse, 791*
宴 *arty, 610*

祭 *estival, 327*

244-C

祭estival on the 際erge of 察nspection 擦crapes for funding 際ccasion...

宀 (cover, lid)

察nspection 察uess

SATSU
inspection, guess, review, scrutiny, inquest, probe, auditing, check

FLIP: 2.0.b. Sort Of (stem)

洞察 *seeing thru, discern* **dōsatsu**
拝察 *inferring, guessing* **haisatsu**
巡察 *inspection round* **junsatsu**
観察 *observing, watching closely* **kansatsu**
監察 *inspection, investigation* **kansatsu**
観察眼 *discerning eye* **kansatsugan**
観察力 *power of observation* **kansatsuryoku**
警察 *police* **keisatsu**
⇒無警察 *anarchy, lawlessness* **mukeisatsu**
⇒治安警察 *security police* **chian keisatsu**
警察官 *police officer* **keisatsukan**
警察犬 *police dog* **keisatsuken**
警察権 *police power* **keisatsuken**
警察署 *police station* **keisatsusho**
賢察 *conjecture, guess, surmise* **kensatsu**
検察 *investigation, inspection* **kensatsu**
検察庁 *Public Prosecutor's Office* **kensatsuchō**
考察 *examine, consider, study* **kōsatsu**
高察 *"your esteemed idea..."* **kōsatsu**

明察 *discernment, perception* **meisatsu**
了察 *taking into consideration* **ryōsatsu**
察知 *guess, surmise, judgement* **sacchi**
査察 *inspection, investigation* **sasatsu**
省察 *reflecting on, introspect* **seisatsu**
診察 *examination, inspection* **shinsatsu**
視察 *inspection, observation* **shisatsu**
推察 *guess, surmise, conjecture* **suisatsu**
偵察 *reconnaissance, scouting* **teisatsu**
偵察機 *reconnaissance plane* **teisatsuki**
透察 *insight, discernment* **tōsatsu**

審 *nspection, 339* | 査 *nspection, 624*
調 *nspection, 280* | 閲 *nspection, 942*
検 *nspection, 939*

祭 *estival, 327*

244-D

祭*estival on the* 際*erge of* 察*nspection* 擦*crapes for funding* 際*ccasion..*

手⇔扌 (hand, manual)

擦*crape* 擦*riction*

su(reru), su(ru), kosu(ru), nasu(ri), SATSU
scrape, friction, rubbing

FLIP: 7.1. Right (Sort Of)

塗擦 *applying an ointment* **tosatsu**
摩擦 *friction, rubbing* **masatsu**
摩擦熱 *frictional heat* **masatsunetsu**
摩擦音 *frictional sound* **masatsuon**
人擦れ *sophisticated personality* **hitozure**
衣擦れ *rustling of clothes* **kinuzure**
耳擦り *whispering* **mimikosuri**
手擦れ *wear & tear damage* **tekosure**
床擦れ *bedsore* **tokozure**
上擦る *speak in a high pitch* **uwazuru**
悪擦れ *oversophistication* **waruzure**
靴擦れ *shoe sore* **kutsuzure**
擦過傷 *graze, abrasion* **sakkashō**
擦り傷 *scratch, scratch* **surikizu**
擦り込む *rub, scrape* **surikomu**
擦り寄る *draw close, edge up* **suriyoru**
擦りガラス *frosted glass* **surigarasu**
擦り減らす *wear down, rub off* **suriherasu**

擦り切れる *wear out, be worn away* **surikireru**
擦り付ける *lay, daub, rub, smear* **suritsukeru**
ほう擦り *cheek-to-cheek rubbing* **hōzuri**
擦り合う *blame each other* **nasuriau**
阿婆擦れ *hussy, extra burden* **abazure**
当て擦り *insinuation, innuendo* **atekosuri**
貿易摩擦 *trade conflict, -friction* **bōeki masatsu**
擦り剥く *scrape, skin, abrade* **kosurimuku**
擦れ合う *rub against each other* **sureau**
擦れ違う *pass by each other* **surechigau**
擦れ擦れ *passing by; barely* **suresure**
擦れっ枯らし *hussy, extra burden* **surekkarashi**

磨*rush, 166*	漆*arnish, 611*
摩*crape, 331*	熱*eat, 153*

察*nspect, 328*

245-A

Words of 敬*espect in* 警*arnings quite* 驚*urprising...*

攵 (action)

敬*espect* 敬*steem*

uyama(u), KEI
respect, esteem, homage, revere, adore, cherish, courtesy

FLIP: 7.1. Right (Sort Of)

愛敬 *love & respect* **aikei, aikyō**
不敬 *disrespect, impiety* **fukei**
畏敬 *reverence, esteem* **ikei**
自敬 *self-respect* **jikei**
敬愛 *respect, love, esteem* **keiai**
敬慕 *adoration, veneration, devotion* **keibo**
敬遠 *avoidance, shunning* **keien**
敬服 *admiration, respect* **keifuku**
敬語 *words-, terms of respect* **keigo**
敬具 *"yours sincerely..."* **keigu**
敬白 *"yours sincerely..."* **keihaku**
敬意 *respect, regard* **keii**
敬虔 *pious, devout, faithful* **keiken**
敬礼 *salute, salutation, bow* **keirei**
敬老 *respect for the aged* **keirō**
敬老の日 *respect-for-the-aged day* **keirō no hi**
敬神 *piety, devoutness, pious* **keishin**
敬称 *honorific title, terms of respect* **keishō**
恭敬 *respect & reverence* **kyōkei**

失敬 *rude, discourteous* **shikkei**
尊敬 *respect, esteem* **sonkei**
崇敬 *adoration, veneration* **sūkei**
最敬礼 *highest respects* **saikeirei**
表敬訪問 *courtesy call, ~visit* **hyōkei hōmon**

恭*espect, 620*	尚*espect, 99*
仰*espect, 706*	崇*espect, 879*
謹*espect, 962*	礼*espect, 685*

歌*oem, 878*

245-B

Words of 敬espect in 警arnings quite 驚urprising...

言 (speaking)

警arning　警recaution

imashi(meru), KEI

warning, precaution, dissuasion

FLIP: 4.0.a. Bottom (flat)

警備　*private security* **keibi**
警棒　*truncheon, nightstick* **keibō**
警防　*preservation of public order* **keibō**
警部　*police inspector, investigation unit* **keibu**
警衛　*guard, escort* **keiei**
警護　*guard, convoy, escort* **keigo**
警乗　*guarding aboard* **keijō**
警巡　*patrol* **keijun**
警戒　*precaution, caution, warning* **keikai**
警戒網　*police dragnet* **keikaimō**
警戒線　*"police line: do not cross..."* **keikaisen**
警官　*police officer* **keikan**
⇒婦人警官　*lady cop* **fujin keikan**
警官隊　*police force* **keikantai**
警告　*precaution, caution, warning* **keikoku**
警句　*witty remark, wisecrack, aphorism* **keiku**
警急　*emergency, crisis* **keikyū**
警務　*police affairs* **keimu**
警察　*police* **keisatsu**

警察官　*police officer* **keisatsukan**
警察権　*police power* **keisatsuken**
警察犬　*police dog* **keisatsuken**
警世　*warning to the society* **keisei**
警世家　*prophet, visionary* **keiseika**
警視　*police superintendent* **keishi**
警視庁　*metropolitan police agency* **keishichō**
警鐘　*alarm, siren* **keishō**
警手　*guard, sentry* **keishu**
警笛　*whistle, alarm* **keiteki**
夜警　*night watchman* **yakei**

驚*care, 330*	戒*dmonish, 493*
威*uthority, 520*	諭*dmonish, 922*
権*uthority, 804*	律*egulation, 731*

警*urprise, 330*

245-C

Words of 敬espect in 警arnings quite 驚urprising...

馬 (horse)

驚urprise　驚care

odoro(ku), odoro(kasu), KYŌ

surprise, scare, threaten, frighten, intimidate, menace, panicking

Facing: 3.0. ☞☜ Across

驚き　*surprise, astonishment, wonder* **odoroki**
驚かせる　*frighten, surprise* **odorokaseru**
吃驚　*astonishment, disbelief* **bikkuri, kikkyō**
一驚　*astonishment, baffling* **ikkyō**
喫驚　*astonishment, disbelief* **kikkyō**
驚愕　*astonishment, amazement* **kyōgaku**
驚異　*wonder, marvel, fascination* **kyōi**
驚異的　*marvellous, wonderful* **kyōiteki**
驚喜　*joy, delight, amazement* **kyōki**
驚嘆　*admiration, amazement* **kyōtan**
驚倒　*earth-shaking, sensational* **kyōtō**
驚天動地　*earth-shaking* **kyōten dōchi**

威*hreat, 520*	脅*hreaten, 577*
嚇*hreat, 261*	急*udden, 868*
虞*hreat, 889*	瞬*link, 921*

警*arning, 330*

246-A

麻emp-plants & lemons for 摩ubbing off 魔emons...

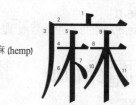

麻 (hemp)

麻emp-plant   麻umb

asa, MA
hemp plant, numb

FLIP: 8.0.b. Inner (stem)

マニラ麻 *Manila hemp, abaca* **maniraasa**
亜麻 *flax, linen* **ama**
亜麻仁 *linseed* **amani**
麻袋 *jute sack* **asabukuro**
麻糸 *hemp thread* **asaito**
麻縄 *hempen rope* **asanawa**
麻布 *hemp cloth* **asanuno**
胡麻 *sesame* **goma**
黄麻 *jute* **kōma**
麻雀 *mah-jong* **maajan**
麻雀屋 *mah-jong parlour* **maajanya**
麻痺 *paralysis, numbness* **mahi**
⇒脳性麻痺 *cerebral palsy* **nōsei mahi**
麻疹 *measles* **mashin**
麻酔 *anaesthesia, narcotic* **masui**
⇒局部麻酔 *local anaesthesia* **kyokubu masui**
麻酔薬 *anaesthetic, narcotic drugs* **masuiyaku**
乱麻 *anarchy, mob rule, chaos* **ranma**
製麻 *hemp-, flax spinning* **seima**

大麻 *cannabis, marijuana, joint* **taima**
麻薬 *drug, dope, narcotic* **mayaku**
麻薬中毒 *drug addiction* **mayaku chūdoku**
麻薬常習者 *narcotic, junkie, drug addict*
  mayaku jōshūsha
麻薬密売人 *drug-, dope pusher*
  mayaku mitsubainin
麻薬取締り *narcotic control*
  mayaku torishimari
麻の葉 *hemp leaf* **asanoha**
蕁麻疹 *hives, urticaria* **jinmashin**

木*ree, 461*	菜*egetable, 915*
繊*iber, 803*	植*egetation, 783*
植*lant, 783*	畑*lantation, 482*

林*oods, 526*

246-B

麻emp plants & lemons for 摩ubbing off 魔emons...

手⇔扌 (hand, manual)

摩crape   摩ubbing

MA, su(ru)
scrape, rub-off, rubbing

FLIP: 8.0.b. Inner (stem)

按摩 *massage* **anma**
減摩 *friction reduction* **genma**
護摩 *sacred fire of invocation* **goma**
護摩の灰 *passenger-disguised thief* **goma no hai**
摩滅 *wearing away* **mametsu**
摩耗 *abrasion, bruise* **mamō**
摩羅 *male organ, penis* **mara**
摩擦 *friction, rub* **masatsu**
⇒貿易摩擦 *trade friction, ~dispute* **bōeki masatsu**
摩擦音 *friction noise* **masatsuon**
摩擦熱 *frictional heat* **masatsunetsu**
摩擦抵抗 *frictional resistance* **masatsu teikō**
摩損 *wearing away, ~out* **mason**
揣摩 *conjecture, speculation* **shima**
摩天楼 *skyscraper, skyline* **matenrō**
薩摩藩 *Satsuma clan (Kagoshima Pref.)* **satsumahan**
薩 摩芋 *sweet potato* **satsumaimo**
摩り替える *substitute, replacement* **surikaeru**
摩訶不思議 *awesome mystery* **makafushigi**

擦*riction, 329*	磨*rush, 166*
研*olish, 951*	漆*arnish, 611*
錬*olish, 718*	熱*eat, 153*

磨*rush, 166*

246-C
麻emp plants & lemons for 摩ubbing off 魔emons...

鬼 (spirits)

魔emon   魔evil

MA
demon, devil

FLIP: 8.0.b. Inner (stem)

悪魔 devil, demon **akuma**
病魔 strange disease **byōma**
邪魔 hindrance, obstruction **jama**
邪魔者 nuisance, annoyance, irksome **jamamono**
魔道 path of evil **madō**
魔法 magic, wizardry, sorcery **mahō**
魔法瓶 thermos, vacuum bottle **mahōbin**
魔法使い wizard, sorcerer, witch **mahōtsukai**
魔神 evil spirit, demon **majin**
魔女 witch, hag, sorceress **majo**
魔女狩り witch-hunt **majogari**
魔術 magic, spell, enchantment **majutsu**
魔界 evil empire **makai**
魔境 demon-infested **makyō**
魔球 diabolical, demonic **makyū**
魔物 evil spirit, demon **mamono**
魔王 Lucifer, Satan **maō**
魔力 magic, charm **maryoku**
魔性 evil, demonic **mashō**

魔手 clutches of evil **mashū**
夢魔 nightmare, bad dream **muma**
色魔 sex maniac, pervert **shikima**
白魔 white devil, snowstorm **shiroma, hakuma**
睡魔 drowsiness, sleepiness **suima**
水魔 disastrous flood **suima**
天魔 demon, evil spirit **tenma**
伏魔殿 beehive of demons **fukumaden**
放火魔 firebug, pyromaniac **hōkama**
魔除け charm against evil **mayoke**
通り魔 phantom killer **toorima**

悪vil, 389	鬼evil, 935
凶vil, 80	罪riminal, 289
邪vil, 58	犯riminal, 640

磨rush, 166

247-A
副ice mayor's 富ortune for a very 福ucky baboon...

刀⇔刂 (blade, cutting)

副eputy   副ice

FUKU
deputy, second-in-rank, vice-

FLIP: 6.0.a. Left (flat)

副木 splint, brace **fukuboku**
副長 company vice president **fukuchō**
副題 sub-title **fukudai**
副業 side business, moonlighting **fukugyō**
副本 duplicate copy **fukuhon**
副因 secondary cause **fukuin**
副腎 adrenal glands **fukujin**
副官 aide-de-camp **fukukan, fukkan**
副詞 adverb **fukushi**
副詞句 adverbial phrase **fukushiku**
副詞節 adverbial clause **fukushisetsu**
副使 deputy envoy, ~emissary **fukushi**
副署 countersignature **fukusho**
副賞 supplementary prize **fukushō**
副将 adjutant general **fukushō**
副食 side dish **fukushoku**
副手 assistant, deputy **fukute**
副知事 vice governor **fukuchiji**
副代表 deputy representative **fukudaihyō**

副読本 supplementary reading **fukudokuhon**
副学長 university vice president **fukugakuchō**
副次的 secondary, alternative **fukujiteki**
副会長 vice chairman **fukukaichō**
副産物 by-product, derivative **fukusanbutsu**
副作用 side effect **fukusayō**
副社長 executive vice president **fukushachō**
副収入 secondary income **fukushunnyū**
副葬品 items buried with the dead **fukusōhin**
副都心 sub-centre, sub-city **fukutoshin**
副大統領 Vice President **fukudaitōryō**

次ext, 460	第[order], 102
佐elper, 310	二econd, 457
順equence, 959	嗣uccessor, 836

幅idth, 640

247-B

副ice mayor's 富ortune for a very 福ucky baboon...

ウ (cover, lid)

富*ortune* 富*ealth*

FLIP: 1.0.a. Whole (flat)

tomi, to(mu), FU, FŪ
fortune, wealth, money, opulence, riches

富岳 *Mt. Fuji, Fuji mountain* **fugaku**
富源 *national resources, source of wealth* **fugen**
富豪 *rich, wealthy* **fugō**
富家 *wealthy family* **fuka**
富貴 *rich & noble* **fūki**
富鉱 *high-grade ore* **fukō**
富国 *rich nation* **fukoku**
富強 *rich & powerful* **fukyō**
富農 *rich farmer* **funō**
富力 *power of money, financial sway* **furyoku**
富者 *rich person* **fusha**
富商 *wealthy merchant* **fushō**
富裕 *wealth, riches, fortune* **fuyū**
富有 *wealthy & affluent* **fuyū**
貧富 *wealth & poverty, rich & poor* **hinpu**
豊富 *rich, abundant, plentiful* **hōfu**
豊満 *plump, abundant* **hōman**
国富 *nations treasure, national wealth* **kokufu**
巨富 *enormous wealth* **kyofu**

富札 *lotto ticket* **tomifuda**
富籤 *lotto ticket* **tomikuji**
富山 *Toyama City, Toyama Prefecture* **toyama**
富山県 *Toyama Prefecture* **toyama-ken**
富士額 *hairline resembling mt. fuji* **fujibitai**
富士絹 *fuji silk fabric* **fujiginu**
富士川 *Fujikawa River, Shizuoka Pref.* **fujikawa**
富士山 *Mt. Fuji, Fuji mountain* **fujisan**
逆さ富士 *inverted reflection of Mt. Fuji (on water)* **sakasafuji**

豊*bundance*, 965		隆*rosperity*, 133	
裕*ffluence*, 758		盛*rosperity*, 244	
繁*rosperity*, 434		益*rofit*, 622	

福*ucky*, 333

247-C

副ice mayor's 富ortune for a very 福ucky baboon...

示⇔ネ (display, show)

福*ortunate* 福*oodluck*

FLIP: 7.0.a. Right (flat)

FUKU
fortunate, goodluck

万福 *all health & happiness* **banpuku**
大福 *rice cake & bean jam* **daifuku**
艶福 *love success* **enpuku**
福音 *Gospel, glad tidings* **fukuin**
福音書 *Gospel* **fukuinsho**
福神 *god of fortune* **fukujin**
福寿 *happiness & long life* **fukuju**
福寿草 *adonis* **fukujusō**
福耳 *plump ears (said to be money luck)* **fukumimi**
福利 *welfare, well-being* **fukuri**
福祉 *welfare, well-being* **fukushi**
福祉政策 *welfare policy, ~measures* **fukushi seisaku**
福相 *happy-looks* **fukusō**
福徳 *happiness & well-being* **fukutoku**
福運 *happiness & good fortune* **fukuun**
禍福 *fortune & misfortune* **kafuku**
慶福 *blessings, happiness* **keifuku**
幸福 *happiness & well-being* **kōfuku**
冥福 *"repose of one's soul..."* **meifuku**

民福 *citizen welfare* **minpuku**
清福 *happiness* **seifuku**
至福 *supreme bliss, perfect happiness* **shifuku**
祝福 *blessing, benediction* **shukufuku**
追福 *memorial services* **tsuifuku**
裕福 *affluence, fortune, wealth* **yūfuku**
福引き *lottery, lotto* **fukubiki**
福岡市 *fukuoka city, fukuoka pref.* **fukuoka-shi**
七福神 *seven gods of fortune* **shichi fukujin**
多福豆 *large beans* **tafukumame**
天福時代 *Tenpuku Era (1233-1234)* **tenpuku jidai**

祉*elfare*, 193		賜*estow*, 150	
義*ighteous*, 341		催*ponsor*, 416	
善*ighteous*, 450		贈*onation*, 838	
施*estow*, 649		献*onation*, 414	

富*ortune*, 333

248-A

替eplacement by net fibres, 賛pproved by scuba 潜ivers...

日 (sunlight, daytime)

替eplace 替ubstitute

ka(eru); ka(waru), TAI

replace, substitute, supplant, switch with, alternate with, exchange, in place of, in lieu of

FLIP: 1.0.a. Whole (flat)

替えズボン spare trousers **kaezubon**
代替 substitution, replacement **daitai**
振替 money remittance **furikae**
為替 foreign currency exchange **kawase**
交替 change, replacement, substitution **kōtai**
両替 exchange for same amount **ryōgae**
隆替 rise & fall, changing fortunes **ryūtai**
引替え exchange, convert **hikikae**
言替え reword, say in other words **iikae**
替え玉 substitute, replacement **kaedama**
替え歌 parody, mimicry, voice imitation **kaeuta**
書替え rewrite, write in another way **kakikae**
着替え fresh clothes **kigae**
荷為替 documentary bill **nigawase**
小為替 money-, postal order **kogawase**
衣替え seasonal change of clothes **koromogae**
立替え pay for another, pay in advance **tatekae**
宿替え change of lodging quarter **yadogae**
吹き替え sound-, voice dubbing **fukikae**

張り替え re-cover, re-paper, re-upholster **harikae**
入れ替え shift, replacement **irekae**
買い替え rebuild, renew **kaikae**
掛け替え replace, substitute **kakekae**
組み替え rearrangement, readjustment **kumikae**
摩り替え substitute, exchange, change **surikae**
建て替え rebuild, reconstruct **tatekae**
付け替え replacement, substitute **tsukekae**
作り替え remake, rebuild, reconstruct **tsukurikae**
詰め替え repack, repackage, rebottle **tsumekae**
植え替え re-planting **uekae**

換eplace, 819 | 遷hange, 603
代eplace, 96 | 変hange, 581

賛pproval, 334

248-B

替eplacement by net fibres, 賛pproved by scuba 潜ivers...

貝 (shell, old money)

❶賛raise ❷賛pproval

SAN

praise, accolade; approval, concur, consent

FLIP: 1.O.b. Whole (stem)

❶画賛 written dedication on a photo **gasan**
自賛 self-praise, self-admiration **jisan**
熱賛 enthusiastic praise **nessan**
礼賛 praise, worship **raisan**
論賛 commentary in praise of **ronsan**
賛美 praise, glorification **sanbi**
賛美歌 hymn **sanbika**
賛美歌集 hymnal book **sanbi kashū**
賛辞 praise, eulogy **sanji**
賛歌 hymn, paean **sanka**
賛嘆 extol, praise, admire **santan**
称賛 praise, admiration, applause **shōsan**
称賛者 admirer, supporter **shōsansha**
賞賛 praise, admire **shōsan**
絶賛 highest praise **zessan**
自画賛 praise one's self-portrait **jigasan**

賛同 consent, approval **sandō**
賛意 consent, approval **san'i**
賛助 support, patronage **sanjo**
賛否 yes-or-no, approval, consent **sanpi**
賛成 approval, agreement **sansei**
賛成派 supporters, proponents **sanseiha**
賛成者 in favour, supporter **sanseisha**
賛成演説 speech in support **sansei enzetsu**
賛成投票 favourable vote **sansei tōhyō**
翼賛 support, assistance **yokusan**

褒raise, 552 | 承pproval, 117 | 諾onsent, 277
可pproval, 15 | 認ecognize, 535 | 肯onsent, 616

替eplace, 334

❷協賛 support, cooperation **kyōsan**
協賛金 money in support **kyōsankin**

248-C

替eplacement by net fibres, 贊pproved by scuba 潜ivers...

潜ubmerge   潜iving

水⇔氵 (water)

FLIP: 7.0.a. Right (flat)

mogu(ru), hiso(mu), kugu(ru), SEN
submerge, diving, lurking behind, underwater

潜り dive, plunge into the water **moguri**
潜り込む creep, get in **mogurikomu**
沈潜 sinking, submersion **chinsen**
原潜 nuclear submarine **gensen**
潜没 submerge, dive **senbotsu**
潜血 occult blood-letting **senketsu**
潜行 underwater navigation **senkō**
潜航 submarine ship **senkō**
潜航艇 submarine **senkōtei**
潜熱 latent heat **sennetsu**
潜入 infiltration, sneaking in **sennyū**
潜伏 concealed, hidden, submerged **senpuku**
潜伏期 incubation period **senpukuki**
潜流 undercurrent **senryū**
潜心 meditation, contemplation, reflection **senshin**
潜水 diving, submersion **sensui**
潜水病 caisson disease **sensuibyō**
潜水夫 sea diver **sensuifu**
潜水艦 submarine, sub **sensuikan**

潜在 latency, potential **senzai**
潜在的 latent, potential **senzaiteki**
潜在意識 subconscious mind **senzai ishiki**
潜在需要 potential demand **senzai juyō**
潜像 latent-, lingering image **senzō**
対潜 anti-submarine **taisen**
潜り戸 wicket, gate **kugurido**
駆潜艇 anti-submarine vessel **kusentei**
潜勢力 latent power, potential **senseiryoku**
潜望鏡 periscope **senbōkyō**
掻い潜る dodge through **kaikuguru**

沈inking, 719	浸mmerse, 770
没inking, 744	透ransparency, 383
礁unken, 920	隠idden, 840

替eplace, 334

249-A

錯ixed-up 借oan 籍egistry 散cattered in misery...

錯ixed-up   錯crambling

金 (metal)

FLIP: 7.0.a. Right (flat)
FLIP: 5.0.a. Left & Right

SAKU
mixed-up, scrambling, complicated

介錯 assisting in a suicide **kaishaku**
交錯 mixed, intricate **kōsaku**
錯覚 illusion, wrong thinking **sakkaku**
錯角 alternate angles **sakkaku**
錯誤 mistake, error, blunder **sakugo**
⇒試行錯誤 trial & error **shikō sakugo**
錯乱 derangement, distraction **sakuran**
錯綜 complication, intricacy **sakusō**
錯雑 complicated, intricate, confound **sakuzatsu**
倒錯 perversion, aberration **tōsaku**
倒錯者 pervert, sick mind, maniac **tōsakusha**
盤根錯節 knotty & thorny, messy **bankon sakusetsu**

混ixture, 38	迷onfusion, 904
乱onfusion, 686	慌anic, 507
争onflict, 231	雑ssortment, 776

鋳intage, 440

249-B

錯*ixed-up* 借*oan* 籍*egistry* 散*cattered in misery...*

借*orrow*　借*oan*　借*ebt*

人⇔イ (person)

FLIP: 7.0.a. Right (flat)

ka(riru), SHAKU
borrow, loan, debt, credit, debenture

賃借 *renting, rental* **chinshaku**
拝借 *borrowing, quotation* **haishaku**
仮借 *pardon, excuse, mercy* **kashaku**
家借 *house for rent* **kashaku**
連借 *joint debt, consolidated loan* **renshaku**
借款 *debt, loan, borrowings* **shakkan**
借金 *debt, loan, borrowings* **shakkin**
借金取り *debt collector* **shakkintori**
借地 *leased land, land for lease* **shakuchi**
借地人 *tenant, leaseholder* **shakuchinin**
借家 *rental house, house-for-rent* **shakuya**
借用 *borrowing, loan* **shakuyō**
借財 *debt, loan* **shakuzai**
租借 *lease* **soshaku**
租借権 *leasehold rights* **soshakuken**
寸借 *small loan* **sunshaku**
貸借 *assets & liabilities* **taishaku**
転借 *tenancy, lease* **tenshaku**
借り店 *rented shop* **karidana**

借り方 *way of borrowing; debtor* **karikata**
借り物 *borrowed articles, loaned item* **karimono**
借り主 *borrower, debtor* **karinushi**
借り手 *borrower, debtor* **karite**
借り出す *borrow, take out a loan* **karidasu**
借り越し *outstanding debt, balance due* **karikoshi**
借り上げる *take over, requisition* **kariageru**
円借款 *yen-denominated loan* **enshakkan**
前借り *receiving a loan in advance* **maegari**
間借り *renting a room* **magari**
又借り *borrowing from a borrower* **matagari**

貸*ental, 145*	払*ayment, 682*
賃*ayment, 145*	料*ayment, 194*
納*ayment, 296*	債*orrow, 823*

惜*egret, 281*

249-C

錯*ixed-up* 借*oan* 籍*egistry* 散*cattered in misery...*

籍*egistry*　籍*ecord*

竹 (bamboo)

FLIP: 6.2. Left Bottom
FLIP: 7.3.a. Right Bottom (flat)

SEKI
registry, record, roster

地籍 *land registration* **chiseki**
学籍 *school register, ~enrolment* **gakuseki**
原籍 *permanent residence* **genseki**
軍籍 *military records, ~registry* **gunseki**
版籍 *registry of land & people* **hanseki**
兵籍 *military roster* **heiseki**
本籍 *permanent residence* **honseki**
本籍地 *permanent residence site* **honsekichi**
移籍 *transfer of registry* **iseki**
除籍 *removal from the register, disowning* **joseki**
漢籍 *Chinese classics* **kanseki**
鬼籍 *death roster* **kiseki**
国籍 *citizenship, nationality* **kokuseki**
⇒重国籍 *dual-, multiple citizenship* **jūkokuseki**
戸籍 *census registration* **koseki**
戸籍法 *family registration law* **kosekihō**
戸籍抄本 *abridged family register* **koseki shōhon**
戸籍謄本 *official copy of family register* **koseki tōhon**
入籍 *entry in the family registry by marriage* **nyūseki**

落籍 *absence of registration* **rakuseki**
離籍 *removal from family register* **riseki**
船籍 *ships registry* **senseki**
臣籍 *status as commoner* **shinseki**
史籍 *history book* **shiseki**
書籍 *books, writings, publications* **shoseki**
送籍 *registry of new address* **sōseki**
典籍 *classical books* **tenseki**
党籍 *party register, ~registry* **tōseki**
在籍 *being registered, as listed* **zaiseki**
族籍 *class & domicile* **zokuseki**

帳*egistry, 641*	簿*ecord, 64*
記*ecord, 728*	録*ecord, 841*

錯*ixed-up, 335*

249-D

錯ixed-up 借oan 籍egistry 散cattered in misery...

散catter 散pread-out

文 (action)

chi(rakasu), chi(rakarau), chi(ru), chi(rasu), SAN
scatter, spread-out, disperse

FLIP: 6.0.b. Left (stem)

分散 *dispersal, diffusion* **bunsan**
発散 *emission, dispersal* **hassan**
放散 *radiation, emission* **hōsan**
解散 *breaking up, dispersal* **kaisan**
拡散 *diffusion, proliferation* **kakusan**
閑散 *dull, slack, sluggish* **kansan**
離散 *scatter, dispersal* **risan**
散文 *literary prose* **sanbun**
散超 *excessive disbursement* **sanchō**
散逸 *dissipation, diffusion* **san'itsu**
散会 *adjournment, closing* **sankai**
散開 *deployment, stationing* **sankai**
散見 *appearing frequently* **sanken**
散漫 *haphazard, sloppy, shoddy* **sanman**
散発 *sporadic-, spontaneous occurrence* **sanpatsu**
散髪 *getting a haircut* **sanpatsu**
散歩 *walk, stroll* **sanpo**
散票 *scattered votes, spoiled ballot* **sanpyō**

散乱 *dispersal, scattering* **sanran**
散策 *walk, stroll* **sansaku**
散失 *scattered & lost* **sanshitsu**
散水 *sprinkling with water* **sansui**
散薬 *powdered medicine* **sanyaku**
散在 *scatter, being dotted* **sanzai**
散財 *wasteful spending, squandering* **sanzai**
四散 *dispersal, scatter* **shisan**
消散 *evaporation, vanishing* **shōsan**
退散 *being dispersed, running away* **taisan**
散兵線 *skirmish line, line-of-fire* **sanpeisen**
砕け散る *break into pieces* **kudakechiru**

敷catter, 170   遍idespread, 43
拡nlarge, 205

敬espect, 329

250-A

Revised 藩uedal 翻ranslation, after a 番umber of 審nspections...

⺾ (grass)

藩eudal clan

HAN
feudal clan

FLIP: 7.3.a. Right Bottom (flat)

脱藩 *samurai leaving one's lord* **dappan**
藩閥 *clanship, favouritism* **hanbatsu**
藩学 *school for the samurai clan* **hangaku**
藩儒 *Daimyo scholar* **hanju**
藩校 *samurai school for clan family* **hankō**
藩侯 *feudal lord, Daimyo* **hankō**
藩内 *within the feudal system* **hannai**
藩老 *clan elder* **hanrō**
藩札 *feudal paper money* **hansatsu**
藩士 *clansman, retainer* **hanshi**
藩主 *feudal lord* **hanshu**
藩邸 *Daimyo palace (Edo Era)* **hantei**
旧藩 *former clan* **kyūhan**
列藩 *various clans* **reppan**
親藩 *Tokugawa vassals* **shinpan**
廃藩 *abolition of clan system* **haihan**
廃藩置県 *replacement of clans by prefectures*
   haihan chiken
薩摩藩 *Satsuma clan* **satsumahan**

封eudal, 890
殿ordship, 522

番umber, 338

250-B

Revised 藩uedal 翻ranslation, after a 番umber of 審nspections...

羽 (feathers, wings)

翻ranslate 翻urn-over

hirugae(su), hirugae(ru), HON
translate, interpret, turn-over

FLIP: 6.2. Left Bottom

翻案 *adaptation, adoption, modification* **hon'an**
翻意 *context translation; change of mind* **hon'i**
翻字 *transliteration* **honji**
翻刻 *reprint, reprinting* **honkoku**
翻弄 *frivolous, petty, trifle* **honrō**
翻訳 *translation, interpretation* **honyaku**
⇒逐次翻訳 *literal translation* **chikuji honyaku**
翻訳家 *translator, interpreter* **honyakuka**
翻訳権 *translation rights* **honyakuken**
翻訳書 *translation text* **honyakusho**
翻然 *suddenly, all of a sudden* **honzen**

文*iteracy, 558*	代*eplace, 96*
訳*ranslate, 752*	遷*hange, 603*
替*eplace, 334*	変*hange, 581*
換*eplace, 819*	稿*anuscript, 435*

番*umber, 338*

250-C

Revised 藩uedal 翻ranslation, after a 番umber of 審nspections...

田 (cultivated field)

❶番umber ❷番atch

tsugai, BAN
number, count; view, watch

FLIP: 4.0.a. Bottom (flat)
FLIP: 2.0.a. Sort Of (flat)

❶番地 *house number* **banchi**
番外 *extra, special issue* **bangai**
番号 *number* **bangō**
番号札 *numbered ticket, ~plate* **bangōfuda**
出番 *one's turn, ~role* **deban**
非番 *off duty, on leave* **hiban**
品番 *inventory, stock number* **hinban**
本番 *actual performance* **honban**
一番 *the most~, the best~, number one* **ichiban**
⇒春一番 *first gale of spring* **haruichiban**
順番 *order, turn* **junban**
欠番 *missing number* **ketsuban**
交番 *nearby police outpost* **kōban**
局番 *exchange number* **kyokuban**
店番 *tending, tender* **miseban**
門番 *gatekeeper, porter* **monban**
遅番 *late shift at work, night shift* **osoban**
先番 *one's turn to move (game)* **senban**
輪番制 *rotation system* **rinbansei**

❷番茶 *coarse-, unrefined tea* **bancha**
番組 *TV programme, ~show* **bangumi**
番犬 *watchdog* **banken**
番人 *watchman, guard, sentry* **bannin**
番兵 *sentry, guard* **banpei**
番卒 *sentry, guard* **bansotsu**
番頭 *head clerk* **bantō**
番付 *ranking list* **banzuke**
玄関番 *doorkeeper, gatekeeper* **genkanban**
留守番 *stay in place as caretaker* **rusuban**
番狂わせ *unexpected result, upset* **bankuruwase**
当番 *one's turn to watch* **tōban**

号*umber, 866*	第*[order], 102*
数*umber, 156*	算*alculate, 141*
順*equence, 959*	

雷*hunder, 136*

250-D

Revised 藩uedal 翻ranslation, after a 番umber of 審nspections...

宀 (cover, lid)

審rial　　審nspection

SHIN
trial, inspection, scrutiny, inquest, probe

FLIP: 2.0.a. Sort Of (flat)

陪審 *jury, juror* **baishin**
陪審員 *jury member, juror* **baishin'in**
副審 *assistant umpire* **fukushin**
覆審 *retrial, court review* **fukushin**
不審 *doubt, suspicion, disbelief* **fushin**
不審者 *mysterious person* **fushinsha**
原審 *original trial, first hearing* **genshin**
誤審 *misjudgement, erroneous verdict* **goshin**
一審 *first trial, first hearing* **isshin**
結審 *trial conclusion* **kesshin**
球審 *chief umpire* **kyūshin**
塁審 *base umpire* **ruishin**
再審 *retrial, review* **saishin**
線審 *line man (tennis referee)* **senshin**
審美 *aesthetic appreciation* **shinbi**
審美眼 *sense of beauty* **shinbigan**
審美的 *aesthetic, beautiful* **shinbiteki**
審議 *deliberation, discussion* **shingi**
審議会 *council, assembly* **shingikai**

審問 *inquiry, hearing* **shinmon**
審判 *judge, umpire, referee* **shinpan**
審判官 *umpire, referee* **shinpankan**
審理 *trial, litigation, court suit* **shinri**
審査 *inspection, examination* **shinsa**
審査員 *jury member, juror* **shinsain**
初審 *original trial, first hearing* **shoshin**
主審 *head umpire, chief referee* **shushin**
対審 *cross examination* **taishin**
予審 *preliminary hearing* **yoshin**
第二審 *retrial, second hearing* **dainishin**
控訴審 *court-, judicial appeal* **kōsoshin**

察nspection, 328	検nspection, 939
審nspection, 339	閲nspection, 942
調nspection, 280	

番umber, *338*

251-A

憶emory caught a 億undred-million 意houghts...

心⇔忄 (heart, feelings)

憶emory　　憶ecollection

OKU
memory, recollection, remembrance, speculate

FLIP: 7.2.a. Right Top (flat)

記憶 *memory, reminiscence, recollection* **kioku**
記憶術 *mnemonics, art of memorizing* **kiokujutsu**
記憶力 *memory ability* **kiokuryoku**
記憶喪失 *amnesia, memory lapse* **kioku sōshitsu**
記憶容量 *memory capacity* **kioku yōryō**
憶病 *timid, meek, docile* **okubyō**
憶断 *conjecture, guessing* **okudan**
憶念 *constant thought* **okunen**
憶説 *conjecture, hypothesis* **okusetsu**
憶測 *guess, conjecture* **okusoku**
追憶 *recollection, reminiscence* **tsuioku**

簿ecord, 64	歴istory, 595
録ecord, 841	暦alendar, 595
史istory, 85	

億undred million, *340*　　意hought, *340*

251-B

憶*emory caught a* 億*undred-million* 意*houghts...*

人⇔亻 (person)

億*undred million*

OKU

one hundred million

億劫	*bother, hassle, nuisance* **okkū**
億兆	*great number of* **okuchō**
億万	*great number of* **okuman**
億年	*one hundred million years* **okunen**
一億	*one hundred million* **ichioku**
数億	*hundreds of millions* **sūoku**
何億もの	*hundreds of millions* **nan'okumono**
億万長者	*billionaire, very wealthy person* **okumanchōja**

FLIP: 7.2.a. Right Top (flat)

一*ne, 858*	千*housand, 74*
十*en, 344*	万*en thousand, 465*
百*undred, 14*	零*ero, 874*

意*hought, 340*	億*undred million, 340*

251-C

憶*emory caught a* 億*undred-million* 意*houghts...*

心⇔忄 (heart, feelings)

意*hought* 意*dea* 意*ill*

I

thought, idea, will, concept, mind, meaning

悪意	*ill will, malice, evil intent* **akui**
注意	*warning, caution* **chūi**
同意	*consent, agreement* **dōi**
鋭意	*wholeheartedly, zealous, zestful* **eii**
合意	*agreement, consent* **gōi**
極意	*secret, mysteries* **gokui**
配意	*consideration, thoughtfulness* **haii**
意義	*meaning, significance* **igi**
意見	*opinion, view, comment* **iken**
意気	*spirits, willpower* **iki**
意向	*intention, opinion, wishes* **ikō**
意味	*meaning, intent* **imi**
意志	*will, intention* **ishi**
意識	*consciousness, awareness* **ishiki**
意欲	*volition, willingness* **iyoku**
辞意	*intention to resign* **jii**
決意	*determination, resolution* **ketsui**
好意	*favour, goodwill* **kōi**
作意	*intention, volition* **sakui**

FLIP: 3.0.a. Top (flat)

戦意	*fighting spirit, espirit-de-corps* **sen'i**
真意	*real intention, true meaning* **shin'i**
失意	*disappointment, despair* **shitsui**
総意	*consensus, collective decision* **sōi**
敵意	*hostility, acrimony, animosity* **tekii**
得意	*favourite, pride, strength* **tokui**
用意	*preparation, arrangements* **yōi**
反意語	*antonym, opposite meaning* **han'igo**
意外性	*unexpectedness, suddenness* **igaisei**
意地悪	*"picking on someone..."* **ijiwaru**
意加減	*haphazard, random, unreliable* **ikagen**
意固地	*obstinate, hard-headed* **ikoji**

想*dea, 524*	考*hinking, 392*
念*dea, 182*	志*ntention, 426*
慮*houghts, 70*	

章*adge, 324*	音*ound, 314*

252-A

義n-laws led 議iscussions on 儀ites of 義ighteous 犠acrifice...

羊 (sheep)

❶義*ighteous* ❷義*n-laws*

GI

righteous, goodness, virtue, meaning; in-laws

FLIP: 3.0.a. Top (flat)

❶ 忠義 *loyalty, faithfulness* **chūgi**
道義 *morality, morals, virtues* **dōgi**
義憤 *indignation, fury* **gifun**
義眼 *artificial-, glass eye* **gigan**
義挙 *noble deed* **gikyo**
義務 *duty, obligation* **gimu**
義理 *debt-of-gratitude, moral debt* **giri**
義肢 *artificial limb* **gishi**
義歯 *artificial-, false tooth* **gishi**
義手 *artificial arm, ~hand* **gishu**
義足 *artificial leg* **gisoku**
義絶 *break off relations* **gizetsu**
仁義 *humanity, humanism* **jingi**
講義 *lecture, lesson* **kōgi**
名義 *person's name* **meigi**
奥義 *secrets, concealed matters* **ōgi, okugi**
恩義 *kindness, favour* **ongi**
正義 *justice, righteous* **seigi**
徳義 *morality, morals, virtues* **tokugi**

義援金 *monetary contribution, donation* **gienkin**
義侠心 *chivalry, courage, valour* **gikyōshin**
民衆主義 *democracy* **minshū shugi**
社会主義 *socialism* **shakai shugi**

❷ 義母 *mother-in-law* **gibo**
義父 *father-in-law* **gifu**
義兄 *brother-in-law* **gikei**
義兄弟 *brother-in-law* **gikyōdai**
義妹 *younger sister-in-law* **gimai**
義姉 *sister-in-law* **gishi**
義弟 *brother-in-law* **gitei**

善*ighteous*, 450	礼*itual*, 685	家*amily*, 909
儀*itual*, 342	徳*irtue*, 844	縁*inship*, 675

善*ighteous*, 450

252-B

義n-laws led 議iscussions on 儀ites of 義ighteous 犠acrifice...

言 (speaking)

議*iscussion* 議*onference*

GI

discussion, conference, deliberate

FLIP: 7.2.a. Right Top (flat)
FLIP: 6.0.a. Left (flat)

謀議 *conspiracy, plot* **bōgi**
議案 *bill, measure* **gian**
議長 *presiding officer, chairperson* **gichō**
議員 *Diet member, lawmaker* **giin**
議院 *house, Diet, legislature* **giin**
⇒衆議院 *Diet upper house* **shūgiin**
議事 *proceedings, minutes* **giji**
議場 *assembly hall, chamber* **gijō**
議会 *Diet, congress, parliament* **gikai**
議決 *decision, resolution* **giketsu**
議決権 *right to vote, suffrage* **giketsuken**
議論 *discussion, deliberation* **giron**
議了 *conclusion of a deliberation* **giryō**
評議 *conference, discussion* **hyōgi**
異議 *objection, protest* **igi**
会議 *meeting, discussion* **kaigi**
閣議 *cabinet meeting* **kakugi**
建議 *proposal, suggestion* **kengi**
決議 *decision, resolution* **ketsugi**

抗議 *protest, object* **kōgi**
密議 *secret conference* **mitsugi**
内議 *secret conference* **naigi**
論議 *discussion, debate* **rongi**
再議 *reconsideration, new deliberation* **saigi**
審議 *deliberation, consideration* **shingi**
衆議 *public discussion, ~hearing* **shūgi**
争議 *labour dispute, strike, walkout* **sōgi**
討議 *discussion, deliberation* **tōgi**
不思議 *mysterious, incomprehensible* **fushigi**
参議院 *Diet lower house* **sangiin**

会*eeting*, 864	論*iscussion*, 786	談*alks*, 308
講*ecture*, 226	弁*peech*, 570	渉*ross-over*, 273

義*ighteous*, 341

252-C

義n-laws led 議iscussions on 儀ites of 義ighteous 犠acrifice...

人⇔亻 (person)

儀*itual*   儀*eremony*

GI

ritual, ceremony, protocol, solemnity

FLIP: 7.2.a. Right Top (flat)

儀文 *formalistic language* **gibun**
儀法 *rule* **gihō**
儀表 *paragon, paradigm, model* **gihyō**
儀型 *pattern, model* **gikei**
儀礼 *ceremony, courtesy* **girei**
儀礼的 *formalistic, ceremonial* **gireiteki**
儀式 *ceremony, rite* **gishiki**
儀典 *protocol, rules of decorum* **giten**
儀刀 *ritual sword* **gitō**
威儀 *dignity, solemnity* **igi**
辞儀 *bow, greeting* **jigi**
婚儀 *wedding ceremony* **kongi**
難儀 *hardships, difficulties* **nangi**
律儀 *faithfulness, honesty* **richigi**
略儀 *informal* **ryakugi**
祭儀 *festival* **saigi**
仕儀 *circumstances, conditions* **shigi**
祝儀 *congratulatory, gift, ~present* **shūgi**
葬儀 *funeral, memorial service* **sōgi**

葬儀屋 *mortician, funeral director* **sōgiya**
余儀 *another way, alternative* **yogi**
余儀ない *inevitable, unavoidable* **yoginai**
儀仗兵 *honour guard, military escort* **gijōhei**
羅釘儀 *compass* **rashingi**
風儀 *manners, etiquette* **fūgi**
儀容 *manners, etiquette, decorum* **giyō**
行儀 *manners, etiquette, decorum* **gyōgi**
⇒不行儀 *rudeness, bad manners* **fugyōgi**
礼儀 *etiquette, manners* **reigi**
流儀 *way, fashion, manner* **ryūgi**

礼*itual*, 685	祈*rayer*, 184	式*tyle*, 418
聖*acred*, 617	拝*rayer*, 636	飾*rnament*, 664

義*ighteous*, 341

252-D

義n-laws led 議iscussions on 儀ites of 義ighteous 犠acrifice...

牛⇔牛 (cattle)

犠*acrifice*   犠*ictim*

GI

sacrifice, victim, martyr, prey, pawn

FLIP: 7.2.a. Right Top (flat)

犠打 *sacrificial batting (baseball)* **gida**
犠牛 *sacrificial bullock* **gigyū**
犠牲 *sacrifice, victim* **gisei**
犠牲者 *victim, casualty, fatality* **giseisha**
犠牲的 *sacrificial, martyrdom* **giseiteki**
犠羊 *sacrificial lamb* **giyō**

牲*ictim*, 883	逝*eath*, 54	栄*lory*, 580
死*eath*, 513	亡*eath*, 72	誉*onour*, 252

義*ighteous*, 341

253-A

顧econsider 雇mployment on pay increments...

頁 (large shell, page)

顧elf-reflect　　顧onsider

kaeri(miru), KO
self-reflect, consider, ponder, contemplate

顧みる　reflect upon, pay attention　**kaerimiru**
愛顧　patronage, custom　**aiko**
一顧　glance, look　**ikko**
一顧もしない　"I don't give a damn..."　**ikko mo shinai**
回顧　recollection, retrospection　**kaiko**
回顧録　reminiscences, memoirs　**kaikoroku**
回顧的　retrospective　**kaikoteki**
後顧　after one's death　**kōko**
顧客　client, customer　**kokyaku**
顧問　consultant, advisor　**komon**
顧問弁護士　legal consultant　**komon bengoshi**
顧問医　medical adviser　**komon'i**
顧問官　councillor　**komonkan**
顧慮　taking into consideration　**koryo**
恩顧　favour, patronage　**onko**
三顧　all courtesies　**sanko**
四顧　looking all around　**shiko**
左顧右眄　vacillation, wavering　**sako uben**
右顧左眄　vacillation, wavering　**uko saben**

FLIP: 7.0.b2. Right (stem)

後顧の憂い　"concern for others when one is safe..."
kōko no urei

意 dea, 340	慮 hought, 70
想 dea, 524	念 hought, 182
念 dea, 182	省 elf-reflect, 572
妄 houghtless, 34	

雇mploy, 343

253-B

顧econsider 雇mployment on pay increments...

隹 (long-tailed birds)

雇mploy　雇ecruit

yato(u), KO
employ, recruit, hiring, career, engage services

雇い口　job employment　**yatoiguchi**
雇い人　employee　**yatoinin**
雇い主　employer　**yatoinushi**
雇い入れる　engage in employment　**yatoiireru**
解雇　dismissal, discharge　**kaiko**
解雇手当　separation pay　**kaiko teate**
解雇通知　dismissal notice, pink slip　**kaiko tsūchi**
雇員　employee, staff member　**koin**
雇用　employment, hiring, recruitment　**koyō**
⇒完全雇用　full employment　**kanzen koyō**
⇒終身雇用　life-time employment　**shūshin koyō**
雇庸　employment, hiring, recruitment　**koyō**
雇用条件　terms of employment　**koyō jōken**
雇用関係　employment relationship　**koyō kankei**
雇用契約　employment contract　**koyō keiyaku**
雇用主　employer　**koyōnushi**
雇用者　employer　**koyōsha**
日雇い　daily labourer　**hiyatoi**
常雇い　regular employee　**jōyatoi**

Facing: 2.1. East ☞ (H)

定雇い　full-time employee　**teiyatoi**
月雇い　monthly labourer　**tsukiyatoi**
臨時雇い　temporary staff　**rinjiyatoi**

勤 mploy, 962	務 mploy, 454	稼 ake-a-living, 824
採 mploy, 915	就 mploy, 719	仕 ervice, 9
抱 mploy, 503	職 mploy, 855	労 abour, 351

扇 olding-fan, 677

254-A

Noodle 汁oup or lemon 汁uice cost 十en cents to produce...

水 ⇔ 氵 (water)

汁uice　　汁oup

shiru, JŪ
juice, soup, extracts

FLIP: 7.0.b1. Right (stem)

灰汁 *lye, harshness* **aku**
墨汁 *Indian ink, Chinese ink* **bokujū**
豚汁 *pork & veggies miso soup* **butajiru**
毒汁 *poisonous juice* **dokujū**
液汁 *juice; sap* **ekijū**
鼻汁 *nasal mucus* **hanajiru**
汁液 *fruit juice* **jūeki**
果汁 *fruit juice* **kajū**
苦汁 *brine, bittern* **kujū**
煮汁 *soup, broth* **nijiru**
肉汁 *meat juice* **nikujū**
汁気 *juice, juiciness* **shiruke**
汁粉 *rice cake on sweet red-bean soup* **shiruko**
汁物 *soup, broth* **shirumono**
多汁 *juicy, succulent* **tajiru**
胆汁 *bile, gall* **tanjū**
膿汁 *pus, purulent* **umijiru**
出し汁 *broth, soup* **dashijiru**
味噌汁 *miso soup* **miso shiru**

澄し汁 *clear soup* **sumashijiru**
研ぎ汁 *rice-washed water* **togijiru**
野菜汁 *vegetable soup, ~broth* **yasaijiru**
茹で汁 *broth, soup* **yudejiru**
一汁一菜 *simple meal (soup & vegetable)*
　　ichijū issai

滴xtract, 799	飲rink, 255	液iquid, 508
搾queeze, 722	湯ot-water, 932	
食uisine, 255	果ruit, 287	

汁asculine, 367

254-B

Noodle 汁oup or lemon 汁uice cost 十en cents to produce...

十 (cross)

十en　　②十ross

tō, to, JŪ, JI
ten; Christianity, cross

FLIP: 1.0.b. Whole (stem)

❶十戒 *Ten Commandments* **jikkai**
十回 *ten times* **jikkai, jukkai**
十分 *satisfactory, sufficient* **jūbun**
十代 *teenage years, adolescence, puberty* **jūdai**
十月 *October* **jūgatsu**
十能 *utensil for live charcoals* **jūnō**
十両 *second highest division in sumo* **jūryō**
十指 *the ten fingers* **jusshi**
十全 *thorough, exhaustive, perfect* **jūzen**
数十 *dozens* **sūjū**
十日 *10th day of a month* **tooka, jūnichi**
五十音 *Japanese syllabary* **gojūon**
十角形 *decagon* **jikkakukei, jukkakei**
十進法 *decimal system* **jisshinhō, jusshinhō**
十五夜 *full moon night* **jūgoya**
十一月 *November* **jūichigatsu**
十二月 *December* **jūnigatsu**
十姉妹 *lovebirds; society flinch* **jūshimatsu, jūshimai**
三十路 *one's thirtyish, 30~39 years old* **misoji**

八十八夜 *best planting season* **hachijūhachiya**
十中八九 *in all likelihood, in 9-to-10*
　　jicchūhakku
十二指腸 *duodenum* **jūnishichō**
十人十色 *"too many cooks spoil the soup..."*
　　jūnintoiro
十手 *short metal truncheon (used in edo era)* **jitte**
❷十字 *Holy Cross, Crucifix* **jūji**
⇒白十字 *white cross* **hakujūji**
⇒赤十字 *Red Cross* **sekijūji**
十字軍 *Crusade* **jūjigun**
十字路 *crossroads, juncture* **jūjiro**
十文字 *cross* **jūmonji**

一ne, 858	万en thousand, 465
百undred, 14	億undred-million, 340
千housand, 74	零ero, 874

255-A

French culinary 団*roup* 寸*easured the soup...*

団*roup*   団*ssociation*

□ (enclosure)

DAN, TON

group, association, syndicate, assemblage

Facing: 1.0. 👈 West (W)

団地 *public housing, residential district* **danchi**
団子 *sweet rice dumpling* **dango**
団子鼻 *snub nose, snubbish*
    dangobana, dangoppana
団結 *union, solidarity* **danketsu**
団交 *collective bargaining* **dankō**
団欒 *family bosom* **danran**
団体 *group, assembly* **dantai**
営団 *corporation* **eidan**
布団 *beddings, futon, mattress* **futon**
楽団 *orchestra* **gakudan**
劇団 *drama troupe* **gekidan**
軍団 *military corps, army corps* **gundan**
兵団 *military corps, army corps* **heidan**
一団 *group, assembly* **ichidan**
解団 *disbanding a group* **kaidan**
公団 *government corporation* **kōdan**
球団 *baseball team* **kyūdan**
旅団 *brigade* **ryodan**

星団 *constellation, cluster of stars* **seidan**
船団 *naval fleet, armada* **sendan**
師団 *army division* **shidan**
集団 *group, squad* **shūdan**
団扇 *hand fan, folding fan* **uchiwa**
財団 *foundation, fund* **zaidan**
母集団 *mother's group* **boshūdan**
調査団 *inquiry commission* **chōsadan**
外交団 *diplomatic corps* **gaikōdan**
院外団 *lobby group, interest party* **ingaidan**
記者団 *press corps, media* **kishadan**
座布団 *cushion, buffer* **zabuton**

組*roup, 138*	盟*lliance, 21*	員*ember, 410*
会*ssembly, 864*	連*lliance, 305*	協*ooperate, 577*

図*ketch, 47*

255-B

French culinary 団*roup* 寸*easured the soup...*

寸 *(measurement)*

寸 *[3 cm]*   寸*easurement*

SUN

[3 cm], measurement, calibration, length

Facing: 1.0. 👈 West (W)

同寸 *same size* **dōsun**
原寸 *actual-, original size* **gensun**
原寸大 *actual-, original size* **gensundai**
一寸 *about 3.03 cm; "just a little..."* **issun, chotto**
一寸先 *move by an inch* **issunsaki**
採寸 *taking body measurement* **saisun**
尺寸 *a little bit* **sekisun, shakusun**
寸分 *at all, in sum, entirety* **sunbun**
寸描 *concise sketch* **sunbyō**
寸秒 *speedy, immediate* **sunbyō**
寸断 *cutting off; cancelled train stops* **sundan**
寸土 *a square inch of land* **sundo**
寸劇 *skit, short play* **sungeki**
寸言 *short remark, quip* **sungen**
寸時 *momentarily, immediately* **sunji**
寸暇 *spare moment, idle time* **sunka**
寸刻 *a brief time* **sunkoku**
寸法 *dimension, size* **sunpō**
寸評 *short review* **sunpyō**

寸借 *borrowing small money* **sunshaku**
寸志 *token-of-gratitude* **sunshi**
寸心 *small token of gratitude* **sunshin**
寸進 *move by an inch* **sunshin**
寸書 *short note, scribbling* **sunsho**
寸鉄 *barehanded; small weapon* **suntetsu**
寸前 *"just before, on the verge..."* **sunzen**
寸胴 *cylindrical container, no shape* **zundō**
一寸見 *a glimpse of, at first sight* **chottomi**
五寸釘 *long nails* **gosunkugi**
寸詰まり *shrinking, downsizing* **sunzumari**

計*easurement, 692*	尺*easurement, 574*
算*alculate, 141*	数*umber, 156*
測*easurement, 291*	

才*ears old, 185*

256-A

学tudy of 字etters made the 字istrict prosper...

学tudy　　学cholar

子 (child)

mana(bu), GAKU
study, scholar, learning, education, academic

FLIP: 3.0.b. Top (stem
Facing: 1.0. ☞ West (W)

大学 university, college **daigaku**
独学 self-learning, self-study **dokugaku**
学科 subject, department **gakka**
学会 academic conference **gakkai**
学界 academic circles, academe **gakkai**
学期 academic term, semester, quarter **gakki**
学校 school **gakkō**
学究 scholar, academic **gakkyū**
学級 class, grade **gakkyū**
学長 university president **gakuchō**
学園 university town; educational institute **gakuen**
学位 university degree **gakui**
学院 academy, institute **gakuin**
学術 academics, scholarly **gakujutsu**
学歴 academic achievement **gakureki**
学力 academic ability **gakuryoku**
学生 university student **gakusei**
法学 law, jurisprudence **hōgaku**
医学 medical science, medicine **igaku**

見学 observation, study tour **kengaku**
共学 co-education **kyōgaku**
入学 university admission, ~enrolment **nyūgaku**
理学 science **rigaku**
留学 studying overseas **ryūgaku**
私学 private university, ~school **shigaku**
数学 mathematics **sūgaku**
向学心 intellectual thirst **kōgakushin**
教育学 pedagogy, study of education **kyōikugaku**
理化学 physics & chemistry **rikagaku**
奨学金 scholarship **shōgakukin**

教ducate, 385	卒raduate, 109
習earning, 238	考hinking, 392
校chool, 773	勉fforts, 527

字etter, 346

256-B

学tudy of 字etters made the 字istrict prosper...

❶字etter　　❷字istrict

子 (child)

aza, JI
letter, writing system; district, zone

FLIP: 3.0.b. Top (stem
Facing: 1.0. ☞ West (W)

❶赤字 deficit, loss, "in the red..." **akaji**
題字 title, headline **daiji**
英字 alphabet letters **eiji**
太字 bold-type letter **futoji**
誤字 misspelling, misprint, typo **goji**
印字 printing letters **inji**
字義 word meaning **jigi**
字画 number of strokes **jikaku**
字句 words & phrases, wording **jiku**
字幕 translation subtitles **jimaku**
字体 typeface, penmanship style **jitai**
十字 Holy Cross, Crucifix **jūji**
漢字 Chinese characters **kanji**
黒字 profit, surplus, in the black **kuroji**
文字 letter, character **moji**
⇒頭文字 initials, large caps **kashiramoji**
⇒暗号文字 cipher, cryptograph **angō moji**
⇒表意文字 ideograph, ideogram **hyōi moji**
⇒象形文字 Hieroglyphics **shōkei moji**

苗字 surname, family name, last name **myōji**
略字 simplified Kanji **ryakuji**
植字 typesetting for printing **shokuji**
植字工 compositor, typesetter **shokujikō**
習字 writing style, calligraphy, penmanship **shūji**
数字 numbers, numerals **sūji**
点字 Braille codes **tenji**
字引き dictionary **jibiki**
斜字体 italic, italized letters **shajitai**
生き字引 walking encyclopaedia **ikijibiki**
写真植字 photo-typesetting **shashin shokuji**
❷大字 rural district **ōaza**

書ritings, 116	句hrase, 16	文iteracy, 558
言ord, 251	漢anji, 926	読eading, 260

字uterspace, 81

257--A
Tired 体ody takes a 休est in Buenos Aires...

人⇔亻 (person)

体ody　　体hysical

karada, TAI, TEI
body, physical, composition, form

FLIP: 7.0.b1. Right (stem)

文体 *literary style* **buntai**
物体 *solid substance, matter* **buttai**
大体 *generally, on the whole* **daitai**
団体 *group, association* **dantai**
液体 *liquid, fluid* **ekitai**
字体 *penmanship, writing style* **jitai**
実体 *essence, substance* **jittai**
解体 *dissolution, disbanding* **kaitai**
固体 *solid matter, hard object* **kotai**
球体 *spherical object, sphere* **kyūtai**
身体 *torso, body* **shintai**
死体 *corpse, cadaver, dead body* **shitai**
書体 *penmanship, writing style* **shotai**
体位 *physique, posture* **taii**
体育 *physical education* **taiiku**
体重 *body weight* **taijū**
体格 *physique, build, body frame* **taikaku**
体型 *figure, form* **taikei**
体系 *system, organization* **taikei**

体温 *temperature* **taion**
体温計 *clinical thermometer* **taionkei**
体力 *physical strength* **tairyoku**
容体 *body condition* **yōdai**
具体化 *materialization, become tangible* **gutaika**
弱体化 *weakening, deterioration* **jakutaika**
立方体 *cube* **rippōtai**
世間体 *appearance in the society* **sekentei**
体感的 *sensible, sensual, sensous* **taikanteki**
体よく *polite, tactful* **teiyoku**
肉体関係 *blood relationship* **nikutai kankei**

身*ody, 504*　　容*ppearance, 492*
形*hape, 951*　　構*osture, 714*
型*attern, 536*　　物*bjects, 647*
姿*ppearance, 609*

休*ecess, 347*

257-B
Tired 体ody takes a 休est in Buenos Aires...

人⇔亻 (person)

休ecess　　休est　　休acation

yasu(mu), yasu(meru), yasu(maseru), KYŪ
recess, rest, vacation

FLIP: 7.0.b1. Right (stem)

代休 *paid leave, vacation* **daikyū**
半休 *half-day* **hankyū**
休演 *stage absence* **kyūen**
休学 *temporary school leave* **kyūgaku**
休業 *business holiday, "closed..."* **kyūgyō**
休日 *day off, holiday* **kyūjitsu**
休暇 *vacation, paid leave* **kyūka**
休会 *adjournment, recess* **kyūkai**
休刊 *publication suspension* **kyūkan**
休館 *"library-, hall closed..."* **kyūkan**
休憩 *rest, recess* **kyūkei**
休講 *class suspension, "no classes..."* **kyūkō**
休戦 *ceasefire, armistice, truce* **kyūsen**
休止 *dormant, standstill* **kyūshi**
休息 *rest, recess, stop* **kyūsoku**
休廷 *court adjournment* **kyūtei**
休養 *recuperation, recovery, convalescence* **kyūyō**
無休 *open 365 days* **mukyū**
連休 *serial holidays* **renkyū**

臨休 *special holiday* **rinkyū**
産休 *maternity leave, childbirth leave* **sankyū**
週休 *weekly off, weekends* **shūkyū, shukyū**
定休 *regular holiday* **teikyū**
運休 *suspension of transport service* **unkyū**
冬休み *winter vacation* **fuyuyasumi**
昼休み *noon recess, lunch break* **hiruyasumi**
公休日 *national holiday, day off* **kōkyūbi**
休診日 *doctor's day off* **kyūshinbi**
中休み *rest, break, respite* **nakayasumi**
夏休み *summer vacation* **natsuyasumi**
臨時休業 *labour holidays* **rinji kyūgyō**

憩*elaxation, 169*　　暇*ree time, 653*
閑*eisure, 283*　　健*ealthy, 390*
悠*eisure, 898*　　緩*oosening, 821*

体*ody, 347*

258-A

When 引ulling in 弓rchery, don't you hurry...

引ulling   引xtract

弓 (archery bow)

hi(ku), hi(keru), IN
pulling, extract, draw

FLIP: 7.0.b1. Right (stem)
Facing: 1.2. 🔄 West (V)

強引	by force, coercive, compulsive	**gōin**
引航	tow, tug	**inkō**
引力	gravitational force	**inryoku**
引責	take responsibility	**inseki**
引率	take command, leadership	**insotsu**
引退	retire, withdraw, quit, leave	**intai**
引用	quotation, quoting	**inyō**
吸引	absorption, pull, suck in	**kyūin**
索引	index	**sakuin**
誘引	temptation, enticement, luring	**yūin**
細引き	cord, rope	**hosobiki**
万引き	shoplifting	**manbiki**
長引く	be prolonged, drag on	**nagabiku**
値引き	discount, bargain	**nebiki**
手引き	manual, guide, handbook	**tebiki**
綱引き	tug-of-war	**tsunahiki**
引き合い	reference, quotation, inquiry	**hikiai**
引き払う	move out from one's house	**hikiharau**
引き逃げ	hit-&-run crime	**hikinige**

引き続き	continuation, serial	**hikitsuzuki**
引き受け	undertaking, accepting	**hikiuke**
引き渡し	delivery, transfer	**hikiwatashi**
引っ越し	relocation of residence	**hikkoshi**
生き字引	walking encyclopaedia	**ikijibiki**
地引き網	dragnet	**jibikiami**
取り引き	dealings, transactions	**torihiki**
割り引く	discount, reduced price	**waribiku**
引き起こす	pull up, cause, arise	**hikiokosu**
証券取引所	stock exchange	**shōken torihikijo**
代金引き替え	cash on delivery	**daikin hikikae**

押*ushing*, 37	圧*ressure*, 632
張*xert*, 274	力*orce*, 351

弔*ourning*. *538*

258-B

When 引ulling in 弓rchery, don't you hurry...

弓rchery   弓ow

弓 (archery bow)

yumi, KYŪ
archery, bow

Facing: 1.0. 🔄 West (W)
Facing: 1.0. 🔄 West (W)

大弓	bow & archery	**daikyū**, **taiyumi**
半弓	small bow	**hankyū**
石弓	cross bow	**ishiyumi**
胡弓	Oriental fiddle	**kokyū**
弓馬	archery on horsemanship	**kyūba**
弓道	Japanese archery	**kyūdō**
弓弦	bowstring	**kyūgen**
弓状	bow-shaped object	**kyūjō**
弓術	archery skills	**kyūjutsu**
洋弓	Western arrow	**yōkyū**
弓場	archery ground	**yumiba**
弓張り	paper lantern w/ bow-shaped handle	**yumihari**
弓張り月	crescent moon	**yumiharizuki**
弓形	arch, curve, bow shape	**yumigata**, **kyūkei**
弓師	bow maker, archery craftman	**yumishi**
弓矢	bow & arrow	**yumiya**
弓手	left hand	**yunde**

矢*rrow*, 18	射*hoot*, 504
抽*ulling*, 37	

己*elf*, *5*

259-A

Machine for 写opying 与applied with ink...

写opy　写epict　写ortray

冖 (cover)

写

utsu(su), utsu(ru), SHA

copy, depict, duplicate, portray, replicate

FLIP: 3.0.b. Top (stem)
Facing: 2.1. East ☞ (H)

描写	description, depiction, portrayal	**byōsha**
映写	film projection	**eisha**
複写	reproduction, duplication, copy	**fukusha**
複写機	copying machine	**fukushaki**
被写体	subject (photography)	**hishatai**
実写	instant photos	**jissha**
模写	copy, facsimile, replica	**mosha**
念写	psychic photography	**nensha**
臨写	copying	**rinsha**
接写	close-up photo	**sessha**
写譜	copy a musical score	**shafu**
写本	manuscript, original text	**shahon**
写経	copied Sutra	**shakyō**
写生	drawing, sketch	**shasei**
写真	photo, picture	**shashin**
写真機	camera	**shashinki**
写真植字	phototypesetting	**shashin shokuji**
写像	mapping	**shazō**
試写	film preview	**shisha**

縮写	reduced copy, miniature replica	**shukusha**
縮写図	reduced drawing	**shukushazu**
手写	copying by hand	**shusha**
速写	snapshot, quick copying	**sokusha**
転写	transcribe, copy	**tensha**
特写	exclusive photo	**tokusha**
透写	tracing	**tōsha**
青写真	architectural plan, blueprint	**aojashin**
書き写す	copy by handwriting	**kakiutsusu**
写実的	realistic, life story, true-to-life	**shajitsuteki**
謄写版	mimeograph	**tōshaban**

撮hotograph, 423	図rawing, 47	複opy, 830
絵rawing, 143	描rawing, 271	芸rts, 619

与upply, 349

259-B

Machine for 写opying 与applied with ink...

与upply　与rovide

一 (one, single)

与

ata(eru), YO

supply, provide, give, dispense, make available

Facing: 2.0. East ☞ (W)

分与	allocation, distribution	**bunyo**
賦与	endowment, presentation	**fuyo**
付与	give, grant, provide	**fuyo**
譲与	transfer, concession, cession	**jōyo**
授与	awarding, conferment	**juyo**
授与式	presentation ceremony	**juyoshiki**
関与	participation, engaging	**kanyo**
恵与	present, bestow, grant	**keiyo**
寄与	academic journal; contribution	**kiyo**
供与	grant, granting	**kyōyo**
給与	salary, stipend, allowance	**kyūyo**
参与	participate, engage in	**sanyo**
賞与	salary bonus	**shōyo**
貸与	debt, loan, lend	**taiyo**
天与	heaven-sent, divine gift	**tenyo**
党与	colleagues, companions	**tōyo**
投与	prescribe medicine	**tōyo**
与圧	pressurization	**yoatsu**
与奪	give-or-take away (power)	**yodatsu**

与件	postulate, datum	**yoken**
与信	lending, loaning	**yoshin**
与太	foolish, silly	**yota**
与太話	silly talk, foolish gossip	**yotabanashi**
与太者	hooligan, hoodlum	**yotamono**
与太郎	fool, idiot, stupid	**yotarō**
与党	ruling party, party in power	**yotō**
贈与	donation, presentation	**zōyo**
贈与者	giver, donor, contributor	**zōyosha**
与野党	ruling & opposition parties	**yoyatō**
分け与える	distribute, divide	**wakeataeru**

給upply, 143	届eliver, 631	
充upply, 884	頒istribution, 835	
納upply, 296	源rigin, 431	

写opy, 349

260-A

安afety is never 安heap for 女omen trailed by creeps...

宀 (cover, lid)

❶安afety ❷安heap

yasu(i), AN
safety, security; cheap, bargain, budget price, low-priced, discount

FLIP: 3.0.b. Top (stem)
Facing: 1.1. ⟵ West (H)

❶
安直 plain & simple **anchoku**
安易 easygoing, easy lifestyle **an'i**
安逸 idle living, ~lifestyle **an'itsu**
安住 peaceful living, quiet lifestyle **anjū**
安眠 sound sleep **anmin**
安寧 peace & order, well-being **annei**
安穏 peace & quiet **an'on**
安否 safety, welfare **anpi**
安楽 at ease, comfortable **anraku**
安楽死 euthanasia, mercy killing **anrakushi**
安心 relief, security **anshin**
安定 stable, secure **antei**
安産 easy childbirth **anzan**
安全 safe, secure **anzen**
⇒交通安全 safe driving **kōtsū anzen**
治安 peace & order situation **chian**
不安 worry, anxiety, uneasiness **fuan**
平安 peace, tranquillity, welfare **heian**
保安 preservation of peace & order **hoan**

慰安 comfort, consolation, recreation **ian**
公安 public peace, safety, security **kōan**
目安 standard, aim **meyasu**
気安い cordial, familiar, friendly **kiyasui**
心安い friendly, familiar **kokoroyasui**

❷安価 cheap, inexpensive **anka**
円安 cheap yen, weak yen **enyasu**
激安 extremely cheap, good buy **gekiyasu**
格安 bargain, good buy **kakuyasu**
安値 cheap, inexpensive **yasune**
安売り selling cheap **yasuuri**

低ow, 700	寧uiet, 967
静uiet, 230	秩ublic order, 730

妄houghtless, 34

260-B

安afety is never 安heap for 女omen trailed by creeps...

女 (woman)

女oman 女emale

onna, me, JO, NYO, NYŌ
woman, female

Facing: 2.0. East ☞ (W)

美女 pretty woman **bijo**
長女 eldest daughter **chōjo**
婦女 women **fujo**
侍女 lady-in-waiting, ladys maid **jijo**
女中 maid, lady servant **jochū**
女医 female physician, lady doctor **joi**
女権 women's rights **joken**
女傑 heroine **joketsu**
女王 queen **jōō**
女性 female, lady, woman **josei**
女優 actress **joyū**
彼女 she; girlfriend **kanojo**
魔女 witch **majo**
女神 goddess, lady diety **megami**
女官 court lady **nyokan**
女腹 sonless mother (all daughters) **onnabara**
女手 feminine handwriting **onnade**
女形 Kabuki actor playing female **onnagata**
女嫌い misogynist, woman-hater **onnagirai**

女癖 womaniser, philanderer **onnaguse**
乙女 maiden, virgin **otome**
才女 talented, intelligent woman **saijo**
処女 virgin, maiden **shojo**
少女 little girl **shōjo**
淑女 lady, young woman **shukujo**
貞女 faithful woman **teijo**
雪女 snow fairy, fairy mother **yukionna**
女学生 schoolgirl, university girl **jogakusei**
女の人 female, lady, woman **onna no hito**
女文字 ① feminine handwriting **onnamoji**
女文字 ② "a woman who raised two sons by
　herself..." **onnamoji**

姉lder sister, 114	嬢oung girl, 854
妹ounger sister, 114	婆ld woman, 32
叔oung aunt, 510	母other, 90

261-A

労abourers' 力trength go to extreme lengths...

力 (strength, force)

労abour　労orker

RŌ
labour, worker, proletariat

馬労 *horse trader* **bakurō**	
御苦労様 *"a job well done..."* **gokurōsama**	
漁労 *fishing, fishery* **gyorō**	
疲労 *fatigue, work stress* **hirō**	
報労 *labour reward* **hōrō**	
慰労 *work recognition* **irō**	
過労死 *overworking to death* **karōshi**	
勤労 *work, labour, service* **kinrō**	
勤労意欲 *work vigour, work vitality* **kinrō iyoku**	
功労 *meritorious services* **kōrō**	
苦労 *hardship, difficulty, burden* **kurō**	
労賃 *wages, salaries* **rōchin**	
労働 *work, labour* **rōdō**	
労働組合 *labour union, workers union* **rōdō kumiai**	
労働者 *labourer, worker* **rōdōsha**	
労役 *toiling, tilling* **rōeki**	
労苦 *pains, toil, labour* **rōku**	
苦労保障 *disability insurance* **kurō hoshō**	
労災保険 *employment insurance* **rōsai hoken**	

FLIP: 3.0.b. Top (stem)
Facing: 2.2. East ☞ (V)

労作 *laborious work* **rōsaku**
労使 *labour & management* **rōshi**
労資 *capital & labour* **rōshi**
労使紛争 *labour dispute* **rōshi funsō**
労使交渉 *labour & mgt. talks* **rōshi kōshō**
労組 *labour union* **rōkumi, rōso**
労務 *labour, work, service* **rōmu**
労力 *effort, labour ability* **rōryoku**
心労 *anguish, anxiety* **shinrō**
就労 *work, job* **shūrō**
足労 *burden of going to a place* **sokurō**
取り越し苦労 *belabour* **torikoshi gurō**

動*ovement, 422*	産*roduce, 883*
赴*roceed-to-work, 706*	造*roduce, 267*
作*roduce, 724*	雇*mploy, 343*

芳*ragrance, 533*

261-B

労abourers' 力trength go to extreme lengths...

力 (strength, force)

力trength　力orce

chikara, RYOKU, RIKI
strength, force, power, energy

暴力 *violence, physical force* **bōryoku**
動力 *effort, endeavour, undertaking* **dōryoku**
兵力 *force-of-arms* **heiryoku**
筆力 *"power of the pen.."* **hitsuryoku**
実力 *real ability, actual capability* **jitsuryoku**
権力 *power, authority, influence* **kenryoku**
金力 *financial strength* **kinryoku**
効力 *effect, force, validity* **kōryoku**
協力 *cooperation, participation* **kyōryoku**
念力 *willpower, determination* **nenriki**
能力 *ability, competence* **nōryoku**
力学 *dynamics* **rikigaku**
力作 *meticulous, painstaking work* **rikisaku**
力説 *emphasis, laying stress* **rikisetsu**
力士 *sumo wrestler* **rikishi**
勢力 *power, force* **seiryoku**
死力 *desperate, frantic, despondent* **shiryoku**
主力 *main force* **shuryoku**
底力 *real ability, actual capability* **sokojikara**

Facing: 2.0. East ☞ (W)

体力 *physical strength* **tairyoku**
有力 *influential, significant* **yūryoku**
力一杯 *lots of strength* **chikaraippai**
力持ち *physically-strong person* **chikaramochi**
力強い *strong & powerful* **chikarazuyoi**
直感力 *intuition, hunch* **chokkanryoku**
表現力 *power of expression* **hyōgenryoku**
購買力 *purchasing power* **kōbairyoku**
説得力 *convincing, persuasive* **settokuryoku**
想像力 *imaginative, creativity* **sōzōryoku**

動*ovement, 422*	産*roduce, 883*
赴*roceed-to-work, 706*	造*roduce, 267*
作*roduce, 724*	労*abour, 351*

刀*lade, 353*　九*ine, 73*

262-A

Hands caught 窃tealing to be 切ut in the evening...

穴 (hole, cave)

窃*tealing*　窃*obbery*

SETSU
stealing, robbery, theft, looting, burglary, heist, larceny

FLIP: 3.0.b. Top (stem)

剽窃 *plagiarism, literary theft* **hyōsetsu**
窃取 *stealing, larceny* **sesshu**
窃用 *embezzlement, absconding* **setsuyō**
窃盗 *theft, robbery, larceny* **settō**
窃盗犯 *thief, burglar* **settōhan**
窃盗罪 *theft, larceny crime* **settōzai**

侵*iolate, 769*	悪*vil, 389*
盗*tealing, 621*	凶*vil, 80*
奪*natch, 162*	犯*riminal, 640*
賊*iracy, 160*	罪*riminal, 289*

切*utting. 352*

262-B

Hands caught 窃tealing to be 切ut in the evening...

刀⇔刂 (blade, cutting)

切*utting*

ki(ru), ki(reru), SETSU
cutting, chopping

Facing: 3.0. ☞☜ Across

切符 *ticket, coupon, voucher* **kippu**
切手 *postage stamp* **kitte**
切開 *incision, section* **sekkai**
切腹 *suicide by disembowelment* **seppuku**
切に *sincerely, earnestly, eagerly* **setsu(ni)**
切断 *cut off* **setsudan**
親切 *kind, cordial, friendly, amicable* **shinsetsu**
大切 *important, significant* **taisetsu**
適切 *appropriate, suitable, proper* **tekisetsu**
切っ先 *the point* **kissaki**
小切手 *bank cheque* **kogitte**
首切り *decapitation; job dismissal, ~firing* **kubikiri**
区切り *stop, full stop, end* **kugiri**
千切り *long strips of cut vegetables* **sengiri**
切実に *sincerely, earnestly* **setsujitsu(ni)**
切なる *earnest, eager* **setsunaru**
裏切り *betrayal, treachery, duplicity* **uragiri**
ワン切 *one ring phone call* **wangiri**
踏み切り *inseparable; railroad crossing* **fumikiri**

切り回す *deal with, manage, run* **kirimawasu**
切り下げる *reduce, cut* **kirisageru**
切りつける *slash, cut* **kiritsukeru**
切り詰める *reduce, cut down* **kiritsumeru**
食い切る *tear, bite off* **kuikiru**
締め切り *deadline, target date* **shimekiri**
白を切る *pretend ignorance* **shira o kiru**
売り切れ *"sold-out..."* **urikire**
肉切り包丁 *butcher's knife* **nikugiri bōchō**
思い切った *drastic, thorough* **omoikitta**
数え切れない *countless* **kazoekirenai**
食べ切れない *unable to finish eating* **tabekirenai**

刃*word, 75*	鋭*harp, 943*
剣*word, 939*	削*harpen, 118*
刀*lade, 353*	

刀*lade, 353*

263-A

初*irst, sharpen the* 刀*nife's* 刀*lade then* 初*tart the raid...*

刀⇔刂 (blade, cutting)

初*tart*   初*irst*

hatsu, haji(me), SHO
start, first, begin, commence, initiate

Facing: 1.2. West (V)

初めまして *"nice to meet you..."* **hajimemashite**
原初 *origin, source* **gensho**
初子 *one's first child* **hatsugo**
初氷 *first freezing in the year* **hatsugōri**
初恋 *one's first love* **hatsukoi**
初孫 *first grandchild* **hatsumago**
初詣 *first visit to the shrine* **hatsumōde**
初荷 *first cargo of the New Year* **hatsuni**
初霜 *first frost of the year* **hatsushimo**
初雪 *first snow of the year* **hatsuyuki**
初演 *premiere, first screening* **shoen**
初版 *first-, initial printing* **shohan**
初夏 *beginning of summer* **shoka**
初回 *beginning, start* **shokai**
初見 *first sighting, first viewing* **shoken**
初期 *beginning, initial stages* **shoki**
初期化 *initialisation* **shokika**
初校 *first proof, draft paper* **shokō**
初婚 *first marriage* **shokon**

初級 *beginner-level class* **shokyū**
初日 *opening day, first day* **shonichi**
初診 *first medical check-up* **shoshin**
初審 *first trial, first hearing* **shoshin**
初手 *first move, first strike* **shote**
初産 *woman's first childbirth* **uizan**, **shosan**
初乗り *first ride, base fare* **hatsunori**
初学者 *beginner, plebe student* **shogakusha**
初一念 *original idea, intention* **shoichinen**
初任給 *one's first paycheck* **shoninkyū**
初対面 *first meeting* **shotaimen**
初初しい *innocent, naïve* **uiuishii**

始*tart, 210*	先*head, 478*	元*rigin, 195*
発*tart, 368*	前*efore, 118*	原*riginal, 431*

辺*icinity, 93*

263-B

初*irst, sharpen the* 刀*nife's* 刀*lade then* 初*tart the raid...*

刀⇔刂 (blade, cutting)

刀*nife*   刀*lade*

katana, TŌ
knife, blade

Facing: 1.0. West (W)

木刀 *wooden practice sword* **bokutō**
血刀 *blood-stained sword* **chigatana**
鈍刀 *dull-, unsharpened sword* **dontō**
懐刀 *brain, right hand; dagger* **futokorogatana**
軍刀 *sabre, military sword* **guntō**
牛刀 *butcher knife* **gyūtō**
宝刀 *treasured-, precious sword* **hōtō**
快刀 *sharp sword* **kaitō**
剃刀 *barber razor* **kamisori**
銘刀 *sword made by noted craftsmen* **meitō**
名刀 *famous sword* **meitō**
竹刀 *bamboo sword* **shinai**
執刀 *surgery operation* **shittō**
太刀 *sword* **tachi**
太刀魚 *scabbard fish* **tachiuo**
帯刀 *wearing of sword* **taitō**
短刀 *dagger, short sword* **tantō**
刀剣 *sword* **tōken**
刀工 *swordsmith* **tōkō**

刀身 *sword blade* **tōshin**
刀匠 *sword maker, swordsmith* **tōshō**
刀傷 *sword wound* **tōshō**, **katanakizu**
日本刀 *Japanese sword* **nihontō**
二刀流 *two-sword fencing* **nitōryū**
秋刀魚 *saury fish, mackerel* **sanma**
青竜刀 *Chinese broadsword* **seiryūtō**
彫刻刀 *chisel* **chōkokutō**
解剖刀 *surgery scalpel, doctor's knife* **kaibōtō**
助太刀 *loyal supporter* **sukedachi**
押っ取り刀 *neck-breaking speed* **ottorigatana**

刃*lade, 75*	侍*amurai, 249*	鋭*harp, 943*
士*ighter, 8*	切*utting, 352*	削*harpen, 118*

辺*icinity, 93*

264-A

In every 危anger, 厄isaster's no stranger...

危anger   危eril

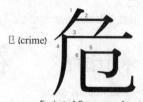

巳 (crime)

Facing: 4.0. 🔁 Apart

abu(nai), aya(ui), aya(bumu), KI
danger, peril, hazard, jeopardy, risky

安危 safety-or-danger **anki**
危地 "danger zone..." **kichi**
危害 harm, injury **kigai**
危惧 misgivings, apprehension, uneasiness **kigu**
危険 danger, risk, hazard, peril **kiken**
危険物 hazardous elements **kikenbutsu**
危険性 danger, risk **kikensei**
危険区域 "danger zone..." **kiken kuiki**
危険信号 distress signal, SOS **kiken shingō**
危険思想 dangerous thoughts **kiken shisō**
危機 crisis, emergency, exigency **kiki**
危局 critical situation **kikyoku**
危急 emergency, crisis **kikyū**
危急存亡 a matter of life-or-death **kikyū sonbō**
危難 danger, peril, hazard **kinan**
危殆 danger, peril, hazard **kitai**
危篤 critically ill **kitoku**

敢aring, 449	勝ictory, 406	警arning, 330
挑hallenge, 214	失ailure, 19	驚care, 330
功uccess, 635	敗ailure, 137	

色olour, 403

264-B

In every 危anger, 厄isaster's no stranger...

厄isaster   厄ragedy

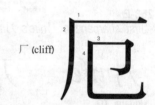

厂 (cliff)

Facing: 2.1. East ☞ (H)

YAKU
disaster, misfortune, tragedy

後厄 year after a disastrous one **atoyaku**
前厄 year before a critical one, unlucky age **maeyaku**
災厄 sudden-, unexpected misfortune **saiyaku**
大厄 great calamity, ~disaster **taiyaku**
厄介 troublesome, annoying, irritating **yakkai**
⇒荷厄介 cumbersome, burdensome **niyakkai**
厄介者 burden, nuisance, bothersome **yakkaimono**
厄日 unlucky-, critical day **yakubi**
厄年 unlucky year, evil age **yakudoshi**
厄難 unexpected misfortune **yakunan**
厄落し exorcism, driving out evils **yakuotoshi**
厄払い exorcism, driving out evils **yakubarai**
厄除け amulet, talisman, charm **yakuyoke**

禍ragedy, 799	傷njury, 933
惨ragedy, 396	障njury, 325
悲ragedy, 289	損njury, 410
災isaster, 571	痛njury, 60
害njury, 904	哀orrows, 374

反gainst, 537

265-A

After 依equest for 衣lothes, donations flowed...

依*equest* 依*etition*

人⇔亻 (person)

I, E

request, petition, pleading, depend on, solicit, entreaty

Facing: 4.0. ⟲⟳ Apart

依願 *one's request* **igan**
依願免官 *retirement at one's request* **igan menkan**
依拠 *"based on..."* **ikyo**
依頼 *request, something asked for* **irai**
依頼状 *written request, official request* **iraijō**
依頼人 *client* **irainin**
依頼心 *parasitic mentality* **iraishin**
依然 *"as before, still..."* **izen**
依然として *still, as yet* **izentoshite**
依存 *dependence, reliance* **izon**
⇒相互依存 *mutual dependence* **sōgo izon**
依存性 *dependency, parasitism* **izonsei**
帰依 *embrace, become a believer* **kie**
依怙地 *obstinacy, hard-headed* **ikoji**

願*equest, 964*	望*esire, 618*
求*equest, 256*	欲*esire, 892*
請*equest, 791*	志*ntention, 426*
頼*equest, 562*	尋*nquire, 868*

衣*lothes, 355*

265-B

After 依equest for 衣lothes, donations flowed...

衣*lothes* 衣*ardrobe*

衣⇔衤 (clothing)

koromo, I

clothes, wardrobe, garment, outfit, garments

Facing: 2.0. East ☞ (W)

便衣 *one's daily wear* **ben'i**
着衣 *one's clothes* **chakui**
脱衣 *undressing, stripping* **datsui**
脱衣所 *dressing room, fitting room* **datsuijo**
胴衣 *jacket, vest* **dōi**
衣文 *clothes, wear, outfit* **emon**
外衣 *outer wardrobe* **gaii**
獄衣 *person clothes* **gokui**
軍衣 *military uniform* **gun'i**
御衣 *imperial clothes* **gyoi**
羽衣 *robe of feathers* **hagoromo**
白衣 *white uniform (hospital)* **hakui, byakui**
法衣 *judge robe, lawyer robe* **hōe**
衣服 *garment, dress, costume* **ifuku**
衣類 *clothes, garments* **irui**
衣料 *clothes, garments* **iryō**
衣糧 *food & clothing* **iryō**
衣装 *clothes, dress, wardrobe* **ishō**
⇒花嫁衣装 *bridal gown* **hanayome ishō**

⇒婚礼衣装 *wedding attire* **konrei ishō**
黒衣 *black robe, ~garments* **kokui**
羅衣 *thin kimono* **rai**
衣魚 *clothes moth, bookworm* **shimi**
僧衣 *Buddhist priests robe* **sōi**
浴衣 *summer kimono* **yukata**
衣食住 *food, clothing & shelter* **ishokujū**
衣擦れ *rustling of clothes* **kinuzure**
更衣室 *locker-, dressing room* **kōishitsu**
衣替え *seasonal change of clothes* **koromogae**
糖衣錠 *sugar-coated tablet* **tōijō**

縫*ewing, 779*	布*loth, 208*	織*nitting, 855*
繰*pinning, 851*	裁*lothes, 802*	編*nitting, 42*
紡*pinning, 735*	服*lothes, 734*	糸*hread, 375*

依*equest, 355*

266-A

To the 沼wamp was 召ummoned Monte Cristo's Edmond...

水 ⇔ 氵 (water)

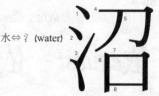

沼wamp   沼arshland

numa, SHŌ

swamp, marshland, wetland, muddy pond

FLIP: 7.3.a. Right Bottom (flat)

泥沼 *deadlock, stalemate, stand-off* **doronuma**
湖沼 *lakes & marshes* **koshō**
沼地 *swampy-, marshy-, wetland* **numachi**
沼田 *marshy rice field* **numata**
沼気 *methane, marsh gas* **shōki**
沼湖 *swamps & lakes* **shōko**
沼沢 *swamp, marsh land* **shōtaku**

沢*wamp, 753*	潜*ubmerge, 335*	泥*lay, 302*
礁*unken, 920*	没*inking, 744*	

召*ummon, 356*

266-B

To the 沼wamp was 召ummoned Monte Cristo's Edmond...

口 (mouth)

召ummon

me(su), SHŌ

summon, call out

FLIP: 4.0.a. Bottom (flat)

召使 *servant, maid, domestic help* **meshitsukai**
応召 *military draft, ~conscription* **ōshō**
応召兵 *military draftee* **ōshōhei**
応召者 *draftee, conscript, recruit* **ōshōsha**
召状 *invitation letter* **shōjō**
召還 *recall, summons* **shōkan**
召喚 *summons, subpoena* **shōkan**
召喚状 *summons, subpoena* **shōkanjō**
召集 *convoke, assemble* **shōshū**
召集令 *draft order* **shōshūrei**
御召し *summons, subpoena* **omeshi**
召し物 *food, drink, clothes (polite)* **meshimono**
召し換え *changing clothes* **meshikae**
召し出す *summon, call* **meshidasu**
召し使う *employing a servant* **meshitsukau**
召し上がる *eat, dine (honorific)* **meshiagaru**
召し入れる *call in, summon* **meshiireru**
召し抱える *hire, recruit, employ* **meshikakaeru**
思し召し *"as one pleases..."* **oboshimeshi**

聞こし召す *drink, eat, dine out* **kikoshimesu**

喚*ummon, 820*	吏*uthority, 463*
令*ommand, 362*	威*uthority, 520*
権*uthority, 804*	官*ublic official, 105*
宣*nnouncement, 899*	

沼*wamp, 356*

267-A

Food 例amples in Khartoum, many wait in 列olumns...

人⇔イ (person)

例xample　例pecimen

tato(eru), REI
example, specimen, given

Facing: 1.2. ☞ West (V)

悪例　bad precedent, ~example **akurei**
文例　model sentence **bunrei**
凡例　explanatory notes **hanrei**
範例　sample, specimen **hanrei**
比例　proportion, symmetry **hirei**
法例　legal precedents **hōrei**
一例　example, instance **ichirei**
異例　exceptional case **irei**
実例　concrete example, specific case **jitsurei**
条例　regulations, ordinance, law **jōrei**
慣例　custom, practice, precedent **kanrei**
恒例　established norm, ~practice **kōrei**
例文　example, illustrative sentence **reibun**
例題　example, exercise **reidai**
例外　exception, excluded case **reigai**
例言　explanatory notes **reigen**
例示　illustration, given example **reiji**
例日　regular days, weekday **reijitsu**
例会　regular meeting **reikai**

例解　illustration, example **reikai**
例刻　usual time **reikoku**
例年　average year, every year **reinen**
類例　parallel, similar instance **ruirei**
作例　example, illustration **sakurei**
症例　case of illness, medical case **shōrei**
定例　established norm, ~practice **teirei**
適例　good example **tekirei**
前例　precedent, parallel **zenrei**
例え話　allegory, parable, fable **tatoe banashi**
具体例　concrete example, specific case **gutairei**

範xample, 584	塑attern, 896
鑑attern, 857	柄attern, 213
型attern, 536	模attern, 827

倒verthrow, 496

267-B

Food 例amples in Khartoum, many wait in 列olumns...

刀⇔刂 (blade, cutting)

列ows　列olumn

RETSU
rows, column, queue

Facing: 1.2. ☞ West (V)

分列　filing off **bunretsu**
陳列　display, exhibition **chinretsu**
直列　series, serial **chokuretsu**
中列　middle row **chūretsu**
行列　procession, march, parade **gyōretsu**
配列　arrangement, order **hairetsu**
並列　parallel, running across **heiretsu**
陣列　battle formation **jinretsu**
序列　order, rank **joretsu**
順列　permutation, transfer **junretsu**
縦列　columns, files, rows **jūretsu**
系列　affiliate companies; succession **keiretsu**
後列　backrow **kōretsu**
羅列　enumeration, listing **raretsu**
列記　shortlisted candidates **rekki**
列国　all countries, the world **rekkoku**
列挙　enumeration, listing **rekkyo**
列強　great powers, colonial powers **rekkyō**
列席　attendance (formal occasion) **resseki**

列車　train, monorail **ressha**
列伝　series of biographies **retsuden**
列次　sequence, order **retsuji**
列島　islands, archipelago **rettō**
参列　attendance, participation **sanretsu**
整列　standing in line, queue **seiretsu**
戦列　line of battle, frontline **senretsu**
葬列　funeral procession, ~march **sōretsu**
数列　math series **sūretsu**
隊列　line of soldiers **tairetsu**
前列　front row **zenretsu**

行extline, 79	並arallel, 444
線ine, 531	沿longside, 756

死eath, 513

268-A
Hear 弦tring-instruments' 玄rofound moments...

弓 (archery bow)

弦usical string

tsuru, GEN
musical string

Facing: 4.0. Apart

調弦 *tuning (string instrument)* **chōgen**
弦楽 *string music* **gengaku**
弦楽器 *string instrument* **gengakki**
弦楽合奏 *string ensemble* **gengaku gassō**
弦月 *crescent moon* **gengetsu**
弦歌 *singing with string instruments* **genka**
弦管 *wind instruments* **genkan**
弦声 *sound of strings* **gensei**
弦線 *violin string* **gensen**
弦材 *chord member* **genzai**
補弦 *supplementary chord* **hogen**
上弦 *dichotomy; first quarter (moon)* **jōgen**
下弦 *last quarter (moon)* **kagen**
管弦 *wind & string instruments* **kangen**
管弦楽 *orchestra music* **kangengaku**
管弦楽団 *symphony orchestra* **kangen gakudan**
弓弦 *bowstring* **kyūgen**
三弦 *three-string instrument* **sangen**
正弦 *sine of an angle* **seigen**

弦音 *vibrating string instrument* **tsuruoto**
余弦 *calculus cosine* **yogen**
一弦琴 *single-string instrument* **ichigenkin**

歌*inging, 878*
曲*elody, 476*
奏*usic play, 579*
譜*usical note, 455*
琴*ither, 907*
娯*musement, 453*
興*musement, 867*
楽*leasure, 447*

強*trong, 894*

268-B
Hear 弦tring-instruments' 玄rofound moments...

玄 (darkness)

玄rofound 玄ystery

GEN
profound, mystery, enigma, mirage

Facing: 2.0. East (W)

玄麦 *coarse-, unpolished barley* **genbaku**
玄関 *main entrance* **genkan**
⇒表玄関 *front door, main entrance* **omote genkan**
玄関番 *doorman, doorkeeper* **genkanban**
玄関先 *front door, main entrance* **genkansaki**
玄関払い *refusal to meet a visitor* **genkanbarai**
玄黄 *black & yellow silk* **genkō**
玄米 *unpolished rice* **genmai**
玄妙 *occult, mystical* **genmyō**
玄翁 *bush hammer* **gennō**
玄理 *abstruse theory* **genri**
玄孫 *great-great grandchild* **genson**
玄冬 *winter* **gentō**
玄人 *professional, specialist, expert* **kurōto**
玄人筋 *professional, specialist, expert* **kurōtosuji**
幽玄 *mystery, profundity* **yūgen**
玄武岩 *basalt* **genbugan**
信玄袋 *cloth bag, sack* **shingenbukuro**

幻*antasy, 88*
著*tark, 279*
光*hining, 77*
照*hining, 529*

糸*hread, 375*

269-A

版ublished 片artiality breaches equality...

片 (board, woodblock)

版rinting 版ublishing

HAN
printing, publishing

FLIP: 7.3.b. Right Bottom (stem)
Facing: 2.2. East ☞ (V)

銅版 *copper plate* **dōban**
鉛版 *stereotype, conventional* **enban**
原版 *original plate* **genban**
版画 *block-printed cards* **hanga**
版木 *printing block* **hangi**
版権 *copyrights, publishing rights* **hanken**
版元 *book publisher* **hanmoto**
版下 *block print copy* **hanshita**
版図 *territory, domain, turf* **hanto**
重版 *second printing* **jūhan**
改版 *revision, updating* **kaihan**
活版 *letterpress, typography* **kappan**
木版 *woodblock printing* **mokuhan**
再版 *reprinting, republishing* **saihan**
製版 *printing plate-making* **seihan**
石版 *lithograph* **sekiban**
新版 *new publication* **shinpan**
初版 *maiden-, first edition* **shohan**
出版 *publishing, publication* **shuppan**

絶版 *out-of-print* **zeppan**
普及版 *popular edition* **fukyūban**
原色版 *heliotype printing* **genshokuban**
限定版 *limited edition* **genteiban**
豪華版 *deluxe edition* **gōkaban**
決定版 *definitiv edition* **ketteiban**
組み版 *printing form* **kumihan**
廉価版 *cheap edition* **renkaban**
縮刷版 *pocket-, compact edition* **shukusatsuban**
謄写版 *mimeograph* **tōshaban**
凸版印刷 *relief printing* **toppan insatsu**

刷*rinting*, 760	校*roof-reading*, 773
刊*ublication*, 687	訂*diting*, 174
掲*ublish*, 810	著*uthor*, 279
載*ublish*, 802	書*ritings*, 116

片*ne-sided*, 359

269-B

版ublished 片artiality breaches equality...

片 (board, woodblock)

片artial 片ne-sided

片

kata, HEN
partial, onerous, one-sided, one-half, one of two, unilateral

Facing: 2.0. East ☞ (W)

阿片 *opium, narcotics* **ahen**
断片 *fragment, flak, shrapnel* **danpen**
破片 *fragment, scrap* **hahen**
薄片 *flake, peel, thin layer* **hakuhen**
片雲 *scattered clouds* **hen'un**
火片 *sparks* **kahen**
片足 *one-legged* **kataashi**
片側 *one-sided* **katagawa**
片刃 *single-blade sword* **kataha**
片肌 *one side of the shoulder* **katahada**
片肌を脱ぐ *"lend a help..."* **katahada o nugu**
片端 *one edge, ~side* **katahashi**
片膝 *one knee* **katahiza**
片方 *one edge, ~side* **katahō**
片言 *speaking in broken language* **katakoto**
片目 *one-eyed* **katame**
片面 *one-sided* **katamen**
片身 *one-sided* **katami**
片道 *one way* **katamichi**

片親 *single parent* **kataoya**
片鱗 *single scale* **katarin**
片隅 *nook, corner* **katasumi**
片手 *one hand* **katate**
片時 *moment, short time* **katatoki**
片腕 *one arm* **kataude**
細片 *fragment, splinter* **saihen**
雪片 *snowflake* **seppen**
紙片 *paper slip* **shihen**
鉄片 *scrap iron, ~metal* **teppen**
片意地 *obstinacy, stubbornness* **kataiji**
片田舎 *remote rural area* **katainaka**
片仮名 *katakana characters* **katakana**
片手間 *sparetime* **katatema**
片思い *unrequited-, frustrated love* **kataomoi**

偏*artial*, 43	側*ide*, 291

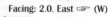
方*irection*, 533

270-A

法udiciary for the Mafia Dons, not to 去bandon...

法*egal*　　法*aw*　　法*ethod*

水 ⇔ 氵 (water)

HŌ, HO, HA

legal, law, judicial, juridical, method

法 FLIP: 7.2.b. Right Top (stem)
Facing: 2.2. East ☞ (V)

便法　makeshift, temporary **benpō**
合法　legality, lawfulness **gōhō**
不法　illegal, unlawful **fuhō**
兵法　strategy, tactics **heihō**
秘法　secret method **hihō**
筆法　penmanship, writing style **hippō**
法案　legislative bill, ~measure **hōan**
法衣　barrister's robe **hōe**
法外　unreasonable, excessive **hōgai**
法学　law, jurisprudence **hōgaku**
法事　Buddhist memorial service **hōji**
法人　corporation, juridical body **hōjin**
法科　law department **hōka**
法規　regulations, laws, rules **hōki**
法王　Roman Catholic Pope **hōō**
法王庁　Vatican, Holy See **hōōchō**
法令　laws & ordinances **hōrei**
法律　laws **hōritsu**
法廷　court of law **hōtei**

法典　statutes, code of laws **hōten**
違法　illegal, unlawful **ihō**
順法　law observance **junpō**
刑法　criminal law, penal code **keihō**
憲法　constitution, basic law **kenpō**
魔法　magic, sorcery, witchcraft **mahō**
療法　treatment, remedy, cure **ryōhō**
司法　administration of justice **shihō**
話法　narration **wahō**
税法　tax laws, tax code **zeihō**
倒置法　upside down, inversion **tōchihō**
特許法　patent law **tokkyohō**

廷*mperial court*, 26	裁*udgement*, 802
定*ertain*, 550	判*udgement*, 949
決*ecide*, 699	

去*eave-out*, 360

270-B

法udiciary for the Mafia Dons, not to 去bandon...

去*bandon*　　去*y-gone*

ム (oneself)

去

sa(ru), KYO, KO

abandon, by-gone, leave-out, go away

FLIP: 3.0.a. Top (flat)
Facing: 2.0. East ☞ (W)

辞去　leaving, quitting, retiring **jikyo**
除去　removal, taking down, elimination **jokyo**
過去　past, bygone's **kako**
過去帳　death registry, death notices **kakochō**
薨去　dying, death, passing away **kōkyo**
去年　last year, the year past **kyonen**
去来　recurrence, relapse **kyorai**
去勢　castration, emasculation, gelding **kyosei**
去勢牛　bullock, castrated bull **kyoseigyū**
去就　course-of-action, attitude **kyoshū**
逝去　death, passing away **seikyo**
死去　death, passing away **shikyo**
消去　withdrawal, elimination **shōkyo**
退去　evacuation, leaving, quitting **taikyo**
撤去　removal, abolition, dismantlement **tekkyo**
吹き去る　blow away **fukisaru**
葬り去る　bury, inter **hōmurisaru**
消し去る　wipe away, vanish, remove **keshisaru**
消え去る　disappear, vanishing **kiesaru**

崩れ去る　collapse, downfall **kuzuresaru**
持ち去る　take away, make off with **mochisaru**
逃げ去る　run off, run away **nigesaru**
抜き去る　overtake, surpass **nukisaru**
置き去り　leaving behind, abandonment **okizari**
捨て去る　forsake **sutesaru**
飛び去る　fly away **tobisaru**
遠去かる　become distant, fade away **toozakaru**
取り去る　get rid of, eliminate **torisaru**
連れ去る　take by force, kidnap, abduct **tsuresaru**
忘れ去る　completely forget **wasuresaru**

遺*eave-behind*, 914	退*ithdraw*, 770
置*eave-behind*, 420	撤*ithdraw*, 843
却*ithdraw*, 387	罷*ithdraw*, 322

広*arge*, 205

271-A

Old garden 囲*nclosed, a wishing* 井*ell of ghosts...*

☐ (enclosure)

2 5 6
1 3
4
7

囲*nclose*   囲*ncircle*

FLIP: 2.0.a. Sort Of (flat)

kako(mu), kako(u), I
enclose, encircle, scope, confines, spanning

腹囲 *girth of abdomen* **fukui**
外囲 *surroundings, periphery, environs* **gaii**
範囲 *range, scope & limitation* **han'i**
⇒広範囲 *wide range, wide area* **kōhan'i**
⇒勢力範囲 *sphere-of-influence* **seiryoku han'i**
範囲内 *within the scope, ~range* **han'inai**
包囲 *siege, encirclement, encroachment* **hōi**
囲碁 *Go game* **igo**
重囲 *close siege* **jūi**
攻囲 *laying seize, under attack* **kōi**
胸囲 *chest size* **kyōi**
四囲 *circumstances, situation* **shii**
周囲 *circumference, girth, periphery* **shūi**
頭囲 *girth of head* **tōi**
腰囲 *hip measurement* **yōi**
雰囲気 *atmosphere, mood* **fun'iki**
囲炉裏 *open hearth* **irori**
板囲い *board fence* **itagakoi**
囲い者 *mistress, concubine* **kakoimono**

霜囲い *frost protection* **shimogakoi**
外囲い *enclosure, confines* **sotogakoi**
雪囲い *snow shed* **yukikakoi**
取り囲む *surround, besiege* **torikakomu**

郭*nclose, 398*	境*oundary, 839*
周*icinity, 280*	奥*nside, 903*
辺*icinity, 93*	内*nside, 297*
近*earby, 184*	限*oundary, 771*
限*imit, 771*	含*nclude, 183*

井*ater well, 361*

271-B

Old garden 囲*nclosed, a wishing* 井*ell of ghosts...*

二 (two, second)

3 4
1
2

井*ater well*

FLIP: 2.0.b. Sort Of (stem)

i, SEI, SHŌ
water well

ガス井 *gas well* **gasusei**
井戸 *water well* **ido**
井戸端会議 *housewives' gossip (hang-out)*
   idobata kaigi
井戸水 *well water* **idomizu**
井桁 *well crib* **igeta**
井守 *newt, eft* **imori**
井筒 *well curb* **izutsu**
鑿井 *oil drilling* **sakusei**
井目 *Go game main points* **seimoku**
井水 *water from well* **seisui**
市井 *common streets* **shisei**
天井 *ceiling* **tenjō**
天井灯 *ceiling lights* **tenjōtō**
天井裏 *space between ceiling & roof* **tenjōura**
筒井 *well curb* **tsutsui**
油井 *oil well* **yusei**
青天井 *infinity, "sky's-the-limit..."* **aotenjō**
福井県 *Fukui Prefecture* **fukui-ken**

古井戸 *old well* **furuido**
車井戸 *well pulley* **kuruma'ido**

扉*oor, 678*	掘*igging, 211*
門*ate, 286*	溝*aterway, 226*
口*pening, 458*	槽*ater-tank, 327*
関*arrier, 284*	

共*ogether, 302*

272-A

命estiny's highest prize: 令ommand of one's 命ife...

口 (mouth)

❶命ife   ❷命estiny

inochi, MEI, MYŌ
life; destiny, fate, order

FLIP: 2.0.b. Sort Of (stem)

❶
亡命 *asylum, exile, defection* **bōmei**
長命 *long life, longevity* **chōmei**
厳命 *strict orders* **genmei**
拝命 *appointment to a higher post* **haimei**
命拾い *escape from death* **inochibiroi**
命綱 *life line* **inochizuna**
人命 *human life* **jinmei**
寿命 *life expectancy, life span* **jumyō**
革命 *revolution, reform* **kakumei**
革命政府 *revolutionary government* **kakumei seifu**
産業革命 *industrial revolution* **sangyō kakumei**
懸命 *strenuous, eager* **kenmei**
命中 *hit, being it* **meichū**
命題 *proposition, thesis* **meidai**
命名 *naming, christening* **meimei**
命脈 *life line* **meimyaku**
命日 *death anniversary* **meinichi**
命令 *order, command* **meirei**
露命 *scanty lifestyle* **romei**

生命 *human life, life* **seimei**
社命 *company orders* **shamei**
使命 *mission, appointed task* **shimei**
存命 *living, survival* **zonmei**
致命傷 *fatal-, mortal wound* **chimeishō**

❷
死命 *fate, deliverance* **shimei**
宿命 *fate, destiny* **shukumei**
待命 *awaiting orders, on call* **taimei**
短命 *early death, short life* **tanmei**
特命 *specially-appointed* **tokumei**
運命 *fate, destiny* **unmei**

生*ife, 474*	産*hildbirth, 883*
誕*hildbirth, 515*	

卵*gg, 971*

272-B

命estiny's highest prize: 令ommand of one's 命ife...

人⇔亻 (person)

令ommand   令rder

REI
command, decree, edict, order, instruction

FLIP: 2.0.b. Sort Of (stem)

勅令 *imperial command* **chokurei**
布令 *official announcement, public notice* **furei**
号令 *command, order* **gōrei**
軍令 *military order* **gunrei**
発令 *issuance of an order* **hatsurei**
法令 *laws & ordinances* **hōrei**
威令 *authority, official power* **irei**
辞令 *letter of appointment* **jirei**
条令 *law, ordinance, regulation* **jōrei**
禁令 *injunction, prohibition* **kinrei**
訓令 *instructions, orders* **kunrei**
命令 *order, command* **meirei**
⇒執行命令 *order of execution* **shikkō meirei**
⇒逮捕命令 *arrest warrant* **taiho meirei**
命令書 *written order, writ, warrant* **meireisho**
年令 *age* **nenrei**
令嬢 *daughter, young lady* **reijō**
令状 *warrant, written order* **reijō**
⇒捜査令状 *search warrant* **sōsa reijō**

令名 *outstanding reputation* **reimei**
令息 *your son (honorific)* **reisoku**
制令 *regulations, rules* **seirei**
政令 *government ordinance* **seirei**
指令 *order, instructions* **shirei**
司令 *command, order, instruction* **shirei**
司令官 *military commander* **shireikan**
司令塔 *command-, control tower* **shireitō**
省令 *ministerial order* **shōrei**
動員令 *deployment order* **dōinrei**
戒厳令 *martial law, military occupation* **kaigenrei**

帥*ommander, 483*	領*overn, 874*
督*ommander, 911*	統*overn, 885*
威*uthority, 520*	府*overnment, 429*
権*uthority, 804*	

分*ivide, 518*

273-A

拓*learing-up* 石*tones, yielded dead bones...*

手⇔扌 (hand, manual)

拓*lear-up*　　拓*evelop*

TAKU
clear-up, develop

Facing: 4.0. 🖙🖙 Apart
FLIP: 7.3.a. Right Bottom (flat)

魚拓 *fish image print* **gyotaku**
開拓 *reclamation, clearing of land* **kaitaku**
⇒未開拓 *uncultivated, undeveloped* **mikaitaku**
開拓者 *settler, pioneer, developer* **kaitakusha**
干拓 *reclamation by drainage* **kantaku**
干拓地 *reclaimed land* **kantakuchi**
干拓工事 *reclamation works* **kantaku kōji**
拓地 *land development, ~cultivation* **takuchi**
拓本 *rubbed copy* **takuhon**
拓殖 *colonization, settlement* **takushoku**
拓殖者 *colonist, land developer* **takushokusha**

開*evelop, 284*	革*eform, 39*
整*djust, 31*	新*ew, 668*
改*eform, 725*	更*new, 402*

招*nvite, 956*

273-B

拓*learing-up* 石*tones, yielded dead bones...*

石 (stone)

石*tone*　　石*ock*

ishi, SEKI, SHAKU, KOKU
rock, stone

FLIP: 4.0.a. Bottom (flat)

岩石 *coastal rock* **ganseki**
碁石 *Go piece (Japanese chess)* **goishi**
墓石 *tombstone, gravesite marker* **hakaishi, boseki**
宝石 *jewelry, precious gem* **hōseki**
石文 *stone monument* **ishibumi**
腎石 *kidney stone* **jinseki**
磁石 *magnet* **jishaku**
定石 *Shōgi chess move* **jōseki**
懐石 *tea lunch* **kaiseki**
鉱石 *mineral, ore* **kōseki**
庭石 *garden stone* **niwaishi**
落石 *falling rocks* **rakuseki**
採石 *quarrying (marble)* **saiseki**
石版 *lithography* **sekiban**
石炭 *coal* **sekitan**
石油 *oil, petroleum* **sekiyu**
石像 *stone statue* **sekizō**
石化 *fosilized, petrify* **sekika, sekka**
石鹸 *soap* **sekken**

石工 *stone craftman* **sekkō**
敷石 *paving stone, flagstone* **shikiishi**
礎石 *cornerstone* **soseki**
胆石 *gallstone* **tanseki**
投石 *throwing stone* **tōseki**
薬石 *"all the medical care..."* **yakuseki**
大盤石 *"solid as rock..."* **daibanjaku**
大理石 *marble* **dairiseki**
石焼き *stone-grilled barbequing* **ishiyaki**
捨て石 *sacrifice, sacrificial stone* **suteishi**
誕生石 *birth stone* **tanjōseki**
飛び石 *stepping stone* **tobiishi**

岩*ock, 29*
砂*ands, 643*

右*ight-side, 87*

274-A

姻arriage 如quals a new heritage...

女 (woman)

姻arriage 姻atrimony

IN

marriage, matrimony, nuptials, wedding, getting hitch

FLIP: 7.0.a. Right (flat)

姻戚 relative by marriage, in-laws **inseki**
姻族 relative by marriage, in-laws **inzoku**
婚姻 marriage **kon'in**

夫usband, 83	家amily, 909
妻ife, 611	族amily, 649
婦ife, 785	扶amily-support, 97
婚arriage, 637	任bligation, 709

如qual, 364

274-B

姻arriage 如quals a new heritage...

女 (woman)

如

如qual   如uch as

goto(shi), JO, NYO

equal to, equivalent, as is, such as

FLIP: 7.0.a. Right (flat)

一如 oneness **ichi'nyo**
如何 how come, how **ikaga**, **ikan**
如何程 how many, how much **ikahodo**
如何物 phoney-, fake articles, imitation **ikamono**
如何なる every, any **ikanaru**
如何様① hoax, fraud **ikasama**
如何様② how, what kind **ikayō**
如何許り how much **ikabakari**
如上 "the above-mentioned..." **jojō**
欠如 insufficiency, deficiency **ketsujo**
如月 February, second lunar month **kisaragi**
如法 Buddhist fidelity **nyohō**
如意 Buddhist monk servants **nyoi**
如実 realistic, true-to-life, factual **nyojitsu**
如来 Buddha **nyorai**
真如 absolute reality **shinnyo**
突如 suddenly, unexpectedly **totsujo**
躍如 vivid, lifelike, zestful **yakujo**
不如意 hardship, contrary to one's will **fu'nyoi**

如雨露 watering can **jōro**, **joro**
如才ない tactful, suave, savvy **josainai**

均qual, 470	同imilar, 245
斉qual, 112	平lain, 488
似imilar, 472	

加ddition, 201

275-A

Sea 界orld of 介hellfish, 介ediation in Atlantis...

田 (cultivated field)

界orld 界ircle

KAI
world, circle, field, bounds, profession

FLIP: 1.0.b. Whole (stem)

外界 outer-, outside world **gaikai**
学界 academic world, academe **gakkai**
眼界 field of vision **gankai**
限界 limit, bounds **genkai**
業界 business world **gyōkai**
塵界 mundane life **jinkai**
界隈 neighbourhood, vicinity **kaiwai**
角界 world of sumo wrestling **kakkai**
各界 various professions **kakkai**
苦界 "world of sufferings..." **kukai**
境界 boundary, border **kyōkai**
球界 baseball profession **kyūkai**
内界 inner world, one's mind **naikai**
霊界 spiritual world **reikai**
臨界 critical, turning point **rinkai**
政界 political world, ~circles **seikai**
世界 world, earth **sekai**
⇒第三世界 Third World nations, developing countries **daisan sekai**

斯界 expert, this field **shikai**
視界 range of vision, visibility **shikai**
他界 death, passing away **takai**
財界 financial world, ~circles **zaikai**
俗界 earthly life, secular life **zokkai**
芸能界 showbiz, entertainment world **geinōkai**
法曹界 legal giants **hōsōkai**
医学界 medical profession **igakukai, igakkai**
工業界 industrial circles, ~world **kōgyōkai**
教育界 academic world, academe **kyōikukai**
音楽界 musical circles **ongakukai**
全世界 the whole world **zensekai**

世orld, 411　　衆opulace, 766
公ublic, 180

果esult, 287

275-B

Sea 界orld of 介hellfish, 介ediation in Atlantis...

人⇔亻 (person)

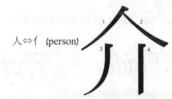

❶介ediate ❷介hellfish

KAI
mediate, intercede, intervene, meddle; shellfish

FLIP: 1.0.b. Whole (stem)

❶媒介 mediation, convey **baikai**
媒介物 medium, carrier **baikaibutsu**
仲介 mediation, intercession **chūkai**
仲介物 medium **chūkaibutsu**
仲介者 intermediary, mediator, go-between **chūkaisha**
一介の mere, only **ikkai no**
介護 care, nursing **kaigo**
介抱 care, nursing **kaihō**
介意 caring for, nursing **kaii**
介助 help, assistance, support **kaijo**
介入 intervention, intercession, stepping in **kainyū**
介錯 helping one commit suicide **kaishaku**
介在 intervention, interposition **kaizai**
狷介 obstinate, stubborn, hard-headed **kenkai**
紹介 introduction, recommendation **shōkai**
⇒自己紹介 self-introduction **jiko shōkai**
⇒新刊紹介 book review **shinkan shōkai**
紹介状 letter of introduction **shōkaijō**
紹介者 introducer **shōkaisha**

厄介 troublesome, annoying, disturbing **yakkai**
厄介者 nuisance, troublesome **yakkaimono**
不介入 non-intervention **fukainyū**
介添え best man, bridesmaid **kaizoe**
荷厄介 burden, nuisance, troublesome **niyakkai**

❷魚介 seafoods, marine products **gyokai**
鱗介 seafoods, marine products **rinkai**

媒ediator, 292　　談alks, 308
渉ross-over, 273　　魚ishes, 49

今OW, 182

276-A

狩*unters* 守*bide to* 守*rotect the wild...*

犭 (beast)

狩*unting*　狩*icking fruits*

ka(ri), ka(ru), SHU
hunting, picking (fruits)

FLIP: 7.2.b. Right Top (stem)
Facing: 1.2. ☞ West (V)

狩出す　*hunt out, round up* **karidasu**
狩り込み　*hunting, rounding up* **karikomi**
狩り集める　*gather, muster* **kariatsumeru**
蛍狩り　*firefly-catching* **hotarugari**
首狩り　*head hunting* **kubigari**
熊狩り　*bear hunting* **kumagari**
山狩り　*mountain hunting* **yamagari**
葡萄狩り　*grape picking* **budōgari**
魔女狩り　*witch-hunt* **majogari**
猛獣狩り　*big game hunting* **mōjūgari**
紅葉狩り　*autumn-leaves viewing* **momijigari**
暴力団狩り　*rounding up of gangsters* **bōryokudangari**
狩猟　*hunting, shooting* **shuryō**
狩猟場　*hunting ground* **shuryōba**
狩猟家　*hunter, huntsman, huntress* **shuryōka**
狩猟期　*hunting season* **shuryōki**
潮干狩　*shellfish gathering, ~collecting* **shiohigari**

猟*unting, 657*	畜*aising, 528*
獣*east, 846*	牧*asture, 647*
飼*aising, 835*	捕*eizure, 812*

将*eneral, 521*

276-B

狩*unters* 守*bide to* 守*rotect the wild...*

宀 (cover, lid)

❶守*bide*　❷守*efence*

mamo(ru), mamori, SHU, SU
abide, adhere; defence, protect

FLIP: 3.0.b. Top (stem)
Facing: 1.1. ☞ West (H)

❶墨守　*devotion, adherence, commitment* **bokushu**
鎮守　*village shrine* **chinju**
厳守　*strict observance* **genshu**
保守　*conservatism* **hoshu**
保守党　*conservative party* **hoshutō**
導守　*law observance* **junshu**
順守　*abide with the law* **junshu**

❷門守　*gatekeeper, watchman* **kadomori**
看守　*guard, jailer, gaoler* **kanshu**
子守　*baby-sitting, nursing* **komori**
子守り歌　*lullaby, nursery song* **komoriuta**
固守　*persistent defence* **koshu**
攻守　*offence & defence* **kōshu**
見守る　*look after, watch over* **mimamoru**
宮守　*shrine keeper* **miyamori**
留守　*absence, not present* **rusu**
留守番　*stay in place as caretaker* **rusuban**
占守　*occupying, holding* **senshu**

拙守　*weak defence* **sesshu**
死守　*defending to the death* **shishu**
守備　*defence, fielding* **shubi**
守備兵　*garrison-, sentry guards* **shubihei**
守衛　*guard, door-keeper* **shuei**
守護　*protection, guarding* **shugo**
守旧　*conservatism* **shukyū**
守勢　*defensive posture* **shusei**
守戦　*defensive war* **shusen**
太守　*governor-general, viceroy* **taishu**
灯台守　*lighthouse keeper* **tōdaimori**
守銭奴　*miser, niggard, frugal* **shusendo**

保*ecure, 552*	護*rotect, 828*
衛*rotect, 796*	防*rotect, 736*

守*etter, 346*

277-A

荘olemn 荘illa for a 壮asculine gorilla...

-艹- (grass)

❶荘illa   ❷荘olemn

SŌ
villa; solemn, dignified

FLIP: 7.0.a. Right (flat)
FLIP: 7.3.a. Right Bottom (flat)

❶別荘　vacation-, retreat house **bessō**
⇒貸し別荘　rental vacation cottage **kashi bessō**
雀荘　mah-jong parlor **jansō**
山荘　mountain villa **sansō**
荘園　manor house, mansion **shōen, sōsen**
荘司　manor manager **sōji**

❷荘厳　solemnity, sacredness **shōgon, sōgon**
　荘重　solemnity, sacredness **sōchō**

閑eisure, 283	遊njoy, 650
悠eisure, 898	聖acred, 617
憩elaxation, 169	神ivine, 712
喫njoy, 900	祈rayer, 184
享njoy, 398	拝rayer, 636

壮asculine, 367

277-B

荘olemn 荘illa for a 壮asculine gorilla...

士 (samurai, warrior)

壮asculine   壮agnificent

SŌ
masculine, magnificent, grandeur, heroic, vigorous

FLIP: 7.0.a. Right (flat)

豪壮　magnificent, gorgeous **gōsō**
悲壮　tragic & brave, heroic **hisō**
宏壮　magnificent-looking **kōsō**
広壮　grand-looking, high & mighty **kōsō**
宏壮　magnificent, spectacular **kōsō**
強壮　strong, sturdy, robust **kyōsō**
老壮　young & old **rōsō**
壮夫　good physique man **shōfu**
少壮　young & vigorous **shōsō**
壮美　splendour, grand, magnificent **sōbi**
壮大　grand, magnificent **sōdai**
壮言　magnificent words **sōgen**
壮快　thrilling, exciting, stirring **sōkai**
壮観　magnificent scene **sōkan**
壮健　healthy, robust **sōken**
壮行　rousing, stirring **sōkō**
壮挙　daring endeavour, heroic attempt **sōkyo**
壮年　one's finest years, primehood **sōnen**
壮齢　prime of one's life **sōrei**

壮麗　grand, magnificent **sōrei**
壮烈　heroic, glorious **sōretsu**
壮者　one's primehood **sōsha**
壮士　brave, heroic, daring **sōshi**
壮志　burning ambition, will **sōshi**
壮丁　conscription age **sōtei**
壮途　ambitious attempt **sōto**
壮図　grand project **sōto**
壮絶　heroic, life-&-death situation **sōzetsu**
雄壮　brave, courageous, heroic **yūsō**
勇壮　brave, courageous, heroic **yūsō**

男asculine, 597	郎asculine, 404
僕asculine, 157	偉agnificent, 797
雄asculine, 775	敢auntless, 449

汁uice, 344

278-A

Slavery 廃bolition 発tarted Southern sedition...

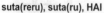

广 (rooftop)

廃bolish　廃liminate

suta(reru), suta(ru), HAI
abolish, eliminate, dispose of, discard, discontinue, thrash, waste

FLIP: 8.0.b. Inner (stem)

廃案 *rejected bill, defeated bill* **haian**
廃嫡 *disinheritance, disowning* **haichaku**
廃液 *waste water, liquid waste* **haieki**
廃語 *obsolete-, dead word* **haigo**
廃合 *abolition & merging, restructuring* **haigō**
廃業 *going out of business, insolvency* **haigyō**
廃品 *junk, waste materials* **haihin**
廃位 *dethronement, unseating* **haii**
廃人 *handicapped-, disabled person* **haijin**
廃家 *extinct family* **haika**
廃刊 *defunct publication* **haikan**
廃棄 *scrapping, abrogation, repeal* **haiki**
廃坑 *abandoned mine* **haikō**
廃却 *scrapping, abolition* **haikyaku**
廃去 *abandon, withdraw from* **haikyo**
廃熱 *wasted heat* **hainetsu**
廃船 *decommissioned ship* **haisen**
廃線 *discontinued train-, bus line* **haisen**
廃車 *scrap car, abandoned car* **haisha**

廃止 *abolition, eradication* **haishi**
廃水 *waste water, sewer water* **haisui**
廃山 *abandoned mine site* **haizan**
改廃 *alteration & abolition, reorganization* **kaihai**
興廃 *rise & fall, vicissitudes* **kōhai**
荒廃 *devastation, ruins, desolation* **kōhai**
老廃 *wasted, useless, futile* **rōhai**
存廃 *continuity-or-abolition* **sonpai**
退廃 *decadence, ruin* **taihai**
撤廃 *abolition, removal, discarding* **teppai**
全廃 *total abolition* **zenpai**

絶radicate, 403	外emove, 188
消elete, 265	脱emove, 941
抹ross-out, 13	止erminate, 192

発tart, 368

278-B

Slavery 廃bolition 発tarted Southern sedition...

戏 (depart)

発tart　発mit

HATSU, HOTSU
start, originate, begin, leave from, emit

FLIP: 1.0.b. Whole (stem)

爆発 *explosion, detonation* **bakuhatsu**
偶発 *accidental occurrence* **gūhatsu**
発火 *catch fire, ignite* **hakka**
発見 *discovery, detection* **hakken**
発生 *occurrence, outgrowth* **hassei**
発想 *conception, creativity* **hassō**
発案 *proposal, suggestion* **hatsuan**
発芽 *germination, budding* **hatsuga**
発言 *outburst, utterance* **hatsugen**
発育 *growth, development* **hatsuiku**
発明 *invention, discovery* **hatsumei**
発音 *pronunciation, reading* **hatsuon**
発令 *announcement, public notice* **hatsurei**
発展 *progress, development* **hatten**
併発 *coincidence, by-chance* **heihatsu**
家発 *time leaving one's house* **iehatsu**
蒸発 *evaporation, vaporization* **jōhatsu**
開発 *development, innovation* **kaihatsu**
活発 *dynamic, lively, animated* **kappatsu**

啓発 *enlightenment, illumination* **keihatsu**
揮発 *volatilisation* **kihatsu**
先発 *start in advance, start ahead* **senpatsu**
始発 *first plane, first train, first bus* **shihatsu**
触発 *touching off, setting off* **shokuhatsu**
摘発 *disclosure, exposure, revelation* **tekihatsu**
誘発 *causing, inducing, setting off* **yūhatsu**
続発 *succession, continuity* **zokuhatsu**
挑発的 *provocative, inciteful* **chōhatsuteki**
発祥地 *birthplace, cradle of* **hasshōchi**
東京発 *flight from Tōkyō* **tōkyō hatsu**

始tart, 210
初tart, 353

登limb, 437

279-A

独erman scientists have known that 虫nsects 独lone can live
in a nuclear zone...

犭 (beast)

❶独lone   ❷独ermany

hito(ri), DOKU
alone, independent; Germany

FLIP: 7.1. Right (Sort Of)
Facing: 4.0. ⟨⟨⟩⟩ Apart

❶独りぼっち *alone, solitary, solitude* **hitoribocchi**
独断 *arbitrary, partial, unjust* **dokudan**
独泳 *solo swimming* **dokuei**
独演 *solo performance, ~recital* **dokuen**
独学 *self-study, self-learning* **dokugaku**
独眼 *one-eyed* **dokugan**
独語 *monologue, soliloquy* **dokugo**
独白 *monologue, soliloquy* **dokuhaku**
独話 *talking to oneself, thinking aloud* **dokuwa**
独自 *original, unique, peculiar* **dokuji**
独立 *independence, self-government* **dokuritsu**
独力 *single-handedly, sole effort* **dokuryoku**
独裁 *dictatorship, despotism* **dokusai**
独占 *monopoly, oligopoly* **dokusen**
独身 *single life, unmarried* **dokushin**
独習 *self-learning, self-teaching* **dokushū**
独走 *easy win, cakewalk* **dokusō**
独奏 *solo performance (piano, violin)* **dokusō**
独創 *creativity, originality* **dokusō**

独特 *unique, peculiar, original* **dokutoku**
独善 *self-righteousness* **dokuzen**
孤独 *loneliness, solitary, solitude* **kodoku**
⇒天涯孤独 *completely alone* **tengai kodoku**
単独 *sole, individual, single* **tandoku**
独り言 *mutter, murmur, utter* **hitorigoto**
独り立ち *self-sustaining* **hitoridachi**
独り占め *monopoly, oligopoly* **hitorijime**
独り暮らし *living alone* **hitorigurashi**
独り善がり *self-conceited* **hitoriyogari**
❷独文 *German literature* **dokubun**

身elf, 504	孤olitary, 148	唯olitary, 642
己elf, 5	専xclusive, 514	
自elf, 462	寡lone, 161	

拐idnap, 956

279-B

独erman scientists have known that 虫nsects 独lone can live
in a nuclear zone...

虫 (insect)

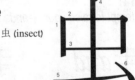

虫nsect

mushi, CHŪ
insect, fly

FLIP: 2.0.a. Sort Of (flat)

油虫 *plant louse* **aburamushi**
赤虫 *blood worm* **akamushi**
防虫 *insect-protection* **bōchū**
虫垂 *appendix* **chūsui**
益虫 *beneficial insect* **ekichū**
船虫 *sea slater* **funamushi**
害虫 *harmful insect, vermin* **gaichū**
芋虫 *caterpillar* **imomushi**
毛虫 *caterpillar* **kemushi**
甲虫 *beetle* **kōchū**
昆虫 *insect* **konchū**
松虫 *grasshopper, cricket* **matsumushi**
虫歯 *decayed tooth, dental cavity* **mushiba**
苦虫 *sour face, sullen look* **nigamushi**
鈴虫 *cricket* **suzumushi**
玉虫 *scarab beetle* **tamamushi**
田虫 *ringworm* **tamushi**
幼虫 *larva* **yōchū**
捕虫網 *insect net* **hochūami**

髪切虫 *longhorn beetle* **kamikirimushi**
寄生虫 *parasite* **kiseichū**
黄金虫 *gold beetle, goldbug* **koganemushi**
虫干し *airing, letting air in* **mushiboshi**
虫下し *vermifuge* **mushikudashi**
虫食い *worm-eaten hole* **mushikui**
虫眼鏡 *magnifying glass* **mushimegane**
虫除け *insecticide, insect killer* **mushiyoke**
泣き虫 *cry baby, blubberer* **nakimushi**
南京虫 *bedbug* **nankinmushi**
天道虫 *ladybird* **tentōmushi**

昆nsect, 38
蚊osquito, 654
蛍irefly, 628

史istory, 85

280-A

挙*ttempt to raise your* 手*ands if police demands...*

手⇔扌 (hand, manual)

挙*ecite*　　挙*ttempt*

a(geru), a(garu), KYO
recite, attempt, enumerate, nominate, raise

FLIP: 3.0.b. Top (stem)
FLIP: 2.0.b. Sort Of (stem)

挙句 *finally, in the end* **ageku**
美挙 *praiseworthy deed* **bikyo**
暴挙 *hasty-, reckless attempt* **bōkyo**
義挙 *heroic attempt* **gikyo**
愚挙 *silly undertaking, stupid attempt* **gukyo**
快挙 *splendid feat, inspiring feat* **kaikyo**
軽挙 *hasty-, impulsive action* **keikyo**
検挙 *arrest, round-up, raid* **kenkyo**
挙動 *behaviour, conduct, attitude* **kyodō**
挙兵 *armed uprising, rebellion* **kyohei**
挙行 *performance, celebration* **kyokō**
挙国 *whole nation* **kyokoku**
挙止 *demeanour, bearing* **kyoshi**
挙式 *ceremony, decorum* **kyoshiki**
挙証 *presenting evidence* **kyoshō**
挙手 *show of hands, acclamation* **kyoshu**
挙用 *appointment, promotion* **kyoyō**
枚挙 *enumeration, listing* **maikyo**
列挙 *enumeration, listing* **rekkyo**

再挙 *renewed attempt* **saikyo**
盛挙 *great endeavour, grand undertaking* **seikyo**
選挙 *election* **senkyo**
⇒普通選挙 *universal suffrage, one-man-one-vote*
　futsū senkyo
壮挙 *heroic attempt* **sōkyo**
推挙 *recommendation, endorsement* **suikyo**
大挙 *full force, en masse* **taikyo**
鉄挙 *hand fist* **tekken**
言挙げ *verbal expression* **kotoage**

轄*ontrol, 968*
管*ontrol, 917*
操*perate, 851*

手*and, 370*

280-B

挙*ttempt to raise your* 手*ands if police demands...*

手⇔扌 (hand, manual)

手*and*　　手*anual*

te, ta, SHU
hand, manual, *expert suffix*

Facing: 1.0. 🢐 West (W)
FLIP: 2.0.b. Sort Of (stem)

相手 *counterpart, companion* **aite**
握手 *handshake* **akushu**
義手 *artificial hand, fake arm* **gishu**
拍手 *applause, handclapping* **hakushu**
下手① *unskilled, clumsy* **heta**
下手② *lower part of the stage* **shimote**
上手① *skilled, excellent* **jōzu**
上手② *upper part of the stage* **kamite**
切手 *postage stamp* **kitte**
元手 *capital, funds* **motode**
両手 *both hands* **ryōte**
選手 *athlete, player* **senshu**
手芸 *handicraft, hand-made goods* **shugei**
手術 *surgery, operation* **shujutsu**
手話 *sign language (deaf & mute)* **shuwa**
手袋 *hand gloves* **tebukuro**
手帳 *notebook, memos* **techō**
手紙 *letter* **tegami**
話し手 *the person speaking* **hanashite**

働き手 *worker, driving force* **hatarakite**
手当て *allowance, stipend; medical cure* **teate**
手振り *hand gesture, hand mannerism* **teburi**
手違い *mistake, error* **techigai**
手一杯 *full, very busy, occupied* **teippai**
手荷物 *carry-on baggage* **tenimotsu**
手の内 *intention, will, volition* **tenouchi**
手の掌 *palm of the hand* **tenohira**
手の甲 *back of the hand* **tenokō**
手作業 *manual, by hand, labourious* **tesagyō**
大手企業 *conglomerate, big corporation* **oote kigyō**
御手洗い *washroom, lavatory* **otearai**
手に取る *take in one's hand* **te(ni)toru**

指*inger, 242*　管*ontrol, 917*　握*rasp, 427*
轄*ontrol, 968*　持*olding, 249*　肢*ppendage, 200*

毛*kin hair, 468*

281-A

遮*ntercepted letters, all about* 庶*eneral-matters...*

辶 (transport)

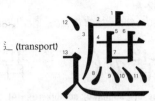

遮*ntercept*　遮*nterrupt*

saegi(ru), SHA
intercept, interrupt, blocking, obstruct
遮断 *interception, blockage, isolation* **shadan**
遮断機 *"train crossing" gate* **shadanki**
遮蔽 *covering, sheltering* **shahei**
遮光 *blocking a light* **shakō**
遮光側 *unseen-, covered side* **shakōgawa**
遮二無二 *reckless, clumsy* **shani muni**

FLIP: 8.0.b. Inner (stem)
Facing: 4.0. ⟱⟱ Apart

妨*indrance, 734*
阻*mpede, 756*

庶*llegitimate, 371*

281-B

遮*ntercepted letters, all about* 庶*eneral-matters...*

广 (rooftop)

庶

❶庶*anifold* ❷庶*llegitimate child*

SHO
manifold, various; illegitimate, lovechild

FLIP: 8.0.b. Inner (stem)

❶庶事 *various matters* **shoji**
庶幾 *wish, desire* **shoki**
庶民 *inhabitant, people* **shomin**
庶務 *general administration* **shomu**
庶務課 *administrative section* **shomuka**
庶政 *all phases of government* **shosei**
衆庶 *masses, common people* **shūsho**

❷庶系 *illegitimate family branch* **shokei**
庶流 *illegitimate family branch* **shoryū**
庶生 *illegitimate birth* **shosei**
庶姓 *illegitimacy* **shosei**
庶子 *illegitimate child* **shoshi**
庶出 *illegitimate birth* **shoshutsu**

雑*arious, 776*　常*egular, 94*
諸*arious, 794*　普*ommon, 455*
般*egular, 323*　嫡*egitimate, 966*

焦*ocus, 919*

282-A

Cadaver's 背ack to face 北orth for luck...

背*ack*　　　背*osterior*

肉⇔月 (flesh, body part)

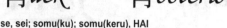

se, sei; somu(ku); somu(keru), HAI
back, posterior, rear

FLIP: 2.0.b. Sort Of (stem)

中背 *medium height* **chūzei**
腹背 *front & back* **fukuhai**
背部 *back, rear part* **haibu**
背馳 *inconsistent, incoherent* **haichi**
背泳 *backstroke swimming* **haiei**
背後 *back, rear, behind* **haigo**
背反 *contrary, oppose, against* **haihan**
背景 *background, scenery* **haikei**
背教 *renouncing one's religion, apostasy* **haikyō**
背面 *rear, reverse side* **haimen**
背任 *breach-of-trust, betrayal* **hainin**
背理 *irrationality, absurdity* **hairi**
背信 *breach-of-faith, betrayal* **haishin**
背走 *running backwards* **haisō**
背徳 *immorality, vice* **haitoku**
違背 *offence, violation* **ihai**
光背 *halo* **kōhai**
猫背 *stoop* **nekoze**
背広 *business suit, ~attire* **sebiro**

背骨 *backbone, spinal column* **sebone**
背革 *leather back* **segawa**
背中 *body back* **senaka**
背筋 *back, spine* **sesuji**
背丈 *height, stature* **setake**
背番号 *uniform number* **sebangō**
背格好 *height, build* **sekakkō**
背伸び *overstretching, aiming too high* **senobi**
背負う *responsibility, burden* **seō**
背泳ぎ *backstroke swimming* **seoyogi**
背水の陣 *"one's last stand..."* **haisui no jin**

肩*houlder, 678*	首*ead, 311*
首*eck, 311*	胴*orso, 867*

皆*veryone, 39*

282-B

Cadaver's 背ack to face 北orth for luck...

北*orthern*

ヒ (spoon)

kita, HOKU
north

FLIP: 2.0.b. Sort Of (stem)

敗北 *defeat, losing* **haiboku**
北海 *north sea* **hokkai**
北光 *aurora lights* **hokkō**
北境 *northern boundary* **hokkyō**
北極 *North Pole, Arctic* **hokkyoku**
北米 *northern America* **hokubei**
北岸 *northern coast* **hokugan**
北限 *northern limit* **hokugen**
北緯 *north latitude* **hokui**
北欧 *north Europe, Scandinavia* **hokuō**
北西 *northwest* **hokusei**
北鮮 *North Korea* **hokuchō**
北進 *advancing north* **hokushin**
北空 *nothern skies* **hokuten, kitazora**
北洋 *northern seas* **hokuyō**
以北 *north* **ihoku**
華北 *northern China* **kahoku**
北側 *northern side* **kitagawa**
北風 *northern winds* **kitakaze**

真北 *directly facing north* **makita**
南北 *North-South (civil war)* **nanboku**
北京 *Beijing, Peking* **pekin**
台北 *Taipei, Taiwan* **taipei**
北上中 *proceeding north* **hokujōchū**
北朝鮮 *North Korea* **kita chōsen**
北向き *facing north* **kitamuki**
西北西 *west northwest* **seihokusei**
東北東 *east northeast* **tōhokutō**
北回帰線 *tropic of cancer* **kitakai kisen**
北枕で寝る *sleep facing north*
　　kitamakura de neru

南*outhern, 414*	西*estern, 18*
東*astern, 220*	方*irection, 533*

比*ompare, 466*

283-A

草*rass so curly to be cut* 早*-arly...*

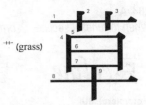

-艹- (grass)

草*rass*

kusa, SŌ
grass

FLIP: 1.0.b. Whole (stem)

青草 *young grass* **aokusa**
牧草 *grass, pasturage, hay* **bokusō**
毒草 *poisonous plant* **dokusō**
干し草 *dry grass, hay* **hoshikusa**
海草 *sea weeds* **kaisō**
枯れ草 *dry grass, hay* **karekusa**
草花 *flower, flowering plant* **kusabana**
草いきれ *grass smell* **kusaikire**
草刈り *lawn mowing* **kusakari**
草競馬 *amateur horse race* **kusakeiba**
草木 *plant, vegetation* **kusaki, sōmoku**
草の根 *grassroots level* **kusanone**
草取り *weeding-out* **kusatori**
草分け *pioneer, settler* **kusawake**
草野球 *amateur baseball, minor league* **kusayakyū**
草山 *grassy hills, grassy mountains* **kusayama**
夏草 *summer grass* **natsukusa**
桜草 *primrose* **sakurasō**
草案 *rough draft, draft plan* **sōan**

草原 *prairie, pampas, savannah* **sōgen**
草稿 *draft, manuscript* **sōkō**
草書 *cursive style* **sōsho**
草本 *manuscript; herbs* **sōhon**
煙草 *cigarette, tobacco* **tabako**
浮き草 *floating plants, duckweed* **ukikusa**
若草 *young grass* **wakakusa**
薬草 *wild grass, herb* **yakusō**
野草 *wild grass* **yasō**
雑草 *weeds* **zassō**
草履 *sandals* **zōri**

芝*awn, 84*	植*egetation, 783*
竹*amboo, 79*	培*ultivate, 698*
緑*reen, 841*	耕*ultivate, 655*

早*-arly.* 373

283-B

草*rass so curly to be cut* 早*-arly...*

日 (sunlight, daytime)

早*arly*   早*remature*

haya(i), haya(meru), SŌ, SA
early, premature, quick

FLIP: 1.0.b. Whole (stem)

足早 *fast-, brisk walker* **ashibaya**
早出 *attending early* **hayade**
早鐘 *alarm bell* **hayagane**
早死に *early death, die young* **hayaji(ni)**
早飯 *eating early* **hayameshi**
早道 *shortcut* **hayamichi**
早耳 *quick ears, good listener* **hayamimi**
早寝 *sleeping early* **hayane**
早業 *quick work, feat* **hayawaza**
口早 *quick tongue, fast talker* **kuchibaya**
早速 *right away, immediately* **sassoku**
尚早 *too early, premature* **shōsō**
早晩 *sooner-or-later, "one of these days..."* **sōban**
早朝 *early morning* **sōchō**
早暁 *dawn, daybreak* **sōgyō**
早計 *premature, hasty, rush* **sōkei**
早期 *early stage* **sōki**
早婚 *early marriage* **sōkon**
早急 *immediate, urgent, quick* **sōkyū**

早老 *premature ageing* **sōrō**
早世 *early death, short life, die young* **sōsei**
早退 *leaving early* **sōtai**
早産 *premature birth* **sōzan**
早稲 *early rice crop* **wase**
朝早く *early morning* **asahayaku**
早立ち *early start* **hayadachi**
早起き *early rising* **hayaoki**
早送り *fast forward* **hayaokuri**
早とちり *hasty, impulsive* **hayatochiri**
遅かれ早かれ *sooner-or-later* **osokare hayakare**

宵*arly evening, 264*	暁*aybreak, 818*
朝*orning, 662*	遅*ardy, 944*

 草*rass.* 373

284-A

When fortunes 衰ecline, 衰orrows incline...

衣⇔ネ (clothing)

衰ecline   衰egenerate

otoro(eru), SUI
decline, degenerate, decadence

FLIP: 3.0.a. Top (flat)

減衰 *decline, decadence* **gensui**
衰え *decline, failing* **otoroe**
老衰 *senility, feebleness, old age* **rōsui**
盛衰 *rise & fall, vicissitudes* **seisui**
⇒栄枯盛衰 *rise & fall, vicissitudes* **eiko seisui**
衰微 *decline, waning* **suibi**
衰亡 *decline, ruin* **suibō**
衰弱 *weakness, debility* **suijaku**
⇒神経衰弱 *nervous breakdown* **shinkei suijaku**
衰滅 *decline, extinction* **suimetsu**
衰勢 *decline, waning* **suisei**
衰退 *decline, decay* **suitai**
衰退期 *period of decadence* **suitaiki**
衰運 *declining-, falling fortune* **suiun**
衰残 *worn-out, emaciated* **suizan**

古*ither, 477*	陥*all-down, 893*
枯*ither, 960*	堕*all-down, 807*
減*ecrease, 46*	落*all-down, 826*
耗*essen, 655*	低*inimum, 700*

衷*nner feelings, 119*

284-B

When fortunes 衰ecline, 哀orrows incline...

口 (mouth)

哀orrows   哀adness

awa(re), awa(remu), kana(shii), AI
sorrows, sadness, melancholy

FLIP: 3.0.a. Top (flat)

哀れみ *pity, mercy* **awaremi**
哀れっぽい *plaintive, pleading* **awareppoi**
哀しみ *sorrow, grief, sadness* **kanashimi**
哀別 *sad farewell* **aibetsu**
哀調 *sentimental melody* **aichō**
哀願 *imploring, invoking* **aigan**
哀号 *whining, wailing, moaning* **aigō**
哀情 *sorrows, sadness* **aijō**
哀歌 *sorrowful song* **aika**
哀歓 *joys & sorrows* **aikan**
哀感 *sad feeling* **aikan**
哀哭 *mourning, wailing, grieving* **aikoku**
哀楽 *sorrow & happiness* **airaku**
⇒喜怒哀楽 *feelings, emotions, passions* **kido airaku**
哀憐 *compassion, mercy* **airen**
哀惜 *death sorrow, grief* **aiseki**
哀切 *pathos, pathetic story* **aisetsu**
哀史 *tragic history* **aishi**
哀詩 *elegy, pathetic poem* **aishi**

哀傷 *deep sorrows* **aishō**
哀愁 *grave-, deep sorrows* **aishū**
哀訴 *appeal, enjoin* **aiso**
哀悼 *condolence, sympathy* **aitō**
哀話 *pathetic story* **aiwa**
悲哀 *sorrow, grief, sadness* **hiai**
可哀相 *pitiful, poor, sad* **kawaisō**
物の哀れ *pathos-of-things* **mono no aware**

愁*orrows, 415*	惨*ragedy, 396*
悲*orrows, 289*	悲*ragedy, 289*
禍*ragedy, 799*	厄*ragedy, 354*

京*apital, 386*

285-A

索earch for 索ope found 糸hread instead...

糸 (thread, continuity)

❶索earch ❷索ope

SAKU
search, look-for, finding; rope

FLIP: 7.2.a. Right Top (flat)

❶ 軸索 axis cylinder **jikusaku**
繋索 moorings, anchorage **keisaku**
検索 search, reference **kensaku**
模索 grope, fumbling **mosaku**
索莫 bleak, desolate **sakubaku**
索具 rigging, implements **sakugu**
索引 index, reference, notes **sakuin**
索敵 enemy searching **sakuteki**
詮索 search, inquiry **sensaku**
思索 contemplation, meditation **shisaku**
捜索 search, manhunt **sōsaku**
総索引 general index **sōsakuin**
捜索状 search warrant **sōsakujō**
捜索隊 search party **sōsakutai**
探索 search, inquiry **tansaku**

❷ 鋼索 cable, wire rope **kōsaku**
索道 cable way, rope way **sakudō**
索条 cable, rope **sakujō**

鉄索 cable, wire rope **tessaku**

捜earch, 36	調nspection, 280
探earch, 787	検nspection, 939
討nvestigate, 691	査nspection, 624
察nspection, 328	閲nspection, 942
審nspection, 339	

素lement, 578

285-B

索earch for 索ope found 糸hread instead...

糸 (thread, continuity)

糸hread

ito, SHI
thread

Facing: 2.0. East ☞ (W)

抜糸 taking-out wound stitches **basshi**
一糸 a string **isshi**
糸口 beginning, clue **itoguchi**
糸車 spinning wheel **itoguruma**
糸巻 spool, reel **itomaki**
糸目 fine thread **itome**
糸底 bottom rim **itosoko**
糸杉 cypress **itosugi**
糸柳 weeping willow **itoyanagi**
毛糸 woollen yarn **keito**
生糸 raw silk **kiito**
金糸 golden thread **kinshi**
絹糸 silk thread **kinuito, kenshi**
綿糸 cotton **menshi**
道糸 fishing line **michiito**
縫糸 sewing thread **nuiito**
蚕糸 silk culture, silk raising **sanshi**
製糸 spinning, silk reeling **seishi**
縦糸 warp **tateito**

横糸 weft, woof **yokoito**
糸案内 thread guide **itoannai**
糸切れ thread breaks, thread strands **itogire**
糸入り silkpaper with cotton threads **itoiri**
糸押え thread presser **itoosae**
刺繍糸 embroidery thread **shishūito**
釣り糸 fishing line **tsuriito**
糸切り歯 eye-tooth, canine **itokiriba**

縫ewing, 779	衣lothes, 355
繰pinning, 851	裁lothes, 802
紡pinning, 735	服lothes, 734
布loth, 208	絹ilk, 158

糸escendants, 262

286-A

With respectful erses reside travel guides...

言 (speaking)

詞hrase   詞erse

SHI
phrase, verse, words

FLIP: 6.0.a. Left (flat)
FLIP: 8.0.a. Inner (flat)

分詞 *word participle* **bunshi**
動詞 *verb, action words* **dōshi**
副詞 *adverb* **fukushi**
賀詞 *congratulatory speech* **gashi**
品詞 *part of speech* **hinshi**
助詞 *word particle* **joshi**
序詞 *foreword, preface, prologue* **joshi**
冠詞 *word article* **kanshi**
⇒定冠詞 *definite word article* **teikanshi**
歌詞 *song lyrics, musical lyrics* **kashi**
詞書 *prefect, foreword* **kotobagaki**
祝詞 *congratulatory speech* **norito**
作詞 *lyrics writing, ~composition* **sakushi**
誓詞 *oath, pledge, vow* **seishi**
台詞 *words, one's line, ~part* **serifu**
詞宗 *laureate, literary master* **shishō**
詞章 *prose & poetry* **shishō**
賞詞 *praise, adulation* **shōshi**
祝詞 *congratulatory words* **shukushi**

名詞 *noun* **meishi**
⇒抽象名詞 *abstract noun* **chūshō meishi**
⇒普通名詞 *common noun* **futsū meishi**
訳詞 *lyrics translation* **yakushi**
疑問詞 *interrogative, question* **gimonshi**
自動詞 *intransitive verb* **jidōshi**
間投詞 *interjective word* **kantōshi**
詞華集 *anthology, selected works* **shikashū**
他動詞 *transitive verb* **tadōshi**
前置詞 *word preposition* **zenchishi**
捨て台詞 *parting shot* **sutezerifu**

言*ord*, 251	弁*peech*, 570
語*ord*, 780	句*hrase*, 16
文*iterature*, 558	

伺*nquire*, 101

286-B

With respectful 詞erses 司reside travel guides...

口 (mouth)

司dminister   司reside

SHI
administer, preside, officiate, control

FLIP: 8.0.a. Inner (flat)
Facing: 1.0. West (W)

宮司 *shrine chief priest* **gūji**
行司 *sumo referee* **gyōji**
上司 *one's boss, ~superior* **jōshi**
門司 *Moji City, Fukuoka* **moji**
祭司 *officiating priest* **saishi**
社司 *Shintō priest* **shashi**
司直 *judge, judiciary* **shichoku**
司法 *administration of justice* **shihō**
司法権 *judicial power, jurisdiction* **shihōken**
司会 *master of ceremonies, emcee* **shikai**
司教 *bishop, archbishop* **shikyō**
司教区 *diocese* **shikyōku**
司令 *command, order, instruction* **shirei**
司令部 *military headquarters* **shireibu**
司令部 *command, headquarters* **shireibu**
⇒軍司令部 *military headquarters* **gunshireibu**
司令官 *commander* **shireikan**
⇒総司令官 *supreme commander* **sōshireikan**
司祭 *priest, rabbi* **shisai**

司祭職 *priesthood, clergy vocation* **shisaishoku**
司書 *librarian* **shisho**
寿司 *fresh raw fish on rice cutlets* **sushi**
寿司屋 *sushi bar, sushi chef* **sushiya**
有司 *competent authorities, officials* **yūshi**
曹司 *children of noble family* **zōshi**
保護司 *probation officer* **hogoshi**
立行司 *head sumo referee* **tategyōji**
大司教 *Catholic cardinal* **daishikyō**
握り寿司 *Nigiri sushi* **nigirizushi**

掌*dminister*, 614	管*ontrol*, 917
轄*ontrol*, 968	導*uidance*, 312

同*like*, 245

287-A

Indian cooks 宰upervise blending of 辛pice...

宰*anage*   宰*upervise*

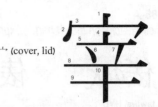

宀 (cover, lid)

SAI
manage, supervise, preside

宰領 *supervision, guidance* **sairyō**
宰相 *prime minister, premier* **saishō**
主宰 *presiding over* **shusai**
主宰者 *presiding chairperson* **shusaisha**
大宰府 *ancient headquarters in Kyūshū* **dazaifu**

FLIP: 1.0.b. Whole (stem)

旨*nstruct, 242*   導*uidance, 312*
領*overn, 874*   営*anagement, 580*

亭*estaurant, 393*

287-B

Indian cooks 宰upervise blending of 辛pice...

辛*picy*   辛*ungent*

辛 (bitter; spicy)

kara(i), tsura(i), SHIN
spicy, pungent, chilli, hot-taste, hardship

辛い *hard & tough* **tsurai**
激辛 *fiery hot, devil spice* **gekikara**
辛辛 *barely, merely* **karagara**
辛口 *salty taste; dry (beer)* **karakuchi**
辛目 *salty, saltiness* **karame**
辛味 *hot-, pungent-, spicy* **karami**
辛子 *mustard* **karashi**
辛党 *drinker* **karatō**
辛抱 *patience, perseverance* **shinbō**
辛抱強い *patient, persevering* **shinbōzuyoi**
辛気 *fretful, whining* **shinki**
辛気臭い *boring, dull, monotonous* **shinkikusai**
辛苦 *hardship, trials, pains* **shinku**
⇒粒粒辛苦 *perseverence, painstaking*
  ryūryū shinku
辛辣 *bitter, pungent* **shinratsu**
辛労 *toil, trouble, travails* **shinrō**
辛労 *hardship, trials, struggle* **shinrō**
辛酸 *hardship, trials, pains* **shinsan**

FLIP: 1.0.b. Whole (stem)

辛勝 *narrow victory, near defeat* **shinshō**
塩辛 *salted fish innards* **shiokara**
塩辛い *salty* **shiokarai**
甘辛い *salty & sweet* **amakarai**
唐辛子 *red pepper* **tōgarashi**
聞き辛い *unapproacable, aloof* **kikizurai**
香辛料 *spices & flavouring* **kōshinryō**
世知辛い *hard to live, ~get by* **sechigarai**
辛うじて *narrowly, barely, hardly* **karōjite**

塩*alt, 621*   味*aste, 871*
甘*weet, 395*   食*uisine, 255*

辛*appiness, 268*   音*ound, 314*

288-A

Rice 俵acks on the 表hart, 表xpressions of the heart...

人 ⇔ 亻 (person)

俵ack   **俵ushel**

tawara, HYŌ
sack, straw sack, bushel

FLIP: 7.2.a. Right Top (flat)

土俵 *sumo arena ring; sandbag* **dohyō**
⇒初土俵 *sumo wrestler's debut* **hatsudohyō**
土俵際 ① *brink of, critical moment* **dohyōgiwa**
土俵際 ② *edge of the ring* **dohyōgiwa**
土俵入り *sumo opening rituals* **dohyōiri**
俵数 *number of straw bags* **hyōsū**
一俵 *one sackload* **ippyō**
米俵 *sackload of rice* **komedawara**
桟俵 *straw lids of a sack* **sandawara**
炭俵 *sackload of charcoal* **sumidawara**
俵物 *products in a sack* **tawaramono**

袋*ack, 629*   粒*rains, 656*
穀*rains, 41*   収*ollect, 178*
穂*rains, 545*   倉*torage, 399*

情*ondition, 793*

288-B

Rice 俵acks on the 表hart, 表xpressions of the heart...

衣 ⇔ 衤 (clothing)

❶表xpression ❷表hart

omote, arawa(reru), arawa(su), HYŌ
expression, outlook, disposition, show up; chart, diagram, table, tabulation

FLIP: 3.0.a. Top (flat)

❶墓表 *grave marker* **bohyō**
表現 *expression* **hyōgen**
表具 *wall display, ~decorations* **hyōgu**
表示 *indicate, manifest* **hyōji**
表決 *decision, vote* **hyōketsu**
表記 *indication, symbol* **hyōki**
表明 *express, demonstrate* **hyōmei**
表面 *one's expression, complexion* **hyōmen**
表裏 *duplicity* **hyōri**
表彰 *award, commendation* **hyōshō**
意表 *beyond expectations* **ihyō**
辞表 *letter of resignation* **jihyō**
中表 *inside-out* **nakaomote**
表口 *front entrance, main gate* **omoteguchi**
裏表 *front & back side, pros & cons* **uraomote**
表玄関 *front door, main gate* **omotegenkan**
表向き *formality, protocol, outwardly* **omotemuki**
表敬訪問 *courtesy call, visit* **hyōkei hōmon**
表意文字 *ideograph, ideogram* **hyōi moji**

❷別表 *attached list* **beppyō**
表題 *headline, caption* **hyōdai**
表札 *nameplate, nametag* **hyōsatsu**
表紙 *book-, magazine cover* **hyōshi**
年表 *chronological list, chronology* **nenpyō**
時間表 *time chart, schedule* **jikanhyō**
値段表 *price list* **nedanhyō**
料金表 *tariff, price list* **ryōkinhyō**
正誤表 *list of errata* **seigohyō**
定価表 *price list* **teikahyō**
統計表 *statistical scale* **tōkeihyō**
通知表 *school record, ~transcript* **tsūchihyō**
座席表 *seating list, seating order* **zasekihyō**

顔*acial, 833*   姿*ppearance, 609*
面*urface, 36*   算*ompute, 141*

寿*ongevity, 440*

289-A
Stone 畝oof-ridge, 久ong-lasting indeed...

田 (cultivated field)

畝oof-ridge

se, une, BŌ
roof ridge

十畝 *about 10 acres* **jisse, jūsse**
畝間 *space between ridges* **unema**
畝溝 *furrow ridges* **unemizo**
畝織り *ribbed fabrics* **uneori**
畝立て *ridge building, furrowing* **unedate**

FLIP: 6.0.a. Left (flat)
Facing: 1.2. 🖙 West (V)

棟oof-ridge, 221
建uilding, 390
築onstruct, 907

敏lert, 434

289-B
Stone 畝oof-ridge, 久ong-lasting indeed...

丿 (katakana の)

久ternal   久ong-lasting

hisa(shii), KYŪ, KU
eternal, long-lasting, endless, immortal

久し振り *"a long time since then..."* **hisashiburi**
永久 *permanent, eternal* **eikyū**
永久歯 *permanent tooth* **eikyūshi**
久久 *long-awaited* **hisabisa**
持久 *endurance, perseverance* **jikyū**
持久戦 *war of attrition* **jikyūsen**
恒久 *permanence, everlasting* **kōkyū**
恒久化 *perpetuation* **kōkyūka**
恒久的 *permanent, everlasting* **kōkyūteki**
恒久平和 *eternal peace* **kōkyū heiwa**
久遠 *eternity, immortality* **kuon**
久闊 *failure to keep in touch* **kyūkatsu**
耐久 *durability, long lasting* **taikyū**
耐久力 *durability, endurance* **taikyūryoku**
耐久性 *durability, tenacity* **taikyūsei**
耐久戦 *war of attrition* **taikyūsen**
耐久寿命 *endurance, longevity* **taikyū jumyō**
悠久 *eternal, everlasting* **yūkyū**
半永久的 *semi-permanent* **han'eikyūteki**

Facing: 1.0. 🖙 West (W)

久留米市 *Kurume City, Fukuoka Pref.* **kurume-shi**
文久時代 *Bunkyū Era (1861-1864)* **bunkyū jidai**
長久時代 *Chōkyū Era (1040-1044)*
  chōkyū jidai
延久時代 *Enkyū Era (1069-1074)* **enkyū jidai**
元久時代 *Genkyū Era (1204-1206)*
  genkyū jidai
承久時代 *Jōkyū Era (1219-1222)* **jōkyū jidai**
健久時代 *Kenkyū Era (1190-1199)* **kenkyū jidai**
久安時代 *Kyūan Era (1145-1151)* **kyūan jidai**
久寿時代 *Kyūju Era (1154-1156)* **kyūju jidai**

長ong, 273   寿ongevity, 440
永ternal, 10   永ong-lasting, 10

勺[18ml], 470

290-A

御onorables don't wail missing a 卸holesale...

御[honorific]

彳 (stroll)

御

Facing: 4.0. 🔁☞ Apart

on, GYO, GO
[honorific]

姉御	boss wife; woman boss	**anego**
御幣	Shintō paper strips	**gohei**
御飯	boiled rice	**gohan**
御難	misfortune, adversity, tragedy	**gonan**
御覧	"look at, take a look..."	**goran**
御所	imperial palace	**gosho**
御殿	palace, court	**goten**
御用	business, order, request	**goyō**
御邸	imperial villa	**goyōtei**
御用始め	first business day of the year	**goyō hajime**
御用納め	last business day of the year	**goyō osame**
御意	your pleasure	**gyoi**
御者	driver, coachman	**gyosha**
御者台	driver's seat	**gyoshadai**
御門	emperor; palace gates	**mikado**
御霊	spirit of the dead	**mitama**
御萩	rice cake with bean jam	**ohagi**
御釜	homosexual; iron pot	**okama**
御社	your company, you	**onsha**

御大	boss, one's superior	**ontai**
御宅	you, your home (honorific)	**otaku**
制御	control, manage	**seigyo**
御馳走	dinner, treat	**gochisō**
御自身	you yourself (honorific)	**gojishin**
御両親	your parents	**goryōshin**
御成功	your success	**goseikō**
御存じ	know, aware of	**gozonji**
御影石	granite	**mikageishi**
御供え	offering, presentation	**osonae**
御転婆	high-spirited, boisterous	**otenba**

様[honorific], 944	尚espect, 99
恭espect, 620	崇espect, 879
仰espect, 706	礼espect, 685
謹espect, 962	敬espect, 329

卸holesale, 380

290-B

御onorables don't wail missing a 卸holesale...

卸holesale   卸n masse

卩 (joint; stamp)

卸

Facing: 2.2. East ☞ (V)

oro(su), oroshi
wholesale, gross, en masse

荷卸	unloading, discharge	**nioroshi**
卸値	wholesale price	**oroshine**
卸商	wholesaler	**oroshishō**
卸相場	wholesale market	**oroshi sōba**
棚卸し	inventory counting	**tanaoroshi**
卸し問屋	wholesale merchant	**oroshitonya**
卸し売り	wholesale	**oroshiuri**
卸し売り店	wholesale store	**oroshiuriten**
卸し売り市場	wholesale market	**oroshiuri shijō**

広arge, 205	業usiness, 124
市arket, 304	商usiness, 135
購urchase, 714	頒etail, 835
買urchase, 516	販elling, 137

御[honorific], 380

291-A

致*ring-about the* 至*tmost barbeque roast...*

至 (arriving)

致*arry-out*　　致*ring-about*

ita(su), CHI
carry-out, bring-about, do humbly, effectuate

FLIP: 6.2. Left Bottom
Facing: 3.0. ☞☜ **Across**

致死 *lethal, manslaughter* **chishi**
⇒過失致死 *involuntary manslaughter*
　　kashitsu chishi
⇒傷害致死 *death by beating* **shōgai chishi**
致仕 *resignation; 70 years old* **chishi**
風致 *scenic beauty* **fūchi**
合致 *agreement, consent, approval* **gachi**
雅致 *elegance, grace* **gacchi**
筆致 *writing style, penmanship* **hicchi**
一致 *agreement, consent, approval* **icchi**
⇒不一致 *inconsistency, incoherence* **fuicchi**
⇒挙国一致 *national unity* **kyokoku icchi**
⇒満場一致 *unanimity* **manjō icchi**
⇒霊肉一致 *"one body, one soul..."* **reiniku icchi**
⇒全会一致 *unanimity, collective decision*
　　zenkai icchi
一致点 *point of agreement* **icchiten**
引致 *taking into custody* **inchi**
韻致 *elegance, excellence* **inchi**

致す *perform, execute* **itasu**
極致 *the highest, the finest* **kyokuchi**
拉致 *abduction, taking into custody* **rachi**
拉致事件 *abduction case* **rachi jiken**
招致 *invitation, summons, subpoena* **shōchi**
送致 *sending to the police* **sōchi**
誘致 *attraction, invitation* **yūchi**
致死量 *lethal dose, deadly dosage* **chishiryō**
致命傷 *fatal wound, mortal injury* **chimeishō**
致命的 *fatal, mortal, deadly* **chimeiteki**
致し方 *ways & means* **itashikata**
致し方ない *"no other choice..."* **itashikatanai**

執*arry-out*, 268	践*ractice*, 671	達*each*, 267
行*erform*, 79	事*ction*, 116	守*bide*, 366

致*ring-about*, *381*

291-B

致*ring-about the* 至*tmost barbeque roast...*

至 (arriving)

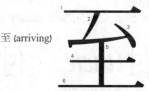

至*eading-to*　　至*tmost*

ita(ru), SHI
leading-to, come to, utmost

FLIP: 4.0.a. Bottom (flat)

夏至 *summer solstice* **geshi**
必至 *inevitable, unavoidable* **hisshi**
至便 *most convenient* **shiben**
至福 *supreme bliss, perfect happiness* **shifuku**
至芸 *masterpiece artwork* **shigei**
至言 *wise saying, famous proverb* **shigen**
至極 *extreme, excessive, ultimate* **shigoku**
至宝 *greatest treasure* **shihō**
至情 *genuine feelings* **shijō**
至上 *supreme, the highest* **shijō**
至上命令 *direct order from the top* **shijō meirei**
至近 *close range, point blank* **shikin**
至高 *supremacy, domination* **shikō**
至孝 *utmost filiality* **shikō**
至幸 *supreme bliss* **shikō**
至急 *immediately, without delay* **shikyū**
至妙 *extraordinarily fine* **shimyō**
至難 *utmost difficulty* **shinan**
至難の技 *utmost difficulty* **shinan no waza**

至楽 *utmost pleasure* **shiraku**
至論 *convincing argument* **shiron**
至誠 *extreme devotion* **shisei**
至心 *sincerity* **shishin**
至当 *reasonable, just* **shitō**
至要 *essential, paramount* **shiyō**
冬至 *winter solstice* **tōji**
至る所 *all over, everywhere* **itaru tokoro**
至公至平 *utterly just* **shikō shihei**
若げの至り *youthful inexperience* **wakage no itari**
至れり尽くせり *"more than satisfactory..."*
　　itareri tsukuseri

方*irection*, 533	窮*xtreme*, 876
端*ndpoint*, 974	極*xtreme*, 947
最*aximum*, 423	甚*xtreme*, 293

到*rrive*, *496*

292-A
The"B" in Kanji 附ttach, clearly 付ttached...

附*ttach*　　　附*elong*

阝⇔阜 (village=left)

tsu(keru), tsu(ku), FU
attach, belong, adjoin

Facing: 3.0. ☞☜ Across

附着	adherence, conformity **fuchaku**
附言	postscript, additional remarks **fugen**
附票	label **fuhyō**
附近	neighbourhood, vicinity **fukin**
附録	supplement, appendix, extra **furoku**
附箋	label, tag **fusen**
附則	supplementary rule **fusoku**
附帯	incidental, concomitant **futai**
附託	commitment, devotion **futaku**
附表	attached chart **fūhyō**
附票	label, tag **fūhyō**
附属	accessory, belonging to **fuzoku**
附属病院	affiliated hospital **fuzoku byōin**
附属学校	affiliated school **fuzoku gakkō**
附属書類	attached documents **fuzoku shorui**
附属図書館	affiliated library **fuzoku toshokan**
附図	attached chart **fuzu**
附随	accompany, detailed to **fuzui**
寄附	donation, contribution **kifu**

交附 *handing over, handover* **kōfu**
見附 *final approach to the castle* **mitsuke**
添附 *attaching, annexing* **tenpu**

付*ttach*, 382	伴*ccompany*, 949
随*ccompany*, 807	括*asten*, 954
添*ccompany*, 620	合*ogether*, 232

付*ttach*, 382

292-B
The"B" in Kanji 附ttach, clearly 付ttached...

付*ttach*　　　付*ppend*

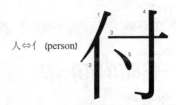

人⇔亻 (person)

tsu(ku), tsu(keru), FU
attach, append, belong, fasten, adjoining

Facing: 1.2. ☜ West (V)

付言	additional remarks **fugen**
付記	additional writing **fuki**
付近	surroundings, vicinity **fukin**
付属	affiliated, belonging to **fuzoku**
付随	accompanying, escorting **fuzui**
配付	distribution, delivery **haifu**
返付	returning, giving up **henpu**
日付	date **hizuke**
還付	return, give up **kanpu**
給付	benefit, payment, provisions **kyūfu**
納付	payment, delivery **nōfu**
送付	sending, remittance **sōfu**
添付	annex, appending **tenpu**
味付け	seasoning, flavouring **ajitsuke**
家付き	heir, heiress **ietsuki**
感付く	feel, sense **kanzuku**
寄付金	cash donation, donated money **kifukin**
根付く	take root, rooting **nezuku**
受け付	registration counter **uketsuke**

組み伏せ *holding, grappling down* **kumifuse**
目に付く *lock into one's eyes* **menitsuku**
燃え付く *catch fire* **moetsuku**
結び付き *connexion, link* **musubitsuki**
付け足す *addition, supplement* **tsuketasu**
付き合い *acquaintance, love relationship* **tsukiai**
付き添い *escort, chaperon, usher* **tsukisoi**
付け替える *change, replace* **tsukekaeru**
付け込む *take advantage of* **tsukekomu**
付け回す *follow around, tail* **tsukemawasu**
付け落とし *omission, deletion* **tsukeotoshi**

附*ttach*, 382	伴*ccompany*, 949
随*ccompany*, 807	括*asten*, 954
添*ccompany*, 620	合*ogether*, 232

代*poch*, 96

293-A

透 *ransparency of cash reserves, accounting* 秀 *uperb...*

辶 (transport)

透 *ransparent* 透 *ranslucent*

su(ku), su(kasu), su(keru), too(shi), too(ru), TŌ
transparent, translucent, pass thru

Facing: 1.1. 🔄 West (H)

透ける *transparent, clarity* **sukeru**
透かし絵 *transparent drawing* **sukashie**
透き間 *crevice, gap, opening, space* **sukima**
透き見 *steal a glance, peep* **sukimi**
透き通る *become transparent* **sukitooru**
滲透 *permeation, infiltration, osmosis* **shintō**
浸透 *permeation, infiltration* **shintō**
透過 *permeation, penetration* **tōka**
透明 *transparency, translucence* **tōmei**
透明度 *transparency degree, translucence* **tōmeido**
透明人間 *invisible person* **tōmei ningen**
透察 *insight, impression* **tōsatsu**
透析 *kidney dialysis* **tōseki**
透写 *tracing, sketching* **tōsha**
透視 *clairvoyance, extra-sensory* **tōshi**
透視画法 *prototype drawing* **tōshi gahō**
透視力 *clairvoyant power* **tōshiryoku**
透水 *water permeability* **tōsui**
透徹 *clarity, permeation* **tōtetsu**

不透明 *opaque, unclear, vague* **futōmei**
浸透圧 *osmotic pressure* **shintōatsu**
素透し *transparent* **sudooshi**
手透き *leisure time, idle time* **tesuki**
透磁率 *magnetic permeability* **tōjiritsu**
明け透け *frank, straightforward* **akesuke**
肩透かし *dodge, duck* **katasukashi**
見え透く *obvious, transparent* **miesuku**
見え透く *transparent, translucent* **miesuku**
染み透る *impress, sink deep* **shimitooru**
透かし彫り *openwork* **sukashibori**

明 *lear, 22*	晴 *lear-up, 792*
朗 *lear, 800*	澄 *ake clear, 437*

逓 *onvey, 304*

293-B

透 *ransparency of cash reserves, accounting* 秀 *uperb...*

禾 (tree branch)

秀 *uperb* 秀 *xcellence*

hii(deru), SHŪ
superb, excellence, superiority

Facing: 1.1. 🔄 West (H)

閨秀 *successful woman* **keishū**
閨秀作家 *successful female novelist* **keishū sakka**
秀抜 *excellent work* **shūbatsu**
秀吟 *excellent haiku* **shūgin**
秀逸 *excellence, superiority* **shūitsu**
秀歌 *excellent poem* **shūka**
秀句 *wisecrack, quip, witty remark* **shūku**
俊秀 *genius, prodigy* **shunshū**
秀麗 *graceful, beautiful, elegant* **shūrei**
⇒眉目秀麗 *good-looking face* **bimoku shūrei**
秀才 *brilliant-, talented person* **shūsai**
秀作 *excellent work* **shūsaku**
優秀 *excellent, outstanding* **yūshū**
最優秀 *the very best, the finest* **saiyūshū**

傑 *xcellence, 921*	妙 *uperb, 726*
優 *xcellence, 556*	最 *aximum, 423*
偉 *minent, 797*	

香 *ragrance, 895*

294-A
据*et-in-place*, 居*esidential space...*

据*et-in-place*　据*nstall*

手⇔扌 (hand, manual)

su(eru), su(waru), KYO
set-in-place, install, situate

据え膳 *reserved meal* **suezen**
据え風呂 *bathtub with water heater* **suefuro**
据え置き *deferment, postponement* **sueoki**
据え置き期間 *period of deferment* **sueoki kikan**
据え置く *defer, postpone, delay* **sueoku**
据え付け *installation* **suetsuke**
据え付け工事 *installation works* **suetsuke kōji**
拮据 *hard work, diligence* **kikkyo**
見据える *look hard, gaze at* **misueru**
腹を据える *decide, make-up one's mind* **hara o sueru**
打ち据える *whip (horse)* **uchisueru**
睨み据える *glare at* **niramisueru**

FLIP: 7.3.a. Right Bottom (flat)
Facing: 4.0. ⟲⟳ Apart

置*ut-on, 420*	存*xist, 634*
居*xist, 384*	有*xist, 617*
在*xist, 634*	占*ccupy, 223*

握*rasp, 427*

294-B
据*et-in-place*, 居*esidential space...*

居*esidence*　居*xist*

尸 (corpse)

i(ru), KYO
residence, exist, housing, staying, shelter

別居 *husband & wife residing apart* **bekkyo**
同居 *living together* **dōkyo**
群居 *live gregariously* **gunkyo**
居所 *whereabouts, address* **idokoro**
居間 *living-, sitting room* **ima**
隠居 *retirement, retired lifestyle* **inkyo**
居候 *parasite, freeloader* **isōrō**
住居 *residence, domicile, dwelling* **jūkyo**
閑居 *quiet-, retired life* **kankyo**
穴居 *cave dwelling* **kekkyo**
皇居 *imperial palace* **kōkyo**
居住 *residence, domicile, dwelling* **kyojū**
旧居 *one's former house* **kyūkyo**
長居 *overstaying one's visit* **nagai**
仲居 *waitress* **nakai**
入居 *moving into a house* **nyūkyo**
芝居 *play, drama* **shibai**
⇒道化芝居 *fraudulent, bogus, phoney* **dōke shibai**
敷居 *threshold, door sills* **shikii**

FLIP: 4.0.a. Bottom (flat)

転居 *change of residence* **tenkyo**
鳥居 *shrine gate* **torii**
雑居 *multi-families living in one house* **zakkyo**
居心地 *snug, cozy, comfortable* **igokochi**
居直る *make a threatening look* **inaoru**
居眠り *dozing off, falling asleep* **inemuri**
居残る *remain behind* **inokoru**
居座る *stay, settle down* **isuwaru**
居着く *stay on, settle down* **itsuku**
居酒屋 *bar, tavern, pub, saloon* **izakaya**
紙芝居 *picture-story show* **kamishibai**

軒*[houses], 710*	邸*esidence, 860*
住*esidence, 750*	在*taying, 634*
宅*esidence, 82*	

局*ureau, 573*

295-A

教eachings on 孝ilial-obedience take 教eligious precedence...

父 (action)

❶教ducate ❷教eligion

oshi(eru), oso(waru), KYŌ
educate, inculcate, teaching; religion

FLIP: 7.1. Right (Sort Of)
Facing: 1.2. ☞ West (V)

❶教案 *lesson plan, teaching plan* **kyōan**
教育 *education* **kyōiku**
教員 *faculty staff, educator, academe* **kyōin**
教授 *university professor* **kyōju**
教訓 *moral lesson, moral story* **kyōkun**
教師 *teacher, instructor* **kyōshi**
教職 *faculty staff, educator, academe* **kyōshoku**
教卓 *teacher's classroom desk* **kyōtaku**
教程 *school curriculum* **kyōtei**
教諭 *teacher (pre-university teacher)* **kyōyu**
教材 *teaching materials* **kyōzai**
教科書 *school textbook* **kyōkasho**
❷仏教 *Buddhism* **bukkyō**
調教 *training* **chōkyō**
布教 *propagation, missionary work* **fukyō**
異教 *paganism, heathenism* **ikyō**
教会 *church* **kyōkai**
邪教 *heretical religion, blasphemy* **jakyō**
儒教 *Confucianism* **jukyō**

殉教 *martyrdom, sacrificial death* **junkyō**
回教 *Islam, Moslem, Muslim* **kaikyō**
旧教 *Catholic church, Catholicism* **kyūkyō**
政教 *religion & politics* **seikyō**
説教 *sermon, preaching* **sekkyō**
説教師 *preacher, pastor* **sekkyōshi**
司教 *bishop, archbishop* **shikyō**
信教 *religion, faith, religious belief* **shinkyō**
新教 *Protestantism* **shinkyō**
宗教 *religion, faith, religious belief* **shūkyō**
清教徒 *Puritan* **seikyōto**
宣教師 *missionary* **senkyōshi**

習earning, 238	講ecture, 226
修aster, 898	徒isciple, 497

赦orgive, 262

295-B

教eachings on 孝ilial-obedience take 教eligious precedence...

子 (child)

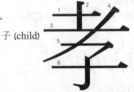

孝ilial 孝arental love

KŌ
filial, parental love

Facing: 1.1. ☞ West (H)

忠孝 *filial piety, ~obedience* **chūkō**
不孝 *unfilial-, ungrateful child* **fukō**
孝道 *filial obedience* **kōdō**
孝女 *devoted daughter* **kōjo**
孝順 *filial obedience* **kōjun**
孝行 *filial duty* **kōkō**
孝子 *Confucius; filial child* **kōshi**
孝心 *filial love* **kōshin**
孝養 *duties to one's parents* **kōyō**
至孝 *utmost filial piety* **shikō**
親不孝 *unfilial-, ungrateful child* **oyafukō**
親孝行 *filial obedience* **oyakōkō**

親arent, 669	幼hildhood, 88
父ather, 467	子hild, 456
母other, 90	童hild, 564
児hild, 464	懇ntimacy, 164
稚hild, 776	徳irtue, 844

考hinking, 392

296-A
涼ool-winds in the 京apital of Montreal...

涼ool-temperature

suzu(shii), suzu(mu), RYŌ
cool temperature

涼み台 *bench for evening-cool strollers* **suzumidai**
涼み客 *evening-cool strollers* **suzumi kyaku**
朝涼 *morning breeze* **asasuzumi**
晩涼 *evening breeze* **banryō**
荒涼 *bleak, desolate, deserted* **kōryō**
納涼 *cool breeze, balmy wind* **nōryō**
冷涼 *coolness* **reiryō**
涼風 *cool breeze* **ryōfū**
涼感 *cool feeling, ~look* **ryōkan**
涼気 *cool air, balmy wind* **ryōki**
涼味 *coolness* **ryōmi**
涼秋 *cool autumn; September* **ryōshū**
涼雨 *cooling rain* **ryōu**
清涼 *cool, refreshing* **seiryō**
清涼飲料 *carbonated beverage* **seiryō inryō**
夕涼み *evening breeze* **yūsuzumi**

水 ⇔ 氵 (water)

FLIP: 7.0.b1. Right (stem)

寒hilly, 121	冬inter, 397
冷hilly, 684	氷ce, 10

涼ool-temperature, 386

296-B
涼ool winds in the 京apital of Montreal...

京apital

KYŌ, KEI
capital

中京 *Nagoya City* **chūkyō**
英京 *London, England* **eikyō**
上京 *going to Tōkyō* **jōkyō**
京浜 *Tōkyō & Yokohama* **keihin**
京城 *Seoul, Korea* **keijō**
帰京 *return to Tōkyō* **kikyō**
京都 *Kyōto City* **kyōto**
南京 *Nanjing, China* **nankin**
南京袋 *gunny sacks* **nankinbukuro**
南京錠 *padlock* **nankinjō**
南京虫 *bedbug* **nankinmushi**
北京 *Beijing, Peking* **pekin**
北京原人 *Peking man* **pekin genjin**
北京語 *Mandarin language* **pekingo**
離京 *leaving Tōkyō* **rikyō**
西京 *Western capital* **saikyō**
滞京 *staying in Tōkyō* **taikyō**
退京 *leaving Tōkyō* **taikyō**
帝京 *capital where the emperor lives* **teikyō**

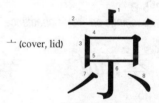

一 (cover, lid)

FLIP: 1.0.b. Whole (stem)

東京 *Tōkyō City* **tōkyō**
東京都 *Tōkyō metropolitan government* **tōkyōto**
在京 *staying in Tōkyō* **zaikyō**
平安京 *ancient Kyōto* **heiankyō**
平城京 *ancient Nara* **heijōkyō**

都etropolis, 694	府overnment, 429
市ity, 304	業usiness, 124
街istrict, 107	商usiness, 135
区istrict, 80	皇mperor, 113

哀orrows, 374

297-A

For athletes' 脚egs, 却ithdraw ham & eggs...

肉⇔月 (flesh, body part)

脚*eg*　　　　脚*ppendage*

ashi, KYAKU, KYA
leg, appendage

FLIP: 8.0.a. Inner (flat)
Facing: 2.2. East ☞ (V)

雨脚 *rain density* **amaashi**
行脚 *travelling on foot* **angya**
脚荷 *cargo ballast* **ashini**
後脚 *hind legs* **atoashi**
馬脚 *horse legs; true intent* **bakyaku**
火脚 *encroaching fire* **hiashi**
日脚 *long days, long wait* **hiashi**
飛脚 *express messenger* **hikyaku**
開脚 *legs astride* **kaikyaku**
脚気 *beriberi, vitamin b deficiency* **kakke**
健脚 *good walker, brisk walker* **kenkyaku**
脚絆 *gaiters, leggings* **kyahan**
脚半 *leggings, gaiters* **kyahan**
脚下 *at one's heels, ~feet* **kyakka**
脚光 *footlights, spotlight, limelight* **kyakkō**
脚注 *footnote, endnote* **kyakuchū**
脚本 *play, drama, scenario* **kyakuhon**
脚本家 *playwright, scriptwriter* **kyakuhonka**
脚韻 *word rhyme* **kyakuin**

脚力 *foot power, walking ability* **kyakuryoku**
脚色 *portrayal, depiction* **kyakushoku**
脚立 *stepladder* **kyatatsu**
橋脚 *bridge pier* **kyōkyaku**
立脚 *based on* **rikkyaku**
立脚点 *standpoint, viewpoint* **rikkyakuten**
三脚 *tripod, object with 3 legs* **sankyaku**
失脚 *out-balance, downfall* **shikkyaku**
鉄脚 *iron legs* **tekkyaku**
脚線美 *beautiful legs* **kyakusenbi**
両脚規 *artist's compass* **ryōkyakuki**

足*eg, 481*	交*rossing, 467*
歩*alk, 272*	行*rip, 79*
往*ome & go, 749*	通*assing, 59*

勝*ictory, 406*

297-B

For athletes' 脚egs, 却ithdraw ham & eggs...

卩 (joint; stamp)

却*ithdraw*　　　　却*etreat*

kae(tte), KYAKU
withdraw, retreat, eliminate, disengage

FLIP: 6.1. Left Top
Facing: 2.2. East ☞ (V)

却って *"all the more, rather..."* **kaette**
売却 *sale, selling* **baikyaku**
売却済み *"already sold..."* **baikyakuzumi**
没却 *disregard, belittle, ignore* **bokkyaku**
忘却 *oblivion, forgetfulness* **bōkyaku**
脱却 *breakaway, getting rid of* **dakkyaku**
廃却 *scrapping, disposal, discarding* **haikyaku**
返却 *return, repayment* **henkyaku**
除却 *exclusion, elimination* **jokyaku**
閑却 *negligence, oversight* **kankyaku**
過冷却 *super-cooling* **kareikyaku**
棄却 *rejection, dismissal* **kikyaku**
困却 *distress, predicament* **konkyaku**
却下 *dismissal, rejection* **kyakka**
冷却 *cooling, refrigeration* **reikyaku**
冷却器 *refrigerator, freezer, car radiator* **reikyakuki**
消却 *erasure, deletion* **shōkyaku**
償却 *repayment, refund* **shōkyaku**

⇒減価償却 *price depreciation, deflation*
　genka shōkyaku
焼却 *burning up, incineration* **shōkyaku**
退却 *retreat, withdrawal, retirement*
　taikyaku
⇒総退却 *general retreat* **sōtaikyaku**
却部 *table legs* **kyakubu**

引|*xtract, 348*	撤*ithdraw, 843*
抽*xtract, 37*	罷*ithdraw, 322*
摘*luck, 800*	還*eturn, 165*
退*ithdraw, 770*	返*eturn, 537*

脚*egs, 387*

298-A

捨*hrown in a jail* 舍*uarter, a well-known reporter...

手⇔扌 (hand, manual)

捨*hrow-away*   捨*hrow-out*

su(teru), SHA

throw-away, throw-out, thrashing, discard, get rid of, thrashing

FLIP: 7.O.a. Right (flat)

捨て鉢 *despair, desperation* **sutebachi**
捨て所 *place to kill oneself* **sutedokoro**
捨て金 *wasted money* **sutegane**
捨て子 *abandoned child* **sutego**
捨て石 *sacrifice, victim* **suteishi**
捨て値 *sacrificial price* **sutene**
捨て置く *leave alone, overlook* **suteoku**
捨て台詞 *parting shot* **suteserifu**
捨て売り *sacrifice sale, fire sale* **suteuri**
捨て書き *splattered writing* **sutegaki**
用捨 *adoption-or-rejection* **yōsha**
喜捨 *alms-giving, charity* **kisha**
捨象 *abstraction, conceptual* **shashō**
捨身① *risking one's life for others* **sutemi**
捨身② *enter monkhood* **shashin**
取捨 *adoption-or-rejection* **shusha**
掛け捨て *default on instalment* **kakezute**
聞き捨て *inexcusable, unpardonable* **kikisute**
見捨てる *abandon, desert, forsake* **misuteru**

四捨五入 *rounding off numbers* **shisha gonyū**
呼び捨て *not using "-san" for a person* **yobisute**
世捨て人 *reclusive, hermit* **yosutebito**
振り捨てる *abandon, desert* **furisuteru**
掃き捨てる *sweep away* **hakisuteru**
言い捨てる *say with anger, spit out* **iisuteru**
書き捨てる *write & throw away* **kakisuteru**
切り捨てる *discard, omit, cut-down* **kirisuteru**
投げ捨てる *throw away, discard* **nagesuteru**
脱ぎ捨てる *throw-, cast-, kick off* **nugisuteru**
焼き捨てる *burn, throw into the fire* **yakisuteru**

投*hrow, 745*	排*ejection, 795*
拾*hck up, 231*	断*ejection, 958*
斥*ejection, 424*	否*ejection, 300*

拾*ick-up, 231*

298-B

捨*hrown in a jail* 舍*uarter, a well-known reporter...

人⇔亻 (person)

舍*uarters*

SHA

quarters, building

FLIP: 1.O.a. Whole (flat)

牧舍 *cattle shed, cow barn* **bokusha**
病舍 *hospital ward, infirmary* **byōsha**
畜舍 *cattle shed, cow barn* **chikusha**
庁舍 *government building* **chōsha**
営舍 *barracks, garrison* **eisha**
駅舍 *small train station* **ekisha**
学舍 *school house* **gakusha**
獄舍 *prison house* **gokusha**
牛舍 *cattle shed, cow barn* **gyūsha**
兵舍 *barracks, garrison* **heisha**
田舍 *countryside, rural* **inaka**
田舍育ち *countryside-bred* **inaka sodachi**
官舍 *official residence* **kansha**
鶏舍 *poultry house, chicken barn* **keisha**
犬舍 *dog house* **kensha**
校舍 *school house* **kōsha**
公舍 *official residence* **kōsha**
客舍 *hotel, inn* **kyakusha**
旅舍 *hotel, inn* **ryosha**

寮舍 *dormitory, boarding house* **ryōsha**
舍営 *quarters, dwelling* **shaei**
舍監 *dormitory superintendent* **shakan**
舍利 *Buddhist bone's* **shari**
舍宅 *house, dwelling* **shataku**
舍弟 *one's younger brother* **shatei**
精舍 *monastery, convent* **shōja**
宿舍 *lodgings, hotel accommodation* **shukusha**
片田舍 *"end of the world place..."* **katainaka**
市庁舍 *townhall office* **shichōsha**

庫*torage, 306*	蔵*torage, 565*
倉*torage, 399*	貯*torage, 967*

金*etal, 25*

299-A

No 悪vils among 亜sian eels...

心 ⇔ 忄 (heart, feelings)

悪*vil* 悪*alice*

FLIP: 3.0.a. Top (flat)

waru(i), AKU, O
evil, malice, worsen

悪化 *deterioration, aggravation* **akka**
悪漢 *villain, bad guy* **akkan**
悪文 *poor penmanship, ~illegible writing* **akubun**
悪道 *evil way* **akudō**
悪疫 *plague, disaster, calamity* **akueki**
悪意 *ill will, malice* **akui**
悪魔 *devil, Satan, Lucifer* **akuma**
悪運 *bad luck, ill fortunate* **akuun**
悪例 *bad example, ~precedent* **akurei**
悪徳 *immorality, vice* **akutoku**
悪友 *undesirable friend; real friend* **akuyū**
害悪 *evil-, harmful influence* **gaiaku**
悪戯 *mischief, prank* **itazura**
改悪 *change for the worse, deterioration* **kaiaku**
奸悪 *wicked-, crook person* **kan'aku**
凶悪 *heinous, atrocious, barbarity, horrendous* **kyōaku**
悪寒 *chills, bad cold* **okan**
劣悪 *poor, inferiority, mediocrity* **retsuaku**

最悪 *"in the worst case, worst of all..."* **saiaku**
粗悪 *inferior, coarse, crude* **soaku**
悪気 *malice, ill will, evil intent* **warugi**
罪悪 *sin, crime, guilt* **zaiaku**
善悪 *good & evil, right & wrong* **zen'aku**
憎悪 *abhorrence, aversion* **zōo**
悪影響 *bad influence* **akueikyō**
極悪人 *devil, fiend* **gokuakunin**
必要悪 *necessary evil* **hitsuyōaku**
社会悪 *social evil, ~cancer* **shakaiaku**
悪賢い *wily, cunning, crafty* **warugashikoi**
悪酔い *"sick & tired of drinking..."* **waruyoi**

罪*riminal, 289*	鬼*evil, 935*	虐*trocity, 870*
犯*riminal, 640*	魔*evil, 332*	酷*trocity, 266*

亜*sia, 389*

299-B

No 悪vils among 亜sian eels...

二 (two, second)

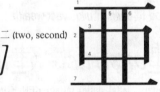

sia ²亜*honetic [a]*

A
Asia; phonetic [A]

FLIP: 1.0.a. Whole (flat)

❶東亜 *Far East, East Asia* **tōa**
亜細亜 *Asia* **ajia**
大東亜 *Greater East Asia* **daitōa**
露西亜 *Russia* **roshia**
亜米利加 *America* **amerika**

❷亜鉛化 *zinc oxide* **aenka**
亜鉛メッキ *zinc plating* **aenmekki**
亜科 *sub-order* **aka**
亜麻 *flax* **ama**
亜麻仁 *linseed* **amani**
亜麻布 *linen* **amanuno**
亜麻製 *flaxen, linen* **amasei**
亜鈴 *dumbbells* **arei**
亜流 *imitation, phoney* **aryū**
亜種 *sub specie* **ashu**
亜炭 *lignite* **atan**
亜炭化物 *subcarbide* **atan kabutsu**
亜族 *tribe branch* **azoku**

白亜 *white chalk; white wall* **hakua**
白亜紀 *Cretaceous period* **hakuaki**
亜砒酸 *arsenic acid* **ahisan**
亜寒帯 *sub-arctic-, sub-antarctic zone* **akantai**
亜熱帯 *subtropical-, semi-tropical zone* **anettai**
亜音速 *subsonic speed* **aonsoku**
亜燐酸 *phosphorous acid* **arinsan**
亜硫酸 *sulphurous acid* **aryūsan**
亜硝酸 *nitrous acid* **ashōsan**
亜大陸 *subcontinent* **atairiku**

次*ext, 460*	中*hina, 85*
順*equence, 959*	華*hina, 40*
第*[order], 102*	日*apan, 14*
号*umber, 866*	東*astern, 220*

悪*vil, 389*

300-A
Good 健ealth 建uilds vast wealth...

人⇔イ (person)

健ealthy   健obust

ta(teru), ta(tsu), suko(yaka), KEN, KON
healthy, robust, sturdy

FLIP: 7.2.b. Right Top (stem)
Facing: 1.2. ☜ West (V)

健やかさ *healthiness, soundness* **sukoyakasa**
頑健 *robust physique, ~build* **ganken**
剛健 *sturdiness, robustness* **gōken**
保健 *healthcare, health upkeep* **hoken**
健気 *diligent, admirable, laudable* **ken'age**
健忘 *oblivious, short memory* **kenbō**
健忘症 *forgetfulness, absent-minded* **kenbōshō**
健児 *vigorous youth* **kenji**
健康 *health, well-being* **kenkō**
健康美 *beauty of health* **kenkōbi**
健康体 *healthy body* **kenkōtai**
健康保険 *health insurance* **kenkō hoken**
健康状態 *health condition* **kenkō jōtai**
健康診断 *physical check-up, medical exam*
    kenkō shindan
健脚 *strong legs* **kenkyaku**
健筆 *good-, prolific writer* **kenpitsu**
健勝 *good health* **kenshō**
健闘 *good fight* **kentō**

健在 *fine & healthy* **kenzai**
健全 *perfect health, sound health* **kenzen**
強健 *strong health* **kyōken**
穏健 *moderate, sound* **onken**
穏健派 *moderates* **onkenha**
壮健 *healthy, robust physique* **sōken**
勇健 *sound health, robust* **yūken**
不健康 *unhealthy* **fukenkō**
健胃剤 *stomach medicine* **ken'izai**
世界保健機構 *World Health Organization*
    sekai hoken kikō

力*trength, 351*	勢*igour, 153*	丈*obust, 463*
康*ealthy, 881*	精*igour, 792*	剛*trong, 975*
康*obust, 881*	強*trong, 894*	

建*uilding, 390*

300-B
Good 健ealth 建uilds vast wealth...

廴 (stretch)

建onstruct   建uilding

ta(teru), ta(te), da(te), ta(tsu), KEN, KON
construct, building, edifice, structure

FLIP: 7.1. Right (Sort Of)
Facing: 1.2. ☜ West (V)

建具 *fittings, equipment, tools* **tategu**
建値 *market-, price quotation* **tatene**
建坪 *floor space* **tatetsubo**
円建て *price in Japanese yen* **endate**
建て前 *theory, principle, pretext* **tatemae**
建て網 *fish trap net* **tateami**
仮建築 *temporary construction (pre-fab)*
    karikenchiku
建て増し *extension of a building* **tatemashi**
建て直し *reconstruction, restoration* **tatenaoshi**
建て売り *build & sell* **tateuri**
建て売り住宅 *newly-built house for sale*
    tateuri jūtaku
建て掛け *half-built* **tatekake**
土建 *building, structure* **doken**
封建 *feudalism, vassalage* **hōken**
建築 *architecture, building design* **kenchiku**
⇒防火建築 *fireproof building* **bōka kenchiku**
建築家 *architect* **kenchikuka**

建議 *proposal, suggestion* **kengi**
建議書 *recommendation in writing* **kengisho**
建軍 *establishment of the armed forces* **kengun**
建国 *founding of a nation* **kenkoku**
建国記念日 *National Foundation Day*
    (11 February) **kenkoku kinenbi**
建白 *petition, appeal* **kenpaku**
建設 *construction* **kensetsu**
建材 *construction-, building materials* **kenzai**
建造 *building, construction* **kenzō**
建立 *erection, building* **konryū**
再建 *reconstruction, rebuilding* **saiken**
二本建て *dual system, double standard* **nihondate**
建て替える *rebuild, reconstruct* **tatekaeru**

立*uild, 234*	起*rise, 754*	築*rchitect, 907*

津*arbour, 731*

301--A

Earth 圏*phere* 巻*rapped, in Ozone trap...*

□ (enclosure)

FLIP: 8.0.b. Inner (stem)

KEN

sphere, circle, bloc, orbit

圏外 *outside the sphere* **kengai**
圏内 *within the sphere* **kennai**
気圏 *atmosphere* **kiken**
大圏 *large sphere, big circle* **taiken**
暴風圏 *storm-ravaged area* **bōfūken**
文化圏 *cultural sphere* **bunkaken**
電離圏 *ionosphere* **denriken**
英語圏 *English-speaking nations* **eigoken**
北極圏 *Arctic Circle* **hokkyokuken**
磁気圏 *magnetosphere* **jikiken**
共産圏 *communist bloc* **kyōsanken**
共栄圏 *co-prosperity sphere* **kyōeiken**
南極圏 *antarctic circle, ~zone* **nankyokuken**
生物圏 *biosphere* **seibutsuken**
成層圏 *stratosphere* **seisōken**
首都圏 *metropolitan area* **shutoken**
台風圏 *typhoon-ravaged area* **taifūken**
大東亜共栄圏 *Greater East Asia Co-Prosperity Sphere*
   daitōa kyōeiken

囲*nclose, 361*	盟*lliance, 21*
限*imit, 771*	連*lliance, 305*
球*phere, 257*	同*imilar, 245*
玉*phere, 11*	

巻*oll-up, 391*

301-B

Earth 圏*phere* 巻*rapped, in Ozone trap...*

巻*oll-up*　　巻*oiling*

己 (self)

maki, ma(ku), KAN

roll-up, coiling, volume

FLIP: 3.0.b. Top (stem)

圧巻 *highlight* **akkan**
葉巻 *cigar* **hamaki**
腹巻 *belly band* **haramaki**
補巻 *supplementary volume* **hokan**
一巻 *one reel, one roll* **ikkan**
糸巻 *spool, reel* **itomaki**
巻尾 *book appendix, ~reference* **kanbi**
巻雲 *cirrus* **ken'un**
巻紙 *rolled paper sheet* **makigami**
寝巻 *bedclothes, pyjamas* **nemaki**
席巻 *sweep over enemy lines* **sekken**
渦巻 *spiral, coiled, scrolled* **uzumaki**
全巻 *whole volume, ~reel* **zenkan**
絵巻物 *picture scroll* **emakimono**
襟巻き *muffler, scarf* **erimaki**
鉢巻き *headband* **hachimaki**
春巻き *egg roll, spring roll* **harumaki**
息巻く *argue furiously* **ikimaku**
巻き毛 *ringlet, curled hair* **makige**

巻き尺 *tape measure* **makijaku**
逆巻く *rage, surge, roll* **sakamaku**
遠巻き *encircle from a distance* **toomaki**
巻き返し *rollback, rolling back* **makikaeshi**
巻き込む *implicate, drag, embroil* **makikomu**
巻き戻し *tape rewinding* **makimodoshi**
巻き物 *roll, scroll* **makimono**
巻き取る *reel, rewind* **makitoru**
巻き添え *complexity, quagmire* **makizoe**
巻き付ける *wind, coil* **makitsukeru**
巻き上げる *cheat, roll up, swindle* **makiageru**
一巻の終り *be finished* **ikkan no owari**
太巻き *thick sushi roll* **futomaki**
鉄火巻き *tuna sushi roll* **tekkamaki**
かっぱ巻き *cucumber sushi roll* **kappamaki**

包*rapping, 503*	括*undle, 954*
束*undle, 502*	把*undle, 717*

己*elf, 5*

302-A

拷ortured 考hinking, after severe beating...

手⇔扌 (hand, manual)

拷orture   拷logging

GŌ
torture, flogging

Facing: 4.0. 🔚🔜 Apart

拷器 *torture device* **gōki**
拷問 *torture* **gōmon**
拷問台 *torture platform* **gōmondai**
拷問具 *torture device* **gōmongu**
拷問室 *torture chamber* **gōmonshitsu**

酷*ruelty, 266*	痛*njury, 60*	害*njury, 904*
虐*yranny, 870*	障*njury, 325*	傷*njury, 933*
苦*nguish, 477*	損*njury, 410*	被*uffer, 715*
悩*nguish, 48*	被*njury, 715*	

持*olding, 249*

302-B

拷ortured 考hinking, after severe beating...

耂 (person)

考hinking   考ontemplate

kanga(eru), KŌ
thinking, contemplate, conjecture, deduce, ponder, consider

Facing: 2.0. East ☞ (W)

備考 *note, reference* **bikō**
一考 *consider, re-think, ponder* **ikkō**
熟考 *careful consideration* **jukkō**
考案 *idea, device, plan* **kōan**
考案者 *designer, originator* **kōansha**
考課 *evaluation of one's records* **kōka**
考古学 *archaeology, paleohiistory* **kōkogaku**
考古学者 *archaeologist* **kōko gakusha**
考慮 *consideration, re-thinking* **kōryo**
考量 *consider, ponder, contemplate* **kōryō**
考査 *examination, test* **kōsa**
考察 *consideration, examination* **kōsatsu**
考証 *research, investigation* **kōshō**
黙考 *meditation, contemplation* **mokkō**
無考え *thoughtless, unthinking* **mukangae**
論考 *a study, a research* **ronkō**
再考 *reconsider, rethink* **saikō**
参考 *reference, quotation* **sankō**
思考 *thinking, consideration* **shikō**

思考力 *power of thinking* **shikōryoku**
私考 *private opinion* **shikō**
追考 *after thoughts, second thoughts* **tsuikō**
考え物 *problem to think about* **kangaemono**
考え事 *something to think about* **kangaegoto**
沈思黙考 *deep meditation* **chinshi mokkō**
考え違い *mistaken thinking* **kangaechigai**
考え出す *think out, invent, devise* **kangaedasu**
考え込む *think hard, brood over* **kangaekomu**
考え直す *reconsider, rethink* **kangaenaosu**
素人考え *shallow thinking* **shirōto kangae**
考え回らす *ponder* **kangaemegurasu**

意*hought, 340*	慮*hought, 70*
想*hought, 524*	志*ntention, 426*
念*hought, 182*	

考*hinking, 392*

303-A

停top by the 亭estaurant for another croissant...

停top   停alting

人⇔亻 (person)

TEI

stop, halting, put an end, cease, discontinue

FLIP: 7.1. Right (Sort Of)

バス停 *bus stop, bus waiting area* **basutei**
調停 *mediation, arbitration* **chōtei**
⇒労使調停 *labour arbitration* **rōshi chōtei**
電停 *street car stop* **dentei**
急停 *sudden stop (car)* **kyūtei**
停会 *adjournment, suspension* **teikai**
停学 *school suspension* **teigaku**
停止 *stop, suspension, cancellation* **teishi**
⇒営業停止 *business suspension* **eigyō teishi**
停止線 *finish line, stop line* **teishisen**
停止信号 *stop signal, red signal* **teishi shingō**
停止不良 *defective manufacture* **teishi furyō**
停車 *halting-, stopping a car* **teisha**
⇒無停車 *non-stop train* **muteisha**
⇒各駅停車 *local train stop* **kakueki teisha**
停車所 *bus stop, waiting area* **teishajo**
停車場 *taxi stand, waiting area* **teishajō**
停職 *suspension from office* **teishoku**
停戦 *cease-fire, truce, armistice* **teisen**

停船 *stop sailing, decommissioned ship* **teisen**
停滞 *stagnation, accumulation* **teitai**
停電 *blackout, power outage* **teiden**
停頓 *deadlock, standoff, impasse* **teiton**
停年 *age limit* **teinen**
停泊 *anchoring, berthing* **teihaku**
停留 *stopping, discontinuance* **teiryū**
停戦会談 *cease-fire negotiations* **teisen kaidan**
停戦協定 *armistice, cease-fire* **teisen kyōtei**

止*top, 192*	抹*ross out, 13*
絶*radicate, 403*	終*inish, 397*
消*elete, 265*	了*inish, 456*
廃*bolish, 368*	

亭*estaurant, 393*

303-B

停top by the 亭estaurant for another croissant...

亭estaurant

宀 (cover, lid)

TEI

restaurant, cafeteria, canteen

FLIP: 2.0.b. Sort Of (stem)

地亭 *lakeside arbour* **chitei**
園亭 *gazebo* **entei**
旗亭 *small restaurant, inn* **kitei**
料亭 *high-class Japanese restaurant* **ryōtei**
亭主 *host, inn-keeper; husband* **teishu**
亭主関白 *aristocratic husband* **teishu kanpaku**
亭亭 *lofty, high & mighty* **teitei**
勘亭流 *Kanji style used in Sumo & Kabuki* **kanteiryū**

宴*anquet, 610*	豪*plendour, 910*
興*ntertainment, 867*	貴*recious, 913*
客*uest, 559*	特*pecial, 250*
賓*uest, 161*	殊*pecialty, 234*
食*uisine, 255*	酒*iquor, 789*

高*igh, 435*

304-A

控efraining travel agency kept the 空kies 空mpty...

❶控efrain 控bstain ❷控otes

手⇔扌 (hand, manual)

hika(eru), KŌ
refrain, abstain, desist, hold back; notes

FLIP: 7.0.a. Right (flat)

❶控え所 *waiting room* **hikaejo**
控え目 *moderate, modest* **hikaeme**
控え室 *waiting-, reception room* **hikaeshitsu**
控え見本 *duplicate sample* **hikae mihon**
控え選手 *substitute-, alternate athlete* **hikae senshu**
控え屋敷 *villa, retreat* **hikae yashiki**
控除 *subtraction, deduction* **kōjo**
控除額 *deducted sum* **kōjogaku**
控制 *checking, controlling* **kōsei**
控訴 *court appeal* **kōso**
控訴院 *appellate court* **kōsoin**
控訴状 *petition of appeal* **kōsojō**
控訴権 *right to appeal* **kōsoken**
控訴審 *appeal trial* **kōsoshin**
主控え *mainstay, principal* **shubikae**
売り控える *refrain from selling* **urihikaeru**
買い控える *refrain from buying* **kaihikaeru**
差し控える *cease & desist* **sashihikaeru**

❷控え帳 *notebook* **hikaechō**
控え書き *memo, notes* **hikaegaki**
手控え *note, memo* **tebikae**
手控える *reserve, cut down* **tebikaeru**

意hought, 340	慮houghts, 70
想hought, 524	志ntention, 426
念hought, 182	

空mpty, 394

304-B

控efraining travel agency kept the 空kies 空mpty...

穴 (hole, cave)

❶空ky ❷空mpty

sora, a(keru), a(ku), kara, KŪ
sky; empty

FLIP: 1.0.a. Whole (flat)

❶青空 *blue sky* **aozora**
冬空 *wintry-, winter sky* **fuyuzora**
星空 *starlit sky, starry sky* **hoshizora**
空手 *karate martial arts* **karate**
航空 *airline, aviation* **kōkū**
虚空 *open space, the air* **kokū**
空間 *space, room* **kūkan**
⇒宇宙空間 *outer space* **uchū kūkan**
空気 *air* **kūki**
空港 *airport* **kūkō**
空想 *fantasy, daydreaming* **kūsō**
領空 *territorial air, air space* **ryōkū**
寒空 *cold weather, wintry sky* **samuzora**
空涙 *fake tears, crocodile tears* **soranamida**
低空 *low altitude, ~sky* **teikū**
天空 *sky, heavens* **tenkū**
夜空 *night sky* **yozora**
雪空 *snowy sky* **yukizora**
制空権 *battle for the skies* **seikūken**

対空ミサイル *anti-aircraft missile* **taikū misairu**

❷空談 *idle talk, gossip, rumour* **kūdan**
空白 *blank, empty space* **kūhaku**
空費 *wasting money, squandering* **kūhi**
空き瓶 *empty bottle* **akibin**
空き地 *vacant land, ~lot* **akichi**
空き缶 *empty can, empty tin* **akikan**
空き巣 *sneak thieving, burglar* **akisu**
空き家 *vacant-, empty house* **akiya**
空っ風 *dry wind* **karakkaze**
空っぽ *empty, broke, vacant* **karappo**

天eaven, 83	青lue colour, 115
雲loud, 154	零ero, 874
無othing, 49	

突reak-thru, 576

305-A

Berries so 紺ark-blue, how 甘weet to chew...

糸 (thread, continuity)

紺*ark blue*　　紺*avy blue*

KON
dark blue, navy blue

紺色 *navy-, dark-, deep blue* **kon'iro**
紺地 *dark blue cloth* **konji**
紺青 *dark blue* **konjō**
紺碧 *azure* **konpeki**
紺屋 *dyer, dyers shop* **kōya, konya**
濃紺 *navy-, dark-, deep blue* **nōkon**
紫紺 *blue purple* **shikon**
花紺青 *royal blue* **hanakonjō**
茄子紺 *dusky purple* **nasukon**

FLIP: 7.0.a. Right (flat)

青*lue colour, 115*	色*olour, 403*
太*hick, 6*	彩*olour, 914*
濃*hick, 446*	染*olouring, 607*

組*roup, 138*

305-B

Berries so 紺ark-blue, how 甘weet to chew...

甘 (sweet)

甘*weet*　　甘*ugary*

ama(i), ama(eru), ama(yakasu), KAN
sweet, sugary

甘っちょろい *easygoing, carefree* **amacchoroi**
甘茶 *sweet tea, sweetened tea* **amacha**
甘えん坊 *spoiled child, brat* **amaenbō**
甘栗 *roasted sweet chestnuts* **amaguri**
甘塩 *lightly salted* **amajio**
甘皮 *pellicle, coat, film* **amakawa**
甘口 *sweet taste* **amakuchi**
甘草 *liquorice* **amakusa**
甘煮 *sugar-boiled* **amani**
甘食 *sweet foodstuff* **amashoku**
甘党 *non-drinker, abstemious, teethtotaler* **amatō**
甘酒 *fermented rice drink* **amazake**
甘酢 *sweet vinegar (mirin)* **amazu**
甘酸っぱい *sour-sweet taste* **amazuppai**
甘美 *sweet taste* **kanbi**
甘言 *flattery words, sweet talk* **kangen**
甘受 *submission, resignation* **kanju**
甘苦 *joys & sorrows* **kanku**
甘味 *sweetness* **kanmi**

FLIP: 1.0.a. Whole (flat)

甘夢 *pleasant dreams* **kanmu**
甘露 *nectar, sugar-coated food* **kanro**
甘酸 *sweet & sour* **kansan**
甘心 *satisfaction, fulfilment* **kanshin**
甘薯 *sweet potato* **kansho**
甘蔗 *sugar cane* **kansho**
甘く見る *underestimate, make light of* **amakumiru**
甘納豆 *azuki-, sugared beans* **amanattō**
甘味料 *sweetener, sugar* **kanmiryō**

糖*ugar, 439*	甘*weet, 395*
菓*weets, 123*	味*aste, 871*

且*urther, 500*

306-A

惨*iserable hobbit came for a* 参*emple-visit...*

心⇔忄 (heart, feelings)

惨*iserable* 惨*ragedy*

miji(me), SAN, ZAN
miserable, tragedy, misfortune, cruelty

悲惨 *misery, tragedy* **hisan**
陰惨 *ghastly, horrible, chilling* **insan**
惨め *miserable, cruel, tragic* **mijime**
無惨 *merciless, pitiless* **muzan**
惨害 *havoc, ravage, disaster* **sangai**
惨劇 *tragedy, tragic event* **sangeki**
惨事 *disaster, tragedy* **sanji**
惨状 *miserable condition* **sanjō**
惨禍 *calamity, disaster* **sanka**
惨苦 *misery, tragedy* **sanku**
惨落 *sudden fall* **sanraku**
惨烈 *horrible, atrocious, cruel* **sanretsu**
惨憺 *terrible, horrible, miserable* **santan**
惨絶 *cruel, merciless, brutal* **sanzetsu**
凄惨 *ghastly, horrible, frightening* **seisan**
惨酷 *cruel, merciless, brutal* **zankoku**
惨敗 *crushing defeat, shut-out* **zanpai**
惨殺 *grisly murder* **zansatsu**
惨殺者 *killer, murderer* **zansatsusha**

Facing: 2.2. ☞ East (V)
Facing: 4.0. 〜☜☞〜 Apart

惨殺体 *mangled-, mutilated corpse*
　　zansatsutai
惨殺死体 *mangled-, mutilated corpse*
　　zansatsu shitai
惨死 *tragic death, chilling death* **zanshi**
惨死体 *mangled-, mutilated corpse* **zanshitai**

虞*nxiety, 889*	害*njury, 904*
煩*nxiety, 832*	傷*njury, 933*
禍*ragedy, 799*	障*njury, 325*
悲*ragedy, 289*	損*njury, 410*
厄*ragedy, 354*	痛*njury, 60*

修*aster, 898*

306-B

惨*iserable hobbit came for a* 参*emple-visit...*

ム (oneself)

参*emple-visit* 参*articipate*

mai(ru), SAN
temple-visit, visit a holy place, partake, participate

墓参 *visiting ancestral graves* **bosan**
遅参 *late comer, tardy* **chisan**
代参 *visiting of behalf of* **daisan**
不参 *non-attendance, absence* **fusan**
不参加 *non-participation* **fusanka**
持参 *bringing on a visit* **jisan**
見参 *meeting, seeing* **kenzan**
帰参 *return to one's lord* **kisan**
古参 *seniority, old-timer, old hand* **kosan**
降参 *surrender, submission, capitulation* **kōsan**
日参 *daily visits* **nissan**
参謀 *officer-level, executive* **sanbō**
参内 *visiting a palace* **sandai**
参賀 *visit a palace* **sanga**
参事 *counsellor, adviser* **sanji**
参加 *participation, taking part* **sanka**
参画 *planning participation* **sankaku**
参考 *reference, consultation* **sankō**
参入 *entry, enter into* **sannyū**

FLIP: 2.0.b. Sort Of (stem)

参拝 *worship, shrine visit* **sanpai**
参列 *attendance, presence* **sanretsu**
参政 *participating in government* **sansei**
参照 *reference, bibliography* **sanshō**
参与 *taking part, participation* **sanyo**
参禅 *practice of Zen meditation* **sanzen**
新参 *newcomer, new face* **shinzan**
墓参り *tomb visit* **hakamairi**
寒参り *shrine visit on cold nights* **kanmairi**
宮参り *infant's first shrine visit* **miyamairi**
参観日 *parental visiting day (school)* **sankanbi**

寺*emple, 248*	神*ivine, 712*
祈*rayer, 184*	拝*rayer, 636*
信*aith, 252*	宗*eligion, 879*
聖*acred, 617*	加*articipate, 201*

惨*iserable, 396*

307-A

To 終inish by 冬inter, training of sprinters...

糸 (thread, continuity)

終inish   終omplete

o(waru), o(eru), SHŪ
finish, complete, come to end, finish, closure, terminate, terminal, cease

臨終 *one's end, death* **rinjū**
始終 *always, constantly, all the time* **shijū**
終映 *last film showing, final screening* **shūei**
終業 *closing of work, ~school* **shūgyō**
終発 *last service (train)* **shūhatsu**
終日 *all day long* **shūjitsu**
終刊 *last issue* **shūkan**
終結 *conclusion, end* **shūketsu**
終期 *expiration, end-of-term* **shūki**
終航 *last flight-, voyage* **shūkō**
終極 *final-, ultimate purpose* **shūkyoku**
終局 *end, close* **shūkyoku**
終曲 *finale, final performance* **shūkyoku**
終幕 *"the end..." (show)* **shūmaku**
終末 *conclusion, end* **shūmatsu**
終了 *completion, end* **shūryō**
終生 *lifetime, lifeterm* **shūsei**
終戦 *end of war, war conclusion* **shūsen**
終車 *last bus, last train* **shūsha**

FLIP: 7.1. Right (Sort Of)
Facing: 3.0. ☞☜ **Across**

終始 *from beginning to the end* **shūshi**
終止 *end, stop, close* **shūshi**
終身 *lifetime, lifeterm* **shūshin**
終身雇用 *life-time employment* **shūshin koyō**
終身刑 *life imprisonment, ~sentence* **shūshinkei**
終息 *last breath* **shūsoku**
終点 *terminal end, final stop* **shūten**
終夜 *all night long* **shūya**
有終 *glorious end* **yūshū**
最終的 *the very last* **saishūteki**
終盤戦 *end game* **shūbansen**
終業式 *completion ceremony* **shūgyōshiki**

止*top, 192*	末*atter-part, 13*
停*top, 393*	了*inish, 456*
済*ettle, 961*	完*omplete, 196*

経*ime-lapse, 791*

307-B

To 終inish by 冬inter, training of sprinters...

冬⇔夂 (winter)

冬inter

fuyu, TŌ
winter

晩冬 *delayed winter* **bantō**
仲冬 *mid-winter* **chūto**
暖冬 *warm winter* **dantō**
越冬 *wintering, hibernation* **ettō**
冬場 *wintertime* **fuyuba**
冬服 *winter clothes, ~wear* **fuyufuku**
冬着 *winter clothes, ~wear* **fuyugi**
冬物 *winter clothes, ~wear* **fuyumono**
冬山 *mountain in winter* **fuyuyama**
冬空 *wintry sky, winter sky* **fuyuzora**
厳冬 *severe winter* **gentō**
玄冬 *winter* **gentō**
真冬 *dead of winter* **mafuyu**
忍冬 *honeysuckle* **nindō**
立冬 *start of winter season* **rittō**
昨冬 *last winter* **sakutō**
初冬 *early winter* **shotō**
冬至 *winter solstice* **tōji**
冬期 *winter, wintertime* **tōki**

FLIP: 2.0.b. Sort Of (stem)
Facing: 1.1. ☜ **West (H)**

冬季 *winter season* **tōki**
冬眠 *hibernation, winter sleep* **tōmin**
冬天 *wintry sky, winter sky* **tōten**
冬枯れ *withering in winter* **fuyugare**
冬籠り *hibernation, winter sleep* **fuyugomori**
冬越し *passing the winter* **fuyugoshi**
冬支度 *winter preparation* **fuyujitaku**
冬向き *"for use in winter..."* **fuyumuki**
冬将軍 *general winter* **fuyushōgun**
冬休み *winter vacation* **fuyuyasumi**
春夏秋冬 *four seasons, all-year round*
  shunka shūtō

冷*hilly, 684*	氷*reeze, 10*
氷*ce, 10*	寒*hills, 121*
凍*reeze, 221*	

尺*xhaust, 574*

308-A

Garden 郭nclosed, 享njoy poetry & prose...

阝⇔阜 (village-right)

郭

郭*nclose*   **郭***onfines*

KAKU
enclose, confines,

外郭 *outer fence* **gaikaku**
外郭団体 *affiliate group, aggrupation* **gaikaku dantai**
一郭 *city section* **ikkaku**
城郭 *castle walls* **jōkaku**
郭公 *cuckoo* **kakkō**
郭公鳥 *cuckoo* **kakkōdori**
郭清 *purification, purging, cleansing* **kakusei**
胸郭 *thorax, chest* **kyōkaku**
輪郭 *outline, features, contours* **rinkaku**
遊郭 *amusement area; red-light district* **yūkaku**

FLIP: 6.1. Left Top

囲*nclose, 361*	限*oundary, 771*
奥*nside, 903*	涯*imit, 890*
内*nside, 297*	限*imit, 771*
境*oundary, 839*	最*aximum, 423*

部*ection, 957*

308-B

Garden 郭nclosed, 享njoy poetry & prose...

宀 (cover, lid)

享

享*njoy*   **享***leasure*

u(keru), KYŌ
enjoy, pleasure, delight

享受 *enjoyment, pleasure* **kyōju**
享年 *age at death* **kyōnen**
享楽 *enjoyment, pleasure* **kyōraku**
享楽主義 *Epicureanism, Hedonism* **kyōraku shugi**
享有 *birthright possession* **kyōyū**
長享時代 *Chōkyō Era (1487-1489)* **chōkyō jidai**
永享時代 *Eikyō Era (1429-1441)* **eikyō jidai**
延享時代 *Enkyō Era (1744-1748)* **enkyō jidai**
元亨時代 *Genkō Era (1321-1324)* **genkō jidai**
貞享時代 *Jōkyō Era (1684-1688)* **jōkyō jidai**
享保時代 *Kyōho Era (1716-1736)* **kyōho jidai**
享禄時代 *Kyōroku Era (1528-1532)* **kyōroku jidai**
京徳時代 *Kyōtoku Era (1452-1454)* **kyōtoku jidai**
享和時代 *Kyōwa Era (1801-1804)* **kyōwa jidai**

FLIP: 3.0.a. Top (flat)

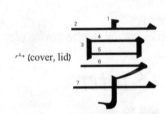

喫*njoy, 900*	愉*leasure, 922*
遊*njoy, 650*	楽*leasure, 447*
悦*leasant, 942*	興*ntertainment, 867*
快*leasant, 699*	閑*eisure, 283*
歓*leasure, 667*	悠*eisure, 898*
娯*leasure, 453*	娯*musement, 453*

京*apital, 386*

309-A

創reativity, 倉torage of infinity...

創reativity　創riginality

刀⇔刂 (blade, cutting)

tsuku(ru), SŌ
creativity, originality, innovation, imagination

独創 creativity, originality, novelty **dokusō**
独創性 originality, creativity **dokusōsei**
銃創 bullet wound **jūsō**
創案 original idea **sōan**
創業 founding, establishment **sōgyō**
創意 originality, innovation **sōi**
創刊 first publication **sōkan**
創刊号 publication's first issue **sōkangō**
創見 original view **sōken**
創立 founding, establishment **sōritsu**
創立者 founder, founding father **sōritsusha**
創作 creative work, novelty **sōsaku**
創作力 originality, creativity **sōsakuryoku**
創成 creation **sōsei**
創製 invention **sōsei**
創設 establishment, founding **sōsetsu**
創始 origination, foundation **sōshi**
創始者 originator, creator **sōshisha**
創傷 wound, injury **sōshō**

FLIP: 6.2. Left Bottom
Facing: 3.0. ☞☜ Across

創出 creation **sōshutsu**
草創 inception, beginning **sōsō**
創造 Genesis, creation **sōzō**
創世期 initial stage, early period **sōseiki**
創世記 Genesis, creation **sōseiki**

初 *irst*, 353	意 *dea*, 340
元 *rigin*, 195	想 *dea*, 524
源 *rigin*, 431	念 *dea*, 182
原 *riginal*, 431	殊 *nique*, 234

倉 *torage*, 399

309-B

創reativity, 倉torage of infinity...

倉torage　倉arehouse

人⇔イ (person)

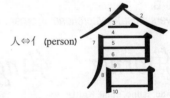

kura, SŌ
storage, storehouse, warehouse, depository

弾倉 bullet magazine **dansō**
営倉 guardhouse, stockade **eisō**
小倉 Kokura City, Fukuoka Prefecture **kokura**
穀倉 granary **kokusō**, **kokugura**
米倉 rice granary **komegura**
倉荷 warehouse goods **kurani**
倉主 warehouse owner **kuranushi**
倉敷 Kurashiki City, Okayama Pref. **kurashiki-shi**
胸倉 breast, lapels **munagura**
船倉 ship hatch **sensō**
倉庫 warehouse, storage **sōko**
土倉 basement warehouse **tsuchigura**
校倉 log-built storehouse **azekura**
武器倉 weapon storage, armoury **bukigura**
常平倉 granary **jōheisō**
重営倉 maximum security detention **jūeisō**
倉渡し direct from warehouse **kurawatashi**
穀倉地帯 granary region **kokusō chitai**

FLIP: 4.0.a. Bottom (flat)

庫 *torage*, 306	給 *upply*, 143
蔵 *torage*, 565	納 *upply*, 296
貯 *torage*, 967	与 *upply*, 349
保 *reserve*, 552	充 *upply*, 884

創 *reativity*, 399

310-A

Drivers must 解omprehend 角orners' dead end...

角 (horns)

❶解omprehend　　❷解issolve

to(ku), to(keru), to(kasu), KAI, GE
comprehend, fathom, figure out, grasp, understand; dissolve, melting

Facing: 1.2. ☜ West (V)

❶ 弁解　*excuse, pretext, alibi* **benkai**
分解　*analysis, dissection; breaking down* **bunkai**
注解　*note, explanatory, comment* **chūkai**
誤解　*misunderstanding, miscomprehension* **gokai**
解放　*full tide* **kaihō** *release*
解決　*solution, answer (problem question)* **kaiketsu**
解明　*elucidation, clarification* **kaimei**
解析　*analysis, critical thinking* **kaiseki**
解説　*explanation, clarification* **kaisetsu**
解釈　*interpretation, questioning* **kaishaku**
解答　*correct answers* **kaisetsu**
見解　*opinion, viewpoint* **kenkai**
難解　*difficult, laborious, painstaking* **nankai**
理解　*understanding, comprehension* **rikai**
了解　*approval, agreement* **ryōkai**
正解　*correct answer* **seikai**
詳解　*detailed-, meticulous explanation* **shōkai**
和解　*compromise, settlement* **wakai**
図解　*diagram, illustration* **zukai**

❷ 氷解　*melting away, thawing, de-icing* **hyōkai**
解剖　*autopsy, dissection* **kaibō**
解団　*disband* **kaidan**
解除　*cancel, annul, rescind* **kaijo**
解禁　*lifting of a prohibition* **kaikin**
解散　*firing, dismissal, discharge* **kaiko**
解雇　*break up, dismissal* **kaisan**
解体　*dismantling, breaking up* **kaitai**
解約　*account cancellation* **kaiyaku**
溶解　*dissolution, melting, solution* **yōkai**
融解　*fusion, melting, dissolution* **yūkai**
雪解け　*thawing, de-icing, de-freezing* **yukidoke**
解き放す　*untie, let loose, set free* **tokihanasu**

分*nderstand, 518*　　認*ecognize, 535*
肯*ffirmative, 616*　　識*ecognize, 856*

鮮*resh, 679*

310-B

Drivers must 解omprehend 角orners' dead end...

角 (horns)

角orner　　角ngle

kado, tsuno, sumi, KAKU
corner, angle, curve, horn

Facing: 1.0. ☜ West (W)

直角　*right angle* **chokkaku**
鈍角　*obtuse angle* **donkaku**
鋭角　*acute angle* **eikaku**
外角　*exterior angle* **gaikaku**
牛角　*cattle horns* **gyūkaku**
方角　*direction* **hōgaku**
一角　*one corner* **ikkaku**
角店　*store on the corner* **kadomise**
角帽　*college cap, mortarboard* **kakubō**
角度　*angle* **kakudo**
角膜　*cornea* **kakumaku**
角材　*square lumber, ~timber* **kakuzai**
街角　*street corner* **machikado**
内角　*interior angle* **naikaku**
六角　*hexagon* **rokkaku**
三角　*triangle* **sankaku**
折角　*"since it's already done..."* **sekkaku**
視角　*visual angle* **shikaku**
四角　*square* **shikaku**

死角　*blind spot, unseen spot* **shikaku**
触角　*feeler, antenna* **shokkaku**
角笛　*horn, bugle* **tsunobue**
角隠し　*Shintō bridal hood* **tsunokakushi**
五角形　*pentagon* **gokakkei**
八角形　*octagon* **hakkakukei**
十角形　*decagon* **jūkakkei**
角刈り　*crew cut, flattop* **kakugari**
傾斜角　*inclination angle* **keishakaku**
四つ角　*crossroads* **yotsukado**
広角レンズ　*wide-angle lens* **kōkakurenzu**

隅*orner, 816*　　曲*urve, 476*
礎*ornerstone, 166*

用*urpose, 409*

311-A
Motorbiking with no 帽*eadgear, either* 冒*ourage or fear...*

巾 (cloth, fabric)

帽*eadgear*　　　帽*at*

BŌ
headgear, hat

FLIP: 5.0.a Left & Right

赤帽 *red cap, porter* **akabō**
帽子 *hat, cap, bonnet* **bōshi**
⇒夏帽子 *summer cap* **natsubōshi**
⇒綿帽子 *Shintō bride veil* **watabōshi**
⇒麦藁帽子 *straw hat* **mugiwara bōshi**
帽子掛け *hat rack, hat tree* **bōshikake**
帽子屋 *hat store, hatter* **bōshiya**
帽章 *hat-, cap badge* **bōshō**
着帽 *"put your hats on..."* **chakubō**
脱帽 *taking off one's hat* **datsubō**
学帽 *school cap* **gakubō**
軍帽 *military cap, graduation hat* **gunbō**
角帽 *square college cap* **kakubō**
無帽 *bare-headed, without hat* **mubō**
略帽 *ordinary cap* **ryakubō**
制帽 *hat-wearing regulation* **seibō**
正帽 *uniform cap* **seibō**
学生帽 *student cap* **gakuseibō**
飛行帽 *pilot cap, aviator hat* **hikōbō**

海水帽 *ocean swimming cap* **kaisuibō**
中折帽 *felt hat* **nakaorebō**
潜水帽 *diving cap* **sensuibō**
戦闘帽 *military cap* **sentōbō**
水泳帽 *swimming cap* **suieibō**
登山帽 *climber's hat* **tozanbō**
運動帽 *athletic cap* **undōbō**
山高帽 *derby hat* **yamatakabō**

首*ead, 311*	防*rotect, 736*
頭*ead, 832*	衛*rotect, 796*
安*afety, 350*	護*rotect, 828*

冒*ourage, 401*

311-B
Motorbiking with no 帽*eadgear, either* 冒*ourage or fear...*

目 (eyesight, visual)

冒*ourage*　　　冒*isky*

oka(su), BŌ
courage, risky, venturesome

FLIP: 1.0.a. Whole (flat)

冒険 *adventure, risk* **bōken**
冒険家 *adventurer, explorer* **bōkenka**
冒険者 *adventurer, explorer* **bōkensha**
冒険心 *spirit of adventure* **bōkenshin**
冒頭 *beginning, opening* **bōtō**
冒頭陳述 *opening statement* **bōtō chinjutsu**
冒讀 *blasphemy, profanity, heresy* **bōtoku**
冒険談 *tales of adventures* **bōkendan**
冒険的 *adventurous, venturesome, risky* **bōkenteki**
冒険好き *adventurous, venturesome, risky* **bōkensuki**
感冒 *common cold* **kanbō**

敢*ourage, 449*	勇*ourage, 59*
胆*ourage, 740*	雄*ourage, 775*
挑*hallenge, 214*	敢*aring, 449*

宣*nnounce, 899*

312-A

Old shoulders of Mr. Magoo 硬ardening 更new...

石 (stone)

硬

1 6 11
2 8
7
4 10
3 12
5

FLIP: 7.1. Right (Sort Of)

硬ardness 硬tiffness

kata(i), KŌ
hardness, stiffness, firmness, rigidity

硬い *hard, stiff; nervous* **katai**
硬調 *contrast* **kōchō**
硬直 *stiffening, rigidity* **kōchoku**
⇒死後硬直 *hardening of a corpse* **shigo kōchoku**
硬度 *hardness, solidity* **kōdo**
硬玉 *jadeite* **kōgyoku**
硬派 *hard-line, diehards, hawkists* **kōha**
硬筆 *pen-or-pencil* **kōhitsu**
硬化 *hardening, stiffening* **kōka**
⇒動脈硬化 *hardening of arteries* **dōmyaku kōka**
硬貨 *coins, minted money* **kōka**
硬骨 *backbone, skeleton* **kōkotsu**
硬球 *hardball* **kōkyū**
硬軟 *hardness-or-softness* **kōnan**
硬性 *hardness* **kōsei**
硬質 *hardness* **kōshitsu**
硬水 *hard water* **kōsui**
強硬 *strong, firm, hard* **kyōkō**
強硬派 *diehards, hardliners* **kyōkōha**

生硬 *crudeness, rough, raw* **seikō**
肝硬変 *liver cirrhosis* **kankōhen**
硬化症 *sclerosis* **kōkashō**

緊*ard, 599*
固*ard, 491*
凝*arden, 57*

更*new, 402*

312-B

Old shoulders of Mr. Magoo 硬ardening 更new...

日 (sunlight, daytime)

更

1
2 3 6
4
5
7

FLIP: 2.0.b. Sort Of (stem)

更new 更oreover

sara(ni), fu(kasu), fu(keru), KŌ
anew, moreover, afresh, renewal

更ける *become late, grow old* **fukeru**
更なる *"more, further..."* **saranaru**
変更 *modification, alteration, revision* **henkō**
⇒名義変更 *transfer of ownership (purchase)*
  meigi henkō
今更 *"at this time, as of now..."* **imasara**
殊更 *particularly, especially; deliberately* **kotosara**
更改 *renewal, alteration, updating* **kōkai**
更生 *rebirth, rehabilitation* **kōsei**
更生品 *reconditioned-, renovated goods* **kōseihin**
更新 *renewal, renovation* **kōshin**
更迭 *re-shuffle, reorganization* **kōtetsu**
満更 *"not really..."* **manzara**
尚更 *"all the more..."* **naosara**
更更 *"at all..."* **sarasara**
深更 *dead of the night* **shinkō**
初更 *first watch of the night* **shokō**
衣更え *seasonal changing of clothes* **koromogae**
夜更かし *staying late the night* **yofukashi**

更衣室 *locker-, dressing room* **kōishitsu**
更年期 *menopause, new womanhood* **kōnenki**

且*urther, 500*   新*ew, 668*
尚*urther, 99*   革*eform, 39*

便*onvenience, 480*

313-A

Job of censors: 絶*radicate* 色*rotic* 色*olours...*

糸 (thread, continuity)

絶*radicate*　　　絶*liminate*

ta(eru), ta(yasu), ZETSU
eradicate, eliminate, squash, discard, break-off, obliterate

Facing: 3.0. ☞☜ Across

超絶 *transcend, exceed, surpass* **chōzetsu**	
中絶 *abortion, pregnancy termination* **chūzetsu**	
断絶 *severance, rupture* **danzetsu**	
隔絶 *isolation, separation* **kakuzetsu**	
気絶 *faint, pass out, black out* **kizetsu**	
根絶 *eradication, extermination* **konzetsu**	
拒絶 *refusal, rejection, denial* **kyozetsu**	
謝絶 *refusal, declination, denial* **shazetsu**	
死絶 *extinction* **shizetsu**	
途絶 *stop, ceasing, discontinuance* **tozetsu**	
途絶える *be interrupted, break off* **todaeru**	
絶佳 *superb, excellent* **zekka**	
絶景 *magnificent view, ~scenery* **zekkei**	
絶交 *breaking off an relationship* **zekkō**	
絶句 *dying words, last words* **zekku**	
絶叫 *scream, yell, shouting* **zekkyō**	
絶版 *out-of-print* **zeppan**	
絶賛 *admiration, high praise, accolade* **zessan**	
絶世 *peerless, unrivalled* **zessei**	

絶食 *fasting, food abstinence* **zesshoku**
絶息 *dying breathe* **zessoku**
絶美 *absolutely beautiful* **zetsubi**
絶望 *despair, hopelessness* **zetsubō**
絶大 *grandest, greatest* **zetsudai**
絶命 *death, demise* **zetsumei**
絶滅 *extermination, extinction* **zetsumetsu**
絶妙 *miraculous, act-of-god* **zetsumyō**
絶対 *absolute, definitely* **zettai**
死に絶える *die out, extinct* **shi(ni)taeru**
絶海の孤島 *far solitary island* **zekkai no kotō**

消*elete, 265*	外*emove, 188*	停*top, 393*
廃*bolish, 368*	脱*emove, 941*	終*inish, 397*
抹*ross-out, 13*	止*erminate, 192*	了*inish, 456*

緑*reen, 841*　　　給*upply, 143*

313-B

Job of censors: 絶*radicate* 色*rotic* 色*olours...*

色 (colour)

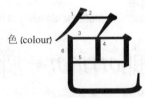

❶色*olour*　　❷色*rotic*

iro, SHOKU, SHIKI
colour, paint; erotic

Facing: 4.0. ☜☞ Apart

❶暮色 *dusk, twilight* **boshoku**
茶色 *brown* **chairo**
着色 *coloration, colouring* **chakushoku**
調色 *mixed colours* **chōshoku**
暖色 *warm colours* **danshoku**
原色 *original colour* **genshoku**
敗色 *signs of defeat* **haishoku**
変色 *discolourization, colour change* **henshoku**
異色 *unique, novel* **ishoku**
寒色 *cold colours* **kanshoku**
顔色 *facial complexion* **kaoiro**
景色 *view, landscape, scenery* **keshiki**
血色 *complexion* **kesshoku**
気色 *mood, feelings* **kishoku**
明色 *bright colours* **meishoku**
音色 *tone, timbre* **neiro**
才色 *beauty & brains* **saishoku**
生色 *fresh-looking* **seishoku**
色盲 *colour blindness* **shikimō**

色彩 *colouring, hue* **shikisai**
色素 *colouring pigment* **shikiso**
褪色 *be discoloured, fade out* **taishoku**
特色 *characteristics* **tokushoku**
容色 *looks, beauty* **yōshoku**
色合い *colour, shade* **iroai**
色褪せ *fade out, be discoloured* **iroaseru**
色鉛筆 *colour pencil* **iroenpitsu**
❷男色 *sodomy* **danshoku**
色気 *sex appeal* **iroke**
色目 *pervert glance, suggestive look* **irome**
色情 *sexual lust* **shikijō**
色狂い *sex pervert, sex maniac* **irogurui**

白*hite, 15*	青*lue colour, 115*
黒*lack, 320*	黄*ellow, 197*
赤*ed colour, 261*	緑*reen, 841*

角*orner, 400*

314-A

郎asculine matador standing in the 廊orridor...

β ⟷ 阜 (village-right)

郎asculine

RŌ

masculine suffix, young man

Facing: 2.2. East ☞ (V)

下郎 *servant, valet* **gerō**
一郎 *Ichiro (first name)* **ichirō**
女郎 *prostitute, whore, hooker* **jorō**
女郎屋 *brothel, whore house* **jorōya**
郎等 *vassals, retainer* **rōdō, rōtō**
郎君 *young lord* **rōkun**
郎党 *vassals, retainer* **rōtō, rōdō**
⇒一族郎党 *all in the family, nepotism* **ichizoku rōtō**
新郎 *bride & groom* **shinrō**
新郎新婦 *bride & groom* **shinrō shinpu**
外郎 *rice jelly sweets* **uirō**
野郎 *fool, idiot, stupid* **yarō**
悪太郎 *naughty boy* **akutarō**
源五郎 *Japanese water beetle* **gengorō**
与太郎 *fool, idiot* **yotarō**
雪女郎 *snow fairy* **yukijorō**
夜郎自大 *arrogant, haughty, overbearing* **yarō jidai**

壮asculine, 367	雄asculine, 775
男asculine, 597	彼 [third person], 224
僕asculine, 157	

朗lear, 800

314-B

郎asculine matador standing in the 廊orridor...

广 (rooftop)

廊orridor 廊allway

RŌ

corridor, hallway, passageway

Facing: 2.1. East ☞ (H)

画廊 *art gallery* **garō**
歩廊 *corridor, passage* **horō**
回廊 *corridor, passage* **kairō**
廊下 *corridor, hall way* **rōka**
通廊 *hallway, corridor, pathwalk* **tsūrō**
渡り廊下 *arcade, roofed passage* **watari rōka**

歩alk, 272	道oad, 312
道ath, 312	路oad, 405
通assing, 59	往ome & go, 749

郎asculine, 404

315-A

露xposed to heavy 露ew, 露ussian 路oads will do...

雨 (weather)

❶露xposure ❷露ew ❸露ussia

tsuyu, RO
exposure, disclosure, revelation; dew; Russia

FLIP: 3.0.b. Top (stem)

❶暴露 exposure, revelation **bakuro**
白露 White Russia, Belarus **hakuro**
発露 manifestation, expression **hatsuro**
披露 announcement, public notice **hirō**
披露宴 wedding party **hirōen**
露悪 boasting one's vices **ro'aku**
露盤 pagoda roof **roban**
露台 balcony, veranda **rodai**
露営 camping out, encampment **roei**
露地 plain ground **roji**
露見 exposure, disclosure, leak out **roken**
露光 light exposure (film) **rokō**
露骨 plain, frank, open **rokotsu**
露命 transient life, temporal world **romei**
露出 exposure, disclosure, leak out **roshutsu**
露呈 exposure, revelation **rotei**
露天 open air **roten**
露店 street stall, ~booth **roten**
露頭 outcrop **rotō**

流露 outpouring of feelings **ryūro**
吐露 expression, laying bare **toro**
露店商 booth-, stall keeper **rotenshō**
露天風呂 open-air hot springs **rotenburo**
❷朝露 morning dew **asatsuyu**
雨露 rain & dew **ametsuyu, uro**
甘露 nectar, honeydew **kanro**
甘露煮 caramelized food **kanroni**
露滴 dewdrop **roteki**
露点 dew point **roten**
夜露 evening dew **yotsuyu**
❸日露 Japan-Russia **nichiro**
露帝 Czar of Russia **rotei**

霧oggy, 454	雰oggy, 518
霜rost, 615	暴xpose, 561
曇oggy, 154	公ublic, 180

霧isty, 454

315-B

露xposed to heavy 露ew, 露ussian 路oads will do...

足 (feet, legs)

路oad 路oute

ji, michi, RO
road, route, highway

FLIP: 7.3.a. Right Bottom (flat)
Facing: 3.0. ☞☜ Across

断路 "road closed..." **danro**
遠路 long route **enro**
復路 return trip **fukuro**
風路 air route, air duct **fūro**
街路 street, avenue **gairo**
販路 market **hanro**
遍路 pilgrimage, pilgrim **henro**
一路 one road; straight, directly **ichiro**
順路 route **junro**
回路 circuit **kairo**
岐路 crossroads, forked road **kiro**
空路 airway, aircraft route **kūro**
末路 the end, last days **matsuro**
迷路 maze, labyrinth, snarl **meiro**
波路 sea route, sea lanes **namiji**
路傍 roadside, wayside **robō**
路地 alley **roji**
路上 on the road **rojō**
路肩 road shoulder **rokata**

路線 line, route **rosen**
路程 distance, mileage **rotei**
路頭 street, way **rotō**
線路 rail, railroad line **senro**
針路 course **shinro**
走路 track, course **sōro**
退路 escape route, exit path **tairo**
闇路 dark road, untrekked path **yamiji**
要路 authorities, officials **yōro**
十字路 crossroads **jūjiro**
滑走路 airport runway **kassōro**

道ath, 312	軌ailroad, 660
畔ice-field path, 484	通assing, 59
岐orked-road, 704	往ome & go, 749

跡elics, 672

316-A

勝ictory in cricket to earn new 券icket...

勝ictory 勝inning

力 (strength, force)

ka(tsu), masa(ru), sugu(reru) SHŌ
victory, winning, excel, success, triumph

FLIP: 7.2.b. Right Top (stem)

圧勝 overwhelming-, landslide victory **asshō**
必勝 certain victory **hisshō**
快勝 sweeping victory **kaishō**
完勝 complete victory **kanshō**
勝手 not mindful of others, arbitrary **katte**
景勝 picturesque, scenic **keishō**
健勝 good health, robust health **kenshō**
連勝 consecutive winning **renshō**
辛勝 narrow victory **shinshō**
勝負 match, victory-or-defeat **shōbu**
勝敗 outcome, victory-or-defeat **shōhai**
勝機 chance of victory **shōki**
勝利 beat, win, exceed **shōri**
勝算 winning chances, odds of **shōsan**
勝者 winner **shōsha**
勝訴 winning a lawsuit **shōso**
祝勝 victory celebration **shukushō**
殊勝 laudable, commendable, praiseworthy **shushō**

大勝 great victory **taishō**
優勝 victory, win **yūshō**
全勝 win all rounds, clean sweep **zenshō**
勝ち目 winning chances, odds of **kachime**
丸勝ち complete victory **marugachi**
我勝ち "to each his own..." **waregachi**
判定勝ち win by split decision **hanteigachi**
勝ち得る win, gain, earn **kachieru**
勝ち負け victory-or-defeat **kachimake**
勝ち取る gain, obtain, win **kachitoru**
二勝三敗 two wins & three defeats **nishō sanpai**
打ち勝つ overcome, resist, get over **uchikatsu**

功uccess, 635	利dvantage, 686
得dvantage, 940	挑hallenge, 214

券icket, 406

316-B

勝ictory in cricket to earn new 券icket...

券icket 券oupon

刀⇔刂 (blade, cutting)

KEN
ticket, coupon, stub, voucher, certificate

FLIP: 3.0.b. Top (stem)

馬券 horse race betting ticket **baken**
発券 issue tickets, notes **hakken**
株券 stock certificate **kabuken**
金券 gold certificate **kinken**
沽券 dignity, honour, nobility **koken**
旅券 passport, travel document **ryoken**
債券 bond, debenture **saiken**
車券 bicycle race betting ticket **shaken**
質券 pawn ticket **shichiken**
証券 bill, bond, securities **shōken**
⇒船荷証券 bill-of-lading **funani shōken**
⇒有価証券 securities, stocks & bonds
yūka shōken
証券取引所 securities-, stock exchange
shōken torihikijo
食券 food coupon **shokken**
傍聴券 entrance-, admission ticket **bōchōken**
抽選券 lotto ticket **chūsenken**
銀行券 bank note, bank bill **ginkōken**

乗車券 train ticket **jōshaken**
券売機 ticket-selling machine **kenbaiki**
急行券 express train ticket **kyūkōken**
日銀券 Bank of Japan bonds **nichiginken**
入場券 entrance-, admission ticket **nyūjōken**
診察券 medical check-up card **shinsatsuken**
招待券 invitation card **shōtaiken**
定期券 regular pass (train) **teikiken**
搭乗券 boarding pass **tōjōken**
福引き券 lotto ticket **fukubikiken**
引き換え券 coupon, voucher **hikikaeken**
座席指定券 reserved-seat ticket **zaseki shiteiken**

符ark, 582	標ign, 549
札abel, 685	符ign, 582

巻oll-up, 391

317-A

Blood 循*irculation* 盾*hields cell mutation...*

循*irculation*

イ (stroll)

JUN
circulation

FLIP: 8.0.a. Inner (flat)

因循 *conservative, irresolute* **injun**
循環 *circulation, rotation* **junkan**
⇒血液循環 *blood circulation* **ketsueki junkan**
循環バス *loop-line bus* **junkan basu**
循環論法 *circular argument* **junkan ronpō**
循環系 *circulatory system* **junkankei**
循環器 *circulation organ* **junkanki**
悪循環 *vicious cycle, endless vile* **akujunkan**

回*irculate, 458*	旋*otate, 651*
脈*eins, 766*	管*ontrol, 917*
筒*ipe, 51*	続*ontinue, 260*

律*egulation, 731*

317-B

Blood 循*irculation* 盾*hields cell mutation...*

盾*hield*

目 (eyesight, visual)

tate, JUN
shield, protection, covering

FLIP: 8.0.a. Inner (flat)
FLIP: 4.0.a. Bottom (flat)

小盾 *small shield* **kodate**
矛盾 *contradiction, inconsistency* **mujun**
盾突く *resist, defy, oppose* **tatetsuku**
後ろ盾 *backing, support, assistance* **ushirodate**

衛*rotect, 796*	防*rotect, 736*
護*rotect, 828*	守*efence, 366*

看*ook after, 623*

318-A

Keeping lockets of 髪air, 友riendship's loving care...

髟 (long hair)

髪*air*

kami, HATSU
hair

弁髪 *pigtail* **benpatsu**
長髪 *long hair* **chōhatsu**
調髪 *getting a haircut* **chōhatsu**
断髪 *bobbed hair* **danpatsu**
怒髪 *rage, anger* **dohatsu**
銀髪 *silver hair, grey hair* **ginpatsu**
蓬髪 *untidy-, unkempt hair* **hōhatsu**
遺髪 *locket of deceased hair (memento)* **ihatsu**
髪型 *hairstyle, hairdo* **kamigata**
金髪 *blonde hair, blondie* **kinpatsu**
黒髪 *black hair* **kurokami**
前髪 *frontal hair* **maegami**
毛髪 *hair* **mōhatsu**
散髪 *haircut, hairdressing* **sanpatsu**
整髪 *haircut, hairdressing* **seihatsu**
洗髪 *hairwashing* **senpatsu**
白髪 *white hair, grey hair* **shiraga**
束髪 *pompadour hairstyle* **sokuhatsu**
短髪 *short hair* **tanpatsu**

Facing: 3.0. Across
FLIP: 4.0.b. Bottom (stem)

頭髪 *head hair* **tōhatsu**
洋髪 *Western hairstyle* **yōhatsu**
髪の毛 *hair* **kaminoke**
髪切虫 *long-horned beetle* **kamikirimushi**
間一髪 *narrowly, "by a hairline..."* **kan'ippatsu**
切り髪 *hair cut* **kirigami**
乱れ髪 *untidy-, unkempt hairstyle* **midaregami**
共白髪 *spouses ageing together* **tomoshiraga**
後ろ髪 *back head hair* **ushirogami**
若白髪 *premature greying* **wakashiraga**

毛*kin hair, 468*	膚*kin, 69*
羽*eather, 240*	皮*kin, 224*
翼*eather, 239*	肌*kin, 747*

318-B

Keeping lockets of 髪air, 友riendship's loving care...

又 (again)

友*riendship*   友*ellowship*

tomo, YŪ
friendship, fellowship, buddy, amity

悪友 *true friend; undesirable friend* **akuyū**
病友 *hospital wardmate* **byōyū**
知友 *close friend, buddy* **chiyū**
益友 *reliable friend* **ekiyū**
学友 *school friend, school buddy* **gakuyū**
朋友 *friend, colleague* **hōyū**
校友 *school friend* **kōyū**
級友 *classmate, grademate* **kyūyū**
旧友 *old friend, long-time friend* **kyūyū**
盟友 *sworn friend* **meiyū**
僚友 *colleague, officemate* **ryōyū**
清友 *refined friend* **seiyū**
政友 *political ally* **seiyū**
戦友 *comrade-in-arms, war buddy* **senyū**
社友 *close officemate* **shayū**
親友 *close friend* **shinyū**
詩友 *poetry friend* **shiyū**
友達 *friend, buddy, chum* **tomodachi**
友達付き合い *get along with* **tomodachi tsukiai**

FLIP: 4.0.b. Bottom (stem)

友愛 *friendship, fellowship* **yūai**
友誼 *friendly relations* **yūgi**
友軍 *friendly army, ~force* **yūgun**
友邦 *friendly nation* **yūhō**
友人 *friend, buddy, chum* **yūjin**
友情 *friendship, fellowship* **yūjō**
友好 *friendship, friendliness, goodwill* **yūkō**
友党 *allied political party* **yūtō**
血友病 *haemophilia* **ketsuyūbyō**
竹馬の友 *childhood friend* **chikuba no tomo**
飲み友達 *drinking buddy* **nomi tomodachi**

歓*oodwill, 42*	親*ntimate, 669*
懇*ntimacy, 164*	仲*olleague, 695*
善*ighteous, 450*	

反*gainst, 537*

319-A

備*repare for a* 用*urpose to* 用*tilize your utmost...*

人⟺イ (person)

備*repare for*   備*rovide for*

sona(eru), sona(waru), BI
prepare for, provide for, make available, provision

FLIP: 8.0.b. Inner (stem)
Facing: 4.0. 🐟🐟 Apart

備忘 *reminder* **bibō**
備忘録 *memorandum, memo* **bibōroku**
備蓄 *stockpile, arsenal, cache* **bichiku**
備品 *furnishings, fixtures, fittings* **bihin**
備考 *note, reference* **bikō**
防備 *defence, self-protection, security* **bōbi**
武備 *armaments, defences* **bubi**
不備 *unprepared, lack of preparations* **fubi**
具備 *equipment, implements, tools* **gubi**
軍備 *armaments, rearming* **gunbi**
配備 *deployment, stationing, emplacement* **haibi**
常備 *standing, regular* **jōbi**
準備 *preparation, readying* **junbi**
準備金 *reserve funds* **junbikin**
完備 *fully-equipped* **kanbi**
警備 *security, guarding* **keibi**
警備艇 *coast guard boat* **keibitei**
兼備 *two things simultaneously (rich & smart)* **kenbi**
後備 *second reserve* **kōbi**

整備 *maintenance, check up* **seibi**
戦備 *war preparations* **senbi**
設備 *equipment, facilities* **setsubi**
守備 *defence, fielding* **shubi**
守備兵 *guards, sentry troops* **shubihei**
装備 *equipment, implements, facilities* **sōbi**
予備 *spare, reserve* **yobi**
全備 *fully-geared, fully-equipped* **zenbi**
金準備 *gold reserves* **kinjunbi**
再軍備 *re-armament, arms build-up* **saigunbi**

与*rovide, 349*	擁*upport, 151*
賄*rovide, 806*	支*upport, 201*
給*upply, 143*	貢*upport, 625*
納*upply, 296*	援*upport, 820*

偏*ncline, 43*

319-B

備*repare for a* 用*urpose to* 用*tilize your utmost...*

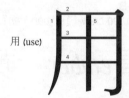

用 (use)

用*urpose*   用*tilize*

mochi(iru), YŌ
purpose, utilize, function, avail-of, things-to-do

FLIP: 2.0.b. Sort Of (stem)

服用 *"to be taken internally..."* **fukuyō**
御用 *business, order* **goyō**
併用 *combination, mixture, blending* **heiyō**
費用 *cost, expenses* **hiyō**
器用 *clever, skillful* **kiyō**
雇用 *employment* **koyō**
効用 *effect, use, utility* **kōyō**
公用 *official use* **kōyō**
利用 *use, avail of* **riyō**
採用 *employment, hiring* **saiyō**
信用 *trust, confidence* **shinyō**
私用 *private use* **shiyō**
使用 *use, apply, employ* **shiyō**
転用 *divert, convert* **tenyō**
盗用 *plagiarism, literary theft* **tōyō**
用談 *business talks* **yōdan**
用語 *term, terminology* **yōgo**
用具 *tool, implement* **yōgu**
用意 *preparation, alertness* **yōi**

用事 *business, purpose* **yōji**
用心 *carefulness, preparedness* **yōjin**
用件 *case, matter* **yōken**
用紙 *form, sheet* **yōshi**
用水 *irrigation water* **yōsui**
用材 *lumber, timber* **yōzai**
副作用 *side effects* **fukusayō**
御用足し *delivery, purveyor* **goyōtashi**
慣用句 *idiom, efigurative speech* **kanyōku**
用向き *"for business purposes..."* **yōmuki**
用足し *errand; going to the restroom* **yōtashi**
算用数字 *Arabic numbers* **sanyō sūji**

使*tilize, 480*	要*ecessity, 419*
利*dvantage, 686*	備*urnish, 409*
得*dvantage, 940*	賄*urnish, 806*

田*arm field, 482*

320-A

損njured crew 員embers can't remember...

損njury 損amage

soko(nau), soko(neru), SON
injury, damage, harm, hurting

手⇔扌 (hand, manual)

FLIP: 7.0.b2. Right (stem)

減損 decrease, depreciation, degrading **genson**
破損 damage, disaster, harm **hason**
海損 sea damage **kaison**
欠損 deficiency, loss **kesson**
毀損 damage, injury **kison**
丸損 total loss **maruzon**
摩損 wearing down, wear & tear **mason**
大損 heavy damage, incremental loss **oozon**
汚損 stain, dirt, soiled **oson**
両損 loss for both sides, no-win situation **ryōzon**
差損 balance sheet loss **sason**
損益 profit & loss, loss & gain **son'eki**
損害 damage, injury, loss **songai**
損害保険 hazard insurance **songai**
損金 financial loss **sonkin**
損耗 wear & tear **sonmō**
損保 damage insurance, non-life insurance **sonpo**
損率 loss factor **sonritsu**
損料 rental fee **sonryō**

損失 loss, failure **sonshitsu**
損傷 damage, injury **sonshō**
損得 loss & gain, profit & loss **sontoku**
雑損 miscellaneous losses **zasson**
全損 total loss **zenson**
骨折り損 waste of time, vain efforts **honeorizon**
見損なう fail to see, oversight **misokonau**
言い損なう fail to say, misspeak **iisokonau**
数え損なう miscount **kazoesokonau**
成り損なう unable to become **narisokonau**
逃げ損なう unable to escape **nigesokonau**
死に損なう fail to die (suicide), outlive one's time **shi(ni) sokonau**

害njury, 904	痛njury, 60
傷njury, 933	禍alamity, 799
障njury, 325	災alamity, 571

慣et used to, 532

320-B

損njured crew 員embers can't remember...

員ember 員taff

IN
member, staff, affiliate, constituent

口 (mouth)

FLIP: 1.0.b. Whole (stem)

部員 club member, staff member **buin**
団員 group member **dan'in**
駅員 station employee **ekiin**
幅員 road width, ship width **fukuin**
減員 staff reduction, labour downsizing **gen'in**
議員 legislator, lawmaker **giin**
委員 committee member **iin**
員数 number of persons **inzū**
海員 sailor, seaman **kaiin**
会員 member, membership **kaiin**
係員 office clerk **kakariin**
欠員 job vacancy, job recruitment **ketsuin**
雇員 temporary staff, tempt **koin**
工員 factory worker, ~worker **kōin**
満員 full, "no seats available..." **man'in**
船員 ship crew, sailor, seamen **sen'in**
社員 staff member, employee, workforce **shain**
所員 staff member, employee, workforce **shoin**
職員 staff member, employee, workforce **shokuin**

総員 total membership **sōin**
定員 regular limit, fixed capacity **teiin**
店員 salesclerk **ten'in**
役員 executive, officer-level **yakuin**
要員 staff, work force **yōin**
全員 everyone in the group **zen'in**
調査員 examiner, investigator **chōsain**
代議員 representative, delegate **daigiin**
銀行員 bank clerk, ~employee **ginkōin**
医局員 medical staff **ikyokuin**
事務員 office clerk **jimuin**

人erson, 2	組roup, 138
家xpert, 909	団roup, 345
師xpert, 483	協ooperate, 577

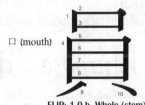

買urchase, 516   貝hellfish, 516

321-A
Green 葉eaves fill the 世orld of Adam & Eve...

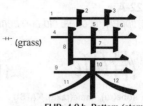

葉*eaf*   葉*oliage*

-#- (grass)

ha, YŌ
leaf, foliage

FLIP: 4.0.b. Bottom (stem)
FLIP: 3.0.b. Top (stem)

青葉 *young leaves* **aoba**
中葉 *in the middle of* **chūyō**
枝葉 *branches & leaves* **edaha**
葉蜂 *sawfly* **habachi**
葉書 *postcard* **hagaki**
葉巻 *cigar* **hamaki**
葉巻き入れ *cigar case* **hamakiire**
葉桜 *sakura leaf* **hazakura**
葉末 *tip of a leaf* **hazue**
葉月 *august, month of autumn* **hazuki**
言葉 *word, phrase* **kotoba**
黄葉 *yellow leaves* **kōyō**
紅葉 *autumn leaves* **kōyō**, **momiji**
草葉 *one's gravesite* **kusaba**
松葉 *pine needle* **matsuba**
落葉 *fallen leaves* **rakuyō**
単葉 *single leaf* **tanyō**
若葉 *young leaves* **wakaba**
葉芽 *leaf bud* **yōga**

葉柄 *leafstalk, petiole* **yōhei**
葉脈 *vein, artery, nerve* **yōmyaku**
葉身 *leaf blade* **yōshin**
前葉 *previous page* **zenyō**
花言葉 *flowery language, high falutin* **hanakotoba**
落ち葉 *fallen leaves* **ochiba**
押し葉 *preserved-, pressed leaf* **oshiba**
針葉樹 *conifer, needle-leaf tree* **shinyōju**
葉緑素 *chlorophyll* **yōryokuso**
話し言葉 *spoken language* **hanashikotoba**
書き言葉 *written language, literary* **kakikotoba**

木*ree, 461*	植*egetation, 783*
植*lant, 783*	畑*lantation, 482*
菜*egetable, 915*	緑*reen, 841*

棄*bandon, 608*

321-B
Green 葉eaves fill the 世orld of Adam & Eve...

一 (one, single)

世*orld*   世*ociety*

yo, SEI, SE
world, society, public, age

Facing: 2.0. East ☞ (W)

治世 *reign, rule* **chisei**
中世 *Medieval Ages* **chūsei**
濁世 *"this corrupt world..."* **dakusei**
現世 *present life* **gense**
一世 *first generation; a lifetime* **issei**
辞世 *demise, death, passing away* **jisei**
時世 *"these times..."* **jisei**
来世 *life after death* **raise**
乱世 *anarchy, mob rule* **ransei**
世評 *reputation; public opinion* **sehyō**
世紀 *century* **seiki**
世事 *worldly affairs* **seji**
世界 *world* **sekai**
世界観 *view-of-life, world view* **sekaikan**
世界史 *world history* **sekaishi**
世界平和 *world peace* **sekai heiwa**
世間 *public, society-at-large* **seken**
世間話 *chattering, gossip* **seken banashi**
世話 *care, aid, help, minding* **sewa**

世俗 *worldly affairs, secular life* **sezoku**
処世 *conduct of life* **shosei**
出世 *life success, success story* **shusse**
渡世 *making a living, getting by* **tosei**
世論 *public opinion* **yoron**, **seron**
絶世 *unsurpassed, peerless* **zessei**
顔見世 *showing one's face; debut* **kaomise**
創世記 *Genesis, creation* **sōseiki**
浮き世 *transient world, this world* **ukiyo**
世の中 *the public, society-at-large* **yo no naka**
世継ぎ *heir, heiress, successor* **yotsugi**
俗世間 *the world, everyday life* **zokuseken**

界*orld, 365*	公*ublic, 180*
衆*opulace, 766*	公*ommunity, 180*

屯*eployment, 198*

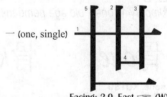

322-A

滑lippery 骨ones, old age bemoans...

滑 slide   滑 lippery

水 ⇔ 氵 (water)

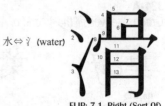

FLIP: 7.1. Right (Sort Of)

sube(ru), name(raka), KATSU
slide, slippery, skidding, smooth

滑らす *letting one slip, ~slide* **suberasu**
円滑 *smooth, seamless* **enkatsu**
平滑 *smooth, seamless* **heikatsu**
潤滑 *lubrication, smooth* **junkatsu**
潤滑油 *lubricating oil* **junkatsuyu**
滑降 *descent, fall* **kakkō**
滑空 *gliding, hovering* **kakkū**
滑石 *talc* **kasseki**
滑石粉 *talcum powder* **kassekiko**
滑車 *pulley, block* **kassha**
滑走 *gliding, sliding* **kassō**
滑走輪 *landing gear* **kassōrin**
滑走路 *airport runway* **kassōro**
滑弁 *slide valve* **katsuben**
滑脱 *adapting to circumstances* **katsudatsu**
⇒円転滑脱 *versatile, tactful, discreet*
　　enten katsudatsu
滑落 *slip, slide* **katsuraku**
滑剤 *lubricant, grease* **katsuzai**

滑稽 *comical, funny; joke* **kokkei**
滑子 *Nameko mushroom* **nameko**
滑り台 *playground slide* **suberidai**
滑り出し *start sliding, ~slipping* **suberidashi**
滑り止め *skid, tire chain* **suberidome**
滑り込み *sliding, slipping* **suberikomi**
滑り落ちる *slip, slip down* **suberiochiru**
直滑降 *straight descent, nosedive* **chokkakkō**
動滑車 *mobile pulley* **dōkassha**
地滑り *landslide, mudslide* **jisuberi**
上滑り *shallow, superficial, flimsy* **uwasuberi**
横滑り *sideslip, skid* **yokosuberi**

| 転roll over, 661 | 堕all-down, 807 |
| 陥all-down, 893 | 落all-down, 826 |

骨one, 412

322-B

滑lippery 骨ones, old age bemoans...

骨 one   骨 keleton

骨 (bone)

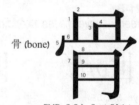

FLIP: 2.0.b. Sort Of (stem)

hone, KOTSU
bone, orthopaedics, skeleton

鼻骨 *nasal bone* **bikotsu**
分骨 *partial laying of ashes* **bunkotsu**
恥骨 *pubic bone's* **chikotsu**
白骨 *bleached bone's, skeleton* **hakkotsu**
骨細 *small-boned* **honeboso**
遺骨 *bone & ashes of the dead* **ikotsu**
人骨 *human bone, ~skeleton* **jinkotsu**
気骨 *backbone, soul, spirit* **kikotsu**
筋骨 *muscles & bone's* **kinkotsu**
骨格 *build, framework* **kokkaku**
骨灰 *bone ashes* **koppai**
骨折 *bone fracture* **kossetsu**
骨子 *main point, gist* **kosshi**
骨盤 *pelvis region* **kotsuban**
骨肉 *"one's flesh & blood..."* **kotsuniku**
骨髄 *bone marrow* **kotsuzui**
埋骨 *burial of bone ashes* **maikotsu**
納骨 *entombment of ashes* **nōkotsu**
露骨 *plain, frank, open* **rokotsu**

鎖骨 *collarbone* **sakotsu**
背骨 *backbone, spinal column* **sebone**
接骨 *bone-setting* **sekkotsu**
鉄骨 *steel frame, iron frame* **tekkotsu**
土性骨 *guts, courage* **doshōbone**
骨組み *framework, outline, frame* **honegumi**
骨接ぎ *bone-setting, bone-setter* **honetsugi**
骨休め *rest, relaxation* **honeyasume**
骨上げ *gathering ashes of the dead* **kotsuage**
頭蓋骨 *skull, skeleton head* **zugaikotsu**
骨折り損 *futile, vain efforts* **honeorizon**
骨っぽい *bony, backbone, skinny* **honeppoi**
骨董品 *antique goods* **kottōhin**
骨年齢 *one's bone age* **kotsunenrei**
骨粗鬆症 *bone old age disease* **kotsososhōshō**

| 髄 one-marrow, 806 |

過 xcessive, 798

323-A

晚vening curfew 免xemption led to defection...

日 (sunlight, daytime)

晚vening   晚ightfall

BAN

evening, nightfall, night time

FLIP: 6.0.a. Left (flat)
Facing: 1.2. ⟲ West (V)

朝晩	day & night	**asaban**
晩学	late learning, late education	**bangaku**
晩熟	late bloomer	**banjuku**
晩夏	delayed summer	**banka**
晩景	night scenery	**bankei**
晩期	final stage, latter part	**banki**
晩婚	late marriage	**bankon**
晩飯	supper, dinner	**banmeshi**
晩年	one's later years, twilight years	**bannen**
晩餐	dinner, supper, evening meal	**bansan**
晩餐会	dinner party, dinner	**bansankai**
晩成	late bloomer	**bansei**
晩節	noble living, honourable life	**bansetsu**
晩酌	night cap, dinner drink	**banshaku**
晩鐘	evening prayer bell	**banshō**
晩秋	late autumn, latter autumn	**banshū**
晩春	late spring, latter spring	**banshun**
晩霜	late frost	**bansō**
晩冬	late winter, latter winter	**bantō**

一晩	overnight, one night	**hitoban**
隔晩	every other evening	**kakuban**
今晩	this evening	**konban**
毎晩	every night	**maiban**
明晩	tomorrow evening	**myōban**
歳晩	one's final years, twilight years	**saiban**
昨晩	last night	**sakuban**
早晩	sooner-or-later	**sōban**
翌晩	tomorrow evening	**yokuban**
晩御飯	dinner, supper	**bangohan**

夕ightfall, 187	眠leeping, 495
夜ightfall, 508	寝leeping, 769
宿leep-over, 448	睡leeping, 948

映eflect, 217

323-B

晚vening curfew 免xemption led to defection...

儿 (human legs)

免xempt   免icense

manuka(reru), MEN

exempt, exception, license

Facing: 1.0. ⟲ West (W)

減免	mitigating circumstance; tax cut	**genmen**
御免	"sorry, excuse me..."	**gomen**
御免なさい	"I'm sorry, pardon me..."	**gomennasai**
罷免	dismissal, discharge, firing	**himen**
放免	custody release	**hōmen**
免疫	immunity, exemption	**men'eki**
免役	exemption from military draft	**men'eki**
免疫性	immunity, exemption	**men'ekisei**
免除	exemption, remission	**menjo**
⇒兵役免除	exempt from military service	**heieki menjo**
⇒債務免除	non-liability	**saimu menjo**
免状	license, certification	**menjō**
免官	dismissal, discharge	**menkan**
免許	license, permit	**menkyo**
免許状	license certificate	**menkyojō**
免許料	license fees	**menkyoryō**
免許証	license card	**menkyoshō**
免責	immunity, exemption	**menseki**
免職	dismissal, discharge	**menshoku**

⇒懲戒免職	disciplinary dismissal
	chōkai menshoku
⇒依願免職	resign voluntarily **igan menshoku**
⇒論旨免職	officially-hinted resignation
	yushi menshoku

免訴	acquittal, "not guilty"	**menso**
免罪	acquittal, indulgence	**menzai**
免税	tax exemption	**menzei**
免税品	duty-free goods	**menzeihin**
免税店	duty-free shop	**menzeiten**
任免	appointment & dismissal	**ninmen**
赦免	pardon, indulgence	**shamen**
特免	special license	**tokumen**

外utside, 188	異ifferent, 239
他nother, 688	許llow, 180

勉fforts, 527   逸eviate, 527

324-A
ODA 献onations go to 南outhern nations...

献onation 献ontribution

犬⇔犭 (dog; beast)

KEN, KON
donation, contribution, offer

FLIP: 6.0.b. Left (stem)

文献 *literature, writings* **bunken**
奉献 *offering, dedication* **hōken**
一献 *cup of sake* **ikkon**
献木 *lumber donated for shrine construction* **kenboku**
献茶 *powder tea offering, tea gift* **kencha**
献言 *offering one's views* **kengen**
献辞 *dedication, commitment* **kenji**
献上 *presentation, offering* **kenjō**
献花 *floral offering, flower giving* **kenka**
献血 *blood donation* **kenketsu**
献金 *contribution, donation* **kenkin**
⇒政治献金 *political donation* **seiji kenkin**
献物 *offering, dedication, present* **kenmotsu**
献納 *donation, contribution* **kennō**
献納品 *gift, present, offering* **kennōhin**
献納者 *donor, presenter* **kennōsha**
献杯 *offering a cup of wine* **kenpai**
献本 *complimentary book* **kenpon**
献策 *suggestion, proposal* **kensaku**

献酌 *offering drinks* **kenshaku**
献身 *devoting oneself* **kenshin**
献身的 *devoted, painstaking* **kenshinteki**
献酬 *exchange of sake cups* **kenshū**
献体 *organ donation upon death* **kentai**
献呈 *gift presentation* **kentei**
献灯 *votive lantern* **kentō**
貢献 *contribution, services* **kōken**
献立 *menu; arrangement, programme* **kondate**

贈*onation, 838*	賜*estow, 150*
施*estow, 649*	催*ponsor, 416*

就*mploy, 719*

324-B
ODA 献onations go to 南outhern nations...

南outhern

十 (cross)

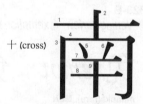

minami, NAN, NA
southern

FLIP: 1.0.b. Whole (stem)

南瓜 *pumpkin, squash* **kabocha**
真南 *directly facing south* **maminami**
南中 *acupuncture meridian line* **nanchū**
南風 *southern wind* **nanpū**
南限 *southern limit* **nangen**
南国 *southern nation* **nanngoku**
南緯 *south latitude* **nan'i**
南下 *going south* **nanka**
南海 *southern seas* **nankai**
南京 *Nanjing, China* **nankin**
南京錠 *padlock* **nankinjō**
南京虫 *bedbug* **nankinmushi**
南航 *sail south* **nankō**
南極 *South Pole, Antarctic* **nankyoku**
南面 *facing south* **nanmen**
南欧 *southern Europe* **nan'ō**
南方 *tropics, southward* **nanpō**
南西 *southwest* **nansei**
南端 *southernmost tip* **nantan**

南天 *mandin, southern stars* **nanten**
南洋 *southern seas* **nanyō**
指南 *instruct, coach* **shinan**
南半球 *southern hemisphere* **minami hankyū**
南向き *facing south* **minamimuki**
南極海 *Antarctic ocean* **nankyokukai**
南極圏 *Antarctic zone* **nankyokuken**
南極点 *South Pole* **nankyokuten**
東南東 *east southeast* **tōnantō**
南北戦争 *US civil war (1861-1865)*
  nanboku sensō
南極大陸 *Antarctic continent, Antarctica*
  nankyoku tairiku
南十字星 *southern cross* **minami jūjisei**

北*orthern, 372*	東*astern, 220*
西*estern, 18*	

真*incere, 487*

325-A

愁rief in 秋utumn came brief for Tom...

心⇔忄 (heart, feelings)

愁rief　　愁orrows

ure(i), ure(eru), SHŪ
grief, sorrows, gloomy, melancholy, sadness

Facing: 3.0. ☞☜ Across

哀愁 *grave-, deep sorrows* **aishū**
悲愁 *sorrow, pathos* **hishū**
郷愁 *homesickness, longing to come home* **kyōshū**
離愁 *sorrows of separation* **rishū**
旅愁 *journey loneliness, ~sickness* **ryoshū**
愁眉 *worried look, anxious face* **shūbi**
愁思 *grief, worry, distress* **shūshi**
愁傷 *extreme sorrow, painful grief* **shūshō**
愁色 *worried look, sullen face* **shūshoku**
愁嘆 *tragic, disaster* **shūtan**
愁嘆場 *scene of disaster, tragic scene* **shūtanba**
愁雲 *gloomy atmosphere* **shūun**
憂愁 *gloom, melancholy* **yūshū**
幽愁 *gloom, melancholy* **yūshū**
愁傷様 *"my heart-felt sympathy..."* **shūshōsama**
愁訴 *symptoms, signs of* **shūso**
⇒不定愁訴 *indeterminate symptoms* **futei shūso**

悲orrows, 289	禍ragedy, 799
哀orrows, 374	惨ragedy, 396
憂loomy, 556	厄ragedy, 354
暗loomy, 315	虐ruelty, 870

然s such, 445

325-B

愁rief in 秋utumn came brief for Tom...

禾 (tree branch)

秋

秋utumn　　秋all

aki, SHŪ
autumn, fall

FLIP: 7.1. Right (Sort Of)

秋口 *start of autumn* **akiguchi**
秋草 *autumn flowers* **akigusa**
秋風 *autumn breeze* **akikaze**
秋作 *autumn crops* **akisaku**
秋雨 *autumn rain* **akisame**
秋山 *mountains in autumn* **akiyama**
晩秋 *delayed autumn* **banshū**
暮秋 *late autumn* **boshū**
仲秋 *middle of autumn* **chūshū**
今秋 *this fall, this autumn* **konshū**
立秋 *start of autumn* **risshū**
清秋 *clear autumn skies* **seishū**
新秋 *early autumn* **shinshū**
初秋 *start of autumn* **shoshū**
秋分 *autumnal equinox* **shūbun**
秋分の日 *Autumnal Equinox Day* **shūbun no hi**
秋波 *indecent stare* **shūha**
秋日 *autumn day* **shūjitsu**
秋季 *autumn, fall* **shūki**

春秋 *spring & autumn, spring & fall* **shunjū**
秋冷 *autumn chill* **shūrei**
秋声 *autumn wind noise* **shūsei**
秋霜 *autumn frost* **shūsō**
残秋 *final days of autumn* **zanshū**
秋晴れ *nice autumn day* **akibare**
秋蒔き *planting in autumn* **akimaki**
秋植え *planting in autumn* **akiue**
秋刀魚 *saury fish, mackerel* **sanma**
千秋楽 *last day, last night* **senshūraku**
秋の夜長 *autumn long night* **aki no yonaga**

葉eaf, 411	彩olour, 914
赤ed colour, 261	色olour, 403
丹ed colour, 78	

科aculty, 194

326-A
催ponsored summit drew only 仙ermits...

人⇔亻 (person)

催ponsor 催uspices

moyō(su), SAI

sponsor, auspices, patronage, press for

FLIP: 7.2.a. Right Top (flat)

開催 opening a convention **kaisai**
開催中 "meeting in session..." **kaisaichū**
共催 joint auspices, co-sponsorship **kyōsai**
催事 exhibition, display **saiji**
催告 notification, announcement **saikoku**
催眠 hypnosis, trance, mesmerism **saimin**
催涙弾 tear-gas grenade **sairuidan**
催涙ガス tear gas **sairui gasu**
催促 demand, pressing, urging **saisoku**
主催 sponsorship, auspices **shusai**
主催者 sponsor **shusaisha**
雨催い signs of rain **amemoyoi**
居催促 stay until debt is paid **izaisoku**
催し物 entertainment, auspices **moyōshimono**
催馬楽 Gagaku song **saibara**
催淫剤 aphrodisiac, sleeping pills **saiinzai**
雪催い signs of snow **yukimoyoi**

施estow, 649 | 献onation, 414
賜estow, 150 | 贈onation, 838

備urnish, 409

326-B
催ponsored summit drew only 仙ermits...

人⇔亻 (person)

仙ermit 仙izard

SEN

hermit, supernatural, wizard, fairy, immortal mountain

FLIP: 7.0.a. Right (flat)

歌仙 master-, great poet **kasen**
銘仙 famous silk products **meisen**
仙台 Sendai City (Miyagi Prefecture) **sendai**
仙術 supernatural skills **senjutsu**
仙界 abode of immortals **senkai**
仙骨 sacrum; philosophic mind **senkotsu**
仙境 abode of immortals **senkyō**
仙郷 abode of immortals **senkyō**
仙人 hermit, mountain person **sennin**
仙薬 magical medicines, elixir **senyaku**
仙女 fairy maiden, mountain maiden **sennyo**
神仙 supernatural **shinsen**
詩仙 great poet **shisen**
酒仙 heavy drinker, alcoholic **shusen**
水仙 narcissus; daffodil **suisen**
登仙 becoming a saint **tōsen**
画仙紙 drawing paper **gasenshi**
鳳仙花 balsam, "touch-me-not..." **hōsenka**
仙人掌 cactus **saboten**

雲仙岳 Mt. Unzen (Nagasaki Pref.) **unzendake**

翁ld man, 238 | 独lone, 369
寡lone, 161 | 唯olitary, 642
孤lone, 148 | 寂onely, 911

拙lumsy, 172

327-A

電lectricity in the 雨ain struck a walking cane...

雨 (weather)

電lectricity　　電ower

FLIP: 2.0.a. Sort Of (flat)

DEN
electricity, energy, power

弔電	condolence telegram	**chōden**
電圧	voltage, electric pressure	**den'atsu**
電位	electric potential	**den'i**
電化	electrification	**denka**
電解	electrolysis	**denkai**
電機	electronics	**denki**
電気	electricity, light	**denki**
電報	telegram	**denpō**
電力	electric power, electricity	**denryoku**
電車	electric train	**densha**
電子	electron	**denshi**
電灯	flashlight, torch	**dentō**
配電	electric supply	**haiden**
受電	electric re-charge	**juden**
充電	electric re-charging	**jūden**
起電	electricity generation	**kiden**
来電	telegram	**raiden**
漏電	short circuit electricity	**rōden**
節電	electricity conservation	**setsuden**

祝電	congratulatory telegram	**shukuden**
停電	blackout, power failure, ~outage	**teiden**
蓄電池	storage battery	**chikudenchi**
超電導	superconductor	**chōdendō**
電磁気	electromagnet	**denjiki**
発電機	electric generator, dynamo	**hatsudenki**
乾電池	dry cell, dry battery	**kandenchi**
豆電球	micro bulb	**mamedenkyū**
静電気	static electricity	**seidenki**
陽電気	positive electric charge	**yōdenki**
留守番電話	voice mail	**rusuban denwa**

雷*hunder, 136*	源*ource, 431*
力*orce, 351*	発*tart, 368*
熱*eat, 153*	

雷*hunder, 136*	雪*now, 136*

327-B

電lectricity in the 雨ain struck a walking cane...

雨 (weather)

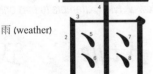

雨aining　　雨ainfall

ame, ama, U
raining, rainfall, rainwater

FLIP: 2.0.b. Sort Of (stem)

雨戸	sliding door, shutter	**amado**
雨樋	gutter	**amadoi**
雨傘	umbrella	**amagasa**
雨具	rainwear	**amagu**
雨雲	rain cloud	**amagumo**
雨靴	rain boots, galoshes	**amagutsu**
雨水	rainwater	**amamizu**
雨空	rainy skies	**amazora**
白雨	rain shower	**hakuu**
春雨	spring rain, bean threads	**harusame**
氷雨	cold rain	**hisame**
一雨	shower, rainfall	**hitoame**
霧雨	drizzle, misty rain	**kirisame**
長雨	long spell of rains	**nagaame**
大雨	rain pour	**ooame**
雷雨	thunderstorm, ~shower	**raiu**
晴雨	weather, climate	**seiu**
時雨	wintry-, autumn shower	**shigure**
梅雨	rainy season	**tsuyu**

雨季	rainy season, wet season	**uki**
雨天	rainy skies	**uten**
雨垂れ	raindrop	**amadare**
雨乞い	rain prayer	**amagoi**
雨宿り	taking shelter from rain	**amayadori**
雨降り	rainfall	**amefuri**
雨模様	signs of rain	**amemoyō**
降雨量	rainfall volume	**kōuryō**
酸性雨	acid rain	**sanseiu**
照り雨	raining on sunshine	**teriame**
通り雨	rain shower	**tooriame**

水*ater, 9*	空*ky, 394*
候*eather, 122*	雷*hunder, 136*
雲*loud, 154*	季*eason, 583*

両*air, 567*

328-A

New 式tyle 試ttempts to hire only temps....

試*ttempt*   試*rial*

言 (speaking)

kokoro(miru), tame(su), tame(shi), SHI
attempt, endeavour, trial

FLIP: 6.0.a. Left (flat)
FLIP: 8.0.a. Inner (flat)

入試 *entrance examination* **nyūshi**
試合 *game, match, contest* **shiai**
試案 *tentative plan, proposal* **shian**
試売 *trial marketing* **shibai**
試着 *clothes fitting* **shichaku**
試補 *probationer, freshman* **shiho**
試乗 *test ride* **shijō**
試験 *examination, test, quiz* **shiken**
⇒筆記試験 *written examination* **hikki shiken**
⇒国家試験 *national licensing exam* **kokka shiken**
試験管 *test tube* **shikenkan**
試験地獄 *examination ordeal* **shiken jigoku**
試掘 *prospecting, speculating* **shikutsu**
試供 *offer as a specimen, ~sample* **shikyō**
試練 *trial, probation* **shiren**
試論 *tentative, experimental* **shiron**
試作 *trial manufacture* **shisaku**
試算 *checking a calculation* **shisan**
試刷 *proof printing* **shisatsu**

試写 *preview showing (film)* **shisha**
試射 *test firing, target shooting* **shisha**
試食 *taste sampling* **shishoku**
試用 *trial, try-out* **shiyō**
追試 *make-up test, remedial test* **tsuishi**
腕試し *trying one's ability* **udetameshi**
運試し *trying one's luck* **undameshi**
力試し *physical test* **chikaratameshi**
泥試合 *mudslinging contest* **dorojiai**
試金石 *touchstone, bedrock* **shikinseki**
試運転 *trial run, test drive* **shiunten**

挑*hallenge, 214*	執*arry-out, 268*
貫*arry out, 532*	致*arry-out, 381*
行*erform, 79*	事*ction, 116*

式*tyle, 418*

328-B

New 式tyle 試ttempts to hire only temps....

式*tyle*   式*ormality*

弋 (ceremony)

SHIKI
style, formality, convention, ceremony

FLIP: 6.2. Left Bottom
Facing: 1.0. West (W)

仏式 *Buddhist rites* **busshiki**
儀式 *ceremony, rite, function* **gishiki**
本式 *regular, orthodox* **honshiki**
方式 *form, method, mode, style* **hōshiki**
形式 *form, formality* **keishiki**
旧式 *old style* **kyūshiki**
礼式 *etiquette, good manners* **reishiki**
略式 *informality, casualness* **ryakushiki**
正式 *formality, formal* **seishiki**
式服 *ceremonial dress* **shikifuku**
式辞 *ceremony speech* **shikiji**
式場 *place for ceremonies* **shikijō**
式典 *ceremony, formality* **shikiten**
葬式 *funeral-, memorial service* **sōshiki**
数式 *formula, numerical expression* **sūshiki**
等式 *equality, parity* **tōshiki**
和式 *Japanese-style* **washiki**
様式 *manner, style* **yōshiki**
図式 *diagram, chart, graph* **zushiki**

調印式 *signing ceremony* **chōinshiki**
方程式 *mathematical equation* **hōteishiki**
授賞式 *awards ceremony* **jushōshiki**
化学式 *chemical formula* **kagakushiki**
開会式 *opening ceremony* **kaikaishiki**
結婚式 *wedding, marriage ceremony* **kekkonshiki**
起工式 *ground-breaking rites* **kikōshiki**
洗礼式 *baptism, christening* **senreishiki**
卒業式 *graduation exercise* **sotsugyōshiki**
贈呈式 *presentation ceremony* **zōteishiki**
株式会社 *corporation, incorporated*
  kabushiki kaisha

的*tyle, 696*	態*ppearance, 322*
風*tyle, 894*	容*ppearance, 492*
姿*ppearance, 609*	儀*eremony, 342*

戒*dmonish, 493*

329-A
Weak 腰elvis 要ecessitates dialysis...

腰elvis   腰aist

肉⇔月 (flesh, body part)

koshi, YŌ
pelvis, pelvic joint, waist

FLIP: 7.2.a. Right Top (flat)

足腰 *legs & loins* **ashikoshi**
中腰 *semi-seated posture* **chūgoshi**
本腰 *earnestly, seriously, diligent* **hongoshi**
細腰 *slender hips* **hosogoshi**
小腰 *slight bow* **kogoshi**
腰骨 *hipbone; persevere* **koshibone**
腰高 *insolent, unstable, top heavy* **koshidaka**
腰刀 *shorter sword* **koshigatana**
腰巻 *waist cloth* **koshimaki**
腰元 *lady-in-waiting* **koshimoto**
腰肉 *sirloin* **koshiniku**
腰弱 *weak back* **koshiyowa**
腰湯 *hip-level filled bath* **koshiyu**
丸腰 *unarmed, weaponless* **marugoshi**
物腰 *movements, body mechanism* **monogoshi**
強腰 *firm posture* **tsuyogoshi**
柳腰 *slim waist, slender figure* **yanagigoshi**
腰部 *waist & hips* **yōbu**
腰囲 *hip size* **yōi**

腰間 *hips area* **yōkan**
腰痛 *lower back pain, lumbago* **yōtsū**
腰椎 *lumbar* **yōtsui**
弱腰 *weak attitude, weak bones* **yowagoshi**
腰上げ *waistline tucking* **koshiage**
腰張り *wainscot* **koshibari**
腰巾着 *shadow, hanger-on* **koshiginchaku**
腰掛け *seat, chair, bench, stool* **koshikake**
腰抜け *coward, weak-kneed, sissy* **koshinuke**
逃げ腰 *preparing to escape* **nigegoshi**
浮き腰 *floating loin* **ukigoshi**

筋 *oint, 584*	脚 *egs, 387*
筋 *uscle, 584*	足 *egs, 481*

勝 *ictory, 406*

329-B
Weak 腰elvis 要ecessitates dialysis...

要ecessity   要ssential

西⇔西 (western)

i(ru), kaname, YŌ
necessity, basic, essential, important, requirement

FLIP: 3.0.a. Top (flat)

概要 *outline, summary* **gaiyō**
需要 *demand, need* **juyō**
肝要 *essential, vital* **kanyō**
緊要 *very important* **kinyō**
紀要 *academic journal* **kiyō**
強要 *coercion, forcible* **kyōyō**
大要 *summary, outline, gist* **taiyō**
提要 *summary, compendium* **teiyō**
摘要 *summary, gist* **tekiyō**
要望 *request, demand* **yōbō**
要談 *important talk* **yōdan**
要害 *stronghold, bedrock* **yōgai**
要撃 *ambush, surprise attack* **yōgeki**
要員 *staff, work force* **yōin**
要因 *factor, cause* **yōin**
要人 *leading figure, vip* **yōjin**
要訣 *essentials, basics, fundamentals* **yōketsu**
要項 *essential points, gist, outline* **yōkō**
要綱 *summary, summation* **yōkō**

要務 *urgent business, pressing matter* **yōmu**
要塞 *fortress, fortification, stronghold* **yōsai**
要請 *request, demand, asking for* **yōsei**
要旨 *point, gist, essence* **yōshi**
要衝 *important-, strategic point* **yōshō**
要職 *important post* **yōshoku**
要素 *component, constituent* **yōso**
要用 *important matters* **yōyō**
必要 *necessity, indispensability* **hitsuyō**
要件 *necessary condition, prerequisite* **yōken**
要求 *requirement, demand, needs* **yōkyū**

素 *lement, 578*	拠 *asis, 473*
用 *vail of, 409*	基 *asis, 590*
使 *tilize, 480*	先 *head, 478*

票 *lection, 549*

330-A

Clues 置eft-behind 直irectly point to Mr. Rhind...

冖 (net, eye crown)

置ut-on   置eave-behind

o(ku), CHI
put-on, place, leave-behind

FLIP: 3.0.a. Top (flat)
FLIP: 2.0.a. Sort Of (flat)

安置	*enshrinement*	**anchi**
置換	*substitution, replacement*	**chikan**
代置	*replace*	**daichi**
布置	*arrangement, adjustment*	**fuchi**
配置	*posting, arrangement*	**haichi**
廃置	*abolish-or-establish*	**haichi**
併置	*juxtaposition, side-by-side*	**heichi**
位置	*location, position, place*	**ichi**
引置	*take custody of*	**inchi**
常置	*permanent, standing*	**jōchi**
拘置	*confinement, detention*	**kōchi**
置屋	*Geisha house*	**okiya**
留置	*custody, detention*	**ryūchi**
設置	*establishment, foundation*	**secchi**
処置	*treatment, measures, disposal*	**shochi**
措置	*measure, step, action*	**sochi**
装置	*device, equipment, apparatus*	**sōchi**
対置	*contraposition, facing across*	**taichi**
定置	*fixed, stationary*	**teichi**

転置	*transposition*	**tenchi**
倒置	*upside down, inversion, turtle turn*	**tōchi**
物置き	*closet, storage*	**mono'oki**
置き物	*ornament, decoration*	**okimono**
置き場	*place to put something*	**okiba**
買い置き	*stock, inventory*	**kaioki**
置き換え	*substitution, replacement*	**okikae**
据え置き	*deferment, postponement*	**sueoki**
捨て置く	*leave alone, overlook*	**suteoku**
留め置く	*hold, lock up, leave, detain*	**tomeoku**
取って置く	*save, keep, hold, reserve*	**totteoku**

履ut-on, 442	履ear, 442
装ear, 629	据et-in-place, 384
着ear, 589	残emain, 767

直irect, 420

330-B

Clues 置eft-behind 直irectly point to Mr. Rhind...

目 (eyesight, visual)

直irect   直traight

nao(su), nao(ru), tada(chi)ni, CHOKU, JIKI
direct, linear, straight, fixing

FLIP: 3.0.a. Top (flat)
FLIP: 2.0.a. Sort Of (flat)

直々	*directly; in person, personally*	**jikijiki**
直角	*right angle*	**chokkaku**
直覚	*intuition, hunch, sixth sense*	**chokkaku**
直轄	*direct control, ~administration*	**chokkatsu**
直径	*diameter*	**chokkei**
直系	*direct descendant*	**chokkei**
直行	*direct, non-stop*	**chokkō**
直球	*straight pitch*	**chokkyū**
直売	*direct sale, "for sale by owner..."*	**chokubai**
直便	*direct flight, non-stop flight*	**chokubin**
直営	*direct management*	**chokuei**
直後	*just after, right after*	**chokugo**
直立	*stand upright, ~erect*	**chokuritsu**
直線	*direct line*	**chokusen**
直進	*moving straight*	**chokushin**
直前	*right before*	**chokuzen**
剛直	*upright, standing up*	**gōchoku**
直納	*direct supply*	**jikinō**
直答	*direct answer*	**jikitō**

硬直	*stiffening, rigidity*	**kōchoku**
司直	*judiciary, judicature*	**shichoku**
正直	*honest, sincere*	**shōjiki**
宿直	*night duty*	**shukuchoku**
率直	*frank, candid, straightforward*	**socchoku**
垂直	*vertical, perpendicular*	**suichoku**
素直	*gentle, mind*	**sunao**
居直る	*behave menacingly*	**inaoru**
色直し	*changing of wedding gowns*	**ironaoshi**
仲直り	*reconciliation, resettlement*	**nakanaori**
直感力	*power of intuition*	**chokkanryoku**
向き直る	*turn around, ~toward*	**mukinaoru**
作り直し	*rebuilding*	**tsukurinaoshi**
考え直す	*reconsider, rethink*	**kangaenaosu**

線inear, 531	行extline, 79

値rice, 783

331-A
Cash 節*onserved* 即*mmediately reserved...*

竹 (bamboo)

❶ 節*onserve* ❷ 節*eason* ❸ 節*not*

fushi, SETSU
conserve, saving, moderation; season, period; knot

Facing: 2.2. East ☞ (V)
Facing: 4.0. ☞☞ Apart

❶ 晩節 *noble living* **bansetsu**
節制 *moderation, self-restraint* **sessei**
節食 *eating moderately, dieting* **sesshoku**
節酒 *drinking moderately* **sesshu**
節操 *integrity, fidelity, constancy* **sessō**
節水 *water conservation* **sessui**
節電 *power conservation, saving electricity* **setsuden**
節度 *sobriety, moderation, temperance* **setsudo**
節煙 *cigarette-, tobacco moderation* **setsuen**
節減 *reduction, curtailment* **setsugen**
節約 *economizing, conservation* **setsuyaku**
節用 *thrift, frugality; dictionary* **setsuyō**
貞節 *fidelity, chastity, abstinence* **teisetsu**
❷ 時節 *season, occasion* **jisetsu**
季節 *season* **kisetsu**
苦節 *unrelenting drive* **kusetsu**
末節 *frivolous-, petty-, trivial details* **massetsu**
節句 *season festival* **sekku**
節分 *day before spring* **setsubun**

使節 *delegate, envoy, emissary* **shisetsu**
章節 *chapters & sections* **shōsetsu**
当節 *popular, these days* **tōsetsu**
削り節 *dried-bonito flavouring* **kezuribushi**
腕っ節 *physical strength* **udeppushi**
分節 *partition, division* **bunsetsu**
❸ 関節 *joint, connecting point* **kansetsu**
結節 *knotting, node* **kessetsu**
音節 *syllable* **onsetsu**
節穴 *knothole* **fushiana**
節目 *knot, tie* **fushime**

季*eason, 583*	秋*utumn, 415*
冬*inter, 397*	春*pring, 579*
夏*ummer, 606*	候*limate, 122*

管*ontrol, 917*

331-B
Cash 節*onserved* 即*mmediately reserved...*

卩 (joint; stamp)

即*mmediate* 即*nstantly*

sunawachi, SOKU
immediate, instantly, forthwith

Facing: 2.2. East ☞ (V)

即決 *swift-, prompt decision* **sokketsu**
即決裁判 *summary trial* **sokketsu saiban**
即金 *ready cash, cold cash* **sokkin**
即金払い *cash payment, cash deal* **sokkinbarai**
即行 *quick-, immediate execution* **sokkō**
即効 *quick-, immediate effect* **sokkō**
即刻 *instant, at once, immediate* **sokkoku**
即今 *at this moment, right now* **sokkon**
即効性 *quick-, immediate effect* **sokkōsei**
即興 *improvisation, impromptu* **sokkyō**
即売 *direct sale, spot sale* **sokubai**
即題 *theme subject for improvisation* **sokudai**
即諾 *immediate consent* **sokudaku**
即断 *immediate decision* **sokudan**
即吟 *improvisation, impromptu* **sokugin**
即位 *enthronement, coronation* **sokui**
即位式 *enthronement, coronation rites* **sokuishiki**
即時 *instant, at once, immediate* **sokuji**
即日 *same day* **sokujitsu**

即妙 *immediate wisdom* **sokumyō**
即納 *prompt payment* **sokunō**
即応 *adaptation, conformity* **sokuō**
即製 *ready-made, instant* **sokusei**
即席 *impromptu, immediate* **sokuseki**
即死 *instant death* **sokushi**
即答 *immediate reply* **sokutō**
即夜 *same evening, same night* **sokuya**
即座 *instant, immediate* **sokuza**
展示即売会 *sale & exhibit* **tenji sokubaikai**

既*lready, 316*	現*resent, 814*
終*inish, 397*	済*onsummate, 961*
今*ow, 182*	途*urrently, 882*

即*asculine, 404*

332-A

働*abour* 動*ovement for job improvement...*

人⇔亻 (person)

働*abour* 働*orker*

hatara(ku), DŌ
labour, worker, hard work, proletariat

働き *labour, work, function* **hataraki**
働き蟻 *worker ant* **hatarakiari**
働き蜂 *workaholic, worker bee* **hatarakibachi**
働き口 *job, position* **hatarakiguchi**
働き掛ける *work on, commence work* **hatarakikakeru**
働き者 *hard worker, labourer* **hatarakimono**
働き手 *worker, driving force* **hatarakite**
働き盛り *prime of one's working age* **hatarakizakari**
実働 *actual working time* **jitsudō**
重労働 *heavy-, hard labour* **jūrōdō**
軽労働 *light work* **keirōdō**
気働き *work agility, ~dexterity* **kibataraki**
協働 *collaborative work* **kyōdō**
糠働き *futile work, fruitless labour* **nukabataraki**
労働 *labour, work* **rōdō**
⇒頭脳労働 *brain-, mental work* **zunō rōdō**
労働組合 *labour union* **rōdō kumiai**
労働力 *labour power* **rōdōryoku**

Facing: 4.0. ⟳⟲ Apart

労働者 *labourer, worker* **rōdōsha**
労働党 *labour party* **rōdōtō**
節句働き *"lazy man has no time for rest..."* **sekkubataraki**
下働き *assistant, helper; subordinate work* **shitabataraki**
立ち働き *work* **tachihataraki**
只働き *work without pay, free work* **tadabataraki**
共働き *husband & wife income* **tomobataraki**

労*orkforce, 351*	産*roduce, 883*
赴*roceed-to-work, 706*	造*roduce, 267*
作*roduce, 724*	稼*ake-a-living, 824*

動*ovement, 422*

332-B

働*abour* 動*ovement for job improvement...*

力 (strength, force)

動*ovement* 動*ction*

ugo(ku), ugokasu), DŌ
movement, action, activity, shift

微動 *tremor, slight quiver* **bidō**
動物 *animal* **dōbutsu**
動員 *deployment, mobilization* **dōin**
動機 *motive* **dōki**
動向 *trend, inclination* **dōkō**
動作 *movement* **dōsa**
動詞 *verb, action words* **dōshi**
動揺 *tremble, shake* **dōyō**
激動 *turbulence, agitation* **gekidō**
波動 *wave motion, undulation* **hadō**
発動 *put into motion* **hatsudō**
移動 *transfer, move, re-locate* **idō**
稼動 *operation, work, control* **kadō**
活動 *action, activities, projects* **katsudō**
鼓動 *beat, pulsation, pulse beating* **kodō**
行動 *action, attitude, behaviour* **kōdō**
挙動 *action, movement, behaviour* **kyodō**
鳴動 *rumbling, deep sound* **meidō**
脈動 *pulsation, pulse beating* **myakudō**

Facing: 4.0. ⟳⟲ Apart

能動 *active, dynamic, animated* **nōdō**
律動 *rhythm, rhythmic movement* **ritsudō**
策動 *maneuver, scheme* **sakudō**
扇動 *instigation, agitation, incitement* **sendō**
始動 *start, first* **shidō**
震動 *shake, tremor* **shindō**
衝動 *impulse, urge* **shōdō**
騒動 *disturbance, dispute* **sōdō**
運動 *sports; movement* **undō**
躍動 *throbbing pulse, stirring* **yakudō**
揺動 *wavering, flickering* **yōdō**
不動産 *real estate, realty* **fudōsan**
動物園 *zoo* **dōbutsuen**
自動車 *vehicle, automobile, car* **jidōsha**
運動会 *sports meet* **undōkai**

事*ction, 116*	活*ction, 237*

働*abour, 422*

333-A

撮hotos 撮ummarize 最uperlatives of any size...

手⇔扌 (hand, manual)

撮hotograph　撮ummarize

FLIP: 7.2.a. Right Top (flat)

to(ru), tsuma(mu), SATSU
photograph, summarize

撮土 pinch of earth **satsudo**
撮要 compendium, outline **satsuyō**
撮み洗い partial laundry to remove stains **tsumamiarai**
撮み出す pick out, drag out **tsumamidasu**
撮み食い eating with hands **tsumamigui**
撮み物 alcohol snacks, finger food **tsumamimono**
空撮 aerial photography **kūsatsu**
撮影 photography, shooting **satsuei**
撮影所 photography studio **satsueijo**
特撮 special camera effects **tokusatsu**
撮像管 camera image tube **satsuzōkan**
撮り方 way of taking photos **torikata**
夜間撮影 night photography **yakan satsuei**
隠し撮り sneak shot, candid shot **kakushidori**

写ortray, 349	略ummary, 825
絵rawing, 143	策easure, 875
図rawing, 47	抄ummary, 726
描rawing, 271	積stimate, 822

最aximum, 423

333-B

撮hotos 撮ummarize 最uperlatives of any size...

日 (sunlight, daytime)

最uperlative　最aximum

motto(mo), SAI
superlative, maximum, paramount, utmost, ultimate, supreme

FLIP: 3.0.a. Top (flat)

最早 "by now, already, about this time..." **mohaya**
最も the most, fully **mottomo**
最愛 "my dearest..." **saiai**
最悪 worst, worst case **saiaku**
最長 the longest **saichō**
最大 the largest, the biggest **saidai**
最期 one's end, death **saigo**
最後 final end **saigo**
最上 the highest, the finest **saijō**
最近 recently, lately **saikin**
最古 the oldest record, the oldest **saiko**
最高 maximum, the highest **saikō**
最強 the strongest **saikyō**
最良 the very best, the finest **sairyō**
最新 the newest **saishin**
最深 the deepest **saishin**
最少 the fewest, the least in number **saishō**
最小 the smallest, minimum **saishō**
最終 the final, the last **saishū**

最多 the most number of **saita**
最短 the shortest **saitan**
最低 the lowest, minimum **saitei**
最適 the most suitable **saiteki**
最雑 the most assorted, ~varied **saizatsu**
最善 the very best, the finest **saizen**
最寄り nearby place **moyori**
最重要 the most important **saijūyō**
最優秀 superior, the very best **saiyūshū**
最戦線 battle frontlines **saizensen**
真っ最中 right in the middle of **massaichū**

窮xtreme, 876	端ndpoint, 974
極xtreme, 947	超xceed, 664
甚xtreme, 293	越vertake, 663

撮hotograph, 423

334-A

訴awsuit on 訴ppeal, plaintiffs 斥eject the deal...

言 (speaking)

訴awsuit 訴ppeal

utta(eru), SO

lawsuit, appeal, court suit, indictment, charges, legal complaint, accusation, allegation

FLIP: 6.0.a. Left (flat)
Facing: 2.2. East ☞ (V)

哀訴 *appeal to a higher court* **aiso**
敗訴 *losing a lawsuit* **haiso**
反訴 *countersuit* **hanso**
直訴 *direct appeal* **jikiso**
上訴 *appeal to a higher court* **jōso**
受訴 *court acceptance of lawsuit* **juso**
起訴 *prosecution, indictment* **kiso**
⇒不起訴 *not prosecuted, not indicted* **fukiso**
告訴 *accusation, lawsuit* **kokuso**
公訴 *prosecution, indictment* **kōso**
控訴 *appeal, petition* **kōso**
免訴 *acquittal, "not guilty..."* **menso**
応訴 *reply to a complaint* **ōso**
勝訴 *winning a lawsuit* **shōso**
主訴 *principal complaint* **shuso**
愁訴 *appeal, entreaty* **shūso**
訴願 *decision, appeal* **sogan**
訴願人 *appellee, petitioner* **sogannin**
訴因 *charge, complaint* **soin**

訴状 *filing a petition* **sojō**
訴求 *business solicitation* **sokyū**
訴人 *plaintiff, complainant* **sonin**
⇒被上訴人 *appellee, petitioner* **hijō sonin**
訴訟 *lawsuit, court suit* **soshō**
⇒刑事訴訟 *criminal complaint* **keiji soshō**
訴訟手続 *legal proceedings* **soshō tetsuzuki**
訴追 *impeachment judge* **sotsui**
提訴 *lawsuit, court suit* **teiso**
追訴 *additional indictment* **tsuiso**
被起訴者 *indictee, complainant* **hikisosha**

訟*ccusation, 181*	決*udgement, 699*
廷*ourt-of-law, 26*	裁*udgement, 802*
法*egal, 360*	判*udgement, 949*

斥*eject, 424*

334-B

訴awsuit on 訴ppeal, plaintiffs 斥eject the deal...

斤 (axe)

斥eject 斥xclude

SEKI

reject, exclude, expel, remove

Facing: 2.0. East ☞ (W)

排斥 *exclude, expel, reject* **haiseki**
賓斥 *exclude, expel, reject* **hinseki**
除斥 *exclude, expel, reject* **joseki**
斥力 *repulsive force* **sekiryoku**
斥候 *scouting the enemy* **sekkō**

排*ejection, 795*	除*xclude, 501*
断*ejection, 958*	排*xclude, 795*
否*ejection, 300*	外*utside, 188*

丘川, *106*

335-A

銘*ignatures claim* 銘*recepts of great* 名*ames to respect...*

金 (metal)

銘*ignature* ² **銘***recepts*

MEI
signature, inscription; precepts, motto

FLIP: 6.0.a. Left (flat)
FLIP: 7.3.a. Right Bottom (flat)

❶ 墓銘 *tombstone epitaph* **bomei**
碑銘 *tombstone epitaph* **himei**
感銘 *deeply touched, ~moving* **kanmei**
記銘 *engraving* **kimei**
銘板 *nameplate* **meiban**
銘木 *precious wood* **meiboku**
銘文 *inscription, engraving* **meibun**
銘茶 *famous tea brand* **meicha**
銘柄 *brand, trademark* **meigara**
銘柄品 *top-brand goods* **meigarahin**
銘柄売買 *sale by trademark* **meigara baibai**
銘菓 *high-quality cake* **meika**
銘記 *keeping-, bearing in mind* **meiki**
銘銘 *each, every, per piece* **meimei**
銘銘伝 *biographies* **meimeiden**
銘銘皿 *small plate* **meimeizara**
銘仙 *high-class silk cloth* **meisen**
銘酒 *high-quality sake* **meishu**
銘酒屋 *whorehouse, brothel* **meishuya**

銘刀 *famous sword brand* **meitō**
無銘 *anonymous, unknown* **mumei**
銘打つ *call; inscription* **meiutsu**
墓碑銘 *tombstone epitaph* **bōimei**
墓誌銘 *tombstone epitaph* **bōshimei**

❷ 座右の銘 *personal motto* **zayū no mei**

署*ignature, 614*
称*itular, 130*
名*ame, 425*

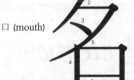
鈴*ell, 683*

335-B

銘*ignatures claim* 銘*recepts of great* 名*ames to respect...*

口 (mouth)

名*urname* 名*ame*

na, MEI, MYŌ
name, surname, family name

FLIP: 4.0.a. Bottom (flat)

別名 *alias, pseudonym, pen name* **betsumei**
題名 *title, theme, subject* **daimei**
大名 *feudal lord* **daimyō**
芸名 *screen name* **geimei**
本名 *one's real name* **honmyō**
名案 *good idea* **meian**
名簿 *name list, roster* **meibo**
名画 *famous painting, masterpiece* **meiga**
名言 *wise proverb, famous saying* **meigen**
名義 *registered owner* **meigi**
名人 *expert* **meijin**
名歌 *famous, poem, song* **meika**
名鑑 *directory, name list* **meikan**
名句 *wise proverb, noted saying* **meiku**
名曲 *masterpiece music* **meikyoku**
命名 *naming, christening* **meimei**
名目 *alibi, excuse, pretext* **meimoku**
名作 *masterpiece work* **meisaku**
名声 *fame, popularity* **meisei**

名詞 *noun* **meishi**
名刺 *name card, business card* **meishi**
名称 *title, rank, status* **meishō**
名所 *famous places* **meisho**
名誉 *honour* **meiyo**
名札 *nameplate, name tag* **nafuda**
名前 *name* **namae**
姓名 *surname, family name* **seimei**
氏名 *name* **shimei**
署名 *signature, sign* **shomei**
有名 *famous, well-known, popular* **yūmei**
名産品 *special product, delicacy* **meisanhin**
平仮名 *Hiragana* **hiragana**
片仮名 *Katakana* **katakana**
名氏 *celebrity, famous person* **meishi**

氏*urname, 489*　　姓*urname, 638*

各*very, 498*

336-A

誌hronicle of inventions had simple 志ntentions...

言 (speaking)

誌hronicle   誌ecord

shirushi, SHI
chronicle, record, magazine

FLIP: 6.0.a. Left (flat)
FLIP: 7.2.a. Right Top (flat)

米誌 *American magazine* **beishi**
墓誌 *life story inscribed on tomb* **boshi**
地誌 *local topography* **chishi**
英誌 *English magazine* **eishi**
語誌 *word root, etymology* **goshi**
本誌 *this magazine* **honshi**
日誌 *daily journal, diary* **nisshi**
⇒航海日誌 *ship logbook* **kōkai nisshi**
誌上 *in this magazine* **shijō**
誌面 *in a magazine* **shimen**
誌友 *fellow subscriber* **shiyū**
書誌 *bibliography, references* **shoshi**
雑誌 *magazine, journal* **zasshi**
⇒同人雑誌 *small magazine* **dōjin zasshi**
⇒婦人雑誌 *ladies magazine* **fujin zasshi**
⇒娯楽雑誌 *popular magazine* **goraku zasshi**
⇒機関雑誌 *agency publication* **kikan zasshi**
⇒総合雑誌 *general-interest magazine* **sōgō zasshi**

月刊誌 *monthly magazine* **gekkanshi**
機関誌 *bulletin, organ* **kikanshi**
季刊誌 *quarterly magazine* **kikanshi**
植物誌 *magazine on flowers* **shokubutsushi**
週刊誌 *weekly magazine, weekly* **shūkanshi**

記*ecord, 728*		録*ecord, 841*	史*istory, 85*
簿*ecord, 64*		紀*eriod, 727*	歴*istory, 595*

読*eading, 260*

336-B

誌hronicle of inventions had simple 志ntentions...

心⇔忄 (heart, feelings)

志ntention   志otive

kokorozashi, kokoroza(su), SHI
intention, motive, volition, ulterior aim, ambition

FLIP: 3.0.a. Top (flat)

薄志 *feeble-minded, weak-willed* **hakushi**
芳志 *kindness, good-hearted* **hōshi**
遺志 *dying-, last wish* **ishi**
意志 *will, volition, motive* **ishi**
決志 *resolve, determination* **kesshi**
厚志 *kindness, good-hearted* **kōshi**
立志 *setting one's life aim* **risshi**
立志伝 *success story* **risshiden**
志望 *wish, aspiration, ambition* **shibō**
志望校 *school of choice* **shibōkō**
志望者 *applicant, candidate* **shibōsha**
志願 *volunteering, application* **shigan**
志願兵 *volunteer conscripts, ~soldiers* **shiganhei**
志願者 *applicant, candidate* **shigansha**
志気 *determination, burning will* **shiki**
志向 *intention, inclination* **shikō**
志士 *noble patriot* **shishi**
志操 *purpose, principle, constancy* **shisō**
初志 *original intention, primary aim* **shoshi**

夙志 *long-cherished dream* **shukushi**
素志 *long-cherished dream* **soshi**
寸志 *little token of gratitude* **sunshi**
大志 *ambition, aspiration* **taishi**
篤志 *charity, benevolence* **tokushi**
篤志家 *philanthropist, charitable person* **tokushika**
闘志 *fighting spirit, espirit-de-corps* **tōshi**
有志 *interest, concern* **yūshi**
雄志 *lofty ambition* **yūshi**
青雲の志 *noble-, lofty ambitions*
　　　seiun no kokorozashi

意*dea, 340*		提*roposal, 313*
想*dea, 524*		慮*hought, 70*
念*dea, 182*		案*roposal, 609*

忘*orget, 34*

337-A

握*ripped by folklore, reader sleeps in a book* 屋*tore...*

手⇔扌 (hand, manual)

握*rasp*　　握*rip*　　握*old*

nigi(ru), AKU
grasp, grip, clinch, clutches, glutches, hold

握り飯 *rice-ball* **nigirimeshi**
握り屋 *tight-fisted* **nigiriya**
握り鮨 *Nigiri sushi* **nigirizushi**
握り潰す *shelve, crush* **nigiritsubusu**
握り寿司 *Nigiri sushi* **nigirizushi**
握りこぶし *handfist* **nigirikobushi**
握り締める *grasp tightly, grip hard* **nigirishimeru**
握力 *grip, hold, grasp* **akuryoku**
握力計 *hand dynamometer* **akuryokukei**
握手 *handshake* **akushu**
把握 *grasping, understanding* **haaku**
一握 *"a handful of..."* **ichiaku**
一握り *"a handful of..."* **hitonigiri**
掌握 *commandeering, seizure* **shōaku**

FLIP: 7.3.a. Right Bottom (flat)
Facing: 4.0. ☜☞ Apart

持*olding, 249*　　轄*ontrol, 968*
取*ake, 229*　　管*ontrol, 917*
摂*ake over, 612*　　捕*eizure, 812*

据*et-in-place, 384*

337-B

握*ripped by folklore, reader sleeps in a book* 屋*tore...*

尸 (corpse)

❶屋*ouse*　　❷屋*tore*

ya, OKU
house, shelter; outlet, shop, small store

❶廃屋 *abandoned house* **haioku**
部屋 *room, flat* **heya**
平屋 *one-story house, bungalow* **hiraya**
火屋 *lamp cover* **hoya**
家屋 *house* **kaoku**
仮屋 *temporary shelter* **kariya**
水屋 *water basin at a shrine* **mizuya**
長屋 *row houses* **nagaya**
屋外 *open air, outdoors* **okugai**
屋上 *roof, rooftop* **okujō**
屋内 *inside, interior* **okunai**
霊屋 *mausoleum* **tamaya**
屋根 *roof* **yane**
屋敷 *mansion, manor house* **yashiki**
屋根裏部屋 *attic* **yaneurabeya**
❷屋台 *stand, stall, booth* **yatai**
花屋 *flower shop, florist* **hanaya**
本屋 *bookstore, book dealer* **honya**
紺屋 *dyer's shop* **konya**

FLIP: 4.0.a. Bottom (flat)
Facing: 2.1. East ☞ (H)

薬屋 *drugstore, pharmacy* **kusuriya**
飯屋 *cheap eatery* **meshiya**
店屋 *shop, store* **miseya**
餅屋 *rice cake dealer* **mochiya**
肉屋 *butcher, meat shop* **nikuya**
魚屋 *fish dealer, fish store* **sakanaya**
鮨屋 *sushi bar, ~restaurant* **sushiya**
畳屋 *tatami maker (straw floormat)* **tatamiya**
闇屋 *black marketeer* **yamiya**
屋号 *store name* **yagō**
殺し屋 *assassin, gun-for-hire* **koroshiya**
飲み屋 *bar, pub house* **nomiya**
裏長屋 *back alley row houses* **uranagaya**
呼び屋 *promoter* **yobiya**

店*tore, 222*　　舗*tore, 813*

握*rasp, 427*

338-A

声oices of tenor, behind the 戸oor...

士 (samurai, warrior)

声oice　声ocals

koe, kowa, SEI, SHŌ
voice, vocals

FLIP: 3.0.a. Top (flat)

濁声 thick-, stentorian voice **dakusei**
怒声 furious-, angry voice **dosei**
鼻声 nasal voice **hanagoe**
発声 vocalization, verbalizing **hassei**
砲声 roaring of a gunfire **hōsei**
銃声 gunshot noise **jūsei**
歓声 shout of joy, cheers **kansei**
声色 voice impersonation, mimicry **kowairo**
名声 fame, popularity **meisei**
涙声 crying voice, sobs **namidagoe**
肉声 bare voice (without microphone) **nikusei**
音声 voice, sound **onsei**
声望 reputation, popularity, fame **seibō**
声調 tone of voice **seichō**
声援 encouragement, cheering **seien**
声楽 vocal music, chorus **seigaku**
声価 reputation, honour **seika**
声明 statement, declaration **seimei**
声量 volume of voice **seiryō**

声帯 vocal cords **seitai**
声優 voice actor, voice actress **seiyū**
嘆声 sight-of-relief, ~admiration **tansei**
震え声 trembling voice **furuegoe**
擬声語 onomatopoeic word **giseigo**
掛け声 shout, call **kakegoe**
拡声器 loudspeaker **kakuseiki**
鳴き声 song, cry, chirp **nakigoe**
泣き声 crying-, tearful voice, sobbing **nakigoe**
叫び声 shout, scream, shriek **sakebigoe**
喚き声 shout, scream, yell, shriek **wamekikoe**
笑い声 laughter, laughing **waraigoe**

音ound, 314	話peech, 236
曲elody, 476	弁peech, 570
叫cream, 693	伝onvey, 619
鳴owling, 842	

戸oor, 428

338-B

声oices of tenor, behind the 戸oor...

戸 (doorway)

戸oor　戸ousehold

to, he, KO
door, entrance, household

Facing: 2.0. East ☞ (W)

雨戸 sliding door, shutter **amado**
網戸 screen door, window screen **amido**
江戸 old name for Tōkyō (1603-1867) **edo**
下戸 non-drinker, teetotaller, abstemious **geko**
井戸 water well **ido**
岩戸 cave door **iwato**
上戸 drinker **jōgo**
木戸 wicket, garden gate **kido**
戸別 door-to-door **kobetsu**
戸外 outdoors, open air **kogai**
戸籍 family register **koseki**
戸主 head of the family **koshu**
戸数 number of houses **kosū**
門戸 door, opening; possibility **monko**
納戸 storehouse **nando**
戸袋 shutter box **tobukuro**
戸棚 closet, cupboard **todana**
戸口 doorway, entrance **toguchi**
八戸市 Hachinohe City, Aomori Pref. **hachinohe-shi**

引き戸 sliding door **hikido**
開き戸 hinged door **hirakido**
神戸市 Kōbe City, Hyōgo Prefecture **kōbe-shi**
格子戸 lattice door **kōshido**
潜り戸 wicket **kugurido**
繰り戸 sliding door **kurido**
瀬戸際 brink, verge, critical moment **setogiwa**
瀬戸物 china, porcelain, pottery **setomono**
戸惑う be perplexed, be baffled **tomadō**
泣き上戸 sentimental drunkard **nakijōgo**
戸締まり door lock **tojimari**
笑い上戸 good laugher, merry drinker **waraijōgo**

扉oor, 678	入nter, 2
門ate, 286	出xit, 173
口pening, 458	

所ocation, 676

339-A
腐otten & 腐poiled, a 府overnment roiled...

腐otten　　腐poiled

肉⇔月 (flesh, body part)

FLIP: 4.0.b. Bottom (stem)

kusa(ru), kusa(reru), kusa(rasu), FU
rotten, spoiled, decay, mouldering

防腐 *preserving, embalming* **bōfu**
防腐剤 *anti-septic, preservative* **bōfuzai**
陳腐 *hackneyed, stereotyped* **chinpu**
腐敗 *rot, decay, spoiling* **fuhai**
腐儒 *unworthy scholar* **fuju**
腐刑 *castration, gelding* **fukei**
腐刻 *etching* **fukoku**
腐朽 *decay, rottening* **fukyū**
腐肉 *spoiled meat* **funiku**
腐乱 *decomposition, rottening* **furan**
腐卵 *rotten egg* **furan**
腐爛 *ulcer* **furan**
腐心 *tremendous efforts* **fushin**
腐食 *corrosion, rottening away* **fushoku**
腐臭 *rotten odour* **fushū**
豆腐 *bean curd* **tōfu**
⇒氷豆腐 *chilled toufu* **kooridōfu**
⇒焼き豆腐 *grilled toufu* **yakitōfu**
⇒奴豆腐 *tofu cubes* **yakkodōfu**

⇒湯豆腐 *boiled bean curd* **yutōfu, yudōfu**
豆腐屋 *bean curd maker, ~shop* **tōfuya**
腐葉土 *leaf mould* **fuyōdo**
腐植土 *humus* **fushokudo**
腐れ縁 *undesirable bond* **kusareen**
目腐れ *bleary-eyed* **mekusare**
目腐れ金 *alms for the poor* **mekusaregane**
腐乱死体 *rotten corpse* **furan shitai**
不貞腐れ *spiteful, sulky* **futekusare**
立ち腐れ *rottening on the vine* **tachigusare**
蒸れ腐され *dry rottening* **muregusare**

菌*acteria, 52*
汚*irty, 737*
毒*oison, 578*

府*overnment, 429*

339-B
腐otten & 腐poiled, a 府overnment roiled...

府overnment

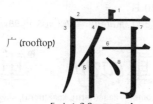

广 (rooftop)

Facing: 3.0. 👉👈 Across

FU
government, urban prefecture

幕府 *Shogunate government* **bakufu**
府庁 *urban prefectural office* **fuchō**
府下 *suburbia, suburb districts* **fuka**
府会 *urban prefectural assembly* **fukai**
府警 *prefectural police* **fukei**
府県 *prefectures* **fuken**
⇒都道府県 *prefectural system* **todōfuken**
学府 *academic elite, intelligentsia* **gakufu**
⇒最高学府 *highest educational institution*
　　　saikō gakufu
覇府 *Shogunate government* **hafu**
国府 *ancient provincial capital* **kokufu**
冥府 *world of the dead* **meifu**
政府 *government* **seifu**
政府間 *government-to-government* **seifukan**
首府 *nations capital* **shufu**
枢府 *privy council* **sūfu**
別府市 *Beppu City (Oita Prefecture)* **beppu-shi**
鎮守府 *naval station* **chinjufu**

大宰府 *ancient headquarters in Kyūshū* **dazaifu**
軍政府 *military government* **gunseifu**
反政府 *rebel, renegade, anti-government*
　　　hanseifu
仮政府 *provisional government* **kariseifu**
甲府市 *Kōfu City, Yamanishi Prefecture* **kōfu-shi**
京都府 *Kyōto City government* **kyōto-fu**
大阪府 *Ōsaka municipal government* **oosaka-fu**
立法府 *law-making body, legislature* **rippōfu**
総理府 *prime minister's office* **sōrifu**
総督府 *governor-general's office* **sōtokufu**

政*olitics, 725*　　領*overn, 874*
国*ation, 92*　　民*eople, 495*
統*overn, 885*　　衆*opulace, 766*

付*ttach, 382*

340-A

種eed 種ariety 重verlaps 重eavily...

❶種ariety ❷種eedling

禾 (tree branch)

FLIP: 7.1. Right (Sort Of)

tane, SHU

variety, type, kind, genre, classification, category; seedling

❶ 断種 sterilization, castration, gelding **danshu**
業種 industry category, ~classification **gyōshu**
変種 variety, miscellaneous **henshu**
品種 variety, breed, kind **hinshu**
異種 different kind, variety **ishu**
人種 human race, mankind **jinshu**
各種 various, assortment **kakushu**
良種 good quality **ryōshu**
接種 inoculation, vaccination, immunization **sesshu**
新種 new variety, new breed **shinshu**
職種 job category, ~classification **shokushu**
種別 classification, kind **shubetsu**
種目 event, item **shumoku**
種類 kind, type **shurui**
種痘 inoculation, vaccination, immunization **shutō**
種族 race, species, tribe **shuzoku**
種火 pilot burner, ~light **tanebi**
種馬 stallion, studhorse **taneuma**
種牛 stud bull **taneushi**

特種 scoop, exclusive **tokudane**
雑種 crossbreed, hybrid, mongrel **zasshu**
言い種 remarks, excuse, alibi **iigusa**
純血種 thorough-bred **junketsushu**
種切れ out-of-materials (seeds) **tanegire**
種蒔き sowing, seeding **tanemaki**
笑い種 laughingstock, ~matter **waraigusa**
変わり種 variety, miscellaneous **kawaridane**

❷ 種子 seed, seedling **shushi**
種油 seed oil, vegetable oil **taneabura**
種畑 seed garden **tanebatake**

類ype, 156	諸arious, 794
雑arious, 776	芽prout, 57

重eavy, 430

340-B

種eed 種ariety 重verlaps 重eavily...

❶重eavy ❷重verlap

里 (hometown)

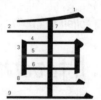

FLIP: 2.0.a. Sort Of (flat)

omo(i); kasa(naru), kasa(neru), shige, e, JŪ, CHŌ

heavy, hefty, weighty; overlap, pile-up, duplicate

❶ 厳重 strict, close, severe **genjū**
偏重 overwhelming importance **henchō**
自重 prudence, promptness **jichō**
重罰 severe punishment **jūbatsu**
重病 serious illness, gravely sick **jūbyō**
重大 serious, grave, severe **jūdai**
重犯 felony, crime **jūhan**
重砲 heavy artillery, ~bombardment **jūhō**
重重 "very much, extremely..." **jūjū**
重任 heavy responsibility **jūnin**
重量 weight, load capacity **jūryō**
重力 gravitational force, gravity **jūryoku**
重責 heavy responsibility **jūseki**
重心 centre of gravity **jūshin**
重障 serious handicap, ~disability **jūshō**
重傷 serious injury **jūshō**
重症 serious illness **jūshō**
重点 important points **jūten**
重役 executive, director, officer-level **jūyaku**

重要 important, essential **jūyō**
重税 heavy taxation **jūzei**
荷重 load, cargo **kajū**
過重 overweight **kajū**
貴重 precious, valuable, priceless **kichō**
気重 heavy hearted **kiomo**
慎重 careful, discreet **shinchō**
尊重 respect, esteem **sonchō**
体重 body weight **taijū**
❷ 重婚 bigamy, polygamy **jūkon**
重盗 double steal (baseball) **jūtō**
二重 double, two-fold **nijū**
丁重 courteous, polite, respectful **teichō**
重国籍 dual-, multiple citizenship **jūkokuseki**

軽ightweight, 790	激ntense, 170

垂ang down, 505

341-A

源*ource phenomenal when* 原*riginal...*

源*ource*　　源*rigin*

水 ⇔ 氵 (water)

minamoto, GEN
source, origin, beginning

FLIP: 8.0.b. Inner (stem)

電源 *source of electricity, power switch* **dengen**
富源 *source of wealth* **fugen**
源流 *source, origin* **genryū**
源泉 *principal source* **gensen**
源泉所得税 *withholding income tax*
　　　gensen shotokuzei
語源 *etymology, root word* **gogen**
本源 *origin, source* **hongen**
字源 *origin of a Kanji character* **jigen**
起源 *origin, beginning* **kigen**
光源 *illuminant, light source* **kōgen**
根源 *root, source* **kongen**
熱源 *heat source* **netsugen**
音源 *sound source* **ongen**
資源 *resources (natural)* **shigen**
⇒地下資源 *underground resources* **chikashigen**
⇒鉱物資源 *mineral resources* **kōbutsu shigen**
⇒森林資源 *forest resources* **shinrin shigen**
⇒天然資源 *natural resources* **tennen shigen**

水源 *water source, maritime resources* **suigen**
財源 *revenue source* **zaigen**
税源 *source of tax revenue* **zeigen**
病源菌 *pathogenic bacteria, germ* **byōgenkin**
動力源 *power source* **dōryokugen**
栄養源 *nutrient source* **eiyōgen**
情報源 *information sources* **jōhōgen**
供給源 *source of supplies* **kyōkyūgen**
震源地 *epicentre, ground zero* **shingenchi**
収入源 *source of income* **shūnyūgen**
桃源郷 *Shangri-la, paradise* **tōgenkyō**
源氏物語 *tale of genji* **genji monogatari**

| 給*upply, 143* | 納*upply, 296* |
| 充*upply, 884* | 与-*upply, 349* |

原*riginal, 431*

341-B

源*ource phenomenal when* 原*riginal...*

❶原*riginal*　❷原*lain*

厂 (cliff)

hara, GEN
original, first-hand; plain

FLIP: 8.0.b. Inner (stem)

❶病原 *cause of an illness* **byōgen**
原案 *original plan, ~bill* **gen'an**
原爆 *atom-, atomic bomb* **genbaku**
原注 *original notes* **genchū**
原画 *original picture* **genga**
原義 *original meaning* **gengi**
原語 *root word, ~language* **gengo**
原因 *cause, factor* **gen'in**
原価 *cost, price* **genka**
原型 *prototype, model* **genkei**
原形 *original shape* **genkei**
原稿 *manuscript, article* **genkō**
原告 *plaintiff, complainant, accuser* **genkoku**
原理 *fundamental cause* **genri**
原料 *raw materials, fuel* **genryō**
原作 *original works* **gensaku**
原子 *atom, molecule* **genshi**
原審 *first court trial* **genshin**
原則 *principle, general rule, policy* **gensoku**

原話 *original story* **genwa**
原油 *crude oil* **genyu**
原罪 *original sin* **genzai**
河原 *river bank, ~beach* **kawara**
原産地 *place of origin* **gensanchi**

❷高原 *plateau, high plains* **kōgen**
野原 *field, plain, the greens* **nohara**
雪原 *snowfield* **setsugen**
草原 *prairie, pampas, savannah* **sōgen**
青海原 *blue sea* **aounabara**
原っぱ *plain, field* **harappa**

| 元*rigin, 195* | 平-*lains, 488* |
| 源*rigin, 431* | 野*lains, 873* |

泉*prings, 531*

342-A

締onclude treaties to 締ighten fire of the 帝mpire...

糸 (thread, continuity)

❶締ighten ❷締onclude

shi(maru), shi(meru), shi(me), TEI
tighten; conclude

FLIP: 7.0.b1. Right (stem)

❶ 締まり *tightness* **shimari**
締り屋 *thrifty, miser, close-fisted* **shimariya**
締め金 *tightening claps* **shimegane**
締め具 *bindings* **shimegu**
締め出し *tighten* **shimedashi**
締め上げる *tighten up* **shimeageru**
締め込む *tighten, compress* **shimekomu**
締め殺す *death by strangulation* **shimekorosu**
締め付け *shutting out* **shimetsuke**
音締 *melody fine-tuning* **nejime**
胴締め *waistband* **dōjime**
元締め *manager, controller* **motojime**
緒締め *pouchbag strings* **ojime**
総締め *over-all total* **sōjime**
抱き締める *tight embrace* **dakishimeru**
踏み締める *step firmly* **fumishimeru**
羽交い締め *full nelson (wrestling)* **hagaijime**
引き締める *tighten, stiffen* **hikishimeru**
握り締める *tight grasp, hold tight* **nigirishimeru**

締め切り *deadline, target date* **shimekiri**
締め切り時間 *closing day* **shimekiri jikan**
締め切り期日 *deadline date* **shimekirikijitsu**
締め切る *closing hour* **shimekiru**
締め括り *conclusion, end* **shimekukuri**
❷ 締結 *conclude, contract* **teiketsu**
締盟 *enter into a treaty* **teimei**
締盟国 *treaty-signatory nation* **teimeikoku**
締約 *conclusion of a treaty* **teiyaku**
戸締り *house-closing for the night* **tojimari**
取締役 *company official* **torishimariyaku**

抄ummary, 726	裁udgement, 802
撮ummarize, 423	判udgement, 949
決udgement, 699	

続ontinue, 260

342-B

締onclude treaties to 締ighten fire of the 帝mpire...

巾 (cloth, fabric)

帝mpire   帝mperial

TEI
empire, imperial

FLIP: 1.0.b. Whole (stem)

廃帝 *ex-monarch, deposed emperor* **haitei**
女帝 *female emperor, empress* **jotei**
上帝 *God* **jōtei**
皇帝 *emperor* **kōtei**
露帝 *Czar of Russia* **rotei**
先帝 *deceased emperor* **sentei**
大帝 *great emperor* **taitei**
帝位 *throne, crown* **teii**
帝冠 *imperial crown* **teikan**
帝国 *empire* **teikoku**
⇒大英帝国 *the Great British Empire* **daiei teikoku**
⇒大日本帝国 *Empire of Japan* **dainippon teikoku**
帝国主義 *imperialism* **teikoku shugi**
帝王 *emperor, monarch* **teiō**
帝王切開 *caesarean delivery, c-section* **teiō sekkai**
帝陵 *imperial mausoleum* **teiryō**
帝政 *imperial government* **teisei**
帝室 *imperial household* **teishutsu**
帝都 *imperial capital* **teito**

天帝 *lord of heaven* **tentei**

皇mperor, 113	国ation, 92
克onquer, 204	帥ommander, 483
征onquer, 31	督ommander, 911
覇egemony, 603	領overn, 874

帯egion, 557

343-A

総otal rainbows, unseen from the 窓indows...

総eneral　総otal

糸 (thread, continuity)

Facing: 2.2. East ☞ (V)

sube(te), SŌ
general, total, summation

総長	general president	**sōchō**
総譜	full score	**sōfu**
総額	total amount, sum total	**sōgaku**
総合	synthesis; general, universal	**sōgō**
総意	collective will	**sōi**
総員	all members, everyone	**sōin**
総会	general assembly	**sōkai**
⇒株主総会	shareholder's meeting	**kabunushi sōkai**
総括	generalization, summarization	**sōkatsu**
総計	total amount, sum total	**sōkei**
総見	meeting a large contingent	**sōken**
総局	general affairs office	**sōkyoku**
総務	general affairs	**sōmu**
総覧	looking thru papers, skimming	**sōran**
総理	prime minister	**sōri**
総量	total weight, ~load	**sōryō**
総力	general efforts	**sōryoku**
総裁	president, chairperson	**sōsai**
総説	general remarks	**sōsetsu**

総身	whole body	**sōshin**
総則	general rules	**sōsoku**
総数	total number	**sōsū**
総帥	supreme commander	**sōsui**
総体	wholly, generally	**sōtai**
総点	total score	**sōten**
総菜	daily dishes, side dish	**sōzai**
総勢	"in all, all told..."	**sōzei**
総攻撃	all-out strike, general attack	**sōkōgeki**
総花式	across-the-board	**sōbanashiki**
総辞職	mass resignation	**sōjishoku**

皆verything, 39	毎very, 241
全ntire, 24	完omplete, 196

窓indow, 433

343-B

総otal rainbows, unseen from the 窓indows...

窓indow

穴 (hole, cave)

FLIP: 3.0.b. Top (stem)

mado, SŌ
window

窓ガラス	window glass, ~pane	**madogarasu**
出窓	bayview window	**demado**
船窓	porthole	**funamado**
学窓	studying, learning	**gakusō**
舷窓	porthole	**gensō**
獄窓	prison window	**gokusō**
風窓	air hole	**kazemado**
小窓	small window	**komado**
窓台	window sill	**madodai**
窓側	window side	**madogawa**
窓際	by the window; fence-sitter	**madogiwa**
窓口	window counter, contact person	**madoguchi**
窓枠	window frame, window sash	**madowaku**
丸窓	round window	**marumado**
車窓	car window, train window	**shasō**
深窓	secluded inner room; over-protected girl	**shinsō**
窓外	outside the window	**sōgai**
天窓	skylight, bay window	**tenmado**
鉄窓	iron grill window, prison window	**tessō**

裏窓	rear window	**uramado**
鎧窓	louver window	**yoroimado**
陳列窓	shop window, ~display	**chinretsumado**
同窓会	alumni association	**dōsōkai**
同窓生	fellow alumnus, schoolmate	**dōsōsei**
引き窓	trap door	**hikimado**
開き窓	casement window	**hirakimado**
飾り窓	window display	**kazarimado**
格子窓	lattice window	**kōshimado**
窓掛け	window curtains, blinds	**madokake**
窓際族	"sitting until retirement..."	**madogiwazoku**
窓明かり	lights from windows	**madoakari**

観cenery, 667	口pening, 458
景cenery, 546	目ye, 462
眺cenery, 215	眼yesight, 771

密ecret, 220

344-A

繁rosperity in search for those 敏lert...

糸 (thread, continuity)

繁rosperity　繁ffluence

shige(ru), shige(ku), HAN
prosperity, affluence, bountiful, thriving

繁忙　very busy, very full, occupied **hanbō**
繁栄　prosperity, flourishing, thriving **han'ei**
繁劇　busy, preoccupied **hangeki**
繁盛　prosperity, thriving, flourishing **hanjō**
繁華　flourishing, thriving **hanka**
繁華街　downtown, commercial district **hankagai**
繁閑　business slack **hankan**
繁簡　simplicity & complexity **hankan**
繁茂　getting thick, luxuriance **hanmo**
繁殖　breeding, propagation **hanshoku**
繁殖期　breeding season **hanshokuki**
繁多　busy, preoccupied **hanta**
繁雑　complicate, intricate **hanzatsu**
頻繁　frequent, often **hinpan**
農繁　prosperous harvest **nōhan**
繁繁　very frequent, very often **shigeshige**
農繁期　prosperous harvest season **nōhanki**
繁文縟礼　tedious formality **hanbun jokurei**

Facing: 3.0. ☞☜ Across

富ortune, 333	益rofit, 622
豊bundance, 965	進rogress, 51
裕ffluence, 758	展rogress, 522
隆rosperity, 133	歩rogress, 272
盛rosperity, 244	

敏lert, 434

344-B

繁rosperity in search for those 敏lert...

攵 (action)

敏lert　敏stute

BIN
alert, agile, astute, sensitive, nimble

敏感　sensitive, touchy, delicate **binkan**
敏活　quick, alert, keen **binkatsu**
敏捷　agility, dexterity **binshō**
敏速　promptness, alacrity **binsoku**
敏達　wise, alert **bintatsu**
敏達天皇　Emperor Bintatsu (572-585) **bintatsu tennō**
敏腕　agile person **binwan**
敏腕家　doer, go-getter, action-oriented **binwanka**
鋭敏　sharp, keen, astute **eibin**
不敏　dull, inept **fubin**
過敏　sensitive, touchy, delicate **kabin**
⇒神経過敏　oversensitive, "on one's nerves..." **shinkei kabin**
過敏症　hyper-sensitivity **kabinshō**
機敏　astute, alert, keen **kibin**
明敏　sagacious, incisive, perceptive **meibin**
俊敏　quick, alert, keen **shunbin**
目敏い　quickness, alacrity, keenness **mezatoi**

FLIP: 7.1. Right (Sort Of)
Facing: 1.2. ☜ West (V)

迅uick, 95	迅peedy, 95
速uick, 502	速peedy, 502
鋭harp, 943	

每very, 241

345-A

Epic 稿*anuscript,* 高*igh price picked...*

禾 (tree branch)

FLIP: 7.0.b2. Right (stem)

稿*anuscript*   稿*rticle*

KŌ
manuscript, article, discourse, essay, treatise, writings

脱稿 *manuscript completion* **dakkō**
画稿 *sketch* **gakō**
原稿 *manuscript, draft* **genkō**
原稿料 *writing fee* **genkōryō**
原稿用紙 *Japanese manuscript paper* **genkō yōshi**
遺稿 *posthumous manuscripts* **ikō**
歌稿 *draft poem* **kakō**
起稿 *commence writing a manuscript* **kikō**
寄稿 *manuscript writing* **kikō**
稿本 *manuscript* **kōhon**
稿料 *manuscript-, writing fee* **kōryō**
詩稿 *draft poem* **shikō**
草稿 *draft manuscript* **sōkō**
送稿 *sending a manuscript for publication* **sōkō**
投稿 *manuscript contribution (newspaper)* **tōkō**
投稿欄 *readers column* **tōkōran**
投稿者 *manuscript contributor* **tōkōsha**
続稿 *serialized manuscript* **zokkō**
決定稿 *final manuscript* **ketteikō**

生原稿 *draft manuscript* **namagenkō**

校*roof-reading, 773*	著*uthor, 279*
訂*diting, 174*	書*ritings, 116*
編*diting, 42*	

矯*eformatory, 163*	橋*ridge, 163*

345-B

Epic 稿*anuscript,* 高*igh price picked...*

高 (high)

FLIP: 1.0.b. Whole (stem)

高*igh*   高*levated*

taka(i), taka, taka(maru), taka(meru), KŌ
high, elevated, altitude

円高 *strong yen* **endaka**
標高 *altitude, elevation from the sea* **hyōkō**
高圧 *high pressure, ~voltage* **kōatsu**
高地 *high lands, highly-elevated* **kōchi**
高度 *altitude, elevation from the sea* **kōdo**
高遠 *lofty, high, noble* **kōen**
高原 *plateau, high plains* **kōgen**
高位 *high rank, high status* **kōi**
高価 *expensive, costly* **kōka**
高校 *high school* **kōkō**
高級 *high class, ~level* **kōkyū**
高熱 *scorching heat* **kōnetsu**
高温 *high temperature* **kōon**
高音 *high-pitch, ~tone, soprano* **kōon**
高速 *high-speed, fast* **kōsoku**
最高 *maximum, the highest* **saikō**
高波 *tall-, high waves* **takanami**
割高 *relatively high* **waridaka**
座高 *seated height* **zakō**

残高 *outstanding-, running balance* **zandaka**
漁獲高 *fishing catch* **gyokakudaka**
鼻高々 *proudly, boastfully* **hanatakadaka**
捕獲高 *fishing catch* **hokakudaka**
高血圧 *high blood pressure* **kōketsuatsu**
高齢化 *ageing, greying society* **kōreika**
収穫高 *harvest, crop* **shūkakudaka**
高円宮 *Prince Takamado (1955-2002)*
    takamado-no-miya
棒高跳び *pole jump, ~vault* **bōtakatobi**
超高層ビル *skyscraper, skyline towers*
    chōkōsō biru
走り高跳び *running high jump* **hashiritakatobi**

上*pper, 859*	最*aximum, 423*
貴*recious, 913*	登*scend, 437*

亭*estaurant, 393*

346-A

Stop 戯lirting, that's 虚utile perverting...

戯*lirting*　　戯*ntic*　　戯*rick*

戈 (spear)

FLIP: 8.0.a. Inner (flat)
Facing: 2.2. East ☞ (V)

tawamu(reru), GI, GE
flirting, antic, prank, trick, sport, jocular, jest

愛戯 *love play* **aigi**
戯作 *fiction, novella* **gesaku**
戯作者 *fiction writer, novelist* **gesakusha**
戯文 *humorous writing* **gibun**
戯画 *caricature, cartoon* **giga**
戯評 *lampoon, caricature* **gihyō**
戯曲 *drama, play* **gikyoku**
戯曲作家 *dramatist, playwright* **gikyoku sakka**
悪戯 *mischief, trick, prank* **itazura, akugi**
児戯 *mischief, trick, prank* **jigi**
嬉戯 *frisk, frolic* **kigi**
球戯 *billiards, pool* **kyūgi**
遊戯 *playing & dancing, amusement* **yūgi**
⇒桃色遊戯 *sex scene* **momoiro yūgi**
⇒室内遊戯 *indoor games* **shitsunai yūgi**
戯言 *rubbish-, silly talk* **zaregoto**
前戯 *foreplay, prelude* **zengi**
戯け物 *fool, idiot* **tawakemono**

遊戯場 *playground* **yūgijō**
遊戯室 *playroom* **yūgishitsu**
遊戯的 *prankish, tricky* **yūgiteki**

楽*njoy, 447*	閑*eisure, 283*
喫*njoy, 900*	悠*eisure, 898*
享*njoy, 398*	遊*lay, 650*

蔵*torage, 565*

346-B

Stop 戯lirting, that's 虚utile perverting...

虚*utile*　　虚*alse*

虍 (tiger)

FLIP: 4.0.a. Bottom (flat)
Facing: 2.1. East ☞ (H)

KYO, KO
futile, false, vain, void

廃虚 *remains, ruins* **haikyo**
謙虚 *modesty, humility* **kenkyo**
虚空 *space, room, air* **kokū**
空虚 *empty, vacant, hollow* **kūkyo**
虚伝 *false rumour* **kyoden**
虚栄 *vanity, showiness, self-conceit* **kyoei**
虚言 *lies, falsehood, untrue* **kyogen**
虚偽 *lie, lying* **kyogi**
虚業 *risky business* **kyogyō**
虚報 *false report, fabrication* **kyohō**
虚位 *titular post, nominal rank* **kyoi**
虚弱 *weak, delicate, fragile* **kyojaku**
虚辞 *falsehood, untrue* **kyoji**
虚実 *truth-or-fiction* **kyojitsu**
虚構 *fiction, fabrication* **kyokō**
虚根 *imaginary root* **kyokon**
虚名 *empty reputation* **kyomei**
虚妄 *falsehood, untrue* **kyomō**
虚無 *nihility, nothingness* **kyomu**

虚礼 *empty gestures* **kyorei**
虚勢 *bluff, bluster* **kyosei**
虚式 *imaginary expression* **kyoshiki**
虚心 *disinterest, indifference* **kyoshin**
虚飾 *show, vanity, ostentation* **kyoshoku**
虚数 *imaginary number* **kyosū**
虚誕 *trumped up* **kyotan**
虚像 *virtual-, false image* **kyozō**
虚無僧 *flute-playing zen monk* **komusō**
虚脱感 *despondency, desperation* **kyodatsukan**
虚仮威し *bluff, bluster* **kokeodoshi**

| 無*othing, 49* |
| 不*[negative], 300* |
| 非*[negative], 288* |

虐*ruelty, 870*

347-A

To 澄ake-clear: No 登limbing with fear...

澄*ake clear*　　澄*harp*

水⇔氵 (water)

su(mu); su(masu), CHŌ
make clear, sharp, lucid, limpid

FLIP: 7.0.a. Right (flat)

澄ませる *listen, purify* **sumaseru**
澄まし顔 *uncaring-, dismissive look* **sumashigao**
澄まし屋 *smug, prude, prim* **sumashiya**
澄し汁 *clear soup* **sumashijiru**
澄み切り *crystal clear* **sumikiri**
澄み渡る *be perfectly clear* **sumiwataru**
澄明 *clear, bright* **chōmei**
澄徹 *clear, transparent* **chōtetsu**
明澄 *clear, distinct* **meichō**
清澄 *clear, lucid; serene* **seichō**
上澄み *scooping up* **uwasumi**
見澄ます *watching intently, ~attentively* **misumasu**
水澄まし *whirligig beetle* **mizusumashi**
研ぎ澄ます *sharpen well* **togisumasu**
取り澄ます *put on air* **torisumasu**
聞き澄ます *listen intently* **kikisumasu**
狙い澄ます *take careful aim* **neraisumasu**

朗 *lear, 800*	解 *omprehend, 400*
照 *hining, 529*	分 *omprehend, 518*
光 *hining, 77*	輝 *parkling, 296*

登*limb, 437*

347-B

To 澄ake-clear: No 登limbing with fear...

登*limb*　　登*scend*

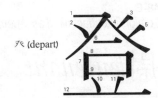

癶 (depart)

nobo(ru), TŌ, TO
climb, ascend, elevate, scale, upward

FLIP: 1.0.a. Whole (flat)

登坂 *uphill slope, hill climbing* **noborizaka, tohan**
登板 *taking to the mound (baseball)* **tōban**
登頂 *reaching the peak, ~summit* **tōchō**
登庁 *assumption of public office* **tōchō**
登第 *passing an exam* **tōdai**
登壇 *taking the podium, ~stage* **tōdan**
登院 *attending a parliament session* **tōin**
登場 *appearance, entrance, presence* **tōjō**
登城 *go to a castle* **tōjō**
登記 *registration, signing up* **tōki**
登記簿 *registry, registration list* **tōkibo**
登記所 *registry office* **tōkisho**
登校 *attending school* **tōkō**
登校拒否 *refusal to attend school* **tōkō kyohi**
登臨 *throne ascension* **tōrin**
登録 *registration, signing up* **tōroku**
登載 *record, registration, listing* **tōsai**
登仙 *sainthood* **tōsen**
登塔 *climb up a tower* **tōtō**

登用 *job promotion* **tōyō**
登山 *mountaineering, mountain climbing* **tozan**
登山帽 *mountaineering headgear* **tozanbō**
登山道 *mountain trail, ~path* **tozandō**
登山家 *mountaineer, alpinist* **tozanka**
山登り *mountain climbing* **yamanobori**
不登校 *non-attendance (school)* **futōkō**
木登り *tree climbing* **kinobori**
滝登り *waterfalls climbing* **takinobori**
登竜門 *"gate to success..."* **tōryūmon**

昇 *scend, 299*	山 *ountain, 172*
上 *scend, 859*	岳 *ountain peak, 28*
高 *levated, 435*	峰 *ountain peak, 779*

発 *tart, 368*

348-A

慰omfort attendant hired as 尉ieutenant...

心 ⇔ 忄 (heart, feelings)

慰omfort 慰onsole

nagusa(meru), nagusa(mu), I

comfort, console

慰み物 *diversion of sorrows* **nagusamimono**
慰み半分 *"partly for the pleasure..."* **nagusamihanbun**
弔慰 *condolence, sympathy, commiseration* **chōi**
弔慰金 *condolence money* **chōikin**
慰安 *comfort, consolation, recreation* **ian**
慰安婦 *WWII forced-prostitute* **ianfu**
慰安旅行 *recreational trip* **ian ryokō**
慰撫 *soothing, placating, mollifying* **ibu**
慰問 *consolation, sympathy, commiseration* **imon**
慰問状 *letter of condolence* **imonjō**
慰労 *acknowledgement, recognition* **irō**
慰留 *persuade not to resign* **iryū**
慰謝 *consolation, comfort* **isha**
慰藉 *consolation, solace* **isha**
慰謝料 *compensation money* **isharyō**
自慰 *masturbation* **jii**
慰霊碑 *cenotaph, memorial tower* **ireihi**
慰霊祭 *memorial service* **ireisai**

FLIP: 8.0.b. Inner (stem)
Facing: 3.0. ☞☜ **Across**

慰霊塔 *memorial tower* **ireitō**
口慰む *talking to beat boredom* **kuchinagusamu**
言い慰める *words of condolence* **iinagusameru**

憩 *elaxation, 169*	緩 *oosening, 821*
閑 *eisure, 283*	悠 *eisure, 898*

尉 *ieutenant, 438*

348-B

慰omfort attendant hired as 尉ieutenant...

寸 (measurement)

尉ieutenant

I

lieutenant, company officer

中尉 *first lieutenant* **chūi**
尉官 *officers below rank of major* **ikan**
准尉 *warrant officer* **jun'i**
少尉 *second lieutenant, midshipman* **shōi**
大尉 *army captain, navy lieutenant* **taii**

Facing: 3.0. ☞☜ **Across**
FLIP: 8.0.b. Inner (stem)

軍 *oldier, 295*	兵 *oldier, 490*
卒 *oldier, 109*	曹 *ergeant, 326*

慰 *omfort, 438*

349-A
No fake 糖*ugar mixed with* 唐*hinese vinegar...*

糖ugar　　糖lucose

米 (grains, rice)

TŌ
　sugar, glucose

FLIP: 6.0.b. Left (stem)
FLIP: 7.3.a. Right Bottom (flat)

果糖　*fructose, fruit sugar* **katō**
血糖　*blood sugar* **kettō**
無糖　*unsweetened, sugar-free* **mutō**
乳糖　*milk sugar, lactose* **nyūtō**
砂糖　*sugar* **satō**
砂糖黍　*sugar cane* **satōkibi**
砂糖大根　*sugar beet* **satō daikon**
精糖　*sugar refining* **seitō**
製糖　*sugar manufacturing* **seitō**
蔗糖　*cane sugar, sucrose* **shotō**
粗糖　*coarse-, unrefined sugar* **sotō**
糖分　*sugar content* **tōbun**
糖度　*sugar level* **tōdo**
糖衣　*sugar-coating* **tōi**
糖衣錠　*sugar-coated tablet* **tōijō**
糖化　*saccharification* **tōka**
糖菓　*candies, sweets* **tōka**
糖蜜　*syrup, molasses* **tōmitsu**
糖類　*saccharine, artificial sugar* **tōrui**

糖質　*glucide* **tōshitsu**
赤砂糖　*brown sugar* **akazatō**
麦芽糖　*malt sugar, maltose* **bakugatō**
葡萄糖　*dextrose, grape sugar* **budōtō**
角砂糖　*sugar cubes* **kakuzatō**
粉砂糖　*powdered sugar* **konazatō**
氷砂糖　*rock-, sugar candy* **koorizatō**
黒砂糖　*unrefined-, brown sugar* **kurozatō**
精白糖　*refined sugar* **seihakutō**
精糖業　*sugar industry* **seitōgyō**
白砂糖　*white-, refined sugar* **shirozatō**
糖尿病　*diabetes, high blood sugar* **tō'nyōbyō**

甘*weet, 395*　　　　味*aste, 871*
菓*weets, 123*

唐*hinese, 439*

349-B
No fake 糖*ugar mixed with* 唐*hinese vinegar...*

唐hinese　　唐athay

口 (mouth)

kara, TŌ
　Chinese, Tang Dynasty, Cathay

FLIP: 4.0.a. Bottom (flat)

唐戸　*Chinese-style door* **karado**
唐風　*Chinese-style design* **karafū**
唐船　*Tang dynasty ship* **karafune**
唐画　*Chinese movies, ~painting* **karaga**
唐芋　*sweet potato* **karaimo**
唐糸　*Chinese yarn* **karaito**
唐紙　*sliding door paper* **karakami**
唐金　*bronze* **karakane**
唐傘　*oil paper umbrella* **karakasa**
唐子　*Chinese classical doll* **karako**
唐紅　*scarlet* **karakurenai**
唐松　*larch tree* **karamatsu**
唐物　*Chinese goods* **karamono**
唐門　*Chinese-style gate* **karamon**
唐墨　*Chinese inking* **karasumi**
唐手　*Karate martial arts* **karate**
唐様　*Chinese-style design* **karayō**
唐朝　*Tang dynasty* **tōchō**
唐土　*Cathay, China* **tōdo**

唐人　*Chinese person* **tōjin, karabito**
唐音　*Tang dynasty reading of Kanji* **tōon**
唐詩　*tang poèm* **tōshi**
唐突　*unexpected, sudden* **tōtotsu**
唐臼　*mortar for hulling* **tōusu**
唐言葉　*Chinese language* **karakotoba**
毛唐人　*hairy barbarian, ~foreigner* **ketōjin**
唐辛子　*red pepper* **tōgarashi**
唐変木　*dunce, dullard, moron* **tōhenboku**
唐草模様　*arabesque design* **karakusa moyō**
荒唐無稽　*absurd, non-sensical* **kōtō mukei**

漢*anji, 926*　　　中*hina, 85*
呉*[Wu dynasty], 453*　華*hina, 40*
東*riental, 220*

康*ranquility, 881*

350-A

Coin 鋳intage, 寿ongevity envisaged...

鋳asting　鋳intage

金 (metal)

i(ru), CHŪ
casting, mintage

鋳貨　coin mintage **chūka**
鋳塊　ingot **chūkai**
鋳金　metal casting **chūkin**
鋳鋼　cast steel **chūkō**
鋳鉄　cast iron **chūtetsu**
鋳造　metal casting **chūzō**
鋳像　cast image **chūzō**
電鋳　electrotyping **denchū**
鋳型　metal casting mould **igata**
鋳物　casting, cast metal **imono**
改鋳　recasting, re-minting **kaichū**
再鋳　recasting, mending **saichū**
新鋳　newly-minted **shinchū**
鋳込む　cast moulding **ikomu**
鋳直し　recasting, re-minting **inaoshi**
鋳潰す　meltdown **itsubusu**
鋳造所　foundry, mintage **chūzōsho**
鋳掛ける　recasting, mending **ikakeru**
鋳掛け屋　tinsmith **ikakeya**

FLIP: 6.0.a. Left (flat)
Facing: 4.0. ⊂⊃⊂⊃ Apart

銭oins, 767
鉄ron, 155
燃urning, 445

銭oins, 767

350-B

Coin 鋳intage, 寿ongevity envisaged...

寸 (measurement)

寿ongevity

kotobuki, kotoho(gu), JU
longevity, long-lasting, congratulate

Facing: 3.0. ⊂⊃⊂⊃ Across

米寿　eighty-eight birthday **beiju**
長寿　longevity, long life **chōju**
延寿　long life, longevity **enju**
福寿　happiness & longevity **fukuju**
福寿草　Adonis armour **fukujusō**
白寿　ninety-nine years old **hakuju**
寿命　life expectancy, life span **jumyō**
⇒耐久寿命　long life, longevity **taikyū jumyō**
寿齢　long life, longevity **jurei**
喜寿　one's seventy-seventh birthday **kiju**
高寿　advanced age **kōju**
聖寿　emperor's age **seiju**
頌寿　birthdays on the 60th, 70th, 80th & 90th **shōju**
卒寿　one's ninetieth birthday **sotsuju**
寿司　sushi, raw fish cuisine **sushi**
⇒握り寿司　Nigiri sushi **nigirizushi**
⇒稲荷寿司　rice stuffed tofu **inarizushi**
寿司屋　sushi shop, sushi bar **sushiya**
天寿　natural lifetime span **tenju**

寿老人　god of longevity **jurōjin**
新年の寿　New Year's greetings
　shinnen no kotobuki
久寿時代　Kyūji Era (1154-1156) **kyūju jidai**
万寿時代　Manju Era (1024-1028) **manju jidai**
仁寿時代　Ninju Era (851-854) **ninju jidai**

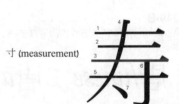

永ong-lasting, 10
久ong-lasting, 379
長ong, 273

浅hallow, 768

351-A

嘱ntrusted gong to the temple 属elongs...

嘱ntrust 嘱onsign

口 (mouth)

SHOKU
entrust, authorize, consign, charge with

委嘱 commission, appointment **ishoku**
依嘱 entrust with **ishoku**
依託 request **itaku**
嘱望 expectation, hope **shokubō**
嘱目 special attention **shokumoku**
嘱託 part-time employment **shokutaku**

FLIP: 6.0.a. Left (flat)
Facing: 3.0. ☞☜ Across

預ntrust, 569	任ntrust, 709
委ntrust, 583	信aith, 252
託ntrust, 82	

属elong, 441

351-B

嘱ntrusted gong to the temple 属elongs...

属elong 属ffiliate

尸 (corpse)

ZOKU
belong, affiliate, auxiliary

部属 section, division **buzoku**
直属 directly attached **chokuzoku**
付属 attached, belonging to **fuzoku**
軍属 civilian staff in the military **gunzoku**
配属 assignment, posting **haizoku**
卑属 collateral descendant **hizoku**
従属 subordination, yielding **jūzoku**
金属 metal, metallic **kinzoku**
帰属 revert, relapse, regress **kizoku**
隷属 subordination, subservience **reizoku**
専属 belonging exclusively **senzoku**
属望 pinning on one's hopes **shokubō**
属目 paying attention **shokumoku**
所属 belong to, affiliation **shozoku**
尊属 ascendant, succession **sonzoku**
転属 transfer, move location **tenzoku**
属官 subordinate, underling **zokkan**
属国 dependent nation, protectorate **zokkoku**
属地 territory, possession **zokuchi**

Facing: 2.1. East ☞ (H)

属格 genitive case **zokukaku**
属名 generic name **zokumei**
属領 territory, possession **zokuryō**
属差 generic difference **zokusa**
属性 attribute, trait, quality **zokusei**
属島 territorial island **zokushima**, **zokutō**
非金属 non-metallic **hikinzoku**
卑金属 base metal **hikinzoku**
重金属 heavy metal **jūkinzoku**
軽金属 light metal **keikinzoku**
貴金属 precious metal **kikinzoku**
無所属 independent, neutral **mushozoku**

付ttach, 382	伴ccompany, 949
附ttach, 382	共ogether, 302
随ccompany, 807	合ogether, 232
添ccompany, 620	

嘱ntrust, 441

441

352-A

履ut-on crayons for art 復estoration...

履ut-on   履ear

ha(ku), RI
put-on, wear

履き物 footwear, shoes **hakimono**
履き違える wear by mistake, miswear **hakichigaeru**
木履 wooden clog **bokuri**
不履行 non-fulfilment, default **furikō**
幣履 worn-out sandals **heiri**
履行 fulfilment, performance **rikō**
履行不能 impossibility, unlikelihood **rikō funō**
履歴 resume, curriculum vitae **rireki**
履歴書 written resume, curriculum vitae **rirekisho**
履修 completion, going thru **rishū**
履修単位 academic unit, course credit **rishū tan'i**
草履 Japanese sandals **zōri**
草履虫 paramecium **zōrimushi**
草履取り slippers carrier (house servant) **zōritori**
革草履 leather slippers **kawazōri**
下履き outdoor footwear **shitabaki**
上履き pair of slippers **uwabaki**
上草履 indoors sandals **uwazōri**

尸 (corpse)

履

Facing: 3.0. ☞☜ Across

履中天皇 Emperor Richū (400-405) **richū tennō**
下駄履き住宅 apartment-store building
　　getabaki jūtaku

装ear, 629
着ear, 589
置ut-on, 420

復ecovery.442

352-B

履ut-on crayons for art 復estoration...

復ecovery   復estoration

FUKU
recovery, restoration

彳 (stroll)

復

Facing: 1.2. ☜ West (V)

復刊 reprint, re-publishing **fukkan**
復活 restoration, revival **fukkatsu**
復活祭 Easter **fukkatsusai**
復権 restoration of rights, rehabilitation **fukken**
復帰 reversion, reinstatement **fukki**
復古 restoration of previous regime **fukko**
復興 reconstruction **fukkō**
復航 return flight **fukkō**
復刻 reproduction **fukkoku**
復旧 restoration, comeback **fukkyū**
復調 recovery, recuperation **fukuchō**
復縁 marital reconciliation, ~settlement **fukuen**
復元 original restoration **fukugen**
復原 restoration of former state-of-affairs **fukugen**
復配 resumption of dividends **fukuhai**
復員 demobilization, repatriation **fukuin**
復命 report to one's superior **fukumei**
復任 reappointment, reinstatement **fukunin**
復路 return trip, homecoming **fukuro**

復籍 returning to one's family register **fukuseki**
復申 reply, response **fukushin**
復職 work reinstatement, job recall **fukushoku**
復習 lesson review **fukushū**
復党 rejoining the party **fukutō**
復答 reply, response **fukutō**
反復 repetition, redundancy **hanpuku**
報復 retaliation, revenge, getting back at **hōfuku**
回復 recuperation, recovery, convalescence **kaifuku**
克復 conquer, conquest **kokufuku**
往復 going & returning, round trip **ōfuku**

元rigin, 195　　　帰eturn, 784
原riginal, 431　　返eturn, 537
還eturn, 165

復ultiply. 830

353-A

To 餓tarve thy 我elf, plead no help..!

餓*tarve*　　餓*unger*

食 (food)

GA

starve, hunger, famine

餓鬼 *mischievous child, brat* **gaki**
餓鬼道 *hell for hungry demons* **gakidō**
餓鬼大将 *street boys gang* **gakidaishō**
餓死 *death by starvation* **gashi**
飢餓 *starvation, hunger* **kiga**
施餓鬼 *memorial service for orphans* **segaki**

Facing: 3.0. ☞☜ Across

| 飢*tarve, 746* |
| 食*uisine, 255* |
| 糧*oodstuff, 451* |

| 我*elf, 443* |

353-B

To 餓tarve thy 我elf, plead no help..!

我*[we]*　　我*elf*

戈 (spear)

ware, wa, GA

[we], [I], self

忘我 *self-oblivion; trance* **bōga**
没我 *selflessness, sacrificial* **botsuga**
我意 *obstinacy, hard-headed* **gai**
我慢 *patience, self-control* **gaman**
⇒痩せ我慢 *endurance for one's pride*
　　yasegaman
我利 *self-interests, egotism* **gari**
我利我利亡者 *greedy-, avaricious* **garigari mōja**
我流 *according to one's way* **garyū**
我執 *egocentricity, idiosyncrasy* **gashū**
我欲 *self-interests, egotism* **gayoku**
彼我 *he & I; they & we* **higa**
自我 *self, ego, one's person* **jiga**
怪我 *injury, wound, bruises* **kega**
無我 *selfless, unselfish* **muga**
小我 *smaller ego, little self* **shōga**
主我 *ego, self* **shuga**
我が *our, our own, us* **waga**
我事 *one's own business* **wagakoto**

Facing: 4.0. ☜☞ Apart

我儘 *selfish, egotistical, wilful* **wagamama**
我等 *we, us* **warera**
我我 *we, us* **wareware**
我が国 *our country, Japan* **wagakuni**
我が身 *oneself* **wagami**
我が物 *our property* **wagamono**
我乍ら *"if it's us, if it's me..."* **warenagara**
我先に *"me first..."* **waresaki(ni)**
我武者羅 *reckless, irresponsible* **gamushara**
我勝ちに *"each to one's own..."* **waregachi(ni)**
我知らず *selfless, sacrificial* **wareshirazu**
唯我独尊 *conceited, self-glory* **yuiga dokuson**

| 身*elf, 504* | 自*elf, 462* |
| 己*elf, 5* | 独*lone, 369* |

| 弍*WO, 100* |

354-A

霊*pirit* 並*arallels one's laurels...*

霊*pirit* 霊*oul*

雨 (weather)

tama, REI, RYŌ
spirit, ghost, soul, supernatural

FLIP: 1.0.a. Whole (flat)

悪霊	*evil spirits* **akuryō**	霊薬	*miraculous medicine* **reiyaku**
亡霊	*spirit, ghost* **bōrei**	霊山	*sacred mountain* **reizan**
英霊	*spirit of dead soldiers* **eirei**	霊前	*spirit of the dead* **reizen**
交霊	*conversation with the dead* **kōrei**	聖霊	*Holy Ghost, Holy Spirit* **seirei**
言霊	*spirit of words* **kotodama**	心霊	*psychic, spiritual* **shinrei**
御霊	*spirit of the dead* **mitama**	神霊	*spirit, soul* **shinrei**
怨霊	*vindictive ghost* **onryō**	死霊	*spirit of the dead* **shiryō**
霊媒	*spiritual medium* **reibai**	精霊	*pure-, sacred spirits* **seirei**
霊地	*sacred grounds, holy land* **reichi**	幽霊	*ghost, apparition* **yūrei**
霊長	*lord of spirits* **reichō**	全霊	*exerting one's heart & soul* **zenrei**
霊園	*cemetery, gravesite* **reien**	慰霊祭	*memorial service* **ireisai**
霊峰	*sacred mountain* **reihō**	守護霊	*guardian angel* **shugorei**
霊域	*sacred grounds* **reiiki**	霊柩車	*hearse, funeral car* **reikyūsha**
霊界	*spiritual world* **reikai**		
霊感	*inspiration, spirits* **reikan**		
霊験	*miracle, act-of-God* **reiken**		
霊魂	*soul, spirit* **reikon**		
霊泉	*therapeutic hot springs* **reisen**		
霊芝	*Reishi mushroom* **reishi**		

魂*oul, 936*　　逝*eath, 54*
死*eath, 513*　　亡*eath, 72*

需*emand, 548*

354-B

霊*pirit* 並*arallels one's laurels...*

並*arallel* 並*longside*

一 (one, single)

nara(bu), nara(beru), nara(bi)ni, HEI
parallel, alongside, side-by-side, align

FLIP: 1.0.a. Whole (flat)

並びに	*"as well as..."* **narabi(ni)**	並びない	*unrivalled, incomparable* **narabinai**
並置	*juxtaposition, placing next to* **heichi**	並並	*ordinary, commonplace* **naminami**
並行	*going side by side* **heikō**	並並ならぬ	*out-of-the-ordinary* **naminami naranu**
並列	*parallel arrangement* **heiretsu**	並肉	*medium-quality meat* **naminiku**
並立	*standing along with* **heiritsu**	人並み	*average-, common people* **hitonami**
並存	*co-existence, "let & let live..."* **heizon**	手並み	*one's skills, one's forte* **tenami**
穂並	*wave of grain* **honami**	並製品	*medium-quality goods* **namiseihin**
町並	*streets, towns & houses* **machinami**	並大抵	*ordinary, regular, common* **namitaitei**
並木	*row of trees* **namiki**	並外れる	*extraordinary,* **namihazureru**
並木道	*tree-lined road* **namikimichi**	人間並み	*average folks* **ningennami**
足並み	*cadence, pace* **ashinami**	並み外れて	*extraordinarily, outstandingly*
歯並び	*teeth alignment* **hanarabi**		**namihazurete**
毛並み	*hair contours; family level* **kenami**		
軒並み	*row of houses* **nokinami**		
並み足	*going for a walk, strolling* **namiashi**		
五目並べ	*Japanese checkers* **gomoku narabe**		
並べ換え	*replacement, substitution* **narabekae**		
立ち並び	*stand in line, fall in line* **tachinarabi**		
並べ立てる	*enumerate, read off* **narabetateru**		

横*idewards, 197*
沿*longside, 756*

普*ommon, 455*

355-A
燃urning allure of Mother 然ature...

火⇔灬 (fire)

燃urning 燃laze

mo(eru), mo(yasu), mo(su), NEN
burning, blaze, combustion

Facing: 4.0. ☜☞ Apart

防燃 *fire resistant* **bōnen**
不燃 *non-combustible, non-flammable* **funen**
発熱 *heat temperature* **hatsunetsu**
内燃 *internal combustion* **nainen**
難燃 *non-combustible* **nannen**
燃費 *fuel efficiency* **nenpi**
燃料 *fuel, energy* **nenryō**
⇒液体燃料 *liquid fuel, liquefied fuel* **ekitai nenryō**
⇒固体燃料 *solid fuel* **kotai nenryō**
燃料補給 *refuelling* **nenryō hokyū**
燃焼 *combustion, flaming* **nenshō**
⇒完全燃焼 *perfect combustion* **kanzen nenshō**
燃焼性 *combustibility, flammability* **nenshōsei**
再燃 *returning to the fore, comeback* **sainen**
核燃料 *nuclear fuel* **kakunenryō**
可燃物 *combustible, inflammable* **kanenbutsu**
可燃性 *combustibility, flammability* **kanensei**
燃え殻 *cinder, ashes* **moegara**
燃え出す *catch fire, flare up* **moedasu**

燃え残り *burning remains, embers* **moenokori**
燃え思い *burning passion* **moeomoi**
燃え盛る *blaze, burn brightly* **moesakaru**
燃え差し *burning remains, embers* **moesashi**
燃え立つ *blaze, flame* **moetatsu**
燃え付く *catch, catch fire* **moetsuku**
燃え移る *spread, scatter* **moeutsuru**
燃え易い *easily flammable* **moeyasui**
燃え上がる *flare up* **moeagaru**
燃え広がる *spread of a fire* **moehirogaru**
燃え尽きる *lose stream, burn out* **moetsukiru**

火 *ire, 3*	災 *isaster, 571*
煙 *moke, 644*	厄 *isaster, 354*
焼 *oasting, 817*	

然 *ature, 445*

355-B
燃urning allure of Mother 然ature...

火⇔灬 (fire)

然ature 然s such

shika(ri), ZEN, NEN
nature, as such, as is

Facing: 4.0. ☜☞ Apart

暗然 *overcome with grief* **anzen**
断然 *firmly, resolutely* **danzen**
同然 *"as good as, same as..."* **dōzen**
厳然 *undeniable, strict, severe* **genzen**
傲然 *arrogance, overbearing, haughty* **gōzen**
偶然 *accident, coincidence, by chance* **gūzen**
判然 *clear, distinct, evident* **hanzen**
平然 *calm, cool, quiet* **heizen**
必然 *necessary, inevitable* **hitsuzen**
本然 *natural, inborn, innate* **honzen**
隠然 *latent, secret* **inzen**
依然 *still, as yet* **izen**
純然 *absolute, pure, sheer* **junzen**
画然 *sharp distinction, clear difference* **kakuzen**
果然 *as expected, predictably* **kazen**
公然 *open, public* **kōzen**
猛然 *fiercely, vehemently, ferociously* **mōzen**
冷然 *indifference, cold treatment* **reizen**
歴然 *self-evident, unmistakable, clear* **rekizen**

整然 *orderly, systematic* **seizen**
自然 *nature, environment* **shizen**
粛然 *solemn, quiet* **shukuzen**
天然 *natural, inborn, innate, act-of-god* **tennen**
突然 *sudden, abrupt, unexpected* **totsuzen**
当然 *naturally, expectedly, a given* **tōzen**
悠然 *calm, at ease, serene* **yūzen**
雑然 *disorderly, untidy, disorganized* **zatsuzen**
全然 *"at all, entirely..."* **zenzen**
敢然と *resolutely, determinedly* **kanzento**
未然に *before happening* **mizen(ni)**

緑 *nvironment, 841*	質 *ature, 627*
環 *nvirons, 165*	性 *ature, 474*

燃 *urning, 445*

356-A

濃hick & 濃ense 農griculture, farmers' grandeur...

濃hick　　濃ense

水 ⇔ 氵 (water)

ko(i), NŌ

thick, dense, rich, condensed

FLIP: 7.2.a. Right Top (flat)

濃紫　deep purple **komurasaki**
濃度　density, richness (colour) **nōdo**
濃艶　alluring, glamorous, gorgeous **nōen**
濃化　thickening, enrichment **nōka**
濃厚　thick, deep, rich **nōkō**
濃紺　navy blue, dark blue **nōkon**
濃密　dense, thick fog **nōmitsu**
濃霧　dense fog, thick fog **nōmu**
濃緑　dark green **nōryoku**
濃縮　concentration, enrichment **nōshuku**
濃縮ウラン　enriched-, concentrated uranium
　　　nōshuku uran
濃縮ジューズ　rich-, thick juice, juice concentrate
　　　nōshuku jūsū
濃淡　light & shade **nōtan**
濃い茶　thick green tea **koicha**
濃褐色　dark brown **nōkasshoku**
濃紅色　deep red, crimson **nōkōshoku**

濃青色　dark blue **nōseishoku**
濃溶液　concentrated solution **nōyōeki**
油っ濃い　greasy, fatty, oily **aburakkoi**
脂っ濃い　greasy, rich (foods) **aburakkoi**

| 塗aint, 882 | 太hick, 6 |
| 厚hick, 964 | 油etroleum, 540 |

農griculture, 446

356-B

濃hick & 濃ense 農griculture, farmers' grandeur...

農arming　農griculture

辰 (dragon)

NŌ

farming, agriculture

FLIP: 3.0.a. Top (flat)

大農　large-scale farming **dainō**
営農　farming, agriculture **einō**
富農　wealthy farmer **funō**
豪農　wealthy farmer **gōnō**
半農　part-time farming **hannō**
貧農　poor farmer **hinnō**
帰農　back-to-the-farm **kinō**
農地　agricultural land, farmland **nōchi**
農道　rice paddy path, farm road **nōdō**
農園　farm, plantation **nōen**
農学　agriculture science, agronomy **nōgaku**
農芸　agriculture & horticulture **nōgei**
農具　farm implements, farm tools **nōgu**
農業　agriculture, farming **nōgyō**
農兵　peasant militia, farmer conscripts **nōhei**
農場　farm, plantation, ranch **nōjō**
農家　farmer, peasant **nōka**
農期　farming season **nōki**
農耕　farming, cultivation, tillage **nōkō**

農協　agricultural co-operative **nōkyō**
農民　farmer, peasant **nōmin**
農作　farming, cultivating **nōsaku**
農産　agriculture production, harvest **nōsan**
農相　minister of agriculture **nōso**
農村　farming village **nōson**
農薬　farming chemicals **nōyaku**
酪農　dairy farming **rakunō**
離農　quit farming for another work **rinō**
小作農　tenant farmer **kosakunō**
農閑期　slack farming season **nōkanki**
農機具　farming machines & implements **nōkigu**

野ield, 873	稲ice plant, 893
畑lantation, 482	畔ice-field path, 484
植lant, 783	米ice, 77
田ice field, 482	

豊bundance, 965

357-A
薬rugs for cure, not for 楽leasure...

⁺⁺ (grass)

薬rugs　　薬edicine

kusuri, YAKU
drugs, medication, medicine, pharmacy, pill, tablet

FLIP: 1.0.b. Whole (stem)

爆薬 explosives, flammable, combustible **bakuyaku**
弾薬 ammunition & explosives **danyaku**
毒薬 poisonous drug, poison **dokuyaku**
劇薬 lethal drug, deadly poison **gekiyaku**
鼻薬 bribe, kickback, hush money **hanagusuri**
火薬 gunpowder **kayaku**
傷薬 wound ointment **kizugusuri**
粉薬 powdered medicine **konagusuri**
薬箱 medicine box **kusuribako**
薬瓶 medicine bottle **kusuribin**
薬屋 drugstore, pharmacy **kusuriya**
薬指 fourth finger **kusuriyubi**
麻薬 drug, dope, narcotic **mayaku**
妙薬 wonder drug **myōyaku**
農薬 farm chemicals **nōyaku**
硝薬 gunpowder **shōyaku**
薬局 drugstore, pharmacy **yakkyoku**
薬物 medicine, drug, medication **yakubutsu**
薬毒 toxic element in medicine **yakudoku**

薬学 study of pharmacy, pharmacology **yakugaku**
薬品 medicine, drug, chemical **yakuhin**
薬味 spice, flavour **yakumi**
薬草 herb, herbal drugs **yakusō**
薬用 medicinal value, ~use **yakuyō**
薬剤 medicine, drug **yakuzai**
座薬 suppository **zayaku**
漢方薬 Chinese medicine **kanpōyaku**
眠り薬 sleeping pill, ~aid **nemurigusuri**
塗り薬 ointment, liniment, unguent **nurigusuri**
通じ薬 laxative, sedative **tsūjigusuri**

剤rugs, 961	患ickness, 475
治ecuperate, 210	症ickness, 788
癒ecuperate, 923	病ickness, 213
療ecuperate, 67	医edicine, 19

楽njoy, 447

357-B
薬rugs for cure, not for 楽leasure...

木 (wooden)

楽njoy　　楽leasure

tano(shimu), tano(shii), GAKU, RAKU
enjoy, pleasure, delight

FLIP: 1.0.b. Whole (stem)

道楽 hobby, pleasure, amusement **dōraku**
雅楽 Japanese court music **gagaku**
楽屋 dressing room **gakuya**
極楽 paradise **gokuraku**
娯楽 amusement, recreation **goraku**
神楽 sacred Shintō dance **kagura**
快楽 pleasure, enjoyment **kairaku**
歓楽 pleasure, enjoyment **kanraku**
苦楽 joy & sorrow **kuraku**
享楽 pleasure, enjoyment **kyōraku**
能楽 Noh play, Noh drama **nōgaku**
楽観 optimism, positive outlook **rakkan**
楽観視 optimistic view, positive outlook **rakkanshi**
楽観的 optimistic, positive outlook **rakkanteki**
楽園 paradise **rakuen**
楽天 positivism, optimistic **rakuten**
安楽死 euthanasia, mercy killing **anrakushi**
千秋楽 last day **senshūraku**
楽器 musical instrument **gakki**

楽譜 musical scoring **gakufu**
楽聖 master musician, maestro **gakusei**
楽隊 musical-, brass band **gakutai**
弦楽 string musical instrument **gengaku**
軍楽 military band **gungaku**
邦楽 Japanese music **hōgaku**
器楽 instrumental music **kigaku**
音楽 music, song **ongaku**
⇒軽音楽 light melody **keiongaku**
声楽 vocal music, chorus **seigaku**
奏楽 musical performance **sōgaku**
洋楽 Western music **yōgaku**

興ntertainment, 867	快leasant, 699
享njoy, 398	歓leasure, 667
遊njoy, 650	娯leasure, 453
悦leasant, 942	愉leasure, 922

薬rugs, 447

358-A

縮hrinking 宿odging, lodgers dodging...

糸 (thread, continuity)

縮hrink　　縮ownsize

chiji(maru), chiji(mu), chiji(meru), chiji(rasu), chiji(reru), SHUKU
shrink, downsize, minimize, reduce

FLIP: 7.3.a. Right Bottom (flat)

縮み織り *cotton crepe* **chijimiori**
縮み上がる *cower, huddle up* **chijimiagaru**
圧縮 *compression* **asshuku**
圧縮機 *compressor* **asshukuki**
縮緬 *crape, crepe* **chirimen**
軍縮 *disarmament, arms reduction* **gunshuku**
凝縮 *condensation* **gyōshuku**
畏縮 *flinching, shrinking* **ishuku**
緊縮 *retrenchment, austerity* **kinshuku**
緊縮政策 *austerity policy, belt-tightening*
　　　kinshuku seisaku
恐縮 *gratitude, shame* **kyōshuku**
濃縮 *concentration, condensation* **nōshuku**
伸縮 *stretch, spread, expansion* **shinshuku**
縮減 *reduction, cutting down* **shukugen**
縮刷 *printing in reduced size* **shukusatsu**
縮刷版 *pocket-, compact edition* **shukusatsuban**
縮写 *reduced-, miniature copy* **shukusha**
縮尺 *measurement scale* **shukushaku**

縮小 *reduction, downsizing* **shukushō**
縮約 *abbreviation, acronym* **shukuyaku**
縮図 *reduced drawing, epitome* **shukuzu**
収縮 *contraction, shrinkage* **shūshuku**
短縮 *reduction, shortening* **tanshuku**
⇒操業短縮 *operations downsizing*
　　　sōgyō tanshuku
縮れ毛 *curly hair, curls* **chijirege**
伸び縮み *expansion & contraction* **nobichijimi**

減*ecrease, 46*	寡*ittle, 161*
幾*ew, 547*	若*ittle, 276*
少*ew, 459*	耗*essen, 655*
微*light, 62*	

績*chievement, 822*

358-B

縮hrinking 宿odging, lodgers dodging...

宀 (cover, lid)

宿odging　　宿oarding

yado(ru), yado(su), yado, SHUKU, JUKU
lodging, boarding, sleep-over, stay-overnight, accommodation, billeting

FLIP: 7.3.a. Right Bottom (flat)

宿す *to get pregnant* **yadosu**
分宿 *lodging separately* **bunshuku**
合宿 *lodging together* **gasshuku**
下宿 *lodging, boarding* **geshuku**
定宿 *one's usual hotel* **jōyado**
寄宿 *board & lodging* **kishuku**
民宿 *bed & breakfast inn* **minshuku**
無宿 *homeless, vagabond* **mushuku**
野宿 *sleeping outdoors* **nojuku**
星宿 *constellation, cluster of stars* **seishuku**
新宿 *Shinjuku, Tōkyō* **shinjuku**
宿場 *stage* **shukuba**
宿便 *long feces* **shukuben**
宿望 *old wish, old desire* **shukubō**
宿坊 *temple lodgings* **shukubō**
宿直 *night duty* **shukuchoku**
宿題 *homework, assignment* **shukudai**
宿怨 *grudge, bad blood, revenge* **shukuen**
宿縁 *fate, destiny* **shukuen**

宿願 *long-cherished dream* **shukugan**
宿泊 *sleeping overnight, sleepover* **shukuhaku**
宿意 *long-held opinion; old grudges* **shukui**
宿命 *fate, destiny* **shukumei**
宿舎 *hotel, lodgings* **shukusha**
宿酔 *alcohol hang-over* **shukusui**
宿敵 *old enemy, blood enemy* **shukuteki**
宿賃 *lodging charges* **yadochin**
宿主 *hotel owner, inn owner* **yadonushi**
宿屋 *inn, hotel* **yadoya**
安宿 *cheap hotel* **yasuyado**
宿無し *homeless, vagabond* **yadonashi**
宿借り *hermit crab* **yadokari**
宿り木 *mistletoe, parasite, freeloader* **yadorigi**
宿割り *allotment of lodgings* **yadowari**

| 泊*leep-over, 742* | 室*oom, 485* |

百*undred, 14*

359-A

厳*evere training for the* 敢*old &* 敢*aring...*

厳*evere*　　　厳*arsh*　　　厳*ntense*

厂 (cliff)

kibi(shii), ogoso(ka), GEN, GON
severe, harsh, intense, ruthless, stinging, unsparing

厳罰 *severe punishment, heavy servitude* **genbatsu**
厳重 *strict, severe, unsparing* **genjū**
厳戒 *heavy guard, strict observation* **genkai**
厳格 *stern, rigid, strict* **genkaku**
厳寒 *intense cold* **genkan**
厳刑 *severe punishment* **genkei**
厳禁 *strictly forbidden, ~prohibited* **genkin**
厳命 *strict order* **genmei**
厳密 *strict, severe, unsparing* **genmitsu**
厳父 *your father, strict father* **genpu**
厳封 *tight sealing (documents)* **genpū**
厳正 *strictness, severity* **gensei**
厳選 *painstaking selection* **gensen**
厳暑 *blistering heat* **gensho**
厳守 *strict observance* **genshu**
厳粛 *solemnity, gravity* **genshuku**
厳存 *stern existence* **genson**
厳冬 *severe winter* **gentō**
厳然 *undeniable, strict* **genzen**

FLIP: 7.3.b. Right Bottom (stem)
Facing: 3.0. ☞ ☜ Across

威厳 *dignity, decorum* **igen**
戒厳令 *martial law, military occupation* **kaigenrei**
寛厳 *leniency-or-severity* **kangen**
謹厳 *serious, grave, severe, unsparing* **kingen**
冷厳 *grim, stern, strict* **reigen**
森厳 *solemn, sublime* **shingen**
峻厳 *strict, harsh, severe* **shungen**
荘厳 *solemn, sublime* **sōgon**
尊厳 *dignity, majesty, sanctity* **songen**
端厳 *solemnity & serenity* **tangen**

| 烈*evere, 585* | 猛*ierce, 657* |
| 激*ierce, 170* | 獣*east, 846* |

| 敢*ourage, 449* | |

359-B

厳*evere training for the* 敢*old &* 敢*aring...*

敢*aring*　　　敢*ourage*

父 (action)

ae(te), KAN
daring, courage, bold, bravery, dauntless, valour

敢えて *particularly, willingly; anyway* **aete**
敢えない *tragic, fateful* **aenai**
果敢 *daring, bold, dauntless* **kakan**
⇒勇猛果敢 *daring, bold, dauntless* **yūmō kakan**
果敢ない *vain, empty* **hakanai**
取り敢えず *immediately; for the time being* **toriaezu**
敢為 *daring, bold, dauntless* **kan'i**
敢然 *firmly, resolutely, determined* **kanzen**
勇敢 *brave, courageous* **yūkan**
敢行 *decisive action, execution* **kankō**
敢闘 *fighting courageously* **kantō**
敢闘賞 *fighting-spirit award* **kantōshō**
敢闘精神 *fighting spirit, determination* **kantō seishin**

FLIP: 7.1. Right (Sort Of)
Facing: 1.2. ☜ West (V)

| 胆*ourage, 740* | 勇*ourage, 59* |
| 冒*ourage, 401* | 雄*ourage, 775* |

| 乾*rying, 661* | |

360-A

繕*ending & forgiveness, that's* 善*ighteousness...*

糸 (thread, continuity)

繕*epair*　繕*ending*

tsukuro(u), ZEN

repair, mending, remedy, servicing

営繕　*building & repairs* **eizen**
修繕　*repair, servicing* **shūzen**
身繕い　*dress up well* **mitsukuroi**
見繕い　*decide well* **mizukuroi**
繕い物　*things to be mended* **tsukuroimono**
言い繕い　*gloss over* **iitsukuroi**
取り繕い　*repair, mend, patch up* **toritsukuroi**

FLIP: 7.0.a. Right (flat)

整*ectify, 31*	改*eform, 725*
革*eform, 39*	更*new, 402*

善*ighteous, 450*

360-B

繕*ending & forgiveness, that's* 善*ighteousness...*

口 (mouth)

善*ighteous*　善*oodness*

yo(i), ZEN

righteous, goodness

独善　*self-righteousness* **dokuzen**
不善　*misdeed, mischief* **fuzen**
偽善　*hypocrisy, fake kindness* **gizen**
慈善　*charity, benevolence* **jizen**
慈善家　*charitable, philanthropist* **jizenka**
改善　*improvement, reforming* **kaizen**
最善　*the very best, the finest* **saizen**
親善　*goodwill, friendship* **shinzen**
小善　*little kindness* **shōzen**
善悪　*good & evil, right-or-wrong* **zen'aku**
善美　*gorgeous, superb* **zenbi**
善玉　*good man* **zendama**
善道　*virtuous path* **zendō**
善導　*proper guidance* **zendō**
善意　*good intentions, good will* **zen'i**
善果　*favourable results* **zenka**
善行　*good deed, good conduct* **zenkō**
善人　*good person* **zennin**
善隣　*good neighbours* **zenrin**

FLIP: 1.0.a. Whole (flat)

善良　*honest-to-goodness* **zenryō**
善政　*good administration* **zensei**
善戦　*exerting one's best* **zensen**
善心　*conscience, righteousness* **zenshin**
善処　*dealing with properly* **zensho**
善用　*good use* **zenyō**
善後策　*relief measure, remedial* **zengosaku**
次善の策　*second best thing, the alternative*
　　jizen no saku
善し悪し　*good & evil, right-or-wrong* **yoshiashi**
善男善女　*pious men & women* **zennan zennyo**
独り善がり　*self-conceited* **hitori yogari**

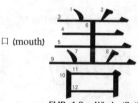

義*ighteous, 341*	款*oodwill, 42*
懇*ntimacy, 164*	友*riendship, 408*
親*ntimacy, 669*	徳*irtue, 844*

差*ifference, 589*

361-A

糧oodstuff 量uantity plenty in Djibouti...

米 (grains, rice)

糧oodstuff 糧ood supply

kate, RYŌ, RŌ
foodstuff, food supply

FLIP: 5.0.a Left & Right

馬糧 fodder, feeds **baryō**
兵糧 military food provisions **hyōrō**
衣糧 food & clothing **iryō**
口糧 food rations **kōryō**
糧道 supply lines, ~route **ryōdō**
糧秣 provisions & feeds **ryōmatsu**
糧食 food supplies, provision **ryōshoku**
食糧 food, foodstuffs **shokuryō**
心の糧 food-for-thought **kokoro no kate**
日日の糧 one's daily bread **hibi no kate**

食uisine, 255	多lenty, 187
飯ooked rice, 256	豊lenty, 965
炊ooking, 865	健ealthy, 390

量uantity, 451

361-B

糧oodstuff 量uantity plenty in Djibouti...

里 (hometown)

量uantity 量mount

haka(ru), RYŌ
quantity, amount, volume, aggregate

FLIP: 1.0.a. Whole (flat)

物量 amount of materials **butsuryō**
雅量 generosity, kind-hearted **garyō**
重量 weight, load **jūryō**
計量 measure, weight **keiryō**
器量 personal appearance **kiryō**
広量 generosity; broadminded **kōryō**
考量 consideration, pondering **kōryō**
極量 maximum load, ~dosage **kyokuryō**
量販 sales volume **ryōhan**
量感 massiveness, enormity **ryōkan**
量刑 reasonable punishment **ryōkei**
量産 mass production **ryōsan**
量的 quantitative **ryōteki**
裁量 discretion, opinion **sairyō**
声量 voice loudness, sound volume **seiryō**
酌量 consideration, thoughtfulness **shakuryō**
思量 thought, consideration **shiryō**
質量 mass, quality & quantity **shitsuryō**
測量 survey, sounding, surveying **sokuryō**

数量 volume, quantity **sūryō**
大量 vast quantity, large volume **tairyō**
適量 proper-, suitable amount **tekiryō**
用量 capacity, amount in use **yōryō**
容量 capacity, volume **yōryō**
致死量 lethal dose, deadly dosage **chishiryō**
貯水量 volume of stored water **chosuiryō**
度量衡 measurement system **doryōkō**
許容量 acceptable limit **kyoyōryō**
量子論 quantum theory **ryōshiron**
推し量る guess, presume, surmise **oshihakaru**

額mount, 559	材aterials, 186
桟rame, 768	料aterials, 194
枠rame, 761	多lenty, 187

童hildren, 564

362-A

響chos of my 郷ometown heard in downtown...

音 (sound) 響

❶ 響cho **❷ 響ffect**

hibi(ku), hibi(ki), KYŌ

echo, reverberation; effect, outcome

FLIP: 4.0.a. Bottom (flat)

❶ 反響 *echo, reverberation* **hankyō**
交響 *reverberation* **kōkyō**
交響楽 *symphony music* **kōkyōgaku**
交響曲 *symphony melody* **kōkyōkyoku**
音響 *sound* **onkyō**
⇒大音響 *loud noise* **daionkyō**
音響学 *acoustics science* **onkyōgaku**
残響 *lingering sound (gonging of bells)* **zankyō**
地響き *rumblings of the earth* **jihibiki**
音響効果 *sound effects* **onkyō kōka**
鳴り響く *resound, echo, ring* **narihibiku**
響き渡り *reverberation, echo; repercussion* **hibikiwatari**
交響楽団 *symphony orchestra* **kōkyō gakudan**

声oice, 428	効ffect, 645
音oise, 314	因ause, 862
騒oise, 924	果esult, 287

郷ometown, 452

❷ 影響 *influence, effect* **eikyō**
影響力 *influence, effect* **eikyōryoku**
悪影響 *bad influence, harmful effect* **akueikyō**
影響下 *"under the influence of..."* **eikyōka**
差し響く *affect, influence* **sashihibiku**

362-B

響chos of my 郷ometown heard in downtown...

阝⟷阜 (village-right) 郷

郷ometown **郷irthplace**

KYŌ, GŌ

hometown, birthplace, homeland

Facing: 2.2. East ☞ (V)

愛郷 *hometown affection* **aikyō**
望郷 *homesickness, nostalgia* **bōkyō**
同郷 *same hometown, ~birthplace* **dōkyō**
故郷 *hometown, birthplace* **furusato, kokyō**
郷社 *village shrine* **gōsha**
郷士 *countryside samurai, ~warrior* **gōshi**
郷村 *villages* **gōson**
異郷 *foreign country, strange land* **ikyō**
家郷 *family ancestral home* **kakyō**
帰郷 *coming home* **kikyō**
近郷 *neighbouring towns* **kingō**
郷土 *hometown, native land* **kyōdo**
郷土史 *folk history* **kyōdoshi**
郷土芸術 *folk art, craft* **kyōdo geijutsu**
郷関 *hometown, birthplace* **kyōkan**
郷里 *native town, birthplace* **kyōri**
郷愁 *homesickness, longing to come home* **kyōshū**
郷党 *townmates* **kyōtō**
郷俗 *folk customs* **kyōzoku**

離郷 *leaving one's hometown* **rikyō**
水郷 *riveredge town* **suigō**
他郷 *strange land, foreign country* **takyō**
在郷 *staying in one's town* **zaigō, zaikyō**
郷土料理 *local dishes* **kyōdo ryōri**
郷土芸能 *local performing arts* **kyōdo geinō**

里ometown, 321	誕hildbirth, 515
村illage, 690	産hildbirth, 883
帰eturn, 784	幼hildhood, 88

響cho, 452

363-A

娯*musement not easy for the* 呉*[Wu dynasty]...*

娯*leasure*   娯*musement*

女 (woman)

GO
pleasure, amusement, entertainment, enjoyment, merriment, recreation

FLIP: 7.2.a. Right Top (flat)

娯楽 *amusement, pastime* **goraku**
娯楽室 *recreation hall* **goraku shitsu**
娯楽街 *amusement town* **gorakugai**
娯楽品 *amusement object, plaything* **gorakuhin**
娯楽場 *amusement place* **gorakujō**
娯楽番組 *entertainment show* **goraku bangumi**
娯楽映画 *amusing movie* **goraku eiga**
娯楽機関 *recreational facilities* **goraku kikan**
娯楽施設 *amusement facilities* **goraku shisetsu**
娯楽雑誌 *popular magazine* **goraku zasshi**

悦*leasant, 942*	歓*leasure, 667*
快*leasant, 699*	喫*leasure, 900*
楽*leasure, 447*	愉*leasure, 922*

呉*[Wu dynasty], 453*

363-B

娯*musement not easy for the* 呉*[Wu dynasty]...*

呉*[Wu dynasty]*

口 (mouth)

kure, GO
[Wu dynasty]

FLIP: 3.0.a. Top (flat)

呉れる *give something* **kureru**
呉越 *Wu & Yue (rival states in ancient China)* **goetsu**
呉越同舟 *"rivals on the same boat..."* **goetsu dōshū**
呉服 *kimono fabric* **gofuku**
呉服屋 *kimono shop, ~dealer* **gofukuya**
呉音 *Wu Chinese reading* **goon**

華*hina, 40*	唐*hinese, 439*
中*hina, 85*	東*riental, 220*

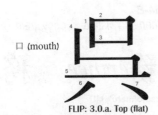

娯*musement, 453*

364-A

When its 霧isty & 霧oggy, train 務ervice is sloppy...

雨 (weather)

霧*oggy*　　霧*isty*

kiri, MU
foggy, misty, fuzzy

FLIP: 3.0.b. Top (stem)

朝霧 *misty morning* **asagiri**
煙霧 *smoke & fog* **enmu**
海霧 *ocean fog* **kaimu**
川霧 *misty river* **kawagiri**
霧雨 *drizzle, misty rain* **kirisame**
霧中 *in the fog* **muchū**
⇒五里霧中 *"groping in the dark..."* **gori muchū**
霧氷 *frost, ice* **muhyō**
霧散 *dispersal, dissipation* **musan**
霧笛 *foghorn alarm* **muteki**
濃霧 *dense-, thick fog* **nōmu**
狭霧 *mist, fog* **sagiri**
雲霧 *foggy clouds* **unmu**
薄霧 *light mist* **usugiri**
山霧 *misty mountain* **yamagiri**
夜霧 *night fog, foggy evening* **yogiri**
夕霧 *misty evening* **yūgiri**
噴霧器 *spray, vaporizer* **funmuki**
霧吹き *water spray, spray jet* **kirifuki**

雲散霧消 *"disappear in the mist..."* **unsan mushō**

霜*rost*, 615
曇*oggy*, 154
雰*oggy*, 518

露*ew*, 405

364-B

When its 霧isty & 霧oggy, train 務ervice is sloppy...

力 (strength, force)

務*ervice*　　務*mploy*

tsuto(meru), MU
service, serve, employ

Facing: 3.0. ⎙ Across
Facing: 4.0. ⎙ Apart

服務 *public service, ~duties* **fukumu**
学務 *academic affairs* **gakumu**
激務 *hectic-, arduous work* **gekimu**
義務 *duty, obligation* **gimu**
業務 *business, service* **gyōmu**
事務所 *office, workplace* **jimusho**
常務 *general manager* **jōmu**
警務 *police affairs* **keimu**
兼務 *additional task, concurrent posts* **kenmu**
勤務 *service, work, duty* **kinmu**
工務 *engineering works* **kōmu**
急務 *urgent business, pressing matter* **kyūmu**
内務 *internal affairs* **naimu**
任務 *duty, obligation* **ninmu**
債務 *debt, loan, borrowings* **saimu**
責務 *duty, obligation, responsibility* **sekimu**
専務 *special task, ~assignment* **senmu**
職務 *duty function, job description* **shokumu**
総務 *general affairs* **sōmu**

用務 *business matter* **yōmu**
財務 *financial matters* **zaimu**
残務 *remaining job, unfinished job* **zanmu**
雑務 *miscellaneous affairs* **zatsumu**
俗務 *mundane affairs* **zokumu**
外務省 *ministry of foreign affairs* **gaimushō**
刑務所 *prison, jail, gaol* **keimusho**
国務省 *US State Department* **kokumushō**
公務員 *civil servant, government employee* **kōmuin**
税務署 *tax agency* **zeimusho**
国連事務局 *United Nations Secretariat*
　　kokuren jimukyoku

勤*ervice*, 962　　労*abour*, 351
仕*ervice*, 9　　任*bligation*, 709
働*abour*, 422

矛*albsrd*, 568

365-A

Flat 譜usical-notes for 普ommon throats...

譜usical note

言 (speaking)

FU

musical note

FLIP: 5.0.a Left & Right

暗譜 *memorizing a musical note* **anpu**
読譜 *reading a musical note* **dokufu**
譜代 *successive generations* **fudai**
譜代大名 *Daimyo dynasty* **fudai daimyō**
譜面 *musical score* **fumen**
画譜 *album, photo book* **gafu**
楽譜 *musical score* **gakufu**
楽譜台 *music sheet stand* **gakufudai**
家譜 *family lineage, kinship* **kafu**
花譜 *flower album* **kafu**
系譜 *genealogy, kinship* **keifu**
棋譜 *Shōgi game records* **kifu**
曲譜 *musical score* **kyokufu**
年譜 *chronological listing* **nenpu**
音譜 *musical score* **onfu, onpu**
略譜 *brief musical score, melody* **ryakufu**
採譜 *copying a tune* **saifu**
写譜 *copying a musical sheet* **shafu**
氏譜 *genealogy, kinship* **shifu**

総譜 *full musical score* **sōfu**
五線譜 *notes on musical score* **gosenfu**
皇統譜 *imperial family record* **kōtōfu**

快*leasant, 699*	享*leasure, 398*
悦*leasure, 942*	楽*leasure, 447*

普*ommon, 455*

365-B

Flat 譜usical-notes for 普ommon throats...

普ommon 普rdinary

日 (sunlight, daytime)

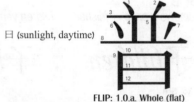

FU

common, ordinary, plain, average

FLIP: 1.0.a. Whole (flat)

普段 *usual, ordinary times* **fudan**
普段着 *daily clothes, casual wear* **fudangi**
普遍 *universal, general* **fuhen**
普遍性 *universality, general applicability* **fuhensei**
普遍的 *universal, generic* **fuhenteki**
普及 *diffusion, spreading* **fukyū**
普及版 *popular edition* **fukyūban**
普選 *universal suffrage* **fusen**
普請 *building, repairs* **fushin**
⇒橋普請 *building construction* **hashibushin**
⇒仮普請 *temporary building* **karibushin**
⇒道普請 *road repair, road maintenance* **michibushin**
⇒安普請 *cheaply-built (house)* **yasubushin**
普通 *usual, common, regular* **futsū**
普通列車 *local train, slow train* **futsū ressha**
普通料金 *ordinary rate, regular fee* **futsū ryōkin**
普通選挙 *universal suffrage, one-man one-vote*
　　futsū senkyo
普通預金 *regular savings account* **futsū yokin**

普通郵便 *ordinary mail, ~post* **futsū yūbin**

庸*ediocre, 906*	般*egular, 323*
凡*rdinary, 78*	

並*arallel, 444*

366-A

Homework once 了inished, 子hildren vanish...

了inish   了omplete

RYŌ
finish, complete, ending, closure, comprehend

了 (hook, barb)

丁 Facing: 1.0. West (W)

読了 *finish reading* **dokuryō**
議了 *end of deliberation* **giryō**
完了 *completion (construction)* **kanryō**
⇒過去完了 *past perfect* **kako kanryō**
⇒建設完了 *"construction finished..."*
　　kensetsu kanryō
結了 *end, completed, finished* **ketsuryō**
校了 *final proof reading* **kōryō**
満了 *expiry, expiration, maturity* **manryō**
魅了 *fascination, charm, appeal* **miryō**
魅了的 *charm, appeal, beauty* **miryōteki**
未了 *unfinished, incomplete* **miryō**
了知 *understanding, awareness* **ryōchi**
了解 *approval, agreement* **ryōkai**
⇒暗黙了解 *tacit approval, acquiescence*
　　anmoku ryōkai
了解事項 *agreed matters, "done deal..."* **ryōkai jikō**
了見 *intention, idea, judgement* **ryōken**
了簡 *idea; discretion; forgive* **ryōken**

了簡違い *mistaken idea; indiscretion*
　　ryōken chigai
了察 *consideration, thinking* **ryōsatsu**
了承 *acknowledgement, consent* **ryōshō**
終了 *completion, finishing* **shūryō**
修了 *completion, finishing* **shūryō**
投了 *giving up, accepting defeat* **tōryō**
訳了 *finish translation* **yakuryō**

完omplete, 196	止erminate, 192
終inish, 397	締onclude, 432

子hildren, 456

366-B

Homework once 了inished, 子hildren vanish...

子 (child)

子hildren   子ittle

ko, SHI
children, offspring, little, *noun suffix*

Facing: 1.0. West (W)

母子 *mother & child* **boshi**
帽子 *hat, cap* **bōshi**
電子 *electron* **denshi**
弟子 *pupil, apprentice* **deshi**
父子 *father & son* **fushi**
双子 *twins* **futago**
原子 *atom* **genshi**
黒子 *mole, beauty spot* **hokuro**
子種 *offspring, child* **kodane**
子供 *child, children* **kodomo**
子供服 *children's wear* **kodomofuku**
子供部屋 *children's room* **kodomobeya**
子犬 *puppy, little dog* **koinu**
子守 *baby-sitter, baby-sitting* **komori**
親子 *parent & child* **oyako**
里子 *foster child* **satogo**
子音 *consonant syllable* **shiin**
子宮 *womb, uterus* **shikyū**
子細 *details, circumstances* **shisai**

子爵 *viscount* **shishaku**
太子 *crown prince* **taishi**
店子 *store tenant* **tanako**
養子 *adopted child, foster child* **yōshi**
遺伝子 *gene, DNA* **idenshi**
案山子 *scarecrow* **kakashi**
隠し子 *illegitimate child* **kakushigo**
子会社 *subsidiary company* **kogaisha**
子山羊 *baby goat, young goat* **koyagi**
車椅子 *wheelchair* **kurumaisu**
教え子 *pupil, student* **oshiego**
子午線 *meridian line (acupuncture)* **shigosen**

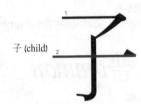

児hildren, 464	童hildren, 564
稚hildren, 776	孫randchild, 263
幼hildhood, 88	若oung, 276

了omplete, 456

367-A

Chapter 二wo, all about 仁 irtue...

二 (two, second)

二wo

futa(tsu), futa, NI
two

FLIP: 1.0.a. Whole (flat)

二子 *twins* **futago**
二心 *duplicity, double-dealing* **futagokoro**
二股 *forked, bifurcation* **futamata**
二親 *both parents, father & mother* **futaoya**
二人 *two persons; a couple* **futari**
二日 *second day of the month* **futsuka**
二つ目 *second (in a series)* **futatsume**
無二 *unrivalled, "unlike another..."* **muni**
二番 *second* **niban**
二分 *two halves* **nibun, nifun**
二度 *second time, twice* **nido**
二月 *February* **nigatsu**
二言 *duplicity, double-dealing* **nigon**
二扁 *second edition* **nihen**
二百 *two hundred* **nihyaku**
二次 *secondary* **niji**
二回 *twice; double* **nikai**
二階 *second floor* **nikai**
二期 *two terms, semestral* **niki**

二極 *bi-polar, two extremes* **nikyoku**
二塁 *second base* **nirui**
二世 *(~Charles II)* **nisei**
二割 *twenty percent* **niwari**
二十歳 *twenty-years old* **hatachi**
二十日 *20th day of the month* **hatsuka**
二年生 *second grade, sophomore* **ninensei**
二輪車 *two-wheeled (push cart)* **nirinsha**
二酸化 *dioxide* **nisanka**
一石二鳥 *"hit two birds by a stone..."* **isseki nichō**
二院制度 *two-chamber system* **niin seido**
二ヶ国語 *bilingual* **nikakokugo**

弐wo, 100	次ext, 460
両air, 567	副eputy, 332
乙econd group,	双win, 177

仁irtue, 457

367-B

Chapter 二wo, all about 仁 irtue...

人⇔亻 (person)

仁irtue   仁enevolence

JIN, NI
virtue, benevolence, goodness, righteous

FLIP: 7.0.a. Right (flat)

同仁 *impartial benevolence* **dōjin**
不仁 *cold-hearted, heartless* **fujin**
御仁 *personage, dignitary, luminary* **gojin**
裕仁 *Emperor Showa (posthumous name)* **hirohito**
仁愛 *benevolence, philanthropy* **jin'ai**
仁義 *humanity & justice* **jingi**
仁人 *benevolent person* **jinjin**
仁術 *selfless deed, benevolent act* **jinjutsu, ninjutsu**
仁兄 *friend, buddy, chum* **jinkei**
仁君 *benevolent ruler* **jinkun**
仁政 *benevolent rule* **jinsei**
仁者 *virtuous man* **jinsha**
仁心 *benevolent, humanity* **jinshin**
仁徳 *benevolence, magnanimity* **jintoku**
核仁 *nucleus, core* **kakujin**
寛仁 *magnanimous* **kanjin**
杏仁 *apricot kernel* **kyōnin**
仁王 *two Deva kings* **niō**
仁王立ち *standing proud* **niōdachi**

親仁 *one's father* **oyaji**
親仁方 *elderly, old person* **oyajikata**
亜麻仁 *linseed* **amani**
朴念仁 *moron, stick, dunce* **bokunenjin**
元仁時代 *Gennin Era (1224-1225)* **gennin jidai**
弘仁時代 *Kōnin Era (810-824)* **kōnin jidai**
仁安時代 *Nin'an Era (1166-1169)* **nin'an jidai**
仁寿時代 *Ninju Era (851-854)* **ninju jidai**
仁平時代 *Ninpei Era (1151-1154)* **ninpei jidai**
応仁時代 *Ōnin Era (1467-1469)* **ōnin jidai**
暦仁時代 *Ryakunin Era (1238-1239)* **ryakunin jidai**
天仁時代 *Tennin Era (1108-1110)* **tennin jidai**

徳irtue, 844	善ighteous, 450
倫thics, 787	孔onfucius, 684
義ighteous, 341	儒onfucius, 548

二econd, 457

368-A
Word-of- □ outh 回irculates doubts...

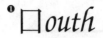

□ (mouth)

¹□*outh* ²□*pening*

kuchi, KŌ, KU
mouth; opening, aperture

FLIP: 1.0.a. Whole (flat)

❶ 口外 *revelation, disclosure* **kōgai**
口語 *spoken language, colloquial* **kōgo**
口述 *oral dictation* **kōjutsu**
口腔 *mouth, oral cavity* **kōkū**
口論 *argument, bickering* **kōron**
口元 *mouth, lips* **kuchimoto**
口止め *forbidden to speak* **kuchidome**
口汚い *verbally-abusive, foul-mouthed* **kuchigitanai**
口癖 *way of saying* **kuchiguse**
口コミ *word-of-mouth* **kuchikomi**
口煩い *nagging, persistent* **kuchiurusai**
口添え *recommendation* **kuchizoe**
口説く *persuade, convince* **kudoku**
飲み口 *oral digestion, oral intake* **nomikuchi**
裏口入学 *fraudulent university admission*
　　uraguchi nyūgaku
❷ 秋口 *early autumn* **akiguchi**
別口 *another topic, separate matter* **betsukuchi**
糸口 *beginning, clue* **itoguchi**

人口 *population* **jinkō**
銃口 *gun muzzle* **jūkō**
陰口 *backbiting, backtalking* **kageguchi**
火口 *crater* **kakō**
河口 *mouth of a river* **kakō**
軽口 *light jest, talkativeness* **karukuchi**
傷口 *wound, bruise* **kizuguchi**
口径 *diameter* **kōkei**
口座 *bank account* **kōza**
口紅 *lipstick, rouge* **kuchibeni**
口火 *pilot light, fuse, origin* **kuchibi**
表口 *front door, main entrance* **omoteguchi**
裏口 *rear entrance, backdoor* **uraguchi**
入口 *entrance, opening* **iriguchi**

開*pen, 284*	披*pen, 104*

回*irculate, 458*

368-B
Word-of- □ outh 回irculates doubts...

□ (enclosure)

回*irculate* 回*otate*

mawa(su), mawa(ru), KAI, E
circulate, gyrate, rotate, turnaround, time(s)

FLIP: 1.0.a. Whole (flat)

次回 *next time* **jikai**
巡回 *round, patrol* **junkai**
回復 *recovery, rehabilitation* **kaifuku**
回帰 *recurrence, revolution* **kaiki**
回顧 *retrospection, reminiscence* **kaiko**
回航 *navigation, cruise* **kaikō**
回教 *Islam, Moslem, Muslim* **kaikyō**
回路 *circuit (electric)* **kairo**
回廊 *corridor, hallway* **kairō**
回診 *doctor's hospital rounds* **kaishin**
回収 *collection, reclaiming* **kaishū**
回送 *"returning to bus station..."* **kaisō**
回数 *frequency, number of times* **kaisū**
回転 *rotating, revolving* **kaiten**
旋回 *turning, circling* **senkai**
初回 *beginning, start* **shokai**
転回 *turning, circling, rotating* **tenkai**
回し者 *spy, secret agent* **mawashimono**
何回も *many times, often* **nankaimo**

利回り *yield, return, interest* **rimawari**
遠回り *roundabout way, detour* **toomawari**
歩き回る *walk around* **arukimawaru**
振り回す *show off, swing, brandish* **furimawasu**
走り回る *run around* **hashirimawaru**
引き回す *take around, draw* **hikimawasu**
転げ回る *tumble, writhe* **korogemawaru**
回りくどい *circumvent, roundabout* **mawarikudoi**
乗り回す *drive around, ride about* **norimawasu**
飛び回る *flutter, romp about* **tobimawaru**
動き回る *move around* **ugokimawaru**

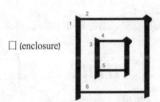

旋*evolve, 651*	循*irculation, 407*
輪*ircle, 786*	巡*atrol, 571*
丸*ound, 73*	往*ome & go, 749*
周*ap, 280*	

口*outh, 458*

369-A

Too 小mall too 少ew, vaccines for flu...

小mall   小ittle

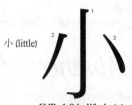

小 (little)

FLIP: 1.0.b. Whole (stem)

chii(sai), ko, o, SHŌ
small, little

小豆 *adzuki beans* **azuki**
微小 *slight, minute* **bishō**
極小 *minimum* **gokushō**
小人 *dwarf, midget person* **kobito**
小形 *small-sized* **kogata**
小言 *fault-finding, complaining* **kogoto**
小麦 *wheat* **komugi**
小雨 *drizzling, light rain* **kosame**
小唄 *ditty, ballad* **kouta**
小売 *retail, retailing* **kouri**
小屋 *hut, shack* **koya**
小指 *little finger* **koyubi**
小皿 *small plate* **kozara**
小便 *urine, urination, pee* **shōben**
小異 *minor difference* **shōi**
小事 *frivolous-, petty-, trifle matters* **shōji**
小寒 *period of mild chill* **shōkan**
小康 *state of remission* **shōkō**
小冊 *booklet, pamphlet* **shōsatsu**

小説 *novel, short story* **shōsetsu**
縮小 *reduction, down-sizing* **shukushō**
短小 *small, little, short* **tanshō**
小さ目 *a little bit, small serving* **chiisame**
犬小屋 *kennel, dog house* **inugoya**
小文字 *small letters, lower caps* **komoji**
小荷物 *parcel, small package* **konimotsu**
小学校 *elementary school* **shōgakkō**
小児科 *pediatrics, children doctor* **shōnika**
小委員会 *sub-committee* **shōiinkai**

寡*ittle, 161*	少*ew, 459*
若*ittle, 276*	子*hild, 456*
幾*ew, 547*	微*light, 62*

水*ater, 9*

369-B

Too 小mall too 少ew, vaccines for flu...

少ew   少carce

小 (little)

FLIP: 2.0.b. Sort Of (stem)

suko(shi); suku(nai), SHŌ
few, scarce, insufficient, scanty, slight, deficient, inadequate

少ない *small, little, scarce* **sukunai**
微少 *slight, infinitesmal, microscopic* **bishō**
減少 *decrease, decline, reduction* **genshō**
弱小 *young, youth* **jakushō**
過少 *too little, too few* **kashō**
寡少 *little, scanty* **kashō**
軽少 *slight, trifle* **keishō**
希少 *rare, scarce, uncommon* **kishō**
年少 *young person* **nenshō**
老少 *young & old* **rōshō**
最少 *the fewest, the least in number* **saishō**
鮮少 *a few, little* **senshō**
少額 *small sum, small amount* **shōgaku**
少尉 *2nd lieutenant, midshipman* **shōi**
少女 *little young girl* **shōjo**
少憩 *short break, recess* **shōkei**
少年 *little boy, young boy* **shōnen**
少量 *small amount* **shōryō**
少差 *narrow margin* **shōsa**

少佐 *major, lieutenant commander* **shōsa**
少々 *a moment, a little* **shōshō**
少将 *brigadier general* **shōshō**
少食 *eating little* **shōshoku**
少壮 *young & vigorous* **shōsō**
少数 *a few, minority* **shōsū**
多少 *a little, a few* **tashō**
幼少 *childhood, infancy, young* **yōshō**
青少年 *youth, young adults* **seishōnen**
少しだけ *just a little* **sukoshidake**
少しずつ *little by little* **sukoshizutsu**

寡*ittle, 161*	幾*ew, 547*
若*ittle, 276*	微*light, 62*

小*mall, 459*

370-A

欠bsence of what's 次ext, consult your Rolex...

欠 (lacking)

欠bsence 欠issing

ka(ku), ka(keru), KETSU
absence, deficient, inadequate, missing, lacking, scarce, slight, scanty

Facing: 1.0. 🐦 West (W)

欠伸 *yawn, gape* **akubi**
長欠 *long absence* **chōketsu**
補欠 *alternate, substitute, replacement* **hoketsu**
間欠 *intermittent, interval, alternate* **kanketsu**
欠格 *disqualification, forfeiture* **kekkaku**
欠陥 *defect, flaw, shortcomings* **kekkan**
欠勤 *work absence, ~leave* **kekkin**
欠航 *suspension of transport service* **kekkō**
欠配 *non-delivery, non-arrival* **keppai**
欠本 *missing volume, ~book* **keppon**
欠席 *absence, non-attendance* **kesseki**
欠食 *skipping meals, food abstinence* **kesshoku**
欠損 *deficit, in-the-red* **kesson**
欠番 *missing number* **ketsuban**
欠便 *cancelled flight* **ketsubin**
欠乏 *shortage, lacking, deficiency* **ketsubō**
欠員 *vacant position, job opening* **ketsuin**
欠字 *missing letter* **ketsuji**
欠場 *absence, non-attendance* **ketsujō**

欠講 *cancelled lecture* **kekkō**
欠落 *shortage, lacking, deficiency* **ketsuraku**
欠礼 *new year non-observance due to mourning* **ketsurei**
欠点 *weak point, weakness* **ketten**
金欠 *lack of money, financial difficulty* **kinketsu**
無欠 *flawless, lacking none* **muketsu**
酸欠 *lack of oxygen* **sanketsu**
出欠 *attendance-or-absence* **shukketsu**
事欠く *lack of, short of* **kotokaku**
不可欠 *indispensable, essential* **fukaketsu**
満ち欠け *waxing & waning* **michikake**

無othing, 49	非[negative], 288
敗ailure, 137	不[negative], 300

次ext, 460

370-B

欠bsence of what's 次ext, consult your Rolex...

欠 (lacking)

次ext 次ubsequent

tsugi, tsu(gu), JI, SHI
next, subsequent, ensuing, succeeding

Facing: 1.2. 🐦 West (V)

逐次 *one after another, in order, serial* **chikuji**
次長 *deputy, second from the top* **jichō**
次代 *succeeding generations* **jidai**
次元 *dimension, level* **jigen**
次号 *next issue, next number* **jigō**
次女 *second eldest daughter* **jijo**
次回 *next time, second time around* **jikai**
次官 *vice-minister, under-secretary* **jikan**
次兄 *second eldest brother* **jikei**
次期 *next term* **jiki**
次記 *"as follows, the following..."* **jiki**
次男 *second eldest son* **jinan**
次席 *next in line, second ranking* **jiseki**
次席 *second place* **jiseki**
次週 *next week* **jishū**
次点 *borderline, boundary* **jiten**
次善 *second best, best alternative* **jizen**
順次 *one after another, serial, consecutive* **junji**
高次 *high level* **kōji**

今次 *this time, now, for the time being* **konji**
目次 *table of contents* **mokuji**
年次 *annual, yearly* **nenji**
席次 *seating order, ~list* **sekiji**
次第に *gradually* **shidai(ni)**
数次 *several times, multiple* **sūji**
副次的 *secondary, alternative* **fukujiteki**
二次会 *second party (drinking party)* **nijikai**
野次る *jeer, hoot, boo, heckle* **yajiru**
四次元 *four dimensions* **yojigen**
野次馬 *nosy person* **yajiuma**

亜ext to, 389	続ontinue, 260
順equence, 959	継ontinuity, 958
第[order], 102	翌ucceeding, 237
号umber, 866	

欠bsence, 460

371-A
Save rees & 木ood, 本ain 本ook concludes...

木 (wooden)

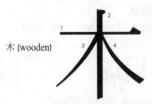

木ree　木ood

ki, ko, MOKU, BOKU
tree, wood

FLIP: 1.0.b. Whole (stem)

木剣 *wooden sword* **bokken**
樹木 *trees, woods* **jumoku**
木戸 *wicket, garden gate* **kido**
木口 *cut end* **kiguchi**
木苺 *raspberry* **kiichigo**
木霊 *spirit of a tree* **kodama**
木陰 *tree shade* **kokage**
草木 *plant, vegetation* **kusaki, sōmoku**
木琴 *xylophone* **mokkin**
木工 *carpentry, woodwork* **mokkō**
木魚 *wooden gong* **mokugyo**
木版 *woodblock printing* **mokuhan**
木食 *dieting on fruits* **mokujiki**
木星 *Planet Jupiter* **mokusei**
木製 *wooden products, woodcraft* **mokusei**
木材 *lumber, wood, timber* **mokuzai**
木像 *wooden image* **mokuzō**
木綿 *cotton cloth* **momen**
庭木 *garden tree* **niwaki**

垂木 *wodden raft* **taruki**
材木 *lumber, timber* **zaimoku**
枯れ木 *decayed-, withered tree* **kareki**
木の実 *nut, berry* **kinomi**
木切れ *wood chip* **kigire**
木の芽 *bud, sprout* **konome**
木曜日 *thursday* **mokuyōbi**
接ぎ木 *grafting, grated tree* **tsugiki**
積み木 *building blocks* **tsumiki**
木枯らし *cold winter wind* **kogarashi**
止まり木 *wooden perch* **tomarigi**

材 *oods, 186*	葉 *eaf, 411*
林 *oods, 526*	緑 *reen, 841*
森 *orest, 526*	

本 *ook, 461*

371-B
Save 木rees & 木ood, ain 本ook concludes...

木 (wooden)

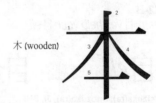

❶本ain　❷本ook

moto, HON
main, basis, true; book

FLIP: 1.0.b. Whole (stem)

❶本業 *main profession, full-time job* **hongyō**
本位 *principle, basics, fundamentals* **hon'i**
本館 *main building, ~hall* **honkan**
本家 *main family* **honke**
本件 *this case, ~affair* **honken**
本気 *earnestness, serious* **honki**
本拠 *headquarters, base* **honkyo**
本局 *head office, headquarters* **honkyoku**
本給 *basic salary, base wage* **honkyū**
本元 *origin, source* **honmoto**
本音 *real intention* **honne**
本能 *instinct, intuition* **honnō**
闘争本能 *fighting spirit* **tōsō honnō**
本俸 *basic salary* **honpō**
本社 *head-, main office* **honsha**
本心 *real intention* **honshin**
本性 *real character* **honshō**
本筋 *main thread, ~subject* **honsuji**
本意 *will, intention, volition* **hon'i**

本科 *regular course* **honka**
本学 *this university, ~school* **hongaku**
本当 *real, true, genuine* **hontō**
標本 *specimen, sample* **hyōhon**
見本 *sample, specimen* **mihon**
本歌 *original song* **motouta**
本会議 *plenary session* **honkaigi**
本格的 *fundamental, real stuff* **honkakuteki**

❷本屋 *bookstore, ~dealer* **honya**
献本 *complimentary copy from author* **kenpon**
脚本家 *playwright, script writer* **kyakuhonka**
漫画本 *comic book* **mangabon**
抄本 *abridged copy, ~edition* **shōhon**
謄本 *certified copy* **tōhon**
贈呈本 *complimentary copy* **zōteibon**

冊 *[books], 20*	真 *incere, 487*
読 *eading, 260*	誠 *incere, 245*

木 *ree, 461*

372-A
Sharp 目 yes help your 自 elf...

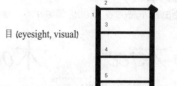

目 (eyesight, visual)

 ❶目*ye* ❷目*oint*

me, ma, MOKU, BOKU
eye, vision, visual; point, degree, item

FLIP: 1.0.a. Whole (flat)

❶注目 *focus of attention, concentration* **chūmoku**
眼目 *main point, gist* **ganmoku**
細目 *details, particulars* **hosome**
耳目 *eyes & ears, one's attention* **jimoku**
科目 *course subject, academic subject* **kamoku**
目玉 *centre of attention, eyeball* **medama**
名目 *pretext, excuse, alibi* **meimoku**
面目 *face, prestige, honour* **menmoku, menboku**
目次 *table of contents* **mokuji**
目算 *anticipation, expectation* **mokusan**
盲目 *blind person* **mōmoku**
大目 *large serving (food)* **oome**
大目に見る *overlook* **oome(ni) miru**
大目玉 *scolding, dressing down* **oomedama**
鳥目 *night blindness* **torime**
裏目 *disappointment, despair, misgivings* **urame**
勝ち目 *winning chance, odds* **kachime**
目の毒 *eyesore, unbearable sight* **menodoku**
目立つ *stand out, be noticed* **medatsu**

目の前 *"before one's eyes..."* **menomae**
目移り *puzzled, baffled* **meutsuri**
目指す *aim, target* **mezasu**
種目 *event, item* **shumoku**
死に目 *verge of death, dying bed* **shinime**
素人目 *untrained eyes* **shirōtome**
題目 *theme, title, subject matter* **daimoku**
❷駄目 *no good, wrong, inferior* **dame**
目的 *purpose, objective, aim* **mokuteki**
目標 *purpose, objective, aim* **mokūyō**
役目 *duty, function, role* **yakume**
真面目 *serious, no-nonsense* **majime**
目的地 *travel destination* **mokutekichi**
変わり目 *change, turning point* **kawarime**

眼 *yesight, 771*   見 *eeing, 307*

目 *urther, 500*

372-B
Sharp 目 yes help your 自 elf...

自*elf*   自*tself*

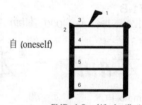

自 (oneself)

mizuka(ra), onozuka(ra), JI, SHI
self, one's own, automatic, itself

FLIP: 1.0.a. Whole (flat)

独自 *original, inherent, peculiar* **dokuji**
自愛 *self-regard, self-love* **jiai**
自爆 *suicide bombing, self-explosion* **jibaku**
自弁 *paying for oneself, Dutch treat* **jiben**
自分 *oneself, one's person* **jibun**
自衛 *self-defence, self-protection* **jiei**
自我 *ego, self, pride* **jiga**
自白 *confession, penance* **jihaku**
自発 *spontaneous, sporadic* **jihatsu**
自発的 *spontaneous, sporadic* **jihatsuteki**
自慰 *masturbation* **jii**
自浄 *self-purification, ~cleansing* **jijō**
自戒 *self-discipline* **jikai**
自壊 *disintegrate, fall apart* **jikai**
自覚 *consciousness, awareness* **jikaku**
自決 *suicide; self-determination* **jiketsu**
自慢 *pride, honour* **jiman**
自殺 *suicide, killing oneself* **jisatsu**
自薦 *self-recommendation* **jisen**

自首 *voluntary surrender* **jishu**
自習 *self-study, one's research* **jishū**
⇒自学自習 *self-study, self-learning* **jigaku jishū**
自粛 *impose self-control, ~restraint* **jishuku**
自由 *freedom, liberty* **jiyū**
各自 *respectively, each, every* **kakuji**
自然 *nature, environment, greens* **shizen**
自営業 *self-employed* **jieigyō**
自衛権 *right of self-defence* **jieiken**
自衛隊 *self-defence force* **jieitai**
自画像 *self-portrait* **jigazō**
自意識 *self-consciousness* **ji'ishiki**

己 *elf, 5*   寡 *lone, 161*
独 *lone, 369*   孤 *lone, 148*

目 *ye, 462*

373-A

Our health 丈*obust,* 吏*fficials to trust...*

一 (one, single)

丈*obust*   丈*turdy*

take, JŌ
robust, sturdy, strong, stout, stature

Facing: 2.0. East ☞ (W)

万丈 *unlimited, "sky's the limit..."* **banjō**
⇒波瀾万丈 *ups & downs, checkered* **haran banjō**
⇒気炎万丈 *high spirits, spirited* **kien banjō**
⇒気焔万丈 *high spirits, spirited* **kien banjō**
頑丈 *sturdy, strong, firm, robust* **ganjō**
方丈 *chief priest quarters* **hōjō**
丈夫 *strong, durable, sturdy, robust* **jōbu**
丈余 *over 10 feet, over three metres* **jōyo**
気丈 *stout-hearted* **kijō**
気丈夫 *re-assuring, comforting* **kijōbu**
気丈者 *stout-hearted person* **kijōmono**
着丈 *kimono length* **kitake**
草丈 *crop size, ~height* **kusatake**
身丈 *one's height, garment length* **mitake**
軒丈 *eaves height* **nokitake**
背丈 *height, stature* **setake**
袖丈 *sleeve length* **sodetake**
其丈 *"all the more..."* **soredake**
桁丈 *sleeve length* **yukidake, yukitake**

美丈夫 *good features, good looks* **bijōfu**
大丈夫 *"all right, safe, OK, fine..."* **daijōbu**
八丈島 *Hachijō Island (near Tōkyō City)*
　　　hachijōjima
偉丈夫 *great exploits* **ijōfu**
居丈高 *domineering, manipulative* **itakedaka**
威丈高 *domineering, manipulative* **itakedaka**
女丈夫 *heroine* **jojōbu**
心丈夫 *strong-hearted, iron will* **kokorojōbu**
首っ丈 *fascinated, obsessed with* **kubittake**
黒八丈 *thick black silk* **kurohachijō**
有りっ丈 *"all there is..."* **arittake**

強*trong, 894*	筋*uscle, 584*
剛*trong, 975*	力*orce, 351*
健*ealthy, 390*	張*xert, 274*

吏*fficial, 463*

373-B

Our health 丈*obust,* 吏*fficials to trust...*

口 (mouth)

吏*fficial*   吏*uthority*

RI
official, authority, dignitary, officialdom, top brass

FLIP: 2.0.b. Sort Of (stem)

幕吏 *Shōgunate official* **bakuri**
獄吏 *prison official* **gokuri**
捕吏 *apprehending-, arresting officer* **hori**
官吏 *civil servant, public employee* **kanri**
下吏 *rank & file official* **kari**
刑吏 *executioner, hangman* **keiri**
酷吏 *corrupt official* **kokuri**
公吏 *government officials* **kōri**
能吏 *able officer* **nōri**
廉吏 *honest official* **renri**
吏員 *officer, official* **riin**
吏人 *officials, authorities* **rijin**
吏臭 *officialdom* **rishū**
老吏 *ageing official* **rōri**
良吏 *conscientious official* **ryōri**
小吏 *petty officer* **shōri**
廷吏 *court official* **teiri**
税吏 *tax official* **zeiri**
⇒徴税吏 *tax collector* **chōzeiri**

⇒収税吏 *tax official* **shūzeiri**
俗吏 *petty officer* **zokuri**
官公吏 *government officials* **kankōri**
執行吏 *court official* **shikkōri**
税関吏 *customs officer* **zeikanri**

役*fficial, 746*	臣*etainer, 542*
官*ublic official, 105*	相*inister, 524*
庁*ubic office, 633*	

使*tilize, 480*

374-A

旧*ormerly a* 児*hild, no longer wild...*

日 (sunlight, daytime)

旧*ormerly*   旧*revious*

furu(i), KYŪ

formerly, previous, erstwhile, before, defunct

FLIP: 5.0.a Left & Right

旧ソビエト *former Soviet Union* **kyū sobieto**	旧作 *old work* **kyūsaku**
懐旧 *memories, reminiscences* **kaikyū**	旧姓 *maiden name* **kyūsei**
旧悪 *past misdeeds, old sins* **kyūaku**	旧跡 *historic ruins, relics* **kyūseki**
旧聞 *old news, old story* **kyūbun**	旧師 *one's former teacher* **kyūshi**
旧知 *old acquaintance* **kyūchi**	旧式 *old style, old technique* **kyūshiki**
旧型 *old model* **kyūgata**	旧態 *former state of things* **kyūtai**
旧劇 *classical play* **kyūgeki**	旧友 *old friend, close friend* **kyūyū**
旧弊 *old abuses, past sins* **kyūhei**	新旧 *old and new* **shinkyū**
旧家 *good old family* **kyūka**	守旧 *conservative, orthodox* **shukyū**
旧観 *former appearance* **kyūkan**	旧字体 *old Kanji characters* **kyūjitai**
旧交 *old friendship, long acquaintance* **kyūkō**	旧教徒 *Roman Catholic* **kyūkyōto**
旧居 *one's former house* **kyūkyo**	旧約聖書 *Old Testament* **kyūyaku seisho**
旧派 *old school, old timer* **kyūha**	
旧年 *last year* **kyūnen**	
旧恩 *old debt of gratitude* **kyūon**	
旧来 *conventional, regular* **kyūrai**	
旧暦 *lunar calendar* **kyūreki**	
旧領 *former territory* **kyūryō**	
旧債 *old unpaid debt* **kyūsai**	

先*efore, 478*	去*eave-out, 360*
前*efore, 118*	枯*ither, 960*
昔*lden-times, 281*	

日*ay, 14*

374-B

旧*ormerly a* 児*hild, no longer wild...*

儿 (human legs)

児*hildren*   児*uvenile*

ko, JI, NI

children, juvenile, kiddie, kiddo, young child

FLIP: 7.2.a. Right Top (flat)

愛児 *one's favourite child* **aiji**	胎児 *foetus, embryo* **taiji**
病児 *sickly child* **byōji**	蕩児 *prodigal son, debauchee* **tōji**
寵児 *favourite son, ~daughter* **chōji**	幼児 *infant, little child* **yōji**
男児 *little boy* **danji**	⇒乳幼児 *infant, baby* **nyūyōji**
園児 *kindergrader* **enji**	肥満児 *obese child* **himanji**
遺児 *posthumous child* **iji**	混血児 *child of mixed race* **konketsuji**
育児 *child care* **ikuji**	未熟児 *premature baby* **mijukuji**
児童 *child, pupil* **jidō**	問題児 *problem child* **mondaiji**
児戯 *children play* **jigi**	熱血児 *hot-blooded, mercurial* **nekketsuji**
児女 *little girl & a woman* **jijo**	私生児 *love-, illegitimate child* **shiseiji**
児孫 *next generations* **jison**	小児科 *paediatrics, children's clinic* **shōnika**
女児 *little girl* **jijo**	早生児 *premature baby* **sōseiji**
健児 *healthy-, robust child* **kenji**	
孤児 *orphan* **koji**	
孤児院 *orphanage* **kojiin**	
迷児 *lost child* **maigo**	
乳児 *suckling, baby* **nyūji**	
蚕児 *silkworm* **sanji**	
死児 *dead-born child* **shiji**	

稚*hildren, 776*	若*oung, 276*
幼*hildhood, 88*	小*mall, 459*
子*hildren, 456*	童*hildren, 564*

旧*ormerly, 464*

375-A

万 en-thousand audience 励 ncourage 励 iligence...

一 (one, single)

万

万 en thousand

yorozu, MAN, BAN
ten thousand, 10,000

Facing: 2.0. East ☞ (W)

万物 *all things, creation* **banbutsu**	万華鏡 *kaleidoscope* **mangekyō**
万事 *everything, all things* **banji**	万年筆 *fountain pen* **mannenhitsu**
万丈 *overwhelming, overpowering* **banjō**	万能選手 *well-rounded athlete* **bannō senshu**
万感 *all kinds of feelings, flood of emotions* **bankan**	万歳三唱 *banzai three cheers, hurray!*
万能 *all-around* **bannō**	**banzai sanshō**
万福 *all the health & happiness* **banpuku, manpuku**	永万時代 *Eiman Era (1165-66)* **eiman jidai**
万雷 *thunderous applause* **banrai**	万延時代 *Man'en Era (1860-61)* **man'en jidai**
万策 *every means* **bansaku**	万治時代 *Manji Era (1658-61)* **manji jidai**
万死 *sure death, no chance to live* **banshi**	万寿時代 *Manju Era (1024-28)* **manju jidai**
万障 *all obstacles, at any cost* **banshō**	百万長者 *millionaire, wealthy* **hyakuman chōja**
万全 *thorough, assured, fool-proof* **banzen**	億万長者 *billionaire, very rich* **okuman chōja**
万病 *all kinds of diseases* **manbyō**	千変万化 *innumerable changes* **senpen banka**
万言 *lengthy talk* **mangen**	
万一 *"in the event of, in case of..."* **man'ichi**	一ne, 858 　千housand, 74
万金 *tons of cash* **mankin**	十en, 344 　億undred-million, 340
万年 *perpetuity, eternity* **mannen**	百undred, 14 　零ero, 874
万人 *everyone, all persons* **mannin**	
万国旗 *flags of all nations* **bankokki**	方irection, 533
万引き *shoplifting* **manbiki**	

375-B

万 en-thousand audience 励 ncourage 励 iligence...

力 (strength, force)

励

❶励 ncourage　❷励 iligence

hage(mu), hage(mi), hage(masu), REI
encourage, cheer-up, embolden, motivate, inspire, prodding, prompt; diligence, forbearance

Facing: 2.2. East ☞ (V)

❶励み *encouragement, inspiration* **hagemi**
励み合う *mutual encouragement* **hagemiau**
激励 *encouragement, inspiration* **gekirei**
励起 *excitement, agitation* **reiki**
励行 *observance, practice* **reikō**
奨励 *encouragement, promotion* **shōrei**
奨励金 *bounty, subsidy* **shōreikin**
他励 *other inspiration* **tarei**
督励 *encouragement, inspiration* **tokurei**

❷勉励 *diligence, perseverance* **benrei**
奮励 *strenuous, determined* **funrei**
励声 *hoarse-, strained voice* **reisei**
精励 *diligence, industriousness* **seirei**

奨ncourage, 521	努fforts, 44	労abour, 351
促ncourage, 481	勉fforts, 527	張xert, 274

万 en thousand, 465

376-A

比*ompare before you* 批*riticize the* 比*hilippine price...*

比 (compare)

❶比ompare ❷比hilippines

kura(beru), HI
compare; Philippines

Facing: 1.2. ☜ West (V)

❶逆比 *inverse proportion* **gyakuhi**
比価 *parity, equality, reciprocity* **hiatai**
比重 *relative-, comparative importance* **hijū**
比重計 *hydrometer* **hijūkei**
比価 *parity, equality* **hika**
比較 *comparison, contrast* **hikaku**
比肩 *equal, tantamount* **hiken**
比況 *similar conditions* **hikyō**
比熱 *specific heat* **hinetsu**
比例 *proportion, symmetry* **hirei**
比隣 *vicinity, environs* **hirin**
比倫 *peer, equal, match* **hirin**
比率 *ratio, percentage* **hiritsu**
比類 *match, equal* **hirui**
比翼 *lovebirds* **hiyoku**
公比 *common ratio* **kōhi**
比物 *comparison, analogy* **kurabemono**
無比 *unrivalled, matchless* **muhi**
類比 *analogy, comparison* **ruihi**

正比 *direct ratio* **seihi**
対比 *comparison, contrast* **taihi**
等比 *equal ratio* **tōhi**
等比級数 *geometric series* **tōhi kyūsū**
等比数列 *geometric progression* **tōhi sūretsu**
恵比寿 *god of wealth (Ebisu)* **ebisu**
反比例 *inverse* **hanpirei**
根比べ *endurance game* **konkurabe**
腕比べ *competition, match* **udekurabe**
比電荷 *specific electric charge* **hidenka**
❷比島 *The Philippines, Philippine Islands* **hitō**
比律賓 *The Philippines* **firipin**

較*ompare, 774*	調*nspection, 280*
察*nspection, 328*	検*nspection, 939*
審*nspection, 339*	査*nspection, 624*

北*orthern, 372*

376-B

比*ompare before you* 批*riticize the* 比*hilippine price...*

手⇔扌 (hand, manual)

批riticize 批ensure

HI
criticize, castigate, censure, lambaste

Facing: 4.0. ☜☞ Apart

批議 *blame, criticize* **higi**
批判 *criticism, critique* **hihan**
⇒無批判 *non-critical* **muhihan**
批判的 *critical, questioning* **hihanteki**
批評 *criticism, critique, commentary* **hihyō**
⇒本文批評 *critique, commentary* **honbun hihyō**
⇒匿名批評 *anonymous criticism* **tokumei hihyō**
批評眼 *critical-, discerning eye* **hihyōgan**
批評家 *critic, reviewer* **hihyōka**
批准 *ratification, adoption* **hijun**
批准書 *instruments of ratification* **hijunsho**
批難 *blame, criticize* **hinan**
批点 *proof-reader's correction notes* **hiten**
高批 *"your esteemed criticism..."* **kōhi**

評*ommentary, 701*	決*udgement, 699*
価*alue, 35*	裁*udgement, 802*
値*alue, 783*	判*udgement, 949*

比*ompare, 466*

377-A

父ather lost in 交rossing when streets are confusing...

父 (father)

父ather   父addy

chichi, FU
father, daddy, paternal, papa

FLIP: 1.0.b. Whole (stem)

亡父	one's late father	**bōfu**
父方	father's side	**chichikata**
父親	one's father	**chichioya**
父上	father (honorific)	**chichiue**
父母	parents, father & mother	**fubo, chichihaha**
父系	paternal, father's side	**fukei**
父兄	parents, guardians	**fukei**
父兄会	parents-teachers' association	**fukeikai**
父権	paternal rights	**fuken**
父性	paternity	**fusei**
父子	father & son	**fushi**
岳父	one's father-in-law	**gakufu**
厳父	your (his) father	**genpu**
義父	father-in-law	**gifu**
異父	different father	**ifu**
異父兄弟	siblings by different fathers	**ifu kyōdai**
実父	one's real father, biological father	**jippu**
継父	stepfather	**keifu**
国父	father of the nation	**kokufu**

教父	baptism godfather	**kyōfu**
叔父	uncle younger than parent	**oji**
伯父	uncle older than parent	**oji**
親父	one's own father	**oyaji**
老父	one's old man	**rōfu**
神父	catholic priest, father	**shinpu**
祖父	grandfather	**sofu**
尊父	your father	**sonpu**
外祖父	mother's father	**gaisofu**
小父さん	gentleman, sir	**ojisan**
お祖父さん	grandfather	**ojiisan**

母other, 90	扶amily support, 97
子hild, 456	任bligation, 709
家amily, 909	男asculine, 597

交rossing, 467

377-B

父ather lost in 交rossing when streets are confusing...

⼇ (cover, lid)

交rossing   交nterchange

ma(jiru), maji(eru), ma(zeru), ka(u), ka(wasu), KŌ
crossing, interchange

FLIP: 1.0.b. Whole (stem)

断交	breaking-off relations	**dankō**
団交	collective bargaining	**dankō**
外交	diplomacy	**gaikō**
情交	sexual affair, ~intercourse	**jōkō**
交番	nearby police outpost	**kōban**
交互	alternation, vacillation, oscillation	**kōgo**
交配	cross-breeding, mating	**kōhai**
交換	exchange, substitution	**kōkan**
国交	diplomatic relations	**kōkkō**
交歓	exchange of courtesies, ~pleasantries	**kōkan**
交交	one after another	**komogomo**
混交	mixture, blending	**konkō**
交霊	talking with the dead	**kōrei**
交流	cultural exchange	**kōryū**
交叉	intersection, crossing	**kōsa**
交差	crossing	**kōsa**
交際	keeping relations with	**kōsai**
⇒援助交際	compensated dating	**enjo kōsai**
交線	intersecting line	**kōsen**

交戦	combat, exchange-of-fire	**kōsen**
交信	exchange of talks	**kōshin**
交渉	negotiations, bargaining	**kōshō**
交通	road traffic	**kōtsū**
交友	acquaintance, casual friendship	**kōyū**
交遊	associate with	**kōyū**
旧交	old friendship	**kyūkō**
乱交	group sex, orgy	**rankō**
性交	sexual intercourse	**seikō**
親交	friendship, friendly relations	**shinkō**
手交	hand over, deliver	**shukō**
絶交	breaking off relations	**zekkō**
交差点	intersection, crossing	**kōsaten**
交代交代	taking turns with another	**kōtai kōtai**

行rip, 79	旅ravel, 650
通assing, 59	来oming, 871

衣lothes, 355

378-A

毛 kin-hair on trail points to a camel's 尾 ail...

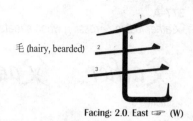

毛 *kin hair*

毛 (hairy, bearded)

ke, MŌ
skin hair, feather, down

Facing: 2.0. East ☞ (W)

刷毛 *brush* **hake**
鼻毛 *nostril hair* **hanage**
育毛 *hair restoration* **ikumō**
陰毛 *genital-, pubic hair* **inmō**
純毛 *pure wool* **junmō**
毛穴 *hair pore* **keana**
毛足 *hair length* **keashi**
毛羽 *nap, fluff* **keba**
毛皮 *fur* **kegawa**
毛色 *hair colour* **keiro**
毛糸 *woollen yarn* **keito**
毛虫 *caterpillar* **kemushi**
毛筋 *hairline* **kesuji**
毛布 *blanket* **mōfu**
毛髪 *hair* **mōhatsu**
毛筆 *writing brush* **mōhitsu**
毛根 *hair root* **mōkon**
胸毛 *chest hair* **munage**
植毛 *hair transplant* **shokumō**

旋毛 *hair whorl, curl* **tsumuji**
羽毛 *feather, plume* **umō**
和毛 *downy hair* **wake**
綿毛 *down feather* **watage**
羊毛 *wool* **yōmō**
縮れ毛 *curly hair, curls* **chijirege**
髪の毛 *hair* **kaminoke**
毛深い *hairy* **kebukai**
毛抜き *tweezers, hair puller* **kenuki**
巻き毛 *ringlet, curled hair* **makige**
毛細管 *capillary vessel* **mōsaikan**

髪 *air, 408*	膚 *kin, 69*
羽 *eather, 240*	皮 *kin, 224*
翼 *eather, 239*	肌 *kin, 747*

手 *and, 370*

378-B

毛 kin-hair on trail points to a camel's 尾 ail...

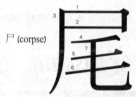

尾 *ail*

尸 (corpse)

o, BI
tail, endpoint

Facing: 2.1. East ☞ (H)

尾部 *tail section* **bibu**
尾錠 *buckle* **bijō**
尾錠金 *metal clasp, buckle* **bijōgane**
尾行 *following, tailing, dogging* **bikō**
尾籠 *tail plane* **birō**
尾灯 *tail light, tail lamp* **bitō**
尾翼 *tail plane* **biyoku**
語尾 *end of a word* **gobi**
艦尾 *stern of a ship* **kanbi**
巻尾 *book appendix* **kanbi**
結尾 *ending, conclusion* **ketsubi**
交尾 *copulation, mating* **kōbi**
末尾 *ending, closure* **matsubi**
鳩尾 *stomach pit* **mizoochi, kyūbi**
尾花 *Japanese pampas* **obana**
尾羽 *reduced circumstances* **obane**
尾鰭 *tail & fins, caudal-, tail fin* **obire**
尾籠 *indecency, immorality* **okago**
尾根 *ridge* **one**

尻尾 *tail* **shippo**
首尾 *head-to-tail, start-to-finish* **shubi**
掉尾 *ending, closure* **tōbi**
追尾 *pursuit, trail* **tsuibi**
牛尾 *cow tail* **ushio**
尾骶骨 *coccyx* **biteikotsu**
不首尾 *failure, blunder, fiasco* **fushubi**
上首尾 *great success* **jōshubi**
尾白鷲 *white-tailed eagle* **ojirowashi**
最後尾 *end of the line* **saikōbi**
有尾目 *tailed amphibians* **yūbimoku**

背 *osterior, 372*
裏 *osterior, 872*
後 *osterior, 897*

尿 *rine, 573*

379-A
心eart 応esponds in seconds...

心⇔忄 (heart, feelings)

心eart　心ardiac

kokoro, SHIN
heart, cardiac

Facing: 2.0. East ☞ (W)

安心 *at ease, relief* **anshin**
童心 *childish mind* **dōshin**
関心 *interest, concern* **kanshin**
恋心 *love, affection* **koigokoro**
心根 *true feelings, real emotions* **kokorone, shinkon**
親心 *parental love, filial affection* **oyagokoro**
良心 *conscience, righteousness* **ryōshin**
専心 *devotion, concentration* **senshin**
心外 *unexpected, sudden* **shingai**
心眼 *mind's eye* **shingan**
信心 *faith, devotion* **shinjin**
心情 *feelings, emotions* **shinjō**
心血 *heart & soul* **shinketsu**
心境 *frame of mind, mental state* **shinkyō**
心配 *worry, bother, concern* **shinpai**
心理 *mental state, psychology* **shinri**
心象 *mental image* **shinshō**
心臓 *heart organ* **shinzō**
私心 *selfishness, selfish motive* **shishin**

下心 *hidden intention, ulterior motive* **shitagokoro**
傷心 *grief, sorrow, heartache* **shōshin**
得心 *satisfaction, fulfillment* **tokushin**
用心 *carefulness, alertness, keeness* **yōjin**
出来心 *impulse, whim* **dekigokoro**
依頼心 *parasitic mind* **iraishin**
向学心 *intellectual thirst* **kōgakushin**
向上心 *ambition, aspiration* **kōjōshin**
好奇心 *curiosity, keen interest* **kōkishin**
心構え *frame-of-mind* **kokorogamae**
心強い *reassuring, encouraging* **kokorozuyoi**

感*eelings, 45*	情*eelings, 793*
気*eelings, 98*	央*entral, 218*

必*bsolutely, 218*

379-B
心eart 応esponds in seconds...

心⇔忄⇔小 (feelings)

応esponse　応nswer

kotae(ru), Ō
response, answer

Facing: 2.1. East ☞ (H)

反応 *response, reaction* **hannō**
一応 *as of now, in the meantime* **ichiō**
順応 *adaptation, adjustment* **junnō**
感応 *sympathetic reply* **kannō**
供応 *wining & dinning, banquet* **kyōō**
応募 *application, enlistment* **ōbo**
応分 *based on one's ability* **ōbun**
応諾 *consent, approval* **ōdaku**
応援 *cheer, support, encourage* **ōen**
応変 *expediency, convenience* **ōhen**
応報 *retribution, requital* **ōhō**
応力 *physical response* **ōryoku**
応戦 *return fire, battle response* **ōsen**
応接 *receiving visitors* **ōsetsu**
応接間 *drawing-, reception room* **ōsetsuma**
応射 *return fire, battle response* **ōsha**
応召 *military conscription, ~draft* **ōshō**
応手 *counter-move, counter-act* **ōshu**
応酬 *exchange, reply, response* **ōshū**

応訴 *reply to a complaint, countersuit* **ōso**
応対 *reception, treatment* **ōtai**
応答 *response, reply, answer* **ōtō**
応用 *practical application, ~benefit* **ōyō**
照応 *correspondence, agreement* **shōō**
即応 *adaptation, conformity* **sokuō**
対応 *counter-measure, counter-action* **taiō**
適応 *adaptability, suitability, fitness* **tekiō**
応急策 *emergency measure* **ōkyūsaku**
手応え *response, effect* **tegotae**

答*esponse, 232*	尋*nquire, 868*
問*uestion, 283*	聞*nquire, 282*
伺*nquire, 101*	遵*bedience, 544*
諮*nquire, 865*	従*bedience, 551*

忘*orget, 34*

380-A

勺*[18 ml] is* 均*qual to* 勺*[18 ml]...*

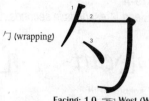

勺 (wrapping)

勺*[18 ml]*

SHAKU
[18 millilitre]

一勺 *0.033 sqm.* **isshaku**
勺飲 *little water to drink* **shakuin**
勺薬 *peony, small medicine* **shakuyaku**

Facing: 1.0. 🧭 West (W)

升*[1.8 ltr], 298*	坪*[3.3 sqm], 488*
旬*[10 day], 494*	匁*[3.75 gm], 75*
斗*[18 ltr], 195*	尺*[30 cm], 574*
寸*[3 cm], 345*	斤*[600 gm], 471*

夕*vening, 187*

380-B

勺*[18 ml] is* 均*qual to* 勺*[18 ml]...*

土 (ground, soil)

均

均*qual*　　均*ymmetrical*

hito(shii), KIN
equal, symmetrical

平均 *average, mode, median* **heikin**
平均点 *average mark, median grade* **heikinten**
均圧 *equal pressure* **kin'atsu**
均分 *equal division* **kinbun**
均一 *standard, uniform* **kin'itsu**
均衡 *balance, proportional, equilibrium* **kinkō**
均整 *balance, symmetry* **kinsei**
均斉 *symmetry, balance* **kinsei**
均質 *homogeneous, uniform* **kinshitsu**
均質化 *homogenisation, standardization* **kinshitsuka**
均質性 *homogeneity, uniformity* **kinshitsusei**
均等 *equality, parity* **kintō**
⇒機会均等 *equal opportunity* **kikai kintō**
均等割り *per capita rate* **kintōwari**
不均衡 *disproportionate, unbalance* **fukinkō**
不均斉 *asymmetrical, lop-sided* **fukinsei**
手風金 *accordion* **tefūkin**
均整美 *proportional beauty* **kinseibi**
踏み均す *trample upon with feet* **fuminarasu**

Facing: 1.2. 🧭 West (V)

掻き均す *rake smooth* **kakinarasu**
均質相和す *happily-married* **kinshitsu aiwasu**

斉*qual, 112*	同*imilar, 245*
如*qual, 364*	平*lain, 488*
似*imilar, 472*	

勺*[18ml], 470*

381-A

斤 *[600 gm] of socks wrongly* 折 *olded got Fred badly scolded...*

斤 (axe)

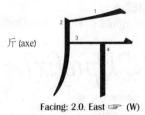

斤 *[600 gm]*

KIN
[600 gram]

一斤 *600 gram* **ikkin**
⇒食パン一斤 *one loaf of bread* **shokupan ikkin**
半斤 *half a loaf of bread* **hangin**
斤目 *weight in catties* **kinme**
斤量 *weight* **kinryō**

Facing: 2.0. East ☞ (W)

升 *[1.8 ltr]*, 298	寸 *[3 cm]*, 345
旬 *[10 day]*, 494	坪 *[3.3 sqm]*, 488
斗 *[18 ltr]*, 195	匁 *[3.75 gm]*, 75
勺 *[18 ml]*, 470	尺 *[30 cm]*, 574

析 *nalysis*, 185	不 *[negative]*, 300

381-B

斤 *[600 gm] of socks wrongly* 折 *olded got Fred badly scolded...*

手⇔扌 (hand, manual)

折 *old*   折 *reak*

o(reru), o(ru), ori, SETSU
fold, break

折り箱 *cardboard box* **oribako**
折り戸 *folding door* **orido**
折り紙 *folded paper figurines* **origami**
折り板 *fold plate* **oriita**
折り目 *crease, fold* **orime**
折り鶴 *folded paper crane* **orizuru**
折り合い *terms-of-agreement* **oriai**
折り込み *insertion, fold out* **orikomi**
折り曲げ *folding* **orimage**
折り畳む *fold into two, double* **oritatamu**
折り詰め *boxed lunch* **orizume**
骨折 *bone fracture* **kossetsu**
屈折 *refraction, indentation* **kussetsu**
曲折 *ups & downs, vicissitudes* **kyokusetsu**
左折 *left turn, turning left* **sasetsu**
左折禁止 *"no left turn..."* **sasetsu kinshi**
右折禁止 *"no right turn..."* **usetsu kinshi**
折衷 *proposed compromise* **secchū**
折角 *"since its already done..."* **sekkaku**

Facing: 4.0. ☜☞ Apart

折半 *equal sharing, fifty-fifty* **seppan**
折衝 *negotiations, bargaining* **sesshō**
右折 *right turn, turning right* **usetsu**
夭折 *premature death, short life* **yōsetsu**
挫折 *baffling, frustrating* **zasetsu**
指折り *prominent, eminent, foremost* **yubiori**
針折れ *bent needle* **hariore**
端折る *cut short, leave out, tuck up* **hashoru**
骨折り損 *vain efforts* **honeorizon**
菓子折り *box of cake* **kashiori**
四つ折り *folding into quarters* **yottsuori**

裂 *plit-up*, 585	曲 *ending*, 476
壊 *reak-down*, 847	巻 *oll-up*, 391
破 *estroy*, 715	

析 *nalysis*, 185

382-A
以*refixes* 似*imilar sound familiar...*

以*[prefix]* 以*y-way-of*

人⇔イ (person)

motte, I
[prefix], by-way-of, means of

以遠 *beyond, further* **ien**
以外 *others, exception* **igai**
以後 *from now on, after that* **igo**
以北 *northern* **ihoku**
以上 *as mentioned, above; "that's all..."* **ijō**
以下 *following, below* **ika**
以降 *rest, since then* **ikō**
以内 *within, less than, and under* **inai**
以南 *southern* **inan**
以来 *after that, since then* **irai**
以西 *westward* **isei**, **isai**
以東 *eastward* **itō**
以前 *before, once, in the past* **izen**
所以 *reason, cause, why* **yuen**
今以て *until now, up to the present* **imamotte**
以心伝心 *mental telepathy* **ishin denshin**
前以って *at the outset, beforehand* **maemotte**
以ての外 *inexcusable, outrageous* **motte no hoka**
尚以って *still more, all the more* **naomotte**

Facing: 2.0. East ☞ (W)

有史以来 *"as old as history..."* **yūshi irai**

方*irection, 533*	境*oundary, 839*
限*imit, 771*	限*oundary, 771*
定*efinite, 550*	時*ime, 653*

似*imilar, 472*

382-B
以*refixes* 似*imilar sound familiar...*

似*imilar* 似*esemble*

人⇔イ (person)

ni(ru), JI
similar, alike, look-alike, resemble, replica

擬似 *false, fake, imitation* **giji**
擬似的 *suspected, imitative* **gijiteki**
擬似軍事 *paramilitary* **giji gunji**
近似 *approximation, estimation* **kinji**
近似値 *approximation, estimation* **kinjichi**
酷似 *close resemblance, ~similarity* **kokuji**
真似 *imitation, mimicry* **mane**
真似事 *imitation, mimicry* **manegoto**
似顔 *portrait, likeness* **nigao**
似顔絵 *portrait, likeness* **nigaoe**
類似 *resemblance, similarity* **ruiji**
類似品 *counterfeit, imitation goods* **ruijihin**
類似性 *resemblance, similarity* **ruijisei**
類似点 *similarity, similar point* **ruijiten**
猿似 *chance resemblance* **saruni**
相似 *resemblance, similarity* **sōji**
相似形 *similarities (geometry)* **sōjikei**
空似 *accidental resemblance* **sorani**
人真似 *mimicking, impersonating* **hitomane**

Facing: 3.0. ☞☜ Across
Facing: 4.0. ☜☞ Apart

口真似 *mimicking, voice imitation* **kuchimane**
物真似 *imitation, mimicry* **monomane**
似合う *suit, match* **niau**
似通う *resemble, look alike* **nikayō**
似寄り *similar, look alike* **niyori**
猿真似 *"see-do-hear-no-evil-monkeys..."* **sarumane**
手真似 *hand gestures imitation* **temane**
歌真似 *imitating a popular singer* **utamane**
不似合い *inaptitude, incongruity* **funiai**
泣き真似 *fake-, crocodile tears* **nakimane**
他人の空似 *strangers' resemblance*
　　tanin no sorani

同*imilar, 245*	較*ompare, 774*
違*ifference, 796*	比*ompare, 466*
異*ifferent, 239*	

以*[prefix], 472*

383-A
Clients 処reatment 拠asis good at Macy's...

処reatment 　処andling

几 (table; windy)

tokoro, SHO
treatment, handling, deal with

彼処 *there, that place* **asoko**
何処 *where* **doko, izuko**
偶処 *living together* **gūsho**
此処 *here, this place* **koko**
目処 *outlook, potential, prospects* **medo**
死処 *place of death* **shinidokoro**
処罰 *punishment, penalty* **shobatsu**
処分 *disposal, punishment* **shobun**
⇒仮処分 *temporary disposition* **karishobun**
⇒懲戒処分 *disciplinary punishment* **chōkai shobun**
処置 *deal with, take measures* **shochi**
処遇 *treatment, handling* **shogū**
処方 *medical prescription* **shohō**
処女 *virgin, maiden* **shojo**
処女地 *virgin soil* **shojochi**
処女作 *one's first published writing* **shojosaku**
処女航海 *maiden voyage* **shojo kōkai**
処刑 *execution, punishment* **shokei**
処決 *settle, decide* **shoketsu**

Facing: 1.1. ☞ West (H)
FLIP: 7.1. Right (Sort Of)

処理 *dispose, manage, deal with* **shori**
⇒熱処理 *heat treatment* **netsushori**
処世 *conduct of life* **shosei**
処世術 *street smart* **shoseijutsu**
処世訓 *instructions on worldly wisdom* **shoseikun**
出処 *origin, source* **shussho, dedokoro**
其処 *there, that place* **soko**
対処 *dealing with a difficult problem* **taisho**
善処 *dealing with properly* **zensho**
止め処 *termination, conclusion* **tomedokoro**

療reatment, 67	営anagement, 580
宰anage, 377	策olicy, 875
扱reatment, 189	

拠asis, 473

383-B
Clients 処reatment 拠asis good at Macy's...

拠asis 　拠oundation

手⇔扌 (hand, manual)

KYO, KO
basis, foundation, groundwork, underpinning

本拠 *headquarters, base* **honkyo**
依拠 *based on* **ikyo**
準拠 *based on* **junkyo**
割拠 *territorial defence* **kakkyo**
⇒群雄割拠 *rival local barons* **gunyū kakkyo**
根拠 *basis, foundation, authority* **konkyo**
根拠地 *base, foundation* **konkyochi**
拠金 *money contribution* **kyokin**
拠守 *defence, security* **kyoshu**
拠出 *financial offer* **kyoshutsu**
拠点 *position, point, base* **kyoten**
論拠 *ground, basis* **ronkyo**
占拠 *occupation, take-over* **senkyo**
証拠 *proof, evidence* **shōko**
⇒状況証拠 *circumstantial evidence* **jōkyō shōko**
証拠物 *physical evidence* **shōkobutsu**
証拠人 *witness, eyewitness* **shōkonin**
証拠書類 *documented evidence* **shōko shorui**
証拠立てる *substantiate, corroborate* **shōkodateru**

Facing: 1.2. ☞ West (V)
FLIP: 7.1. Right (Sort Of)

典拠 *source, authority* **tenkyo**
拠り所 *ground, authority* **yoridokoro**

基asis, 590	素lement, 578
根oot, 772	

処reatment, 473

384-A

The 性ature of 性ex 生auses 生aw 生ife complex...

生 (life, birth)

⁰生ife ⁰生aw ⁰生tudent

i(kiru), i(kasu), u(mu), u(mareru), ha(yasu), ha(eru), nama, ki, SEI, SHŌ
life; raw; student

FLIP: 2.0.a. Sort Of (flat)

- ❶一生 *lifetime, lifespan* **isshō**
- 人生 *human life* **jinsei**
- 寄生 *paratism, parasite* **kisei**
- 康生 *welfare, healthcare* **kōsei**
- 生別 *personal background, childhood* **seibetsu**
- 生物① *living things* **seibutsu, ikimono**
- 生物② *uncooked, perishables* **namamono**
- 生家 *one's birth house* **seika**
- 生活 *living, lifestyle, livelihood* **seikatsu**
- 生気 *fresh, terrible, vivid* **seiki**
- 生命 *life, lifeline* **seimei**
- 生民 *people, subjects* **seimin**
- 生産 *production, manufacture* **seisan**
- 生死 *life & death* **seishi**
- 生息 *live, subsist* **seisoku**
- 生徒 *student, pupil* **seito**
- 生前 *in one's lifetime* **seizen**
- 生体 *living organism, live being* **seitai**

- 先生 *teacher, master* **sensei**
- 芝生 *lawn, grass, turf* **shibafu**
- 生涯 *one's lifetime* **shōgai**
- 終生 *rest of one's life, lifetime* **shūsei**
- 実習生 *intern, trainee* **jisshūsei**
- 浪人生 *university entrance exam flunker* **rōninsei**
- 生理日 *menstruation period* **seiribi**
- 誕生日 *birthday* **tanjōbi**
- 生き残る *survive, outlive* **ikinokoru**
- 生年月日 *date of birth* **seinen gappi**
- 生ビール *draft beer* **namabi-ru**
- ❷生放送 *live broadcast, spot relay* **namahōsō**
- ❸学生 *university student* **gakusei**

> 性*ature, 474* 人*uman, 2* 産*hildbirth, 883*
> 命*ife, 362* 誕*hildbirth, 515*

> 牛*attle, 179*

384-B

The 性ature of 性ex 生auses 生aw 生ife complex...

心⇔忄 (heart, feelings)

⁰性ature ⁰性ex

saga, SEI, SHŌ
nature, composition, essence, quality; sex, coitus, gender

FLIP: 7.1. Right (Sort Of)

- ❶活性 *activation, liveliness, dynamism* **kassei**
- 根性 *disposition, nature* **konjō**
- 個性 *individuality* **kosei**
- 慢性 *chronic* **mansei**
- 理性 *reason, rationale, logic* **risei**
- 性格 *personal character, personality* **seikaku**
- 性向 *character, personality* **seikō**
- 性根 *nature* **seikon**
- 性能 *performance, efficiency* **seinō**
- 性質 *nature, property, character* **seishitsu**
- 野性 *wild, unruly, undisciplined* **yasei**
- 意外性 *unexpectedness, upset* **igaisei**
- 可能性 *possibility, likelihood* **kanōsei**
- 類似性 *resemblance, similarity* **ruijisei**
- 相互性 *mutuality, reciprocity* **sōgosei**
- 適応性 *adaptability, flexibility* **tekiōsei**
- 特異性 *peculiarity, singularity* **tokuisei**
- 話題性 *topicality, thematic* **wadaisei**

- ❷母性 *maternity, motherhood* **bosei**
- 男性 *man, masculine* **dansei**
- 父性 *paternity, fatherhood* **fusei**
- 女性 *woman, female, feminine* **josei**
- 両性 *both sexes* **ryōsei**
- 性別 *gender, male-or-female* **seibetsu**
- 性病 *sexual disease* **seibyō**
- 性状 *nature; one's disposition* **seijō**
- 性器 *sex organ, genitals* **seiki**
- 性交 *sexual intercourse* **seikō**
- 性欲 *sexual appetite* **seiyoku**
- 性同一性 *one's gender identity* **seidōitsusei**
- 同性愛 *homosexuality, lesbianism* **dōseiai**

> 色*rotic, 403*
> 質*ature, 627*

> 性*ictim, 883*

385-A

忠oyalty amidst 患ickness, charmed Her Highness...

心⇔忄 (heart, feelings)

忠oyalty   忠aithful

CHŪ
loyalty, faithful, allegiance

FLIP: 3.0.b. Top (stem)

忠愛 *loyalty, devotion* **chūai**
忠僕 *loyal servant, acolyte* **chūboku**
忠言 *advice, counsel* **chūgen**
忠義 *loyalty, devotion* **chūgi**
忠義者 *loyal person* **chūgimono**
忠実 *faithful, loyal* **chūjitsu**
忠純 *unwavering loyalty* **chūjun**
忠順 *obedience, allegiance, loyalty* **chūjun**
忠犬 *faithful dog* **chūken**
忠勤 *faithfulness, loyalty* **chūkin**
忠孝 *filial piety, loyalty to one's parents* **chūkō**
忠告 *advice, counsel* **chūkoku**
忠魂 *loyal dead* **chūkon**
忠魂碑 *monument to the loyal dead* **chūkonhi**
忠君 *loyalty to the sovereign* **chūkun**
忠烈 *unwavering loyalty* **chūretsu**
忠良 *loyal, faithful* **chūryō**
忠誠 *loyalty, allegiance* **chūsei**
忠節 *loyalty, allegiance, fidelity* **chūsetsu**

忠臣 *loyal retainer* **chūshin**
忠信 *loyalty, faithfulness* **chūshin**
忠貞 *fidelity, loyalty* **chūtei**
忠勇 *loyalty & bravery* **chūyū**
不忠 *disloyal, ungrateful* **fuchū**
尽忠 *loyal, faithful* **jinchū**
誠忠 *loyalty, allegiance* **seichū**
忠霊塔 *war dead monument* **chūreitō**
忠誠心 *loyalty, allegiance* **chūseishin**
忠義立て *act of loyalty* **chūgidate**

爵oyalty, 593	師eacher, 483
徒isciple, 497	訓eachings, 959
教ducate, 385	孝ilial, 385

仲olleague, 695

385-B

忠oyalty amidst 患ickness, charmed Her Highness...

心⇔忄 (heart, feelings)

患ickness   患llness

wazura(u), KAN
sickness, illness, infection

FLIP: 3.0.b. Top (stem)

病患 *illness, sickness* **byōkan**
外患 *external problem* **gaikan**
⇒内憂外患 *internal & external problems* **naiyū gaikan**
肺患 *lung disease* **haikan**
重患 *serious illness* **jūkan**
禍患 *disaster, tragedy, calamity* **kakan**
患部 *afflicted body part* **kanbu**
患者 *patient, sick person* **kanja**
⇒外来患者 *outpatient* **gairai kanja**
⇒肺病患者 *lung disease patient* **haibyō kanja**
⇒結核患者 *tuberculosis patient* **kekkaku kanja**
恋患い *lovesick, love struck* **koiwazurai**
後患 *harmful side, repercussion* **kōkan**
後患 *future illness* **kōkan**
国患 *nation-wide problem* **kokkan**
急患 *emergency case* **kyūkan**
内患 *internal problem* **naikan**
罹患 *virus-infected, disease-stricken* **rikan**
疾患 *disease, ailment, illness* **shikkan**

⇒胸部疾患 *chest disease* **kyōbu shikkan**
宿患 *long illness* **shukkan**
通患 *common problem* **tsūkan**
憂患 *grief, sorrow, sadness* **yūkan**
長患い *long illness* **nagawazurai**
新患者 *newly-admitted patient* **shinkanja**

症ickness, 788	治ecuperate, 210
病ickness, 213	癒ecuperate, 923
医edicine, 19	療ecuperate, 67

忠oyalty, 475

386-A

曲elody's fools, 曲ending of music 典ules...

❶曲elody **❷曲ending** **曲urve**

日 (sunlight, daytime)

FLIP: 1.0.a. Whole (flat)

ma(geru), ma(garu), KYOKU
melody, hymn; bending, curve, twisting

- ❶ 舞曲 *dance music* **bukyoku**
- 楽曲 *musical composition* **gakkyoku**
- 戯曲 *drama, play* **gikyoku**
- 悲曲 *elegy, sad song* **hikyoku**
- 序曲 *overture* **jokyoku**
- 歌曲 *song, singing* **kakyoku**
- 曲調 *composition title* **kyokuchō**
- 曲譜 *musical score* **kyokufu**
- 曲名 *famous melody* **kyokumei**
- 名曲 *masterpiece music* **meikyoku**
- 作曲 *musical composition* **sakkyoku**
- 夜曲 *serenade* **yakyoku**
- 謡曲 *Noh chanting* **yōkyoku**
- 鎮魂曲 *requiem, funeral music* **chinkonkyoku**
- 幻想曲 *fantasia* **gensōkyoku**
- 課題曲 *set piece* **kadaikyoku**
- 歌謡曲 *popular song, pop music* **kayōkyoku**
- 器楽曲 *instrumental piece* **kigakukyoku**
- 交響曲 *symphony music* **kōkyōkyoku**

- 即興曲 *impromptu, improvisation* **sokkyōkyoku**
- ❷ 屈曲 *bend, curve* **kukkyoku**
- 曲者 *suspicious-looking, rascal* **kusemono**
- 曲解 *perversion, misinterpretation* **kyokkai**
- 曲馬 *circus horse* **kyokuba**
- 曲芸 *acrobatics* **kyokugei**
- 曲毛 *curly-, wavy hair* **kyokumo, kusuge**
- 曲線 *curve, curvy line* **kyokusen**
- 曲折 *rise & fall, vicissitudes* **kyokusetsu**
- 湾曲 *curving, bend* **wankyoku**
- 曲り角 *street corner* **magarikado**
- 折り曲げ *folding* **orimage**

屈ending, 212	興ntertainment, 867
伏end down, 702	楽leasure, 447

典ules, 476

386-B

曲elody's fools, 曲ending of music 典ules...

典ode **典ule**

八 (eight, divisible)

FLIP: 1.0.b. Whole (stem)

TEN
code, maxim, rule, standard work

- 仏典 *Buddhist sutras* **butten**
- 栄典 *honour, glory* **eiten**
- 楽典 *musical grammar* **gakuten**
- 原典 *original text, ~works* **genten**
- 儀典 *protocol, rules of decorum* **giten**
- 宝典 *precious book; thesaurus* **hōten**
- 辞典 *dictionary* **jiten**
- ⇒百科事典 *encyclopaedia* **hyakka jiten**
- ⇒漢和辞典 *Japanese Kanji dictionary* **kanwa jiten**
- ⇒和英辞典 *Japanese-English dictionary* **waei jiten**
- 事典 *encyclopaedia* **jiten**
- 香典 *cash offer for a dead spirit* **kōden**
- 国典 *national rites & ceremonies* **kokuten**
- 古典 *classic* **koten**
- 教典 *canonical laws* **kyōten**
- 経典 *sacred book, scripture* **kyōten**
- 恩典 *special favour, ~request* **onten**
- 礼典 *rules of etiquette* **reiten**
- 祭典 *festival, feast* **saiten**

- 聖典 *sacred book, scripture* **seiten**
- 盛典 *magnificent ceremony* **seiten**
- 式典 *ceremony, rites* **shikiten**
- 祝典 *celebration, thanksgiving* **shukuten**
- 大典 *great ceremony* **taiten**
- 典型 *model, type, paragon* **tenkei**
- 典拠 *source, authority* **tenkyo**
- 典範 *model, standard, exemplar* **tenpan**
- 典麗 *graceful, elegant* **tenrei**
- 典礼 *ceremony, rites* **tenrei**
- 特典 *privilege, special favour* **tokuten**

規tandard, 814
法aw, 360
廷mperial court, 26

曲elody, 476

387-A

古*ither in the cold,* 苦*uffer the* 古*ld...*

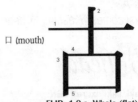

口 (mouth)

FLIP: 1.0.a. Whole (flat)

古*ld*　　　古*ither*

furu(i), furu(su), KO
old, wither

復古 *restoration, rehabilitation* **fukko**
古顔 *familiar face, old-timer* **furugao**
古本 *old books* **furuhon**
古株 *old-timer, old stump* **furukabu**
懐古 *retrospection, nostalgia, reminiscences* **kaiko**
古米 *old rice* **kamai**
古代 *ancient times* **kodai**
古風 *old style, customs* **kofū**
古墳 *ancient tomb, tumulus* **kofun**
古雅 *classical grace* **koga**
古語 *archaic word* **kogo**
古豪 *veteran, expert, professional* **kogō**
古希 *one's seventyish, 70~79 years old* **koki**
古今 *all ages, all times* **kokon**
古参 *seniority, old-timer, old hand* **kosan**
古跡 *ruins, remains, relics* **koseki**
古銭 *ancient coins* **kosen**
古式 *old rite, ancient ceremony* **koshiki**
古書 *rare books* **kosho**

古色 *antique-looking* **koshoku**
古典 *the classics, classical literature* **koten**
最古 *the oldest* **saiko**
太古 *ancient times* **taiko**
古臭い *old-fashioned, outdated* **furukusai**
着古し *old clothes* **kifurushi**
考古学 *archaeology* **kōkogaku**
古生物 *extinct species* **koseibutsu**
名古屋 *Nagoya City, Aichi Prefecture* **nagoya**
言い古す *say repeatedly* **iifurusu**
古めかしい *old-fashioned* **furumekashii**
使い古す *wear & tear, wear out* **tsukaifurusu**

歳*ears old, 111*	枯*ither, 960*
齢*ears old, 553*	朽*ecay, 738*
昔*lden-times, 281*	枯*ecay, 960*

舌*ongue, 236*

387-B

古*ither in the cold,* 苦*uffer the* 古*ld...*

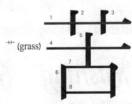

艹 (grass)

FLIP: 1.0.a. Whole (flat)

苦*uffer*　　苦*nguish*

kuru(shimu), kuru(shimeru), kuru(shii), niga(i), niga(ru), KU
suffer, anguish, misery, bitter, agony

病苦 *illness pains* **byōku**
貧苦 *poverty hardships* **hinku**
困苦 *difficulty, adversity* **konku**
苦衷 *dilemma, distress* **kuchū**
苦学 *studying difficulties* **kugaku**
苦言 *candid-, honest advice* **kugen**
苦行 *penance, asceticism* **kugyō**
苦杯 *"agony of defeat..."* **kuhai**
苦境 *difficulties, adversities* **kukyō**
苦悶 *agony, anguish, anxiety* **kumon**
苦難 *suffering, misery* **kunan**
苦悩 *adversity, dilemma* **kunō**
苦楽 *joy & sorrow* **kuraku**
苦労 *worrying, anxiety* **kurō**
苦慮 *thorough thinking, pondering* **kuryo**
苦節 *unflagging efforts* **kusetsu**
苦痛 *pain, agony* **kutsū**
苦手 *one's weakness, vulnerability* **nigate**
苦瓜 *balsam* **nigauri**

苦笑い *bitter smile* **nigawarai**
苦み走る *stern face* **nigamibashiru**
労苦 *pains, toil, labour* **rōku**
惨苦 *misery, tragic difficulties* **sanku**
辛苦 *trials & tribulations* **shinku**
痛苦 *anguish, distress, perplexity* **tsūku**
責め苦 *ordeal, torments* **semeku**
暑苦しい *stuffy, sultry* **atsukurushii**
息苦しい *choking, suffocating* **ikigurushii**
堅苦しい *formal, ceremonious* **katakurushii**
心苦しい *feel uneasy* **kokorogurushii**
胸苦しい *tormented feelings* **munagurushii**
寝苦しい *sleeping difficulties* **negurushii**
苦苦しい *disgusting, unpleasant* **niganigashii**

悩*nguish, 48*	痛*njury, 60*
損*njury, 410*	障*njury, 325*

古*ld, 477*

388-A

先irst comes 洗ashing 先head of anything...

先head　　先efore

儿 (human legs)

saki, saki(nzuru), SEN
ahead, before, erstwhile, first, precedent, primary, primer

FLIP: 2.0.b. Sort Of (stem)

足先 foot, toe **ashisaki**
歯先 gear teeth **hasaki**
矛先 tip of a sword **hokosaki**
店先 store front, shop front **misesaki**
幸先 omen, foreboding, premonition **saisaki**
先着 first arrival **senchaku**
先月 last month **sengetsu**
先日 the other day, the previous day **senjitsu**
先見 foresight, vision **senken**
先決 decide first, determine **senketsu**
先行 precede, go first **senkō**
先客 previous guest **senkyaku**
先輩 one's senior, elder colleague **senpai**
先頭 precede, go ahead **sentō**
先生 teacher, expert, doctor **sensei**
祖先 ancestors, forebears, progenitors **sosen**
率先 initiate, take the lead **sossen**
矢先 arrowhead **yasaki**
優先 priority, preference **yūsen**

行き先 destination, whereabouts **ikisaki, yukisaki**
老い先 one's remaining years **oisaki**
送り先 destination, recipients address **okurisaki**
旅行先 travel destination **ryokōsaki**
先回り reaching ahead, anticipation **sakimawari**
先駆者 pioneer, innovator **senkusha**
先々月 two months ago **sensengetsu**
先進国 industrialized nations **senshinkoku**
勤め先 workplace, office **tsutomesaki**
真っ先に "before anything else..." **massaki(ni)**
先駆ける lead, go ahead **sakigakeru**
問い合せ先 call center **toiawasesaki**

前efore, 118	昨revious, 722
方irection, 533	将uture, 521

失ailure, 19

388-B

先irst comes 洗ashing 先head of anything...

洗ashing　　洗aundry

水⇔氵 (water)

ara(u), SEN
washing, laundry, cleaning with water

FLIP: 7.1. Right (Sort Of)

酸洗 pickling, pickle-making **sansen**
洗眼 eye-washing **sengan**
洗顔 face-washing **sengan**
洗浄 washing, laundry **senjō**
洗浄薬 soap, laundry detergent **senjōgusuri**
洗浄器 washer, syringe **senjōki**
洗米 washed rice **senmai**
無洗米 unwashed rice **musenmai**
洗脳 brainwashing **sennō**
洗髪 hair-washing, shampooing **senpatsu**
洗礼 baptism, christening **senrei**
洗礼式 baptism, christening rites **senreishiki**
洗練 refinement **senren**
洗車 car wash **sensha**
洗濯 washing, laundry **sentaku**
洗濯機 washing machine **sentakuki**
洗剤 detergent, cleanser **senzai**
水洗 flush toilet **suisen**
洗い熊 racoon **araiguma**

洗い物 dishes, laundry clothes **araimono**
丸洗い washing the whole thing **maruarai**
皿洗い dish washing, dishwasher **saraarai**
洗面所 washroom, bathroom **senmenjo**
洗面器 washing basin **senmenki**
手洗い hand-washing **tearai**
洗い出す dig up, excavate **araidasu**
洗い流す wash away, wash off **arainagasu**
洗い直す reconsider, wash again **arainaosu**
洗い晒し shabby, worn-out **araizarashi**
洗い落とす wash away, wash off **araiotosu**
洗い立てる rake up **araitateru**
洗いざらい one & all, everything **araizarai**

掃leaning, 785	服lothes, 734
裁lothes, 802	衣lothes, 355

先head, 478

389-A

逐riven-out 逐ne-by-one, peace 遂inally 遂chieved by the gun...

辶 (transport)

❶ 逐rive-out **❷ 逐ne-by-one**

CHIKU
drive-out; one-by-one

Facing: 1.1. West (H)

❶ 逐電 *run away with, abscond* **chikuden, chikuten**
放逐 *banishment, expulsion, exile* **hōchiku**
角逐 *competition, rivalry* **kakuchiku**
駆逐 *expelling, driving out* **kuchiku**
駆逐艦 *destroyer ship* **kuchikukan**

走 *unning, 497*	追 *ursue, 108*
奔 *un-away, 120*	尽 *ursue, 574*
逃 *scape, 216*	追 *ress for, 108*

逐 *chieve, 479*

❷ 逐語的 *literal, verbatim, word-for-word* **chikugoteki**
逐語訳 *word-for-word translation* **chikugoyaku**
逐一 *one-by-one, in detail* **chikuichi**
逐次 *one after another, sequential* **chikuji**
逐次的 *sequential* **chikujiteki**
逐次変換 *sequential transformation* **chikuji henkan**
逐次翻訳 *sequential translation* **chikuji honyaku**
逐日 *day to day* **chikujitsu**
逐条 *item-by-item* **chikujō**
逐条審議 *article-by-article deliberation* **chikujō shingi**
逐年 *year-by-year* **chikunen**

389-B

逐riven-out 逐ne-by-one, peace 遂inally 遂chieved by the gun...

辶 (transport)

遂 *chieve* 遂 *ccomplish*

to(geru), tsui(ni), SUI
achieve, accomplish, consummate, perpetrate

Facing: 1.1. West (H)

遂げる *realize, achieve, attain* **togeru**
遂に *"at last, finally, in the end..."* **tsui(ni)**
完遂 *successful execution* **kansui**
既遂 *perpetrated, consummated* **kisui**
遂行 *accomplishment, achievement* **suikō**
自殺未遂 *attempted suicide* **jisatsu misui**
殺人未遂 *attempted murder* **satsujin misui**
やり遂げる *carry out, accomplish, execute* **yaritogeru**
成し遂げる *accomplish, achieve, attain* **nashitogeru**
添い遂げる *lifetime marriage* **soitogeru**

完 *ulfil, 196*	終 *inish, 397*
満 *ulfil, 567*	了 *inish, 456*

逐 *rive-out, 479*

390-A

使nvoys wrongly 使tilized, 便onvenience paid the price...

人⇔亻 (person)

❶使tilize   **❷使nvoy**

tsuka(u), SHI

utilize, expend; diplomat, emissary, envoy

FLIP: 7.1. Right (Sort Of)
Facing: 4.0. 〜〜 Apart

❶ 酷使   work hard, overwork **kokushi**
行使   seeking recourse **kōshi**
駆使   "good command of..." **kushi**
召使   servant, maid **meshitsukai**
労使   labour & management **rōshi**
使役   employment, service **shieki**
使命   mission, task, assignment **shimei**
使丁   servant, maid, attendant **shitei**
使徒   apostle, disciple **shito**
使途   purpose, objective **shito**
使用   avail, make use of, utilize **shiyō**
天使   angel **tenshi**
金使い   way of spending money **kanezukai**
使い道   ways of using **tsukaimichi**
使い手   end-user, consumer **tsukaite**
使い走り   errand boy, runner **tsukaibashiri**
使い古す   wear out **tsukaifurusu**
使い残す   leave unspent, ~unused **tsukainokosu**
使い慣らす   break in **tsukainarasu**

魔法使い   magician, wizard, sorcerer **mahōtsukai**
❷ 副使   deputy envoy, ~emissary **fukushi**
軍使   military envoy, ~emissary **gunshi**
国使   envoy, diplomat, delegate, emissary **kokushi**
公使   minister plenipotentiary **kōshi**
急使   express messenger **kyūshi**
密使   secret emissary, ~envoy **misshi**
使節   delegate, envoy, mission **shisetsu**
使者   messenger, envoy, ~emissary **shisha**
大使   ambassador, envoy, ~emissary **taishi**
特使   special envoy, ~emissary **tokushi**

用 vail of, 409	採 mploy, 915
伝 onvey, 619	抱 mploy, 503
逓 onvey, 304	

吏 fficial, 463

390-B

使nvoys wrongly 使tilized, 便onvenience paid the price...

人⇔亻 (person)

便onvenience   **便xpedience**

tayo(ri), BEN, BIN

convenience, betterment, expedience, amenity, post

FLIP: 7.1. Right (Sort Of)
Facing: 4.0. 〜〜 Apart

便宜   convenience, advantage, comfort **bengi**
便所   toilet, rest room, wash room **benjo**
便器   toilet stool, toilet **benki**
便口   speaking smooth **benkō**
便秘   constipation, alimentary stoppage **benpi**
便法   expediency, ways & means **benpō**
便利   convenience, advantage, comfort **benri**
便通   bowel movement **bentsū**
便座   toilet stool, toilet seat **benza**
便便   idle life, do-nothing, easy lifestyle **benben**
便乗   getting a lift, giving a ride **binjō**
便覧   manual, handbook, guide **binran**
便箋   writing paper, notepaper **binsen**
大便   faeces, excrement, pooh **daiben**
船便   sea mail, surface mail **funabin**
排便   defecation **haiben**
方便   expediency, ways & means **hōben**
簡便   handy, simple & easy **kanben**
検便   stool analysis **kenben**

欠便   "flight cancelled..." **ketsubin**
後便   letter to be sent later **kōbin**
穏便   gentle, amicable **onbin**
至便   greatly convenient **shiben**
小便   urine, pee **shōben**
郵便   mail, postage **yūbin**
郵便局   post office, mail station **yūbinkyoku**
増便   increased flights **zōbin**
航空便   air-mail, aeromail, aerogramme **kōkūbin**
寝小便   bed-wetting **neshōben**
宅急便   home delivery **takkyūbin**

宜 onvenience, 500	用 urpose, 409
益 enefit, 622	為 urpose, 509
得 enefit, 940	易 imple, 933

更 new, 402

391-A

足oot work & 足ufficient raw eggs 促rompt Rocky's 足egs...

足 (feet, legs)

⁰足oot   ⁰足ufficient

ashi, ta(ru) ta(riru), ta(su), SOKU
foot, leg, appendage; sufficient, addition

FLIP: 3.0.a. Top (flat)
Facing: 2.0. East ☞ (W)

❶足場 foothold, footing, scaffold **ashiba**
足首 ankle **ashikubi**
足下 foot, step, footstep **ashimoto**
足許 foot place **ashimoto**
足元 one's walking, one's feet **ashimoto**
足音 footstep **ashioto**
足先 foot, toe **ashisaki**
遠足 field trip, excursion **ensoku**
義足 artificial leg, fake leg **gisoku**
片足 one legged person **kataashi**
両足 both legs, both feet **ryōashi**
足跡 footprint, tracks **sokuseki, ashiato**
足袋 Japanese socks **tabi**
足の甲 instep **ashi no kō**
足取り step, pace **ashidori**
足かせ fetters **ashikase**
足並み style of walking **ashinami**
偏平足 flat-footed **henpeisoku**
足掛かり foothold **ashigakari**

足慣らし warming up, practice **ashinarashi**
❷不足 insufficiency, lacking **fusoku**
発足 starting off **hassoku, hossoku**
補足 supplementary, addition **hosoku**
自足 self-sufficiency **jisoku**
充足 sufficiency, enough **jūsoku**
足止め accidental prevention **ashidome**
足固め groundwork, preparations **ashigatame**
足し算 addition, adding **tashizan**
用足し errand, going to the restroom **yōtashi**
付け足し addition, supplement **tsuketashi**
満ち足りる be satisfied **michitariru**

歩alk, 272	往ome & go, 749
走unning, 497	満atisfy, 567
脚egs, 387	飽atiate, 665

号umber, 866

391-B

足oot work & 足ufficient raw eggs 促rompt Rocky's 足egs...

人⇔亻 (person)

促rompt   促ncourage

unaga(su), SOKU
prompt, encourage, hasten, motivate, spur, prodding

Facing: 4.0. ☜☞ Apart

催促 pressed for time, busy **akusoku**
催促 demand, pressing, urging **saisoku**
促音 Japanese double consonant (っ) **sokuon**
促成 forced cultivation **sokusei**
促成栽培 forced cultivation **sokusei saibai**
促進 promotion, encouragement **sokushin**
⇒販売促進 sales promotion **hanbai sokushin**
促進剤 hastening agent, catalyst **sokushinzai**
督促 pressing, demand, urging **tokusoku**
督促状 demand note, letter-of-demand **tokusokujō**

奨ncourage, 521	薦ecommend, 68
励ncourage, 465	勧ecommend, 666
起rise, 754	推ecommend, 777

足oot, 481

392-A

田 ice-field 畑 lantations feed Asian nations...

田 (cultivated field)

田 ice field   田 arm field

ta, DEN
rice field, farm field

FLIP: 1.0.a. Whole (flat)

浅田 *shallow field* **asada**
田地 *rice farm, rice field* **denchi**
田園 *country, rural districts* **den'en**
田夫 *peasant* **denpu**
田作 *rice toiling, rice cultivation* **densaku**
田野 *cultivated field, plantation* **denya**
塩田 *salt field, salt farm* **enden**
半田 *electric soldering* **handa**
票田 *political bailiwick, vote-rich* **hyōden**
稲田 *rice field, rice paddy* **inada**
田舎 *rural, countryside* **inaka**
瓜田 *melon farm* **kaden**
帰田 *return to farming* **kiden**
沼田 *marshy-, swampy field* **numata**
小田 *small rice field* **oda**
新田 *newly-cultivated farm* **shinden**
桑田 *mulberry field* **sōden**
田畑 *farm, fields* **tahata**
田虫 *ringworm* **tamushi**

田圃 *rice paddy* **tanbo**
棚田 *terraced field* **tanada**
炭田 *coal field* **tanden**
田螺 *mud snail* **tanishi**
田植 *rice planting* **taue**
田植時 *rice planting season* **tauedoki**
油田 *oil field* **yuden**
田舎道 *rural road* **inakamichi**
田舎者 *bumpkin (derogatory)* **inakamono**
片田舎 *"end of the world place..."* **katainaka**
真田虫 *tapeworm* **sanadamushi**
田打ち *farming, field toiling* **tauchi**

畑 *lantation, 482*		農 *arming, 446*	
原 *lains, 431*		植 *lant, 783*	
野 *lains, 873*		食 *oods, 255*	

田 *eason, 540*

392-B

田 ice-field 畑 lantations feed Asian nations...

田 (cultivated field)   畑

畑 lantation   畑 arm field

hata, hatake
plantation, farm field

FLIP: 7.0.a. Right (flat)

茶畑 *tea farm, tea plantation* **chabatake**
花畑 *flower garden* **hanabatake**
畑地 *farmland* **hatachi**
畑物 *farm products* **hatakemono**
畑作 *non-paddy farming* **hatasaku**
桑畑 *mulberry field* **kuwabatake**
麦畑 *wheat-, barley field* **mugibatake**
田畑 *farm, fields* **tahata**
種畑 *seed garden* **tanebatake**
梅畑 *plum orchard* **umebatake**
葡萄畑 *vineyard* **budōbatake**
段々畑 *farm terraces* **dandanbatake**
畑違い *not one's line of specialty* **hatakechigai**
畑水練 *"learning by the books..."* **hatakesuiren**
畑打ち *farm plowing* **hatauchi**
焼き畑 *slash & burn farming* **yakihata**
野菜畑 *vegetable garden* **yasaibatake**

田 *ice field, 482*		農 *arming, 446*	
原 *lain, 431*		植 *lant, 783*	
野 *lains, 873*			

田 *ice field, 482*

393-A
For every 帥ommander, an 師xpert 師eacher...

巾 (cloth, fabric)

帥ommander

sochi, sotsu, SUI
commander

FLIP: 7.0.b1. Right (stem)

元帥 *general of the army, fleet admiral* **gensui**
軍帥 *supreme commander* **gunsui**
将帥 *commander* **shōsui**
総帥 *commander-in-chief* **sōsui**
統帥 *high command* **tōsui**
統帥権 *supremo's prerogative* **tōsuiken**
大元帥 *supreme commander* **daigensui**

令 *ommand, 362*	軍 *oldier, 295*
督 *ommander, 911*	威 *uthority, 520*
将 *eneral, 521*	権 *uthority, 804*
導 *uidance, 312*	領 *overn, 874*
兵 *oldier, 490*	

師 *eacher, 483*

393-B
For every 帥ommander, an 師xpert 師eacher...

巾 (cloth, fabric)

師eacher   師xpert

SHI
teacher, expert, specialist, master

FLIP: 7.0.b1. Right (stem)

牧師 *pastor, vicar, reverend* **bokushi**
技師 *engineer, technician* **gishi**
軍師 *military strategist* **gunshi**
針師 *acupuncturist* **harishi**
医師 *medical doctor, physician* **ishi**
講師 *assistant professor, lecturer* **kōshi**
教師 *teacher, instructor* **kyōshi**
庭師 *gardener, horticulturist* **niwashi**
恩師 *mentor, ex-teacher* **onshi**
漁師 *fisherman* **ryōshi**
猟師 *hunter, huntsman* **ryōshi**
師団 *army division* **shidan**
師範 *teacher, master* **shihan**
師事 *becoming pupil* **shiji**
師匠 *great teacher* **shishō**
師弟 *teacher & student* **shitei**
師走 *December, the year end* **shiwasu**
業師 *technician, craftsman, expert* **wazashi**
弓師 *bow maker, archery craftsman* **yumishi**

占い師 *fortune-teller* **uranaishi**
美容師 *cosmetician, beautician* **biyōshi**
道化師 *clown, jester, pierrot* **dōkeshi**
看護師 *male or female nurse* **kangoshi**
軽業師 *acrobat, circus performer* **karuwazashi**
講釈師 *storyteller, narrator* **kōshakushi**
魔術師 *magician* **majutsushi**
漫才師 *comedian* **manzaishi**
詐欺師 *swindler, con artist, cheat* **sagishi**
説教師 *preacher* **sekkyōshi**
宣教師 *missionary* **senkyōshi**
薬剤師 *pharmacist* **yakuzaishi**

授 *eaching, 539*	博 *xpertise, 514*
訓 *eachings, 959*	巧 *xpertise, 738*
教 *ducate, 385*	修 *xpertise, 898*
家 *xpert, 909*	導 *uidance, 312*

帥 *ommander, 483*

394-A

半alf the 畔ice-paths had gold karats...

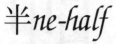 半ne-half   半artial

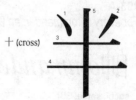

十 (cross)

FLIP: 1.0.b. Whole (stem)

naka(ba), HAN
one-half, partial, fifty-fifty, semi-

半 right in the middle **ainakaba**
半円 semi-circle **han'en**
半額 half price, 50% discount **hangaku**
半減 cutting into, reducing by half **hangen**
半壊 partial destruction **hankai**
半径 radius **hankei**
半旗 flag at half-mast **hanki**
半期 half year, half term **hanki**
半球 hemisphere **hankyū**
半面 face profile **hanmen**
半農 part-time farming **hannō**
半音 semi-tone, half step **han'on**
半拍 half-tone, half-note **hanpaku**
半紙 Japanese writing paper **hanshi**
半身 half of one's body **hanshin**
半神 demigod **hanshin**
半島 peninsula **hantō**
半月 half moon **hantsuki, hangetsu**
後半 second half, second term **kōhan**

折半 go fifty-fifty, share & share alike **seppan**
大半 majority, greater part **taihan**
前半 first half of the term **zenhan, zenpan**
半殺し near death **hangoroshi**
半端物 left-over things **hanpamono**
過半数 majority, greater half **kahansū**
生半可 superficial, flimsy, frivolous **namahanka**
半永久的 semi-permanent **han'eikyūteki**
半死半生 half dead, half alive **hanshi hanshō**
一知半解 superficial, flimsy, frivolous **icchi hankai**
一言半句 dumbfounded, "left speechless..."
  ichigon-, ichigen hanku

準emi-, 919	中iddle, 85
未ot yet, 12	途urrently, 882

伴ccompany, 949

394-B

半alf the 畔ice-paths had gold karats...

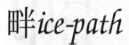 畔ice-path   畔aterside

田 (cultivated field)

FLIP: 5.0.b. Left & Right

aze, HAN
rice-path, waterside

畔道 ridge, footpath (between ricefields) **azemichi**
池畔 edge of a pond **chihan**
河畔 riverside, riverbank **kahan**
湖畔 lakeside, lakeshore **kohan**
橋畔 either side of a bridge **kyōhan**

農arming, 446	田ice field, 482
野ield, 873	稲ice plant, 893
畑lantation, 482	米ice, 77
植lant, 783	耕ultivate, 655

半ne-half, 484

395-A

室oom with 窒itrogen 窒uffocates often...

室oom　　室hamber

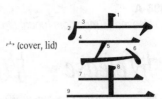

宀 (cover, lid)

muro, SHITSU
room, chamber, cubicle

病室 *hospital room* **byōshitsu**
茶室 *tea-ceremony room* **chashitsu**
岩室 *stone stove* **iwamuro**
個室 *single room, individual room* **koshitsu**
客室 *guest room, cabin* **kyakushitsu**
教室 *classroom, lecture room* **kyōshitsu**
教室 *empty room* **kūshitsu**
満室 *"no vacant rooms..."* **manshitsu**
密室 *hidden room, secret room* **misshitsu**
室蘭 *Muroran City (Hokkaidō)* **muroran**
温室 *greenhouse, hothouse* **onshitsu**
隣室 *next room* **rinshitsu**
船室 *ship cabin* **senshitsu**
寝室 *bedroom, sleeping quarters* **shinshitsu**
室外 *outdoors* **shitsugai**
私室 *private room* **shishitsu**
室内 *inside, indoors* **shitsunai**
退室 *leaving a room* **taishitsu**
和室 *tatami room* **washitsu**

FLIP: 3.0.b. Top (stem)
FLIP: 4.0.a. Bottom (flat)

浴室 *bathroom, shower room* **yokushitsu**
洋室 *Western-style room* **yōshitsu**
防音室 *soundproofed room* **bōonshitsu**
談話室 *lounge, reception room* **danwashitsu**
控え室 *waiting room* **hikaeshitsu**
拷問室 *torture chamber* **gōmon shitsu**
準備室 *preparation room* **junbishitsu**
研究室 *professor's room* **kenkyūshitsu**
機関室 *engine room* **kikanshitsu**
更衣室 *changing room (clothes)* **kōishitsu**
職員室 *staff room, office room* **shokuinshitsu**
図書室 *reading room, mini-library* **toshoshitsu**
役員室 *executive office, VIP room* **yakuinshitsu**
室町時代 *Muromachi era* **muromachi jidai**

房*luster, 676*

窒*itrogen, 485*

395-B

室oom with 窒itrogen 窒uffocates often...

❶窒uffocate　❷窒itrogen

穴 (hole, cave)

CHITSU
suffocate; nitrogen

❶窒死 *death by suffocation* **chisshi**
窒息 *choking, suffocation* **chissoku**
窒息死 *death by suffocation* **chissokushi**
窒息性ガス *blackdamp* **chissokusei gasu**

❷窒素 *nitrogen* **chisso**
窒素肥料 *nitrogenous fertilizer* **chisso hiryō**
窒化物 *nitride* **chikkabutsu**

FLIP: 3.0.b. Top (stem)
FLIP: 4.0.a. Bottom (flat)

毒*oison, 578*
息*reathe, 586*

室*oom, 485*

396-A

放eleased 倣mpostors thought to be doctors...

文 (action)

放

放elease   放et-go

hana(tsu), hana(su), hana(reru), HŌ
release, let go, set free, liberate, emancipate

FLIP: 7.1. Right (Sort Of)
Facing: 3.0. ☞☜ Across

放談 *random-, free-wheeling talks* **hōdan**
放映 *broadcasting, televising* **hōei**
放言 ① *careless-, unthoughtful remark* **hōgen**
放言 ② *random talks* **hōgen**
放縦 *self-indulgence, self-gratification* **hōjū**
放火 *arson, incendiary fire* **hōka**
放棄 *renunciation, capitulation* **hōki**
放校 *school expulsion* **hōkō**
放光 *light emission* **hōkō**
放漫 *careless, irresponsible* **hōman**
放免 *custody release* **hōmen**
放熱 *heat radiation* **hōnetsu**
放任 *non-intervention, "let it be..."* **hōnin**
奔放 *unrestrained, unrestricted* **honpō**
放列 *battery, column, row* **hōretsu**
放浪 *wandering, roaming* **hōrō**
放流 *discharge, release* **hōryū**
放散 *radiate, emit, diffuse* **hōsan**
放射 *radiation* **hōsha**

放心 *absent-mindedness* **hōshin**
放送 *broadcasting, relay* **hōsō**
放胆 *boldness, fearless* **hōtan**
解放 *liberation, emancipation* **kaihō**
釈放 *release, setting free* **shakuhō**
粗放 *careless, clumsy, sloppy* **sohō**
放課後 *after school* **hōkago**
野放し *leave free, do nothing* **nobanashi**
解き放す *untie, set free, let loose* **tokihanasu**
開けっ放し *"leaving open what was closed..."*
   akeppanashi
脱ぎっ放し *"leaving one's worn clothes anywhere..."*
   nugippanashi

| 開*pen, 284* | 披*pen, 104* | 口*pening, 458* |

倣*mitate, 486*

396-B

放eleased 倣mpostors thought to be doctors...

人⇔亻 (person)

倣

倣mitate   倣imulate

nara(u), HŌ
imitate, simulate, counterfeit, disguise, mimicry, copy

FLIP: 7.1. Right (Sort Of)
Facing: 3.0. ☞☜ Across

摸倣 *imitation, mimicry, impersonating* **mohō**
模倣屋 *copycat, imitator, impersonator* **mohōya**
倣う *follow, imitate* **narau**
先例に倣う *follow a precedent* **senrei (ni) narau**

| 擬*mitate, 56* | 同*imilar, 245* |
| 似*imilar, 472* | 装*retend, 629* |

放*elease, 486*

397-A

Among 具ools, only the 真ruth rules...

具*ools*　　具*mplements*

八 (eight, divisible)

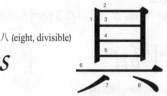

sona(eru), GU
tools, implements, utensils, apparatus

FLIP: 1.0.b. Whole (stem)

雨具 *rainwear, rain gear* **amagu**
馬具 *horseriding gear* **bagu**
武具 *arms, weapons, munitions* **bugu**
文具 *stationery, office supplies* **bungu**
仏具 *Buddhist altar fittings* **butsugu**
道具 *tools, utensils* **dōgu**
具合 *condition, convenience* **guai**
具備 *equipment, apparatus* **gubi**
具現 *embodiment, realization* **gugen**
具申 *detailed report, full report* **gushin**
具象 *concrete expression* **gushō**
表具 *mounted picture* **hyōgu**
家具 *furniture* **kagu**
金具 *metal fittings* **kanagu**
敬具 *"sincerely yours..."* **keigu**
器具 *utensil, implement, instrument* **kigu**
⇒避妊器具 *contraceptive device* **hinin kigu**
工具 *tool, implement, utensil* **kōgu**
民具 *daily wares* **mingu**

猟具 *hunting equipment, ~gear* **ryōgu**
寝具 *bedding, bedclothes* **shingu**
装具 *outfit, fittings, equipment* **sōgu**
建具 *fittings, equipment, tools* **tategu**
夜具 *bedding, bedclothes* **yagu**
用具 *tool, implement, outfit* **yōgu**
絵の具 *colouring tools* **enogu**
具体案 *concrete plan, definite plan* **gutaian**
具体的 *concrete, actual, real* **gutaiteki**

器*evice, 902*	工*rtisan, 176*
材*aterials, 186*	匠*rtisan, 106*
料*aterials, 194*	

具*hellfish, 516*

397-B

Among 具ools, only the 真ruth rules...

真*incere*　　真*ruth*

目 (eyesight, visual)

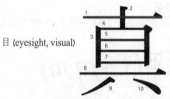

ma, SHIN
sincere, truth, genuine, authentic

FLIP: 1.0.b. Whole (stem)

迫真 *realistic, life-like, true-to-life* **hakushin**
純真 *purity & sincerity* **junshin**
真顔 *serious look, mean-looking* **magao**
真際 *just as, right in the middle of* **magiwa**
真昼 *midday, broad daylight, high noon* **mahiru**
真夏 *midsummer* **manatsu**
真似 *imitation, copying, impersonation* **mane**
真上 *just right above of* **maue**
真横 *side, lateral* **mayoko**
写真 *photograph, picture* **shashin**
真偽 *authenticity, genuineness* **shingi**
真意 *real intention, true meaning* **shin'i**
真因 *real cause* **shin'in**
真珠 *pearl* **shinju**
真価 *true value, real worth* **shinka**
真剣 *serious, determined* **shinken**
真否 *true-or-false* **shinpi**
真筆 *one's handwriting, penmanship* **shinpitsu**
真性 *genuine, real* **shinsei**

天真 *naïvete, simplicity* **tenshin**
真ん中 *right in the middle* **mannaka**
真暗闇 *complete darkness* **makkurayami**
青写真 *architectural plan, blueprint* **aojashin**
真っ赤 *red, deep red, crimson* **makka**
真っ暗 *dark, pitch-dark, hopeless* **makkura**
真っ黒 *black, total darkness* **makkuro**
真ん前 *right in front, in the face of* **manmae**
真っ青 *pale blue* **massao**
真っ白 *snow-white, pure-white* **masshiro**
真っ先に *first of all, before anything* **massaki(ni)**
真っ最中 *middle, in the midst of* **massaichū**
真っ盛り *at one's best* **massakari**

誠*incere, 245*	純*urity, 199*
実*ruth, 121*	浄*urity, 230*
潔*urity, 901*	料*urity, 762*

具*ools, 487*

398-A

平-*lat house of 100* 坪*[3.3 sqm] built for beavers...*

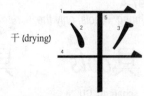

干 (drying)

平*lat*   平*lain*

tai(ra), hira, HEI, BYŌ
flat, plain

FLIP: 1.0.b. Whole (stem)

平等	*equality, fairness, impartiality* **byōdō**		平野	*plain field, open meadows* **heiya**
平安	*peace, tranquillity, calm* **heian**		平然	*cool, calm* **heizen**
平凡	*simple & common, nothing special* **heibon**		平幕	*rank-&-file* **hiramaku**
平方	*square metre* **heihō**		平屋	*one-story house, bungalow* **hiraya**
平易	*easiness, plainness, simplicity* **heii**		開平	*extract the square root* **kaihei**
平日	*weekdays (Monday-thru-Fridays)* **heijitsu**		公平	*fair, impartial, non-partisan* **kōhei**
平常	*normal, regular* **heijō**		平壌	*Pyongyang, Korea* **pyonyan**
平価	*parity, par value* **heika**		水平	*horizontal, flat* **suihei**
平価切下げ	*price cut, ~reduction* **heika kirisage**		平泳ぎ	*breaststroke swimming* **hiraoyogi**
平滑	*smooth & unruffled* **heikatsu**		偏平足	*flat-footed* **henpeisoku**
平気	*coolness, calmness, normality* **heiki**		平社員	*entry-level staff* **hirashain**
平均	*average* **heikin**		平カット	*flat cut* **hirakatto**
平均点	*average point* **heikinten**		平仮名	*Hiragana* **hiragana**
平行	*parallel* **heikō**		太平洋	*Pacific Ocean* **taiheiyō**
平衡	*equilibrium, balance* **heikō**		手の平	*palm of the hand* **tenohira**
平面	*flat surface, plain* **heimen**			
平穏	*calmness, quietness, serenity* **heion**			
平静	*calm, cool, composed* **heisei**			
平定	*suppress, repress* **heitei**			

野*lains, 873*	面*urface, 36*

呼*alling, 701*

398-B

平-*lat house of 100* 坪*[3.3 sq m] built for beavers...*

土 (ground, soil)

坪*[3.3 sq m]*

tsubo
[3.3 square metre]

FLIP: 5.0.b. Left & Right

一坪	*3.3 square metres* **hitotsubo**
地坪	*ground area, acreage* **jitsubo**
建坪	*floor space* **tatetsubo**
立坪	*about 6 cubic meters* **tatetsubo**
坪数	*area measurement* **tsubosū**
⇒延べ坪数	*total floor unit area* **nobe tsubosū**
坪当たり	*per space, ~area* **tsubo atari**
坪壱万円	*ten thousand yen per unit area* **tsubo ichiman'en**

升*[1.8 ltr], 298*	寸*[3 cm], 345*
旬*[10 day], 494*	匁*[3.75 gm], 75*
斗*[18 ltr], 195*	尺*[30 cm], 574*
勺*[18 ml], 470*	斤*[600 gm], 471*

平*lat, 488*

399-A

氏*urname on* 紙*aper, the serial raper...*

氏 (clan)

氏*urname*   氏*amily name*

uji, SHI
family name, surname

某氏	*a certain person*	**bōshi**
同氏	*the said person*	**dōshi**
彼氏	*boyfriend, lover*	**kareshi**
華氏	*fahrenheit*	**kashi**
両氏	*both men*	**ryōshi**
姓氏	*surname, last name*	**seishi**
摂氏	*centigrade, celsius*	**sesshi**
氏譜	*genealogy, parentage, kinship*	**shifu**
氏名	*full name*	**shimei, ujina**
氏名点呼	*roll call*	**shimei tenko**
失名氏	*unknown person, anonymous*	**shitsumeishi**
氏族	*family, clan*	**shizoku**
氏族制度	*clan system, nepotism*	**shizoku seido**
諸氏	*ladies & gentlemen*	**shoshi**
氏寺	*clan temple*	**ujidera**
氏神	*tutelary deity, guardian angel*	**ujigami**
氏人	*clansman*	**ujihito**
氏子	*shrine layman*	**ujiko**
無名氏	*unknown person, anonymous*	**mumeishi, nanashi**

Facing: 2.0. East ☞ (W)

姓*urname, 638*	縁*inship, 675*
名*urname, 425*	呼*alling, 701*
家*amily, 909*	称*itular, 130*
族*amily, 649*	

民*eople, 495*

399-B

氏*urname on* 紙*aper, the serial raper...*

糸 (thread, continuity)

紙*aper*

kami, SHI
paper, writing sheet

外紙	*foreign-, non-Japanese newspaper*	**gaishi**
白紙	*blank-, white paper*	**hakushi, shirakami**
半紙	*Japanese writing paper*	**hanshi**
表紙	*book cover, paper binding*	**hyōshi**
印紙	*documentary stamp*	**inshi**
壁紙	*wallpaper*	**kabegami**
紙箱	*paper carton*	**kamibako**
紙袋	*paperbag, brown paperbag*	**kamibukuro**
紙屑	*wastepaper*	**kamikuzu**
帯紙	*paper band on a book*	**obigami**
製紙	*paper making, ~manufacture*	**seishi**
紙幣	*paper money*	**shihei**
紙片	*white paper strips (Shintō shrine)*	**shihen**
紙面	*paper surface*	**shimen**
紙質	*paper quality*	**shishitsu**
手紙	*letter*	**tegami**
薄紙	*thin paper*	**usugami**
用紙	*form, sheet*	**yōshi**
英字紙	*English-language newspaper*	**eijishi**

Facing: 2.2. East ☞ (V)

紙粘土	*paper-mache*	**kaminendo**
紙製品	*paper products*	**kamiseihin**
紙芝居	*picture-story show*	**kamishibai**
紙包み	*paper parcel*	**kamizutsumi**
紙縒り	*paper string*	**koyori**
日刊紙	*daily newspapers, dailies*	**nikkanshi**
再生紙	*recycled paper*	**saiseishi**
方眼紙	*graph-, plotting paper*	**hōganshi**
包装紙	*wrapping paper*	**hōsōshi**
紙コップ	*paper cup*	**kamikoppu**
紙ナプキン	*paper napkin*	**kaminapukin**
紙オムツ	*diaper*	**kamiomutsu**

書*ritings, 116*	誌*ecord, 426*
読*eading, 260*	記*ecord, 728*
字*etter, 346*	枚*[sheets], 724*

氏*urname, 489*

400-A

兵*oldiers on the* 浜*each guarding a sea witch...*

兵*oldier*   兵*ilitary*

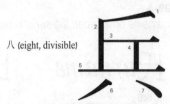

八 (eight, divisible)

HEI, PEI, HYŌ
soldier, military, troops, uniformed service, armed forces

Facing: 2.1. East ☞ (H)

番兵 *sentry, guard* **banpei, banhei**
募兵 *military recruitment* **bohei**
徴兵 *military conscription* **chōhei**
伏兵 *ambush squad* **fukuhei**
派兵 *troop deployment* **hahei**
兵団 *corps, troops* **heidan**
兵役 *military service* **heieki**
兵学 *military science, ~academy* **heigaku**
兵法 *strategy, tactics* **heihō**
兵員 *troop strength, soldiers* **heiin**
兵器 *weapon, arms* **heiki**
兵力 *force-of-arms* **heiryoku**
兵舎 *barracks* **heisha**
兵士 *soldier, private* **heishi**
兵卒 *soldier, private* **heisotsu**
兵隊 *soldier, sailor, troops* **heitai**
砲兵 *artillery soldiers, artillery* **hōhei**
兵糧 *provisions, food supplies* **hyōrō**
騎兵 *cavalry troops* **kihei**

民兵 *armed civilians, militias* **minpei**
撤兵 *troop withdrawal, ~military retreat* **teppei**
増兵 *reinforcement* **zōhei**
護衛兵 *guard, escort, bodyguard* **goeihei**
核兵器 *nuclear weapons* **kakuheiki**
憲兵隊 *WWII Japanese secret police* **kenpeitai**
志願兵 *volunteer soldier* **shiganhei**
傷病兵 *corps of invalids* **shōbyōhei**
守備兵 *guards, garrison* **shubihei**
用兵術 *military strategy, ~tactics* **yōheijutsu**
兵器産業 *arms-, weapons industry* **heiki sangyō**

隊*quad, 543*	衛*rotect, 796*
軍*oldier, 295*	護*rotect, 828*
卒*oldier, 109*	防*rotect, 736*
戦*ighting, 517*	守*efence, 366*

岳*ountain peak, 28*

400-B

兵*oldiers on the* 浜*each guarding sea witch...*

浜*each*   浜*eashore*

水 ⇔ 氵 (water)

hama, HIN
beach, coastal, seashore, seaside

Facing: 2.2. East ☞ (V)

浜辺 *seashore, beach, coast* **hamabe**
浜風 *beach breeze, ~wind* **hamakaze**
浜面 *beach, seashore* **hamazura**
海浜 *seashore, beach, coast* **kaihin**
京浜 *Tōkyō-Yokohama region* **keihin**
白浜 *white beach* **shirahama**
砂浜 *sand beach* **sunahama**
横浜 *Yokohama City, Kanagawa Prefecture* **yokohama**
浜茄子 *sweet brier* **hamanasu**
浜焼き *grilling at the beach* **hamayaki**
浜昼顔 *sea bells* **hamahirugao**
浜地鳥 *shore plover* **hamachidori**
浜木綿 *crinum* **hamayū**

浦*eashore, 813*	海*cean, 241*
涯*eashore, 890*	洋*cean, 247*
岸*eashore, 30*	

兵*oldier, 490*

401-A

固ardened criminals are not plain 個ndividuals...

olid   ard

□ (enclosure)

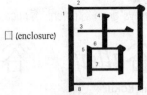

FLIP: 1.0.a. Whole (flat)

kata(i), kata(maru), kata(meru), KO
solid, hard, rigid, firm

安固 firm, secure, fixed **anko**
断固 firm, determined **danko**
頑固 stubborn, hard-headed **ganko**
拳固 clenched fist **genko**
凝固 congelation, co-agulation **gyōko**
確固 resolute, firm, determined **kakko**
堅固 strong-willed, unyielding **kengo**
禁固 imprisonment, confinement **kinko**
固着 adherence, persistence, tenacity **kochaku**
固辞 categorical refusal, emphatic denial **koji**
固持 persistence, insistence **koji**
固化 solidification, hardening **koka**
固形 solidity, hardness **kokei**
固形食 solid food **kokeishoku**
固執 persistence, fixation **koshitsu**
固疾 chronic illness **koshitsu**
固守 tenacious defence **koshu**
固体 solid matter **kotai**
固定 fixation, set-up **kotei**

固有 inherent, indigenous **koyū**
強固 strong, firm **kyōko**
足固め groundwork, preparation **ashigatame**
意固地 obstinacy, tenacity **ikoji**
地固め ground-level preparation **jigatame**
証拠固め evidence gathering **shōkogatame**
凝り固まる be intolerant, fanatical **korikatamaru**
練り固める harden by kneading **nerikatameru**
押し固める pressing together **oshikatameru**
差し固める hold firmly; stern warning
　　　sashikatameru

| 堅olid, 599 | 凝arden, 57 |
| 締ighten, 432 | 物bjects, 647 |

周ap, 280

401-B

固ardened criminals are not plain 個ndividuals...

個ndividual   個rivate

人⇔亻 (person)

FLIP: 7.0.a. Right (flat)

KO
individual, private, separate, apart, detached; general counter

別個 different, another **bekko**
一個 one piece, one item **ikko**
一個人 private person **ichi kojin**
各個 everyone, all persons **kakko**
個所 spot, point, passage **kasho**
個別 separate, private **kobetsu**
個人 individual, personal **kojin**
個人タクシー privately-owned taxi **kojin takushii**
個人差 individuality, personal difference **kojinsa**
個人経営 private management **kojin keiei**
個人教授 private lessons **kojin kyōju**
個個 individuals **koko**
個性 individuality, uniqueness **kosei**
個室 private room **koshitsu**
個数 number, piece **kosū**
個体 individual, singular **kotai**
個展 private exhibition **koten**
好個 excellence, superiority, superb **kōko**

数個 several objects **sūko**

私[I], 682	自elf, 462
我elf, 443	身elf, 504
己elf, 5	別eparate, 866

固ard, 491

402-A

谷*alleys' grain* 容*ontent,* 容*ppears affluent...*

谷*alley*   谷*avine*

谷 (valley)

tani, KOKU
valley, ravine, gorge

渓谷 *valley, glen, gorge* **keikoku**
空谷 *empty valley* **kūkoku**
峡谷 *ravine, gorge, canyon* **kyōkoku**
谷川 *mountain stream* **tanigawa**
谷風 *valley breeze* **tanikaze**
谷間 *valley, ravine* **tanima**
谷水 *water in the valley* **tanimizu**
谷底 *bottom of a ravine* **tanizoko**
幽谷 *deep ravine* **yūkoku**
⇒深山幽谷 *deep mountains & valleys* **shinzan yūkoku**

FLIP: 1.0.a. Whole (flat)

峡*avine, 763*	山*ountain, 172*
渓*avine, 97*	岳*ountain peak, 28*
丘*lope, 106*	峰*ountain peak, 779*
崎*lope, 270*	峠*ountain trail, 646*

合*ogether, 232*

402-B

谷*alleys' grain* 容*ontent,* 容*ppears affluent...*

❶容*ontent*   ❷容*ppearance*

宀 (cover, lid)

i(reru), YŌ
content, volume; appearance, configuration

❶内容 *content, capacity* **naiyō**
容器 *container, vessel* **yōki**
容認 *approval, admit, tolerance* **yōnin**
容量 *capacity, volume* **yōryō**
容積 *capacity, volume* **yōseki**
全容 *complete story* **zenyō**
捕虜収容所 *POW camp* **horyo shūyōjo**

❷変容 *change in appearance* **henyō**
包容 *tolerance, magnanimity* **hōyō**
偉容 *noble-looking, dignified appearance* **iyō**
威容 *noble-looking, dignified appearance* **iyō**
陣容 *battle formation* **jinyō**
受容 *receiving, acceptance, treatment* **juyō**
寛容 *tolerance, generosity* **kanyō**
許容 *permission, authorization* **kyoyō**
許容量 *acceptable limit* **kyoyōryō**
収容 *guest seating admittance* **shūyō**
容貌 *looks, face* **yōbō**

FLIP: 1.0.a. Whole (flat)

容体 *one's condition* **yōdai**
容体 *patient's condition* **yōdai**
容疑 *suspicion, doubts* **yōgi**
容疑者 *crime suspect* **yōgisha**
容易 *easy, simple* **yōi**
容喙 *meddling, interference* **yōkai**
容共 *pro-communist* **yōkyō**
容赦 *pardon, forgiveness* **yōsha**
容赦ない *merciless, unsparing, ruthless* **yōshanai**
容姿 *figure, appearance, looks* **yōshi**
容色 *looks, beauty, appearance* **yōshoku**
美容師 *cosmetician, beautician* **biyōshi**

姿*ppearance, 609*	限*imit, 771*
態*ppearance, 322*	現*ppear, 814*
涯*imit, 890*	

谷*avine, 492*

403-A

Workers 戒dmonished when 械achine was unpolished...

戈 (spear)

戒dmonish　戒hastise

imashi(meru), KAI
  admonish, chastise, caution

Facing: 2.0. East ☞ (W)
FLIP: 6.2. Left Bottom

戒める *reprove, rebuke, censure* **imashimeru**
懲戒 *censure, reprimand, reproach* **chōkai**
懲戒免職 *disciplinary dismissal* **chōkai menshoku**
懲戒処分 *disciplinary action* **chōkai shobun**
厳戒 *heavy guard, strict observation* **genkai**
破戒 *commandment violation* **hakai**
破戒僧 *sinful monk, corrupt priest* **hakaisō**
遺戒 *last will* **ikai**
自戒 *self-admonition, self-reproach* **jikai**
浄戒 *precepts, commandments* **jōkai**
受戒 *Buddhist confirmation* **jukai**
十戒 *Ten Commandments* **jūkkai, jikkai**
戒壇 *temple ordination platform* **kaidan**
戒厳 *alertness, one's guard* **kaigen**
戒厳令 *martial law, military occupation* **kaigenrei**
戒告 *warning, reprimand, censure* **kaikoku**
戒名 *one's posthumous Buddhist name* **kaimyō**
戒律 *religious precepts* **kairitsu**
戒心 *precaution, care* **kaishin**

警戒 *precaution, caution, lookout, guard* **keikai**
警戒網 *police dragnet* **keikaimō**
警戒線 *"police line: do not cross..."* **keikaisen**
警戒心 *alertness, one's guard* **keikaishin**
警戒警報 *precaution, warning* **keikai keihō**
警戒水位 *dangerous water level* **keikai suii**
禁戒 *commandment, prohibition* **kinkai**
訓戒 *admonition, warning* **kunkai**
教戒 *exhortation, preaching* **kyōkai**
斎戒 *purification, sterilization* **saikai**
哨戒 *patrol, guard* **shōkai**

諭dmonish, 922　権uthority, 804
驚care, 330　警arning, 330
威uthority, 520

械achine, 493

403-B

Workers 戒dmonished when 械achine was unpolished...

木 (wooden)

械achine　械echanics

KAI
  machine, mechanics

Facing: 2.2. East ☞ (V)
FLIP: 8.0.b. Inner (stem)

器械 *instrument, equipment, apparatus* **kikai**
機械 *machine, mechanized device* **kikai**
⇒工作機械 *machine tools* **kōsaku kikai**
機械学 *study of machines* **kikaigaku**
機械化 *mechanization* **kikaika**
機械的 *mechanical* **kikaiteki**
機械屋 *machinist* **kikaiya**
機械工学 *mechanical engineering* **kikai kōgaku**
機械体操 *gymnastics apparatus* **kikai taisō**
手械 *handcuffs, manacles* **tekase**

機achine, 547　作roduce, 724
具mplements, 487　産roduce, 883
器evice, 902　造roduce, 267
匠rtisan, 106　品roducts, 901

戒dmonish, 493

404-A

In 旬en-days, 殉artyr to cast away...

日 (sunlight, daytime)

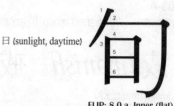

旬 *[10 day]*

JUN, SHUN
[ten days]

中旬 *middle ten days of a month* **chūjun**
下旬 *last ten days of a month* **gejun**
上旬 *first ten days of a month* **jōjun**
旬日 *period of ten days* **junjitsu**
旬間 *period of ten days* **junkan**
旬刊 *journal issued every 10 days* **junkan**
旬報 *bulletin issued every 10 days* **junpō**
初旬 *first ten days of a month* **shojun**
四旬節 *Holy Lent* **shijunsetsu**
旬の野菜 *vegetables in season* **shun no yasai**

FLIP: 8.0.a. Inner (flat)

日 *ay, 14*	月 *onth, 22*
曜 *eekday, 849*	年 *ear, 27*
週 *eekly, 279*	

句 *hrase, 16*

404-B

In 旬en-days, 殉artyr to cast away...

歹 (dried bones)

殉artyr   殉acrifice

jun(zuru), JUN
martyr, victim, sacrifice, prey, pawn

殉国 *patriotic urge, martyrdom* **junkoku**
殉教 *martyrdom, sacrificial death* **junkyō**
殉教者 *martyr, victim* **junkyōsha**
殉死 *death on duty* **junshi**
殉職 *dying on duty* **junshoku**
殉職者 *"dead in the line of duty..."* **junshokusha**
殉難 *martyrdom* **junnan**
殉難者 *martyr, victim* **junnansha**

FLIP: 8.0.a. Inner (flat)
Facing: 1.2. ☜ West (V)

犠 *acrifice, 342*	亡 *eath, 72*
死 *eath, 513*	栄 *lory, 580*
逝 *eath, 54*	誉 *onour, 252*

旬 *[10 day]. 494*

405-A

氏eople always 眠sleep, nothing to reap...

氏 (clan)

氏eople　氏itizen

tami, MIN

people, citizen, inhabitant, resident

Facing: 2.0. East ☞ (W)

漁民	fisherman, fisher folk	**gyomin**
平民	commoner, subject	**heimin**
貧民	poor-, needy person	**hinmin**
人民	people, citizens	**jinmin**
住民	resident, inhabitant	**jūmin**
官民	government & people	**kanmin**
県民	prefectural residents	**kenmin**
国民	people, citizens	**kokumin**
公民	community residents	**kōmin**
民営	private management	**min'ei**
民意	will of the people, popular mandate	**min'i**
民家	private house	**minka**
民間	civilian, ordinary people	**minkan**
民権	civil rights	**minken**
民兵	armed civilians, militias	**minpei**
民法	civil law, civil code	**minpō**
民政	civilian government, municipality	**minsei**
民心	public sentiments, pulse of the people	**minshin**
民衆	common people, masses	**minshū**

民宿	board & lodging	**minshuku**
民話	folktale, folklore	**minwa**
民族	natives, locals	**minzoku**
民俗	folk customs, folklore	**minzoku**
難民	refugee, asylee, evacuee	**nanmin**
選民	chosen people	**senmin**
市民	citizens, people	**shimin**
臣民	subjects, colonial people	**shinmin**
島民	islander, island residents	**tōmin**
避難民	evacuee, refugee	**hinanmin**
植民地	colony, territory, doman	**shokuminchi**
民主主義	democracy	**minshu shugi**

票uffrage, 549	方erson, 533
衆opulace, 766	選hoice, 303
人eople, 2	択hoice, 753

氏urname, 489

405-B

氏eople always 眠sleep, nothing to reap...

目 (eyesight, visual)

眠leeping　眠rowsy

nemu(ru), nemu(i), MIN

sleeping, snoozing, drowse, drowsy

FLIP: 6.0.a. Left (flat)

安眠	sound sleep	**anmin**
惰眠	lethargy, idleness	**damin**
永眠	eternal rest, death	**eimin**
不眠	lack of sleep, insomnia	**fumin**
不眠症	insomnia, sleeping disorder	**fuminshō**
不眠不休	lack of sleep & restlessness	**fumin fukyū**
熟眠	sound sleep	**jukumin**
快眠	sound-, pleasant sleep	**kaimin**
仮眠	catnap, nap, siesta	**kamin**
夏眠	aestivation	**kamin**
休眠	dormancy, idleness	**kyūmin**
眠気	sleepiness, drowsiness	**nemuke**
眠気覚まし	something to wake one up	
	nemukezamashi	
催眠	hypnosis, hypnotizing	**saimin**
催眠術	hypnotism, mesmerism	**saimin jutsu**
催眠術師	hypnotist, mesmerizer	**saimin jutsushi**
催眠療法	hypnotic-, mesmeric treatment	
	saimin ryōhō	

春眠	springtime sleep (pleasant)	**shunmin**
就眠	go to sleep, go to bed	**shūmin**
睡眠	sleep, sleeping	**suimin**
睡眠薬	sleeping pill, ~aid	**suiminyaku**
睡眠不足	lack of sleep, insomnia	**suimin busoku**
睡眠時間	sleeping hours	**suimin jikan**
冬眠	hibernation, winter sleep	**tōmin**
一眠り	catnap, nap, siesta	**hitonemuri**
居眠り	sleeping, dozing off	**inemuri**
眠り病	sleeping disorder, ~debility	**nemuribyō**
眠り草	mimosaceae	**nemurigusa**
眠り薬	sleeping pill, ~aid	**nemurigusuri**
空眠り	pretending to be asleep	**soranemuri**

寝leep, 769	泊leep-over, 742
睡leeping, 948	宿odging, 448

眼yesight, 771

406-A

Rebels 到rriving to 倒verthrow the King...

刀⇔刂 (blade, cutting)

到rrive　　到estination

TŌ

arrive, destination, landing, reach

FLIP: 6.2. Left Bottom

未到 *unreached, unaccomplished* **mitō**
⇒人生未到 *unreached in one's life* **jinsei mitō**
⇒前人未到 *unreached by human* **zenjin mitō**
殺到 *rushing, stampede* **sattō**
精到 *meticulous, detailed* **seitō**
周到 *scrupulous, meticulous* **shūtō**
⇒用意周到 *thorough, rigorous, careful* **yōi shūtō**
想到 *think, ponder, consider* **sōtō**
到着 *arrival, landing* **tōchaku**
到着駅 *arrival station* **tōchakueki**
到着時刻 *arrival time* **tōchaku jikoku**
到来 *arrival, incoming, advent* **tōrai**
到達 *arrival, attainment, reaching* **tōtatsu**
到達地 *destination* **tōtatsuchi**
到達港 *port of arrival* **tōtatsukō**
到底 *utterly, absolutely* **tōtei**
到頭 *at last, finally* **tōtō**

着rrive, 589	訪isit, 737
来rrive, 871	賓isitor, 161
踏tep on, 672	客isitor, 559

至eading-to, 381

406-B

Rebels 到rriving to 倒verthrow the King...

人⇔イ (person)

倒verthrow　　倒opple-down

tao(reru), tao(su), TŌ

overthrow, topple down, depose, dethrone, subvert, throw out

Facing: 3.0. ☞☜ Across
FLIP: 8.0.b. Inner (stem)

罵倒 *denounce, condemn, lambaste* **batō**
打倒 *overthrow a government* **datō**
傾倒 *devotion, faith, commitment* **keitō**
驚倒 *earth-shaking* **kyōtō**
面倒 *troublesome, annoying* **mendō**
卒倒 *fainting, passing out, collapse* **sottō**
倒幕 *overthrowing the Shōgunate* **tōbaku**
倒木 *fallen tree* **tōboku**
倒置 *upside down, inversion, turtle turn* **tōchi**
倒影 *inverted image, reflection* **tōei**
倒壊 *collapse, falling down* **tōkai**
倒閣 *overthrowing a cabinet* **tōkaku**
倒句 *inversion of word order* **tōku**
倒立 *handstand* **tōritsu**
倒錯 *perversion, aberration, regression* **tōsaku**
倒産 *bankruptcy, insolvency* **tōsan**
横倒し *falling sideways* **yokodaoshi**
圧倒的 *overwhelming, sweeping* **attōteki**
前倒し *accelerated payment* **maedaoshi**

共倒れ *falling together* **tomodaore**
吹き倒す *blow down* **fukitaosu**
踏み倒す *evade, trample down* **fumitaosu**
引き倒す *drag down, pull down* **hikitaosu**
行き倒れ *dying on the road* **ikidaore**
貸し倒れ *uncollectible loan, bad debt* **kashidaore**
殴り倒す *knock down* **naguritaosu**
拝み倒す *entreat* **ogamitaosu**
将棋倒し *domino effect collapse* **shōgidaoshi**
突き倒す *push away, shove* **tsukitaosu**
見かけ倒し *gimcrack, pretense* **mikakedaoshi**

斥ejection, 424	陥ollapse, 893
排ejection, 795	崩ollapse, 912
断ejection, 958	落ollapse, 826
否ejection, 300	破estroy, 715

到rrive, 496

407-A

徒*isciples willingly* 走*un their master's errand...*

走 (running)

FLIP: 3.0.a. Top (flat)

走*unning* 走*printing*

hashi(ru), SŌ
running, sprinting

伴走	escort, chaperon	**bansō**
暴走	running-, driving recklessly	**bōsō**
独走	running solo	**dokusō**
敗走	rout, flight, escape	**haisō**
背走	running backward	**haisō**
帆走	sailing, gliding	**hansō**
奔走	effort, good offices	**honsō**
縦走	traversing, running thru	**jūsō**
快走	fast running	**kaisō**
滑走	gliding, sliding, taxiing	**kassō**
滑走路	airport runway	**kassōro**
継走	relay race	**keisō**
競走	race, sprint	**kyōsō**
力走	"running like hell..."	**rikisō**
疾走	scamper, scud	**shissō**
師走	December, the year end	**shiwasu**
走破	running full-course	**sōha**
走法	running style	**sōhō**
走行	running, moving	**sōkō**

走馬灯	revolving lantern	**sōmatō**
走路	track, course	**sōro**
走塁	base running	**sōrui**
走査	scanning, browsing	**sōsa**
走者	runner	**sōsha**
遁走	flight, escape	**tonsō**
逃走	escape, running away, fleeing	**tōsō**
御馳走	dinner, food treat	**gochisō**
口走る	blurt out	**kuchibashiru**
徒競走	foot race	**tokyōsō**
突っ走る	run at full speed	**tsuppashiru**
東奔西走	being concerned with	**tōhon seisō**

奔	un-away, 120	尽	ursue, 574
逃	scape, 216	逐	rive-out, 479
追	ursue, 108	猟	hasing, 657

徒*isciple, 497*

407-B

徒*isciples willingly* 走*un their master's errand...*

彳 (stroll)

FLIP: 7.2.a. Right Top (flat)

徒*isciple* 徒*ollower*

itazura, TO
disciple, follower, adherent, subaltern

徒に	in vain	**itazura(ni)**
徒心	fickle-hearted	**adagokoro**
博徒	gambler	**bakuto**
暴徒	rioters, mob	**bōto**
学徒	student, disciple	**gakuto**
逆徒	rebels, renegade, traitor	**gyakuto**
反徒	rebels, renegade	**hanto**
凶徒	rioters, mob, hooligans	**kyōto**
門徒	sect follower	**monto**
徒言	useless discussion, idle talk	**mudagoto**
聖徒	saint, disciple, apostle	**seito**
生徒	student, pupil	**seito**
信徒	faithful, believer	**shinto**
使徒	apostle, disciple	**shito**
酒徒	drinking buddy	**shuto**
宗徒	sect follower	**shūto**
囚徒	prisoner, convict, felon	**shūto**
徒歩	walk, go on foot	**toho**
徒刑	penal servitude	**tokei**

徒労	futile-, vain effort	**torō**
徒論	arguing in vain, futile discussion	**toron**
徒死	dying in vain, meaningless death	**toshi**
徒食	idle lifestyle	**toshoku**
徒弟	apprentice, instructee, acolyte	**totei**
徒党	crime syndicate	**totō**
仏教徒	Buddhist	**bukkyōto**
異教徒	pagan, heathen, heretic	**ikyōto**
邪教徒	heretic, blasphemy	**jakyōto**
回教徒	Muslim, Moslem, Islamic	**kaikyōto**
旧教徒	Roman Catholic	**kyūkyōto**
清教徒	Puritan	**seikyōto**

教	ducate, 385	爵	oyalty, 593
師	eacher, 483	忠	oyalty, 475
訓	eachings, 959	孝	ilial, 385

徒*bey, 551*

408-A

各*very foetus, a possible* 格*tatus...*

口 (mouth)

各*very*

ono-ono, KAKU
every, each

FLIP: 2.0.a. Sort Of (flat)

各階 *every floor, all floors* **kakukai**
各個 *everyone, all* **kakko**
各戸 *each household, door-to-door* **kakko**
各行 *each line (text)* **kakugyō**
各項 *each item in the agenda* **kakkō**
各国 *each nation, all countries* **kakkoku**
各部 *each section, every department* **kakubu**
各地 *each area, various places* **kakuchi**
各駅 *each station, every station* **kakueki**
各派 *every faction, each sect* **kakuha**
各般 *all, each, every* **kakuhan**
各位 *everyone, all* **kakui**
各員 *each member, each of you* **kakuin**
各自 *each person, everyone* **kakuji**
各人 *each person, everyone* **kakujin**
各人各様 *"so many men, so many ways..."*
    kakujin kakuyō
各界 *all professions* **kakukai**
各論 *details, particulars* **kakuron**

各所 *everywhere, every place* **kakusho**
各省 *each ministry, all ministries* **kakushō**
各種 *various, several, diverse* **kakushu**
各種学校 *vocational-, finishing school*
    kakushu gakkō
各層 *each class, every stratum* **kakusō**
各各 *each, every, all* **onoono**
各方面 *each & every direction* **kakuhōmen**
関係者各位 *"to whom it may concern..."*
    kankeisha kakui

皆*verything, 39*	完*omplete, 196*
全*ntire, 24*	個*ndividual, 491*
毎*very, 241*	総*otality, 433*

名*ame, 425*

408-B

各*very foetus, a possible* 格*tatus...*

木 (wooden)

格*tatus*

KAKU, KŌ
status, state, ranking, norm

FLIP: 7.1. Right (Sort Of)

同格 *same ranking, ~qualification* **dōkaku**
風格 *noble-looking* **fūkaku**
厳格 *strict, severe, mean* **genkaku**
合格 *passing an exam* **gōkaku**
品格 *dignity, grace; quality* **hinkaku**
人格 *character, personality* **jinkaku**
価格 *price of commodities, ~goods* **kakaku**
格好 *shape, figure, appearance* **kakkō**
格別 *exceptional, special, unique* **kakubetsu**
格調 *tone, style* **kakuchō**
格言 *saying, proverb, maxim* **kakugen**
格差 *gap, differential, disparity* **kakusa**
格式 *formality, decorum* **kakushiki**
格闘 *fight, grapple* **kakutō**
格安 *bargain, good buy* **kakuyasu**
規格 *standard, regulation* **kikaku**
降格 *demotion, downgrading* **kōkaku**
骨格 *frame, build, frame work* **kokkaku**
格子 *lattice, grille, cross stripes* **kōshi**

性格 *character, personality, demeanour* **seikaku**
資格 *qualification, competence* **shikaku**
失格 *disqualification, failure* **shikkaku**
昇格 *promotion, status elevation* **shōkaku**
主格 *nominative, subjective case* **shukaku**
体格 *physique, build, body frame* **taikaku**
定格 *standard, conventional* **teikaku**
本格的 *expert, full-scale, genuine* **honkakuteki**
格上げ *upgrading, raising, promoting* **kakuage**
格段に *remarkably, by far* **kakudan(ni)**

位*tatus, 235*	準*evel, 919*
級*evel, 189*	段*tep, 555*
等*rade, 251*	階*evel, 129*

各*very, 498*

409-A

On the 卓*able* 悼*rieves* 卓*rominent Steve...*

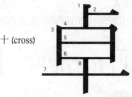

十 (cross)

❶卓*able*   **❷卓***rominence*

TAKU
table; prominence

FLIP: 2.0.b. Sort Of (stem)
FLIP: 4.0.b. Bottom (stem)

❶ 円卓 *round table* **entaku**
教卓 *teacher's classroom desk* **kyōtaku**
食卓 *dining table* **shokutaku**
食卓用 *for table use* **shokutakuyō**
卓球 *table tennis, ping-pong* **takkyū**
卓上 *"on the table..."* **takujō**
卓上ランプ *desk lamp* **takujō ranpu**
座卓 *low table* **zataku**
卓袱台 *low dining table* **chabudai**

台*latform, 209*	席*eating, 91*
級*evel, 189*	座*eating, 109*
準*evel, 919*	学*tudy, 346*

早*arly, 373*

❷電卓 *electronic calculator* **dentaku**
卓見 *foresight, clear-sightedness* **takken**
卓抜 *excellent, prominent* **takubatsu**
卓越 *excellence, superiority* **takuetsu**
卓立 *outstanding, excellent* **takuritsu**
卓論 *excellent-, sound opinion* **takuron**
卓説 *excellent-, sound opinion* **takusetsu**
卓絶 *excellent, prominent* **takuzetsu**

409-B

On the 卓*able* 悼*rieves* 卓*rominent Steve...*

心⇔忄⇔小 (feelings)

悼*ament*   **悼***rieve*

ita(mu), TŌ
lament, grieve, mourning, bereavement, funeral

FLIP: 7.1. Right (Sort Of)
FLIP: 7.3.b. Right Bottom (stem)

哀悼 *condolence, sympathy* **aitō**
悼辞 *letter of condolence* **tōji**
追悼 *mourning, grieving, wailing* **tsuitō**
追悼会 *memorial-, funeral service* **tsuitōkai**
追悼歌 *requiem, elegy* **tsuitōka**

愁*rief, 415*	忌*ourning, 6*
嘆*rieve, 927*	喪*ourning, 119*
愁*orrows, 415*	弔*ourning, 538*
悲*orrows, 289*	

卓*able, 499*

410-A

且*urther* 宜*onvenience, a business sense...*

且*urther* 且*oreover*

ka(tsu)
further, moreover, besides, as well
且つ *"besides, moreover..."* **katsu**
且つ又 *"furthermore, moreover..."* **katsumata**
なお且つ *"besides, furthermore..."* **naokatsu**

一 (one, single)

FLIP: 1.0.a. Whole (flat)

更 *new, 402*
尚 *urther, 99*

具 *ye, 462*

410-B

且*urther* 宜*onvenience, a business sense...*

宜*onvenience* 宜*xpedience*

mube, yoro(shii), yoro(shiku),GI
convenience, expedience, betterment, amenity, right
宜しい *"it's fine with me..."* **yoroshii**
宜しく *"my best regards..."* **yoroshiku**
便宜 *convenience, advantage, benefit* **bengi**
便宜上 *convenience sake* **bengijō**
便宜的 *temporary, stop-gap* **bengiteki**
便宜主義 *opportunism* **bengi shugi**
時宜 *the right time, opportune time* **jigi**
機宜 *chance, opportunity* **kigi**
禰宜 *rank & file Shintō priest* **negi**
適宜 *proper, suitable, fitting* **tekigi**

宀 (cover, lid)

FLIP: 1.0.a. Whole (flat)

便 *onvenience, 480*　得 *enefit, 940*
用 *vail of, 409*　得 *dvantage, 940*
益 *enefit, 622*　利 *dvantage, 686*

且 *urther, 500*

411-A
When 余urplus 除xcluded, profits clouded...

余*urplus* 余*xtra*

人⇔亻 (person)

ama(ru), ama(su), YO
surplus, extra, excess, remaining

FLIP: 1.0.b. Whole (stem)

窮余 *last resort, final alternative* **kyūyo**
余病 *illness complications* **yobyō**
余地 *margin, room* **yochi**
余談 *diverting from the topic* **yodan**
余弦 *math cosine* **yogen**
余技 *hobby, past time* **yogi**
余波 *after-effects* **yoha**
余白 *margin, blank space* **yohaku**
余韻 *lingering note, ~sound* **yoin**
余事 *other things, ~affairs* **yoji**
余剰 *surplus, excess* **yojō**
余暇 *leisure, spare time* **yoka**
余寒 *lingering cold* **yokan**
余計 ① *all the more; surplus* **yokei**
余計 ② *none of one's business* **yokei**
余光 *afterglow* **yokō**
余興 *entertainment, amusement* **yokyō**
余念 *total devotion, ~commitment* **yonen**
余力 *surplus energy* **yoryoku**

余生 *one's remaining years, twilight years* **yosei**
余震 *aftershocks, reverberations* **yoshin**
余色 *complementary colours* **yoshoku**
余徳 *good reputation* **yotoku**
余得 *extra benefits* **yotoku**
余話 *gossip, rumour* **yowa**
余財 *surplus funds* **yozai**
残余 *leftovers, remains* **zanyo**
余り物 *remains, ruins, relics* **amarimono**
剰余金 *surplus funds* **jōyokin**
刑余者 *ex-convict, freed felon* **keiyosha**
有り余る *super-abundant, overflowing* **ariamaru**

剰*urplus, 511*	繁*rosperity, 434*
豊*bundance, 965*	隆*rosperity, 133*
富*ortune, 333*	盛*lourishment, 244*
裕*ffluence, 758*	多*lenty, 187*

金*etal, 25*

411-B
When 余urplus 除xcluded, profits clouded...

除*xclude* 除*emove*

阝⇔阜 (village=left)

nozo(ku), JO, JI
exclude, expulsion, remove, take off

FLIP: 7.0.b1. Right (stem)

排除 *exclusion, removal, expulsion* **haijo**
除外 *exception, exemption* **jogai**
乗除 *multiplication & division* **jōjo**
除去 *removal, elimination* **jokyo**
除幕 *unveiling, opening, inauguration* **jomaku**
除籍 *removal from the register, delisting* **joseki**
除雪 *snow ploughing* **josetsu**
除湿 *dehumidification* **joshitsu**
除霜 *defrosting, de-icing, thawing* **josō**
除草 *weeding out* **josō**
除草剤 *herbicide, weed killer* **josōzai**
除数 *divisor number* **josū**
除隊 *discharge, removal* **jotai**
除夜 *New Year's eve* **joya**
除氷 *defrosting, de-icing, thawing* **jōyō**
解除 *cancel, remove, lift* **kaijo**
控除 *tax deduction, tax break* **kōjo**
駆除 *eliminate, exterminate* **kujo**
免除 *exemption, remission* **menjo**

⇒兵役免除 *draft exemption* **heieki menjo**
⇒債務免除 *acquittal, non-liability* **saimu menjo**
削除 *elimination, deletion* **sakujo**
整除 *divisibility* **seijo**
掃除 *cleaning, cleansing* **sōji**
掃除婦 *cleaning lady* **sōjifu**
掃除機 *vacuum cleaner* **sōjiki**
泥除け *fender, mudguard, wing* **doroyoke**
虫除け *insecticide, mothball* **mushiyoke**
霜除け *frost proofing* **shimoyoke**
雪除け *snowshed* **yukiyoke**

排*xclude, 795*	断*ejection, 958*
斥*ejection, 424*	否*ejection, 300*
排*ejection, 795*	外*emove, 188*

険*teep, 938*

412-A
束*undle of sticks burn* 速*uick...*

束*undle*　束*ie-up*

木 (wooden)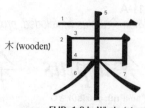

taba, taba(neru), SOKU
bundle, bunch, tie-up

FLIP: 1.0.b. Whole (stem)

束の間 *brief intermission, interlude* **tsukanoma**
不束 *unrefined, ill-bred* **futsutsuka**
花束 *floral bouquet* **hanataba**
幣束 *Shintō ornaments(rope & paper)* **heisoku**
一束 *a bundle* **hitotaba, issoku**
磁束 *magnetic flux* **jisoku**
鍵束 *bunch of keys* **kagitaba**
検束 *confinement, detention, arrest* **kensoku**
結束 *banding together* **kessoku**
光束 *luminous flux* **kōsoku**
拘束 *restraint, custody* **kōsoku**
拘束時間 *entire time spent* **kōsoku jikan**
拘束力 *binding force* **kōsokuryoku**
大束 *large bundle of* **ootaba**
札束 *roll of bills, wads of cash* **satsutaba**
装束 *attire, costume, clothes* **shōzoku**
収束 *gather & bundle up* **shūsoku**
束縛 *restraints, limitations* **sokubaku**
束髪 *pompadour hairstyle* **sokuhatsu**

束線 *binding wire* **sokusen**
束帯 *old ceremonial attire* **sokutai**
束子 *scrubbing brush* **tawashi**
束柱 *roof ridge pillar* **tsukabashira**
約束 *promise, appointment* **yakusoku**
約束事 *promise, appointment* **yakusokugoto**
約束手形 *promissory note* **yakusoku tegata**
覚束ない *frivolous, precarious* **obotsukanai**
黒装束 *"all in black clothes..."* **kuroshōzoku**
白装束 *"all in white clothes..."* **shiroshōzoku**

括*undle, 954*	合*ogether, 232*
把*undle, 717*	包*rapping, 503*
締*onclude, 432*	集*ather, 50*

克*onquer, 204*

412-B
束*undle of sticks burn* 速*uick...*

速*uick*　速*peedy*

辶 (transport)

haya(i), haya(meru), sumi(yaka), SOKU
quick, speedy, swift, brisk, rapid, haste

FLIP: 3.0.b. Top (stem)

秒速 *speed per second* **byōsoku**
減速 *speed reduction, deceleration* **gensoku**
迅速 *rapid, quick, speedy* **jinsoku**
快速 *high speed* **kaisoku**
加速 *speed acceleration* **kasoku**
急速 *swift, rapid, fast* **kyūsoku**
音速 *speed of sound* **onsoku**
早速 *"at once, immediately..."* **sassoku**
拙速 *done fast & sloppily* **sessoku**
失速 *getting stalled, ~jammed* **shissoku**
速乾 *quick drying up* **sokkan**
速記 *shorthand, stenography* **sokki**
速攻 *swift attack* **sokkō**
速効 *quick effect, immediate effect* **sokkō**
速断 *hasty-, impulsive conclusion* **sokudan**
速度 *speed* **sokudo**
⇒戻り速度 *return speed* **modori sokudo**
⇒最高速度 *maximum speed* **saikō sokudo**
⇒制限速度 *speed limit* **seigen sokudo**

速度計 *speedometer* **sokudokei**
速読 *speed reading* **sokudoku**
速報 *flash bulletin, news flash* **sokuhō**
速筆 *speed writing, scribbling* **sokuhitsu**
速算 *fast calculation* **sokusan**
速写 *snapshot* **sokusha**
速修 *learning quick, fast learner* **sokushū**
速達 *express delivery* **sokutatsu**
速達郵便 *express mail* **sokutatsu yūbin**
超音速 *supersonic speed* **chōonsoku**
速射砲 *rapid-firing gun* **sokushahō**
高速道路 *highway, express way* **kōsodōro**

疾*peedy, 681*	運*riving, 295*
迅*peedy, 95*	走*unning, 497*
早*arly, 373*	動*ovement, 422*

遠*istant, 916*

413-A

包rapped in Dad's 抱mbrace, Baby Grace...

ク (wrapping)

包rapping 包nveloping

tsutsu(mu), HŌ
wrapping, enveloping, sheath, covering, encompassing

Facing: 1.1. West (H)

包丁 *kitchen-, butcher's knife* **hōchō**
⇒肉切り包丁 *meat knife* **nikugiri bōchō**
包含 *inclusion, implication* **hōgan**
包皮 *foreskin* **hōhi**
包皮切断 *circumcision* **hōhi setsudan**
包囲 *siege, encirclement, raid* **hōi**
包括 *inclusion, siege, encirclement* **hōkatsu**
包括的 *comprehensive, sweeping* **hōkatsuteki**
包茎 *phimosis* **hōkei**
包摂 *subsuming, connotation* **hōsetsu**
包装 *packaging, packing, wrapping* **hōsō**
包装紙 *wrapping-, packing paper* **hōsōshi**
包帯 *bandage, dressing, gauze* **hōtai**
包容 *tolerance, magnanimity, generosity* **hōyō**
包蔵 *contain; implying* **hōzō**
梱包 *packaging, packing, wrapping* **konpō**
空包 *blank gun cartridge* **kūhō**
内包 *connotation, implication* **naihō**
薬包 *bullet cartridge* **yakuhō**

薬包紙 *medicine paper wrapper* **yakuhōshi**
紙包み *paper parcel, paper-wrapped* **kamizutsumi**
薦包み *straw mat wrapper* **komozutsumi**
小包み *parcel, small package* **kozutsumi**
上包み *wrapping cover* **uwazutsumi**
包み隠し *concealing, hidden* **tsutsumikakushi**
包み飾り *ostentatious display* **tsutsumikazari**
包み込む *wrapping-, packing up* **tsutsumikomu**
包み直す *rewrapping, repacking* **tsutsuminaosu**

囲nclose, 361	合ogether, 232
郭nclose, 398	括undle, 954
巻oll-up, 391	集ather, 50

已elf, 5

413-B

包rapped in Dad's 抱mbrace, Baby Grace...

手⇔扌 (hand, manual)

❶抱mbrace ❷抱mploy

da(ku); ida(ku); kaka(eru), HŌ
embrace, hugging; employ

Facing: 1.2. West (V)

❶抱っこ *hug, hold in one's arms* **dakko**
抱き合う *embrace, hold each other* **dakiau**
抱き込む *win over another, bribe* **dakikomu**
抱き付く *hug another's arms* **dakitsuku**
抱き合わせ *bundling, tie in* **dakiawase**
抱き抱える *carry in one's arms* **dakikakaeru**
抱き起こす *raise in one's arms* **dakiokosu**
抱き締める *hold, hug, embrace,* **dakishimeru**
抱き竦める *tight embrace* **dakisukumeru**
抱き止める *hold (someone) back* **dakitomeru**
抱き寄せる *hug onto one's breast* **dakiyoseru**
抱き上げる *take up in one's arms* **dakiageru**
一抱え *"an armful of..."* **hitokakae**
抱負 *ambition, wish* **hōfu**
抱懐 *harbour, cherish* **hōkai**
抱括 *inclusive, sweeping* **hōkatsu**
抱卵 *incubation, hatchery* **hōran**
抱擁 *embrace, hug* **hōyō**
介抱 *care, nursing* **kaihō**

抱え込む *be perplexed, be puzzled* **kakaekomu**
辛抱 *patience, indulgence* **shinbō**
丸抱え *full provider* **marugakae**
抱腹絶倒 *roaring laughter* **hōfuku zettō**
辛抱強い *patient, persevering* **shinbōzuyoi**

❷抱え主 *employer* **kakaenushi**
召し抱える *hire, recruit* **meshikakaeru**

採mploy, 915	伝onvey, 619
使tilize, 480	逓onvey, 304
用urpose, 409	受eceive, 539

泡ubbles, 689

414-A

Dead 身ody after 射hooting 身elf in a tragedy...

❶身elf　　**❷身ody**

身 (self, body)

mi, SHIN
self, one's person; body

Facing: 1.0. ☞ West (W)

❶護身 *self-protection, defence* **goshin**
変身 *personal transformation* **henshin**
保身 *self-protection, self-preservation* **hoshin**
身頃 *body, oneself* **migoro**
身近 *familiar, common* **mijika**
身元 *personal identity* **mimoto**
終身 *remainder of one's life, for life* **shūshin**
出身 *native of~ (Tōkyō-born)* **shusshin**
前身 *one's previous life* **zenshin**
献身的 *charity, giving to others* **kenshinteki**
身構え *posture, attitude* **migamae**
身の上話 *life story* **minouebanashi**
自分自身 *oneself, one's person* **jibun jishin**
身の回り *personal belongings* **mi no mawari**
身びいき *nepotism, favouritism* **mibiiki**
身の代金 *ransom money* **minoshirokin**
身分 *identity, self, status* **mibun**
身分証明書 *identification card* **mibun shōmeisho**
❷脂身 *body fat* **aburami**

病身 *illness, sickness* **byōshin**
銃身 *barrel of a gun* **jūshin**
肩身 *face, honour* **katami**
黄身 *egg yoke* **kimi**
身長 *height, body length* **shinchō**
心身 *mind & body* **shinshin**
身体 *human body* **shintai**
全身 *whole body* **zenshin**
身寄り *relatives, relation* **miyori**
刺し身 *fresh raw fish cuisine* **sashimi**
打ち身 *wound, bruise* **uchimi**
受け身 *apathy, passiveness, lethargy* **ukemi**
肩身が狭い *feeling ashamed* **katami ga semai**
肩身が広い *feeling proud* **katami ga hiroi**

我elf, 443	自elf, 462	己elf, 5

自elf, 462

414-B

Dead 身ody after 射hooting 身elf in a tragedy...

射hooting　　**射rojectile**

寸 (measurement)

i(ru), SHA
shoot, projectile, splash, hurling, thrusting

Facing: 1.2. ☞ West (V)

直射 *direct rays* **chokusha**
注射 *injection, hypodermic, inoculation* **chūsha**
注射液 *injection fluid* **chūshaeki**
注射器 *syringe, injection device* **chūshaki**
噴射 *jet speed* **funsha**
誤射 *accidental firing, "friendly fire..."* **gosha**
反射 *reflection, contemplation* **hansha**
⇒条件反射 *conditioned response* **jōken hansha**
発射 *firing, shooting* **hassha**
放射 *radiation, emission* **hōsha**
射手 *marksman, sharpshooter* **shashu**
射手座 *Sagittarius, archer* **iteza**
射止める *shoot, win* **itomeru**
騎射 *horseback archery* **kisha**
猛射 *heavy gunfire* **mōsha**
日射 *solar radiation* **nissha**
乱射 *indiscriminate firing, trigger-happy* **ransha**
射爆 *fire bomb, incendiary bomb* **shabaku**
射撃 *firing, shooting* **shageki**

射殺 *shooting to death* **shasatsu**
射精 *ejaculation, organism, climax, coming* **shasei**
射程 *shooting range, target range* **shatei**
射的 *target shooting* **shateki**
試射 *test firing, target shooting* **shisha**
照射 *irradiation, radiation* **shōsha**
速射 *rapid firing* **sokusha**
掃射 *machine-gunning* **sōsha**
投射 *projection* **tōsha**
射抜く *shoot thru* **inuku**
熱射病 *heatstroke, sunstroke* **nesshabyō**

泉prings, 531
打trike, 636

謝pology, 876

415-A

垂angling 錘pindle, hopes rekindle...

 垂angle   垂ang down

土 (ground, soil)

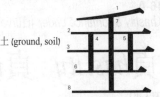

FLIP: 2.0.a. Sort Of (flat)

ta(reru), ta(rasu), SUI
dangle, hang down, flapping

垂らす *drip, hang down* **tarasu**
虫垂 *appendix* **chūsui**
虫垂炎 *appendicitis* **chūsuien**
下垂 *dangle, hang down* **kasui**
懸垂 *chinning, chin-up* **kensui**
枝垂れ柳 *weeping willow* **shidareyanagi**
枝垂れ桜 *weeping cherry* **shidarezakura**
垂直 *vertical, perpendicularity* **suichoku**
垂直面 *vertical surface* **suichokumen**
垂直線 *perpendicular line* **suichokusen**
垂範 *set a good example* **suihan**
垂迹 *Buddhist manifestation for humanity* **suijaku**
垂下 *dangle, hang down* **suika**
垂訓 *teaching, instruction* **suikun**
垂線 *perpendicular line* **suisen**
垂死 *verge of death, dying moments* **suishi**
垂心 *orthocentre* **suishin**
垂涎 *watering mouth* **suizen**
垂髪 *hair drooping down* **taregami**

垂木 *rafter, float, buoy* **taruki**
雨垂れ *raindrops* **amadare**
胃下垂 *gastroptosis* **ikasui**
耳垂れ *running ears* **mimidare**
垂れ幕 *curtain, veil* **taremaku**
垂れ流し *effluence, discharge* **tarenagashi**
垂れ耳 *flopped ears* **taremimi**
前垂れ *apron* **maedare**
項垂れる *drooping one's head* **unadareru**
潮垂れる *shed lots of tears* **shiotareru**
脳下垂体 *pituitary gland* **nōka suitai**

掛*ang up, 107*   懸*anging, 566*
架*anging, 202*

乗*ide on, 511*   郵*ostal office, 948*

415-B

垂angling 錘pindle, hopes rekindle...

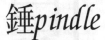 錘pindle

金 (metal)

FLIP: 7.1. Right (Sort Of)

tsumu, omori, SUI
spindle

紡錘 *spindle* **bōsui**
紡錘形 *spindle form, ~shape* **bōsuikei**
鉛錘 *plumb* **ensui**
休錘 *unused spindles* **kyūsui**
錘状 *spindle-shaped* **suijō**
平衡錘 *counterweight* **heikōsui**

針*eedle, 692*   紡*pinning, 735*
縫*ewing, 779*   回*otate, 458*
繰*pinning, 851*

錠*adlock, 550*

416-A

貞 *hastity & romance under* 偵 *urveillance...*

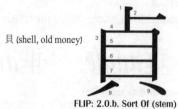

貝 (shell, old money)

貞 *hastity*   貞 *idelity*

TEI, JŌ
fidelity, chastity, puritanism, continence

FLIP: 2.0.b. Sort Of (stem)

忠貞 chastity, fidelity, faithfulness **chūtei**
童貞 virginity, chastity (male) **dōtei**
不貞 unfaithful, adulterous **futei**
不貞寝 stay in bed sulking **futene**
不貞腐れる be spiteful, scornful **futekusareru**
貞婦 chaste, virtuous woman **teifu**
貞実 devoted, faithful, loyal **teijitsu**
貞女 chaste, virtuous woman **teijo**
貞潔 chaste, virtuous **teiketsu**
貞烈 chaste, virtuous **teiretsu**
貞節 chastity, faithfulness **teisetsu**
貞淑 virtue, chastity **teishuku**
貞操 chastity, fidelity, faithfulness **teisō**
貞操帯 chastity belt **teisōtai**
安貞時代 Antei Era (1227-1229) **antei jidai**
貞永時代 Jōei Era (1232-1233) **jōei jidai**
貞観時代 Jōgan Era (859-877) **jōgan jidai**
貞治時代 Jōji Era (1362-1368) **jōji jidai**
貞享時代 Jōkyō Era (1684-1688) **jōkyō jidai**

貞応時代 Jōō Era (1222-1224) **jōō jidai**

爵 oyalty, 593	愛 ove, 593
忠 oyalty, 475	恋 ove, 581
孝 ilial, 385	徳 irtue, 844

貝 *hellfish, 516*

416-B

貞 *hastity & romance under* 偵 *urveillance...*

人⇔亻 (person)

偵 *urveillance*   偵 *spionage*

TEI
surveillance, detective, espionage, spy

FLIP: 7.1. Right (Sort Of)

密偵 spy, secret agent **mittei**
内偵 conducting secret inquiries **naitei**
探偵 detective work **tantei**
探偵小説 detective novel **tantei shōsetsu**
偵知 spying, surveillance **teichi**
偵察 reconnaissance, scouting **teisatsu**
偵察機 reconnaissance plane **teisatsuki**
偵察隊 reconnaissance squad **teisatsutai**

察 nspection, 328	検 nspection, 939
審 nspection, 339	査 nspection, 624
調 nspection, 280	閲 nspection, 942

貞 *hastity, 506*

417-A
荒ough 慌anic, abandon the Titanic...!

++ (grass)

荒ough　荒urbulent

ara(i), a(reru), a(rasu), KŌ
rough, turbulent, untamed, wild, brusque

荒っぽい　unrefined-, rough, crude **arappoi**
荒れ地　waste land, barren **arechi**
荒れ野　wilderness, the wilds **areno**
荒れ狂う　rage, fury, madness **arekurū**
荒れ果てる　be desolated **arehateru**
荒家　dilapidated-, run down house **abaraya**
荒肝　"frightened to the liver..." **aragimo**
荒行　austerity, discipline **aragyō**
荒物　wild-, despondent person **aramono**
荒波　violent waters, rough seas **aranami**
荒縄　straw rope **aranawa**
荒荷　rough cargo **arani**
荒馬　wild-, untamed horse **arauma**
荒海　rough sea, roaring waves **araumi**
荒技　rough-, raw technique **arawaza**
備荒　famine preparedness **bikō**
荒土　waste land, barren **kōdo**
荒廃　devastation, ruins, desolation **kōhai**
荒淫　debauchery **kōin**

Facing: 4.0. ⟿⟾ Apart
FLIP: 3.0.b. Top (stem)

荒城　ruined castle **kōjō**
荒天　stormy-, rough weather **kōten**
荒野　waste land, barren **kōya**
荒稼ぎ　profiteering, make a killing **arakasegi**
一荒れ　burst of rage **hitoare**
荒仕事　arm-twisting work **arashigoto**
荒くれ男　roughneck **arakureotoko**
吹き荒ぶ　blow hard, storm violently **fukisusabu**
踏み荒らす　trample, ravage **fumiarasu**
食い荒らす　eating like a beast **kuiarasu**

慌anic, 507	虞nxiety, 889
濁urbid, 924	煩nxiety, 832
争onflict, 231	暴ampage, 561

流current, 781

417-B
荒ough 慌anic, abandon the Titanic...!

慌anic　慌renzy　慌urried

心⟷忄⟷⺗ (feelings)

awa(teru), awa(tadashii), KŌ
panic, frenzy, hurried, hysteria, pandemonium, stampede

慌ただしい　unsettled, hurried, flushed **awatadashii**
慌てふためく　panic, frenzy **awatefutameku**
慌て者　scattered brain, absent-mindedness **awatemono**
恐慌　panic, hysteria, pandemonium **kyōkō**
大慌て　hot haste **ōawate**
大恐慌　① great panic, pandemonium **daikyōkō**
大恐慌　② Great Depression **daikyōkō**

Facing: 4.0. ⟿⟾ Apart
FLIP: 7.2.b. Right Top (stem)

荒urbulent, 507	虞nxiety, 889
濁urbid, 924	煩nxiety, 832
争onflict, 231	暴ampage, 561

荒urbulent, 507

418-A

Icebergs solid, by summer 夜*venings* 液*iquid...*

夕 (evening, night)

夜*vening*　夜*ightfall*

yoru, yo, YA
evening, nightfall, night time

FLIP: 7.1. Right (Sort Of)
Facing: 1.1. 🕊 West (H)

昼夜 *day & night* **chūya**
一夜 *one night, all night long* **ichiya, hitoya, hitoyo**
今夜 *this evening, tonight* **konya**
昨夜 *last night* **sakuya**
深夜 *midnight, dead-of-the-night* **shinya**
徹夜 *staying up all night* **tetsuya**
夜学 *night-, evening school* **yagaku**
夜具 *bedding, bedclothes* **yagu**
夜陰 *nights darkness* **yain**
夜会 *soiree, evening party* **yakai**
夜会服 *evening dress, formal attire* **yakaifuku**
夜間 *night, night time* **yakan**
夜景 *night scenery* **yakei**
夜警 *night watchman* **yakei**
夜勤 *night duty, ~shift, ~work* **yakin**
夜勤手当 *night work allowance* **yakin teate**
夜目 *in the dark* **yome**
夜中 *midnight, dead-of-the-night* **yonaka**
夜空 *night sky, evening sky* **yozora**

昼も夜も *day & night, 24 hours* **hirumo yorumo**
星月夜 *starlight night, starry night* **hoshizukiyo**
十五夜 *night of a full moon* **jūgoya**
夜明け *daybreak, dawn* **yoake**
夜汽車 *night train* **yogisha**
夜なべ *night work* **yonabe**
夜泣き *crying at night* **yonaki**
夜逃げ *flee at night* **yonige**
秋の夜長 *long autumn nights* **aki no yonaga**
夜郎自大 *arrogant, haughty, egoistic* **yarōjidai**
夜な夜な *night after night* **yonayona**

夕 *vening*, 187	眠 *leeping*, 495
晩 *vening*, 413	寝 *leeping*, 769
月 *oon*, 22	睡 *leeping*, 948

液 *iquid*, 508

418-B

Icebergs solid, by summer 夜*venings* 液*iquid...*

水⇔氵 (water)

液*iquid*　液*luid*　液*atery*

EKI
liquid, fluid, watery

FLIP: 7.1. Right (Sort Of)
Facing: 1.1. 🕊 West (H)

唾液 *saliva* **daeki**
毒液 *poison liquid* **dokueki**
液状 *liquidness, liquidity* **ekijō**
液汁 *juice; sap* **ekijū**
液化 *liquefaction, liquidization* **ekika**
液量 *liquid amount* **ekiryō**
液晶 *liquid crystal* **ekishō**
液晶テレビ *LCD television* **ekishō terebi**
液体 *liquid, fluid* **ekitai**
液体燃料 *liquid fuel* **ekitai nenryō**
液剤 *liquid medicine* **ekizai**
廃液 *waste water, liquid waste* **haieki**
排液 *drainage* **haieki**
胃液 *gastric juice* **ieki**
樹液 *sap, tree juice (rubber)* **jueki**
血液 *blood* **ketsueki**
血液型 *blood type* **ketsueki gata**
粘液 *mucus, viscous liquid* **nen'eki**
乳液 *milky lotion, latex* **nyūeki**

精液 *semen, sperm* **seieki**
体液 *body fluids* **taieki**
薬液 *liquid medicine* **yakueki**
溶液 *solution, liquid* **yōeki**
⇒飽和溶液 *saturated solution* **hōwa yōeki**
培養液 *cultured fluid, ~solution* **baiyōeki**
注射液 *injection (liquid)* **chūshaeki**
不凍液 *anti-freeze* **futōeki**
消毒液 *anti-septive solution* **shōdokueki**
消化液 *digestive juices* **shōkaeki**
水溶液 *aqueous solution* **suiyōeki**

水 *ater*, 9	透 *ransparency*, 383
雨 *aining*, 417	

夜 *vening*, 508

419-A

為n order to go abroad, commit no 偽raud...

為n order to   為urpose

火⇔灬 (fire)

tame, na(su), I
in order to, purpose, function

Facing: 2.0. East ☞ (W)

為政 governing, administering **isei**
敢為 daring, bold, audacious **kan'i**
為替 money order, exchange **kawase**
⇒円為替 yen currency exchange **enkawase**
⇒小為替 postal money order **kogawase**
⇒荷為替 documentary bill **nigawase**
⇒郵便為替 postal money order **yūbin kawase**
為替管理 currency exchange controls **kawase kanri**
為替相場 exchange rate **kawase sōba**
為替手形 bill-of-exchange, draft **kawase tegata**
行為 conduct, act **kōi**
⇒性行為 sexual intercourse **seikōi**
⇒越権行為 arrogation, abuse of power **ekken kōi**
⇒不正行為 cheating, irregularity **fusei kōi**
⇒背徳行為 immoral conduct **haitoku kōi**
⇒犯罪行為 criminal act, felony **hanzai kōi**
⇒違法行為 illegal act **ihō kōi**
⇒汚職行為 malversation, embezzlement **oshoku kōi**
⇒侵略行為 act of aggression **shinryaku kōi**

⇒敵対行為 hostility, antagonism **tekitai kōi**
⇒残虐行為 cruel act, atrocity, barbarity
　　 zangyaku kōi
無為 idleness, lethargy **mui**
無為無策 lack of policy, ~direction **mui musaku**
無作為 unintentional, accidental **musakui**
作為 intentional behaviour **sakui**
為所 "in the meantime..." **shidokoro**
有為 promising, talented, capable **yūi**
為残す leave something unfinished **shinokosu**
人為的 artificial, man-made **jin'iteki**
為遂げる complete one's job **shitogeru**

用tilize, 409	措easures, 282
応omply, 469	策olicy, 875
従omply, 551	略ummary, 825

偽raud, 509

419-B

為n order to go abroad, commit no 偽raud...

偽raudulent   偽eceit

人⇔亻 (person)

itsuwa(ru), nise, GI
bogus, cheating, deceit, dupe, fraudulent, phony, pseudo, deception, trickery

Facing: 4.0. ☜☞ Apart

偽り lie, falsehood **itsuwari**
偽り者 hypocrite, pretender **itsuwarimono**
偽悪 pretending to be bad **giaku**
偽物 imitation, phoney, impostor **gibutsu, nisemono**
偽版 pirated copy **gihan**
偽筆 forged handwriting **gihitsu**
偽印 fake seal, forged seal **giin**
偽名 false name, alias, nom-de-guerre **gimei**
偽作 counterfeit, fake, forgery, phoney **gisaku**
偽史 fake history **gishi**
偽書 fake-, falsified documents **gisho**
偽称 stolen identity, impostor **gishō**
偽証 false evidence, perjury **gishō**
偽証罪 perjury, false statement **gishōzai**
偽装 disguise, dummy **gisō**
偽装殺人 fake murderer **gisō satsujin**
偽善 hypocrisy, fake behaviour **gizen**
偽善者 hypocrite, pretender **gizensha**
偽善的 hypocritical, feigned behaviour **gizenteki**

偽造 forgery, fabrication **gizō**
偽造罪 forgery, sham, fabrication **gizōzai**
虚偽 lie, falsehood **kyogi**
偽金 counterfeit coins **nisegane**
偽薬 placebo, fake drugs **nisegusuri**
偽膜 false membrane **nisemaku**
偽者 impostor, fake **nisemono**
偽札 forged paper money **nisesatsu**
真偽 genuine-or-fake, authenticity **shingi**
偽学生 bogus student **nisegakusei**

欺raudulent, 658	邪vil, 58
詐raudulent, 723	凶vil, 80
罪riminal, 289	悪vil, 389
犯riminal, 640	

為n order to, 509

420-A

叔ounger-uncles & 叔ounger-aunts can be so 淑legant...

又 (again)

^❶叔*ounger uncle* ^❷叔*ounger aunt*

SHUKU

young uncle; young aunt *(younger sibling of one's parent)*

FLIP: 7.0.b2. Right (stem)

❶伯叔 *brothers & uncle* **hakushuku**
叔父 *uncle (younger than parent)* **oji**
大叔父 *grand uncle* **ōoji**
叔世 *age of decline* **shukusei**

❷叔母 *aunt (younger than parent)* **oba**, **shukubo**
大叔母 *grand aunt* **ōoba**

若*oung, 276*	妹*ounger sister, 114*
嬢*oung girl, 854*	伯*lder-uncle, 741*
弟*ounger brother, 102*	伯*lder-aunt, 741*

叔*arrate, 648*

420-B

叔ounger-uncles & 叔ounger-aunts can be so 淑legant...

水⇔氵 (water)

淑*raceful*　　淑*legant*

shito(yaka), SHUKU

graceful, elegant

FLIP: 7.0.b2. Right (stem)

私淑 *adoration, reverence* **shishuku**
淑女 *lady, young woman* **shukujo**
淑徳 *feminine elegance, ~grace* **shukutoku**
貞淑 *chastity, fidelity, faithfulness* **teishuku**

韻*raceful, 315*	麗*eautiful, 68*
雅*raceful, 58*	佳*eauty, 891*
美*eautiful, 124*	女*oman, 350*

叔*oung uncle, 510*

421-A
Load 乗board the 剰urplus of gourds...

丿 (katakana の)

乗board   乗ide on

no(ru), no(seru), JŌ
aboard, ride on, get on, loading

FLIP: 2.0.b. Sort Of (stem)

便乗 *getting a ride, taking advantage* **binjō**
同乗 *take advantage, avail of* **dōjō**
乗馬 *horseriding, equestrian* **jōba**
乗除 *multiplication & division* **jōjo**
乗客 *passenger* **jōkyaku**
乗数 *multiplier* **jōsū**
階乗 *factorial* **kaijō**
二乗 *multiply by itself* **nijō**
試乗 *test ride, trial run* **shijō**
搭乗 *riding, boarding, embarking* **tōjō**
船乗り *sailor, seaman, mariner* **funanori**
乗務員 *vehicle crew* **jōmuin**
曲乗り *air stunt, aerobatics* **kyokunori**
波乗り *surfing, surfboarding* **naminori**
乗り気 *interest, enthusiasm, eagerness* **noriki**
乗り手 *passenger, rider* **norite**
只乗り *stolen ride, free loading* **tadanori**
添乗員 *tour conductor, ~guide* **tenjōin**
搭乗員 *crew, member* **tōjōin**

乗車券 *transporation ticket* **jōshaken**
搭乗券 *boarding pass* **tōjōken**
搭乗者 *passenger* **tōjōsha**
遠乗り *long-distance ride, ~drive* **toonori**
乗り合い *riding together* **noriai**
乗り換え *transfer, change trains* **norikae**
乗り越す *ride past* **norikosu**
乗り降り *getting on & off* **noriori**
乗り移る *transfer, change into* **noriutsuru**
乗っ取り *hijacking, commandeering* **nottori**
乗っ取る *hijack, take over* **nottoru**
乗り越える *overcome, surmount* **norikoeru**

荷*reight, 877*   搭*reight, 146*
貨*reight, 191*   車*ehicle, 306*

垂*ang down, 505*

421-B
Load 乗board the 剰urplus of gourds...

刀⇔刂 (blade, cutting)

剰urplus   剰xtra

amatsusa(e), JŌ
surplus, extra, besides

Facing: 1.2. ☜ West (V)

剰語 *word redundancy, verbose* **jōgo**
剰語 *word redundancy, verbose* **jōgo**
剰費 *unnecessary expenses* **jōhi**
剰員 *superfluous member* **jōin**
剰余 *surplus, excess* **jōyo**
剰余金 *surplus fund* **jōyokin**
剰余価値 *surplus value* **jōyo kachi**
過剰 *surplus, excess, extra* **kajō**
余剰 *surplus, excess, extra* **yojō**
余剰物資 *excess goods* **yojō busshi**
余剰人員 *excess workers* **yojō jin'in**
自意識過剰 *overly self-conscious* **jiishiki kajō**

余*urplus, 501*   繁*rosperity, 434*
豊*bundance, 965*   隆*rosperity, 133*
富*ortune, 333*   盛*lrosperity, 244*
裕*ffluence, 758*   多*lenty, 187*

乗*ide on, 511*

422-A

洪*loods in Ann Arbor stopped by* 港*arbour...*

水⇔氵 (water)

洪*looding* 洪*nundation*

KŌ
flooding, inundation, deluge

FLIP: 7.0.b2. Right (stem)

洪大 *vast-, immense flooding* **kōdai**
洪荒 *flood, inundation, deluge* **kōkō**
洪水 *flooding, inundation, deluge* **kōzui**
洪積世 *diluvial epoch* **kōsekisei**
洪積層 *diluvium* **kōsekisō**

港*arbour, 512*	川*iver, 76*
津*arbour, 731*	堤*mbankment, 314*
河*iver, 877*	州*andbank, 76*

浜*each, 490*

422-B

洪*loods in Ann Arbor stopped by* 港*arbour...*

水⇔氵 (water)

港*arbour* 港*ort*

minato, KŌ
harbour, port

FLIP: 7.2.b. Right Top (stem)

母港 *home port* **bokō**
築港 *harbour construction* **chikkō**
軍港 *naval port* **gunkō**
漁港 *fishing port* **gyokō**
香港 *Hong Kong, China* **honkon**
開港 *open port* **kaikō**
寄港 *port call (visiting ships)* **kikō**
帰港 *returning to one's port* **kikō**
港口 *harbour entrance* **kōkō**
港門 *harbour entrance* **kōmon**
港内 *in the harbour* **kōnai**
港都 *port city* **kōto**
港湾 *harbour, port* **kōwan**
港税 *harbour fees* **kōzei**
空港 *airport* **kūkō**
港町 *port town* **minatomachi**
内港 *inner harbour* **naikō**
入港 *entering port* **nyūkō**
商港 *trading port* **shōkō**

出港 *leave port, sailing* **shukkō**
要港 *strategic port* **yōkō**
船積港 *port-of-shipment, ~origin* **funazumikō**
不凍港 *ice-free port* **futōkō**
河口港 *estuary harbour* **kakōkō**
寄港地 *port-of-call* **kikōchi**
港祭り *harbour festival* **minatomatsuri**
陸揚港 *port-of-discharge, ~unloading* **rikuagekō**
商業港 *trading port* **shōgyōkō**
輸出港 *export port, out port* **yushutsukō**
積み出し港 *port-of-origin* **tsumidashikō**

津*arbour, 731*	搭*reight, 146*	船*hip, 757*
輸*hipment, 660*	丸*[ships], 73*	舶*hip, 742*
荷*reight, 877*	隻*[ships], 50*	帆*ailing, 641*
貨*reight, 191*	舟*oat, 90*	

湾*ulf, 909*

423-A

死ead man's 葬urial seemed unreal...

死eath   死emise

歹 (dried bones)

死

shi(nu), SHI
death, dead, demise, dying, passing away

Facing: 4.0. 🕳️🕳️ Apart

圧死 crushed to death **asshi**
病死 death by illness **byōshi**
餓死 starved to death, famine **gashi**
獄死 die in prison **gokushi**
必死 desperate, despondent **hisshi**
情死 lovers' suicide **jōshi**
殉死 death on duty **junshi**
脳死 brain dead **nōshi**
戦死 death in combat, killed in action **senshi**
死亡 death, demise, passing away **shibō**
死骸 cadaver, corpse, carcass **shigai**
死後 after one's death **shigo**
死因 cause of death **shiin**
死児 born dead, dead baby **shiji**
死海 Dead Sea **shikai**
死角 blind spot, hidden angle **shikaku**
死活 life & death **shikatsu**
死活問題 matter of life-or-death **shikatsu mondai**
死刑 death penalty, capital punishment **shikei**

死期 hour, time of death **shiki**
死去 death, passing away **shikyo**
惨死 tragic-, painful death **zanshi**
安楽死 euthanasia, mercy killing **anrakushi**
死に花 glorious death **shi(ni)bana**
死に顔 dead face **shi(ni)gao**
死に目 deathbed **shi(ni)me**
死に水 alcohol poured on the dead (funeral)
　　shi(ni)mizu
若死に early death, short life, die young **wakaji(ni)**
死にかける kill almost, near death **shi(ni)kakeru**
死に絶える die out, extinct **shi(ni)taeru**

逝eath, 54	患ickness, 475
亡eath, 72	症ickness, 788
葬urial, 513	病ickness, 213

港arbour, 512

423-B

死ead man's 葬urial seemed unreal...

葬urial   葬nterment

艹 (grass)

葬

hōmu(ru), SŌ
burial, interment, entomb

FLIP: 3.0.b. Top (stem)
Facing: 4.0. 🕳️🕳️ Apart

仏葬 Buddhist funeral **bussō**
鳥葬 leaving a corpse to the vultures **chōsō**
土葬 ground burial, interment **dosō**
風葬 leaving a corpse to the elements **fūsō**
合葬 joint funeral **gōsō**
軍葬 military funeral **gunsō**
本葬 formal funeral **honsō**
改葬 reburial, reinterment **kaisō**
会葬 funeral service **kaisō**
海葬 ocean interment, sea burial **kaisō**
仮葬 temporary interment **kasō**
火葬 cremation **kasō**
国葬 state funeral **kokusō**
埋葬 burial, interment **maisō**
密葬 private funeral **missō**
社葬 funeral at workplace **shasō**
神葬 Shintō funeral **shinsō**
葬儀 funeral service **sōgi**
葬儀場 funeral hall **sōgijō**

葬儀屋 mortician, funeral director **sōgiya**
葬具 funeral ornaments (Buddhist) **sōgu**
葬礼 funeral **sōrei**
葬列 funeral march, ~procession **sōretsu**
葬祭 funeral service **sōsai**
⇒冠婚葬祭 ceremonial occasion **kankon sōsai**
葬式 funeral ceremony **sōshiki**
葬送 funeral attendance, paying last respect **sōsō**
水葬 ocean interment, sea burial **suisō**
大葬 imperial-, royal funeral **taisō**
葬り去る bury, inter **hōmurisaru**

亡eath, 72	喪ourning, 119
死eath, 513	悼ourning, 499
逝eath, 54	弔ourning, 538
忌ourning, 6	

死eath, 513

424-A

専xclusively for artists with high 博xpertise...

専xclusive 専pecialty

寸 (measurement)

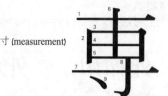

moppa(ra), SEN
exclusive, specialty

FLIP: 3.0.a. Top (flat)

専売 monopoly **senbai**
専売品 specialty goods **senbaihin**
専断 arbitrary-, one-sided decision **sendan**
専業 full-time job, ~occupation **sengyō**
専業農家 full-time farmer **sengyō nōka**
専一 utmost importance **sen'itsu**
専従 full-time work **senjū**
専科 special course **senka**
専管 exclusive jurisdiction, ~administration **senkan**
専権 abuse of power, ~authority **senken**
専攻 specialty, specialization, majoring **senkō**
専門 expertise, specialty, profession **senmon**
専門家 specialist, professional **senmonka**
専門店 specialty store **senmonten**
専門学校 specialization school **senmon gakkō**
専念 devotion, concentration **sennen**
専任 regular staff, full time **sennin**
専横 high-handed, arbitrary, one-sided **sen'ō**
専制 despotism, autocracy, tyranny **sensei**

専制的 despotic, autocratic **senseiteki**
専制君主 autocrat, despot, tyrant **sensei kunshu**
専制主義 absolutism, despotism **sensei shugi**
専心 devotion, concentration **senshin**
専修 special course, ~study **senshū**
専用 exclusive use **senyō**
⇒女性専用 "reserved for women..." **josei senyō**
専用機 private jet, personal plane **senyōki**
専有 exclusive possession **senyū**
専属 belonging exclusively **senzoku**
専攻科目 course specialization **senkō kamoku**

家xpert, 909	修aster, 898
師xpert, 483	巧killful, 738
博xpertise, 514	術kills, 110

博xpertise, 514

424-B

専xclusively for artists with high 博xpertise...

博xpertise 博rofessional

十 (cross)

HAKU, BAKU
expertise, professional, proficiency, forte, mastery

FLIP: 7.2.a. Right Top (flat)

博打 gambling, betting **bakuchi**
博労 horse trading **bakurō**
博徒 gambler, bettor **bakuto**
万博 world fair, world expo **banpaku**
該博 extensive-, profound knowledge **gaihaku**
博士 doctorate, doctoral **hakase, hakashi**
⇒法学博士 doctor of laws **hōgaku hakushi**
⇒医学博士 doctor of medicine, M.D. **igaku hakushi**
博士号 doctorate, Ph.D. **hakasegō, hakushigō**
博士課程 doctoral course **hakashi katei**
博愛 philanthropy, charity **hakuai**
博物学 natural history **hakubutsugaku**
博物館 museum **hakubutsukan**
博大 thorough, extensive, encompassing **hakudai**
博雅 extensive knowledge **hakuga**
博学 broad knowledge, extensive study **hakugaku**
博覧 extensive reading; public exhibit **hakuran**

博覧会 expo, fair, exhibition **hakurankai**
⇒万国博覧会 international exposition
  bankoku hakurankai
博識 extensive-, profound knowledge **hakushiki**
賭博 gambling, betting **tobaku**
博士論文 doctoral dissertation **hakushi ronbun**

専xclusive, 514	術kills, 110
家xpert, 909	学tudy, 346
師xpert, 483	教ducate, 385
修aster, 898	習earning, 238
巧killful, 738	特pecial, 250

専xclusive, 514

425-A

Life 延xtension, on 誕irthday occasion...

廴 (stretch)

延rolong 延xtend

no(basu) no(beru) no(biru), EN
prolong, extend, lengthen, protract, stretch, delay

Facing: 4.0. ◁▷ Apart

圧延	*extended pressure* **atsuen**
遅延	*delay, postponement* **chien**
延着	*delay, late arrival* **enchaku**
延長	*extension, deferment* **enchō**
延引	*delay, postponement* **en'in**
延会	*postponement, adjournment* **enkai**
延期	*postponement, adjournment* **enki**
延命	*prolonged existence, longevity* **enmei**
延納	*deferred payment* **ennō**
延発	*prolonged departure* **enpatsu**
延性	*ductility, elasticity* **ensei**
延焼	*spread of fire* **enshō**
延滞	*arrears, overdue payment* **entai**
外延	*extension, prolongation* **gaien**
延縄	*trawl line* **haenawa**
順延	*postponement, deferment* **jun'en**
蔓延	*spread; prevail* **man'en**
日延べ	*postpone, extend, delay* **hinobe**
間延び	*slow, dull* **manobi**

延べ坪	*total floor space* **nobe tsubo**
延べ払い	*deferred payment* **nobe barai**
延べ時間	*man-hours* **nobe jikan**
延べ人員	*total man-days* **nobe jin'in**
延べ日数	*total number of days* **nobe nissū**
延び延び	*postponement* **nobinobi**
生き延びる	*live, outlive, survive* **ikinobiru**
繰り延べる	*postpone, delay* **kurinoberu**
落ち延びる	*escape safely* **ochinobiru**

伸*tretch, 713*	力*trength, 351*
張*tretch, 274*	勢*igour, 153*
努*fforts, 44*	精*igour, 792*
勉*fforts, 527*	将*uture, 521*

延*ourt-of-law, 26*

425-B

Life 延xtension, on 誕irthday occasion...

言 (speaking)

誕irthday 誕hildbirth

TAN
birthday, childbirth, nativity

FLIP: 6.0.a. Left (flat)
Facing: 4.0. ◁▷ Apart

降誕	*Nativity, birth of Jesus Christ* **kōtan**
荒誕	*silly, nonsense* **kōtan**
虚誕	*made-up, trumped-up* **kyotan**
生誕	*birthday, nativity* **seitan**
聖誕祭	*Christmas Day* **seitansai**
誕生	*birth* **tanjō**
誕生日	*birthday* **tanjōbi**
誕生地	*birthplace* **tanjōchi**
誕生家	*birth house* **tanjōka**
誕生石	*birth stone* **tanjōseki**
誕生祝い	*birthday celebration* **tanjōiwai**
誕辰	*birthday* **tanshin**

生*ife, 474*	産*hildbirth, 883*
命*ife, 362*	人*uman, 2*
性*ature, 474*	

延*rolong, 515*

426-A

Figurine 貝 hells encased, all 買 urchased...

貝 (shell, old money)

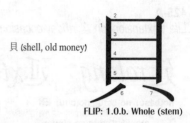

貝 *hellfish*

kai
shellfish

赤貝 *ark shell* **akagai**
青貝 *mother-of-pearl* **aogai**
蝶貝 *pearl oyster* **chōgai**
灰貝 *ivory shell* **haikai**
貽貝 *sea mussels* **igai**
角貝 *tusk shell* **kadokai**
貝柱 *adductor muscle, scallop* **kaibashira**
貝殻 *shell, seashell* **kaigara**
貝殻追放 *ostracism, disowning* **kaigara tsuihō**
貝殻骨 *shoulder blade* **kaigarabone**
貝類 *shellfish* **kairui**
貝塚 *kitchen midden, shell mound* **kaizuka**
烏貝 *freshwater mussel* **karasugai**
生貝 *raw shellfish* **namagai**
桜貝 *tellinacean, cherry shell* **sakuragai**
宝貝 *cowry* **takaragai**
鳥貝 *cockle shell* **torigai**
帆立貝 *scallop* **hotategai**

FLIP: 1.0.b. Whole (stem)

貝殻虫 *insect, louse* **kaigaramushi**
貝焼き *grilled shells* **kaiyaki**
貝細工 *shellwork* **kaizaiku**
馬刀貝 *razor clam shell* **mategai**
真珠貝 *pearl oyster* **shinjugai**
阿古屋貝 *pearl oyster* **akoyagai**

魚 *ishes, 49*	食 *oods, 255*
金 *oney, 25*	洋 *cean, 247*
海 *cean, 241*	

貝 *ools, 487*

426-B

Figurine 貝 hells encased, all 買 urchased...

貝 (shell, old money)

買 *urchase*   買 *uying*

ka(u), BAI
purchase, buying, acquire with money, pay for

売買 *purchase, sale, buy & sell* **baibai**
買価 *purchase price* **baika**
買収 *purchase, buying* **baishū**
購買 *purchase, buying* **kōbai**
購買力 *purchasing power* **kōbairyoku**
仲買 *brokerage, middleman* **nakagai**
買い得 *bargain, good buy* **kaidoku**
買い方 *buyer; how to buy* **kaikata**
買い気 *bullish sentiments* **kaiki**
買戻し *buy back, refund* **kaimodoshi**
買い値 *buying price, purchase price* **kaine**
買い主 *buyer, purchaser* **kainushi**
買い手 *buyer, purchaser* **kaite**
盲買い *buying blind* **mekuragai**
先買い *buying in advance* **sakigai**
不買運動 *sale boycott* **fubai undō**
買い漁る *buy in sequence* **kaiasaru**
買い食い *eating on the way home* **kaigui**
買い入れ *purchase, buying* **kaiire**

FLIP: 1.0.b. Whole (stem)

買い切る *buy up, buy out* **kaikiru**
買い込む *buy in, purchase* **kaikomu**
買い置き *stocks, inventories* **kaioki**
買い占め *corner, buying up* **kaishime**
買い叩く *beat down* **kaitataku**
買い取る *buy, purchase* **kaitoru**
衝動買い *impulsive buying* **shōdōgai**
買い上げる *purchase, buy* **kaiageru**
買い集める *buy up* **kaiatsumeru**

販 *elling, 137*	金 *oney, 25*
市 *arket, 304*	商 *usiness, 135*
購 *urchase, 714*	

買 *arry out, 532*

427-A

単*imple rattles start bloody* 戦*attles...*

単*imple* 単*nitary*

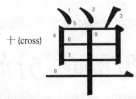

十 (cross)

FLIP: 1.0.b. Whole (stem)

TAN
simple, unitary, basic

単衣 *simple-designed kimono* **hitoe**
簡単 *easy, simple* **kantan**
単文 *simple sentence* **tanbun**
単調 *monotonous, one-kind* **tanchō**
単独 *single, individual* **tandoku**
単眼 *monocular, one-eyed* **tangan**
単元 *academic unit, credit* **tangen**
単語 *word, vocabulary* **tango**
単位 *academic unit, credit* **tan'i**
単純 *simplicity & plainness* **tanjun**
単価 *unit price, unit cost* **tanka**
単記 *single entry, one-liner* **tanki**
単軌 *monorail, light rail* **tanki**
単音 *monotone, monosyllable* **tan'on**
単発 *single engine (plane)* **tanpatsu**
単品 *one-of-a-kind article* **tanpin**
単利 *simple interest (loan)* **tanri**
単彩 *monochrome* **tansai**
単作 *single crop* **tansaku**

単声 *lone voice* **tansei**
単線 *single track (railroad)* **tansen**
単車 *motorcycle, bicycle* **tansha**
単式 *single-entry accounting* **tanshiki**
単身 *away from one's family* **tanshin**
単身赴任 *working away from one's family*
 tanshin funin
単色 *single colour* **tanshoku**
単座 *one seater (plane)* **tanza**
単一化 *simplification, standardization* **tan'itsuka**
単行本 *pocket book* **tankōbon**
単細胞 *single cell, simple-minded* **tansaibō**

測*easurement, 291*	尺*easurement, 574*
計*easurement, 692*	寸*easurement, 345*

戦*attle, 517*

427-B

単*imple rattles start bloody* 戦*attles...*

戦*attle* 戦*ighting*

戈 (spear)

FLIP: 6.0.b. Left (stem)

tataka(u), ikusa, SEN
battle, fighting, combat, struggle, warfare

挑戦 *challenge, provocation* **chōsen**
激戦 *fierce battle* **gekisen**
敗戦 *defeat, loss, vanquished* **haisen**
非戦 *anti-war, peace movement* **hisen**
交戦 *exchange of fire* **kōsen**
抗戦 *armed resistance* **kōsen**
内戦 *civil war* **naisen**
応戦 *return fire, battle response* **ōsen**
乱戦 *fighting confusion, dogfight* **ransen**
戦後 *post war (1945~48)* **sengo**
戦意 *fighting spirit, espirit-de-corps, morale* **sen'i**
戦場 *battlefield, war theatre* **senjō**
戦果 *military exploits, spoils-of-war* **senka**
戦火 *flames of war, war ravages* **senka**
戦禍 *war damages* **senka**
戦艦 *battleship, warship* **senkan**
戦況 *war conditions* **senkyō**
戦犯 *war criminal* **senpan**
戦歴 *military history* **senreki**

戦災 *war damage, ~ravages* **sensai**
戦線 *battle lines, frontlines* **sensen**
宣戦 *declaration of war, war proclamation* **sensen**
戦史 *war history* **senshi**
戦士 *soldier, combatant, warrior* **senshi**
戦死 *killed in combat, death in action* **senshi**
戦傷 *combat wounds, war injury* **senshō**
戦闘 *combat, battle* **sentō**
戦友 *comrade-in-arms, war buddy* **senyū**

激*ierce, 170*	死*eath, 513*	闘*ombat, 946*
猛*ierce, 657*	逝*eath, 54*	武*ombatant, 100*
烈*ierce, 585*	亡*eath, 72*	

単*imple, 517*

428-A

Minds 分ivided can't 分nderstand 雰tmosphere in 雰oggy lands...

刀⇔刂 (blade, cutting)

❶分ivide ❷分nderstand ❸分inute

wa(keru), wa(katsu), wa(kareru), wa(karu), BUN, FUN, BU

divide, partition, portion; understand, comprehend, fathom, figure out, grasp; minute

FLIP: 2.0.b. Sort Of (stem)

❶分別 *classify, sort out* **bunbetsu**
分科 *branch, section* **bunka**
分解 *dismantle, take it apart, disassemble* **bunkai**
分割 *split up, partition, divide up* **bunkatsu**
分泌 *secretion, excretion* **bunpi**
分裂 *fission, splitting* **bunretsu**
分離 *share, separate, divide* **bunri**
分類 *classification, sorting out* **bunrui**
分析 *analysis, dissection* **bunseki**
分子 *atom, molecule* **bunshi**
分身 *share, divide* **bunshin**
分野 *field of study* **bunya**
配分 *distribution, allocating, dividing up* **haibun**
自分 *oneself, one's person* **jibun**
充分 *sufficient, enough* **jūbun**
気分 *mood, feeling* **kibun**
親分 *big boss, the big guy* **oyabun**
成分 *ingredient, component* **seibun**
処分 *punish, dispose* **shobun**

寸分 *at all, entirety* **sunbun**
多分 *perhaps, maybe* **tabun**
糖分 *sugar content* **tōbun**
随分 *exceptionally, considerably* **zuibun**
分担金 *financial share, allotment* **buntankin**
不十分 *insufficient, lacking, not enough* **fujūbun**
百分率 *percentage* **hyakubunritsu**
仮処分 *provisional disposition* **karishobun**
分れ目 *turning point, crossroad* **wakareme**
山分け *sharing a large amount* **yamawake**
分かれ道 *forked road* **wakaremichi**
❷分かり安い *easily-understandable* **wakariyasui**
❸一分 *one minute* **ippun**

切*utting, 352*	部*art, 957*

今*ow, 182*	介*ediate, 365*

428-B

Minds 分ivided can't 分nderstand 雰tmosphere in 雰oggy lands...

雨 (weather)

雰tmosphere 雰oggy

FUN

atmosphere, aura, surroundings, foggy, fuzzy

FLIP: 3.0.b. Top (stem)

雰囲気 *atmosphere, mood, ambiance* **fun'iki**
雰虹 *rainbow* **funkō**

環*urroundings, 165*	候*eather, 122*
曇*oggy, 154*	節*eason, 421*
霧*oggy, 454*	季*eason, 583*

零*ero, 874*

429-A

Black 豆eans for 痘mallpox genes...

豆eans

mame, TŌ, ZU
beans

豆 (beans)

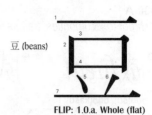

FLIP: 1.0.a. Whole (flat)

青豆 *green peas* **aomame**
小豆 *adzuki beans, tiny beans* **azuki**
血豆 *blood blister* **chimame**
大豆 *soybean* **daizu**
枝豆 *green soybeans* **edamame**
黒豆 *black soybean, black beans* **kuromame**
豆銀 *Edo coins* **mamegin**
豆本 *miniature book* **mamehon, mamebon**
豆炭 *oval charcoal briquette* **mametan**
豆粒 *little dot* **mametsubu**
蜜豆 *concealed beans, bean hoarding* **mitsumame**
納豆 *fermented soybeans* **nattō**
煮豆 *boiled beans* **nimame**
塩豆 *salted beans* **shiomame**
底豆 *foot blisters* **sokomame**
空豆 *broad bean* **soramame**
豆腐 *bean curd* **tōfu**
豆腐屋 *bean curd store, ~maker* **tōfuya**

豆乳 *soybean milk* **tōnyū**
隠元豆 *kidney bean* **ingenmame**
豆電球 *miniature bulb* **mamedenkyū**
豆鉄砲 *peashooter, beanshooter* **mamedeppō**
豆撒き *bean-scattering* **mamemaki**
豆人形 *miniature dolls* **mameningyō**
豆台風 *weak typhoon* **mametaifū**
南京豆 *peanuts* **nankinmame**
湯豆腐 *boiled bean curd* **yudōfu**
伊豆半島 *Izu Peninsula* **izu hantō**
豆自動車 *mini car* **mamejidōsha**
焼き豆腐 *broiled tofu* **yakidōfu**

種*eedling, 430*	芽*prout, 57*
根*oot, 772*	苗*prout, 270*

登*limb, 437*

429-B

Black 豆eans for 痘mallpox genes...

痘mallpox

TŌ
small pox

广 (sickness)

FLIP: 8.0.a. Inner (flat)

痘痕 *pockmark* **abata**
牛痘 *cattle pox, vaccinia* **gyūtō**
種痘 *smallpox inoculation, vaccination* **shutō**
水痘 *chickenpox, varicella* **suitō**
痘苗 *smallpox vaccine* **tōbyō**
痘瘡 *smallpox disease* **tōsō**
天然痘 *smallpox, varicella* **tennentō**
痘痕もえくぼ *"love is blind..."* **abatamoekubo**

患*ickness, 475*	療*ecuperate, 67*
症*ickness, 788*	剤*rugs, 961*
病*ickness, 213*	薬*rugs, 447*
治*ecuperate, 210*	医*edicine, 19*
癒*ecuperate, 923*	菌*acteria, 52*

痴*oolish, 681*

430-A

威*hreat* to 威*uthorities*, traitors to 滅*erish*...

女 (woman)

❶威*hreat* **❷威*uthority***

odo(su), odo(kasu), I
threat; authority, officialdom, might

Facing: 2.1. East ☞ (H)

❶威張る *boast, arrogant, haughty* **ibaru**
威丈高 *overbearing, high-handed* **itakedaka**
暴威 *tyranny, despotism* **bōi**
威圧 *coercion, high-handedness* **iatsu**
威圧的 *coercive, high-handed* **iatsuteki**
威嚇 *intimidation, threat, menace* **ikaku**
威嚇射撃 *warning shot* **ikaku shageki**
示威 *show-of-force, demonstration* **jii**
示威運動 *demonstration, protest rally* **jii undō**
脅威 *menace, threat* **kyōi**
猛威 *rage, violence* **mōi**
虚仮威し *bluff, ruse* **kokeodoshi**

❷威望 *fame & influence* **ibō**
威武 *power & force* **ibu**
威風 *majesty, dignity, nobility* **ifū**
威服 *yielding, submission* **ifuku**
威厳 *dignity, nobility* **igen**
威儀 *dignity, solemnity* **igi**

威権 *authority, power* **iken**
威光 *authority, power* **ikō**
威名 *renown, prestige* **imei**
威令 *authority, power* **irei**
威力 *power, authority* **iryoku**
威勢 *spirits, vigour, zest* **isei**
威信 *prestige, dignity, repute* **ishin**
威容 *dignified-, noble looking* **iyō**
権威 *authority, power* **ken'i**
権威筋 *authoritative source* **ken'isuji**
国威 *national prestige, ~dignity* **kokui**
神威 *mandate of heaven, divine rights* **shin'i**

権*uthority*, 804	諭*dmonish*, 922
戒*dmonish*, 493	警*recaution*, 330

成*chieve*, 244

430-B

威*hreat* to 威*uthorities*, traitors to 滅*erish*...

水⇔氵 (water)

滅*erish* 滅*xterminate*

horo(biru); horo(bosu), METSU
perish, exterminate, annihilate, destroy

Facing: 2.2. East ☞ (V)

撲滅 *eradication, uprooting* **bokumetsu**
仏滅 *Buddha's death, unlucky day* **butsumetsu**
不滅 *immortality, perpetuity, everlasting* **fumetsu**
撃滅 *destruction, extermination* **gekimetsu**
幻滅 *disillusionment, disenchantment* **genmetsu**
破滅 *wreck, ruin, destruction* **hametsu**
必滅 *doomed to extinction* **hitsumetsu**
隠滅 *extinction, destruction* **inmetsu**
自滅 *self-destruction, ~annihilation* **jimetsu**
壊滅 *destruction, annihilation* **kaimetsu**
摩滅 *wearing away, withering away* **mametsu**
明滅 *flickering, glimmer* **meimetsu**
滅菌 *sterilization, pasteurisation* **mekkin**
滅却 *extinguish, destroy* **mekkyaku**
滅亡 *downfall, extinction* **metsubō**
入滅 *entering Nirvana, supreme bliss* **nyūmetsu**
死滅 *extinction, destruction* **shimetsu**
消滅 *extinction, disappearance* **shōmetsu**
掃滅 *extermination, annihilation* **sōmetsu**

衰滅 *decline & fall* **suimetsu**
点滅 *blinking lights, off-&-on lights* **tenmetsu**
全滅 *extermination, genocide, massacre* **zenmetsu**
絶滅 *extermination, annihilation* **zetsumetsu**
滅入る *feel gloomy* **meiru**
滅多に *seldom, rarely* **metta(ni)**
罪滅ぼし *atonement for sins* **tsumihoroboshi**
滅茶苦茶 *reposterous; mess, wreck* **mechakucha**
滅相もない *absurd, preposterous* **messōmonai**
滅多矢鱈 *recklessly, clumsily* **mettayatara**

絶*radicate*, 403	禍*ragedy*, 799
破*estroy*, 715	惨*ragedy*, 396
廃*bolish*, 368	悲*ragedy*, 289
壊*estroy*, 847	厄*ragedy*, 354

減*ecrease*, 46

431-A

将uture 将enerals 奨ncourage liberals...

❶将eneral　❷将uture

SHŌ

general; future, coming years

寸 (measurement)

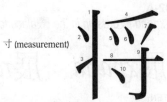

Facing: 1.2. 🢂 West (V)

❶武将 *general, military commander* **bushō**
知将 *resourceful general* **chishō**
中将 *lieutenant general; deputy admiral* **chujō**
副将 *second in command* **fukushō**
軍将 *army general* **gunshō**
敗将 *beaten general* **haishō**
名将 *noted commander* **meishō**
女将 *landlady, proprietress* **okami**
王将 *king in Shōgi game* **ōshō**
陸将 *lieutenant general* **rikushō**
将棋 *Japanese chess* **shōgi**
将棋倒し *domino effect collapse* **shōgidaoshi**
将軍 *Shōgun* **shōgun**
⇒冬将軍 *general winter* **fuyushōgun**
将軍職 *Shōgunate* **shōgunshoku**
将兵 *officers & men* **shōhei**
将官 *flag officer* **shōkan**
将校 *military academy* **shōkō**
将士 *officers & men* **shōshi**

少将 *major general, rear admiral* **shōshō**
将卒 *officers & men* **shōsotsu**
主将 *navy captain, army colonel; team captain* **shushō**
大将 *general, admiral* **taishō**
⇒総大将 *commander-in-chief* **sōdaishō**
⇒餓鬼大将 *bully, thug, hooligan* **gaki taishō**
敵将 *enemy general* **tekishō**
闘将 *courageous general* **tōshō**
❷将来 *future* **shōrai**
将来性 *future prospects* **shōraisei**
将来的 *futuristic, in the future* **shōraiteki**

系 *osterity, 262*　永 *ternal, 10*　時 *ime, 653*
後 *fter, 897*　入 *ternal, 379*　経 *ime-lapse, 791*

受 *eceive, 539*

431-B

将uture 将enerals 奨ncourage liberals...

奨ncourage　奨rompt

SHŌ

encourage, prompt, propel, spur, inspire, prodding, cheer-up, embolden, motivate

大 (grand)

FLIP: 4.0.b. Bottom (stem)

報奨 *reward, pay, fee* **hōshō**
報奨金 *reward, bonus* **hōshōkin**
勧奨 *encouragement, endorsement* **kanshō**
選奨 *recommendation, nomination* **senshō**
奨励 *encouragement, promotion* **shōrei**
奨励金 *bounty, subsidy* **shōreikin**
⇒輸出奨励金 *export bounty* **yushutsu shōreikin**
奨学生 *scholar* **shōgakusei**
奨学金 *scholarship* **shōgakukin**

促 *ncourage, 481*　薦 *ecommend, 68*
励 *ncourage, 465*　勧 *ecommend, 666*
努 *fforts, 44*　推 *ecommend, 777*
勉 *fforts, 527*

将 *uture, 521*

432-A

展xpand 殿ordship in the 殿alace for Czar Nicholas...

展xpand 展rogress

尸 (corpse)

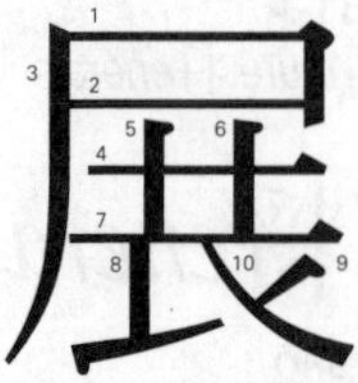

TEN

expand, progress, unfold, display

Facing: 2.1. East ☞ (H)
FLIP: 8.0.a. Inner (flat)

発展 *development, progress* **hatten**
⇒海外発展 *overseas development* **kaigai hatten**
⇒経済発展 *economic development* **keizai hatten**
発展性 *development potential* **hattensei**
発展途上国 *developing nations, Third World* **hatten tojōkoku**
個展 *private exhibition* **koten**
進展 *development, evolution* **shinten**
親展 *private & confidential* **shinten**
親展書 *"confidential letter..."* **shintensho**
展望 *prospect, outlook, view* **tenbō**
展望台 *observation deck* **tenbōdai**
展示 *exhibition, display* **tenji**
展示物 *goods on exhibit* **tenjibutsu**
展示場 *exhibition place* **tenjijō**
展示会 *exhibition, exposition* **tenjikai**
展示即売会 *exhibition sale* **tenjisoku baikai**
展開 *development, evolution* **tenkai**
展観 *exhibition, display, exposition* **tenkan**
展覧 *exhibition* **tenran**
展覧物 *exhibited articles* **tenranbutsu**
展覧会 *exhibition, show* **tenrankai**
展覧室 *exhibition room* **tenranshitsu**
展覧会場 *exhibition gallery* **tenran kaijō**
展性 *malleability, elasticity* **tensei**

進rogress, 51	盛ffluence, 244
歩rogress, 272	繁ffluence, 434
化ecome, 192	裕ffluence, 758
成ecome, 244	富ortune, 333

殿ordship, 522

432-B

展xpand 殿ordship in the 殿alace for Czar Nicholas...

❶殿alace ❷殿ordship

殳 (pike)

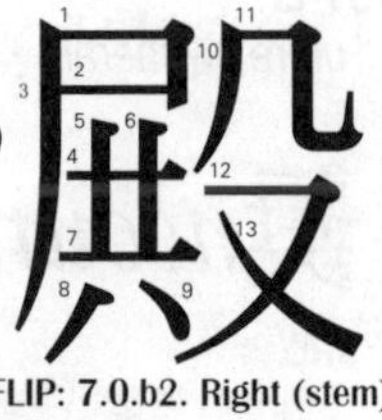

tono, dono, DEN

palace, chateau; lordship

FLIP: 7.0.b2. Right (stem)

❶仏殿 *Buddhist temple building* **butsuden**
沈殿 *precipitation, sedimentation* **chinden**
沈殿物 *precipitate, sediment* **chindenbutsu**
殿中 *inside the palace* **denchū**
殿堂 *palace, sanctuary* **dendō**
殿堂入り *entry to the Hall of Fame* **dendōiri**
殿軍 *imperial guards* **dengun**
御殿 *palace, imperial court* **goten**
拝殿 *worship hall* **haiden**
本殿 *main shrine* **honden**
宮殿 *imperial palace* **kyūden**
内殿 *inner shrine* **naiden**
霊殿 *shrine, sanctuary* **reiden**
祭殿 *shrine, sanctuary* **saiden**
社殿 *main hall of a shrine* **shaden**
神殿 *shrine* **shinden**
寝殿 *main house* **shinden**

❷殿下 *His-, Her Imperial Highness* **denka**
貴殿 *you (honorific)* **kiden**
殿方 *"gentlemen..."* **tonogata**
殿御 *gentleman* **tonogo**
殿様 *feudal lord* **tonosama**
若殿 *young lord* **wakatono**
若殿原 *young samurais* **wakatonobara**
湯殿 *bathroom* **yudono**
妃殿下 *Her Imperial Highness* **hidenka**
宝物殿 *treasure house* **hōmotsuden**
奥御殿 *inner palace* **okugoten**
白亜の殿堂 *white hall* **hakua no dendō**
皇太子殿下 *His Imperial Highness, the Crown Prince* **kōtaishi denka**

宮alace, 105	王onarch, 12
妃rincess, 728	皇mperor, 113
姫rincess, 542	后mpress, 87

展xpand, 522

433-A

A 竜ragon call from the 滝aterfall...

竜*ragon*

tatsu, RYŪ
dragon

臥竜	declining fame	**garyū**
魚竜	ichthyosaur	**gyoryū**
飛竜	flying dragon	**hiryū**
恐竜	dinosaur, reptile monster	**kyōryū**
土竜	mole	**mogura**
竜胆	gentian	**rindō**
竜骨	keel	**ryūkotsu**
竜眼	longan	**ryūgan**
竜顔	emperor's countenance	**ryūgan**
竜宮	dragons palace	**ryūgū**
竜神	dragon deity	**ryūjin**
竜虎	mighty, fierce	**ryūko**
竜骨	keel, hull	**ryūkotsu**
竜目	dragon horse	**ryūme**
竜脳	borneol	**ryūnō**
竜王	dragon king	**ryūō**
竜頭	crown, stem	**ryūtō**
竜口	dragon's mouth	**tatsu no kuchi**
針土竜	spiny anteater, echidna	**harimogura**

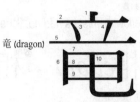

竜 (dragon)

FLIP: 2.0.a. Sort Of (flat)

竜騎兵	dragoon	**ryūkihei**
竜舌蘭	agave	**ryūzetsuran**
青竜刀	Chinese broadsword	**seiryūtō**
竜巻き	tornado, whirlwind	**tatsumaki**
竜田姫	goddess of autumn season	**tatsutahime**
登竜門	"gate to success..."	**tōryūmon**
烏竜茶	Chinese red tea	**ūroncha**
竜宮城	dragon king palace	**ryugūjo**
画竜点睛	finishing touches	**garyō tensei**
竜頭蛇尾	great start-but-poor finish	**ryūtō dabi**
竜の落し子	sea horse	**tatsu no otoshigo**

巨*iant*, 206	烈*ierce*, 585
激*ierce*, 170	玄*ystery*, 358
猛*ierce*, 657	炎*lames*, 309

意*dea*, *340*

433-B

A 竜ragon call from the 滝aterfall...

滝*aterfall*

taki
waterfall

雄滝	waterfalls bigger side	**odaki**
白滝	white konnyaku	**shirataki**
滝川	rapids, cascade	**takigawa**
滝口	waterfalls crest	**takiguchi**
滝壷	waterfalls bed	**takitsubo**
湯滝	hot-water falls, hot shower	**yudaki**
滝登り	waterfalls climbing	**takinobori**
滝飲み	"drink bottoms up..."	**takinomi**

水⇔氵 (water)

FLIP: 7.1. Right (Sort Of)

峡*avine*, 763	川*iver*, 76
渓*avine*, 97	潟*agoon*, 870
谷*avine*, 492	湖*ake*, 801
河*iver*, 877	

竜*ragon*, *523*

434-A

相*ellow* 相*inisters had no* 想*dea about the media...*

相*ellow* **相***inister* **相***hase*

目 (eyesight, visual)

ai, SŌ, SHŌ
fellow; minister; phase

FLIP: 5.0.a. Left & Right

❶ 相子 *a tie, a draw* **aiko**
相席 *table sharing, seated together* **aiseki**
相手 *counter-part, partner, ~mate* **aite**
首相 *prime minister, premier* **shushō**
相愛 *mutual love* **sōai**
相談 *consultation, counselling* **sōdan**
相伝 *inheritance, legacy, bequest* **sōden**
相互 *mutuality, reciprocity* **sōgo**
相違 *difference, discrepancy, disparity* **sōi**
相関 *correlation, relativity* **sōkan**
相殺 *offsetting, counterbalance* **sōsatsu, sōsai**
粗相 *careless act, clumsy attitude* **sosō**
相対 *relativity, relativeness* **sōtai**
相続 *inheritance, legacy, bequest* **sōzoku**
相撲 *sumo wrestling* **sumō**
相弟子 *fellow pupils, ~acolytes* **aideshi**
❷ 外相 *foreign minister* **gaishō**
宰相 *premier* **saishō**
蔵相 *finance minister* **zōshō**

❸ 形相 *look, expression, appearance* **gyōsō**
貧相 *shabby, poor-looking* **hinsō**
皮相 *shallow, outward look* **hisō**
位相 *phase, topology* **isō**
実相 *real situation, actual condition* **jissō**
寝相 *sleeping position* **nezō**
死相 *dead-looking person* **shisō**
様相 *aspect, phase, condition* **yōsō**
相次ぐ *continuous, uninterrupted* **aitsugu**
円相場 *yen exchange rate* **ensōba**
為替相場 *foreign exchange rate* **kawase sōba**

仲*ellow, 695*	僚*ellow, 66*
奴*ellow, 44*	省*inistry, 572*
輩*ellow, 290*	臣*etainer, 542*

租*rop, 755*	組*roup, 138*

434-B

相*ellow* 相*inisters had no* 想*dea about the media...*

想*dea* **想***hought*

心 ⇔ 忄 (heart, feelings)

SŌ
idea, thought, abstraction, concept, inkling, notion

FLIP: 6.1. Left Top
FLIP: 7.2.a. Right Top (flat)

愛想 *amiability, cordiality, friendliness* **aisō**
着想 *idea, thought, concept* **chakusō**
断想 *random thoughts* **dansō**
幻想 *fantasy, illusion* **gensō**
発想 *concept, thought, idea* **hassō**
回想 *reminiscence, recollection* **kaisō**
感想 *impression, feelings* **kansō**
仮想 *supposition, hypothesis* **kasō**
奇想 *fantastic thoughts* **kisō**
構想 *plan, plot, idea* **kōsō**
空想 *fantasy, illusion* **kūsō**
瞑想 *meditation, contemplation* **meisō**
黙想 *minute-of-silence* **mokusō**
妄想 *delusion, wild fancy* **mōsō**
夢想 *dream, vision, fancy* **musō**
連想 *stream of thoughts* **rensō**
理想 *ideal, exemplar, model* **risō**
思想 *idea, thought, concept* **shisō**
詩想 *poetic thoughts* **shisō**

想起 *remembering, recollection* **sōki**
想念 *idea, thought, concept* **sōnen**
想定 *hypothesis, premise* **sōtei**
想到 *think of, ponder on, consider* **sōtō**
想像 *imagination, creativity* **sōzō**
想像力 *imaginative, creativity* **sōzōryoku**
追想 *reminiscence, recollection* **tsuisō**
予想 *prospect, expectation* **yosō**
予想外 *unexpected, surprise* **yosōgai**
随想 *random thoughts* **zuisō**
想像上 *imaginary* **sōzōjō**
想定内 *"within consideration..."* **sōteinai**
想定外 *"out of consideration..."* **sōteigai**

意*dea, 340*	慮*hought, 70*
念*dea, 182*	考*hinking, 392*

想*dea, 524*

435-A

兼oncurrently 廉onest, 廉ncorruptible Elliot Ness...

八 (eight, divisible)

兼oncurrent 兼ual post

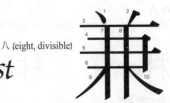

ka(neru), KEN
concurrent, dual post, two jobs

FLIP: 2.0.b. Sort Of (stem)

兼ねる *serve concurrently* **kaneru**
兼ね合い *balance, equilibrium* **kaneai**
兼備 *two things simultaneously (rich & smart)* **kenbi**
兼題 *poetry theme* **kendai**
兼営 *dual managerial task* **ken'ei**
兼業 *side business, moonlighting* **kengyō**
兼業農家 *farmer with a side job* **kengyō nōka**
兼官 *additional public post* **kenkan**
兼勤 *additional work, extra job* **kenkin**
兼行 *dual-, concurrent job* **kenkō**
兼務 *holding an additional job* **kenmu**
兼任 *concurrent-, additional post* **kennin**
兼職 *simultaneous holding of posts* **kenshoku**
兼修 *extra study* **kenshū**
兼帯 *dual use* **kentai**
兼用 *combined usage, dual purpose* **kenyō**
兼有 *simultaneous possession* **kenyū**
気兼ね *constraints, hesitation* **kigane**
見兼ねる *"cannot just do nothing..."* **mikaneru**

申し兼ねる *"sorry about the extra work..."*
  mōshikaneru
仕兼ねる *"cannot be done..."* **shikaneru**
待ち兼ねる *"cannot wait for..."* **machikaneru**
堪り兼ねる *unbearable, intolerable* **tamarikaneru**
有り兼ねない *"not impossible..."* **arikanenai**

途urrently, 882	伴ccompany, 949
似imilar, 472	並arallel, 444
同imilar, 245	今ow, 182
随ccompany, 807	現resent, 814

善ighteousness, 450

435-B

兼oncurrently 廉onest, 廉ncorruptible Elliot Ness...

广 (rooftop)

廉onest 廉ncorrupt

kado, REN
honest, incorruptible

FLIP: 7.1. Right (Sort Of)

一廉 *respectable, upright* **hitokado**
廉売 *bargain-, clearance sale* **renbai**
廉直 *upright, standing up* **renchoku**
廉価 *cheap, low-price* **renka**
廉価版 *cheap edition* **renkaban**
廉価品 *low-priced goods* **renkahin**
廉潔 *integrity, upright* **renketsu**
廉吏 *incorruptible official* **renri**
廉正 *pure-hearted* **rensei**
廉士 *uncovetous* **renshi**
清廉 *honest, incorruptible* **seiren**
清廉潔白 *unquestionable integrity* **seiren keppaku**
低廉 *cheap, inexpensive* **teiren**
破廉恥 *shameless, embarrassing* **harenchi**
廉恥心 *sense of honour* **renchishin**

誠incere, 245	仁irtue, 457
真incere, 487	徳irtue, 844
実ruth, 121	善oodness, 450

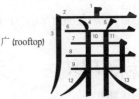

兼oncurrent, 525

436-A

林ood in the 森orest, plenty in Bucharest...

林oods 林rove

木 (wooden)

FLIP: 5.0.b. Left & Right

hayashi, RIN
woods, grove, thicket

梅林 *plum grove* **bairin**
営林 *forest management* **eirin**
辞林 *dictionary* **jirin**
樹林 *forest* **jurin**
松林 *pine grove* **matsubayashi**
密林 *thick-, dense forest* **mitsurin**
農林 *agriculture & forestry* **nōrin**
林木 *forest & trees* **rinboku**
林道 *forest trail, ~path* **rindō**
林学 *forestry* **ringaku**
林檎 *apple* **ringo**
林檎酒 *apple cider* **ringoshu**
林業 *forestry* **ringyō**
林立 *bristling* **rinritsu**
林産 *forest products* **rinsan**
林政 *forestry management* **rinsei**
林野 *forests & fields* **rinya**
林野庁 *forestry agency* **rinyachō**
緑林 *mountain bandits* **ryokurin**

山林 *mountains & forests* **sanrin**
森林 *woods, forest* **shinrin**
植林 *re-forestation, tree-planting* **shokurin**
書林 *bookstore* **shorin**
竹林 *bamboo grove* **takerin, chikurin**
禅林 *Zen temple* **zenrin**
造林 *re-forestation, tree-planting* **zōrin**
原生林 *virgin forest* **genseirin**
熱帯林 *tropical forest* **nettairin**
林務官 *forest officer* **rinmukan**
林間学校 *open-air school* **rinkan gakkō**

材*oods, 186*
木*ood, 461*
森*orest, 526*

材*aterials, 186*

436-B

林ood in the 森orest, plenty in Bucharest...

森orest 森hicket

木 (wooden)

FLIP: 1.0.b. Whole (stem)

mori, SHIN
forest, thicket

森陰 *forest shade* **morikage**
森厳 *awesome, solemn* **shingen**
森閑 *reign of silence* **shinkan**
森林 *woods, forest* **shinrin**
森森 *forest depths, deep forest* **shinshin**
青森県 *Aomori Prefecture* **aomori-ken**
青森市 *Aomori city, Aomori Prefecture* **aomori-shi**
森林学 *forestry science* **shinringaku**
森林帯 *forest zone* **shinrintai**
森林浴 *energizing moments in the forest* **shinrinyoku**
森羅万象 *all things in the universe* **shinra banshō**
森林保護 *forest preservation* **shinrin hogo**
森林公園 *forest park* **shinrin kōen**

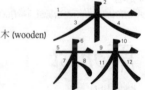

木*ood, 461* 緑*reen, 841*
材*oods, 186* 岳*ountain peak, 28*
林*oods, 526* 峰*ountain peak, 779*

林*oods, 526*

437-A

勉fforts negate when minds 逸eviate...

力 (strength, force)

勉*ffort*   勉*iligence*

tsuto(meru), BEN
effort, diligence, endeavour, forbearance

勉学 *studying, learning* **bengaku**
勉強 *study, work, lesson* **benkyō**
⇒糞勉強 *cramming* **kusobenkyō**
⇒俄勉強 *cramming* **niwakabenkyō**
勉強会 *study group, study meeting* **benkyōkai**
勉励 *hard work* **benrei**
勤勉 *diligent, persevering* **kinben**
猛勉 *scholars tenacity, diligent study* **mōben**
不勉強 *fail to study, lesson unpreparedness* **fubenkyō**
がり勉 *studious, scholarly* **gariben**
勤勉家 *hard worker, industrious labourer* **kinbenka**
勤勉性 *diligence, perseverance* **kinbensei**

Facing: 4.0. 🖙 Apart

働*abour, 422*	伸*tretch, 713*
労*abour, 351*	張*tretch, 274*
努*fforts, 44*	精*igour, 792*
張*xert, 274*	

免*xempt, 413*

437-B

勉fforts negate when minds 逸eviate...

辶 (transport)

逸*eviate*   逸*et-apart*

ITSU
deviate, set-apart, let slip

逸する *pass up a chance; deviate* **issuru**
安逸 *idle living, ~lifestyle* **an'itsu**
独逸 *Germany* **doitsu**
放逸 *self-indulgence* **hōitsu**
飄逸 *buoyant, aloof* **hyōitsu**
逸物 *one's precious belongings* **ichimotsu**
逸機 *lost chance, missed opportunity* **ikki**
逸興 *very amusing* **ikkyō**
逸球 *muffed ball* **ikkyū**
隠逸 *seclusion, solitude* **in'itsu**
逸品 *excellent piece, rarity* **ippin**
逸書 *lost writings, unfound book* **issho**
逸出 *escape; excel* **isshutsu**
逸走 *scamper away, escape* **issō**
逸足 *fast mover, doer; prodigy* **issoku**
逸文 *missing writings* **itsubun**
逸聞 *widely unknown* **itsubun**
逸脱 *deviation, departure* **itsudatsu**
逸事 *anecdote* **itsuji**

Facing: 1.1. 🖙 West (H)

逸民 *retired person, recluse* **itsumin**
逸楽 *idle pleasure* **itsuraku**
逸話 *anecdote, strange tale* **itsuwa**
逸材 *talented person* **itsuzai**
散逸 *scattered & lost* **san'itsu**
秀逸 *excellence, superiority* **shūitsu**
俊逸 *excellence, genius* **shun'itsu**
逸早く *quickly, promptly* **ichihayaku**
逸速く *quickly, promptly* **ichihayaku**
逸れ弾 *stray bullet* **soredama**
逸れ矢 *stray arrow* **soreya**

違*ifference, 796*	免*xempt, 413*
差*ifference, 589*	専*xclusive, 514*
異*ifferent, 239*	殊*pecial, 234*

免*xempt, 413*

527

438-A

畜*reeding pigs in a* 蓄*torage eating porridge...*

田 (cultivated field)

畜*reeding* 畜*aising*

CHIKU
breeding, raising, livestock, hatchery

FLIP: 4.0.a. Bottom (flat)

牧畜 *stock raising* **bokuchiku**
牧畜業者 *livestock farmer* **bokuchiku gyōsha**
畜殺 *slaughter, butcher* **chikusatsu**
畜犬 *pet dog* **chikuken**
畜類 *domestic beast* **chikurui**
畜産 *livestock industry* **chikusan**
畜産物 *livestock by-products* **chikusanbutsu**
畜産業 *stock raising* **chikusangyō**
畜舎 *animal barn* **chikusha**
畜生 *beast, brute; "damn it..."* **chikushō**
畜生道 *incest* **chikushōdō**
役畜 *domestic beast, wild animal* **ekichiku**
人畜 *human-or-animal* **jinchiku**
家畜 *domestic animals* **kachiku**
鬼畜 *brute, savage, barbaric* **kichiku**
有畜 *with livestock* **yūchiku**
無畜 *without livestock* **muchiku**
種畜 *stock breeding, stock raising* **shuchiku**

飼*aising, 835*	牛*attle, 179*
養*aising, 253*	鶏*hicken, 842*
牧*asture, 647*	豚*ig, 910*
群*erd, 259*	羊*heep, 247*

蓄*toring, 528*

438-B

畜*reeding pigs in a* 蓄*torage eating porridge...*

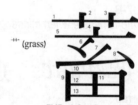

艹 (grass)

蓄*toring* 蓄*torage*

takuwa(eru), CHIKU
storage, storing, depository

FLIP: 4.0.a. Bottom (flat)

備蓄 *stockpile, storage* **bichiku**
蓄電 *electricity storage* **chikuden**
蓄電池 *storage battery* **chikudenchi**
蓄電器 *electric capacitor* **chikudenki**
蓄膿症 *empyema* **chikunōshō**
蓄積 *accumulation, amassing* **chikuseki**
蓄妾 *keeping a mistress* **chikushō**
蓄財 *accumulated wealth* **chikuzai**
貯蓄 *savings* **chochiku**
貯蓄心 *frugality, thrift, saving mentality* **chochikushin**
電蓄 *phonograph, gramophone* **denchiku**
含蓄 *significance, implication* **ganchiku**
蓄音器 *phonograph, gramophone* **chikuonki**

庫*torage, 306*	給*upply, 143*
倉*torage, 399*	納*upply, 296*
蔵*torage, 565*	与*upply, 349*
貯*torage, 967*	充*upply, 884*

畜*reeding, 528*

439-A
What 昭rightly 照hines can 照mbarrass or divine...

日 (sunlight, daytime)

昭*right*   昭*uminous*

SHŌ
bright, luminous, radiant
昭代 *enlightened era* **shōdai**
孝昭天皇 *Emperor Kōshō (475-393 BC)*
　　kōshō tennō
昭和元年 *first year of Emperor Showa's reign (1926)*
　　shōwa gannen
昭和時代 *Showa Era (1926-1989)* **shōwa jidai**
昭和天皇 *Emperor Hirohito* **shōwa tennō**
昭和基地 *Emperor Hirohito Base in South Pole*
　　shōwa kichi

FLIP: 6.0.a. Left (flat)
FLIP: 7.3.a. Right Bottom (flat)

照*hine, 529*	明*right, 22*
光*hining, 77*	英*rilliance, 217*
澄*ake clear, 437*	輝*parkling, 296*

沼*wamp, 356*

439-B
What 昭rightly 照hines can 照mbarrass or divine...

火⇔灬 (fire)

①照*hine*   ②照*mbarrass*

te(ru), te(rasu), te(reru), SHŌ
shining, glowing, illuminate; embarrass, ridicule
❶晩照 *sunset* **banshō**
辺照 *reflected light* **hanshō, henshō**
引照 *reference, bibliography* **inshō**
観照 *meditation, contemplation* **kanshō**
日照 *sunshine, sunlight* **nisshō**
日照権 *right to sunlight* **nisshōken**
参照 *reference, bibliography* **sanshō**
照度 *illumination degree* **shōdo**
照合 *collation* **shōgō**
照準 *one's aim, one's purpose* **shōjun**
照会 *inquiry, reference* **shōkai**
照明 *illumination, luminescence* **shōmei**
⇒舞台照明 *stage lighting* **butai shōmei**
照応 *correspondence, agreement* **shōō**
照覧 *witnessing, clearly seeing* **shōran**
照査 *verification; collation* **shōsa**
照星 *front sight, frontal view* **shōsei**
照射 *irradiation, radiation* **shōsha**
対照 *contrast, comparison* **taishō**

FLIP: 6.1. Left Top

残照 *afterglow, lingering glow* **zanshō**
油照り *muggy-, sultry weather* **aburaderi**
火照り *glow, heat, luminosity* **hoteri**
探照灯 *searchlight, floodlight* **tanshōtō**
照り返し *reflected light* **terikaeshi**
照葉樹林 *evergreen forest* **shōyō jurin**
照る照る坊主 *rainmaker dolls* **teruterubōzu**
天照大神 *sun goddess* **amaterasu oomikami**
❷照れ屋 *overly-shy person* **tereya**
照れ隠し *laugh to cover oneself* **terekakushi**
照れ臭い *embarrassed, ashamed* **terekusai**
照れ笑い *embarrassed laughter* **terewarai**
照れ性 *overly shy* **tereshō**

光*hining, 77*	英*rilliance, 217*
昭*right, 529*	輝*parkling, 296*
明*right, 22*	辱*mbarrass, 588*

昭*right, 529*

440-A

象*lephants'* 象*mage* & 像*tatue, what a view...*

豕 (pig)

❶象*mage* ❷象*lephant*

SHŌ, ZŌ
image, phenomenon; elephant

Facing: 1.0. West (W)

❶ 万象 *all things in the universe* **banshō**
物象 *inanimate object* **busshō**
抽象 *abstraction, metaphysical* **chūshō**
抽象論 *abstract argument, ~opinion* **chūshōron**
現象 *phenomenon* **genshō**
⇒老化現象 *ageing phenomena* **rōka genshō**
⇒社会現象 *social phenomenon* **shakai genshō**
具象 *embodiment, personification* **gushō**
表象 *abstract painting, ~picture* **hyōshō**
印象 *impression, idea* **inshō**
⇒第一印象 *first impression* **daiichi inshō**
印象的 *impressive, stirring, inspirational* **inshōteki**
観象 *atmospheric observation* **kanshō**
形象 *shape, form* **keishō**
気象 *weather conditions* **kishō**
海象 *walrus* **seiuchi**
捨象 *abstraction* **shashō**
心象 *mental image* **shinshō**
象徴 *symbol, emblem* **shōchō**

象徴的 *symbolic, emblemic* **shōchōteki**
象限 *quadrant* **shōgen**
対象 *object, aim, purpose* **taishō**
天象 *atmospheric conditions* **tenshō**
天象儀 *planetarium* **tenshōgi**
象眼 *in-laying* **zōgan**
象牙 *ivory* **zōge**
象牙の塔 *ivory tower* **zōge no tō**
象虫 *weevil* **zōmushi**
象形文字 *Hieroglyphic letters* **shōkei moji**
❷象亀 *elephant, tortoise* **zōgame**

映*eflect, 217*	意*dea, 340*	形*hape, 951*
鑑*irror, 857*	想*dea, 524*	図*rawing, 47*
鏡*irror, 839*	念*dea, 182*	描*rawing, 271*

免*xempt, 413*

440-B

象*lephants'* 象*mage* & 像*tatue, what a view...*

人⇔イ (person)

像*tatue* 像*ikeness*

ZŌ
statue, likeness, portrait

Facing: 1.2. West (V)

銅像 *bronze statue* **dōzō**
仏像 *Buddhist statue* **butsuzō**
映像 *projected image, screening* **eizō**
影像 *portrait, painting, likeness* **eizō**
胸像 *bust statue* **kyōzō**
巨像 *colossus, giant statue* **kyozō**
群像 *group* **gunzō**
偶像 *idol* **gūzō**
結像 *image forming in the mind* **ketsuzō**
画像 *image, picture* **gazō**
想像 *imagination* **sōzō**
想像力 *power of imagination, creativity* **sōzōryoku**
想像妊娠 *imagined pregnancy* **sōzō ninshin**
残像 *lingering image in the mind* **zanzō**
写像 *mapping* **shazō**
心像 *mental image* **shinzō**
裸像 *nude sculpture* **razō**
現像 *photo film processing* **genzō**
塑像 *plastic figure* **sozō**

絵像 *portrait* **ezō**
肖像 *portrait, likeness, painting* **shōzō**
実像 *real image* **jitsuzō**
聖像 *sacred image* **seizō**
座像 *seated figure* **zazō**
彫像 *statue* **chōzō**
石像 *stone image* **sekizō**
虚像 *virtual image, pretence* **kyozō**
木像 *wooden statue* **mokuzō**
自画像 *self-portrait* **jigazō**
騎馬像 *horse riding-, equestrian statue* **kibazō**

形*hape, 951*	図*rawing, 47*
象*mage, 530*	

象*lephant, 530*

441-A

泉ot-springs by the finish 線ine filled with sake wine...

水 ⇔ 氵 (water)

泉prings　泉ountain

izumi, SEN
springs, fountain

FLIP: 3.0.a. Top (flat)

噴泉 water fountain **funsen**
源泉 principal source **gensen**
源泉課税 principal income tax **gensen kazei**
源泉所得税 principal taxation **gensen shotokuzei**
飛泉 waterfalls **hisen**
泉熱 scarlet fever **izuminetsu**
渓泉 valley spring **keisen**
鉱泉 mineral spring, ~water **kōsen**
熱泉 hot springs **nessen**
温泉 hot springs, hot spa **onsen**
温泉場 spa, hot spring **onsenba**
温泉卵 hot spring-dipped egg **onsen tamago**
温泉郷 hot springs town **onsenkyō**
温泉療法 hot spring cure treatment **onsen ryōhō**
霊泉 therapeutic hot springs **reisen**
冷泉 cold springs **reisen**
清泉 clear-water spring **seisen**
泉下 hades; the next world **senka**
泉石 springs & rocks in a garden **senseki**

泉水 fountain, mini pond **sensui**
黄泉 netherland, land of the dead **yomi**
間欠泉 geyser, intermittent spring **kanketsusen**
硫黄泉 sulphur springs **iōsen**
鉄鉱泉 rusty-water springs **tekkōsen**

浴shower, 891	水ater, 9
射shoot, 504	源ource, 431

線ine, 531

441-B

泉ot-springs by the finish 線ine filled with sake wine...

糸 (thread, continuity)

線inear　線ining

SEN
linear, lining, cable

FLIP: 7.0.b1. Right (stem)

傍線 underline, sideline **bōsen**
直線 straight line, direct line **chokusen**
断線 breaking of lines (railway) **dansen**
電線 electric wire **densen**
伏線 anticipation, underplot **fukusen**
外線 outside phone call, external line **gaisen**
光線 rays of light **kōsen**
幹線 trunk line, main line **kansen**
架線 wire, wiring **kasen**
活線 live electric wire **kassen**
曲線 curve, curving line **kyokusen**
無線 wireless, radio **musen**
内線 phone extension, inside call **naisen**
路線 railway route **rosen**
線画 drawing lines **senga**
線上 "on the borderline..." **senjō**
線香 candle stick, incense stick **senkō**
戦線 battle line, frontline **sensen**
線審 line man (tennis referee) **senshin**

線路 railway route **senro**
斜線 slanted line **shasen**
支線 branch line **shisen**
視線 glance, gaze, stare **shisen**
点線 dotted line **tensen**
前線 front, frontline **zensen**
平行線 parallel lines **heikōsen**
補給線 pipe line **hokyūsen**
警戒線 "police line: do not cross..." **keikaisen**
境界線 boundary, border line **kyōkaisen**
垂直線 perpendicular line **suichokusen**
停止線 finish line, stop line **teishisen**
等温線 isotherm **tōonsen**
宇宙線 cosmic rays **uchūsen**

行rip, 79	直traight, 420	緯orizontal, 797
形hape, 951	縦ertical, 551	並arallel, 444

泉prings, 531

442-A

Ears to 貫*ierce,* 慣*abit passed upon for many years...*

貝 (shell, old money)

貫*enetrate* 　貫*arry out*

tsuranu(ku), KAN
penetrate, pierce, run thru, carry-out

FLIP: 1.0.b. Whole (stem)

一貫 *coherence, consistency* **ikkan**
⇒裸一貫 *"no property but one's body..."* **hadaka ikkan**
⇒首尾一貫 *logical, coherent* **shubi ikkan**
⇒終始一貫 *consistent, constant* **shūshi ikkan**
縦貫 *running thru, traversing* **jūkan**
縦貫道路 *road running across* **jūkan dōro**
縦貫鉄道 *railroad running across* **jūkan tetsudō**
貫首 *chief priest* **kanju**
貫目 *old word for weight measurement* **kanme**
貫入 *penetration, piercing* **kannyū**
貫禄 *presence, dignity* **kanroku**
貫流 *flowing thru, underlying* **kanryū**
貫籍 *census registration* **kanseki**
貫徹 *accomplishment, attainment* **kantetsu**
貫通 *penetration, piercing* **kantsū**
満貫 *highest score* **mangan**
突貫 *rush, overflow, storm* **tokkan**
指貫 *thimble* **yubinuki**
貫き通す *fulfil one's wish* **tsuranukitoosu**

打ち貫く *pierce thru* **uchinuku**

刺*ierce*, 875	行*erform*, 79
徹*ierce-thru*, 843	執*arry-out*, 268
挿*nsert*, 126	致*arry-out*, 381

買*urchase*, 516

442-B

Ears to 貫*ierce,* 慣*abit passed upon for many years...*

心 ⇔ 忄 ⇔ 小 (feelings)

慣*abitual* 　慣*et used to*

na(reru), na(rasu), KAN
habitual, get used to, accustom, behaviour, character, attitude, customary

FLIP: 7.0.b2. Right (stem)

慣行 *custom, practice, habitual* **kankō**
慣行犯 *habitual crime* **kankōhan**
慣例 *custom, precedent* **kanrei**
慣例上 *by tradition, by convention* **kanreijō**
慣性 *inertia, latent energy* **kansei**
慣習 *custom, convention* **kanshū**
慣習風袋 *customary tare* **kanshū fūtai**
慣用 *common use* **kanyō**
慣用語 *idiomatic language* **kanyōgo**
慣用句 *idiom, figurative speech* **kanyōku**
慣用手段 *usual measures* **kanyō shudan**
旧慣 *old ways of doing things* **kyūkan**
習慣 *habit, custom* **shūkan**
不慣れ *inexperience, amateur, greenhorn* **funare**
食習慣 *food habits, eating habits* **shokushūkan**
商慣習 *commercial custom* **shōkanshū**
足慣らし *workout, warming up, practice* **ashinarashi**
肩慣らし *warming-up* **katanarashi**
口慣らし *oral drill* **kuchinarashi**

耳慣れる *get used to hearing* **miminareru**
見慣れる *familiar sight, get used to see* **minareru**
物慣れる *get used to it* **mononareru**
手慣れる *used to handling* **tenareru**
世慣れる *become street-smart* **yonareru**
飼い慣らす *get used to tame* **kainarasu**
聞き慣れる *familiar sounding* **kikinareru**
耳慣れない *"never heard..."* **miminarenai**
住み慣れる *"feel at home..."* **suminareru**

癖*abitual*, 65	事*ction*, 116
仕*ction*, 9	活*ction*, 237

貫*arry out*, 532

443-A

Sweet 方erson's 芳ragrance, her 方irection glanced...

方 (direction)

❶方*irection* ❷方*erson*

kata, HŌ
direction; person, individual, somebody, someone

Facing: 2.0. East ☞ (W)

❶地方 *countryside, rural* **chihō**
出方 *attitude, move* **dekata**
方便 *expediency, means* **hōben**
方方① *"here and there..."* **hōbō**
方角 *direction* **hōgaku**
方言 *dialect, local language* **hōgen**
方法 *method, way, means* **hōhō**
方位 *direction* **hōi**
方向 *direction* **hōkō**
方面 *direction, "this way to..."* **hōmen**
方血 *blood-letting* **hōketsu**
方策 *scheme, measures* **hōsaku**
方式 *form, method* **hōshiki**
方針 *policy, measures* **hōshin**
一方 *"on the otherhand, also..."* **ippō**
快方 *better condition* **kaihō**
彼方 *far, distance* **kanata**
味方 *taking side with, align with* **mikata**
両方 *both sides* **ryōhō**

仕方 *way, method, means* **shikata**
他方 *other side* **tahō**
裏方 *behind the scenes* **urakata**
夕方 *evening, night* **yūgata**
明け方 *dawn, daybreak* **akegata**
方眼紙 *graph paper, plotting paper* **hōganshi**
方程式 *mathematical equation* **hōteishiki**
書き方 *writing-, literary style* **kakikata**
漢方薬 *Chinese herbal medicine* **kanpōyaku**
解き方 *way of dealing with problems* **tokikata**
遣り方 *way of doing things* **yarikata**
❷方方② *all persons, everyone* **katagata**
親方 *sumo owner; master carpenter* **oyakata**
親方日の丸 *"gov't to pay the bill..."*
　　oyakata hinomaru

者*erson, 278*　人*erson, 2*　道*ath, 312*

万*en thousand, 465*

443-B

Sweet 方erson's 芳ragrance, her 方irection glanced...

艹 (grass)

芳*ragrance*　　芳*avourable*

kanba(shii), kaguwa(shii),HŌ
fragrance, scent, sweet smell; favourable

Facing: 2.1. East ☞ (H)
FLIP: 3.0.b. Top (stem)

芳しい *good, sweet smell* **kanbashii, kaguwashii**
芳眉 *pretty eyebrows* **hōbi**
芳情 *"your kindness..."* **hōjō**
芳醇 *rich; mellow* **hōjun**
芳紀 *young girl's age, sweet sixteen* **hōki**
芳気 *young age* **hōki**
芳香 *fragrance, perfume, aroma* **hōkō**
芳名 *your name, (honorific)* **hōmei**
芳名録 *guest list* **hōmeiroku**
芳烈 *aroma* **hōretsu**
芳志 *"your kindness..."* **hōshi**
芳草 *fragrant herb* **hōsō**
芳墨 *scented ink* **hōboku**
芳墨帳 *autographed album* **hōbokuchō**
芳心 *good wishes, kindness, goodwill* **hōshin**
芳信 *"your esteemed letter..."* **hōshin**
芳書 *"your esteemed letter..."* **hōsho**
遺芳 *"in honour of the dead..."* **ihō**

薫*ragrance, 934*　　香*ragrance, 895*
鼻*ose, 169*　　　　花*lower, 191*
臭*mell, 586*　　　　華*lower, 40*

方*erson, 533*

444-A

制ystematic 製anufacture, due to workers' tenure...

刀⇔刂 (blade, cutting)

制ystem　　制ontrol

SEI

system, control, regulation, process

Facing: 3.0. ⟲⟳ Across

圧制 oppression, tyranny **assei**	先制 headstart, leeway, edge **sensei**
現制 present-, existing system **gensei**	専制 despotism, autocracy, tyranny **sensei**
兵制 military system **heisei**	節制 moderation, self-restraint **sessei**
編制 forming an organization **hensei**	体制 organization, composition **taisei**
管制 regulation, restriction **kansei**	帝制 imperial system **teisei**
禁制 prohibition, forbidden, unlawful **kinsei**	統制 regulation, control **tōsei**
規制 regulation, restriction **kisei**	抑制 repression, restraint, control **yokusei**
強制 compulsion, coercion **kyōsei**	税制 taxation, tax imposition **zeisei**
産制 birth control **sansei**	二院制 bicameral system **niinsei**
制圧 control, ascendancy, mastery **seiatsu**	輪番制 rotation system **rinbansei**
制度 system, institution, organization **seido**	制球力 control, strength **seikyūryoku**
制服 uniform, work clothes **seifuku**	天皇制 emperor system **tennōsei**
制限 limitation, restriction **seigen**	
制御 control, strength **seigyo**	
制令 regulation, supervision **seirei**	決ecide, 699　規tandard, 814　律egulation, 731
制裁 sanctions, punitive measures **seisai**	定efinite, 550　則egulation, 290　協ooperate, 577
制作 film production **seisaku**	
制止 restraint, control **seishi**	刺ierce, 875
制定 enactment, establishment **seitei**	

444-B

制ystematic 製anufacture, due to workers' tenure...

衣⇔衤 (clothing)

製anufacture　　製abricate

SEI

manufacture, assemble, fabricate

Facing: 2.1. East ☞ (H)

調製 made-to-order, custom-made **chōsei**	製糸 spinning, silk reeling **seishi**
縫製 sewing, stitching **hōsei**	製紙 paper manufacture **seishi**
官製 government-manufactured **kansei**	製薬 drug manufacture **seiyaku**
既製 ready-made **kisei**	製油 oil manufacture **seiyu**
鋼製 steel manufacture **kōsei**	製材 lumber, timber **seizai**
薫製 food smoking process **kunsei**	即製 on the spot processing **sokusei**
木製 wooden products **mokusei**	粗製 crude manufacture **sosei**
再製 reprocessing, recycling **saisei**	手製 hand-made, handicraft **tesei**
製茶 tea processing **seicha**	特製 specially-made for **tokusei**
製塩 salt-making **seien**	
製粉 flour manufacture **seifun**	造anufacture, 267　　造roduce, 267
製版 plate-making **seihan**	作roduce, 724　　品roducts, 901
製品 manufactured goods **seihin**	産roduce, 883　　制ystem, 534
製本 book binding **seihon**	
製菓 confectionery, sweets-making **seika**	制ystem, 534
製靴 shoemaking **seika**	
製麺 noodle-making **seimen**	
製作 production (film) **seisaku**	
精製 refining (sugar) **seisei**	

445-A

忍oncealed 忍erseverance 認ecognized as endurance...

心⇔忄 (heart, feelings)

❶忍ersevere **❷忍onceal**

shino(bu), shino(baseru), NIN
persevere, holding fast, persisting, steadfast, bear with, tenacity; conceal, hidden, secret

Facing: 4.0. ⤙⤚ Apart

❶忍び足 *stealthy steps* **shinobiashi**
忍び音 *subdued sobbing* **shinobine**
忍び難い *unbearable* **shinobigatai**
隠忍 *patience, endurance* **innin**
堪忍 *patience, forgiveness* **kannin**
堅忍 *indomitable, unrelenting* **kennin**
忍冬 *Japanese honeysuckle* **nindō, suikazura**
忍従 *patient submission* **ninjū**
忍苦 *patient endurance* **ninku**
忍耐 *endurance, perseverance* **nintai**
忍耐力 *endurance, perseverance* **nintairyoku**
忍耐強い *patience, steadfast* **nintaizuyoi**
耐え忍ぶ *bear, stand, put up with* **taeshinobu**
残忍 *cruel, harsh, brutal* **zannin**

❷忍び声 *whisper* **shinobigoe**
忍び入る *sneak in* **shinobiiru**
忍び込む *steal, sneak* **shinobikomu**

忍び泣き *sobbing, burst into tears* **shinobinaki**
忍び姿 *disguise, incognito* **shinobisugata**
忍び笑い *giggle, chuckle* **shinobiwarai**
忍び寄る *creep up, draw near* **shinobiyoru**
忍び逢い *secret meeting* **shinobiai**
忍者 *spy samurai* **ninja**
忍術 *art of stealth & espionage* **ninjutsu**
忍法 *being invisible* **ninpō**

匿onceal, 277	隠idden, 840
覆onceal, 602	秘idden, 219
陰idden, 864	耐ndure, 974

刀lade, 353

445-B

忍oncealed 忍erseverance 認ecognized as endurance...

言 (speaking)

認ecognize **認cknowledge**

mito(meru), NIN
recognize, acknowledge, certify, confirm, verify

FLIP: 6.0.a. Left (flat)

誤認 *misconception, misunderstanding* **gonin**
否認 *denial, disapproval, repudiation* **hinin**
自認 *admission of failures* **jinin**
確認 *confirmation, verification* **kakunin**
検認 *probation, inspection* **kennin**
公認 *official recognition, ~authorization* **kōnin**
認印 *seal of approval, official seal* **mitomein**
黙認 *overlook, acquiescence* **mokunin**
認知 *recognition, acknowledgement* **ninchi**
認諾 *approve, assent* **nindaku**
認可 *permission, approval* **ninka**
認可者 *licensor* **ninkasha**
認可証 *certificate, license* **ninkasho**
認否 *arrangement, adjustment* **ninpi**
認識 *recognition, awareness* **ninshiki**
認識論 *epistemology, metaphysics* **ninshikiron**
認識不足 *lack of recognition, ~appreciation*
　　　　　ninshiki busoku
認証 *authentication, authorization* **ninshō**

認定 *authorization, recognition* **nintei**
再認 *permit renewal, ~extension* **sainin**
信認 *acknowledge, acceptance* **shinnin**
承認 *approval, consent, agreement* **shōnin**
追認 *post-facto confirmation* **tsuinin**
容認 *approval, accept, admit* **yōnin**
是認 *approval, admission, approbation* **zenin**
不認可 *rejection, non-approval* **funinka**
未確認 *unconfirmed, unverified* **mikakunin**
認め合う *mutual understanding* **mitomeau**
再確認 *reconfirmation, reaffirmation* **saikakunin**
罪状認否 *arraignment, court plea* **zaijō ninpi**

知wareness, 103	受ccept, 539
識wareness, 856	可pproval, 15
覚emember, 307	承pproval, 117

誌hronicle, 426

446-A

Death 刑*enalty* 型*attern, Amnesty's concern..!*

刀⇔刂 (blade, cutting)

刑*enalty*　　　　刑*unishment*

KEI
penalty, punishment, retribution, punitive

FLIP: 6.0.b. Left (stem)

減刑　*commutation, reduced sentence* **genkei**
実刑　*prison sentence, punishment* **jikkei**
銃刑　*death by firing squad, musketry* **jūkei**
重刑　*excessive punishment* **jūkei**
火刑　*be burned at stake* **kakei**
刑罰　*punishment, penalty* **keibatsu**
刑具　*punishment device* **keigu**
刑法　*criminal law, penal code* **keihō**
刑法学者　*criminologist* **keihō gakusha**
刑事　*detective, investigator* **keiji**
刑事犯　*criminal offence* **keijihan**
刑事事件　*crime, penal case* **keiji jiken**
刑事責任　*criminal liability* **keiji sekinin**
刑事訴訟　*criminal litigation* **keiji soshō**
刑場　*place of execution* **keijō**
刑期　*prison term, jail sentence* **keiki**
刑吏　*executioner, hangman* **keiri**
刑死　*execution of death sentence* **keishi**
極刑　*death penalty, capital punishment* **kyokkei**

求刑　*prosecution, plaintiff, accuser* **kyūkei**
流刑　*banishment, exile* **rukei**
私刑　*death by lynching* **shikei**
死刑　*death penalty, capital punishment* **shikei**
処刑　*execution of a sentence* **shokei**
主刑　*main punishment* **shukei**
体刑　*penal servitude, punishment* **taikei**
天刑　*divine punishment* **tenkei**
刑務所　*prison, jail, gaol* **keimusho**
絞首刑　*death by hanging* **kōshukei**
終身刑　*life sentence, ~imprisonment* **shūshinkei**

懲*unishment, 63*		罪*riminal, 289*	
罰*unishment, 759*		犯*riminal, 640*	
囚*risoner, 863*		凶*vil, 80*	

形*orm, 951*

446-B

Death 刑*enalty* 型*attern, Amnesty's concern..!*

土 (ground, soil)

型*attern*　　　　型*odel*

kata, KEI
pattern, model, prototype, type

FLIP: 4.0.a. Bottom (flat)

母型　*matrix, form, cast* **bokei**
文型　*sentence pattern* **bunkei**
同型　*same pattern* **dōkei**
原型　*prototype, model* **genkei**
歯型　*toothprint, toothmarks* **hagata**
鋳型　*casting mould* **igata**
髪型　*hairstyle* **kamigata**
型紙　*dressmaking pattern* **katagami**
型式　*model, pattern* **keishiki**
木型　*wood pattern* **kigata**
旧型　*old model* **kyūgata**
模型　*model* **mokei**
並型　*ordinary size* **namigata**
大型　*extra-large, supersize* **oogata**
類型　*type, pattern, prototype* **ruikei**
成型　*cast, pressing* **seikei**
紙型　*paper pattern* **shikei**
新型　*new pattern* **shingata**
体型　*figure, form, build* **taikei**

定型　*fixed form* **teikei**
典型　*model, type, paragon* **tenkei**
典型的　*typical* **tenkeiteki**
煩型　*complainer, fault-finder* **urusagata**
造型　*moulding* **zōkei**
努力型　*hard-working type* **doryokugata**
標準型　*standard type* **hyōjungata**
型破り　*unconventional, unique* **katayaburi**
血液型　*blood type* **ketsuekigata**

鑑*attern, 857*		範*odel, 584*	
塑*attern, 896*		形*hape, 951*	
柄*attern, 213*		製*anufacture, 534*	

刑*enalty, 536*

447-A

None 反gainst, 返eturn of stolen grains...

反gainst　　反ppose

又 (again)

反

so(ru), so(rasu), HAN, HON, TAN
against, oppose, contrary, counter

FLIP: 4.0.b. Bottom (stem)

反米 *anti-US sentiments* **hanbei**
反動 *reaction, counter action* **handō**
反映 *reflection, contemplation* **han'ei**
反撃 *counter-attack, retaliatory strike* **hangeki**
反逆 *treason, rebellion* **hangyaku**
反逆者 *traitor, rebel, renegade, quisling* **hangyakusha**
反核 *anti-nuclear* **hankaku**
反感 *antipathy, hostility, animosity* **hankan**
反抗 *resistance, opposition* **hankō**
反響 *sensation, echo, response* **hankyō**
反共 *anti-communism* **hankyō**
反面 *"on the otherhand..."* **hanmen**
反目 *antagonism, animosity, hostility* **hanmoku**
反日 *anti-Japanese* **hannichi**
反応 *response, reaction* **hannō**
反発 *repulsion, revulsion* **hanpatsu**
反落 *decline in reaction* **hanraku**
反乱 *return question, retort* **hanran**
反論 *rebuttal, rejoinder, retort* **hanron**

反省 *reflection; reconsideration* **hansei**
反戦 *anti-war, peace movement* **hansen**
反射 *reflection, contemplation* **hansha**
⇒条件反射 *conditioned reflex* **jōken hansha**
反照 *reflection, contemplation* **hanshō**
反対 *opposition, resistance* **hantai**
反転 *turtle turn, upside down* **hanten**
反吐 *vomiting, puke, throwing up* **hedo**
違反 *offence, violation* **ihan**
⇒憲法違反 *unconstitutional* **kenpō ihan**
反物 *kimono fabric, ~cloth* **tanmono**
造反 *rebellion, uprising* **zōhan**
仰け反る *bend back oneself* **nokezoru**

逆pposite, 896	争onflict, 231
抗esistance, 749	戦attle, 517
抵esistance, 700	

友riendship, 408

447-B

None 反gainst, 返eturn of stolen grains...

返eturn　　返ome-back

辶 (transport)

返

kae(ru), kae(su), HEN
return, come back, revert

FLIP: 8.0.b. Inner (stem)
Facing: 4.0. Apart

返電 *reply telegram* **henden**
返事 *answer, reply* **henji**
⇒二つ返事 *immediate reply, readily* **futatsu henji**
返上 *return, giving back* **henjō**
返還 *return, revert* **henkan**
返金 *refund, repayment* **henkin**
返却 *return a borrowed item* **henkyaku**
返納 *payback, refund* **hennō**
返品 *returned goods* **henpin**
返報 *retaliation, revenge, getting back at* **henpō**
返本 *returned book* **henpon**
返礼 *gift in return* **henrei**
返済 *repayment, payback* **hensai**
返済期限 *repayment schedule* **hensai kigen**
返信 *reply, answer* **henshin**
返送 *"return to sender..."* **hensō**
返答 *answer in reply, retort* **hentō**
宙返り *somersault, loop-the-loop* **chūgaeri**
送り返す *send back, return* **okurikaesu**

照り返し *reflection (light or heat)* **terikaeshi**
揺り返し *aftershock, reverberation* **yurikaeshi**
返り咲き *comeback, grand return* **kaerizaki**
跳ね返す *reject, repulse, bounce* **hanekaesu**
混ぜ返す *interrupt; stir up* **mazekaesu**
蒸し返す *steam again, rehash* **mushikaesu**
追い返す *send away, drive back* **oikaesu**
読み返す *read again, re-reading* **yomikaesu**

換eplace, 819	還eturn, 165
替eplace, 334	帰eturn, 784
代eplace, 96	戻eturn, 541

坂lope, 733

448-A

Heinous murder 弔ourns with 沸oiling horns...

弓 (archery bow) 3

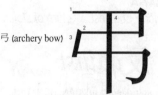

弔ourning 弔uneral

tomura(u), CHŌ
mourning, funeral, condole, bereavement

Facing: 1.0. 🔁 West (W)

弔文 *letter of condolence, ~sympathy* **chōbun**
弔電 *sympathy-, condolence telegram* **chōden**
弔砲 *funeral salute* **chōhō**
弔意 *condolence, mourning, commiseration* **chōi**
弔慰 *condolence, sympathy, commiseration* **chōi**
弔辞 *condolence message* **chōji**
弔歌 *dirge, requiem, elegy* **chōka**
弔花 *funeral flowers* **chōka**
弔旗 *black mourning flag, flag at half mast* **chōki**
弔問 *condolence visit* **chōmon**
弔問客 *condolence visitor* **chōmonkyaku**
弔詞 *condolence message* **chōshi**
弔鐘 *funeral bell* **chōshō**
慶弔 *congratulations & condolences* **keichō**
弔慰金 *condolence money* **chōikin**
弔い合戦 *avenging battle* **tomurai gassen**

喪*ourning, 119*	死*eath, 513*
忌*ourn, 6*	逝*eath, 54*
愁*orrows, 415*	亡*eath, 72*
悲*orrows, 289*	哀*adness, 374*

弓*ulling, 348*

448-B

Heinous murder 弔ourns with 沸oiling horns...

水⇔氵 (water) 2

沸oiling 沸immering

wa(ku), wa(kasu), FUTSU
boiling, simmering

Facing: 1.2. 🔁 West (V)

沸かす *excite, heat, boil* **wakasu**
沸き返る *boil up; be excited* **wakikaeru**
沸き立つ *boil up, arise, seethe* **wakitatsu**
湯沸かし *boiling kettle, boiling pot* **yuwakashi**
湯沸かし器 *water heater* **yuwakashiki**
沸き上がる *arise, well up* **wakiagaru**
沸き起こる *burst, arise* **wakiokoru**
沸石 *zeolite* **fusseki**
沸騰 *boiling, seething, scalding* **futtō**
沸騰点 *boiling point* **futtōten**
煮沸 *boiling, seething, scalding* **shafutsu**
煮沸消毒 *sterilization by boiling* **shafutsu shōdoku**
沸点 *boiling point* **futten**

煮*oiling, 278*
燃*urning, 445*
湯*ot-water, 932*

津*arbour, 731*

449-A

受*eceive no study* 授*rants,* 授*eaching post vacant...*

又 (again)

受*eceive*   受*ccept*

u(keru), u(karu), JU
receive, accept, obtain, pass an exam

FLIP: 4.0.b. Bottom (stem)

傍受 *pick up, intercept, monitor* **bōju**
拝受 *receipt of* **haiju**
受諾 *consent to* **judaku**
授受 *give & take, exchange* **juju**
受験 *entrance examination* **juken**
受講 *attend a lecture* **jukō**
受難 *sufferings, difficulties* **junan**
受領 *acceptance, receipt* **juryō**
受信 *receipt of message, ~e-mail* **jushin**
受診 *consult a doctor* **jushin**
受章 *receive an award, medal* **jushō**
甘受 *submission, resignation* **kanju**
享受 *enjoyment, pleasure* **kyōju**
受刑者 *convicted felon* **jukeisha**
買受人 *purchaser, auction winner* **kaiukenin**
感受性 *sensibility, sensuality* **kanjusei**
受け身 *passiveness, apathy* **ukemi**
受け皿 *pan, plate* **ukezara**
受け入れ *acceptance, treatment* **ukeire**

受け持ち *charge, taking charge* **ukemochi**
受け流す *parry* **ukenagasu**
受け取る *receive, accept, get, take* **uketoru**
受け継ぐ *inherit, succeed, take over* **uketsugu**
受け渡し *delivery, handing over* **ukewatashi**
郵便受け *mailbox, letter box* **yūbin'uke**
待ち受ける *wait for* **machiukeru**
受け止める *catch, react to* **uketomeru**
受け付ける *accept, receive* **uketsukeru**
譲り受ける *inherit, succeed* **yuzuriukeru**

請*emand, 791*
頂*eceive, 134*
採*dopt, 915*

愛*ove, 593*

449-B

受*eceive no study* 授*rants,* 授*eaching post vacant...*

手⇔扌 (hand, manual)

❶授*eaching* ❷授*rant*

sazu(keru), sazu(karu), JU
teaching, educate, instruction, lecture, inculcate; grant

FLIP: 7.3.b. Right Bottom (stem)

❶伝授 *initiation, instruction* **denju**
授業 *class, lesson* **jugyō**
授業料 *tuition, school fees* **jugyōryō**
授業時間 *lesson-, class hours* **jugyō jikan**
授受 *transfer, exchange* **juju**
授戒 *Buddhist initiation rites* **jukai**
口授 *oral instruction, ~lessons* **kōju**
教授 *university professor* **kyōju**
⇒個人教授 *private lessons* **kojin kyōju**
⇒交換教授 *exchange professor* **kōkan kyōju**
⇒名誉教授 *professor emeritus* **meiyo kyōju**
⇒助教授 *associate professor* **jokyōju**
教授団 *faculty* **kyōjudan**
教授法 *teaching methodology* **kyōjuhō**

❷授粉 *pollination* **jufun**
授乳 *breast-feeding, lactation* **ju'nyū**
授乳期 *lactation period* **ju'nyūki**
授産 *recruitment, hiring* **jusan**

授精 *fertilization, pollination* **jusei**
授爵 *confer nobility, ~peerage* **jushaku**
授賞 *awarding a prize, citation* **jushō**
授賞式 *awards ceremony* **jushōshiki**
授与 *awarding, conferment* **juyo**
神授 *divine gift* **shinju**
天授 *in-born gifts* **tenju**
授権資本 *authorized capital stock* **juken shihon**
授かり物 *gift, blessing, boon* **sazukarimono**

教*ducate, 385*　　習*earning, 238*
修*aster, 898*　　読*eading, 260*
徒*isciple, 497*　　書*ritings, 116*
師*eacher, 483*　　文*iteracy, 558*

採*dopt, 915*

450-A

By 由eason of 油etroleum, prices in premium...

由eason   由ogic

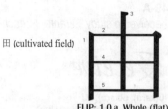

田 (cultivated field)

FLIP: 1.0.a. Whole (flat)

yoshi, YU, YŪ, YUI
reason, logic, rationale, dialectic

由々しい *grave, serious* **yuyushii**
因由 *cause & effect* **inyu**
自由 *freedom, liberty* **jiyū**
事由 *reason, cause* **jiyū**
自由放任 *non-intervention* **jiyū hōnin**
自由自在 *free existence, independent* **jiyū jizai**
自由の女神 *Statue of Liberty* **jiyū no megami**
自由形 *freestyle swimming* **jiyūgata**
自由業 *self-employed* **jiyūgyō**
自由化 *liberalization* **jiyūka**
経由 *via, by way of, detour, stopover* **keiyu**
理由 *reason, rationale, logic* **riyū**
由縁 *reason, relationship* **yuen**
由緒 *history, lineage* **yuisho**
由来 *origin, cause, source* **yurai**

理*eason, 872*	哲*hilosophy, 53*
故*eason, 960*	賢*isdom, 598*

田*ice field, 482*

450-B

By 由eason of 油etroleum, prices in premium...

油etroleum

水⇔氵 (water)

FLIP: 7.0.a. Right (flat)

abura, YU
petroleum, oil, black gold

油絵 *oil painting* **aburae**
油紙 *oil-paper* **aburagami**
油気 *greasiness, oiliness* **aburake**
油虫 *cockroach, plant louse* **aburamushi**
油菜 *rape oil, rapeseed* **aburana**
注油 *oiling, lubrication, grease* **chūyu**
鯨油 *whale oil* **geiyu**
原油 *crude oil, petroleum* **genyu**
給油 *lubrication, oiling, greasing* **kyūyu**
採油 *oil drilling, oil pumping* **saiyu**
搾油 *oil extraction, oil drilling* **sakuyu**
製油 *oil refining, oil processing* **seiyu**
送油 *oil pumping, oil extraction* **sōyu**
種油 *seed oil, vegetable oil* **taneabura**
灯油 *kerosene, paraffin oil* **tōyu**
油圧 *oil-, hydraulic pressure* **yuatsu**
油断 *carelessness, clumsiness* **yudan**
油田 *oil field* **yuden**
油煙 *lampblack, soot* **yuen**

油井 *oil well* **yusei**
油性 *oil, grease* **yusei**
油脂 *oils & fats* **yushi**
油槽 *oil tank* **yusō**
油層 *oil stratum, oil deposits* **yusō**
油剤 *ointment* **yuzai**
油差し *oil can* **aburasashi**
潤滑油 *lubricating oil* **junkatsuyu**
機械油 *machine oil* **kikai abura**
菜種油 *rapeseed oil* **natane abura**

商*ommerce, 135*	業*usiness, 124*
燃*urning, 445*	商*usiness, 135*
液*iquid, 508*	電*nergy, 417*

抽*xtract, 37*

451-A
戻eturned after 24 years, five with lots of 涙ears...

戻eturn   戻omeback

戸 (doorway)

modo(ru), modo(su), REI
return, comeback, revert

FLIP: 8.O.b. Inner (stem)

暴戻 atrocity, tyranny, heinous **bōrei**
背戻 disobey, defy, ignore **hairei**
返戻 return, give back **henrei**
後戻り turning back, returning **atomodori**
出戻り return to one's parents home **demodori**
逆戻り retrogression, turn back **gyakumodori**
早戻し rewinding a tape **hayamodoshi**
小戻り moving back a little **komodori**
戻り道 one's way back, return trip **modorimichi**
戻り速度 return speed **modorisokudo**
戻し税 tax refund **modoshizei**
積戻し send back, re-ship **tsumimodoshi**
払い戻し refund, repayment **haraimodoshi**
買い戻す repurchase, buy back **kaimodosu**
繰り戻し put back **kurimodoshi**
舞い戻り return, go back **maimodori**
巻き戻し rewinding a tape **makimodoshi**
押し戻し push back, reject **oshimodoshi**
差し戻し send back **sashimodoshi**

立ち戻り return to, go back to **tachimodori**
取り戻す take back, restore **torimodosu**
突き戻し thrust back **tsukimodoshi**
連れ戻す escorting back **tsuremodosu**
請け戻し redemption, repayment **ukemodoshi**
売り戻し re-sale **urimodoshi**
割り戻し rebate, return **warimodoshi**
割戻し金 rebate price **warimodoshikin**
焼き戻し iron tempering **yakimodoshi**
呼び戻し recall, call back **yobimodoshi**
揺り戻し swinging back **yurimodoshi**

先efore, 478	還eturn, 165	元rigin, 195
前efore, 118	帰eturn, 784	源rigin, 431
返eturn, 537	原riginal, 431	

房luster, 676

451-B
戻eturned after 24 years, five with lots of 涙ears...

涙ears   涙rying

水⇔氵 (water)

namida, RUI
tears, crying, shedding tears, wailing, weeping, whimpering, sobbing

FLIP: 8.O.b. Inner (stem)

暗涙 silent tears, quiet sobbing **anrui**
感涙 moving to tears **kanrui**
血涙 bitter tears **ketsurui**
紅涙 feminine tears **kōrui**
涙雨 sprinkling rainfall **namida ame**
涙声 crying voice, sobs **namidagoe**
涙雲 move to tears **namidagumo**
涙顔 tearful face, crying face **namidagao**
涙金 consolation money **namidakin**
涙脆い easily moved to tears **namidamoroi**
熱涙 hot tears **netsurui**
落涙 shedding tears **rakurui**
涙管 tear duct **ruikan**
涙嚢 tear sac **ruinō**
涙腺 lachrymal gland **ruisen**
声涙 tearful voice **seirui**
空涙 fake-, crocodile tears **soranamida**
催涙弾 tear-gas canister **sairuidan**
悔し涙 tears of regret **kuyashinamida**

嬉し涙 tears-of-joy **ureshinamida**
有り難涙 tears of gratitude **arigata namida**
不覚の涙 crying in spite of oneself **fukaku no namida**
催涙ガス tear gas **sairuigasu**
涙具ましい touching **namidagumashii**

泣rying, 235	哀orrows, 374
感eelings, 45	愁orrows, 415
気eelings, 98	悲orrows, 289
情eelings, 793	愁rief, 415

戻eturn, 541

452-A

臣ubjects & 臣etainers serve 姫rincess sisters...

°臣etainer °臣ubjects

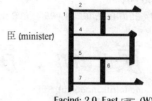

臣 (minister)

Facing: 2.0. East ☞ (W)

SHIN, JIN
retainer, serf, vassal; subjects

❶大臣 *cabinet minister* **daijin**
⇒外務大臣 *minister of foreign affairs* **gaimu daijin**
⇒郵政大臣 *minister of posts & telecommunications*
　　yūsei daijin
⇒財務大臣 *finance minister* **zaimu daijin**
⇒内閣総理大臣 *prime minister* **naikaku sōri daijin**
総理大臣 *the prime minister* **sōri daijin**
陪臣 *vassal retainer* **baishin**
忠臣 *loyal subject, faithful retainer* **chūshin**
群臣 *entire officialdom* **gunshin**
愚臣 *foolish retainer; "this humble vassal..."* **gushin**
逆臣 *rebel subject, renegade* **gyakushin**
侍臣 *courtier, attendant* **jishin**
重臣 *chief retainer* **jūshin**
家臣 *vassal, serf* **kashin**
下臣 *low-ranking retainer* **kashin**
乱臣 *traitorous vassal, quisling* **ranshin**
老臣 *senior vassal* **rōshin**
臣道 *way of a loyal subject* **shindō**

臣事 *retainers services* **shinji**
臣従 *retainers services* **shinjyū**
臣子 *retainers & their children* **shinshi**
臣属 *vassalage, subjects* **shinzoku**
使臣 *envoy, messenger* **shishin**
小臣 *lower-ranking vassal* **shōshin**
廷臣 *official retainer* **teishin**
❷君臣 *ruler & subject* **kunshin**
臣下 *subject, retainer* **shinka**
臣民 *subjects, colonial peoples* **shinmin**
臣服 *obey, follow, abide* **shinpuku**

府overnment, 429	宮alace, 105
役fficial, 746	殿alace, 522
吏fficial, 463	民eople, 495

巨iant, 206

452-B

臣ubjects & 臣etainers serve 姫rincess sisters...

姫rincess　　姫oble girl

女 (woman)

Facing: 2.2. East ☞ (V)

hime
princess, noble girl

姫蜂 *ichneumon* **himebachi**
姫君 *princess* **himegimi**
姫萩 *milkwort* **himehagi**
姫路 *Himeji City, Hyogo Prefecture* **himeji**
姫鏡 *model young lass* **himekagami**
姫松 *small pine tree* **himematsu**
姫宮 *princess* **himemiya**
姫様 *princess* **himesama**
姫鵜 *pelagic cormorant* **himeu**
舞姫 *female dancer* **maihime**
乙姫 *younger princess* **otohime**
歌姫 *female singer, ~vocalist* **utahime**
山姫 *mountain fairy, ~goddess* **yamahime**
姫小松 *small pine tree* **himekomatsu**
姫百合 *red star lily* **himeyuri**
織り姫 *Star Vega* **orihime**

王onarch, 12	殿alace, 522
皇mperor, 113	城astle, 243
后mpress, 87	妃rincess, 728

娠regnancy, 61

453-A

Kamikaze 隊quads *to* 墜escend *at all odds...*

ß ↔ 阜 (village=left)

隊*quad* 隊*roops*

TAI

squad, troops, platoon

Facing: 3.0. ☞ ☜ Across

部隊 *military unit, corps* **butai**
中隊 *army platoon* **chūtai**
大隊 *battalion, corps* **daitai**
楽隊 *musical band* **gakutai**
原隊 *one's original unit* **gentai**
軍隊 *soldier, troops* **guntai**
兵隊 *soldier* **heitai**
編隊 *formation (flight)* **hentai**
本隊 *main force* **hontai**
除隊 *military, discharge* **jotai**
縦隊 *column-, file of soldiers* **jūtai**
艦隊 *fleet, squadron* **kantai**
連隊 *regiment* **rentai**
戦隊 *squadron, flotilla* **sentai**
船隊 *naval fleet, armada* **sentai**
隊員 *platoon member, soldier* **taiin**
隊形 *formation, squadron* **taikei**
隊列 *column-, file of soldiers* **tairetsu**
デモ隊 *demonstrators, rallyists* **demotai**

軍楽隊 *military-, navy band* **gungakutai**
砲兵隊 *artillery corps* **hōheitai**
自衛隊 *self-defence force* **jieitai**
警官隊 *police squad* **keikantai**
憲兵隊 *WWII Japanese secret police* **kenpeitai**
先遣隊 *advance troops* **senkentai**
親衛隊 *bodyguards* **shin'eitai**
守備隊 *barracks, garrison* **shubitai**
捜索隊 *search party* **sōsakutai**
探検隊 *exploration party* **tankentai**
登山隊 *mountaineering party* **tozantai**

兵*oldier, 490*	戦*ighting, 517*	防*rotect, 736*
軍*oldier, 295*	衛*rotect, 796*	守*efence, 366*
卒*oldier, 109*	護*rotect, 828*	戦*attle, 517*

塚*ound, 825*

453-B

Kamikaze 隊quads *to* 墜escend *at all odds...*

土 (ground, soil)

墜*escent* 墜*ollapse*

TSUI

descent, collapse, downfall, founder

FLIP: 4.0.a. Bottom (flat)

撃墜 *shooting down* **gekitsui**
失墜 *fall, loss* **shittsui**
墜落 *fall, crash* **tsuiraku**
墜死 *falling to one's death* **tsuishi**

降*escend, 133*	落*ollapse, 826*
堕*escent, 807*	陥*ollapse, 893*

隊*quad, 543*

454-A

尊*steemed audience showed* 遵*bedience ...*

寸 (measurement)

尊*steem*   尊*espect*

FLIP: 3.0.a. Top (flat)

tatto(bu), tōto(bu), tatto(i), tōto(i), SON
esteem, respect, homage, honour, cherish, revere, adore

本尊 *main image of worship* **honzon**
⇒守り本尊 *patron saint* **mamori honzon**
自尊 *self-esteem, self-respect* **jison**
自尊心 *pride, self-respect* **jisonshin**
女尊 *respect for women* **joson**
釈尊 *Gautama Buddha* **shakuson**
尊重 *respect, esteem, reverence* **sonchō**
尊大 *arrogance, haughtiness* **sondai**
尊顔 *your countenance* **songan**
尊厳 *dignity, majesty* **songen**
尊号 *honorific title* **songō**
尊攘 *"revere the emperor..."* **sonjō**
尊敬 *respect, esteem, praise* **sonkei**
尊貴 *revered person* **sonki**
尊名 *your name (honorific)* **sonmei**
尊王 *imperial reverence* **sonnō**
尊王党 *imperialists, royalists* **sonnōtō**
尊卑 *the revered & the lowly* **sonpi**
尊父 *your father (honorific)* **sonpu**

尊者 *one's superior* **sonsha**
尊称 *honorific title* **sonshō**
尊崇 *veneration, reverence* **sonsū**
尊体 *your health (honorific)* **sontai**
尊宅 *your esteemed house (honorific)* **sontaku**
尊属 *ascendants, forebears, progenitors* **sonzoku**
尊属殺人 *patricide, matricide, parricide*
    sonzoku satsujin
尊像 *your portrait (honorific)* **sonzō**
男尊女卑 *male priority* **danson jōi**
女尊男卑 *female priority* **joson danpi**

恭*espect, 620*	敬*espect, 329*	礼*espect, 685*
仰*espect, 706*	尚*espect, 99*	仁*irtue, 457*
謹*espect, 962*	崇*espect, 879*	徳*irtue, 844*

遵*bedience, 544*

454-B

尊*steemed audience showed* 遵*bedience ...*

辶 (transport)

遵*bedience*   遵*ompliance*

FLIP: 3.0.a. Top (flat)

shitaga(u), JUN
obedience, compliance, conformity, deference

遵行 *obey, abide, follow* **junkō**
遵法 *law abiding* **junpō**
遵奉 *observance, abiding* **junpō**
遵守 *observance* **junshu**

礼*espect, 685*	仁*irtue, 457*
忠*oyalty, 475*	徳*irtue, 844*
孝*ilial, 385*	敬*espect, 329*

尊*steem, 544*

455-A
恵*lessed are the* 穂*rains when it rains...*

心 ⇔ 忄 ⇔ 灬 (feelings)

恵*lessing*　恵*avour*

megu(mu), KEI, E
blessing, favour, privilege, heaven-sent, divine gift

FLIP: 3.0.a. Top (flat)

知恵 *wisdom, intelligence* **chie**
知恵の輪 *puzzling ring* **chie no wa**
恵方 *lucky direction* **ehō**
恵方参り *new years visit to a shrine* **ehōmairi**
互恵 *reciprocity, mutuality* **gokei**
互恵的 *reciprocal, mutuality* **gokeiteki**
慈恵 *charity, altruism* **jikei**
仁恵 *gracious, benevolent* **jinkei**
恵沢 *blessing, favour* **keitaku**
恵与 *giving, bestowing* **keiyo**
恵贈 *presentation, offering* **keizō**
恵み *mercy, charity, alms, favour* **megumi**
恩恵 *favour, benefit* **onkei**
天恵 *heavenly-sent, divine blessing* **tenkei**
特恵 *preferential treatment, priority* **tokkei**
浅知恵 *shallow-mind, narrow thinking* **asajie**
後智恵 *hindsight* **atojie**
智恵歯 *wisdom tooth* **chieba**
智恵袋 *close advisers* **chiebukuro**

知恵者 *clever, wise, brilliant* **chiesha**
恵比寿 *god of wealth* **ebisu**
遅知恵 *retarded, slow-learner* **osojie**
遅知恵 *slow wisdom* **osojie**
最恵国 *most-favoured nation* **saikeikoku**
猿知恵 *shallow cunning* **sarujie**
悪知恵 *cunning, guile, macabre* **warujie**
知恵遅れ *mentally retarded* **chieokure**
恵比須顔 *smiling face* **ebisugao**
入れ知恵 *hint, suggestion* **irejie**

吉*ortunate, 227*	繁*rosperity, 434*
豊*bundance, 965*	隆*rosperity, 133*
富*ortune, 333*	得*dvantage, 940*
裕*ffluence, 758*	利*dvantage, 686*

東*astern, 220*

455-B
恵*lessed are the* 穂*rains when it rains...*

禾 (tree branch)

穂*rain*　穂*ice plant*

ho, SUI
grain, rice plant, spike

FLIP: 7.2.a. Right Top (flat)

初穂 *season's first crop* **hatsuho**
穂波 *waves of riceplants* **honami**
穂並み *waves of riceplants* **honami**
穂先 *spearhead, grain tip* **hosaki**
稲穂 *ears of riceplants* **inaho**
刈穂 *harvested rice ears* **kariho**
花穂 *grain spike* **kasui**
瑞穂 *ears of riceplants* **mizuho**
穂状 *ear-shaped grain* **suijō**
穂高岳 *Mt. Hodakatake* **hodakadake**
黒穂病 *smut, blight* **kurohobyō**
落ち穂 *gleanings* **ochibo**
落ち穂拾い *picking up fallen rice ears*
　　ochibohiroi
出穂期 *sprouting season* **shussuiki**
接ぎ穂 *graft, slip* **tsugiho**

麦*arley, 606*	稲*ice plant, 893*
穀*rain, 41*	耕*ultivate, 655*
粒*rain, 656*	培*ultivate, 698*

穏*ranquil, 840*

456-A
景cenic 影hadows, fantastic meadows...

景*cenery* 景*iew*

日 (sunlight, daytime)

FLIP: 1.0.b. Whole (stem)

KEI
scenery, view, vista, spectacle

美景 beautiful scenery **bikei**
盆景 miniature landscape (bonsai) **bonkei**
遠景 distant view, horizon **enkei**
風景 scenery, scene, landscape **fūkei**
風景画 landscape picture **fūkeiga**
背景 background, scenery, setting **haikei**
実景 actual view **jikkei**
情景 scene, sight, scenery **jōkei**
海景 ocean view **kaikei**
佳景 beautiful scenery **kakei**
景物 seasons natural features **keibutsu**
景品 premium, gift **keihin**
景観 view, vista, scenery **keikan**
景気 robust, ~brisk economy **keiki**
景況 situation, circumstances **keikyō**
景勝 picturesque, scenic **keishō**
景色 view, landscape, scenery **keshiki**
近景 foreground, panorama **kinkei**
光景 sight, view, scene **kōkei**

勝景 beautiful scenery **shōkei**
雲景 cloud view **unkei**
夜景 night view, nightline **yakei**
絶景 fantastic view **zekkei**
前景 foreground, forefront **zenkei**
全景 panorama, horizon **zenkei**
春景色 spring landscape, ~view **harukeshiki**
好景気 prosperity, good times **kōkeiki**
雪景色 snow landscape, snow view **yukigeshiki**
日本三景 Japan's 3 famous views **nihon sankei**
天下の景 speculative view **tenkanokei**

観*cenery*, 667	佳*eauty*, 891
眺*cenery*, 215	魅*eauty*, 969
観*iew*, 667	美*eautiful*, 124

星*tar*, 113

456-B
景cenic 影hadows, fantastic meadows...

影*hadow* 影*hade*

彡 (hair ornament)

FLIP: 6.0.b. Left (stem)

kage, EI
shadow, shade

暗影 gloom, dark shadow **an'ei**
影響 influence, effort **eikyō**
影像 portrait, likeness **eizō**
幻影 vision, illusion **gen'ei**
片影 glimpse, speck, sign **hen'ei**
日影 sunshine **hikage**
人影 person's shadow **hitokage**
火影 light, flicker of light **hokage**
星影 starlight **hoshikage**
陰影 shadow, shade **in'ei**
印影 imprint of a seal **in'ei**
人影 human shadow **jin'ei, hitokage**
影絵 shadow picture **kagee**
影印 photo reproduction **kagejirushi**
影身 person's shadow **kagemi**
孤影 solo figure **koei**
御影石 granite **mikageishi**
面影 image, face, shadow **omokage**
撮影 photography, shooting **satsuei**

撮影所 photography studio **satsueijo**
射影 image projection (film) **shaei**
島影 island's shadow **shimakage**
灯影 camp fire shadows **tōei**
投影 projection, shadow **tōei**
投影図 projection chart **tōeizu**
月影 moonlight, moonshine **tsukikage**
残影 traces, remains, ruins **zan'ei**
造影 contrast media **zōei**
悪影響 bad influence, harmful effect **akueikyō**

陰*hadows*, 864	眺*cenery*, 215
象*mage*, 530	観*iew*, 667
観*cenery*, 667	暗*ark*, 315

彰*itation*, 325

457-A

幾ow much 機hance would a 幾ew old 機achines run
out of balance?

玄 (short thread)

①幾ow much **②幾ew**

iku, KI
how much; few, scanty, some

Facing: 2.1. East ☞ (H)

❶幾許 *how much, how many* **ikubaku**
幾程 *how much, how many* **ikuhodo**
幾時 *what time* **ikuji**
幾時間 *a few hours, some hours* **ikujikan**
幾万 *tens of thousands* **ikuman**
幾昔 *how primitive* **ikumukashi**
幾ら *how much* **ikura**
幾才 *how old* **ikusai**
幾多 *many, various, diverse* **ikuta**
幾つ *how many* **ikutsu**
幾月 *how many months* **ikutsuki**
幾何 *geometry* **kika**
幾何学 *geometry* **kikagaku**

❷幾分 *somehow, somewhat* **ikubun**
幾重 *repeatedly, earnestly* **ikue**
幾日 *a few days* **ikunichi**

幾度 *a few times* **ikudo, ikutabi**
幾人 *a few persons* **ikunin**
幾夜 *a few nights* **ikuyo**
幾年 *a few years, some years* **ikutose, ikunen**
幾千 *thousands* **ikusen**
庶幾 *hope, desire, wish* **shoki**

少*ew, 459*	価*rice, 35*
寡*ittle, 161*	額*rice, 559*
若*ittle, 276*	値*rice, 783*

機*achine, 547*

457-B

幾ow much 機hance would a 幾ew old 機achines run
out of balance?

木 (wooden)

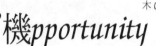

①機achine **②機pportunity**

hata, KI
machine, mechanics; opportunity, chance

Facing: 2.2. East ☞ (V)

❶電機 *electronics* **denki**
動機 *motive, intention, volition* **dōki**
機械 *machine, machinery* **kikai**
機関 *organ, institution, machine* **kikan**
危機 *crisis, emergency* **kiki**
機構 *structure, organisation* **kikō**
機密 *secret, secrecy, covert* **kimitsu**
機能 *function, role* **kinō**
有機 *organic substance* **yūki**
編み機 *knitting machine* **amiki**
電算機 *electronic calculator* **densanki**
飛行機 *aircraft, airplane* **hikōki**
印刷機 *printing press, ~machine* **insatsuki**
録音機 *recording device, dictaphone* **rokuonki**
両替機 *money changer* **ryōgaeki**
製本機 *book binder* **seihonki**
扇風機 *electric fan* **senpūki**
写真機 *camera* **shashinki**
昇降機 *elevator, lift* **shōkōki**

掃除機 *vacuum cleaner* **sōjiki**
探査機 *probe, investigation* **tansaki**
❷心機一転 ① *change-of-heart* **shinki itten**
心機一転 ② *"make a fresh start..."* **shinki itten**
時機 *chance, opportunity, occasion* **jiki**
契機 *opportunity, chance* **keiki**
機会 *opportunity, chance* **kikai**
機運 *opportunity, chance* **kiun**
好機 *good chance, ~opportunity* **kōki**
勝機 *chance of victory* **shōki**
枢機 *state-of-affairs* **sūki**
待機 *standing by, wait & see* **taiki**

械*achine, 493*	作*roduce, 724*
具*mplements, 487*	産*roduce, 883*
器*evice, 902*	造*roduce, 267*
匠*rtisan, 106*	品*roducts, 901*

幾*ew, 547*

458-A

Heavy 需*emands for virtues to please* 儒*onfucius...*

需*emand*

雨 (weather)

JU
demand

FLIP: 1.0.b. Whole (stem)

外需 *foreign demand* **gaiju**
軍需 *war materials, munitions* **gunju**
軍需景気 *war-led prosperity* **gunju keiki**
実需 *actual demand* **jitsuju**
需給 *supply & demand* **jukyū**
需給関係 *supply & demand relationship* **jukyū kankei**
需要 *demand, needs* **juyō**
⇒潜在需要 *potential demand* **senzai juyō**
需要家 *consumer, customer* **juyōka**
民需 *civilian needs* **minju**
民需用 *publicly-owned, for public use* **minjuyō**
内需 *domestic demand* **naiju**
特需 *special procurements* **tokuju**
必需品 *necessity, basic goods* **hitsujuhin**

徴*emand, 62* 業*usiness, 124*
要*ecessity, 419* 商*usiness, 135*

電*lectricity, 417*

458-B

Heavy 需*emands for virtues to please* 儒*onfucius...*

儒*onfucius*

人⇔亻 (person)

JU
Confucius

FLIP: 7.0.b2. Right (stem)

大儒 *great scholar* **daiju, taiju**
藩儒 *Daimyo scholar* **hanju**
儒仏 *Confucianism & Buddhism* **jubutsu**
儒学 *Confucianism studies* **jugaku**
儒家 *Confucian scholar* **juka**
儒教 *Confucianism* **jukyō**
儒生 *Confucian scholar* **jusei**
儒者 *Confucianist* **jusha**
犬儒 *cynicism, distrust, acrimony* **kenju**
侏儒 *pygmy, dwarf* **shuju**

孔*onfucius, 684* 義*ighteous, 341*
仁*irtue, 457* 善*ighteous, 450*
徳*irtue, 844* 篤*ighteous, 317*
倫*thics, 787*

需*emand, 548*

459-A

Democratic voting with 票uffrage 標arkings...

示⇔ネ (display, show)

❶票uffrage   ❷票lip

HYŌ
suffrage, election, voting; slip, sheet

FLIP: 1.0.b. Whole (stem)

❶ 青票 *opposing vote, blue ballot* **aohyō**
軍票 *military currency* **gunpyō**
白票 *blank vote, spoiled ballot* **hakuhyō**
票田 *voting bailiwick* **hyōden**
票決 *voting, casting a vote* **hyōketsu**
票決権 *right of voting, suffrage* **hyōketsuken**
票差 *vote margin* **hyōsa**
票数 *number of votes* **hyōsū**
票灯 *pilot lamp, sign lamp* **hyōtō**
一票 *one vote, your vote* **ippyō**
開票 *vote counting, opening the ballots* **kaihyō**
満票 *unanimous vote, unanimity* **manpyō**
里票 *milestone* **rihyō**
散票 *scattered votes, spoiled ballot* **sanpyō**
死票 *wasted vote* **shihyō**
集票 *collecting votes, campaigning* **shūhyō**
投票 *voting, going to the polls* **tōhyō**
⇒賛成投票 *favourable vote* **sansei tōhyō**
投票日 *election day* **tōhyōbi**

投票区 *voting district* **tōhyōku**
投票率 *election turn-out* **tōhyōritsu**
灯票 *light buoy* **tōhyō**
得票 *votes gained* **tokuhyō**
得票数 *number of votes polled* **tokuhyōsū**
無投票 *without vote, by acclamation* **mutōhyō**
❷ 入金票 *deposit slip, ~ticket* **nyūkinhyō**
伝票 *slip, note, ticket* **denpyō**
附票 *label* **fuhyō**
付票 *label, tag* **fuhyō**
証票 *voucher, coupon* **shōhyō**
調査票 *questionnaire sheet* **chōsahyō**
閲覧票 *call slip* **etsuranhyō**
住民票 *residence certificate* **jūminhyō**

| 選hoice, 303 | 衆opulace, 766 |
| 択hoice, 753 | 決udgement, 699 |

要ssential, 419

459-B

Democratic voting with 票uffrage 標arkings...

木 (wooden)

標arking   標ymbol

shime, HYŌ
marking, symbol, sign

FLIP: 7.0.b1. Right (stem)

墓標 *tombstone, gravemarker* **bohyō**
道標 *guidepost* **dōhyō**
浮標 *buoy, float mark* **fuhyō**
標榜 *advocate, proponent* **hyōbō**
標木 *wooden signpost, grave marker* **hyōboku**
標題 *title, headline, caption* **hyōdai**
標語 *slogan, catch phrase* **hyōgo**
標本 *specimen, sample* **hyōhon**
⇒植物標本 *botanical specimen*
    shokubutsu hyōhon
標準 *standard, level* **hyōjun**
標準語 *standard language (accent)* **hyōjungo**
標記 *mark, heading* **hyōki**
標旗 *symbol flag* **hyōki**
標高 *height from sea level* **hyōkō**
標札 *nameplate, mark* **hyōsatsu**
標識 *sign, mark, beacon* **hyōshiki**
標章 *emblem, ensign* **hyōshō**
標的 *target, mark* **hyōteki**

目標 *aim, goal, objective* **mokuhyō**
音標 *phonetic sign* **onpyō**
指標 *index, sign, market* **shihyō**
商標 *trademark, brand name* **shōhyō**
通標 *tablet, market* **tsūhyō**
座標 *coordinates, interconnecting points* **zahyō**
境界標 *boundary marker* **kyōkaihyō**
里程標 *milestone, epoch* **riteihyō**

| 符ark, 582 | 称itular, 130 |
| 札abel, 685 | 挙numerate, 370 |

票uffrage, 549

460-A

定scertain that all gates are blocked with 錠adlocks...

定ertain 定efinite

宀 (cover, lid)

sada(meru), sada(maru), sada(ka), TEI, JŌ
certain, ascertain, definite, determined, fixed

Facing: 2.1. ☞ East (H)

断定 decision, conclusion **dantei**
不定 indefinite, unsettled fujō, **futei**
限定 limitation, qualification **gentei**
判定 decision, judgement, ruling, verdict **hantei**
否定 denial, refusal, rejection **hitei**
評定 evaluation, assessment **hyōtei**
定規 ruler **jōgi**
確定 decision, confirmation **kakutei**
勘定 invoice, bill, accounts **kanjō**
決定 decision, conclusion **kettei**
既定 pre-arrangement, preparations **kitei**
規定 regulation, prescription **kitei**
肯定 affirmation, consent, approval **kōtei**
認定 authorization, recognition **nintei**
裁定 ruling, judgement, verdict, decision **saitei**
策定 decision, ruling, judgement, verdict **sakutei**
算定 calculation, estimate, appraisal **santei**
査定 assessment, revision **satei**
制定 enactment, establishment **seitei**

設定 settings, defaults **settei**
指定 designation, appointment **shitei**
推定 presumption, assumption **suitei**
定額 fixed-, specified amount **teigaku**
定員 regular limit, fixed capacity **teiin**
定住 settle down, live permanently **teijū**
定価 list price, fixed price **teika**
定格 standard, regular, normal **teikaku**
定款 articles of incorporation **teikan**
定期 fixed term, ~period, (train pass) **teiki**
予定 schedule, plan **yotei**
暫定 temporary condition **zantei**

確erify, 804   察nspection, 328   検nspection, 939
決ecide, 699   審nspection, 339   査nspection, 624
限imit, 771   調nspection, 280   閲nspection, 942

走unning, 497

460-B

定scertain that all gates are blocked with 錠adlocks...

❶錠adlock   ❷錠ablet

金 (metal)

JŌ
padlock, blocked, closure, lock up; tablet, pill

FLIP: 6.0.a. Left (flat)
Facing: 2.2. ☞ East (V)

❶尾錠 buckle belt **bijō**
尾錠金 buckle, clasp **bijōgane**
蝦錠 padlock **ebijō**
錠前 lock, pad lock, key **jōmae**
錠前屋 locksmith **jōmaeya**
施錠 locking **sejō**
手錠 handcuff **tejō**
海老錠 padlock **ebijō**
南京錠 padlock **nankinjō**

❷錠剤 tablet, pill **jōzai**
糖衣錠 sugar-coated tablet **tōijō**
ビタミン剤 vitamin pill **bitaminjō**

閉lose, 285   妨indrance, 734   剤rugs, 961
鎖hain, 665   遮nterrupt, 371   医edicine, 19
阻mpede, 756   禁rohibit, 560   治ecuperate, 210

定ertain, 550

461-A

Captured troops 従*omply fine on a* 縦*ertical-line...*

従*ompliance* 従*bedience*

イ (stroll)

Facing: 4.0. 〜〜〜 Apart

shitaga(u), shitaga(eru), JŪ
compliance, obedience, conformity, deference, follow

従って *"therefore, accordingly..."* **shitagatte**
服従 *obey, submit, comply* **fukujū**
侍従 *chamberlain* **jijū**
従僕 *servant, minder, acolyte* **jūboku**
従物 *accessory item* **jūbutsu**
従軍 *going to the frontlines* **jūgun**
従軍記者 *war correspondent* **jūgun kisha**
従犯 *crime accessory, ~participant* **jūhan**
従因 *secondary clause* **jūin**
従事 *being engaged, ~occupied* **jūji**
従順 *subordinate, submissive* **jūjun**
従来 *"so far, up to now, until now..."* **jūrai**
従者 *follower, minder, acolyte* **jūsha**
従卒 *orderly, officers servant* **jūsotsu**
従前 *so far, up to now, until now* **jūzen**
従属 *subordination, dependency* **jūzoku**
従属国 *dependent nation, protectorate* **jūzokukoku**
家従 *butler, house servant* **kajū**
屈従 *submission, yielding, giving up* **kutsujū**

盲従 *blind obedience* **mōjū**
忍従 *patient submission* **ninjū**
隷従 *slave* **reijū**
従容 *calm, composed* **shōyō**
主従 *master & servant* **shujū**
追従 *flattery, adulation, accolade* **tsuijū**
随従 *follow the lead* **zuijū**
従兄弟 *cousin* **itoko**
従業員 *employee, staff member* **jūgyōin**
従価税 *ad valorem tax, value-added tax* **jūkazei**
専従者 *full-time worker, regular staff* **senjūsha**

応*omply, 469*	則*egulation, 290*
措*easures, 282*	制*egulation, 534*
策*olicy, 875*	律*egulation, 731*

従*isciple, 497*

461-B

Captured troops 従*omply fine on a* 縦*ertical-line...*

縦*ertical* 縦*pbright*

糸 (thread, continuity)

Facing: 2.2. East ☞ (V)

tate, JŪ
vertical, upbright

放縦 *self-indulgence* **hōjū**
縦断 *traversing, travelling across* **jūdan**
縦陣 *column of soldiers* **jūjin**
縦貫 *running thru, traversing* **jūkan**
縦横 *"in all directions..."* **jūō, tateyoko**
縦覧 *inspection, review* **jūran**
縦列 *column, file* **jūretsu**
縦線 *vertical line* **jūsen**
縦射 *raking fire* **jūsha**
縦走 *running thru, traversing* **jūsō**
縦隊 *column of soldiers* **jūtai**
縦続 *cascade* **jūzoku**
操縦 *operation, control* **sōjū**
操縦席 *airplane cockpit* **sōjūseki**
縦穴 *pit, shaft* **tateana**
縦笛 *recorder* **tatebue**
縦糸 *warp, knot* **tateito**
縦軸 *vertical axis, spindle* **tatejiku**
縦縞 *vertical stripes, pin stripes* **tatejima**

縦長 *oblong, semi-circle* **tatenaga**
縦波 *longitudinal wave* **tatenami**
縦線 *vertical line* **tatesen**
縦令 *"even if, even though..."* **tatoi**
縦書き *vertical writing* **tategaki**
縦向き *lengthwise, lengthsize* **tatemuki**
縦結び *vertical knot* **tatemusubi**
縦送り *tack width* **tateokuri**
縦割り *slivers, splinter* **tatewari**
縦揺れ *pitch, pitching angle* **tateyure**
縦座標 *y-coordinate, horizontal line* **tatezahyō**

立*tand up, 234*	直*inear, 420*
起*rise, 754*	線*inear, 531*
並*arallel, 444*	

従*omply, 551*

462-A
保*reserve* & 保*bide*, 褒*xtolled far & wide...*

保*reserve* 保*ecure*

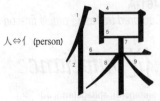

人⇔亻 (person)

FLIP: 7.0.b1. Right (stem)

tamo(tsu), HO
preserve, secure, safe-keeping

保安 *order & public safety* **hoan**
保母 *nursery teacher* **hobo**
保父 *male nurse* **hofu**
保護 *care for, protect* **hogo**
保護者 *child's guardian, parents* **hogosha**
保育 *child care* **hoiku**
保育園 *nursery, kindergarten* **hoikuen**
保持 *maintain, preserve* **hoji**
保管 *storage, custody, charge* **hokan**
保健 *healthcare, health upkeep* **hoken**
保険 *insurance* **hoken**
保健所 *healthcare office* **hokenjo**
保温 *heating, keeping warm* **hoon**
保線 *rail maintenance, ~management* **hosen**
保釈 *out-on-bail, bail bond* **hoshaku**
保身 *self-protection, personal security* **hoshin**
保証 *guarantee, warranty* **hoshō**
保証人 *guarantor, loan co-signer* **hoshōnin**
保養 *relaxation, recuperation* **hoyō**

保有 *possess, hold* **hoyū**
保全 *conservation, preservation* **hozen**
保存 *preserve, save* **hozon**
確保 *securing, safeguarding* **kakuho**
留保 *reservation* **ryūho**
損保 *non-life insurance* **sonpo**
担保 *mortgage collateral* **tanpo**
安保理 *security council* **anpori**
日保ち *for a long time* **himochi**
保菌者 *bacillus-, germ carrier* **hokinsha**
保守党 *conservative party* **hoshutō**
目の保養 *feast for the eyes* **menohoyō**

守*bide*, 366	護*rotect*, 828 蔵*torage*, 565
衛*rotect*, 796	防*rotect*, 736 倉*torage*, 399

俣*odest*, 938

462-B
保*reserve* & 保*bide*, 褒*xtolled far & wide...*

褒*xtoll* 褒*raise*

衣⇔衤 (clothing)

Facing: 2.1. East ☞ (H)
FLIP: 8.0.b. Inner (stem)

home(ru), HŌ
extol, praise, commend

褒美 *reward, prize, citation* **hōbi**
褒貶 *praise & censure* **hōhen**
褒辞 *words of praise* **hōji**
褒状 *certificate of merit* **hōjō**
褒章 *medal, ribbon* **hōshō**
褒賞 *prize, award, citation* **hōshō**
過褒 *excessive praise, undue adulation* **kahō**
褒め言葉 *words of praise* **homekotoba**
褒め上げる *high praise* **homeageru**
褒め立てる *extol excessively* **hometateru**

賛*raise*, 334	彰*ward*, 325
可*pproval*, 15	賞*ward*, 554
承*pproval*, 117	栄*lory*, 580
賛*pproval*, 334	誉*onour*, 252

保*reserve*, 552

463-A

By one's 歯eeth, 齢ears-old can be told...

歯eeth 歯ental

止 (stopping)

FLIP: 4.0.a. Bottom (flat)

ha, SHI
teeth, dental

抜歯 *tooth extraction* **basshi**
義歯 *artificial teeth, false teeth* **gishi**
歯型 *toothprint, toothmarks* **hagata**
歯茎 *gums* **haguki**
歯黒 *teeth blackening* **haguro**
歯車 *gear, cogwheels* **haguruma**
歯先 *gear teeth* **hasaki**
犬歯 *canine tooth* **kenshi**
門歯 *incisor tooth* **monshi**
虫歯 *decayed tooth, dental cavity* **mushiba**
乳歯 *milk tooth, baby tooth* **nyūshi**
奥歯 *molar tooth* **okuba**
羊歯 *fern, lacy plant* **shida**
歯牙 *teeth & tusks* **shiga**
歯科 *dentistry, dental medicine* **shika**
歯石 *tartar* **shiseki**
歯ブラシ *toothbrush* **haburashi**
知恵歯 *wisdom tooth* **chieba**
出っ歯 *protruding tooth, bucktooth* **deppa**

永久歯 *permanent tooth* **eikyūshi**
歯止め *brake, drag* **hadome**
歯痒い *feel impatient, annoying* **hagayui**
歯ぎしり *grinding one's teeth* **hagishiri**
歯医者 *dentist, dental doctor* **haisha**
歯磨き *tooth brushing* **hamigaki**
入れ歯 *artificial teeth, false teeth* **ireba**
反っ歯 *protruding tooth, bucktooth* **soppa**
八重歯 *double tooth* **yaeba**
歯磨き粉 *toothpaste* **hamigakiko**
糸切り歯 *eye-tooth, canine* **itokiriba**
味噌っ歯 *decayed tooth* **misoppa**

口*outh, 458*
食*uisine, 255*

歳*ears old, 111*

463-B

By one's 歯eeth, 齢ears-old can be told...

齢ears old 齢ge

歯 (teeth)

FLIP: 6.2. Left Bottom

yowai, REI
years old, age

馬齢 *wasted years, squandered youth* **barei**
学齢 *school age* **gakurei**
月齢 *age of the moon* **getsurei**
弱齢 *young age* **jakurei**
樹齢 *tree age* **jurei**
寿齢 *long life, longevity* **jurei**
艦齢 *warships age* **kanrei**
妙齢 *bloom of womanhood* **myōrei**
年齢 *age* **nenrei**
⇒結婚年齢 *marriageable age* **kekkon nenrei**
老齢 *old age, senility* **rōrei**
船齢 *ship age* **senrei**
壮齢 *prime of life* **sōrei**
適齢 *proper age, suitable age* **tekirei**
余齢 *one's twilight years* **yorei**
幼齢 *young age* **yōrei**
高齢化 *ageing, greying society* **kōreika**
高齢者 *old age, senior citizens* **kōreisha**
暦年齢 *chronological age* **rekinenrei**

馬齢を重ねる *"growing old without achieving anything worthwhile..."* **barei o kasaneru**

才*ears old, 185*
歳*ears old, 111*
翁*ld man, 238*
婆*ld woman, 32*

耐*ongevity, 974*
永*ong-lasting, 10*
久*ong-lasting, 379*
寿*ong-lasting, 440*

歯*eeth, 553*

464-A

Winner takes the 賞rize while the loser 償ndemnifies...

貝 (shell, old money)

賞*rize*   賞*ward*

SHŌ

prize, award, conferment, accolade

FLIP: 1.0.b. Whole (stem)

ノーベル賞 *Nobel Prize* **nōberushō**
副賞 *supplementary prize* **fukushō**
激賞 *high praise, extolling, accolade* **gekishō**
褒賞 *admiration, praise, citation* **hōshō**
授賞 *awarding a prize, prize presentation* **jushō**
授賞式 *award-giving ceremony* **jushōshiki**
鑑賞 *appreciation, commendation* **kanshō**
観賞 *appreciate, enjoy, relish* **kanshō**
懸賞 *prize, reward* **kenshō**
懸賞論文 *prize essay* **kenshō ronbun**
正賞 *top award, main prize, first place* **seishō**
賞罰 *reward-or-punishment* **shōbatsu**
賞杯 *trophy, prize cup* **shōhai**
賞品 *non-cash prize* **shōhin**
賞状 *certificate of merit* **shōjō**
賞金 *prize money, reward* **shōkin**
賞味 *tasting, appreciation, relish* **shōmi**
賞賛 *admiration, praise, citation* **shōsan**
賞与 *salary bonus* **shōyo**

推賞 *admiration, praise* **suishō**
大賞 *top award, main prize, first place* **taishō**
嘆賞 *admiration, high praise, accolade* **tanshō**
特賞 *special prize, ~award* **tokushō**
努力賞 *prize for effort* **doryokushō**
技能賞 *technique prize* **ginōshō**
一等賞 *first place, top prize* **ittōshō**
二等賞 *second place* **nitōshō**
三等賞 *third place* **santōshō**
皆勤賞 *perfect attendance reward* **kaikinshō**
敢闘賞 *fighting-spirit prize* **kantōshō**
功労賞 *distinguished service award* **kōrōshō**
殊勲賞 *outstanding award* **shukunshō**

酬*eward*, 670	彰*ward*, 325
慶*ongratulate*, 69	

員*ember*, 410

464-B

Winner takes the 賞rize while the loser 償ndemnifies...

人⇔亻 (person)

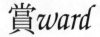

償*ndemnity*   償*ompensation*

tsuguna(u), SHŌ

indemnity, compensation, recompense, remuneration, reparation

FLIP: 7.0.b2. Right (stem)

賠償 *compensation, reparation* **baishō**
⇒損害賠償 *loss compensation, damages*
    songai baishō
賠償金 *indemnity, reparations* **baishōkin**
賠償交渉 *reparation talks* **baishō kōshō**
賠償協定 *reparation treaty* **baishō kyōtei**
弁償 *indemnity, reparation, compensation* **benshō**
弁償金 *indemnity-, reparation money* **benshōkin**
代償 *payment on behalf of* **daishō**
補償 *indemnification, reparation* **hoshō**
⇒労災補償 *disability compensation* **rōsai hoshō**
⇒災害補償 *casualty compensation* **saigai hoshō**
⇒失業補償 *unemployment stipend*
    shitsugyō hoshō
報償 *indemnity, reparation, compensation* **hōshō**
報償金 *remuneration payment* **hōshōkin**
無償 *gratis, free-of-charge* **mushō**
償還 *repayment, redemption* **shōkan**
償還期限 *term of redemption* **shōkan kigen**

償金 *indemnification money* **shōkin**
償却 *repayment, redemption* **shōkyaku**
⇒減価償却 *depreciation, devaluation*
    genka shōkyaku
有償 *with compensation, indemnify* **yūshō**

賠*ndemnify*, 698	障*njury*, 325	料*ayment*, 194
害*njury*, 904	損*njury*, 410	納*ayment*, 296
傷*njury*, 933	痛*njury*, 60	払*ayment*, 682

賞*rize*, 554

465-A

段*teps of* 鍛*iscipline* 鍛*emper the soul clean...*

段*tep*　　段*evel*

夋 (pike)

FLIP: 7.0.b2. Right (stem)

DAN
step, level, ranking

段々 *gradually, steadily, little-by-little* **dandan**
段々畑 *terraced farm, ~plantation* **dandan batake**
段ボール *large carton box* **danbōru**
別段 *particular, peculiar, special* **betsudan**
段平 *broadsword* **danbira**
段袋 *large sack* **danbukuro**
段車 *steeped pulley* **danguruma**
段階 *step, stride* **dankai**
段落 *paragraph* **danraku**
段差 *difference in rank; elevation bump* **dansa**
普段 *usual, ordinary, non-special* **fudan**
石段 *stone steps* **ishidan**
階段 *stairs, steps* **kaidan**
格段 *remarkable progress* **kakudan**
高段 *high-ranking, high officials* **kōdan**
無段 *yet-to-be-done, unfinished* **mudan**
値段 *price, cost* **nedan**
算段 *management, contrivance* **sandan**
初段 *beginner rank, entry-level* **shodan**

昇段 *job promotion* **shōdan**
手段 *ways & means* **shudan**
⇒常套手段 *old trick* **jōtō shudan**
全段 *entire page* **zendan**
大上段 *brandishing a sword* **daijōdan**
段違い *different class, ~level* **danchigai**
段取り *plan, course-of-action* **dandori**
段飾り *dolls arrayed on stairs* **dankazari**
踏み段 *step, stair* **fumidan**
有段者 *grade holder* **yūdansha**
三段跳び *"hop, step & jump..."* **sandan tobi**

級*evel, 189*	階*evel, 129*
準*evel, 919*	位*tatus, 235*
等*rade, 251*	

投*hrow, 745*	役*fficial, 746*

465-B

段*teps of* 鍛*iscipline* 鍛*emper the soul clean...*

❶鍛*emper*　❷鍛*iscipline*

金 (metal)

FLIP: 6.0.a. Left (flat)
FLIP: 7.0.b2. Right (stem)

kita(eru), TAN
temper; discipline

❶鍛冶 *swordsmith, blacksmith* **kaji**
鍛冶屋 *blacksmith, ~shop* **kajiya**
鍛工 *metal works* **tankō**
鍛工所 *foundry* **tankōsho**
鍛鋼 *forge steel* **tankō**
鍛接 *forge welding* **tansetsu**
鍛鉄 *tempering iron* **tantetsu**
鍛治 *metal forging* **tanya**
鍛造 *metal forging* **tanzō**
可鍛性 *malleability* **katansei**

❷鍛え上げる *become highly-trained* **kitaeageru**
鍛練 *training, discipline, temper* **tanren**
鍛成 *training, discipline, cultivation* **tansei**

倹*odest, 938*	教*eaching, 385*
慎*odest, 831*	授*eaching, 539*
謙*odesty, 805*	訓*eachings, 959*

段*tep, 555*

466-A

憂xcellent 優ctress in 憂istress over ripped dress...

心⇔忄 (heart, feelings)

憂*loomy* 憂*istress*

FLIP: 3.0.b. Top (stem)

ure(eru), ure(e), ure(i), u(i), YŪ
gloomy, distress, dismal, anxiety

同憂 *shared anxiety, common distress* **dōyū**
杞憂 *imagined fear, phobia* **kiyū**
喜憂 *joys & sorrows* **kiyū**
内憂 *marital-, domestic problems* **naiyū**
深憂 *serious anxiety* **shinyū**
憂患 *distress, sorrows, anxiety* **yūkan**
憂国 *patriotism, love of country* **yūkoku**
憂苦 *distress, sorrows, anxiety* **yūku**
憂悶 *mental anxiety, psychological stress* **yūmon**
憂慮 *perplexity, worry, concern* **yūryo**
憂心 *grieving heart* **yūshin**
憂色 *anxious-looking* **yūshoku**
憂愁 *gloom, melancholy, misery* **yūshū**
憂鬱 *depressing, gloomy, miserable* **yūutsu**
憂鬱症 *melancholia, depression* **yūutsushō**
憂鬱質 *depression-prone* **yūutsushitsu**
物憂い *gloom & doom* **monoui**
憂き目 *hardships, misfortune* **ukime**
憂き身 *absolute devotion* **ukimi**

憂い顔 *distressful look, anxious face* **ureigao**
一喜一憂 *joys & sorrows* **ikki ichiyū**
憂さ晴らし *diversion, distraction* **usabarashi**

暗 *loomy, 315*	禍 *ragedy, 799*
哀 *orrows, 374*	惨 *ragedy, 396*
愁 *orrows, 415*	厄 *ragedy, 354*
悲 *orrows, 289*	哀 *adness, 374*

賞 *ward, 554*

466-B

優xcellent 優ctress in 憂istress over ripped dress...

人⇔亻 (person)

❶優*xcellence* ❷優*cting*

FLIP: 7.2.b. Right Top (stem)

sugu(reru), yasa(shii), YŪ
excellence, superiority, superiority; acting

❶優形 *slender-, delicate figure* **yasagata**
優女 *gentle woman* **yasaonna**
優男 *slender male* **yasaotoko**
優美 *graceful, elegant* **yūbi**
優長 *leisure, ease* **yūchō**
優艶 *beauty, elegance* **yūen**
優越 *superiority, excellence* **yūetsu**
優越感 *superiority complex* **yūetsukan**
優雅 *elegance, grace* **yūga**
優遇 *kind treatment, preferred* **yūgū**
優位 *predominance, superiority, excellence* **yūi**
優劣 *merits & demerits* **yūretsu**
優良 *excellent, superior* **yūryō**
優性 *dominance, prepotence* **yūsei**
優勢 *superiority, excellence* **yūsei**
優先 *priority, preferred* **yūsen**
優先株 *preferred stocks, ~shares* **yūsenkabu**
優者 *superior, outstanding person* **yūsha**
優勝 *victory, winning* **yūshō**

優秀 *excellent, superior* **yūshū**
優退 *retiring at one's primehood* **yūtai**
優待 *warm reception, hospitality* **yūtai**
優等 *.excellence, superior* **yūtō**
優生学 *eugenics* **yūseigaku**
優柔不断 *indecisive, gullible* **yūjūfudan**
優性遺伝 *dominant inheritance* **yūsei iden**

❷男優 *male actor* **danyū**
俳優 *actor, actress* **haiyū**
女優 *actress* **joyū**
名優 *famous artist, ~star* **meiyū**
声優 *voice actor, voice actress* **seiyū**

傑 *xcellence, 921*	秀 *uperiority, 383*
秀 *xcellence, 383*	最 *uperlative, 423*

憂 *loomy, 556*

467-A

帯ash of pigeons, keepsake of 滞tay in the 帯egion...

❶帯egion ❷帯ash

巾 (cloth, fabric)

obi, o(biru), TAI
region; sash, wear, belt

FLIP: 1.0.b. Whole (stem)

❶ 地帯 zone, belt, area **chitai**
暖帯 subtropics **dantai**
付帯 incidental, ancillary, secondary **futai**
拐帯 fraud, absconding, deceit, shenanigan **kaitai**
寒帯 frigid zone's, cold region **kantai**
熱帯 tropics, tropical zone **nettai**
声帯 vocal cords **seitai**
世帯 family household **setai**
所帯 family household **shotai**
帯電 electrification **taiden**
時間帯 time zone, time slot **jikantai**
帯域幅 bandwidth **taiikihaba**
❷ 着帯 pregnancy-, maternity belt **chakutai**
腹帯 belly-, waist band **fukutai, haraobi**
眼帯 eye bandage **gantai**
包帯 bandage, dressing, gauze **hōtai**
角帯 male obi sash **kadoobi**
携帯 portable, carry on, mobile **keitai**
携帯品 personal effects, ~belongings **keitaihin**

黒帯 black belt **kuroobi**
丸帯 kimono obi sash **maruobi**
帯揚げ obi bustle **obiage**
帯留 sash clip **obidome**
連帯 alliance, confederacy **rentai**
妻帯 finding a wife **saitai**
止血帯 tourniquet **shiketsutai**
帯剣 sabre, sword **taiken**
帯出 taking out books (library) **taishutsu**
帯刀 wearing a sword **taitō**
貞操帯 chastity belt **teisōtai**

域egion, 139	地arth, 688
所ocation, 676	域erritory, 139
場ocation, 147	

帯mpire, 432

467-B

帯ash of pigeons, keepsake of 滞tay in the 帯egion...

滞taying 滞rrears

水⇔氵 (water)

todokō(ru), TAI
staying, arrears, stagnate

FLIP: 7.0.b1. Right (stem)

沈滞 stagnation, inactivity **chintai**
遅滞 delay, arrears **chitai**
延滞 arrears, late payment **entai**
延滞金 overdue debt, loan arrears **entaikin**
延滞税 tax arrears **entaizei**
延滞利子 overdue interest, late charges **entai rishi**
延滞通知 overdue-, delinquent notice **entai tsūchi**
凝滞 delay, late **gyōtai**
渋滞 traffic congestion, ~jam **jūtai**
結滞 intermittent (pulsebeat) **kettai**
食滞 undigested in one's stomach **shokutai**
滞米 staying in America **taibei**
滞陣 encampment, staying **taijin**
滞貨 accumulation of goods **taika**
滞空 duration, length of time **taikū**
滞京 staying in the capital **taikyō**
滞郷 living in one's native place **taikyō**
滞日 one's stay in Japan **tainichi**
滞納 non-payment, arrears **tainō**

滞納者 defaulter, delinquent **tainōsha**
滞納処分 disposition for non-payment
　tainō shobun
滞留 accumulated goods **tairyū**
滞船 demurrage, holding charges **taisen**
滞在 stay, residing **taizai**
滞在地 present residence **taizai chi**
滞在中 during one's stay **taizai chū**
滞在客 hotel-, homestay guest **taizai kyaku**
滞在者 sojourner, visitor **taizai sha**
停滞 stagnation, accumulation **teitai**

留taying, 128	住esidence, 750
残emain, 767	宅esidence, 82
居esidence, 384	邸esidence, 860

帯egion, 557

468-A

In English 文iterature, the royal 紋rest endure...

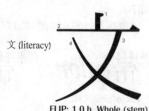

文 (literacy)

文iteracy 文ritings

fumi, aya, BUN, MON
literacy, writings, read-&-write, letters

FLIP: 1.0.b. Whole (stem)

文案 *draft text, ~manuscript* **bun'an**
文学 *literature* **bungaku**
文豪 *literary genius, prolific writer* **bungō**
文人 *literary person, man of letters* **bunjin**
文化 *culture* **bunka**
文明 *civilization* **bunmei**
文脈 *literary context* **bunmyaku**
文法 *grammar, syntax* **bunpō**
文書 *text, writing* **bunsho**
文章 *writing, sentence* **bunshō**
文集 *anthology* **bunshū**
弔文 *funeral address* **chōbun**
注文 *purchase order* **chūmon**
英文 *English sentence* **eibun**
序文 *preface, foreword, prologue* **jobun**
条文 *text, provision* **jōbun**
漢文 *Kanji writing, ~text* **kanbun**
空文 *dead letter* **kūbun**
文字 *letters, characters* **moji**

文句 *complaint; phrase* **monku**
文盲 *illiteracy, no-read-no-write* **monmō**
例文 *example sentence* **reibun**
論文 *thesis, dissertation* **ronbun**
作文 *essay, composition* **sakubun**
正文 *official text* **seibun**
和文 *Japanese text* **wabun**
訳文 *translation, translated text* **yakubun**
暗号文 *cryptograph, encryption code* **angōbun**
命令文 *imperative sentence* **meireibun**
声明文 *explanation text, statement* **seimeibun**

書ritings, 116		読eading, 260
言ord, 251		教ducate, 385
字etter, 346		習earning, 238

又gain, 177	父ather, 467

468-B

In English 文iterature, the royal 紋rest endure...

糸 (thread, continuity)

紋rest 紋mprint

MON
crest, imprint

FLIP: 7.0.b2. Right (stem)

衣紋 *kimono neck* **emon**
衣紋掛け *coat hanger* **emonkake**
風紋 *wavelines on sand* **fūmon**
波紋 *water ripple; sensation ring* **hamon**
斑紋 *speckle, spot* **hanmon**
地紋 *woven-, weaving pattern* **jimon**
定紋 *official crest* **jōmon**
家紋 *family crest* **kamon**
小紋 *excellent pattern; kimono cloth* **komon**
紋日 *holiday* **monbi**
紋所 *family crest* **mondokoro**
紋服 *family-crested clothes* **monpuku**
紋章 *crest, coat of arms* **monshō**
紋付 *crested kimono* **montsuki**
紋様 *crest pattern* **monyō**
無紋 *without a family crest* **mumon**
声紋 *voiceprint, sonogram* **seimon**
指紋 *fingerprint* **shimon**
掌紋 *palm print* **shōmon**

水紋 *water ripples pattern* **suimon**
裏紋 *informal family crest* **uramon**
蛇紋石 *serpentine* **jamonseki**
書き紋 *hand-drawn family crest* **kakimon**
紋織り *figured fabrics* **mon'ori**
紋白蝶 *cabbage butterfly* **monshirochō**
縫い紋 *embroidered family crest* **nuimon**
衣紋掛け *coat-, dress hanger* **emonkake**
紋切り型 *conventional* **monkirigata**
紋切り形 *conventional* **monkirigata**

菊hrysanthemum, 903		標ign, 549
花lower, 191		符ign, 582
華lower, 40		誉onour, 252

級rade, 189

469-A

客ustomers surprised at the bargain 額rice...

宀 (cover, lid)

客ustomer　客lient　客uest

KYAKU, KAKU
customer, client, guest, visitor

FLIP: 2.0.a. Sort Of (flat)

珍客 *unexpected visitor, ~caller* **chinkyaku**
乗客 *passenger* **jōkyaku**
観客 *tourist, spectator* **kankyaku**
剣客 *fencer, swordsman* **kenkyaku**
顧客 *client, customer* **kokyaku**
客足 *customers, clientele* **kyakuashi**
客演 *guest appearance* **kyakuen**
客員 *guest, visitor, client* **kyakuin**
客人 *guest, caller, visitor* **kyakujin**
客観 *objectivity, impartiality* **kyakkan**
客間 *guest room, reception room* **kyakuma**
客席 *visitors seat* **kyakuseki**
客船 *passenger boat, liner* **kyakusen**
客室 *guest room, cabin* **kyakushitsu**
客体 *object* **kyakutai**
客用 *"for use of guest only..."* **kyakuyō**
来客 *visitor, caller, guest* **raikyaku**
旅客 *passenger, traveller* **ryokaku, ryokyaku**
船客 *ship passenger* **senkyaku**

先客 *previous visitor* **senkyaku**
刺客 *assassin, gun-for-hire* **shikyaku, shikaku**
弔問客 *condolence visitor* **chōmonkyaku**
避暑客 *summer visitor* **hishokyaku**
訪問客 *visitor, guest, caller* **hōmonkyaku**
固定客 *regular customer, ~client* **koteikyaku**
客待ち *waiting for customers* **kyakumachi**
滞在客 *guest, visitor, caller* **taizaikyaku**
泊まり客 *hotel guest, house guest* **tomarikyaku**
立ち見客 *stand-in spectator* **tachimikyaku**
冷やかし客 *window-shopper* **hiyakashikyaku**

迎*elcome, 705*	宴*arty, 610*
篤*ordial, 317*	屋*tore, 427*
興*ntertainment, 867*	店*tore, 222*

宮*hrine, 105*

469-B

客ustomers surprised at the bargain 額rice...

頁 (large shell, page)

❶額mount　❷額rame

hitai, GAKU
amount, price, cost; frame, encasing

FLIP: 7.0.b2. Right (stem)

❶倍額 *double the amount* **baigaku**
同額 *same amount* **dōgaku**
額面 *face value, par value* **gakumen**
額装 *picture frame mounting* **gakusō**
減額 *decreased amount, reduced price* **gengaku**
月額 *monthly sum, ~amount* **getsugaku**
半額 *half price, 50% discount* **hangaku**
価額 *amount, value, price* **kagaku**
金額 *amount of money* **kingaku**
高額 *large amount of money* **kōgaku**
巨額 *vast sum* **kyogaku**
満額 *full amount, total balance* **mangaku**
年額 *annual sum, yearly amount* **nengaku**
差額 *margin, difference* **sagaku**
産額 *production output, productivity* **sangaku**
少額 *small sum* **shōgaku**
総額 *total sum, sum total* **sōgaku**
多額 *large amount* **tagaku**
低額 *small amount of money* **teigaku**

定額 *fixed amount, ~sum* **teigaku**
残額 *balance, remainder* **zangaku**
税額 *tax amount* **zeigaku**
全額 *full amount, total price* **zengaku**
増額 *increased amount* **zōgaku**
募集額 *fund-raising amount* **boshūgaku**
超過額 *surplus, excess, extra* **chōkagaku**
額際 *"by the hairline..."* **hitaigiwa**
査定額 *assessed-, appraised value* **sateigaku**
請求額 *amount requested* **seikyūgaku**
送金額 *remittance amount* **sōkingaku**
❷額縁 *frame, structure* **gakubuchi**
富士額 *mountain-shaped forehead* **fujibitai**

賃*ayment, 145*	料*ayment, 194*
納*ayment, 296*	価*rice, 35*
払*ayment, 682*	値*rice, 783*

顕*bvious, 931*

470-A

禁rohibited for scholars, high 襟eck collars...

示⇔ネ (display, show)

禁rohibit 禁orbid

KIN

prohibit, forbid, inhibit, restriction, disallow, forestall

FLIP: 1.0.b. Whole (stem)

厳禁 "strictly prohibited..." **genkin**
解禁 lifting of a prohibition **kaikin**
監禁 imprisonment, detention **kankin**
禁圧 suppression, prohibition **kin'atsu**
禁断 prohibition, forbiddance **kindan**
禁断症状 withdrawal symptom **kindan shōjō**
禁煙 "no smoking..." **kin'en**
禁煙車 no-smoking car (train) **kin'ensha**
禁獄 imprisonment, detention **kingoku**
禁忌 taboo, contra-indication **kinki**
禁固 imprisonment, confinement **kinko**
禁句 taboo word, ~phrase **kinku**
禁物 forbidden, taboo **kinmotsu**
禁令 prohibition, embargo, sanction **kinrei**
禁漁 "no fishing..." **kinryō**
禁猟 "no hunting..." **kinryō**
禁制 prohibition, restriction **kinsei**
禁止 prohibition, injunction, cease & desist **kinshi**
禁止命令 prohibition order **kinshi meirei**

禁書 prohibited books **kinsho**
禁酒 alcohol abstinence **kinshu**
禁酒家 teetotaller, abstemious, non-drinker
　　 kinshuka
禁足 confinement, staying inside **kinsoku**
禁則 prohibition, forbiddance **kinsoku**
禁欲 sexual abstinence **kinyoku**
禁輸 trade embargo **kinyu**
拘禁 detention, custody **kōkin**
国禁 government-banned **kokkin**
軟禁 lenient imprisonment, house arrest **nankin**
失禁 incontinence, debauchery **shikkin**

法aw, 360　典ules, 476　　懲unishment, 63
規ule, 814　刑unishment, 536　罰unishment, 759

襟eck collar, 560

470-B

禁rohibited for scholars, high 襟eck collars...

衣⇔ネ (clothing)

襟eck collar 襟ape

eri, KIN

neck collar, nape

FLIP: 7.0.b1. Right (stem)

襟足 head back hair **eriashi**
襟髪 hair around the nape **erigami**
襟腰 neck length **erigoshi**
襟首 nape of the neck **erikubi**
襟元 neck **erimoto**
襟章 collar pin, collar badge **erishō**
半襟 neck piece **han'eri**
開襟 wing-collared **kaikin**
襟度 magnanimity **kindo**
襟懐 inner heart, real intention **kinkai**
胸襟 heart-to-heart talk **kyōkin**
裏襟 neckband lining **uraeri**
襟留め breast pin **eridome**
襟飾り neckwear **erikazari**
襟巻き muffler, scarf **erimaki**
掛け襟 kimono collar **kakeeri**
折り襟 folded collar **orieri**
立ち襟 stand-up collar **tachieri**
詰め襟 stand-up collar **tsumeeri**

襟を正す straighten-up oneself **eri o tadasu**

首eck, 311　　　　服lothes, 734
肩houlder, 678　　裁lothes, 802

禁rohibit, 560

471-A

Scandals once 暴xposed, 暴iolence 爆xplodes...

日 (sunlight, daytime)

❶暴iolence ❷暴xpose

aba(reru), aba(ku), BŌ, BAKU
violence, rampage; expose, disclosure, revelation

FLIP: 2.0.b. Sort Of (stem)

❶
暴れ馬	*unruly-, wild horse* **abareuma**
暴圧	*coercive pressure, compulsion* **bōatsu**
暴風	*violent wind, storm* **bōfū**
暴言	*abusive words, verbal abuse* **bōgen**
暴虐	*cruelty, tyranny* **bōgyaku**
暴発	*explosion, discharge* **bōhatsu**
暴威	*tyranny, cruel violence* **bōi**
暴飲	*excessive-, heavy drinking* **bōin**
暴飲暴食	*overdrinking & overeating* **bōin bōshoku**
暴漢	*bully, thug, hooligan* **bōkan**
暴行	*violence, use-of-force* **bōkō**
暴君	*tyrant, despot* **bōkun**
暴挙	*violence, outrage* **bōkyo**
暴慢	*rude, overbearing, haughty* **bōman**
暴落	*sudden fall, nosedive* **bōraku**
暴利	*excessive profiting, price gorging* **bōri**
暴論	*wild remark, undue claim* **bōron**
暴力	*physical force, violence* **bōryoku**
暴政	*tyrannical rule* **bōsei**

暴食	*over-eating, gluttony, avarice* **bōshoku**
暴走	*running-, driving recklessly* **bōsō**
暴走運転	*reckless driving* **bōsō unten**
暴徒	*rioters, mob rule* **bōto**
暴投	*wild pitch (baseball)* **bōtō**
暴騰	*sudden rise, upsurge* **bōtō**
暴動	*erratic movement* **bōdō**
凶暴	*violent, atrocious, brutal* **kyōbō**
狂暴	*violent, atrocious, brutal* **kyōbō**
横暴	*tyrannical, despotic* **ōbō**
乱暴	*violence, coercion, use-of-force* **ranbō**
❷暴露	*expose, damning revelation* **bakuro**

露*xposure, 405*	壊*estroy, 847*
慌*anic, 507*	破*estroy, 715*

最*aximum, 423*

471-B

Scandals once 暴xposed, 暴iolence 爆xplodes...

火⇔灬 (fire)

爆xplosion 爆emolition

BAKU
explosion, demolition, detonation

FLIP: 7.1. Right (Sort Of)

爆竹	*firecracker, small fireworks* **bakuchiku**
爆沈	*exploding & sinking* **bakuchin**
爆弾	*bomb, explosives* **bakudan**
爆煙	*smoke from explosion* **bakuen**
爆風	*blast, detonation, explosion* **bakufū**
爆撃	*bombing, detonation* **bakugeki**
爆破	*blast, blowing up* **bakuha**
爆発	*explosion, blasting* **bakuhatsu**
⇒核爆発	*nuclear explosion, ~detonation* **kakubakuhatsu**
爆発的	*explosive, "explosive potential..."* **bakuhatsuteki**
爆音	*explosion, whir, roar* **bakuon**
爆雷	*depth charge* **bakurai**
爆裂	*blast, detonation, explosion* **bakuretsu**
爆砕	*blast, detonation, explosion* **bakusai**
爆睡	*"sleep like a dog..."* **bakusui**
爆死	*death by explosion, bomb fatality* **bakushi**
爆心	*epicentre of bombing, ground zero* **bakushin**

爆心地	*epicentre, ground zero* **bakushinchi**
爆笑	*roaring laughter* **bakushō**
爆傷	*injury by explosion* **bakushō**
爆薬	*explosives, bomb* **bakuyaku**
原爆	*atom-, atomic bomb* **genbaku**
被爆	*being bombed* **hibaku**
被爆者	*bomb victim (atomic)* **hibakusha**
自爆	*suicide bombing, self-explosion* **jibaku**
起爆	*ignition, setting off* **kibaku**
空爆	*aerial bombardment* **kūbaku**
猛爆	*intensive bombing* **mōbaku**
盲爆	*indiscriminate-, carpet bombing* **mōbaku**
射爆	*fire bomb, incendiary bomb* **shabaku**
水爆	*hydrogen bomb* **suibaku**

壊*estroy, 847*	陥*ollapse, 893*	落*ollapse, 826*
破*estroy, 715*	崩*ollapse, 912*	死*eath, 513*

暴*ampage, 561*

472-A

頼equest to close the 瀬apids foiled a stampede...

頁 (large shell, page)

頼equest   頼eliance

tano(mu),tano(moshii), tayo(ru), RAI

request, reliance, depend on, asking, pleading, solicit

FLIP: 5.0.b. Left & Right

頼み request, favour, entreaty **tanomi**
頼みの綱 last resort, only hope **tanomi no tsuna**
頼み入る earnest request **tanomiiru**
頼み込む earnest request **tanomikomu**
頼み少ない helpless, hopeless **tanomisukunai**
頼り reliance, trust **tayori**
頼りない unreliable, untrustworthy **tayorinai**
無頼 villain, scoundrel **burai**
無頼漢 villain, scoundrel **buraikan**
力頼み relying on someone **chikaradanomi**
人頼み relying on others **hitodanomi**
神頼み seeking divine help **kamidanomi**
心頼み relying on someone **kokorodanomi**
又頼み requesting on behalf of another **matadanomi**
空頼み vain hope, false hope **soradanomi**
依頼 request, dependence **irai**
依頼人 client, customer **irainin**
⇒弁護依頼人 lawyer's client **bengo irainin**
依頼状 written request **iraijō**

信頼 trust, confidence, reliance **shinrai**
信頼感 sense of trusting others **shinraikan**
信頼性 trust, reliability **shinraisei**
依頼心 parasitic attitude **iraishin**
頼信紙 telegram form paper **raishinshi**
頼母子講 mutual financing assoc. **tanomoshikō**

陳etition, 132	求equest, 256
依equest, 355	請equest, 791
願equest, 964	

頭ead, 832

472-B

頼equest to close the 瀬apids foiled a stampede...

水⇔氵 (water)

瀬apids   瀬hallows

se

rapids, shallows

FLIP: 7.0.b2. Right (stem)
FLIP: 8.0.b. Inner (stem)

浅瀬 shoal, ford **asase**
早瀬 swift current, rapids **hayase**
川瀬 shallows, rapids **kawase**
逢瀬 lovers' tryst **ōse**
瀬戸 strait, channel **seto**
瀬戸際 brink, verge, edge **setogiwa**
瀬戸物 porcelain, chinaware **setomono**
瀬戸物屋 china shop **setomonoya**
潮瀬 sea tides **shiose, shioze**
高瀬 shallows **takase**
高瀬舟 riverboat **takasebune**
瀬踏み sounding out, measuring **sebumi**
立つ瀬 one's grounds, turf **tatsuse**
年の瀬 final days of the year **toshi no se**
歳の瀬 year's end **toshi no se**
浮かぶ瀬 lucky breaks **ukabuse**
遣る瀬ない dreary, gloomy **yarusenai**

浅hallow, 768	浪urrent, 254
波urrent, 32	流urrent, 781

頼equest, 562

473-A

Curtain 維ope & quilt made from a 羅hin-silk...

維*ope*

I
    rope, cord

維持 *maintenance, preservation* **iji**
⇒治安維持 *preservation of public order* **chian iji**
維持費 *maintenance-, upkeep expenses* **ijihi**
維新 *restoration, renovation* **ishin**
⇒明治維新 *Meiji Restoration (1868)* **meiji ishin**
繊維 *fiber* **sen'i**
⇒化学繊維 *chemical fibre* **kagaku sen'i**
繊維質 *fibre quality* **sen'ishitsu**
線維束 *fascicle* **sen'isoku**
繊維工業 *textile industry* **sen'i kōgyō**
維管束 *vascular bundle* **ikansoku**
繊維製品 *textile products* **sen'i seihin**

糸 (thread, continuity)

Facing: 2.2. East ☞ (V)

糸*hread, 375*	布*loth, 208*
綱*ope, 159*	衣*lothes, 355*
縄*ope, 158*	裁*lothes, 802*
綱*ord, 159*	服*lothes, 734*
縫*ewing, 779*	織*nitting, 855*
繰*pinning, 851*	編*nitting, 42*
紡*pinning, 735*	

稚*hildren, 776*

473-B

Curtain 維ope & quilt made from a 羅hin-silk...

羅*hin silk*

RA
    thin silk, fine silk

雀羅 *sparrow net* **jakura**
綺羅 *dazzling clothes* **kira**
綺羅星 *twinkling-, glittering stars* **kiraboshi**
甲羅 *shell, husk (turtle)* **kōra**
伽羅 *Japanese yew* **kyara**
魔羅 *male organ, penis* **mara**
網羅 *comprehend, encompass* **mōra**
羅衣 *thin kimono* **rai**
羅列 *enumeration, listing* **raretsu**
羅紗 *woollen cloth* **rasha**
羅針 *compass needle* **rashin**
羅針盤 *magnetic compass* **rashinban**
羅典 *Latin* **raten**
修羅 *bloodshed scene, tragic scene* **shura**
修羅場 *scene of a carnage* **shurajō, shuraba**
阿羅漢 *attaining nirvana* **arakan**
阿修羅 *absolute frenzy* **ashura**
婆羅門 *Brahman* **baramon**
一張羅 *one's favourite clothes* **icchōra**

罒 (net, eye crown)

FLIP: 3.0.a. Top (flat)

曼陀羅 *Mandala* **mandara**
羅漢 *Arhat, attaining Nirvana* **rakan**
羅漢柏 *hiba arborvitae* **rakanhaku**
天婦羅 *deep-fried breaded cuisine* **tenpura**
森羅万象 *all things in the universe*
    shinra banshō
我武者羅 *recklessly, clumsily* **gamushara**

絹*ilk, 158*	紡*pinning, 735*	服*lothes, 734*
蚕*ilkworm, 628*	布*loth, 208*	織*nitting, 855*
縫*ewing, 779*	衣*lothes, 355*	編*nitting, 42*
繰*pinning, 851*	裁*lothes, 802*	糸*hread, 375*

維*ope, 563*

474-A

童hild with a silver 鐘ell playing well...

童hildren   童uvenile

warabe, DŌ
children, juvenile, kiddie, kiddo, young child

立 (standing)

FLIP: 1.0.a. Whole (flat)

悪童 *brat, naughty-, prankish child* **akudō**
牧童 *cowboy, sheppered* **bokudō**
童画 *children's photos* **dōga**
童顔 *baby face, pretty boy* **dōgan**
童子 *little child* **dōji**
童児 *child, boy, girl, pupil* **dōji**
童女 *little girl* **dōjo**
童心 *child mind, heart* **dōshin**
童貞 *virginity, chastity (male)* **dōtei**
童話 *fairy tale, nursery story* **dōwa**
童話劇 *children show* **dōwageki**
童謡 *nursery rhyme, children's song* **dōyō**
学童 *school children* **gakudō**
児童 *child, boy, girl, pupil* **jidō**
怪童 *monster child* **kaidō**
河童 *river goblin, good swimmer* **kappa**
大童 *great efforts* **ōwarawa**
神童 *child prodigy* **shindō**
小童 *little boy, little girl* **shōdō**

村童 *village child* **sondō**
天童 *heaven-sent child* **tendō**
童歌 *children's song* **warabeuta**
幼童 *little child* **yōdō**

稚hildren, 776	児hildren, 464
幼hildhood, 88	孫randchild, 263
子hildren, 456	若oung, 276

量uantity, 451

474-B

童hild with a silver 鐘ell playing well...

鐘ell

kane, SHŌ
bell, chime, gong

金 (metal)

FLIP: 5.0.a Left & Right

鐘突き *bell tolling* **kanetsuki**
鐘撞き *bell tolling* **kanetsuki**
鐘撞き堂 *bell tower, belfry* **kanetsukidō**
晩鐘 *evening bell* **banshō**
梵鐘 *Buddhist bell* **bonshō**
弔鐘 *funeral bell* **chōshō**
半鐘 *small hanging bell; temple-, camp bell* **hanshō**
早鐘 *alarm bell, warning bell* **hayagane**
時鐘 *time bell* **jishō**
警鐘 *alarm bell, warning bell* **keishō**
鐘楼 *bell tower, belfry* **shōrō**
鐘声 *bell-ringing* **shōsei**
釣り鐘 *hanging bell, temple bell* **tsurigane**
釣り鐘堂 *belfry, bell tower* **tsuriganedō**
釣り鐘草 *bellflower* **tsuriganesō**
破れ鐘 *cracked bell* **waregane**
鐘乳洞 *limestone cave, ~cavern* **shōnyūdō**
鐘乳石 *stalactite* **shōnyūseki**
明けの鐘 *bell-ringing at dawn* **ake no kane**

除夜の鐘 *New Year's midnight bell-ringing* **joya no kane**

鈴ell, 683	曲elody, 476
音ound, 314	呼alling, 701

鏡irror, 839

475-A

蔵torage of pagans for 臓ody organs...

蔵torage　蔵arehouse

艹 (grass)

kura, ZŌ
storage, warehouse, depository

FLIP: 3.0.b. Top (stem)
Facing: 2.1. East ☞ (H)

愛蔵 *cherished possessions* **aizō**
穴蔵 *cellar* **anagura**
西蔵 *Tibet* **chibetto**
貯蔵 *storage, preservation* **chozō**
貯蔵物 *stores, supplies, provision* **chozōbutsu**
土蔵 *storehouse* **dozō**
腹蔵 *"without reservations..."* **fukuzō**
秘蔵 *precious, favourite* **hizō**
秘蔵っ子 *favourite pupil, ~child* **hizōkko**
包蔵 *involving something else* **hōzō**
蔵番 *warehouse keeper* **kuraban**
蔵米 *warehoused rice* **kuramai**
蔵元 *warehouse owner* **kuramoto**
経蔵 *scripture house* **kyōzō**
埋蔵 *buried underground* **maizō**
内蔵 *keeping concealed, inherent* **naizō**
酒蔵 *wine cellar* **sakagura**
私蔵 *privately storage* **shizō**
所蔵 *owning, possessing* **shozō**

収蔵 *storing away, warehousing* **shūzō**
退蔵 *hoarding, illegal storing* **taizō**
蔵版 *copyrights owner* **zōhan**
蔵書 *collection of books, private library* **zōsho**
貯蔵庫 *storehouse* **chozōko**
蔵出し *direct from warehouse* **kuradashi**
蔵入れ *warehousing, storing* **kuraire**
埋蔵金 *buried gold* **maizōkin**
大蔵省 *finance ministry* **ookurashō**
冷蔵庫 *cold storage, refrigerator* **reizōko**

庫*torage, 306*	収*ollect, 178*
倉*torage, 399*	集*ollect, 50*
貯*torage, 967*	給*upply, 143*
積*ccumulate, 822*	納*upply, 296*

歳*ears old, 111*

475-B

蔵torage of pagans for 臓ody organs...

臓ody organs

肉⇔月 (flesh, body part)

ZŌ
body organs

五臓 *five viscera (organs)* **gozō**
腎臓 *kidney organ* **jinzō**
肝臓 *liver organ* **kanzō**
肝臓病 *liver disease* **kanzōbyō**
内臓 *internal organs, the insides* **naizō**
心臓 *heart organ* **shinzō**
臓器 *internal organs* **zōki**
臓物 *giblets, guts, nerves, mettle* **zōmotsu**
臓腑 *viscera, entrails* **zōfu**
心臓形 *heart-shaped* **shinzōgata**
心臓炎 *heart inflammation* **shinzōen**
心臓部 *heart organ* **shinzōbu**
心臓病 *heart illness* **shinzōbyō**
心臓麻痺 *heart failure, heart attack* **shinzō mahi**
脾臓 *spleen* **hizō**
腎臓炎 *kidney inflammation* **jinzōen**
腎臓病 *kidney illness* **jinzōbyō**
膵臓 *pancreas* **suizō**
膵臓病 *pancreatic disorder* **suizōbyō**

Facing: 4.0. ☜☞ Apart
FLIP: 7.2.b. Right Top (stem)

膵臓炎 *pancreatic inflammation* **suizōen**
肝臓炎 *hepatitis* **kanzōen**

血*lood, 20*	腸*ntestine, 150*
肺*ungs, 305*	腰*elvis, 419*
腹*tomach, 830*	

蔵*torage, 565*

476-A
県*refecture* 懸*angs final* 懸*ffer to pro golfer..*

県*refecture*

agata, KEN
prefecture

目 (eyesight, visual)

FLIP: 2.0.b. Sort Of (stem)
FLIP: 3.0.a. Top (flat)

同県 *same prefecture* **dōken**
府県 *prefectures* **fuken**
⇒都道府県 *local governments* **todō fuken**
群県 *counties & prefectures* **gunken**
県庁 *prefectural office* **kenchō**
県道 *prefectural road, ~highway* **kendō**
県営 *prefectural management* **ken'ei**
県営球場 *prefectural baseball stadium* **ken'ei kyūjō**
県議会 *prefectural assembly* **kengikai**
県警 *prefectural police* **kenkei**
県民 *prefectural residents* **kenmin**
県民税 *prefecture citizen tax* **kenminzei**
県知事 *prefectural governor* **kenchiji**
県立 *prefecture-owned* **kenritsu**
近県 *neighbouring prefectures* **kinken**
分県地図 *map of prefectures* **bunken chizu**
廃藩置県 *replacement of clans with prefectures*
    haihan chiken

市*ity, 304*	丁*lock-of-houses, 173*
町*own, 174*	民*eople, 495*
区*istrict, 80*	

目*ye, 462*

476-B
県*refecture* 懸*angs final* 懸*ffer to pro golfer...*

懸*anging* 懸*uspension*

ka(karu), ka(keru), KEN, KE
hanging, suspending

心⇔忄 (heart, feelings)

Facing: 2.1. East ☞ (H)

懸案 *pending-, unresolved problems* **ken'an**
懸吊 *suspension, hanging* **kenchō**
懸濁 *suspension, hanging* **kendaku**
懸崖 *precipice, overhanging a cliff* **kengai**
懸軍 *expeditionary troops* **kengun**
懸隔 *difference, discrepancy, disparity* **kenkaku**
懸命 *strenuous, exhaustive, vigorous* **kenmei**
⇒一所懸命 *with utmost effort, for life* **issho kenmei**
⇒一生懸命 *with utmost effort, for life* **isshō kenmei**
懸念 *fear, anxiety, worry* **kenen**
懸賞 *prize, reward* **kenshō**
懸賞品 *non-cash reward, goods prizes* **kenshōhin**
懸賞金 *monetary reward, money prize* **kenshōkin**
懸賞論文 *winning essay* **kenshō ronbun**
懸垂 *hanging, suspension* **kensui**
懸絶 *great difference, extreme disparity* **kenzetsu**
懸想 *falling in love* **kesō**
懸想文 *love letter* **kesōbun**
命懸け *desperate, despondent* **inochigake**

懸け橋 *suspension bridge; pipeline* **kakehashi**
神懸り *"in the divine hands..."* **kamigakari**
手懸り *handhold; clue, hint* **tegakari**
気懸かり *anxiety, worry, concern* **kigakari**
懸賞募集 *collection of prize entries*
    kenshō boshū
躍り懸かり *spring upon, jump at* **odorikakari**
懸け離れる *have a wide gap with* **kakehanareru**

掛*ang up, 107*	橋*ridge, 163*
架*anging, 202*	高*levated, 435*

県*refecture, 566*

477-A

両oth groom & bride happily 満atisfied...

一 (one, single)

両oth　両air　両ual

RYŌ
both, pair, dual

FLIP: 1.0.b. Whole (stem)

両足 *both legs, ~feet* **ryōashi**
両替 *money changing* **ryōgae**
両替機 *coin machine* **ryōgaeki**
為替両替 *currency exchange* **kawase ryōgae**
両眼 *both eyes* **ryōgan**
両側 *both sides* **ryōgawa**
両義 *double meaning* **ryōgi**
両方 *both* **ryōhō**
両院 *bicameral, two-chamber* **ryōin**
両国 *both countries* **ryōkoku**
両国民 *both peoples (two countries)* **ryōkokumin**
両極 *north & south poles* **ryōkyoku**
両極端 *extremes, polarized* **ryōkyokutan**
両面 *both sides* **ryōmen**
両立 *compatibility, consistency* **ryōritsu**
両性 *both sexes, male & female* **ryōsei**
両者 *both persons* **ryōsha**
両親 *parents, father & mother* **ryōshin**
両端 *both ends* **ryōtan**

両手 *both hands* **ryōte**
両得 *serving two ends, win-win* **ryōtoku**
両様 *both, same ways...* **ryōyō**
両用 *dual use, dual purpose* **ryōyō**
両翼 *both wings, both flanks* **ryōyoku**
両全 *win-win for both sides* **ryōzen**
両損 *lose-lose situation, no-win situation* **ryōzon**
車両 *motor vehicle* **sharyō**
両三日 *a few days, 2-3 days* **ryōmikka**
両生類 *amphibian, sea-land (animal)* **ryōseirui**
両性的 *bi-sexual* **ryōseiteki**

双oth, 177	二wo, 457	再epeat, 225
双win, 177	弐wo, 100	

丙hird class, 212

477-B

両oth groom & bride happily 満atisfied...

水⇔氵 (water)

満atisfy　満ulfil　満ill-up

mi(chiru), mi(tasu), MAN
satisfy, fulfil, fill-up, saturate

FLIP: 7.0.b2. Right (stem)

不満 *unsatisfactory, insufficiency* **fuman**
肥満 *growing fat, ~stout, ~obese* **himan**
肥満児 *obese-, overweight child* **himanji**
豊満 *plump, abundant, rich* **hōman**
飽満 *eating to the full* **hōman**
充満 *maximum load, full capacity* **jūman**
干満 *ebb & flow, tide* **kanman**
満潮 *high tide* **manchō**
満悦 *contentment & pleasure* **man'etsu**
満額 *full payment, full amount* **mangaku**
満款 *highest score* **mangan**
満月 *full moon* **mangetsu**
満員 *full capacity, "no seats available..."* **man'in**
満場 *whole audience* **manjō**
満開 *full bloom, full blossom* **mankai**
満期 *expiration, maturity date* **manki**
満喫 *full satisfaction, ~enjoyment* **mankitsu**
満腔 *wholehearted sympathy* **mankō**
満面 *whole face* **manmen**

満杯 *filled up, full to the limit* **manpai**
満票 *unanimous vote* **manpyō**
満載 *full load, maximum capacity* **mansai**
満車 *"no parking available..."* **mansha**
満身 *whole body* **manshin**
満室 *"no vacant rooms..."* **manshitsu**
満水 *filled up with water* **mansui**
満タン *gasoline full tank* **mantan**
満点 *perfect score, 100%* **manten**
満足 *satisfaction* **manzoku**
二十歳未満 *below 20 years old* **hatachi miman**

全ntire, 24	慶ejoice, 69
喜appiness, 965	賀elebration, 202
祥appiness, 248	祝elebration, 716
幸appiness, 268	完omplete, 196

両oth, 567

478-A

柔oft iceberg struck by a 矛alberd...

矛 (spear)

矛alberd

hoko, MU
halberd

Facing: 1.0. ⟜ West (W)

矛先 *direction, way* **hokosaki**
矛盾 *contradiction, inconsistency* **mujun**

武*arrior, 100*	盾*hield, 407*
戦*ighting, 517*	侍*amurai, 249*
闘*ombat, 946*	武*artial, 100*

予*dvance, 569*

478-B

柔oft iceberg struck by a 矛alberd...

木 (wooden)

柔oft   柔lexible

yawa(rakai), yawa(raka), JŪ, NYŪ
flexible, soft, elastic

FLIP: 4.0.b. Bottom (stem)

軟*oft, 659*	固*ard, 491*
緊*ard, 599*	緩*oosening, 821*

矛*alberd, 568*

柔道 *judo martial arts* **jūdō**
柔皮 *tanned leather* **jūhi**
柔順 *compliant, docile, meek, submissive* **jūjun**
柔術 *jujitsu martial arts* **jūjutsu**
柔毛 *soft hair* **jūmō**
柔軟 *flexible, soft* **jūnan**
柔軟性 *flexibility, malleability* **jūnansei**
柔軟体操 *callisthenics* **jūnan taisō**
柔道家 *judo martial arts expert* **jūdōka**
懐柔 *conciliation, appeasement* **kaijū**
懐柔策 *conciliatory policy, peace overture* **kaijūsaku**
柔弱 *weak, feeble, invertebrate* **nyūjaku**
柔和 *mild, gentle, weak* **nyūwa**
柔肌 *soft skin* **yawahada**
柔柔 *softly, gently* **yawayawa**
物柔らか *mild, gentle, soft* **monoyawaraka**
手柔らか *soft hands, feminine hands* **teyawaraka**
柔らか物 *silks* **yawarakamono**
優柔不断 *indecisive, vacillating, wavering* **yūjū fudan**

479-A

Money 予dvanced, 預ntrust to chance...

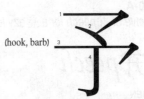

予dvanced   予revious

」(hook, barb)

YO

advanced, previous, ahead, beforehand, preceding

予備 *spare, reserve, second-* **yobi**
予防 *prevention, forestalling, arresting* **yobō**
予知 *foresight, foreknowledge, premonition* **yochi**
予兆 *bad omen* **yochō**
予断 *foresight, prediction* **yodan**
予言 *prophecy, foretell, prediction* **yogen**
予後 *convalescence, recovery, recuperation* **yogo**
予報 *forecast, prediction* **yohō**
予示 *signs of, appearance of* **yoji**
予価 *expected price* **yoka**
予科 *beginners-, preparatory course* **yoka**
予覚 *foreboding, premonition* **yokaku**
予感 *foreboding, premonition* **yokan**
予見 *foresight, prediction* **yoken**
予期 *expectation, anticipation* **yoki**
予行 *rehearsal, trial run* **yokō**
予告 *foreknowledge, foretelling* **yokoku**
予鈴 *warning, bell-ringing* **yorei**
予算 *budget, estimate* **yosan**

Facing: 1.0. West (W)

予選 *provisional voting, ~election* **yosen**
予診 *preliminary medical check-up* **yoshin**
予審 *preliminary examination* **yoshin**
予震 *foreshocks, pre-tremours* **yoshin**
予習 *lesson preparation, advanced study* **yoshū**
予想 *anticipation, expectation* **yosō**
予測 *prediction, estimate* **yosoku**
予定 *time schedule, plan* **yotei**
予約 *reservation, appointment* **yoyaku**
予予 *"for a long time...."* **yoyo**
猶予 *postponement, deferment* **yūyo**

先efore, 478	初tart, 353
前efore, 118	発tart, 368
始egin, 210	一irst, 858

予alberd, 568

479-B

Money 予dvanced, 預ntrust to chance...

預ntrust   預eposit

頁 (large shell, page)

azu(keru), azu(karu), YO
entrust, deposit

FLIP: 7.0.b2. Right (stem)

預言 *prophecy, prediction* **yogen**
預血 *blood donation* **yoketsu**
預金 *savings deposits, money saved* **yokin**
預金通帳 *bankbook, passbook* **yokin tsūchō**
預金利子 *interest on money deposited* **yokinrishi**
預金者 *depositor, account holder* **yokinsha**
銀行預金 *bank savings* **ginkō yokin**
預託 *bank deposit, entrusted money* **yotaku**
預貯金 *bank deposit, bank savings* **yochokin**
預かり金 *entrusted money* **azukarikin**
預かり物 *deposited items, entrusted things* **azukarimono**
預かり人 *person entrusted of belongings)* **azukarinin**
預かり主 *owner of entrusted belongings* **azukarinushi**
預かり所 *cloakroom, baggage room* **azukarisho**
預かり証 *bag check, luggage receipt* **azukarishō**
預け入れる *deposit (money)* **azukeireru**

金oney, 25	嘱ntrust, 441
幣oney, 171	託ntrust, 82
委ntrust, 583	任ntrust, 709

予dvance, 569

480-A
弁alve of 弁peech for a 怠azy leech...

廾 (clasped hands)

❶ 弁peech   **❷ 弁alve**

BEN
speech, articulate, eloquent; valve

FLIP: 4.0.b. Bottom (stem)
Facing: 4.0. ⟲⟳ Apart

❶買弁 *purchasing agent* **baiben**
弁別 *knowing right from wrong* **benbetsu**
弁解 *excuse, alibi, pretext* **benkai**
弁明 *explanation, vindication* **benmei**
弁髪 *pigtail hairstyle* **benpatsu**
弁済 *repayment, settlement* **bensai**
弁士 *speaker, narrator, orator* **benshi**
弁当 *Japanese meal-in-a-box* **bentō**
手弁当 *pay one's expense* **tebentō**
弁舌 *speech, address* **benzetsu**
代弁 *delegate, proxy, on behalf of* **daiben**
駅弁 *boxed lunch (train station)* **ekiben**
合弁 *joint management* **gōben**
自弁 *paying own expense, Dutch treat* **jiben**
花弁 *flower petal* **kaben**
勘弁 *pardon, excuse, endurance* **kanben**
活弁 *silent film narrator* **katsuben**
抗弁 *protest, plea, complaint, grievance* **kōben**
強弁 *far-fetched arguments* **kyōben**

熱弁 *impassioned speech* **netsuben**
論弁 *argument* **ronben**
思弁 *speculation, prospect* **shiben**
答弁 *answer, reply, explanation* **tōben**
雄弁 *eloquence, fluency, articulateness* **yūben**
雄弁家 *eloquent speaker* **yūbenka**
弁護士 *defence counsel, ~lawyer* **bengoshi**
弁理士 *patent lawyer* **benrishi**
弁償金 *compensation, indemnity* **benshōkin**
減圧弁 *regulator, transformer* **gen'atsuben**
東京弁 *Tōkyō-accent* **tōkyōben**
❷排気弁 *exhaust valve* **haikiben**

言*alking*, 251   口*outh*, 458   筒*ipe*, 51
談*alks*, 308   話*peak*, 236   管*ipe*, 917

惨*iserable*, 396

480-B
弁alve of 弁peech for a 怠azy leech...

心⟷忄⟷小 (feelings)

怠aziness   **怠dleness**

nama(keru); okota(ru), TAI
laziness, idleness, indolence, lackadaisical

FLIP: 8.0.a. Inner (flat)

怠け者 *lazy, lazybones, laggard* **namakemono**
緩怠 *laxity, negligence* **kantai**
過怠 *negligence, fault* **katai**
倦怠 *fatigue, weariness, lethargy* **kentai**
懈怠 *lazy, laggard, negligent* **ketai**
怠惰 *lazy, lazybones, laggard* **taida**
怠業 *work slowdown strike* **taigyō**
怠屈 *boredom, boring* **taikutsu**
怠慢 *negligence, carelessness* **taiman**
倦怠期 *boring times* **kentaiki**
倦怠感 *fatigue, weariness, lethargy* **kentaikan**

惰*azyness*, 311   閑*eisure*, 283
飽*oredom*, 665   悠*eisure*, 898
暇*ree time*, 653   鈍*tagnate*, 199

治*ecuperate*, 210

481-A

巡round the area of 災isaster, 巡atrols search faster...

《《⇔川 (river)

巡atrol　巡round

巡

megu(ru), JUN
patrol, around, scouting

Facing: 4.0. ⌐☞ Apart

一巡 *patrol rounds* ichijun
一巡り *a turn around : one full year* hitomeguri
巡演 *tour performance (concert)* jun'en
巡閲 *inspection tour* jun'etsu
巡業 *performance tour* jungyō
巡回 *round, patrol, tour* junkai
巡航 *cruising, sailing* junkō
巡行 *tour rounds, patrol* junkō
巡航 *cruising, sailing* junkō
巡幸 *imperial tour* junkō
巡拝 *pilgrimage* junpai
巡覧 *tour, sightseeing* junran
巡礼 *pilgrimage* junrei
巡歴 *visit of historic sites* junreki
巡査 *police officer, cop, constable* junsa
巡察 *inspection rounds* junsatsu
巡視 *inspection rounds* junshi
巡洋 *cruise tour* junyō
巡洋艦 *cruiser vessel* junyōkan

巡遊 *tour, sightseeing* junyū
逡巡 *hesitate, vacillate, waver* shunjun
巡り歩く *walk around* meguriaruku
血の巡り *blood circulation* chi no meguri
堂々巡り *going round in circles* dōdōmeguri
駆け巡る *run about, run around* kakemeguru
巡り合い *unexpected meeting* meguriai
聖地巡礼 *pilgrimage rounds* seichi junrei
思い巡らす *random thinking* omoimegurasu
張り巡らす *stretch out, -around* harimegurasu

481-B

巡round the area of 災isaster, 巡atrols search faster...

火⇔灬 (fire)

災isaster　災alamity

災

wazawa(i), SAI
disaster, calamity, catastrophe

Facing: 2.1. East ☞ (H)

防災 *disaster protection, ~preparedness* bōsai
風災 *wind damage, tornado* fūsai
人災 *man-made disasters* jinsai
火災 *fire disaster* kasai
火災警報 *fire alarm* kasai keihō
罹災 *suffering from a disaster* risai
労災 *workers' disaster relief* rōsai
災害 *disaster, calamity, accident* saigai
災害地 *stricken-, disaster area* saigaichi
災害保険 *casualty insurance* saigai hoken
災害救助 *disaster relief, ~assistance* saigai kyūjo
災害対策 *measures against disasters* saigai taisaku
災禍 *calamity, disaster, catastrophe* saika
災難 *calamity, disaster, catastrophe* sainan
災厄 *calamity, disaster, catastrophe* saiyaku
戦災 *war damage, ~ravages* sensai
戦災者 *war disaster victims* sensaisha
震災 *earthquake disaster* shinsai
震災地 *earthquake disaster area* shinsaichi

息災 *good health, safe & sound* sokusai
天災 *natural catastrophe, calamity* tensai
大震災 *1923 Tōkyō earthquake* daishinsai
被災地 *disaster-stricken area* hisaichi
坑内火災 *pit fire* kōnai kasai
無病息災 *perfect health* mubyōsokusai
不測の災い *unexpected disaster*
　　fusoku no wazawai

禍ragedy, 799		死eath, 513	
惨ragedy, 396		逝eath, 54	
悲ragedy, 289		亡eath, 72	
厄ragedy, 354		障njury, 325	

災aint, 309

482-A

省*elf-reflection*, not 劣*nferior* in the 省*inistry of Interior*...

目 (eyesight, visual)

❶省*elf-reflect* **❷省***inistry*

kaeri(miru), habu(ku), SEI, SHŌ
self-reflect, introspect, contemplate; Ministry, Cabinet office

FLIP: 4.0.a. Bottom (flat)

❶反省 *soul-searching, deep-reflection* **hansei**
自省 *self-examination, ~reflection* **jisei**
帰省 *returning home* **kisei**
猛省 *sincere-, serious reflection* **mōsei**
内省 *inner reflection* **naisei**
三省 *introspection, reflection* **sansei**
省察 *self-reflection* **seisatsu, shōsatsu**
省筆 *abbreviation, simplified Kanji strokes* **shōhitsu**
省略 *abbreviation, acronym* **shōryaku**
省みる *reflect, reconsider* **kaerimiru**
省力化 *staff reduction, labour downsizing* **shōryokuka**
人事不省 *absent-mindedness, lethargic* **jinji fusei**

❷法務省 *Ministry of Justice* **hōmushō**
海軍省 *Ministry of the Navy (pre-war)* **kaigunshō**
官省 *government office* **kanshō**
建設省 *Ministry of Construction* **kensetsushō**
宮内省 *Imperial Household Ministry* **kunaishō**
文部省 *Ministry of Education* **monbushō**

大蔵省 *Ministry of Finance* **ookurashō**
陸軍省 *Ministry of the Army (pre-war)* **rikugunshō**
省庁 *government ministry office* **shōchō**
各省大臣 *all cabinet ministers* **kakushō daijin**
省営 *Ministry-managed* **shōei**
省令 *ministerial order* **shōrei**
広東省 *Guandong, China* **kantonshō**

顧*elf-reflect, 343*	役*fficial, 746*
府*overnment, 429*	公*ublic, 180*
庁*ubic office, 633*	政*dministration, 725*
吏*fficial, 463*	署*ublic-office, 614*

首*eck, 311*

482-B

省*elf-reflection*, not 劣*nferior* in the 省*inistry of Interior*...

力 (strength, force)

劣*nferior* 劣*ediocre*

oto(ru), RETSU
inferior, lousy, mediocre, frail, paltry, shoddy, shoddy, sleazy, weakling

Facing: 3.0. ☞☜ Across

下劣 *base, gross, vulgar* **geretsu**
愚劣 *stupidity, folly* **guretsu**
卑劣 *mean, dirty* **hiretsu**
卑劣漢 *sneaky fellow* **hiretsukan**
見劣り *compare negatively* **miotori**
劣化 *deterioration, worsening* **rekka**
劣勢 *inferiority, mediocrity* **ressei**
劣性 *recessiveness* **ressei**
劣性遺伝 *recessive gene* **ressei iden**
劣悪 *inferior, poor* **retsuaku**
劣弱 *low, inferior* **retsujaku**
劣情 *lust, wild passions* **retsujō**
劣等感 *inferiority complex* **rettōkan**
劣等生 *inferior-, dull student* **rettōsei**
劣等 *inferiority, mediocrity* **rettō**
陋劣 *mean, despicable* **rōretsu**
拙劣 *clumsy, unskilful* **setsuretsu**
低劣 *cheap & trashy* **teiretsu**
庸劣 *mediocre, inferior, foolish* **yōretsu**

優劣 *superiority-or-inferiority, ability* **yūretsu**
優秀劣敗 *"winner takes all..."* **yūshū reppai**
負けず劣らず *"no less than..."*
makezu otorazu

負*efeat, 625*	弱*eakling, 908*
失*ailure, 19*	

少*ew, 459*

483-A

尿*rine test at the* 局*ureau led to a* 局*ituation for Ichirō...*

尸 (corpse)

尿*rine*   尿*ee*

NYŌ
　　urine, pee

道尿 *catheterise* **dō'nyō**
糞尿 *excrements, faeces, pooh* **funnyō**
排尿 *urinating, peeing* **hainyō**
頻尿 *frequent urination* **hinnyō**
放尿 *urinary discharge, urine* **hō'nyō**
遺尿 *bed-wetting* **i'nyō**
検尿 *urine test, urine analysis* **kennyō**
血尿 *bloody-, bleeding urine* **ketsu'nyō**
血尿症 *haematuria* **ketsu'nyōshō**
尿道 *urethra* **nyōdō**
尿道炎 *urethritis, urethra inflammation* **nyōdōen**
尿意 *urge to urinate* **nyōi**
尿器 *urinal, bedpan, pisspot* **nyōki**
尿路 *urinary tract* **nyōro**
尿酸 *uric acid* **nyōsan**
尿石 *urinary stone* **nyōseki**
尿素 *urea* **nyōso**
利尿 *diuretic* **ri'nyō**
尿瓶 *urinal, bedpan, pisspot* **shibin**

Facing: 3.0. ☞☜ Across

尿尿 *excrements, faeces* **shin'yō**
泌尿器 *urinary organs* **hi'nyōki**
泌尿器科 *urology* **hi'nyōkika**
尿毒症 *urine poisoning, uraemia* **nyōdokushō**
尿検査 *urinalysis, urine analysis* **nyōkensa**
糖尿病 *diabetes* **tō'nyōbyō**
夜尿症 *bed-wetting* **ya'nyōshō**
輸尿管 *ureter* **yu'nyōkan**

胆*all bladder, 740*
排*ejection, 795*

尾*ail, 468*

483-B

尿*rine test at the* 局*ureau led to a* 局*ituation for Ichirō...*

尸 (corpse)

❶局*ureau*   ❷局*ituation*

KYOKU
　　bureau, outpost; situation, condition

❶破局 *collapse, ruin, end* **hakyoku**
本局 *head-, main office* **honkyoku**
医局 *medical office* **ikyoku**
局番 *area number* **kyokuban**
⇒市外局番 *phone area code* **shigai kyokuban**
局部 *limited part* **kyokubu**
局地 *locality* **kyokuchi**
局長 *bureau director, postmaster* **kyokuchō**
局限 *confining, limiting* **kyokugen**
局員 *post office staff* **kyokuin**
局所 *limited part* **kyokusho**
支局 *branch office* **shikyoku**
対局 *Go game* **taikyoku**
当局 *concerned authorities* **tōkyoku**
薬局 *drugstore, pharmacy* **yakkyoku**
事務局 *executive office, secretariat* **jimūkyoku**
局留め *general delivery, poste restante* **kyokudome**
局外者 *onlooker, passerby* **kyokugaisha**
政治局 *politburo, central committee* **seijikyoku**

Facing: 3.0. ☞☜ Across
FLIP: 8.0.a. Inner (flat)

郵便局 *post office, mailing station* **yūbinkyoku**
❷時局 *current situation* **jikyoku**
局面 *situation, phase, aspect* **kyokumen**
事局 *situation, circumstances* **jikyoku**
結局 *"after all, in the end..."* **kekkyoku**
難局 *difficult, grave, severe* **nankyoku**
政局 *political situation* **seikyoku**
戦局 *war situation, state-of-war* **senkyoku**
選局 *tuning in (radio)* **senkyoku**
終局 *conclusion, endgame* **shūkyoku**
大局 *general situation* **taikyoku**
全局 *general-, overall situation* **zenkyoku**

庁*ublic office, 633*
署*ublic-office, 614*
所*ocation, 676*

居*xist, 384*

484-A

尽xhausted making 尺[30 cm] harpoon by high 昼oon...

尸 (corpse)

尽xhaust 尽ursue

tsu(kusu), tsu(kiru), tsu(kasu), JIN
exhaust, pursue, strive for, use up

Facing: 2.0. East ☞ (W)
FLIP: 2.0.b. Sort Of (stem)

大尽 extravagant, luxurious **daijin**
不尽 "yours sincerely..." **fujin**
金尽く financial sway **ganetsuku**
自尽 suicide, killing oneself **jijin**
尽忠 loyalty, devotion, fidelity **jinchū**
尽日 whole day; last day of the month **jinjitsu**
尽力 endeavour, effort, labour **jinryoku**
尽瘁 absolute devotion **jinsui**
無尽 inexhaustible, unlimited **mujin**
無尽蔵 inexhaustible supply **mujinzō**
食尽 maximum eclipse **shokujin**
蕩尽 squander, dissipate **tōjin**
尽未来 eternity, perpetuity, forever **jinmirai**
理不尽 ridiculous, unreasonable, absurd **rifujin**
力尽きる exhaust one's strength **chikaratsukiru**
心尽くし kindness, consideration **kokorotsukushi**
見尽くす "see to the end..." **mitsukusu**
物尽くす exhaustive, thorough **monotsukusu**
言い尽くす "empty one's chest, say it all..." **iitsukusu**

買い尽くす buy out, buy it all **kaitsukusu**
食い尽くす consume, eat up **kuitsukusu**
燃え尽きる burn out **moetsukiru**
論じ尽くす discuss exhaustively **ronjitsukusu**
知り尽くす know thoroughly **shiritsukusu**
立ち尽くす remain standing **tachitsukusu**
取り尽くす taking all **toritsukusu**
使い尽くす use to the last **tsukaitsukusu**
売り尽くす selling to the last item **uritsukusu**
焼き尽くす burn up, use up **yakitsukusu**
遣り尽くす exert best efforts **yaritsukusu**

追ursue, 108	励iligence, 465
逐rive-out, 479	搾queeze, 722
追ress for, 108	張xert, 274

冬inter, 397

484-B

尽xhausted making 尺[30 cm] harpoon by high 昼oon...

尸 (corpse)

尺[30 cm] 尺easurement

SHAKU
[30 centimetres], length, measurement

Facing: 2.0. East ☞ (W)
FLIP: 2.0.b. Sort Of (stem)

矩尺 carpentry square **kanejaku**
着尺 kimono standard measurement **kijaku**
鯨尺 about 37.8 centimetres **kujirajaku**
曲尺 carpentry square **magarijaku**
間尺 unworthy, wasted **mashaku**
六尺 palanquin bearer, six footer **rokushaku**
尺骨 thumb ulna **shakkotsu**
尺骨 ulna **shakubone**
尺地 small parcel of land **shakuchi**
尺度 measure, criterion, standard **shakudo**
尺八 Japanese bamboo flute **shakuhachi**
尺寸 a little bit, small amount **shakusun, sekisun**
尺余 in excess of a foot **shakuyo**
照尺 gun sights **shōshaku**
縮尺 measuring scale **shukushaku**
計算尺 slide ruler **keisanjaku**
巻き尺 tape measure **makijaku**
生半尺 half-done, half-baked **namahanjaku**
折り尺 folding ruler **orijaku**

三尺帯 children's obi sash **sanjakuobi**
尺貫法 Japanese weights & measures
  shakkanhō
尺取虫 inch worm **shakutorimushi**

升[1.8 ltr], 298	寸[3 cm], 345
旬[10 day], 494	坪[3.3 sqm], 488
斗[18 ltr], 195	匁[3.75 gm], 75
勺[18 ml], 470	斤[600 gm], 471

尽xhaust, 574

484-C

尺xhausted making 尺 *[30 cm] harpoon by high* 昼oon...

日 (sunlight, daytime)

昼aytime   昼oon

昼

FLIP: 2.0.a. Sort Of (flat)
FLIP: 4.0.a. Bottom (flat)

hiru, CHŪ
daytime, noon, midday, meridian

昼食 *luncheon, midday meal* **chūshoku**
昼食会 *luncheon, lunch meeting* **chūshokukai**
昼食時間 *lunch break, lunch hour*
   chūshoku jikan
昼餐 *luncheon* **chūsan**
昼夜 *day & night* **chūya**
昼夜兼行 *24 hours, round the clock*
   chūya kenkō
昼夜帯び *double-sided obi* **chūyaobi**
白昼 *broad daylight* **hakuchū**
昼顔 *bindweed* **hirugao**
昼餉 *lunch* **hiruge**
昼後 *a little after noon* **hirugo**
昼頃 *about noon, around 12 o'clock a.m.* **hirugoro**
昼間 *daytime, broad daylight* **hiruma, chūkan**
昼前 *a little before noon* **hirumae**
昼飯 *lunch* **hirumeshi**
昼寝 *nap, siesta, afternoon sleep* **hirune**
小昼 *a little before noon* **kohiru**

真昼 *high noon, 12 o'clock a.m.* **mahiru**
夜昼 *day & night, night & day* **yoruhiru**
昼行灯 *"futile as a daytime lantern..."* **hiruandon**
昼日中 *broad daylight* **hiruhinaka**
昼興行 *matinee show* **hirukōgyō**
昼休み *noon recess, lunch break* **hiruyasumi**
真昼間 *broad daylight* **mappiruma**
昼下がり *early afternoon* **hirusagari**

日*ay, 14*	朝*orning, 662*
暁*aybreak, 818*	陽*un, 932*

尺xhaust, *574*

485-A

究esearch on 窯eramics 突hrusted new dynamics...

穴 (hole, cave)

究esearch

究

FLIP: 3.0.b. Top (stem)

kiwa(meru), KYŪ
research, study enquiry, findings, investigate

学究 *academic research* **gakkyū**
学究的 *academic, scholarly* **gakkyūteki**
研究 *research, study* **kenkyū**
⇒地域研究 *area studies* **chiiki kenkyū**
研究費 *research money, ~grant* **kenkyūhi**
研究家 *research scholar, researcher* **kenkyūka**
研究科 *graduate course* **kenkyūka**
研究者 *researcher* **kenkyūsha**
研究心 *probing mind* **kenkyūshin**
研究室 *professor's-, research room* **kenkyūshitsu**
研究所 *research institute* **kenkyūsho**
研究開発 *research & development*
   kenkyū kaihatsu
研究論文 *treatise, dissertation*
   kenkyū ronbun
研究資料 *research materials, ~data*
   kenkyū shiryō
攻究 *study, investigate, research* **kōkyū**
講究 *specialized research* **kōkyū**

究明 *study, investigation* **kyūmei**
究理 *philosophical reasoning* **kyūri**
論究 *thorough & exhaustive discussion* **ronkyū**
推究 *inference, inferring* **suikyū**
探究 *inquiry, research* **tankyū**
探究心 *probing mind* **tankyūshin**
追究 *inquiry, research* **tsuikyū**
究極的 *ultimate, final* **kyūkyokuteki**

教*ducate, 385*	考*hinking, 392*
習*earning, 238*	勉*fforts, 527*
修*astery, 898*	討*nvestigate, 691*

突*reak-thru, 576*

485-B

究esearch on 窯eramics 突hrusted new dynamics...

穴 (hole, cave)

窯eramics　　　**窯ottery**

FLIP: 1.0.b. Whole (stem)

kama, YŌ
ceramics, pottery, earthenware, kiln

窯印 potter's imprint, ~seal **kamajirushi**
窯元 potter-making place **kamamoto**
官窯 government-owned kiln **kanyō**
炭窯 charcoal kiln **sumigama**
土窯 clay oven, brick oven **tsuchikama**
窯業 ceramic industry **yōgyō**
石塊窯 lime kiln **sekkaigama**

陶orcelain, 811	工raft, 176
磁orcelain, 54	匠raftsman, 106
皿late, 21	芸rts, 619
泥irt, 302	

突reak-thru, 576

485-C

究esearch on 窯eramics 突hrusted laws new dynamics...

穴 (hole, cave)

突hrust　　　突reak-thru

FLIP: 3.0.b. Top (stem)

tsu(ku), TOTSU
thrust, break-thru, dash, penetrate

突き指 sprained finger **tsukiyubi**
突き傷 knife-, stabbing wound **tsukikizu**
突き刺す stick, pierce **tsukisasu**
突き進む advance, thrust thru **tsukisusumu**
突き倒す push away, shove **tsukitaosu**
突き通す pierce, thrust, skewer **tsukitoosu**
突き破る break thru, pierce, crash **tsukiyaburu**
突き出す thrust, stick out, protrude **tsukidasu**
猪突 rushing recklessly **chototsu**
煙突 chimney, funnel, smokestack **entotsu**
激突 crash, collision, concussion **gekitotsu**
剣突 rebuff, retort, rejoinder **kentsuku**
衝突 collision, conflict **shōtotsu**
突角 convex angle **tokkaku**
突貫 charge, dash **tokkan**
突破 breaking in, piercing thru **toppa**
突発 bursting out **toppatsu**
突飛 wild, extravagant **toppi**
突風 gust of wind **toppū**

突進 charge, dash **tosshin**
突出 portruding, dangling **tosshutsu**
唐突 unexpected, abrupt, sudden **tōtotsu**
突撃 charge, sudden attack **totsugeki**
突如 all of a sudden, abruptly **totsujo**
突入 rushing in, plunging in **totsunyū**
⇒再突入 atmosphere re-entry **saitotsunyū**
突端 tip, point **tottan**
突堤 breakwater, sea wall, embankment **tottei**
追突 coming from behind, side entry **tsuitotsu**
盾突く defy, disobey, oppose **tatetsuku**

刺ierce, 875	挿nsert, 126
徹ierce-thru, 843	穴avity, 4

空ky, 394

486-A

脅hreatened by pirates to 協ooperate...

肉⇔月 (flesh, body part)

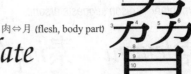

脅hreaten　脅ntimidate

obiya(kasu), odo(kasu) odo(su), KYŌ
threaten, intimidate, menace, terror, bully

脅迫 *threat, intimidation, menace* **kyōhaku**
脅迫状 *threatening letter* **kyōhakujō**
脅迫的 *threatening, intimidating* **kyōhakuteki**
脅迫電話 *phone threat* **kyōhaku denwa**
脅威 *menace, threat* **kyōi**
脅喝 *threat, intimidation, menace* **kyōkatsu**
脅し文句 *verbal threat* **odoshimonku**

FLIP: 4.0.b. Bottom (stem)
Facing: 4.0. 🐟🐟 Apart)

威*hreat, 520*	驚*care, 330*
嚇*hreat, 261*	怖*cary, 209*
虞*hreat, 889*	恐*cary, 906*
恐*enace, 906*	振*remble, 60*

協*ooperate, 577*

486-B

脅hreatened by pirates to 協ooperate...

十 (cross)

協ooperate　協articipate

KYŌ
cooperate, participate, partake, collaborate

妥協 *compromise, concession* **dakyō**
漁協 *fishery cooperative* **gyokyō**
協調 *cooperation, collaboration* **kyōchō**
協調性 *one's spirit of cooperation* **kyōchōsei**
協同組合 *co-operative, association*
　　kyōdō kumiai
協議 *conference, discussion* **kyōgi**
協議員 *delegate, meeting participant* **kyōgiin**
協議会 *conference, council* **kyōgikai**
協議事項 *agenda, item for discussion*
　　kyōgi jikō
協業 *collaborative work* **kyōgyō**
協会 *association, society* **kyōkai**
協力 *cooperation, participation* **kyōryoku**
協力者 *co-worker, collaborator* **kyōryokusha**
協賛 *support, cooperation* **kyōsan**
協賛金 *project-support fund* **kyōsankin**
協商 *commercial agreement* **kyōshō**
協奏曲 *concert, concierto* **kyōsōkyoku**

Facing: 2.2. East ☞ (V)

協定 *agreement* **kyōtei**
協定価格 *agreed price* **kyōtei kakaku**
紳士協定 *gentlemen's agreement*
　　shinshi kyōtei
停戦協定 *armistice, ceasefire* **teisen kyōtei**
協和 *harmony* **kyōwa**
協約 *agreement* **kyōyaku**
農協 *agricultural cooperative* **nōkyō**
和協 *harmony & cooperation* **wakyō**

加*articipate, 201*	可*pproval, 15*
携*articipate, 151*	承*pproval, 117*
共*ogether, 302*	諾*pproval, 277*
和*armony, 103*	賛*pproval, 334*

脅*hreaten, 577*

487-A

素lementary 毒oison suggests arson...

素lement   素imple

糸 (thread, continuity)

FLIP: 3.0.a. Top (flat)

moto, SO, SU
element, simple, basic, plain

窒素 nitrogen **chisso**
毒素 toxic substance, ~element **dokuso**
塩素 chlorine **enso**
元素 chemical element **genso**
簡素 simple & frugal **kanso**
酵素 enzyme **kōso**
酸素 oxygen **sanso**
色素 colour pigment **shikiso**
素面 soberness, sobriety **shirafu**
素人 amateur, novice, greenhorn **shirōto**
質素 frugal, plain, simple **shisso**
素因 primary factor, main cause **soin**
素行 conduct, behaviour **sokō**
素麺 thin white noodles **sōmen**
素子 element **soshi**
素質 quality; talent, genius **soshitsu**
素数 prime number **sosū**
素材 material, subject matter **sozai**
素足 barefooted **suashi**

素手 bare hands **sude**
素顔 face without cosmetics **sugao**
素肌 bare hands, ~skin **suhada**
素裸 stark, naked **suhadaka, suppadaka**
水素 hydrogen **suiso**
素直 frank, honest **sunao**
素敵 lovely, splendid, superb **suteki**
炭素 carbon, carbonated **tanso**
要素 component, constituent **yōso**
栄養素 nutrient, vitamins **eiyōso**
葉緑素 chlorophyll **yōryokuso**

素lement, 578	工raft, 176
単imple, 517	匠raftsman, 106
要ssential, 419	芸rts, 619

素earch, 375   毒oison, 578

487-B

素lementary 毒oison suggests arson...

毒oison   毒enom

毋 (mother)

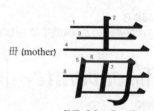

FLIP: 3.0.a. Top (flat)

DOKU
poison, venom

毒づく curse, expletive, swearing **dokuzuku**
毒ガス poison gas **dokugasu**
毒々しい gaudy, malicious **dokudokushii**
毒物 toxic-, poisonous substance **dokubutsu**
毒蛇 poisonous-, venomous snake **dokuhebi**
毒牙 poison fang **dokuga**
毒言 verbal abuse, abusive words **dokugen**
毒魚 poisonous fish **dokugyo**
毒刃 assassin's dagger **dokujin**
毒気 poisonous air, malice **dokuke**
毒消し antidote, counter-actant **dokukeshi**
毒味 poison food tasting **dokumi**
毒殺 poisoned to death **dokusatsu**
毒性 toxicity, venomous **dokusei**
毒手 dirty trick **dokushu**
毒素 toxin, poisonous substance **dokuso**
毒草 poisonous plant **dokusō**
毒矢 poisoned arrow **dokuya**
毒薬 poison, poison drugs **dokuyaku**

毒舌 spiteful tongue, foul-mouthed **dokuzetsu**
鉛毒 lead poisoning **endoku**
害毒 evil, poison, harm **gaidoku**
解毒 antidote, counter-actant **gedoku**
鉱毒 mineral poisoning **kōdoku**
無毒 harmless person **mudoku**
消毒 sanitize, disinfect **shōdoku**
薬毒 toxic substance **yakudoku**
気の毒 disgusting, sickening **kinodoku**
目の毒 eyesore, unbearable sight **menodoku**
服毒自殺 suicide poisoning **fukudoku jisatsu**

死eath, 513	亡eath, 72	被njury, 715
逝eath, 54	殺urder, 744	害njury, 904

責ondemn, 115   青lue colour, 115

488-A

春pring 奏usicale turned comical...

日 (sunlight, daytime)

春pring　　春rimehood

haru, SHUN
spring, primehood

FLIP: 1.0.a. Whole (flat)

晚春 *delayed spring* **banshun**
売春 *prostitution* **baishun**
迎春 *New Year greetings; pleasant spring* **geishun**
春霞 *spring haze* **harugasumi**
春着 *spring wear* **harugi**
春風 *spring breeze, ~wind* **harukaze**
春先 *early spring* **harusaki**
春雨 *spring rain, bean threads* **harusame**
今春 *this spring* **konshun**
明春 *next-, coming spring* **myōshun**
来春 *next-, coming spring* **raishun**
立春 *start of spring season* **risshun**
昨春 *spring last* **sakushun**
青春 *youth, juvenile* **seishun**
春暖 *warm-, mild spring* **shundan**
春画 *pornographic photos* **shunga**
春情 *sexual passion, lust* **shunjō**
春秋 *spring & autumn; promising future* **shunjū**
春景 *spring scenery* **shunkei**

春季 *spring, springtime* **shunki**
春本 *pornographic book* **shunpon**
春雷 *spring thunder* **shunrai**
春闘 *spring offensive (labour)* **shuntō**
常春 *eternal spring* **tokoharu**
陽春 *springtime* **yōshun**
売春婦 *prostitute, whore, hooker* **baishunfu**
春一番 *first gale of spring* **haruichiban**
春景色 *snow landscape, snow view* **harugeshiki**
春休み *spring vacation* **haruyasumi**
思春期 *puberty, adolescence* **shishunki**
春分の日 *Vernal Equinox Day* **shunbun no hi**

花*lower, 191*	秋*utumn, 415*	冬*inter, 397*
華*lower, 40*	夏*ummer, 606*	季*eason, 583*

香*ragrance, 895*

488-B

春pring 奏usicale turned comical...

大 (grand)

奏usic play　　奏nsemble

kana(deru), SŌ
music play, ensemble

FLIP: 1.0.b. Whole (stem)

伴奏 *musical accompaniment* **bansō**
伴奏者 *accompanist player* **bansōsha**
弾奏 *performance, concert* **dansō**
伝奏 *deliver a report to the emperor* **densō**
独奏 *solo performance (piano, violin)* **dokusō**
演奏 *musical recital, ~concert* **ensō**
演奏法 *musical rendition* **ensōhō**
伏奏 *report to the emperor* **fukusō**
合奏 *ensemble* **gassō**
⇒弦楽合奏 *string ensemble* **gengaku gassō**
弦楽 *string music* **gengaku**
序奏 *prelude, overture music* **josō**
上奏 *report to the emperor* **jōsō**
重奏 *instrumental ensemble* **jūsō**
後奏 *postlude* **kōsō**
協奏曲 *concerto* **kyōsōkyoku**
内奏 *secret report to the emperor* **naisō**
連奏 *musical ensemble* **rensō**
節奏 *rhythm* **sessō**

奏楽 *musical performance, ~concert* **sōgaku**
奏上 *report to the emperor* **sōjō**
奏功 *success, favourable outcome* **sōkō**
奏効 *effectiveness, efficacy* **sōkō**
奏請 *petition to the emperor* **sōsei**
奏者 *musical performer* **sōsha**
⇒木琴奏者 *xylophonist* **mokkin sōsha**
吹奏 *playing a wind instrument* **suisō**
前奏 *prelude, overture music* **zensō**
五重奏 *quintet* **gojūsō**
変奏曲 *musical variation* **hensōkyoku**

弦*usical string, 358*	曲*elody, 476*
譜*usical note, 455*	歌*inging, 878*

泰*alm, 612*

489-A

営*anagerial* 栄*lory for Mubarak began in the* 営*arracks...*

口 (mouth)

❶ 営*anagement*   **❷** 営*arracks*

itona(mu), EI
management, administration, oversee; barracks

FLIP: 1.0.a. Whole (flat)

❶ 直営 *direct management, ~control* **chokuei**
営団 *corporation, business entity* **eidan**
営営 *unrelenting work* **eiei**
営農 *farm management* **einō**
営利 *money-making, profit-making* **eiri**
営林 *forestry management* **eirin**
本営 *management headquarters* **hon'ei**
経営 *management, operation* **keiei**
公営 *public management* **kōei**
国営 *government-managed* **kokuei**
民営 *private management* **min'ei**
私営 *private management* **shiei**
市営 *city-managed* **shiei**
都営 *city-managed* **toei**
運営 *management, operation* **un'ei**
自営業 *family business, self-employed* **jieigyō**
❷ 造営 *construction, building* **zōei**
営造物 *building, structure* **eizōbutsu**
脱営 *deserting (soldier), awol* **datsuei**

営舎 *barracks, garrison* **eisha**
営繕 *building & repairs* **eizen**
軍営 *military camp, ~base* **gun'ei**
兵営 *barracks, garrison* **heiei**
陣営 *athletes camp* **jin'ei**
入営 *enlisting in the military* **nyūei**
露営 *camping out, encampment* **roei**
設営 *construction, arrangement* **setsuei**
宿営 *billeting, lodging* **shukuei**
敵営 *enemy camp* **tekiei**
野営 *camping out, encampment* **yaei**

業*usiness, 124*	領*ontrol, 874*
商*ommerce, 135*	旨*nstruct, 242*
株*orporation, 130*	統*overn, 885*

宮*hrine, 105*

489-B

営*anagerial* 栄*lory for Mubarak began in the* 営*arracks...*

木 (wooden)

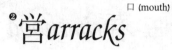

栄*lory*   栄*restige*

ha(e), ha(eru), saka(eru), EI
glory, prestige, distinction

FLIP: 1.0.b. Whole (stem)

栄華 *glory, prosperity* **eiga**
栄位 *dignified rank* **eii**
栄辱 *honour & disgrace, rise & fall* **eijoku**
栄冠 *crown, garland* **eikan**
栄枯 *flourish & wither away* **eiko**
栄光 *glory, honour* **eikō**
栄進 *promotion, advancement* **eishin**
栄達 *distinguished, renowned* **eitatsu**
栄転 *promotion, advancement* **eiten**
栄誉 *honour, glory, distinction* **eiyo**
栄養 *nutrition, nutrients, nourishment* **eiyō**
栄養学 *dietetics, nutrition* **eiyōgaku**
栄養価 *nutritive value* **eiyōka**
栄養士 *nutritionist, dietician,* **eiyōshi**
栄養素 *nutrient, vitamins* **eiyōso**
栄養分 *nutrient, vitamins* **eiyōbun**
栄養剤 *nutrient, vitamins* **eiyōzai**
栄養不良 *undernourished, malnourished* **eiyō furyō**
繁栄 *prosperity, flourishing* **han'ei**

光栄 *honour, glory, distinction* **kōei**
虚栄 *vanity, conceit, ostentation* **kyoei**
共栄 *mutual prosperity, co-prosperity* **kyōei**
見栄 *showing off, ostentation* **mie**
栄螺 *turban shell* **sazae**
清栄 *prosperity, good times, affluence* **seiei**
余栄 *posthumous glory* **yoei**
虚栄心 *vanity, conceit, ostentation* **kyoeishin**
聞き栄え *"worth hearing about..."* **kikibae**
栄枯盛衰 *rise & fall* **eiko seisui**
代わり栄え *change for the better* **kawaribae**

誉*onour, 252*
誇*ride, 947*
名*ame, 425*

学*tudy, 346*

490-A

恋ove & 恋omance does not 変hange by chance...

心 ⇔ 忄 ⇔ 小 (feelings)

恋omance　　恋ove

koi, ko(u), koi(shii), REN
romance, love, amorous

FLIP: 3.0.b. Top (stem)
Facing: 3.0. ☞ ☜ Across

初恋　first love **hatsukoi**
悲恋　tragic love **hiren**
色恋　love **irokoi**
邪恋　forbidden love **jaren**
片恋　unrequited love, frustrated love **katakoi**
眷恋　deep attachment **kenren**
恋人　boyfriend, girlfriend **koibito**
恋文　love letter **koibumi**
恋敵　love rival **koigataki**
恋心　falling in love **koigokoro**
恋路　love & romance **koiji**
恋風　zephyr of love **koikaze**
恋仲　falling in love **koinaka**
恋歌　love song **koiuta, renka**
恋愛　love for the opposite sex **ren'ai**
恋慕　falling in love **renbo**
恋情　love, attachment **renjō**
恋々　fond attachment **renren**

失恋　unrequited love, frustrated love **shitsuren**
妻恋　love for one's wife **tsumagoi**
恋煩い　love sickness **koiwazurai**
恋愛中　in love **ren'aichū**
恋愛観　philosophy of love **ren'aikan**
横恋慕　forbidden love, illicit love **yokorenbo**
恋の悩み　torments-of-love **koi no nayami**
恋焦がれる　love obsession **koikogareru**

愛ove, 593	姻arriage, 364
感eelings, 45	婚arriage, 637
気eelings, 98	貞idelity, 506
情eelings, 793	忠oyalty, 475

変hange, 581

490-B

恋ove & 恋omance does not 変hange by chance...

夂 ⇔ 夂 (winter)

❶変hange　　❷変bnormal

ka(waru), ka(eru), HEN
change, alter, modify, switch, shift, transform, variation; abnormal

FLIP: 2.0.b. Sort Of (stem)

❶不変　unchanging, steadfast **fuhen**
劇変　violent change **gekihen**
変圧　transformation **hen'atsu**
変動　change, fluctuation **hendō**
変位　displacement, dislocation **hen'i**
変異　variation, mutation **hen'i**
変移　transition, change **hen'i**
変化　change, variety **henka**
変革　change, reform **henkaku**
変換　conversion, transformation **henkan**
変形　transformation **henkei**
変更　change, renewal, update **henkō**
⇒名義変更　ownership transfer (purchase)
　　meigi henkō
変心　change-of-heart **henshin**
変身　physical transformation **henshin**
変質　qualitative change **henshitsu**
変体　variation, disparity **hentai**
変態　pervert, sex maniac **hentai**

変転　change, new transformation **henten**
変容　change in appearance **henyō**
改変　alteration, reforming **kaihen**
黄変　turning yellowish **ōhen**
可変性　variability, adjustability **kahensei**
声変わり　voice changing **koegawari**
❷変人　eccentric person **henjin**
変節　treachery, betrayal **hensetsu**
変死　unnatural death **henshi**
変則　irregular, abnormality **hensoku**
変造　forgery, fake, fabrication, phoney **henzō**
大変　difficult, problematic; very much **taihen**

遷hange, 603	換eplace, 819
化ecome, 192	替eplace, 334

恋omance, 581

491-A

"Kick me" 符*ags pinned by* 笑*aughing hags...*

竹 (bamboo)

符*ign*   符*arking*

FU
sign, marking, label, symbol

Facing: 1.1. West (H)

合符 *baggage claim stub* **aifu**
符丁 *sign, code, password* **fuchō**
符牒 *mark, code, symbol* **fuchō**
符合 *coincidence, correspondence* **fugō**
符号 *sign, symbol* **fugō**
⇒省略符号 *apostrophe mark* **shōryaku fugō**
⇒呼び出し符号 *call sign* **yobidashi fugō**
符節 *corresponding, tallying with* **fusetsu**
護符 *amulet, talisman, charm* **gofu**
呪符 *amulet, talisman, charm* **jufu**
切符 *ticket, stub, coupon* **kippu**
⇒往復切符 *round-trip-, return ticket* **ōfuku kippu**
⇒通し切符 *pass ticket* **tooshi kippu**
⇒乗り越し切符 *fare-adjustment ticket* **norikoshi kippu**
音符 *musical note* **onpu**
⇒長音符 *long-vowel mark* **chōonpu**
⇒全音符 *whole musical note* **zen'onpu**
⇒八分音符 *eighth musical note* **hachibu onpu**

⇒二分音符 *half note musical note* **nibun onpu**
⇒四分音符 *quarter musical note* **shibun onpu, shibu onpu**
神符 *amulet, talisman, charm* **shinpu**
割符 *tally, check* **warifu**
赤切符 *third-class ticket* **akagippu**
疑問符 *question mark* **gimonfu**
引用符 *quotation mark* **inyōfu**
感嘆符 *exclamation point* **kantanfu**
休止符 *rest (music)* **kyūshifu**
免罪符 *indulgence, leniency, tolerance* **menzaifu**
終止符 *period, full stop* **shūshifu**

標*ign, 549*   券*icket, 406*
札*abel, 685*

策*olicy, 875*

491-B

"Kick me" 符*ags pinned by* 笑*aughing hags...*

竹 (bamboo)

笑*augh*   笑*mile*

wara(u), e(mu), SHŌ
laugh, smile, ridicule, chuckle, giggle

Facing: 1.1. West (H)

微笑み *smile, smiling face* **hohoemi**
苦笑い *bitter smile* **nigawarai**
高笑い *roaring laughter* **takawarai**
薄笑い *faint smile* **usuwarai**
笑い話 *funny story, joke, gag, jest* **waraibanashi**
笑い顔 *smiling face* **waraigao**
笑い声 *laughter, chuckling* **waraigoe**
笑い事 *laughing matter* **waraigoto**
笑い草 *object of ridicule, butt of jokes* **waraigusa**
笑い者 *laughing stock* **waraimono**
馬鹿笑い *mad laughter* **bakawarai**
含み笑い *suppressed laughter* **fukumiwarai**
泣き笑い *tearful smile* **nakiwarai**
可笑しい *"funny, something wrong..."* **okashii**
忍び笑い *silent titter, giggle, chuckle* **shinobiwarai**
作り笑い *forced laugh, feigned smile* **tsukuriwarai**
爆笑 *roar of laughter* **bakushō**
微笑 *smile, beaming* **bishō**
嘲笑 *laugh at, make fun of* **chōshō**

談笑 *friendly talks, chatting* **danshō**
笑顔 *smile, smiling face* **egao**
艶笑 *seductive smile* **enshō**
苦笑 *feigned smile* **kushō**
冷笑 *macabre smile, grin, sneer* **reishō**
失笑 *burst of laughter* **shisshō**
笑劇 *comedy, satire, farce* **shōgeki**
笑気 *laughing gas, nitrous oxide* **shōki**
笑納 *receive with laughter* **shōnō**
笑殺 *dismiss with laughter* **shōsatsu**
笑止 *ridiculous, absurd* **shōshi**

唇*ips, 588*   祥*appiness, 248*
喜*appiness, 965*   慶*ejoice, 69*
幸*appiness, 268*

符*ign, 582*

492-A
Next boxing 季*eason to* 委*ntrust Robinson...*

子 (child)

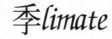
季*eason*　　季*limate*

KI
season, climate

Facing: 1.1. 🔜 West (H)

時季 *season (winter, spring, summer & fall)* **jiki**
夏季 *summertime* **kaki**
乾季 *dry season* **kanki**
季題 *seasonal theme* **kidai**
季語 *seasonal word (haiku)* **kigo**
季刊 *quarterly magazine, quarterly* **kikan**
季候 *season* **kikō**
季節 *season* **kisetsu**
季節風 *seasonal wind, monsoon* **kisetsufū**
季節感 *sense of the season* **kisetsukan**
季節的 *seasonal, seasonable* **kisetsuteki**
年季 *experienced-, professional hand* **nenki**
四季 *four seasons, all-year round* **shiki**
秋季 *autumn, fall* **shūki**
春季 *spring, springtime* **shunki**
冬季 *winter season* **tōki**
雨季 *rainy season, wet season* **uki**

節*eason, 421*	秋*utumn, 415*
冬*inter, 397*	春*pring, 579*
夏*ummer, 606*	候*limate, 122*

秀*xcellence, 383*

492-B
Next boxing 季*eason to* 委*ntrust Robinson...*

女 (woman)

委*ntrust*　　委*andate*

yuda(neru), I
entrust, mandate, authorize, commit, delegate

Facing: 3.0. 👉👈 Across

委付 *relinquishing one's rights* **ifu**
委員 *committee member, commissioner* **iin**
⇒論説委員 *editorial writer, lead writer*
　　ronsetsu iin
委員長 *committee chairperson* **iinchō**
委員会 *committee, commission* **iinkai**
⇒小委員会 *sub-committee* **shōiinkai**
⇒懲罰委員会 *disciplinary committee*
　　chōbatsu iinkai
⇒常設委員会 *standing committee* **jōsetsu iinkai**
⇒準備委員会 *preparation committee* **junbi iinkai**
⇒査問委員会 *fact-finding committee* **samon iinkai**
⇒執行委員会 *executive committee* **shikkō iinkai**
⇒審査委員会 *screening committee* **shinsa iinkai**
⇒運営委員会 *steering committee* **un'ei iinkai**
委譲 *transfer of rights (new ownership)* **ijō**
委棄 *consign, waive one's rights* **iki**
委曲 *details, particulars* **ikyoku**
委任 *delegation of authority, power of attorney* **inin**

委任統治 *mandate* **inin tōchi**
委任状 *authorization certificate* **ininjō**
委任者 *power of attorney issuer* **ininsha**
委細 *details, particulars* **isai**
委嘱 *commission, appointment* **ishoku**
委縮 *contraction, shrivelling* **ishuku**
委託 *trust, consignment* **itaku**
委託販売 *consignment sale* **itaku hanbai**
委託品 *consignment goods* **itakuhin**
委託金 *money-in-trust* **itakukin**

嘱*ntrust, 441*	忠*oyalty, 475*
託*ntrust, 82*	貞*idelity, 506*
任*ntrust, 709*	預*ntrust, 569*

季*eason, 583*

493-A

Sports 範odels flex their 筋uscles...

範*xample* 範*odel*

HAN
example, model, specimen

竹 (bamboo)

FLIP: 6.2. Left Bottom

文範 *draft composition* **bunpan**
範疇 *category, classification* **hanchū**
範囲 *range, scope & limitation* **han'i**
⇒勢力範囲 *sphere-of-influence* **seiryoku han'i**
範囲内 *within the scope, ~range* **han'inai**
範例 *example* **hanrei**
規範 *standard, norm, model* **kihan**
軌範 *model, exemplar* **kihan**
規範的 *model, exemplary* **kihanteki**
広範 *broad, extensive* **kōhan**
模範 *model, exemplar* **mohan**
模範生 *model-, honour student* **mohansei**
模範的 *model, exemplary* **mohanteki**
師範 *instructor, teacher* **shihan**
師範学校 *teacher's college* **shihan gakkō**
典範 *model, standard* **tenpan**

例*xample, 357*	塑*attern, 896*
鑑*attern, 857*	柄*attern, 213*
型*attern, 536*	模*attern, 827*

箱*OX, 616*

493-B

Sports 範odels flex their 筋uscles...

筋*uscle* 筋*oint*

suji, KIN
muscle, joint, threadlike

竹 (bamboo) 筋

Facing: 4.0. ⬅➡ Apart

青筋 *blue veins, ~arteries* **aosuji**
粗筋 *rough outline* **arasuji**
血筋 *blood relationship* **chisuji**
腹筋 *abdominal muscle* **fukkin**
鼻筋 *nose* **hanasuji**
本筋 *main subject, ~theme* **honsuji**
川筋 *river* **kawasuji**
毛筋 *minor details* **kesuji**
筋炎 *muscle inflammation* **kin'en**
筋骨 *muscles & bone's* **kinkotsu**
筋肉 *muscle* **kinniku**
金筋 *gold stripes* **kinsuji**
首筋 *scruff of the neck* **kubisuji**
客筋 *clientele, customers* **kyakusuji**
道筋 *route, course* **michisuji**
背筋 *spinal column* **sesuji, haikin**
心筋 *heart muscle* **shinkin**
筋金 *backbone* **sujigane**
筋子 *salmon roe* **sujiko**

筋道 *reason, logic, the beef* **sujimichi**
鉄筋 *reinforcing bars* **tekkin**
手筋 *lines on the palm* **tesuji**
関係筋 *competent sources* **kankeisuji**
権威筋 *authoritative source* **ken'isuji**
玄人筋 *well-informed* **kurōtosuji**
筋合い *reason* **sujiai**
筋張る *serious, sinewy* **sujibaru**
筋書き *synopsis, outline* **sujigaki**
随意筋 *skeletal muscle* **zuiikin**
筋向かい *across the street* **sujimukai**

力*trength, 351*	丈*trong, 463*
伸*tretch, 713*	強*trong, 894*
張*tretch, 274*	剛*trong, 975*

節*eason, 421*

494-A

Heat so 烈ntense, it 裂plit the fence...

火⇔灬 (fire)

烈ntense　　烈ehement

RETSU
intense, vehement, fierce, severe, stinging, aggressive

Facing: 1.2. ☜ West (V)

忠烈　unwavering loyalty **chūretsu**
激烈　fierce, violent, ferocious **gekiretsu**
義烈　nobility, valour, heroism **girestu**
芳烈　aroma, fresh smell **hōretsu**
苛烈　hard-fought, intense struggle **karetsu**
酷烈　intense, severe, rigorous **kokuretsu**
強烈　intense, severe **kyōretsu**
猛烈　intense, severe **mōretsu**
熱烈　fierce, fervent, vehement **netsuretsu**
烈火　rage, fury, ire, wrath **rekka**
烈開　burst open, break loose **rekkai**
烈婦　virtuous woman **reppu**
烈夫　patriot, hero **reppu**
烈風　violent wind, gale **reppū**
烈士　patriot, hero **resshi**
烈震　intense earthquake, severe jolt **resshin**
烈日　scorching sun **retsujitsu**
烈女　strong-willed woman **retsujo**
烈烈　fierce, fervent, vehement **retsuretsu**

惨烈　atrocious, horrible **sanretsu**
鮮烈　vivid, striking, stark **senretsu**
熾烈　keen, fierce **shiretsu**
峻烈　sharp, severe, fierce **shunretsu**
壮烈　heroic, courageous **sōretsu**
貞烈　undiluted chastity **teiretsu**
痛烈　severe, fierce **tsūretsu**
勇烈　brave, daring, fearless **yūretsu**
奇天烈　strange, funny **kiteretsu**
武烈天皇　Emperor Būretsu (498-506)
　　būretsu tennō

厳evere, 449	猛ierce, 657
激ierce, 170	獣east, 846

裂plit-up, 585

494-B

Heat so 烈ntense, it 裂plit the fence...

衣⇔衤 (clothing)

裂plit-up　裂reak-apart

sa(keru), sa(ku), RETSU
split-up, tear-up, break-apart

Facing: 3.0. ☞☜ Across

爆裂　explosion, detonation, blasting **bakuretsu**
爆裂弾　bombs, explosives **bakuretsudan**
分裂　split apart, break up **bunretsu**
⇒核分裂　nuclear fission **kakubunretsu**
破裂　explosion, detonation, blasting **haretsu**
決裂　ruptures, cracking **ketsuretsu**
亀裂　crack, crevice, clef, cranny **kiretsu**
滅裂　chaotic, incoherent **metsuretsu**
裂傷　lacerations, bleeding wound **resshō**
裂け目　crack, tear, rip, cranny **sakeme**
炸裂　explode, burst **sakuretsu**
炸裂弾　explosives **sakuretsudan**
釘裂き　tearing clothes (on nail) **kugizaki**
八裂き　tear incessantly **yatsuzaki**
張り裂き　burst, split apart **harizaki**
引き裂く　tear up, rip apart **hikisaku**
鉤裂き　tear, crack, cranny **kagizaki**
四分五裂　disruption, breaking, splitting
　　shibu goretsu, shibun goretsu

折reak, 471	分ivide, 518
壊reak-down, 847	剖ivide, 950
破estroy, 715	割ivide, 968

製anufacture, 534

495-A

臭*tinky rum* 息*reathe his* 息*on...*

臭*ad smell*　　臭*dour*

自 (oneself)

kusa(i), SHŪ
bad smell, odour, stench, stinky, whiff

FLIP: 1.0.b. Whole (stem)

悪臭　*offensive odour, stinky* **akushū**
防臭　*deodorization, deodorizing* **bōshū**
脱臭　*deodorization* **dasshū**
腐臭　*rotten odour* **fushū**
激臭　*offensive odour* **gekishū**
異臭　*nasty odour* **ishū**
口臭　*bad breath* **kōshū**
生臭　*worldly interests* **namagusa**
死臭　*rotten corpse odour* **shishū**
臭覚　*sense of smell* **shūkaku**
臭気　*bad odour* **shūki**
臭気止め　*deodorizer, deodorant* **shūkidome**
臭味　*offensive odour, stink* **shūmi**
体臭　*body odour* **taishū**
腋臭　*body odour* **wakiga**
俗臭　*vulgarity, gross, crudeness* **zokushū**
青臭い　*inexperienced, naïve, greenhorn* **aokusai**
汗臭い　*perspiration odour* **asekusai**
乳臭い　*immatured; inexperienced* **chichikusai**

泥臭い　*unrefined, earth smell* **dorokusai**
古臭い　*old-fashioned, hackneyed* **furukusai**
黴臭い　*musty odour* **kabikusai**
水臭い　*to be reserved* **mizukusai**
男臭い　*masculine bad odour* **otokokusai**
酒臭い　*alcohol odour* **sakekusai**
土臭い　*dirt odour* **tsuchikusai**
けち臭い　*stingy, cheap, miser* **kechikusai**
焦げ臭い　*burnt-, charred odour* **kogekusai**
辛気臭い　*boring, dull, monotonous* **shinkikusai**
照れ臭い　*feel embarrassed* **terekusai**

鼻*ose, 169*	芳*ragrance, 533*
薫*ragrance, 934*	花*lower, 191*
香*ragrance, 895*	華*lower, 40*

息*reathe, 586*

495-B

臭*tinky rum* 息*reathe his* 息*on...*

❶息*reathe*　　❷息*on*

心⟷忄⟷⺗ (feelings)

iki, SOKU
breathe, inhale, exhale; son

FLIP: 3.0.a. Top (flat)

❶安息　*rest, repose* **ansoku**
窒息　*suffocation, choking* **chissoku**
鼻息　*snort, nasal breathing* **hanaiki**
一息　*breathe, respiration* **hitoiki**
息吹　*breath of spring* **ibuki**
気息　*breath, inhale, respire* **kisoku**
休息　*rest, repose* **kyūsoku**
寝息　*sound sleep, fast asleep* **neiki**
生息　*living beings* **seisoku**
消息　*news, whereabouts* **shōsoku**
終息　*one's last breath* **shūsoku**
息災　*good health* **sokusai**
溜息　*sigh, deep sigh* **tameiki**
嘆息　*sigh-of-grief* **tansoku**
吐息　*sigh, deep breath* **toiki**
喘息　*asthma* **zensoku**
絶息　*stop breathing* **zessoku**
息切れ　*breathing difficulties* **ikigire**
息臭い　*bad breath, foul breath* **ikikusai**

息巻く　*be furious, ~enraged* **ikimaku**
息抜き　*rest, relaxation* **ikinuki**
息遣い　*breathing* **ikizukai**
息苦しい　*choking, suffocating* **ikigurushii**

❷愛息　*one's beloved son* **aisoku**
愚息　*"my foolish son..." (humble)* **gusoku**
息子　*son, boy* **musuko**
利息　*interest payment* **risoku**
⇒無利息　*interest-free* **murisoku**
令息　*"your son..."* **reisoku**
息女　*daughter* **sokujo**

肺*ungs, 305*	婿*on-in-law, 638*
父*ather, 467*	誕*hildbirth, 515*
母*other, 90*	産*hildbirth, 883*

憩*elaxation, 169*　　鳥*irds, 125*

496-A

傍*ayside* eye 接*ontact*, drivers distract...

人⇔亻 (person)

傍*eside*　　傍*ayside*

soba, katawa(ra), BŌ
  beside, wayside, sideward

FLIP: 7.2.a. Right Top (flat)

傍聴 *hearing, listening* **bōchō**
傍聴券 *entrance ticket* **bōchōken**
傍聴人 *audience, listener* **bōchōnin**
傍聴席 *public gallery* **bōchōseki**
傍注 *marginal notes* **bōchū**
傍題 *subtitle* **bōdai**
傍白 *white side* **bōhaku**
傍人 *bystander* **bōjin**
傍受 *monitoring, intercepting* **bōju**
傍観 *looking on, standing by* **bōkan**
⇒袖手傍観 *onlookers with folded arms*
　　shūshu bōkan
傍観者 *onlookers, bystanders*
　　bōkansha
傍系 *collateral line* **bōkei**
傍流 *branch, side* **bōryū**
傍線 *underline, sideline* **bōsen**
傍視 *looking from the sides* **bōshi**

傍証 *circumstantial evidence* **bōshō**
傍点 *dotted marks, dots* **bōten**
傍目 *casual observing, onlooking* **hatame, okame**
傍輩 *colleagues, companions* **hōbai**
近傍 *neighbourhood, vicinity* **kinbō**
路傍 *roadside, wayside* **robō**
傍論 *obiter dictum* **sobaron**
傍焼き *be jealous of* **okayaki**
傍若無人 *insolent, arrogant* **bōjaku bujin**

沿*longside*, 756	横*ateral*, 197
並*arallel*, 444	伴*ogether*, 949
合*ogether*, 232	共*ogether*, 302

倍*ultiply*, 950

496-B

傍*ayside* eye 接*ontact*, drivers distract...

手⇔扌 (hand, manual)

接*ontact*　　接*onnexion*

tsu(gu), SETSU
  contact, connexion, touch

FLIP: 7.2.a. Right Top (flat)

直接 *direct* **chokusetsu**
外接 *circumscribing, circumventing* **gaisetsu**
骨接ぎ *bone-setting, bone-setter* **honetsugi**
間接 *indirect connexion* **kansetsu**
近接 *neighbouring* **kinsetsu**
面接 *interview, inquiry* **mensetsu**
密接 *close, intimate* **missetsu**
内接 *inscription* **naisetsu**
応接 *reception, treatment* **ōsetsu**
隣接 *adjoining, neighbouring* **rinsetsu**
接見 *audience (with the emperor)* **sekken**
接近 *approach, access* **sekkin**
接骨 *bone-setting* **sekkotsu**
接客 *waiting for customers* **sekkyaku**
接吻 *kiss* **seppun**
接線 *tangent line* **sessen**
接戦 *close fight* **sessen**
接写 *close-up photo* **sessha**
接触 *touch, contact* **sesshoku**

接種 *inoculation, vaccination, immunization* **sesshu**
接収 *requisition, taking over* **sesshū**
接岸 *along the coastline* **setsugan**
接合 *union, connection, joining* **setsugō**
接辞 *affix, append, fasten* **setsuji**
接受 *accepting, receiving* **setsuju**
接続 *connexion, joining* **setsuzoku**
接待 *reception, welcome; serving, offering* **settai**
接点 *contact point, point-of-intersection* **setten**
接ぎ木 *grafting, grated tree* **tsugiki**
溶接 *metal welding* **yōsetsu**

触*ouch*, 923	続*ontinue*, 260
結*onnect*, 227	継*ontinuity*, 958
連*lliance*, 305	答*esponse*, 232

摘*luck*, 800

497-A

唇 *ips that berate surely* 辱 *umiliate...*

口 (mouth)

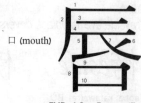

唇 *ips*   唇 *abia*

kuchibiru, SHIN
lips, labia

読唇 *reading another's lips* **dokushin**
陰唇 *labia* **inshin**
欠唇 *cleflip, harelip* **kesshin**
紅唇 *red lips* **kōshin**
口唇 *lips* **kōshin**
唇音 *labial sound* **shin'on**
下唇 *lower lip* **shitakuchibiru**
兎唇 *cleflip, harelip* **toshin**
上唇 *upper lip* **uwakuchibiru**

FLIP: 4.0.a. Bottom (flat)

弁 *peech, 570*	言 *alking, 251*
笑 *mile, 582*	語 *alking, 780*
歯 *eeth, 553*	口 *pening, 458*

唇 *umiliate, 588*

497-B

唇 *ips that berate surely* 辱 *umiliate...*

辰 (dragon)

辱 *umiliate*   辱 *nsult*

hazakashi(meru), JOKU
humiliate, insult, embarrass

侮辱 *insult, contempt, affront* **bujoku**
恥辱 *shame, disgrace* **chijoku**
栄辱 *honour & disgrace, fame* **eijoku**
辱知 *desirable friend* **jokuchi**
国辱 *national shame* **kokujoku**
屈辱 *humiliation, insult, indignity* **kutsujoku**
屈辱的 *humiliating, shameful* **kutsujokuteki**
汚辱 *shame, disgrace, dishonour* **ojoku**
陵辱 *insult, affront, indignity* **ryōjoku**
凌辱 *insult, affront* **ryōjoku**
雪辱 *vindication, revenge* **setsujoku**
雪辱戦 *vindication struggle* **setsujokusen**

Facing: 4.0. ～ Apart

恥 *isgrace, 229*

唇 *ips, 588*

498-A

着utting-on a seatbelt until 着rrival is the 差ifferential...

羊⇔羊 (sheep)

❶着rrive　**❷着ut-on**

ki(ru), ki(seru), tsu(ku), tsu(keru), CHAKU
arrive, landing; put-on, wear

FLIP: 4.0.a. Bottom (flat)
FLIP: 3.0.a. Top (flat)

❶着工　*start, starting* **chakkō**
着駅　*destination station (train)* **chakueki**
着服　*embezzlement, absconding* **chakufuku**
着眼　*aim, viewpoint* **chakugan**
着実　*firm, steady* **chakujitsu**
着席　*taking one's seat, sitting down* **chakuseki**
着信　*mail delivery, ~arrival* **chakushin**
着色　*colouration, colouring* **chakushoku**
着想　*idea, conception* **chakusō**
沈着　*deposition, sworn statement* **chinchaku**
延着　*delayed-, late arrival* **enchaku**
発着　*departure & arrival* **hacchaku**
漂着　*drifting ashore* **hyōchaku**
決着　*conclusion, decision* **kecchaku**
着物　*Japanese kimono, clothes* **kimono**
到着　*arrival, landing, loading* **tōchaku**
❷着用　*wearing, putting on* **chakuyō**
着衣　*clothes, clothing, wear* **chakui**
肌着　*underclothes, underwear* **hadagi**

吸着　*absorption, suction* **kyūchaku**
粘着　*adhesion, stickiness* **nenchaku**
接着　*adhesion, sticking together* **secchaku**
先着　*first to arrive* **senchaku**
執着　*attachment, persistence* **shūchaku**
下着　*underwear, undergarments* **shitagi**
装着　*installation, facilities* **sōchaku**
薄着　*thin clothing, light clothing* **usugi**
溶着　*welding* **yōchaku**
癒着　*adhesion, sticking together* **yuchaku**
柔道着　*judo uniform* **jūdōgi**
追い着く　*catch up, overtake* **oitsuku**

到*rrive, 496*	装*ear, 629*
帰*eturn, 784*	履*ear, 442*
履*ut-on, 442*	服*lothes, 734*

差*ifference, 589*

498-B

着utting-on a seatbelt until 着rrival is the 差ifferential...

工 (craftmanship)

差ifference　**差apse**

sa(su), SA
difference, lapse, disparity, gap

FLIP: 3.0.a. Top (flat)

段差　*difference in rank; elevation gap* **dansa**
誤差　*error, mistake* **gosa**
偏差　*deviation, veering-away* **hensa**
票差　*margin of votes* **hyōsa**
格差　*gap, difference* **kakusa**
較差　*range (in between)* **kakusa**
僅差　*narrow, slim margin* **kinsa**
交差　*crossing, intersection, interchange* **kōsa**
落差　*water level* **rakusa**
差別　*discrimination* **sabetsu**
⇒男女差別　*gender discrimination* **danjo sabetsu**
⇒人類差別　*race discrimination, bigotry* **jinrui sabetsu**
差動　*differential, gap, disparity* **sadō**
差益　*profit margin* **saeki**
差額　*price differential* **sagaku**
差異　*gap, difference, disparity* **sai**
差遣　*dispatch, deployment* **saken**
差金　*money difference* **sakin**
大差　*big difference, ~gap, ~disparity* **taisa**

点差　*difference in points* **tensa**
油差し　*oil can* **aburasashi**
地域差　*regional differences* **chiikisa**
個人差　*individuality, personal difference* **kojinsa**
眼差し　*way of looking* **manazashi**
目差す　*aim at* **mezasu**
根差す　*take root, come* **nezasu**
指差す　*point one's finger, pinpoint* **yubisasu**
時差ボケ　*jet lag* **jisaboke**
差し引き　*plus minus, equal, even* **sashihiki**
等差数列　*arithmetic progression* **tōsa sūretsu**
雲泥の差　*great difference* **undei no sa**

隔*nterval, 963*	間*nterval, 286*
違*isparity, 796*	距*istance, 207*

着*rrive, 589*

499-A

基asis of 碁[Go]: Never say "no..."

基oundation   基asis

土 (ground, soil)

FLIP: 1.0.a. Whole (flat)

moto, motoi, KI
foundation, basis, groundwork, underpinning

基づく　*founded on* **motozuku**
塩基　*basicity, salinity* **enki**
基石　*foundation stone* **goishi, kiseki**
開基　*foundation-laying* **kaiki**
基板　*circuit board (electric)* **kiban**
基盤　*base, foundation* **kiban**
基部　*base, foundation* **kibu**
基地　*military base, ~installation* **kichi**
基調　*base, foundation* **kichō**
基源　*origin, source* **kigen**
基本　*basis, foundation* **kihon**
基本給　*basic salary, ~wage, ~pay* **kihonkyū**
基本原理　*fundamental theory* **kihon genri**
基軸　*standard, criterion* **kijiku**
基準　*standard, datum* **kijun**
基幹　*nucleus* **kikan**
基形　*basic form* **kikei**
基金　*fund, foundation* **kikin**
基音　*keynote* **kion**

基督　*Jesus Christ* **kirisuto**
基線　*baseline, bottomline* **kisen**
基色　*background colour* **kishoku**
基礎　*basis, foundation* **kiso**
基数　*cardinal number* **kisū**
基底　*base, foundation* **kitei**
基点　*cardinal-, basic point* **kiten**
根基　*radical* **konki**
培養基　*culture medium* **baiyōki**
遊離基　*free radical* **yūriki**

拠*asis, 473*
根*oot, 772*
礎*ornerstone, 166*

碁*hess, 590*

499-B

基asis of 碁[Go]: Never say "no..."

碁[Go]   碁heckers

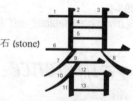

石 (stone)

FLIP: 3.0.a. Top (flat)

GO
Japanese checkers, Go game

碁盤　*Go board* **goban**
碁盤縞　*checkerboard pattern* **gobanjima**
碁盤割　*checkerboard-like partitioning* **gobanwari**
碁打　*Go player* **gouchi**
碁石　*Go piece, ~stone* **goishi**
碁会　*Go club* **gokai**
碁会所　*Go parlour* **gokaisho**
碁客　*Go player* **gokaku**
囲碁　*Go, ancient Japanese game* **igo**
持碁　*stalemate in Go game* **jigo**
西洋碁　*checkers game* **seiyōgo**

棋*hess [Shōgi], 819*

暮*ivelihood, 601*

500-A
愚*tupidity* 遇*ncounters more blunders...*

愚*tupid*　　　愚*diotic*

心 ⇔ 忄 (heart, feelings)

FLIP: 3.0.b. Top (stem)

oro(ka), GU
stupid, idiotic, moron, imbecile, booboo, folly

愚か者 *fool, foolish person* **orokamono**
暗愚 *imbecile, moron, stupid* **angu**
痴愚 *imbecile, moron, stupid* **chigu**
頑愚 *hard-headed fool* **gangu**
愚案 *"in my humble view..."; stupid plan* **guan**
愚痴 *murmurs, grumble* **guchi**
愚直 *stupid honesty* **guchoku**
愚鈍 *imbecility, stupidity, folly* **gudon**
愚意 *"in my humble opinion..."* **gui**
愚人 *fool, stupid person* **gujin**
愚見 *"in my humble opinion..."* **guken**
愚行 *foolish act, stupid behaviour* **gukō**
愚挙 *silly attempt* **gukyo**
愚昧 *stupidity & ignorance* **gumai**
愚民 *"the foolish masses..."* **gumin**
愚問 *silly-, foolish question* **gumon**
愚劣 *stupidity, folly, imbecility* **guretsu**
愚弄 *mockery, derision, ridicule* **gurō**
愚論 *absurd opinion* **guron**

愚妻 *"my foolish wife..." (humble)* **gusai**
愚作 *poor-, trash, worthless work* **gusaku**
愚策 *stupid plan* **gusaku**
愚説 *silly opinion* **gusetsu**
愚臣 *foolish retainer; this humble vassal* **gushin**
愚息 *"my foolish son..." (humble)* **gusoku**
愚図 *fret about, grumble, whine* **guzu**
賢愚 *wise-or-foolish* **kengu**
衆愚 *mob, vulgar* **shūgu**
大愚 *very idiot person* **taigu**
愚連隊 *gangsters, hooligans* **gurentai**

妄*houghtless, 34*
劣*nferior, 572*

遇*ncounter, 591*

500-B
愚*tupidity* 遇*ncounters more blunders...*

遇*ncounter*　　　遇*reatment*

辶 (transport)

FLIP: 3.0.b. Top (stem)

a(u), GŪ
encounter, treatment, stumble, chance upon, coincidental

知遇 *favourable treatment* **chigū**
寵遇 *special favour, patronage* **chōgū**
不遇 *obscure, unfortunate* **fugū**
薄遇 *cold treatment, aloofness* **hakugū**
奇遇 *chance meeting* **kigū**
厚遇 *hospitality, warm reception* **kōgū**
酷遇 *maltreatment, abusive* **kokugū**
境遇 *circumstances, environment* **kyōgū**
礼遇 *courteous reception* **reigū**
冷遇 *cold treatment, aloofness* **reigū**
処遇 *treatment, reception* **shogū**
殊遇 *special favour, cordial treatment* **shugū**
遭遇 *encounter, coming across* **sōgū**
待遇 *treatment, reception* **taigū**
優遇 *priority treatment, preference* **yūgū**
遇不遇 *happiness & sorrows* **gūfugū**
千載一遇 *"chance of a lifetime..."* **senzai ichigū**

遭*ncounter, 326*
会*eeting, 864*
合*ogether, 232*

過*xcessive, 798*

501-A
Bodyguards 覧ook-over, not just 監atching-over...

見 (seeing)

覧ook at　覧bserve

RAN
look at, observe, discern

FLIP: 4.0.b. Bottom (stem)
FLIP: 8.0.a. Inner (flat)

便覧 *manual, handbook* **benran**
便覧 *handbook, manual, guide* **binran**
閲覧 *reading, perusal* **etsuran**
博覧 *extensive knowledge* **hakuran**
博覧会 *expo, fair, exhibition* **hakurankai**
一覧 *a glance, a look* **ichiran**
一覧表 *table, chart, list* **ichiranhyō**
上覧 *emperor's inspection* **jōran**
熟覧 *scrutiny* **jukuran**
縦覧 *tour inspection* **jūran**
回覧 *circulation, rotating* **kairan**
観覧 *viewing, watching* **kanran**
観覧車 *Ferris Wheel* **kanransha**
貴覧 *"your inspection..." (polite)* **kiran**
高覧 *"your inspection..." (polite)* **kōran**
供覧 *show, display, exhibition* **kyōran**
内覧 *preview, premiere presentation* **nairan**
借覧 *reading borrowed books* **shakuran**
照覧 *"your inspection..." (honorific)* **shōran**

笑覧 *"your inspection..." (honorific)* **shōran**
収覧 *grasp; winning over* **shūran**
総覧 *looking thru papers, skimming* **sōran**
天覧 *emperor's inspection* **tenran**
通覧 *glancing over* **tsūran**
要覧 *summary, outline* **yōran**
遊覧 *sight-seeing, leisure travel* **yūran**
遊覧地 *amusement site* **yūranchi**
遊覧客 *visitors, leisure clients* **yūrankyaku**
展覧物 *items on exhibit* **tenranbutsu**
展覧会 *exhibition, show* **tenrankai**

捜*earch, 36*　探*earch, 787*　視*bserve, 815*
索*earch, 375*　監*atch over, 592*　番*atch, 338*

賢*ntelligent, 598*

501-B
Bodyguards 覧ook-over, not just 監atching-over...

皿 (plate)

監atch-over　監upervise

KAN
watch-over, supervise, oversee

FLIP: 4.0.a. Bottom (flat)

学監 *school director* **gakkan**
技監 *chief engineer* **gikan**
監房 *prison, jail, gaol* **kanbō**
監獄 *prison, jail, gaol* **kangoku**
監事 *inspector, auditor* **kanji**
監禁 *imprisonment, detention* **kankin**
監査 *inspection, audit* **kansa**
⇒会計監査 *auditing, books inspection* **kaikei kansa**
監察 *inspection, audit* **kansatsu**
監察官 *government auditor* **kansatsukan**
監査役 *auditor, inspector* **kansayaku**
監製 *supervised manufacturing* **kansei**
監視 *watch, observe, monitor* **kanshi**
監視人 *guard, watchman* **kanshinin**
監視所 *guard station* **kanshisho**
監守 *watch, observe, monitor* **kanshu**
監修 *supervision, guidance* **kanshū**
監督 *supervisor, proctor* **kantoku**
⇒美術監督 *art director* **bijutsu kantoku**

⇒舞台監督 *stage director* **butai kantoku**
⇒試験監督 *test proctoring* **shiken kantoku**
監督下 *"under the jurisdiction of..."* **kantokuka**
監督官 *supervisor* **kantokukan**
監訳 *supervised translation* **kanyaku**
舎監 *dormitory superintendent* **shakan**
収監 *confinement, imprisonment* **shūkan**
総監 *chief auditor, inspector-general* **sōkan**
監守人 *custodian* **kanshunin**
監修者 *supervisor, director* **kanshūsha**

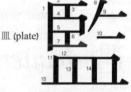

番*atch, 338*　　覧*ook at, 592*
看*ook after, 623*　供*ook-after, 303*
構*ook after, 714*　視*bserve, 815*

覧*ook at, 592*

502-A

In true 愛ove, 爵obility is not above...

心 ⇔ 忄 ⇔ 㣺 (feelings)

愛ove 愛omance

AI
love, romance, amorous

Facing: 4.0. ⇔ Apart

愛玩 *make a pet* **aigan**
愛護 *protection, care, support* **aigo**
愛人 *boyfriend, girlfriend* **aijin**
愛嬢 *one's beloved daughter* **aijō**
愛情 *love, romantic feelings* **aijō**
愛犬 *pet dog* **aiken**
愛顧 *patronage, custom* **aiko**
愛好 *liking, affection* **aikō**
愛敬 *charm, amiability, cordiality* **aikyō**
愛息 *one's beloved son* **aisoku**
愛憎 *love & hate* **aizō**
忠愛 *loyalty, devotion, obsession* **chūai**
博愛 *philanthropy, charity* **hakuai**
偏愛 *partiality, favouritism* **hen'ai**
慈愛 *love, affection, kindness* **jiai**
純愛 *platonic-, pure love* **jun'ai**
敬愛 *respect, love, veneration* **keiai**
求愛 *courting, courtship* **kyūai**
熱愛 *passionate love* **netsuai**

友愛 *friendship, fellowship* **yūai**
愛読者 *voracious reader* **aidokusha**
愛煙家 *chain-, heavy smoker* **aienka**
愛国心 *patriotism, love of country* **aikokushin**
母性愛 *maternal love, motherly love* **boseiai**
夫婦愛 *marital love* **fūfuai**
愛し子 *beloved child* **itoshigo**
可愛い *pretty, cute, charming* **kawaii**
兄弟愛 *brotherly-, fraternal love* **kyōdaiai**
郷土愛 *love of hometown* **kyōdoai**

恋 *ove, 581*	姻 *arriage, 364*	
感 *eelings, 45*	婚 *arriage, 637*	
気 *eelings, 98*	貞 *idelity, 506*	
情 *eelings, 793*	忠 *oyalty, 475*	

受 *eceive, 539*

502-B

In true 愛ove, 爵obility is not above...

爫 (claws, nails)

爵obility 爵ristocrat

SHAKU
nobility, aristocrat

FLIP: 8.0.a. Inner (flat)
Facing: 3.0. ⇨ Across

男爵 *baron* **danshaku**
⇒女男爵 *baroness* **onna danshaku**
男爵夫人 *baroness* **danshaku fujin**
伯爵 *count, earl* **hakushaku**
伯爵夫人 *countess* **hakushaku fujin**
叙爵 *conferment of peerage* **joshaku**
授爵 *nobility, aristocracy* **jushaku**
侯爵 *marquis, marquess* **kōshaku**
公爵 *duke, prince* **kōshaku**
公爵夫人 *duchess, princess* **kōshaku fujin**
勲爵 *order of merit & peerage* **kunshaku**
爵位 *nobility title, royalty* **shakui**
子爵 *viscount* **shishaku**
子爵夫人 *viscountess* **shishaku fujin**
有爵 *with peerage* **yūshaku**
侯爵夫人 *marchioness* **kōshaku fujin**

姫 *rincess, 542*	侯 *obility, 122*	
妃 *rincess, 728*	曹 *obility, 326*	

受 *eceive, 539*

503-A

貧 *auper panhandling a* 盆 *ray on* 盆 *uddhist souls' day...*

貝 (shell, old money)

FLIP: 4.0.b. Bottom (stem)

貧 *overty* 貧 *estitute*

mazu(shii), HIN, BIN
poverty, destitute, impoverished, indigent, pauper, flat broke

貧しさ *poverty, destitution* **mazushisa**
貧乏 *poor, pauper, destitute* **binbō**
貧乏くじ *blank, unlucky number* **binbōkuji**
貧乏神 *god of poverty* **binbōgami**
貧乏人 *poor person, pauper* **binbōnin**
極貧 *extreme poverty, ~destitution* **gokuhin**
貧打 *poor batting (baseball)* **hinda**
貧者 *poor person* **hinja**
貧弱 *poor, feeble* **hinjaku**
貧家 *poor person's home, slum* **hinka**
貧血 *anaemia* **hinketsu**
貧困 *poverty, penury, impoverishment* **hinkon**
貧攻 *weak baseball batting* **hinkō**
貧鉱 *low-grade ore* **hinkō**
貧苦 *poverty hardships* **hinku**
貧窮 *poverty, penury, destitution* **hinkyū**
貧民 *poor, needy* **hinmin**
貧民宿 *slums, shanty* **hinminkutsu**
貧農 *poor peasant, destitute farmer* **hinnō**

貧富 *wealth & poverty, rich & poor* **hinpu**
貧富の差 *rich & poor gap* **hinpu no sa**
貧相 *shabby, poor-looking* **hinsō**
貧欲 *greedy, avaricious, covetous* **hinyoku**
じり貧 *slow decline* **jirihin**
寒貧 *absolute poverty* **kanpin**
救貧 *poverty alleviation* **kyūhin**
清貧 *poor but honest* **seihin**
赤貧 *poor but honest* **sekihin**
素寒貧 *pauper, poor, destitute* **sukanpin**
脳貧血 *cerebral anaemia* **nōhinketsu**

乏 *overty, 84*	飢 *tarve, 746*
少 *carce, 459*	低 *inimum, 700*
餓 *tarve, 443*	無 *othing, 49*

盆 *uddhist Feast, 594*

503-B

貧 *auper panhandling a* 盆 *ray on* 盆 *uddhist souls' day...*

皿 (plate)

FLIP: 4.0.a. Bottom (flat)

❶ 盆 *ray* ❷ 盆 *uddhist Feast*

BON
tray; Buddhist summer feast

❶ 盆地 *basin, hollow, valley* **bonchi**
盆画 *tray landscape* **bonga**
盆景 *miniature garden on a tray* **bonkei**
盆栽 *bonsai, potted plant* **bonsai**
盆石 *miniature garden on a tray* **bonseki**
茶盆 *tea tray* **chabon**
初盆 *first Bon after one's death* **hatsubon**
角盆 *square tray* **kakubon**
菓子盆 *confectionery tray* **kashibon**
塗り盆 *varnished-, lacquered tray* **nuribon**

❷ 新盆 *first bon after one's death* **niibon**
お盆 *Bon summer festival* **obon**
盆暮れ *Buddhist festival of the dead* **bonkure**
盆祭り *Buddhist festival of the dead* **bonmatsuri**
盆踊り *Buddhist summer dance* **bon'odori**
盂蘭盆 *Buddhist festival of the dead* **urabon**

皿 *ish, 21*	僧 *uddhist monk, 836*
盤 *isk, 324*	坊 *uddhist monk, 736*
鉢 *owl, 666*	禅 *en Buddhism, 782*
仏 *uddha, 683*	

盗 *obbery, 621*

504-A

歴istory's neither a radar, nor a 暦alendar...

止 (stopping)

歴istory

REKI
history

FLIP: 8.0.b. Inner (stem)

病歴 *medical history, ~record* **byōreki**
学歴 *scholastic record, ~achievement* **gakureki**
犯歴 *criminal record* **hanreki**
遍歴 *travels, pilgrimage* **henreki**
披歴 *express (one's opinion)* **hireki**
経歴 *personal history, curriculum vitae* **keireki**
来歴 *history, origin* **raireki**
⇒故事来歴 *origin & history* **koji raireki**
歴代 *succeeding generations* **rekidai**
歴訪 *visit, making a call* **rekihō**
暦年 *year after year* **rekinen**
歴任 *work history, job experience* **rekinin**
歴歴① *VIPs, big shots* **rekireki**
歴歴② *clear, obvious* **rekireki**
歴史 *history* **rekishi**
歴史学 *history studies* **rekishigaku**
歴史家 *historian, history scholar* **rekishika**
歴史観 *view of history* **rekishikan**
歴史小説 *history-based novel* **rekishi shōsetsu**

歴遊 *tour* **rekiyū**
歴然 *self-evident, obvious* **rekizen**
履歴 *personal history, background* **rireki**
履歴書 *resume, curriculum vitae* **rirekisho**
略歴 *brief resume* **ryakureki**
戦歴 *military history* **senreki**
社歴 *company history* **shareki**
職歴 *work history, job experience* **shokureki**
前歴 *personal record, personal history* **zenreki**
既往歴 *patient's medical history* **kiōreki**
逮捕歴 *arrest record, criminal record* **taihoreki**

史*istory, 85*	紀*arration, 727*
暦*alendar, 595*	簿*ecord, 64*
記*ecord, 728*	昔*lden-times, 281*
録*ecord, 841*	

暦*alendar, 595*

504-B

歴istory's neither a radar, nor a 暦alendar...

日 (sunlight, daytime)

暦alendar 暦hronology

koyomi, REKI
calendar, chronology

FLIP: 8.0.a. Inner (flat)

花暦 *floral calendar* **hanagoyomi**
柱暦 *wall calendar* **hashira goyomi**
陰暦 *lunar calendar* **inreki**
改暦 *New Year resolution* **kaireki**
還暦 *sixtieth birthday* **kanreki**
旧暦 *lunar calendar* **kyūreki**
暦法 *calendar method* **rekihō**
暦日 *calendar day* **rekijitsu**
暦年 *chronological age* **rekinen**
暦年齢 *calendar year* **rekinenrei**
暦数 *calendar calculation; fate* **rekisū**
西暦 *Western calendar, A.D.* **seireki**
新暦 *Western calendar* **shinreki**
梅暦 *harbinger of spring (plum)* **ume goyomi**
陽暦 *solar calendar* **yōreki**
暦改正 *calendar reform* **koyomi kaisei**
教会暦 *church calendar* **kyōkaireki**
太陰暦 *lunar calendar* **taiinreki**
太陽暦 *solar calendar* **taiyōreki**

史*istory, 85*	録*ecord, 841*
歴*istory, 595*	紀*arration, 727*
記*ecord, 728*	昔*lden-times, 281*
簿*ecord, 64*	

歴*istory, 595*

505-A

思hinking of 累umulative points, 男asculine pitcher dove into third 塁ase, his 胃tomach grazed...

心⇔忄 (heart, feelings)

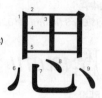

思hinking   思ontemplate

omo(u), SHI

thinking, contemplate, deduce, consider, ponder, conjecture

FLIP: 3.0.a. Top (flat)

思惑 expectation, anticipation **omowaku**
思案 consider, reflect, contemplate **shian**
思弁 speculation, prospect **shiben**
思潮 stream of thoughts **shichō**
思惟 speculation, prospect **shii**
思考 thinking, pondering **shikō**
思慮 thought, consideration **shiryo**
思慮深い thoughtful, considerate **shiryobukai**
思索 think ahead, speculate **shisaku**
思想 idea, concept, thought **shisō**
片思い unrequited love, frustrated love **kataomoi**
無思慮 indiscretion, misconduct **mushiryo**
思い出 memories, reminiscences **omoide**
親思い filial love, parental affection **oyaomoi**
沈思黙考 deep meditation **chinshi mokkō**
思し召し "as you like..." **oboshimeshi**
思し残す regret, misgivings **omoinokosu**
思い違い misunderstanding **omoichigai**
思い込む believe in completely **omoikomu**

思い知る realize, come to know **omoishiru**
思いつく think of, hit upon **omoitsuku**
思いやる think well, consider, ponder **omoiyaru**
思い上がる flatter oneself **omoiagaru**
思い当たる think correctly **omoiataru**
思い止まる give up an idea **omoidomaru**
思い巡らす contemplate, ponder **omoimegurasu**
思い乱れる mental distraction **omoimidareru**
思い起こす remember, recall **omoiokosu**
思い詰める brood over, consider **omoitsumeru**
思いも寄らない "not in my wildest dream..." **omoi mo yoranai**

考hinking, 392	省elf-reflect, 572
顧elf-reflect, 343	意dea, 340

男asculine, 597

505-B

思hinking of 累umulative points, 男asculine pitcher dove into third 塁ase, his 胃tomach grazed...

糸 (thread, continuity)

累umulative   累ver-all

RUI

cumulative, over-all

FLIP: 3.0.a. Top (flat)

煩累 annoyance, concerns, troubles **hanrui**
係累 affinity, kinship, relatives **keirui**
連累 implication, complicity **renrui**
累代 successive generations **ruidai**
累減 regressive, retrogressive, reactionary **ruigen**
累犯 repeat offence, recidivist **ruihan**
累次 successive, repeated **ruiji**
累日 day-by-day **ruijitsu**
累乗 involution, complication **ruijō**
累加 progressive increase **ruika**
累計 cumulative total **ruikei**
累年 successive years **ruinen**
累卵 imminent danger **ruiran**
累算 cumulative total **ruisan**
累算温度 cumulative temperature **ruisan ondo**
累世 succeeding generations **ruisei**
累積 accumulation, cumulation **ruiseki**
累積赤字 accumulated deficit **ruiseki akaji**
累進 successive promotions, ~advance **ruishin**

累進課税 progressive taxation **ruishin kazei**
累増 cumulation, increase **ruizō**

総otality, 433	加ddition, 201
計easurement, 692	完omplete, 196
算alculate, 141	全omplete, 24

異fferent, 239

505-C

思*hinking of* 累*umulative points,* 男*asculine pitcher dove into third* 塁*ase, his* 胃*tomach grazed...* 田 (cultivated field)

男*asculine* 男*anhood*

otoko, DAN, NAN
masculine, manhood, guy, macho

FLIP: 3.0.a. Top (flat)

東男 *man from eastern Japan* **azuma otoko**
美男 *handsome man* **binan**
醜男 *ugly man* **buotoko**
嫡男 *legitimate son* **chakunan**
長男 *eldest son* **chōnan**
男児 *baby boy, pretty boy* **danji**
男女 *both sexes, male & female* **danjo**
男女平等 *gender-, sexual equality* **danjo byōdō**
男女差別 *gender-, sex discrimination* **danjo sabetsu**
男工 *male labourer* **dankō**
男根 *male organ, penis* **dankon**
男声 *male voice* **dansei**
男性 *masculine* **dansei**
男爵 *baron* **danshaku**
男娼 *male prostitute* **danshō**
男色 *homosexuality* **danshoku**
男囚 *male prisoner* **danshū**
男優 *male actor* **danyū**
男気 *masculine heart, macho* **otokogi**

男心 *masculine heart, macho* **otokogokoro**
男前 *macho-looking, manly* **otokomae**
作男 *farm helper* **sakuotoko**
男子校 *boys school* **danshikō**
男の人 *male, gentleman* **otoko no hito**
男の子 *little boy* **otoko no ko**
男文字 *masculine handwriting* **otokomoji**
男盛り *prime of manhood* **otokozakari**
男っぽい *manly, masculine* **otokoppoi**
男やもめ *widower* **otokoyamome**
善男善女 *pious men & women* **zennan zennyo**

士*entleman, 8*	僕*asculine, 157*
紳*entleman, 713*	雄*asculine, 775*
兄*lder-brother, 203*	郎*asculine, 404*
壮*asculine, 367*	侍*amurai, 249*

思*hink, 596*

505-D

思*hinking of* 累*umulative points,* 男*asculine pitcher dove into third* 塁*ase, his* 胃*tomach grazed...* 土 (ground, soil)

塁*mall base* 塁*ase*

RUI
small base, base, rampart

FLIP: 1.0.a. Whole (flat)

防塁 *fortress, stronghold* **bōrui**
土塁 *earthwork, fieldwork* **dorui**
本塁 *homebase* **honrui**
本塁打 *homerun* **honruida**
堡塁 *fortress, stronghold* **horui**
一塁 *first base* **ichirui**
城塁 *fortress, stronghold* **jōrui**
堅塁 *fortress, stronghold* **kenrui**
孤塁 *isolated base* **korui**
満塁 *loaded base* **manrui**
二塁 *second base* **nirui**
塁打 *base hit* **ruida**
塁壁 *ramparts* **ruiheki**
塁審 *base umpire, ~referee* **ruishin**
塁手 *baseman* **ruishu**
三塁 *third base* **sanrui**
三塁打 *triple hit* **sanruida**
三塁手 *third baseman* **sanruishu**
進塁 *advancing to the next base* **shinrui**

出塁 *base landing* **shutsurui**
走塁 *base running* **sōrui**
敵塁 *enemy's position* **tekirui**
盗塁 *base stealing* **tōrui**
残塁 *stuck between two bases* **zanrui**

基*asis, 590*	根*oot, 772*
拠*asis, 473*	柱*illar, 751*

異*ifferent, 239*

505-E

思hinking of 累umulative points, 男asculine pitcher dove into third 塁ase, his 胃tomach grazed...

肉⇔月 (flesh, body part)

胃tomach　　胃bdomen

I

stomach, abdomen, belly, tummy

胃部 stomach part **ibu**
胃袋 stomach, craw **ibukuro**
胃病 stomach illness **ibyō**
胃腸 digestion **ichō**
胃腸病 digestion disorder **ichōbyō**
胃腸薬 indigestion drug **ichōyaku**
胃液 gastric juice **ieki**
胃炎 gastritis, ulcer **ien**
胃癌 stomach cancer **igan**
胃壁 stomach lining **iheki**
胃弱 dyspepsia, indigestion **ijaku**
胃鏡 gastroscope **ikyō**
胃熱 gastric fever **inetsu**
胃酸 acidic stomach **isan**
胃散 drug powder for stomach **isan**
胃痛 stomach ache, ~pain **itsū**
胃潰瘍 stomach-, gastric ulcer **ikaiyō**
胃拡張 gastric dilatation **ikakuchō**

FLIP: 1.0.b. Whole (stem)

胃下垂 gastroptosis **ikasui**
胃痙攣 stomach cramps **ikeiren**
健胃剤 stomach medicine **ken'izai**

腹tomach, 830	食oods, 255
腸ntestine, 150	飲rinking, 255

界orld, 365

506-A

賢ntelligent & 緊ight, a 堅olid knight...

貝 (shell, old money)

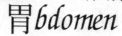

賢ntelligent　　賢isdom

kashiko(i), KEN

intelligent, wisdom

遺賢 wise men left out **iken**
賢母 wise mother **kenbo**
⇒良妻賢母 good wife & wise mother **ryōsai kenbo**
賢愚 wise-or-foolish **kengu**
賢者 wise man, sage **kenja**
賢人 wise person **kenjin**
賢兄 wise elder brother, ~friend **kenkei**
賢明 wise, clever **kenmei**
賢婦 wise lady **kenpu**
賢慮 clever idea **kenryo**
賢才 wise & agile **kensai**
賢妻 wise wife **kensai**
賢察 conjecture, guess, inference **kensatsu**
賢主 wise lord, wise ruler **kenshu**
賢弟 wise younger brother, ~friend **kentei**
賢哲 sage, wise man **kentetsu**
後賢 future clever men **kōken**
聖賢 sages & saints **seiken**
先賢 ancient wisdom **senken**

FLIP: 4.0.b. Bottom (stem)

七賢 seven wise men (ancient Greece) **shichiken**
諸賢 "gentlemen..." **shoken**
大賢 sage, wise man **taiken**
賢夫人 wise wife **kenpujin**
猿賢い cunning, mischievous **sarugashikoi**
悪賢い wily, cunning, crafty, sly **warugashikoi**
小賢しい smart, wise, clever **kozakashii**
仁賢天皇 Emperor Ninken (488-498) **ninken tennō**

哲isdom, 53
寛agnanimity, 308

覧ook at, 592

506-B
賢ntelligent & 緊ight, a 堅olid knight...

糸 (thread, continuity)

①緊*ight* ②緊*xigent*

KIN
tight, firm, hard, rigid; exigent

FLIP: 7.2.b. Right Top (stem)

① 緊縛 *tightly-bound* **kinbaku**
緊張 *strain, tension, stress* **kinchō**
緊張緩和 *stress relaxation* **kinchōkanwa**
緊密 *closed-door, confidential, secret* **kinmitsu**
緊迫 *tension, strain* **kinpaku**
緊縮 *austerity, retrenchment* **kinshuku**
緊縮政策 *austerity measures, belt-tightening*
　　kinshuku seisaku
緊縮予算 *reduced budget* **kinshuku yosan**
緊縮財政 *financial austerity* **kinshuku zaisei**

緊切 *urgent, pressing* **kinsetsu**
緊要 *very important, significant* **kinyō**
喫緊事 *matters of great importance* **kikkinji**
緊褌一番 *bracing oneself for* **kinkon ichiban**

> 固*olid, 491*　　　　堅*olid, 599*
> 凝*arden, 57*

> 堅*olid, 599*

② 緊急 *urgent, emergency* **kinkyū**
緊急動議 *urgent motion, ~appeal* **kinkyū dōgi**
緊急避難 *emergency evacuation* **kinkyū hinan**
緊急事態 *state of emergency* **kinkyū jitai**
緊急問題 *urgent-, burning question*
　　kinkyū mondai
緊急措置 *emergency measure* **kinkyū sochi**

506-C
賢ntelligent & 緊ight, a 堅olid knight...

土 (ground, soil)

堅*olid*　　堅*ard object*

kata(i), KEN
solid, hard object

FLIP: 4.0.a. Bottom (flat)
FLIP: 7.2.b. Right Top (stem)

中堅 *nucleus, backbone, mainstay* **chūken**
堅気 *serious, staid* **katagi**
堅木 *hardwood, oak* **katagi**
堅人 *honest & serious person* **katajin**
堅塩 *rock salt* **katashio**
堅炭 *hard charcoal* **katazumi**
堅調 *steady, firm, certain* **kenchō**
堅固 *strong, sturdy, robust* **kengo**
堅持 *holding fast, sticking* **kenji**
堅陣 *stronghold, bedrock* **kenjin**
堅実 *steadiness, stability* **kenjitsu**
堅城 *impregnable castle* **kenjō**
堅果 *nut (hard fruit)* **kenka**
堅忍 *unrelenting will* **kennin**
堅牢 *solid, strong* **kenrō**
堅塁 *stronghold, bedrock* **kenrui**
堅志 *iron will, strong-willed* **kenshi**
堅守 *strong defence* **kenshu**
堅材 *hardwood* **kenzai**

義理堅い *dutiful mind* **girigatai**
堅苦しい *formal, stiff, rigid* **katakurushii**
堅太り *plump & solid* **katabutori**
堅信礼 *catholic confirmation rites* **kenshinrei**
口堅い *discreet, tight-lipped* **kuchigatai**
物堅い *honest, faithful, reliable* **monogatai**
底堅い *hardrock bottom* **sokogatai**
手堅い *solid, strong, firm, reliable* **tegatai**

> 固*olid, 491*
> 凝*arden, 57*
> 緊*ard, 599*

> 緊*ard, 599*

507-A

慕earn-for a job 募ecruit with good 暮ivelihood, lest you
幕nveil a 墓omb in the woods...

心⇔忄⇔小 (feelings)

慕earn for　慕dore

shita(u), BO
yearn for, adore, affection

愛慕 *love, affection, adoration* **aibo**
慕情 *longing for, yearning* **bojō**
敬慕 *adoration, homage* **keibo**
恋慕 *love, attachment* **renbo**
思慕 *deep attachment* **shibo**
追慕 *cherishing a dead's memory* **tsuibo**
横恋慕 *forbidden love* **yokorenbo**
慕い寄る *approach with adoration* **shitaiyoru**

FLIP: 3.0.a. Top (flat)

依*equest, 355*	請*equest, 791*
願*equest, 964*	頼*equest, 562*
求*equest, 256*	望*esire, 618*

幕*nveil, 601*

507-B

慕earn-for a job 募ecruit with good 暮ivelihood, lest you
幕nveil a 墓omb in the woods...

力 (strength, force)

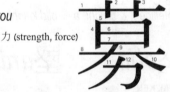

募ecruit　募olicit

tsuno(ru), BO
recruit, solicit, hiring enlist, enrolment

FLIP: 3.0.a. Top (flat)

募兵 *military recruitment* **bohei**
募金 *fund raising* **bokin**
⇒街頭募金 *street fund raising* **gaitō bokin**
募金運動 *fund-raising drive* **bokin undō**
募債 *bond flotation, raising a loan* **bosai**
募集 *recruitment* **boshū**
⇒懸賞募集 *prize contest solicitation*
　　kenshō boshū
募集中 *"now hiring...", urgent recruitment*
　　boshūchū
募集額 *amount to be raised* **boshūgaku**
募集要項 *list of entrance requirements*
　　boshū yōkō
徴募 *enlistment; recruitment* **chōbo**
公募 *public solicitation* **kōbo**
急募 *urgent hiring, immediate hiring* **kyūbo**
応募 *application, enlistment* **ōbo**
応募者 *applicant, candidate* **ōbosha**
大募集 *mass recruitment* **daiboshū**

吹き募る *blowing hard* **fukitsunoru**
言い募る *incessant arguing* **iitsunoru**
思い募る *incessant thinking, obsession*
　　omoitsunoru

依*equest, 355*	請*equest, 791*
願*equest, 964*	頼*equest, 562*
求*equest, 256*	雇*mploy, 343*

慕*ffectionate, 600*

507-C

慕*earn-for a job* 募*ecruit with good* 暮*ivelihood, lest you* 幕*nveil a* 墓*omb in the woods...*

暮*ivelihood*   暮*wilight*

日 (sunlight, daytime)

FLIP: 1.0.a. Whole (flat)

ku(reru), ku(rasu), BO
livelihood, living, subsistence; twilight, dusk

暮らし *life, living, livelihood* **kurashi**
⇒独り暮らし *living alone* **hitorigurashi**
暮らし向き *making a living, livelihood* **kurashimuki**
泣き暮らす *living in sorrow* **nakikurasu**
言い暮らす *killing time by talking* **iikurasu**
暮れ方 *dusk, evening* **kuregata**
暮れ六つ *evening bell (six o'clock)* **kuremutsu**
暮色 *dusk, twilight* **boshoku**
暮春 *delayed spring, late spring* **boshun**
暮夜 *night, evening* **boya**
朝暮 *day & night* **chōbo**
薄暮 *dusk, twilight* **hakubo**
野暮 *boorish, clumsy, churlish* **yabo**
野暮天 *boorish, clumsy, churlish* **yaboten**
日暮れ *nightfall, sunset* **higure**
お歳暮 *year-end gift to one's superior* **oseibo**
夕暮れ *night, evening* **yūgure**
行き暮れる *"still on the way at nightfall..."* **yukikureru**

明け暮れる *day & night, all the time* **akekureru**
遊び暮らす *spend all day in idleness* **asobikurasu**
暮れ果てる *get completely dark* **kurehateru**
待ち暮らす *waiting all the day long* **machikurasu**

稼*ake-a-living*, 824	住*esidence*, 750
生*ife*, 474	食*uisine*, 255
命*ife*, 362	労*abour*, 351

幕*nveil*, 601

507-D

慕*earn-for a job* 募*ecruit with good* 暮*ivelihood, lest you* 幕*nveil a* 墓*omb in the woods...*

❶幕*nveil*   ❷幕*hogunate*

巾 (cloth, fabric)

FLIP: 1.0.a. Whole (flat)

MAKU, BAKU
unveil, inaugurate; Shogunate

❶ 幕営 *camping out, encampment* **bakuei**
幕僚 *staff, work force, employee* **bakuryō**
弾幕 *artillery barrage* **danmaku**
煙幕 *smokescreen* **enmaku**
銀幕 *silverscreen, movies* **ginmaku**
閉幕 *curtain closing* **heimaku**
平幕 *rank-and-file* **hiramaku**
字幕 *film-, movie subtitles* **jimaku**
序幕 *opening scene, prelude* **jomaku**
除幕 *unveiling, inauguration, opening* **jomaku**
除幕式 *unveiling ceremony* **jomakushiki**
開幕 *curtain raising, opening* **kaimaku**
剣幕 *threatening look* **kenmaku**
黒幕 *black curtain; curtain raiser* **kuromaku**
幕間 *intermission, interlude, interval* **makuai**
幕開け *opening, inauguration* **makuake**
幕下 *low-ranked sumo wrestler* **makushita**
幕内 *first-class sumo wrestler* **makuuchi**
幔幕 *curtain* **manmaku**

入幕 *rising to the top of sumo world* **nyūmaku**
終幕 *ending, last scene* **shūmaku**
天幕 *tent* **tenmaku**
内幕 *inside facts* **uchimaku, naimaku**
引き幕 *curtain raising* **hikimaku**
幕切れ *ending, closing* **makugire**
垂れ幕 *curtain* **taremaku**
❷幕府 *Shogunate government* **bakufu**
幕末 *Tokugawa Shogunate's last days* **bakumatsu**
佐幕 *pro-Shogunate* **sabaku**
倒幕 *anti-Shogunate* **tōbaku**

始*tart*, 210	藩*eudal clan*, 337
開*pen*, 284	殿*ordship*, 522
披*pen*, 104	

墓*omb*, 602

507-E

慕earn-for a job 募ecruit with good 暮ivelihood, lest you
幕nveil a 墓omb in the woods...

土 (ground, soil)

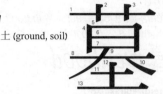

墓*omb*　　墓*ravesite*

haka, BO
tomb, gravesite, cemetery, crypt, sepulchre

FLIP: 1.0.a. Whole (flat)

墓参り *tomb visit* **hakamairi**
墓地 *graveyard, cemetery* **bochi**
墓碑 *gravestone, tombstone* **bohi**
墓碑銘 *tombstone epitaph* **bohimei**
墓表 *grave marker* **bohyō**
墓標 *grave marker* **bohyō**
墓穴 *grave, tomb* **boketsu**
墓銘 *tombstone epitaph* **bomei**
墓参 *visiting a grave, cemetery visit* **bosan**
墓誌 *tombstone inscription, epitaph* **boshi**
墓前 *"before the tomb of..."* **bozen**
墳墓 *grave, tomb* **funbo**
墳墓の地 *ancestral tomb* **funbo no chi**
墓跡 *dolmen, cromlech* **hakaato**
墓場 *graveyard, cemetery* **hakaba**
墓堀 *grave digging* **hakahori**
墓石 *tombstone, gravestone* **hakaishi, boseki**
墓守 *gravekeeper* **hakamori**
陵墓 *imperial mausoleum* **ryōbo**

碑*ombstone, 937*	逝*eath, 54*
葬*urial, 513*	亡*eath, 72*
死*eath, 513*	永*ternal, 10*

幕*nveil, 601*

508-A

覆oncealed warships 遷elocating south waning 覇upremacy
漂loating-about...

西⇔西 (western)

❶覆*onceal*　　❷覆*verturn*

ō(u), kutsugae(ru), kutsugae(su), FUKU
conceal, covering, cover-up, mask; overturn

FLIP: 3.0.a. Top (flat)

❶覆い被さる *fall, cover* **ooikabusaru**
覆い被せる *cover* **ooikabuseru**
覆刻 *reproduction, replication* **fukkoku**
覆土 *covering seeds with soil* **fukudo**
覆面 *facial mask* **fukumen**
覆面子 *anonymous author* **fukumenshi**
覆滅 *eliminate, annihilate* **fukumetsu**
覆輪 *ornamental ring* **fukurin**
被覆 *covering, lid, cap* **hifuku**
日覆 *sunscreen* **hioi**
雨覆い *rain cover* **amaooi**
耳覆い *earmuffs* **mimiooi**

陰*idden, 864*	忍*onceal, 535*
隠*idden, 840*	裏*everse, 872*
秘*idden, 219*	逆*everse, 896*
匿*onceal, 277*	

履*ut-on, 442*

❷覆没 *capsizing & sinking* **fukubotsu**
覆審 *judicial review, retrial* **fukushin**
覆奏 *reinvestigate & report* **fukusō**
反覆 *re-doing, repeating* **hanpuku**
転覆 *overthrow, turning over* **tenpuku**
顛覆 *overthrow, turning over* **tenpuku**

508-B

覆*oncealed warships* 遷*elocating south waning* 覇*upremacy*
漂*loating-about...*

辶 (transport)

遷*elocate* 遷*hange*

SEN
relocate, change

変遷	*transformation, transition*	**hensen**
左遷	*demotion, relegation*	**sasen**
遷延	*delay, deferment, procrastination*	**sen'en**
遷化	*death of a high priest*	**senge**
遷移	*transition, change location*	**sen'i**
遷幸	*emperor's leaving the capital*	**senkō**
遷都	*transfer of the capital*	**sento**
遷座	*transfer of a Buddha statue*	**senza**
遷宮式	*dedication of a new shrine*	**sengūshiki**

FLIP: 3.0.a. Top (flat)

移*ransfer, 188*	場*ocation, 147*
譲*ransfer, 853*	所*ocation, 676*
変*hange, 581*	

覇*egemony, 603*

508-C

覆*oncealed warships* 遷*elocating south waning* 覇*upremacy*
漂*loating-about...*

西⇔襾 (western)

覇*egemony* 覇*upremacy*

HA
hegemony, supremacy, domineering

覇道	*martial law, military government*	**hadō**
覇府	*Shogunate*	**hafu**
覇業	*domination, hegemony*	**hagyō**
覇権	*supremacy, hegemony*	**haken**
覇気	*spirit of ambition*	**haki**
覇者	*conqueror, champion*	**hasha**
連覇	*consecutive winnings, straight victories*	**renpa**
制覇	*conquest, domination*	**seiha**
那覇市	*Naha City, Okinawa Prefecture*	**naha-shi**
争覇戦	*power struggle*	**sōhasen**

FLIP: 3.0.a. Top (flat)

克*onquest, 204*	有*ossess, 617*
征*onquer, 31*	勝*ictory, 406*
抑*uppress, 705*	戦*attle, 517*

覆*onceal, 602*

508-D

覆 *oncealed warships* 遷 *elocating south waning* 覇 *egemony*
漂 *loating-about...*

水 ⇔ 氵 (water)

FLIP: 7.0.b1. Right (stem)

漂 *rift-about*　　漂 *loat-about*

tadayo(u), HYŌ
drift-about, float about

漂着 *drifting ashore* **hyōchaku**
漂白 *bleaching, bleach* **hyōhaku**
漂白剤 *bleaching agent, whitener* **hyōhakuzai**
漂泊 *wander, drift, vagabond* **hyōhaku**
漂浪 *wandering, vagabond* **hyōrō**
漂流 *driftage, drifting* **hyōryū**
漂流物 *drift, flotsam, driftage* **hyōryūbutsu**
漂流記 *castaway stories* **hyōryūki**
漂流民 *shipwrecked survivors; castaways* **hyōryūmin**
漂流船 *drifting ship, ~boat* **hyōryūsen**
漂流者 *shipwrecked persons; castaways* **hyōryūsha**
漂砂 *drift sand* **hyōsa**
漂失 *drift away, wander out* **hyōshitsu**

浪 *rifting,* 254	浮 *loat,* 970
波 *urrent,* 32	方 *irection,* 533
流 *urrent,* 781	妄 *houghtless,* 34

票 *uffrage,* 549

TEST YOUR IQ IN KANJI CHARACTERS

Find out which one doesn't belong in the group: a, b, c, or d. Concentrate on the core meaning. Correct answers are found on page 1126.

	a	b	c	d		a	b	c	d
1].	海	石	山	空	18].	町	家	県	市
2].	男	木	女	子	19].	竹	字	学	校
3].	雨	日	月	星	20].	川	海	鳥	湖
4].	目	耳	人	手	21].	竹	草	木	猫
5].	白	川	赤	黒	22].	白	行	帰	出
6].	四	十	百	千	23].	人	起	方	生
7].	上	下	中	左	24].	北	南	右	東
8].	歩	見	聞	話	25].	虫	外	内	中
9].	風	車	雨	天	26].	父	花	母	子
10].	車	船	馬	書	27].	春	夏	天	秋
11].	泣	本	書	字	28].	兄	家	姉	妹
12].	無	有	非	不	29].	蛇	馬	豚	鳥
13].	長	高	心	短	30].	昼	夜	火	朝
14].	木	金	林	森	31].	歌	踊	考	走
15].	飲	言	語	聞	32].	体	考	思	意
16].	食	貝	飲	寝	33].	雨	水	雪	雷
17].	中	日	島	米	34].	声	音	休	鳴

35].	a. 寒	b. 冷	c. 氷	d. 厚		68].	a. 盟	b. 伴	c. 添	d. 随
36].	a. 舌	b. 手	c. 頭	d. 足		69].	a. 寡	b. 独	c. 到	d. 孤
37].	a. 教	b. 口	c. 習	d. 学		70].	a. 着	b. 発	c. 到	d. 来
38].	a. 遠	b. 近	c. 草	d. 行		71].	a. 佐	b. 助	c. 匠	d. 援
39].	a. 紙	b. 話	c. 絵	d. 描		72].	a. 伐	b. 攻	c. 撃	d. 守
40].	a. 買	b. 商	c. 金	d. 売		73].	a. 容	b. 態	c. 績	d. 姿
41].	a. 牛	b. 豚	c. 鳥	d. 比		74].	a. 煩	b. 憎	c. 苦	d. 美
42].	a. 走	b. 道	c. 通	d. 路		75].	a. 進	b. 戒	c. 論	d. 警
43].	a. 幸	b. 泣	c. 喜	d. 楽		76].	a. 得	b. 利	c. 負	d. 益
44].	a. 働	b. 造	c. 遊	d. 作		77].	a. 美	b. 雅	c. 昇	d. 佳
45].	a. 砂	b. 好	c. 愛	d. 情		78].	a. 衣	b. 裁	c. 服	d. 調
46].	a. 負	b. 勝	c. 敗	d. 失		79].	a. 唐	b. 華	c. 台	d. 中
47].	a. 役	b. 事	c. 官	d. 吏		80].	a. 始	b. 完	c. 終	d. 了
48].	a. 式	b. 風	c. 活	d. 様		81].	a. 謡	b. 乱	c. 吟	d. 唱
49].	a. 死	b. 去	c. 昔	d. 前		82].	a. 勇	b. 敢	c. 栓	d. 雄
50].	a. 守	b. 防	c. 葉	d. 保		83].	a. 敢	b. 希	c. 望	d. 欲
51].	a. 歯	b. 舌	c. 骨	d. 血		84].	a. 侮	b. 嫌	c. 喜	d. 憎
52].	a. 華	b. 払	c. 税	d. 買		85].	a. 亡	b. 死	c. 生	d. 逝
53].	a. 職	b. 学	c. 労	d. 働		86].	a. 隠	b. 示	c. 匿	d. 忍
54].	a. 児	b. 童	c. 先	d. 稚		87].	a. 乳	b. 況	c. 情	d. 状
55].	a. 和	b. 軍	c. 戦	d. 闘		88].	a. 遠	b. 疎	c. 周	d. 距
56].	a. 悪	b. 犯	c. 意	d. 囚		89].	a. 楽	b. 恥	c. 遊	d. 享
57].	a. 感	b. 理	c. 論	d. 意		90].	a. 痢	b. 疾	c. 症	d. 病
58].	a. 照	b. 輝	c. 伝	d. 光		91].	a. 違	b. 差	c. 難	d. 異
59].	a. 伝	b. 告	c. 読	d. 語		92].	a. 託	b. 編	c. 任	d. 預
60].	a. 期	b. 来	c. 時	d. 季		93].	a. 猛	b. 烈	c. 薫	d. 激
61].	a. 人	b. 衆	c. 官	d. 民		94].	a. 情	b. 恵	c. 感	d. 気
62].	a. 聖	b. 祈	c. 座	d. 参		95].	a. 釣	b. 漁	c. 狩	d. 魚
63].	a. 聖	b. 婦	c. 妻	d. 夫		96].	a. 穫	b. 粒	c. 穂	d. 穀
64].	a. 候	b. 節	c. 術	d. 季		97].	a. 乱	b. 統	c. 領	d. 府
65].	a. 財	b. 貴	c. 安	d. 宝		98].	a. 察	b. 調	c. 辱	d. 審
66].	a. 輩	b. 敵	c. 仲	d. 僚		99].	a. 雄	b. 妻	c. 僕	d. 郎
67].	a. 楼	b. 峰	c. 底	d. 眺		100].	a. 祥	b. 幸	c. 悲	d. 喜

509-A
夏*ummer* 麦*arley won't make us burly...*

夏*ummer*

natsu, KA, GE
summer

夏ばて *heat exhaustion* **natsubate**
晩夏 *delayed summer* **banka**
仲夏 *middle of summer* **chūka**
夏至 *summer solstice* **geshi**
半夏 *final days of seed-sowing* **hange**
夏期 *summertime* **kaki**
夏眠 *aestivations* **kamin**
真夏 *midsummer* **manatsu**
夏場 *summer season* **natsuba**
夏鳥 *summer bird* **natsudori**
夏服 *summer clothes* **natsufuku**
夏着 *summer wear* **natsugi**
夏雲 *summer clouds* **natsugumo**
夏草 *summer grass* **natsukusa**
夏物 *summer clothes, ~wear* **natsumono**
夏作 *summer crop* **natsusaku**
夏山 *summer mountaineering* **natsuyama**
冷夏 *cool summer* **reika**
立夏 *first day of summer* **rikka**

夂⇔夊 (winter)

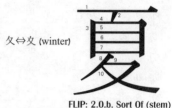

FLIP: 2.0.b. Sort Of (stem)

昨夏 *summer last* **sakunatsu**
盛夏 *middle of summer* **seika**
初夏 *start of summer season* **shoka**
常夏 *ever-lasting summer* **tokonatsu**
残夏 *final days of summer* **zanka**
夏時間 *daylight saving time* **natsujikan**
夏風邪 *summer cold* **natsukaze**
夏負け *yielding to summer heat* **natsumake**
夏ミカン *Chinese citron* **natsumikan**
夏向き *"for summer use..."* **natsumuki**
夏休み *summer vacation* **natsuyasumi**

節*eason, 421*	秋*utumn, 415*
冬*inter, 397*	春*pring, 579*
暑*ot weather, 615*	候*limate, 122*

真*incere, 487*

509-B
夏*ummer* 麦*arley won't make us burly...*

麦*arley*   麦*heat*

mugi, BAKU
barley, wheat

麦芽 *malt, wheat germ* **bakuga**
麦芽糖 *malt sugar, maltose* **bakugatō**
麦秋 *wheat harvest time* **bakushū**
麦酒 *beer* **bakushu, biiru**
米麦 *rice & barley* **beibaku**
燕麦 *oats* **enbaku**
裸麦 *rye* **hadakamugi**
鳩麦 *tear grass* **hatomugi**
冷麦 *chilled noodles* **hiyamugi**
烏麦 *oats* **karasumugi**
小麦 *wheat, corn* **komugi**
小麦色 *brownish barley colour* **komugiiro**
麦畑 *wheat field, barley field* **mugibatake**
麦笛 *wheat-straw whistle* **mugibue**
麦茶 *barley tea* **mugicha**
麦粉 *baking flour, wheat flour* **mugiko**
麦飯 *boiled rice & barley* **mugimeshi**
麦作 *wheat cultivating* **mugisaku**
麦藁 *straw* **mugiwara**

麦 (barley)

FLIP: 2.0.b. Sort Of (stem)

麦湯 *barley tea* **mugiyu**
大麦 *barley* **oomugi**
精麦 *barley wheat* **seibaku**
蕎麦 *buckwheat* **soba**
麦搗き *wheat polishing* **mugitsuki**
麦打ち *wheat threshing* **mugiuchi**
麦焦がし *parched barley flour* **mugikogashi**
蕎麦殻 *buckwheat shell* **sobagara**
蕎麦屋 *noodle shop* **sobaya**
掛け蕎麦 *buckwheat noodle soup* **kakesoba**
麦わら帽子 *straw hat* **mugiwara bōshi**

穀*rain, 41*	農*arming, 446*
穂*rain, 545*	耕*arming, 655*
粒*rain, 656*	培*arming, 698*

表*hart, 378*

510-A

条*rticles on* 桑*ulberry* 染*ye caught my eye...*

条*rticle*　条*lause*

木 (wooden)

JŌ
article, clause, section

FLIP: 2.0.b. Sort Of (stem)

別条 *separate clause* **betsujō**
条文 *text, proviso, stipulation, caveat* **jōbun**
条款 *provisions, stipulations, articles* **jōkan**
条件 *condition, term* **jōken**
⇒妥結条件 *terms-of-agreement* **daketsu jōken**
⇒希望条件 *conditions desired* **kibō jōken**
⇒交換条件 *bargaining point* **kōkan jōken**
⇒雇用条件 *terms of employment* **koyō jōken**
条件付 *conditional, ~attached* **jōkentsuki**
条件反射 *conditioned response* **jōken hansha**
条項 *clauses, items, stipulations* **jōkō**
条目 *article, stipulation, proviso, caveat* **jōmoku**
条例 *regulation, ordinance* **jōrei**
条令 *order, ordinance, regulation* **jōrei**
条理 *logic, reason* **jōri**
条章 *provisions, stipulations, articles* **jōshō**
条約 *treaty, pact* **jōyaku**
⇒仮条約 *provisional treaty* **karijōyaku**
⇒修好条約 *friendship treaty* **shūkō jōyaku**

条約国 *treaty-signatory nation* **jōyakukoku**
条約改正 *treaty revision* **jōyaku kaisei**
箇条 *article, clause, item* **kajō**
信条 *principle, creed, credo* **shinjō**
前条 *preceding clause* **zenjō**
星条旗 *US flag, Star-Spangled Banner* **seijōki**

款*rticle, 42*　契*romise, 900*
句*hrase, 16*　約*romise, 697*

架*anging, 202*

510-B

条*rticles on* 桑*ulberry* 染*ye caught my eye...*

染*yeing*　染*olouring*

木 (wooden)

so(meru), so(mu), so(maru), shi(miru), shi(mi), SEN
dyeing, colouring

FLIP: 4.0.b. Bottom (stem)

媒染 *colouring, colour fixing* **baisen**
伝染 *contagion, infection* **densen**
伝染病 *epidemic, contagious disease* **densenbyō**
感染 *infection, contagion* **kansen**
捺染 *textile printing, fabric colouring* **nassen**
汚染 *pollution, contamination* **osen**
先染め *dyed yarn* **sakizome**
染髪 *hair dyeing, hair colouring* **senpatsu**
染料 *dyestuff, colouring solution* **senryō**
染色 *dyeing* **senshoku**
染織 *dyeing & weaving* **senshoku**
油染み *oil stain, oil dirt* **aburajimi**
汗染み *sweat stains, sweat odour* **asejimi**
紅染め *red stains* **benizome**
血染め *blood stains, specks of blood* **chizome**
色染め *dyeing, colouring* **irozome**
幼馴染 *childhood friend* **osananajimi**
染毛剤 *hair dyeing, hair colouring* **senmōzai**
染色体 *chromosome* **senshokutai**

染め型 *dyeing frame* **somegata**
染め粉 *dyeing powder* **someko**
染め物 *dyed goods, ~fabrics* **somemono**
墨染め *dyeing black* **sumizome**
環境汚染 *environmental pollution* **kankyō osen**
顔馴染み *familiar face* **kaonajimi**
煮染める *boiling in soy sauce* **nishimeru**
染み出す *ooze out* **shimidasu**
染み込む *imbue, soak* **shimikomu**
染み透る *be impressed, sink deep* **shimitooru**

彩*olour, 914*　衣*lothes, 355*
色*olour, 403*　裁*lothes, 802*
布*loth, 208*　服*lothes, 734*

案*roposal, 609*

510-C

条rticles on 桑ulberry 染ye caught my eye...

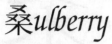

桑 (wooden)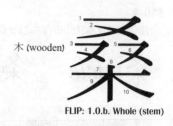

桑ulberry

kuwa, SŌ
mulberry

FLIP: 1.0.b. Whole (stem)

桑原	mulberry field	**kuwabara**
桑畑	mulberry field	**kuwabatake**
桑田	mulberry orchard	**sōden**
桑園	blueberry farm, ~orchard	**sōen**
桑門	Buddhist priesthood	**sōmon**
桑摘み	mulberry picking	**kuwatsumi**
真桑瓜	Oriental melon	**makuwauri**
桑原桑原	"Heaven forbid!..."	**kuwabara kuwabara**

桃each, 215
果ruit, 287

察nspect, 328

511-A

棄bandon 案roposal for garbage disposal...

木 (wooden)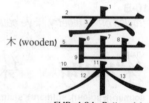

棄bandon   棄bolish

su(teru), KI
abandon, abolish, discontinue, dispose of, eliminate, thrash, discard

FLIP: 4.0.b. Bottom (stem)

唾棄	abhor; spew out	**daki**
廃棄	abrogation, scrapping, repeal	**haiki**
廃棄物	waste, emission	**haikibutsu**
破棄	annulment, abrogation, breach	**haki**
放棄	renunciation, relinquishment	**hōki**
遺棄	abandoning, desertion	**iki**
自棄	desperation, desolation	**jiki, yake**
⇒自暴自棄	self-destruction, desperation	**jibōjiki**
棄権	abstention, renunciation	**kiken**
棄権者	absentee, deserter	**kikensha**
棄却	rejection, dismissal	**kikyaku**
棄約	breaking one's promise	**kiyaku**
投棄	throwing away, discarding	**tōki**
自棄酒	drinking to forget one's sadness	**yakezake**

退bandon, 770   絶radicate, 403
撤bandon, 843   消elete, 265
辞uitting, 954   抹ross-out, 13

葉eaf, 411

511-B

棄*bandon* 案*roposal for garbage disposal...*

木 (wooden)

案*roposal*   案*uggestion*

AN
proposal, proposition, suggestion

FLIP: 4.0.b. Bottom (stem)

案外 *on the contrary, against one's wishes* **angai**
案件 *issue, matter, case* **anken**
案内 *guidance, information, pamphlet* **annai**
案内状 *invitation card* **annaijō**
案出 *devise, invent* **anshutsu**
文案 *draft proposal* **bun'an**
代案 *alternative plan, plan B* **daian**
原案 *original plan, plan a* **gen'an**
議案 *legislative bill, ~measure* **gian**
法案 *legislative bill, measure* **hōan**
翻案 *adaptation* **hon'an**
懸案 *pending matter, matter-in-question* **ken'an**
考案 *idea, plan, thought* **kōan**
名案 *brilliant idea* **meian**
思案 *idea, proposal* **shian**
私案 *personal plan* **shian**
試案 *provisional-, tentative plan* **shian**
新案 *new idea, patent device* **shin'an**
草案 *draft, rough draft* **sōan**

対案 *counter-proposal* **taian**
提案 *proposal, suggestion* **teian**
答案 *answer sheet* **tōan**
図案 *design, plan* **zuan**
案の定 *"sure enough, as expected..."* **annojō**
案じる *anxious, worry, perflexity* **anjiru**
具体案 *concrete, definite plan* **gutaian**
案山子 *scarecrow; figurehead* **kakashi**
道案内 *road map, road guide* **michiannai**
答申案 *report draft* **tōshin'an**
予算案 *budget bill* **yosan'an**

提*roposal*, 313	念*dea*, 182
意*dea*, 340	勧*ecommend*, 666
想*dea*, 524	推*ecommend*, 777

棄*bandon*, 608

512-A

姿*ppearance of* 妥*ontentment with no resentment...*

女 (woman)

姿*ppearance*   姿*igure*

sugata, SHI
appearance, figure, configuration, posture, form

Facing: 3.0. ☞ ☜ Across

英姿 *heroic-, gallant looks* **eishi**
絵姿 *portrait, likeness* **esugata**
風姿 *demeanour, appearance, looks* **fūshi**
初姿 *new clothes for the New Year* **hatsusugata**
嬌姿 *lovely appearance* **kyōshi**
寝姿 *sleeping position* **nesugata**
荷姿 *packaged appearance* **nisugata**
麗姿 *beautiful looks* **reishi**
姿勢 *posture, attitude, carriage* **shisei**
姿態 *figure, shape, form* **shitai**
姿容 *form, appearance* **shiyō**
姿絵 *portrait, likeness* **sugatae**
姿見 *full-length mirror* **sugatami**
旅姿 *travelling clothes* **tabisugata**
優姿 *graceful looks* **yasasugata**
容姿 *figure, appearance, looks* **yōshi**
勇姿 *valiant figure* **yūshi**
雄姿 *magnificent view* **yūshi**
舞台姿 *stage appearance* **butaisugata**

高姿勢 *high profile, high & mighty* **kōshisei**
忍び姿 *phoney, disguise* **shinobisugata**
立ち姿 *tanding position* **tachisugata**
後ろ姿 *back posture* **ushirosugata**

容*ppearance*, 492	構*osture*, 714
態*ppearance*, 322	形*hape*, 951

桜*herry blossom*, 127

512-B

姿ppearance of 妥-ontentment with no resentment...

女 (woman)

妥ontentment   妥ompromise

DA

contentment, compromise, conciliate, settlement

妥結 compromise, settlement **daketsu**
妥結条件 terms-of-agreement **daketsu jōken**
妥協 compromise, bargaining **dakyō**
妥協案 compromise proposal **dakyōan**
妥協点 point of compromise **dakyōten**
妥当 suitable, appropriate **datō**
妥当性 suitability, propriety **datōsei**

Facing: 2.1. East ☞ (H)
Facing: 3.0. ☞☜ Across

満atisfy, 567
穏ranquillity, 840
康ranquillity, 881

委ntrust, 583

513-A

宴anquet hosted by your 妻ife had no table knife...

宀 (cover, lid)

宴anquet   宴arty

utage, EN

banquet, party, feast, soiree, gala dinner

別宴 farewell party **betsuen**
宴会 feast, party, banquet **enkai**
宴会場 banquet hall **enkaijō**
宴楽 feast & merry-making **enraku**
宴席 banquet seat, dinner seat **enseki**
宴遊 feast & merry-making **enyū**
賀宴 banquet **gaen**
御宴 palace banquet **gyoen**
饗宴 feast, banquet **kyōen**
球宴 all-star baseball game **kyūen**
内宴 private party **naien**
盛宴 grand banquet **seien**
賜宴 palace banquet **shien**
小宴 small party **shōen**
酒宴 drinking party **shuen**
祝宴 banquet in honour of **shukuen**
披露宴 wedding party **hirōen**
歓迎宴 welcome party **kangeien**

FLIP: 3.0.a. Top (flat)

喫njoy, 900   快leasant, 699
享njoy, 398   歓leasure, 667
遊njoy, 650   娯leasure, 453
悦leasant, 942 愉leasure, 922

妻arried lady, 611

513-B

妻anquet hosted by your 妻ife had no table knife...

女 (woman)

妻ife　　妻arried lady

tsuma, SAI
wife, married-lady, lady of the house

Facing: 3.0. ☞ ☜ Across

愛妻	*beloved wife, love for one's wife* **aisai**
悪妻	*bad wife, irresponsible wife* **akusai**
亡妻	*deceased wife* **bōsai**
病妻	*sick wife, invalid wife* **byōsai**
夫妻	*married couple, Mr. & Mrs.* **fusai**
後妻	*second wife* **gosai**
愚妻	*"my foolish wife..." (humble)* **gusai**
人妻	*married woman* **hitozuma**
本妻	*lawful wife, one's real wife* **honsai**
稲妻	*flash of lightning* **inazuma**
賢妻	*intelligent wife* **kensai**
切妻	*gable, ridge, end wall* **kirizuma**
無妻	*unmarried man, old bachelor* **musai**
内妻	*common-law wife* **naisai**
新妻	*newly-married woman* **niizuma**
良妻	*good wife* **ryōsai**
妻女	*one's wife & daughters* **saijo**
妻子	*wife & children, one's family* **saishi**
妻室	*one's wife* **saishitsu**

妻帯	*getting married, betrothal* **saitai**
妻帯者	*married man* **saitaisha**
正妻	*lawful wife, one's real wife* **seisai**
先妻	*ex-wife, former wife* **sensai**
手妻	*fingertips; sleight of hand* **tezuma**
妻戸	*pair of panel doors* **tsumado**
妻恋	*love for one's wife* **tsumagoi**
若妻	*very young wife* **wakazuma**
有妻	*man with a wife, married man* **yūsai**
恐妻家	*henpecked husband* **kyōsaika**

婦*ife*, 785	家*amily*, 909
姻*arriage*, 364	族*amily*, 649
婚*arriage*, 637	任*bligation*, 709

婆*ld woman*, 32

514-A

漆acquer depicting 黍alm used to embalm...

水⇔氵 (water)

漆acquer　　漆arnish

urushi, SHITSU
lacquer, varnish, enamel, glossy

FLIP: 7.0.b1. Right (stem)

乾漆	*dry lacquer* **kanshitsu**
黒漆	*black lacquer* **kokushitsu**
漆器	*lacquer ware, ~work* **shikki**
漆工	*lacquer ware, ~work* **shikkō**
漆黒	*pitch black* **shikkoku**
漆喰	*plaster, stucco, mortar* **shikkui**
漆絵	*lacquer painting* **urushie**
漆屋	*lacquer shop, ~artist* **urushiya**
漆負け	*lacquer poisoning* **urushimake**
漆塗り	*lacquer coating* **urushinuri**
漆細工	*lacquer ware, ~work* **urushizaiku**

塗*aint*, 882	図*rawing*, 47
画*ainting*, 35	描*rawing*, 271
絵*rawing*, 143	輝*hining*, 296

淡*ale*, 309

514-B

漆acquer depicting 泰alm used to embalm...

水 ⇔ 氵 (water)

泰alm　　泰erenity

TAI

calm, serenity, placidity, sobriety, stillness, tranquillity

FLIP: 2.0.b. Sort Of (stem)

安泰 tranquillity, serenity **antai**
泰安 peace, tranquillity **taian**
泰平 peace, tranquillity **taihei**
泰国 Kingdom of Thailand **taikoku**
泰西 west, occident **taisei**
泰斗 leading authority, expert **taito**
泰然 calm, self-possessed **taizen**
泰然自若 imperturbability, composure **taizen jijaku**

穏alm, 840	康ranquillity, 881
鎮alm, 831	静uiet, 230
穏ranquillity, 840	寧uiet, 967

奏usic play, 579

515-A

摂aking over 渋eluctance, that's perseverance...

手 ⇔ 扌 (hand, manual)

摂ake over　摂ct as regent

to(ru), SETSU

take over, take in, act as regent, subsume

FLIP: 7.1. Right (Sort Of)

包摂 subsumption **hōsetsu**
兼摂 holding an additional post **kensetsu**
摂関 regents & advisers **sekkan**
摂関家 line of regents **sekkanke**
摂家 line of regents & advisers **sekke**
摂行 acting on behalf of another **sekkō**
摂生 caring for one's health **sessei**
摂氏 centigrade, Celsius **sesshi**
摂政 regent, regency **sesshō**
摂取 ingestion, assimilation **sesshu**
摂取量 intake, input **sesshuryō**
摂動 gravitational perturbation **setsudō**
摂理 providence, destiny, fate **setsuri**
摂理的 providential, opportune **setsuriteki**
摂養 taking care of one's health **setsuyō**
不摂生 disregard one's health **fusessei**
摂護腺 prostate gland **setsugosen**

令ommand, 362	覇egemony, 603
帥ommander, 483	轄ontrol, 968
督ommander, 911	管ontrol, 917
導uidance, 312	替eplace, 334

渋stringent, 613

515-B

摂*aking over* 渋*eluctance, that's perseverance...*

水 ⇔ 氵 (water)

渋*stringent*   渋*eluctance*

shibu(i), shibu, shibu(ru), JŪ
astringent, reluctance, hesitance, acrid, unwillingness, *with some difficulty*

FLIP: 7.3.b. Right Bottom (stem)

渋ちん *stingy, miser, frugal* **shibuchin**
渋色 *tan colour* **shibuiro**
渋皮 *inner skin* **shibukawa**
渋味 *astringency, refinement* **shibumi**
渋渋 *reluctantly, hesitantly* **shibushibu**
渋抜き *removing astringency* **shibunuki**
渋り腹 *gripes, tenesmus* **shiburibara**
鉄渋 *rusty taste* **tetsushibu**
茶渋 *tea incrustation* **chashibu**
渋面 *grimace, wince, sullen* **jūmen**
渋っ面 *sullen look, scowl* **shibuttsura**
渋滞 *traffic jam, ~congestion* **jūtai**
晦渋 *difficult to understand* **kaijū**
苦渋 *distressed-looking* **kujū**
難渋 *difficulty, hardship* **nanjū**
渋柿 *astringent persimmon* **shibugaki**
渋紙 *astringent-treated paper* **shibugami**
出し渋る *grudge, bad blood* **dashishiburu**
言い渋る *hesitate to say* **iishiburu**

売り渋る *unwilling to sell inner skin*
　(chestnut) **urishiburu**
渋谷区 *Shibuya-ward* **shibuya-ka**

美*eautiful*, 124	韻*raceful*, 315
麗*eautiful*, 68	雅*raceful*, 58
佳*eauty*, 891	淑*raceful*, 510

渋*ross-over*, 273

516-A

Enemy 撃*ttack and blast, too late to* 掌*rasp...*

手 ⇔ 扌 (hand, manual)

撃*ttack*   撃*ssault*   撃*trike*

u(tsu), GEKI
attack, assault, strike, charging, hitting, offence, storming, raiding

FLIP: 6.1. Left Top

爆撃 *bombing offensive* **bakugeki**
直撃 *direct hit, bulls eye* **chokugeki**
電撃 *electric shock* **dengeki**
迎撃 *interception, blockade* **geigeki**
撃破 *defeating, destruction* **gekiha**
撃滅 *destruction, extermination* **gekimetsu**
撃退 *repulse, repel, drive back* **gekitai**
撃墜 *shooting down* **gekitsui**
排撃 *rejection, interception, blockade* **haigeki**
反撃 *counterattack, retaliatory strike* **hangeki**
砲撃 *fire, bombardment* **hōgeki**
銃撃 *shooting down* **jūgeki**
攻撃 *attack, assault, offence* **kōgeki**
挟撃 *attack on both flanks* **kyōgeki**
急撃 *surprise attack, sudden blow* **kyūgeki**
猛撃 *hard blow, severe blow* **mōgeki**
雷撃 *lightning strike, torpedo attack* **raigeki**
射撃 *firing, shooting* **shageki**
進撃 *advance strike, first strike* **shingeki**

衝撃 *shock, impact* **shōgeki**
衝撃波 *shock wave* **shōgekiha**
襲撃 *surprise attack, ambush* **shūgeki**
狙撃 *sniper fire* **sogeki**
突撃 *charge, dash* **totsugeki**
痛撃 *painful blow* **tsūgeki**
追撃 *follow-up attack* **tsuigeki**
要撃 *ambush, assassination* **yōgeki**
遊撃 *search & kill, trigger-happy* **yūgeki**
目撃者 *eyewitness, survivor* **mokugekisha**
総攻撃 *all-out offence, general strike* **sōkōgeki**

攻*ttack*, 635	討*ttack*, 691	争*trife*, 231
襲*ttack*, 630	伐*ttack*, 96	撲*trike*, 157

暫*nterim*, 928

516-B

Enemy 撃ttack and blast, too late to 掌rasp...

手⇔扌 (hand, manual)

掌rasp 掌alm

tenohira, SHŌ
grasp, palm (hand), take charge, administer, clinch, clutches, glutches, oversee

FLIP: 3.0.a. Top (flat)

分掌 *division of duties* **bunshō**
合掌 *linking hands in prayer* **gasshō**
管掌 *in-charge, administrator* **kanshō**
管掌術 *palm-reading* **kanshōjutsu**
車掌 *train conductor* **shashō**
車掌室 *train conductor's room* **shashōshitsu**
掌握 *grasp, seize, have at hand* **shohaku**
掌中 *on hand, in the hand* **shōchū**
掌中本 *pocketbook size* **shōchūbon**
掌大 *palm size* **shōdai**
掌編 *short story, short novel* **shōhen**
職掌 *duty, work* **shokushō**
掌理 *presiding over* **shōri**
掌状 *shape of a hand* **shōjō**
掌管 *manage, handling* **shōkan**
掌典 *ritual, rite* **shōten**
仙人掌 *cactus plants* **saboten**
手の掌 *palm of the hand* **tenohira**

司]*dminister, 376*	執*rasp, 268*
政*dministration, 725*	解*rasp, 400*
管*ontrol, 917*	握*rasp, 427*
操*perate, 851*	

常*ormal,94*

517-A

署ublic-office demanded 署ignature on 署ot-weather expenditure...

罒 (net, eye crown)

❶署*ignature* ❷署*ublic-office*

SHO
signature, autograph, sign; public office

FLIP: 3.0.a. Top (flat)

❶代署 *proxy signature, "signed for by..."* **daisho**
副署 *countersignature* **fukusho**
連署 *joint signature, co-signatory* **rensho**
親署 *emperor's signature* **shinsho**
署名 *signature, autograph* **shomei**
署名国 *treaty signatory nation* **shomeikoku**
署名者 *signatory, contracting party* **shomeisha**
署名運動 *signature-, petition campaign* **shomei undō**

❷分署 *branch office* **bunsho**
部署 *post assignment* **busho**
本署 *headquarters, principal office* **honsho**
自署 *autograph, signature* **jisho**
公署 *public offices* **kōsho**
支署 *branch office* **shisho**
署長 *chief, head* **shochō**
署員 *staff member, clerk* **shoin**
消防署 *fire station* **shōbōsho**
官公署 *municipal office* **kankōsho**

警察署 *police station* **keisatsusho**
税務署 *tax office, Japanese irs* **zeimusho**
税務署長 *chief tax officer* **zeimu shochō**
税務署員 *tax collector* **zeimu shoin**

銘*ignature, 425*
庁*ubic office, 633*
官*ublic official, 105*

者*erson,278*

517-B

署ublic-office demanded 署ignature on 署ot-weather expenditure...

日 (sunlight, daytime)

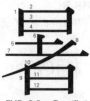

署ot weather   署ot climate

FLIP: 3.0.a. Top (flat)

atsu(i), SHO
hot weather, hot climate, hot temperature, summer heat, thermal

炎暑 *intense-, scorching heat* **ensho**
激暑 *intense heat, severe summer* **gekisho**
厳暑 *intense-, scorching heat* **gensho**
極暑 *intense-, scorching heat* **gokusho**
避暑 *spending the summer* **hisho**
避暑地 *summer resort* **hishochi**
避暑客 *summer visitor* **hishokyaku**
寒暑 *cold & hot, winter & summer* **kansho**
酷暑 *intense heat, swelter* **kokusho**
猛暑 *intense-, scorching heat* **mōsho**
暑中 *midsummer* **shochū**
暑中見舞い *summertime greetings* **shochū mimai**
暑寒 *hot & cold weather* **shokan**
暑気 *heat, hotness, heat wave* **shoki**
暑熱 *summer heat* **shonetsu**
大暑 *intense-, scorching heat* **taisho**
残暑 *lingering summer heat* **zansho**
暑苦しい *stuffy, sultry* **atsukurushii**
暑さ凌ぎ *relief from heat* **atsusashinogi**

暑がり屋 *heat-sensitive person* **atsugariya**
蒸し暑い *stifling, muggy, sultry* **mushiatsui**
暑行天皇 *Emperor Keikō (71-130)*
　　keikō tennō

温*ot temperature, 622*	夏*ummer, 606*
湯*ot-water, 932*	汗*erspire, 710*
熱*eat, 153*	傘*mbrella, 142*

署*ublic-office, 614*

518-A

霜rost in a 箱ox kept in Halifax...

雨 (weather)

霜rosty   霜rigid

FLIP: 3.0.b. Top (stem)

shimo, SŌ
frosty, frigid, shivers

晩霜 *late frost, night frost* **bansō**
風霜 *wind & frost* **fūsō**
初霜 *first frost of the year* **hatsushimo**
除霜 *defrosting, de-icing, thawing* **jōsō**
降霜 *snowfall, snowing* **kōsō**
大霜 *heavy frosting* **ooshimo**
遅霜 *spring frost* **osojimo**
星霜 *bygone years, the past* **seisō**
霜柱 *ice needles, frost columns* **shimobashira**
霜月 *November* **shimotsuki**
霜夜 *evening frost, frosty night* **shimoyo**
秋霜 *autumn frost* **shūsō**
秋霜烈日 *withering frost & scorching heat*
　　shūsō retsujitsu
霜害 *frost damage* **sōgai**
霜雪 *frost & snow* **sōsetsu**
露霜 *frozen dew* **tsuyujimo**
霜解け *thaw, de-ice, defrost* **shimodoke**
霜降り *checkered-, salt & pepper pattern* **shimofuri**

霜囲い *straw cover* **shimogakoi**
霜枯れ *wintry & frosty, frost withered* **shimogare**
霜取り *defrosting, de-icing, thawing* **shimotori**
霜焼け *frostbite, chilblains* **shimoyake**

曇*oggy, 154*
霧*oggy, 454*
雰*oggy, 518*

箱*ox, 616*

518-B

霜rost in a 箱ox kept in Halifax...

竹 (bamboo)

箱ox　　箱eceptacle

hako

box, bin, container, receptacle

FLIP: 7.3.a. Right Bottom (flat)

豚箱	jail, police cell **butabako**	道具箱	tool box **dōgubako**
茶箱	tea box, chest box **chabako**	絵の具箱	paint box **enogubako**
文箱	box for letters **fubako, fumibako**	箱入り	put in boxes, encase **hakoiri**
筆箱	pen case **fudebako**	箱入り娘	overprotected girl **hakoiri musume**
箱舟	noah's ark **hakobune**	箱詰め	packing, boxing **hakozume**
箱庭	miniature garden **hakoniwa**	救急箱	first-aid kit **kyūkyūbako**
箱師	train pickpocket **hakoshi**	料金箱	fee box **ryōkinbako**
箱柳	Japanese aspen **hakoyanagi**	玉手箱	pandora's box; treasure box **tamatebako**
針箱	sewing kit **haribako**	跳び箱	vaulting horse **tobibako**
本箱	book case, book shelf **honbako**	郵便箱	mailbox **yūbinbako**
紙箱	carton **kamibako**	私書箱	PO box **shishobako**
木箱	wooden box **kibako**		
小箱	small box **kobako**		
薬箱	medicine chest **kusuribako**		
外箱	slip case **sotobako**		
巣箱	bird house, hive **subako**		
手箱	box for personal effects **tebako**		
空き箱	empty box **akibako**		
貯金箱	piggy bank **chokinbako**		

容ontent, 492	内nside, 297
包rapping, 503	奥nside, 903

相ellow, 524

519-A

肯ffirm soul 有xistence based on evidence...

肉⇔月 (flesh, body part)

肯ffirmative　　肯ositive

KŌ

affirmative, positive, approval, assent, concur, consent

FLIP: 4.0.b. Bottom (stem)

肯綮	"right on the mark..." **kōkei**
肯定	affirmation **kōtei**
肯定文	affirmative sentence **kōteibun**
肯定的	affirmative, positive **kōteiteki**
首肯	consent, approval **shukō**

可pproval, 15
承pproval, 117
賛pproval, 334

青lue colour, 115

519-B

肯 ffirm soul 有 xistence based on evidence...

有 ossess   有 xist

肉⇔月 (flesh, body part)

a(ru), YŪ, U
possess, exist, have

FLIP: 4.0.b. Bottom (stem)

含有	containing, in place **ganyū**
現有	present ownership **genyū**
併有	have two simultaneously **heiyū**
保有	possession, maintenance **hoyū**
享有	possession, ownership **kyōyū**
領有	possession, ownership **ryōyū**
占有	possession, occupancy **senyū**
占有権	right of possession **senyūken**
専有	exclusive possession **senyū**
私有	private possession **shiyū**
所有	own, possess, hold **shoyū**
有無	existence, presence, "yes or no..." **umu**
有益	useful, helpful, instructive **yūeki**
有害	harmful, injurious **yūgai**
有配	dividends, yields **yūhai**
有機	organic substance **yūki**
有名	famous, well-known, popular **yūmei**
有理	rationale, reason, logic **yūri**
有利	beneficial, advantage, useful **yūri**

有力	strong & powerful **yūryoku**
有識	knowledgeable, well-informed **yūshiki**
有り金	all the money **arigane**
有意義	meaningful, significant **yūigi**
有り得る	be possible, probable, likely **ariuru**
有り余る	superabundant, overflowing **ariamaru**
有り合わせ	stuff on hand **ariawase**
有り難い	grateful, thankful **arigatagai**
有限会社	limited company **yūgen gaisha**
有事の際	in case of~ **yūji no sai**
有線テレビ	cable TV **yūsen terebi**

在 xist, 634	持 olding, 249
存 xist, 634	握 rasp, 427
居 xist, 384	

肯 ffirmative, 616

520-A

聖 acred 望 esire, bishop's 呈 ffer to retire...

聖 acred   聖 oly   聖 ivine

耳 (ears)

hijiri, SEI
sacred, holy, divine, pious, sacrosanct, saintly, sanctified, solemn, consecrated, hallowed

FLIP: 4.0.a. Bottom (flat)

楽聖	master musician, maestro **gakusei**
聖別	consecration, sanctity **seibetsu**
聖母	Holy Mother, Virgin Mary **seibo**
聖地	sacred ground, holy land **seichi**
聖壇	altar; pulpit **seidan**
聖断	emperor's decision, judgement **seidan**
聖域	sacred-, holy precincts **seiiki**
聖人	saint, canonized person **seijin**
聖日	Holy Day of Sabbath **seijitsu**
聖女	saintly woman **seijo**
聖火	Olympic flame, Olympic torch **seika**
聖歌	hymnal, gospel songs **seika**
聖賢	saints & sages **seiken**
聖訓	sacred teachings **seikun**
聖教	sacred teachings **seikyō**
聖恩	imperial favour **seion**
聖霊	holy ghost, Holy Spirit **seirei**
聖跡	biblical sites, holy land **seiseki**
聖戦	holy war, crusade, jihad **seisen**

聖書	Holy Bible, holy scripture **seisho**
聖職	holy orders, vocation **seishoku**
聖水	blessed water, holy water **seisui**
聖典	sacred book, scripture **seiten**
聖徒	saint, disciple, apostle **seito**
聖夜	Christmas eve, holy night **seiya**
聖油	blessed oil, chrism **seiyu**
聖像	sacred image, icon **seizō**
神聖	sacredness, holiness **shinsei**
詩聖	master poet **shisei**

信 aith, 252	祈 rayer, 184
神 ivine, 712	宗 eligion, 879
拝 rayer, 636	純 urity, 199

望 esire, 618

520-B

聖*acred* 望*esire*, bishop's 呈*ffer to retire...*

肉⇔月 (flesh, body part)

望*esire*　望*spiration*

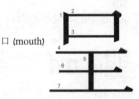

FLIP: 4.0.a. Bottom (flat)

nozo(mu), BŌ, MŌ
desire, aspiration, craving, urge, wish, liking, look afar

望外	unexpected, unpredictable	**bōgai**
望見	watching at a distance	**bōken**
望郷	homesickness, nostalgia	**bōkyō**
眺望	view, prospect, desire	**chōbō**
遠望	far-, distant view	**enbō**
願望	wish, desire	**ganbō**
非望	improper desire	**hibō**
本望	real desire, hidden intention	**honmō**
人望	popularity, public acclaim	**jinbō**
観望	observing developments	**kanbō**
渇望	yearning, longing, eagerness	**katsubō**
希望	wish, hope, want, look for	**kibō**
好望	promising, potential	**kōbō**
懇望	earnest request, solicitation	**konmō**
声望	reputation, popularity	**seibō**
切望	yearning, longing, eagerness	**setsubō**
志望	wish, aspiration, desire	**shibō**
信望	prestige, popularity	**shinbō**
失望	disappointment, despair	**shitsubō**

嘱望	expectation, anticipation	**shokubō**
宿望	long-cherished wish	**shukubō**
大望	aspiration, ambition	**taibō, taimō**
展望	view, prospect, desire	**tenbō**
徳望	renowned virtues	**tokubō**
要望	wish, hope, want	**yōbō**
欲望	desire, ambition, greed	**yokubō**
有望	promising, hopeful	**yūbō**
絶望	despair, hopelessness	**zetsubō**
望遠鏡	telescope, binoculars	**bōenkyō**
望祖父	one's late grandfather	**bōsofu**
待ち望む	"look forward to..."	**machinozomu**

希 *reference, 208*	欲 *esire, 892*
頼 *equest, 562*	志 *ntention, 426*

聖 *acred, 617*

520-C

聖*acred* 望*esire*, bishop's 呈*ffer to retire...*

口 (mouth)

呈*ffering*　呈*edication*

FLIP: 1.0.a. Whole (flat)

TEI
offering, dedication, donation, oblation, present

拝呈	gift presentation	**haitei**
奉呈	presentation to the emperor	**hōtei**
献呈	presentation, offering	**kentei**
謹呈	dedication, presentation copy	**kintei**
露呈	revelation, exposure, disclosure	**rotei**
進呈	offering (flowers)	**shintei**
進呈本	complimentary book	**shinteihon**
進呈者	donor, presentator, giver	**shinteisha**
送呈	sending a complimentary copy	**sōtei**
呈示	present, exhibit	**teiji**
呈上	presentation, offering	**teijō**
呈色	colouring, colouration	**teishiki, teishoku**
贈呈	presentation, presenting	**zōtei**
贈呈本	complimentary book	**zōteibon**
贈呈品	present, gift	**zōteihin**
贈呈者	donor, presenter, giver	**zōteisha**
贈呈式	presentation ceremony	**zōteishiki**
書呈	presentation, offering	**shotei**
⇒案内書呈	guidebook presentation	**annai shotei**

奉 *ffer, 275*	仕 *ervice, 9*
献 *onation, 414*	勤 *ervice, 962*
催 *ponsor, 416*	務 *ervice, 454*

皇 *mperor, 113*

521-A

What 芸rt 伝onveys, hearts obey...

芸rt   芸esign

++- (grass)

GEI
art, design

FLIP: 3.0.b. Top (stem)
Facing: 2.1. East ☞ (H)

武芸 *martial arts* **bugei**
文芸 *literary arts* **bungei**
珍芸 *uncommon-, unusual trick* **chingei**
演芸 *entertainment, performance* **engei**
園芸 *gardening, horticulture* **engei**
芸談 *art discussion* **geidan**
芸術 *fine arts* **geijutsu**
芸名 *stage-, screen name* **geimei**
芸人 *professional entertainer* **geinin**
芸能 *public entertainment, showbiz* **geinō**
芸能人 *entertainer, celebrity* **geinōjin**
芸者 *Geisha girl* **geisha**
芸当 *performance, feat, stunt* **geitō**
腹芸 *subtle communication* **haragei**
工芸 *industrial arts, craft* **kōgei**
曲芸 *stunt, acrobatics* **kyokugei**
民芸 *folk art, handicraft, folk craft* **mingei**
水芸 *water tricks* **mizugei**
無芸 *unaccomplished artist* **mugei**

農芸 *agriculture & horticulture* **nōgei**
才芸 *talents & accomplishments* **saigei**
至芸 *first class art* **shigei**
手芸 *handicraft, hand-made goods* **shugei**
陶芸 *ceramic art, ceramics, pottery* **tōgei**
裏芸 *performance tricks* **uragei**
話芸 *art of storytelling* **wagei**
遊芸 *art & dance* **yūgei**
隠し芸 *parlour trick, stunt* **kakushigei**
素人芸 *amateur entertainment* **shirōtogei**
旅芸人 *roving-, strolling entertainer* **tabigeinin**

| 巧killful, 738 | 工rtisan, 176 | 佳eauty, 891 |
| 術kills, 110 | 匠rtisan, 106 | 魅eauty, 969 |

芝awn, 84

521-B

What 芸rt 伝onveys, hearts obey...

伝onvey   伝ommunicate

人⇔イ (person)

tsuta(eru), tsuta(waru), tsuta(u), DEN
convey, communicate, tell, transmit, leave message

Facing: 4.0. ☜☞ Apart

伝聞 *hearsay, rumour* **denbun**
伝導 *transmission, conductivity* **dendō**
伝道 *religious propagation, preaching* **dendō**
伝言 *message, notice* **dengon**
伝授 *initiation, instruction* **denju**
伝記 *biography, life story* **denki**
伝票 *slip of paper, memo* **denpyō**
伝令 *messenger, courier* **denrei**
伝染 *infection, contagion* **densen**
伝染病 *epidemic, contagious disease* **densenbyō**
伝説 *legend, tradition, folklore* **densetsu**
伝承 *tradition, transmission* **denshō**
伝達 *transmission, notification* **dentatsu**
伝統 *tradition, custom* **dentō**
駅伝 *long-distance relay race* **ekiden**
誤伝 *misinformation, misreporting* **goden**
秘伝 *secret, mysteries* **hiden**
評伝 *critical biography* **hyōden**
遺伝 *heredity, genetic* **iden**

自伝 *autobiography* **jiden**
直伝 *pass down directly* **jikiden**
家伝 *family tradition* **kaden**
皆伝 *full proficiency* **kaiden**
列伝 *serialized life story* **retsuden**
略伝 *brief biography* **ryakuden**
宣伝 *advertisement, propaganda* **senden**
⇒逆宣伝 *negative advertisement* **gyakusenden**
史伝 *historical legend* **shiden**
相伝 *inheritance* **sōden**
以心伝心 *mental telepathy* **ishin denshin**

告eport, 266	知wareness, 103
報eport, 733	識wareness, 856
逓onvey, 304	

会ssembly, 864

522-A

恭*espect that* 添*ppends hardly ends...*

恭*espect*　　恭*evere*

uya'uya(shii), KYŌ
respect, revere, courtesy, homage

恭順 *fealty, allegiance* **kyōjun**
恭敬 *respect, reverence* **kyōkei**
恭謙 *modesty, humility* **kyōken**
恭倹 *modest & respectful* **kyōken**
恭賀 *respectful congratulations* **kyōga**
恭賀新年 *Happy New Year* **kyōga shinnen**

心 ⇔ 忄 ⇔ 小 (feelings)

FLIP: 2.0.b. Sort Of (stem)

仰*espect, 706*	礼*espect, 685*
謹*espect, 962*	申*peak humble, 89*
敬*espect, 329*	御*[honorific], 380*
尚*espect, 99*	様*[honorific], 944*
崇*espect, 879*	

洪*looding, 512*

522-B

恭*espect that* 添*ppends hardly ends...*

添*ppend*　　添*ccompany*

so(eru); so(u), TEN
append, accompany, adjoining, add to

水 ⇔ 氵 (water)

FLIP: 7.3.b. Right Bottom (stem)
Facing: 1.2. ☞ West (V)

添字 *subscript, index* **soeji**
添え文 *accompanying letter* **soebumi**
添え木 *splint* **soegi**
添え状 *accompanying letter* **soejō**
添え物 *supplement, garnish* **soemono**
添え役 *secondary role* **soeyaku**
添え書き *note, postscript* **soegaki**
添え言葉 *advice, encouragement* **soekotoba**
添い臥 *sleeping together* **soibushi**
添い寝 *sleeping together* **soine**
添い遂げる *lifetime marriage* **soitogeru**
添乗 *accompany, guide* **tenjō**
添乗員 *tour guide* **tenjōin**
添加 *addition, annexing* **tenka**
添加物 *additive, preservative, seasoning* **tenkabutsu**
添付 *attachment, appendage* **tenpu**
添削 *correction, revision* **tensaku**
添書 *attached letter* **tensho**
力添え *help, support, assistance* **chikarazoe**

介添え *assistant, helper* **kaizoe**
心添え *advice, counsel* **kokorozoe**
口添え *advice, recommendation* **kuchizoe**
後添い *second wife* **nochizoi**
山添い *along the mountain* **yamazoi**
巻き添え *entanglement, quagmire* **makizoe**
差し添え *one's shorter sword* **sashisoe**
付き添う *escort, accompany* **tsukisō**
連れ添う *be married to* **tsuresō**
寄り添う *nestle* **yorisō**
申し添える *"in addition to that..."* **mōshi soeru**

付*ttach, 382*	伴*ccompany, 949*
附*ttach, 382*	加*ddition, 201*
随*ccompany, 807*	伴*ogether, 949*

恭*espect, 620*

523-A
盗tolen 塩alt mixed with malt...

盗obbery　盗tealing

皿 (plate)

nusu(mu), TŌ
robbery, stealing, theft, looting, burglary, heist, larceny

FLIP: 4.0.a. Bottom (flat)

盗み　stealing, theft, robbery **nusumi**
盗み出す　stealing, theft, robbery **nusumidasu**
盗み聞き　eavesdropping, wiretapping **nusumigiki**
盗み見る　looking on private matters **nusumimiru**
盗み読み　reading someone's letter **nusumiyomi**
盗心　kleptomaniac **nusumigokoro, tōshin**
強盗　theft, robbery, burglary **gōtō**
⇒銀行強盗　bank robbery, ~heist **ginkō gōtō**
重盗　double steal (baseball) **jūtō**
怪盗　phantom thief **kaitō**
盗人　thief, burglar, robber **nusubito, nusutto**
窃盗　theft, thief **settō**
窃盗犯　thief, robbery crime **settōhan**
窃盗罪　theft, larceny **settōzai**
⇒現行窃盗罪　open theft **genkō settōzai**
盗聴　wire-tapping, bugging **tōchō**
盗聴器　wiretap device **tōchōki**
盗癖　kleptomaniac **tōheki**
盗品　stolen goods **tōhin**

盗掘　illegal diggings **tōkutsu**
盗難　theft, robbery, burglary **tōnan**
盗難品　stolen goods **tōnanhin**
盗難届け　robbery report **tōnan todoke**
盗難事件　case of theft, ~robbery **tōnan jiken**
盗塁　stolen base (baseball) **tōrui**
盗作　plagiarism, literary theft **tōsaku**
盗犯　thief, robbery crime **tōhan**
盗用　plagiarism, literary theft **tōyō**
盗賊　thief, burglar, robber **tōzoku**
夜盗　night thief **yatō**

罪riminal, 289	凶vil, 80
犯riminal, 640	邪vil, 58
悪vil, 389	侵iolate, 769

盛lourishment, 244

523-B
盗tolen 塩alt mixed with malt...

塩alt　塩aline

土 (ground, soil)

shio, EN
salt, saline

FLIP: 4.0.a. Bottom (flat)

塩梅　seasoning; circumstances **anbai**
塩分　base salinity **enbun**
塩田　salt field, ~paddy **enden**
塩害　salt water-damaged~ **engai**
塩化　chlorination **enka**
塩基　base salinity **enki**
塩基性　base, basicity **enkisei**
塩酸　muriatic acid **ensan**
塩素　chlorine **enso**
塩水　salt water **ensui**
苦塩　brine **nigashio, nigari**
製塩　salt making **seien**
製塩所　salt factory **seienjo**
塩味　saltiness, salty taste **shioaji**
塩辛　salty & spicy **shiokara**
塩気　saltiness, salty taste **shioke**
塩水　salt water **shiomizu, ensui**
塩鮭　salted salmon **shiozake**
食塩　table salt **shokuen**

低塩　low-salt **teien**
手塩　"with great care..." **teshio**
塩出し　soaking with salt **shiodashi**
塩焼き　grilled salted fish **shioyaki**
塩漬け　salted food **shiozuke**
胡麻塩　toasted sesame; greyish hair **gomashio**
硫酸塩　sulphate **ryūsan'en**
塩加減　seasoning, flavouring **shiokagen**
硝酸塩　nitrate **shōsan'en**
炭酸塩　carbonate **tansan'en**
天然塩　natural salt **tennen'en**

海cean, 241	味aste, 871
洋cean, 247	

盗obbery, 621

524-A

益rofit & 益enefit from sale of 温arm outfits...

益enefit　　**益rofit**

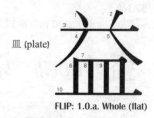

皿 (plate)

FLIP: 1.0.a. Whole (flat)

EKI, YAKU
benefit, profit, gains, returns, yields, plus

便益 one's convenience **ben'eki**
益鳥 beneficial bird **ekichō**
益虫 beneficial insect **ekichū**
益金 profit, gain, advantage **ekikin**
減益 profit reduction **gen'eki**
裨益 benefit, gain, advantage **hieki**
実益 net profit, utility, benefit **jitsueki**
純益 net earnings, pure profits **jun'eki**
公益 public interest, ~welfare **kōeki**
国益 national interest **kokueki**
益々 even more, greatly **masumasu**
無益 useless, futile, empty **mueki**
年益 annual profit **nen'eki**
利益 profit, gain, benefit **rieki**
⇒不利益 without profit **furieki**
利益配当 profit distribution **rieki haitō**
差益 profit margin **saeki**
私益 personal gain, ~interest **shieki**
収益 profit, earnings **shūeki**

収益金 earnings, yields, profits **shūekikin**
収益率 earning rate, rate of returns **shūekiritsu**
総益 gross profit **sōeki**
損益 profit & loss, loss & gain **son'eki**
損益分岐点 break-even margin **son'eki bunkiten**
用益 use & benefit, usufruct **yōeki**
用益権 usufruct **yōekiken**
有益 useful, helpful, instructive **yūeki**
増益 profit increase **zōeki**
受益者 beneficiary, receiving end **juekisha**
既得権益 vested interests **kitoku ken'eki**

得rofit, 940　進rogress, 51	便onvenience, 480
利rofit, 686　展rogress, 522	宜onvenience, 500

盗obbery, 621

524-B

益rofit & 益enefit from sale of 温arm outfits...

温ot temperature　　**温hermal**

水⇔氵 (water)

FLIP: 7.0.a. Right (flat)

atata(kai), atata(ka), atata(maru), atata(meru), ON
hot temperature, thermal, warm

温もり warmth **nukumori**
温々 comfortably warm, snug; brazen **nukunuku**
保温 heating, keeping warm **hoon**
常温 normal temperature **jōon**
検温 body temperature taking **ken'on**
気温 weather temperature **kion**
高温 high temperature **kōon**
温暖 warm, mild **ondan**
温度 temperature (degrees) **ondo**
⇒臨界温度 critical temperature **rinkai ondo**
温度計 thermometer **ondokei**
温情 sympathy, empathy, compassion **onjō**
温順 docile, meek, compliant **onjun**
温厚 gentle, mild-mannered **onkō**
温泉 hot springs, spa **onsen**
温室 greenhouse **onshitsu**
温床 hotbed **onshō**
温水 warm water **onsui**
温水プール heated swimming pool **onsui pūru**

温和 mild, temperate **onwa**
温存 preservation, retention **onzon**
室温 room temperature **shitsuon**
水温 water temperature **suion**
体温 temperature **taion**
体温計 clinical thermometer **taionkei**
低温 low temperature **teion**
適温 suitable temperature **tekion**
温湿布 hot compress **onshippu**
三寒四温 cycle of three cold & four warm days **sankan shion**
温故知新 learning from the past **onko chishin**

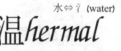

暑ot weather, 615	熱eat, 153
湯ot-water, 932	暖armth, 821

湿amp, 931

525-A

看 *ook-after the* 盲 *lind walking behind...*

目 (eyesight, visual)

看*ook after*   看*ursing*

FLIP: 4.0.a. Bottom (flat)

mi(ru), KAN
look-after, nursing, caring, watch for

准看 *pre-nurse, sub-nurse* **junkan**
看板 *sign, billboard* **kanban**
⇒表看板 *billboard in front (store)* **omote kanban**
⇒一枚看板 *one's only suit* **ichimai kanban**
⇒立て看板 *standing billboard* **tatekanban**
看板娘 *showcase girl* **kanban musume**
看板屋 *billboard painter* **kanbanya**
看病 *nursing, caring* **kanbyō**
看病疲れ *nurse's fatigue* **kanbyō tsukare**
看護 *nursing, care* **kango**
看護婦 *female nurse* **kangofu**
看護兵 *medic, military nurse* **kangohei**
看護人 *male nurse* **kangonin**
看護士 *male nurse* **kangoshi**
看護師 *male-or-female nurse* **kangoshi**
看護婦長 *head nurse, matron* **kango fuchō**
看過 *overlooking a mistake* **kanka**
看破 *penetrating, translucent* **kanpa**

看視 *watching, looking out* **kanshi**
看守 *guard, jailer, gaoler* **kanshu**
看取 *perceive, detect* **kanshu**
金看板 *gold-coloured signboard* **kinkanban**
看做す *consider as, regard as* **minasu**
看取る① *nurse, tend, care* **mitoru**
看取る② *dying in peace with family at one's*
　 side **mitoru**

臨*ttend, 902*	患*ickness, 475*
供*ook-after, 303*	症*ickness, 788*
護*rotect, 828*	病*ickness, 213*

盲*lind, 623*

525-B

看 *ook-after the* 盲 *lind walking behind...*

目 (eyesight, visual)

盲*lind*   盲*ightless*

FLIP: 4.0.a. Bottom (flat)

mekura, me(shii), MŌ
blind, sightless

文盲 *illiteracy, "no-read no-write..."* **bunmō, monmō**
群盲 *blind masses, illiterate masses* **gunmō**
盲穴 *blind spot, blind hole* **mekuraana**
盲判 *blind endorsement* **mekuraban**
盲買 *buying w/o seeing the merchandize* **mekuragai**
盲唖 *blind & mute* **mōa**
盲愛 *blind love, infatuation* **mōai**
盲爆 *carpet bombing* **mōbaku**
盲腸 *appendix, cecum* **mōchō**
盲腸炎 *appendicitis* **mōchōen**
盲断 *blind judgement* **mōdan**
盲動 *act blindly* **mōdō**
盲人 *blind person* **mōjin**
盲従 *blind obedience* **mōjū**
盲管 *cul-de-sac* **mōkan**
盲目 *blindness* **mōmoku**
盲信 *blind belief, ~obedience* **mōshin**
盲進 *blind advance, ~attack* **mōshin**
盲想 *wild ideas, weird thinking* **mōsō**

盲点 *blind spot, scotoma* **mōten**
雪盲 *snowblindness* **setsumō**
色盲 *colour blindness* **shikimō**
全盲 *total blindness* **zenmō**
明き盲 *illiterate, unschooled* **akimekura**
盲打ち *hitting blindly* **mekurauchi**
盲撃ち *trigger-happy* **mekurauchi**
盲導犬 *seeing-eye dog* **mōdōken**
盲学校 *school for the blind* **mōgakkō**
夜盲症 *night blindness* **yamōshō**

黒*lack, 320*	眼*yesight, 771*
暗*ark, 315*	目*ye, 462*

看*ook after, 623*

526-A

査nspection map for 畳:atami-mats already 畳:olded-up...

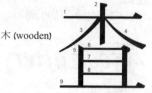

木 (wooden)

査nspection 査heck

SA

inspection, check, review, scrutiny, inquest, probe, look into

FLIP: 1.0.a. Whole (flat)

調査 *investigation, inquiry, research* **chōsa**
⇒秘密調査 *secret investigation* **himitsu chōsa**
⇒世論調査 *poll survey* **yoron chōsa**
巡査 *police officer, cop, constable* **junsa**
監査 *inspection, audit* **kansa**
⇒会計監査 *auditing, books inspection* **kaikei kansa**
検査 *inspection, examination* **kensa**
⇒尿検査 *urinalysis, urine analysis* **nyōkensa**
⇒血液検査 *blood test* **ketsueki kensa**
検査役 *inspector, examiner* **kensayaku**
考査 *examination, inspection* **kōsa**
査閲 *inspection, investigation* **saetsu**
査問 *inquiry, inquisition, hearing* **samon**
査察 *inspection, investigation* **sasatsu**
査証 *visa, permission to disembark* **sashō**
査収 *checking & receiving* **sashū**
査定 *assessment, revision* **satei**
査定額 *assessed value, appraised worth* **sateigaku**
精査 *detailed examination* **seisa**

審査 *examination, inspection* **shinsa**
審査員 *judge, juror, jury member* **shinsain**
照査 *verification, confirmation* **shōsa**
主査 *chief detective* **shusa**
走査 *scanning, going over* **sōsa**
捜査 *search, investigation* **sōsa**
捜査員 *detective, investigator* **sōsain**
捜査令状 *search warrant* **sōsa reijō**
探査 *investigation, inquiry, probe* **tansa**
踏査 *field survey, ocular inspection* **tōsa**

察nspection, 328	検nspection, 939
審nspection, 339	閲nspection, 942
調nspection, 280	

者erson, 278

526-B

査nspection map for 畳:atami-mats already 畳:olded-up...

田 (cultivated field)

畳atami 畳old up

tatami, tata(mu), JŌ

tatami floormat, fold up

FLIP: 1.0.a. Whole (flat)

畳む *keep, close, fold* **tatamu**
畳み込む *bear, fold, stand, endure* **tatamikomu**
青畳 *fresh-, new tatami mat* **aodatami**
重畳 *piled-up after another* **chōjō**
半畳 *half-size tatami mat* **hanjō**
一畳 *one tatami mat* **ichijō**
石畳 *stone pavement* **ishidatami**
畳語 *repetitive wording, verbose* **jōgo**
畳表 *tatami front face* **tatami omote**
畳針 *tatami needle* **tatamibari**
畳目 *tatami mesh* **tatamime**
畳屋 *tatami maker (straw mat)* **tatamiya**
畳替え *replacing old with new tatami* **tatamigae**
畳水練 *"armchair learning..."* **tatami suiren**
折り畳む *fold, double* **oritatamu**
折り畳み式 *foldable, collapsible* **oritatamishiki**
畳み掛ける *press, urge, plead* **tatami kakeru**

床loor, 633	宜onvenience, 500
便onvenience, 480	

宜onvenience, 500

527-A

負*wing* 負*efeat,* 貢*ributes paid complete...*

負*efeat*　　負*we*

貝 (shell, old money)

FLIP: 4.0.b. Bottom (stem)

ma(keru), ma(kasu), o(u), FU
defeat, owe, burden, obligated, bear with

負号	minus, negative sign **fugō**
負荷	load, cargo **fuka**
負極	negative pole **fukyoku**
負量	negative amount **furyō**
負債	debts, liabilities, loans **fusai**
負債者	debtor, borrower, lender **fusaisha**
負傷	injury, hurt, wound **fushō**
負傷者	wounded person, injured party **fushōsha**
負数	negative number **fusū**
負託	mandate, trust **futaku**
負担	burden, load **futan**
抱負	ambition, aspiration **hōfu**
自負	flatter oneself, take pride in **jifu**
負革	sling, strap (rifle) **oikawa**
正負	plus & minus **seifu**
勝負	contest, victory-or-defeat **shōbu**
請負	contracting, outsourcing **ukeoi**
負け犬	defeated, loser, beaten **makeinu**
負け色	signs of defeat **makeiro**

根負け	endurance limit **konmake**
負け星	mark of a loss **makeboshi**
負い目	indebtedness, obligation **oime**
大負け	crushing defeat **oomake**
手負い	wounded, injured **teoi**
判定負け	lose by split decision **hanteimake**
勝ち負け	victory-or-defeat, at issue **kachimake**
負け嫌い	unrelenting, unyielding **makegirai**
負けじ魂	"never give-up spirit..." **makeji damashii**
負け越し	more losses than wins **makekoshi**
請け負う	contract, undertake **ukeō**

敗*efeat*, 137	失*issing*, 19
失*ailure*, 19	欠*issing*, 460

貝*ember*, 410

527-B

負*wing* 負*efeat,* 貢*ributes paid complete...*

貢*upport*　　貢*ribute*

貝 (shell, old money)

FLIP: 1.0.b. Whole (stem)

mitsu(gu), KŌ, KU
support, tribute, aide, contribution, backing, help

朝貢	imperial court tribute **chōkō**
朝貢国	tributary nation **chōkōkoku**
貢調	payment of tribute **kōchō**
貢腑	tribute & taxes **kōfu**
貢献	contribution, services **kōken**
貢進	payment of tribute **kōshin**
貢租	tribute, levy **kōso**
貢物	tribute, levy **mitsugimono**
年貢	annual tribute **nengu**
年貢米	yearly rice in lieu of tax **nengumai**
入貢	payment of tribute **nyūkō**
進貢	payment of tribute **shinkō**

援*upport*, 820	協*ooperate*, 577
支*upport*, 201	擁*upport*, 151
助*upport*, 953	

貝*ember*, 410

528-A

費*pending on Earth's* 資*esources to protect* 質*ature's forces...*

貝 (shell, old money)

費*pending*   費*xpenditure*

FLIP: 4.0.b. Bottom (stem)

tsui(yasu), tsui(eru), HI
spending, expenditure, expense

学費	*school expenses*	**gakuhi**
費目	*itemized expenses*	**himoku**
費消	*spending, using up*	**hishō**
費用	*cost, expenses*	**hiyō**
実費	*expenses incurred*	**jippi**
会費	*membership dues*	**kaihi**
官費	*government expense*	**kanpi**
経費	*expenses, upkeep*	**keihi**
国費	*public expenditure*	**kokuhi**
空費	*wasting money, squandering*	**kūhi**
巨費	*grossly expensive, prohibitive cost*	**kyohi**
燃費	*fuel efficiency*	**nenpi**
乱費	*wasteful spending*	**ranpi**
浪費	*waste, extravagance*	**rōhi**
歳費	*annual expenditure*	**saihi**
戦費	*war expenditure*	**senpi**
私費	*own expenses, paying for oneself*	**shihi**
失費	*unforeseen-, unexpected expenses*	**shippi**
消費	*consumption, using, availing*	**shōhi**

消費税	*consumption tax, sales tax*	**shōhizei**
食費	*food expenses*	**shokuhi**
出費	*expenses, disbursements*	**shuppi**
雑費	*miscellaneous expense*	**zappi**
営業費	*operating expenses*	**eigyōhi**
維持費	*upkeep-, maintenance cost*	**ijihi**
育児費	*child-care expenses*	**ikujihi**
研究費	*research funds*	**kenkyūhi**
生活費	*living expenses, cost of living*	**seikatsuhi**
運営費	*operational cost*	**un'eihi**
養育費	*child-rearing expenses*	**yōikuhi**

賃*ayment, 145*	払*ayment, 682*
納*ayment, 296*	料*ayment, 194*

質*ature, 627*

528-B

費*pending on Earth's* 資*esources to protect* 質*ature's forces...*

貝 (shell, old money)

資*esources   資herewithal*

FLIP: 4.0.b. Bottom (stem)

SHI
resources, wherewithal

米資	*US capital*	**beishi**
物資	*goods, supplies, materials*	**busshi**
英資	*fine character*	**eishi**
外資	*foreign capital*	**gaishi**
学資	*school expenses, ~fees*	**gakushi**
減資	*capital decrease, ~reduction*	**genshi**
合資	*joint stocks*	**gōshi**
軍資	*military funds, war chest*	**gunshi**
軍資金	*war chest, war funds*	**gunshikin**
放資	*investment, seed money*	**hōshi**
労資	*capital & labour*	**rōshi**
資源	*resources*	**shigen**
資本	*capital, financial investment*	**shihon**
資本金	*capital, investment money*	**shihonkin**
資本主義	*capitalism, capitalist ideology*	**shihon shugi**
資格	*qualification, competence*	**shikaku**
資金	*fund, money, finance*	**shikin**
⇒育英資金	*scholarship*	**ikuei shikin**
資料	*materials, data, relevant papers*	**shiryō**

資力	*financial means, ~strength*	**shiryoku**
資産	*property, fortune, assets, wealth*	**shisan**
師資	*asking for tutorial lesson*	**shishi**
資質	*nature, disposition*	**shishitsu**
資材	*materials, ingredients*	**shizai**
出資	*financing, investment*	**shusshi**
天資	*nature, talent*	**tenshi**
投資	*investment, capital*	**tōshi**
⇒海外投資	*foreign investment*	**kaigai tōshi**
融資	*loan, finance*	**yūshi**
増資	*capital increase*	**zōshi**

材*aterials, 186*	金*oney, 25*
料*aterials, 194*	財*inance, 186*

質*ature, 627*

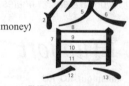

528-C

費*pending on Earth's* 資*esources to protect* 質*ature's forces...*

貝 (shell, old money)

❶質*ature* **❷質***ostage*

SHITSU, SHICHI
nature, quality, matter, substance; hostage, pawn shop, captive

FLIP: 4.0.b. Bottom (stem)

❶ 美質 *good quality, virtue* **bishitsu**
物質 *substance, matter* **busshitsu**
土質 *soil nature* **doshitsu**
同質 *homogeneous, same quality* **dōshitsu**
品質 *product quality* **hinshitsu**
本質 *essence, reality* **honshitsu**
異質 *heterogeneous* **ishitsu**
実質 *substance, matter,* **jisshitsu**
均質 *homogeneous* **kinshitsu**
硬質 *hardness, solidness* **kōshitsu**
音質 *sound quality* **onshitsu**
良質 *good quality* **ryōshitsu**
性質 *nature, character* **seishitsu**
紙質 *paper quality* **shishitsu**
資質 *nature, disposition* **shishitsu**
質素 *frugal, plain, simple* **shisso**
質朴 *plain & simple* **shitsuboku**
質疑 *interrogation, interpellation* **shitsugi**
質感 *feel of the material* **shitsukan**

質問 *question, inquiry* **shitsumon**
質問書 *questionnaire sheet* **shitsumonsho**
質量 *mass, quality & quantity* **shitsuryō**
質的 *qualitative* **shitsuteki**
素質 *quality, makings, talent* **soshitsu**
対質 *interrogation, cross-examination* **taishitsu**
体質 *physique, build, body frame* **taishitsu**
材質 *quality of materials used* **zaishitsu**
繊維質 *fibres* **sen'ishitsu**
神経質 *nervousness, sensitivity* **shinkeishitsu**
❷ 人質 *hostage, kidnap victim* **hitojichi**
質屋 *pawnshop, pawnbroker* **shichiya**
質流れ *forfeited pawned item* **shichinagare**

性*ature, 474*	捕*atch, 812*
然*ature, 445*	囚*risoner, 863*

貿*arter, 128*

529-A

蛮*arbarians steal* 蚕*ilkworm but* 蛍*ireflies conform...*

虫 (insect)

蛮*arbarian* **蛮***avage*

BAN
barbarian, savage, boorish

Facing: 3.0. ☞ ☜ Across

蛮カラ *unrefined-, ill-mannered* **bankara**
蛮地 *barbaric lands* **banchi**
蛮風 *barbarous, savage ways* **banfū**
蛮語 *barbarian language, foul mouth* **bango**
蛮人 *barbarian* **banjin**
蛮行 *brutality, barbarous acts* **bankō**
蛮骨 *brute courage* **bankotsu**
蛮境 *barbarian turf* **bankyō**
蛮民 *barbaric people* **banmin**
蛮力 *brute force* **banryoku**
蛮声 *coarse tone, ~voice* **bansei**
蛮習 *barbaric customs* **banshū**
蛮勇 *recklessness, brute force* **banyū**
蛮族 *savage tribe* **banzoku**
南蛮 *southern barbarians* **nanban**
南蛮人 *southern barbarians* **nanbanjin**
野蛮 *barbaric, savage* **yaban**
野蛮人 *barbaric, savage foreigners* **yabanjin**

激*ierce, 170*	虐*ruelty, 870*
猛*ierce, 657*	酷*ruelty, 266*
烈*ierce, 585*	族*ribe, 649*
獣*east, 846*	

蛍*irefly, 628*

529-B

蚕*arbarians steal* 蚕*ilkworm, but* 蛍*ireflies conform...*

虫 (insect)

蚕*ilkworm*

kaiko, ko, SAN
silkworm

FLIP: 2.0.a. Sort Of (flat)
FLIP: 3.0.b. Top (stem)

春蚕	spring silkworm	**harugo**
蚕飼	silkworm raising	**kogai**
蚕業	silkworm cultivation	**sangyō**
蚕児	silkworm	**sanji**
蚕卵	silkworm egg	**sanran**
蚕糸	silk thread	**sanshi**
蚕紙	silkworms eggs paper	**sanshi**
蚕室	silkworm-breeding room	**sanshitsu**
蚕食	encroachment, inroads	**sanshoku**
蚕種	silkworm egg	**sanshu**
蚕豆	fava bean	**santō, soramame**
秋蚕	autumn silkworm	**shūsan**
養蚕	sericulture, silkworm cultivation	**yōsan**
蚕卵紙	silkworm-egg paper	**sanranshi**
天蚕糸	silken gut fishing lines	**tensanshi**
蚕糸業	silk reeling industry	**sanshigyō**
養蚕業	silkworm-breeding industry	**yōsangyō**
養蚕地	silkworm-breeding region	**yōsanchi**

絹*ilk, 158*
羅*hin silk, 563*

蛮*arbarian, 627*

529-C

蚕*arbarians steal* 蚕*ilkworm, but* 蛍*ireflies conform...*

虫 (insect)

蛍*irefly*

hotaru, KEI
firefly

FLIP: 2.0.a. Sort Of (flat)

蛍袋	bellflower	**hotaru bukuro**
蛍火	glow of a firefly	**hotarubi**
蛍石	luminous stone	**hotaruishi, keiseki**
蛍火	firefly slow	**keika**
蛍光	fluorescence	**keikō**
蛍光灯	fluorescent light, ~lamp	**keikōtō**
蛍光塗料	luminous paint	**keikō toryō**
土蛍	glow worm	**tsuchibotaru**
蛍狩り	firefly-catching	**hotarugari**
蛍烏賊	luminous squid	**hotaruika**
蛍雪の功	fruits of diligent study	**keisetsu no kō**

蚊*osquito, 654*	明*right, 22*
昆*nsect, 38*	英*rilliance, 217*
虫*nsect, 369*	光*hining, 77*
昭*right, 529*	輝*parkling, 296*

堂*ltar, 94*

530-A

装*earing rice* 袋*acks,* 襲*ttackers stole rice crackers...*

衣⇔ネ (clothing)

❶装*ear*　❷装*retend*

yosoo(u), SŌ, SHŌ
wear, dress, fit out; pretend

FLIP: 7.2.a. Right Top (flat)

❶武装 armaments **busō**
服装 dress, attire **fukusō**
軍装 military equipment **gunsō**
包装 wrapping, packaging **hōsō**
舗装 surfacing, pavement **hosō**
衣装 costume, wardrobe, attire **ishō**
改装 remodel, renovate **kaisō**
革装 leather-covered **kawasō**
礼装 full dress, gala attire **reisō**
略装 informal clothes, daily wear **ryakusō**
旅装 travelling outfit **ryosō**
盛装 gala attire **seisō**
正装 formal dress, ~attire **seisō**
新装 refurbishing, redecoration **shinsō**
装束 costume, dress **shōzoku**
装備 equipment, implements **sōbi**
装置 device, apparatus **sōchi**
装弾 loading up bullets **sōdan**
装具 outfit, fittings, equipment **sōgu**

装甲 armour **sōkō**
装飾 decoration, ornament **sōshoku**
装丁 cover design, binding **sōtei**
装填 loading, changing **sōten**
塗装 paint, coating **tosō**
和装 Japanese clothes, kimono **wasō**
洋装 Western clothes **yōsō**
❷男装 disguise as a male **dansō**
偽装 fake, phoney, imitation **gisō**
変装 disguise, impostor **hensō**
仮装 disguise clothes **kasō**

履ut-on, 442	擬mitation, 56
着ear, 589	倣mitation, 486
履ear, 442	

袋ack, 629

530-B

装*earing rice* 袋*acks,* 襲*ttackers stole rice crackers...*

衣⇔ネ (clothing)

袋*ack*　袋*ushel*

fukuro, TAI
sack, bag, bushel

Facing: 2.1. East ☞ (H)

網袋 net bag **amibukuro**
茶袋 tea bag **chabukuro**
段袋 large sack **danbukuro**
餌袋 crop, gizzard **esabukuro**
袋帯 double-sewn obi **fukuro obi**
袋網 bag net **fukuroami**
袋耳 retentive memory **fukuromimi**
袋物 bags, sacks & pouches **fukuromono**
風袋 packing, packaging **fūtai**
⇒慣習風袋 customary tare **kanshū fūtai**
蛍袋 bellflower **hotarubukuro**
布袋 pot-bellied god of wealth **hotei**
胃袋 stomach, craw **ibukuro**
状袋 letter envelope **jōbukuro**
紙袋 paper bag **kamibukuro**
革袋 leather bag **kawabukuro**
氷袋 ice bag **kooribukuro**
寝袋 sleeping bag **nebukuro**
製袋 bag making **seitai**

砂袋 sandbag **sunabukuro**
足袋 kimono socks **tabi**
手袋 hand gloves **tebukuro**
天袋 storage above closet **tenbukuro**
戸袋 shutter box **tobukuro**
郵袋 postal sack **yūtai**
袋小路 dead end, blind alley **fukuro kōji**
袋叩き gang up & beat up **fukurodataki**
袋縫い double sewing **fukuronui**
袋織り double knitting **fukuroori**
浮き袋 life buoy, float **ukibukuro**

俵ack, 378	穂rains, 545
穀rains, 41	粒rains, 656

装retend, 629

530-C

装earing rice 袋acks, 襲ttackers stole rice crackers...

衣⇔ネ (clothing)

襲ttack   襲ssault

FLIP: 6.1. Left Top

oso(u), SHŪ
attack, assault, offence, charging, strike, storming, raiding

襲い掛かる	attack, jump, pounce on **osoikakaru**
珍襲	treasured item **chinshū**
逆襲	counterattack, retort **gyakushū**
因襲	convention, customs **inshū**
奇襲	surprise-, sudden attack **kishū**
空襲	air raid, aerial attack **kūshū**
強襲	fierce attack **kyōshū**
急襲	sudden attack **kyūshū**
猛襲	fierce attack **mōshū**
来襲	assault, attack **raishū**
世襲	hereditary, genetic **seshū**
世襲財産	inherited estate **seshū zaisan**
襲撃	attack, assault, raid **shūgeki**
襲衣	wear clothes over another **shūi**
襲名	name succession **shūmei**
襲来	attack, invasion, raid **shūrai**
襲用	follow, adopt **shūyō**
敵襲	enemy attack **tekishū**
踏襲	observing old tradition **tōshū**

夜襲 night raid, ~assault **yashū**

責 ondemn, 115	討 ttack, 691
撃 ttack, 613	伐 ttack, 96
攻 ttack, 635	打 trike, 636

袋 ack 629

531-A

笛lute 笛histled with grace 届eliver 届otice to 宙uterspace...

竹 (bamboo)

笛lute   笛histle

FLIP: 4.0.a. Bottom (flat)

fue, TEKI
flute, whistle

葦笛	reed whistle **ashibue**
牧笛	shepherd's flute **bokuteki**
銀笛	flageolet **ginteki**
号笛	horn, whistle, siren **gōteki**
警笛	alarm whistle **keiteki**
汽笛	steam whistle, siren **kiteki**
鼓笛	drums & fifes **koteki**
鼓笛隊	drum & fife band **kotekitai**
口笛	whistle **kuchibue**
草笛	leaf flute **kusabue**
牧笛	shepherd's flute **makibue**
魔笛	magic flute **mateki**
麦笛	oaten flute **mugibue**
霧笛	foghorn **muteki**
喉笛	wind flute **nodobue**
柴笛	young leaf flute **shibabue**
縦笛	recorder, upright flute **tatebue**
笛声	flute-, whistling sound **tekisei**
角笛	horn, bugle **tsunobue**

横笛	flute, fife **yokobue**
指笛	finger-whistling **yubibue**
笛吹き	flute piper **fuefuki**
虎落笛	winter wind thru the fence **mogaribue**

風 ind, 894	曲 elody, 476
息 reathe, 586	音 ound, 314

宙 elestial, 631

531-B

笛*lute* 笛*histled with grace* 届*eliver* 届*otice to* 宙*uterspace...*

届*otice*   届*eliver*

尸 (corpse)

todo(ku), todo(keru)
notice, deliver, arrive

FLIP: 4.0.a. Bottom (flat)

無届 *without notice* **mutodoke**
届出 *official notice, written report* **todokede**
届書 *official notice, written report* **todokesho**
遅刻届 *tardiness report* **chikoku todoke**
紛失届 *report of lost article* **funshitsu todoke**
不届き *outrageous, insolent, rude* **futodoki**
欠勤届 *report of absences* **kekkin todoke**
未届け *failure to report* **mitodoke**
離婚届 *divorce application, ~notice* **rikon todoke**
死亡届 *report of death* **shibō todoke**
出産届 *birth registration* **shussan todoke**
退学届 *school expulsion notice* **taigaku todoke**
退会届 *withdrawal notice* **taikai todoke**
届け出 *notification; arrival* **todokede**
届け出る *hand over, notify, report* **todokederu**
届け物 *delivered goods* **todokemono**
届け先 *receivers address* **todokesaki**
結婚届け *report of marriage* **kekkon todoke**
欠席届け *report of absences* **kesseki todoke**

寄留届け *report of temporary stay* **kiryū todoke**
婚姻届け *marriage registration* **kon'in todoke**
出生届け *report of birth* **shussei todoke**
盗難届け *burglary report* **tōnan todoke**
付け届け *tip; bribe, grease money* **tsuketodoke**
行き届く *attentive, mindful, observant*
  yukitodoku
聞き届ける *grant, conform, adhere* **kikitodokeru**
送り届ける *take, send, deliver* **okuri todokeru**
不行き届き *remiss, negligent* **fuyukitodoki**

送*ending, 708*	来*rrive, 871*
着*rrive, 589*	告*nnounce, 266*
到*rrive, 496*	伝*onvey, 619*

届*xist, 384*

531-C

笛*lute* 笛*histled with grace* 届*eliver* 届*otice to* 宙*uterspace...*

宀 (cover, lid)

宙*elestial*   宙*uter space*

CHŪ
celestial, outer space, mid-air, cosmos, deep space, extra-terrestrial, universe, galaxy

FLIP: 1.0.a. Whole (flat)

航宙 *space flight* **kōchū**
小宇宙 *microcosm, infinitesimal* **shōuchū**
宙返り *somersault, loop-the-loop* **chūgaeri**
宙乗り *aerial stunts* **chūnori**
宙吊り *dangling in mid-air* **chūzuri**
大宇宙 *the great universe* **daiuchū**
宇宙 *outer space, celestial bodies* **uchū**
宇宙学 *astronomy, cosmology* **uchūgaku**
宇宙塵 *cosmic dust* **uchūjin**
宇宙人 *extra-terrestrial aliens* **uchūjin**
宇宙論 *cosmology* **uchūron**
宇宙線 *cosmic rays* **uchūsen**
宇宙船 *spaceship* **uchūsen**
宇宙中継 *satellite broadcast* **uchū chūkei**
宇宙衛星 *space satellite* **uchū eisei**
宇宙飛行 *space flight* **uchū hikō**
宇宙飛行士 *astronaut, cosmonaut* **uchū hikōshi**
宇宙科学 *space science* **uchū kagaku**
宇宙科学者 *space scientist* **uchū kagakusha**

宇宙空間 *outer space, celestial bodies*
  uchū kūkan
宇宙遊泳 *space walk* **uchū yūei**
宇宙ロケット *space rocket* **uchū roketto**

宇*elestial, 81*	天*eaven, 83*
星*tars, 113*	空*ky, 394*

再*epeat, 225*

532-A

Volcanic 圧*ressure spews* 灰*shes to the bushes...*

土 (ground, soil)

圧*ressure*　圧*orce*

FLIP: 8.0.a. Inner (flat)

ATSU
pressure, force, energy

圧巻 *highlight, focal point, key point* **akkan**
圧迫 *pressure, oppression* **appaku**
圧砕 *crushing* **assai**
圧搾 *compression* **assaku**
圧制 *oppression, tyranny* **assei**
圧死 *crushed to death* **asshi**
圧勝 *landslide victory* **asshō**
圧縮 *compression* **asshuku**
圧力 *pressure, compelling force* **atsuryoku**
鎮圧 *suppression, repression* **chin'atsu**
弾圧 *suppression, oppression* **dan'atsu**
電圧 *voltage, electric pressure* **den'atsu**
風圧 *wind pressure* **fūatsu**
外圧 *external pressure* **gaiatsu**
変圧 *transformation* **hen'atsu**
威圧 *coercion, compulsion* **iatsu**
血圧 *blood pressure* **ketsuatsu**
気圧 *atmosphere pressure* **kiatsu**

⇒蒸気圧 *steam pressure* **jōkiatsu**
内圧 *internal pressure* **naiatsu**
制圧 *ascendancy, supremacy* **seiatsu**
指圧 *finger pressure massage* **shiatsu**
水圧 *water-, hydraulic pressure* **suiatsu**
耐圧 *pressure resistance* **taiatsu**
抑圧 *oppression, suppression* **yokuatsu**
油圧 *oil pressure, hydraulic pressure* **yuatsu**
圧倒的 *overwhelming, overriding* **attōteki**
浸透圧 *osmotic pressure* **shintōatsu**
低気圧 *atmospheric depression* **teikiatsu**
等圧線 *isobar* **tōatsusen**

吸*uction, 190*
力*orce, 351*

灰*shes, 632*

532-B

Volcanic 圧*ressure spews* 灰*shes to the bushes...*

火⇔灬 (fire)

灰*shes*　灰*inders*

FLIP: 8.0.b. Inner (stem)

hai, KAI
ashes, cinders

灰汁 *lye, harshness* **aku**
灰篩 *ash sifter* **haifurui**
灰殻 *ashes* **haigara**
灰色 *grey* **haiiro**
灰色っぽい *greyish* **haiiroppoi**
灰落とし *ashtray* **haiotoshi**
灰皿 *ashtray* **haizara**
重灰 *thick, heavy ashes* **jūkai**
灰分 *ashes content* **kaibun**
灰燼 *ashes* **kaijin**
灰塵 *dust & ashes* **kaijin**
灰滅 *burn up, be ruined* **kaimetsu**
木灰 *burnt charcoals* **kibai**
骨灰① *dead bone ashes* **kobbai, kokkai**
骨灰② *breaking into bone powder* **koppai, kotsubai**
石灰 *lime, quicklime* **sekkai**
石灰岩 *limestone* **sekkaigan**
石灰水 *limewater* **sekkaisui**
死灰 *cremated ashes* **shikai**

藁灰 *straw ash* **warabai**
凝灰岩 *tuff* **gyōkaigan**
灰神楽 *cloud of ashes* **haikagura**
灰受け *ashtray* **haiuke**
灰白色 *light grey* **kaihakushoku**
懐炉灰 *pocket-heater fuel* **kairobai**
灰緑色 *greenish grey* **kairyokushoku**
火山灰 *volcano ashes* **kazanbai**
生石灰 *lime, calcium oxide* **seisekkai**
死の灰 *radioactive fallout* **shinohai**
護摩の灰 *passenger-disguised thief* **gomanohai**

煙*moke, 644*
災*isaster, 571*
熱*eat, 153*
火*ire, 3*
葬*urial, 513*
燃*urning, 445*

炭*oal, 29*

533-A

庁*ublic-office* 床*loor with shiny colour...*

庁*ublic office*

CHŌ
public office, government agency

庁舎 *government building* **chōsha**
府庁 *urban prefectural office* **fuchō**
開庁 *inauguration of a public office* **kaichō**
官庁 *government office* **kanchō**
⇒管轄官庁 *competent authorities*
    kankatsu kanchō
官庁街 *government office district* **kanchōgai**
県庁 *prefectural government* **kenchō**
公庁 *government agency* **kōchō**
政庁 *government office* **seichō**
支庁 *prefectural branch office* **shichō**
省庁 *ministries & government offices* **shōchō**
退庁 *leaving a public office* **taichō**
都庁 *metropolitan government* **tochō**
⇒東京都庁 *Tōkyō Metropolitan Government*
    tōkyō tochō
登庁 *attendance in a public office* **tōchō**
防衛庁 *Japan Defence Agency* **bōeichō**
法王庁 *Vatican, Holy See* **hōōchō**

广 *(rooftop)*

FLIP: 8.0.b. Inner (stem)
Facing: 3.0. ☞ 🔁 Across

官公庁 *government & municipal offices*
    kankōchō
環境庁 *Environment Agency* **kankyōchō**
警視庁 *Metropolitan Police Office* **keishichō**
検察庁 *Public Prosecutor's Office*
    kensatsuchō
宮内庁 *Imperial Household Agency* **kunaichō**
林野庁 *Forestry Agency* **rinyachō**
市庁舎 *townhall office* **shichōsha**
特許庁 *Patent Office* **tokkyochō**

署*ublic-office*, 614	政*dministration*, 725
更*fficial*, 463	官*uthority*, 105
役*fficial*, 746	権*uthority*, 804

圧*ressure*, 632

533-B

庁*ublic-office* 床*loor with shiny colour...*

床*loor*   床*ed*

toko, yuka, SHŌ
floor, bed

病床 *sickbed* **byōshō**
着床 *implantation* **chakushō**
道床 *roadbed* **dōshō**
岩床 *bedrock* **ganshō**
銃床 *gunstock* **jūshō**
髪床 *barber, hairdresser* **kamidoko**
金床 *anvil* **kanadoko**
川床 *riverbed, riverfloor* **kawadoko**
起床 *getting up, rising from bed* **kishō**
鉱床 *mineral deposits* **kōshō**
苗床 *nursery, seedbed* **naedoko**
寝床 *berthing, taxiing* **nedoko**
温床 *hotbed* **onshō**
臨床 *clinical* **rinshō**
離床 *leaving one's sick bed* **rishō**
床几 *folding stool* **shōgi**
就床 *sleep, go to bed, retire* **shūshō**
床店 *stall, booth* **tokomise**
床屋 *barber, hairdresser* **tokoya**

广 *(rooftop)*

FLIP: 8.0.b. Inner (stem)

床山 *sumo hairdresser* **tokoyama**
床板 *flooring, floor board* **yukaita**
床下 *under the floor* **yukashita**
床上 *flooded, inundated, underwater* **yukaue**
床払い *leaving one's sick bed* **tokobarai**
床張り *flooring, floor space* **tokobari, yokobari**
床入り *marital consummation* **tokoiri**
床擦れ *bedsore, oversleeping pains* **tokozure**
奥床しい *graceful, elegant* **okuyukashii**
床面積 *floor space* **yukamenseki**

畳*old-up*, 624	家*ouse*, 909
歩*alk*, 272	建*onstruct*, 390
屋*ouse*, 427	

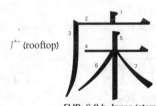

応*omply*, 469

534-A

在*xistence of* 存*nowledge leads to courage...*

在*xist*   在*taying*

a(ru), ZAI
exist, be, staying

土 (ground, soil)

FLIP: 7.3.a. Right Bottom (flat)

駐在 *residing, being posted* **chūzai**
不在 *absent, away from work* **fuzai**
外在 *omnipresence, all-present* **gaizai**
偏在 *ubiquitous, omnipresent* **henzai**
介在 *intervention, interposition* **kaizai**
健在 *alive & well, fine & healthy* **kenzai**
混在 *mixing, blending* **konzai**
内在 *inherence, dwelling in* **naizai**
潜在 *latency, potentiality* **senzai**
所在 *whereabouts, location* **shozai**
存在 *existence, presence* **sonzai**
存在理由 *reason for being, raison d'etre* **sonzai riyū**
滞在 *stay, residing* **taizai**
点在 *being dotted, scattering* **tenzai**
在学 *enrolled in school* **zaigaku**
在住 *residence, domicile* **zaijū**
在住者 *resident, dweller, house occupant* **zaijūsha**
在家 *laity, laymen* **zaike**
在勤 *being in office, working* **zaikin**

在庫 *in stock, available* **zaiko**
在庫品 *goods-in-stock, available stock* **zaikohin**
在日 *residing in Japan* **zainichi**
在籍 *enrolment, enlisting, registered* **zaiseki**
在職 *office tenure* **zaishoku**
在宅 *staying home, at home* **zaitaku**
在り処 *whereabouts, location* **arika**
在り方 *proper way, right thing to do* **arikata**
顕在化 *clarification, elucidation* **kenzaika**
変幻自在 *ever-changing* **hengen jizai**
在外邦人 *Japanese overseas residents*
    zaigai hōjin

居*xist, 384*	有*xist, 617*
据*et-in-place, 384*	現*resent, 814*

布*loth, 208*

534-B

在*xistence of* 存*nowledge leads to courage...*

❶存*xist*   ❷存*nowledge*

SON, ZON
exist; knowledge

子 (child)

Facing: 3.0. ☞☜ Across

❶厳存 *stern-, stark reality* **genson**
併存 *co-existence, "live-and-let-live..."* **heizon**
保存 *saving, preserving* **hozon**
依存 *dependence, reliance* **izon**
⇒相互依存 *interdependence* **sōgo izon**
自存 *self-existence, exist for itself* **jison**
実存 *actual existence* **jitsuzon**
既存 *already existing* **kizon**
共存 *co-existence, "live-and-let-live..."* **kyōzon**
温存 *preservation, continuity* **onzon**
生存 *existence, survival* **seizon**
⇒適者生存 *survival-of-the-fittest* **tekisha seizon**
存亡 *fate, destiny, life-or-death* **sonbō**
存廃 *retain-or-abolish* **sonpai**
存否 *existence or non-existence* **sonpi**
存立 *existence, present & existing* **sonritsu**
存在 *existence, presence, being* **sonzai**
存在理由 *reason-for-being, raison d'tre* **sonzai riyū**
存続 *continuance, lasting, permanence* **sonzoku**

残存 *remains, surviving, subsisting* **zanzon**
存分に *to the heart's content* **zonbun(ni)**
存外 *beyond expectation, unanticipated* **zongai**
存生 *existence, be alive* **zonjō**
存命 *living, survival, existing* **zonmei**
一存 *personal judgement* **ichizon**
❷異存 *objection, another opinion* **izon**
所存 *opinion, intention* **shozon**
御存じ *know, aware of* **gozonji**
存じる *think (polite)* **zonjiru**

居*xist, 384*	慮*dea, 70*
有*xist, 617*	念*dea, 182*
在*xist, 634*	意*dea, 340*
現*resent, 814*	想*dea, 524*

在*xist, 634*

535-A

功*erits to the police* 攻*ttack ended a hijack...*

功*erits*　　功*ttainment*

力 (strength, force)

isao, KŌ, KU
merits, attainment, exploits

Facing: 2.2. East ☞ (V)
FLIP: 6.0.a. Left (flat)

微功 *minor achievement* **bikō**
武功 *battle exploits, war success* **bukō**
軍功 *military exploits, gains of war* **gunkō**
偉功 *great achievement, ~exploits* **ikō**
寄功 *phenomenal success* **kikō**
功過 *merits & demerits* **kōka**
功勲 *meritorious service* **kōkun**
功名 *great achievement, ~exploits* **kōmyō**
功名心 *ambition, aspiration* **kōmyōshin**
功利 *utility, advantage, benefit* **kōri**
功利主義 *utilitarianism* **kōri shugi**
功利的 *utilitarian, practical, pragmatic* **kōriteki**
功労 *meritorious deed* **kōrō**
功績 *meritorious achievement* **kōseki**
功臣 *worthy retainer* **kōshin**
功罪 *merits & demerits* **kōzai**
功徳 *pious act, charity* **kudoku, kōtoku**
勲功 *brilliant exploits* **kunkō**
功力 *merits of piety* **kuriki, kōryoku**

年功 *length of service, seniority* **nenkō**
論功 *merit evaluation* **ronkō**
成功 *success, accomplishment* **seikō**
戦功 *military exploits, gains of war* **senkō**
竣功 *construction completion* **shunkō**
奏功 *success, accomplishment* **sōkō**
大功 *meritorious service* **taikō**
特功 *special efficacy* **tokkō**
年の功 *wisdom of age* **toshinokō**
有功 *meritorious, advantageous* **yūkō**

勝*ictory, 406*	賀*elebration, 202*
果*ruit, 287*	祝*elebration, 716*
慶*ejoice, 69*	勲*xploits, 934*

幼*hildhood,* 88

535-B

功*erits to the police* 攻*ttack ended a hijack...*

攻*ttack*　　攻*trike*

攵 (action)

se(meru), KŌ
attack, strike, assault, charging, hitting, offence, storming, raiding

Facing: 1.2. ☜ West (V)
FLIP: 6.0.a. Left (flat)

反攻 *counter attack, ~offence* **hankō**
攻防 *offence & defence* **kōbō**
攻防戦 *offensive & defensive battle* **kōbōsen**
攻撃 *attack, offence, strike* **kōgeki**
⇒総攻撃 *all-out attack, general offensive*
　　sōkōgeki
⇒波状攻撃 *attack in waves* **hajō kōgeki**
⇒側面攻撃 *flank attack* **sokumen kōgeki**
⇒毒ガス攻撃 *poison gas attack*
　　dokugasu kōgeki
攻撃力 *offensive power* **kōgekiryoku**
攻撃的 *aggressive, offensive* **kōgekiteki**
攻略 *conquest, subjugation* **kōryaku**
攻勢 *offensive, attacking* **kōsei**
攻守 *offence & defence* **kōshu**
攻伐 *subjugation, conquest* **kōbatsu**
攻囲 *siege* **kōi**
攻究 *master, study, research* **kōkyū**
猛攻 *violent attack* **mōkō**

内攻 *internal strike, "inside job..."* **naikō**
正攻法 *fair & square tactics* **seikōhō**
攻め入る *invade, penetrate* **semeiru**
攻め手 *attacker, assailant, offender* **semete**
先攻 *first strike* **senkō**
専攻 *major, specialization* **senkō**
専攻科目 *one's major, course specialization*
　　senkō kamoku
進攻 *attack, offence, strike* **shinkō**
侵攻 *invasion, conquest* **shinkō**
速攻 *swift attack, surgical strike* **sokkō**

| 撃*ttack, 613* | 討*ttack, 691* | 撲*trike, 157* |
| 襲*ttack, 630* | 伐*ttack, 96* | 打*trike, 636* |

功*erits,* 635

536-A

Better 拝*ray before* 打*triking day...*

手⇔扌 (hand, manual)

拝*rayer*　　拝*orship*

oga(mu), HAI
prayer, worship, humbly

FLIP: 7.0.b1. Right (stem)

伏し拝む *kneel & pray* **fushiogamu**
拝眉 *pleasure of meeting* **haibi**
拝聞 *listen, hear* **haibun**
拝聴 *listening, hearing* **haichō**
拝殿 *hall of worship* **haiden**
拝読 *sacred-, solemn reading* **haidoku**
拝謁 *audience with the emperor* **haietsu**
拝復 *"in reply to your letter..."* **haifuku**
拝賀 *greetings, congratulations* **haiga**
拝顔 *receiving an imperial audience* **haigan**
拝受 *accepting with humility* **haiju**
拝観 *seeing, visiting, looking* **haikan**
拝啓 *"Dear, My dear..."* **haikei**
拝見 *looking, seeing, watching* **haiken**
拝金 *money worship, financial obsession* **haikin**
拝命 *official appointment, recognition* **haimei**
拝礼 *worship, prayer* **hairei**
拝領 *one's lord* **hairyō**
拝察 *sincere prayers* **haisatsu**

拝借 *borrowing, quotation* **haishaku**
拝承 *"I am informed that ..."* **haishō**
拝呈 *presentation* **haitei**
巡拝 *pilgrimage* **junpai**
礼拝 *worship, service* **reihai, raihai**
礼拝堂 *house of worship* **reihaidō, raihaidō**
参拝 *worship, praying* **sanpai**
崇拝 *worship, adoration* **sūhai**
⇒偶像崇拝 *idol worship, idolatry* **gūzō sūhai**
⇒祖先崇拝 *ancestral worship* **sosen sūhai**
拝み倒す *entreat into consenting* **ogamitaosu**

寺*emple, 248*	神*ivine, 712*	頼*equest, 562*
参*emple-visit, 396*	祈*rayer, 184*	堂*ltar, 94*

持*olding. 249*

536-B

Better 拝*ray before* 打*triking day...*

手⇔扌 (hand, manual)

打

打*trike*　　打*itting*

u(tsu), DA
strike, hitting, offence, attack, charging

Facing: 3.0. ☞☜ Across
FLIP: 7.0.b1. Right (stem)

打撲 *stroke, blow, punch* **daboku**
打撃 *strike, beating, hit* **dageki**
打開 *break, opening* **dakai**
打率 *one's batting average (baseball)* **daritsu**
打算 *calculation, selfishness* **dasan**
打席 *one's batting turn (baseball)* **daseki**
打線 *batting line-up (baseball)* **dasen**
打診 *sounding out, tapping* **dashin**
打倒 *overthrowing, beating* **datō**
猛打 *heavy hit, intense blow* **mōda**
殴打 *strike, beating, hit* **ōda**
乱打 *striking violently* **randa**
相打ち *"hitting each other simultaneously..."* **aiuchi**
銘打つ *call, call out* **meiutsu**
耳打ち *whisper, murmur* **mimiuchi**
手打ち *"slaying with one's own hands..."* **teuchi**
裏打ち *lining, backing; rear attack* **urauchi**
不意打ち *surprise attack, ambush* **fuiuchi**
組み打ち *grapple, wrestle* **kumiuchi**

追い打ち *attacking a fleeing enemy* **oiuchi**
一網打尽 *roundup; mass arrest* **ichimō dajin**
打ち上げ *launch, lift off* **uchiage**
打ち合い *exchange of blows* **uchiai**
打ち合せ *arrangements, preparations* **uchiawase**
打ち出し *come out with~* **uchidashi**
打ち勝つ *overcome, resist, get over* **uchikatsu**
打ち消し *denial, negation, refusal* **uchikeshi**
打ち殺す *beaten to death, shoot dead* **uchikorosu**
打ち崩し *knock out, strike down* **uchikuzushi**
打ち取る *get; slay, kill* **uchitoru**
打ち漏らす *unable to kill* **uchimorasu**
打ち解ける *make friends with* **uchitokeru**

撲*trike, 157*	攻*ttack, 635*	討*ttack, 691*
撃*ttack, 613*	襲*ttack, 630*	伐*ttack, 96*

灯*amplight. 175*

537-A

好*iking thru old age, a lasting* 婚*arriage...*

女 (woman)

好*iking*　　　好*reference*

kono(mu), kono(mashii), su(ku), KŌ
liking, preference, desire, fondness, favourable

Facing: 3.0. ☞☜ Across

愛好	liking, affection	**aikō**
同好	same interests & likes	**dōkō**
格好	shape, figure, appearance	**kakkō**
好悪	likes & dislikes	**kōaku**
好演	good performance	**kōen**
好学	love of learning, intellectual thirst	**kōgaku**
好配	good news, glad tidings	**kōhai**
好捕	catching well	**kōho**
好評	favourable comment	**kōhyō**
好感	good feeling, impression	**kōkan**
好機	chance, opportunity, opportune time	**kōki**
好期	the right time, good timing	**kōki**
好況	prosperity, good times	**kōkyō**
好手	good move, smart move	**kōshu**
好適	suitable, proper	**kōteki**
好転	change for the better	**kōten**
好投	good pitch	**kōtō**
良好	satisfied, excellent, favourable	**ryōkō**
友好	friendliness, friendship	**yūkō**

絶好	best, perfect, finest	**zekkō**
出好き	extrovert, gregarious, sociable	**dezuki**
程好い	suitable, moderate, modest	**hodoyoi**
好景気	prosperity, good times	**kōkeiki**
好奇心	curiosity, deep interest	**kōkishin**
見好い	pleasant to watch	**miyoi**
仲好し	good friends, bosom buddies	**nakayoshi**
背格好	height, build, body frame	**sekakkō**
好き嫌い	likes & dislikes, preference	**sukikirai**
選り好み	fastidiousness	**yorigonomi**
お好み焼き	meat & vegetable pancake **okonomiyaki**	

希*reference*, 208	欲*esire*, 892
望*esire*, 618	頼*equest*, 562

妊*regnancy*, 709

537-B

好*iking thru old age, a lasting* 婚*arriage...*

女 (woman)

婚*arriage*　　婚*atrimony*

KON
marriage, matrimony, nuptials, getting hitch

FLIP: 7.3.a. Right Bottom (flat)

晩婚	late marriage	**bankon**
銀婚式	silver wedding anniversary	**ginkonshiki**
重婚	bigamy, polygamy	**jūkon**
結婚	marriage, wedding, matrimony	**kekkon**
既婚	married, wedded	**kikon**
既婚者	married person	**kikonsha**
婚儀	wedding	**kongi**
婚姻	marriage	**kon'in**
婚姻届け	marriage application	**kon'in todoke**
婚家	one's in-laws	**konka**
婚期	marriageable age	**konki**
婚礼	wedding ceremony	**konrei**
婚礼衣装	wedding gown, ~dress	**konrei ishō**
婚約	marital engagement, betrothal	**konyaku**
婚約者	fiance, fiancee, engaged person	**konyakusha**
婚約指輪	engagement ring, betrothal ring **konyaku yubiwa**	
婚前	premarital, before marriage	**konzen**
求婚	marriage proposal	**kyūkon**

求婚者	marriage suitor	**kyūkonsha**
未婚	unmarried, single	**mikon**
離婚	divorce, annulment, marital break-up	**rikon**
離婚届	divorce application, ~notice	**rikon todoke**
離婚手当	alimony, child support	**rikon teate**
離婚手続	divorce paperwork	**rikon tetsuzuki**
再婚	remarriage	**saikon**
成婚式	imperial wedding	**seikonshiki**
新婚	newly-married	**shinkon**
新婚旅行	honeymoon	**shinkon ryokō**
初婚	first marriage	**shokon**
早婚	early marriage	**sōkon**

姻*arriage*, 364	家*amily*, 909
妻*arried lady*, 611	族*amily*, 649
婦*arried-lady*, 785	愛*ove*, 593

姻*arriage*, 364

538-A

姓*urname* of 婿*on-in-law* that of Zorro...

女 (woman)

姓*urname*　　姓*amily name*

SEI, SHŌ
surname, family name

同姓 *same surname* **dōsei**
本姓 *original surname* **honsei**
百姓 *peasant, farmer* **hyakushō**
百姓一揆 *peasant uprising* **hyakushōikki**
異姓 *different surname* **isei**
改姓 *change of name, new surname* **kaisei**
小姓 *page to nobility* **koshō**
旧姓 *former-, maiden name* **kyūsei**
姓名 *surname, family name* **seimei**
姓氏 *full name* **seishi**
庶姓 *illegitimate child* **shosei**
素姓 *birth, parentage, affinity, kinship* **sujō**
他姓 *another surname, alias* **tasei**
俗姓 *monks' secular name* **zokusei**
土百姓 *soil peasant* **dobyakushō**
鈍百姓 *stupid peasant* **donbyakushō**
小百姓 *petty peasant* **kobyakushō**

Facing: 3.0. ☞☜ Across
FLIP: 7.1. Right (Sort Of)

氏*urname, 489*	族*amily, 649*
名*urname, 425*	係*elative, 263*
家*amily, 909*	縁*inship, 675*

姉*lder sister, 114*

538-B

姓*urname* of 婿*on-in-law* that of Zorro...

女 (woman)

婿*on-in-law*

muko, SEI
son-in-law

愛婿 *favourite son-in-law* **aisei**
姉婿 *brother-in-law* **anemuko**
花婿 *bridge groom* **hanamuko**
女婿 *son-in-law* **josei**
娘婿 *son-in-law, bridegroom* **musumemuko**
令婿 *"your son-in-law..."* **reisei**
入り婿 *acceptance into the wife family* **irimuko**
婿選び *looking for a son-in-law* **mukoerabi**
婿入り *acceptance into the wife family* **mukoiri**
婿探し *looking for a son-in-law* **mukosagashi**
婿養子 *son-in-law, bridegroom* **mukoyōshi**
婿取り娘 *adoption of daughter's husband*
　　mukotori musume

FLIP: 7.3.b. Right Bottom (stem)

姻*arriage, 364*	夫*usband, 83*
婚*arriage, 637*	妻*ife, 611*
家*amily, 909*	婦*ife, 785*
族*amily, 649*	縁*inship, 675*

婚*arriage, 637*

539-A

狂razy cardinal in 獄rison with 犯riminals...

犬⇔犭 (dog; beast)

狂razy　狂nsane

kuru(u), kuru(oshii), KYŌ
crazy, insane, psychopathic, psychotic, lunatic, whacko, maniac, madness

FLIP: 7.0.a. Right (flat)

風狂 *insanity, madness* **fūkyō**
発狂 *going mad, ~insane* **hakkyō**
偏狂 *monomaniac* **henkyō**
狂暴 *wild & violent* **kyōbō**
狂暴性 *violence, madness* **kyōbōsei**
狂炎 *fierce flames, conflagration* **kyōen**
狂風 *violent wind* **kyōfū**
狂言 *farce, sham* **kyōgen**
狂言自殺 *fake suicide* **kyōgen jisatsu**
狂奔 *busy, occupied, engaged* **kyōhon**
狂人 *maniac, lunatic* **kyōjin**
狂女 *madwoman, hag* **kyōjo**
狂歌 *comic-, satirical poem* **kyōka**
狂犬 *mad dog, hound dog* **kyōken**
狂犬病 *rabies, dog bites* **kyōkenbyō**
狂喜 *exultation, rapture, ecstasy* **kyōki**
狂気 *crazy, insanity, madness, delusion* **kyōki**
狂乱 *madness, insanity* **kyōran**
狂死 *dying mad* **kyōshi**

狂信 *fanaticism, extremism* **kyōshin**
狂騒 *pandemonium, mad uproar* **kyōsō**
狂態 *shameful conduct* **kyōtai**
狂的 *fanatical, radical, extremist* **kyōteki**
熱狂 *enthusiasm, excitement* **nekkyō**
熱狂的 *enthusiastic, frantic, wild* **nekkyōteki**
色狂い *sex maniac* **irogurui**
女狂い *womaniser, philanderer* **onnagurui**
男狂い *self-indulgent; flirtation w/ men* **otokogurui**
荒れ狂う *rage, fury, ferocity* **arekurū**
番狂わせ *unexpected, upset* **bankuruwase**

慌*anic, 507*	凶*vil, 80*
幻*antasy, 88*	悪*vil, 389*

性*ature, 474*

539-B

狂razy cardinal in 獄rison with 犯riminals...

犬⇔犭 (dog; beast)

獄

獄rison　獄ailhouse

GOKU
prison, jailhouse, lock-up, penitentiary, stockade, calaboose, detention, dungeon, incarceration

FLIP: 8.0.a. Inner (flat)

脱獄 *jailbreak, prison escape* **datsugoku**
下獄 *sending to prison* **gegoku**
疑獄 *graft, scandal* **gigoku**
獄中 *imprisoned, jailed* **gokuchū**
獄衣 *prison clothes, jail uniform* **gokui**
獄門 *prison gate, jail* **gokumon**
獄内 *imprisoned, jailed* **gokunai**
獄吏 *prison officials* **gokuri**
獄舎 *prison house, ~building* **gokusha**
獄死 *dying in prison* **gokushi**
獄囚 *prisoner, detainee* **gokushū**
獄則 *prison rules* **gokusoku**
獄卒 *prison warden, gaoler* **gokusotsu**
獄屋 *prison, jail, gaol* **gokuya**
破獄 *jailbreak, prison escape* **hagoku**
地獄 *hell, inferno* **jigoku**
⇒生き地獄 *"living hell..."* **ikijigoku**
⇒試験地獄 *examination ordeal* **shiken jigoku**
⇒焦熱地獄 *hell, inferno* **shōnetsu jigoku**

監獄 *prison, jail, gaol* **kangoku**
禁獄 *imprisonment, detention* **kingoku**
入獄 *being imprisoned* **nyūgoku**
煉獄 *purgatory* **rengoku**
牢獄 *prison, jail, gaol* **rōgoku**
大獄 *mass arrest, mass round up* **taigoku**
典獄 *prison officials* **tengoku**
投獄 *imprisonment, detention* **tōgoku**
獄道者 *scoundrel* **gokudōsha**
出獄者 *released convict* **shutsugokusha**
在獄中 *during imprisonment* **zaigokuchū**

囚*risoner, 863*	罰*unishment, 759*
刑*unishment, 536*	罪*riminal, 289*
懲*unishment, 63*	犯*riminal, 640*

徴*emand, 62*

539-C

犴razy cardinal in 獄rison with 犯riminals...

犬⇔犭 (dog; beast)

犯riminal   犯elony

oka(su), HAN
criminal, felony, offence

Facing: 4.0. ⇦⇨ Apart

防犯 *crime prevention* **bōhan**
犯意 *criminal intent* **han'i**
犯行 *crime, felony* **hankō**
⇒計画的犯行 *premeditated crime*
    keikakuteki hankō
犯人 *criminal, convict, felon* **hannin**
⇒放火犯人 *arsonist* **hōka hannin**
⇒拐帯犯人 *absconderer, con artist* **kaitai hannin**
犯歴 *criminal record* **hanreki**
犯跡 *crime evidence* **hanseki**
犯則 *rule violation, breach* **hansoku**
犯罪 *crime, offence, sin* **hanzai**
⇒性犯罪 *sexual crime* **seihanzai**
⇒完全犯罪 *perfect crime* **kanzen hanzai**
⇒凶悪犯罪 *heinous crime, atrocity* **kyōaku hanzai**
犯罪隠匿 *conceal a crime* **hanzai intoku**
犯罪行為 *crime, felony* **hanzai kōi**
違犯 *violation, offence* **ihan**
事犯 *criminal offence* **jihan**

常習犯 *habitual crime, recidivist* **jōshūhan**
従犯 *accessory, accomplish, conspirator* **jūhan**
重犯 *heavy offence, felony, serious crime* **jūhan**
共犯 *conspiracy, plot, collusion* **kyōhan**
累犯 *repeated offence, recidivist* **ruihan**
正犯 *principal offence* **seihan**
戦犯 *war criminal* **senpan**
侵犯 *violation, infringement* **shinpan**
初犯 *first crime, first-time offender* **shohan**
刑事犯 *criminal offence, felony* **keijihan**
殺人犯 *murder felony* **satsujinhan**
窃盗犯 *thief, burglar, robber* **settōhan**

悪*vil, 389*	罰*unishment, 759*	懲*unishment, 63*
凶*vil, 80*	罪*riminal, 289*	刑*unishment, 536*

仰espect, *706*

540-A

Boat 幅idth in 帳egistry 帆ailing to victory...

巾 (cloth, fabric)

幅idth   幅easurement

haba, FUKU
width, measurement, breadth, margin, calibration, spanning

FLIP: 5.0.a Left & Right

幅員 *road width, ship width* **fukuin**
画幅 *hanging picture, ~scroll* **gafuku**
歩幅 *step, stride* **hohaba**
一幅 *scroll* **ippuku**
恰幅 *body build, physique* **kappuku**
肩幅 *shoulder width* **katahaba**
川幅 *river width* **kawahaba**
小幅 *small margin, narrow limit* **kohaba**
満幅 *full breadth* **manpuku**
身幅 *kimono width* **mihaba**
胸幅 *chest width* **munehaba**
中幅 *medium width* **nakahaba**
値幅 *price range* **nehaba**
利幅 *profit margin* **rihaba**
船幅 *ship beam* **senpuku**
紙幅 *paper width* **shifuku**
手幅 *hand width* **tehaba**
横幅 *breadth, wideness* **yokohaba**
幅跳び *broad jump, long jump* **habatobi**

幅寄せ *loop guide* **habayose**
走り幅跳び *long-jump running* **hashiri habatobi**
広幅 *very wide, broad, extensive* **hirohaba**
大幅 *substantial, enormous* **oohaba**
振幅 *amplitude, vibration swing* **shinpuku**
震幅 *seismic amplitude* **shinpuku**
全幅 *entire breath, all-encompassing* **zenpuku**
増幅 *amplification, magnification* **zōfuku**
幅広い *extensive, wide, broad* **habahiroi**
幅利き *influential person* **habakiki**
幅対応 *appropriate width* **habataiō**

横*ateral, 197*	測*easurement, 291*
拡*nlarge, 205*	計*easurement, 692*
広*arge, 205*	

福elfare, *333*

540-B
Boat 幅idth in 帳egistry 帆ailing to victory...

帆 (cloth, fabric)

帆*ailing*

ho, HAN
sailing

帆船 *sailboat* **hansen**
帆走 *sailing, gliding* **hansō**
帆柱 *sailboat mast* **hobashira**
帆桁 *sail boom, yard* **hogeta**
帆影 *boat in sight, sailing image* **hokage**
帆蓮 *sailing mast* **homushiro**
帆布 *sailing canvas* **honuno**
帆綱 *halyard* **hozuna**
片帆 *reef sailing* **kataho**
帰帆 *homebound sailboat* **kihan**
孤帆 *solo sailing; solitary sailboat* **kohan**
真帆 *spread out sailing* **maho**
三角帆 *jib sailing* **sankakuho**
白帆 *white sail* **shiraho**
出帆 *sailing, leaving port* **shuppan**
帆掛け舟 *sailboat* **hokakebune**
帆前船 *sailing ship* **homaesen**
帆立貝 *scallop shellfish* **hotategai**

FLIP: 6.0.b. Left (stem)

機帆船 *motor sailboat* **kihansen**
順風満帆 *favourable wind* **junpū manpan**

舶*hip, 742*	船*hip, 757*
舟*hip, 90*	海*cean, 241*
航*avigation, 748*	洋*cean, 247*

卵*gg, 971*

540-C
Boat 幅idth in 帳egistry 帆ailing to victory...

巾 (cloth, fabric)

帳*egistry*   帳*emo*

CHŌ
registry, memo, logbook, roster, notebook, ledger

帳合 *balancing the books* **chōai**
帳場 *counter, front desk* **chōba**
帳簿 *account book, ledger* **chōbo**
帳簿係 *accountant, bookkeeper* **chōbogakari**
帳尻 *balance of accounts* **chōjiri**
帳面 *notebook, books* **chōmen**
帳元 *promoter, manager; bookie* **chōmoto**
台帳 *ledger, registry, journal* **daichō**
画帳 *photo album* **gachō**
蚊帳 *mosquito net* **kaya**
記帳 *journal entry, make a record* **kichō**
⇒日記帳 *diary notes* **nikkichō**
⇒雑記帳 *notebook, scrapbook* **zakkichō**
元帳 *ledger, register* **motochō**
手帳 *passbook, notebook* **techō**
⇒母子手帳 *pregnancy notebook* **boshi techō**
通帳 *notebook, passbook* **tsūchō**
⇒貯金通帳 *bankbook, passbook* **chokin tsūchō**
⇒銀行通帳 *bankbook, passbook* **ginkō tsūchō**

FLIP: 6.0.b. Left (stem)

⇒預金通帳 *bankbook, passbook* **yokin tsūchō**
宿帳 *hotel registry* **yadochō**
帳付け *bookkeeper; bookkeeping* **chōtsuke**
電話帳 *telephone directory, phone book*
　　denwachō
過去帳 *death registry* **kakochō**
練習帳 *workbook, practice book* **renshūchō**
写生帳 *sketchbook* **shaseichō**
写真帳 *photo album* **shashinchō**
単語帳 *wordbook* **tangochō**
捕り物帳 *detective story* **torimonochō**
受け取り帳 *receipt logbook* **uketorichō**

籍*egistry, 336*	文*iteracy, 558*
記*ecord, 728*	書*ritings, 116*
録*ecord, 841*	稿*ritings, 435*

張*tretch, 274*　　脹*welling, 274*

541-A

吹*lowing of horns brings* 唯*olitary scorns...*

吹*lowing*

口 (mouth)

FLIP: 6.0.a. Left (flat)
Facing: 1.2. 🐦 West (V)

fu(ku), SUI
blowing, blustery, windy

吹聴 *announcing in public* **fuichō**
息吹 *breathe, breathing* **ibuki**
鼓吹 *inspire, cheer up* **kosui**
吹鳴 *whistle-blowing* **suimei**
吹奏 *playing a wind instrument* **suisō**
山吹 *yellow rose* **yamabuki**
笛吹き *piper* **fuefuki**
吹き手 *braggart* **fukite**
吹き矢 *blow dart, blow gun* **fukiya**
花吹雪 *falling cherry blossoms* **hanafubuki**
霧吹き *spray, spraying* **kirifuki**
芽吹く *bud, sprout* **mebuku**
吹き消す *blow out (candlelight)* **fukikesu**
吹き込む *blow in, inspire, record* **fukikomu**
吹き抜け *well, stairwell* **fukinuke**
吹き降り *driving rain* **fukiburi**
吹き出す *shoot forth; burst into laughter* **fukidasu**
吹き替え *voice dubbing* **fukikae**
吹き荒ぶ *blow hard, storm violently* **fukisusabu**

吹き倒す *blow down* **fukitaosu**
吹き飛ぶ *be dispelled, be blown off* **fukitobu**
吹き出物 *pimple, skin rash* **fukidemono**
吹き上げる *blow up, puff up* **fukiageru**
吹き荒れる *blow hard & strong* **fukiareru**
吹き散らす *blow away, spread about* **fukichirasu**
吹き掛ける *spray, blow, breathe* **fukikakeru**
吹き下ろす *blow down* **fukiorosu**
吹き飛ばす *overcome, dispel, blow off* **fukitobasu**
吹き付ける *blow, spray* **fukitsukeru**
吹き寄せる *blow near* **fukiyoseru**

風*ind, 894*
笛*lute, 630*

叫*cream, 693*

541-B

吹*lowing of horns brings* 唯*olitary scorns...*

唯*olitary* 唯*ingular*

口 (mouth)

FLIP: 6.0.a. Left (flat)
Facing: 2.2. East ☞ (V)

YUI, I
solitary, singular, one-of-a-kind

唯一 *only, sole, one-and-only* **yuiitsu**
唯今 *"now, at this time..."* **tadaima**
唯美的 *aesthetic, esthetic* **yuibiteki**
唯美主義 *aestheticism* **yuibishugi**
唯物論 *materialism* **yuibutsuron**
唯物的 *materialistic, worldliness* **yuibutsuteki**
唯物史観 *historical materialism (Hegel)*
　yuibutsu shikan
唯物主義 *materialism* **yuibutsushugi**
唯我尊 *vanity, self-conceited, self-glory* **yuigazon**
唯我独尊 *vanity, self-conceited, self-glory*
　yuigadokuson
唯識 *Buddhist spiritualism* **yuishiki**
真唯中 *"right in the midst of..."* **mattadanaka**
唯名論 *nominalism* **yuimeiron**
唯理論 *rationalism* **yuiriron**
唯心論 *spiritualism, idealism* **yuishinron**
唯心論者 *spiritualist, idealist* **yuishin ronsha**
唯唯諾諾 *readily, willingness, obligedly* **iidakudaku**

孤*olitary, 148*　　　殊*pecial, 234*
専*xclusive, 514*　　特*pecial, 250*
選*hoice, 303*　　　異*ifferent, 239*
択*hoice, 753*　　　他*ifferent, 688*

雅*raceful, 58*

542-A
In the 砂ands abandon an old war 砲anon...

石 (stone)

砂ands   砂ravel

suna, SA, SHA
sands, gravel

Facing: 3.0. ☞✎ Across

土砂 *earth & sand* **dosha**
土砂崩れ *washout, landslide* **dosha kuzure**
砂利 *gravel* **jari**
硅砂 *quartz sand, silica* **keisha**
黄砂 *yellow sand* **kōsa**
熱砂 *burning sand* **nessa**
流砂 *quick sand* **ryūsa**
砂漠 *desert, barren, sahara* **sabaku**
砂防 *soil erosion prevention* **sabō**
砂岩 *sandstone* **sagan**
砂塵 *dust powder* **sajin**
砂金 *gold dust, gold powder* **sakin**
砂丘 *sand hill, dune* **sakyū**
砂州 *sandbank* **sasu**
砂鉄 *iron sand* **satetsu**
砂糖 *sugar* **satō**
砂嵐 *sand storm* **sunaarashi**
砂場 *sandbox, sandpit* **sunaba**
砂袋 *sandbag* **sunabukuro**

砂地 *sandy soil* **sunachi**
砂絵 *sketch on the sand* **sunae**
砂肝 *gizzards, insides* **sunagimo**
砂子 *sand; silver dust* **sunago**
砂浜 *sandy beach* **sunahama**
砂煙 *cloud of dust* **sunakemuri**
砂山 *sand hill, dune* **sunayama**
角砂糖 *lump sugar* **kakuzatō**
氷砂糖 *rock-, sugar candy* **koorizatō**
砂風呂 *sand bathing* **sunaburo**
砂時計 *sandglass* **sunadokei**

石 *tone, 363*	浜 *eashore, 490*
岩 *ock, 29*	涯 *eashore, 890*
浦 *eashore, 813*	岸 *eashore, 30*

秒 *econds, 727*

542-B
In the 砂ands abandon an old war 砲anon...

石 (stone)

砲annon   砲rtillery

HŌ
cannon, artillery, heavy guns

Facing: 3.0. ☞✎ Across

弔砲 *funeral salute* **chōhō**
号砲 *signal gun* **gōhō**
発砲 *firing, shooting* **happō**
砲台 *cannon platform, ~battery* **hōdai**
砲弾 *cannonball* **hōdan**
砲煙 *artillery smoke, ~fume* **hōen**
砲丸 *artillery fire, cannon fire* **hōgan**
砲眼 *gun sight, gunport* **hōgan**
砲撃 *bombardment* **hōgeki**
砲兵 *artillery soldiers* **hōhei**
砲兵隊 *artillery corps, ~troops* **hōheitai**
砲術 *gunnery* **hōjutsu**
砲火 *gunfire* **hōka**
⇒対空砲火 *anti-aircraft* **taikū hōka**
砲艦 *gunboat* **hōkan**
砲声 *roaring of a gun, gunshot* **hōsei**
砲車 *gun carriage* **hōsha**
砲手 *artilleryman* **hōshu**
銃砲 *guns, firearms* **jūhō**

重砲 *heavy artillery* **jūhō**
艦砲 *ship artillery* **kanpō**
巨砲 *heavy artillery* **kyohō**
礼砲 *21-gun salute* **reihō**
祝砲 *21-gun salute* **shukuhō**
大砲 *cannon, artillery* **taihō**
鉄砲 *handgun, sidearm* **teppō**
高射砲 *anti-aircraft artillery* **kōshahō**
豆鉄砲 *pea-, beanshooter* **mamedeppō**
水鉄砲 *water pistol* **mizudeppō**
速射砲 *rapid-fire gunshot* **sokushahō**

戦 *ighting, 517*	傷 *njury, 933*
武 *arrior, 100*	障 *njury, 325*
爆 *xplosion, 561*	損 *njury, 410*
害 *njury, 904*	痛 *njury, 60*

破 *estroy, 715*

543-A

Billowing 煙moke from 炉urnaces choke...

煙*moke*　　煙*ume*

火⇔灬 (fire)

FLIP: 7.0.a. Right (flat)

kemuri, kemu(ru), kemu(i), EN
smoke, fume, smoulder

煤煙	*soot & smoke*	**baien**
爆煙	*smoke from explosion*	**bakuen**
防煙	*smoke proofing, ~protection*	**bōen**
血煙	*blood spurting, heavy bleeding*	**chikemuri**
煙害	*smoke-induced damage*	**engai**
煙幕	*smoke screen*	**enmaku**
煙霧	*smoke & fog*	**enmu**
煙死	*death by suffocation*	**enshi**
煙硝	*powder*	**enshō**
煙突	*chimney, funnel*	**entotsu**
噴煙	*smoke, smoulder, smudge*	**fun'en**
排煙	*exhaust smoke*	**haien**
発煙	*smoke emission*	**hatsuen**
砲煙	*artillery smoke*	**hōen**
嫌煙	*smoking aversion*	**ken'en**
嫌煙権	*non-smokers rights*	**ken'enken**
禁煙	*smoking prohibited, "no smoking..."*	**kin'en**
禁煙車	*no-smoking car (train)*	**kin'ensha**
喫煙室	*smoking room*	**kitsuenshitsu**

黒煙	*black smoke*	**kokuen**
猛煙	*thick-, heavy smoke*	**mōen**
無煙	*smokeless*	**muen**
節煙	*smoking reduction*	**setsuen**
紫煙	*tobacco smoke*	**shien**
硝煙	*powder smoke*	**shōen**
煙草	*cigarette, tobacco*	**tabako**
土煙	*cloud of dust*	**tsuchi kemuri**
油煙	*lampblack, soot*	**yuen**
雪煙	*snow spray*	**yukikemuri**
愛煙家	*chain-, habitual smoker*	**aienka**

汽*team, 98*	燃*urning, 445*
蒸*team, 117*	火*ire, 3*

焼*arbeque, 817*

543-B

Billowing 煙moke from 炉urnaces choke...

炉*urnace*　　炉*urner*

火⇔灬 (fire)

Facing: 2.2. East ☞ (V)

RO
furnace, burner

暖炉	*fireplace, furnace, stove*	**danro**
平炉	*open hearth furnace, ~burner*	**hiraro**
懐炉	*body warmer*	**kairo**
懐炉灰	*portable cookware*	**kairobai**
火炉	*furnace*	**karo**
香炉	*incense burner*	**kōro**
高炉	*blast furnace, ~burner*	**kōro**
炉端	*by the fireside, ~fireplace*	**robata**
炉棚	*mantelpiece*	**rodana**
炉辺	*fireside sweet talks*	**rohen, robata**
炉心	*reactor core*	**roshin**
炉床	*hearth, fireplace*	**roshō**
炉頭	*around the hearth*	**rotō**
転炉	*revolving furnace, ~burner*	**tenro**
電気炉	*electric furnace, ~burner*	**denkiro**
原子炉	*atomic reactor*	**genshiro**
反射炉	*reverbating furnace, ~burner*	**hansharo**
囲炉裏	*open hearth*	**irori**
乾燥炉	*drying furnace, ~burner*	**kansōro**

軽水炉	*light-water reactor*	**keisuiro**
燃焼炉	*combustion furnace*	**nenshōro**
溶鉱炉	*smelter, smelting furnace*	**yōkōro**
鎔鉱炉	*blast furnace, ~burner*	**yōkōro**
増殖炉	*breeder reactor*	**zōshokuro**
核反応路	*nuclear reactor*	**kakuhannōro**
炉辺談話	*fireside sweet talks*	**rohen danwa**

燃*urning, 445*	火*ire, 3*
焼*oasting, 817*	薪*irewood, 668*
熱*eat, 153*	力*nergy, 351*
煙*moke, 644*	

炊*ooking, 865*

544-A
Noisy 郊uburbs 効ffectively disturb...

郊 ⇔ 阜 (village-right)

郊uburbs   郊utskirts

KŌ
suburbs, outskirts

近郊 *suburbs, outskirts* **kinkō**
郊外 *suburbs, outskirts* **kōgai**
郊外電車 *suburban train, shuttle train* **kōgai densha**
郊野 *suburban fields* **kōya**
西郊 *western suburbs* **seikō**
秋郊 *autumn fields* **shūkō**
断郊競走 *cross-country race* **dankō kyōsō**

FLIP: 6.0.b. Left (stem)
Facing: 2.2. East ☞ (V)

外*utside, 188*	京*apital, 386*
村*illage, 690*	都*etropolis, 694*
郷*ometown, 452*	緑*nvironment, 841*
里*ometown, 321*	環*nvirons, 165*

効*ffect, 645*

544-B
Noisy 郊uburbs 効ffectively disturb...

力 (strength, force)

効ffect   効alidate

ki(ku), KŌ
effect, outcome, validate

遅効 *late-, slow effect* **chikō**
発効 *coming into effect* **hakkō**
偉効 *great effect* **ikō**
実効 *practical effect, ~benefits* **jikkō**
時効 *time prescription* **jikō**
効き目 *efficacious, effectiveness* **kikime**
寄効 *remarkable effect* **kikō**
効果 *effect, result, outcome* **kōka**
⇒逆効果 *opposite effect, backfire* **gyaku kōka**
⇒即効薬 *quick remedy* **sokkōyaku**
⇒舞台効果 *stage effects* **butai kōka**
⇒演出効果 *stage effects* **enshutsu kōka**
⇒限界効用 *marginal utility* **genkai kōyō**
⇒音響効果 *sound effects* **onkyō kōka**
効験 *effect, efficacy, efficaciousness* **kōken**
効能 *effect, virtue* **kōnō**
効能書き *statement of virtues* **kōnōgaki**
効率 *efficiency, efficacious, effectiveness* **kōritsu**
効力 *effect, force, validity* **kōryoku**

FLIP: 6.0.b. Left (stem)
Facing: 2.2. East ☞ (V)

効用 *effect, use, utility* **kōyō**
無効 *annulment, invalidity, cancellation* **mukō**
失効 *invalidation, cancellation* **shikkō**
速効 *quick-, instant effect* **sokkō**
即効性 *instant-, immediate effect* **sokkōsei**
奏効 *effectual, effectivity, efficacy* **sōkō**
特効 *special efficacy* **tokkō**
薬効 *medicinal effect, ~value* **yakkō**
有効 *effective, valid* **yūkō**
有効期間 *validity period, time effectivity*
　　yūkō kikan

響*ffect, 452*	期*eriod, 658*
因*ause, 862*	経*ime-lapse, 791*
果*esult, 287*	肯*ffirmative, 616*

郊*uburbs, 645*

545-A

Follow the 峠ountain-trail to the 岬ape of Whales...

ountain trail

tōge
mountain trail

峠道 *mountain trail* **tōgemichi**

山 (mountain)

FLIP: 6.0.a. Left (flat)

岬ape, 646
山ountain, 172
岳ountain peak, 28

崎lope, 270

545-B

Follow the 峠ountain-trail to the 岬ape of Whales...

岬ape   岬romontory

misaki
cape, promontory

潮岬 *southern tip of Kii Peninsula* **shio no misaki**
足摺岬 *southern tip of Shikoku* **ashizurimisaki**
知床岬 *eastern tip of Hokkaidō* **shiretokomisaki**
宗谷岬 *northern tip of Hokkaidō* **sōyamisaki**
岬の突端 *tip of a cape* **misaki no tottan**

山 (mountain)

FLIP: 5.0.b. Left & Right

峠ountain trail, 646
岳ountain peak, 28
山ountain, 172

ress, 37

546-A

物bjects of 牧asture, old days to recapture...

牛⇔牛 (cattle)

物bjects   物hings

mono, BUTSU, MOTSU
objects, things, property, possession

Facing: 1.2. ☜ West (V)

物価 *commodity prices* **bukka**
物産 *product, produce* **bussan**
物理 *physics, natural law* **butsuri**
動物 *animal* **dōbutsu**
現物 *actual product* **genbutsu**
本物 *real stuff, genuine* **honmono**
貨物 *freight, cargo* **kamotsu**
見物 *sight-seeing, observation* **kenbutsu**
果物 *fruit* **kudamono**
名物 *specialty, famous product* **meibutsu**
物音 *sound, noise* **monooto**
物語 *story, tale, legend* **monogatari**
荷物 *baggage, luggage, suitcase* **nimotsu**
偽物 *fake, imitation, copy, phoney* **nisemono**
私物 *private property* **shibutsu**
植物 *plant, vegetation* **shokubutsu**
書物 *books, papers, writings* **shomotsu**
宝物 *treasure, heirloom* **takaramono, hōmotsu**
薬物 *medicine, drug* **yakubutsu**

暗記物 *something to memorize* **ankimono**
預り物 *something to entrust* **azukarimono**
絵巻物 *picture scroll* **emakimono**
物干し *drying clothes pole* **monohoshi**
物覚え *memory ability* **monooboe**
飲み物 *drink, beverage, liquor* **nomimono**
農産物 *agricultural produce* **nōsanbutsu**
調べ物 *something to verify* **shirabemono**
作り物 *man-made, artificial* **tsukurimono**
忘れ物 *forgotten belongings* **wasuremono**
読み物 *reading materials* **yomimono**

箇*[objects]*, 52
荷*argo*, 877
何*omething*, 101

牧*asture*, 647

546-B

物bjects of 牧asture, old days to recapture...

牛⇔牛 (cattle)

牧asture   牧reeding

maki, BOKU
pasture, breeding, hatchery

Facing: 1.2. ☜ West (V)

牧歌 *pastoral song* **bokka**
牧地 *pasture, meadow* **bokuchi**
牧畜 *stock-breeding, ~raising* **bokuchiku**
牧童 *cowboy, shepherd boy* **bokudō**
牧夫 *herdsman, shepherd* **bokufu**
牧人 *herdsman, shepherd* **bokujin**
牧場 *stock farm, meadow* **bokujō**
牧民 *governing, ruling* **bokumin**
牧舎 *farm house* **bokusha**
牧師 *pastor, vicar, reverend* **bokushi**
牧師館 *rectory* **bokushikan**
牧神 *satyr, pan* **bokushin**
牧草 *grass, pasturage, hay* **bokusō**
牧草地 *pasture, meadow* **bokusōchi**
牧笛 *shepherds flute* **bokuteki**
牧野 *pasture, meadow* **bokuya**
牧羊 *sheep, lamb* **bokuyō**
放牧 *grazing, pasturing* **hōboku**
放牧地 *pasture land, meadow* **hōbokuchi**

農牧 *agriculture & stock breeding* **nōboku**
農牧地 *farming & grazing land* **nōbokuchi**
遊牧 *wandering-, nomadic lifestyle* **yūboku**

牛*attle*, 179   養*reeding*, 253
飼*reeding*, 835   酪*airy*, 670
畜*reeding*, 528   羊*heep*, 247

物bjects, 647

547-A

Bullet 斜rajectory in 叙arration kept the sensation...

斗 (amount)

斜iagonal　　斜rajectory

nana(me), SHA
diagonal, trajectory, slanting, oblique

FLIP: 6.0.b. Left (stem)

斜め *diagonal, oblique* **naname**
傾斜 *inclination, slope* **keisha**
傾斜度 *gradient, slope* **keishado**
傾斜角 *inclination angle* **keishakaku**
傾斜面 *slope, inclined plane* **keishamen**
斜影 *oblique shadow* **shaei**
斜辺 *oblique side* **shahen**
斜角 *oblique angle* **shakaku**
斜光 *slanting rays* **shakō**
斜坑 *inclined shaft* **shakō**
斜面 *slope, slant* **shamen**
斜線 *slanted line* **shasen**
斜視 *slanted-eyed* **shashi**
斜視図 *perspective* **shashizu**
斜塔 *leaning tower* **shatō**
斜陽 *setting sun, declining* **shayō**
斜陽族 *declining elite family* **shayōzoku**

斜陽産業 *sunset-, declining industry* **shayō sangyō**
斜交い *diagonal, oblique* **hasukai**
急傾斜 *steep slope* **kyūkeisha**
斜字体 *italized letters, italics* **shajitai**
斜投影 *oblique projection* **shatōei**

偏 *artial, 43*	緯 *orizontal, 797*
片 *artial, 359*	縦 *ertical, 551*
直 *traight, 420*	並 *arallel, 444*

針 *eedle, 692*

547-B

Bullet 斜rajectory in 叙arration kept the sensation...

又 (again)

叙arration　　叙escription

JO
narration, description

FLIP: 5.0.b. Left & Right

叙位 *rank conferment* **joi**
叙事 *narration, story-telling* **joji**
叙事文 *description, narration* **jojibun**
叙事詩 *epic, heroic story* **jojishi**
叙情 *lyricism* **jojō**
叙情詩 *lyrical poetry* **jojōshi**
叙情詩人 *lyrical poet* **jojō shijin**
叙述 *narration, depiction, portrayal* **jojutsu**
叙景 *scenery description* **jokei**
叙勲 *decoration, award, citation* **jokun**
叙任 *post appointment, job assumption* **jonin**
叙説 *explanation, interpretation* **josetsu**
略叙 *brief narration, short description* **ryakujo**
平叙文 *declarative sentence* **heijobun**
自叙伝 *auto-biography* **jijoden**

紀 *arration, 727*	告 *eport, 266*
逓 *onvey, 304*	報 *eport, 733*
伝 *onvey, 619*	記 *ecord, 728*
談 *onverse, 308*	語 *alking, 780*

叔 *oung uncle, 510*

548-A

施*estow* 族*amily* 旅*ravel to the* 族*ribe of Abel...*

①施*estow* ②施*acilities*

方 (direction)

hodoko(su), SHI, SE
bestow, endow, carry out; facilities

Facing: 2.2. East ☞ (V)

❶ 布施 *alms for the poor, dole outs* **fuse**
布施市 *Fuse City, Ōsaka* **fuse-shi**
実施 *implement, enforce, execute* **jisshi**
施肥 *fertilization* **sehi**
施錠 *locking, padlocking* **sejō**
施工 *execution, carrying out* **sekō, shikō**
施米 *rice given for charity* **semai**
施物 *alms for the poor, dole outs* **semotsu**
施療 *free medical treatment* **seryō**
施主 *bereaved family* **seshu**
施薬 *free drugs, ~medicine* **seyaku**
施術 *surgical operation* **shijutsu**
施行 *enforcement, execution* **shikō, sekō**
施策 *policy, measures* **shisaku**
施政 *administration, governance* **shisei**
施政方針 *administrative policy, ~measure*
  shisei hōshin
❷ 施設 *facilities, complex* **shisetsu**
⇒ 福利施設 *welfare facilities* **fukuri shisetsu**

⇒ 福祉施設 *welfare facilities*
  fukushi shisetsu
⇒ 娯楽施設 *recreational facilities*
  goraku shisetsu
⇒ 厚生施設 *welfare facilities* **kōsei shisetsu**
⇒ 養護施設 *institution for the disabled*
  yōgo shisetsu
⇒ 遊技施設 *recreation facilities* **yūgi shisetsu**
施し物 *alms, charity, dole out* **hodokoshimono**
未実施 *not carried out, undone* **mijisshi**
施餓鬼① *memorial service for orphans* **segaki**
施餓鬼② *Buddhist rite of feeding hungry ghosts*
  segaki

立 *tand up,* 234	建 *onstruct,* 390
整 *djust,* 31	祉 *elfare,* 193

旋 *evolve,* 651

548-B

施*estow* 族*amily* 旅*ravel to the* 族*ribe of Abel...*

①族*amily* ②族*ribe*

方 (direction)

ZOKU
family; tribe

Facing: 3.0. ☞ Across

❶ 語族 *family of languages* **gozoku**
豪族 *powerful & influential family* **gōzoku**
姻族 *in-laws* **inzoku**
遺族 *bereaved family* **izoku**
華族 *noble family* **kazoku**
家族 *family, one's family* **kazoku**
⇒ 扶養家族 *family dependants* **fuyō kazoku**
血族 *blood relatives* **ketsuzoku**
貴族 *aristocrat, nobility* **kizoku**
皇族 *imperial family class* **kōzoku**
王族 *royal family, ~blood* **ōzoku**
親族 *close relative, close kin* **shinzoku**
氏族 *family, clan* **shizoku**
士族 *samurai clan* **shizoku**
族長 *family patriarch, ~matriarch* **zokuchō**
族滅 *family massacre* **zokumetsu**
族籍 *class & domicile* **zokuseki**
族称 *noble, samurai or commoner class* **zokushō**
核家族 *core-, immediate family* **kakukazoku**

斜陽族 *declining upper-class family* **shayōzoku**
❷ 亜族 *sub-tribe* **azoku**
蛮族 *savage tribe* **banzoku**
閥族 *savage tribe* **batsuzoku**
部族 *tribal group, tribe* **buzoku**
同族 *same tribe, ~family* **dōzoku**
民族 *tribal group, tribe* **minzoku**
⇒ 農耕民族 *agricultural folks* **nōkō minzoku**
暴走族 *motorcycle gang* **bōsōzoku**
種族 *race, tribe, species* **shuzoku**
水族 *aquatic animals* **suizoku**
一族郎党 *"all in the family..."* **ichizoku rōtō**

家 *amily,* 909	子 *hildren,* 456
父 *ather,* 467	縁 *inship,* 675
母 *other,* 90	孫 *randchild,* 263

旋 *evolve,* 651

548-C

施*estow* 族*amily* 旅*ravel to the* 族*ribe of Abel...*

方 (direction)

旅*ravel*　　旅*xcursion*

tabi, RYO
travel, trip, sightseeing, excursion, tourism

Facing: 3.0. ☞☜ Across

船旅	*sea voyage*	**funatabi**
旅籠	*inn, motel*	**hatago**
股旅	*vagabond life*	**matatabi**
長旅	*long travel*	**nagatabi**
旅団	*tour group, brigade*	**ryodan**
旅費	*travel expense*	**ryohi**
旅情	*urge to travel, travel mood*	**ryojō**
旅客	*traveller, tourist*	**ryokaku, ryokyaku**
旅館	*Japanese inn*	**ryokan**
旅券	*passport, travel document*	**ryoken**
旅行	*trip, travel*	**ryokō**
⇒団体旅行	*group tour, ~excursion*	**dantai ryokō**
⇒世界旅行	*world tour*	**sekai ryokō**
⇒修学旅行	*school excursion*	**shūgaku ryokō**
旅行家	*seasoned traveller, tourist*	**ryokōka**
旅行先	*travel destination*	**ryokōsaki**
旅行者	*tourist, traveller*	**ryokōsha**
旅舎	*inn, motel*	**ryosha**
旅愁	*journey loneliness*	**ryoshū**

旅程	*itinerary, travel plans*	**ryotei**
旅人	*traveller*	**tabibito, tabito, tabinin**
旅心	*urge to travel*	**tabigokoro**
旅寝	*travel inn, motel*	**tabine**
旅所	*resting place for palanquins*	**tabisho**
旅僧	*traveling monk*	**tabisō**
旅の空	*away from home*	**tabi no sora**
旅芸人	*strolling entertainer, ~artist*	**tabigeinin**
旅回り	*tour, travel*	**tabimawari**
旅戻り	*return trip*	**tabimodori**
旅疲れ	*travel fatigue*	**tabizukare**

行*rip, 79*	出*ome-out, 173*
来*oming, 871*	訪*isit, 737*
往*ome & go, 749*	外*utside, 188*

族*amily, 649*

549-A

Children at 遊*lay on* 旋*evolving rides they stay...*

辶 (transport)

遊*njoy*　　遊*lay*

aso(bu), YŪ
enjoy, play, leisure

Facing: 3.0. ☞☜ Across

浮遊	*floating, hovering*	**fuyū**
外遊	*foreign travels*	**gaiyū**
豪遊	*spree, revelry, frolic*	**gōyū**
回遊	*excursion, field trip*	**kaiyū**
漫遊	*excursion, field trip*	**manyū**
来遊	*dropping in, dropping by*	**raiyū**
周遊	*excursion, field trip*	**shūyū**
遊牧	*wandering-, nomadic lifestyle*	**yūboku**
遊泳	*leisure swimming*	**yūei**
⇒宇宙遊泳	*space walk*	**uchū yūei**
遊学	*educational-, learning tour*	**yūgaku**
遊撃	*search & kill*	**yūgeki**
遊戯	*playing & dancing*	**yūgi**
遊技	*amusement, past time*	**yūgi**
遊軍	*reservist corps*	**yūgun**
遊女	*prostitute, whore, hooker*	**yūjo**
遊金	*idle funds, play money*	**yūkin**
遊興	*merrymaking, revelry, party*	**yūkyō**
遊民	*idle-, leisure persons*	**yūmin**

遊覧	*excursion, sightseeing*	**yūran**
遊歴	*excursion, field trip*	**yūreki**
遊離	*isolation, seclusion*	**yūri**
遊資	*idle capital, ~funds*	**yūshi**
遊説	*campaigning, electioneering*	**yūzei**
園遊会	*garden-, lawn party*	**enyūkai**
舟遊び	*rowing, boating*	**funaasobi**
夢遊病	*sleepwalking, somnambulism*	**muyūbyō**
遊園地	*amusement park, theme park*	**yūenchi**
遊戯場	*playground, children's park*	**yūgijō**
遊び	*play, playing*	**asobi**
遊びに来る	*casual visit, dropping by*	**asobi(ni)kuru**

楽*njoy, 447*	享*njoy, 398*	悠*eisure, 898*
喫*njoy, 900*	閑*eisure, 283*	悦*leasant, 942*

族*amily, 649*

549-B

Children at 遊lay on 旋evolving rides they stay...

旋*evolve*　旋*otate*

SEN
revolve, rotate, circulate, gyrate, turnaround

斡旋 *good offices, mediation* **assen**
⇒就職斡旋 *job placement, recruitment*
　　shūshoku assen
斡旋者 *mediator, intermediary* **assensha**
凱旋 *victor's return, triumphal return* **gaisen**
凱旋門 *arch of triumph* **gaisenmon**
回旋 *turning, circling, rotating* **kaisen**
螺旋 *screw* **neji, rasen**
⇒木螺旋 *wooden screw* **mokuneji**
旋盤 *lathe* **senban**
旋盤工 *turner, lathe worker* **senbankō**
旋盤工場 *turnery* **senban kōjō**
旋回 *turning, circling, rotating* **senkai**
旋回飛行 *circular flying* **senkai hikō**
旋風 *whirlwind, cyclone, tornado* **senpū**
旋律 *melody, lathe* **senritsu**
旋転 *gyration, whirling* **senten**
周旋 *good offices, agency* **shūsen**
周旋業 *brokerage industry* **shūsengyō**

方 (direction)

Facing: 2.2. East ☞ (V)

周旋料 *broker's fee, commission* **shūsenryō**
周旋屋 *broker, commission agency* **shūsenya**
旋毛 *hair whorl, curl* **tsumuji, senmō**
旋毛曲がり *cranky person* **tsumujimagari**

回*otate, 458*	転*oll over, 661*
巡*round, 571*	繰*pinning, 851*

旅*ravel, 650*

550-A

腕rms, 胸hest & 胎terus saved from virus by 腕alents of
　　Dr. Malthus...

肉⇔月 (flesh, body part)

❶腕*rm*　❷腕*alent*

ude, WAN
arm; talent, skills, ability

❶細腕 *thin arm* **hosoude**
剛腕 *strong arm* **gōwan**
上腕 *upper arm* **jōwan**
片腕 *one-arm* **kataude**
右腕 *right arm, ~hand* **migiude, uwan**
左腕 *left-handed* **hidariude, sawan**
鉄腕 *strong arm* **tetsuwan**
腕木 *cross arm* **udegi**
腕首 *hand wrist* **udekubi**
腕枕 *resting head on one's arms* **udemakura**
腕輪 *hand bracelet* **udewa**
腕白 *prank, mischief, naughtiness* **wanpaku**
腕力 *physical strength* **wanryoku**
腕章 *arm band* **wanshō**
前腕 *forearm* **zenwan**
利き腕 *dominant hand* **kikiude**
二の腕 *upper arm* **ninoude**
押え腕 *presser arm* **osaeude**
腕時計 *wristwatch, watch* **udedokei**

FLIP: 7.2.b. Right Top (stem)
Facing: 3.0. ☞☜ Across

腕組み *folding of arms* **udegumi**
腕捲り *rolling up one's sleeves* **udemakuri**
腕っ節 *physical strength* **udeppushi**
腕相撲 *arm wrestling* **udezumō**
❷敏腕 *shrewd, capable, agile* **binwan**
才腕 *ability, skill* **saiwan**
手腕 *skill, ability, capability* **shuwan**
凄腕 *cracker jack, go-getter* **sugoude**
腕前 *skill, ability* **udemae**
腕利き *able person* **udekiki**
腕比べ *competition, contest* **udekurabe**
腕次第 *"depending on one's ability..."* **udeshidai**

能*bility, 321*	力*trength, 351*
巧*killful, 738*	博*xpertise, 514*
術*kills, 110*	修*xpertise, 898*

脚*legs, 387*

550-B

腕rms, 胸hest & 胎terus saved from virus by 腕alents of
Dr. Malthus...

肉⇔月 (flesh, body part)

胸hest 胸reast

mune, muna, KYŌ
chest, breast

Facing: 1.2. ☜ West (V)
FLIP: 8.0.a. Inner (flat)

度胸	nerve, guts, mettle, courage	**dokyō**
鳩胸	chicken breast	**hatomune**
豊胸	fulsome breasts	**hōkyō**
気胸	pneumothorax	**kikyō**
胸部	chest, breast	**kyōbu**
胸中	innermost feelings	**kyōchū**
胸泳	breaststroke swimming	**kyōei**
胸壁	chest wall	**kyōheki**
胸囲	chest size	**kyōi**
胸郭	thorax, chest	**kyōkaku**
胸襟	heart organ	**kyōkin**
胸腔	thorax cavity	**kyōkō**
胸骨	breast bone	**kyōkotsu**
胸裏	bosom, heart, feelings	**kyōri**
胸底	innermost feelings	**kyōtei**
胸痛	chest pains	**kyōtsū**
胸像	bust, sculpture	**kyōzō**
胸高	wearing high obi	**munadaka**
胸毛	chest hair	**munage**

胸倉	lapel	**munagura**
胸板	breast	**munaita**
胸元	breast, chest	**munamoto**
胸幅	chest width	**munehaba**
膿胸	pyothorax	**nōkyō**
大胸	main gist, main point	**oomune**
胸苦しい	tormented feelings	**munagurushii**
胸騒ぎ	premonition, foreboding	**munasawagi**
胸算用	mental calculation	**munazanyō**
胸当て	chest shield	**muneate**
胸三寸	"do as you please..."	**munesanzun**
胸焼け	heartburn, heartache	**muneyake**

肺ungs, 305	吹lowing, 642
息reathe, 586	風ind, 894

脳rain, 47

550-C

腕rms, 胸hest & 胎terus saved from virus by 腕alents of
Dr. Malthus...

肉⇔月 (flesh, body part)

胎terus 胎eotus

TAI
uterus, feotus, womb

FLIP: 7.3.a. Right Bottom (flat)

母胎	mother's womb	**botai**
堕胎	artificial abortion	**datai**
奪胎	adaptations	**dattai**
脱胎	artificial abortion	**dattai**
胚胎	embryo conception	**haitai**
受胎	conception, pregnancy	**jutai**
懐胎	conceiving a child, "in the way..."	**kaitai**
死胎	dead foetus	**shitai**
胎盤	placenta	**taiban**
胎動	foetal movement	**taidō**
胎毒	eczema at birth	**taidoku**
胎芽	propagule	**taiga**
胎児	foetus, embryo	**taiji**
胎中	conceiving a child, "in the way..."	**taijū, taichū**
胎教	foetal care, ~education	**taikyō**
胎内	inside the womb	**tainai**
胎生	viviparity	**taisei**
胎生学	embryology	**taiseigaku**
胎生動物	viviparous animals	**taisei dōbutsu**

誕hildbirth, 515	命ife, 362
産hildbirth, 883	娠regnancy, 61
生ife, 474	妊regnancy, 709

昭right, 529

551-A

暇*ree-time, too precious* 時*ime...*

日 (sunlight, daytime)

暇*ree time*　暇*eisure*

hima, KA
  free time, leisure, idle time, spare time

FLIP: 6.0.a. Left (flat)

閑暇 *leisure-, spare-, free time* **kanka**
休暇 *vacation, rest & recreation* **kyūka**
⇒育児休暇 *child-care leave* **ikuji kyūka**
⇒夏期休暇 *summer vacation, ~leave* **kaki kyūka**
⇒有給休暇 *paid leave, compensatory time-off*
  yūkyū kyūka
休暇願い *request for vacation* **kyūkanegai**
請暇 *request for vacation* **seika**
賜暇 *leave of absence, furlough* **shika**
寸暇 *spare moment, idle time* **sunka**
余暇 *leisure, spare time* **yoka**
暇乞い *taking a leave of absence* **itomagoi**
暇取る *take a break, respite* **himatoru**
暇潰し *killing time, whiling away*
  himatsubushi

閑*eisure,* 283	喫*njoy,* 900
悠*eisure,* 898	享*njoy,* 398
楽*njoy,* 447	遊*njoy,* 650

始*egin, 210*

551-B

暇*ree-time, too precious* 時*ime...*

日 (sunlight, daytime)

時*ime*　時*our*

toki, JI
  time, hour, duration

FLIP: 6.0.a. Left (flat)
FLIP: 7.2.a. Right Top (flat)

時めく *agitated heart-beat* **tokimeku**
時ならぬ *suddenly, untimely* **tokinaranu**
同時 *at the same time, simultaneously* **dōji**
平時 *peace time, normal time* **heiji**
一時 *one-time, temporary* **ichiji, hitotoki**
時代 *era, time, age, period* **jidai**
時評 *comments on current events* **jihyō**
時事 *time, occasion* **jiji**
時下 *recently, lately* **jika**
時価 *current-, market price* **jika**
時間 *time, hour* **jikan**
⇒拘束時間 *entire time spent* **kōsoku jikan**
時間割り *schedule, timetable* **jikanwari**
時期 *time, period* **jiki**
時機 *chance, occasion* **jiki**
時刻 *time, hour* **jikoku**
時給 *hourly wage, pay by the hour* **jikyū**
常時 *always, all the time* **jōji**
零時 *twelve high noon* **reiji**

臨時 *temporary, stop-gap* **rinji**
時雨 *wintry-, autumn shower* **shigure**
時化 *storm, poor catch of fish* **shike**
瞬時 *moment* **shunji**
当時 *that time, that same day* **tōji**
時計 *clock, watch* **tokei**
時々 *occasionally, now & then* **tokidoki**
随時 *at any time, when necessary* **zuiji**
娘時代 *girlhood years* **musumejidai**
田植時 *rice planting season* **tauedoki**
平安時代 *Heian Era (794-1185)* **heian jidai**

秒*econds,* 727	週*eekly,* 279
日*ay,* 14	月*onth,* 22
曜*eekday,* 849	年*ear,* 27

待*aiting. 940*

552-A
蚊osquito & 蛇nake frolic on the lake...

蚊osquito

虫 (insect)

FLIP: 7.0.b2. Right (stem)

ka, BUN
mosquito

家蚊 *mosquito house* **ieka**
蚊針 *fishing fly* **kabari**
蚊柱 *swarming mosquitoes* **kabashira**
蚊鉤 *fishing fly* **kakagi**
蚊屋 *mosquito net* **kaya**
蚊帳 *mosquito net* **kaya, kachō**
大蚊 *crane fly* **ooka**
藪蚊 *aedine mosquito* **yabuka**
揺蚊 *midge* **yuka**
羽斑蚊 *anopheles* **hamadaraka**
飛蚊症 *myodesopsia* **hibunshō**
蚊燻し *smoking-out mosquitoes* **kaibushi**
蚊蜻蛉 *crane fly* **katonbo**
蚊遣り *mosquito-repellent incense* **kayari**
蚊取り線香 *mosquito-repellent incense* **katori senkō**

昆 *nsect, 38*	蛍 *irefly, 628*
虫 *nsect, 369*	

蛇 *nake, 654*

552-B
蚊osquito & 蛇nake frolic on the lake...

蛇nake

虫 (insect)

Facing: 2.2. East ☞ (V)

hebi, JA, DA
snake

蛇革 *snakeskin* **hebikawa**
蛇遣い *snake tamer* **hebizukai**
長蛇 *long snake* **chōda**
長蛇の列 *long queue, long line* **chōda no retsu**
大蛇 *large serpent* **daija**
蛇蝎 *serpent & scorpion* **dakatsu**
蛇行 *meanderings* **dakō**
蛇足 *redundancy, needless repetition* **dasoku**
毒蛇 *poison snake* **dokuja, dokuhebi**
蛇腹 *bellows, cornice* **jabara**
蛇毒 *snake poison* **jadoku**
蛇口 *faucet, tap* **jaguchi**
蛇管 *watering hose* **jakan**
蛇体 *serpentine* **jatai**
金蛇 *Japanese grass lizard* **kanehebi**
水蛇 *water snake* **mizuhebi**
錦蛇 *python-, harlequin snake* **nishikihebi**
縞蛇 *Japanese rat snake* **shimahebi**
海蛇 *sea snake* **umihebi**

藪蛇 *causing needless troubles* **yabuhebi**
蛇皮線 *snake skin samisen* **jabisen**
蛇紋石 *serpentine* **jamonseki**
蛇の目 *bulls eye design; umbrella* **janome**
眼鏡蛇 *cobra* **meganehebi**
竜頭蛇尾 *great start-but-poor finish* **ryūtō dabi**

毒 *oison, 578*	猛 *ierce, 657*
細 *lender, 138*	烈 *ierce, 585*
長 *ong, 273*	獣 *east, 846*
激 *ierce, 170*	

蚊 *osquito, 654*

553-A
耕*ultivation to* 耗*essen when soil worsens...*

耒 (plow)

耕*ultivate*　　耕*arming*

tagaya(su), KŌ
 cultivate, farming, tilling

FLIP: 5.0.b. Left & Right

馬耕 *tilling land with a horse* **bakō**
筆耕 *copying-by-hand; stencil* **hikkō**
帰耕 *return to agriculture* **kikō**
耕地 *cultivated-, arable land* **kōchi**
耕土 *arable land* **kōdo**
耕具 *farming tools, ~implements* **kōgu**
耕作 *cultivation, farming* **kōsaku**
耕作物 *farm produce* **kōsakubutsu**
耕作地 *arable land, arable field* **kōsakuchi**
耕作者 *tiller, farmer* **kōsakusha**
耕耘 *cultivation, farming* **kōun**
農耕 *farming, cultivation, tillage* **nōkō**
農耕民族 *agricultural people, farming folk*
  nōkō minzoku
深耕 *deep ploughing* **shinkō**
退耕 *quit farming* **taikō**
水耕法 *fish farming, aquaculture* **suikōhō**

墾*ultivate, 164*	稲*ice plant, 893*
培*ultivate, 698*	畑*lantation, 482*
植*lant, 783*	農*griculture, 446*

耗*essen, 655*

553-B
耕*ultivation to* 耗*essen when soil worsens...*

耒 (plow)

耗*essen*　　耗*xpend*

MŌ, KŌ
 lessen, expend, wear away

FLIP: 6.0.b. Left (stem)

減耗 *natural decrease* **genmō**
摩耗 *abrasion, bruise* **mamō**
消耗 *wear & tear* **shōmō**
消耗品 *expendable supplies* **shōmōhin**
消耗戦 *war of attrition* **shōmōsen**
損耗 *wear & tear* **sonmō**

減*ecrease, 46*	少*ew, 459*
縮*hrink, 448*	微*light, 62*
幾*ew, 547*	

耕*ultivate, 655*

554-A
Rice 粒 rains 粧 dorn the wide plains...

米 (grains, rice)

粒 *rain*　　　粒 *ranule*

tsubu, RYŪ
grain, granule

FLIP: 5.0.a Left & Right

雨粒　*raindrops* **amatsubu**
泡粒　*bubble* **awatsubu**
一粒　*a grain of~* **hitotsubu**
一粒種　*only child* **hitotsubudane**
顆粒　*granules, granulated* **karyū**
穀粒　*grains* **kokuryū**
米粒　*rice grain* **kometsubu**
小粒　*small grains, ~drops* **kotsubu**
豆粒　*"like dots of beans..."* **mametsubu**
飯粒　*cooked rice grains* **meshitsubu**
大粒　*large grains, ~drops* **ootsubu**
粒度　*grain size* **ryūdo**
粒状　*granular, granulated* **ryūjō**
粒界　*grain boundary* **ryūkai**
粒径　*grain diameter* **ryūkei**
粒子　*atomic particle* **ryūshi**
粒食　*eating rice* **ryūshoku**
細粒　*granules* **sairyū**
砂粒　*sand gravel* **sunatsubu**

粒銀　*small silver coins* **tsubugin**
粒選　*good pick, well-selected* **tsubusen**
粒粒　*grains, lumps* **tsubutsubu, ryūryū**
粒剤　*granules, granulated* **tsubuzai**
粟粒　*millet grains* **zokuryū, awatsubu**
微粒子　*fine grains* **biryūshi**
芥子粒　*poppy seed; thinny tiny* **keshitsubu**
素粒子　*elementary particle* **soryūshi**
粒立つ　*grainy, foamy* **tsubudatsu**
粒選り　*"the chosen one..."* **tsubuyori**
粒揃い　*uniform excellence* **tsubuzoroi**

穀 *rain*, 41	麦 *arley*, 606	芽 *prout*, 57
穂 *rain*, 545	種 *eedling*, 430	苗 *prout*, 270

粧 *dorn*, 656

554-B
Rice 粒 rains 粧 dorn the wide plains...

米 (grains, rice)

粧 *dorn*　　　粧 *ecorate*

SHŌ
adorn, decorate, beautify, apply make up

FLIP: 6.0.b. Left (stem)

美粧　*beautiful make-up* **bishō**
美粧院　*beauty saloon, ~parlour* **bishōin**
化粧　*cosmetics, make-up* **keshō**
化粧箱　*make-up kit* **keshōbako**
化粧品　*cosmetics, make-up* **keshōhin**
厚化粧　*heavy make-up* **atsugeshō**
薄化粧　*light make-up* **usukeshō, usugeshō**
夕化粧　*evening make-up* **yūgeshō**
雪化粧　*snow blanket* **yukigeshō**

飾 *ecorate*, 664	麗 *retty*, 68
姿 *ppearance*, 609	美 *retty*, 124
態 *ppearance*, 322	佳 *retty*, 891
容 *ppearance*, 492	

粒 *rain*, 656

555-A

Beasts so 猛ierce, 猟unted by spears...

猛ierce   猛erocious

犬⇔犭 (dog; beast)

take, MŌ

fierce, ferocious, savage, bestial, aggressive

FLIP: 7.3.a. Right Bottom (flat)

獰猛	fierce, ferocious **dōmō**
猛爆	intensive bombing **mōbaku**
猛勉	intensive studying **mōben**
猛鳥	bird of prey **mōchō**
猛打	heavy hit **mōda**
猛打者	heavy batter, slugger **mōdasha**
猛毒	deadly poison **mōdoku**
猛煙	thick-, heavy smoke **mōen**
猛撃	fierce attack, heavy assault **mōgeki**
猛威	rage, violence **mōi**
猛獣	beast of prey, wild animal **mōjū**
猛火	raging flames, conflagration **mōka**
猛犬	fierce dog **mōken**
猛禽	bird of prey **mōkin**
猛攻	violent attack **mōkō**
猛烈	violent, vehement **mōretsu**
猛者	strong & bold man **mosa**
猛省	serious reflection **mōsei**
猛進	rushing recklessly **mōshin**

猛暑	intense-, scorching heat **mōsho**
猛将	valiant general **mōshō**
猛襲	fierce attack, heavy assault **mōshū**
猛追	hot pursuit, hot trail **mōtsui**
猛雨	heavy rainpour, downpour **mōu**
猛然	fiercely, ferociously **mōzen**
勇猛	bold, valiant **yūmō**
勇猛果敢	dauntless, daring **yūmō kakan**
猛練習	intensive training **mōrenshū**
猛反撃	fierce counter-attack **mōhangeki**
猛猛しい	ferocious, fierce **takedakeshii**

激ierce, 170	烈evere, 585
烈ierce, 585	蛮avage, 627
厳evere, 449	酷avagery, 266

猟unting, 657

555-B

Beasts so 猛ierce, 猟unted by spears...

猟unting   猟hase

犬⇔犭 (dog; beast)

RYŌ

hunting, chase

FLIP: 7.1. Right (Sort Of)

不猟	poor catch **furyō**
漁猟	fishing & hunting **gyorō**
銃猟	hunting gun, shotgun **jūryō**
猟人	hunter, huntsman, huntress **karyūdo**
禁猟	"no hunting!..." **kinryō**
密猟	poaching **mitsuryō**
猟場	hunting ground **ryōba**
猟銃	hunting gun, shotgun **ryōjū**
猟犬	hunting dog, hound dog **ryōken**
猟期	hunting season **ryōki**
猟李	hunting season **ryōki**
猟奇	hunting, chasing **ryōki**
猟師	hunter, huntsman **ryōshi**
猟色	lewdness, lustful **ryōshoku**
猟官	job hunting for a public office **ryōkan**
猟刀	hunting knife **ryōtō**
渉猟	voracious reading **shōryō**
狩猟	hunting, shooting **shuryō**
狩猟場	hunting ground **shuryōba**

狩猟家	hunter, huntsman, huntress **shuryōka**
狩猟期	hunting season **shuryōki**
狩猟解禁日	"hunting season open..." **shuryō kaikinbi**
狩猟禁止期	"hunting season closed..." **shuryō kinshiki**
出猟	going out hunting **shutsuryō**
大猟	large catch **tairyō**
遊猟	hunting **yūryō**
遊猟家	hunter **yūryōka**
御猟場	imperial hunting grounds **goryōba**

狩unting, 366	畜aising, 528
獣east, 846	牧asture, 647
飼aising, 835	捕eizure, 812

猶elay, 790

556-A
期*eriodic* 欺*raud stopped by Inspector Maude...

期*eriod* 期*xpect*

肉⇔月 (flesh, body part)

KI, GO

period, expect, season, term, duration

延期	*postponement, adjournment* **enki**
学期	*term, semester* **gakki**
半期	*half year, half term* **hanki**
一期	*in one's lifetime; one term* **ichigo**
時期	*time, period* **jiki**
夏期	*summer season* **kaki**
刑期	*prison term, jail sentence* **keiki**
期限	*time limit, period, expiry date* **kigen**
期日	*appointed date, time limit* **kijitsu**
期間	*period, term* **kikan**
期末	*end of term* **kimatsu**
期待	*expectation, anticipation* **kitai**
好期	*right time, good timing* **kōki**
後期	*second half* **kōki**
婚期	*marriageable age* **konki**
今期	*this term, this session* **konki**
満期	*expiration, expiry, maturity* **manki**
任期	*term of office, length of service* **ninki**
納期	*delivery time-limit* **nōki**

FLIP: 6.0.b. Left (stem)

最期	*one's last moments* **saigo**
死期	*hour of death, time of death* **shiki**
初期	*beginning, initial stages* **shoki**
周期	*period, cycle* **shūki**
早期	*early stage, early term* **sōki**
定期	*fixed-term* **teiki**
冬期	*winter, wintertime* **tōki**
前期	*first half year, first term* **zenki**
渇水期	*dry season* **kassuiki**
更年期	*menopause* **kōnenki**
幼児期	*infancy, childhood* **yōjiki**

時*ime, 653*	効*ffect, 645*
経*ime-lapse, 791*	果*ffect, 287*

欺*raudulent, 658*

556-B
期*eriodic* 欺*raud stopped by Inspector Maude...

欺*raudulent* 欺*eceit*

欠 (lacking)

azamu(ku), GI

bogus, fraudulent, deceit, phoney, pseudo, spurious

欺瞞	*swindle, deceit, fraud, shenanigan* **giman**
欺瞞者	*swindler, con artist, fraud* **gimansha**
欺瞞的	*deceitful, fraudulent, cheat* **gimanteki**
詐欺	*swindle, fraud, shenanigan* **sagi**
詐欺師	*swindler, con artist, fraud* **sagishi**
詐欺罪	*false pretext, deceit, deception* **sagizai**
詐欺譲渡	*fraudulent transfer, ~assignment* **sagi jōto**

FLIP: 6.0.b. Left (stem)

偽*raudulent, 509*	犯*riminal, 640*
詐*raudulent, 723*	悪*vil, 389*
罪*riminal, 289*	

散*catter, 337*

557-A

軸xle in 軟oft manuever, 軌ailroad 輸hipments 転oll-over...

車 (vehicle, wheel)

FLIP: 5.0.a Left & Right

JIKU
axle, axis

地軸	*earth axis*	**chijiku**
長軸	*major axis*	**chōjiku**
中軸	*axis, pivot*	**chūjiku**
動軸	*driving axle*	**dōjiku**
同軸	*same axle*	**dōjiku**
軸足	*pivotal leg*	**jikuashi**
軸箱	*axle box*	**jikubako**
軸木	*scroll roller*	**jikugi**
軸物	*scroll picture*	**jikumono**
軸索	*axis cylinder*	**jikusaku**
軸線	*axis line*	**jikusen**
軸装	*scroll mounting*	**jikusō**
花軸	*flower stalk*	**kajiku**
機軸	*axle, shaft, pivot, spindle*	**kijiku**
基軸	*criterion, standard*	**kijiku**
車軸	*axle, shaft, pivot, spindle*	**shajiku**
死軸	*dead axle*	**shijiku**
主軸	*principal axis*	**shujiku**
枢軸	*pivotal point*	**sūjiku**

短軸	*minor axis*	**tanjiku**
縦軸	*vertical axis, spindle*	**tatejiku**
横軸	*horizontal axis*	**yokojiku**
軸受け	*ball bearings*	**jikuuke**
回転軸	*revolution axis*	**kaitenjiku**
掛け軸	*hanging scroll*	**kakejiku**
巻き軸	*scroll roller*	**makijiku**
左右軸	*lateral axis*	**sayūjiku**
対称軸	*symmetry axis*	**taishōjiku**
座標軸	*co-ordinate axis*	**zahyōjiku**
玉軸受け	*ball bearings*	**tamajikuuke**

枢*ivot, 952*
轄*edge, 968*

抽*xtract,37*

557-B

軸xle in 軟oft manuever, 軌ailroad 輸hipments 転oll-over...

車 (vehicle, wheel)

FLIP: 6.0.b. Left (stem)

yawa(rakai), yawa(raka), NAN
soft, flexible, elastic

柔軟	*supple, flexible*	**jūnan**
柔軟性	*suppleness, pliability*	**jūnansei**
硬軟	*hardness-or-softness*	**kōnan**
軟便	*loose stool, watery faeces*	**nanben**
軟調	*weakness, bearish*	**nanchō**
軟泥	*ooze, slim, mire*	**nandei**
軟風	*gentle wind*	**nanfu, nanpū**
軟弱	*soft, feeble, pale*	**nanjaku**
軟弱外交	*weak-kneed diplomacy*	**nanjaku gaikō**
軟化	*softening, mollification*	**nanka**
軟禁	*lenient detention, house arrest*	**nankin**
軟膏	*ointment, salve*	**nankō**
軟鋼	*mild steel, soft iron*	**nankō**
軟骨	*cartilage, soft bone*	**nankotsu**
軟球	*softball*	**nankyū**
軟毛	*soft hairs, soft feathers*	**nanmō**
軟派	*moderate party; flirt*	**nanpa**
軟論	*weak argument*	**nanron**
軟性	*soft, elastic*	**nansei**

軟質	*soft, flexible*	**nanshitsu**
軟水	*soft water*	**nansui**
軟鉄	*soft iron*	**nantetsu**
軟投	*slow pitch*	**nantō**
軟文学	*simple literature*	**nanbungaku**
軟着陸	*soft-, smooth landing*	**nanchakuriku**
軟口蓋	*soft palate*	**nankōgai**
陸軟風	*land-to-sea breeze*	**riku nanfu, -nanpū**
軟式庭球	*softball tennis*	**nanshiki teikyū**
軟式野球	*rubber-ball baseball*	**nanshiki yakyū**
軟体動物	*mollusc*	**nantai dōbutsu**

柔*oft, 568*
弱*eakling, 908*
劣*nferior, 572*

較*ompare,774*

557-C

軸*xle in* 軟*oft manuever*, 軌*ailroad* 輸*hipments* 転*oll-over...*

車 *(vehicle, wheel)*

軌*ailroad* 軌*ailway*

KI

railroad, railway, track

不軌 *lawlessness, anarchy* **fuki**
常軌 *proper way, suitable method* **jōki**
軌道 *orbit, line, track* **kidō**
⇒無軌道 *"without a trace..."* **mukidō**
軌道修正 *railway-, railroad repair* **kidō shūsei**
軌範 *model, exemplar* **kihan**
規範的 *model, exemplary* **kihanteki**
軌条 *railway, railroad* **kijō**
軌間 *railroad track gauge* **kikan**
軌跡 *path, route* **kiseki**
広軌 *broad gauge* **kōki**
広軌鉄道 *broad-gauge railway* **kōki tetsudō**
狭軌 *narrow gauge* **kyōki**
単軌 *monorail, light rail* **tanki**

FLIP: 6.0.b. Left (stem)

交*rossing, 467*	運*ransport, 295*
行*rip, 79*	搬*ransport, 323*
通*assing, 59*	輸*ransport, 660*
旅*ravel, 650*	配*ransport, 754*

軒*[houses]*, 710

557-D

軸*xle in* 軟*oft manuever*, 軌*ailroad* 輸*hipments* 転*oll-over...*

車 *(vehicle, wheel)*

輸*hipment* 輸*elivery*

YU

shipment, delivery, hand-over, transport

禁輸 *embargo, prohibition* **kinyu**
禁輸品 *contraband goods, banned imports* **kinyuhin**
空輸 *air transport, air shipment* **kūyu**
密輸 *smuggling* **mitsuyu**
密輸団 *smuggling ring* **mitsuyudan**
運輸 *transportation, trucking* **unyu**
輸液 *transfusion* **yueki**
輸銀 *export-import bank* **yugin**
輸血 *blood transfusion* **yuketsu**
輸出 *export* **yushutsu**
輸出税 *export tariff, duties* **yushutsuzei**
輸出業 *export business* **yushutsugyō**
輸出港 *port of origin* **yushutsukō**
輸出入 *export & import* **yushutsunyū**
輸出入品 *import-export goods*
　　yushutsunyūhin
輸送 *transportation, trucking* **yusō**
⇒陸上輸送 *surface mail* **rikujō yusō**
輸送機 *transport plane* **yusōki**

FLIP: 6.0.b. Left (stem)

輸卒 *transport troops* **yusotsu**
直輸出 *direct export* **chokuyushutsu**
逆輸出 *re-export* **gyakuyushutsu**
金輸出 *gold export* **kinyushutsu**
輸尿管 *ureter* **yunyōkan**
輸入品 *import goods* **yunyūhin**
輸入港 *port of entry* **yunyūkō**
輸入税 *import tariff, duties* **yunyūzei**
輸卵管 *fallopian tube* **yurankan**
輸精管 *spermatic duct* **yuseikan**
貨物輸送機 *cargo plane* **kamotsu yusōki**

搬*ransport, 323*	荷*reight, 877*
送*ending, 708*	貨*reight, 191*
届*eliver, 631*	搭*reight, 146*

諭*dmonish*, 922

557-E

軸*xle in* 軟*oft manuever*, 軌*ailroad* 輸*hipments* 転*oll-over...*

車 (vehicle, wheel)

転*oll over* 転*verturn*

FLIP: 6.0.b. Left (stem)

koro(bu), koro(garu), koro(geru), koro(gasu), ten(zuru), TEN
roll over, overturn, capsize, topple down, tumbling

栄転	*job promotion* **eiten**	転校	*school transfer* **tenkō**
逆転	*reversal, about-face, U-turn* **gyakuten**	転向	*about-face, conversion* **tenkō**
変転	*change, transition* **henten**	転任	*change of post* **tennin**
一転	*one single turn* **itten**	転入	*moving in* **tennyū**
一転二転	*keeps on changing, unreliable* **itten niten**	転落	*falling down* **tenraku**
⇒心機一転	*change-of-heart* **shinki itten**	転籍	*residence transfer* **tenseki**
自転車	*bicycle, bike* **jitensha**	転進	*change of course* **tenshin**
回転	*revolution, rotation* **kaiten**	転出	*jobsite transfer, re-assignment* **tenshutsu**
好転	*improvement, change for the better* **kōten**	転転	*rolling, bouncing* **tenten**
急転	*sudden change* **kyūten**	転属	*transfer of section* **tenzoku**
捻転	*twisting, writhing* **nenten**	運転	*driving (motor vehicle)* **unten**
横転	*falling sideways* **ōten**		
転義	*figurative meaning* **tengi**		

滑*lide, 412*　　落*all-down, 826*
陥*all-down, 893*　衰*ecline, 374*
堕*all-down, 807*　倒*verthrow, 496*

軽*ightweight, 790*

転業 *changing career, ~profession* **tengyō**
転位 *transposition* **ten'i**
転移 *transfer, spread, change* **ten'i**
転化 *change, transformation* **tenka**
転記 *altering written entries* **tenki**
転勤 *job transfer, change of workplace* **tenkin**

558-A

乾*ried* 幹*ree-trunks from* 朝*ynasty Ming arrived this* 朝*orning...*

乙⇔乚 (fish hook)

乾*rying*　　乾*esiccate*

FLIP: 6.0.b. Left (stem)

ho(su), kawa(ku), kawa(kasu), KAN
drying, desiccate

乾魚	*dried fish* **hizakana**	乾坤	*heaven & earth* **kenkon**
乾咳	*dry cough* **inuiseki, karaseki**	乾坤一擲	*"all-or-nothing..."* **kenkon itteki**
乾物	*groceries, dry goods* **kanbutsu, himono**	速乾	*quick drying* **sokkan**
乾裂	*cracking due to dryness* **kanretsu**	干乾し	*starving, hungry, famish* **hiboshi**
乾田	*dry rice field* **kanden**	陰乾し	*drying in the shade* **kageboshi**
乾果	*dried fruits* **kanka**	乾干し	*dried fish, ~vegetables* **karaboshi**
乾季	*dry season* **kanki**	乾電池	*dry cell, dry battery* **kandenchi**
乾期	*dry season* **kanki**	乾拭き	*wiping clean with dry cloth* **karabuki**
乾麺	*dry noodles* **kanmen**	生乾き	*semi-drying* **namagawaki**
乾杯	*toast, cheers* **kanpai**	乾元時代	*Kengen Era (1302-1303)* **kengen jidai**
乾板	*dry plate* **kanpan**	乾涸びる	*drying thoroughly* **hikarabiru**
乾瓢	*dried gourd strip* **kanpyō**		
乾酪	*cheese* **kanraku**		

燥*rying, 852*
干*rying, 74*

幹*ree trunk, 662*

乾留 *carbonisation, distillation* **kanryū**
乾式 *drying process* **kanshiki**
乾漆 *dry lacquer* **kanshitsu**
乾燥 *dryness, desiccation* **kansō**
乾燥季 *dry season* **kansōki**
乾燥剤 *drying agent, desiccant* **kansōzai**

558-B

乾*ried* 幹*ree-trunks from* 朝*ynasty Ming arrived this* 朝*orning...*

干 (drying)

幹*ree trunk* 幹*runk*

miki, KAN
tree trunk, trunk

FLIP: 5.0.b. Left & Right

語幹 *word stem* **gokan**
樹幹 *trunk, shaft* **jukan**
幹部 *executive, officer* **kanbu**
幹部会 *executive-level meeting* **kanbukai**
幹事 *master of ceremonies, emcee* **kanji**
幹事長 *chief secretary, chief rapporteur* **kanjichō**
幹線 *main line, trunk line* **kansen**
幹線道路 *main road, trunk road* **kansen dōro**
基幹 *nucleus, core, basic (industries)* **kikan**
骨幹 *body built, physique* **kokkan**
根幹 *basis, foundation* **konkan**
才幹 *ability, talent* **saikan**
枝幹 *trunk & branches* **shikan**
主幹 *head, chief, boss* **shukan**
材幹 *ability, talent* **zaikan**
新幹線 *bullet train* **shinkansen**

枝*ree-branch, 704*	葉*eaf, 411*
木*ree, 461*	緑*reen, 841*
支*ranch, 201*	環*nvirons, 165*

軒*[houses], 710*

558-C

乾*ried* 幹*ree-trunks from* 朝*ynasty Ming arrived this* 朝*orning...*

肉⇔月 (flesh, body part)

❶朝*orning* ❷朝*ynasty*

asa, ashita, CHŌ
morning; dynasty, *North Korea*

FLIP: 6.0.b. Left (stem)

❶朝晩 *mornings & evenings, always* **asaban**
朝顔 *morning-glory flower* **asagao**
朝方 *toward the morning* **asagata**
朝曇 *morning clouds* **asagumori**
朝日 *morning sun, rising sun* **asahi**
朝風 *morning breeze* **asakaze**
朝飯 *breakfast, morning meal* **asameshi**
朝凪 *morning calm in the ocean* **asanagi**
朝潮 *morning tide* **asashio**
朝湯 *morning hotbath* **asayu**
朝刊 *morning newspaper* **chōkan**
朝来 *"since this morning..."* **chōrai**
朝礼 *office morning rites* **chōrei**
朝食 *breakfast, morning meal* **chōshoku**
早朝 *early morning* **sōchō**
朝開け *daybreak, dawn* **asaake**
朝立ち *early morning departure* **asadachi**
朝帰り *coming home in the morning* **asagaeri**
朝早く *early in the morning* **asahayaku**

朝寝坊 *late riser, oversleeping* **asanebō**
朝起き *early riser, waking up early* **asaoki**
朝焼け *morning glow* **asayake**

❷朝見 *imperial audience* **chōken**
朝政 *imperial government* **chōsei**
朝臣 *court nobility* **chōshin**
朝廷 *imperial court* **chōtei**
王朝 *dynasty* **ōchō**
清朝 *Manchu dynasty* **shinchō**
朝鮮 *entire Korea* **chōsen**
朝鮮半島 *Korean peninsula* **chōsen hantō**

日*un, 14*	明*right, 22*
日*ay, 14*	英*rilliance, 217*
暁*aybreak, 818*	東*riental, 220*

朝*orning, 662*

559-A

趣urpose 超xceeds and 越vertakes in 越ietnam's wake...

走 (running)

❶ 趣urpose　　**❷ 趣lavour**

omomuki, SHU
purpose; flavour

風趣 *natural beauty, ~charm* **fūshu**
雅趣 *elegance, grace* **gashu**
意趣 *intention; grudge* **ishu**
意趣返し *retaliation, getting even* **ishugaeshi**
情趣 *taste, flavour* **jōshu**
興趣 *elegance, flavour, interest* **kyōshu**
妙趣 *beauty & charm* **myōshu**
詩趣 *beauty of poetry* **shishu**
趣意 *aim, purpose, objective* **shui**
趣意書 *prospectus, catalogue* **shuisho**
趣向 *idea, device, plan* **shukō**
趣味 *hobby, liking, past time* **shumi**
⇒骨董趣味 *antiquarianism* **kottō shumi**
趣旨 *purpose, aim; meaning* **shushi**
野趣 *countryside beauty, rural scene* **yashu**
俗趣 *vulgar taste* **zokushu**
悪趣味 *vulgar taste, bad habit* **akushumi**
没趣味 *insipid, dull* **bosshumi**

FLIP: 6.1. Left Top
Facing: 2.2. East ☞ **(V)**

無趣味 *unsophisticated, lack of taste* **mushumi**
多趣味 *variety of interests* **tashumi**
新趣向 *fresh ideas, new plan* **shinshukō**

焦ocus, 919	慣abit, 532
目oint, 462	癖abitual, 65
優xcellence, 556	希esire, 208

越vertake, 663

559-B

趣urpose 超xceeds and 越vertakes in 越ietnam's wake...

走 (running)

❶ 越vertake　　**❷ 越ietnam**

ko(su), ko(eru), ETSU
overtake, exceed, pass-over, go beyond, transgress, skip over; Vietnam

❶超越 *transcendence, exceeding* **chōetsu**
越権 *abuse of power, arrogation* **ekken**
越境 *border transgression* **ekkyō**
越年 *outlive, outlast* **etsunen**
越冬 *wintering, hibernation* **ettō**
越冬隊 *wintering party* **ettōtai**
激越 *vehemence, fervour* **gekietsu**
卓越 *excellence, prominence* **takuetsu**
優越 *superiority, excellence* **yūetsu**
優越感 *superiority complex* **yūetsukan**
川越し *crossing a river* **kawagoshi**
垣越し *jumping the fence* **kakigoshi**
頭越し *by-passing one's boss* **atamagoshi**
葉越し *see thru the leaves* **hagoshi**
年越し *bidding the year out* **toshikoshi**
見越す *foresee, anticipate* **mikosu**
山越え *crossing mountains* **yamagoe**
引っ越し *transfer of residence, moving in* **hikkoshi**
勝ち越し *ahead with so many wins* **kachikoshi**

FLIP: 6.1. Left Top
Facing: 2.2. East ☞ **(V)**

借り越し *outstanding debt* **karikoshi**
繰り越し *transfer, move locations* **kurikoshi**
申し越し *request, application* **mōshikoshi**
追い越し *overpassing, overtaking* **oikoshi**
取り越し *do in advance* **torikoshi**
罷り越す *visit, call* **makarikosu**
持ち越す *carry over, bring over* **mochikosu**
乗り越す *overpass one's destination* **norikosu**
通り越す *overpass, overtake* **toorikosu**
踏み越える *overstep, step across* **fumikoeru**
飛び越える *jump, leap, hop* **tobikoeru**
❷日越 *Japan-Vietnam* **nichietsu**

過xcessive, 798	窮xtreme, 876
濫xcessive, 856	極xtreme, 947
超xceed, 664	甚xtreme, 293

趣nterest, 663

559-C

趣*urpose* 超*xceeds and* 越*vertakes in* 越*ietnam's wake...*

走 (running)

超*xceed* 超*uper*

ko(su), ko(eru), CHŌ
exceed, super, extraordinary, surpass

FLIP: 6.1. Left Top
FLIP: 7.3.a. Right Bottom (flat)

超凡 *uncommon, extraordinary* **chōbon**
超脱 *transcendence* **chōdatsu**
超越 *transcendence* **chōetsu**
超人 *superhuman, supernatural* **chōjin**
出超 *trade surplus* **shucchō**
超過 *excess, surplus* **chōka**
⇒輸出超過 *trade surplus* **yushutsu chōka**
超過額 *surplus-, excess amount* **chōkagaku**
超過勤務 *overtime work* **chōka kinmu**
超克 *surmount, overcome* **chōkoku**
超然 *aloof, indifferent* **chōzen**
超絶 *transcendence, exceeding* **chōzetsu**
超俗 *aloof, indifferent* **chōzoku**
入超 *excessive importation* **nyūchō**
散超 *excessive disbursement* **sanchō**
超ベリバ *extremely bad (slang)* **chōberiba**
超電導 *superconductor* **chōdendō**
超伝導 *superconductor* **chōdendō**
超満員 *crowded beyond capacity* **chōman'in**

超音波 *supersonic waves* **chōonpa**
超音速 *supersonic speed* **chōonsoku**
超大型 *extra large, supersize* **chōoogata**
超小型 *extra small, micro-* **chōkogata**
超大国 *superpower nation* **chōtaikoku**
超短波 *ultra-short waves* **chōtanpa**
超党派 *non-partisan* **chōtōha**
超特急 *super high-speed train* **chōtokkyū**
超特作 *special film* **chōtokusaku**
超高速度 *super high-speed* **chōkōsokudo**
超高層ビル *skyscraper* **chōkōsō biru**
超自然的 *supernatural* **chōshizenteki**
超現実主義 *surrealism* **chōgenjitsu shugi**

過*xcessive*, 798   越*vertake*, 663   極*xtreme*, 947
濫*xcessive*, 856   窮*xtreme*, 876   甚*xtreme*, 293

超*xceed*, 664

560-A

飾*ecorating at random leads to* 飽*oredom...*

食 (food)

飾*ecorate* 飾*dorn*

kaza(ru), SHOKU
decorate, adorn, beautify, bedeck, embellish, festoon, ornament

FLIP: 7.1. Right (Sort Of)

飾り *accessories, ornaments* **kazari**
⇒髪飾り *hair ornament* **kamikazari**
⇒着飾る *dress up, wear, put on (clothes)* **kikazaru**
⇒首飾り *necklace* **kubikazari**
⇒松飾り *Japanese New Year ornaments*
matsukazari
⇒耳飾り *earrings* **mimikazari**
⇒店飾り *window dressing* **misekazari**
⇒胸飾り *buttonhole, brooch* **munekazari**
⇒床飾り *alcove art objects* **tokokazari**
⇒羽ね飾り *feather on the lapel* **hanekazari**
飾り気 *showiness, pretentious, ostentation* **kazarike**
飾り窓 *display window* **kazarimado**
飾り物 *ornament, figurehead* **kazarimono**
飾り付け *decoration, ornament* **kazaritsuke**
飾り立てる *decorate, deck* **kazaritateru**
文飾 *flowery words, rhetorical* **bunshoku**
電飾 *decorative lights* **denshoku**
服飾 *fashion accessories* **fukushoku**

服飾品 *accessories, ornaments* **fukushokuhin**
粉飾 *bogus-, made-up stories* **funshoku**
粉飾決算 *ghost-, bogus accounts*
funshoku kessan
宝飾 *jewels & ornaments* **hōshoku**
潤飾 *embellishment, ornaments* **junshoku**
虚飾 *show, vanity, ostentation* **kyoshoku**
落飾 *tonsure* **rakushoku**
修飾 *ornamentation, decoration* **shūshoku**
修飾語 *word modifier* **shūshokugo**
装飾 *decoration, ornament* **sōshoku**
⇒室内装飾 *interior design* **shitsunai sōshoku**
装飾品 *decoration, ornament* **sōshokuhin**

潤*mbellish*, 930   容*ppearance*, 492
姿*ppearance*, 609   佳*eauty*, 891
態*ppearance*, 322   魅*eauty*, 969

師*xpert*, 483

560-B

飾ecorating at random leads to 飽oredom...

飽oredom 飽onotony

a(kiru), a(kasu), HŌ
boredom, monotony, get tired of, satiate, saturate

飽きる *get tired of, get bored* **akiru**
飽き性 *getting bored of* **akishō**
飽き飽き *get sick & tired of* **akiaki**
飽きっぽい *getting bored easily* **akippoi**
飽き足らない *discontented, unsatisfied*
  akitaranai
飽き足りない *discontented, unsatisfied* **akitarinai**
飽く迄も *"even in the worst case..."* **akumademo**
飽く無き *insatiable, untiring* **akunaki**
飽満 *satiety, gluttony* **hōman**
飽食 *satiety, gluttony* **hōshoku**
飽和 *saturation, congestion* **hōwa**
飽和点 *saturation point* **hōwaten**
光飽和 *light saturation* **hikarihōwa**
光飽和点 *light saturation point* **hikarihōwaten**
見飽きる *get tired of seeing* **miakiru**
過飽和 *oversaturation* **kahōwa**
聞き飽きる *"sick & tired of hearing..."* **kikiakiru**

食 (food)

Facing: 3.0. ☞☜ Across

惰 *dleness, 311*
怠 *azyness, 570*
暇 *ree time, 653*

飼 *reeding, 835*

561-A

鎖hained to a food 鉢owl, prisoner cried foul...

鎖hain   鎖losed

kusari, SA
chain, closed, locked, manacle, sealed

鎖網 *chain stitching* **kusariami**
鎖題 *chain-like poems* **kusaridai**
鎖鎌 *chain & sickle (communist symbol)* **kusarigama**
鎖車 *sprocket wheel* **kusariguruma**
鎖止め *sprocket* **kusaridome**
鎖歯車 *sprocket wheel* **kusari haguruma**
鎖伝動 *chain drive* **kusari dendō**
錨鎖 *hawser, chain cable* **byōsa**
封鎖 *blockade, blocking up* **fūsa**
閉鎖 *closing, shutting down* **heisa**
閉鎖的 *insular, exclusive, unsociable* **heisateki**
一鎖 *sole passage* **hitokusari**
金鎖 *gold chain* **kanagusari, kingusari**
連鎖 *chain, linkage* **rensa**
連鎖店 *chain store* **rensaten**
連鎖反応 *chain reaction* **rensa hannō**
鎖状 *chain-like* **kusarijō, sajō**
鎖状分子 *chain molecule* **sajō bunshi**
鎖国 *national isolation, reclusive state* **sakoku**

金 (metal)

FLIP: 5.0.b. Left & Right

鎖国主義 *national isolation, autarkism*
  sakoku shugi
鎖骨 *collarbone* **sakotsu**
鎖港 *"harbours closed..."* **sakō**
測鎖 *measuring chain* **sokusa**
鉄鎖 *iron chain* **tessa**

錠 *adlock, 550*   妨 *indrance, 734*
閉 *lose, 285*   遮 *nterrupt, 371*
阻 *mpede, 756*   禁 *rohibit, 560*

錯 *ixed-up, 335*

530-B

鎖*hained to a food* 鉢*owl, prisoner cried foul...*

鉢*owl*

金 (metal)

FLIP: 5.0.b. Left & Right

hachi, HATSU
bowl, pot

鉢物 *food bowl* **hachimono**
火鉢 *charcoal brazier* **hibachi**
衣鉢 *master's secret* **ihatsu**
小鉢 *small bowl* **kobachi**
乳鉢 *mortar* **nyūbachi**
お鉢 *rice bowl; around the crater* **ohachi**
托鉢 *religious mendicancy* **takuhatsu**
鉄鉢 *beggar priests bowl* **teppatsu**
鉢の花 *flower in a pot* **hachi no hana**
鉢合せ *chance meeting, meet with~* **hachiawase**
鉢巻き *headband* **hachimaki**
鉢植え *potted plant* **hachiue**
箱火鉢 *boxed brazier* **hakohibachi**
菓子鉢 *candy bowl* **kashibachi**
菊二鉢 *two pots of chrysanthemums* **kikufutahachi**
金魚鉢 *goldfish bowl* **kingyobachi**
捏ね蜂 *kneading thru* **konebachi**
盛り鉢 *bowl, pot* **moribachi**
長火鉢 *oblong brazier* **nagahibachi**

瀬戸鉢 *earthenware pot* **setobachi**
擂り鉢 *earthenware mortar* **suribachi**
捨て鉢 *throw-away bowl; in despair* **sutebachi**
釣り鉢 *hanging flowerpot* **tsuribachi**
植木鉢 *flowerpot* **uekibachi**
手洗い鉢 *wash basin* **tearaibachi**

盤*isk, 324*	食*oods, 255*
盆*ray, 594*	飯*eal, 256*
皿*ish, 21*	

鉗*eedle, 692*

562-A

Most 勧*ecommended* 歓*leasure,* 観*iewing one's treasure...*

勧*ecommend*   勧*dvice*

力 (strength, force)

Facing: 2.2. East ☞ (V)

susu(meru), KAN
recommend, advice, counsel, urge

勧め *advice, recommendation* **susume**
勧銀 *hypothecary bank* **kangin**
勧業 *industrialization, promotion of industries* **kangyō**
勧進 *fund-raising for temple construction* **kanjin**
勧進元 *promoter, sponsor* **kanjinmoto**
勧告 *advice, recommendation, counsel* **kankoku**
勧奨 *recommendation, advice* **kanshō**
勧誘 *invitation, solicitation, canvass* **kanyū**
勧誘員 *canvasser, solicitor* **kanyūin**
勧善懲悪 *rewarding good & punishing evil*
    kanzen chōaku

推*ecommend, 777*	承*pproval, 117*
薦*ecommend, 68*	賛*pproval, 334*
可*pproval, 15*	諾*pproval, 277*

歓*leasure, 667*

562-B

Most 勧ecommended 歓leasure, 観iewing one's treasure...

欠 (lacking)

歓*leasure*   歓*ordial*

KAN
pleasure, cordial, amicable, delight, joyous

Facing: 3.0. ☞☜ Across

哀歓 *joys & sorrows* **aikan**
合歓 *enjoying together* **gōkan**
歓談 *pleasant chat, friendly talks* **kandan**
歓迎 *welcome, cordial reception* **kangei**
歓迎会 *welcome party, reception* **kangeikai**
歓喜 *joy, delight, ecstasy* **kanki**
歓呼 *cheer, joy* **kanko**
歓楽 *pleasure, joy, delight* **kanraku**
歓楽街 *amusement area* **kanrakugai**
歓声 *shout-of-joy, cheers* **kansei**
歓心 *joy, pleasant* **kanshin**
歓心を買う *curry a favour* **kanshin o kau**
歓送 *send-off, farewell* **kansō**
歓送会 *farewell party* **kansōkai**
歓待 *hospitality, welcome* **kantai**
交歓 *exchange-of-courtesies* **kōkan**
交歓会 *welcome-, reception party* **kōkankai**
合歓木 *silk tree* **nemunoki**
大歓迎 *"sincerest welcome..."* **daikangei**

交歓試合 *goodwill-, friendship games* **kōkan jiai**

悦*leasant,* 942	喫*leasure,* 900
快*leasant,* 699	娯*leasure,* 453
楽*leasure,* 447	愉*leasure,* 922

勧*ecommend,* 666

562-C

Most 勧ecommended 歓leasure, 観iewing one's treasure...

見 (seeing)

観*iew*   観*cenery*

mi(ru), KAN
view, scenery, spectacle, vista

FLIP: 7.1. Right (Sort Of)

美観 *beautiful view, scenic view* **bikan**
傍観 *looking on, standing by* **bōkan**
直観 *intuition, hunch, sixth sense* **chokkan**
外観 *outward appearance* **gaikan**
概観 *surveying, approximating* **gaikan**
拝観 *seeing, visiting, looking* **haikan**
悲観 *pessimism, cynicism* **hikan**
偉観 *majestic-, magnificent view* **ikan**
観閲 *troops inspection parade* **kanetsu**
観劇 *going to the theatre* **kangeki**
観光 *tourism, sightseeing* **kankō**
観客 *audience, spectators* **kankyaku**
観念 *idea, conviction* **kannen**
観音 *goddess of mercy* **kannon**
観察 *observation, watching* **kansatsu**
観賞 *admiration, enjoyment* **kanshō**
観点 *point of view, standpoint* **kanten**
景観 *view, vista, panorama* **keikan**
客観 *objectivity, impartiality* **kyakkan**

楽観 *optimism, positive outlook* **rakkan**
盛観 *magnificent sight* **seikan**
静観 *wait & see* **seikan**
史観 *historical view* **shikan**
主観 *subjectivity, partiality* **shukan**
壮観 *magnificent scene* **sōkan**
達観 *philosophical view* **takkan**
人生観 *view-of-life* **jinseikan**
観覧車 *ferris wheel* **kanransha**
参観日 *parental visiting day (school)* **sankanbi**
世界観 *view-of-the-world* **sekaikan**

景*cenery,* 546	眼*yesight,* 771
眺*cenery,* 215	覧*bserve,* 592
見*eeing,* 307	視*bserve,* 815

親*ntimate,* 669

563-A

新resh, 新rand-new 薪irewood, 親ntimate 親arents approve...

斤 (axe)

新ew　　新resh　　新ovelty

atara(shii), ara(ta), SHIN
new, fresh, brand new, novelty

FLIP: 6.0.b. Left (stem)

革新 innovation, reform **kakushin**
更新 renewal, revising, updating **kōshin**
最新 the newest~ **saishin**
刷新 reform, renovation **sasshin**
新案 novel idea, unique idea **shin'an**
新聞 newspapers, dailies **shinbun**
新着 new arrivals, newcomers **shinchaku**
新鋭 new & powerful **shin'ei**
新顔 newcomer, ~face, fresh arrival **shingao**
新月 new moon **shingetsu**
新刊 new publication, ~issue **shinkan**
新館 new building, annex **shinkan**
新香 pickled vegetables **shinko, shinkō**
新婚 newly-married **shinkon**
新芽 sprout, shoot, bud **shinme**
新任 newly-appointed **shinnin**
新品 brand new, all-new **shinpin**
新来 new comer **shinrai**
新鮮 fresh goods **shinsen**

新卒 fresh graduate **shinsotsu**
新訂 new revision **shintei**
新造 newly-built **shinzō**
新潟県 Niigata Prefecture **niigata-ken**
新学期 new academic term **shingakki**
新幹線 bullet train **shinkansen**
新年会 New Year party **shinnenkai**
新商品 new products **shinshōhin**
明治維新 Meiji Restoration (1868) **meiji ishin**
耳新しい "never heard..." **mimiatarashii**
新郎新婦 bride & groom **shinrō shinpu**

鮮resh, 679	発tart, 368
始tart, 210	源ource, 431
初tart, 353	春pring, 579

親ntimate, 669

563-B

新resh, 新rand-new 薪irewood, 親ntimate 親arents approve...

艹 (grass)

薪irewood

takigi, maki, SHIN
firewood

FLIP: 6.2. Left Bottom

薪水 cooking **shinsui**
薪炭 firewood & charcoal **shintan**
薪割り wood chopping **makiwari**
薪拾い firewood gathering **takigihiroi**

燃urning, 445	材oods, 186
炊ooking, 865	林oods, 526
木ood, 461	

新resh, 668

563-C

新*resh*, 新*rand-new* 薪*irewood*, 親*ntimate* 親*arents approve...*

見 (seeing)

FLIP: 6.0.b. Left (stem)

❶親*arent* **❷親***ntimate*

oya, shita(shii), shita(shimu), SHIN
parent, folks; endear, fondness, intimate, bonding

❶ 仮親 *adoptive parents, foster parents* **karioya**
片親 *single parent* **kataoya**
肉親 *blood relatives* **nikushin**
親分 *big boss* **oyabun**
親玉 *gang boss, ringleader* **oyadama**
親心 *parental love, filial affection* **oyagokoro**
親父 *one's father* **oyaji**
親子 *parent & child* **oyako**
親元 *parental home* **oyamoto**
親指 *thumb, big toe* **oyayubi**
両親 *parents, father & mother* **ryōshin**
里親 *foster parent, adoptive parent* **satooya**
親権 ① *parental rights (child custody)* **shinken**
親王 *imperial prince* **shinnō**
親類 *blood relatives* **shinrui**
親政 *direct rule of the emperor* **shinsei**
親戚 *blood relatives* **shinseki**
等親 *first-degree relative* **tōshin**
継親 *step parent* **tsugioya, mamaoya**

親不孝 *ungrateful-, unfilial child* **oyafukō**
親殺し *parricide, patricide, matricide* **oyagoroshi**
育ての親 *foster parent* **sodate no oya**
親愛 *"dear, beloved..."* **shin'ai**
❷ 親交 *friendship, friendly relations* **shinkō**
親権 ② *formal complaint* **shinken**
親日 *pro-Japanese* **shinnichi**
親告 *formal complaint in person* **shinkoku**
親切 *kind, friendly, cordial* **shinsetsu**
親書 *autographed letter* **shinsho**
親展 *private & confidential letter* **shinten**
親善 *goodwill* **shinzen**
懇親会 *get-together, social gathering* **konshinkai**

懇*ntimacy, 164* 友*riendship, 408* 族*amily, 649*
款*oodwill, 42* 善*ighteous, 450* 家*amily, 909*

観*cenery, 667*

564-A

酵*ermentation* 酬*eward offered at* 酪*airy barnyard...*

酉 (liquor)

酵*erment* **酵***east*

KŌ
ferment, yeast, acidify, latter

FLIP: 6.0.a. Left (flat)

発酵 *fermentation* **hakkō**
発酵素 *yeast, ferment* **hakkōso**
酵母 *yeast, leaven* **kōbo**
酵母菌 *yeast bacteria* **kōbokin**
酵素 *enzyme* **kōso**

乳*airy, 970* 保*reserve, 552*
酪*airy, 670*

酸*cid, 764*

564-B

酵*ermentation* 酬*eward offered at* 酪*airy barnyard...*

酉 (liquor)

酬*eward*　　酬*eciprocate*

FLIP: 6.0.a. Left (flat)

muku(iru), SHŪ
reward, remuneration, reciprocate

報酬 *reward, pay, fee* **hōshū**
⇒無報酬 *free-of-charge, gratis* **muhōshū**
献酬 *exchange of sake cups (Shintō wedding)* **kenshū**
応酬 *reply, retort, response* **ōshū**

賞*ward, 554*	納*ayment, 296*
彰*ward, 325*	払*ayment, 682*
慶*ongratulate, 69*	料*ayment, 194*
賃*ayment, 145*	

州*rovince, 76*

564-C

酵*ermentation* 酬*eward offered at* 酪*airy barnyard...*

酉 (liquor)

酪*airy*　　酪*ilk products*

FLIP: 6.0.a. Left (flat)

RAKU
dairy, milk products

牛酪 *butter* **gyūraku**
乾酪 *cheese* **kanraku**
乳酪 *dairy products* **nyūraku**
酪牛 *dairy-, milking cow* **rakugyū**
酪農 *dairy farming* **rakunō**
酪農場 *dairy, dairy farm* **rakunōjō**
酪農家 *dairy farmer* **rakunōka**
酪農製品 *dairy products* **rakunō seihin**
酪酸 *butyric acid* **rakusan**

牛*attle, 179*	乳*airy, 970*
乳*ilk, 970*	牧*asture, 647*

酵*erment, 669*

565-A

踐*ctual* 踊*ance improves body balance...*

足 (feet, legs)

踐*ctual*　　踐*ractice*

SEN

actual, practice, implement

実践 *put into practice* **jissen**
実践的 *practical, applicable* **jissenteki**
践言 *keep-, bear in mind* **sengen**
践踏 *trample down* **sentō**

Facing: 2.2. East ☞ (V)

| 実*ruth, 121* | 執*arry-out, 268* |
| 真*ruth, 487* | 致*arry-out, 381* |

| 銭*oins, 767* |

565-B

踐*ctual* 踊*ance improves body balance...*

足 (feet, legs)

踊*ancing*

odo(ru), odo(ri), YŌ

dancing

踊り *dance, dancing* **odori**
踊り場 *dance area* **odoriba**
踊り字 *repetition character [々]* **odoriji**
踊り子 *dancer, ballet dancer* **odoriko**
踊り手 *dancer, dancing girl* **odorite**
踊り出す *dance* **odoridasu**
踊り込む *jump in, rush in* **odorikomu**
踊り回る *dance about, dance around* **odorimawaru**
躍り懸かる *spring upon* **odorikakaru**
舞踊 *dance, dancing* **buyō**
舞踊劇 *drama dance* **buyōgeki**
踊躍 *jumping with joy* **yōyaku**
民踊 *folk dance* **minyō**
盆踊り *Buddhist festival dance* **bon'odori**
小躍り *jumping with joy* **koodori**
素踊り *dancing without costumes* **suodori**
手踊り *posture dance* **teodori**
舞い踊る *dance* **maiodoru**
踊り狂う *crazy dancing* **odorikurū**

Facing: 3.0. ☞☜ Across
FLIP: 7.3.b. Right Bottom (stem)

舞*ancing, 167*	賀*elebration, 202*
跳*eaping, 216*	祝*elebration, 716*
興*ntertainment, 867*	足*eg, 481*
慶*ejoice, 69*	

| 躍*opping, 850* |

566-A

踏tepping on 跡elics convinced the skeptics...

足 (feet, legs)

FLIP: 7.1. Right (Sort Of)

踏tep on   踏ased on

fu(mu), fu(maeru), TŌ
step on, based on, tread on

踏み跡	footprint	**fumiato**
踏み台	stepping stone	**fumidai**
踏み段	step, stair	**fumidan**
踏み石	stepping stone	**fumiishi**
踏み出す	step forward	**fumidasu**
踏み外す	lose one's footing, go astray	**fumihazusu**
踏み切り	take-off, stepping out	**fumikiri**
踏み込む	raid, break-in, charge	**fumikomu**
踏み均す	beat, trample upon with feet	**fuminarasu**
踏み躙る	trample, crush, tread	**fuminijiru**
踏み抜く	step, tread thru	**fuminuku**
踏み潰す	crush underfoot, trample	**fumitsubusu**
踏み倒す	evade, trample down	**fumitaosu**
踏み荒らす	trample, tread, devastate	**fumiarasu**
踏み入れる	set, step in, tread on	**fumiireru**
踏み越える	overcome, step	**fumikoeru**
踏み鳴らす	stamp on	**fuminarasu**
踏み締める	step firmly, treat firmly	**fumishimeru**
踏み止まる	remain, hold back, stay	**fumitodomaru**

踏み付ける	trample upon	**fumitsukeru**
舞踏	dance, dancing	**butō**
高踏	high-standing, elevated	**kōtō**
未踏	untrodden, undefeated, unbeaten	**mitō**
踏破	travelling on foot, tramping	**tōha**
踏査	survey, exploration	**tōsa**
踏襲	following suit, pursuit	**tōshū**
雑踏	crowd, throng	**zattō**
足踏み	step, tread	**ashibumi**
値踏み	quotation, appraisal, estimate	**nebumi**
瀬踏み	sounding out, measuring depths	**sebumi**

基asis, 590	根oot, 772
拠asis, 473	脚egs, 387
礎ornerstone, 166	足egs, 481

踊ancing, 671

566-B

踏tepping on 跡elics convinced the skeptics...

足 (feet, legs)

FLIP: 7.1. Right (Sort Of)
Facing: 3.0. ⟸⟹ Across

跡elics   跡uins

ato, SEKI
relics, ruins, remains, trace

足跡	footprint, tracks	**ashiato, sokuseki**
跡地	site, location	**atochi**
跡形	traces, vestiges	**atokata**
跡目	successor as family head	**atome**
病跡	pathology	**byōseki**
犯跡	crime evidence	**hanseki**
秘跡	sacrament, holy rites	**hiseki**
筆跡	handwriting, penmanship	**hisseki**
遺跡	ruins, remains	**iseki**
人跡	human traces	**jinseki**
形跡	evidence, traces, marks	**keiseki**
軌跡	path, route, trail	**kiseki**
奇跡	miracle, wonder	**kiseki**
傷跡	scar, bruise, wound	**kizuato**
痕跡	traces, vestiges	**konseki**
古跡	old ruins	**koseki**
口跡	one's line in a script	**kōseki**
航跡	remains of a decrepit ship	**kōseki**
旧跡	historic site, ruins	**kyūseki**

名跡	famous historic site	**myōseki, meiseki**
聖跡	sacred historical place	**seiseki**
戦跡	old battlefield	**senseki**
城跡	castle-, palace ruins	**shiroato**
史跡	historic spot, ~relics	**shiseki**
失跡	disappearance, vanishing	**shisseki**
追跡	pursuit, chase	**tsuiseki**
罪跡	guilt evidence	**zaiseki**
跡継ぎ	successor, heir, heiress	**atotsugi**
跡付け	investigation, findings	**atozuke**

史istory, 85	残emain, 767
歴istory, 595	証vidence, 789
昔lden-times, 281	物hings, 647

踏ased on, 672

567-A

驗xamine a 騎orse-ride in the far & wide...

馬 (horse)

驗*xamine*　　驗*esting*

KEN, GEN
examine, testing, experience

FLIP: 7.0.b2. Right (stem)

実験 *clinical trial, experiment* **jikken**
受験 *exam preparation* **juken**
受験票 *examinee ticket* **jukenhyō**
受験科 *exam review course* **jukenka**
受験料 *exam fee* **jukenryō**
受験生 *exam reviewee* **jukensei**
受験者 *examinee, testee* **jukensha**
核実験 *nuclear test* **kakujikken**
経験 *experience* **keiken**
経験論 *empiricism* **keikenron**
経験者 *experienced person* **keikensha**
経験則 *"rule of the thumb..."* **keikensoku**
経験的 *by experience, empirical* **keikenteki**
験算 *account verification* **kenzan**
効験 *effect, efficacy* **kōken**
霊験 *miracle, act-of-God* **reiken**
試験 *examination, test, quiz* **shiken**
⇒筆記試験 *written examination* **hikki shiken**
⇒検定試験 *licensure exam* **kentei shiken**

⇒期末試験 *term examination* **kimatsu shiken**
⇒模擬試験 *reviewer exam* **mogi shiken**
⇒卒業試験 *graduation exam* **sotsugyō shiken**
試験官 *examiner* **shikenkan**
試験管 *test tube* **shikenkan**
試験紙 *litmus paper* **shikenshi**
試験疑獄 *torturous exams* **shiken jigoku**
体験 *experience* **taiken**
体験談 *talks on one's experience* **taikendan**
先験的 *transcendental* **senkenteki**
被験者 *examinee, testee* **hikensha**

貫*arry out, 532*	致*arry-out, 381*
行*erform, 79*	覚*emember, 307*
執*arry-out, 268*	記*hronicle, 728*

騒*oise, 924*

567-B

驗xamine a 騎orse-ride in the far & wide...

馬 (horse)

騎*orse ride*

KI
horse ride

FLIP: 7.2.b. Right Top (stem)
Facing: 3.0. ☞ ☜ Across

一騎 *one horseman, lone rider* **ikki**
一騎当千 *unmatched, invincible* **ikkitōsen**
一騎打ち *man-to-man combat, handfighting* **ikkiuchi**
従騎 *attendants on horseback* **jūki**
騎馬 *horse-mounted, horseriding* **kiba**
騎馬戦 *piggyback-, chicken fight* **kibasen**
騎馬隊 *cavalry soldiers* **kibatai**
騎兵 *cavalry, horseman* **kihei**
騎兵隊 *cavalry soldiers* **kiheitai**
騎乗 *on horseback, horse-mounted* **kijō**
騎銃 *carbine rifle* **kijū**
騎虎 *decided course-of-action* **kiko**
騎行 *travel by horse* **kikō**
騎射 *archery on horseback* **kisha**
騎士 *knight* **kishi**
騎士道 *chivalry* **kishidō**
騎手 *jockey, horseman* **kishu**
単騎 *lone horserider* **tanki**
軽騎兵 *light cavalry* **keikihei**

竜騎兵 *dragoon* **ryūkihei**
槍騎兵 *lancer* **sōkihei**
騎虎の勢 *"cannot quit..." momentum*
　　　kiko no ikioi

馬*orse, 318*	運*ransport, 295*
駄*orseload, 674*	搬*ransport, 323*
駆*alloping, 674*	輸*ransport, 660*
駅*rain station, 318*	配*ransport, 754*

騒*oise, 924*

568-A

Heavy 駄orseloads put horses in 駆alloping mode...

馬 (horse)

駄orseload 駄ood-for-nothing

DA

horse load, good-for-nothing

FLIP: 7.1. Right (Sort Of)

足駄 *rain clogs* **ashida**
駄馬 *pack horse* **daba**
駄弁 *idle talk, rubbish talk* **daben**
駄文 *poor writing, illegible penmanship* **dabun**
駄賃 *tip, reward* **dachin**
駄駄 *peevishness, whiny* **dada**
駄駄っ子 *fretful child* **dadakko**
駄犬 *mongrel, mutt* **daken**
駄句 *poor poem* **daku**
駄目 *"no good, hopeless..."* **dame**
駄作 *poor work, trash, worthless* **dasaku**
下駄 *Japanese wooden clogs* **geta**
無駄 *waste, futility, in vain* **muda**
無駄足 *useless trip* **mudaashi**
無駄話 *empty talk* **mudabanashi**
無駄骨 *vain efforts* **mudabone**
無駄金 *wasted money* **mudagane**
無駄口 *idle talk, rubbish talk* **mudaguchi**
無駄毛 *unwanted hair* **mudage**

無駄飯 *idle lifestyle; food leftovers* **mudameshi**
無駄死に *senseless death* **mudaji(ni)**
荷駄 *horseload* **nida**
雪駄 *leather-soled clogs* **setta**
駄法螺 *boastful talk* **dabora**
駄菓子 *cheep sweets* **dagashi**
駄洒落 *poor pun, cheap joke* **dajare**
韋駄天 *lightning quick* **idaten**
駒下駄 *low wooden clogs* **komageta**
高下駄 *high wooden clogs* **takageta**
税金無駄使い *waste of taxpayer's money*
　　zeikin mudazukai

馬orse, 318	駆alloping, 674
騎orse ride, 673	駅rain station, 318

騎orse ride, 673	駆alloping, 674

568-B

Heavy 駄orseloads put horses in 駆alloping mode...

馬 (horse)

駆alloping 駆orseride

ka(keru), ka(ru), KU

galloping, horseride

Facing: 2.2. East ☞ (V)

駆け足 *run, gallop* **kakeashi**
駆け出し *novice, beginner, greenhorn* **kakedashi**
駆け引き *bargaining, tactics* **kakehiki**
駆けっこ *race, running contest* **kakekko**
駆け込む *rush in, dash, charge* **kakekomu**
駆け回る *get busy, run around* **kakemawaru**
駆け落ち *elopement, runaway* **kakeochi**
駆け寄る *run up* **kakeyoru**
駆け降りる *run down* **kakeoriru**
駆け付ける *rush, hurry, run* **kaketsukeru**
駆け上がる *run up* **kakeagaru**
駆け抜ける *run thru (fence)* **kakenukeru**
馳駆 *exert oneself, dash around* **chiku**
長駆 *long horseride journey* **chōku**
駆逐 *expulsion, being driven away* **kuchiku**
駆動 *operating, driving* **kudō**
駆除 *extermination, getting rid of* **kujo**
駆使 *adroit, "good command of..."* **kushi**
疾駆 *ride fast on a horse* **shikku**

朝駆け *early morning ride; attack at dawn* **asagake**
駆虫剤 *insecticides, insect-repellent* **kuchūzai**
駆潜艇 *submarine chaser* **kusentei**
先駆け *pioneer, forerunner, innovator* **sakigake**
先駆者 *pioneer, forerunner, innovator* **senkusha**
遠駆け *long ride, long march* **toogake**
駆り出す *lead, dash out, start running* **karidasu**
抜け駆け *scoop, "stealing the thunder..."* **nukegake**
駆り立てる *drive, pursue* **karitateru**
駆り集める *gather* **kariatsumeru**
前駆症状 *premonitory symptoms* **zenku shōjō**

馬orse, 318	駄orse load, 674
騎orse ride, 673	駅rain station, 318

騎orse ride, 673	

569-A

Feudal 縁elations govern 綿otton plantations...

糸 (thread, continuity)

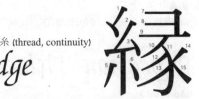

縁elationship

縁dge

Facing: 3.0. ☞☜ Across

fuchi, enishi, EN
relationship, edge, kinship

悪縁	*undesirable bond*	**akuen**
縁談	*marriage proposal*	**endan**
縁側	*veranda, porch*	**engawa**
縁起	*omen, luck*	**engi**
縁故	*connexion, relation*	**enko**
縁日	*fair, festival, feast*	**ennichi**
縁先	*veranda edge*	**ensaki**
縁戚	*relative, kinship*	**enseki**
復縁	*reconciliation, rapprochement*	**fukuen**
船縁	*side of ship, ship deck*	**funaberi**
銀縁	*silver rim*	**ginbuchi**
因縁	*fate, relation*	**innen**
血縁	*blood relationship, kinship*	**ketsuen**
奇縁	*strange coincidence*	**kien**
金縁	*gold rim*	**kinbuchi**
無縁	*unknown, x-factor*	**muen**
内縁	*common-law marriage*	**naien**
良縁	*good match*	**ryōen**
宿縁	*fate, destiny*	**shukuen**

遠縁	*distant relationship*	**tooen**
由縁	*relationship, reason, rationale*	**yuen**
絶縁	*breaking off relations, disowning*	**zetsuen**
俗縁	*worldly ties*	**zokuen**
縁の下	*space under the floor*	**en no shita**
縁遠い	*far removed; no chance to marry*	**endooi**
縁組み	*adoption, marriage*	**engumi**
縁取り	*edge hemming*	**fuchidori**
縁引き	*relation, connexion*	**enbiki**
腐れ縁	*undesirable bond*	**kusareen**
離縁状	*letter of divorce*	**rienjō**

系*osterity,* 262	祖*ncestor,* 953
係*elative,* 263	血*lood,* 20
系*escendants,* 262	継*ontinuity,* 958

緑*reen,* 841   線*ine,* 531

569-B

Feudal 縁elations govern 綿otton plantations...

糸 (thread, continuity)

綿otton

wata, MEN
cotton

FLIP: 7.0.b1. Right (stem)

原綿	*raw cotton*	**genmen**
石綿	*asbestos*	**ishiwata, sekimen**
純綿	*pure cotton, 100% cotton*	**junmen**
海綿	*sponge*	**kaimen**
真綿	*silk floss*	**mawata**
綿棒	*cotton spinning*	**menbō**
綿花	*raw cotton*	**menka**
綿綿	*unceasing, endless*	**menmen**
綿密	*detailed, itemized*	**menmitsu**
綿布	*cotton cloth*	**menpu**
綿服	*cotton clothes*	**menpuku**
綿糸	*cotton yarn*	**menshi**
綿羊	*sheep cotton*	**menyō**
木綿	*cotton cloth*	**momen**
連綿	*uninterrupted, consecutive*	**renmen**
綿油	*cottonseed oil*	**wataabura**
綿飴	*cotton candy*	**wataame**
綿種	*cotton seeds*	**watadane**
綿毛	*down*	**watage**

綿雲	*fleecy clouds*	**watagumo**
綿雪	*large snowflakes*	**watayuki**
綿入れ	*wadded garment, ~quilt*	**wataire**
綿繰り	*cotton ginning*	**watakuri**
綿抜き	*unpadded kimono*	**watanuki**
綿打ち	*cotton willowing*	**watauchi**
綿火薬	*cotton for gunpowder*	**menkayaku**
木綿糸	*cotton thread*	**momen'ito**
綿織物	*cotton fabrics, ~cloth*	**men'orimono**
綿製品	*cotton goods*	**menseihin**
綿菓子	*cotton candy*	**watagashi**

布*loth,* 208	糸*hread,* 375
衣*lothes,* 355	縫*ewing,* 779
裁*lothes,* 802	繰*pinning,* 851
服*lothes,* 734	紡*pinning,* 735

線*ine,* 531

570-A

所*ocation of special* 房*lusters for* 啓*nlightened masters...*

戸 (doorway)

所*ocation* 所*lace*

tokoro, SHO
location, place, venue, locality; nominalization

Facing: 2.2. East ☞ (V)

場所 *place, room* **basho**
便所 *toilet, rest room, wash room* **benjo**
茶所 *tea-growing area* **chadokoro**
台所 *kitchen* **daidokoro**
居所 *whereabouts, address* **idokoro**
住所 *address, residence* **jūsho**
近所 *neighbour* **kinjo**
空所 *empty space* **kūsho**
名所 *famous place, tourist site* **meisho**
死所 *death place* **shinidokoro**
所業 *deed, work, feat* **shogyō**
所員 *staff member* **shoin**
所持 *possession, property* **shoji**
所感 *impression, opinion* **shokan**
所管 *jurisdiction, administration* **shokan**
所轄 *jurisdiction, administration* **shokatsu**
所見 *views, opinion, comment* **shoken**
所望 *desire, request* **shomō**
所産 *product, fruits* **shosan**

所説 *one's explanation* **shosetsu**
所信 *belief, conviction* **shoshin**
所帯 *household, family* **shotai**
所有 *ownership, possession* **shoyū**
所在 *whereabouts, address* **shozai**
短所 *behaviour, conduct, action* **tansho**
要所 *strategic point* **yōsho**
所以 *reason, why* **yuen**
随所 *everywhere, any place* **zuisho**
研究所 *research institute* **kenkyūsho**
裁判所 *court of law* **saibansho**
市役所 *city hall, municipal hall* **shiyakusho**

場*ocation, 147*	居*esidence, 384*
箇*[places], 52*	住*esidence, 750*
宅*esidence, 82*	

房*luster, 676*

571-B

所*ocation of special* 房*lusters for* 啓*nlightened masters...*

戸 (doorway)

房*luster* 房*hamber*

fusa, BŌ
cluster, chamber, tassel, room

Facing: 2.1. East ☞ (H)

房中 *in the bedroom* **bōchū**
房事 *bedroom privacy* **bōji**
厨房 *kitchen, galley* **chūbō**
暖房 *heating* **danbō**
暖房装置 *heating system* **danbō sōchi**
同房 *same cell* **dōbō**
独房 *solitary cell* **dokubō**
房房 *bushy hair* **fusafusa**
房毛 *tuft, tassel* **fusage**
蜂房 *beehive, apiary* **hōbō**
官房 *secretariat* **kanbō**
官房長官 *cabinet chief secretary* **kanbō chōkan**
監房 *prison cell* **kanbō**
閨房 *bedroom, sleeping quarter* **keibō**
工房 *studio, atelier* **kōbō**
黒房 *sumo black tassel* **kurobusa**
女房 *one's wife* **nyōbō**
女房役 *helper* **nyōbōyaku**
女房持ち *married man* **nyōbōmochi**

乳房 *breast nipples* **nyūbō, chibusa**
冷房 *air conditioning, cooler* **reibō**
冷房中 *"air-condition on..."* **reibōchū**
船房 *cabin* **senbō**
子房 *plant ovary* **shibō**
書房 *study; bookstore* **shobō**
僧房 *monk dormitory* **sōbō**
左心房 *left heart atrium* **sashinbō**
右心房 *right heart atrium* **ushinbō**
文房具 *stationery, office supplies* **bunbōgu**
文房具屋 *stationery store* **bunbōguya**

室*oom, 485*

戻*eturn, 541*

570-C

所*ocation of special* 房*lusters for* 啓*nlightened masters...*

口 (mouth)

啓*nlighten*　　　　啓*wakening*

hiraku, KEI
enlighten, awakening

FLIP: 4.0.a. Bottom (flat)

中啓 *ritual, ceremonial* **chūkei**
行啓 *imperial presence* **gyōkei**
拝啓 *"Dear sir, Madame..."* **haikei**
還啓 *empress's return* **kankei**
啓発 *enlightenment, edification* **keihatsu**
啓示 *revelation, apocalypse* **keiji**
啓上 *terms-of-respect* **keijō**
啓蒙 *enlightenment, elucidation* **keimō**
啓蒙的 *enlightening, awakening* **keimōteki**
謹啓 *"Dear Sirs, Gentlemen..."* **kinkei**
天啓 *divine revelation, enlightenment* **tenkei**

哲*isdom, 53*	純*urity, 199*
悟*nlighten, 780*	浄*urity, 230*
脳*rains, 47*	粋*urity, 762*

所*ocation, 676*

571-A

扇*olding-fan left by the* 扉*oor, my* 肩*houlders hot no more...*

戸 (doorway)

扇*olding-fan*　　　　扇*an*

ōgi, SEN
folding fan, fan

Facing: 3.0. ☞☜ Across

銀扇 *silver-coloured fan* **ginsen**
白扇 *white folding fan* **hakusen**
金扇 *gold coloured fan* **kinsen**
舞扇 *fan used in a Japanese dance* **maiōgi**
扇形 *sector, group* **ōgigata, senkei**
扇動 *instigation, incitement, agitation* **sendō**
扇動者 *agitator, instigator* **sendōsha**
扇動的 *inflammatory, incendiary* **sendōteki**
扇状 *fan-shaped object* **senjō**
扇情 *inflammatory, provocative* **senjō**
扇情的 *inflammatory, provocative* **senjōteki**
扇子 *hand fan* **sensu**
鉄扇 *iron-lined fan* **tessen**
団扇 *folding fan* **uchiwa**
換気扇 *ventilation fan* **kankisen**
扇状地 *alluvial fan* **senjōchi**
扇風機 *electric fan* **senpūki**
夏炉冬扇 *useless things* **karo tōsen**

風*ind, 894*	手*and, 370*
吹*lowing, 642*	携*andcarry, 151*

扉*oor, 678*

571-B

扇olding-fan left by the 扉oor, my 肩houlders hot no more...

戸 (doorway)

扉oor 　 扉inged door

tobira, HI
door, hinged door

開扉	opening the door	**kaihi**
門扉	doors of a gate	**monpi**
鉄扉	iron door	**teppi**
扉絵	frontispiece (title page)	**tobirae**
裏扉	back leaf (title page)	**uratobira**
防火扉	fire-proof door	**bōkatobira, bōkahi**
防水扉	watertight-door	**bōsuitobira, bōsuihi**
自動扉	automatic door	**jidōtobira**

FLIP: 8.0.b. Inner (stem)

戸 oor, 428	門 ate, 286
扉 oor, 678	口 pening, 458

雇 mploy, 343

571-C

扇olding-fan left by the 扉oor, my 肩houlders hot no more...

肉⇔月 (flesh, body part)

肩houlder

kata, KEN
shoulder

Facing: 3.0. 🖝🖜 Across

比肩	equal, tantamount	**hiken**
肩口	near the shoulders	**kataguchi**
肩車	piggyback, shoulder ride (child)	**kataguruma**
肩幅	shoulder width	**katahaba**
肩越	over one's shoulders	**katagoshi**
肩身	one's stake, face, honour	**katami**
肩先	shoulders	**katasaki**
肩章	shoulder strap, epaulet	**kenshō**
強肩	strong shoulders	**kyōken**
路肩	road shoulder	**rokata**
双肩	shoulders	**sōken**
怒り肩	square shoulder	**ikarigata**
肩上げ	tuck on one's shoulders	**kataage**
肩揚げ	tuck on one's shoulders	**kataage**
肩当て	shoulder pad	**kataate**
肩書き	title, degree	**katagaki**
肩入れ	support, backing	**kataire**
肩掛け	shawl	**katakake**
肩凝り	stiff shoulders	**katakori**

肩脱ぎ	bare one's shoulder	**katanugi**
肩甲骨	shoulder blade, scapula	**kenkōkotsu**
撫で肩	drooping shoulders	**nadegata**
肩代わり	take-over, assume	**katagawari**
肩慣らし	warm-up, preparing	**katanarashi**
肩透かし	dodge, duck, elude	**katasukashi**

首 ead, 311	胴 orso, 867
首 eck, 311	背 ack, 372

肯 ffirmative, 616

572-A

鮮*ivid* 鯨*hales seen in* 鮮*resh Wales...*

鮮*resh*　　鮮*ivid*

aza(yaka), SEN
　　fresh, vivid

生鮮　*fresh* **seisen**
生鮮度　*food freshness* **seisendo**
鮮度　*food freshness* **sendo**
鮮鋭　*clear & sharp* **sen'ei**
鮮魚　*fresh fish, raw fish* **sengyo**
鮮血　*fresh blood* **senketsu**
鮮紅　*scarlet* **senkō**
鮮明　*vivid, clear* **senmei**
⇒不鮮明　*blurry, unclear* **fusenmei**
鮮肉　*fresh meat* **senniku**
鮮麗　*vivid, gorgeous* **senrei**
鮮烈　*striking, vivid* **senretsu**
鮮少　*a few, little* **senshō**
新鮮　*food freshness* **shinsen**
朝鮮　*Korea* **chōsen**
北朝鮮　*North Korea* **kita chōsen**
朝鮮語　*Korean language* **chōsengo**
朝鮮人　*Korean* **chōsenjin**
朝鮮半島　*Korean Peninsula* **chōsen hantō**

魚 (fishes)

FLIP: 7.0.b1. Right (stem)

朝鮮人参　*ginseng* **chōsen ninjin**
北鮮　*North Korea* **hokusen**
南鮮　*South Korea* **nansen**

| 新*resh, 668* | 魚*ishes, 49* |
| 生*aw, 474* | 菜*egetable, 915* |

| 犠*acrifice, 342* |

572-B

鮮*ivid* 鯨*hales seen in* 鮮*resh Wales...*

鯨*hale*

kujira, GEI
　　whale

鯨波　*sky-high waves* **geiha**
鯨飲　*"drinking like a fish..."* **geiin**
鯨骨　*whale bone* **geikotsu**
鯨肉　*whale meat* **geiniku, kujiraniku**
鯨脂　*blubber, lard, tallow* **geishi, kujira abura**
鯨油　*whale oil* **geiyu**
捕鯨　*whaling, whale fishing* **hogei**
捕鯨船　*whaler, whaling vessel* **hogeisen**
鯨尺　*unit of length (37.8 cm)* **kujirajaku**
鯨幕　*black & white curtain* **kujiramaku**
巨鯨　*huge whale* **kyogei**
山鯨　*wild boar* **yamakujira**
抹香鯨　*sperm whale* **makkō kujira**

魚 (fishes)

FLIP: 7.0.b1. Right (stem)

魚*ishes, 49*	巨*iant, 206*
釣*ishing, 697*	洋*cean, 247*
海*cean, 241*	

| 鮮*resh, 679* |

573-A

疫*pidemic* of 疾*peedy* 痢*iarrhoea*--not a 痴*oolish* 疾*isease*, Mama Mia...

疒 (sickness)

疫*pidemic* 疫*ontagious*

EKI, YAKU
epidemic, contagious, communicable, infectious, contamination

FLIP: 8.0.b. Inner (stem)

悪疫 *plague, pestilence* **akueki**
防疫 *epidemics prevention* **bōeki**
疫病 *plague, epidemic, pestilence* **ekibyō, yakubyō**
疫学 *epidemiology* **ekigaku**
疫痢 *children dysentery* **ekiri**
牛疫 *cattle disease epidemic* **gyūeki**
獣疫 *animal-borne epidemic* **jūeki**
検疫 *quarantine inspection* **ken'eki**
検疫官 *quarantine officer* **ken'ekikan**
検疫所 *quarantine station* **ken'ekisho**
免疫 *body immunity* **men'eki**
免疫性 *body immunity* **men'ekisei**
疫病神 *god of plague; disgusting fellow* **yakubyōgami**

患*ickness, 475*	剤*edicine, 961*
病*ickness, 213*	療*ecuperate, 67*
症*ickness, 788*	治*ecuperate, 210*
医*edicine, 19*	癒*ecuperate, 923*
薬*edicine, 447*	

疾*isease, 681*

573-B

疫*pidemic* of 疾*peedy* 痢*iarrhoea*--not a 痴*oolish* 疾*isease*, Mama Mia...

疒 (sickness)

痢*iarrhoea*

RI
diarrhoea

Facing: 3.0. ☞☜ Across

疫痢 *children dysentery* **ekiri**
下痢 *diarrhoea* **geri**
赤痢 *dysentery* **sekiri**

患*ickness, 475*	剤*rugs, 961*
症*ickness, 788*	治*ecuperate, 210*
病*ickness, 213*	癒*ecuperate, 923*
医*edicine, 19*	療*ecuperate, 67*
薬*rugs, 447*	

痴*oolish, 681*

573-C

疫*pidemic* of 疾*peedy* 痢*iarrhoea*--not a 痴*oolish* 疾*isease, Mama Mia...*

疒 (sickness)

痴*oolish*   痴*tupid*

shi(reru), CHI

foolish, stupid, folly, idiotic, imbecile, moron, ignoramus, booboo

Facing: 3.0. ☞☜ Across

痴愚 *imbecility, stupidity* **chigu**
痴呆 *dementia, imbecility* **chihō**
痴人 *idiot, dolt, foolish person* **chijin**
痴情 *blind passion, blind love* **chijō**
痴漢 *pervert, molester* **chikan**
痴態 *foolish act* **chitai**
痴話 *lovers' chat, sweet talk* **chiwa**
痴話喧嘩 *lovers' spat, lovers' quarrel* **chiwa genka**
愚痴 *murmurs, whining, grumble* **guchi**
愚痴る *complain, whimper, grumble* **guchiru**
白痴 *idiot, imbecility, stupidity* **hakuchi**
情痴 *love infatuation, ~obsession* **jōchi**
音痴 *tone-deaf person* **onchi**
⇒運動音痴 *tone-deaf person* **undō onchi**
運痴 *slow-moving, laggard* **unchi**
頓痴気 *idiot, dolt, foolishness* **tonchiki**
酔い痴れる *befuddled, drunk* **yoishireru**

忘*orget, 34*	慢*egligence, 845*
妄*houghtless, 34*	失*ailure, 19*
疎*egligence, 955*	敗*ailure, 137*

痢*iarrhoea, 680*

573-D

疫*pidemic* of 疾*peedy* 痢*iarrhoea*--not a 痴*oolish* 疾*isease, Mama Mia...*

疒 (sickness)

❶疾*isease*   ❷疾*peedy*

SHITSU

disease, infection, illness, sickness; speedy

Facing: 3.0. ☞☜ Across

❶疾っくに *long time ago, well past* **tokku(ni)**
悪疾 *malignant disease* **akushitsu**
眼疾 *vision impairment, eye illness* **ganshitsu**
廃疾 *disability, paralysis* **haishitsu**
耳疾 *ear disease* **jishitsu**
痼疾 *chronic illness* **koshitsu**
淋疾 *gonorrhoea* **rinshitsu**
疾患 *disease, ailment, illness* **shikkan**
⇒胸部疾患 *chest disease* **kyōbu shikkan**
疾病 *illness, disease* **shippei**
疾視 *spitefully gaze* **shisshi**

❷疾呼 *call out, shout* **shikko**
疾駆 *drive fast, dash thru* **shikku**
疾風 *strong wind, rushing gale* **shippū**
疾走 *dashing, scamper* **shissō**

迅*peedy, 95*	徐*lowly, 881*
速*peedy, 502*	鈍*luggish, 199*
早*arly, 373*	

症*isease, 788*

574-A

私rivate 払ayment to a 仏uddhist 仏rench, very urgent...

禾 (tree branch)

❶私rivate ❷私[I]

watakushi, SHI
private; [I]

Facing: 4.0. 🖙 Apart

❶私案 *personal plan* **shian**
私物 *private property* **shibutsu**
私営 *private management* **shiei**
私益 *private gains, interests* **shieki**
私怨 *personal grudge, bad blood* **shien**
私学 *private university, ~school* **shigaku**
私語 *whisper, chattering, murmur* **shigo**
私費 *own expenses, paying for oneself* **shihi**
私意 *private opinion, inner thoughts* **shii**
私事 *private matters* **shiji**
私情 *personal feelings* **shijō**
私家 *private & personal* **shika**
私感 *personal, private feelings* **shikan**
私刑 *lynching* **shikei**
私見 *personal opinion, view* **shiken**
私行 *private conduct* **shikō**
私立 *privately-owned, privately-built* **shiritsu**
私論 *personal theory* **shiron**
私信 *private letter, ~message* **shishin**

私心 *selfishness, ulterior motive* **shishin**
私室 *private room* **shishitsu**
私淑 *adoration, looking up* **shishuku**
私的 *private, personal* **shiteki**
私用 *personal-, private use* **shiyō**
私有 *private property, estate* **shiyū**
私財 *private property, personal wealth* **shizai**
私文書 *private-, personal document* **shibunsho**
私生児 *illegitimate-, love child* **shiseiji**
私生活 *private life, privacy* **shiseikatsu**
私書箱 *post office box, PO Box* **shishobako**
❷私 *the first person "I"* **watashi, watakushi**

個*dividual*, 491	我*elf*, 443	自*elf*, 462
身*elf*, 504	己*elf*, 5	有*ossess*, 617

秒*econds*, 727

574-B

私rivate 払ayment to a 仏uddhist 仏rench, very urgent...

手⇔扌 (hand, manual)

❶払ayment ❷払lear away

hara(u), FUTSU
payment, clear away, get rid of, dispose of

Facing: 4.0. 🖙 Apart

❶後払い *deferred payment* **atobarai**
着払い *payment on delivery, cod* **chakubarai**
不払い *non-payment* **fubarai**
日払い *daily payment* **hibarai**
過払い *overpayment* **kabarai**
靴払い *doormat, shoescraper* **kutsubarai**
未払い *unpaid, outstanding payment* **mibarai**
年払い *annual instalments, ~payments* **nenbarai**
利払い *interest payment* **ribarai**
先払い *advanced payment* **sakibarai**
支払い *payment, account settlement* **shiharai**
内払い *partial payment, instalments* **uchibarai**
現金払い *cash payment, cash deal* **genkinbarai**
払い込み *payment, account settlement* **haraikomi**
払い込む *pay up, settle one's account* **haraikomu**
払い戻し *refund, buy-back* **haraimodoshi**
延べ払い *deferred payment* **nobebarai**
即金払い *cash payment, cash deal* **sokkinbarai**
ボーナス払い *bonus payment* **bōnasubarai**

❷払拭 *wiping away* **fusshoku, fusshiki**
払暁 *dawn, daybreak* **futsugyō**
払底 *shortage, scarcity, insufficiency* **futtei**
足払い *tripping an opponent* **ashibarai**
人払い *clear (the room) of people* **hitobarai**
厄払い *exorcism, driving-out spirits* **yakuharai**
売り払う *selling off* **uriharau**
焼き払う *burn down* **yakiharau**
払い下げ *disposal, discarding* **haraisage**
掻っ払い *snatching* **kapparai**
払い除ける *brush aside, drive away* **harainokeru**
酔っ払い *drunken, drunkard* **yopparai**

賃*ayment*, 145	金*oney*, 25
納*ayment*, 296	買*urchase*, 516
料*ayment*, 194	購*urchase*, 714

北*orthern*, 372

574-C

私rivate 払ayment to a 仏uddhist 仏rench, very urgent...

人⇔亻 (person)

❶仏uddha ❷仏rance

Hotoke, BUTSU
Buddha; France

Facing: 4.0. ☜☞ Apart

❶ 仏陀 *Buddha, Gautama* **budda**
仏閣 *Buddhist temple* **bukkaku**
仏教 *Buddhism, Buddhist religion* **bukkyō**
仏教徒 *Buddhist followers* **bukkyōto**
仏法 *Buddhist teachings, ~analects* **buppō**
仏式 *Buddhist rituals* **busshiki**
仏壇 *Buddhist family altar* **butsudan**
仏殿 *Buddhist temple* **butsuden**
仏道 *Buddhist teachings, ~analects* **butsudō**
仏具 *Buddhist altar items* **butsugu**
仏寺 *Buddhist temple* **butsuji**
仏間 *Buddhist family altar room* **butsuma**
仏滅 *tragic day (Buddha's death)* **butsumetsu**
仏前 *before the dead's tablet* **butsuzen**
仏像 *Buddhist statue* **butsuzō**
仏典 *Buddhist scriptures* **butten**
大仏 *large statue of Buddha* **daibutsu**
仏様 *Almighty Lord Buddha* **Hotokesama**
成仏 *attaining Nirvana* **jōbutsu**

金仏 *Buddha metal statue* **kanabutsu**
念仏 *Buddhist invocation* **nenbutsu**
喉仏 *Adam's apple* **nodobotoke**
石仏 *Buddha stone statue* **sekibutsu**
神仏 *Shintō & Buddhism* **shinbutsu**
仏頂面 *sullen look, sour face* **bucchōzura**

❷ 英仏 *English-French* **eifutsu**
仏領 *French territory* **futsuryō**
日仏 *Japan & France* **nichifutsu**
仏文学 *French literature* **futsubungaku**

盆uddhist Feast, 594	聖acred, 617
僧uddhist monk, 836	神ivine, 712
坊uddhist monk, 736	欧urope, 952

化ecome, 192

575-A

A ringing silver 鈴ell in the 冷hilly 冷old spell...

金 (metal)

鈴ell

suzu, REI, RIN
bell, chime

FLIP: 6.0.a. Left (flat)

亜鈴 *dumb bells* **arei**
⇒鉄亜鈴 *iron dumb bells* **tetsuarei**
電鈴 *electric bell* **denrei**
土鈴 *ceramic bell* **dorei**
風鈴 *wind-bell* **fūrin**
風鈴草 *Canterbury bell* **fūrinsō**
銀鈴 *silver bell* **ginrei**
振鈴 *hand bell* **shinrei**
鈴掛 *plane, sycamore* **suzukake**
鈴鴨 *scaup duck* **suzukamo**
鈴虫 *bell-ring insect, cricket* **suzumushi**
鈴蘭 *lily on the valley* **suzuran**
予鈴 *preliminary bell* **yorei**
馬鈴薯 *Irish potato* **bareisho**
鈴生り *overflowing, cramped* **suzunari**
呼び鈴 *door-, front desk-, counter bell* **yobirin**

鐘ell, 564	曲elody, 476
音ound, 314	呼alling, 701

銘recepts, 425

575-B

A ringing silver 鈴ell in the 冷hilly 冷old spell...

冷*hills*　　　　冷*old*

冫 (freezing, ice)

tsume(tai), sa(masu), sa(meru), hi(eru), hi(ya), REI
chills, cold, shivers

冷性 *coldness, chills* **hieshō**
冷飯 *chilled meal* **hiyameshi**
冷麦 *chilled noodles* **hiyamugi**
冷肉 *chilled meat* **hiyaniku**
寒冷 *coldness, chills* **kanrei**
空冷 *air cooling, refrigeration* **kūrei**
冷房 *air cooling, refrigeration* **reibō**
冷害 *cold weather damage* **reigai**
冷厳 *grim, stern* **reigen**
冷遇 *indifference, callousness* **reigū**
冷評 *unkind criticism* **reihyō**
冷菓 *chilled sweets, ~candies* **reika**
冷夏 *cool summer* **reika**
冷汗 *cold sweats* **reikan**
冷や汗 *cold sweats* **hiyaase**
冷血 *cold-blooded* **reiketsu**
冷気 *cold, coolness, chill* **reiki**
冷酷 *cruel, mean, unkind* **reikoku**
冷却 *cooling, refrigeration* **reikyaku**

FLIP: 7.2.a. Right Top (flat)
FLIP: 7.1. Right (Sort Of)

冷静 *calm, composed* **reisei**
冷戦 *us-soviet cold war* **reisen**
冷笑 *cold smile* **reishō**
冷酒 *chilled sake* **reishu, hiyazake**
冷水 *cold water* **reisui**
冷や水 *cold water* **hiyamizu**
冷淡 *coldness, ~heartedness* **reitan**
冷徹 *cool, realistic* **reitetsu**
冷凍 *refrigeration, freezing* **reitō**
冷雨 *cold rains* **reiu**
冷然 *indifferent, aloof, callous* **reizen**
水冷 *water cooling* **suirei**
湯冷め *chill after taking a bath* **yuzame**

寒*hills, 121*	氷*reeze, 10*	緊*ard, 599*
凍*reeze, 221*	凝*arden, 57*	固*ard, 491*

令*ommand, 362*

576-A

孔onfucius kept 札oney-bills in the South Pole 札abeled in a 孔ole...

❶孔*onfucius*　　　❷孔*ole*

子 (child)

KŌ
Confucius; hole, pore, cavity, cranny, puncture

❶孔孟 *Confucius & Mencius* **kōmō**
孔門 *Confucian school* **kōmon**
孔子 *Confucius* **kōshi**

Facing: 4.0. ⟲⟳ Apart

有孔性 *porosity* **yūkōsei**

❷鼻孔 *nostrils* **bikō**
瞳孔 *eye pupil* **dōkō**
眼孔 *eye socket* **gankō**
毛孔 *pores, opening* **keana**
気孔 *pores, opening* **kikō**
孔穴 *hole* **kōketsu**
孔雀 *peacock, peahen* **kujaku**
耳孔 *earhole* **mimiana**
細孔 *small hole* **saikō**
穿孔 *perforation, hole, vesicle* **senkō**
穿孔機 *perforator* **senkōki**
多孔 *porous* **takō**
覘視孔 *peeping hole* **tenshikō**
通風孔 *ventilation hole, air hole* **tsūfūkō**
通気孔 *ventilation hole, air hole* **tsūkikō**

儒*onfucius, 548*	篤*ighteous, 317*
仁*irtue, 457*	義*ighteous, 341*
徳*irtue, 844*	善*ighteous, 450*
倫*thics, 787*	穴*ole, 4*

乳*airy, 970*

576-B

孔onfucius kept 札oney-bills in the South Pole 札abeled in a 孔ole...

木 (wooden)

❶札Label   ❷札oney-bills

fuda, SATSU
label, tag; money bills

Facing: 2.2. East ☞ (V)

❶ 赤札 red tag **akafuda**
花札 flower cards **hanafuda**
表札 nameplate, doorplate **hyōsatsu**
改札 inspecting tickets **kaisatsu**
鑑札 licence, permit, authorization **kansatsu**
検札 ticket inspection **kensatsu**
門札 nameplate **monsatsu**
名札 nameplate, name tag **nafuda**
値札 price tag **nefuda**
荷札 baggage tag, ~label **nifuda**
納札 voting card (for temple), bidding card **nōsatsu**
入札 bidding, auction **nyūsatsu**
⇒無札入場 entry without ticket **musatsu nyūjō**
応札 placing a bid **ōsatsu**
落札 winning bid, winning in an auction **rakusatsu**
利札 coupon, ticket **risatsu**
正札 price tag **shōfuda**
書札 letter **shosatsu**
集札 ticket collection **shūsatsu**

出札 issuing tickets **shussatsu**
手札 visiting card, name card **tefuda**
富札 lotto ticket **tomifuda**
番号札 numbered ticket **bangōfuda**
入れ札 tender, bid, offer **irefuda**
持ち札 "card in the hand···" **mochifuda**
札幌市 Sapporo City, Hokkaidō **sapporo-shi**
札入れ wallet **satsuire**
偽札 fake paper money **nisesatsu**
❷ 札束 wads of cash, bundle of notes **satsutaba**
新札 new paper bill **shinsatsu**

金oney, 25	納ayment, 296
幣oney, 171	払ayment, 682
賃ayment, 145	料ayment, 194

札espect, 685

577-A

礼ituals without 礼espect, 乱haos to expect...

示 ⇔ ネ (display, show)

❶礼itual   ❷礼espect

REI, RAI
ritual, ceremonial, etiquette; respect, courtesy

Facing: 2.2. East ☞ (V)

❶ 朝礼 office morning rites **chōrei**
儀礼 ceremony, courtesy, respect **girei**
非礼 lacking decorum **hirei**
一礼 bowing **ichirei**
巡礼 pilgrimage **junrei**
⇒聖地巡礼 pilgrimage tour **seichi junrei**
回礼 visiting rounds **kairei**
割礼 circumcision **katsurei**
敬礼 salutation, bow **keirei**
婚礼 wedding ceremony **konrei**
虚礼 useless formalities **kyorei**
黙礼 bow, salute **mokurei**
礼賛 praise, worship **raisan**
礼服 ceremonial dress **reifuku**
礼拝 worship, service **reihai, raihai**
礼装 full dress, full regalia **reisō**
礼典 rituals, rites, ceremony **reiten**
❷ 礼楽 etiquette & music **reigaku**
礼儀 etiquette, manners, politeness **reigi**

礼遇 extending courtesies **reigū**
礼状 letter of appreciation **reijō**
礼金 honorarium, remuneration **reikin**
礼節 courtesy, etiquette **reisetsu**
礼式 etiquette, manners **reishiki**
謝礼 honorarium, remuneration **sharei**
洗礼 baptism, christening **senrei**
洗礼式 baptism, christening **senreishiki**
浸礼 baptism, (immersion) **shinrei**
失礼 rude, impolite, discourteous **shitsurei**
答礼 return salute, return call **tōrei**
お礼参り thanksgiving shrine visit **oreimairi**

恭espect, 620	敬espect, 329
仰espect, 706	尚espect, 99
謹espect, 962	崇espect, 879

札Label, 685

577-B

礼*ituals without* 礼*espect,* 乱*haos to expect...*

乙⇔乚 (fish hook)

乱*haos*　　　乱*onfusion*

mida(su), mida(reru), RAN
chaos, confusion, disorder

Facing: 4.0. ◁▷ Apart

腐乱	decomposition, rottening	**furan**
反乱	revolt, rebellion, riot	**hanran**
波乱	trouble, confusion, difficulties	**haran**
混乱	chaos, disorder	**konran**
乱暴	violent behaviour	**ranbō**
乱打	ferocious strike, ~assault	**randa**
乱獲	indiscriminate hunting	**rankaku**
乱掘	indiscriminate mining	**rankutsu**
乱脈	disorder, discord	**ranmyaku**
乱発	indiscriminate firing, trigger happy	**ranpatsu**
乱作	overproduction of literary works	**ransaku**
乱世	state of anarchy	**ransei**
乱戦	confused fighting, dogfight	**ransen**
乱射	indiscriminate firing, trigger happy	**ransha**
乱視	astigmatism	**ranshi**
乱心	delusion, despondency, madness	**ranshin**
乱数	random numbers	**ransū**
乱闘	free-for-all, rumble, riot	**rantō**
乱雲	nimbus	**ran'un**

乱用	abuse, misuse	**ranyō**
⇒職権乱用	abuse of power	**shokken ranyō**
乱雑	disorder, confusion	**ranzatsu**
乱造	shoddy manufacture	**ranzō**
錯乱	derangement, distraction	**sakuran**
酒乱	drunkard, tipster, alcoholic	**shuran**
騒乱	disturbance, disorder, riot	**sōran**
惑乱	confusion, commotion	**wakuran**
乱れ髪	untidy-, unkempt hair	**midaregami**
乱気流	turbulence, disturbance	**rankiryū**
咲き乱れる	bloom in profusion	**sakimidareru**

争*onflict, 231*	錯*ixed-up, 335*
迷*onfusion, 904*	混*ixture, 38*
慌*anic, 507*	荒*urbulent, 507*

乳*airy, 970*

578-A

利*rofits of hair* 刈*utting stylist to be* 刊*ublished...*

刀⇔刂 (blade, cutting)

利*rofit*　　　利*dvantage*

ki(ku), toshi, RI
profit, advantage, returns, yields, gains, benefit, plus

Facing: 1.2. ◁ West (V)

便利	convenience, comfort, expedience	**benri**
営利	profit-making, money-making	**eiri**
福利	welfare, well-being	**fukuri**
元利	principal plus interest	**ganri**
一利	one advantage, a plus factor	**ichiri**
権利	right, privilege, prerogative	**kenri**
巨利	large profit	**kyori**
利益	profit, gain, advantage, benefit	**rieki**
利益配当	profit distribution	**rieki haitō**
利害	interest, concern, stake	**rigai**
利幅	profit margin	**rihaba**
利権	rights, concession	**riken**
利己	self-interest, selfishness	**riko**
利子	loan interest, savings interest	**rishi**
利息	interest earned, ~incurred	**risoku**
利水	irrigation	**risui**
利点	advantage, benefit	**riten**
利得	gain, profit, advantage, benefit	**ritoku**
利用	availing, utilizing, using	**riyō**

勝利	win, victory	**shōri**
単利	simple interest	**tanri**
徳利	sake bottle	**tokkuri**
有利	beneficial, advantage, useful	**yūri**
地の利	geographical-, territorial advantage	**chinori**
右利き	right-handed person	**migikiki**
利払い	interest payment	**ribarai**
利回り	yield, return, interest, earnings	**rimawari**
利下げ	interest reduction	**risage**
射利心	money-obsessed	**sharishin**
腕利き	able man	**udekiki**

益*rofit, 622*	富*ortune, 333*
得*rofit, 940*	隆*rosperity, 133*
獲*cquire, 829*	盛*rosperity, 244*
豊*rosperous, 965*	繁*rosperity, 434*

刺*ierce, 875*

578-B

利*rofits of hair* 刈*utting stylist to be* 刊*ublished...*

刀⇔刂 (blade, cutting)

刈*utting*   刈*rimming*

ka(ru)
cutting, trimming, mowing, chopping, clipping

FLIP: 6.0.b. Left (stem)

稲刈り *reaping rice, rice harvest* **inekari**
角刈り *crew cut, flattop haircut* **kakugari**
刈り穂 *harvested rice ears* **kariho**
刈り株 *stubble* **karikabu**
刈り手 *mower, reaper* **karite**
草刈り *grass mowing* **kusakari**
草刈り機 *grass mower, mowing machine* **kusakariki**
丸刈り *close-cropped hair, crew cut* **marugari**
芝刈機 *lawn mower* **shibakariki**
下刈り *clearing underbrush* **shitagari**
裾刈り *trimmed haircut* **susogari**
虎刈り *uneven haircut* **toragari**
坊主刈り *crew cut, flattop haircut* **bōzugari**
五部刈り *crew cut, flattop haircut* **gobugari**
刈り干す *cut & dry up* **karihosu**
刈り入れ *crop harvest* **kariire**
刈り込み *trimming, pruning* **karikomi**
刈り取る *mow, cut down, nip* **karitoru**

髪*air, 408*   植*lant, 783*
種*arvest, 829*   畑*lantation, 482*
切*utting, 352*   果*ruit, 287*

凶*vil, 80*

578-C

利*rofits of hair* 刈*utting stylist to be* 刊*ublished...*

刀⇔刂 (blade, cutting)

刊*ublication*   刊*ublishing*

KAN
publication, publishing

FLIP: 6.0.b. Left (stem)

朝刊 *morning newspaper* **chōkan**
復刊 *re-issuing, re-printing* **fukkan**
復刊 *republished, republication* **fukkan**
月刊 *monthly publication* **gekkan**
月刊誌 *monthly magazine* **gekkanshi**
廃刊 *defunct publication* **haikan**
発刊 *publication, publishing* **hakkan**
刊行 *publication, publishing* **kankō**
刊行物 *publication* **kankōbutsu**
既刊 *already-published work* **kikan**
季刊 *quarterly publication* **kikan**
近刊 *soon to be published* **kinkan**
公刊 *publication, publishing* **kōkan**
休刊 *publication holiday* **kyūkan**
休刊日 *newspaper holiday* **kyūkanbi**
未刊 *unpublished work* **mikan**
日刊 *daily publication, daily* **nikkan**
新刊 *new publication* **shinkan**
新刊書 *new book, ~publication* **shinkansho**

新刊紹介 *book review* **shinkan shōkai**
終刊 *terminating a publication* **shūkan**
週刊 *weekly magazine, weekly* **shūkan**
週刊誌 *weekly magazine, weekly* **shūkanshi**
創刊 *starting a publication* **sōkan**
創刊号 *first issue of a publication* **sōkangō**
停刊 *suspending publication* **teikan**
夕刊 *evening paper, ~edition* **yūkan**
増刊 *special issue, extra* **zōkan**
続刊 *serial publication* **zokkan**
伴月刊 *bi-monthly publication* **hangekkan**

掲*ublish, 810*   刷*rinting, 760*
載*ublish, 802*   版*rinting, 359*

判*Judgement, 949*

579-A

他*nother* 地*and,* 他*nother* 池*ond...*

人⇔イ (person)

他*nother*　　他*lse*

hoka, TA
another, else, different, other

Facing: 4.0. 〜☞ Apart

愛他 *altrusim* **aita**
排他 *exclusion* **haita**
他に *"besides, other than that..."* **hoka(ni)**
他聞 *"just between you & me..."* **tabun**
他言 *telling others, revelation, leakage* **tagen, tagon**
他方 *other side* **tahō**
他意 *other intention, hidden mind* **tai**
他所 *another place* **tasho, yoso**
他事 *other matters* **taji**
他日 *some other day* **tajitsu**
他界 *death, passing away* **takai**
他家 *another family* **take**
他見 *confidential, secret* **taken**
他国 *other countries, foreign countries* **takoku**
他国間条約 *multilateral treaty* **takokukan jōyaku**
他面 *other side* **tamen**
他年 *another year* **tanen**
他念 *thinking about something else* **tanen**
他人 *stranger, others, another person* **tanin**

他人の空似 *resemblance of strangers* **tanin no sorani**
他律 *heteronomy* **taritsu**
他流 *another school, outside of the group* **taryū**
他殺 *murder, homicide* **tasatsu**
他社 *other companies* **tasha**
他生 *previous life* **tashō**
他出 *going out* **tashutsu**
他動詞 *transitive verb* **tadōshi**
他ならない *"must be..."* **hokanaranai**
他愛ない *silly, trivial, petty, frivolous* **taainai**
他力本願 *reliance on others* **tariki hongan**

外*utside, 188*	異*ifferent, 239*

地*arth, 688*

579-B

他*nother* 地*and,* 他*nother* 池*ond...*

土 (ground, soil)

地*and*　　地*round*

CHI, JI
land, ground, earth, place

FLIP: 6.0.b. Left (stem)
Facing: 2.2. East ☞ (V)

番地 *house number* **banchi**
地位 *position, status, rank* **chii**
地域 *area, region* **chiiki**
地下 *underground* **chika**
地価 *land price* **chika**
地球 *earth, mother earth* **chikyū**
地理 *geography, topography* **chiri**
地帯 *zone, region* **chitai**
地図 *map, atlas* **chizu**
地獄 *hell, inferno* **jigoku**
地面 *ground, surface* **jimen**
地味 *plain, subdued, conservative* **jimi**
地主 *landlord, landlady* **jinushi**
地震 *earthquake* **jishin**
基地 *military base* **kichi**
高地 *plateau, high ground* **kōchi**
局地 *locality* **kyokuchi**
路地 *alley* **roji**
産地 *place of production* **sanchi**

聖地 *sacred ground, holy land* **seichi**
宅地 *residential area* **takuchi**
土地 *land, property* **tochi**
築地 *reclaimed land* **tsukiji**
裏地 *lining cloth* **uraji**
空き地 *vacant land, empty lot* **akichi**
地の利 *geographical advantage* **chinori**
発祥地 *birthplace, cradle of* **hasshōchi**
意地悪 *ill-tempered, cranky* **ijiwaru**
意気地 *obstinacy, stubbornness* **ikuji, ikiji**
所在地 *location, site* **shozaichi**

土*oil, 8*	界*orld, 365*
陸*and, 140*	世*orld, 411*

池*ond, 689*

579-C
他*nother* 地*and,* 他*nother* 池*ond...*

水 ⇔ 氵 (water)

Facing: 4.0. 🔄 Apart

池*ond*

ike, CHI
pond

墨池	*ink (stone) well*	**bokuchi**
池畔	*edge of a pond*	**chihan**
池心	*center of a pond*	**chishin**
電池	*battery, dry cell*	**denchi**
古池	*old pond*	**furuike**
蓮池	*lotus pond*	**hasuike**
堀池	*artificial pond*	**horiike**
肉池	*ink-pad case*	**nikuchi**
蓄電池	*storage battery, cell*	**chikudenchi**
沈殿池	*settling reservoir*	**chindenchi**
貯水池	*water reservoir*	**chosuichi**
浄水池	*filtration reservoir*	**jōsuichi**
乾電池	*dry cell, dry battery*	**kandenchi**
光電池	*photoelectric cell*	**kōdenchi**
溜め池	*reservoir, cistern*	**tameike**
養殖池	*fish pond*	**yōshokuchi**
用水池	*water reservoir*	**yōsuiike**
酒池肉林	*sumptuous feast*	**shuchi nikurin**

河*iver, 877*
川*iver, 76*

地*arth, 688*

580-A
Protein 泡*ubble dwells in stem* 胞*ells...*

水 ⇔ 氵 (water)

Facing: 1.2. 🔄 West (V)

泡*ubble*

awa, abuku, HŌ
bubble

泡立つ	*bubble, form, lather up*	**awadatsu**
泡立て器	*eggbeater*	**awadateki**
泡立てる	*whip up*	**awadateru**
泡銭	*undeserved money*	**abukuzeni**
泡を食う	*get flurried, lose one's head*	**awa o kū**
泡盛	*millet brandy*	**awamori**
泡粒	*bubble*	**awatsubu**
発泡	*foaming, bubbling*	**happō**
一泡	*frightening, scary*	**hitoawa**
泡沫	*bubble, foam*	**hōmatsu**
泡沫会社	*fly-by-night company*	**hōmatsu gaisha**
気泡	*air bubble*	**kihō**
水泡	*foam, bubble*	**suihō**
水の泡	*futile, useless, worth nothing*	**mizu no awa**
石鹸の泡	*soap bubble*	**sekken no awa**

浮*loat, 970*
泉*prings, 531*

白*hite, 15*
面*urface, 36*

抱*mbrace, 503*

580-B

Protein 泡ubble dwells in stem 胞ells...

肉⇔月 (flesh, body part)

胞*ellular*　胞*lacenta*

HŌ
cellular, placenta, amoebic, membranous sac

Facing: 1.2. 🖢 West (V)

同胞 *countrymen, compatriots* **dōhō**
同胞愛 *brotherly love* **dōhōai**
芽胞 *spore* **gahō**
肺胞 *pulmonary alveoli* **haihō**
胞衣 *placenta, sac* **hōi**
胞子 *spore* **hōshi**
気胞 *air bladder* **kihō**
卵胞 *ovarian follicle* **ranhō**
卵細胞 *ovum, egg cell* **ransaibō**
細胞 *cell* **saibō**
⇒脳細胞 *brain cells* **nōsaibō**
⇒単細胞 *single cell; simple-minded* **tansaibō**
細胞学 *cell science, cytology* **saibōgaku**
小胞 *vesicle* **shōhō**

菌*acteria, 52*
命*ife, 362*
微*inuscule, 62*

胸*hest, 652*

581-A

村illagers 対gainst 討nvestigating 討ttack on Peking ducks...

木 (wooden)

村*illage*　村*amlet*

mura, SON
village, hamlet

Facing: 1.2. 🖢 West (V)

町村 *towns & villages* **chōson**
漁村 *fishing village* **gyoson**
弊村 *"our humble village..."* **heison**
寒村 *out-of-the-way village* **kanson**
江村 *village by the river* **kōson**
村人 *villager, village resident* **murabito**
村雨 *passing rainshower* **murasame**
村境 *village boundary* **murazakai**
農村 *farming village* **nōson**
隣村 *neighbouring village* **rinson**
離村 *village exodus* **rison**
山村 *mountain village* **sanson**
村長 *village chief* **sonchō**
村道 *village road* **sondō**
村童 *village boy* **sondō**
村営 *village management* **son'ei**
村会 *village council* **sonkai**
村民 *villager, village residents* **sonmin**
村費 *village spendings* **sonpi**

村落 *village, hamlet* **sonraku**
村立 *village-built* **sonritsu**
村有 *village-owned* **sonyū**
村税 *village tax* **sonzei**
無医村 *village without a doctor* **muison**
村八分 *ostracism, disowning* **murahachibu**
村祭り *village festival* **muramatsuri**
村役場 *village hall, ~office* **murayakuba**
市町村 *cities, towns & villages* **shichōson**
村夫子 *educated village person* **sonpūshi**
村上天皇 *Emperor Murakami (946-967)*
　　murakami tennō

郷*ometown, 452*　森*orest, 526*　民*nhabitant, 495*
里*ometown, 321*　町*own, 174*　材*oods, 186*

材*aterials, 186*

581-B

村*illagers* 対*gainst* 討*nvestigating* 討*ttack on Peking ducks...*

寸 (measurement)

対*gainst*　　対*cross*

TAI, TSUI
against, across, contrary, opposite, towards, versus

FLIP: 6.0.b. Left (stem)

反対 *contrary, opposition, resistance* **hantai**
応対 *reception, response, reply* **ōtai**
対案 *counterproposal, counter offer* **taian**
対談 *conversation, dialogue* **taidan**
対岸 *opposite side, ~bank* **taigan**
対偶 *companion, friend, partner* **taigū**
対峙 *mountains facing each other* **taiji**
対人 *dealing with other persons* **taijin**
対価 *compensation, payment* **taika**
対角 *opposite angle* **taikaku**
対決 *confrontation, face-off, show-down* **taiketsu**
対抗 *resistance, opposition* **taikō**
対向 *facing opposite, ~across* **taikō**
対局 *game, contest, match* **taikyoku**
対極 *counter situation, ~pole* **taikyoku**
対内 *domestic, internal, in-house* **tainai**
対応 *counter-measure, remedy* **taiō**
⇒幅対応 *appropriate width* **habataiō**
対立 *opposition, resistance* **tairitsu**

対策 *counter measure, remedy* **taisaku**
対戦 *counter offensive, retaliatory strike* **taisen**
対審 *court confrontation* **taishin**
対話 *dialogue, negotiation* **taiwa**
敵対 *hostility, animosity, acrimony* **tekitai**
対句 *anti-thesis* **tsuiku**
絶対 *absolute, unconditional* **zettai**
一対一 *one-to-one* **ittaiichi**
好一対 *well-matched pair* **kōittsui**
対外的 *foreign, external* **taigaiteki**

向*owards, 99*　　方*irection, 533*
反*gainst, 537*　　抗*pposition, 749*

村*illage, 690*

581-C

村*illagers* 対*gainst* 討*nvestigating* 討*ttack on Peking ducks...*

言 (speaking)

討*ttack*　　討*nvestigate*

u(tsu), TŌ
attack, investigate, study, suppress (force)

FLIP: 6.0.a. Left (flat)
Facing: 1.2. ⟵ West (V)

検討 *investigation, examination* **kentō**
征討 *conquest & subjugation* **seitō**
掃討 *mopping up, sweeping operation* **sōtō**
討幕 *anti-Shogunate* **tōbaku**
討伐 *subjugation, suppression* **tōbatsu**
討伐軍 *punitive force* **tōbatsugun**
討伐隊 *punitive force* **tōbatsutai**
討議 *discussion, deliberation* **tōgi**
討究 *study, investigation* **tōkyū**
討論 *debate, discussion* **tōron**
討論会 *panel discussion* **tōronkai**
追討 *tracking down, hot pursuit* **tsuitō**
討手 *pursuers* **utte**
再検討 *re-examination, review* **saikentō**
仇討ち *revenge, retaliatory strike* **adauchi**
敵討ち *retaliation, vengeance* **katakiuchi**
闇討ち *sneak attack, ambush* **yamiuchi**
夜討ち *night attack* **youchi**
返り討ち *"killing one's would-be killer..."* **kaeriuchi**

焼き討ち *setting a fire* **yakiuchi**
同士討ち *sneak attack on one's comrades*
　　dōshiuchi
不意討ち *surprise attack, ambush* **fuiuchi**
討ち入り *raid, storm* **uchiiri**
討ち死に *death in battle* **uchiji(ni)**
騙まし討ち *sneak attack* **damashiuchi**
討ち果たす *kill, slay* **uchihatasu**

評*ommentary, 701*　　論*iscussion, 786*
談*iscussion, 308*　　究*nvestigate, 575*
議*iscussion, 341*

討*diting, 174*　　計*easurement, 692*

582-A

Wrong 針eedle 計easure led to a tailor's closure...

金 (metal)

針eedle

hari, SHIN
needle

FLIP: 5.0.b. Left & Right

秒針	*clock second hand* **byōshin**		短針	*clock hour hand* **tanshin**
長針	*clock long hand* **chōshin**		畳針	*tatami needle* **tatamibari**
針孔	*eye of a needle* **hariana**		運針	*handling of needles* **unshin**
針箱	*sewing kit* **haribako**		釣り針	*fishing hook* **tsuribari**
針金	*wire* **harigane**		編み針	*crochet needle* **amibari**
針鼠	*hedgehog* **harinezumi**		針折れ	*bent needle* **hariore**
針師	*acupuncturist* **harishi**		避雷針	*lightning rod* **hiraishin**
針山	*pincushion* **hariyama**		縫い針	*needle* **nuibari**
絎針	*blindstitching needle* **herihari**		御針子	*seamstress* **ohariko**
方針	*policy, measure* **hōshin**		羅針盤	*magnetic compass* **rashinban**
⇒闘争方針	*hostile policy* **tōsō hōshin**		針葉樹	*conifer, needle-leaf tree* **shinyōju**
磁針	*magnetic needle* **jishin**			
蚊針	*flying fish* **kabari**			
鈎針	*hook* **kagibari**			
検針	*meter reading, ~inspection* **kenshin**			
針術	*acupuncture* **shinjutsu**			
針灸	*acupuncture & moxibustion* **shinkyū**			
針路	*course-of-action* **shinro**			
指針	*index, indicator* **shishin**			

縫 *ewing, 779*		紡 *pinning, 735*
錘 *pindle, 505*		糸 *hread, 375*
繰 *pinning, 851*		結 *onnect, 227*

斜 *iagonal, 648*

582-B

Wrong 針eedle 計easure led to a tailor's closure...

言 (speaking)

計easurement   計lan

haka(ru), haka(rau), KEI
measurement, compute, calculate, accounting, length; plan, scheme

FLIP: 5.0.b. Left & Right

合計	*sum total, grand total* **gōkei**			
会計	*account, payment, finance* **kaikei**		小計	*sub-total* **shōkei**
奸計	*evil plan, ~design* **kankei**		集計	*total, totalling* **shūkei**
計時	*time checking* **keiji**		総計	*grand total* **sōkei**
計画	*plan, programme* **keikaku**		推計	*estimate, appraisal* **suikei**
計器	*meter, gauge, instrument* **keiki**		統計	*statistics* **tōkei**
計略	*plan, strategy* **keiryaku**		余計	*surplus; none of one's business* **yokei**
計量	*weighing, measurement* **keiryo**		柱時計	*wall clock* **hashiradokei**
計算	*calculation, computation* **keisan**		計理士	*accountant, auditor* **keirishi**
計算機	*calculator* **keisanki**		晴雨計	*barometer* **seiukei**
計測	*measurements* **keisoku**		砂時計	*sand glass* **sunadokei**
奇計	*clever plan, wise strategy* **kikei**		体重計	*body weight scale* **taijūkei**
密計	*secret plan* **mikkei**			
妙計	*wise-, brilliant plan* **myōkei**			
日計	*daily journal* **nikkei**			
累計	*sum total, aggregate* **ruikei**			
歳計	*annual account* **saikei**			
生計	*livelihood, living* **seikei**			
設計	*architectural design* **sekkei**			

算 *alculate, 141*		寸 *easurement, 345*
測 *easure, 291*		数 *umber, 156*
尺 *easurement, 574*		

討 *ttack, 691*   計 *easurement, 692*

583-A

糾wist & 叫hout in a dance bout...

糸 (thread, continuity)

糾wist　糾nterrogate

azana(u), KYŪ
twist, interrogate, inquire into

Facing: 3.0. ☞☜ Across

粉糾 complication, entanglement **funkyū**
粉糾 complication, entanglement **funkyū**
糾弾 impeachment, censure **kyūdan**
糾合 calling together, rallying **kyūgō**
糾明 scrutiny, close examination **kyūmei**
糾問 cross-examine, interrogation **kyūmon**

搾queeze, 722	検nspection, 939
察nspection, 328	査nspection, 624
審nspection, 339	閲nspection, 942
調nspection, 280	

純urity, 199

583-B

糾wist & 叫hout in a dance bout...

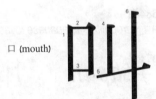

口 (mouth)

叫hout　叫cream

sake(bu), KYŌ
shout, scream, bellow, hollering, outcry, roar

FLIP: 6.0.a. Left (flat)
Facing: 1.2. ☜ West (V)

叫び shout, scream, yell **sakebi**
叫び声 shouting, screaming **sakebigoe**
号叫 calling loud **gōkyō**
叫喚 shout, scream, shriek **kyōkan**
絶叫 scream, yelling **zekkyō**
雄叫び roar, shout, scream **otakebi**
矢叫び archer's shout on release of arrow **yasakebi**
泣き叫ぶ cry out **nakisakebu**

音oise, 314	声oice, 428
騒oise, 924	泣rying, 235
鳴owling, 842	涙rying, 541

糾wist, 693

584-A

A 都etropolitan 邦apanese loves the 邦ountry of Nice...

阝 ⇔ 阜 (village-right)

都*etropolis*

miyako, TO, TSU

metropolis, metropolitan, urban, big city; Tokyo

FLIP: 6.2. Left Bottom
Facing: 2.2. East ☞ (V)

国都 *national capital* **kokuto**
古都 *ancient capital* **koto**
港都 *port city, harbour city* **kōto**
京都 *Kyōto City* **kyōto**
遷都 *transfer of the capital* **sento**
商都 *commercial city, business centre* **shōto**
首都 *capital, metropolis* **shuto**
帝都 *capital of the empire* **teito**
都営 *metropolitan government (Tōkyō)* **toei**
都雅 *refined & graceful* **toga**
都会 *large urban city* **tokai**
都会生活 *urban city life, ~living* **tokai seikatsu**
都会人 *large urban city resident* **tokaijin**
都会化 *urbanization* **tokaika**
都民 *metropolitan residents (Tōkyō)* **tomin**
都政 *city government* **tosei**
都市 *city, town* **toshi**
都市国家 *city state* **toshi kokka**
都心 *centre of a city, inner-city* **toshin**

都督 *governor-general* **totoku**
都税 *metropolitan tax* **tozei**
都度 *every time, all the time* **tsudo**
都合 *convenience, circumstances* **tsugō**
都合悪く *inconveniently* **tsugōwaruku**
都合よく *smoothly, conveniently* **tsugōyoku**
大都会 *big city, metropolis* **daitokai**
副都心 *new city centre* **fukutoshin**
好都合 *favourable situation* **kōtsugō**
都住まい *urban city life, ~living* **miyakozumai**
東京都庁 *Tōkyō Metropolitan government*
　　　tōkyō tochō

京 *apital, 386*	区 *istrict, 80*
市 *ity, 304*	丁 *lock-of-houses, 173*

郵 *ostal office, 948*

584-B

A 都etropolitan 邦apanese loves the 邦ountry of Nice...

阝 ⇔ 阜 (village-right)

❶邦*apan*　❷邦*ountry*

kuni, HŌ

Japan; country

FLIP: 6.0.b. Left (stem)
Facing: 2.2. ☞ East (V)

❶本邦 *"this (our) nation..."* **honpō**
邦文 *Japanese text* **hōbun**
邦文タイプ *Japanese typing* **hōbun taipu**
邦画 *Japanese film, ~movie* **hōga**
邦楽 *Japanese music* **hōgaku**
邦字 *Japanese characters* **hōji**
邦人 *overseas Japanese* **hōjin**
⇒在外邦人 *overseas staying Japanese* **zaigai hōjin**
⇒在留邦人 *overseas staying Japanese* **zairyū hōjin**
邦貨 *Japanese currency* **hōka**
邦訳 *Japanese translation* **hōyaku**

❷万邦 *all countries* **banpō**
邦土 *country, territory* **hōdo**
邦家 *one's country* **hōka**
邦国 *country, nation* **hōkoku**
異邦 *foreign country* **ihō**
盟邦 *allied power, ally nation* **meihō**
隣邦 *neighbouring nation* **rinpō**

東邦 *Oriental nation* **tōhō**
友邦 *friendly-, allied nation* **yūhō**

国 *ountry, 92*	和 *apanese, 103*
京 *apital, 386*	日 *apan, 14*
都 *etropolis, 694*	東 *riental, 220*

非 *[negative], 288*

585-A

仲olleagues 沖ffshore e-mail me no more...

仲olleague 仲ellow

 人⇔亻 (person)

FLIP: 7.0.b1. Right (stem)

naka, CHŪ
colleague, fellow, associate, partner, intermediary

仲夏 *mid-summer* **chūka**
仲介 *mediation, intercession* **chūkai**
仲介物 *medium, go-between* **chūkaibutsu**
仲介者 *intermediary, mediator* **chūkaisha**
仲兄 *second brother* **chūkei**
仲裁 *arbitration, mediation* **chūsai**
仲裁人 *mediator, arbitrator* **chūsainin**
仲裁裁判 *arbitration, mediation* **chūsai saiban**
仲秋 *mid-autumn* **chūshū**
仲春 *mid-spring* **chūshun**
仲冬 *mid-winter* **chūtō**
不仲 *in bad terms, blood bad* **funaka**
伯仲 *good match, suitable partners* **hakuchū**
恋仲 *mutual love, ~affection* **koinaka**
仲買 *brokerage, middleman* **nakagai**
仲買人 *broker, broker agent* **nakagainin**
仲居 *waitress* **nakai**
仲間 *colleague, fellow* **nakama**
⇒遊び仲間 *childhood friend, playmate* **asobinakama**

⇒飲み仲間 *drinking buddy* **nominakama**
⇒釣り仲間 *fishing buddy* **tsurinakama**
仲間入り *take as a friend* **nakamairi**
仲仕 *heaver, docker, stevedore* **nakashi**
仲人 *matchmaker, go-between* **nakōdo**
仲立ち *intermediation, arbitration* **nakadachi**
仲直り *reconciliation, settlement* **nakanaori**
仲違い *estrangement, alienation* **nakatagai**
仲良し *in good terms, intimacy* **nakayoshi**
仲睦まじい *intimate* **nakamutsumajii**
生さぬ仲 *blood relationship* **nasanunaka**

相*ellow*, 524	僚*ellow*, 66
奴*ellow*, 44	友*riendship*, 408
輩*ellow*, 290	

沖*ffshore*, 695

585-B

仲olleagues 沖ffshore e-mail me no more...

沖ffshore 沖ffing

水⇔氵 (water)

FLIP: 7.0.b1. Right (stem)

oki, CHŪ
offshore, offing

沖天 *ascension to heaven* **chūten**
沖合 *coast, open sea* **okiai**
沖辺 *offshore* **okibe**
沖値 *price offshore* **okine**
沖漁 *off-shore fishing* **okiryō**
沖積土 *alluvial soil* **chūsekido**
沖積世 *alluvial epoch* **chūsekisei**
沖積層 *alluvium* **chūsekisō**
沖仲仕 *heaver, docker* **okinakashi**
沖縄県 *Okinawa Prefecture* **okinawa-ken**
沖渡し *off-shore delivery* **okiwatashi**
沖釣り *off-shore fishing* **okizuri**

江*ay*, 176	浦*eashore*, 813
湾*ay*, 909	浜*eashore*, 490
浜*each*, 490	遠*istant*, 916

仲*olleague*, 695

586-A

的tyle of not 酌erving-wine 約romised until 釣ishing is finished...

白 (white)

❶的tyle　　❷的arget

mato, TEKI
style, [descriptive], adjectival suffix; target

FLIP: 6.0.a. Left (flat)

❶便宜的 *temporary, stopgap* **bengiteki**
直観的 *intuitive, perceptive* **chokkanteki**
義務的 *obligatory, perfunctory* **gimuteki**
具体的 *concrete, definite, real* **gutaiteki**
閉鎖的 *insular, unsociable* **heisateki**
感覚的 *sensuous, sensual* **kankakuteki**
活動的 *active, dynamic* **katsudōteki**
計画的 *deliberate, planned* **keikakuteki**
形式的 *formal, ceremonial* **keishikiteki**
規則的 *regular, systematic* **kisokuteki**
基礎的 *fundamental, basic* **kisoteki**
国際的 *international, cosmopolitan* **kokusaiteki**
目的地 *travel destination* **mokutekichi**
肉体的 *sexual, physical* **nikutaiteki**
楽観的 *forward-looking, optimistic* **rakkanteki**
歴史的 *historical, historic* **rekishiteki**
良心的 *conscientious, righteous* **ryōshinteki**
作為的 *intentional, deliberate, willed* **sakuiteki**
産業的 *industrial* **sangyōteki**

世界的 *worldwide, global* **sekaiteki**
多元的 *pluralistic* **tagenteki**
短期的 *short-term, near-term* **tankiteki**
定期的 *regular, periodical* **teikiteki**
❷金的 *bullseye* **kinteki**
的矢 *target & arrow* **matoya**
目的 *purpose, objective, aim* **mokuteki**
射的 *target shooting* **shateki**
的中 *hitting the mark; correct guess* **tekichū**
的確 *precise, accurate* **tekikaku**
的証 *positive proof* **tekishō**

式*tyle, 418*	成*ecome, 244*
化*ecome, 192*	様*anner, 944*

取*ake, 229*

586-B

酌tyle of not 酌erving-wine 約romised until 釣ishing is finished...

酉 (liquor)

酌erve-wine　酌raw water

ku(mu), SHAKU
serve-wine, draw-liquid, ~water, pour-liquid

FLIP: 6.0.a. Left (flat)

媒酌 *match-making* **baishaku**
媒酌人 *matchmaker* **baishakunin**
晩酌 *night cap, dinner drink* **banshaku**
独酌 *solitary drinking, drinking alone* **dokushaku**
お酌 *barmaid, young geisha* **oshaku**
参酌 *take into consideration* **sanshaku**
酌婦 *barmaid, waitress* **shakufu**
酌量 *consideration, thought* **shakuryō**
⇒情状酌量 *extenuation, mitigation*
　　jōjō shakuryō
斟酌 *consideration, thought* **shinshaku**
手酌 *drinking alone* **tejaku**
酌み交わす *drinking together* **kumikawasu**

水*ater, 9*
注*utpour, 750*

配*istribute, 754*

586-C

的*tyle of not* 酌*erving-wine* 約*romised until* 釣*ishing is finished...*

糸 (thread, continuity)

❶約*romise*　❷約*bout*

YAKU

promise, commitment, deal, agreement, contract; about, more-or-less, roughly, approximately **Facing: 3.0.** ☞☜ Across

❶売約 *purchasing agreement* **baiyaku**
破約 *breach of contract* **hayaku**
違約 *contract infringement, ~violation* **iyaku**
条約 *treaty, pact* **jōyaku**
解約 *account closing, ~cancellation* **kaiyaku**
確約 *definite promise* **kakuyaku**
契約 *contract, written obligation* **keiyaku**
倹約 *thrift, frugality, saving money* **kenyaku**
婚約 *wedding engagement, ~betrothal* **konyaku**
口約 *verbal agreement, gentlemen's talk* **kōyaku**
公約 *public pledge, official oath* **kōyaku**
協約 *agreement, contract, promise* **kyōyaku**
盟約 *alliance treaty* **meiyaku**
密約 *secret agreement, hidden deal* **mitsuyaku**
黙約 *tacit agreement, acquiescence* **mokuyaku**
内約 *internal agreement* **naiyaku**
誓約 *oath, pledge, vow* **seiyaku**
先約 *previous agreement* **senyaku**
約款 *clause, stipulations, proviso, caveat* **yakkan**

約定 *contract, agreement* **yakujō**
約束 *promise, appointment* **yakusoku**
予約 *reservation, appointment* **yoyaku**
準契約 *quasi-contract* **junkeiyaku**
簡約 *simplification, conciseness* **kanyaku**
制約 *restriction, limitation* **seiyaku**
❷節約 *economize, conserve* **setsuyaku**
集約 *summing up* **shūyaku**
約分 *reduction of a fraction* **yakubun**
約言 *summarization, summing up* **yakugen**
要約 *summary, gist* **yōyaku**

契*romise, 900*
誓*ledge, 53*

紀*arration, 727*

586-D

的*tyle of not* 酌*erving-wine* 約*romised until* 釣*ishing is finished...*

金 (metal)

釣*ishing*　釣*ngle*

tsu(ru), CHO

fishing, allure, angle

FLIP: 6.0.a. Left (flat)

釣り場 *fishing spot* **tsuriba**
釣り花 *hanging flowers on a vase* **tsuribana**
釣り針 *fishing hook* **tsuribari**
釣り橋 *hanging bridge* **tsuribashi**
釣り堀 *fishing pond* **tsuribori**
釣り船 *fishing boat* **tsuribune**
釣り球 *fishing ball; tempting baseball pitch* **tsuridama**
釣り棚 *hanging shelf* **tsuridana**
釣り床 *hammock* **tsuridoko**
釣り鐘 *hanging-, temple bell* **tsurigane**
釣り糸 *fishing line, ~thread* **tsuriito**
釣り銭 *money change* **tsurisen**
釣り手 *angler* **tsurite**
釣り輪 *fishing ring* **tsuriwa**
釣り竿 *fishing pole* **tsurizao**
釣魚 *fishing, angling* **chōgyo**
釣果 *fishing catch* **chōka**
釣具 *fishing tackle* **tsurigu**
釣瓶 *well bucket* **tsurube**

穴釣り *ice fishing* **anazuri**
陸釣り *fishing from a rock* **okazuri**
沖釣り *off-shore fishing* **okizuri**
魚釣り *fishing* **sakanatsuri, uozuri**
手釣り *hand line fishing* **tezuri**
夜釣り *night fishing* **yozuri**
一本釣り *pole & line fishing* **ipponzuri**
釣り合う *balance, suit* **tsuriau**
釣り込む *draw, tempt, drag, attract* **tsurikomu**
釣り仲間 *fishing buddy* **tsurinakama**
釣り天狗 *proud of one's fishing skills* **tsuritengu**

魚*ishes, 49*　　惑*emptation, 139*
漁*ishing, 48*　　誘*emptation, 895*
海*cean, 241*　　唆*ntice, 764*

酌*raw-liquid, 696*

587-A

培*ultivators' annuity settled an* 賠*ndemnity...*

土 (ground, soil)

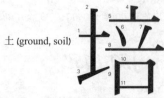

培*ultivate*　培*rowing*

tsuchika(u), BAI
cultivate, growing, farming

FLIP: 5.0.a Left & Right

培地　*culture medium*　**baichi**
培養　*cultivation, culture*　**baiyō**
⇒細菌培養　*bacteria cultivation*　**saikin baiyō**
培養液　*culture fluid, ~solution*　**baiyōeki**
培養基　*culture medium*　**baiyōki**
培養菌　*cultured bacteria*　**baiyōkin**
栽培　*cultivation, growing*　**saibai**
⇒促成栽培　*forced cultivation*　**sokusei saibai**

墾*ultivate, 164*	稲*ice plant, 893*
耕*ultivate, 655*	畑*lantation, 482*
植*lant, 783*	菌*acteria, 52*

倍*ultiply, 950*

587-B

培*ultivators' annuity settled an* 賠*ndemnity...*

貝 (shell, old money)

賠*ndemnity*　賠*ompensation*

BAI
indemnity, compensation, remuneration, reparation

FLIP: 5.0.a Left & Right

賠責　*liability insurance*　**baiseki**
賠償　*compensation, reparation*　**baishō**
⇒損害賠償　*damages, indemnity*　**songai baishō**
賠償金　*indemnity, reparations, damages*　**baishōkin**
賠償交渉　*reparation talks*　**baishō kōshō**
賠償協定　*reparations treaty*　**baishō kyōtei**
代償　*compensation, atonement*　**daishō**
自賠責　*automobile insurance (prefectural)*　**jibaiseki**

侵*iolate, 769*	痛*njury, 60*
害*njury, 904*	俸*emuneration, 276*
傷*njury, 933*	償*emuneration, 554*
障*njury, 325*	酬*emuneration, 670*
損*njury, 410*	

陪*ury-trial, 957*

588-A

Sound 決ecision based on 快leasant conditions ...

水⇔氵 (water)

決ecide   決udgement

ki(meru), ki(maru), KETSU
decide, judgement, conclude, ruling, verdict

Facing: 2.2. East ☞ (V)
Facing: 4.0. ☜☞ Apart

議決 *decision, resolution* **giketsu**
判決 *judgement, ruling, verdict, decision* **hanketsu**
否決 *rejection, voting down* **hiketsu**
票決 *voting, taking a vote* **hyōketsu**
表決 *judgement, ruling, verdict, decision* **hyōketsu**
評決 *judgement, ruling, verdict, decision* **hyōketsu**
一決 *unanimous decision, consensus* **ikketsu**
自決 *suicide; self-determination* **jiketsu**
解決 *solution, remedy, answer* **kaiketsu**
可決 *approval, adoption, passage* **kaketsu**
決壊 *collapse, rip, break, washout* **kekkai**
決起 *rising to action, ~to the occasion* **kekki**
決行 *decisive move* **kekkō**
決裁 *approval, sanction* **kessai**
決算 *accounts settlement, accounting* **kessan**
決戦 *decisive battle, eliminating round* **kessen**
決心 *determination, will power* **kesshin**
決別 *parting with, breaking with* **ketsubetsu**
決議 *resolution, decision* **ketsugi**

決意 *determination, resolution* **ketsui**
決裂 *breakdown, rupture, collapse* **ketsuretsu**
決定 *decision, determination* **kettei**
既決 *decided-, settled matter* **kiketsu**
決まり *rule, decided matter* **kimari**
採決 *vote, roll call, division* **saiketsu**
裁決 *decision, judgement, verdict, ruling* **saiketsu**
先決 *first consideration, initial decision* **senketsu**
即決 *prompt -, summary decision* **sokketsu**
対決 *confrontation, showdown* **taiketsu**
決まり文句 *normative expression* **kimari monku**

> 裁*udgement, 802*
> 判*udgement, 949*
> 定*efinite, 550*

> 沢*arshland, 753*

588-B

Sound 決ecision based on 快leasant conditions ...

心⇔忄⇔忝 (heart, feelings)

快leasant   快oyful

kokoroyo(i), KAI
pleasant, joyful, pleasure, delight

Facing: 1.2. ☜ West (V)
Facing: 4.0. ☜☞ Apart

不快 *unpleasant, disgusting, sickening* **fukai**
豪快 *heroic, tremendous* **gōkai**
快弁 *articulate, eloquence* **kaiben**
快調 *good condition* **kaichō**
快諾 *immediate-, ready consent* **kaidaku**
快復 *recuperation, recovery* **kaifuku**
快報 *good news, glad tidings* **kaihō**
快方 *convalescence, recuperation* **kaihō**
快感 *pleasant, sensual* **kaikan**
快活 *lively, cheerful, merry* **kaikatsu**
快挙 *splendid feat* **kaikyo**
快眠 *pleasant-, sound sleep* **kaimin**
快音 *solid crack, ~cranny* **kaion**
快楽 *pleasure, enjoyment* **kairaku**
快作 *excellent work* **kaisaku**
快晴 *fine weather* **kaisei**
快勝 *sweeping victory* **kaishō**
快食 *good appetite* **kaishoku**
快走 *racing, scudding, sailing* **kaisō**

快速 *fast speed* **kaisoku**
快足 *quick feet* **kaisoku**
快適 *comfortable, pleasant* **kaiteki**
快刀 *sharp sword* **kaitō**
軽快 *light, rhythmical* **keikai**
明快 *clear, lucid, explicit* **meikai**
壮快 *thrilling, exciting* **sōkai**
特快 *express train* **tokkai**
愉快 *enjoyable, pleasant* **yukai**
全快 *complete recovery* **zenkai**
快男児 *cheerful, spirited, zestful* **kaidanji**

> 悦*leasant, 942*   娯*leasure, 453*
> 楽*leasure, 447*   愉*leasure, 922*
> 歓*leasure, 667*   楽*njoy, 447*
> 喫*leasure, 900*

> 決*ecide, 699*

589-A

抵*esistance to snow, a* 低*inimum* 低*ow...*

手⇔扌 (hand, manual)

抵*esistance* 抵*pposition*

TEI
resistance, opposition, objection, repulsion

大抵 *generally, regularly* **taitei**
⇒並大抵 *ordinary* **namitaitei**
抵抗 *resistance, opposition* **teikō**
⇒無抵抗 *non-resistance* **muteikō**
⇒摩擦抵抗 *frictional resistance* **masatsu teikō**
抵抗器 *resistor* **teikōki**
抵触 *conflict, dispute, struggle* **teishoku**
抵当 *mortgage, collateral, security* **teitō**
⇒譲渡抵当 *mortgage, collateral* **jōto teitō**
抵当物 *mortgage, collateral property* **teitōbutsu**
抵当権 *mortgage, hypothec* **teitōken**
抵当流れ *foreclosure* **teitō nagare**

Facing: 4.0. ⟨⟩ Apart

抗*esistance, 749*	戦*ombat, 517*
対*gainst, 691*	闘*ombat, 946*
反*gainst, 537*	武*ombatant, 100*
逆*everse, 896*	

低*inimum, 700*

589-B

抵*esistance to snow, a* 低*inimum* 低*ow...*

人⇔亻 (person)

低*inimum* 低*ow*

hiku(i), hiku(meru), hiku(maru), TEI
minimum, low, slight, least

低目 *minus point, weakness* **hikume**
高低 *high & low, fluctuating* **kōtei**
熱低 *tropical depression, cyclone* **nettei**
最低 *the lowest, minimum* **saitei**
低圧 *low-pressure* **teiatsu**
低地 *low-lying lands* **teichi**
低調 *sluggish, dull* **teichō**
低塩 *low-salt* **teien**
低額 *small sum, ~amount* **teigaku**
低減 *decline, decrease* **teigen**
低位 *low rank* **teii**
低下 *price decline, price fall* **teika**
低価 *low price* **teika**
低回 *loitering, lingering* **teikai**
低空 *low altitude, low sky* **teikū**
低級 *low-class, inferior, substandard* **teikyū**
低能 *feeble-minded, weak-minded* **teinō**
低温 *low temperature* **teion**
低音 *low tone, bass* **teion**

Facing: 4.0. ⟨⟩ Apart

低温殺菌 *pasteurisation* **teion sakkin**
低落 *fall, decline* **teiraku**
低廉 *cheap, inexpensive* **teiren**
低利 *cheap-, low interest* **teiri**
低率 *low rate, ~percentage* **teiritsu**
低湿 *low & marshy* **teishitsu**
低唱 *low-pitch singing* **teishō**
低速 *low-speed, slow moving* **teisoku**
低俗 *vulgar, crude, gross* **teizoku**
低賃金 *cheap wages, ~labour* **teichingin**
低気圧 *atmospheric depression* **teikiatsu**

少*carce, 459*	床*loor, 633*
短*hort, 144*	微*light, 62*
底*ottom, 860*	

抵*esistance, 700*

590-A

呼*alling* for 評*ommentary* on Bill & Hillary...

口 (mouth)

呼*alling*　　呼*nvite*

yo(bu), KO
calling, invite, beckon

FLIP: 5.0.b. Left & Right
Facing: 1.2. 🢀 West (V)

歓呼	*cheer, obviation, applause*	**kanko**
呼号	*"claiming to be as..."*	**kogō**
呼格	*vocative case*	**kokaku**
呼気	*exhalation, respiration*	**koki**
呼吸	*inhalation, breathing*	**kokyū**
呼応	*logical coherent*	**koō**
呼称	*calling, naming*	**koshō**
連呼	*repeated calls*	**renko**
指呼	*a little way from*	**shiko**
称呼	*name designation*	**shōko**
点呼	*roll call*	**tenko**
深呼吸	*deep breathing*	**shinkokyū**
呼び声	*call, cry, rumour*	**yobigoe**
呼び子	*whistle, bird call*	**yobiko**
呼び水	*prime-pumping*	**yobimizu**
呼び物	*special feature*	**yobimono**
呼び値	*nominal price*	**yobine**
呼び鈴	*door-, front desk-, counter bell*	**yobirin**
呼び屋	*promoter*	**yobiya**

呼び合う	*call each other*	**yobiau**
呼び出し	*call, summons, crier*	**yobidashi**
呼び掛け	*appeal, hail, call*	**yobikake**
呼び込み	*calling in*	**yobikomi**
呼び捨て	*calling without "~san"*	**yobisute**
呼び売り	*peddler, street hawker*	**yobiuri**
呼び寄せ	*special offer*	**yobiyose**
呼び上げる	*call out, roll call*	**yobiageru**
呼び集める	*assemble, summon*	**yobiatsumeru**
呼び起こす	*wake up, recall*	**yobiokosu**
呼び止める	*call to stop, challenge*	**yobitomeru**

招*nvite, 956*	賓*uest, 161*
客*uest, 559*	迎*elcome, 705*

評*ommentary, 701*

590-B

呼*alling* for 評*ommentary* on Bill & Hillary...

言 (speaking)

評*ommentary*　　評*ritique*

HYŌ
commentary, critique, appraisal, evaluation, review

FLIP: 5.0.b. Left & Right

概評	*comprehensive-, thorough review*	**gaihyō**
合評	*joint review, ~comments*	**gappyō**
劇評	*drama criticism, ~review*	**gekihyō**
戯評	*lampoon, satire, caricature*	**gihyō**
批評	*criticism, commentary*	**hihyō**
批評眼	*critical-, discerning eye*	**hihyōgan**
品評	*quality assessment, ~appraisal*	**hinpyō**
評判	*reputation, prestige, name-value*	**hyōban**
評注	*comments, annotation, reference*	**hyōchū**
評伝	*critical biography*	**hyōden**
評議	*conference, discussion*	**hyōgi**
評語	*commentary, criticism*	**hyōgo**
評価	*evaluation, estimation, appraisal*	**hyōka**
評決	*verdict, judgement, decision*	**hyōketsu**
評論	*critique, comment, review*	**hyōron**
評論家	*critic, commentator, reviewer*	**hyōronka**
評釈	*annotation, commentary*	**hyōshaku**
評定	*ratings, assessment, review*	**hyōtei**
評点	*ratings, assessment, review*	**hyōten**

時評	*comments on current events*	**jihyō**
高評	*your comment (honorific)*	**kōhyō**
講評	*critique, comment, review*	**kōhyō**
酷評	*brutal criticism, unkind criticism*	**kokuhyō**
冷評	*unkind criticism, cold commentary*	**reihyō**
論評	*comment, criticism*	**ronpyō**
世評	*reputation, public opinion*	**sehyō**
書評	*book review*	**shōyō**
寸評	*short review*	**sunpyō**
定評	*standing reputation*	**teihyō**
適評	*proper criticism*	**tekihyō**

批*riticize, 466*	談*iscussion, 308*
価*alue, 35*	議*iscussion, 341*
値*alue, 783*	論*iscussion, 786*

証*ertificate, 789*

591-A

状onditions for 伏ielding hideout in a building...

犬⇔犭 (dog; beast)

⁰状ondition   ⁰状etter

JŌ

condition, circumstance, situation, form; letter

FLIP: 7.1. Right (Sort Of)

❶ 病状 *illness condition* **byōjō**
現状 *present situation* **genjō**
波状 *wavy, undulated* **hajō**
異状 *irregularity, abnormality* **ijō**
状況 *state of affairs, circumstances* **jōkyō**
状態 *condition, state* **jōtai**
塊状 *monstrous, enormous* **kaijō**
環状 *circle* **kanjō**
形状 *form, shape* **keijō**
鎖状 *chain-like* **kusarijō**
凶状 *crime, felony, serious offence* **kyōjō**
窮状 *distress, anxiety, trouble* **kyūjō**
名状 *"beyond description..."* **meijō**
惨状 *terrible-, miserable scene* **sanjō**
性状 *nature, characteristics* **seijō**
賞状 *certificate of award, citation* **shōjō**
症状 *symptom, illness condition* **shōjō**
敵状 *enemy strength & weakness* **tekijō**
罪状 *crime, guilt, sin* **zaijō**

❷ 免状 *license, diploma, certification* **menjō**
令状 *warrant, written order* **reijō**
⇒搜査令状 *search warrant* **sōsa reijō**
公開状 *open letter* **kōkaijō**
年賀状 *New Year's greeting card* **nengajō**
離縁状 *letter of divorce* **rienjō**
召喚状 *summons, subpoena* **shōkanjō**
祝賀状 *congratulatory message* **shukugajō**
推薦状 *letter of recommendation* **suisenjō**
逮捕状 *arrest warrant* **taihojō**
遺言状 *last will, last testament* **yuigonjō**

況ondition, 716	様anner, 944
情ondition, 793	践ctual, 671
態ondition, 322	現ctual, 814

壮asculine, 367

591-B

状onditions for 伏ielding hideout in a building...

人⇔亻 (person)

伏end down   伏ield

fu(su), fu(seru), FUKU

bend down, yield, capitulate, give-up, grovel, stoop, succumb, prostrate

FLIP: 7.1. Right (Sort Of)

伏せる *face down, keep secret* **fuseru**
伏せ字 *blank, omission, asterisk* **fuseji**
圧伏 *toss out, overpower* **appuku**
伏兵 *ambush squad* **fukuhei**
伏流 *underground stream* **fukuryū**
伏線 *counter-measures* **fukusen**
伏射 *aiming a gunshot* **fukusha**
伏奏 *report to the emperor* **fukusō**
伏在 *pleading guilty* **fukuzai**
伏屋 *cottage, hovel* **fuseya**
平伏 *bowing in respect* **heifuku**
帰伏 *surrender, yielding, capitulation* **kifuku**
起伏 *ups & downs, vicissitudes* **kifuku**
降伏 *capitulation, surrender* **kōfuku**
屈伏 *submission, yielding* **kuppuku**
潜伏 *hidden, covert, concealed* **senpuku**
潜伏期 *incubation period* **senpukuki**
折伏 *preaching down* **shakubuku**
雌伏 *biding one's time* **shifuku**

承伏 *yielding, accepting* **shōfuku**
倒伏 *falling down, collapse* **tōfuku**
伏魔殿 *demon-infested* **fukumaden**
伏し目 *downcast eyes* **fushime**
泣伏す *break down in tears* **nakifusu**
面伏せ *disgraced face* **omobuse**
待ち伏せ *ambush, assassination* **machibuse**
突っ伏す *lying flat facing down* **tsuppusu**
説き伏せる *persuade, convince* **tokifuseru**
腕立て伏せ *push-up* **udetatefuse**

辞uitting, 954
曲end, 476
屈end, 212

状ondition, 702

592-A

社ompany boss of 社ociety wine 吐omitting at a 社hrine...

示⇔ネ (display, show)

❶社ompany   ❷社hrine

yashiro, SHA
company, society; shrine

FLIP: 7.0.a. Right (flat)

❶愛社 *company loyalty* **aisha**
弊社 *(our) company, we* **heisha**
本社 *main office, headquarters* **honsha**
会社 *company, corporation, workplace* **kaisha**
貴社 *your company, (you)* **kisha**
公社 *state-, public corporation* **kōsha**
入社 *joining a company, employment* **nyūsha**
御社 *your company, you* **onsha**
社長 *company president, CEO* **shachō**
社賓 *company guest* **shahin**
社員 *employee, staff member* **shain**
社印 *company seal* **shain**
社訓 *company motto* **shakun**
社命 *company orders* **shamei**
社債 *corporate bonds* **shasai**
社線 *privately-owned railway* **shasen**
社説 *newspaper editorial, ~commentary* **shasetsu**
社史 *company history* **shashi**
社運 *company fortunes* **shaun**

社用 *"on company business..."* **shayō**
社友 *close officemate* **shayū**
支社 *branch office* **shisha**
商社 *big trading firm* **shōsha**
❷神社 *Shintō shrine* **jinja**
寺社 *temples & shrine* **jisha**
社殿 *main shrine building* **shaden**
社会 *society, public-at-large* **shakai**
社会悪 *social evil, ~cancer* **shakaiaku**
社会人 *adult, grown-up* **shakaijin**
社会現象 *social phenomenon* **shakai genshō**

公*ublic, 180*	集*ather, 50*
民*eople, 495*	寺*emple, 248*
衆*opulace, 766*	参*emple-visit, 396*

社*elfare, 193*

592-B

社ompany boss of 社ociety wine 吐omitting at a 社hrine...

口 (mouth)

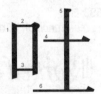

吐omit   吐hrow-up

ha(ku), TO
vomit, throw-up, spew, puke

FLIP: 5.0.a Left & Right

反吐 *vomiting, throwing up* **hedo**
音吐 *loud & clear* **onto**
嘔吐 *vomiting* **ōto**
吐息 *sigh, deep breath* **toiki**
吐血 *blood vomiting* **toketsu**
吐乳 *spitting out milk* **tonyū**
吐露 *expression, laying bare* **toro**
吐瀉 *vomiting & diarrhoea* **tosha**
吐出 *vomit, spit out, confess* **toshutsu**
吐き出す *vomit, spit out, confess* **hakidasu**
吐剤 *emetic* **tozai**
嘘吐き *liar, made-up story* **usotsuki**
吐き気 *nausea, queasiness* **hakike**
吐き下し *vomiting & purging* **hakikudashi**
吐き散らす *throwing up all over* **hakichirasu**

戻*ejection, 541*	斥*ejection, 424*
噴*pew-out, 849*	排*ejection, 795*

叫*hout, 693*

593-A

枝*ree-branch* on 岐*orked-road fell on my abode...*

木 (wooden)

枝*ree-branch*　　枝*ranch*

FLIP: 5.0.b. Left & Right

eda, SHI
tree branch, branch

枝毛　*split hair* **edage**
枝豆　*green soybeans* **edamame**
枝道　*branch road* **edamichi**
小枝　*twig* **koeda**
連枝　*nobleman siblings* **renshi**
整枝　*pruning* **seishi**
枝幹　*trunks & branches* **shikan**
枝葉　*branches & leaves* **shiyō**
枝葉末節　*frivolous-, trifle-, petty* **shiyō massetsu**
若枝　*young branch, shoots* **wakaeda**
楊枝　*toothpick* **yōji**
枝きり　*pruning* **edakiri**
枝接ぎ　*grafting* **edatsugi**
枯れ枝　*dead branch* **kareeda**
爪楊枝　*toothpick* **tsumayōji**
枝枯れ病　*twig blight* **edagarebyō**
枝垂れ柳　*weeping willow* **shidare yanagi**
枝垂れ桜　*weeping cherry* **shidare zakura**

木*ree, 461*
幹*ree trunk, 662*
支*ranch, 201*

技*echnique, 200*

593-B

枝*ree-branch* on 岐*orked-road fell on my abode...*

山 (mountain)

岐*orked-road*　　岐*iverge*

FLIP: 5.0.b. Left & Right

KI
forked road, diverge

分岐　*divergence, branching out* **bunki**
分岐点　*point-of-divergence* **bunkiten**
⇒損益分岐点　*break-even point* **son'eki bunkiten**
岐路　*crossroads, forked road* **kiro**
多岐　*various, diverse, assorted* **taki**
岐阜県　*Gifu Prefecture* **gifu-ken**
隠岐諸島　*cluster of islands (Shimane Prefecture)* **ōki shotō**

挟*orked, 762*　　道*oad, 312*
狭*arrow, 763*　　路*oad, 405*

枝*ree-branch, 704*

594-A
Crime 抑*uppressed,* 迎*elcomed with* 仰*espect...*

手⇔扌 (hand, manual)

抑*uppress* 抑*estrain*

osa(eru), YOKU
suppress, restrain, inhibit, repress, forestall

Facing: 4.0. ☜☞ Apart

抑え難い *irrepressible, uncontrollable* **osaegatai**
抑え付ける *hold down, curb* **osaetsukeru**
取り抑える *catch, capture, seizure* **toriosaeru**
抑抑 *"in the first place; well, now..."* **somosomo**
抑圧 *oppression, repression* **yokuatsu**
抑圧的 *oppressive, repressive* **yokuatsuteki**
抑留 *detention, internment, imprisonment* **yokuryū**
抑留船 *impounded ship* **yokuryūsen**
抑留者 *detainee, internee* **yokuryūsha**
抑制 *repression, restraint* **yokusei**
抑止 *restraint, deterrence* **yokushi**
抑止力 *deterrence, dissuasion* **yokushiryoku**
抑鬱 *dejection, depression* **yokuutsu**
抑揚 *intonation, modulation* **yokuyō**
謙抑 *humbling oneself* **kenyoku**

轄*ontrol, 968*	捕*eizure, 812*
管*ontrol, 917*	獲*eizure, 829*
禁*rohibit, 560*	

仰*espect, 706*

594-B
Crime 抑*uppressed,* 迎*elcomed with* 仰*espect...*

辶 (transport)

迎*elcome* 迎*ordial*

muka(eru), GEI
welcome, cordial, look-up, amicable, greeting

Facing: 4.0. ☜☞ Apart

迎え *facing, meeting, going* **mukae**
迎え火 *fire to welcome departed souls* **mukaebi**
迎え水 *pump-priming* **mukaemizu**
迎え酒 *morning sake* **mukaezake**
迎え撃つ *confront an attack* **mukaeutsu**
迎え入れる *usher in, welcome* **mukaeireru**
迎撃 *interception, blockade* **geigeki**
迎合 *flattery, ingratiation* **geigō**
迎賓 *welcoming guests* **geihin**
迎賓館 *guest house* **geihinkan**
迎接 *meeting & entertaining* **geisetsu**
迎春 *Happy New Year; pleasant spring* **geishun**
迎春花 *New Year seasonal flowers* **geishunka**
奉迎 *imperial welcome greetings* **hōgei**
奉迎門 *welcome arch* **hōgeimon**
歓迎 *welcome, cordial reception* **kangei**
歓迎会 *welcome-, reception party* **kangeikai**
来迎 *coming of Buddha to welcome dead spirits* **raigō**
送迎 *meeting upon arrival & sending off* **sōgei**

魂迎え *welcoming dead spirits* **tamamukae**
呼び迎える *send for* **yobimukaeru**

向*owards, 99*	懇*ordial, 164*
暖*armth, 821*	歓*ordial, 667*

迎*icinity, 93*

594-C

Crime 抑uppressed, 迎elcomed with 仰espect...

仰espect   仰dore   仰ook-up

人⇔亻 (person)

仰

ao(gu), ō(se), GYŌ, KŌ
esteem, adore, look-up, cherish, courtesy, respect

Facing: 4.0. 🔁 Apart

仰ぐ *ask for, look up* **aogu**
仰向く *look up, face up* **aomuku**
仰望 *look up, revere* **gyōbō**
仰臥 *lying on one's back, facing up* **gyōga**
仰仰しい *exaggerated, overstatement* **gyōgyōshii**
仰角 *elevation angle* **gyōkaku**
仰山 *numerous, grandiose* **gyōsan**
仰視 *look up, face up* **gyōshi**
仰天 *astonishment, amazement* **gyōten**
渇仰 *adoration, admiration, veneration* **katsugō**
景仰 *adoration, admiration, veneration* **keigyō**
大仰 *exaggerated, overstatement* **oogyō**
仰せ *words, orders* **ōse**
信仰 *faith, belief, conviction* **shinkō**
信仰告白 *confession of faith* **shinkō kokuhaku**
信仰生活 *monastic-, missionary life* **shinkō seikatsu**
仰け反る *bend back* **nokezoru**
仰せつかる *be ordered, be assigned* **oosetsukaru**

恭espect, 620	尚espect, 99
謹espect, 962	崇espect, 879
敬espect, 329	礼espect, 685

抑uppress, 705

595-A

赴roceeding-to-work, a 朴imple & 朴onest clerk...

走 (running)

赴

赴roceed-to-work

omomu(ku), FU
proceed-to-work, assume office

FLIP: 6.1. Left Top
Facing: 2.2. East ☞ (V)

赴任 *proceeding to one's post* **funin**
赴任地 *workplace, one's post* **funinchi**
赴任先 *workplace, jobsite* **funinsaki**

働abour, 422	勤ervice, 962
労orkforce, 351	任esponsible, 709
務ervice, 454	担esponsible, 739

掛ang up, 107

595-B

赴*roceeding-to-work, a* 朴*imple &* 朴*onest clerk...*

木 (wooden)

朴*imple*　　朴*onest*

BOKU
　simple, honest, basic

朴直	simple & honest	**bokuchoku**
朴訥	ruggedly honest	**bokutotsu**
純朴	innocent, honest, simple	**junboku**
淳朴	innocent, honest, simple	**junboku**
質朴	simple, unsophisticated	**shitsuboku**
素朴	simple, unsophisticated	**soboku**
敦朴	simple & honest	**tonboku**
朴念仁	stick, dunce, unsociable	**bokunenjin**

Facing: 2.2. East ☞ (V)

易*imple, 933*	普*ommon, 455*
簡*imple, 285*	凡*ommon, 78*
素*imple, 578*	劣*nferior, 572*
庸*ediocre, 906*	平*lain, 488*

赴*roceed-to-work, 706*

596-A

咲*looming flowers* 送*ent with* 朕*mperial consent...*

口 (mouth)

咲*looming*　　咲*lowering*

sa(ku)
　blooming, flowering, blossom

FLIP: 5.0.b. Left & Right

早咲き	early bloomer	**hayazaki**
室咲き	hot house flowers	**murozaki**
遅咲き	late blooming	**osozaki**
咲き出す	begin to bloom	**sakidasu**
咲き誇る	glorious blooming	**sakihokoru**
咲き残る	still blooming	**sakinokoru**
咲き揃う	full blooming	**sakisorō**
四季咲き	blooming in all seasons	**shikizaki**
八重咲き	double-blooming	**yaezaki**
返り咲き	comeback, grand return	**kaerizaki**
狂い咲き	flowering out of season	**kuruizaki**
後れ咲き	begin to bloom	**okurezaki**
咲き初める	begin blooming	**sakisomeru**
咲き分ける	blooming in many colours	**sakiwakeru**
咲き乱れる	bloom in profusion	**sakimidareru**
死に花を咲ける	glorious death	**shi(ni) bana o sakaseru**

芳*ragrance, 533*	花*lower, 191*
香*ragrance, 895*	華*lower, 40*
薫*ragrance, 934*	

送*ending, 708*

596-B

咲*looming flowers* 送*ent with* 朕*mperial consent...*

辶 (transport)

送*ending*　送*ispatch*　送*ransmit*

oku(ru), SŌ
sending, dispatch, transmit, posting, shipping

FLIP: 3.0.b. Top (stem)

護送 *escort, convoy* **gosō**
配送 *delivery, shipment* **haisō**
返送 *"return-to-sender..."* **hensō**
放送 *broadcasting* **hōsō**
回送 *mail forwarding; "out-of-service (bus)..."* **kaisō**
歓送 *cordial sending off* **kansō**
後送 *sending later* **kōsō**
密送 *send secretly* **mitsusō, missō**
送別 *seeing off, sending off* **sōbetsu**
送迎 *meet & send-off* **sōgei**
送電 *electricity transmission, ~supply* **sōden**
送風 *ventilation, air conditioning* **sōfū**
送辞 *graduation-, commencement speech* **sōji**
送還 *repatriation, deportation, removal* **sōkan**
送検 *send to trial* **sōken**
送気 *air supply, ventilation* **sōki**
送金 *money remittance, wire transfer* **sōkin**
送稿 *sending manuscript* **sōkō**
壮行 *sending off someone* **sōkō**

送料 *postage fee, mailing cost* **sōryō**
送信 *sending e-mail* **sōshin**
送呈 *complimentary copy, book present* **sōtei**
追送 *send later* **tsuisō**
運送 *transportation, trucking* **unsō**
輸送 *transportation, trucking* **yusō**
郵送 *mail, postal* **yūsō**
送り先 *destination, address* **okurisaki**
見送り *send off, see off* **miokuri**
送り出す *send off, send out* **okuridasu**
送り込む *send, ship out* **okurikomu**

届*eliver, 631*	荷*reight, 877*	
輸*hipment, 660*	貨*reight, 191*	
搬*ransport, 323*	搭*reight, 146*	

送*onfusion, 904*

596-C

咲*looming flowers* 送*ent with* 朕*mperial consent...*

肉⇔月 (flesh, body part)

朕*mperial consent*

CHIN
first-person pronoun reserved for the Emperor of Japan; imperial consent
朕の意 *"Our Imperial Will is..."* **chin no i**

FLIP: 7.0.b2. Right (stem)

璽*mperial seal, 976*	勅*mperial-edict, 955*
詔*mperial-edict, 817*	皇*mperor, 113*

朕*rain, 47*

597-A
妊*regnancy* 任*ntrusts, parental* 任*uties a must...*

女 (woman)

妊*regnancy* 妊*onception*

hara(mu), NIN
pregnancy, conception, child bearing

FLIP: 7.1. Right (Sort Of)
Facing: 3.0. ☞ ☜ Across

不妊 *infertility, sterility* **funin**
避妊 *contraception, birth control* **hinin**
避妊薬 *contraceptive drugs* **hininyaku**
避妊器具 *contraceptive device* **hinin kigu**
懐妊 *pregnancy, conception* **kainin**
妊婦 *pregnant woman* **ninpu**
妊婦服 *pregnancy-, maternity clothes* **ninpufuku**
妊産婦 *pregnant women & midwives* **ninsanpu**
妊娠 *pregnancy, conceiving a child* **ninshin**
⇒想像妊娠 *imagined pregnancy* **sōzō ninshin**
妊娠中絶 *abortion, pregnancy termination*
　　　 ninshin chūzetsu
不妊症 *infertility-, sterility illness* **funinshō**

娠*regnancy, 61*	生*ife, 474*
産*hildbirth, 883*	命*ife, 362*
誕*hildbirth, 515*	系*osterity, 262*

姓*urname, 638*

597-B
妊*regnancy* 任*ntrusts, parental* 任*uties a must...*

人⇔亻 (person)

任*ntrust* 任*esponsible*

maka(seru), maka(su), NIN
entrust, responsible, duty, obligation, authorize, office

FLIP: 7.1. Right (Sort Of)
Facing: 1.2. ☜ West (V)

着任 *assumption of duties* **chakunin**
代任 *acting capacity* **dainin**
赴任 *proceeding to one's post* **funin**
現任 *incumbent, post occupant* **gennin**
放任 *non-intervention, "let it be..."* **hōnin**
委任 *commission, delegation* **inin**
辞任 *resignation, quitting, leaving a job* **jinin**
自任 *self-fascination, narcissism* **jinin**
重任 *heavy-, important responsibility* **jūnin**
兼任 *additional-, concurrent post* **kennin**
帰任 *resumption of duties* **kinin**
降任 *demotion, relegation to a lower post* **kōnin**
任意 *discretionary, optional, voluntary* **nin'i**
任命 *appointment, nomination* **ninmei**
任用 *employing, hiring, recruiting* **ninyō**
来任 *assumption of duties* **rainin**
離任 *leaving one's post* **rinin**
留任 *staying in office, ~on the job* **ryūnin**
再任 *re-appointment, job recall* **sainin**

責任 *responsibility, blame* **sekinin**
専任 *full time job* **sennin**
新任 *newly-appointed, new post* **shinnin**
主任 *in charge of, responsible officer* **shunin**
就任 *appointment to a post* **shūnin**
大任 *important task, responsibility* **tainin**
退任 *retirement* **tainin**
担任 *in charge of, responsible officer* **tannin**
転任 *changing of post, job re-assignment* **tennin**
出任せ *clumsy behaviour* **demakase**
背任罪 *breach of trust, betrayal* **haininzai**
前任者 *predecessor* **zenninsha**

預*ntrust, 569*	勤*ervice, 962*
責*esponsible, 115*	務*ervice, 454*
担*esponsible, 739*	

代*eplace, 96*

598-A

Summer 軒ouses by the river, dwellers 汗weat to their 肝ivers...

車 (vehicle, wheel)

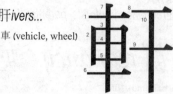

軒 *[houses]*   軒*aves*

FLIP: 5.0.b. Left & Right

noki, KEN
[houses], eaves

一軒 *house, door* **ikken**
一軒家 *one-family house* **ikkenya**
軒別 *house-to-house* **kenbetsu**
軒昂 *in high spirits* **kenkō**
軒高 *in high spirits* **kenkō**
軒数 *number of houses* **kensū**
軒灯 *lantern, door lamp* **kentō**
軒端 *edge of eaves* **nokiba, nokibata**
軒店 *store under the eaves* **nokimise**
軒先 *front of the house* **nokisaki**
軒下 *under the eaves* **nokishita**
軒丈 *eaves height* **nokitake**
二軒家 *two-family house* **nikenya**
二軒立て *duplex, semi-detached house* **nikendate**
軒並み *row of houses* **nokinami**

丁 *lock-of-houses, 173*	住 *esidence, 750*
街 *owntown, 107*	宅 *esidence, 82*
居 *esidence, 384*	邸 *esidence, 860*

幹 *ree trunk, 662*

598-B

Summer 軒ouses by the river, dwellers 汗weat to their 肝ivers...

水 ⇔ 氵 (water)

汗*weat*   汗*erspire*

FLIP: 7.0.b1. Right (stem)

ase, KAN
sweat, perspire

脂汗 *oily-, greasy sweat* **aburaase**
汗水 *heavy sweating* **asemizu**
汗疹 *prickly heat* **asemo**
防汗 *anti-perspirant* **bōkan**
発汗 *sweat, perspire* **hakkan**
汗馬 *sweating horse* **kanba**
汗顔 *sweaty face* **kangan**
汗衣 *underwear; sweaty clothes* **kan'i**
汗血 *sweat & blood* **kanketsu**
汗腺 *sweat glands* **kansen**
生汗 *tense sweat* **namaase**
寝汗 *sleeping perspiration* **nease**
大汗 *heavy sweating* **ooase**
冷汗 *cold sweats* **reikan, hiyaase**
流汗 *sweating, perspiration* **ryūkan**
汗ばむ *slight perspiration* **asebamu**
汗だく *heavily sweating* **asedaku**
汗染み *sweat-stains* **asejimi**
汗かき *frequent sweating* **asekaki**

汗臭い *sweat odour* **asekusai**
汗知らず *prickly baby* **ase shirazu**
汗みずく *heavy sweating* **asemizuku**
汗取り *underwear, underclothes* **asetori**
血の汗 *blood stain* **chi no ase**
冷や汗 *cold sweats* **hiyaase**
多汗症 *excessive sweats* **takanshō**
玉の汗 *perspiration beads* **tama no ase**

働 *abour, 422*	難 *ifficulty, 927*
労 *abour, 351*	走 *unning, 497*
工 *rtisan, 176*	重 *eavy, 430*
匠 *rtisan, 106*	忙 *ectic, 33*

干 *essicate, 74*

598-C

Summer 軒*ouses by the river, dwellers* 汗*weat to their* 肝*ivers...*

肉⇔月 (flesh, body part)

肝*iver*

kimo, KAN
liver

FLIP: 7.0.b1. Right (stem)

肺肝 *innermost heart, liver & gall* **haikan**
肝炎 *hepatitis, liver inflammation* **kan'en**
⇒血清肝炎 *serum hepatitis* **kessei kan'en**
肝心 *main, essential* **kanjin**
肝腎 *main, essential* **kanjin**
肝腎要 *pivotal importance* **kanjinkaname**
肝銘 *deep impressions* **kanmei**
肝胆 *innermost heart, liver & gall* **kantan**
肝要 *main, essential* **kanyō**
肝油 *liver oil* **kanyu**
肝臓 *liver organ* **kanzō**
肝臓病 *liver disease* **kanzōbyō**
肝臓炎 *hepatitis, liver inflammation* **kanzōen**
心肝 *mental attitude* **shinkan**
砂肝 *gizzards, insides* **sunagimo**
胆汁 *bile, gall* **tanjū**
胆嚢 *gall bladder* **tannō**
胆石 *gallstone* **tanseki**
肝硬変 *liver cirrhosis* **kankōhen**

肝試し *testing a person's courage* **kimodameshi**
肝太い *brave, daring, courageous* **kimofutoi**
肝煎り *go-between, mediator* **kimoiri**
肝入り *go-between, mediator* **kimoiri**
肝っ玉 *guts, nerves, mettle, courage* **kimottama**
肝冷やす *"scared to the liver..."* **kimohiyasu**

血*lood, 20*	臓*rgans, 565*
脈*eins, 766*	堪*ndure, 294*
肺*ungs, 305*	耐*ndure, 974*

町*own, 174*

599-A

侮*espise or* 侮*egret but never forget...*

人⇔亻 (person)

侮*espise*　　侮*nsult*

anado(ru), BU
despise, insult, detest, disdain, humiliate

Facing: 1.2. ☜ West (V)

侮蔑 *scorn, contempt, disdain* **bubetsu**
侮言 *insult, indignity, humiliation* **bugen**
侮辱 *insult, contempt, affront* **bujoku**
侮慢 *insult, contempt, affront* **buman**
侮弄 *butt of jokes, ridicule* **burō**
侮笑 *derision, ridicule* **bushō**
軽侮 *scorn, contempt, disdain* **keibu**

憎*atred, 837*	辱*umiliate, 588*
憤*nrage, 848*	恥*isgrace, 229*
嫌*espise, 805*	卑*espise, 936*

梅*lum, 240*

599-B

悔*espise* or 悔*egret* but never forget...

心 ⇔ 忄 ⇔ 小 (feelings)

悔*egret*　　悔*emorse*

ku(iru), ku(yamu), kuya(shii), KAI
regret, remorse, repent, irksome, disappointment, fretful, misgiving

Facing: 1.2. ☜ West (V)

悔やみ　*regret, remorse* **kuyami**
悔しい　*bitter, regret, vexing* **kuyashii**
悔み言　*words of condolence* **kuyamigoto**
悔し涙　*tears of regret* **kuyashinamida**
悔い改め　*repentance, remorse, atonement* **kuiaratame**
悔やみ状　*letter of condolence* **kuyamijō**
悔しがる　*regret, feel chagrined* **kuyashigaru**
悔し紛れ　*out of spite* **kuyashimagire**
悔し泣き　*crying out of remorse* **kuyashinaki**
お悔やみ　*deep condolences, ~sympathy* **okuyami**
悔悟　*repentance, remorse, atonement* **kaigo**
悔恨　*remorse, regret* **kaikon**
悔悛　*repentance, remorse* **kaishun**
後悔　*regret, remorse* **kōkai**
痛切　*sharp, keen, acute* **tsūsetsu**

慨*egret, 316*
憾*egret, 46*
惜*egret, 281*

梅*lum, 240*

600-A

神*od to* 伸*tretch,* 紳*entlemen to fetch...*

示 ⇔ 礻 (display, show)

神*eity*　　神*ivine*　　神*acred*

kami, kan, kō, SHIN, JIN
deity, divine, sacred, God, pious, solemn

FLIP: 7.0.b1. Right (stem)

牧神　*satyr, pan* **bokushin**
阪神　*Ōsaka & Kōbe region* **hanshin**
邪神　*devil, malicious, evil* **jashin**
神宮　*Shintō shrine* **jingū**
神楽　*sacred Shintō dance* **kagura**
神々　*deities, gods* **kamigami**
神風　*divine wind, WWII suicide pilots* **kamikaze**
神業　*act-of-God, divine intervention* **kamiwaza**
敬神　*devoutness, piety, piousness* **keishin**
精神　*mind, mental, spirit* **seishin**
色神　*colour sense* **shikishin**
神罰　*divine punishment, wrath-of-god* **shinbatsu**
神学　*theology, canon laws* **shingaku**
神官　*Shintō priest* **shinkan**
神経　*nerve, sensitivity* **shinkei**
神権　*divine rights* **shinken**
神父　*Catholic priest, father* **shinpu**
神聖　*sacred, holy, divine* **shinsei**
神政　*theocracy* **shinsei**

神式　*Shintō rites* **shinshiki**
心神　*one's mind* **shinshin**
神道　*Shintō religion* **shintō**
神話　*mythology, myth* **shinwa**
天神　*heavenly gods* **tenjin**
神頼み　*praying for something* **kamidanomi**
守り神　*guardian deity, ~angel* **mamorigami**
無神論　*atheism, atheist* **mushinron**
七福神　*seven gods of fortune* **shichifukujin**
死に神　*god of death* **shinigami**
入神の技　*divine talents, ~gift* **nyūshin no waza**

聖*acred, 617*　　信*aith, 252*
祈*rayer, 184*　　宗*aith, 879*
拝*rayer, 636*　　堂*ltar, 94*
仏*uddha, 683*

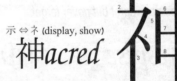

補*upplement, 812*　　伸*tretch, 713*

600-B

神*od to* 伸*tretch,* 紳*entlemen to fetch...*

伸*tretch*   伸*xpand*

人⇔亻 (person)

伸

FLIP: 7.0.b1. Right (stem)

no(biru), no(basu), SHIN
　stretch, expand, exert

欠伸 *yawn, gape* **akubi**
⇒生欠伸 *yawn-at-sight* **namaakubi**
上伸 *upsurge, rise* **jōshin**
屈伸 *expansion & contraction* **kusshin**
急伸 *sudden rise* **kyūshin**
二伸 *postscript, P.S.* **nishin**
伸長 *expansion, elongation* **shinchō**
伸度 *ductility, elasticity* **shindo**
伸筋 *protractor muscle* **shinkin**
伸縮 *stretch, spread* **shinshuku**
伸縮性 *elasticity* **shinshukusei**
伸展 *expansion, extension* **shinten**
追伸 *postscript, P.S.* **tsuishin**
続伸 *continued rise* **zokushin**
背伸び *overstretching, aiming too high* **senobi**
伸し歩く *swaggering, ostentation* **noshiaruku**
伸び縮み *expansion & contraction* **nobichijimi**
伸び悩む *make little progress* **nobinayamu**
伸び伸び *at ease, relax* **nobinobi**

皺伸ばし *smooth out winkles* **shiwanobashi**
引き伸ばす *stretch out, expand* **hikinobasu**
伸び上がる *stand on tiptoe, tiptoe* **nobiagaru**
差し伸べる *hold out* **sashinoberu**

張*tretch, 274*	力*trength, 351*
努*fforts, 44*	勢*igour, 153*
勉*fforts, 527*	精*igour, 792*
延*rolong, 515*	耐*ndure, 974*

神*ivine, 712*

600-C

神*od to* 伸*tretch,* 紳*entlemen to fetch...*

紳*entleman*

糸 (thread, continuity)

紳

FLIP: 7.0.b1. Right (stem)

SHIN
　gentleman

田紳 *countryside gentleman* **denshin**
貴紳 *notable-, reputable man* **kishin**
紳士 *gentleman* **shinshi**
紳士道 *gentlemen's code* **shinshidō**
紳士服 *men's formal attire* **shinshifuku**
紳士靴 *men's shoes* **shinshigutsu**
紳士録 *"who's who..."* **shinshiroku**
紳士的 *gentlemanly* **shinshiteki**
紳士用 *"for men's use..."* **shinshiyō**
紳士協定 *gentlemen's agreement* **shinshi kyōtei**
紳商 *rich merchant* **shinshō**

士*entleman, 8*	僕*asculine, 157*
壮*asculine, 367*	雄*asculine, 775*
男*asculine, 597*	郎*asculine, 404*

伸*tretch, 713*

601-A

On bargain 購*urchase, buy* 構*osture in a haste...*

貝 (shell, old money)

購*urchase* 購*uying*

agana(u), KŌ
purchase, buying, acquire with money

FLIP: 5.0.b. Left & Right

購買 *purchase, buying* **kōbai**
購買力 *purchasing power* **kōbairyoku**
購買組合 *consumers group* **kōbai kumiai**
購読 *subscription, circulation* **kōdoku**
購読者 *subscriber, reader* **kōdokusha**
購入 *purchase, buying* **kō'nyū**
⇒一括購入 *bulk purchase* **ikkatsu kō'nyū**
購入者 *purchaser, buyer* **kō'nyūsha**
購求 *purchase* **kōkyū**
購書 *purchased books* **kōsho**
購読料 *subscription fee* **kōdokuryō**

買*urchase, 516*	払*ayment, 682*
賃*ayment, 145*	料*ayment, 194*
納*ayment, 296*	得*cquire, 940*

講*ecture, 226*

601-B

On bargain 購*urchase, buy* 構*osture in a haste...*

木 (wooden)

構*osture* 構*tance*

kama(eru), kama(u), KŌ
posture, appearance, stance, construct

FLIP: 5.0.b. Left & Right

構える *set up, make, build, take* **kamaeru**
構え手 *caring after another* **kamaete**
結構 *"pretty much, rather..."* **kekkō**
機構 *system, organization, composition* **kikō**
⇒政治機構 *political structure* **seiji kikō**
構文 *sentence construction, syntax* **kōbun**
構築 *building, structure, construction* **kōchiku**
構外 *outside the premises* **kōgai**
構内 *within the premises, ~compounds* **kōnai**
構成 *composition, structure* **kōsei**
構想 *plot, idea, plan* **kōsō**
構材 *construction materials* **kōzai**
構造 *structure, organization* **kōzō**
⇒耐火構造 *fireproof construction* **taika kōzō**
⇒階層構造 *layered structure* **kaisōkōzō**
構造化 *structuralization* **kōzōka**
構造的 *structural* **kōzōteki**
構図 *composition, makeup* **kōzu**
虚構 *fiction, fabrication* **kyokō**

家構え *house appearance* **iegamae**
気構え *readiness, preparedness* **kigamae**
心構え *frame of mind* **kokorogamae**
身構え *be on guard, stand ready* **migamae**
表構え *façade, outward looks* **omotegamae**
外構え *outside appearance* **sotogamae**
面構え *one's face, expression, looks* **tsuragamae**
構成員 *member* **kōseiin**
待ち構え *look forward to, wait for* **machikamae**
三段構え *"A, B, C-preparations..."* **sandangamae**

看*ook after, 623*	態*ppearance, 322*
供*ook-after, 303*	容*ppearance, 492*
姿*ppearance, 609*	現*ppear, 814*

横*idewards, 197*	講*ecture, 226*

602-A

Wars 破estroy, 被ufferings annoy...

石 (stone)

破*estroy*　破*reck*　破*uin*

yabu(ru), yabu(reru), HA
destroy, wreck, ruin, obliterate, damage, hurting, injury, suffer

爆破 *explosion, blast, detonation* **bakuha**
破談 *cancelled negotiations, broken talks* **hadan**
破獄 *jailbreak* **hagoku**
破片 *fragments, broken pieces* **hahen**
破壊 *destruction, wrecking, breaking* **hakai**
破壊力 *destructive power* **hakairyoku**
破壊的 *destructive, destroyer* **hakaiteki**
破戒 *commandment violation* **hakai**
破格 *unprecedented, exceptional* **hakaku**
破棄 *annulment, breach, cancellation* **haki**
破局 *collapse, catastrophe* **hakyoku**
破滅 *ruin, destruction, wreckage* **hametsu**
破門 *expulsion, ejection* **hamon**
発破 *explosion, blast, detonation* **happa**
破産 *bankruptcy, financial insolvency* **hasan**
破線 *broken line* **hasen**
破船 *shipwreck, cast away* **hasen**
破綻 *bankruptcy, financial insolvency* **hatan**
破約 *broken-, unfulfilled promise* **hayaku**

Facing: 2.2. East ☞ (V)
FLIP: 7.3.b. Right Bottom (stem)

看破 *penetrating, seeing thru* **kanpa**
難破 *shipwreck, cast away* **nanpa**
連破 *successive winnings* **renpa**
小破 *slight damage* **shōha**
走破 *running a whole course* **sōha**
踏破 *travelling on foot* **tōha**
突破 *pierce, crash thru* **toppa**
破れ目 *a tear, a break* **yabureme**
道場破り *challenge visit to a training hall (jūdo)*
　　dōjōyaburi
言い破る *refute, confute, contradict* **iiyaburu**
突き破る *pierce, crash thru* **tsukiyaburu**

壊*estroy*, 847	崩*ollapse*, 912	損*amage*, 410
陥*ollapse*, 893	落*ollapse*, 826	害*amage*, 904

砕*ulverize*, 761

602-B

Wars 破estroy, 被ufferings annoy...

衣⇔ネ (clothing)

被*uffer*　被*njury*　被*amage*

kōmu(ru), HI
suffer, injury, damage, harm, hurting

法被 *happi coat* **happi**
被曝 *exposure to radiation* **hibaku**
被爆 *exposure to bombing* **hibaku**
被爆者 *bombing victims* **hibakusha**
被治者 *the governed, the masses* **hichisha**
被弾 *hit by a bullet-or-bomb* **hidan**
被服 *clothing, wardrobe* **hifuku**
被覆 *covering* **hifuku**
被害 *damage, injury, casualty* **higai**
被害地 *afflicted area* **higaichi**
被害者 *victim, aggrieved party* **higaisha**
被害妄想 *persecution complex, paranoia* **higai mōsō**
被告 *defendant, accused* **hikoku**
被告人 *defendant, accused* **hikokunin**
被膜 *capsule* **himaku**
被災 *disaster, tragedy, suffering* **hisai**
被災地 *afflicted area* **hisaichi**
被圧迫 *oppression* **hiappaku**
被疑者 *suspect* **higisha**

FLIP: 7.3.b. Right Bottom (stem)
Facing: 2.2. East ☞ (V)

被験者 *testee, examinee, subject* **hikensha**
被写体 *subject (photography)* **hishatai**
被用者 *employee, staff member* **hiyōsha**
被り物 *something to cover with* **kaburimono**
被保護国 *protectorate nation* **hihogokoku**
被上訴人 *appellee* **hijōsonin**
被起訴人 *indictee, the accused* **hikisosha**
被選挙権 *eligible for election* **hisenkyoken**
被選挙人 *eligible for election* **hisenkyonin**
被子植物 *angiosperm* **hishi shokubutsu**
被推薦者 *shortlisted candidate* **hisuisensha**

苦*uffer*, 477	惨*ragedy*, 396
虞*nxiety*, 889	悲*ragedy*, 289
煩*nxiety*, 832	厄*ragedy*, 354
禍*ragedy*, 799	損*amage*, 410

彼*[third person]*, 224

603-A

Happy 況ituation calls for 祝elebration...

水⇔氵 (water)

況*ituation*　況*ondition*

KYŌ
situation, condition, state

FLIP: 7.0.b2. Right (stem)

況して *"still-, further-, much more..."* **mashite**
不況 *economic recession* **fukyō**
概況 *general outlook, ~situation* **gaikyō**
⇒天気概況 *general weather outlook* **tenki gaikyō**
現況 *present state, status quo* **genkyō**
比況 *comparison, analogy* **hikyō**
悲況 *plight, lamentable state* **hikyō**
況や *"say nothing of, much less..."* **iwanya**
実況 *actual, ~real situation* **jikkyō**
状況 *state of affairs, circumstances* **jōkyō**
状況証拠 *circumstantial evidence* **jōkyō shōko**
情況 *circumstances, state of affairs* **jōkyō**
海況 *sea-faring conditions* **kaikyō**
活況 *dynamic condition, liveliness* **kakkyō**
景況 *the situation, circumstances* **keikyō**
近況 *recent conditions* **kinkyō**
好況 *brisk, flourishing, booming* **kōkyō**
作況 *crop, harvest condition* **sakkyō**
盛況 *prosperity, success, good times* **seikyō**

政況 *political situation* **seikyō**
戦況 *war situation* **senkyō**
市況 *market conditions, the market* **shikyō**
商況 *business situation, the market* **shōkyō**

情*ondition*, 793	様*anner*, 944
状*ondition*, 702	践*ctual*, 671
態*ondition*, 322	現*ctual*, 814

兄*lder-brother*, 203

603-B

Happy 況ituation calls for 祝elebration...

示⇔ネ (display, show)

祝*elebration*　祝*ongratulate*

iwa(u), SHUKU, SHŪ
celebration, congratulate, jubilation, jubilee

FLIP: 7.0.b2. Right (stem)

奉祝 *celebration, thanksgiving* **hōshuku**
慶祝 *congratulation, celebration* **keishuku**
祝詞 ① *address to the gods* **norito**
祝言 *congratulatory words* **shūgen**
祝儀 *celebration, congratulations* **shūgi**
祝文 *congratulatory message* **shukubun**
祝電 *congratulatory telegram* **shukuden**
祝宴 *feast, banquet* **shukuen**
祝福 *blessing, benediction* **shukufuku**
祝賀 *celebration, congratulations* **shukuga**
祝賀会 *celebration, thanksgiving party* **shukugakai**
祝杯 *toast, cheers* **shukuhai**
祝砲 *21-gun salute* **shukuhō**
祝意 *congratulations, celebration* **shukui**
祝辞 *congratulatory address* **shukuji**
祝日 *national-, public holiday* **shukujitsu**
祝詞 ② *congratulatory message* **shukushi**
祝勝 *victory celebration* **shukushō**
祝典 *celebration, festival* **shukuten**

祝い歌 *congratulatory song* **iwaiuta**
祝い酒 *congratulatory drinking* **iwaizake**
前祝い *advance celebration* **maeiwai**
祝祭日 *national-, public holiday* **shukusaijitsu**
内祝い *private celebration* **uchiiwai**
祝い返し *gift in return* **iwaigaeshi**
誕生祝い *birthday celebration* **tanjō iwai**
全快祝い *celebration of full health recovery* **zenkai iwai**

慶*ejoice*, 69	祥*appiness*, 248
賀*elebration*, 202	幸*appiness*, 268
喜*appiness*, 965	宴*anquet*, 610

視*bservation*, 815

604-A

肥*ertilizers in* 把*undles left to idle...*

肉⇔月 (flesh, body part)

肥*ertilize*　　肥*atten*

Facing: 4.0. ☜☞ Apart

koe, futo(ru), ko(yashi), ko(yasu), ko(eru), HI
fertilize, animal feed, fatten

肥やし *fertilizer, manure* **koyashi**
肥え土 *fertile soil, arable land* **koetsuchi**
肥え汲み *carrying night soil* **koekumi**
肥溜め *night soil vat* **koedame**
肥馬 *obese horse* **hiba**
肥大 *fatness, enlargement* **hidai**
肥育 *fattening, growing stout* **hiiku**
肥厚 *skin thickening* **hikō**
肥満 *growing fat, overweight* **himan**
肥満児 *overweight-, obese child* **himanji**
肥満体 *fatness, corpulence* **himantai**
肥料 *fertilizer, manure* **hiryō**
⇒窒素肥料 *nitrogenous fertilizer* **chisso hiryō**
⇒化学肥料 *chemical fertilizer* **kagaku hiryō**
⇒混合肥料 *compound fertilizer* **kongō hiryō**
肥沃 *soil fertility* **hiyoku**
補肥 *fertilizer supplements* **hohi**
金肥 *chemical fertilizer* **kinpi**
原肥 *farm manure* **motogoe**

緑肥 *green manure* **ryokuhi**
施肥 *fertilization* **sehi**
下肥 *human manure* **shimogoe**
水肥 *watery faeces, liquid manure* **suihi**
堆肥 *barnyard manure* **taihi**
追肥 *supplementary fertilizer* **tsuihi**
肥立つ *recover from giving birth* **hidatsu**
寒肥え *winter manure* **kangoe**
小肥り *plump, chubby* **kobutori**
草肥え *fertilizer mixture* **kusagoe**
馬屋肥え *horse shit* **umayagoe**

壌*ertile soil, 853*	畑*lantation, 482*
農*arming, 446*	植*lant, 783*
野*ield, 873*	田*ice field, 482*

暇*ree time, 653*

604-B

肥*ertilizers in* 把*undles left to idle...*

手⇔扌 (hand, manual)

把*undle*　　把*rip*

Facing: 4.0. ☜☞ Apart

HA, WA
bundle, grip, bunch

把握 *grasping, grip, control* **haaku**
把持 *holding on, grasping* **haji**
把手 *grip, handle, knob* **hashu, totte**
把捉 *grasp, comprehend* **hasoku**
一把 *one bundle* **ichiwa**
銃把 *pistol-, handgun grip* **jūha**
二把 *two bundles* **niwa**
三把 *"three bundles of..."* **sanwa**
大雑把 *roughly, approximately* **oozappa**

括*undle, 954*	握*rasp, 427*
束*undle, 502*	擁*mbrace, 151*
略*ummary, 825*	捕*atch, 812*
抄*ummary, 726*	集*ather, 50*

肥*ertilizer, 717*

605-A
錬*rill* & 練*rill, soldiers without meal...*

金 (metal)

錬*olish* 錬*efine*

REN
 polish, refine

FLIP: 5.0.b. Left & Right

百錬 *well-trained* **hyakuren**
錬金術 *alchemy* **renkinjutsu**
錬金術師 *alchemist* **renkin jutsushi**
錬鋼 *wrought steel* **renkō**
錬磨 *training, practice* **renma**
⇒百戦錬磨 *combat-tested* **hyakusen renma**
錬成 *training, drilling* **rensei**
錬鉄 *wrought iron* **rentetsu**
精錬 *gold refining, copper smelting* **seiren**
製錬 *smelting* **seiren**
修錬 *training, practice, drill* **shūren**
鍛錬 *forging, tempering* **tanren**
精錬業 *smelting industry* **seirengyō**
製錬所 *refinery, smelter* **seirenjo**
精錬所 *refinery, smelter* **seirenjō**

練*rill, 718*	授*eaching, 539*
訓*eachings, 959*	習*earning, 238*
師*eacher, 483*	徒*isciple, 497*

鎖*hain, 665*

605-B
錬*rill* & 練*rill, soldiers without meal...*

糸 (thread, continuity)

練*rill* 練*nead*

ne(ru), REN
 drill, exercise, training, knead

FLIP: 7.0.b1. Right (stem)

調練 *drill, training* **chōren**
熟練 *skill, mastery, dexterity* **jukuren**
訓練 *training, drill, exercise* **kunren**
⇒避難訓練 *evacuation drill* **hinan kunren**
⇒職業訓練 *vocational training* **shokugyō kunren**
訓練所 *training school* **kunrenjo**
訓練生 *trainee* **kunrensei**
教練 *military training* **kyōren**
未練 *lingering affection* **miren**
練薬 *ointment* **nerigusuri**
練磨 *practice, drill, training* **renma**
練乳 *condensed milk* **rennyū**
練兵 *military drill, ~exercise* **renpei**
練成 *training, drill, exercise* **rensei**
練習 *practice* **renshū**
練習所 *vocational-, job training school* **renshūjo**
練習曲 *etude* **renshūkyoku**
練習生 *trainee* **renshūsei**
練炭 *charcoal briquette* **rentan**

老練 *experienced, veteran* **rōren**
精練 *highly-polished, ~trained* **seiren**
試練 *trials & tribulations* **shiren**
手練 *skill, dexterity, agility* **shuren**
鍛練 *training, drill, temper* **tanren**
練り絹 *glossy silk* **neriginu**
練り歩く *parade, march* **neriaruku**
練り込む *knead into* **nerikomu**
練り直す *polish, refine, make better* **nerinaosu**
練習試合 *practice game* **renshū jiai**
練達の士 *expert, professional* **rentatsu no shi**

錬*rill, 718*	授*eaching, 539*
践*ractice, 671*	習*earning, 238*

綿*otton, 675*

606-A

就mployment 沈inks when job stinks...

沈inking   沈apsize

水⇔氵 (water)

shizu(mu), shizu(meru), CHIN
sinking, capsize, submerge, submerse, underwater

Facing: 2.2. East ☞ (V)

爆沈 *exploding & sinking* **bakuchin**
沈没 *sinking, submersion* **chinbotsu**
沈没船 *sunken ship* **chinbotsusen**
沈着 *calm, serene, composed* **chinchaku**
沈泥 *silt, residue* **chindei**
沈殿 *precipitation, sedimentation* **chinden**
沈吟 *hum; meditate, muse* **chingin**
沈下 *subsiding, submersion* **chinka**
沈降 *sinking, submerging* **chinkō**
沈黙 *falling into silence* **chinmoku**
沈静 *cooling off, cooling down* **chinsei**
沈積 *sedimentation, bottoming out* **chinseki**
沈潜 *sinking to the bottom* **chinsen**
沈思 *meditation, contemplation, reflection* **chinshi**
沈思黙考 *deep meditation* **chinshi mokkō**
沈滞 *stagnation, inactivity, dullness* **chintai**
沈痛 *grave, serious, severe* **chintsū**
沈鬱 *melancholy, gloomy* **chin'utsu**
沈勇 *calm courage* **chinyū**

浮沈 *rise & fall, vicissitudes* **fuchin**
不沈 *unsinkable, indestructible* **fuchin**
撃沈 *hit & sink* **gekichin**
轟沈 *instant sinking* **gōchin**
自沈 *sinking of one's boat* **jichin**
血沈 *blood sedimentation* **kecchin**
赤沈 *blood sedimentation* **sekichin**
沈丁花 *Daphne* **jinchōge**
意気消沈 *dejected, despondent* **ikishōchin**
打ち沈む *depressed, dejected* **uchishizumu**
浮き沈み *rise & fall, vicissitudes* **ukishizumi**

潜*ubmerge, 335*	没*inking, 744*
礁*unken, 920*	浸*ubmerse, 770*

法*aw, 360*

606-B

就mployment 沈inks when job stinks...

就mployment   就areer

尤 (crippled)

tsu(ku), tsu(keru), SHŪ, JU
employ, career, recruit, hiring, set about

FLIP: 6.0.b. Left (stem)

成就 *fulfil, accomplish, attain* **jōju**
去就 *course-of-action* **kyoshū**
就中 *above all, particularly* **nakanzuku**
就役 *being placed on duty* **shūeki**
就学 *entering a school* **shūgaku**
就学率 *rate of school attendance* **shūgakuritsu**
就学児童 *school children* **shūgaku jidō**
就学年齢 *school age* **shūgaku nenrei**
就業 *job commencement* **shūgyō**
就業率 *employment percentage* **shūgyōritsu**
就業時間 *working hours* **shūgyō jikan**
就業規則 *working regulations* **shūgyō kisoku**
就航 *commissioning of a vessel* **shūkō**
就眠 *going to sleep* **shūmin**
就任 *assumption of office* **shūnin**
就任式 *official oath-taking rites* **shūninshiki**
就労 *employment, working* **shūrō**
就寝 *sleep, go to bed, retire* **shūshin**
就職 *employment, career* **shūshoku**

就職係 *job placement office* **shūshoku gakari**
就職口 *job opening* **shūshokuguchi**
就縛 *catch & tie up* **shūbaku**
就床 *sleep, go to bed, retire* **shūshō**
就職難 *job-hunting difficulties* **shūshokunan**
就職先 *workplace, job site* **shūshokusaki**
就業日数 *days at work* **shūgyō nissū**
就職斡旋 *job placement* **shūshoku assen**

勤*mploy, 962*	務*mploy, 454*
採*mploy, 915*	雇*mploy, 343*
抱*mploy, 503*	職*mploy, 855*

沈*inking, 719*

607-A
珍are 診iagnosis shocked a pharmacist...

王⇔玉 (jewel)

FLIP: 6.0.a. Left (flat)

珍are   珍eldom

mezura(shii), CHIN
rare, seldom

別珍 *velveteen* **becchin**
珍聞 *curious story* **chinbun**
珍物 *curiosity* **chinbutsu**
珍重 *prize, value highly* **chinchō**
珍鳥 *rare bird* **chinchō**
珍談 *anecdote, funny tale* **chindan**
珍芸 *unusual trick* **chingei**
珍事 *unexpected event* **chinji**
珍奇 *rare, strange, odd* **chinki**
珍客 *unexpected visitor* **chinkyaku**
珍味 *delicacy, specialty product* **chinmi**
珍問 *strange question* **chinmon**
珍妙 *odd, fantastic* **chinmyō**
珍品 *rare article, one-of-a-kind* **chinpin**
珍宝 *treasured items, valuables* **chinpō**
珍本 *rare book* **chinpon**
珍説 *odd theory* **chinsetsu**
珍書 *rare book* **chinsho**

珍襲 *treasured, valued, prized* **chinshū**
珍答 *stupid answer, absurd reply* **chintō**
物珍しい *curious* **monomezurashii**
袖珍本 *pocket book* **shūchinbon**
珍現象 *strange phenomenon* **chingenshō**
珍無類 *strange, unique* **chinmurui**

少 *scarce, 459*	頻 *requent, 272*
奇 *trange, 269*	怪 *ubious, 888*

診 *iagnosis, 720*

607-B
珍are 診iagnosis shocked a pharmacist...

言 (speaking)

FLIP: 6.0.a. Left (flat)

診iagnosis   診heck up

mi(ru), SHIN
diagnosis, check-up, examine a patient

聴診 *auscultation* **chōshin**
聴診器 *stethoscope* **chōshinki**
代診 *substitute doctor* **daishin**
打診 *percussion, tapping* **dashin**
誤診 *erroneous diagnosis* **goshin**
受診 *getting a physical check-up* **jushin**
回診 *medical rounds* **kaishin**
検診 *physical check-up* **kenshin**
休診 *"clinic closed..."* **kyūshin**
問診 *medical exam questions* **monshin**
内診 *internal examination* **naishin**
往診 *doctor's visit, home call* **ōshin**
来診 *doctor's visit, home call* **raishin**
診断 *diagnosis, prognosis* **shindan**
⇒早期診断 *early diagnosis* **sōki shindan**
⇒健康診断 *physical check-up* **kenkō shindan**
診断書 *diagnosis report* **shindansho**
診療 *medical treatment* **shinryō**
診療所 *clinic, dispensary* **shinryōjo**

診察 *physical check-up* **shinsatsu**
診察日 *medical check-up day* **shinsatsubi**
視診 *visual examination* **shishin**
触診 *palpitation check-up* **shokushin**
初診 *first medical exam* **shoshin**
宅診 *visiting doctor's diagnosis* **takushin**
予診 *preliminary check-up* **yoshin**

医 *edicine, 19*	病 *ickness, 213*
剤 *edicine, 961*	治 *ecuperate, 210*
患 *ickness, 475*	癒 *ecuperate, 923*
症 *ickness, 788*	療 *ecuperate, 67*

該 *[the said], 973*

608-A

彫 *hiseled on a* 杉 *edar-tree, crest of Robert Lee...*

彡 (hair ornament)

彫 *hisel* 彫 *ngraving*

ho(ru), CHŌ
chisel, carve, engraving

FLIP: 6.0.b. Left (stem)

彫り *engraving, etching, carving* **bori**
彫金 *chasing, metal carving* **chōkin**
彫刻 *sculpture, carving, engraving* **chōkoku**
彫刻家 *sculptor, engraver* **chōkokuka**
彫刻刀 *chisel, incise* **chōkokutō**
彫塑 *plastics, resins* **chōso**
彫琢 *cutting & polishing* **chōtaku**
彫刻師 *sculptor, engraving artist* **chōkokushi**
彫像 *carved statue* **chōzō**
深彫 *deep carving* **fukabori**
木彫 *wood carving* **mokuchō**
粗彫り *rough carving* **arabori**
木彫り *wood carving* **kibori**
丸彫り *round carving* **marubori**
手彫り *hand carving* **tebori**
彫り物 *sculpture, carving* **horimono**
彫り物師 *carver, sculptor* **horimonoshi**
浮き彫り *relief carving, embossed carving* **ukibori**

薄肉彫り *low-embossed carving* **usunikubori**
透かし彫り *openwork carving* **sukashibori**
高浮き彫り *deep-engravings* **takaukibori**

刻 *culpture, 972*	芸 *rts, 619*
像 *tatue, 530*	巧 *kilful, 738*
工 *rtisan, 176*	術 *kills, 110*
匠 *rtisan, 106*	写 *opy, 349*

影 *hadows, 546*

608-B

彫 *hiseled on a* 杉 *edar-tree, crest of Robert Lee...*

木 (wooden)

杉 *edar-tree* 杉 *ryptomeria*

sugi, SAN
cedar-tree, cryptomeria

Facing: 3.0. ☞☜ Across

糸杉 *cypress* **itosugi**
杉箸 *cedar chopsticks* **sugibashi**
杉林 *cedar-, cryptomeria forest* **sugibayashi**
杉戸 *cedar wooden door* **sugido**
杉垣 *cedar-, cryptomeria hedge* **sugigaki**
杉苔 *hair moss* **sugigoke**
杉皮 *cryptomeria bark* **sugikawa**
杉菜 *field horsetail* **sugina**
杉材 *cedar woods materials* **sugizai**
一本杉 *single cedar tree* **ipponsugi**
神代杉 *lignite cedar* **jindaisugi**
杉並木 *cedar tree-lined road, cryptomeria road* **suginamiki**
杉花粉症 *cedar pollen allergy* **sugikafunshō**

柳 *illow-tree, 971*

彩 *olour, 914*

609-A

Grapes 昨*reviously* 搾*queezed made wine to please...*

昨*revious*　　　　昨*rstwhile*

日 (sunlight, daytime)

SAKU

previous, past, erstwhile, before, last

FLIP: 6.0.a. Left (flat)

昨日　*yesterday* **kinō, sakujitsu**
昨今　*lately, nowadays, recently* **sakkon**
昨晩　*last night* **sakuban**
昨朝　*yesterday morning* **sakuchō**
昨暁　*previous daybreak* **sakugyō**
昨夏　*summer last, past summer* **sakunatsu**
昨年　*last year, past year* **sakunen**
昨年度　*last fiscal-, last academic year* **sakunendo**
昨秋　*autumn last, past autumn* **sakushū**
昨春　*spring last, past spring* **sakushun**
昨冬　*winter last, past winter* **sakutō**
昨夕　*last night* **sakuyū**
昨夜　*last night* **yūbe, sakuya**
昨非今是　*"change of heart..."* **sakuhikonze**

昔*ast, 281*	昔*y-gones, 281*
時*ime, 653*	去*y-gones, 360*

作*roduce, 724*

609-B

Grapes 昨*reviously* 搾*queezed made wine to please...*

搾*queeze*　　　　搾*ighten*

手⇔扌 (hand, manual)

shibo(ru), SAKU

squeeze, tighten, compress

FLIP: 7.2.b. Right Top (stem)
Facing: 4.0. Apart

圧搾　*compression* **assaku**
圧搾空気　*compressed air* **assaku kūki**
圧搾ポンプ　*pump compressor* **assaku ponpu**
圧搾器　*air compressor* **assakuki**
乳搾り　*milking* **chichishibori**
搾乳　*milking* **saku'nyū**
搾乳場　*milking barn* **saku'nyūjō**
搾乳器　*milker, milking device* **saku'nyūki**
搾取　*exploitation, squeezing* **sakushu**
搾油　*oil extraction, ~exploration* **sakuyu**
油搾り　*oil press* **aburashibori**
油搾り器　*oil press device* **aburashiboriki**
搾り出す　*squeeze out* **shiboridasu**
搾り取る　*squeeze, wring* **shiboritoru**

滴*xtract, 799*	絞*ighten, 774*
引*xtract, 348*	締*ighten, 432*
抽*xtract, 37*	圧*ressure, 632*

詐*raudulent, 723*

610-A

詐*raudulent* 酢*inegar* 作*roduced by a beggar...*

詐*raudulent*　詐*eceit*

言 (speaking)

SA

fraudulent, deceit, trickery, cheating

詐欺 *fraud, swindle, trickery, cheat* **sagi**
詐欺師 *swindler, con artist, fraud* **sagishi**
詐欺罪 *false pretext, alibi, deceit* **sagizai**
詐欺譲渡 *fraudulent transfer, ~assignment* **sagi jōto**
詐術 *trickery, swindling* **sajutsu**
詐称 *misrepresentation, deception* **sashō**
詐取 *fraud, swindle, trickery* **sashu**

FLIP: 6.0.a. Left (flat)
Facing: 2.2. ☞ East (V)

偽*raudulent, 509*　犯*riminal, 640*
欺*raudulent, 658*　凶*vil, 80*
罪*riminal, 289*　悪*vil, 389*

詐*ppeal, 424*

610-B

詐*raudulent* 酢*inegar* 作*roduced by a beggar...*

酢*inegar*

酉 (liquor)

su, SAKU

vinegar, brine

甘酢 *sweet vinegar* **amazu**
酢酸 *acetic acid* **sakusan**
⇒氷酢酸 *glacial acetic acid* **hyōsakusan**
食酢 *vinegar* **shokusu**
酢豚 *sweet & sour pork* **subuta**
酢蛸 *vinegared octopus* **sudako**
梅酢 *plum vinegar* **umezu**
醸造酢 *brewed vinegar* **jōzōsu**
酢漿草 *wood sorrel* **katabami**
ポン酢 *soy sauce, vinegar & citreous* **ponzu**
三杯酢 *sweet vinegar & soy sauce seasoning* **sanbaizu**
酢味噌 *vinegared miso* **sumiso**
酢の物 *vinegared food* **sunomono**
酢料理 *vinegared cuisine* **suryōri**
酢漬け *pickling in vinegar* **suzuke**

FLIP: 6.0.a. Left (flat)

酸*cid, 764*　漬*ickling, 823*
味*aste, 871*　保*reserve, 552*

酷*ruelty, 266*

610-C

詐*raudulent* 酢*inegar* 作*roduced by a beggar...*

作*aking*　　作*roduce*

人⇔亻 (person)

作

tsuku(ru), SAKU, SA
making, produce, work

Facing: 4.0. 〜〜〜 Apart

著作 *book, writing* **chosaku**
動作 *action, movement* **dōsa**
原作 *original works* **gensaku**
偽作 *counterfeit, fake, forgery, phoney* **gisaku**
愚作 *poor work, trash* **gusaku**
豊作 *rich harvest, bumper crop* **hōsaku**
稲作 *rice plantation, rice crop* **inasaku**
遺作 *posthumous works* **isaku**
改作 *adaptation, rewriting* **kaisaku**
佳作 *fine work, good work* **kasaku**
工作 *handicraft; manuevering* **kōsaku**
耕作 *cultivation, farming* **kōsaku**
凶作 *poor crop, bad harvest* **kyōsaku**
乱作 *overproduction of literary works* **ransaku**
作業 *work, labour* **sagyō**
作家 *writer, author, novelist* **sakka**
作況 *good harvest; harvest condition* **sakkyō**
作曲 *musical composition* **sakkyoku**
作品 *work of art* **sakuhin**

作意 *intention, volition* **sakui**
作為 *fake-, feigned behaviour* **sakui**
作力 *efforts* **saryoku**
製作 *film production* **seisaku**
習作 *study, etude, learning* **shūsaku**
操作 *operation, control* **sōsa**
創作 *creation, creative work* **sōsaku**
盗作 *plagiarism, literary theft* **tōsaku**
造作 *fixtures, fittings, furnishings* **zōsa**
農作物 *harvest* **nōsakumotsu, nōsakubutsu**
処女作 *maiden work* **shojosaku**

産*roduce, 883*	工*raft, 176*	術*kills, 110*
造*roduce, 267*	匠*rtisan, 106*	
品*roducts, 901*	巧*kilful, 738*	

昨*revious, 722*

611-A

枚*heets of* 政*olitical* 改*eform created a firestorm...*

枚*[sheets]*　　枚*[flat things]*

木 (wooden)

枚

MAI
[counter for sheets], [counter for flat things]

FLIP: 7.1. Right (Sort Of)
Facing: 1.2. 〜 West (V)

五枚 *five sheets of paper* **gomai**
一枚 *one sheet of paper* **ichimai**
一枚看板 *one's only suit* **ichimai kanban**
枚挙 *enumerating, counting* **maikyo**
枚数 *number of sheets* **maisū**
何枚 *how many sheets* **nanmai**
大枚 *large bundles of cash* **taimai**
二枚舌 *double dealing, duplicity* **nimaijita**
二枚目 *two-piece suit; handsome guy* **nimaime**
三枚目 *comical person* **sanmaime**
千枚通し *eyeleteer, awl* **senmai dooshi**

紙*aper, 489*
判*aper size, 949*
書*ritings, 116*

枝*ree-branch, 704*

611-B

枚 *heets of* 政 *olitical* 改 *eform created a firestorm...*

攵 (action)

政 *olitics*   政 *dministration*

matsurigoto, SEI, SHŌ
politics, administration, government, regime

Facing: 3.0. ☞☜ Across
FLIP: 7.1. Right (Sort Of)

悪政	misrule, maladministration **akusei**		政令	government ordinance **seirei**
暴政	tyranny, tyrannical rule **bōsei**		政策	policy, measures **seisaku**
軍政	military government **gunsei**		政体	form of government **seitai**
行政	public documentation **gyōsei**		政党	political party **seitō**
仁政	benevolent government **jinsei**		摂政	regent, regency **sesshō**
家政	household management **kasei**		施政	administration, government **shisei**
憲政	constitutional government **kensei**		執政	administration, administrator **shissei**
国政	national government **kokusei**		帝政	monarchic government **teisei**
民政	civilian administration **minsei**		財政	finance, banking circles **zaisei**
内政	domestic governance **naisei**		善政	benevolent government **zensei**
政庁	government office **seichō**		共和政府	republican government **kyōwaseifu**
政府	government, administration **seifu**			
政治	politics, statesmanship **seiji**			
政治家	politician, statesman **seijika**			
政界	political world **seikai**			
政権	government, administration **seiken**			
政見	political view, ~opinion **seiken**			
政教	politics & religion **seikyō**			
政局	political situation **seikyoku**			

庁 *ubic office,* 633   国 *ation,* 92
更 *fficial,* 463   衆 *opulace,* 766
役 *fficial,* 746   民 *eople,* 495

致 *ring-about,* 381

611-C

枚 *heets of* 政 *olitical* 改 *eform created a firestorm...*

攵 (action)

改 *eform*   改 *enewal*

arata(meru), arata(maru), KAI
reform, renewal, renovate, refurbish, improve, upgrade

Facing: 1.2. ☜ West (V)
FLIP: 7.1. Right (Sort Of)

改悪	worsening, deterioration **kaiaku**		改進	progress, reform **kaishin**
改案	revision, rewriting **kaian**		改修	repairs, servicing **kaishū**
改築	reconstruction, re-building **kaichiku**		改宗	convert to another religion **kaishū**
改題	new title, new subject **kaidai**		改組	re-organization, restructuring **kaiso**
改元	new imperial era **kaigen**		改装	remodelling, renovation **kaisō**
改行	starting a new paragraph **kaigyō**		改定	revision, rewriting **kaitei**
改廃	re-organization, restructuring **kaihai**		改訂	revision, rewriting **kaitei**
改版	revision, rewriting **kaihan**		改訳	new translation **kaiyaku**
改変	alteration, changing **kaihen**		改善	improvement, reform **kaizen**
改編	book revision, rewriting **kaihen**		改造	remodelling, renovation **kaizō**
改革	reform, reformation **kaikaku**		更改	renewal, alteration **kōkai**
改憲	constitutional revisions **kaiken**			
改良	improvement, betterment, amelioration **kairyō**			
改作	adaptation, rewrite **kaisaku**			
改正	revision, amendment **kaisei**			
改姓	change of name, new surname **kaisei**			
改選	re-election **kaisen**			
改新	renewal, reformation **kaishin**			
改心	mending of ways **kaishin**			

革 *eform,* 39   且 *oreover,* 500
新 *ew,* 668   尚 *urther,* 99
更 *new,* 402   整 *djust,* 31

放 *elease,* 486

612-A

抄ummary so 妙uperb took 秒econds to be heard...

抄*ummary*　　抄*xcerpt*

手⇔扌 (hand, manual)

SHŌ

summary, excerpt, digest, nutshell, synopsis, gist, abridgement

FLIP: 7.1. Right (Sort Of)
Facing: 1.2. 🢐 West (V)

詩抄 *selected poems* **shishō**
抄物 *commentary, critique, review* **shōmotsu**
抄本 *abridged copy, ~edition* **shōhon**
⇒戸籍抄本 *abridged family register*
　　koseki shōhon
抄録 *extract, abstract* **shōroku**
抄写 *excerpt, quotation* **shōsha**
抄紙 *paper making* **shōshi**
抄出 *excerpts, gist* **shōshutsu**
抄訳 *selected-text translation* **shōyaku**
手抄 *manual copying* **shushō**

撮*ummarize, 423*	括*undle, 954*
略*xcerpt, 825*	束*undle, 502*
簡*oncise, 285*	把*undle, 717*

妙*uperb, 726*

612-B

抄ummary so 妙uperb took 秒econds to be heard...

妙*uperb*　　妙*xquisite*

女 (woman)

tae(naru), MYŌ

superb, exquisite, marvelous

FLIP: 7.1. Right (Sort Of)
Facing: 3.0. 🢒🢐 Across

微妙 *subtle, delicate* **bimyō**
美妙 *exquisite, elegant* **bimyō**
珍妙 *odd, eccentric* **chinmyō**
玄妙 *profound, abstruse* **genmyō**
軽妙 *light & clever* **keimyō**
奇妙 *strange, odd, queer* **kimyō**
巧妙 *excellent, clever* **kōmyō**
妙案 *brilliant idea* **myōan**
妙技 *exquisite skill, feat* **myōgi**
妙計 *ingenious-, clever plan* **myōkei**
妙味 *charm, appeal* **myōmi**
妙音 *exquisite music* **myōon**
妙齢 *young lady, youth* **myōrei**
妙策 *clever scheme* **myōsaku**
妙趣 *exquisite, delicate* **myōshu**
妙手 *expert, master* **myōshu**
妙法 *excellent method* **myōhō**
妙句 *clever wording* **myōku**
妙曲 *excellent music* **myōkyoku**

妙所 *beauty point* **myōsho**
妙薬 *wonder drug* **myōyaku**
奥妙 *mystery, secret* **okumyō**
霊妙 *miraculous, exquisite* **reimyō**
精妙 *exquisite, delicate* **seimyō**
至妙 *extraordinary, exquisite* **shimyō**
神妙 *docile, meek, compliant* **shinmyō**
白妙 *white cloth* **shirotae**, **shirate**
即妙 *instant wit* **sokumyō**
絶妙 *miraculous, act-of-God* **zetsumyō**
妙なる *exquisite, excellent* **taenaru**

秀*uperb, 383*	佳*eauty, 891*
傑*xcellence, 921*	魅*eauty, 969*
優*xcellence, 556*	芸*rts, 619*

抄*ummary, 726*

612-C

抄*ummary so* 妙*uperb took* 秒*econds to be heard...*

禾 (tree branch)

秒*econd(s)*

BYŌ
second(s)

秒間 *second, seconds* **byōkan**
秒差 *difference in seconds* **byōsa**
秒針 *clock second hand* **byōshin**
秒速 *speed per second* **byōsoku**
分秒 *moment* **funbyō**
寸秒 *matter of speed* **sunbyō**
数秒 *few seconds* **sūbyō**
秒読み *countdown, zero hour* **byōyomi**
秒時計 *stopwatch* **byōdokei**

Facing: 1.2. ☜ West (V)

瞬*link, 921*	単*nitary, 517*
分*inute, 518*	微*inuscule, 62*
時*ime, 653*	

秋*utumn, 415*

613-A

Imperial 紀*poch on* 記*ecord by the* 妃*rincess's word...*

糸 (thread, continuity)

紀*eriod*   紀*poch*

KI
period, epoch, era

風紀 *public morals, etiquette* **fūki**
軍紀 *military discipline* **gunki**
芳紀 *age of a young lass* **hōki**
官紀 *official discipline* **kanki**
紀元 *era, epoch, period* **kigen**
⇒一新紀元 *new era, new century* **isshin kigen**
紀元前 *Before Christ, BC* **kigenzen**
紀元後 *Anno Domini, AD, Christian year* **kigengo**
記紀 *Kojiki & Nihonshoki* **kiki**
紀行 *travel notes, ~chronicles* **kikō**
紀行文 *travel notes, ~chronicles* **kikōbun**
紀律 *order, discipline, rule* **kiritsu**
紀要 *academic journal, ~bulletin* **kiyō**
綱紀 *law of the land* **kōki**
校紀 *school discipline* **kōki**
皇紀 *Emperor Jinmu ascension (660 BC)* **kōki**
世紀 *century* **seiki**
⇒現世紀 *this century* **genseiki**
⇒半世紀 *half a century, 50 years* **hanseiki**

Facing: 3.0. ☞☜ Across

⇒一世紀 *one century; first century* **isseiki**
西紀 *Western calendar, amno domini* **seiki**
党紀 *party discipline* **tōki**
新紀元 *new era, new century* **shinkigen**

簿*ecord, 64*	歴*istory, 595*
録*ecord, 841*	暦*alendar, 595*
史*istory, 85*	記*ecord, 728*

糾*nterrogate, 693*

613-B

Imperial 紀poch on 記ecord by the 妃rincess's word...

言 (speaking)

記ecord　　記hronicle

shiru(su), KI
record, chronicle, registry, write down

FLIP: 6.0.a. Left (flat)
Facing: 1.2. ☞ West (V)

暗記 *memorization, memorizing* **anki**
⇒丸暗記 *rote memorization* **maruanki**
簿記 *bookkeeping, accounting record* **boki**
伝記 *biography, life story* **denki**
誤記 *writing error, erratum* **goki**
併記 *putting down, setting forth* **heiki**
次記 *as follows, the following* **jiki**
記号 *sign, mark, symbol* **kigō**
記事 *news article, news item* **kiji**
記述 *description, depiction, portrayal* **kijutsu**
記入 *writing down, record, entry* **kinyū**
記憶 *memory, reminiscence, recollection* **kioku**
記憶術 *mnemonics, art of memorizing* **kiokujutsu**
記録 *records, journal entry* **kiroku**
記載 *mention, entry* **kisai**
記者 *journalist, newspaperman* **kisha**
記者席 *press gallery, journalist box* **kishaseki**
記者会見 *press conference* **kisha kaiken**
記章 *medal, badge* **kishō**

強記 *strong memory* **kyōki**
明記 *clear penmanship* **meiki**
日記 *diary, daily notes* **nikki**
略記 *sketch, outline* **ryakki**
私記 *private-, personal record* **shiki**
書記 *general-secretary* **shoki**
手記 *note, memo* **shuki**
速記 *shorthand, stenography* **sokki**
登記 *registration, signing up* **tōki**
記念日 *memorial-, anniversary day* **kinenbi**
創世記 *Genesis* **sōseiki**

簿ecord, 64	歴istory, 595
録ecord, 841	暦alendar, 595
史istory, 85	紀arration, 727

訳ranslate, 752

613-C

Imperial 紀poch on 記ecord by the 妃rincess's word...

女 (woman)

妃rincess

HI
princess

Facing: 3.0. ☞☜ Across

皇妃 *empress* **kōhi**
后妃 *empress* **kōhi**
公妃 *duchess* **kōhi**
王妃 *queen* **ōhi**
親王妃 *imperial princess* **shinōhi**
妃殿下 *Her Imperial Highness* **hidenka**
皇太子妃 *crown princess* **kōtaishi-hi**

王onarch, 12	殿alace, 522
皇mperor, 113	城astle, 243
后mpress, 87	姫rincess, 542

好iking, 637

614-A

詠oetry about 泳wimming in Wyoming...

言 (speaking)

詠oetry 詠oem

yo(mu), EI
　poetry, poem

詠じる express, recite, compose, chant **eijiru**
詠み人 poem composer, poem writer **yomibito**
詠み人知らず anonymous poet **yomibitoshirazu**
詠み手 poem reader **yomite**
詠み込む recite a poem **yomikomu**
歌詠み poem, poetry **utayomi**
題詠 poetry theme, poem subject **daiei**
詠物 poem on nature **eibutsu**
詠吟 poem delivery, ~recitation **eigin**
詠歌 Buddhist hymn; poetry writing **eika**
詠史 historical poem **eishi**
詠進 Tanka poem presentation, dedication **eishin**
詠唱 chant, poem verse **eishō**
詠草 poem draft **eisō**
詠嘆 admiration, adulation, exclamation **eitan**
詠歎 admiration, adulation, exclamation **eitan**
吟詠 poem reading, poem recitation **gin'ei**
御詠 imperial poetry **gyoei**

FLIP: 6.0.a. Left (flat)
Facing: 1.2. ☞ West (V)

遺詠 poem left by the deceased **iei**
献詠 poetry dedication **ken'ei**
近詠 modern poetry **kin'ei**
朗詠 chanting, reciting **rōei**

> 歌oem, 878
> 詩oetry, 250
> 声oice, 428

> 泳wimming, 729

614-B

詠oetry about 泳wimming in Wyoming...

泳wimming

水⇔氵 (water)

oyo(gu), EI
　swimming

独泳 solo swimming **dokuei**
泳法 swimming style **eihō**
泳者 swimmer **eisha**
遠泳 long-distance swim **en'ei**
背泳 backstroke **haiei**
背泳選手 backstroke swimmer **haiei senshu**
継泳 relay swimming **keiei**
胸泳 breaststroke **kyōei**
競泳 swimming race **kyōei**
競泳大会 swimming contest **kyōei taikai**
力泳 swimming hard **rikiei**
側泳 sidestroke **sokuei**
水泳 swimming **suiei**
⇒寒中水泳 winter swimming **kanchū suiei**
水泳大会 swimming meet **suiei taikai**
水泳帽 swimming cap **suieibō**
水泳着 swimming suit **suieigi**
水泳場 swimming pool **suieijyō**
遊泳 leisure swimming **yūei**

Facing: 1.2. ☞ West (V)

⇒宇宙遊泳 space walk **uchū yūei**
遊泳術 street-smart skills **yūeijjyutsu**
横泳ぎ side stroke **yoko oyogi**
背泳ぎ backstroke **seoyogi**
平泳ぎ breaststroke **hiraoyogi**
犬泳ぎ dog paddle **inu oyogi**
蛙泳ぎ breast stroke **kaeru oyogi**
立ち泳ぎ tread water **tachi oyogi**

川iver, 76	涯eashore, 890
河iver, 877	岸eashore, 30
浦eashore, 813	湖ake, 801
浜eashore, 490	潟agoon, 870

> 詠oetry, 729

615-A

秩ublic-order 迭lternates with people's faith...

秩*ublic order*

禾 (tree branch)

CHITSU
public order, social peace

秩序 *order & discipline* **chitsujo**
⇒無秩序 *chaos, anarchy, mob rule* **muchitsujo**
⇒新秩序 *new order, new society* **shinchitsujo**
⇒安寧秩序 *peace & order* **annei chitsujo**
秩禄 *retainers stipend, ~allowance* **chitsuroku**

FLIP: 7.1. Right (Sort Of)
Facing: 1.2. ☞ West (V)

穏*ranquillity, 840*	黙*uiet, 846*
康*ranquillity, 881*	幽*uiet, 897*
静*uiet, 230*	公*ublic, 180*
寧*uiet, 967*	世*ociety, 411*

株*tocks, 130*	称*itular, 130*

615-B

秩ublic-order 迭lternates with people's faith...

迭*hange*   迭*lternate*

辶 (transport)

TETSU
change, reorganize

更迭 *re-shuffle, reorganization, restructuring* **kōtetsu**

FLIP: 7.1. Right (Sort Of)
Facing: 1.1. ☞ West (H)

整*djust, 31*	改*eform, 725*
遷*hange, 603*	革*eform, 39*
変*hange, 581*	員*taff, 410*

送*ransmit, 708*

616-A

律*egulation inside* 津*arbours, no wild boars...*

律*egulation*   律*hythm*

彳 (stroll)

RITSU, RICHI
regulation, rhythm, rule, law

調律 *tuning (piano)* **chōritsu**
軍律 *military discipline* **gunritsu**
法律 *law, statutes* **hōritsu**
一律 *uniformly, evenly* **ichiritsu**
韻律 *rhythm, meter* **inritsu**
韻律学 *prosody, poem* **inritsugaku**
自律 *self-governing, autonomy, self-rule* **jiritsu**
戒律 *commandments* **kairitsu**
規律 *rule, regulation* **kiritsu**
紀律 *order, discipline* **kiritsu**
音律 *tune, pitch, tone* **onritsu**
律義 *honesty, integrity, honour* **richigi**
律儀 *integrity, honesty* **richigi**
律法 *rule of law* **rippō**
律詩 *Chinese verse* **risshi**
律文 *verse; legal code* **ritsubun**
律動 *rhythmic movement* **ritsudō**
律語 *verse* **ritsugo**
律令 *ancient laws* **ritsuryō**

FLIP: 7.1. Right (Sort Of)
Facing: 1.2. ☞ West (V)

呂律 *articulation* **roretsu**
旋律 *melody, music* **senritsu**
他律 *heteronomy* **taritsu**
定律 *fixed rhythm* **teiritsu**
道徳律 *moral law* **dōtokuritsu**
不文律 *unwritten rule, ~law* **fubunritsu**
因果律 *laws of cause & effect* **ingaritsu**
黄金律 *the golden rule* **ōgonritsu**
律義者 *simple & honest fellow* **richigimono**
自然律 *natural laws* **shizenritsu**
周期律 *periodic law* **shūkiritsu**

則*egulation*, 290	法*aw*, 360
規*ule*, 814	策*olicy*, 875
典*ules*, 476	

津*arbour*, 731

616-B

律*egulation inside* 津*arbours, no wild boars...*

津*arbour*   津*ort*

水⇔氵 (water)

tsu, SHIN
harbour, port

津々 *"full to the brim..."* **shinshin**
津波 *tidal wave* **tsunami**
津浪 *tidal wave* **tsunami**
難波津 *ancient name of Ōsaka City* **naniwatsu**
潮津浪 *tidal bore* **shiotsunami**
綿津見 *god of the seas* **watatsumi**
山津波 *landslide* **yamatsunami**
山津浪 *landslide* **yamatsunami**
興味津津 *very interesting* **kyōmi shinshin**
津津浦浦 *everywhere, here & there* **tsutsu uraura**

FLIP: 7.1. Right (Sort Of)
Facing: 1.2. ☞ West (V)

港*arbour*, 512	貨*reight*, 191
輸*hipment*, 660	搭*reight*, 146
荷*reight*, 877	船*essel*, 757

律*egulation*, 731

617-A

仮emporary bill 板oard on the 坂lopes had 報eports of smuggled 服lothes...

仮*emporary*　仮*rovisional*

人⇔亻 (person)

kari, KA, KE
temporary, provisional, interim, tentative, transient

FLIP: 7.3.b. Right Bottom (stem)

仮題 *temporary title* **kadai**
仮泊 *temporary stay* **kahaku**
仮面 *mask, disguise* **kamen**
仮眠 *catnap, siesta, afternoon sleep* **kamin**
仮親 *adoptive parents* **karioya**
仮屋 *temporary shelter* **kariya**
仮性 *false, fake, psuedo, phoney* **kasei**
仮設 *temporary construction* **kasetsu**
仮説 *hypothesis, supposition* **kasetsu**
仮借 *pardon, parole* **kashaku**
仮死 *suspended animation* **kashi**
仮称 *tentative name* **kashō**
仮想 *tentative impression* **kasō**
仮葬 *temporary burial, ~interment* **kasō**
仮託 *pretext, excuse* **kataku**
仮定 *supposition, premise, hypothesis* **katei**
仮病 *fake illness, malingering* **kebyō**
仮払い *tentative payment* **karibarai**
平仮名 *Hiragana letters* **hiragana**

仮条約 *provisional contract* **karijōyaku**
仮建築 *temporary construction* **karikenchiku**
仮採用 *temporary hire, temp* **karisaiyō**
仮処分 *tentative disposition* **karishobun**
仮出所 *parole, conditional release* **karishussho**
片仮名 *Katakana letters* **katakana**
虚仮威し *bluff, ruse* **kokeodoshi**
仮差押え *sequestration, forfeiture* **karisashiosae**
仮住まい *temporary residence* **karizumai**
振り仮名 *Kana pronunciation, ~reading* **furigana**
送り仮名 *suffix Kana* **okurigana**

短*hort, 144*
時*ime, 653*
経*ime-lapse, 791*

今*resently, 182*
既*lready, 316*

坂*lope, 733*

617-B

仮emporary bill 板oard on the 坂lopes had 報eports of smuggled 服lothes...

板*oard*　板*late*

木 (wooden)

ita, HAN, BAN
board, plate

FLIP: 7.3.b. Right Bottom (stem)

板ガラス *plate-, sheet glass* **itagarasu**
板金 *sheet metal* **bankin**
板書 *blackboard-, chalkboard writing* **bansho**
画板 *drafting board* **gaban**
合板 *plywood, wood sheet* **gōban**
板塀 *fence board, ~divider* **itabei**
板前 *cook, chef* **itamae**
看板 *signboard, billboard* **kanban**
甲板 *deck of a ship* **kanpan**
基板 *circuit board (electric)* **kiban**
鋼板 *steel plate* **kōhan**
黒板 *blackboard, chalkboard* **kokuban**
俎板 *chopping board* **manaita**
胸板 *one's chest* **munaita**
波板 *corrugated roof sheets* **namiita**
鉄板 *steel plate* **teppan**
登板 *taking to the mound (baseball)* **tōban**
床板 *flooring, floor board* **yukaita**
板の間 *wooden flooring* **itanoma**

板囲い *hoarding, boarding* **itagakoi**
案内板 *guide plate* **annaiban**
伝言板 *message-, bulletin board* **dengonban**
羽子板 *battledore* **hagoita**
羽目板 *wainscot, panel* **hameita**
掲示板 *bulletin-, notice board* **keijiban**
送り板 *feed plate* **okuriita**
折り板 *folding plate* **oriita**
支持板 *supporting plate* **shijiita**
敷き板 *wooden base* **shikiita**
殺ぎ板 *wood shingles* **sogiita**

盤*oard, 324*
示*isplay, 878*
告*eport, 266*

枚*[sheets], 724*

617-C

仮*emporary bill* 板*oard on the* 坂*lopes had* 報*eports of*
smuggled 服*lothes...*

土 (ground, soil)

坂*lope*   坂*ills*

saka, HAN
slope, hills

FLIP: 7.3.b. Right Bottom (stem)
Facing: 2.2. East ☞ (V)

急坂 *sudden slope* **kyūhan**
登坂 *uphill slope, hill climbing* **noborizaka**, **tōhan**
男坂 *steeper slope* **otokozaka**
坂道 *slope, hilly* **sakamichi**
山坂 *mountains & hills* **yamasaka**
下り坂 *downward slope* **kudarizaka**
上り坂 *uphill, ascent, elevated* **noborizaka**

丘*lope, 106*	渓*avine, 97*
崎*lope, 270*	谷*avine, 492*
峡*avine, 763*	登*scend, 437*

返*eturn, 537*

617-D

仮*emporary bill* 板*oard on the* 坂*lopes had* 報*eports of*
smuggled 服*lothes...*

土 (ground, soil)

報*eport*   報*nform*

muku(iru), HŌ
report, inform, convey, make known, publicize, requite

FLIP: 6.0.b. Left (stem)

電報 *telegram* **denpō**
画報 *illustrated magazine* **gahō**
学報 *academic journal* **gakuhō**
誤報 *erroneous information* **gohō**
悲報 *tragic news* **hihō**
報知 *information, report* **hōchi**
報道 *report, news, coverage* **hōdō**
報告 *report, notice* **hōkoku**
⇒事後報告 *ex-post facto report* **jigo hōkoku**
報告書 *written report* **hōkokusho**
報労 *reward for one's work* **hōrō**
報奨 *reward, pay, fee* **hōshō**
報奨金 *reward, bonus, bounty* **hōshōkin**
報酬 *reward, salary, bonus* **hōshū**
情報 *information, report* **jōhō**
果報 *luck, fortune* **kahō**
官報 *official gazette* **kanpō**
警報 *warning, caution* **keihō**
吉報 *good news, glad tidings* **kippō**

広報 *public information* **kōhō**
虚報 *false report, erroneous report* **kyohō**
日報 *daily report* **nippō**
朗報 *good news, glad tidings* **rōhō**
詳報 *detailed report* **shōhō**
特報 *flash bulletin, urgent news* **tokuhō**
予報 *forecast, prediction* **yohō**
続報 *subsequent report* **zokuhō**
報償金 *remuneration payment* **hōshōkin**
注意報 *public warning (storm)* **chūihō**
一矢報いる *shoot-back, retort* **isshimukuiru**

告*eport, 266*	載*ublish, 802*
宣*nnouncement, 899*	届*otice, 631*
掲*ublish, 810*	伝*onvey, 619*

執*arry-out, 268*

617-E

仮*emporary bill* 板*oard on the* 坂*lopes had* 報*eports of smuggled* 服*lothes...*

肉⇔月 (flesh, body part)

❶服*lothes* ❷服*ubmit*

FUKU

clothes, uniform, outfit, garments; submit

FLIP: 7.3.b. Right Bottom (stem)
Facing: 4.0. ☜☞ Apart

❶服地 *cloth, dress material* **fukuji**
服務 *job-, duty performance* **fukumu**
服飾 *fashion accessory, ~ornaments* **fukushoku**
服装 *dress, attire, costume* **fukusō**
軍服 *military uniform* **gunpuku**
法服 *judge robe, lawyer's robe* **hōfuku**
衣服 *clothes, garment, costume* **ifuku**
喪服 *funeral attire, mourning dress* **mofuku**
礼服 *ceremonial dress, formal attire* **reifuku**
略服 *ordinary-, informal dress* **ryakufuku**
洋服 *Western clothes, morning attire* **yōfuku**
合い服 *spring-, autumn clothes* **aifuku**
婦人服 *ladies wear, ~clothes* **fujinfuku**
既製服 *ready-to-wear clothes* **kiseifuku**
妊婦服 *pregnancy-, maternity clothes* **ninpufuku**
紳士服 *men's suit, formal attire* **shinshifuku**
宇宙服 *spacesuit* **uchūfuku**
❷圧服 *overpower, overwhelm* **appuku**
服毒 *taking poison* **fukudoku**

服役 *penal sentence, jail term* **fukueki**
服薬 *taking pills* **fukuyaku**
服用 *taking internally* **fukuyō**
服罪 *serving a punishment* **fukuzai**
感服 *admiration, praise* **kanpuku**
敬服 *admiration, praise* **keifuku**
克服 *conquest, invasion* **kokufuku**
征服 *conquest, subjugation* **seifuku**
心服 *admiration, respect, courtesy* **shinpuku**
信服 *convincing a person* **shinpuku**
承服 *consent, approval* **shōfuku**

縫*ewing, 779*	衣*lothes, 355*	編*nitting, 42*
繰*pinning, 851*	裁*lothes, 802*	糸*hread, 375*
紡*pinning, 735*	織*nitting, 855*	

肢*imbs, 200*

618-A

妨*indrance to machine* 紡*pinning now thinning...*

女 (woman)

妨*indrance* 妨*bstacle*

samata(geru), BŌ

hindrance, obstacle, impede, obstruct

Facing: 2.2. East ☞ (V)

妨害 *disturbance, hindrance, obstacle* **bōgai**
⇒営業妨害 *business obstruction* **eigyō bōgai**
⇒議事妨害 *obstruction of proceedings* **giji bōgai**
⇒業務妨害 *business interference* **gyōmu bōgai**
妨害放送 *broadcast jamming* **bōgai hōsō**

衛*rotect, 796*	因*ause, 862*
護*rotect, 828*	困*roblematic, 863*
防*rotect, 736*	難*roblematic, 927*

紡*pinning, 735*

618-B

妨*indrance to machine* 紡*pinning now thinning...*

糸 (thread, continuity)

紡*pinning thread*

tsumu(gu), BŌ
spinning (thread)

Facing: 2.2. East ☞ (V)

- 紡毛 *spinning wool* **bōmō**
- 紡績 *spinning* **bōseki**
- 紡績業 *spinning-, cotton industry* **bōsekigyō**
- 紡績糸 *cotton yarn* **bōsekiito**
- 紡績機械 *spinning machine* **bōseki kikai**
- 紡糸 *spinning* **bōshi**
- 紡織 *spinning & weaving, textile* **bōshoku**
- 紡織工業 *textile industry* **bōshoku kōgyō**
- 紡錘 *spindle* **bōsui**
- 紡錘形 *spindle shape* **bōsuikei**
- 紡車 *spinning wheel* **bōsha**
- 絹紡 *spun silk* **kenbō**
- 混紡 *mixed spinning* **konbō**
- 綿紡 *cotton spinning* **menbō**

布 *loth, 208*	服 *lothes, 734*
縫 *ewing, 779*	織 *nitting, 855*
繰 *pinning, 851*	編 *nitting, 42*
衣 *lothes, 355*	糸 *hread, 375*
裁 *lothes, 802*	錘 *pindle, 505*

妨 *indrance, 734*

619-A

肪*bese* 坊*uddhist-monks* 防*rotect* 訪*isitors with valour...*

肉⇔月 (flesh, body part)

肪*bese*　　　肪*atty*

BŌ
obese, fatty, fatto, burly, plump, corpulent

Facing: 4.0. ☜☞ Apart

- 脂肪 *fat, grease* **shibō**
- ⇒乳脂肪 *butter fat* **nyūshibō**
- ⇒皮下脂肪 *subcutaneous fat* **hika shibō**
- ⇒植物性脂肪 *vegetable fat* **shokubutsusei shibō**
- 脂肪分 *fatty content* **shibōbun**
- 脂肪層 *fat layer* **shibōsō**
- 脂肪酸 *fatty acid* **shibōsan**
- 脂肪質 *fats, lipids* **shibōshitsu**
- 脂肪油 *fatty oil* **shibōyu**
- 脂肪太り *obese person* **shibōbutori**
- 脂肪過多 *excessive fat* **shibōkata**

脂 *nimal fat, 243*	厚 *hick, 964*
太 *bese, 6*	濃 *hick, 446*

肪 *bese, 735*

619-B

坊bese 坊uddhist-monks 防rotect 訪isitors with valour...

◐ ⁰坊onk   ❷ ²坊olloquial name

士 (samurai, warrior)

BŌ, BO
Buddhist monk; colloquial name

❶ 坊主 *shaven head, Buddhist monk* **bōzu**
宿坊 *lodgings for temple pilgrims* **shukubō**
僧坊 *Buddhist monks' living quarters* **sōbō**
坊さん *Buddhist monk* **bōsan**
❷ 三日坊主 *"three-day monk...", quitter* **mikka bōzu**
坊や *little boy, kid* **bōya**
凸坊 *prankish, mischievous boy* **dekobō**
寝坊 *oversleeping, late riser* **nebō**
赤ん坊 *baby, infant* **akanbō**
朝寝坊 *oversleeping, late riser* **asanebō**
茶坊主 *tea servant, flatterer* **chabōzu**
長元坊 *Eurasian kestrel, kestrel* **chōgenbō**
風来坊 *vagabond, wanderer, homeless* **fūraibō**
本因坊 *shogi grand master* **hon'inbō**
小坊主 *little rascal; young priest* **kobōzu**
黒ん坊 *well-tanned complexion* **kuronbō**
丸坊主 *bald, close-cropped haircut* **marubōzu**
見栄坊 *fop, dude* **miebō**
海坊主 *green turtle; sea goblin* **umibōzu**

Facing: 2.2. East ☞ (V)
FLIP: 6.0.a. Left (flat)

甘えん坊 *spoiled child* **amaenbō**
坊ちゃん *"cute little boy, sonny..."* **bocchan**
怒りん坊 *quick-tempered, mercurial* **okorinbō**
卑しん坊 *glutton, avaricious, greedy* **iyashinbō**
立ちん坊 *keep standing* **tachinbō**
通せん坊 *blocking another's way* **toosenbō**
腕白坊主 *prankish child* **wanpaku bōzu**
隠れん坊 *hide-&-seek game* **kakurenbō**
食いしん坊 *glutton, avaricious* **kuishinbō**
お坊っちゃん *overprotected youth* **obocchan**

仏uddha, 683	禅en Buddhism, 782
盆uddhist Feast, 594	寺emple, 248
僧uddhist monk, 836	堂ltar, 94

妨indrance, 734

619-C

坊bese 坊uddhist-monks 防rotect 訪isitors with valour...

防efence   防rotect

阝⇔阜 (village=left)

fuse(gu), BŌ
defence, protect, deterrence, guarding, safeguard

防諜 *counter-espionage* **bōchō**
防潮 *tide protection* **bōchō**
防虫 *insect-protection* **bōchū**
防弾 *bullet-proofing* **bōdan**
防衛 *self-defence, security* **bōei**
防疫 *epidemics prevention* **bōeki**
防煙 *smoke protection* **bōen**
防犯 *crime prevention* **bōhan**
防壁 *protective wall* **bōheki**
防火 *fire prevention* **bōka**
防汗 *anti-perspirant* **bōkan**
防熱 *heat-resistance* **bōnetsu**
防音 *soundproofing* **bōon**
防災 *disaster protection* **bōsai**
防戦 *defensive warfare* **bōsen**
防雪 *snow protection* **bōsetsu**
防止 *prevention, forestalling, precluding* **bōshi**
防振 *anti-vibration* **bōshin**
防食 *corrosion-, rust protection* **bōshoku**

Facing: 2.2. East ☞ (V)

防臭 *deodorization* **bōshū**
風防 *wind protection* **fūbō**
警防 *preservation of peace & order* **keibō**
国防 *national defence, ~security* **kokubō**
攻防 *offence & defence* **kōbō**
砂防 *soil erosion control* **sabō**
消防 *fire fighting* **shōbō**
消防車 *fire truck, fire engine* **shōbōsha**
水防 *flood control* **suibō**
堤防 *levee, embankment* **teibō**
予防 *prevention, forestalling, precluding* **yobō**

衛rotect, 796
護rotect, 828
守efence, 366

坊uddhist monk, 736

619-C

肪 *bese* 坊 *uddhist-monks* 防 *rotect* 訪 *isitors with valour...*

言 (speaking)

訪 *isiting*　　訪 *ravel*

tazu(neru), otozu(reru), HŌ
visiting, travel, courtesy call, touring

FLIP: 6.0.a. Left (flat)
Facing: 2.2. East ☞ (V)

訪ねていく *go to visit* **tazuneteiku**
訪ねてくる *come to visit* **tazunetekuru**
訪米 *visit to America* **hōbei**
訪客 *visitor, guest, caller* **hōkyaku**
訪問 *visit, call* **hōmon**
訪問着 *semi-formal kimono* **hōmongi**
訪問客 *visitor, guest, caller* **hōmonkyaku**
訪問販売 *door-to-door selling* **hōmon hanbai**
訪日 *visit to Japan* **hōnichi**
訪欧 *visit to Europe* **hōō**
往訪 *visit, call* **ōhō**
歴訪 *visit, making a tour* **rekihō**
再訪 *revisiting, homecoming* **saihō**
探訪 *inquiry, investigation* **tanbō**
来訪者 *visitor, guest, caller* **raihōsha**

賓 *isitor, 161*	旅 *ravel, 650*
呼 *nvite, 701*	迎 *elcome, 705*
招 *nvite, 956*	往 *ome & go, 749*
客 *uest, 559*	

訳 *ranslate, 752*

620-A

汚 *irty* 巧 *kills* 朽 *ecay fair play...*

水 ⇔ 氵 (water)

汚 *irty*　　　汚 *ilthy*

kitana(i), kega(rawashii), yogo(reru), yogo(su), kega(reru), kega(su), O
dirty, filthy, nasty, sullied, contaminate

Facing: 2.2. East ☞ (V)

汚物 *excrement, faeces* **obutsu**
汚濁 *pollution, contamination* **odaku**
汚泥 *sludge, mud, slop* **odei**
汚塵 *filth, dirt* **ojin**
汚辱 *disgrace, humiliation, shame* **ojoku**
汚行 *disgraceful conduct, scandal* **okō**
汚垢 *dirt* **okō**
汚名 *indignity, insult, disgrace* **omei**
汚染 *pollution, contamination* **osen**
⇒土壌汚染 *soil pollution, ~contamination* **dojō osen**
⇒環境汚染 *environmental pollution* **kankyō osen**
汚染物質 *pollutant, contaminant* **osen busshitsu**
汚職 *corruption, scandal* **oshoku**
汚職事件 *corruption case* **oshoku jiken**
汚職行為 *malversation, absconding* **oshoku kōi**
汚臭 *foul odour, nasty smell* **oshū**
汚損 *stain, soiling, corruption* **oson**
汚水 *sewage water, sewerage* **osui**
汚水管 *sewage pipe* **osuikan**

汚水処理 *sewage treatment* **osuishori**
汚点 *stain, disgrace, shame* **oten**
腹汚い *dirty-minded* **hara gitanai**
顔汚し *disgrace, discredit* **kao yogoshi**
口汚し *small morsel* **kuchi yogoshi**
口汚い *verbally-abusive* **kuchigitanai**
面汚し *stain, disgrace, shame* **tsurayogoshi**
薄汚い *dirty, filthy, dingy* **usugitanai**
薄汚れ *dirty, sullied, soiled* **usuyogore**
汚れ物 *dirty-, laundry clothes* **yogoremono**
意地汚い *greedy, avaricious* **iji kitanai**

排 *eject, 795*	凶 *vil, 80*	菌 *isease, 52*
罪 *riminal, 289*	邪 *vil, 58*	病 *isease, 213*
悪 *vil, 389*	犯 *riminal, 640*	疾 *isease, 681*

法 *aw, 360*

620-B

汚irty 巧kills 朽ecay fair play...

巧kilful　巧cumen

工 (craftmanship)

uma(i), taku(mi), KŌ
skilful, acumen, agility, expertise, mastery, proficiency, forte

Facing: 2.2. East ☞ (V)
FLIP: 6.0.a. Left (flat)

巧み skilful, clever **takumi**
便巧 flattery, courting favour **benkō**
技巧 skill, craftsmanship **gikō**
技巧的 technical, skillful **gikōteki**
傾巧 flattery, courting favour **keikō**
機巧 cleverness, expertise **kikō**
巧遅 slow & elaborate **kōchi**
巧緻 elaborate, exquisite, dainty **kōchi**
巧知 cleverness, expertise **kōchi**
巧智 cleverness, expertise **kōchi**
巧言 compliments, words of praise **kōgen**
巧技 superb skills, workmanship **kōgi**
巧妙 excellent, clever **kōmyō**
巧拙 skill, workmanship **kōsetsu**
巧者 tact, prudent, discreet **kōsha**
巧手 smart move, clever hand **kōshu**
悧巧 clever, sharp, keen **rikō**
老巧 experienced, veteran, professional **rōkō**
精巧 delicate, sophisticated, exquisite **seikō**

繊巧 detailed craftsmanship **senkō**
大巧 great skills **taikō**
巧い絵 excellent painting **umaie**
悪巧み trickery, ruse, deception **warudakumi**

芸rts, 619		匠rtisan, 106
術kills, 110		腕alent, 651
工rtisan, 176		師xpert, 483

功uccess, 635

620-C

汚irty 巧kills 朽ecay fair play...

朽ecay　朽otten

木 (wooden)

ku(chiru), KYŪ
decay, rotten, mouldering

Facing: 2.2. East ☞ (V)

朽ち葉 withered-, decaying leaves **kuchiba**
朽ち木 withered tree **kuchiki**
朽ち果てる rot away, decay **kuchihateru**
腐朽 decaying, rottening **fukyū**
不朽 immortal, undying, deathless **fukyū**
朽廃 be ruined, ~rotten **kyūhai**
老朽 super-annuation **rōkyū**
老朽化 decaying, rottening **rōkyūka**
老朽船 decrepit ship **rōkyūsen**

枯ither, 960		歳ears old, 111
枯ecay, 960		齢ears old, 553
古ither, 477		昔lden-times, 281

枚[sheets], 724

621-A

但*rovided, patient's father* 担*ears a strong* 胆*all-bladder...*

人⇔亻 (person)

但*roviso* 但*aveat*

tada(shi), TAN
proviso, provided that, caveat, conditional

但し *"however, provided that..."* **tadashi**
但し書き *proviso, caveat, condition* **tadashigaki**
但し付き *proviso, caveat, condition* **tadashitsuki**

FLIP: 7.0.a. Right (flat)

款*rticle, 42*
条*rticle, 607*

恒*lways, 741*

621-B

但*rovided, patient's father* 担*ears a strong* 胆*all-bladder...*

手⇔扌 (hand, manual)

担*esponsible* 担*ear-with*

katsu(gu), nina(u), TAN
responsible, bear-with, accountable, cope-with, bear on shoulder, undertake

分担 *share, allotment* **buntan**
分担金 *financial contribution, allotment* **buntankin**
負担 *burden, load, responsibility* **futan**
加担 *participation, assistance* **katan**
荷担 *participation, assistance* **katan**
荷担者 *participant, accomplice* **katansha**
担架 *stretcher, cot* **tanka**
担任 *officer-in-charge* **tannin**
担保 *collateral, mortgage* **tanpo**
⇒無担保 *unsecured (loan), no collateral* **mutanpo**
担保貸し *secured loan* **tanpokashi**
担保物件 *collateral rights* **tanpo bukken**
担保責任 *mortgage responsibility* **tanpo sekinin**
担子 *palanquin chair; load, cargo* **tanshi**
担子胞子 *basidiospore* **tanshi hōshi**
担子菌類 *basidiomycetes* **tanshi kinrui**
担当 *officer-in-charge* **tantō**
担当官 *official-in-charge, desk officer* **tantōkan**
担当者 *officer-in-charge* **tantōsha**

FLIP: 7.0.a. Right (flat)

担ぎ屋 *peddler, seller, hawker* **katsugiya**
担い手 *bearer, carrier* **ninaite**
御幣担ぎ *superstitious* **gohei katsugi**
担ぎ出す *set up, carry out, choose* **katsugidasu**
差し担い *carry on two persons' shoulders*
　　　　 sashininai
担ぎ上げる *carry up, bring up* **katsugiageru**

任*uty, 709*	預*ntrust, 569*
威*uthority, 520*	勤*ervice, 962*
責*esponsible, 115*	務*ervice, 454*

恒*lways, 741*

621-C

但*rovided, patient's father* 担*ears a strong* 胆*all-bladder...*

肉⇔月 (flesh, body part)

胆*all bladder*　　胆*ourage*

TAN
gall bladder, courage

FLIP: 7.0.a. Right (flat)

大胆　*bold, daring* **daitan**
豪胆　*bold, daring* **gōtan**
放胆　*boldness, fearless, daring* **hōtan**
肝胆　*innermost heart, liver & gall* **kantan**
魂胆　*ulterior design, ~scheme* **kontan**
落胆　*discouragement, disappointment* **rakutan**
竜胆　*bellflower, gentian* **rindō**
心胆　*heart mood* **shintan**
胆汁　*bile, gall* **tanjū**
胆略　*daring & resourcefulness* **tanryaku**
胆力　*nerve, pluck, guts, mettle, courage* **tanryoku**
胆勇　*courage, daring* **tanyū**
胆嚢　*gall bladder* **tannō**
胆石　*gallstone* **tanseki**
胆石病　*gallstone illness, cholelithiasis* **tansekibyō**
海胆　*sea urchin* **uni**

敢*ourage, 449*	雄*ourage, 775*
冒*ourage, 401*	臓*rgans, 565*
勇*ourage, 59*	耐*ndure, 974*

担*ear-with, 739*

622-A

垣*ences around the maze confuse* 恒*lways...*

土 (ground, soil)

垣*ence*　　垣*edge*

kaki
fence, hedge, partition

FLIP: 5.0.a Left & Right
FLIP: 7.0.a. Right (flat)

姫垣　*low fence* **himegaki**
人垣　*crowd, throng* **hitogaki**
斎垣　*shrine fence* **igaki**
生垣　*hedge, quickset* **ikegaki**
石垣　*stone wall* **ishigaki**
板垣　*wooden fence* **itagaki**
垣根　*fence, hedge* **kakine**
腰垣　*hip-high fence* **koshigaki**
袖垣　*low fence (near a gate)* **sodegaki**
竹垣　*bamboo fence* **takegaki**
玉垣　*shrine fence* **tamagaki**
友垣　*friend* **tomogaki**
垣越し　*over the fence* **kakigoshi**
垣間見る　*catch a glimpse* **kaimamiru**
四つ目垣　*lattice fence, trellis* **yotsumegaki**

塀*ence, 887*	周*icinity, 280*
囲*nclose, 361*	辺*icinity, 93*
郭*nclose, 398*	壁*all, 66*

恒*lways, 741*

622-B

垣*ences around the maze confuse* 恒*lways...*

心 ⇔ 忄 ⇔ 灬 (feelings)

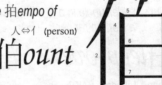

恒*lways*　　恒*onstant*

FLIP: 7.0.a. Right (flat)

KŌ

always, constant, often, incessant, fixed

恒常　*constant, fixed, a given* **kōjō**
恒常的　*constant, fixed, a given* **kōjōteki**
恒久　*perpetuity, eternity* **kōkyū**
恒久的　*everlasting, eternal* **kōkyūteki**
恒久平和　*eternal peace* **kōkyū heiwa**
恒温　*homoiothermal* **kōon**
恒例　*established custom, ~norms* **kōrei**
恒産　*fixed property* **kōsan**
恒星　*fixed star* **kōsei**
恒性　*constancy, permanence* **kōsei**
恒心　*constancy* **kōshin**
恒数　*mathematical constant* **kōsū**
恒久化　*perpetuation, eternal* **kōkyūka**
恒久性　*perpetual, permanence* **kōkyūsei**
恒存　*energy conservation* **kōzon**

| 頻*ften, 272* | 常*egular, 94* |
| 珍*are, 720* | 般*egular, 323* |

| 垣*ence, 740* |

623-A

伯*ount's* 伯*lder-uncle in a* 舶*hip* 泊*leeping-over to the* 拍*empo of a Harlem rapper...*

人 ⇔ 亻 (person)

❶ 伯*lder uncle/aunt*　　❷ 伯*ount*

FLIP: 7.0.a. Right (flat)

HAKU

older uncle, older aunt; count

❶ 画伯　*master painter, great artist* **gahaku**
伯兄　*eldest brother* **hakkei**
伯仲　*suitable match* **hakuchū**
伯楽　*horse trading* **hakuraku**
伯母　*aunt* **oba**
伯父　*uncle* **oji**

❷ 伯爵　*count, earl* **hakushaku**
伯爵夫人　*countess* **hakushaku fujin**

侯*obility, 122*	叔*oung uncle, 510*
曹*obility, 326*	叔*oung aunt, 510*
爵*obility, 593*	

| 拍*empo, 743* |

623-B

伯ount's 伯lder-uncle in a 舶hip 泊leeping-over to the 拍empo of
a Harlem rapper...

舟 (vessel)

舶hip   舶essel

HAKU
  ship, vessel, ocean ship

FLIP: 7.0.a. Right (flat)

舶来 *foreign-made* **hakurai**
舶来品 *foreign-made goods* **hakuraihin**
舶載 *ocean cargo, freight cargo* **hakusai**
舶用 *for shipping, maritime use* **hakuyō**
船舶 *ship, vessel* **senpaku**
船舶業 *maritime industry* **senpakugyō**
船舶法 *maritime laws* **senpakuhō**

舟hip, 90	帆ailing, 641
航avigation, 748	海cean, 241
船hip, 757	洋cean, 247

航avigation, 748

623-C

伯ount's 伯lder-uncle in a 舶hip 泊leeping-over to the 拍empo of
a Harlem rapper...

水⇔氵 (water)

泊leep-over   泊tay-overnight

to(maru), to(meru), HAKU
  sleep-over, stay-overnight

FLIP: 7.0.a. Right (flat)

錨泊 *anchorage* **byōhaku**
外泊 *staying out the night* **gaihaku**
泊地 *anchorage, berthing* **hakuchi**
泊船 *anchoring, berthing* **hakusen**
漂泊 *drifting about, wandering* **hyōhaku**
一泊 *sleepover, overnight stay* **ippaku**
一泊二食付き *overnight lodging & two meals*
  ippaku nishoku tsuki
仮泊 *temporary stay* **kahaku**
民泊 *private lodgings* **minpaku**
宿泊 *lodging, overnight stay* **shukuhaku**
宿泊所 *lodgings* **shukuhakujo**
宿泊人 *lodger, boarder, guest*
  shukuhakunin
宿泊料 *hotel charges* **shukuhakuryō**
淡泊 *indifferent, impersonal* **tanpaku**
停泊 *mooring, berthing* **teihaku**
碇泊 *lie at anchor, be moored* **teihaku**
泊まり番 *night duty* **tomariban**

泊まり賃 *hotel charges* **tomarichin**
泊まり客 *hotel-, house guest* **tomarikyaku**
泊まり掛け *sleep-over, overnight stay*
  tomarigake
碇泊地 *anchorage, berth* **teihakuchi**
休泊所 *rest & sleeping quarters* **kyūhakujo**
寝泊まり *sleep-over, lodge* **netomari**
素泊まり *overnight stay without board* **sudomari**

寝leep, 769	滞taying, 557
眠leep, 495	留taying, 128
睡leeping, 948	宿odging, 448

拍empo, 743

623-D

伯*ount's* 伯*lder-uncle in a* 舶*hip* 泊*leeping-over to the* 拍*empo of a Harlem rapper...*

手⇔扌 (hand, manual)

拍*empo*　　拍*rhythm*

FLIP: 7.0.a. Right (flat)

HAKU, HYŌ
tempo, rhythm, beat

拍動 *pulsebeat, palpitation* **hakudō**
拍車 *spurred into action* **hakusha**
拍手 *applause, handclapping* **hakushu**
拍手喝采 *cheering, handclapping* **hakushu kassai**
拍子 *rhythm, beat, time* **hyōshi**
⇒白拍子 *olden female dancer; prostitute* **shirabyōshi**
⇒手拍子 *beating time with the hand* **tebyōshi**
⇒突拍子 *out-of-tune, exorbitant* **toppyōshi**
⇒足拍子 *beating time with one's foot* **ashibyōshi**
⇒膝拍子 *beating time on one's knee* **hizabyōshi**
拍子木 *handclappers* **hyōshigi**
拍子抜け *discouragement, dismay* **hyōshinuke**
脈拍 *pulsebeat, pulsation* **myakuhaku**
三拍 *three syllables* **sanpaku**
心拍 *heartbeat, pulsation, palpitation* **shinpaku**

鼓*rum, 925*	韻*hyme, 315*
音*ound, 314*	歌*inging, 878*
曲*elody, 476*	

抽*xtract, 37*

624-A

設*et-up for* 殺*urder,* 没*unken cadaver...*

言 (speaking)

設*et-up*　　設*stablish*

FLIP: 5.0.b. Left & Right

mō(keru), SETSU
set-up, establish, initiate, institute

附設 *annex-, adjacent building* **fusetsu**
敷設 *building, laying* **fusetsu**
併設 *annex construction* **heisetsu**
常設 *permanent establishment* **jōsetsu**
開設 *establishment, inauguration* **kaisetsu**
官設 *government-built* **kansetsu**
仮設 *temporary construction* **kasetsu**
架設 *installation, construction* **kasetsu**
建設 *construction, building* **kensetsu**
既設 *existing, already-built* **kisetsu**
公設 *publicly-built* **kōsetsu**
急設 *promptly-installed* **kyūsetsu**
埋設 *laying underground* **maisetsu**
未設 *uninstalled, unconstructed* **misetsu**
濫設 *over-construction* **ransetsu**
設置 *establishment, building* **secchi**
設計 *architectural design, plan* **sekkei**
設備 *equipment, facilities* **setsubi**
設営 *construction, setting up* **setsuei**

設問 *question, query* **setsumon**
設立 *establishment, institution* **setsuritsu**
設定 *settings, defaults* **settei**
新設 *newly-established* **shinsetsu**
施設 *facilities, institution* **shisetsu**
私設 *privately-built, privately-owned* **shisetsu**
創設 *foundation, establishment* **sōsetsu**
特設 *specially-built* **tokusetsu**
増設 *increased construction* **zōsetsu**

立*tand up, 234*	始*tart, 210*
整*djust, 31*	初*tart, 353*
建*onstruct, 390*	発*tart, 368*

説*xplanation, 943*

624-B

設et-up for 殺urder, 没unken cadaver...

殳 (pike)

殺urder   殺illing

FLIP: 5.0.b. Left & Right

koro(su), SATSU, SAI, SETSU
murder, killing, assassinate, slaying

暗殺 *assassination, professional killing* **ansatsu**
撲殺 *death by beating* **bokusatsu**
謀殺 *premeditated murder* **bōsatsu**
忙殺 *crushed to death* **bōsatsu**
毒殺 *murder by poisoning* **dokusatsu**
封殺 *forcing-out, tossing out, overthrowing* **fūsatsu**
虐殺 *slaughter, massacre* **gyakusatsu**
自殺 *suicide, killing oneself* **jisatsu**
銃殺 *shoot to death* **jūsatsu**
絞殺 *death by strangulation* **kōsatsu**
抹殺 *crossing-, wiping out, kill* **massatsu**
黙殺 *total ignoring, avoiding, silence* **mokusatsu**
悩殺 *fascination, enchantment* **nōsatsu**
殺気 *threat, menace, intimidation* **sakki**
殺菌 *sterilization, pasteurisation* **sakkin**
殺傷 *wounding & killing* **sasshō**
殺害 *murder, killing, assassination* **satsugai**
殺害者 *murderer, assassin* **satsugaisha**
殺意 *intent to kill* **satsui**

殺人 *murderer, killer* **satsujin**
殺人鬼 *murderous fiend* **satsujinki**
相殺 *offsetting, counter-balancing* **sōsai**
惨殺 *slaughter, butchery, massacre* **zansatsu**
殺し屋 *killer, murderer, assassin* **koroshiya**
皆殺し *extermination, genocide* **minagoroshi**
殺し文句 *death threat* **koroshimonku**
殴り殺す *death by beating* **nagurikorosu**
刺し殺す *death by stabbing* **sashikorosu**
撃ち殺す *shoot dead, shoot down* **uchikorosu**
打ち殺す *club to death, shoot dead* **uchikorosu**

罪*riminal, 289*	逝*eath, 54*	碑*ombstone, 937*
犯*riminal, 640*	亡*eath, 72*	墓*ravesite, 602*
死*eath, 513*	葬*urial, 513*	悪*vil, 389*

殴*unch, 745*

624-C

設et-up for 殺urder, 没unken cadaver...

水⇔氵 (water)

没inking   没ubmerge

FLIP: 7.0.b2. Right (stem)

BOTSU
sinking, submerge, submerse, underwater

没却 *disregard, getting rid of, effacement* **bokkyaku**
没書 *discarded manuscript* **bossho**
没収 *forfeiture, confiscation* **bosshū**
没我 *selflessness, sacrificial* **botsuga**
没後 *posthumous works* **botsugo**
没年 *age at death* **botsunen**
没入 *being absorbed, ~consumed* **botsunyū**
没落 *ruin, bankruptcy* **botsuraku**
没頭 *devotion, absorption, consumed* **bottō**
病没 *death by illness* **byōbotsu**
沈没 *sinking, going down* **chinbotsu**
沈没船 *sunken ship* **chinbotsusen**
覆没 *capsize & sink* **fukubotsu**
陣没 *death in battle, killed in combat* **jinbotsu**
海没 *sinking into the sea* **kaibotsu**
陥没 *cave-in, sinking* **kanbotsu**
埋没 *burial, fall into oblivion* **maibotsu**
日没 *sunset* **nichibotsu**
生没 *birth & death* **seibotsu**

戦没 *death in battle, killed in combat* **senbotsu**
潜没 *submerge, dive* **senbotsu**
死没 *death* **shibotsu**
出没 *frequenting, coming & going* **shutsubotsu**
水没 *submersion, sinking, capsizing* **suibotsu**
没交渉 *unrelated, irrelevant* **bokkōshō**
没理想 *lack of ideals; realism* **botsu risō**
没趣味 *insipid, prosaic, boring* **bosshumi**
没常識 *lacking common sense* **botsujōshiki**
神出鬼没 *elusive, phantom* **shinshutsu kibotsu**

沈*inking, 719*
潜*ubmerge, 335*
礁*unken, 920*

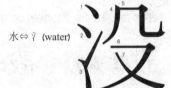

投*hrow, 745*   役*fficial, 746*

625-A

殴*unch* 投*hrown by* 役*fficial facing dismissal...*

殳 (pike)

FLIP: 7.0.b2. Right (stem)

殴*unch*　殴*low*

nagu(ru), Ō
punch, blow, pummel

殴り合い *exchange of blows, scuffle* **naguriai**
殴り合う *exchange of blows, scuffle* **naguriau**
殴り書き *scribble, scrawl* **nagurigaki**
殴り込み *free-for-all, scuffle* **nagurikomi**
殴り殺す *beat to death* **nagurikorosu**
殴り倒す *knock down* **naguritaosu**
殴り付ける *strike, beat* **naguritsukeru**
殴打 *punch, strike, beating* **ōda**
殴殺 *death by beating* **ōsatsu**
横殴り *side punch* **yokonaguri**
ぶん殴る *beat up, mug* **bunnaguru**
書き殴る *scribble writing* **kakinaguru**

打*trike*, 636	痛*ainful*, 60
撲*auling*, 157	障*njury*, 325

欧*urope*, 952

625-B

殴*unch* 投*hrown by* 役*fficial facing dismissal...*

手⇔扌 (hand, manual)

FLIP: 7.0.b2. Right (stem)

投*hrow*　投*itch*

na(geru), TŌ
throw, pitch, send in

快投 *good pitch* **kaitō**
投錨 *anchor dropping* **tōbyō**
投影 *projection image* **tōei**
投影図 *projection chart* **tōeizu**
投合 *agreement, coincidence* **tōgō**
投獄 *imprisonment, detention* **tōgoku**
投票 *vote, voting, suffrage* **tōhyō**
⇒賛成投票 *vote in favour* **sansei tōhyō**
投下 *dropping; investment* **tōka**
投棄 *throwing away, getting rid of* **tōki**
投機 *speculation, prospecting* **tōki**
投降 *surrender, laying down of arms* **tōkō**
投稿 *manuscript contribution (newspaper)* **tōkō**
投入 *investment; throwing in* **tōnyū**
投了 *quitting a game* **tōryō**
投石 *stone throwing* **tōseki**
投射 *screen projection* **tōsha**
投資 *capital investment* **tōshi**
投身 *jumping into one's death* **tōshin**

投書 *manuscript contribution (newspaper)* **tōsho**
投手 *baseball pitcher* **tōshu**
⇒救援投手 *relief pitcher* **kyūen tōshu**
投与 *dosage, medication* **tōyo**
続投 *continue pitching; remain in office* **zokutō**
槍投げ *javelin throwing* **yarinage**
投げ縄 *lariat, lasso* **nagenawa**
投げ槍 *javelin pole* **nageyari**
投げ売り *fire sale, clearance sale* **nageuri**
投げ出す *stretch, give up, fling* **nagedasu**
投げ込む *throw, toss, pitch* **nagekomu**

捨*hrow-away*, 231	断*ejection*, 958
斥*ejection*, 424	否*ejection*, 300
排*ejection*, 795	射*hoot*, 504

段*tep*, 555

625-C

殴unch 投hrown by 役fficial facing dismissal...

イ (stroll)

役fficial   役xecutive

YAKU, EKI
official, executive, managerial, top brass

FLIP: 7.0.b2. Right (stem)

懲役 *imprisonment, detention, confinement* **chōeki**
服役 *penal servitude, ~punishment* **fukueki**
軍役 *military service, ~conscription* **gun'eki**
兵役 *military service, ~conscription* **heieki**
助役 *vice mayor, deputy town head* **joyaku**
重役 *high officials, VIPs* **jūyaku**
顔役 *person of influence, big shot* **kaoyaku**
敵役 *villains role* **katakiyaku**
共役 *conjugate, merge, unify* **kyōyaku**
荷役 *loading & unloading* **niyaku**
側役 *personal attendant, ~servant* **sobayaku**
適役 *highly suitable, ~proper* **tekiyaku**
脇役 *supporting role* **wakiyaku**
役場 *public office* **yakuba**
役柄 *part, position, duty* **yakugara**
役員 *officer, executive, director* **yakuin**
役印 *official seal* **yakuin**
役目 *duty, function, role* **yakume**
役人 *public-, civil servant* **yakunin**

役者 *actor, actress, performer* **yakusha**
役所 *public office, government post* **yakusho**
役職 *post, position* **yakushoku**
役得 *perquisite* **yakutoku**
役割 *role, duty, function* **yakuwari**
雑役 *odd jobs, menial jobs* **zatsueki**
監査役 *auditor, fiscalizer, inspector* **kansayaku**
能役者 *noh actor* **nōyakusha**
市役所 *city hall, municipal hall* **shiyakusho**
役立つ *useful, valuable* **yakudatsu**
憎まれ役 *villain, bad guy* **nikumareyaku**

吏fficial, 463	威uthority, 520
官ublic official, 105	権uthority, 804

後fter, 897

626-A

飢tarving in distress, 肌kinny writer at his 机esk...

食 (food)

飢tarve   飢unger

u(eru), KI
starve, hunger, famine

FLIP: 7.0.b2. Right (stem)
Facing: 1.2. 🍴 West (V)

飢え死に *death by starvation* **ueji(ni)**
飢餓 *famine, starvation* **kiga**
飢寒 *"cold & hungry..."* **kikan**
飢渇 *thirst & hunger* **kikatsu**
飢饉 *famine, starvation* **kikin**
飢民 *starving masses* **kimin**

餓tarve, 443	病ickness, 213
食uisine, 255	患ickness, 475
糧oodstuff, 451	症ickness, 788

飯ooked rice, 256

626-B

飢tarving in distress, 肌kinny writer at his 机esk...

肉⇔月 (flesh, body part)

肌kin   肌erma

hada, KI
skin, derma

石肌 stone surface **ishihada**
肌骨 skin & bone's **kikotsu**
鮫肌 scaly skin, shark-skinned **samehada**
肌膚 skin **kifu**
諸肌 half-naked, bare to the waist **morohada**
山肌 mountain surface **yamahada**
柔肌 tender skin **yawahada**
人肌 human skin **hitohada**
赤肌 abraded-, grazed skin **akahada**
雪肌 snow-white surface **yukihada**
素肌 naked skin, bare skin **suhada**
地肌 ground surface **jihada**
鳥肌 goose bumps **torihada**
肌色 flesh colour **hadairo**
肌身 one's own body **hadami**
肌着 undergarment, underwear **hadagi**
肌理 texture, grain **kiri**
木肌 tree bark **kihada**

FLIP: **7.0.b2. Right (stem)**
Facing: **4.0.** 👁👁 Apart

餅肌 soft skin, velvet skin **mochihada**
荒れ肌 rough surface **arehada**
肌合い getting along **hadaai**
肌脱ぎ half-naked, bare to the waist **hadanugi**
肌寒い chilly, cold **hadazamui**
肌触り soft & comfortable **hadazawari**
競い肌 gallant **kisoihada**
もろ肌 stripped to the waist **morohada**

皮kin, 224
膚kin, 69
毛kin hair, 468

助ssist, 953

626-C

飢tarving in distress, 肌kinny writer at his 机esk...

木 (wooden)

机

机esk   机able

tsukue, KI
desk, table

机辺 around the table **kihen**
机上 on the desk **kijō**
机上の空論 arm chair theory **kijō no kūron**
机下 under the desk **kika**
脇机 cabinet drawer **wakizukue**
床机 folding stool **shōgi**
勉強机 study desk **benkyō zukue**
学習机 study desk **gakushū zukue**

FLIP: **7.0.b2. Right (stem)**

座eating, 109   学tudy, 346
席eating, 91   文iteracy, 558

机esk, 747

627-A

航*avigation maps in a* 坑*haft placed by* 抗*esistance in Gdansk...*

舟 (vessel)

航*avigation*　　航*oyage*

KŌ

navigation, voyage, journey, seafaring, seamanship

FLIP: 7.0.b2. Right (stem)

直航 *direct flight, non-stop flight* **chokkō**
曳航 *towing a ship, ~barge* **eikō**
復航 *return flight* **fukkō**
発航 *departure, flight* **hakkō**
巡航 *cruise, voyage, patrol* **junkō**
回航 *navigation, cruise, sailing* **kaikō**
欠航 *shipping-, flight suspension* **kekkō**
帰航 *homebound flight* **kikō**
航宙 *space flight* **kōchū**
航法 *navigation, maritime laws* **kōhō**
航海 *navigation, voyage, sailing* **kōkai**
航行 *navigation, sailing* **kōkō**
航空 *aviation, airlines* **kōkū**
航程 *cruise, flight* **kōtei**
航路 *flight route, sea passage* **kōro**
航送 *air shipment, send by air* **kōsō**
密航 *stowaway, jumpship* **mikkō**
内航 *coastal flight* **naikō**
難航 *flight difficulties* **nankō**

来航 *visit, visitation* **raikō**
潜航 *submarine voyage, ~navigation* **senkō**
潜航艇 *submarine* **senkōtei**
進航 *on flight, sailing* **shinkō**
出航 *sailing, leaving port* **shukkō**
周航 *circumnavigation* **shūkō**
就航 *transport service, plying* **shūkō**
渡航 *voyaging, going overseas* **tokō**
通航 *navigation, sailing* **tsūkō**
運航 *navigation, flight* **unkō**

艇*oat, 26*		舟*hip, 90*	
丸*[ships], 73*		船*hip, 757*	
隻*[ships], 50*		舶*hip, 742*	

般*eneral, 323*

627-B

航*avigation maps in a* 坑*haft placed by* 抗*esistance in Gdansk...*

土 (ground, soil)

坑*it hole*　　坑*haft*

KŌ

pit hole, shaft

FLIP: 5.0.b. Left & Right (stem)

銅坑 *copper mine* **dōkō**
銀坑 *silver mine* **ginkō**
廃坑 *abandoned minefield* **haikō**
堅坑 *mining shaft, pit* **kenkō, tatekō**
金坑 *gold mine* **kinkō**
坑木 *mine timber* **kōboku**
坑道 *tunnel, shaft, pit* **kōdō**
坑夫 *miner, mine worker* **kōfu**
坑外 *surface, grass* **kōgai**
坑口 *mine entrance, pithead* **kōkō**
坑内 *pit, shaft* **kōnai**
坑内火災 *pit fire, shaft fire* **kōnai kasai**
入坑 *entering a mining field* **nyūkō**
斜坑 *inclined shaft* **shakō**
炭坑 *coal mine shaft* **tankō**
炭坑夫 *coal miner* **tankōfu**
縦坑 *mining shaft, pit* **tatekō**
鉄坑 *iron mine* **tekkō**
石油坑 *oil well* **sekiyukō**

立て坑 *vertical shaft, pit* **tatekō**

狭*arrow, 763*		入*nter, 2*	
穴*ole, 4*		出*xit, 173*	
孔*ole, 684*		口*pening, 458*	

抗*esistance, 749*

627-C

航avigation maps in a 坑haft placed by 抗esistance in Gdansk...

手⇔扌 (hand, manual)

FLIP: 7.0.b2. Right (stem)

抗esistance   抗pposition

KŌ
resistance, opposition, repulsion, objection

抗する *resist, defy, oppose* **kōsuru**
反抗 *opposition, resistance* **hankō**
反抗的 *rebellious, defiant, antagonistic* **hankōteki**
拮抗 *competition, rivalry, antagonism* **kikkō**
抗弁 *protest, grievance, complaint* **kōben**
抗言 *retort, rebuttal* **kōgen**
抗原 *antigen* **kōgen**
抗議 *protest, resistance, objection* **kōgi**
抗議文 *letter of protest* **kōgibun**
抗議デモ *protest rally, demonstration* **kōgi demo**
抗議集会 *protest rally* **kōgi shūkai**
抗議運動 *protest movement* **kōgi undō**
抗菌 *anti-bacterial resistance* **kōkin**
抗告 *protest, appeal* **kōkoku**
抗日 *anti-Japanese* **kōnichi**
抗力 *strength of resistance* **kōryoku**
⇒抵抗力 *power of resistance* **teikōryoku**
⇒不可抗力 *irresistible force* **fuka kōryoku**
抗戦 *resistance, opposition* **kōsen**

抗争 *dispute, struggle, contention* **kōsō**
抗体 *anti-body* **kōtai**
対抗 *opposition, competition* **taikō**
対抗馬 *rival horse; rival candidate* **taikōba**
対抗策 *(counter) measures* **taikōsaku**
抵抗 *opposition, resistance* **teikō**
⇒無抵抗 *non-resistance* **muteikō**
抗毒素 *anti-toxin element* **kōdokuso**
抗生物質 *antibiotic substance* **kōsei busshitsu**
摩擦抵抗 *fake resistance* **masatsu teikō**

対	*gainst, 691*	戦	*ombat, 517*
反	*gainst, 537*	闘	*ombat, 946*
逆	*everse, 896*	武	*arrior, 100*

拡*nlarge, 205*

628-A

往oming-&-going, clients 注ouring into the 住esidence with
huge 柱illars & 駐arking fence...

彳 (stroll)

FLIP: 7.1. Right (Sort Of)

往ome & go   往ack & forth

yuku, Ō
come & go, back & forth, go on

独往 *"my pace...", going one's way* **dokuō**
既往 *past years, bygone years* **kiō**
既往症 *medical case history* **kiōshō**
既往歴 *medical case history* **kiōreki**
往復 *round trip* **ōfuku**
往復切符 *round-trip ticket* **ōfuku kippu**
往復運賃 *round-trip fare* **ōfuku unchin**
往事 *past affairs, ~events* **ōji**
往時 *olden times, the past* **ōji**
往生 *quiet death, being at a loss* **ōjō**
⇒極楽往生 *peaceful death* **gokuraku ōjō**
⇒無理往生 *coerced obedience* **muriōjō**
⇒立ち往生 *standstill, stick* **tachiōjō**
往古 *ancient past* **ōko**
往年 *past years, bygone years* **ōnen**
往来 *traffic, comings & goings* **ōrai**
往診 *doctor's house call, ~home visit* **ōshin**
往診料 *doctor's visiting fee* **ōshinryō**
往診時間 *house visiting hours* **ōshin jikan**

往訪 *visit, call on* **ōhō**
往日 *ancient past* **ōjitsu**
往還 *comings & goings* **ōkan**
往航 *voyage* **ōkō**
往々 *sometimes, on some occasion* **ōō**
往路 *outward journey* **ōro**
往信 *"reply requested..."* **ōshin**
大往生 *dying in peace, quiet death* **daiōjō**
往来止め *"road closed..."* **ōraidome**
往復葉書 *return postcard* **ōfuku hagaki**

出	*ome-out, 173*	還	*eturn, 165*
行	*rip, 79*	帰	*eturn, 784*
旅	*ravel, 650*	戻	*eturn, 541*

注*utpour, 750*

628-B

住*oming-&-going*, clients 注*ouring into the* 住*esidence with huge* 柱*illars &* 駐*arking fence...*

水 ⇔ 氵 (water)

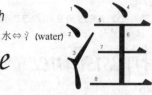

注*utpour*　　注*oncentrate*

soso(gu), CHŪ
outpour, outflow, concentrate

FLIP: 7.1. Right (Sort Of)

傍注 *marginal notes* **bōchū**
注意 *caution, warning* **chūi**
注意事項 *caution, nota bene* **chūi jikō**
注意報 *warning* **chūihō**
注意力 *mental alertness* **chūiryoku**
注解 *note, explanatory, comment* **chūkai**
注記 *annotation, explanatory note* **chūki**
注目 *attention, notice* **chūmoku**
注文 *purchase order* **chūmon**
注文先 *where one places an order* **chūmonsaki**
注文書 *invoice* **chūmonsho**
注入 *pouring in* **chūnyū**
注射 *injection, vaccination, hypodermic* **chūsha**
注射器 *syringe, hypodermic* **chūshaki**
注釈 *commentary, annotation* **chūshaku**
注視 *gaze, stare* **chūshi**
注進 *informing, reporting, warning* **chūshin**
注水 *pouring water on glass* **chūsui**
注油 *oiling & lubrication* **chūyu**

外注 *subcontracting, outsourcing* **gaichū**
原注 *original notes* **genchū**
発注 *sending out orders* **hacchū**
評注 *notes, annotation, commentary* **hyōchū**
受注 *accepting an order* **juchū**
傾注 *devotion, concentration* **keichū**
脚注 *footnote, bibliography* **kyakuchū**
頭注 *headnote, bibliography* **tōchū**
訳注 *translation & annotation* **yakuchū**
注連縄 *New Year rope decoration* **shimenawa**
降り注ぐ *outpour, rain down* **furisosogu**

波*urrent, 32*	流*urrent, 781*
浪*urrent, 254*	荒*urbulent, 507*

住*ome & go, 749*	柱*illar, 751*

628-C

住*oming-&-going*, clients 注*ouring into the* 住*esidence with huge* 柱*illars &* 駐*arking fence...*

人 ⇔ 亻 (person)

住*esidence*　　住*omicile*

su(mu), JŪ
residence, domicile, shelter, abode, dwelling, housing

FLIP: 7.1. Right (Sort Of)

安住 *peaceful living, ~settlement* **anjū**
永住 *permanent residence* **eijū**
永住権 *right of permanent stay* **eijūken**
移住 *migration, emigration* **ijū**
常住 *one's regular residence* **jōjū**
住持 *chief temple priest* **jūji**
住居 *residence, domicile* **jūkyo**
住民 *resident, house occupant* **jūmin**
住人 *inhabitant, resident* **jūnin**
住職 *temple head priest* **jūshoku**
住所 *address, domicile* **jūsho**
住所録 *address book, directory* **jūshoroku**
住宅 *house, residence* **jūtaku**
住宅地 *residential area* **jūtakuchi**
住宅ローン *housing loan* **jūtakurōn**
居住 *residence, domicile* **kyojū**
住家 *residence, household* **sumika**
定住 *settle down, live permanently* **teijū**
転住 *moving one's residence* **tenjū**

在住 *residence, domicile* **zaijū**
住み手 *tenant, occupant* **sumite**
住み心地 *living comfort* **sumigokochi**
住み込む *live together, live in* **sumikomu**
原住民 *aborigine, original inhabitants* **genjūmin**
衣食住 *food, clothing & shelter* **ishokujū**
部屋住み *free-dweller, hanger on* **heyazumi**
住居侵入 *break-in, tresspassing* **jūkyo shinnyū**
住所不明 *"address unknown..."* **jūsho fumei**
町住まい *town life* **machizumai**
都住まい *city life* **miyakozumai**

家*ouse, 909*	宅*esidence, 82*
居*esidence, 384*	

注*utpour, 750*

628-D

往oming-&-going, clients 注ouring into the 住esidence with
huge 柱illars & 駐arking fence...

木 (wooden)

柱*illar* 柱*olumn*

hashira, CHŪ

pillar, column, beam, obelisk, post

FLIP: 7.1. Right (Sort Of)

茶柱	*tea stems in a tea cup* **chabashira**	水柱	*column of water* **mizubashira**
柱状	*column-shaped* **chūjō**	門柱	*gatepost* **monchū**
柱面	*cylindrical surface* **chūmen**	中柱	*pillar in the middle* **nakabashira**
柱石	*cornerstone, bedrock* **chūseki**	男柱	*large pillars at both ends of a bridge*
柱疎	*plinth, brace, pedestal* **chūso**		**otokobashira**
柱頭	*main pillar* **chūtō**	親柱	*main pillar* **oyabashira**
電柱	*electric post* **denchū**	石柱	*stone pillar* **sekichū**
円柱	*cylinder, shaft* **enchū**	脊柱	*spinal column* **sekichū**
花柱	*flower pillar* **hanabashira**	霜柱	*frost pillar* **shimobashira**
鼻柱	*nasal bridge* **hanabashira, bichū**	主柱	*mainstay, main pillar* **shuchū**
柱暦	*wall calendar* **hashiragoyomi**	鉄柱	*steel-, iron pole* **tecchū**
火柱	*column of fire* **hibashira**	床柱	*ornamental alcove* **tokobashira**
人柱	*human shield, sacrifice* **hitobashira**	柱時計	*wall clock* **hashiradokei**
帆柱	*boat-, ship mast* **hobashira**		
氷柱	*icicle, ice pillar* **hyōchū**		
標柱	*post marker* **hyōchū**		
蚊柱	*column of mosquitoes* **kabashira**		
貝柱	*adductor muscle* **kaibashira**		
角柱	*prism (geometry)* **kakuchū**		

基*oundation, 590*	橋*ridge, 163*
礎*ornerstone, 166*	建*onstruct, 390*

住*esidence, 750*

628-E

往oming-&-going, clients 注ouring into the 住esidence with
huge 柱illars & 駐arking fence...

馬 (horse)

駐*arking* 駐*tationing*

CHŪ

parking, stationing

FLIP: 7.1. Right (Sort Of)

駐兵	*deployed-, stationed troops* **chūhei**
駐留	*stay, stationing, posting* **chūryū**
駐留軍	*deployed-, stationed troops* **chūryūgun**
駐車	*vehicle parking* **chūsha**
駐車場	*parking lot, car park* **chūshajō**
駐車違反	*illegal parking* **chūsha ihan**
駐屯	*stationing, deployment* **chūton**
駐屯地	*place of deployment* **chūtonchi**
駐屯軍	*deployed-, stationed troops* **chūtongun**
駐在	*overseas posting, ~assignment* **chūzai**
駐在員	*expatriate, representative* **chūzaiin**
駐在所	*police box, police station* **chūzaijo**
移駐	*troop redeployment* **ichū**
常駐	*permanent deployment* **jōchū**
進駐	*military occupation* **shinchū**
進駐軍	*occupation troops* **shinchūgun**
駐輪場	*bicycle parking spot* **chūrinjō**
駐米大使	*ambassador to the US* **chūbei taishi**
駐英大使	*ambassador to England* **chūei taishi**

駐日大使 *Ambassador to Japan* **chūnichi taishi**

車*ehicle, 306*	止*top, 192*
庫*torage, 306*	停*top, 393*

駆*alloping, 674*

629-A

訳*ranslation* 釈*xplains why the* 沢*wamp was* 択*hosen by Keynes...*

言 (speaking)

❶訳*ranslate* **❷訳***eason*

wake, YAKU

translate, interpret; reason, rationale, logic

FLIP: 6.0.a. Left (flat)
Facing: 1.2. ⚐ West (V)

❶直訳 *literal translation* **chokuyaku**
英訳 *English translation* **eiyaku**
誤訳 *mistranslation* **goyaku**
翻訳 *translation, interpretation* **honyaku**
意訳 *free translation* **iyaku**
改訳 *new translation* **kaiyaku**
完訳 *complete translation* **kanyaku**
監訳 *supervised translation* **kanyaku**
共訳 *joint translation* **kyōyaku**
新訳 *new translation* **shinyaku**
抄訳 *translation of selected works* **shōyaku**
定訳 *generally-accepted translation* **teiyaku**
適訳 *proper translation* **tekiyaku**
点訳 *Braille codes* **tenyaku**
通訳 *translator, interpreter* **tsūyaku**
和訳 *Japanese translation* **wayaku**
訳文 *translated text* **yakubun**
訳注 *translation & annotation* **yakuchū**
訳読 *reading & translation* **yakudoku**

訳語 *equivalent word, ~term* **yakugo**
訳業 *translation circles* **yakugyō**
訳者 *translator, interpreter* **yakusha**
訳詞 *translated lyrics* **yakushi**
訳詩 *translated poem* **yakushi**
訳出 *translate* **yakushutsu**
全訳 *complete translation* **zenyaku**
逐語訳 *word-for-word translation* **chikugoyaku**
❷内訳 *account details* **uchiwake**
訳合 *situation, circumstances* **wakeai**
訳知り *learned in ways of the world* **wakeshiri**

故*eason, 960* 理*eason, 872* 解*omprehend, 400*
由*eason, 540* 翻*ranslate, 338* 哲*isdom, 53*

駅*rain station , 318*

629-B

訳*ranslation* 釈*xplains why the* 沢*wamp was* 択*hosen by Keynes...*

釆 (rice)

釈*xplain* 釈*lucidate*

SHAKU

explain, elucidate, narration

Facing: 4.0. ⚐⚐ Apart

注釈 *annotation, comment, nota bene* **chūshaku**
注釈者 *commentator, annotator* **chūshakusha**
会釈 *slight bow* **eshaku**
語釈 *explanation of a word, phrase* **goshaku**
保釈 *out-on-bail, bail bond* **hoshaku**
評釈 *annotation, footnotes, references* **hyōshaku**
解釈 *interpretation, explanation* **kaishaku**
⇒拡大解釈 *broad interpretation* **kakudai kaishaku**
希釈 *dilution, dissolve* **kishaku**
講釈 *lecture, explanation* **kōshaku**
講釈師 *storyteller, narrator* **kōshakushi**
訓釈 *Kanji reading explanation* **kunshaku**
釈迦 *Buddha, Gautama* **shaka**
釈放 *release, setting free* **shakuhō**
⇒仮釈放 *release on parole* **karishakuhō**
釈明 *vindication, acquittal* **shakumei**
釈然 *satisfactory explanation* **shakuzen**
新釈 *new interpretation* **shinshaku**
通釈 *detailed text explanation* **tsūshaku**

説*xplain, 943* 叙*arrate, 648*
述*ention, 95* 紀*arration, 727*

駅*rain station, 318*

629-C

訳*ranslation* 釈*xplains why the* 沢*wamp was* 択*hosen by Keynes...*

水 ⇔ 氵 (water)

沢*wamp*   沢*arshland*

sawa, TAKU
swamp, marshland

Facing: 4.0. ⟪⟫ Apart

潤沢 *abundance, plentiful, bountiful* **juntaku**
光沢 *gloss, lustre, glow* **kōtaku**
恩沢 *favour, benefit, gain, advantage* **ontaku**
沢辺 *swamp edge* **sawabe**
沢地 *marshy-, swampy, wetland* **sawachi**
沢蟹 *river crab* **sawagani**
沼沢 *swamp, marsh* **shōtaku**
手沢 *soiled from over-handling* **shutaku**
沢山 *plentiful, numerous* **takusan**
⇒子沢山 *large family* **kodakusan**
⇒盛り沢山 *large amount* **moridakusan**
沢庵 *pickled radish* **takuwan, takuan**
徳沢 *grace, blessing, favour* **tokutaku**
余沢 *blessing, benefit, gain* **yotaku**
贅沢 *luxury, extravagance* **zeitaku**
毛沢東 *Mao Zedong (1893-1976)* **mōtakutō**

沼*wamp, 356*	潜*ubmerge, 335*
溝*itch, 226*	没*inking, 744*
礁*unken, 920*	泥*lay, 302*

決*ecide, 699*

629-D

訳*ranslation* 釈*xplains why the* 沢*wamp was* 択*hosen by Keynes...*

手 ⇔ 扌 (hand, manual)

択*hoice*   択*elect*

TAKU
choice, select, pick out, elective, option, alternative

Facing: 4.0. ⟪⟫ Apart

決択 *pick & choose* **kettaku**
採択 *adoption, selection* **saitaku**
選択 *choice, elective* **sentaku**
選択科目 *elective subject, ~course* **sentaku kamoku**
択捉島 *Etorofu islands, Hokkaidō* **etorofutō**
二者択一 *one or the another* **nisha takuitsu**
選択権 *right of choice, option* **sentakuken**
選択肢 *multiple choices* **sentakushi**

選*hoice, 303*	裁*udgement, 802*
決*ecide, 699*	判*udgement, 949*
志*ntention, 426*	

沢*wamp, 753*

630-A

起*wake to* 配*istribute The Times* 配*elivery route...*

走 (running)

起*waken*　　　起*rise*

o(kiru), o(koru), o(kosu), KI
awaken, arise, burst forth, occur, getting-up

FLIP: 6.1. Left Top
Facing: 3.0. ☞☜ Across

縁起 *good omen, luck* **engi**
奮起 *rousing, stirring, exciting* **funki**
早起き *early riser, early birds* **hayaoki**
喚起 *evocation, awakening* **kanki**
決起 *rising to action, ~to the occasion* **kekki**
起案 *draft proposal* **kian**
起爆 *explosion, detonation, blasting* **kibaku**
起動 *starting, upstart* **kidō**
起伏 *ups & downs* **kifuku**
起臥 *getting in & out from bed* **kiga**
起源 *origin, beginning* **kigen**
起因 *origin, root cause* **kiin**
起稿 *start writing* **kikō**
起工式 *ground-breaking ceremony* **kikōshiki**
起居 *daily life-, living* **kikyo**
起立 *standing up, rising* **kiritsu**
起算 *reckoning, retribution* **kisan**
起床 *getting up, rising from bed* **kishō**
起訴 *prosecution, indictment, arraignment* **kiso**

起点 *starting point* **kiten**
起用 *job promotion* **kiyō**
寝起き *waking up, getting up* **neoki**
隆起 *rising up, upheaval, protuberance* **ryūki**
再起 *comeback, recovery, rehabilitation* **saiki**
想起 *remembering, recollection, memory* **sōki**
提起 *bringing forward, lodging* **teiki**
躍起 *eager, mind-set, bent on* **yakki**
起死回生 *revival* **kishi kaisei**
起承転結 *introduction & conclusion*
　　kishō tenketsu
起き上がる *get up, rise, sit up* **okiagaru**

| 立*tand up, 234* | 昇*scend, 299* |
| 覚*wake, 307* | 上*scend, 859* |

| 超*xceed, 664* |

630-B

起*wake to* 配*istribute The Times* 配*elivery route...*

酉 (liquor)

配*istribution*　　配*elivery*

kuba(ru), HAI
distribution, delivery, hand-over, transport

FLIP: 6.0.a. Left (flat)

按配 *disposition, arrangement* **anbai**
遅配 *delayed delivery, late shipment* **chihai**
直配 *direct delivery* **chokuhai**
配備 *troop deployment, ~stationing* **haibi**
配置 *distribution, allocation* **haichi**
配電 *electricity supply* **haiden**
配付 *distribution, allocation* **haifu**
配合 *combination, arrangement* **haigō**
配本 *book distribution, ~allocation* **haihon**
配意 *consideration, rethinking, pondering* **haii**
配管 *pipe, plumbing* **haikan**
配給 *distribution, rationing, allocation* **haikyū**
配慮 *consideration, concern* **hairyo**
配車 *allocating vehicles* **haisha**
配送 *delivery, allocation* **haisō**
配達 *delivery, shipping* **haitatsu**
配点 *allotment of points* **haiten**
配当 *distribution of dividends* **haitō**
配剤 *dispensation, indulgence* **haizai**

欠配 *non-delivery, non-arrival* **keppai**
休配 *delivery off day* **kyūhai**
心配 *anxiety, worry, perplexity* **shinpai**
集配 *collection & delivery* **shūhai**
宅配 *home delivery* **takuhai**
手配 *arrangements, preparations* **tehai**
特配 *extra-delivery* **tokuhai**
増配 *increased ration, ~delivery* **zōhai**
配偶者 *one's spouse* **haigūsha**
急勾配 *steep slope* **kyūkōbai**
目配り *watching over, keeping alert* **mekubari**

届*eliver, 631*	充*upply, 884*
頒*istribution, 835*	納*upply, 296*
給*upply, 143*	与*upply, 349*

| 酌*erve-wine, 696* |

631-A
High 租*evies so* 粗*ough* 阻*mpede our crops...*

禾 (tree branch)

租*and tax*　　租*evy*

SO
land tax, levy

FLIP: 7.0.a. Right (flat)

地租 *land tax* **chiso**
田租 *farmers tax* **denso**
公租 *levy, tax, tribute* **kōso**
貢租 *annual tax* **kōso**
免租 *crop tax exemption* **menso**
租界 *concession, settlement* **sokai**
租借 *lease, rent* **soshaku**
租借地 *land for lease, leased property* **soshakuchi**
租借権 *leasehold rights* **soshakuken**
租庸調 *tax payment in kind* **soyōchō**
租税 *crop taxation* **sozei**
有租地 *taxable land* **yūsochi**

植*lant, 783*	農*arming, 446*
畑*lantation, 482*	獲*cquire, 829*
穫*arvest, 829*	得*cquire, 940*

組*roup, 138*	粗*ough, 755*

631-B
High 租*evies so* 粗*ough* 阻*mpede our crops...*

米 (grains, rice)

粗*ough*　　粗*oarse*

ara(i), SO
rough, coarse, crude, unrefined, unpolished

FLIP: 5.0.a Left & Right

粗金 *unrefined metal, ore* **aragane**
粗壁 *rough-coated wall* **arakabe**
粗方 *almost, nearly, soon* **arakata**
粗皮 *tree bark* **arakawa**
粗木 *lumber, rough timber* **araki**
粗布 *coarse cloth* **aranuno**
粗筋 *rough outline* **arasuji**
粗悪 *inferior, coarse, substandard* **soaku**
粗悪品 *inferior-, substandard goods* **soakuhin**
粗暴 *rough, crude* **sobō**
粗茶 *coarse tea* **socha**
粗大 *rough & large* **sodai**
粗銅 *black copper* **sodō**
粗飯 *frugal meal, cheap food* **sohan**
粗鋼 *crude steel* **sokō**
粗末 *miserable, careless* **somatsu**
粗密 *roughness-or-fineness* **somitsu**
粗製 *crude products* **sosei**
粗製品 *crude-, shoddy goods* **soseihin**

粗製濫造 *crude manufacturing* **sosei ranzō**
粗品 *small gift* **soshina, sohin**
粗食 *poor food, simple diet* **soshoku**
粗酒 *cheap liquor* **soshu**
粗相 *careless thing* **sosō**
粗糖 *raw sugar* **sotō**
粗野 *crude, rough, coarse* **soya**
粗雑 *crude, rough* **sozatsu**
粗目 *granulated sugar* **zarame**
粗塗り *rough coating* **aranuri**
粗探し *faultfinding, complainer* **arasagashi**
粗造り *crude manufacture* **arazukuri**

劣*nferior, 572*	未*ot yet, 12*
弱*eakling, 908*	素*lement, 578*

組*roup, 138*	租*arvest, 755*

631-C

High 租*evies so* 粗*ough* 阻*mpede our crops...*

阻*mpede* 阻*bstruct*

阝 ⇔ 阜 (village=left)

haba(mu), SO
impede, obstruct, inhibit, forestall

FLIP: 7.0.a. Right (flat)

険阻 *steep, rugged* **kenso**
阻害 *obstruction, impediment* **sogai**
阻隔 *estrangement, alienation* **sokaku**
阻止 *obstruction, prevention* **soshi**
阻喪 *discouragement, depression* **sosō**
悪阻 *morning sickness* **tsuwari, akuso**
阻塞気球 *barrage balloon* **sosai kikyū**

妨*indrance, 734*	守*efence, 366*
遮*nterrupt, 371*	防*efence, 736*
困*roblematic, 863*	護*efence, 828*

組*roup, 138*

632-A

沿*long a* 船*hip decrepit, toxic* 鉛*ead creeps...*

沿*longside* 沿*lign*

水 ⇔ 氵 (water)

so(u), EN
align, alongside

FLIP: 7.0.a. Right (flat)

川沿い *along the river, riverside* **kawazoi**
海岸沿い *along the coast* **kaiganzoi**
沿道 *roadside, route* **endō**
沿岸 *coast, shore* **engan**
沿岸漁業 *coastal fishery, ~fishing* **engan gyogyō**
沿海 *coast, shore* **enkai**
沿海州 *maritime provinces* **enkaishū**
沿海漁業 *coastal fishery, ~fishing* **enkai gyogyō**
沿革 *progress, development* **enkaku**
沿線 *along the railroad* **ensen**

並*arallel, 444*	合*ogether, 232*
列*illar, 357*	共*ogether, 302*
直*irect, 420*	伴*ogether, 949*
線*inear, 531*	緯*orizontal, 797*

沿*ecuperate, 210*

632-B

沿*long a* 船*hip decrepit, toxic* 鉛*ead creeps...*

hip   船*essel*

舟 (vessel)

fune, funa, SEN
ship, vessel

FLIP: 7.0.a. Right (flat)

船縁	side of boat, ~of ship	**funaberi**
船出	sailing, leaving port	**funade**
舟守	boat watchman	**funamori**
船荷	cargo, freight, shipload	**funani**
風船	balloon, dirigible, blimp	**fūsen**
漁船	fishing boat, ~vessel	**gyosen**
客船	passenger boat, liner	**kyakusen**
船長	ship captain	**senchō**
船台	shipbuilding berth	**sendai**
船団	fleet, convoy	**sendan**
船員	crewman, seaman, sailor	**sen'in**
船客	ship passenger	**senkyaku**
船室	cabin, ship sleeping quarters	**senshitsu**
船主	shipowner	**senshu**
船首	bow, stem	**senshu**
滞船	late shipping, demurrage	**taisen**
宝船	treasure ship	**takarabune**
用船	chartered vessel	**yōsen**
造船	shipbuilding, ~production	**zōsen**

沈没船	sunken ship	**chinbotsusen**
船大工	ship-building carpenter	**funadaiku**
船会社	shipping company	**funagaisha**
船小屋	boathouse	**funagoya**
船酔い	seasickness, nausea	**funayoi**
船積み	shipment, shipping, loading	**funazumi**
船積港	port-of-shipment, ~origin	**funazumikō**
捕鯨船	whaling ship	**hogeisen**
蒸気船	steamship	**jōkisen**
貨物船	cargo ship, freighter	**kamotsusen**
密航船	smuggling boat	**mikkōsen**
老朽船	decrepit ship	**rōkyūsen**
宇宙船	spaceship, space rocket	**uchūsen**

舟*hip, 90*	艇*oat, 26*	海*cean, 241*
舶*hip, 742*	帆*ailing, 641*	洋*cean, 247*

航*avigation, 748*

632-C

沿*long a* 船*hip decrepit, toxic* 鉛*ead creeps...*

鉛*ead*

金 (metal)

namari, EN
lead

FLIP: 5.0.a Left & Right

亜鉛	zinc	**aen**
亜鉛引き	galvanized iron	**aenbiki**
亜鉛メッキ	zinc plating	**aenmekki**
鉛版	stereotype, conventional	**enban**
鉛直	vertical, perpendicular, upbright	**enchoku**
鉛毒	lead poisoning	**endoku**
鉛塊	lead ingot	**enkai**
鉛管	lead pipe	**enkan**
鉛鉱	lead mine, ~deposits	**enkō**
鉛白	white lead	**enpaku**
鉛筆	pencil	**enpitsu**
鉛筆入れ	pencil box, ~case	**enpitsuire**
鉛筆削り器	pencil sharpener	**enpitsu kezuriki**
鉛錘	sounding lead, plump bob	**ensui**
鉛ざん	poetry writing	**enzan**
白鉛	white lead	**hakuen**
黒鉛	black lead, graphite	**kokuen**
無鉛	lead-free substance	**muen**
鉛色	lead colour	**namariiro**

鉛山	lead mine, ~deposits	**namariyama**
測鉛	sounding lead, plump bob	**sokuen**
鉛中毒	lead poisoning	**enchūdoku**
色鉛筆	colour pencil	**iroenpitsu**

銅*opper, 246*	鉄*ron, 155*
鉱*ineral-ore, 206*	鋼*teel, 975*

鈴*ell, 683*

633-A
Material 裕ffluence can 溶issolve prudence...

衣⇔ネ (clothing)

裕*ffluence*   裕*uxury*

YŪ
affluence, luxury, abundance

富裕 *wealth, affluence* **fuyū**
富裕税 *rich tax, luxury tax* **fuyūzei**
寛裕 *magnanimity, generosity* **kanyū**
余裕 *allowance, room, leeway* **yoyū**
裕度 *tolerance, leniency* **yūdo**
裕福 *rich, wealth, affluence* **yūfuku**

FLIP: 7.0.a. Right (flat)

富*ortune, 333*	隆*rosperity, 133*
豊*bundance, 965*	盛*rosperity, 244*
繁*rosperity, 434*	益*rofit, 622*

溶*ilute, 758*

633-B
Material 裕ffluence can 溶issolve prudence...

水⇔ 氵 (water)

溶*issolve*   溶*ilute*

to(keru), to(kasu), to(ku), YŌ
dissolve, dilute, melting

不溶 *insoluble, non-soluble* **fuyō**
溶暗 *fading out, bleach* **yōan**
溶媒 *solvent* **yōbai**
溶着 *metal welding* **yōchaku**
溶断 *fusion, merger* **yōdan**
溶液 *liquid solution* **yōeki**
溶岩 *volcano lava* **yōgan**
溶岩流 *volcano lava* **yōganryū**
溶化 *melt* **yōka**
溶解 *dissolution, melting* **yōkai**
溶解度 *solubility* **yōkaido**
溶解性 *solubility* **yōkaisei**
溶解点 *melting point* **yōkaiten**
溶血 *haemolysis* **yōketsu**
溶明 *fade-in* **yōmei**
溶性 *soluble* **yōsei**
溶接 *metal welding* **yōsetsu**
溶接工 *welder* **yōsetsukō**
溶出 *elution* **yōshutsu**

FLIP: 7.0.a. Right (flat)

溶融 *melting, fusion* **yōyū**
溶剤 *solvent agent* **yōzai**
可溶性 *soluble, dissolvable* **kayōsei**
濃溶液 *concentrated solution* **nōyōeki**
水溶液 *water solution* **suiyōeki**
水溶性 *water soluble* **suiyōsei**
溶鉱炉 *smelter, smelting furnace* **yōkōro**
溶溶たる *overflowing, spacious* **yōyōtaru**
溶け合う *be mixed, melt into* **tokeau**
溶け込み *adapting oneself, assimilation* **tokekomi**
飽和溶液 *saturated solution* **hōwa yōeki**

融*issolve, 963*	鋳*asting, 440*
混*ixture, 38*	紛*ixture, 778*

答*nswer, 232*

634-A

劇rama script of "Crime & 罰unishment," 刷rinted for comments...

刀⇔刂 (blade, cutting)

劇rama　劇heatre　劇pera

GEKI
drama, theatre, opera, stage play

Facing: 2.2. East ☞ (V)

演劇 drama, play **engeki**
劇団 dramatic troupe **gekidan**
劇毒 lethal-, deadly poison **gekidoku**
劇画 story comic, comic strip **gekiga**
劇変 abrupt-, sudden change **gekihen**
劇評 drama review, ~commentary **gekihyō**
激甚 intense, severe, fierce **gekijin**
劇場 theatre, playhouse **gekijō**
⇒円形劇場 amphitheatre, coliseum **enkei gekijō**
⇒野外劇場 open-air theatre **yagai gekijō**
劇職 extraordinarily busy, preoccupied **gekishoku**
劇痛 sharp pain, searing pain **gekitsū**
劇薬 potent drug, deadly poison **gekiyaku**
繁劇 extremely busy **hangeki**
悲劇 tragedy, disaster **higeki**
歌劇 opera, musical drama **kageki**
観劇 going to the theatre **kangeki**
活劇 action drama **katsugeki**
喜劇 comedy play, satire **kigeki**

黙劇 pantomime, impersonation show **mokugeki**
惨劇 tragedy, tragic event **sangeki**
史劇 historical drama **shigeki**
笑劇 comedy, satire **shōgeki**
寸劇 short play **sungeki**
舞台劇 stage play **butaigeki**
劇映画 movie drama **gekieiga**
劇作家 dramatist, playwright **gekisakka**
悲喜劇 tragicomedy **hikigeki**
神秘劇 mystery drama **shinpigeki**

興ntertainment, 867	聴isten, 844
観iew, 667	聞isten, 282
俳cting, 795	視bserve, 815

戯lirt, 436

634-B

劇rama script of "Crime & 罰unishment," 刷rinted for comments...

罒 (net, eye crown)

罰unishment　罰enalty

BATSU, BACHI
punishment, penalty, retribution, punitive

FLIP: 3.0.a. Top (flat)
FLIP: 6.2. Left Bottom

罰金 fine, penalty **bakkin**
罰杯 "loser-must-drink..." **bappai**
罰俸 withholding of salary as punishment **bappō**
罰則 penal-, prison regulations **bassoku**
罰点 incorrect-, wrong marks **batten**
懲罰 punishment, disciplinary action **chōbatsu**
厳罰 severe punishment **genbatsu**
刑罰 punishment, penalty, sentence **keibatsu**
神罰 divine punishment, wrath-of-God **shinbatsu**
処罰 punishment, penalty, sentence **shobatsu**
賞罰 reward-or-punishment **shōbatsu**
体罰 physical punishment **taibatsu**
天罰 divine punishment, wrath-of-God **tenbatsu**
罰当たり damned, doomed, cursed **bachiatari**
信賞必罰 certain reward-or-punishment
　　shinshō hitsubatsu

刑unishment, 536	獄rison, 639
懲unishment, 63	犯riminal, 640
囚risoner, 863	悪vil, 389

罪riminal, 289

634-C

劇rama script of "Crime & 罰unishment," 刷rinted for comments...

刀⇔刂 (blade, cutting)

刷rinting　刷ress

su(ru), SATSU
printing, press

FLIP: 8.0.b. Inner (stem)
Facing: 3.0. ☞☜ Across

刷り上がる　off-the-press　**suriagaru**
刷り本　printed book to be bounded　**surihon**
刷り立て　freshly-printed book　**suritate**
刷毛　brush, scrub　**hake**
刷子　brush, scrub　**sasshi**
印刷　printing, press work　**insatsu**
⇒凸版印刷　relief printing　**toppan insatsu**
印刷物　printed matter　**insatsubutsu**
刷新　reform, renovation, renewal　**sasshin**
試刷　proof-reading, trial printing　**shisatsu**
失刷　misprinting　**shissatsu**
縮刷　printing in reduced size　**shukusatsu**
縮刷版　pocket book-, compact edition　**shukusatsuban**
増刷　extra printing　**zōsatsu**
別刷り　off printing　**betsuzuri**
色刷り　colour printing　**irozuri**
下刷り　proof-reading　**shitazuri**
手刷り　handprinting, manual press　**tezuri**
校正刷り　proof-reading　**kōseizuri**

抜き刷り　off printing　**nukizuri**

版rinting, 359	載ublish, 802
刊ublication, 687	文iteracy, 558
掲ublish, 810	読eading, 260

制ystem, 534

635-A

酔runkards 砕mashed a photo 枠rame, 粋urely as a game...

酉 (liquor)

酔runk　酔ntoxicate

yo(u), SUI
drunk, intoxicate, tipsy, boozed up

FLIP: 6.0.a. Left (flat)

酔い心地　pleasant drunken mood　**yoigokochi**
酔い覚め　sobering up　**yoizame**
酔っ払い　drunk, drunkard　**yopparai**
酔い痴れる　inebriated, befuddled, drunk　**yoishireru**
酔い潰れる　dead drunk　**yoitsubureru**
泥酔　dead drunk　**deisui**
麻酔　anaesthesia, sedative　**masui**
⇒局部麻酔　partial anaesthesia　**kyokubu masui**
麻酔薬　anaesthetic, sedative drugs　**masuiyaku**
乱酔　dead drunk　**ransui**
心酔　fervent admiration　**shinsui**
酔眼　drunken eyes　**suigan**
酔顔　drunken look　**suigan**
酔歩　tipsy, staggering gait　**suiho**
酔漢　drunk, drunkard　**suikan**
酔客　drunken person　**suikyaku**
酔狂　crazy, stupid act　**suikyō**
酔態　drunkenness, intoxication　**suitai**
酔余　drunken, intoxicated　**suiyo**

大酔　drunken stupor　**taisui**
陶酔　intoxication, fascination　**tōsui**
深酔い　extremely drunk　**fukayoi**
船酔い　seasickness, nausea　**funayoi**
車酔い　road sickness　**kurumayoi**
生酔い　tipsy, drunk, intoxicated　**namayoi**
悪酔い　"sick & tired of drinking..."　**waruyoi**
山酔い　mountain sickness　**yamayoi**
二日酔い　hangover headache　**futsukayoi**
酔生夢死　useless idle life　**suisei mushi**
乗り物酔い　road sickness　**norimonoyoi**

飲rink, 255	閑eisure, 283
酒lcohol, 789	悠eisure, 898

酸cid, 764

635-B

酔runkards 砕mashed a photo 枠rame, 粋urely as a game...

砕mash   砕ulverize

石 (stone)

Facing: 2.2. East ☞ (V)
FLIP: 7.3.b. Right Bottom (stem)

kuda(keru), kuda(ku), SAI
smash, pulverize, shatter, fragmentalize, granulate, powderize

砕け散る *break into pieces* **kudakechiru**
踏み砕く *crush under one's feet* **fumikudaku**
粉骨砕身 *exert one's very best* **funkotsu saishin**
噛み砕く *crunch; simplify* **kamikudaku**
擂り砕く *grind down* **surikudaku**
打ち砕く *break, smash, crush* **uchikudaku**
砕けた態度 *amicable attitude* **kudaketa taido**
爆砕 *break-, explode into pieces* **bakusai**
粉砕 *smashing, shattering, pulverizing* **funsai**
撃砕 *pulverize, shoot to fragments* **gekisai**
玉砕 *glorious death* **gyokusai**
破砕 *crush, smash, crack* **hasai**
砕片 *fragment, splinter* **saihen**
砕氷 *ice-breaking* **saihyō**
砕氷船 *ice-breaking ship* **saihyōsen**
砕石 *quarrying, mining* **saiseki**
腰砕け *weak-kneed* **koshikudake**
砕け米 *deformed rice* **kudakemai**
砕鉱機 *ore crusher* **saikōki**

砕炭機 *coal crusher* **saitanki**
火砕流 *pyroclastic flow* **kasairyū**
砕岩機 *stone crusher* **saiganki**

破*estroy, 715*
壊*estroy, 847*
粉*owder, 778*

破*estroy, 715*

635-C

酔runkards 砕mashed a photo 枠rame, 粋urely as a game...

枠rame   枠asing

木 (wooden)

Facing: 2.2. ☞ East (V)
FLIP: 7.3.b. Right Bottom (stem)

waku
frame, casing, moulding

別枠 *separate matter, ~framework* **betsuwaku**
糸枠 *spool* **itowaku**
型枠 *mould, moulding frame* **katawaku**
黒枠 *black frame* **kurowaku**
窓枠 *window frame, ~sash* **madowaku**
戸枠 *door frame* **towaku**
枠外 *"beyond the limits of..."* **wakugai**
枠内 *"within the framework of..."* **wakunai**
増枠 *increased budget* **zōwaku**
枠組み *putting up frames* **wakugumi**
刺繍枠 *embroidery frame* **shishūwaku**

量*mount, 451*   囲*nclose, 361*
額*mount, 559*   郭*nclose, 398*
桟*rame, 768*

砕*ulverize, 761*

635-D

酔runkards 砕mashed a photo 枠rame, 粋urely as a game...

米 (grains, rice)

粋urity　　　粋xquisite

iki, SUI

purity, exquisite, pristine, refined

FLIP: 6.0.b. Left (stem)
FLIP: 7.3.b. Right Bottom (stem)

抜粋 *extract, excerpt* **bassui**
無粋 *unrefined, unpolished* **busui**
不粋 *unrefined, unpolished* **busui**
純粋 *genuine, pure, unmixed* **junsui**
生粋 *genuine, real thing* **kissui**
小粋 *stylish, good taste* **koiki**
国粋 *national characteristics* **kokusui**
国粋主義 *radical patriotism* **kokusui shugi**
精粋 *selfless, pure* **seisui**
粋人 *person of exquisite taste* **suijin**
粋狂 *whimsical, capricious, vagary* **suikyo**

斎 *urification, 112*	純 *urity, 199*
清 *urify, 793*	浄 *urity, 230*
潔 *urity, 901*	優 *xcellence, 556*

断 *efusal, 958*

636-A

挟orked-road 狭arrows to the 峡avine of sparrows...

手⇔扌 (hand, manual)

挟orked　　　挟cissor

hasa(mu), hasa(maru), KYŌ

forked, pronged, scissor, hold in between

FLIP: 7.0.b2. Right (stem)

挟撃 *attack on both flanks* **kyōgeki**
挟殺 *rundown (baseball)* **kyōsatsu**
挟書 *owning books* **kyōsho**
挟み虫 *earwig* **hasamimushi**
板挟み *predicament, dilemma* **itabasami**
状挟み *letter clip* **jōbasami**
紙挟み *folder; clip* **kamibasami**
氷挟み *ice tongs* **kooribasami**
挟み出す *clip & remove* **hasamidasu**
挟み切る *clip off* **hasamikiru**
挟み込み *insert, put in between* **hasamikomi**
挟み撃ち *attack on both flanks* **hasamiuchi**
差し挟む *insert; harbour, entertain* **sashihasamu**

岐 *orked-road, 704*	道 *ath, 312*
狭 *arrow, 763*	径 *ath, 888*
路 *oad, 405*	細 *lender, 138*

狭 *arrow, 763*

636-B

狭orked-road 狭arrows to the 峡avine of sparrows...

狭arrow　　　狭ramped

犬⇔犭 (dog, beast)

狭

sema(i), seba(maru), seba(meru), KYŌ
narrow, cramped, thin

FLIP: 7.0.b2. Right (stem)

地峡 *isthmus* **chikyō**
狭間 *gorge, rave, mountain depths* **hazama**
偏狭 *narrow-thinking, shallow-minded* **henkyō**
広狭 *wideness & narrowness* **kōkyō**
狭義 *narrow sense, shallow-minded* **kyōgi**
狭軌 *narrow gauge* **kyōki**
狭量 *narrow-minded* **kyōryō**
狭窄 *contraction, stricture* **kyōsaku**
狭小 *narrow & cramped* **kyōshō**
狭霧 *fog, mist* **sagiri**
手狭 *narrow passage, narrows* **tezema**
狭心症 *angina pectoris* **kyōshinshō**
所狭い *crowded area* **tokorosemai**
狭苦しい *cramped, narrow* **semakurushii**

細*lender, 138*	路*oad, 405*
岐*orked-road, 704*	道*ath, 312*
挟*orked, 762*	径*ath, 888*

挟*cissor, 762*

636-C

挟orked-road 狭arrows to the 峡avine of sparrows...

峡avine　　　峡anyon

山 (mountain)

峡

KYŌ
ravine, canyon, gorge

FLIP: 5.0.b. Left & Right

地峡 *isthmus* **chikyō**
海峡 *strait, channel, narrows* **kaikyō**
マラッカ海峡 *Straits of Malacca* **marakka kaikyō**
峡間 *ravine, in-between mountains* **kyōkan**
峡谷 *gorge, ravine, canyon* **kyōkoku**
峡湾 *fjord, fiord* **kyōwan**
山峡 *mountain gorge* **sankyō, yamakai**
峡帯域 *narrow-band* **kyōtaiiki**

渓*avine, 97*	岬*ape, 646*
谷*avine, 492*	山*ountain, 172*
岳*ountain peak, 28*	深*eep, 788*

狭*arrow, 763*

637-A
Rare 酸cid to 唆ntice 俊enius mice...

酸cid   酸xygen

酉 (liquor)

FLIP: 6.0.a. Left (flat)

su(i), SAN
acid, oxygen

塩酸 *hydrochloric-, muriatic acid* **ensan**
蟻酸 *formic acid* **gisan**
砒酸 *arsenic acid* **hisan**
胃酸 *stomach acid* **isan**
核酸 *nucleic acid* **kakusan**
尿酸 *uric acid, urine acid* **nyōsan**
乳酸 *lactic acid* **nyūsan**
酪酸 *butyric acid* **rakusan**
硫酸 *sulphuric-, vitriolic acid* **ryūsan**
酢酸 *acetic acid* **sakusan**
酸鼻 *appalling, horrible* **sanbi**
酸度 *acidity, sourness* **sando**
酸化 *oxidization, oxidation* **sanka**
酸欠 *oxygen shortage* **sanketsu**
酸味 *sourness, acidity* **sanmi**
酸敗 *acidify* **sanpai**
酸類 *acid type* **sanrui**
酸性 *acidity* **sansei**
酸洗 *pickling, pickle-making* **sansen**

酸素 *oxygen* **sanso**
酸雨 *acid rain* **san'u**
青酸 *cyanic-, prussic acid* **seisan**
辛酸 *trials & tribulations* **shinsan**
硝酸 *nitric acid* **shōsan**
蓚酸 *oxalic acid* **shūsan**
耐酸 *acid-resistant substance* **taisan**
炭酸 *carbonic acid* **tansan**
亜硫酸 *sulphurous acid* **aryūsan**
酸っぱい *acid, tart, sour, vinegary* **suppai**
甘酸っぱい *sweet & sour* **amazuppai**

酢*inegar, 723*   保*reserve, 552*
漬*ickling, 823*

酪*airy, 670*

637-B
Rare 酸cid to 唆ntice 俊enius mice...

唆ntice   唆nstigate

口 (mouth)

FLIP: 6.0.a. Left (flat)
Facing: 4.0. ⟐⟐⟐ Apart

sosonoka(su), SA
entice, instigate, inveigle, provoke, tempt, incite

教唆 *instigation, incitement* **kyōsa**
教唆者 *instigator, provocateur* **kyōsasha**
教唆罪 *instigating to a crime* **kyōsazai**
示唆 *suggestion, hint, implication* **shisa**

惑*emptation, 139*   釣*llure, 697*
誘*emptation, 895*   幻*antasy, 88*

俊*enius, 765*

637-C

Rare 酸cid to 唆ntice 俊enius mice...

人⇔亻 (person)

俊*enius*　　俊*rilliant*

SHUN
genius, brilliant, clever, smart

Facing: 4.0. 🐟🐟 Apart

英俊 *talent, gifted person* **eishun**
俊馬 *superior horse* **shunme**
俊抜 *uncommon, superior* **shunbatsu**
俊敏 *quick, keen, sharp* **shunbin**
俊童 *wonder boy, genius child* **shundō**
俊英 *talent, gifted person* **shun'ei**
俊逸 *genius, brilliant* **shun'itsu**
俊傑 *genius, brilliant* **shunketsu**
俊才 *genius, brilliant* **shunsai**
俊秀 *specially-gifted person* **shunshū**
俊足 *fast runner* **shunsoku**
俊徳 *excellent virtues* **shuntoku**

才*enius, 185*	秀*xcellence, 383*
傑*xcellence, 921*	優*xcellence, 556*

唆*ntice, 764*

638-A

派actions of 衆eoples' 脈eins to 派ispatch Citizen Kane...

水⇔氵 (water)

❶派*action*　❷派*ispatch*

HA
faction, clique, sect; dispatch

Facing: 2.2. East ☞ (V)

❶別派 *breakaway sect* **beppa**
分派 *denomination, branch, sect* **bunpa**
学派 *school of thought, ~persuasion* **gakuha**
派閥 *faction, clique* **habatsu**
派手 *showy, gorgeous, gaudy* **hade**
派生 *derive-, stem from* **hasei**
派生語 *derivative word* **haseigo**
派出所 *police box* **hashutsusho**
一派 *sect, demonination* **ippa**
各派 *all parties, all concerned* **kakuha**
硬派 *hard-liners, hawkists* **kōha**
軟派 *moderate party, flirting* **nanpa**
立派 *splendid, fine, magnificent* **rippa**
左派 *left wing* **saha**
宗派 *religious sect, denomination* **shūha**
党派 *party, faction* **tōha**
特派 *special team* **tokuha**
右派 *right wing* **uha**
抽象派 *abstractionism* **chūshōha**

反対派 *opposition, opponents* **hantaiha**
過激派 *radicals, extremists* **kagekiha**
穏健派 *moderates, middle ground* **onkenha**
賛成派 *supporters, proponents* **sanseiha**
戦後派 *post-war generation* **sengoha**
田中派 *Tanaka faction* **tanaka-ha**
❷派米 *dispatch to the US* **habei**
派兵 *troop deployment, ~stationing* **hahei**
派遣 *dispatch, deployment* **haken**
派遣軍 *expeditionary troops* **hakengun**
急派 *emergency squad, rescue mission* **kyūha**
増派 *reinforcement, redeployment* **zōha**

閥*action, 946*	送*ispatch, 708*
盟*lliance, 21*	搬*ransport, 323*
連*lliance, 305*	輸*hipment, 660*

脈*eins, 766*

638-B

派actions of 衆eoples' 脈eins to 派ispatch Citizen Kane...

血 (blood)

衆ultitude　　衆rowd

FLIP: 3.0.a. Top (flat)

SHŪ, SHU
multitude, crowd, populace, throng

聴衆 audience, viewers, listeners **chōshū**
群衆 crowd, throng, multitude **gunshū**
会衆 audience, attendance **kaishū**
観衆 spectators, viewers **kanshū**
公衆 general public **kōshū**
民衆 the people, the masses **minshū**
男衆 male servant **otokoshū**
衆望 public confidence **shūbō**
衆知 common wisdom, popular knowledge **shūchi**
衆議 public discussion **shūgi**
衆愚 mob, vulgar **shūgu**
衆愚政治 mob rule, anarchy **shūgu seiji**
衆評 public opinion **shūhyō**
衆意 "will of the people..." **shūi**
衆人 common masses, common people **shūjin**
衆目 public attention, ~popular acclaim **shūmoku**
衆論 views of the many **shūron**
衆徒 many priests **shūto**
大衆 general public **taishū**

有衆 with popular mandate **yūshū**
民衆化 democratisation **minshūka**
衆議院 diet lower house **shūgiin**
大衆性 political popularity **taishūsei**
若い衆 young men & women **wakaishū**
全民衆 the entire masses **zenminshū**
公衆電話 pay phone **kōshū denwa**
衆議一決 unanimous vote **shūgi ikketsu**
衆口一致 unanimity **shūkō icchi**
アメリカ合衆国 United States of America **amerika gasshūkoku**

世orld, 411	公ublic, 180
界orld, 365	群lock, 259
民eople, 495	

派action, 765

638-C

派actions of 衆eoples' 脈eins to 派ispatch Citizen Kane...

肉⇔月 (flesh, body part)

脈eins　　脈rtery

Facing: 2.2. East ☞ (V)
Facing: 4.0. ☜☞ Apart

MYAKU
veins, artery, pulse

分脈 branch **bunmyaku**
文脈 language context **bunmyaku**
地脈 mineral line deposits **chimyaku**
動脈 artery, vein **dōmyaku**
岩脈 dike **ganmyaku**
語脈 word context, literary meaning **gomyaku**
平脈 normal pulse **heimyaku**
人脈 personal connexion, ~influence **jinmyaku**
静脈 vein, artery **jōmyaku**
静脈瘤 varix **jōmyakuryū**
静脈注射 intravenous injection **jōmyaku chūsha**
血脈 blood vessel, ~artery **ketsumyaku**
気脈 collusion, secret deal **kimyaku**
金脈 financial connexion **kinmyaku**
鉱脈 vein of ore, lode **kōmyaku**
命脈 life, lifeline **meimyaku**
脈管 blood vessel, ~artery **myakkan**
脈動 pulsation, pulse beat **myakudō**
脈拍 pulse, pulse beat **myakuhaku**

脈搏 pulse, pulse beat **myakuhaku**
脈脈 continuous, uninterrupted **myakumyaku**
脈絡 logical connection, coherence **myakuraku**
乱脈 disorder, chaos **ranmyaku**
山脈 mountain ranges **sanmyaku**
死脈 dead pulse, no pulse **shimyaku**
支脈 spur, feeder **shimyaku**
水脈 waterway **suimyaku**
葉脈 vein, artery, nerve **yōmyaku**
中央脈 midrib **chūōmyaku**
不整脈 arrhythmia **fuseimyaku**

血lood, 20	臓rgans, 565
結onnect, 227	肝iver, 711
絡onnect, 826	

派action, 765

639-A

Beneath the 桟*lank-bridge,* 銭*oins of Nemo* 残*emain in a* 浅*hallow...*

金 (metal)

銭*oins* 銭*etal money*

zeni, SEN
coins, metal money

FLIP: 6.0.a. Left (flat)
Facing: 2.2. East ☞ (V)

悪銭 *dirty money, blood money* **akusen**
泡銭 *undeserved money* **abukuzeni**
米銭 *US coins* **beisen**
賃銭 *wages, salary* **chinsen**
銅銭 *copper coins* **dōsen**
端銭 *small coins* **hasen**
橋銭 *tollbridge fee* **hashisen**
日銭 *daily cash flow* **hizeni**
金銭 *money, cash, coins* **kinsen**
古銭 *old coins, numismatics* **kosen**
古銭学 *numismatics* **kosengaku**
口銭 *commission; profit* **kōsen**
小銭 *small coins, loose change* **kozeni**
身銭 *one's own money* **mizeni**
無銭 *penniless, indigent, poor* **musen**
賽銭 *cash offering at shrine* **saisen**
銭貨 *coins* **senka**
銭湯 *public-, cheap bathhouse* **sentō**
寺銭 *gambling fee* **terasen**

釣銭 *loose change, spare coins* **tsurisen**
宿銭 *lodging charges* **yadosen**
湯銭 *public bathhouse fee* **yusen**
銭箱 *cash box* **zenibako**
銭金 *money, coins* **zenikane**
銭儲け *money earner* **zenimōke**
木戸銭 *entrance-, admission fee* **kidosen**
守銭奴 *miser, thrifty, frugal* **shusendo**
渡し銭 *ferryboat fee* **watashisen**
銭入れ *coin purse, wallet* **zeniire**

> 鋳*intage, 440*
> 金*oney, 25*
> 幣*oney, 171*

> 鋳*asting, 440*

639-B

Beneath the 桟*lank-bridge,* 銭*oins of Nemo* 残*emain in a* 浅*hallow...*

歹 (dried bones)

❶残*emain* ❷残*ruelty*

noko(ru), noko(su), ZAN
remain, leave-behind, stay; cruelty

Facing: 4.0. ☜☞ Apart

❶ 敗残 *failure, defeat* **haizan**
残高 *outstanding balance, remainder* **zandaka**
残影 *traces, contours, shadows* **zan'ei**
残骸 *remains, wreckage, ruins* **zangai**
残額 *outstanding balance, remainder* **zangaku**
残業 *overtime work* **zangyō**
残金 *money left, outstanding balance* **zankin**
残光 *sunset afterglow* **zankō**
残念 *disappointment, regrets, misgivings* **zannen**
残飯 *food leftovers* **zanpan**
残品 *remaining stock* **zanpin**
残雪 *remaining snow* **zansetsu**
残暑 *lingering summer heat* **zansho**
残敵 *enemy remnants* **zanteki**
残党 *party remnants* **zantō**
残余 *remainder, the rest* **zanyo**
残像 *lingering image* **zanzō**
残存 *subsisting, surviving, getting by* **zanzon**
居残り *leave behind (a child)* **inokori**

売残り *left unsold merchandise* **urenokori**
言い残す *tell, leave word* **iinokosu**
生き残る *survive, remain alive* **ikinokoru**
書き残す *leave behind in writing* **kakinokosu**
思い残す *regrets, misgivings* **omoinokosu**
使い残す *leave unused* **tsukainokosu**
積み残す *leave unloaded* **tsuminokosu**
❷ 残酷 *cruel, brutal, atrocious* **zankoku**
残忍 *cruelty, atrocity, barbarity* **zannin**
残虐行為 *cruelty, atrocity* **zangyaku kōi**

> 滞*taying, 557* 遺*eave-behind, 914*
> 留*taying, 128* 置*eave-behind, 420*

> 銭*oins, 767*

639-C

Beneath the 桟*lank-bridge,* 銭*oins of Nemo* 残*emain in a* 浅*hallow...*

水 ⇔ 氵 (water)

浅*hallow*　　浅*rivolous*

asa(i), SEN
shallow, frivolous, flimsy

Facing: 4.0. 〜〜 Apart

浅はか　*frivolous, foolish* **asahaka**
浅ましい　*contemptible, shameful* **asamashii**
浅田　*shallow paddy* **asada**
浅手　*minor wounds* **asade**
浅黄　*light yellow* **asagi**
浅葱　*light yellow* **asagi**
浅緑　*light green* **asamidori**
浅蜊　*short-neck clam* **asari**
浅瀬　*shoal, ford* **asase**
浅学　*superficial knowledge* **sengaku**
浅海　*shallow sea, shallow waters* **senkai**
浅見　*shallow view, narrow vision* **senken**
浅紅　*light red, pink* **senkō**
浅薄　*superficiality, flimsy, shallow* **senpaku**
浅慮　*imprudence, narrow-minded* **senryo**
浅才　*incompetence, lack of ability, inept* **sensai**
深浅　*depth, abyss, bottom* **shinsen**
遠浅　*shoal away from the shore* **tooasa**
浅黒い　*dark, tanned* **asaguroi**

浅知恵　*shallow-witted* **asajie**

瀬*hallows, 562*
狭*arrow, 763*

残*emain, 767*

639-D

Beneath the 桟*lank-bridge,* 銭*oins of Nemo* 残*emain in a* 浅*hallow...*

木 (wooden)

桟*lank bridge*

kakehashi, SAN
plank bridge

Facing: 2.2. East ☞ (V)

桟敷　*upper box, ~stand* **sajiki**
⇒天井桟敷　*upper gallery* **tenjō sajiki**
桟橋　*pier, quay, wharf* **sanbashi**
⇒浮き桟橋　*floating pier, ~wharf* **ukisanbashi**
桟俵　*round straw lid (rice sacks)* **sandawara**
桟道　*plank road, hanging bridge* **sandō**
桟梯子　*frame ladder* **sanhashigo**

懸*anging, 566*　　架*anging, 202*
掛*ang up, 107*　　河*iver, 877*

残*emain, 767*

640-A

寝leeping 侵nvader, 浸mmersed in cider...

宀 (cover, lid)

寝leeping

ne(ru), ne(kasu), SHIN
sleeping, drowsy, snoozing

FLIP: 7.3.b. Right Bottom (stem)
Facing: 1.2. ☜ West (V)

寝かす *put to sleep, put to bed* **nekasu**
寝込む *be in bed, fall asleep* **nekomu**
寝つく *fall asleep, hit to the bed* **netsuku**
寝そべる *stretch out in waking up* **nesoberu**
昼寝 *catnap, siesta, afternoon sleep* **hirune**
寝汗 *nocturnal sweat* **nease**
寝袋 *sleeping bag* **nebukuro**
寝床 *bed, sleeping floor* **nedoko**
寝顔 *sleepy face* **negao**
寝言 *talking asleep* **negoto**
寝息 *sound asleep, breathing asleep* **neiki**
寝首 *beheading a sleeping person* **nekubi**
寝酒 *nightcap, last drink before bed* **nezake**
楽寝 *good-, sound sleep* **rakune**
寝具 *beddings, bedclothes* **shingu**
寝室 *bedroom* **shinshitsu**
就寝 *go to sleep* **shūshin**
宵寝 *sleeping early* **yoine**
転寝 *doze, nap* **utatane**

朝寝坊 *oversleeping, late riser* **asanebō**
抱き寝 *sleeping with baby on one's chest* **dakine**
不寝番 *night watchman, ~sentry* **fushinban**
ごろ寝 *sleeping w/o changing clothes* **gorone**
寝苦しい *sleeping difficulties* **negurushii**
寝間着 *pyjamas, bedclothes* **nemaki**
寝起き *awakening, getting up* **neoki**
寝小便 *bed-wetting* **neshōben**
寝煙草 *smoking in bed* **netabako**
雑魚寝 *sleeping crowded on the floor* **zakone**
寝過ごす *oversleep, wake up late* **nesugosu**

眠leeping, 495	泊leep-over, 742
睡leeping, 948	宿odging, 448

浸mmerse, 770

640-B

寝leeping 侵nvader, 浸mmersed in cider...

人⇔亻 (person)

侵iolate   侵nvade

oka(su), SHIN
violate, invade, infringe, intrude, encroach

FLIP: 7.3.b. Right Bottom (stem)

侵奪 *usurpation, arrogation* **shindatsu**
侵害 *infringement, violation* **shingai**
⇒版権侵害 *copyrights infringement, plagiarism*
　　hanken shingai
⇒著作権侵害 *plagiarism, literary piracy*
　　chosakuken shingai
侵撃 *invade & attack* **shingeki**
侵攻 *invasion, encroaching* **shinkō**
侵入 *invasion, incursion, intrusion, trespassing*
　　shinnyū
⇒家宅侵入 *break-in, trespassing* **kataku shinnyū**
侵入者 *invader, intruder, trespasser* **shinnyūsha**
侵犯 *invasion, infringement* **shinpan**
侵略 *aggression, invasion* **shinryaku**
⇒不侵略 *non-aggression* **fushinryaku**
侵略軍 *invading army* **shinryakugun**
侵略国 *aggressor nation* **shinryakukoku**
侵略者 *aggressor, invader* **shinryakusha**
侵略的 *aggressive, domineering* **shinryakuteki**

侵略行為 *act of aggression* **shinryaku kōi**
侵略戦争 *war of aggression*
　　shinryaku sensō
侵食 *infringement, violation* **shinshoku**
侵蝕 *encroachment, corrosion* **shinshoku**
不可侵 *non-aggression, non-hostile* **fukashin**
不可侵条約 *non-aggression pact*
　　fukashin jōyaku
住居侵入罪 *house break-in, trespassing*
　　jūkyo shinnyūzai

禁rohibit, 560	障njury, 325	罪riminal, 289
害njury, 904	損njury, 410	犯riminal, 640
傷njury, 933	痛njury, 60	悪vil, 389

帰oming home, 784

640-C

寝leeping 侵nvader, 浸mmersed in cider.

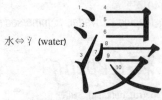

浸mmerse   浸oak

水 ⇔ 氵 (water)

hita(ru), hita(su), SHIN
immerse, soak, submerge, submerse

FLIP: 7.3.b. Right Bottom (stem)

含浸 impregnation **ganshin**
浸潤 permeation, infiltration **shinjun**
浸漬 immerse, dip, soak **shinseki**
浸染 permeate, infiltrate; dye **shinsen**
浸食 erosion, corrosion **shinshoku**
浸蝕 erosion, corrosion **shinshoku**
浸出 percolation, effusion **shinshutsu**
浸水 flooding, inundation **shinsui**
浸水家屋 flooded house **shinsui kaoku**
浸透 penetration, infiltration **shintō**
浸透圧 osmotic pressure **shintōatsu**
肺浸潤 pulmonary tuberculosis **haishinjun**
水浸し flooded, inundated **mizubitashi**
お浸し boiled greens & dressings **ohitashi**
酒浸り drunkenness, intoxication **sakebitari**
入り浸る overstay one's welcome **iribitaru**

漬mmerse, 823	潜ubmerge, 335
沈inking, 719	礁unken, 920

寝leep, 769

641-A

退ithdrawal of age 限imits brightened the 眼yes of hermits...

辶 (transport)

退ithdraw   退etreat

shirizo(ku), shirizo(keru), TAI
withdraw, retreat, vacate, abandon, back off, evacuate

Facing: 4.0. ⟵⟶ Apart

脱退 withdrawal, secession **dattai**
撃退 repulse, setback, retreat **gekitai**
敗退 defeat, retreat, losing a game **haitai**
引退 retirement, separation from work **intai**
隠退 seclusion from society **intai**
辞退 denial, refusal **jitai**
早退 leaving early **sōtai**
衰退 decline, decay, degeneration **suitai**
退部 quitting a school club **taibu**
退団 quitting a group membership **taidan**
退学 quitting a school **taigaku**
退位 royal abdication **taii**
退院 hospital discharge **taiin**
退場 leaving one's place, exit **taijō**
退化 degeneration, decadence **taika**
退官 resignation from a government post **taikan**
退行 regression, retrogression, relapse **taikō**
退却 retreat, withdrawal, retirement **taikyaku**
退去 retreat, withdrawal, leave **taikyo**

退任 retirement, separation from work **tainin**
退路 retreat route, exit route **tairo**
退勢 decline, decay, degeneration **taisei**
退席 leaving one's seat **taiseki**
退職 retirement, separation from work **taishoku**
退色 fading away, fading out **taishoku**
退出 leaving, withdrawal, exit **taishutsu**
退廷 court expulsion **taitei**
撤退 withdrawal, evacuation **tettai**
勇退 voluntary resignation **yūtai**
優退 retiring at one's primehood **yūtai**

却ithdraw, 387	斥ejection, 424
撤ithdraw, 843	排ejection, 795
罷ithdraw, 322	断ejection, 958
去eave-out, 360	否ejection, 300

逮rrest, 880

641-B

退*ithdrawal of age* 限*imits brightened the* 眼*yes of hermits...*

阝 ⇔ 阜 (village=left)

限*imit*　　限*oundary*

kagi(ru), GEN
limit, boundary, restriction, constraints, borderline, bottom-line, ceiling

Facing: 2.2. East ☞ (V)

分限 *percent, ratio* **bungen**
限度 *limit, boundary* **gendo**
限外 *beyond the limits, excess* **gengai**
限界 *limit, boundary* **genkai**
限定 *limitation, qualification* **gentei**
時限 *time limit, deadline* **jigen**
上限 *upper limit, maximum* **jōgen**
下限 *lower limit, minimum* **kagen**
権限 *authority, competence* **kengen**
期限 *time limit, term, period* **kigen**
⇒貸借期限 *loan period, life of a loan* **taishaku kigen**
刻限 *appointed time, ~hour* **kokugen**
極限 *limit, bounds, extremity* **kyokugen**
局限 *confines, limitation* **kyokugen**
門限 *curfew, prohibition hours* **mongen**
無限 *unlimited, limitless* **mugen**
南限 *southern limit* **nangen**
年限 *fixed term of years* **nengen**
⇒兵役年限 *length of military service* **heieki nengen**

⇒修業年限 *period of study* **shūgyō nengen**
日限 *fixed date* **nichigen**
際限 *limits, restrictions* **saigen**
制限 *limitation, restrictions* **seigen**
⇒漢字制限 *limitation of Kanji characters*
　　kanji seigen
象限 *quadrant* **shōgen**
定限 *limitation, restrictions* **teigen**
有限 *finite, limited* **yūgen**
有限会社 *limited partnership, ~company*
　　yūgen gaisha
限り無い *boundless, limitless* **kagirinai**

涯*imit, 890*	満*aturate, 567*	境*oundary, 839*
定*efinite, 550*	最*aximum, 423*	囲*nclose, 361*

根*oot, 772*

641-C

退*ithdrawal of age* 限*imits brightened the* 眼*yes of hermits...*

目 (eyesight, visual)

眼*yesight*　　眼*isual*

manako, me, GAN, GEN
eyesight, visual, optical, vision

FLIP: 6.0.a. Left (flat)

着眼 *aim, objective* **chakugan**
血眼 *bloodshot eye* **chimanako**
複眼 *crossed eyes* **fukugan**
眼科 *ophthalmology, eye medicine* **ganka**
眼界 *field of vision* **gankai**
眼気 *eye disease* **ganki**
眼光 *sight penetration, visibility* **gankō**
眼鏡 *glasses, eyeglasses* **megane, gankyō**
⇒双眼鏡 *binoculars, field glasses* **sōgankyō**
⇒天眼鏡 *magnifying glass* **tengankyō**
眼球 *eyeball* **gankyū**
眼目 *point, main object* **ganmoku**
眼識 *insights, image* **ganshiki**
眼帯 *eye-patch* **gantai**
義眼 *artificial eye, fake eye* **gigan**
銃眼 *loophole, escape clause; crenel* **jūgan**
開眼 *spiritual awakening, enlightenment* **kaigan**
検眼 *eye check up, visual exam* **kengan**
近眼 *near-, short-sightedness* **kingan**

肉眼 *naked eye* **nikugan**
老眼 *presbyopia* **rōgan**
心眼 *minds eye* **shingan**
主眼 *principal object* **shugan**
点眼 *applying eye drops* **tengan**
批評眼 *critical eye* **hihyōgan**
色眼鏡 *coloured-, sun glasses* **iromegane**
眼差し *look, eyes* **manazashi**
虫眼鏡 *magnifying glass* **mushi megane**
千里眼 *clairvoyance, second sight* **senrigan**
審美眼 *sense of beauty, aesthetic* **shinbigan**

目*ye, 462*	眺*aze at, 215*	覧*bserve, 592*
見*eeing, 307*	夢*ream, 167*	視*bserve, 815*

眠*leep, 495*

642-A

根oots of 恨rudges: 銀ilver coins for judges...

根*oot*　　　根*undamental*

木 (wooden)

ne, KON
root, fundamental

Facing: 2.2. East ☞ (V)

病根　disease, evil **byōkon**
大根　radish **daikon**
語根　word origin, root of a word **gokon**
垣根　fence, hedge **kakine**
禍根　root of evil **kakon**
心根　real-, true feelings **kokorone, shinkon**
根源　root, source, origin **kongen**
根元　root, source, origin **kongen**
根性　disposition, nature **konjō**
根気　perseverance, endurance, diligence **konki**
根基　root, source, origin **konki**
根拠　basis, foundation, authority **konkyo**
根本　basis, foundation **konpon**
根粒　root nodule **konryū**
根菜　root crops **konsai**
根底　basis, foundation; bottomline **kontei**
根絶　eradication, extermination **konzetsu**
球根　bulb, tuber **kyūkon**
根城　base of operations **nejiro**

根雪　incessant snow blanket **neyuki**
精根　energy, vigour, vitality **seikon**
性根　perseverance, endurance, diligence **shōkon**
屋根　roof, roofing **yane**
善根　good deeds, altruism, charity **zenkon**
根負け　endurance limit **konmake**
根深い　deep-seated **nebukai**
根分け　parting the roots **newake**
根差す　take root **nezasu**
根付く　take root **nezuku**
根強い　deep-rooted, strong, firm **nezuyoi**

基*oundation*, 590	旨*ain point*, 242
拠*asis*, 473	礎*ornerstone*, 166
本*ain*, 461	要*ecessity*, 419

恨*rudge*, 772

642-B

根oots of 恨rudges: 銀ilver coins for judges...

恨*rudge*　　　恨*ad-blood*

心⇔忄⇔⺗ (feelings)

ura(mu), ura(meshii), KON
grudge, bad blood, ill-will

Facing: 2.2. East ☞ (V)

恨み　grudge, hatred, ill-feeling **urami**
恨み言　bad mouthing behind **uramigoto**
恨む　bear a grudge, be disgusted **uramu**
恨めしい　reproachful, resentful **urameshii**
怨恨　grudge, enmity, bad blood **enkon**
遺恨　grudge, ill will, enmity **ikon**
悔恨　remorse, regret, repentance **kaikon**
恨事　regrettable act **konji**
私恨　personal grudge, bad blood **shikon**
多恨　great discontent **takon**
⇒多情多恨　sensibility, sensitivity **tajō takon**
痛恨　great sorrow, bitter regret **tsūkon**
痛恨事　matter of bitterness **tsūkonji**
片恨み　one-sided grudge (not mutual) **kataurami**
逆恨み　bad blood, grudge, ill will **sakaurami**

嫌*espise*, 805	侮*espise*, 711
卑*espise*, 936	憎*atred*, 837

根*oot*, 772

642-C

根*oots* of 恨*rudges:* 銀*ilver coins for judges...*

金 (metal)

銀*ilver*

shirogane, GIN
silver

FLIP: 6.0.a. Left (flat)
Facing: 2.2. East ☞ (V)

銀メダル *silver medal* **ginmedaru**
銀盤 *silver plate* **ginban**
銀縁 *silver-rimmed glasses* **ginbuchi**
銀河 *galaxy, milky way* **ginga**
銀紙 *aluminium foil* **gingami**
銀貨 *silver coin* **ginka**
銀鉱 *silver mine* **ginkō**
銀行 *bank* **ginkō**
⇒血液銀行 *blood bank* **ketsueki ginkō**
⇒精液銀行 *sperm bank* **seieki ginkō**
銀行員 *bank clerk* **ginkōin**
銀行家 *banker* **ginkōka**
銀幕 *silver screen, movies* **ginmaku**
銀杯 *silver cup* **ginpai**
銀髪 *silver hair, grey hair* **ginpatsu**
銀鈴 *silver bell* **ginrei**
銀輪 *silver ring* **ginrin**
銀星 ① *silver star* **ginsei, ginboshi**
銀星 ② *upset defeat in sumo* **ginsei, ginboshi**

銀賞 *silver award, the second best* **ginshō**
銀座 *Ginza, Tōkyō* **ginza**
白銀 *white silver* **hakugin, shirogane**
銀杏 *ginkgo tree* **ichō, ginnan**
純銀 *pure silver, solid silver* **jungin**
金銀 *gold & silver* **kingin**
日銀 *Bank of Japan* **nichigin**
水銀 *mercury* **suigin**
銀婚式 *silver wedding anniversary* **ginkonshiki**
銀鍍金 *silver-plating* **ginmekki**
硝酸銀 *silver nitrate* **shōsangin**

金*old, 25*　　　金*oney, 25*　　札*oney-bills, 685*
貴*recious, 913*　幣*oney, 171*
宝*reasure, 92*　財*reasury, 186*

録*ecord, 841*

643-A

校*roofreading of* " 校*chool* 較*omparison*" *to end, deadline* 絞*ightened...*

木 (wooden)

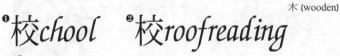

❶校*chool*　❷校*roofreading*

KŌ
school; proofreading, collate

FLIP: 7.0.b2. Right (stem)

❶母校 *alma mater, one's old school* **bokō**
復校 *return to school after a long absence* **fukkō**
学校 *school* **gakkō**
下校 *coming home from school* **gekō**
閉校 *"school closed..."* **heikō**
帰校 *return to school* **kikō**
校長 *school principal, school master* **kōchō**
校外 *off campus* **kōgai**
校医 *school physician* **kōi**
校歌 *school song* **kōka**
校旗 *school flag* **kōki**
高校 *high school* **kōkō**
校訓 *school motto* **kōkun**
校内 *on campus, school premises* **kōnai**
校舎 *school building* **kōsha**
校史 *school history* **kōshi**
校章 *school badge* **kōshō**
校則 *school regulations* **kōsoku**
校庭 *school garden* **kōtei**

将校 *military academy* **shōkō**
登校 *attending school* **tōkō**
男子校 *boys school* **danshikō**
女子校 *girls school* **joshikō**
不登校 *school non-attendance* **futōkō**
姉妹校 *sister school* **shimaikō**
神学校 *seminary, convent* **shingakkō**
❷校本 *annotated text* **kōhon**
校閲 *revision, re-writing, editing* **kōetsu**
校正 *proofreading* **kōsei**
校訂 *revision, re-writing, editing* **kōtei**
再校 *second proof* **saikō**
初校 *first proof* **shokō**

習*earning, 238*　読*eading, 260*　文*iteracy, 558*
教*ducate, 385*　書*ritings, 116*

校*ree-branch, 704*

643-B
校roofreading of " 校chool 較omparison" to end, deadline 絞ightened...

車 (vehicle, wheel)

較*ompare* 較*ontrast*

kura(beru), KAKU, KŌ
compare, contrast

比較 *comparison, contrast* **hikaku**
比較的 *comparatively, relatively* **hikakuteki**
比較級 *comparative degree* **hikakukyū**
比較性 *comparison* **hikakusei**
比較文学 *comparative literature*
　　　hikaku bungaku
比較検討 *comparison, examination*
　　　hikaku kentō
比較言語学 *comparative linguistics*
　　　hikaku gengogaku
較差 *range in between* **kakusa**
較量 *comparison, contrast* **kōryō**
較正 *calibration* **kōsei**

FLIP: 5.0.b. Left & Right

比*ompare, 466*	価*orth , 35*
並*arallel, 444*	値*orth , 783*
横*idewards, 197*	評*ommentary, 701*

絞*ighten, 774*

643-C
校roofreading of " 校chool 較omparison" to end, deadline 絞ightened...

糸 (thread, continuity)

絞*ighten* 絞*queeze*

shi(meru), shi(maru), shi(boru), TEI
squeeze, tighten, compress, strangle, wring

絞刑 *death penalty by hanging* **kōkei**
絞殺 *death by strangulation* **kōsatsu**
絞罪 *death penalty by hanging* **kōzai**
絞り粕 *strained sake lees* **shiborikasu**
絞り出す *press out, squeeze out* **shiboridasu**
絞り込み *focusing, concentrating* **shiborikomi**
絞り染め *tie-dyeing* **shiborizome**
絞り上げる *squeezing money* **shiboriageru**
絞め殺す *death by strangulation* **shimekorosu**
絞首台 *gallows, gibbet, noose* **kōshudai**
絞首刑 *death by hanging* **kōshukei**
豆絞り *splattered spots pattern* **mameshibori**
お絞り *squeezed towelette* **oshibori**
振り絞る① *exert, bring to bear* **furishiboru**
振り絞る② *shriek, scream, cry out, yell* **furishiboru**
引き絞る *draw to the full* **hikishiboru**
知恵を絞る *rack one's mind* **chie o shiboru**

FLIP: 7.0.b2. Right (stem)

締*ighten, 432*
搾*queeze, 722*
圧*ressure, 632*

統*overn, 885*

644-A

雄ourage of 離eparated 雄asculine 稚hildren praised so often...

隹 (long-tailed birds)

❶雄ourage ❷雄asculine

osu,o,YŪ
courage, bravery, heroic; masculine

Facing: 2.2. East ☞ (V)

❶英雄 hero, courageous **eiyū**
群雄 two rival barons **gunyū**
雄弁 eloquence, articulate **yūben**
雄武 courage, bravery **yūbu**
雄大 grand, magnificent **yūdai**
雄断 courageous decision **yūdan**
雄飛 full of ambition, high aspiration **yūhi**
雄峰 majestic peak **yūhō**
雄渾 sublime, bold **yūkon**
雄猛 courageous, daring **yūmō**
雄姿 imposing figure **yūshi**
雄志 lofty ideals **yūshi**
雄心 heroic spirit **yūshin**
雄壮 courageous, gallant **yūsō**
雄図 bold-, daring plan **yūto**
雄略天皇 Emperor Yūryaku (456-479)
　　　 yūryakyu tennō
❷雄花 masculine flower **obana**
雄滝 waterfalls' bigger side **odaki**

雄鳥 rooster, cock **ondori**
雄鶏 rooster, cock **ondori**
雄蕊 stamen **oshibe**
雄蜂 drone **osubachi**
雄犬 male dog **osuinu**
雄馬 stallion, male horse **osuuma**
雄牛 male cattle, ox, bull **oushi**
両雄 two great men **ryōyū**
雌雄 animal gender **shiyū**
雄性 manliness, manhood **yūsei**
雄雄しい manly, macho **ooshii**

壮asculine, 367	郎asculine, 404	冒ourage, 401
男asculine, 597	敢ourage, 449	勇ourage, 59
僕asculine, 157	胆ourage, 740	

稚hildren, 776

644-B

雄ourage of 離eparated 雄asculine 稚hildren praised so often...

隹 (long-tailed birds)

離eparate 離reak-off

hana(reru); hana(su), RI
separate, break-off, detached, take-apart, apart

FLIP: 6.1. Left Top
Facing: 2.2. East ☞ (V)

離れ島 solitary island, remote island **hanarejima**
離れ離れ break up, get scattered **hanare banare**
別離 separation, breaking off **betsuri**
分離 separation, division **bunri**
電離 ionisation **denri**
背離 estrangement, alienation **hairi**
隔離 isolation, quarantine **kakuri**
距離 distance, mileage **kyori**
⇒遠距離 long distance, faraway **enkyori**
離別 leaving, parting, breaking off **ribetsu**
離脱 leaving, seceding **ridatsu**
離縁 divorce, annulment **rien**
離合 alliance, fusion **rigō**
離反 estrangement, alienation **rihan**
離間 estrangement, alienation **rikan**
離婚 divorce, annulment **rikon**
離郷 leaving one's village **rikyō**
離日 leaving Japan for good **rinichi**
離農 quit farming **rinō**

離乳 weaning a baby **rinyū**
離陸 aircraft take-off **ririku**
離散 scatter, dispersal **risan**
離籍 removal from family register **riseki**
離床 leaving one's sick bed **rishō**
離礁 raising a sunken ship **rishō**
離職 quitting one's job, retirement **rishoku**
離山 quitting the temple; sole mountain **rizan**
流離 wandering, roaming **ryūri**
遊離 isolation, seclusion, separation **yūri**
離心率 eccentricity, idiosyncratic **rishinritsu**

別eparate, 866	距istance, 207
違ifference, 796	隔istance, 963
差ifference, 589	悠istant, 898
異ifferent, 239	遠istant, 916

難ifficulty, 927

644-C

雄*ourage of* 離*eparated* 雄*asculine* 稚*hildren praised so often...*

禾 (tree branch)

稚*hildren*　　稚*uvenile*

CHI
children, juvenile, kiddie, kiddo, young child

Facing: 2.2. East ☞ (V)

稚児　*young child* **chigo**
稚魚　*small fry, underling* **chigyo**
稚気　*childishness* **chiki**
稚拙　*childishness* **chisetsu**
丁稚　*apprentice, instructee* **decchi**
丁稚奉公　*apprenticeship* **decchi bōkō**
幼稚園　*kindergarten school* **yōchien**
幼稚園児　*kindergrader* **yōchienji**

児*hildren, 464*	孫*randchild, 263*
幼*hildhood, 88*	縁*inship, 675*
子*hildren, 456*	系*osterity, 262*
童*hildren, 564*	

雄*ourage, 775*

645-A

雑*arious friends* 推*ecommend the* 准*unior trend...*

隹 (long-tailed birds)

雑*ssortment*　　雑*arious*

ZATSU, ZŌ
assortment, various, diverse, variety

FLIP: 6.2. Left Bottom

複雑　*complex, complicated* **fukuzatsu**
繁雑　*complicated, complex, intricate* **hanzatsu**
混雑　*congestion, jamming* **konzatsu**
乱雑　*disorderly, confused* **ranzatsu**
雑貨　*groceries, miscellaneous goods* **zakka**
雑感　*various, diverse thoughts* **zakkan**
雑件　*various, diverse matters* **zakken**
雑記　*miscellaneous notes* **zakki**
雑菌　*various-, diverse germs* **zakkin**
雑穀　*cereals, grain* **zakkoku**
雑居　*multi-families living in one house* **zakkyo**
雑魚　*small fry, unimportant fellow* **zako**
⇒雑魚寝　*sleeping in a huddle* **zakone**
雑費　*miscellaneous expenses* **zappi**
雑誌　*magazine, journal* **zasshi**
雑種　*crossbreed, hybrid, mongrel* **zasshu**
雑草　*weeds* **zassō**
雑損　*miscellaneous losses* **zasson**
雑学　*vast knowledge* **zatsugaku**

雑事　*miscellaneous affairs, routine work* **zatsuji**
雑婚　*communal marriage (tribe)* **zakkon**
雑念　*varied thoughts* **zatsunen**
雑音　*street noise, chattering* **zatsuon**
雑用　*various businesses* **zatsuyō**
雑多　*miscellaneous, mixed* **zatta**
雑沓　*hustle & bustle* **zattō**
雑巾　*floorcloth, duster, mop* **zōkin**
雑煮　*rice cakes & vegetables soup* **zōni**
雑人　*low-class people, the masses* **zōnin**
雑炊　*porridge of rice & vegetables* **zōsui**
雑貨店　*general shop, grocery* **zakkaten**

諸*arious, 794*	紛*ixture, 778*
多*lenty, 187*	類*ategory, 156*
混*ixture, 38*	種*ategory, 430*

雌*emale-animal, 929*

645-B

雑*arious friends* 推*ecommend the* 准*unior trend...*

推*ecommend*　　　推*nfer*

手⇔扌 (hand, manual)

o(su), SUI
recommend, infer, advice

Facing: 4.0. 〰🔲〰 Apart

推し量る *guess, presume* **oshihakaru**
推し進める *push, shove, thrust* **oshisusumeru**
邪推 *baseless accusation* **jasui**
類推 *analogy, guess, judging* **ruisui**
推断 *infer, deduce, conclude* **suidan**
推移 *change, transition, progress* **suii**
推計 *estimate, survey, quotation* **suikei**
推考 *infer, conjecture, imply* **suikō**
推敲 *polish, elaborate* **suikō**
推挙 *recommendation, endorsement* **suikyo**
推理 *inference, deduction* **suiri**
推論 *inference, reasoning* **suiron**
推量 *guess, inference* **suiryō**
推力 *propulsion, driving force* **suiryoku**
推算 *price quotation, estimation* **suisan**
推察 *guess, surmise, conjecture* **suisatsu**
推薦 *recommendation, endorsement* **suisen**
推薦状 *letter of recommendation* **suisenjō**
推進 *promotion, propulsion* **suishin**

⇒噴射推進 *jet propulsion* **funsha suishin**
推進力 *driving force* **suishinryoku**
推称 *praise, admiration* **suishō**
推奨 *recommendation, endorsement* **suishō**
推賞 *praise, extolling, adulation* **suishō**
推測 *guess, conjecture, surmise* **suisoku**
推戴 *"have as president..."* **suitai**
推定 *presumption, assumption* **suitei**
推薬 *propellant, stimulant* **suiyaku**
当て推量 *guesswork* **atezuiryō**
被推薦者 *nominated candidate* **hisuisensha**

勧*ecommend, 666*	承*pproval, 117*	
薦*ecommend, 68*	賛*pproval, 334*	
可*pproval, 15*		

准*atify, 777*

645-C

雑*arious friends* 推*ecommend the* 准*unior trend...*

准*unior*　　　准*ub-*

冫 (freezing, ice)

JUN
junior, sub-

Facing: 2.2. East ☞ (V)

批准 *ratification, adoption* **hijun**
准尉 *warrant officer* **jun'i**
准教員 *teaching assistant* **junkyōin**
准士官 *warrant officer* **junshikan**
准看護婦 *nurse assistant* **junkangofu**

薦*ecommend, 68*	締*onclude, 432*
勧*ecommend, 666*	決*onclude, 699*
推*ecommend, 777*	継*ontinuity, 958*

推*ecommend, 777*

646-A

紛*ixture of curry* 粉*owder,* 紛*istracted my clam chowder...*

糸 (thread, continuity)

紛*ixture*   紛*istract*

magi(reru), magi(rasu), magi(rawasu), magi(rawashii), FUN
mixture, distract, confused

Facing: 3.0. Across

紛れる *get mixed, ~diverted* **magireru**
紛い物 *counterfeit, sham, fake, phoney* **magaimono**
紛らわしい *misleading, ambiguous* **magirawashii**
紛れ込む *get lost among* **magirekomu**
紛れもない *obvious, apparent, evidently* **magiremonai**
紛れもなく *"without a doubt..."* **magiremonaku**
紛議 *discord, controversy* **fungi**
紛擾 *disturbance, trouble* **funjō**
紛糾 *complication, entanglement* **funkyū**
紛紛 *confusion, disarray* **funpun**
粉乱 *confusion, disorder, quagmire* **funran**
紛失 *lost, missing, unfound* **funshitsu**
紛失届 *report of lost article* **funshitsu todoke**
紛失物 *lost-, unfound item* **funshitsubutsu**
紛争 *dispute, strife, trouble* **funsō**
⇒学園紛争 *campus dispute* **gakuen funsō**
⇒労使紛争 *labour dispute, ~unrest* **rōshi funsō**
紛然 *confused, get entangled* **funzen**
内紛 *internal strife, infighting* **naifun**

気紛れ *whim, caprice* **kimagure**
苦し紛れ *distress, desperation* **kurushimagire**
悔し紛れ *vexing, spiteful* **kuyashimagire**
取り紛れる *engaged, entangled* **torimagireru**
言い紛らす *evasive talks, quibbling* **iimagirasu**

混*ixture, 38*
錯*ixed-up, 335*

粉*owder, 778*

646-B

紛*ixture of curry* 粉*owder,* 紛*istracted my clam chowder...*

米 (grains, rice)

粉*owder*

kona, ko, FUN
powder

FLIP: 6.0.b. Left (stem)

粉ミルク *powdered milk, dry milk* **konamiruku**
米粉 *rice flour* **beifun**
微粉 *fine powder* **bifun**
澱粉 *starch* **denpun**
粉末 *powder* **funmatsu**
粉乳 *powdered milk, dry milk* **funnyū**
粉砕 *smashing, crushing* **funsai**
粉飾 *embellishment, decorations* **funshoku**
粉飾決算 *bogus accounts* **funshoku kessan**
石粉 *powdered limestone* **ishiko**
花粉 *flower pollen* **kafun**
花粉症 *hay fever* **kafunshō**
黄粉 *soybean flour* **kinako**
金粉 *gold dust* **kinpun**
紅粉 *rouge & powder* **kōfun**
穀粉 *grain flour* **kokufun**
粉粉 *thinny tiny pieces* **konagona**
粉薬 *powdered drug* **konagusuri**
粉雪 *powdery-, fine snow* **konayuki**

骨粉 *powdered bone's* **koppun**
麦粉 *flour, wheat flour* **mugiko**
鱗粉 *fish scales* **rinpun**
製粉 *flour milling* **seifun**
精粉 *fine powder* **seifun**
脂粉 *cosmetics, makeup* **shifun**
汁粉 *rice cakes on red-bean syrupt* **shiruko**
鉄粉 *iron powder* **teppun**
火の粉 *spark of fire* **hinoko**
洗濯粉 *laundry detergent, ~powder* **sentakuko**
膨らし粉 *baking powder* **fukurashiko**

砕*ulverize, 761*   穀*ranule, 41*
微*light, 62*   粒*ranule, 656*

紛*istract, 778*

647-A

縫ewing kit left at the 峰ummit...

糸 (thread, continuity)

縫ewing　縫titching

nu(u), HŌ
　sewing, stitching

Facing: 3.0. ☞ ☜ Across
FLIP: 7.3.b. Right Bottom (stem)

縫い針 *sewing needle* **nuibari**
縫い箔 *embroidery & foiling* **nuihaku**
縫い方 *style of sewing* **nuikata**
縫い目 *seam, stitch, suture* **nuime**
縫い紋 *embroidered chest* **nuimon**
縫い物 *sewing, needlework* **nuimono**
縫い代 *margin to sew up* **nuishiro**
縫い込み *tucking* **nuikomi**
縫い取り *embroidery* **nuitori**
縫い上げ *a tuck (dress)* **nuiage**
縫いぐるみ *stuffed animal, animal costume* **nuigurumi**
弥縫 *patching up, mending clothes* **bihō**
弥縫策 *contingency-, stopgap measure* **bihōsaku**
縫糸 *sewing thread, thread spool* **nuiito**
裁縫 *sewing, stitching* **saihō**
縫合 *suture, stitching* **hōgō**
縫工 *seamstress, tailor* **hōkō**
縫製 *sewing, stitching* **hōsei**
縫製品 *sowing products* **hōseihin**

粗縫い *basting* **aranui**
縁縫い *hemstitching* **fuchinui**
袋縫い *double-stitching* **fukuronui**
絎縫い *blind stitch* **herinui**
仮縫い *temporary stitching* **karinui**
背縫い *back seam, rear sewing* **senui**
手縫い *hand sewing* **tenui**
伏せ縫い *hemming* **fusenui**
隠し縫い *concealed seams* **kakushinui**
裁ち縫い *sewing, stitching* **tachinui**
天衣無縫 *seamless, flawless* **ten'i muhō**

繰 *pinning*, 851	衣 *lothes*, 355
紡 *pinning*, 735	裁 *lothes*, 802
糸 *hread*, 375	服 *lothes*, 734
布 *loth*, 208	針 *eedle*, 692

峰 *ummit*, 779

647-B

縫ewing kit left at the 峰ummit...

山 (mountain)

峰ummit　峰ountain peak

mine, HŌ
　summit, mountain peak

FLIP: 6.0.a. Left (flat)
FLIP: 7.1. Right (Sort Of)

群峰 *numerous peaks* **gunpō**
高峰 *high mountain, lofty peak* **kōhō**
霊峰 *sacred mountain* **reihō**
連峰 *mountain ranges* **renpō**
主峰 *highest peak* **shuhō**
峻峰 *steep peak* **shunpō**
雄峰 *majestic peak* **yūhō**
喜望峰 *Cape of Good Hope* **kibōhō**
峰打ち *hitting with the back of a sword* **mineuchi**
未踏峰 *unclimbed mountain* **mitōhō**
最高峰 *highest peak, mountain summit* **saikōhō**
処女峰 *unclimbed peak* **shojohō**

岳 *ountain peak*, 28	渓 *avine*, 97
岬 *ape*, 646	谷 *avine*, 492
峡 *avine*, 763	高 *levated*, 435

縫 *ewing*, 779

648-A

語*alks that* 悟*nlighten, never forgotten...*

言 (speaking)

語*alking* 語*anguage*

kata(ru), GO

talking, language, lingo, speak, spoken, verbal, word

FLIP: 6.0.a. Left (flat)
FLIP: 7.3.a. Right Bottom (flat)

外語 *foreign word* **gaigo**
原語 *original word* **gengo**
語学 *linguistics, language study* **gogaku**
語源 *root word, etymology* **gogen**
語意 *word meaning* **goi**
語気 *speaking style* **goki**
語句 *words & phrases* **goku**
卑語 *vulgarism, slang* **higo**
補語 *word complement* **hogo**
熟語 *idiom, idiomatic phrase* **jukugo**
術語 *technical term, terminology* **jutsugo**
敬語 *honorific, term-of-respect* **keigo**
古語 *archaic word* **kogo**
論語 *analects of Confucius* **rongo**
類語 *synonym, same meaning* **ruigo**
略語 *abbreviated word* **ryakugo**
私語 *private chat, whisper* **shigo**
単語 *words* **tango**
訳語 *equivalent, word, term* **yakugo**

用語 *term, terminology* **yōgo**
造語 *coined word, word contraction* **zōgo**
母国語 *native language* **bokokugo**
同意語 *synonym, same meaning* **dōigo**
英語圏 *English-speaking countries* **eigoken**
反意語 *antonym, opposite word* **han'igo**
語り草 *topic, theme* **katarigusa**
語り手 *narrator, the person speaking* **katarite**
統語論 *syntax* **tōgoron**
語り合う *conversation, dialogue* **katariau**
語り継ぐ *word-of-mouth, oral history* **kataritsugu**

言*alking, 251* 口*outh, 458* 伝*onvey, 619*
談*alks, 308* 弁*peech, 570* 聞*isten, 282*

詔*mperial-edict, 817*

648-B

語*alks that* 悟*nlighten, never forgotten...*

心 ⇔ 忄 ⇔ 小 (feelings)

悟*nlighten* 悟*wakening*

sato(ru), GO

enlighten, awakening

FLIP: 7.3.a. Right Bottom (flat)
Facing: 4.0. ⊂⊃⊂⊃ Apart

悟り *spiritual awakening* **satori**
大悟 *enlightenment, awakening* **daigo**
穎悟 *wise, intelligent* **eigo**
悟道 *spiritual enlightenment (Buddhism)* **godō**
悟入 *attain enlightenment in Buddhism* **gonyū**
悟了 *total comprehension* **goryō**
悟性 *wisdom, erudition* **gosei**
悔悟 *repentance, remorse, atonement* **kaigo**
覚悟 *resolution, preparedness* **kakugo**

啓*nlighten, 677* 解*nderstand, 400*
起*waken, 754* 儀*itual, 342*
神*ivine, 712* 礼*itual, 685*
聖*acred, 617* 純*urity, 199*

語*alking, 780*

649-A

硫*ulphur we don't know, poison to* 流*low...*

硫*ulphur*

石 (stone)

RYŪ
sulphur

脱硫 *de-sulphuration* **datsuryū**
硫黄 *sulphur* **iō**
硫黄泉 *sulphur springs* **iōsen**
加硫 *vulcanisation* **karyū**
硫安 *ammonium sulphate* **ryūan**
硫化 *sulphuration, vulcanisation* **ryūka**
硫化ゴム *vulcanised rubber* **ryūkagomu**
硫化水素 *hydrogen sulphide* **ryūkasuiso**
硫酸 *sulphuric-, vitriolic acid* **ryūsan**
硫酸銅 *copper sulphate* **ryūsandō**
硫酸塩 *sulphate* **ryūsanen**
硫酸紙 *parchment paper* **ryūsanshi**
和硫 *vulcanisation* **waryū**
亜硫酸 *sulphurous acid* **aryūsan**
亜硫酸ガス *sulphur dioxide* **aryūsangasu**
希硫酸 *dilute sulphuric acid* **kiryūsan**
低硫黄 *low sulphur* **teiiō**

Facing: 2.2. East ☞ (V)

酸*cid, 764*
毒*oison, 578*

統*overn, 885*

649-B

硫*ulphur we don't know, poison to* 流*low...*

流*urrent*　　流*lowing*

水⇔氵 (water)

naga(reru), naga(su), RYŪ, RU
current, flowing, gushing, streaming, style

物流 *physical distribution* **butsuryū**
潮流 *tide, current* **chōryū**
暖流 *warm current* **danryū**
浮流 *drifting, floating about* **furyū**
風流 *elegant, refined* **fūryū**
漂流 *driftage, drifting* **hyōryū**
上流 *rich class; upper stream* **jōryū**
海流 *ocean current* **kairyū**
寒流 *cold current* **kanryū**
気流 *air current* **kiryū**
交流 *interchange, inter-current* **kōryū**
流罪 *banishment, exile* **ruzai**
流域 *basin, valley* **ryūiki**
流会 *"meeting cancelled..."* **ryūkai**
流血 *bloodshed, bloodletting, carnage* **ryūketsu**
流行 *popular, fashionable* **ryūkō**
流出 *outflow, discharge* **ryūshutsu**
流産 *miscarriage, abortion* **ryūzan**
主流 *main current* **shuryū**

Facing: 2.2. East ☞ (V)

底流 *undercurrent* **teiryū**
流れ者 *wanderer, vagabond, nomad* **nagaremono**
流し台 *kitchen sink* **nagashidai**
流し目 *sidelong glance* **nagashime**
乱気流 *turbulence, agitation* **rankiryū**
流線型 *stream-lined* **ryūsenkei**
洗い流す *wash away* **arainagasu**
流れ作業 *assembly-line operation* **nagare sagyō**
流れ出す *flow out, pour out* **nagaredasu**
流し込む *wash down, pour* **nagashikomu**
流体力学 *fluid dynamics* **ryūtai rikigaku**

波*urrent, 32*　川*iver, 76*　洋*cean, 247*
河*iver, 877*　海*cean, 241*　渦*hirlpool, 798*

荒*anic, 507*

650-A

禅en-Buddhists 弾laying-music, as 弾ullets 弾ounce in the attic...

弓 (archery bow)

禅en Buddhism

ZEN
Zen Buddhism

FLIP: 7.0.b1. Right (stem)

封禅	ancient Chinese sacrificial rite	**hōzen**
参禅	practice of Zen	**sanzen**
座禅	Zen meditation, spiritual meditation	**zazen**
禅寺	Zen temple	**zendera**
禅堂	Zen meditation hall	**zendō**
禅画	Zen painting	**zenga**
禅学	study of Zen Buddhism	**zengaku**
禅譲	abdicating for a virtuous person	**zenjō**
禅杖	stick-beating during Zen meditation	**zenjō**
禅定	concentration during meditation	**zenjō**
禅家	Zen Buddhist monk	**zenka**
禅味	Zen-like	**zenmi**
禅門	entering Zen monk hood	**zenmon**
禅尼	Zen Buddhist nun	**zenni**
禅林	Zen temple	**zenrin**
禅宗	Zen sect	**zenshū**
禅僧	Zen monk	**zensō**
禅話	Zen discourse, dialogue	**zenwa**
禅問答	Zen dialogue	**zenmondō**

仏uddha, 683	聖acred, 617
盆uddhist Feast, 594	神acred, 712
僧uddhist monk, 836	堂ltar, 94
坊uddhist monk, 736	寺emple, 248

裸udity, 288

650-B

禅en-Buddhists 弾laying-music, as 弾ullets 弾ounce in the attic...

弓 (archery bow)

❶弾ullet ❷弾lay music

tama, hi(ku), DAN
bullet, projectile, spring back; play music

FLIP: 7.0.b1. Right (stem)
Facing: 1.1. West (H)

❶爆弾	bomb, explosives	**bakudan**
爆弾投下	bombing, explosion	**bakudan tōka**
防弾	bullet proofing	**bōdan**
弾圧	suppression, oppression	**dan'atsu**
弾着	hit, impact	**danchaku**
弾劾	impeachment	**dangai**
弾劾裁判	impeachment trial	**dangai saiban**
弾丸	bullet, shell	**dangan**
弾幕	artillery barrage	**danmaku**
弾性	elasticity, malleability	**dansei**
弾倉	bullet magazine	**dansō**
弾頭	warhead	**dantō**
弾薬	ammunition, weaponry	**danyaku**
発弾	explosion, detonation	**hatsudan**
⇒不発弾	unexploded bomb, live bomb	**fuhatsudan**
砲弾	shell, cannon ball	**hōdan**
実弾	live ammunition	**jitsudan**
銃弾	bullet, shot	**jūdan**
凶弾	assassin's bullet	**kyōdan**

糾弾	reproach, censure	**kyūdan**
肉弾	human shield, human torpedo	**nikudan**
散弾	gunshot, gunfire	**sandan**
指弾	spurning, rejection	**shidan**
弾道弾	missile	**dandōdan**
流れ弾	stray bullet	**nagaredama**
催涙弾	tear-gas grenade	**sairuidan**
手榴弾	hand grenade	**teryūdan, shuryūdan**
毒ガス弾	gas shell, ~bomb	**dokugasudan**
❷弾奏	playing string instruments	**dansō**
弾き手	piano player, pianist	**hikite**
連弾	piano duet, two playing a piano	**rendan**

奏usic play, 579	曲elody, 476
譜usic note, 455	射hoot, 504
弦usical string, 358	爆xplosion, 561

禅en Buddhism, 782

651-A

Napoleon's 植lants 値rice & 値alue 殖ncreased in Waterloo...

植*lant*   植*egetation*

木 (wooden)

u(eru), u(waru), SHOKU
plant, vegetation

FLIP: 7.1. Right (Sort Of)
Facing: 4.0. ⟵⟶ Apart

扶植 *plant, set-up, establish* **fushoku**
誤植 *misprint, typo* **goshoku**
移植 *transplantation* **ishoku**
入植 *re-settle, immigrate* **nyūshoku**
試植 *plant experiment* **shishoku**
植物 *plant, vegetation, greens* **shokubutsu**
植物病 *plant-borne disease* **shokubutsubyō**
植物園 *botanical garden* **shokubutsuen**
植物学 *botany, study of plants & vegetation*
　　shokubutsugaku
植物誌 *flora, herbal* **shokubutsushi**
植皮 *skin grafting* **shokuhi**
植字 *typesetting* **shokuji**
植樹 *planting trees* **shokuju**
植樹祭 *arbour day* **shokujusai**
植民 *colony, territory* **shokumin**
植民地 *colony, territory* **shokuminchi**
植毛 *hair transplant* **shokumō**
植林 *tree-planting, reforestation* **shokurin**

植生 *greeneries, vegetation* **shokusei**
田植 *rice planting* **taue**
植木 *plant garden* **ueki**
植木屋 *gardener* **uekiya**
穴植え *dibbing* **anaue**
動植物 *plants & animals* **dōshokubutsu**
腐植土 *humus* **fushokudo**
鉢植え *potted plant* **hachiue**
手植え *"planted personally by..."* **teue**
植え替え *transplantation* **uekae**
植え込み *shrubs, hedge* **uekomi**
植え付ける *plant, implant* **uetsukeru**

菜*egetable*, 915	埋*ury*, 319
畑*lantation*, 482	種*eedling*, 430

値*rice*, 783

651-B

Napoleon's 植lants 値rice & 値alue 殖ncreased in Waterloo...

値*alue*   値*rice*

人⇔イ (person)

ne, atai, CHI
value, price, worth

FLIP: 7.1. Right (Sort Of)
Facing: 4.0. ⟵⟶ Apart

着値 *landed price, price quote* **chakune**
同値 *equivalence, parity* **dōchi**
価値 *value, worth, price* **kachi**
元値 *cost price, break-even price* **motone**
中値 *medium price* **nakane**
値段 *price, cost* **nedan**
値札 *price tag* **nefuda**
値幅 *price gap, ~difference* **nehaba**
卸値 *wholesale price* **oroshine**
指値 *price limits* **sashine**
底値 *bottom price, last price* **sokone**
数値 *numerical value* **sūchi**
高値 *high price, expensive* **takane**
売値 *selling price* **urine**
闇値 *price gorging* **yamine**
中央値 *median, midpoint* **chūōchi**
吹値 *sudden price increase* **fukine, fukiatai**
平均値 *mean value* **heikinchi**
買い値 *buying-, purchase price* **kaine**

掛け値 *overcharge, overpayment* **kakene**
値引き *discount, markdown* **nebiki**
値踏み *appraisal, estimate* **nebumi**
値切る *price haggling, bargaining* **negiru**
値崩れ *sudden price decrease* **nekuzure**
値打ち *value, worth, merit* **neuchi**
捨て値 *sacrifice sale, fire sale* **sutene**
呼び値 *nominal price* **yobine**
絶対値 *absolute value* **zettaichi**
値上がり *price increase* **neagari**
値下がり *price fall, depreciation* **nesagari**

価*rice*, 35	幣*oney*, 171
貴*recious*, 913	札*oney-bills*, 685
金*oney*, 25	賃*ayment*, 145

直*irect*, 420

651-C

Napoleon's 植lants 値rice & 値alue 殖ncreased in Waterloo...

殳 (dried bones)

殖ncrease   殖ultiply

fu(eru), fu(yasu), SHOKU
increase, multiply, proliferate

FLIP: 7.2.b. Right Top (stem)
Facing: 4.0. ⟲⟳ Apart

学殖 *learning, scholarship* **gakushoku**	
繁殖 *propagation, spreading* **hanshoku**	
繁殖期 *breeding season* **hanshokuki**	
利殖 *profit earning, money making* **rishoku**	
生殖 *procreation, reproduction* **seishoku**	
生殖器 *reproductive organs* **seishokuki**	
殖民 *colonized peoples, ~inhabitants* **shokumin**	
殖産 *increased productivity* **shokusan**	
殖財 *money making* **shokuzai**	
拓殖 *developing virgin lands* **takushoku**	
拓殖者 *land developer* **takushokusha**	
養殖 *culture; raising* **yōshoku**	
増殖 *increase, multiplication* **zōshoku**	
増殖炉 *breeder reactor* **zōshokuro**	

複*ultiply, 830*	昇*-scend, 299*
倍*ultiply, 950*	上*-scend, 859*
増*ncrease, 837*	登*-limb, 437*
拡*nlarge, 205*	

殉*artyr, 494*

652-A

帰eturning house 婦ife need not 掃weep nor wipe...

刀⇔刂 (blade, cutting)

帰eturn   帰omecoming

kae(ru), kae(su), KI
return, homecoming, come back, coming home

FLIP: 7.3.b. Right Bottom (stem)

不帰 *passing away, death, demise* **fuki**	帰路 *homecoming trip* **kiro**
復帰 *reversion, recovery* **fukki**	帰参 *returning to one's lord* **kisan**
回帰 *recurrence, relapse, revolution* **kaiki**	帰省 *coming back, homecoming* **kisei**
帰着 *come back, return* **kichaku**	帰心 *homesickness, nostalgia* **kishin**
帰朝 *return from a foreign country* **kichō**	帰宅 *return to one's home* **kitaku**
帰依 *faith, embrace; conversion* **kie**	朝帰り *returning home in the morning* **asagaeri**
帰従 *surrender, capitulation* **kijū**	日帰り *coming home same day* **higaeri**
帰順 *returning to the fold of the law* **kijun**	帰り道 *one's way home* **kaerimichi**
帰化 *change of citizenship, naturalization* **kika**	里帰り *visit to parents home* **satogaeri**
帰還 *return, homecoming* **kikan**	持ち帰り *carry home, take-out (food)* **mochikaeri**
帰結 *conclusion, result* **kiketsu**	連れて帰る *take home, bring home* **tsurete kaeru**
帰航 *home-bound voyage* **kikō**	
帰校 *back to school* **kikō**	
帰港 *back to port* **kikō**	
帰国 *returning to one's country* **kikoku**	
帰京 *return to tokyo* **kikyō**	
帰郷 *going home, homecoming* **kikyō**	
帰休 *on leave, furlough* **kikyū**	
帰任 *resumption of duties* **kinin**	

家*ouse, 909*	里*irthplace, 321*
還*eturn, 165*	郷*irthplace, 452*
返*eturn, 537*	元*eginning, 195*
戻*eturn, 541*	

掃*leaning, 785*

652-B

帰*eturning house* 婦*ife need not* 掃*weep nor wipe...*

女 (woman)

婦*ife*　　　　婦*arried-lady*

FU
wife, married-lady, lady of the house

FLIP: 7.3.b. Right Bottom (stem)

毒婦 *wicked woman* **dokufu**
婦長 *head nurse* **fuchō**
夫婦 *married couple* **fūfu**
夫婦愛 *marital love, love in marriage* **fūfuai**
夫婦仲 *marital relationship* **fūfunaka**
夫婦喧嘩 *marital bickering, ~spats* **fūfu genka**
婦人科 *gynaecology, women's doctor* **fujinka**
婦警 *policewoman, lady cop* **fukei**
匹婦 *mediocre woman* **hippu**
情婦 *mistress, concubine* **jōfu**
寡婦 *widow* **kafu**
姦婦 *adulterous-, flirting woman* **kanpu**
妊婦 *pregnant woman* **ninpu**
妊婦服 *pregnancy-, maternity clothes* **ninpufuku**
裸婦 *naked-, nude woman* **rafu**
産婦 *woman nearing childbirth* **sanpu**
新婦 *bride* **shinpu**
娼婦 *prostitute, whore, hooker* **shōfu**
主婦 *housewife, lady of the house* **shufu**

⇒専業主婦 *full-time housewife* **sengyō shufu**
妖婦 *lecherous-, seductive woman* **yōfu**
売春婦 *prostitute, whore, hooker* **baishunfu**
婦女子 *woman, lady* **fujoshi**
婦女暴行 *rape, forcible sex* **fujo bōkō**
助産婦 *midwife* **josanpu**
看護婦 *nurse* **kangofu**
貴婦人 *noble woman* **kifujin**
妊産婦 *pregnant women & midwives* **ninsanpu**
掃除婦 *cleaning woman, ~lady* **sōjifu**
新郎新婦 *bride & groom* **shinrō shinpu**

妻*ife, 611*	婚*arriage, 637*
夫*usband, 83*	家*amily, 909*
姻*arriage, 364*	族*amily, 649*

帰*oming home, 784*

652-C

帰*eturning house* 婦*ife need not* 掃*weep nor wipe...*

手⇔扌 (hand, manual)

掃*weeping*　　　掃*leaning*

ha(ku), SŌ
sweeping, cleaning

FLIP: 7.3.b. Right Bottom (stem)

一掃 *a clean sweep* **issō**
清掃 *cleaning, sweeping* **seisō**
掃除 *cleaning, sweeping* **sōji**
⇒大掃除 *general house-cleaning* **ōsōji**
⇒拭き掃除 *house cleaning* **fukisōji**
⇒掃き掃除 *sweeping & cleaning* **hakisōji**
⇒煙突掃除 *chimney sweeping* **entotsu sōji**
掃除婦 *cleaning woman* **sōjifu**
掃除機 *vacuum cleaner* **sōjiki**
掃除人 *cleaner, sweeper* **sōjinin**
掃除道具 *cleaning-, scrubbing tools* **sōji dōgu**
掃海 *minesweeping* **sōkai**
掃海艇 *minesweeper vessel* **sōkaitei**
掃滅 *annihilation, wiping out* **sōmetsu**
掃射 *machine-gunning, strafing* **sōsha**
⇒機銃掃射 *machine-gunning* **kijū sōsha**
掃討 *wiping out the enemy* **sōtō**
掃蕩 *sweep, clear, mop up* **sōtō**
煤掃き *house cleaning* **susuhaki**

掃き溜め *rubbish heap* **hakidame**
掃き出す *sweep out* **hakidasu**
掃き取る *sweeping off* **hakitoru**
掃き捨てる *sweeping off* **hakisuteru**
掃き寄せる *sweeping up* **hakiyoseru**
掃き集める *sweeping up* **hakiatsumeru**
掃き初め *first sweeping in the year* **hakizome**

洗*ashing, 478*
濯*ashing, 850*

帰*oming home, 784*

653-A

論heory on 倫thics 論iscussed in the 輪ircles of the Olympics...

車 (vehicle, wheel)

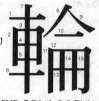

輪ircle   輪ing

wa, RIN
circle, ring, round

輪ゴム *rubber band* **wagomu**
脱輪 *wheels flying out* **datsurin**
銀輪 *silver ring* **ginrin**
鼻輪 *nose ring* **hanawa**
競輪 *bicycle race* **keirin**
口輪 *gun muzzle* **kuchiwa**
年輪 *bygone years, thing of the past* **nenrin**
輪舞 *circular dance* **rinbu**
輪読 *reading alternately* **rindoku**
輪読会 *reader's club* **rindokukai**
輪禍 *traffic accident* **rinka**
輪郭 *outline, contours* **rinkaku**
輪姦 *gang rape* **rinkan**
輪廻 *soul transmigration* **rinne**
輪作 *crop rotation* **rinsaku**
輪生 *verticillation, whorl* **rinsei**
輪唱 *troll, round* **rinshō**
車輪 *wheel* **sharin**
七輪 *mini-charcoal stove* **shichirin**

FLIP: 5.0.b. Left & Right

腕輪 *bracelet* **udewa**
指輪 *ring* **yubiwa**
⇒婚約指輪 *engagement ring* **konyaku yubiwa**
前輪 *front wheel* **zenrin**
駐輪場 *bicycle parking space* **chūrinjō**
一輪車 *wheelbarrow* **ichirinsha**
輪番制 *take turns on something* **rinbansei**
輪転機 *rotary press* **rintenki**
釣り輪 *ring* **tsuriwa**
輪投げ *quoits, discus* **wanage**
知恵の輪 *puzzling ring* **chie no wa**

回otate, 458	囲nclose, 361
丸ound, 73	郭nclose, 398
周ap, 280	

輪hipment, 660

653-B

論heory on 倫thics 論iscussed in the 輪ircles of the Olympics...

言 (speaking)

論iscussion   論heory

RON
discussion, theory, discourse, argue

言論 *speech & writings* **genron**
原論 *principle, fundamental* **genron**
愚論 *foolish opinion, absurd argument* **guron**
反論 *rebuttal, rejoinder, retort* **hanron**
評論 *criticism, critique, review* **hyōron**
序論 *thesis abstract, preface, prologue* **joron**
迷論 *stupid-, absurd argument* **meiron**
理論 *critic, commentator* **riron**
論文 *thesis, dissertation* **ronbun**
論断 *reaching a conclusion* **rondan**
論外 *out-of-the-question* **rongai**
論議 *discussion, argument, debate* **rongi**
論語 *Analects of Confucius* **rongo**
論述 *statement, deposition* **ronjutsu**
論告 *conclusive-, final argument* **ronkoku**
論拠 *ground, basis* **ronkyo**
論及 *reference, quotation* **ronkyū**
論説 *editorial, comment* **ronsetsu**
論旨 *point of argument* **ronshi**

FLIP: 5.0.b. Left & Right

論証 *demonstration, proof* **ronshō**
論点 *point of argument* **ronten**
正論 *sound reasoning* **seiron**
討論 *discussion, debate, dispute* **tōron**
世論 *obiter dictum* **yoron, seron**
俗論 *common view, popular opinion* **zokuron**
抽象論 *abstract argument, ~opinion* **chūshōron**
悲観論 *pessimism, negative outlook* **hikanron**
一般論 *common view, popular opinion* **ippanron**
懐疑論 *scepticism, doubts* **kaigiron**
進化論 *evolution theory, darwinism* **shinkaron**
唯心論 *spiritualism, idealism* **yuishinron**

由ogic, 540	想dea, 524
理ogic, 872	念dea, 182
意dea, 340	談onverse, 308

論dmonish, 922

653-C

論*heory on* 倫*thics* 論*iscussed in the* 輪*ircles of the Olympics...*

倫*thics*　　　　倫*orals*

人⇔イ (person)

RIN

ethics, morals, norms, decorum

FLIP: 7.0.b2. Right (stem)

映倫 *film morality, movie censorship* **eirin**
不倫 *extra-marital, immoral affair* **furin**
五倫 *the five cardinal moral tenets* **gorin**
破倫 *immorality; incest* **harin**
比倫 *peer, match, equal* **hirin**
人倫 *morality, humanism* **jinrin**
乱倫 *immorality, morality breakdown* **ranrin**
倫理 *ethics, morals* **rinri**
倫理学 *study of ethics* **rinrigaku**
倫理的 *ethical, well-mannered* **rinriteki**
絶倫 *peerless, unsurpassed, unrivalled* **zetsurin**

仁*irtue, 457*	善*ighteous, 450*
徳*irtue, 844*	儒*onfucius, 548*
義*ighteous, 341*	孔*onfucius, 684*

論*iscussion, 786*

654-A

探*earching* 深*eep &* 深*ntense with Sherlock's lens...*

探*earch*　　　　探*ook for*

手⇔扌 (hand, manual)

sagu(ru), saga(su), TAN

search, look-for, finding, probe

FLIP: 7.0.b1. Right (stem)

電探 *radar* **dentan**
内探 *private inquiry, secret investigation* **naitan**
探訪 *inquire into, probe* **tanbō**
探聞 *sounding out indirectly* **tanbun**
探知 *detection, espionage* **tanchi**
探知機 *detector* **tanchiki**
探題 *lottery poem themes* **tandai**
探検 *exploration, expedition* **tanken**
探検家 *explorer, adventurer* **tankenka**
探鉱 *mine exploration* **tankō**
探究 *inquiry, investigation* **tankyū**
探究者 *investigator* **tankyūsha**
探求 *fact-finding* **tankyū**
探査 *investigation, inquiry, probe* **tansa**
探査機 *search & rescue plane* **tansaki**
探索 *search, inquiry* **tansaku**
探索パケット *explorer packet* **tansaku paketto**
探勝 *sightseeing* **tanshō**
探測 *sounding out, feeling thru* **tansoku**

探偵 *reconnaissance, spy mission* **tantei**
探照灯 *searchlight* **tanshōtō**
手探り *groping, fumbling* **tesaguri**
粗探し *faultfinding, complainer* **arasagashi**
人探し *person searching* **hitosagashi**
探り足 *groping one's way* **saguriashi**
宝探し *treasure hunting* **takarasagashi**
探り合い *probing each others feelings* **saguriai**
探り回る *grope around* **sagurimawaru**
北極探検 *arctic expedition* **hokkyoku tanken**
探り当てる *grope for* **saguriateru**

索*earch, 375*	調*nspection, 280*
捜*earch, 36*	検*nspection, 939*
察*nspection, 328*	査*nspection, 624*
審*nspection, 339*	閲*nspection, 942*

深*eep, 788*

654-B

探earching 深eep & 深ntense with Sherlock's lens...

深eep   深ntense

水⇔氵 (water)

fuka(i), fuka(meru), fuka(maru), SHIN
deep, intense, stinging

FLIP: 7.0.b1. Right (stem)

深手	severe wound	**fukade**
最深	the deepest	**saishin**
深謀	well-laid plan	**shinbō**
深遠	deep, profound	**shin'en**
深甚	deep~	**shinjin**
深海	deep sea, blue sea	**shinkai**
深更	dead of the night	**shinkō**
深刻	serious, grave	**shinkoku**
深謝	deep gratitude	**shinsha**
深層	the depths	**shinsō**
深夜	dead of the night	**shinya**
深山	mountain depths	**shinzan, miyama**
深入り	go deep into	**fukairi**
毛深い	hairy, bushy	**kebukai**
根深い	deep-rooted, ~seated	**nebukai**
奥深い	profound, deep	**okubukai**
深呼吸	deep breathing	**shinkokyū**
罪深い	sinful, wicked, malicious	**tsumibukai**
欲深い	greedy, avaricious, covetous	**yokubukai**

注意深い	alert, mindful, attentive	**chūibukai**
遠慮深い	reserve, diffident, modest	**enryobukai**
慈悲深い	merciful, pitiful	**jihibukai**
感慨深い	deeply-moved, moving	**kangaibukai**
興味深い	deeply-interested	**kyōmibukai**
迷信深い	superstitious	**meishinbukai**
情け深い	merciful, pitiful	**nasakebukai**
思慮深い	thoughtful, considerate	**shiryobukai**
疑い深い	suspicious, sceptical	**utagaibukai**
用心深い	prudent, cautious	**yōjinbukai**
意味深長	deep meaning	**imi shinchō**

激ntense, 170	洋cean, 247	谷avine, 492
烈ntense, 585	峡avine, 763	
海cean, 241	渓avine, 97	

探earch, 787

655-A

症ickness needs 証vidence for school absence...

症ickness   症isease

疒 (sickness)

SHŌ
sickness, disease, infection, illness

Facing: 2.2. East ☞ (V)

炎症	inflammation	**enshō**
劇症	acute illness, critically-ill	**gekishō**
重症	critical-, serious illness	**jūshō**
軽症	mild illness	**keishō**
脳症	brain fever	**nōshō**
症状	symptoms, patient condition	**shōjō**
⇒禁断症状	withdrawal symptoms	**kindan shōjō**
⇒末期症状	terminal symptoms	**makki shōjō**
症候	symptoms	**shōkō**
症候群	syndrome, symptoms	**shōkōgun**
症例	illness, sickness, disease	**shōrei**
蓄膿症	empyema	**chikunōshō**
不感症	callousness, insensitivity	**fukanshō**
不眠症	insomnia, sleeping disorder	**fuminshō**
敗血症	septicaemia, blood poisoning	**haiketsushō**
自閉症	autism, developmental disorder	**jiheishō**
花粉症	allergy, allergies	**kafunshō**
⇒杉花粉症	cedar pollen allergy	**sugi kafunshō**
健忘症	amnesia, dementia	**kenbōshō**

既往症	medical case history	**kiōshō**
後遺症	sequel, after effects	**kōishō**
恐怖症	morbid fear, phobia	**kyōfushō**
狭心症	angina pectoris	**kyōshinshō**
尿毒症	urine poisoning	**nyōdokushō**
神経症	neurosis, nerve infection	**shinkeishō**
対症剤	specific-, prescribed medicine	**taishōzai**
夜盲症	night blindness	**yamōshō**
夜尿症	bed-wetting	**yanyōshō**
憂鬱症	melancholia	**yūutsushō**
脳軟化症	softening of brain organ	**nōnan kashō**

薬rugs, 447		療ecuperate, 67
剤rugs, 961		患ickness, 475
治ecuperate, 210		病ickness, 213
癒ecuperate, 923		医edicine, 19

病isease, 213

655-B

症*ickness needs* 証*vidence for school absence...*

言 (speaking)

証*vidence* 証*roof*

akashi, SHŌ
evidence, proof, authorization, certificate, verification

FLIP: 6.0.a. Left (flat)
Facing: 2.2. ☞ East (V)

暗証 *code, cipher, encryption* **anshō**
傍証 *circumstantial evidence* **bōshō**
物証 *physical evidence* **busshō**
偽証 *fabricated evidence, perjury* **gishō**
実証 *actual proof* **jisshō**
確証 *conclusive evidence* **kakushō**
検証 *verification, confirmation, attestation* **kenshō**
考証 *research* **kōshō**
公証 *notary public* **kōshō**
認証 *authentication, authorization* **ninshō**
例証 *illustration, example* **reishō**
論証 *demonstration, proof* **ronshō**
査証 *visa, permit to enter a country* **sashō**
心証 *conviction, firm belief* **shinshō**
証言 *testimony, sworn statement* **shōgen**
証票 *voucher* **shōhyō**
証券 *bill, bond, securities* **shōken**
証券取引所 *stock exchange* **shōken torihikijo**
証拠 *proof, evidence* **shōko**

証明 *evidence, proof* **shōmei**
証明書 *written certificate* **shōmeisho**
証人 *sworn witness, person testifying* **shōnin**
証跡 *evidence, traces* **shōseki**
証紙 *documentary stamp* **shōshi**
証書 *bond, deed, certificate* **shōsho**
保証人 *guarantor* **hoshōnin**
許可証 *permit, license* **kyokashō**

| 実*ruth, 121* | 誠*incere, 245* |
| 真*ruth, 487* | 確*onfirm, 804* |

証*ntrust, 82*

656-A

With 酒*lcohol, reflexes* 猶*elay whatever you say...*

酉 (liquor)

酒*lcohol* 酒*iquor*

sake, saka, SHU
alcohol, liquor, booze, cocktails, intoxicant, spirits

FLIP: 7.0.a. Right (flat)

甘酒 *sweetened sake* **amazake**
原酒 *raw sake* **genshu**
飲酒 *drinking alcohol, intoxicated* **inshu**
禁酒 *temperance, abstinence* **kinshu**
生酒 *undiluted sake, draft sake* **kizake**
寝酒 *nightcap, last drink before sleeping* **nezake**
酒場 *bar, barroom, tavern, pub* **sakaba**
酒屋 *wine dealer, liquor store* **sakaya**
酒癖 *drunken behaviour* **sakeguse**
清酒 *sake* **seishu**
節酒 *moderate drinking* **sesshu**
酒毒 *alcohol poisoning* **shudoku**
酒宴 *feast, banquet* **shuen**
酒豪 *heavy drinker, alcoholic* **shugō**
酒気 *alcohol odour* **shuki**
酒乱 *vicious drinker* **shuran**
酒徒 *drinking buddy* **shuto**
酒造 *brewing, distilling* **shuzō**
卵酒 *eggnog with sake* **tamagozake**

梅酒 *plum liqueur* **umeshu**
洋酒 *Western liquors* **yōshu**
酒盛り *drinking party, feast, banquet* **sakamori**
酒臭い *smell of alcohol, reek of liquor* **sakekusai**
酒飲み *drunkard, tippler, boozer, carouser*
sakenomi
居酒屋 *bar, tavern, pub, saloon* **izakaya**
蒸留酒 *distilled liquor* **jōryūshu**
醸造酒 *distilled alcohol* **jōzōshu**
果実酒 *fruit wine* **kajitsushu**
御神酒 *sacred sake, sake offering* **omiki**
雪見酒 *drinking sake in snowfall* **yukimizake**

| 酔*runk, 760* | 閑*eisure, 283* |
| 飲*rink, 255* | 悠*eisure, 898* |

温*ot temperature, 622*

656-B

With 酒lcohol, reflexes 猶elay whatever you say...

犬⇔犭 (dog; beast)

❶猶*elay*　　**❷猶***till more*

YŪ
delay, retard; still more

❶猶予 *postponement, reprieve* **yūyo**
猶子期間 *grace period, suspended term* **yūyo kikan**
執行猶予 *stay of execution, probation* **shikkō yūyo**

❷猶よい *"still better..."* **naoyoi**
猶太人 *Jewish person* **yūdayajin**

FLIP: 7.0.a. Right (flat)

遅*elay, 944*	惰*aziness, 311*
徐*lowly, 881*	怠*aziness, 570*
鈍*tagnate, 199*	

猫*at, 271*

657-A

Boxers 軽ightweight 経anage to 経ass thru unknown fate...

車 (vehicle, wheel)

軽*ightweight*

karu(i), karo(yaka), KEI
lightweight

軽んじる *slight, make little of* **karonjiru**
軽カー *mini-car* **keikaa**
軽口 *light jest, talkativeness* **karukuchi**
軽目 *lightweight* **karume**
軽業 *acrobatics* **karuwaza**
軽便 *convenience, comfort* **keiben**
軽蔑 *disdain, contempt* **keibetsu**
軽微 *slight, negligible* **keibi**
軽減 *reduction, mitigation* **keigen**
軽易 *light & easy* **keii**
軽快 *light, nimble, rhythmical* **keikai**
軽機 *light machine gun* **keiki**
軽挙 *impulsive-, hasty action* **keikyo**
軽量 *lightweight* **keiryō**
軽視 *negligence, making light of* **keishi**
軽震 *weak earthquake* **keishin**
軽信 *gullibility, credulity* **keishin**
軽少 *frivolous, petty, trifle* **keishō**
軽傷 *slight injury* **keishō**

FLIP: 5.0.a Left & Right

軽症 *slight illness* **keishō**
軽食 *light meal* **keishoku**
身軽 *agile, nimble, light* **migaru**
手軽 *easy, plain, simple* **tegaru**
気軽に *"feel free, without reservation..."* **kigaru(ni)**
軽やか *light, not heavy* **karoyaka**
軽軽しい *indifference, aloofness* **karugarushii**
軽合金 *light alloy* **keigōkin**
軽犯罪 *minor offence, misdemeanour* **keihanzai**
軽金属 *light metal* **keikinzoku**
軽工業 *light industries* **keikōgyō**

薄*hin, 63*	重*eavy, 430*
羽*eather, 240*	鳥*irds, 125*
翼*eather, 239*	飛*light, 298*

軒*[houses], 710*

657-B

Boxers 軽ightweight 経anage to 経ass thru unknown fate...

糸 (thread, continuity)

経ass thru　　経anage

he(ru), KEI, KYŌ
pass thru, manage

FLIP: 7.0.a. Right (flat)

月経　*menstruation, menses* **gekkei**
閉経　*menopause* **heikei**
経伝　*writings of saints & sages* **keiden**
経度　*longitude* **keido**
経営　*management, operation* **keiei**
経費　*expenses, costs* **keihi**
経緯　*warp & woof, longitude & latitude* **keii**
経過　*passage of time, lapse of time* **keika**
経験　*experience* **keiken**
経穴　*acupuncture body spots* **keiketsu**
経口　*oral medicine* **keikō**
経歴　*personal history, curriculum vitae* **keireki**
経理　*accounting, bookkeeping* **keiri**
経綸　*govern, manage, administer* **keirin**
経路　*course, route, process* **keiro**
経略　*manage, govern* **keiryaku**
経世　*administration, governing* **keisei**
経線　*meridian line (acupuncture)* **keisen**
経水　*menstruation, menses* **keisui**

経由　*via, by way of, detour, stopover* **keiyu**
経済　*economy, economics* **keizai**
経木　*wood chips, shavings* **kyōgi**
経師　*photo framer* **kyōji**
経典　*sacred books* **kyōten**
政経　*politics & economics* **seikei**
西経　*west longitude* **seikei**
神経　*nerve, sensitivity* **shinkei**
初経　*one's first menstruation* **shokei**
商経　*business & economics* **shōkei**
東経　*east longitude* **tōkei**

期*eriod, 658*	去*eave-out, 360*	済*ettle, 961*
時*ime, 653*	昔*ast, 281*	寿*ongevity, 440*

結*onnect, 227*

658-A

請equest for 晴lear sky-wide, pilots' 精igourous 情eelings 清urified...

言 (speaking)

請equest　　請emand

ko(u), u(keru), SEI, SHIN
request, demand, implore, pleading

FLIP: 5.0.b. Left & Right

電請　*telegram for instructions* **densei**
普請　*construction, building, repairs* **fushin**
懇請　*earnest request* **konsei**
懇請者　*solicitor, requesting person* **konseisha**
強請　*persistent demand, extortion* **kyōsei**
請願　*petition, appeal* **seigan**
請願者　*petitioner* **seigansha**
請願書　*petition* **seigansho**
請暇　*leave request* **seika**
請訓　*request for instructions* **seikun**
請求　*request, claim* **seikyū**
請求書　*bill, invoice* **seikyūsho**
請託　*solicitation, request, appeal* **seitaku**
申請　*application, petition* **shinsei**
申請書　*application form* **shinseisho**
下請け　*subcontract work* **shitauke**
招請　*invitation, call* **shōsei**
店請　*tenants bond* **tanauke**
請負　*contracting, outsourcing* **ukeoi**

請負仕事　*contract work* **ukeoi shigoto**
要請　*request, claim, demand* **yōsei**
茶請け　*sweets served with tea* **chauke**
仮普請　*temporary building* **karibushin**
身請け　*redeem, bail out, ransom* **miuke**
下請け　*sub-contract, outsourcing* **shitauke**
請け判　*surety seal* **ukehan**
請け合い　*guaranteeing* **ukeai**
請け戻し　*redemption* **ukemodoshi**
請け負う　*contract, undertake* **ukeō**
請け取り　*receipt, acceptance* **uketori**
請け売り　*retailing, re-selling* **ukeuri**

受*eceive, 539*	求*equest, 256*
頂*eceive, 134*	頼*equest, 562*
依*equest, 355*	諮*nquire, 865*
願*equest, 964*	尋*nquire, 868*

晴*lear-up, 792*

658-B

請*equest for* 晴*lear sky-wide, pilots'* 精*igourous* 情*eelings* 清*urified...*

日 (sunlight, daytime)

晴*lear-up*   晴*air sky*

晴

ha(reru), ha(rasu), SEI
clear-up, fair sky

FLIP: 5.0.b. Left & Right

快晴 *fine, fair weather* **kaisei**
気晴らし *diversion, pastime* **kibarashi**
好晴 *fair weather, clear sky* **kōsei**
晴曇 *fine & cloudy skies* **seidon**
晴眼 *clear vision, perfect eyesight* **seigan**
晴朗 *fine, serene* **seirō**
晴天 *fair weather, clear sky* **seiten**
青天白日 *clear skies* **seiten hakujitsu**
晴雨 *fair & rainy weather; weather* **seiu**
晴雨計 *barometer* **seiukei**
秋晴れ *nice autumn day* **akibare**
天晴れ *"well done, bravo..."* **appare**
晴れ着 *one's best attire, holiday suit* **haregi**
晴れ間 *lull in the rain, ~before the storm* **harema**
夕晴れ *clear evening* **yūbare**
雪晴れ *clear skies after snowfall* **yukibare**
見晴らし *view of, glimpse of* **miharashi**
日本晴れ *clear Japanese skies* **nihonbare**

五月晴れ *clear skies after rainy season*
　　satsukibare
素晴らしい *"wonderful, marvellous..."*
　　subarashii
憂さ晴らし *diversion, deviation, detour*
　　usabarashi
晴れ上がる *clear up* **hareagaru**
晴れ晴れしい *bright, cheerful, refreshing*
　　harebareshii

明*lear, 22*	英*rilliance, 217*
朗*lear, 800*	澄*ake clear, 437*
昭*right, 529*	空*ky, 394*

請*equest, 791*

658-C

請*equest for* 晴*lear sky-wide, pilots'* 精*igourous* 情*eelings* 清*urified...*

米 (grains, rice)

精*igour*   精*ssence*

精

SEI, SHŌ
vigour, essence, vitality, refine, spirit

FLIP: 5.0.b. Left & Right

遺精 *uncontrolled ejaculation* **isei**
夢精 *wet dream* **musei**
精読 *careful reading* **seidoku**
精鋭 *the best choice, picked* **seiei**
精液 *semen, sperm* **seieki**
精白 *polished, refined* **seihaku**
精兵 *special forces, elite soldiers* **seihei**
精華 *quintessence, epitome* **seika**
精気 *vitality, vigour, high spirits* **seiki**
精勤 *diligence, hard-working* **seikin**
精巧 *exquisite, sophisticated* **seikō**
精根 *energy, strength, vitality* **seikon**
精魂 *whole heart & soul* **seikon**
精米 *refined-, polished rice* **seimai**
精密 *minuteness, precision* **seimitsu**
精励 *diligence, perseverance, tenacity* **seirei**
精錬 *refining, smelting* **seiren**
精力 *vitality, vigour, high spirits* **seiryoku**
精査 *meticulous investigation* **seisa**

精彩 *life, vitality, elan vita* **seisai**
精細 *minuteness, meticulousness* **seisai**
精算 *settlement, calculation* **seisan**
精製 *polishing, refining (sugar, flour, rice)* **seisei**
精精 *"at the most, as much as..."* **seisei**
精子 *sperm, spermatozoon* **seishi**
精神 *mind, spirit, nerve* **seishin**
精粋 *exquisite* **seisui**
精糖 *refined sugar* **seitō**
精油 *refined oil* **seiyu**
精進 *religious asceticism* **shōjin**

勢*igour, 153*	命*ife, 362*
力*trength, 351*	生*ife, 474*
伸*tretch, 713*	力*nergy, 351*
張*tretch, 274*	若*oung, 276*

情*ondition, 793*

658-D

請*equest for* 晴*lear sky-wide, pilots'* 精*igourous* 情*eelings* 清*urified...*

心⇔忄⇔⺗ (feelings)

❶情*eelings* **❷**情*ondition*

nasa(ke), JŌ
feelings, emotions, sentiments; condition, situation, actual

FLIP: 7.0.b2. Right (stem)

❶愛情 *love, romance* **aijō**
慕情 *longing, yearning, love* **bojō**
陳情 *petition, appeal* **chinjō**
同情 *sympathy, commiserate* **dōjō**
激情 *stirring emotions, passion* **gekijō**
表情 *expression, appearance* **hyōjō**
情愛 *affection, sympathy* **jōai**
情火 *flames of love, burning passion* **jōka**
情感 *emotion, feelings, passions* **jōkan**
情景 *sight, scenery, view* **jōkei**
情交 *sexual affair, ~intercourse* **jōkō**
情熱 *passion, strong feelings* **jōnetsu**
情理 *logic & emotions* **jōri**
情死 *lovers' suicide* **jōshi**
情趣 *taste, appreciation* **jōshu**
情操 *sentiment, feelings, emotion* **jōsō**
純情 *pure heart, ~mind* **junjō**
感情 *feeling, sentiment* **kanjō**
熱情 *passion, ardour, fervour* **netsujō**

恩情 *tenderness, warm feelings* **onjō**
私情 *personal-, private feelings* **shijō**
詩情 *poetic sentiments* **shijō**
欲情 *sexual passion, lust, lecherous* **yokujō**
友情 *amicability, friendliness, cordiality* **yūjō**
情け深い *merciful, pitiful* **nasakebukai**
❷事情 *conditions, circumstance* **jijō**
実情 *actual-, real situation* **jitsujō**
情報 *information, news* **jōhō**
情勢 *situation, circumstance* **jōsei**
国情 *state of the nation* **kokujō**

感*eeling*, 45	態*ondition*, 322
気*eelings*, 98	局*ituation*, 573
状*ondition*, 702	

請*equest*, 791

658-E

請*equest for* 晴*lear sky-wide, pilots'* 精*igourous* 情*eelings* 清*urified...*

水⇔氵 (water)

清*urify*　　清*leansing*

kiyo(i), kiyo(meru), kiyo(maru), SEI, SHŌ
purify, purity, cleansing, undiluted, sterilize, pristine, wholesome

FLIP: 7.0.b2. Right (stem)

血清 *blood serum* **kessei**
清聴 *"your kind attention..."* **seichō**
清濁 *purity & impurity* **seidaku**
清栄 *prosperity, affluence* **seiei**
清風 *refreshing breeze* **seifū**
清貧 *"poor but honest..."* **seihin**
清浄 *purity, cleanliness* **seijō**
清純 *purity, innocence* **seijun**
清閑 *quiet, secluded* **seikan**
清潔 *clean, neat, cleanly* **seiketsu**
清音 *unspoken sound* **seion**
清廉 *integrity, honesty* **seiren**
清涼 *cool, refreshing* **seiryō**
清流 *clean stream* **seiryū**
清算 *accounting, bookkeeping* **seisan**
清清 *refreshed feeling* **seisei**
清新 *pure & new* **seishin**
清真 *pure & sincere* **seishin**
清書 *fair copy, copying, copy* **seisho**

清祥 *well & prosperous* **seishō**
清酒 *refined sake* **seishu**
清楚 *neat & clean* **seiso**
清掃 *cleaning, cleansing* **seisō**
清水 *clear-, fresh water* **seisui**
粛清 *purge, purging, cleansing* **shukusei**
岩清水 *spring flowing from rocks* **iwashimizu**
清教徒 *Puritan sect* **seikyōto**
日清戦争 *Sino-Japanese war (1894-1895)*
　　　　nisshin sensō
清浄野菜 *organic vegetables* **seijō yasai**

斎*urification*, 112	浄*urity*, 230
潔*urity*, 901	粋*urity*, 762
純*urity*, 199	

漬*ickling*, 823　　　請*equest*, 791

659-A

諸*arious seatbelt* 緒*traps buckle astronauts' lap...*

諸*arious* 諸*iverse*

言 (speaking)

moro, SHO
various, diverse

FLIP: 6.0.a. Left (flat)
FLIP: 7.3.a. Right Bottom (flat)

諸人	everyone, all persons	**morobito**
諸刃	double-bladed	**moroha**
諸膝	both knees	**morohiza**
諸味	unrefined, coarse	**moromi**
諸諸	various, all kinds	**moromoro**
諸手	both hands	**morote**
諸共	together with	**morotomo**
諸悪	all kinds of evil	**shoaku**
諸芸	accomplishments; various arts	**shogei**
諸行	worldly things	**shogyō**
諸派	various factions	**shoha**
諸般	various, all kinds	**shohan**
諸方	various directions	**shohō**
諸本	various books	**shohon**
諸家	various houses	**shoka**
諸兄	"dear friends..."	**shokei**
諸侯	lords, daimyos	**shokō**
諸国	various countries	**shokoku**
諸君	ladies & gentlemen	**shokun**

諸王	all the kings	**shoō**
諸生	all students	**shosei**
諸説	various stories, diverse views	**shosetsu**
諸姉	"dear ladies..."	**shoshi**
諸氏	everyone, all persons	**shoshi**
諸子	"all of you..."	**shoshi**
諸式	prices	**shoshiki**
諸種	various kinds	**shoshu**
諸相	various aspects	**shosō**
諸島	various islands	**shotō**
諸外国	various foreign countries	**shogaikoku**

多*lenty, 187*	類*ategory, 156*
混*ixture, 38*	種*ategory, 430*
紛*ixture, 778*	雑*ssortment, 776*

請*equest, 791*

659-B

諸*arious seatbelt* 緒*traps buckle astronauts' lap...*

❶緒*trap* ❷緒*utset*

糸 (thread, continuity)

o, SHO, CHO
strap; outset, onset, outbreak

FLIP: 7.3.a. Right Bottom (flat)

❶
鼻緒	clog thong, geta straps	**hanao**
情緒	emotion, atmosphere	**jōcho**
⇒異国情緒	exoticism, extrinsic	**ikoku jōcho**
革緒	sword strap	**kawao**
内緒	secret, private matter	**naisho**
心緒	emotions, feelings; mind	**shinsho**
一緒に	together with, joint	**issho(ni)**
玉の緒	thread of life	**tama no o**
臍の緒	umbilical cord	**heso no o**
息の緒	signs of life	**iki no o**

❷
緒言	foreword, preface, introduction	**shogen, chogen**
緒論	book introduction, forward	**shoron**
緒戦	beginning of a war	**shosen, chosen**
端緒	beginning, start	**tancho**
由緒	distinguished history	**yuisho**

維*ope, 563*	前*efore, 118*
綱*ope, 159*	旧*efore, 464*
縄*ope, 158*	先*efore, 478*

諸*arious, 794*

660-A

俳ctors dare not 排eject a Spielberg project....

人⇔亻 (person)

俳ctor 俳aiku

HAI
actor, acting, Haiku

FLIP: 7.1. Right (Sort Of)

俳文 *Haiku poetry* **haibun**
俳壇 *Haiku world* **haidan**
俳画 *Haiku-inspired picture* **haiga**
俳号 *Haiku poets pen name* **haigō**
俳人 *Haiku poet* **haijin**
俳諧 *joke* **haikai**
俳徊 *loiter around* **haikai**
俳句 *Japanese 17-syllable poem* **haiku**
俳名 *Haiku poets pen name* **haimei**
俳味 *taste for Haiku poetry* **haimi**
俳優 *actor, actress* **haiyū**
⇒映画俳優 *film-, movie actor, ~actress* **eiga haiyū**
⇒喜劇俳優 *comic actor, comedian* **kigeki haiyū**
雑俳 *Haiku-inspired literature* **zappai**

劇*rama, 759* 芸*rts, 619*
興*ntertainment, 867* 娯*musement, 453*
観*iew, 667*

排*xclude, 795*

660-B

俳ctors dare not 排eject a Spielberg project....

手⇔扌 (hand, manual)

排ejection 排xclusion

HAI
rejection, exclusion, discharge

FLIP: 7.1. Right (Sort Of)

排する *reject, expel; push open* **hai(suru)**
按排 *distribute, assign; adjust* **anbai**
排米 *anti-American sentiments* **haibei**
排便 *defecation, faeces, excrement* **haiben**
排英 *anti-British sentiments* **haiei**
排液 *drainage* **haieki**
排煙 *exhaust fumes, ~gas* **haien**
排外 *anti-foreign, xenophobia* **haigai**
排撃 *denunciation, rejection* **haigeki**
排除 *exclusion, elimination* **haijo**
排気 *exhaust, drain* **haiki**
排気管 *exhaust pipe* **haikikan**
排気弁 *exhaust valve* **haikiben**
排気ガス *exhaust fumes* **haikigasu**
排球 *volleyball* **haikyū**
排日 *anti-Japan* **hainichi**
排尿 *urine, pee* **hainyō**
排卵 *ovulation, ovary egg* **hairan**
排列 *disposition, arrangement* **hairetsu**

排斥 *rejection, refusal, denial* **haiseki**
排泄 *excretion, faeces* **haisetsu**
排雪 *snow removal* **haisetsu**
排出 *discharge, exhaustion* **haishutsu**
排水 *sewage water, waste water* **haisui**
排水ポンプ *drain pump* **haisui ponpu**
排他 *exclusive, exclusionary* **haita**
排他的 *clannish, exclusivist* **haitateki**

斥*ejection, 424* 拒*ejection, 207*
断*ejection, 958* 否*ejection, 300*

俳*ctor, 795*

661-A

違ifferent 衛roops on 緯orizontal cadence 衛uarding His 偉minence...

⻌ (transport)

違ifference 違isparity

chiga(u), chiga(eru), I
difference, disparity, gap

Facing: 4.0. 🔁 Apart

違背 *violation, breach, infringement* **ihai**
違反 *violation, offence* **ihan**
違犯 *violation, transgression* **ihan**
違法 *illegal, unlawful* **ihō**
違法行為 *illegal act, violation* **ihō kōi**
違憲 *unconstitutional, constitutional violation* **iken**
違算 *miscalculation, wrong computation* **isan**
違約 *breach of contract, ~of promise* **iyaku**
違約金 *penalty, fine, forfeiture* **iyakukin**
相違 *difference, gap, disparity* **sōi**
間違い *error, mistake, miss* **machigai**
間違いない *certain, unmistakable* **machigainai**
間違い電話 *"dialled wrong..."* **machigai denwa**
勘違い *misunderstanding, misconstruing* **kanchigai**
目違い *wrong judgement* **mechigai**
仲違い *estrangement, alienation* **nakatagai**
手違い *mistake, accident* **techigai**
違和感 *sense of incongruity, ~discrepancy* **iwakan**

行き違い *misunderstand; wrong way* **ikichigai**
入れ違い *misinsertion, misplacing* **irechigai**
考え違い *miscomprehension* **kangaechigai**
見当違い *wrong guess* **kentōchigai**
聞き違う *get wrong, hear wrong* **kikichigau**
間違える *mistake, err* **machigaeru**
思い違い *misunderstanding* **omoichigai**
取り違える *misunderstand* **torichigaeru**
入れ違える *put in the wrong place* **irechigaeru**
履き違える *wear by mistake* **hakichigaeru**
言い違える *say by mistake, misstate* **iichigaeru**

差ifference, 589	較ompare, 774	比ompare, 466
異ifferent, 239	同imilar, 245	距istance, 207
似imilar, 472	並arallel, 444	

衛rotect, 796

661-B

違ifferent 衛roops on 緯orizontal cadence 衛uarding His 偉minence...

行 (going)

衛roops 衛uarding

EI
troops, guarding, protect, defence

Facing: 4.0. 🔁 Apart
Facing: 3.0. 🔁 Across

防衛 *defence, security, self-protection* **bōei**
衛星 *satellite, moon* **eisei**
⇒科学衛星 *scientific research satellite* **kagaku eisei**
⇒宇宙衛星 *space satellite* **uchū eisei**
衛生 *sanitation, hygiene, cleanliness* **eisei**
⇒環境衛生 *environmental hygiene* **kankyō eisei**
衛視 *diet guard, security officer* **eishi**
護衛 *escort, bodyguard* **goei**
護衛兵 *escort, bodyguard* **goeihei**
護衛艦 *convoy vessel, escort ship* **goeikan**
自衛 *self-defence, self-protection* **jiei**
自衛権 *right of self-defence* **jieiken**
自衛隊 *Self-Defence Force* **jieitai**
警衛 *guard, escort* **keiei**
禁衛隊 *imperial guards* **kin'eitai**
後衛 *rear guard* **kōei**
門衛 *gatekeeper, doorkeeper* **mon'ei**
守衛 *guard, door-keeper* **shuei**
前衛 *advance guard, vanguard, front guard* **zen'ei**

衛星係 *health professional* **eiseigakari**
衛生学 *hygiene, hygienic* **eiseigaku**
衛生上 *hygiene, hygienic, sanitary* **eiseijō**
紅衛兵 *Red Guards (China)* **kōeihei**
近衛兵 *imperial guards* **konoehei**
親衛兵 *bodyguard, escort troops* **shin'eihei**
親衛隊 *bodyguard, escort troops* **shin'eitai**
衛星中継 *satellite broadcasting* **eisei chūkei**
衛星放送 *satellite broadcasting* **eisei hōsō**
衛生設備 *health facilities* **eisei setsubi**

護rotect, 828	軍oldier, 295
防rotect, 736	卒oldier, 109
守ide, 366	兵oldier, 490

街owntown, 107

661-C

違*ifferent* 衛*roops on* 緯*orizontal cadence* 衛*uarding His* 偉*minence...*

糸 (thread, continuity)

緯*orizontal*　　緯*atitude*

I

horizontal, latitude

Facing: 2.2. East ☞ (V)

北緯　*north latitude* **hokui**
緯度　*latitude* **ido**
緯線　*parallel to the latitude* **isen**
経緯　*longitude & latitude* **keii**
南緯　*south latitude* **nan'i**
高緯度　*high latitude* **kōido**

並*arallel, 444*	直*inear, 420*
横*idewards, 197*	線*inear, 531*

偉*minent, 797*

661-D

違*ifferent* 衛*roops on* 緯*orizontal cadence* 衛*uarding His* 偉*minence...*

人 ⇔ 亻 (person)

偉*minent*　　偉*agnificent*

era(i), I

eminent, magnificent, grandeur, great

Facing: 4.0. ☜☞ Apart

偉物　*great person* **erabutsu**
偉大　*great, outstanding* **idai**
偉業　*exploits, feat, exploit* **igyō**
偉人　*great person* **ijin**
偉観　*magnificent scene* **ikan**
偉功　*distinguished record* **ikō**
偉効　*great effect* **ikō**
偉勲　*brilliant exploits* **ikun**
偉挙　*great deeds* **ikyo**
偉力　*great talents* **iryoku**
偉才　*exceptional talents* **isai**
偉績　*great accomplishment* **iseki**
偉容　*noble-, dignified-looking* **iyō**
偉材　*greatness, grandeur* **izai**
魁偉　*formidable-looking* **kaii**
雄偉　*grand, magnificent* **yūi**
偉丈夫　*towering & influential person* **ijōfu**
お偉方　*dignified-, noble character* **oeragata**

傑*xcellence, 921*	優*xcellence, 556*
秀*xcellence, 383*	勲*xploits, 934*

違*ifference, 796*

662-A

渦hirlpool of 過xcessive 禍alamity bred a tsunami...

水 ⇔ 氵 (water)

渦*hirlpool*   渦*entrifugal*

uzu, KA
whirlpool, centrifugal, spiral, swirling

FLIP: 7.1. Right (Sort Of)

渦巻き *whirlpool, spiral* **uzumaki**
渦巻く *stir, surge, whirl* **uzumaku**
渦巻模様 *scrollwork* **uzumaki moyō**
渦潮 *whirling current* **uzushio**
渦輪 *whorl, swirl* **uzuwa**
渦中 *maelstrom, vortex* **kachū**
渦動 *vortex* **kadō**
渦状 *spiral, whorl* **kajō**
渦紋 *spiral-, whirlpool design* **kamon**
渦流 *eddy, whirlpool* **karyū**
渦星雲 *spiral nebula* **kaseiun**

禍*alamity*, 799	圧*ressure*, 632
災*alamity*, 571	流*lowing*, 781
波*urrent*, 32	慌*anic*, 507
流*urrent*, 781	力*orce*, 351

禍*alamity*, 799

662-B

渦hirlpool of 過xcessive 禍alamity bred a tsunami...

辶 (transport)

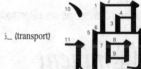

過*xcessive*   過*ass by*

su(giru), su(gosu), KA
excessive, overdone, too much, pass by

Facing: 4.0. ◁▷ Apart
FLIP: 7.1. Right (Sort Of)

超過 *excess, surplus, extra* **chōka**
読過 *finish-, skim reading* **dokuka**
過大 *excessive, unreasonable* **kadai**
過激 *radical, excessive, extreme* **kageki**
過激派 *extremist, radical* **kagekiha**
過言 *exaggeration, overstatement, boasting* **kagon**
過日 *the other day* **kajitsu**
過剰 *surplus, excess* **kajō**
過重 *overweight, overload* **kajū**
過去 *past, bygones* **kako**
過酷 *severe, harsh, cruel* **kakoku**
過密 *overcrowding, congestion* **kamitsu**
過熱 *overheating* **kanetsu**
看過 *looking after, caring* **kanka**
過労 *work fatigue, overworked* **karō**
過労死 *overworked to death* **karōshi**
過料 *penalty, fine* **karyō**
過信 *overconfidence, ego-driven* **kashin**
過失 *error, going overboard* **kashitsu**

過小 *too small* **kashō**
過多 *excessive quantity, ~number* **kata**
過程 *process, procedure* **katei**
過当 *excessive, unreasonable* **katō**
経過 *progress, process* **keika**
濾過 *filtration, filtering* **roka**
透過 *permeation, transmission* **tōka**
罪過 *heinous crime* **zaika**
一過性 *ephemeral, transience* **ikkasei**
過半数 *majority, over 50%* **kahansū**
焼き過ぎる *overgrilling, overroasting* **yakisugiru**

濫*xcessive*, 856	窮*tmost*, 876
超*xceed*, 664	極*tmost*, 947
越*vertake*, 663	端*tmost*, 974

禍*alamity*, 799

662-C

渦*hirlpool of* 過*xcessive* 禍*alamity bred a tsunami...*

示 ⇔ ネ (display, show)

禍*alamity*   禍*ragedy*

FLIP: 7.1. Right (Sort Of)

KA
calamity, tragedy, catastrophe, disaster

災*alamity, 571*	障*njury, 325*
損*njury, 410*	痛*njury, 60*
害*njury, 904*	苦*uffer, 477*
傷*njury, 933*	被*uffer, 715*

渦*hirlpool, 798*

禍禍しい *ominous, foreboding* **magamagashii**
筆禍 *literary repercussions, ~troubles* **hikka**
禍福 *fortune & misfortune* **kafuku**
禍害 *harm, injury, disaster* **kagai**
禍因 *root of a problem* **kain**
禍患 *tragedy, disaster, misfortune* **kakan**
禍根 *root of evil* **kakon**
禍線 *spiral line* **kasen**
黄禍 *Yellow Peril* **kōka**
輪禍 *traffic accident* **rinka**
災禍 *accident, disaster* **saika**
惨禍 *calamity, disaster* **sanka**
赤禍 *Red Peril* **sekka**
戦禍 *war ravages* **senka**
水禍 *flood disaster, drowning* **suika**
薬禍 *harmful drug effects* **yakka**
舌禍 *slip of the tongue* **zekka**
交通禍 *traffic accident* **kōtsūka**

663-A

Rubber 滴*xtracts to be* 摘*lucked from tree cracks...*

水 ⇔ 氵 (water)

滴*xtracts*   滴*rickle*

FLIP: 7.0.b2. Right (stem)

shizuku, shitata(ru), TEKI
extracts, trickle, drop

保*reserve, 552*	漬*mmerse, 823*
浸*mmerse, 770*	潜*ubmerge, 335*

摘*luck, 800*

滴る *drip, drop, trickle* **shitataru**
一滴 *drop, droplet, drippings* **itteki**
露滴 *dewdrops* **roteki**
水滴 *water drops* **suiteki**
数滴 *several droplets* **sūteki**
滴下 *trickle down, drip* **tekika**
滴水 *dripping water* **tekisui**
滴薬 *medicine drops* **tekiyaku**
点滴 *intravenous injection, drippings* **tenteki**
雨滴 *raindrops* **uteki**
余滴 *remaining drippings* **yoteki**

663-B

Rubber 滴xtracts to be 摘lucked from tree cracks...

手⇔扌 (hand, manual)

摘*icking*　　摘*luck*

tsu(mu), TEKI
picking, pluck, tickle

FLIP: 7.0.b2. Right (stem)

摘み草 *herb-, plant picking* **tsumikusa**
摘み取る *pick, nip* **tsumitoru**
摘み切る *nip off, pluck out* **tsumikiru**
指芽 *pointing out, indication* **shiteki**
摘果 *thinning out buds* **tekiga**
摘発 *disclosure, exposure, revelation* **tekihatsu**
摘発者 *informer, whistle blower* **tekihatsusha**
摘録 *summary, gist, excerpts* **tekiroku**
摘載 *summary, gist, excerpts* **tekisai**
摘出 *extraction, removal* **tekishutsu**
摘要 *summary, gist* **tekiyō**
摘記 *summary, gist* **tekki**
全摘 *total removal* **zenchaku**
茶摘み *tea picking* **chatsumi**
鼻摘み *nuisance, irksome, annoyance* **hanatsumi**
花摘み *flower picking* **hanatsumi**
胃摘除 *stomach resection* **itekijo**
桑摘み *mulberry-picking* **kuwatsumi**
掻い摘み *summary, gist, excerpts* **kaitsumami**

引*xtract, 348*	締*ighten, 432*
抽*xtract, 37*	搾*queeze, 722*
絞*ighten, 774*	滴*xtracts, 799*

滴*xtract, 799*

664-A

No 潮urrent in the 湖ake, 朗ladness to a boating date...

肉⇔月 (flesh, body part)

朗*lear*　　朗*lad*

hoga(raka), RŌ
clear, glad, cheerful

Facing: 3.0. ☞☜ Across

明朗 *bright, clear, cheerful* **meirō**
朗読 *recitation, declamation, oratory* **rōdoku**
朗詠 *chanting, reciting* **rōei**
朗吟 *reciting, singing* **rōgin**
朗報 *good news, glad tidings* **rōhō**
朗朗 *clear, sonorous, vibrant* **rōrō**
⇒音吐朗朗 *clear voice* **onto rōrō**
朗唱 *chanting, recitation* **rōshō**
晴朗 *fine, serene* **seirō**
不明朗 *spurious, dubious; bleak* **fumeirō**

英*rilliance, 217*	澄*ake clear, 437*
昭*right, 529*	慶*ejoice, 69*
明*rilliance, 22*	喜*appiness, 965*
輝*parkling, 296*	幸*appiness, 268*
光*hining, 77*	祥*appiness, 248*

郎*asculine, 404*

664-B

No 潮urrent in the 湖ake, 朗ladness to a boating date...

水 ⇔ 氵 (water)

潮*urrent*　潮*ide*

shio, CHŌ
current, tide

FLIP: 8.0.b. Inner (stem)

赤潮 *red tide* **akashio**
防潮 *tide protection, embankment* **bōchō**
血潮 *blood* **chishio**
潮位 *tide level* **chōi**
潮音 *sound waves* **chōon**
潮流 *tide, current* **chōryū**
風潮 *trend, tendency, inclination* **fūchō**
干潮 *low tide, ebb tide* **kanchō**
紅潮 *flush, blushing, reddening* **kōchō**
黒潮 *The Japan Current* **kuroshio**
満潮 *flush, blush, redden* **manchō**
大潮 *flood tide* **ooshio**
親潮 *The Kurile Current* **oyashio**
落潮 *decline, lessening* **rakuchō**
思潮 *stream of thoughts* **shichō**
潮足 *running-, flowing tide* **shioashi**
潮時 *opportunity, occasion* **shiodoki**
潮路 *tide path* **shioji**
潮風 *sea breeze* **shiokaze**

潮気 *salty air* **shioke**
潮煙 *seawater spray* **shiokemuri**
潮騒 *sound of the sea* **shiosai**
潮境 *lines linking two tides* **shiozakai**
初潮 *first menstruation* **shochō**
主潮 *main current* **shuchō**
高潮 *high tide, rough waves* **takashio**
渦潮 *whirling current* **uzushio**
上げ潮 *rising tide, ~current* **ageshio**
最高潮 *high-water mark; climax, peak* **saikōchō**
潮干狩り *shell gathering (low tide)* **shiohigari**

塩*alt, 621*　　洋*cean, 247*
海*cean, 241*

湖*ake, 801*

664-C

No 潮urrent in the 湖ake, 朗ladness to a boating date...

水 ⇔ 氵 (water)

湖*ake*　湖*agoon*

mizu'umi, KO
lake, lagoon, in-let water

FLIP: 8.0.a. Inner (flat)

湖岸 *lakeshore* **kogan**
湖畔 *lakeside, lakeshore* **kohan**
湖上 *on the lake* **kojō**
湖港 *lake harbour* **kokō**
江湖 *society-at-large* **kōko**
湖面 *lake surface* **komen**
湖心 *core of a lake* **koshin**
湖沼 *lakes & marshes* **koshō**
湖水 *lake, inlet waters* **kosui**
湖底 *bottom of a lake, lakebed* **kotei**
潟湖 *lagoon* **sekiko**
沼湖 *swamps & lakes* **shōko**
礁湖 *lagoon* **shōko**
火口湖 *crater lake* **kakōko**
湖沼学 *limnology* **koshō gaku**
淡水湖 *fresh-water lake* **tansuiko**

潟*agoon, 870*　　谷*avine, 492*
峡*avine, 763*　　河*iver, 877*
渓*avine, 97*　　川*iver, 76*

潮*urrent, 801*

665-A

Tales of 裁ustices lavish 裁lothes, 載ublished in 載oads...

衣⇔ネ (clothing)

❶裁*udgement*　❷裁*lothes*

saba(ku), ta(tsu), SAI
judgement, ruling, sentencing, verdict; clothes, garments

FLIP: 6.1. Left Top

❶勅裁　*imperial decision* **chokusai**
仲裁　*arbitration, mediation* **chūsai**
仲裁人　*mediator, arbitrator* **chūsainin**
自裁　*suicide* **jisai**
家裁　*family-, domestic court* **kasai**
決裁　*sanction, approval, consent* **kessai**
公裁　*high court* **kōsai**
裁判　*judgement, court* **saiban**
⇒陪審裁判　*jury trial, trial by jury* **baishin saiban**
⇒弾劾裁判　*impeachment court* **dangai saiban**
⇒民事裁判　*civil court* **minji saiban**
裁判長　*presiding judge, magistrate* **saibanchō**
裁判官　*judge, magistrate* **saibankan**
裁判権　*jurisdiction* **saibanken**
裁断　*cutting; judgement* **saidan**
裁決権　*jurisprudence, jurisdiction* **saiketsuken**
裁量　*legal opinion, discretion* **sairyō**
裁定　*ruling, decision, judgement* **saitei**

制裁　*punishment, sanction, penalty* **seisai**
総裁　*governor-general; Fuehrer* **sōsai**
裁可　*sanction, approval, consent* **saika**
裁決　*decision, judgement* **saiketsu**
❷体裁　*physical appearance* **teisai**
和裁　*Japanese dressmaking* **wasai**
洋裁　*Western dressmaking* **yōsai**
最高裁　*supreme court* **saikōsai**
裁ち板　*tailor's cutting board* **tachiita**
独裁主義　*dictatorship* **dokusai shugi**

判*udgement*, 949	衣*lothes*, 355	
決*udgement*, 699	裁*lothes*, 802	
定*efinite*, 550	服*lothes*, 734	
布*loth*, 208	着*ear*, 589	

裁*aplings*, *803*

665-B

Tales of 裁ustices lavish 裁lothes, 載ublished in 載oads...

車 (vehicle, wheel)

❶載*ublish*　❷載*oading*

no(ru), ta(tsu), SAI
publish; loading

FLIP: 6.2. Left Bottom

❶掲載　*publication, printing* **keisai**
記載　*mention, entry* **kisai**
記載事項　*mentioned items* **kisai jikō**
連載　*serialized publication* **rensai**
載録　*record, journal entry* **sairoku**
所載　*"as published..."* **shosai**
摘載　*summary, excerpts* **tekisai**
転載　*reprinting, reproduction* **tensai**
登載　*publication, printing* **tōsai**
訳載　*translate for publication* **yakusai**
禁転載　*"no copy allowed..."* **kintensai**

積載量　*load capacity* **sekisairyō**
搭載　*loading, equipping* **tōsai**
千載一遇　*chance of a lifetime* **senzai ichigū**

刊*ublication*, 687	搭*oading*, 146	
掲*ublish*, 810	荷*reight*, 877	
版*rinting*, 359	貨*reight*, 191	

蔵*torage*, *565*

❷舶載　*sea transport* **hakusai**
艦載　*freight on board* **kansai**
艦載機　*aircraft carrier plane* **kansaiki**
混載　*mixed, consolidated* **konsai**
休載　*withholding publication* **kyūsai**
満載　*full load, maximum capacity* **mansai**
積載　*loading, piling* **sekisai**

666-A

Pineapple 栽aplings, lots of 繊ibre strings...

木 (wooden)

栽*aplings* 栽*lant*

SAI
saplings, plant

FLIP: 6.1. Left Top
FLIP: 6.2. Left Bottom

盆栽 *miniature-, potted plant* **bonsai**
輪栽 *crop rotation* **rinsai**
栽培 *cultivation, growing* **saibai**
⇒促成栽培 *forced cultivation* **sokusei saibai**
前栽 *garden of trees & flowers* **senzai**
植栽 *tree planting, tree growing* **shokusai**

苗*aplings, 270*	畑*lantation, 482*
植*lant, 783*	田*ice field, 482*
稲*ice plant, 893*	

裁*udgement, 802*

666-B

Pineapple 栽aplings, lots of 繊ibre strings...

糸 (thread, continuity)

繊*ibre* 繊*lender*

SEN
fibre, slender

FLIP: 8.0.a. Inner (flat)

織り手 *weaving person* **orite**
合繊 *synthetic fibre* **gōsen**
化繊 *synthetic fibre* **kasen**
繊度 *silk fineness, ~grade* **sendo**
繊維 *fibre, strand* **sen'i**
⇒合成繊維 *synthetic fibre* **gōsei sen'i**
⇒化学繊維 *chemical fibre* **kagaku sen'i**
繊維質 *fibre quality* **sen'ishitsu**
繊維素 *fibre, cellulose* **sen'iso**
繊維工業 *textile industry* **sen'i kōgyō**
繊維製品 *textiles, fabrics* **sen'i seihin**
繊弱 *frail, weak, delicate* **senjaku**
繊条 *filament, tendril* **senjō**
繊巧 *detailed craftsmanship* **senkō**
繊毛 *cilia, fine hair* **senmō**
繊細 *sensitive, delicate* **sensai**
繊指 *feminine slender fingers* **senshi**
繊手 *delicate hands* **senshu**
繊切り *long strips of cut vegetables* **sengiri**

糸*hread, 375*	紡*pinning, 735*
縫*ewing, 779*	絹*ilk, 158*
繰*pinning, 851*	細*lender, 138*

織*nitting, 855*

667-A

権uthority's might to 確nsure civil 権ights...

木 (wooden)

権*ights*　　権*uthority*

KEN, GON

rights, authority, entitlements, officialdom, perks, prerogative, privilege

Facing: 2.2. East ☞ (V)

権化　*embodiment, personification* **gonge**
版権　*copyrights, publishing rights* **hanken**
威権　*authority, power* **iken**
実権　*actual power* **jikken**
人権　*human rights* **jinken**
権限　*authority, power, competence* **kengen**
権官　*powerful official* **kenkan**
権威　*authority, power* **ken'i**
権利　*right, privilege, prerogative* **kenri**
権力　*power, authority, influence* **kenryoku**
権勢　*power & influence* **kensei**
棄権　*renunciation, relinquishing, forfeiture* **kiken**
金権　*power of money, financial sway* **kinken**
公権　*civil rights* **kōken**
国権　*national sovereignty* **kokken**
政権　*administration, political power* **seiken**
親権　*parental rights (child custody)* **shinken**
神権　*divine rights* **shinken**
職権　*managerial prerogative* **shokken, shokuken**

著作権　*copyrights, author's rights* **chosakuken**
自治権　*autonomy, self-governing* **jichiken**
警察権　*police power* **keisatsuken**
領土権　*territorial rights, domain* **ryōdoken**
留置権　*lien, right of claim* **ryūchiken**
債権者　*creditor, lender* **saikensha**
選挙権　*suffrage, right to vote* **senkyoken**
司法権　*judicial power, jurisdiction* **shihōken**
抵当権　*mortgage rights* **teitōken**
有権者　*right of ownership* **yūkensha**
治外法権　*extra-territorial rights* **chigai hōken**

威*uthority, 520*	自*elf, 462*
利*dvantage, 686*	身*elf, 504*
己*elf, 5*	任*bligation, 709*

確*onfirm, 804*

667-B

権uthority's might to 確nsure civil 権ights...

石 (stone)

確*onfirm*　　確*erify*

tashi(ka), tashi(kameru), KAKU

confirm, verify, affirm, substantiate, validate, assert, authenticate

Facing: 2.2. East ☞ (V)

確固　*firm, steadfast, resolute* **kakko**
確乎　*firm, steadfast, determined* **kakko**
確聞　*learn from proven sources* **kakubun**
確度　*weather forecast accuracy* **kakudo**
確言　*assertion, contention* **kakugen**
確保　*securing, acquiring* **kakuho**
確実　*reliable, certain, steady* **kakujitsu**
確実性　*certainty, absoluteness* **kakujitsusei**
確認　*confirmation, verification* **kakunin**
確率　*probability, likelihood* **kakuritsu**
確立　*establishment, founding* **kakuritsu**
確論　*established theory* **kakuron**
確説　*established theory* **kakusetsu**
確信　*conviction, firm belief* **kakushin**
確執　*discord, feud, rift, dispute* **kakushitsu**
確証　*conclusive-, convincing evidence* **kakushō**
確守　*adherence, loyalty* **kakushu**
確定　*decision, confirmation* **kakutei**
確答　*clear, definite answer* **kakutō**

確約　*definite-, certain promise* **kakuyaku**
明確　*clear, definite* **meikaku**
正確　*accurate, precise, certain* **seikaku**
精確　*accurate, precise, certain* **seikaku**
的確　*precise, exact, accurate* **tekikaku**
不確か　*indefinite, unreliable* **futashika**
不確実　*indefinite, unreliable* **fukakujitsu**
不確定　*uncertain, indefinite* **fukakutei**
不正確　*inaccurate, erroneous* **fuseikaku**
未確認　*unconfirmed, unverified* **mikakunin**
再確認　*reconfirmation, reaffirmation* **saikakunin**

察*nspection, 328*	査*nspection, 624*
審*nspection, 339*	閲*nspection, 942*
検*nspection, 939*	定*ertain, 550*

権*uthority, 804*

668-A

嫌*espise being* 謙*umble, get into trouble...*

女 (woman)

嫌*islike*   嫌*espise*

kira(u), iya, iya(garu), KEN, GEN
dislike despise, detest, hatred, aversion

FLIP: 7.1. Right (Sort Of)
Facing: 3.0. ☞━☜ Across

嫌がる *dislike, hate, aversion* **iyagaru**
嫌らしい *disgusting, indecent, sickening* **iyarashii**
嫌がらせ *annoyance, irksome, nuisance* **iyagarase**
嫌々 *unwillingly, hesitantly, reluctantly* **iyaiya**
嫌気 *boredom, tiredness* **iyake**
嫌味 *cutting remark, irony* **iyami**
嫌煙 *smoking aversion* **ken'en**
嫌煙権 *rights of non-smokers* **ken'enken**
嫌疑 *suspicion, doubt* **kengi**
嫌忌 *dislike, hate, aversion* **kenki**
嫌悪 *hatred, dislike, disgust* **ken'o**
嫌悪感 *sense of hatred, ~dislike, ~disgust* **ken'okan**
機嫌 *mood, temper, disposition* **kigen**
機嫌取り *flatterer, boot-licking* **kigentori**
大嫌い *dislike, aversion, abhorrence* **daikirai**
人嫌い *unsociable, extremely shy* **hitogirai**
毛嫌い *hate, dislike, disgust* **kegirai**
女嫌い *misogynist, woman-hater* **onnagirai**
男嫌い *man-hater* **otokogirai**

嫌気性 *anaerobicity* **kenkisei**
不機嫌 *bad temper, ill humour, cranky* **fukigen**
上機嫌 *high spirits, zestful, cheerful* **jōkigen**
外出嫌い *stay-at-home person* **gaishutsugirai**
人間嫌い *person-hater, anti-social* **ningengirai**
写真嫌い *camera-shy* **shashingirai**
好き嫌い *likes & dislikes, preferences* **sukikirai**
忌み嫌う *hatred, abhorrence, despise* **imikirau**
所嫌わず *anywhere, everywhere* **tokorokirawazu**
負けず嫌い *"never give-up spirit..."* **makezugirai**
食わず嫌い *dislike without tasting* **kuwazugirai**

卑*espise, 936*   侮*espise, 711*
憎*nimosity, 83*   憤*nrage, 848*

嬢*aughter, 854*

668-B

嫌*espise being* 謙*umble, get into trouble...*

言 (speaking)

謙*umble*   謙*odest*

KEN
humble, modest

謙譲 *modesty, humility* **kenjō**
謙虚 *modest, humble* **kenkyo**
謙称 *humble expression* **kenshō**
謙遜 *modesty, humility* **kenson**
謙抑 *humbling oneself* **kenyoku**
恭謙 *modesty, humility* **kyōken**
孝謙天皇 *Lady Emperor Kōken (749-758)*
    kōken tennō

FLIP: 6.0.a. Left (flat)
FLIP: 7.1. Right (Sort Of)

倹*rugal, 938*   申*peak humble, 89*
慎*odest, 831*   弊*umble, 171*

譜*usical note, 455*

669-A
Donor of 髄 *one-marrow to* 賄 *urnish tomorrow...*

骨 (bone)

髄*one-marrow*

ZUI
bone-marrow

延髄	*medulla oblongata*	**enzui**
玉髄	*chalcedony*	**gyokuzui**
骨髄	*bone marrow*	**kotsuzui**
骨髄炎	*osteomyelitis*	**kotsuzuien**
脳髄	*brain organ*	**nōzui**
精髄	*essence, quintessence*	**seizui**
脊髄	*spinal column*	**sekizui**
神髄	*essence, quintessence*	**shinzui**
心髄	*essence, quintessence*	**shinzui**
真髄	*essence, quintessence*	**shinzui**
歯髄	*tooth pulp*	**shizui**
歯髄炎	*pulpitis*	**shizuien**
髄液	*spinal fluid*	**zuieki**
髄虫	*rice borer*	**zuimushi**

FLIP: 6.2. Left Bottom
Facing: 1.2. ☞ West (V)

骨*one, 412*
緊*ard, 599*
固*ard, 491*

骨*one, 412* 賄*urnish, 806*

669-B
Donor of 髄 *one-marrow to* 賄 *urnish tomorrow...*

貝 (shell, old money)

賄*urnish* 賄*rovide*

makana(u), WAI
furnish, provide, make available

賄い	*boarding, meals*	**makanai**
賄い婦	*lady cook*	**makanaifu**
収賄	*bribe taking*	**shūwai**
賄賂	*bribe, bribery, payoff*	**wairo**
贈賄	*bribery, payoff*	**zōwai**
贈賄罪	*bribery crime*	**zōwaizai**
贈収賄	*bribery, payoff*	**zōshūwai**
贈賄事件	*bribery case*	**zōwai jiken**

FLIP: 6.0.a. Left (flat)

備*urnish, 409*	納*upply, 296*
給*upply, 143*	与*upply, 349*
充*upply, 884*	与*rovide, 349*

題*heme, 834* 髄*one-marrow, 806*

670-A

To ruin he went, 随ollowing his Dad's 堕escent...

随 ⟷ 阜 (village=left)

随ollowing   随ccompany

shitaga(u), ZUI
following, accompany

Facing: 3.0. ☞ ☜ Across

付随 *accompaniment, incidental* **fuzui**
附随 *accompaniment, incidental* **fuzui**
気随 *self-indulgence* **kizui**
気随気儘 *"as you please..."* **kizuikimama**
追随 *follow, pursue* **tsuizui**
随分 *exceptionally, considerably* **zuibun**
随伴 *accompaniment* **zuihan**
随筆 *essay, writing, composition* **zuihitsu**
随筆家 *essayist, writer* **zuihitsuka**
随筆集 *collection of essays* **zuihitsushū**
随意 *optional, voluntary* **zuii**
⇒服装随意 *informal attire* **fukusō zuii**
不随意 *involuntary* **fuzuii**
⇒半身不随意 *paralysed partially* **hanshin fuzuii**
⇒全身不随意 *total paralysis* **zenshin fuzuii**
随一 *the most, ~greatest, first* **zuiichi**
随員 *attendant, minder, acolyte* **zuiin**
随時 *any time, whenever* **zuiji**
随従 *follow the lead* **zuijū**

随順 *faithful obedience* **zuijun**
随感 *occasional impressions* **zuikan**
随行 *attendance, accompanying* **zuikō**
随所 *everywhere, in all places* **zuisho**
随処 *everywhere, in all places* **zuisho**
随想 *stray-, random thoughts* **zuisō**
随想録 *essays, memoirs* **zuisōroku**
随意筋 *voluntary-, skeletal muscle* **zuiikin**

伴*ccompany, 949*	附*elong, 382*
添*ccompany, 620*	属*elong, 441*
共*ogether, 302*	合*ogether, 232*

堕*escent, 807*

670-B

To ruin he went, 随ollowing his Dad's 堕escent...

土 (ground, soil)

堕escent   堕egenerate

DA
descent, degenerate

FLIP: 4.0.a. Bottom (flat)

堕する *descend, degenerate* **dasuru**
堕落 *degeneration, decadence* **daraku**
堕力 *inertia, indolence* **daryoku**
堕胎 *artificial abortion, pregnancy termination* **datai**
堕罪 *becoming sinful* **dazai**
自堕落 *easy virtues, dissipation* **jidaraku**

墜*escent, 543*	崩*ollapse, 912*
落*all-down, 826*	衰*ecline, 374*

随*ccompany, 807*

671-A

喝*colding without mercy got my boss so* 渇*hirsty...*

口 (mouth)

喝*colding*　　喝*erate*

KATSU
scolding, berate, chew out, bellow, dress-down, hollering, yell at

大喝 *thunderous shouting* **daikatsu**
恫喝 *threat, intimidation* **dōkatsu**
威喝 *threat, menace, bluff* **ikatsu**
一喝 *shouting, thunder* **ikkatsu**
喝破 *shouting, screaming, yelling* **kappa**
喝采 *applause, cheer, clapping* **kassai**
⇒拍手喝采 *cheering & clapping* **hakushu kassai**
恐喝 *threat, blackmail, intimidation* **kyōkatsu**
脅喝 *threat, blackmail, intimidation* **kyōkatsu**
脅喝罪 *intimidation crime* **kyōkatsuzai**

FLIP: 7.2.a. Right Top (flat)
FLIP: 6.0.a. Left (flat)

叫 *cream, 693*	侮 *espise, 711*
嫌 *espise, 805*	音 *oise, 314*
卑 *espise, 936*	騒 *oise, 924*

渇 *hirsty. 808*

671-B

喝*colding without mercy got my boss so* 渇*hirsty...*

水⇔氵 (water)

渇*hirsty*　　渇*ehydrate*

kawa(ku), KATSU
thirsty, dehydrate, run dry

渇死 *death by dehydration* **kasshi**
渇水 *water shortage* **kassui**
渇水期 *dry season* **kassuiki**
渇望 *longing, eagerness, yearning* **katsubō**
渇仰 *adoration, veneration* **katsugō**
飢渇 *hunger & thirst* **kikatsu**
枯渇 *exhaustion, draining* **kokatsu**
涸渇 *run dry, be drained* **kokatsu**

FLIP: 7.2.a. Right Top (flat)

水 *ater, 9*
飲 *rink, 255*
酒 *lcohol, 789*

掲 *oist(flag), 810*

672-A

謁udience with the Crown after 掲oisting-a-flag that's 褐rown...

言 (speaking)

謁udience with

ETSU
audience with

FLIP: 6.0.a. Left (flat)
FLIP: 7.2.a. Right Top (flat)

謁見　audience, courtesy call　**ekken**
拝謁　imperial audience　**haietsu**
内謁　private audience　**naietsu**
請謁　seeking an audience　**seietsu**
謁見室　courtesy caller room　**ekkenshitsu**

懇ntimacy, 164	誉onour, 252
会eeting, 864	栄lory, 580
談onverse, 308	

渇hirsty, 808

672-B

謁udience with the Crown after 掲oisting-a-flag that's 褐rown...

衣⇔衤 (clothing)

褐rown colour

KATSU
brown colour

FLIP: 7.2.a. Right Top (flat)

褐色　dark brown　**kasshoku**
褐色人種　dark brown peoples　**kasshoku jinshū**
渇藻　brown algae　**kassō**
褐炭　lignite, brown coal　**kattan**
暗褐色　dark brown　**ankasshoku**
茶褐色　brown　**chakasshoku**
黒褐色　black brown　**kokkasshoku**
濃褐色　dark brown　**nōkasshoku**
黄褐色　yellowish brown　**ōkasshoku**
赤褐色　reddish brown　**sekkasshoku**
淡褐色　light brown　**tankasshoku**
鉄褐色　iron grey　**tekkasshoku**

赤ed colour, 261	黒lack, 320
丹ed colour, 78	緑reen, 841
紅carlet, 175	青lue, 115
朱carlet, 233	黄ellow 197

謁udience with, 809

672-C

謁*udience with the Crown after* 掲*oisting-a-flag that's* 褐*rown...*

手⇔扌 (hand, manual)

❶掲*oist (flag)*   **❷掲***ublish*

kaka(geru), KEI
hoist (flag), put up; publish

❶ 掲揚 *hoisting a flag, flag carrier* **keiyō**

❷ 別掲 *"as shown attached..."* **bekkei**
上掲 *"as shown above..."* **jōkei**
掲示 *notice, bulletin* **keiji**
掲示板 *bulletin-, notice board* **keijiban**
掲載 *appearing-, carrying in print* **keisai**
前掲 *"as shown above..."* **zenkei**

FLIP: 7.2.a. Right Top (flat)

刊*ublication, 687*	版*rinting, 359*
載*ublish, 802*	旗*anner, 818*
刷*rinting, 760*	揮*randish, 126*

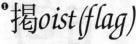
渇*hirsty, 808*

673-A

謡*oh-chantings kept* 陶*orcelains* 揺*haking...*

言 (speaking)

❶謡*hant (Noh)*   **❷謡***opular song*

uta(u), YŌ
Noh chant, incantation, popular song

❶地謡 *Noh chorus* **jiutai**
謡本 *Noh oratorio, ~libretto* **utaibon**
謡物 *Noh recitation, ~chanting* **utaimono**
謡曲 *Noh recitation, ~chanting* **yōkyoku**

❷童謡 *children's song* **dōyō**
歌謡 *song, ballad* **kayō**
民謡 *folk song* **minyō**
里謡 *folk song, ballad* **riyō**
俗謡 *popular folk song* **zokuyō**
歌謡曲 *popular song* **kayōkyoku**

FLIP: 7.1. Right (Sort Of)
FLIP: 6.0.a. Left (flat)

能*[Noh], 321*	曲*elody, 476*
吟*hant, 183*	奏*usic play, 579*
唱*hant, 131*	譜*usical note, 455*

揺*remble, 811*

673-B

謡*oh-chantings kept* 陶*orcelains* 揺*haking...*

陶*orcelain*　　　陶*ottery*

阝⇔阜 (village=left)

TŌ

porcelain, pottery, ceramics, earthenware

Facing: 3.0. ☞ ☜ Across

薫陶 *disciplined, cultured* **kuntō**
製陶 *porcelain pottery* **seitō**
陶土 *pottery clay, kaolin* **tōdo**
陶画 *porcelain drawings* **tōga**
陶芸 *ceramic art, ceramics* **tōgei**
陶芸家 *ceramist, potter* **tōgeika**
陶磁器 *pottery, chinaware* **tōjiki**
陶棺 *earthenware coffin* **tōkan**
陶器 *pottery, chinaware* **tōki**
陶器商 *pottery business* **tōkishō**
陶工 *potter, ceramist* **tōkō**
陶酔 *intoxication, fascination* **tōsui**
陶冶 *cultivation, training* **tōya**
陶然 *enchanted, fascinated, charmed* **tōzen**
鬱陶しい *depressing, gloomy, disheartening* **uttōshii**

磁*orcelain, 54*	匠*rtisan, 106*
窯*ottery, 576*	工*rtisan, 176*
皿*late, 21*	芸*rts, 619*
泥*lay, 302*	

隆*rosperity, 133*	缶*an, 28*

673-C

謡*oh-chantings kept* 陶*orcelains* 揺*haking...*

揺*hake*　　　揺*remble*

手⇔扌 (hand, manual)

yu(reru), yu(rugu), yuru(gasu), yu(ru), yu(suru), yu(suburu), YŌ

shake, tremble, vibrate

FLIP: 7.1. Right (Sort Of)
Facing: 1.2. ☜ West (V)

揺れる *waver, shake, roll, tremble* **yureru**
揺さ振る *shake, swing, sway* **yusaburu**
揺ら揺ら *swaying, flickering* **yurayura**
揺れ動く *waver, flicker, wave, sway* **yureugoku**
揺り椅子 *rocking chair* **yuriisu**
揺り返し *aftershocks, reverberation* **yurikaeshi**
揺りかご *cradle, hammock* **yurikago**
揺り戻し *swinging back* **yurimodoshi**
揺り起こす *shake, swing, sway* **yuriokosu**
揺り落とす *shake down* **yuriotosu**
揺り動かす *shake, swing, sway* **yuriugokasu**
揺るぎ出る *wiggle out* **yurugideru**
揺るぎない *firm, steady, unshaking* **yuruginai**
動揺 *jolting, lurching* **dōyō**
揺動 *rocking, waver, flicker* **yōdō**
揺曳 *flutter, tremble; drag* **yōei**
揺籃 *cradle, beginnings* **yōran**
揺籃期 *infancy, cradle years* **yōranki**
揺蚊 *midge* **yuka**

大揺れ *turbulence, disturbance* **ooyure**
縦揺れ *pitch, pitching* **tateyure**
横揺れ *rolling, revolving* **yokoyure**
貧乏揺すり *mannerism of shaking (foot)*
　　　binbō yusuri

震*remble, 61*	揮*randish, 126*
振*winging, 60*	動*ovement, 422*

援*ssist, 820*

674-A

捕*eizure of store* 補*upplements, owner vehement...*

手⇔扌 (hand, manual)

捕*atching*　捕*eizure*

to(ru), to(raeru), tsuka(maeru), to(rawareru), tsuka(maru), HO
catching, seizure, snatching, grabbing

FLIP: 7.1. Right (Sort Of)

捕縛 *arrest, apprehend* **hobaku**
捕鯨 *whale fishing* **hogei**
捕鯨船 *whaling vessel* **hogeisen**
捕獲 *capture, seizure* **hokaku**
捕獲物 *booty, spoils, plunder* **hokakubutsu**
捕獲高 *fishing catch* **hokakudaka**
捕球 *baseball catcher* **hokyū**
捕吏 *arresting officer* **hori**
捕虜 *prisoner, captive, pow* **horyo**
捕虜収容所 *POW camp* **horyo shūyōjo**
捕殺 *catch & kill* **hosatsu**
捕食 *prey upon* **hoshoku**
捕手 *baseball catcher* **hoshu**
捕捉 *supplement, addition* **hosoku**
逮捕 *arrest, capture, take custody* **taiho**
⇒別件逮捕 *arrest for another crime* **bekken taiho**
逮捕状 *warrant of arrest, arrest warrant* **taihojō**
手捕り *capture, catch with one's hands* **tedori**
捕り物 *under arrest, captive* **torimono**

捕り物帳 *detective story* **torimonochō**
分捕る *seize, plunder* **bundoru**
捕虫網 *insect net* **hochūami**
生け捕る *capture alive* **ikedoru**
搦め捕る *apprehend, arrest* **karametoru**
召し捕る *arrest, apprehend* **meshitoru**
捕らえ所 *the point, meaning* **toraedokoro**
引っ捕らえる *seize, capture, arrest*
　　hittoraeru
捕らvà れの身 *taken captive, prisoner*
　　toraware no mi

拘*rrest, 16*	虜*risoner, 70*
逮*rrest, 880*	囚*risoner, 863*
獄*rison, 639*	

補*upplement, 812*

674-B

捕*eizure of store* 補*upplements, owner vehement...*

衣⇔ネ (clothing)

補*upplement*　補*emedial*

ogina(u), ogina(i), HO
supplement, remedial, replenish

FLIP: 7.1. Right (Sort Of)

補導 *guide, lead* **hodō**
補語 *word complement* **hogo**
補遺 *word supplement* **hoi**
補助 *support, assistance* **hojo**
補充 *replenishment, re-supply* **hojū**
補回 *extra innings in baseball* **hokai**
補角 *supplementary angle* **hokaku**
補完 *complement, supplement* **hokan**
補巻 *supplementary volume* **hokan**
補間 *interpolation* **hokan**
補欠 *alternate, substitute, replace* **hoketsu**
補講 *remedial-, make-up lesson* **hokō**
補強 *reinforcement, strengthening* **hokyō**
補給 *supplies, provisions* **hokyū**
補任 *official appointment* **honin**
補佐 *assistant, aide* **hosa**
補正 *revision, compensation* **hosei**
補償 *indemnity, damages* **hoshō**
補色 *supplementary colours* **hoshoku**

補習 *make-up lesson* **hoshū**
補修 *repair, mending, fixing* **hoshū**
補足 *supplementary, addition* **hosoku**
補則 *supplementary rules* **hosoku**
補訂 *book revision, ~rewriting* **hotei**
官補 *probationary official* **kanho**
候補 *candidate, nominee* **kōho**
試補 *probation officer* **shiho**
転補 *job transfer* **tenpo**
書記補 *assistant clerk* **shokiho**
立候補者 *election candidate* **rikkōhosha**

給*upply, 143*	与*upply, 349*	支*upport, 201*
充*upply, 884*	援*upport, 820*	助*upport, 953*
納*upply, 296*	貢*upport, 625*	擁*upport, 151*

捕*atch, 812*

675-A

A 舗*tore by the* 浦*eashore sells only liquor...*

人 ⇔ 亻 (person)

❶舗*tore*　　**❷舗***ave*

HO
store, shop; pave

FLIP: 6.0.a. Left (flat)
FLIP: 7.1. Right (Sort Of)

❶弊舗 *our store, we* **heiho**
本舗 *main store* **honpo**
名舗 *famous store* **meiho**
老舗 *very old shop* **rōho**, **shinise**
質舗 *pawnshop* **shichiho**
商舗 *store, shop* **shōho**
店舗 *store, shop, stall, booth* **tenpo**
薬舗 *drugstore, pharmacy* **yakuho**
新聞舗 *newspaper delivery store* **shinbunho**

❷舗道 *paved road* **hodō**
舗装 *pavement, surfacing* **hosō**
舗装道路 *pavement, paved road* **hosō dōro**

屋*tore, 427*	売*erchandise, 259*
店*tore, 222*	販*erchandise, 137*

鋳*intage, 440*

675-B

A 舗*tore by the* 浦*eashore sells only liquor...*

水 ⇔ 氵 (water)

浦*eashore*　　浦*oastal*

ura, HO
seashore, seaside, coastal

FLIP: 7.1. Right (Sort Of)

浦辺 *seacoast, seashore* **urabe**
浦人 *seaside villagers* **urabito**
浦路 *coastal road* **uraji**
浦風 *beach wind* **urakaze**
浦波 *wave hitting the beach* **uranami**
浦里 *village by the sea* **urazato**
津津浦浦 *all over places, far & wide* **tsutsu uraura**

岸*eashore, 30*	海*cean, 241*
涯*eashore, 890*	洋*cean, 247*
浜*eashore, 490*	岩*ock, 29*

捕*atch, 812*

676-A

現resent teaching 規tandards, 視bserved at Harvard...

王⇔玉 (jewel)

現resent　　現ctual

現

arawa(reru), arawa(su), GEN
present, actual, obvious, appear, contemporary, currently, existing

FLIP: 7.1. Right (Sort Of)

現場 *actual location, field location* **genba**
現物 *actual goods, "as is" condition* **genbutsu**
現地 *on the spot, field* **genchi**
現役 *active duty* **gen'eki**
現業 *field work* **gengyō**
現実 *reality, actuality* **genjitsu**
現状 *present situation, status-quo* **genjō**
現金 *cash, ready money* **genkin**
現金払い *cash payment* **genkin barai**
現金取引 *cash deal* **genkin torihiki**
現行 *present times, nowadays* **genkō**
現今 *present day, nowadays* **genkon**
現況 *present condition, status quo* **genkyō**
現任 *incumbent official* **gennin**
現品 *actual goods, "as is" condition* **genpin**
現世 *this life, this world* **gense**
現制 *present-, existing system* **gensei**
現象 *phenomenon* **genshō**
現職 *present job* **genshoku**

現出 *appearing, emerging* **genshutsu**
現有 *possession, ownership, holding* **genyū**
現在 *at present, contemporary* **genzai**
現高 *the present amount, running total* **gendaka**
現前 *"in the presence of..."* **genzen**
現像 *film processing, photo development* **genzō**
具現 *embodiment, incarnation* **gugen**
表現 *expression, figurative speech* **hyōgen**
顕現 *manifestation, indicationn* **kengen**
再現 *reproduction; re-enactment* **saigen**
体現 *embodiment, incarnation* **taigen**

今ow, 182	昔lden-times, 281
在xist, 634	将uture, 521
存xist, 634	途urrently, 882

規tandard, 814

676-B

現resent teaching 規tandards, 視bserved at Harvard...

見 (seeing)

規tandard　　規ule

規

KI
standard, rule, policy

FLIP: 7.1. Right (Sort Of)

軍規 *military regulations* **gunki**
法規 *regulations, rules* **hōki**
定規 *ruler, square* **jōgi**
条規 *stipulations, caveat* **jōki**
常規 *established rules* **jōki**
規模 *scope, scale* **kibo**
⇒大規模 *large-scale* **daikibo**
規範 *standard, norm, model* **kihan**
規範的 *standard, model* **kihanteki**
規準 *standard, criterion* **kijun**
規格 *standard, norm, model* **kikaku**
規格品 *standardized goods* **kikakuhin**
規律 *rules & regulations* **kiritsu**
規制 *rules & regulations* **kisei**
規制緩和 *deregulation, rules relaxation* **kisei kanwa**
規正 *improvement, betterment* **kisei**
規則 *rule, regulation* **kisoku**
規則違反 *breach of regulations* **kisoku ihan**
規程 *rule, regulation* **kitei**

規定 *regulation, rules* **kitei**
⇒服務規定 *work regulations* **fukumu kitei**
⇒倫理規定 *code-of-ethics* **rinri kitei**
規約 *terms of agreement* **kiyaku**
校規 *school regulations* **kōki**
内規 *by-laws, regulations* **naiki**
例規 *established rule* **reiki**
正規 *normal procedure* **seiki**
新規 *fresh start, new beginning* **shinki**
宗規 *head of a religion* **shūki**
党規 *party regulations* **tōki**

典ules, 476	策olicy, 875
法aw, 360	常egular, 94
則egulation, 290	般egular, 323
律egulation, 731	

現resent, 814

676-C

現*resent teaching* 規*tandards,* 視*bserved at Harvard...*

視 (seeing)

視*bserve*　　視*atch*

SHI
observe, watch, view, discern, regard

FLIP: 7.1. Right (Sort Of)

注視 *watch closely, gaze steadily* **chūshi**	視点 *point of view, view point* **shiten**
遠視 *farsightedness* **enshi**	視野 *field of vision* **shiya**
凝視 *stare, gaze, watch, observe* **gyōshi**	敵視 *hostility, acrimony, animosity* **tekishi**
弱視 *weak eyesight, ~sight* **jakushi**	透視 *clairvoyance, second sight* **tōshi**
熟視 *intent stare, gazing* **jukushi**	座視 *sit & do-nothing, fence sitting* **zashi**
巡視 *round of inspection* **junshi**	微視的 *microscopic, infinitesimal* **bishiteki**
監視 *watch, observe* **kanshi**	聴視者 *listener, viewer, audience* **chōshisha**
可視 *visibility, clarity* **kashi**	同一視 *equate, correlate* **dōitsushi**
軽視 *negligence, oversight* **keishi**	疑問視 *doubt, distrust, suspicion* **gimonshi**
近視 *near-sightedness* **kinshi**	巨視的 *macroscopic, broad, eclectic* **kyoshiteki**
明視 *clear vision, "20-20"* **meishi**	視聴者 *audience, viewer, listener* **shichōsha**
黙視 *overlook, let go* **mokushi**	
無視 *ignore, disregard, avoid seeing* **mushi**	
乱視 *astigmatism* **ranshi**	
視界 *sight, field of vision* **shikai**	
視覚 *sense of sight, vision* **shikaku**	
視力 *eyesight, vision* **shiryoku**	
視察 *inspection, observation* **shisatsu**	
視線 *one's eyes, glance* **shisen**	

察*nspection, 328*	査*nspection, 624*
審*nspection, 339*	閲*nspection, 942*
検*nspection, 939*	

規*tandard, 814*

677-A

Furious 偶*pouse* 偶*ccasionally at the* 隅*orner of my house...*

人⇔亻 (person)

偶

❶偶*pouse*　❷偶*ccasional*

GŪ, tama
spouse, couple; occasional, by chance

FLIP: 7.2.b. Right Top (stem)

❶
土偶 *earthen figurine, pottery* **dogū**	
偶人 *puppet, doll* **gūjin**	偶偶 *by chance, accidental* **tamatama**
偶力 *"couple of forces..."* **gūryoku**	時偶 *by chance, accidental* **tokitama**
偶作 *impromptu performance* **gūsaku**	
偶成 *contingent, unforeseen, fortuitous* **gūsei**	
偶処 *living together* **gūsho**	
偶数 *even numbers* **gūsū**	
偶像 *idolatry, icons* **gūzō**	
偶像化 *idolatry, icons* **gūzōka**	
偶像視 *iconoclasm* **gūzōshi**	
偶像破壊 *iconoclasm* **gūzō hakai**	
対偶 *contraposition, facing across* **taigū**	
配偶者 *one's spouse* **haigūsha**	
木偶の坊 *wooden icons; good for nothing* **dekunobō**	

夫*usband, 83*	妻*arried lady, 611*
姻*arriage, 364*	婦*arried-lady, 785*
婚*arriage, 637*	遭*hance upon, 326*

隅*orner, 816*

❷
偶発 *accidental-, unforeseen occurrence* **gūhatsu**
偶感 *random thoughts* **gūkan**
偶因 *accidental, unexpected, by chance* **gūin**
偶然 *by chance, accidental* **gūzen**

677-B

Furious 偶pouse 偶ccasionally at the 隅orner of my house...

阝 ⇔ 阜 (village=left)

隅*orner*　隅*ook*

sumi, GŪ
corner, nook

隅っこ　*corner* **sumikko**
一隅　*nook & corner* **ichigū**
片隅　*corner* **katasumi**
隅石　*cornerstone* **sumiishi**
隅木　*corner block* **sumiki**
隅隅　*every nook & corner* **sumizumi**
四隅　*four corners* **yosumi**

FLIP: 7.2.b. Right Top (stem)
Facing: 3.0. ☞☜ Across

角*orner, 400*　　　礎*ornerstone, 166*
曲*urve, 476*

遇*ncounter, 591*

678-A

紹ntroduced by King Federick, fair 詔mperial-edicts...

糸 (thread, continuity)

紹

紹*ntroduce*　紹*resent*

SHŌ
introduce, present

紹介　*introduction, recommendation* **shōkai**
⇒自己紹介　*self-introduction* **jiko shōkai**
⇒新刊紹介　*book review* **shinkan shōkai**
紹介状　*letter of introduction* **shōkaijō**
紹介者　*person introducing another* **shōkaisha**

FLIP: 7.3.a. Right Bottom (flat)
Facing: 3.0. ☞☜ Across

呼*alling, 701*　　　示*isplay, 878*
幕*nveil, 601*

絡*onnect, 826*

678-B

紹ntroduced by King Federick, fair 詔mperial-edicts...

言 (speaking)

詔*mperial-edict*

mikotonori, SHŌ
imperial-edict

詔勅 *imperial message, ~proclamation* **shōchoku**
詔令 *imperial edict, ~rescript* **shōrei**
詔書 *imperial edict, ~rescript* **shōsho**
⇒解散詔書 *Emperor's dissolution of the Diet* **kaisan shōsho**
大詔 *imperial edict, ~rescript* **taishō**

FLIP: 6.0.a. Left (flat)
FLIP: 7.3.a. Right Bottom (flat)

璽*mperial seal, 976*　皇*mperor, 113*
勅*mperial-edict, 955*　朕*mperial consent, 708*

超*xceed, 664*

679-A

焼oasted steak, served at 暁aybreak...

火 ⇔ 灬 (fire)

焼*oasting*　　焼*arbeque*

ya(keru), ya(ku), SHŌ
roasting, barbeque, grilling, burning

延焼 *spreading fire disaster* **enshō**
類焼 *engulfed by fire* **ruishō**
焼酎 *potato & rice wine* **shōchū**
焼却 *incinerate, burn* **shōkyaku**
焼死 *death by burning, burning at stake* **shōshi**
朝焼け *sunrise-, morning glow* **asayake**
石焼き *stone-grilled barbequing* **ishiyaki**
丸焼き *barbecue, roasting* **maruyaki**
胸焼け *heartburn, heartache* **muneyake**
霜焼け *frostbite, chilblains* **shimoyake**
塩焼き *grilled salted fish* **shioyaki**
七宝焼 *cloisonne ware* **shippōyaki**
焼夷弾 *fire bomb, incendiary bomb* **shōidan**
炭焼き *charcoal making* **sumiyaki**
素焼き *unglazed pottery* **suyaki**
卵焼き *omelet, omelette* **tamagoyaki**
夕焼け *sunset-, evening glow* **yūyake**
焼き場 *place for burning* **yakiba**
焼き豚 *roasted pork* **yakibuta**

FLIP: 7.0.b2. Right (stem)

焼き畑 *slash-and-burn* **yakihata**
焼き芋 *baked sweet potato* **yakiimo**
焼き鳥 *barbequed chicken cutlets* **yakitori**
焼き魚 *grilled fish, roasted fish* **yakizakana**
焼き飯 *fried rice* **yakimeshi**
焼き物 *pottery, ceramic, china* **yakimono**
焼き増し *extra printing* **yakimashi**
焼き払う *burn down* **yakiharau**
焼き直し *rehash, adaptation* **yakinaoshi**
焼き蕎麦 *fried noodles & vegetables* **yakisoba**
焼き付け *printing, plating* **yakitsuke**

宴*anquet, 610*　　炎*lames, 309*
牛*attle, 179*　　燃*urning, 445*
豚*ig, 910*　　火*ire, 3*
鶏*hicken, 842*　　食*uisine, 255*

暁*aybreak, 818*

679-B

焼*oasted steak, served at* 暁*aybreak...*

暁*aybreak*　　暁*awn*

akatsuki, GYŌ
daybreak, dawn

日 (sunlight, daytime)

FLIP: 5.0.b. Left & Right

暁に *"in the event of..."* **akatsuki(ni)**
暁闇 *moonless daybreak* **akatsukiyami**
払暁 *daybreak, dawn* **futsugyō**
暁光 *light of daybreak* **gyōkō**
暁星 *morning star, Venus* **gyōsei**
暁天 *dawn, daybreak* **gyōten**
今暁 *daybreak today* **kongyō**
昨暁 *yesterday dawn* **sakugyō**
早暁 *dawn, daybreak* **sōgyō**
通暁 *well-versed, adept with* **tsūgyō**
翌暁 *next morning daybreak* **yokugyō**

日 *ay, 14*	昼 *aytime, 575*
明 *right, 22*	英 *rilliance, 217*
朝 *orning, 662*	翌 *ollowing, 237*

焼 *arbeque, 817*

680-A

旗*anner of* 棋*hess hung in Budapest...*

旗*anner*　　旗*lag*

hata, KI
banner, flag, pennant

方 (direction)

FLIP: 7.3.b. Right Bottom (stem)

赤旗 *red flag, communist flag* **akahata**
軍旗 *military flags* **gunki**
半旗 *flag at half-mast* **hanki**
反旗 *flag of rebellion, ~mutiny* **hanki**
旗日 *national holiday* **hatabi**
旗頭 *leader, chief, boss* **hatagashira**
旗色 *chances of, odds against* **hatairo**
旗印 *motto, slogan* **hatajirushi**
旗本 *Shogun vassal* **hatamoto**
旗竿 *flagstaff, flagpole* **hatazao**
標旗 *marker flag* **hyōki**
旗下 *"under the banner of..."* **kika**
旗艦 *flagship, head vessel* **kikan**
旗鼓 *colours & drums* **kiko**
旗幟 *flag, banner; one's standpoint* **kishi**
旗手 *standard-bearer, flag carrier* **kishu**
小旗 *miniature flag* **kobata**
校旗 *school-, university flag* **kōki**
国旗 *national flag* **kokki**

⇒英国国旗 *Union Jack, British flag* **eikoku kokki**
戦旗 *war flag, battle flag* **senki**
白旗 *flag of surrender* **shirahata**
旗揚げ *flag hoisting* **hataage**
旗振り *waving the flag* **hatafuri**
万国旗 *flags of all nations* **bankokki**
旗行列 *parade of colours* **hatagyōretsu**
国連旗 *United Nations flag* **kokurenki**
日章旗 *Japanese flag* **nisshōki**
星条旗 *US flag, Stars & Stripes* **seijōki**
信号旗 *signal flag* **shingōki**

掲 *oist(flag), 810*	標 *ymbol, 549*
紋 *rest, 558*	号 *ymbol, 866*

棋 *hess, 819*

680-B

旗*anner of* 棋*hess hung in Budapest...*

棋*hess*　　　棋*[shōgi]*

木 (wooden)

KI, GI
chess, Shōgi

FLIP: 7.0.b2. Right (stem)

棋道 *art of Shōgi game* **kidō**
棋譜 *Shōgi game record* **kifu, kifū**
棋風 *way of playing Go* **kifū**
棋界 *Shōgi circles* **kikai**
棋客 *Shōgi player* **kikyaku**
棋聖 *Shōgi master* **kisei**
棋士 *Shōgi player* **kishi**
棋敵 *Shōgi opponent* **kiteki**
将棋 *Japanese chess* **shōgi**
⇒飛び将棋 *Halma* **tobishōgi**
⇒西洋将棋 *Western chess* **seiyō shōgi**
将棋盤 *Shōgi chessboard* **shōgiban**
将棋倒し *domino-effect collapse* **shōgidaoshi**

基*heckers, 590*　　勝*ictory, 406*
競*ompetition, 204*

旗*anner, 818*

681-A

換*eplacing salmon got him police* 喚*ummons...*

換*eplace*　　　換*ubstitute*

手⇔扌 (hand, manual)

ka(eru), ka(waru), KAN
replace, substitute, exchange, switch with

FLIP: 7.3.b. Right Bottom (stem)

置換 *substitution, replacement* **chikan**
不換 *non-convertible* **fukan**
変換 *conversion, transformation* **henkan**
換言 *saying in another way* **kangen**
換価 *monetize, convert into money* **kanka**
換気 *ventilation, change of air* **kanki**
換金 *conversion into cash, monetization* **kankin**
換算 *conversion, exchange* **kansan**
換算表 *exchange table* **kansanhyō**
換算率 *exchange rate* **kansanritsu**
交換 *exchange, substitution* **kōkan**
転換 *conversion, exchange* **tenkan**
互換性 *interchangeability, convertibility* **gokansei**
換気扇 *ventilation fan* **kankisen**
交換台 *switchboard* **kōkandai**
交換手 *telephone operator* **kōkanshu**
交換条件 *bargaining point* **kōkan jōken**
交換教授 *exchange professor* **kōkan kyōju**
物物交換 *barter exchange* **butsubutsu kōkan**

逐次変換 *sequential transformation*
chikuji henkan
引き換え *exchange, conversion* **hikikae**
方向転換 *shift in direction* **hōkō tenkan**
入れ換え *replacement, substitution* **irekae**
書き換え *renewal, rewriting, revision* **kakikae**
気分転換 *refreshing mood* **kibun tenkan**
置き換え *substitution, replacement* **okikae**
乗り換える *change, transfer* **norikaeru**
組み換える *rearrange, recombine* **kumikaeru**
切り換える *exchange; renew* **kirikaeru**
言い換える *reword, paraphrase, restate* **iikaeru**

替*eplace, 334*　遷*hange, 603*　異*ifferent, 239*
変*hange, 581*　代*ubstitute, 96*　他*ifferent, 688*

喚*ummon, 820*

681-B

換eplacing salmon got him police 喚ummons...

喚*ummon* 喚*cream*

口 (mouth)

wame(ku), KAN
summon, call, scream, yell at

FLIP: 7.3.b. Right Bottom (stem)
FLIP: 6.0.a. Left (flat)

喚起 *evocation, awakening* **kanki**
喚呼 *call, cry out* **kanko**
喚問 *summons, subpoena* **kanmon**
喚声 *tears of excitement, joyful tears* **kansei**
叫喚 *scream, yell, cry out* **kyōkan**
召喚 *summons, subpoena* **shōkan**
召喚状 *summons, subpoena* **shōkanjō**
喚き声 *shout, scream, yell, shriek* **wamekigoe**
泣き喚く *scream, cry out* **nakiwameku**
喚き立てる *scream, yell, cry out* **wamekitateru**

召*ummon, 356*	尋*nquire, 868*
伺*nquire, 101*	聞*nquire, 282*
諮*nquire, 865*	威*uthority, 520*

換*eplace, 819*

682-A

援upport once 暖arm, when 緩oosened may harm...

援*upport* 援*ssist*

手⇔扌 (hand, manual)

tasu(keru), EN
support, assist, backing, back-up, help

Facing: 4.0. ⟳ Apart
FLIP: 7.3.b. Right Bottom (stem)

援護 *help, support, backing* **engo**
援軍 *reinforcement troops* **engun**
援助 *help, assistance, aid* **enjo**
⇒技術援助 *technical assistance* **gijutsu enjo**
⇒軍事援助 *military assistance* **gunji enjo**
⇒対外援助 *foreign aid, oda* **taigai enjo**
援兵 *reinforcement army* **enpei**
援用 *invoking, citing, quotation* **enyō**
後援 *support, backing* **kōen**
後援会 *support group* **kōenkai**
救援 *relief, rescue* **kyūen**
救援隊 *rescue party* **kyūentai**
救援物資 *relief goods, ~supplies* **kyūen busshi**
応援 *cheer, support* **ōen**
応援団 *cheering squad* **ōendan**
応援演説 *speech in support* **ōen enzetsu**
来援 *coming to help* **raien**
声援 *cheering, rooting for* **seien**
支援 *support, assistance* **shien**

増援 *reinforcement* **zōen**
増援部隊 *reinforcement troops* **zōen butai**
義援金 *financial contribution, donation* **gienkin**

貢*upport, 625*	擁*upport, 151*
支*upport, 201*	佐*elper, 310*
助*upport, 953*	

緩*oosening, 821*

682-B

援*upport once* 暖*arm, when* 緩*oosened may harm...*

暖*armth*　暖*ordial*

日 (sunlight, daytime)

atata(kai), atata(ka), atata(maru), atata(meru), DAN
warmth, cordial, thermal

FLIP: 6.0.a. Left (flat)
FLIP: 7.3.b. Right Bottom (stem)

暖房 *heating* **danbō**
暖房装置 *heating device* **danbō sōchi**
暖地 *warm region* **danchi**
暖気 *warmth, warm weather* **danki**
暖国 *warm country, warm place* **dankoku**
暖炉 *fireplace, stove* **danro**
暖流 *warm current* **danryū**
暖室 *heated room* **danshitsu**
暖色 *warm colours* **danshoku**
暖帯 *subtropics* **dantai**
暖冬 *warm-, mild winter* **dantō**
寒暖 *temperature, hot & cold* **kandan**
寒暖計 *thermometer, barometer* **kandankei**
暖簾 *good name, goodwill* **noren**
温暖 *mild, warm* **ondan**
春暖 *warm spring* **shundan**
生暖かい *uncomfortably warm* **namaatatakai**
暖取る *warm oneself by the fireside* **dantoru**
冷暖房 *air-conditioning & heating* **reidanbō**

暖冬異変 *strangely warm winter* **dantō ihen**

風*ind, 894*	熱*eat, 153*
涼*ool-temperature, 386*	懇*ntimacy, 164*
篤*ordial, 317*	親*ntimacy, 669*
春*pring, 579*	

腹*tomach, 830*

682-C

援*upport once* 暖*arm, when* 緩*oosened may harm...*

緩*oosening*　緩*often-up*

糸 (thread, continuity)

yuru(mu), yuru(meru), yuru(i), yuru(yaka), KAN
loosening, soften up, relaxation, slack

Facing: 2.2. East ☞ (V)
FLIP: 7.3.b. Right Bottom (stem)

緩み *looseness, carelessness* **yurumi**
緩める *relax, ease, loosen up* **yurumeru**
緩目 *somewhat loose* **yurume**
弛緩 *relax, slack* **chikan, shikan**
緩徐 *gentle & quiet* **kanjo**
緩行 *slow-moving* **kankō**
緩行車 *local train* **kankōsha**
緩急 *speed control* **kankyū**
緩球 *slow pitching (baseball)* **kankyū**
緩慢 *dull, slack, inactive* **kanman**
緩歩 *slow walk, stroll* **kanpo**
緩流 *gentle-, slow current* **kanryū**
緩衝 *shock absorber, buffer* **kanshō**
緩衝器 *shock absorber, buffer* **kanshōki**
緩衝国 *buffer nation* **kanshōkoku**
緩衝地帯 *buffer zone, neutral zone* **kanshō chitai**
緩怠 *laziness, negligence* **kantai**
緩和 *relaxation, detente* **kanwa**

⇒緊張緩和 *détente, relaxation of tension*
　kinchō kanwa
⇒規制緩和 *deregulation, relaxation of rules*
　kisei kanwa
手緩 *lenient, lukewarm* **teyuru**
緩下剤 *laxative, mild cathartic* **kangezai**

憩*elaxation, 169*	悠*eisure, 898*
寛*eniency, 308*	柔*oft, 568*
閑*eisure, 283*	軟*oft, 659*

援*ssist, 820*

683-A

績chievement of 積umulative 債ebt left only 漬ickles in my wallet...

糸 (thread, continuity)

績chievement   績ttainment

SEKI
achievement, attainment, accomplishment

FLIP: 7.0.b2. Right (stem)

紡績 spinning **bōseki**
紡績業 spinning-, cotton industry **bōsekigyō**
紡績糸 spinning yarn **bōsekiito**
治績 administration record **chiseki**
学績 academic achievement **gakuseki**
業績 achievement, attainment **gyōseki**
偉績 brilliant exploits **iseki**
事績 achievements, accomplishments **jiseki**
実績 actual results, ~outcome **jisseki**
功績 achievement, meritorious deed **kōseki**
成績 performance, accomplishment **seiseki**
⇒不成績 disappointing performance **fuseiseki**
⇒好成績 favourable achievements **kōseiseki**
⇒営業成績 business achievement **eigyō seiseki**
⇒勤務成績 job performance record **kinmu seiseki**
成績表 list of achievements **seisekihyō**
成績表 report card **seisekihyō**
戦績 combat record, war record **senseki**

遂chieve, 479	賛raise, 334
成chieve, 244	褒raise, 552
偉minent, 797	勲xploits, 934

積ccumulate, 822

683-B

績chievement of 積umulative 債ebt left only 漬ickles in my wallet...

禾 (tree branch)

積ccumulate   積stimate

tsu(mu), tsu(moru), tsu(mori), SEKI
accumulate, pile-up, estimate

FLIP: 7.0.b2. Right (stem)

蓄積 accumulation, stockpiling **chikuseki**
面積 size, area, acreage **menseki**
累積 accumulation, cumulation **ruiseki**
累積赤字 accumulated deficit **ruiseki akaji**
山積 accumulating, piling up **sanseki**
積悪 long-standing sins **sekiaku**
積分 integrated calculus **sekibun**
積年 accumulated years **sekinen**
積載 loading, storing up **sekisai**
積算 adding up, totalling, summing-up **sekisan**
積雪 accumulated snow **sekisetsu**
積善 accumulated deeds **sekizen**
集積 accumulation, amassing **shūseki**
定積 fixed area; constant volume **teiseki**
容積 capacity, volume, bulk **yōseki**
微積分 differential & integral calculus **bisekibun**
沖積土 alluvial soil, ~ground **chūsekido**
船積み shipment, loading **funazumi**
見積もり price estimate, ~quotation **mitsumori**

積極的 positively, forward-looking **sekkyokuteki**
積み肥 big pile of manure **tsumigoe**
積み荷 load, cargo, freight **tsumini**
積み木 building block **tsumiki**
積み立て reserving, accumulation **tsumitate**
積み出し shipment, forwarding **tsumidashi**
積み重ね accumulation, amassing **tsumikasane**
積み込む put, load, put on board **tsumikomu**
積み残す leave behind **tsuminokosu**
積み降ろし loading & unloading **tsumioroshi**
積み上げる accomplish; pile up **tsumiageru**

収ollect, 178	庫torage, 306	貯torage, 967
集ollect, 50	倉torage, 399	計ompute, 692
重verlap, 430	蔵torage, 565	算ompute, 141

情ondition, 793

683-C

績*chievement of* 積*umulative* 債*ebt left only* 漬*ickles in my wallet...*

人⇔亻 (person)

債*ebt*　　債*oan*

SAI

debt, loan, borrow, credit, debenture

FLIP: 7.0.b2. Right (stem)

募債 *loan flotation, issuance of bonds* **bosai**
負債 *liabilities, debts, loans* **fusai**
負債者 *debtor, borrower* **fusaisha**
外債 *foreign borrowings, external loan* **gaisai**
減債 *partial loan payment* **gensai**
起債 *flotation of bonds* **kisai**
国債 *national debt, government bonds* **kokusai**
公債 *public debt, government borrowings* **kōsai**
旧債 *old loan* **kyūsai**
内債 *domestic borrowings* **naisai**
債券 *bond, debenture* **saiken**
債権 *credit, claim* **saiken**
債権国 *creditor nation* **saikenkoku**
債権者 *creditor, lender* **saikensha**
債鬼 *loan shark, cruel lender* **saiki**
債務 *debt, obligation* **saimu**
債務株 *debenture stock* **saimukabu**
債務国 *debtor nation* **saimukoku**
債務者 *debtor, borrower* **saimusha**

債務免除 *acquittal, "not guilty..."* **saimu menjo**
債務不履行 *loan non-payment, default*
　　saimu furikō
債主 *lender, creditor* **saishu**
戦債 *war bonds, war debts* **sensai**
社債 *corporate bonds, ~borrowings* **shasai**
市債 *municipal bonds* **shisai**
外貨債 *foreign currency loan* **gaikasai**
外国債 *foreign borrowings* **gaikokusai**
公社債 *public corporation bonds* **kōshasai**

借*ebt, 336*	賃*ayment, 145*
金*oney, 25*	納*ayment, 296*
札*oney-bills, 685*	払*ayment, 682*

賃*ayment, 145*

683-D

績*chievement of* 積*umulative* 債*ebt left only* 漬*ickles in my wallet...*

水⇔氵 (water)

漬*ickling*　　漬*mmerse*

tsu(keru), tsu(karu)

pickling, immerse, submerge, submerse

FLIP: 7.0.b2. Right (stem)

漬かる *be pickled, be ready* **tsukaru**
漬ける *pickle, soak* **tsukeru**
漬け込む *pickle* **tsukekomu**
漬物 *pickled vegetables* **tsukemono**
漬物石 *weight used in pickle-making* **tsukemono ishi**
浸漬 *immerse, dip, soak* **shiseki, shinshi**
塩漬け *salted food* **shiozuke**
浅漬け *lightly-pickled* **asazuke**
茶漬け *tea-poured* **chazuke**
古漬け *well-pickled* **furuzuke**
粕漬け *pickled in sake lees* **kasuzuke**
氷漬け *packed in ice, iced* **koorizuke**
生漬け *semi-pickled, weak pickles* **namazuke**
菜漬け *pickled vegetables* **nazuke**
桜漬け *pickled cherry blossoms* **sakurazuke**
酢漬け *pickle-making* **suzuke**
漬け菜 *pickled greens* **tsukena**
漬け梅 *pickled plums* **tsukeume**
矢鱈漬 *mixed-vegetable pickles* **yatarazuke**

大根漬け *pickled radish* **daikonzuke**
福神漬け *soy sauce pickled veggies*
　　fukujinzuke
一夜漬け *pickled overnight; hastily-done*
　　ichiyazuke
芥子漬け *mustard pickles* **karashizuke**
味噌漬け *pickled in miso bean paste* **misozuke**
奈良漬け *sake-pickled* **narazuke**
千枚漬け *pickled slices of radish* **senmaizuke**
沢庵漬け *pickled radish* **takuwanzuke**
山葵漬け *pickled horseradish* **wasabizuke**
糠味噌漬け *pickled w/ rice husk* **nukamisozuke**

保*reserve, 552*	礁*unken, 920*
浸*mmerse, 770*	味*aste, 871*
潜*ubmerge, 335*	

清*urify, 793*

684-A

嫁aughter-in-law found 稼aking-a-living by the 塚ound...

女 (woman)

嫁aughter-in-law

totsu(gu), yome, KA
daughter-in-law, marry (a woman)

嫁ぎ先 *wife's in-laws family* **totsugisaki**
兄嫁 *older brother's wife* **aniyome**
花嫁 *bride* **hanayome**
花嫁御寮 *bride* **hanayome goryō**
花嫁衣装 *bridal gown* **hanayome ishō**
花嫁修業 *training for housewife* **hanayome shugyō**
許嫁 *fiance, fiancee* **iinazuke**
嫁資 *dowry* **kashi**
降嫁 *princess & commoner wedding* **kōka**
弟嫁 *younger brother's wife* **otōtoyome**
再嫁 *remarriage, second marriage* **saika**
転嫁 *blaming others, evading responsibility* **tenka**
嫁御 *bride* **yomego**
嫁菜 *starwort, aster* **yomena**
嫁入り *marriage, wedding* **yomeiri**
嫁入り支度 *marriage preparations* **yomeiri jitaku**
狐の嫁入り *mild rain on sunshine* **kitsune no yomeiri**
嫁いびり *daughter-in-law bullying, ~beating* **yomeibiri**

Facing: 3.0. ☞☜ **Across**
FLIP: 7.2.b. Right Top (stem)

婿*on-in-law, 638*	姻*arriage, 364*
嬢*aughter, 854*	婚*arriage, 637*
娘*aughter, 254*	

塚*ound, 825*　　稼*ake-a-living, 824*

684-B

嫁aughter-in-law found 稼aking-a-living by the 塚ound...

禾 (tree branch)

稼ake-a-living　稼ivelihood

kase(gu), KA
make-a-living, livelihood, subsistence, work

⇒荒稼ぎ *sudden income, big haul* **arakasegi**
⇒出稼ぎ *migrant workers* **dekasegi**
⇒日稼ぎ *daily labourer* **hikasegi**
⇒旅稼ぎ *working away from home* **tabikasegi**
⇒共稼ぎ *dual income family* **tomokasegi**
⇒山稼ぎ *working in the mountains* **yamakasegi**
⇒夜稼ぎ *night worker* **yokasegi**
⇒時間出稼ぎ *hourly-paid migrant workers*
　　jikan dekasegi
稼ぎ人 *breadwinner, family head* **kaseginin**
稼ぎ手 *breadwinner, family head* **kasegite**
稼ぎ高 *income, salary, wage* **kasegidaka**
稼ぎ出す *make money, earn* **kasegidasu**
稼ぎ取る *making a living* **kasegitoru**
稼動 *operation, work* **kadō**
稼業 *business, profession* **kagyō**
⇒役者稼業 *stage career* **yakusha kagyō**

FLIP: 7.2.b. Right Top (stem)
Facing: 1.2. ☜ **West (V)**

扶*amily-support, 97*	暮*ivelihood, 601*
働*abour, 422*	任*bligation, 709*
労*abour, 351*	育*aising, 885*

嫁*aughter-in-law, 824*

684-C

嫁*aughter-in-law found,* 稼*aking-a-living by the* 塚*ound...*

土 (ground, soil)

塚*ound*　　　塚*umulus*

tsuka
mound, tumulus

FLIP: 6.0.b. Left (stem)
Facing: 1.2. ☜ West (V)

蟻塚 *ant hill* **arizuka**
筆塚 *writing brush* **fudezuka**
石塚 *pile of stone's* **ishizuka**
貝塚 *kitchen midden, shell heap* **kaizuka**
塚穴 *grave, tomb* **tsukaana**
比翼塚 *lovers' common grave* **hiyokuzuka**
一里塚 *milestone, landmark, epochal* **ichirizuka**

丘*lope,* 106	崎*lope,* 270
坂*lope,* 733	

稼*ake-a-living* 824

685-A

略*ummary of patients'* 落*ollapse, heart* 絡*onnexions perhaps...*

田 (cultivated field)

略*ummary*　　　略*xcerpt*

RYAKU
summary, excerpt, digest, abridged, strategy

FLIP: 6.0.a. Left (flat)

謀略 *hidden plot, secret plan* **bōryaku**
概略 *outline, summary* **gairyaku**
軍略 *combat strategy, military tactics* **gunryaku**
簡略 *brief, concise, simple* **kanryaku**
計略 *plan, scheme, design* **keiryaku**
攻略 *capture, conquest* **kōryaku**
略記 *sketch, outline* **ryakki**
略文 *abridged sentence* **ryakubun**
略奪 *plunder, pillage, looting* **ryakudatsu**
略伝 *brief biography* **ryakuden**
略画 *sketch, drawing* **ryakuga**
略言 *summary, brief statement* **ryakugen**
略語 *abbreviated word, acronym* **ryakugo**
略号 *code, symbol, sign* **ryakugō**
略字 *simplified Kanji character* **ryakuji**
略述 *summary, outline* **ryakujutsu**
略説 *summary, outline* **ryakusetsu**
略史 *outline, short history* **ryakushi**
略式 *informality, simplicity* **ryakushiki**

略称 *abbreviation, acronym* **ryakushō**
略取 *capture, abduction* **ryakushu**
略体 *simplified Kanji character* **ryakutai**
才略 *clever scheme* **sairyaku**
策略 *stratagem, trick* **sakuryaku**
政略 *political maneuvering, ~scheme* **seiryaku**
戦略 *strategy, tactics* **senryaku**
侵略 *war of aggression, invasion* **shinryaku**
省略 *omission, abbreviation, ellipsis* **shōryaku**
大略 *grand plan; summary, outline* **tairyaku**
要略 *summary, gist* **yōryaku**

策*easure,* 875	概*stimate,* 317
抄*ummary,* 726	積*stimate,* 822
撮*ummarize,* 423	抄*xcerpt,* 726

絡*onnect* 826

685-B

略*ummary of patients'* 落*ollapse, heart* 絡*onnexions perhaps...*

ᵗᵗ (grass)

落*ollapse*　落*all-down*

o(chiru), o(tosu), RAKU
collapse, fall-down, downfall, founder

FLIP: 7.3.a. Right Bottom (flat)
FLIP: 3.0.b. Top (stem)

没落 *ruin, downfall, bankruptcy* **botsuraku**	落涙 *shedding tears* **rakurui**
凋落 *withering away* **chōraku**	落札 *auction winning, successful bid* **rakusatsu**
段落 *paragraph* **danraku**	落成 *completion, fulfilment* **rakusei**
堕落 *degeneration, decadence* **daraku**	落石 *falling rocks* **rakuseki**
脱落 *falling out, ~away* **datsuraku**	零落 *ruin, downfall* **reiraku**
反落 *reactionary fall, ~decline* **hanraku**	低落 *fall, decline, decrease* **teiraku**
陥落 *fall, surrender, collapse* **kanraku**	転落 *downfall, collapse* **tenraku**
滑落 *slipping down* **katsuraku**	当落 *success-or-failure* **tōraku**
欠落 *lacking, shortage, insufficiency* **ketsuraku**	騰落 *ups & downs, fluctuation* **tōraku**
攻落 *hit & sink* **kōraku**	墜落 *fall, crash, descent* **tsuiraku**
急落 *sudden drop, nosedive* **kyūraku**	続落 *continuing fall, ~decline* **zokuraku**
及落 *success-or-failure* **kyūraku**	
落花 *falling flower petals* **rakka**	
落款 *artist signature, ~seal* **rakkan**	
落盤 *caving in, collapse, descent* **rakuban**	
落丁 *missing-, torn pages* **rakuchō**	
落日 *setting sun* **rakujitsu**	
落首 *lampoon, satire, caricature* **rakushu**	
落命 *one's death, demise* **rakumei**	

陥*ollapse, 893*	堕*all-down, 807*
崩*ollapse, 912*	壊*estroy, 847*
降*escend, 133*	破*estroy, 715*

塔*ower, 146*

685-C

略*ummary of patients'* 落*ollapse, heart* 絡*onnexions perhaps...*

糸 (thread, continuity)

絡*ngage*　絡*onnect*

kara(mu), kara(maru), RAKU
engage, connect, linkage, entwine, interlink

FLIP: 7.1. Right (Sort Of)
Facing: 3.0. ☞☜ Across

絡み *entwining, entanglement, quagmire* **karami**	
絡み合う *grapple, entangle, quagmire* **karamiau**	
絡み付く *cling fast, twine* **karamitsuku**	
脈絡 *logical connexion, coherence* **myakuraku**	
連絡 *communication, liaison, contact* **renraku**	
籠絡 *cajole, entice, wean over* **rōraku**	
短絡 *short circuit; simplistic* **tanraku**	

縁*elationship, 675*
係*elative, 263*
連*lliance, 305*

結*onnect, 227*

686-A

膜*embranes X-ray* 模*atterns look too* 漠*bscure to configure...*

肉⇔月 (flesh, body part)

膜*embrane*

MAKU
membrane

FLIP: 7.0.b2. Right (stem)

弁膜 *heart organ valves* **benmaku**	
腹膜 *peritoneum* **fukumaku**	
腹膜炎 *peritonitis* **fukumakuen**	
偽膜 *pseudomembrane* **gimaku**	
薄膜 *thin film* **hakumaku, usumaku**	
皮膜 *membrane* **himaku**	
核膜 *nuclear membrane* **kakumaku**	
隔膜 *diaphragm* **kakumaku**	
角膜 *cornea* **kakumaku**	
角膜炎 *cornea inflammation* **kakumakuen**	
結膜 *conjunctiva* **ketsumaku**	
結膜炎 *conjunctivitis* **ketsumakuen**	
鼓膜 *eardrum* **komaku**	
骨膜 *periosteum* **kotsumaku**	
骨膜炎 *periostitis* **kotsumakuen**	
胸膜 *pleura* **kyōmaku**	
膜状 *membrane-like* **makujō**	
網膜 *eye retina* **mōmaku**	
内膜 *internal membrane* **naimaku**	

粘膜 *mucous membrane* **nenmaku**
脳膜 *meninges* **nōmaku**
脳膜炎 *meningitis, brain fever* **nōmakuen**
肋膜 *pleura* **rokumaku**
横隔膜 *diaphragm* **ōkakumaku**
肋膜炎 *pleuritis* **rokumakuen**
細胞膜 *cell membrane* **saibōmaku**
処女膜 *hymen; maidenhead* **shojomaku**

胞*ellular, 690*	肺*ungs, 305*
脳*rain, 47*	肝*iver, 711*

漠*xpanse, 828*

686-B

膜*embranes X-ray* 模*atterns look too* 漠*bscure to configure...*

木 (wooden)

模*attern*   模*odel*

MO, BO
pattern, model, prototype, template, exemplar, specimen

FLIP: 7.0.b2. Right (stem)

規模 *scale, scope* **kibo**
模擬 *imitation, sham, fake, phoney* **mogi**
模擬戦 *mock battle, fake war* **mogisen**
模擬店 *booth, stand, stall* **mogiten**
模擬法廷 *moot court, kangaroo court* **mogi hōtei**
模擬裁判 *moot court, kangaroo court* **mogi saiban**
模擬試験 *review examination* **mogi shiken**
模範 *model, exemplar* **mohan**
模範生 *model student, ~pupil* **mohansei**
模範的 *exemplary, model* **mohanteki**
模範試合 *exhibition game* **mohan shiai**
模倣 *imitation, copy* **mohō**
模型 *model, prototype, scale design* **mokei**
模形 *scale model, replica* **mokei**
模糊 *dim, vague, opaque* **moko**
模索 *grope, fumbler* **mosaku**
模作 *imitation, sham, fake, phoney* **mosaku**
模写 *reproduction, facsimile* **mosha**
模様 *pattern, design* **moyō**

⇒雨模様 *signs of rain* **amemoyō, amamoyō**
⇒花模様 *floral design, ~background* **hanamoyō**
⇒色模様 *colouring pattern; love scene* **iromoyō**
⇒地模様 *background scene* **jimoyō**
⇒空模様 *looks of the clouds* **soramoyō**
⇒雪模様 *signs of snowfall* **yukimoyō**
⇒染め模様 *dyeing pattern* **somemoyō**
⇒渦巻模様 *scrollwork* **uzumaki moyō**
模様替え *renovation, alteration* **moyōgae**
模造 *imitation, fake, fabrication, phoney* **mozō**
模造品 *imitation-, fake goods* **mozōhin**

鑑*attern, 857*	柄*attern, 213*
型*attern, 536*	例*xample, 357*
塑*attern, 896*	範*xample, 584*

漠*xpanse, 828*

686-C

膜*embranes X-ray* 模*atterns look too* 漠*bscure to configure...*

水 ⇔ 氵 (water)

❶漠*xpanse* ❷漠*bscure*

BAKU
expanse; obscure, opaque, vague

FLIP: 7.0.b2. Right (stem)

❶漠漠 *vast, boundless; vague, obscure* **bakubaku**
空漠 *vast, boundless* **kūbaku**
砂漠 *desert, barren* **sabaku**
砂漠化 *desertification* **sabakuka**
茫漠 *vast, boundless* **bōbaku**
大砂漠 *vast desert* **daisabaku**
広漠 *vast, boundless* **kōbaku**
空空漠漠 *vast & empty* **kūkū bakubaku**

❷漠然と *vaguely, unclear* **bakuzento**
索漠たる *bleak, desolate, dreary* **sakubakutaru**

淡*aint, 309*
薄*hin, 63*

漢*anji, 926*

687-A

護*rotect thy* 穫*arvest &* 獲*cquired interest...*

言 (speaking)

護*rotect* 護*ook after*

mamo(ru), GO
protect, defence, caring, guarding, look-after, safeguard

FLIP: 6.0.a. Left (flat)
FLIP: 7.3.b. Right Bottom (stem)

愛護 *protection, looking after, caring* **aigo**
防護 *protection, defence, security* **bōgo**
援護 *support, backing, assistance* **engo**
掩護 *cover, protection* **engo**
護衛 *bodyguard, escort* **goei**
護衛艦 *convoy vessel* **goeikan**
護符 *amulet, talisman, charm* **gofu**
護憲 *constitutional defence* **goken**
護国 *nations defence, state security* **gokoku**
護身 *self-protection, security* **goshin**
護送 *police escort* **gosō**
護送車 *police wagon, prison bus* **gosōsha**
保護 *care for, protect* **hogo**
⇒母性保護 *motherly care, mothering* **bosei hogo**
⇒環境保護 *environmental protection* **kankyō hogo**
保護区 *sanctuary, safehouse* **hogoku**
保護者 *parents & guardians* **hogosha**
加護 *divine providence, act-of-God* **kago**
介護 *care, nursing* **kaigo**

警護 *guard, convoy, escort* **keigo**
救護 *relief, aid, help* **kyūgo**
守護 *protection, guarding* **shugo**
擁護 *protection, support* **yōgo**
養護 *care, nursing* **yōgo**
養護学校 *school for the disabled* **yōgo gakkō**
弁護士 *attorney, lawyer, barrister* **bengoshi**
看護婦 *female nurse* **kangofu**
看護師 *male-or-female nurse* **kangoshi**
教護院 *juvenile reformatory* **kyōgoin**
如護が島 *isle of amazons* **nyogogashima**

衛*rotect, 796*
防*rotect, 736*
守*efence, 366*

謹*espect, 962*

687-B

護*rotect thy* 穫*arvest &* 獲*cquired interest...*

禾 (tree branch)

穫*arvest*   穫*rop yield*

KAKU
harvest, crop yield, reaping

収穫 *harvest, yield* **shūkaku**
収穫物 *crop, yield* **shūkakubutsu**
収穫時 *harvest time* **shūkakuji**
収穫祭 *harvest feasting* **shūkakusai**
収穫高 *crop harvest* **shūkakudaka**
収穫期 *harvest season* **shūkakuki**
収穫予想 *crop estimate* **shūkaku yosō**

FLIP: 7.2.a. Right Top (flat)
FLIP: 7.3.b. Right Bottom (stem)

刈*utting, 687*	獲*ain, 829*
切*utting, 352*	得*ain, 940*
植*lant, 783*	益*ains, 622*
畑*lantation, 482*	利*ains, 686*
果*ruit, 287*	

獲*cquire, 829*

687-C

護*rotect thy* 穫*arvest &* 獲*cquired interest...*

犬⇔犭 (dog; beast)

獲

獲*cquire*   獲*atch game*

e(ru), KAKU
acquire, catch game

獲物 *catch, capture* **emono**
漁獲 *fishing, fishery* **gyokaku**
漁獲物 *fishing catch* **gyokakubutsu**
漁獲高 *amount of fishing catch* **gyokakudaka**
捕獲 *capture, seizure* **hokaku**
捕獲物 *fishing catch* **hokakubutsu**
捕獲高 *fishing catch* **hokakudaka**
一獲 *one grab, one catch* **ikkaku**
一獲千金 *rich quick scheme* **ikkaku senkin**
獲得 *acquisition, gaining* **kakutoku**
獲得物 *purchase, accession* **kakutokubutsu**
乱獲 *indiscriminate hunting* **rankaku**
濫獲 *overfishing, overhunting* **rankaku**
鹵獲 *capture, seize* **rokaku**
鹵獲物 *spoils, loot* **rokakubutsu**
収穫 *good game, good fight* **shūkaku**

FLIP: 7.2.b. Right Top (stem)
FLIP: 7.3.b. Right Bottom (stem)

益*enefit, 622*
得*dvantage, 940*
利*dvantage, 686*

穫*arvest, 829*

688-A

Size of 腹tomach 複ultiplies with large fries...

肉⇔月 (flesh, body part)

腹tomach   腹bdomen

腹

hara, FUKU
stomach, abdomen, tummy, belly

FLIP: 8.0.a. Inner (flat)

腹ぺこ *starving, hungry, famish* **harapeko**
茶腹 *tea-filled belly* **chabara**
腹筋 *abdominal muscle* **fukkin**
腹案 *idea, plan, thought* **fukuan**
腹部 *stomach, abdomen* **fukubu**
腹膜 *peritoneum* **fukumaku**
腹心 *confidant, confidante* **fukushin**
腹痛 *stomach ache, colic* **fukutsū**
剛腹 *magnanimity, tolerance* **gōfuku**
業腹 *resentment, anger, rancour* **gōhara**
腹芸 *subtle communication* **haragei**
腹子 *fish eggs* **harako**
腹巻 *belly-, waist band* **haramaki**
蛇腹 *bellows, cornice* **jabara**
開腹 *abdomen incision* **kaifuku**
口腹 *true intent, ulterior motive* **kōfuku**
空腹 *empty stomach* **kūfuku**
満腹 *eating to the full* **manpuku**
水腹 *surviving only on water* **mizubara, mizuppara**

女腹 *mother of all girls (no boys)* **onnabara**
男腹 *mother of all boys (no girls)* **otokobara**
立腹 *enrage, infuriate, incense* **rippuku**
切腹 *harakiri, disembowelment* **seppuku**
下腹 *lower abdomen* **shitabara**
裏腹 *opposite of one's words* **urahara**
腹違い *siblings of different mothers* **harachigai**
腹立ち *anger, temper* **haradachi**
腹黒い *malicious, evil-hearted* **haraguroi**
空き腹 *starving, hungry,* **sukibara, sukippara**
太鼓腹 *potbelly, beer-belly* **taikobara**

胃 *tomach, 598*		肺 *ung, 305*
腸 *ntestine, 150*		臓 *rgan, 565*
肝 *iver, 711*		

復 *ecovery, 442*

688-B

Size of 腹tomach 複ultiplies with large fries...

衣⇔ネ (clothing)

複ultiply   複ompound

複

FUKU
multiply, compound, copy, duplicate, reproduce, replicate

FLIP: 8.0.a. Inner (flat)
Facing: 3.0. ☞☜ Across

複文 *complex sentence* **fukubun**
複眼 *crossed eyes* **fukugan**
複合 *compounding* **fukugō**
複合語 *word compound* **fukugōgo**
複合体 *multiple, complex* **fukugōtai**
複合的 *multiple, complex* **fukugōteki**
複合企業 *conglomerate, big business* **fukugō kigyō**
複方 *compound drug prescription* **fukuhō**
複本 *duplicate, copy* **fukuhon**
複衣 *lined garment* **fukui**
複音 *compound sound* **fukuon**
複利 *compounded interest* **fukuri**
複利法 *compound interest method* **fukurihō**
複製 *replica, reproduction* **fukusei**
複線 *double track, two-tiered* **fukusen**
複写 *reproduction, duplication, copy* **fukusha**
複写機 *duplicator, copying machine* **fukushaki**
複写紙 *copying paper, carbon paper* **fukushashi**
複視 *polyopia, compounded vision* **fukushi**

複式 *double-entry accounting* **fukushiki**
複式簿記 *double-entry ledger* **fukushiki boki**
複数 *plural, more than one* **fukusū**
複葉 *compound leaf* **fukuyō**
複座 *two-seater* **fukuza**
複座機 *two-seater plane* **fukuzaki**
複雑 *complicated, complex* **fukuzatsu**
複雑怪奇 *inscrutable* **fukuzatsu kaiki**
複雑化 *complication* **fukuzatsuka**
重複 *overlapping, duplication* **jūfuku, chōfuku**
複十字 *double-crosspiece cross* **fukujūji**

倍 *ultiply, 950*		拡 *nlarge, 205*
殖 *ncrease, 784*		写 *uplicate, 349*
増 *ncrease, 837*		

復 *ecovery, 442*

689-A

鎮*alm* & 慎*iscreet, residents in Crete...*

鎮*acify*　　鎮*alm-down*

金 (metal)

FLIP: 5.0.b. Left & Right

shizu(meru), shizu(maru), CHIN
pacify, calm-down, quell, subside

鎮まる *subside, settle to the bottom* **shizumaru**
文鎮 *paper weight* **bunchin**
鎮圧 *suppression, repression* **chin'atsu**
鎮撫 *pacification, suppression* **chinbu**
鎮台 *garrison* **chindai**
鎮護 *protection, guarding* **chingo**
鎮守 *village shrine* **chinju**
鎮守府 *naval depot* **chinjufu**
鎮火 *extinction, putting out* **chinka**
鎮魂 *repose of souls* **chinkon**
鎮魂曲 *requiem, funeral song* **chinkonkyoku**
鎮魂祭 *memorial-, funeral service* **chinkonsai**
鎮静 *subsiding, calming* **chinsei**
鎮静剤 *sedative, tranquilliser* **chinseizai**
鎮定 *suppression, stifling* **chintei**
鎮痛 *pain reliever* **chintsū**
鎮痛剤 *pain killer, lenitive, analgesic* **chintsūzai**
鎮座 *enshrinement, deitification* **chinza**

風鎮 *hanging scroll weight* **fūchin**
重鎮 *leading figure, main cast* **jūchin**
地鎮祭 *Shintō ground-breaking rites* **jichinsai**
取り鎮める *quiet, quell* **torishizumeru**

康*ranquillity, 881*	黙*uiet, 846*
静*uiet, 230*	幽*uiet, 897*
寧*uiet, 967*	康*olace, 881*

鎖*hain, 665*

689-B

鎮*alm* & 慎*iscreet, residents in Crete...*

慎*iscreet*　　慎*odest*

心 ⇔ 忄 ⇔ 㣺 (feelings)

FLIP: 7.0.b2. Right (stem)

tsutsushi(mu), SHIN
discreet, modest, prudent

慎み *modesty, discretion, prudence* **tsutsushimi**
慎み深い *discreet, prudent* **tsutsushimibukai**
慎ましい *modest, reserved* **tsutsumashii**
戒慎 *cautious, discretion* **kaishin**
謹慎 *good behaviour; temporary absence* **kinshin**
⇒不謹慎 *indiscretion, imprudence* **fukinshin**
慎重 *careful, cautious, prudent* **shinchō**

倹*odest, 938*
申*peak humble, 89*
謙*odesty, 805*

真*incere, 487*

690-A

頭ead 煩nxiety for those fiesty...

頁 (large shell, page)

頭ead　　頭hief

atama, kashira, TŌ, TO, ZU
head, chief, leader, principal, boss

FLIP: 7.0.b2. Right (stem)

頭株 *leader, leading power* **atamakabu**
頭数 *head, chief, boss* **atamakazu**
頭金 *down payment, deposit* **atamakin**
冒頭 *beginning, opening* **bōtō**
没頭 *devotion, absorption* **bottō**
弾頭 *warhead* **dantō**
駅頭 *train station entrance* **ekitō**
陣頭 *lead* **jintō**
会頭 *association president* **kaitō**
鶏頭 *cockscomb* **keitō**
光頭 *bald head* **kōtō**
教頭 *school vice-principal* **kyōtō**
念頭 *mind* **nentō**
乳頭 *breast nipple* **nyūtō**
路頭 *abandoned family* **rotō**
先頭 *forefront, frontal* **sentō**
指頭 *fingertip* **shitō**
台頭 *rise, gaining power* **taitō**
店頭 *store front, stall front* **tentō**

点頭 *nod, move one's head in approval* **tentō**
頭部 *head part* **tōbu**
頭取 *bank president* **tōdori**
頭骨 *forehead* **tōkotsu**
頭上 *overhead, top* **zujō**
頭巾 *hood* **zukin**
頭脳 *brain, head* **zunō**
頭脳流出 *brain drain* **zunō ryūshutsu**
頭痛 *migraine, headache* **zutsū**
偏頭痛 *migraine, headache* **henzutsū**
頭蓋骨 *skull, skeleton head* **zugaikotsu**

首ead, 311	主rincipal, 11
長hief, 273	領overn, 874
導uidance, 312	統overn, 885

頼equest, 562

690-B

頭ead 煩nxiety for those fiesty...

火⇔灬 (fire)

煩nxiety　　煩othersome

wazura(u), wazura(wasu), HAN, GON
anxiety, bothersome, annoyance, distress, vexing

FLIP: 5.0.b. Left & Right

煩がる *get annoyed, ~bothered* **urusagaru**
煩悩 *worldly passions, unholy desires* **bonnō**
煩忙 *pressed with urgent matters* **hanbō**
煩語 *tedious language* **hango**
煩悶 *worry, anxiety, trouble* **hanmon**
煩務 *tedious, laborious* **hanmu**
煩労 *trouble, anxiety* **hanrō**
煩累 *annoyance, nuisance, irksome* **hanrui**
煩瑣 *complex, complicated* **hansa**
煩多 *"too many cooks spoil the soup..."* **hanta**
煩雑 *complex, complicated* **hanzatsu**
煩型 *fastidiousness* **urusagata**
子煩悩 *fond of children* **kobonnō**
恋煩い *lovesickness* **koiwazurai**
小煩い *petty irritation* **kourusai**
口煩い *fault-finding, nagging* **kuchiurusai**
長煩い *long recovery from illness* **nagawazurai**
思い煩い *trouble, anxiety, angst, distress* **omoiwazurai**

虞nxiety, 889	慨egret, 316
苦nguish, 477	憾egret, 46
悩nguish, 48	惜egret, 281
悔egret, 712	困roblematic, 863

慎iscreet, 831

691-A
Smiling 顔ace 傾nclines to gaze...

頁 (large shell, page)

顔ace　　**顔acial**

kao, GAN
face, facial

FLIP: 7.0.b2. Right (stem)

朝顔	*morning glory flower*	**asagao**
童顔	*baby face, young-looking*	**dōgan**
笑顔	*smile, smiling face*	**egao**
古顔	*familiar face*	**furugao**
顔面	*face surface*	**ganmen**
顔料	*pigment, colour, hue*	**ganryō**
拝顔	*face-to-face meeting*	**haigan**
昼顔	*bindweed*	**hirugao**
汗顔	*sweaty face (from shame)*	**kangan**
顔色	*facial complexion*	**kaoiro**
顔役	*influential, big shot*	**kaoyaku**
紅顔	*rosy face*	**kōgan**
丸顔	*round face, moon face*	**marugao**
涙顔	*tearful face*	**namidagao**
寝顔	*sleepy face*	**negao**
温顔	*gentle-looking*	**ongan**
素顔	*face without cosmetics*	**sugao**
酔顔	*drunken face*	**suigan, yoigao**
横顔	*face in profile, side view*	**yokogao**

夕顔	*sleepy face; moonflower*	**yūgao**
顔合わせ	*first meeting, ~get-together*	**kaoawase**
顔触れ	*line-up, personnel*	**kaobure**
顔立ち	*features, looks, semblance*	**kaodachi**
顔負け	*embarrassment, disgrace*	**kaomake**
顔見世	*showing one's face; debut*	**kaomise**
顔つき	*look, countenance*	**kaotsuki**
泣き顔	*tearful face*	**nakigao**
似顔絵	*portrait, likeness*	**nigaoe**
得意顔	*triumphant look*	**tokuigao**
作り顔	*feigned-look*	**zukurigao, tsukurigao**

表xpression, 378		容ppearance, 492
面ace, 36		姿ppearance, 609
態ppearance, 322		

顕bvious, 931

691-B
Smiling 顔ace 傾nclines to gaze...

人⇔亻 (person)

傾ncline　　**傾endency**

katamu(ku), katamu(keru), KEI
incline, tendency, predilection, proclivity, propensity

FLIP: 7.0.b2. Right (stem)

傾き	*inclination, trend, tilt*	**katamuki**
傾聴	*listening intently*	**keichō**
傾注	*devoting oneself*	**keichū**
傾度	*inclination, degree*	**keido**
傾角	*angle of inclination*	**keikaku**
傾国	*beauty; courtesan*	**keikoku**
傾向	*tendency, inclination*	**keikō**
傾功	*flattery, favour-seeking*	**keikō**
傾城	*beauty; courtesan*	**keisei**
傾斜	*inclination, slope*	**keisha**
⇒急傾斜	*steep slope, sudden curve*	**kyūkeisha**
傾斜度	*degree of inclination, gradient*	**keishado**
傾斜角	*angle of inclination*	**keishakaku**
傾斜面	*slope, inclined plane*	**keishamen**
傾倒	*devotion, commitment*	**keitō**
左傾	*leaning to leftist views*	**sakei**
右傾	*leaning to rightist views*	**ukei**
前傾	*forward-bending posture*	**zenkei**

偏ncline, 43		偏artial, 43
斜rajectory, 648		片artial, 359
可ossible, 15		半artial, 484
志ntention, 426		角ngle, 400

頻requent, 272

692-A

A 頑tubborn 題opic: 頒istribution of narcotics...

頁 (large shell, page)

頑tubborn　頑bstinate

GAN, kataku(na)
stubborn, obstinate, recalcitrant, unchanging, headstrong

頑愚	hard-headed fool	**gangu**
頑丈	sturdy, strong, firm	**ganjō**
頑健	robust, excellent health	**ganken**
頑固	stubborn, obstinate	**ganko**
頑固おやじ	obstinate old man	**ganko oyaji**
頑強	stubborn, obstinate	**gankyō**
頑迷	bigot, obstinate, zealot	**ganmei**
頑冥	bigot, obstinate, zealot	**ganmei**
頑張り	persistence, doggedness	**ganbari**
頑張り屋	hard worker, workaholic	**ganbariya**
頑張る	exert one's best, hold out	**ganbaru**
頑是無い	innocent & harmless	**ganzenai**

FLIP: 5.0.b. Left & Right

緊ard, 599	硬ardness, 402
固ard, 491	強trong, 894
凝arden, 57	剛trong, 975

傾ncline, 833

692-B

A 頑tubborn 題opic: 頒istribution of narcotics...

頁 (large shell, page)

題heme　題opic　題itle

DAI
theme, topic, title, problem, subject

傍題	subtitle	**bōdai**
勅題	imperial poem contest	**chokudai**
題言	title, headline	**daigen**
題意	meaning of the title	**daii**
題辞	epigraph	**daiji**
題字	book title	**daiji**
題名	subject title	**daimei**
題目	subject, theme, title	**daimoku**
題材	theme, subject, topic	**daizai**
演題	theme, subject, topic	**endai**
副題	subtitle	**fukudai**
放題	"(eat) all you can..."	**hōdai**
本題	main theme	**hondai**
標題	title, headline, caption	**hyōdai**
表題	title, headline, caption	**hyōdai**
課題	subject, theme, task	**kadai**
仮題	provisional theme	**kadai**
解題	bibliography	**kaidai**
季題	seasonal subject	**kidai**

FLIP: 7.0.b2. Right (stem)
FLIP: 6.1. Left Top

命題	proposition, resolution	**meidai**
問題	problem, question, trouble	**mondai**
⇒死活問題	matter of life-or-death	
	shikatsu mondai	
⇒程度問題	question of degree	
	teido mondai	
無題	untitled, no title	**mudai**
難題	problem proposal	**nandai**
例題	lesson exercise, ~drill	**reidai**
類題	theme classification	**ruidai**
宿題	homework, assignment	**shukudai**
即題	impromptu, extemporaneous	**sokudai**
話題	topic, subject, theme	**wadai**

件ubject, 179	
問atter, 283	

顕bvious, 931

692-C

A 頒tubborn 題opic; 頒istribution of narcotics...

頁 (large shell, page)

頒istribution   頒etail

HAN
distribution, retail

頒価　retail price, distribution price　**hanka**
頒行　distribution, circulation　**hankō**
頒白　grey hair, silver hair　**hanpaku**
頒布　distribution, circulation　**hanpu**

FLIP: 7.0.b2. Right (stem)

配istribute, 754	輸hipment, 660
届eliver, 631	荷reight, 877
送ending, 708	貨reight, 191
運ransport, 295	搭reight, 146
搬ransport, 323	

頑tubborn, 834

693-A

Sheep 飼reeding to soar for King's 嗣uccessor...

食 (food)

飼reeding   飼aising

ka(u), SHI
breeding, raising, hatchery

飼い葉　feed, fodder　**kaiba**
飼い葉桶　manger, feed rack　**kaibaoke**
飼い鳥　poultry, chicken farm　**kaidori**
飼い草　hay　**kaigusa**
飼い犬　pet dog, house dog　**kaiinu**
飼い猫　pet cat, house cat　**kaineko**
飼い主　pet owner, ~master　**kainushi**
飼い桶　manger, feed rack　**kaioke**
飼い殺し　keeping a servant-for-life　**kaigoroshi**
飼い馴らす　tame, domesticate　**kainarasu**
蚕飼　silkworm raising　**kogai**
飼育　raising, breeding　**shiiku**
飼育係　animal breeder, stock farmer　**shiikugakari**
飼育場　livestock farm　**shiikujō**
飼育者　animal breeder, stock farmer　**shiikusha**
飼料　animal feed　**shiryō**
⇒配合飼料　mixed-, assorted feed　**haigōshiryō**
飼養　raising, breeding　**shiyō**
羊飼い　shepherd　**hitsujikai**

Facing: 3.0. ☞☜ Across
FLIP: 8.0.a. Inner (flat)

子飼い　raising from an early age　**kogai**
手飼い　raising from an early age　**tegai**
鵜飼い　cormorant fishing　**ukai**

畜reeding, 528	馬orse, 318
養reeding, 253	猫at, 271
牛attle, 179	犬og, 7
鶏hicken, 842	

飽oredom, 665

693-B

Sheep 飼reeding to soar for King's 嗣uccessor...

口 (mouth)

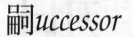

嗣uccessor   嗣nherit

yotsugi, SHI
successor, inherit

FLIP: 6.0.b. Left (stem)

継嗣 *successor to the throne* **keishi**
後嗣 *imperial heir, heiress* **kōshi**
皇嗣 *crown prince, imperial heir* **kōshi**
令嗣 *"Your, His, Her Majesty..."* **reishi**
嗣子 *heir, heiress* **shishi**
⇒皇帝の嗣子 *emperor's heir*
　　kōtei no shishi

嫡eirling, 966	乙econd group, 5
副eputy, 332	次ext, 460
後fter, 897	継ontinuity, 958

銅opper, 246

694-A

A 僧uddhist-monk once said: 増ncrease of 憎atred consumes the hater instead...

人⇔亻 (person)

僧

SŌ
Buddhist monk

FLIP: 7.0.a. Right (flat)

悪僧 *evil monk* **akusō**
伴僧 *monk assistant* **bansō**
学僧 *scholarly monk* **gakusō**
下僧 *low-ranking monk* **gesō**
怪僧 *evil monk* **kaisō**
貴僧 *esteemed monk* **kisō**
小僧 *young monk* **kozō**
客僧 *travelling monk* **kyakusō**
名僧 *famous monk* **meisō**
尼僧 *nun, sister* **nisō**
女僧 *Buddhist nun* **nyosō**
老僧 *old monk* **rōsō**
僧房 *monks dormitory* **sōbō**
僧堂 *meditation hall* **sōdō**
僧服 *monk robe* **sōfuku**
僧号 *Buddhist name* **sōgō**
僧兵 *armed monk* **sōhei**
僧衣 *monk robe* **sōi**
僧院 *monastery, convent* **sōin**

僧正 *archbishop, bishop* **sōjō**
僧門 *priesthood* **sōmon**
僧尼 *monks & nuns* **sōni**
僧侶 *Buddhist priest* **sōryo**
僧籍 *monk hood, monasticism* **sōseki**
僧職 *monk hood, monasticism* **sōshoku**
若僧 *youngster, brat* **wakazō**
役僧 *assistant priest* **yakusō**
禅僧 *Zen Buddhist monk* **zensō**
大僧正 *cardinal, high-ranking monk* **daisōjō**
破戒僧 *sinful-, corrupt monk* **hakaisō**

仏uddha, 683	禅en Buddhism, 782
盆uddhist Feast, 594	祈rayer, 184
坊uddhist monk, 736	拝rayer, 636

増ncrease, 837

694-A

A 僧uddhist-monk once said: 増ncrease of 憎atred consumes
   the hater instead...

土 (ground, soil)

増ncrease   増ultiply

ma(su), fu(eru), fu(yasu), ZŌ
increase, multiply, proliferate

FLIP: 5.0.a Left & Right

倍増	doubling, multiplication	**baizō**
激増	sudden increase, swelling	**gekizō**
純増	net increase, ~increment	**junzō**
累増	cumulation, progressive increase	**ruizō**
年増	mature woman	**toshima**
漸増	gradual increase	**zenzō**
増便	increase in flight service	**zōbin**
増値	establishing more offices	**zōchi**
増長	presumptuous, arrogant	**zōchō**
増大	increase, enlargement	**zōdai**
増援	reinforcement, strengthening	**zōen**
増額	increase, adding, raising	**zōgaku**
増配	increased rations	**zōhai**
増兵	reinforcement, fresh troops	**zōhei**
増員	staff increase	**zōin**
増加	increase, rise, grow	**zōka**
増刊	special issue, extra	**zōkan**
増結	addition, summing up	**zōketsu**
増血	blood increase	**zōketsu**

増強	reinforcement, build-up	**zōkyō**
増量	increased weight, dosage	**zōryō**
増産	increased production	**zōsan**
増刷	increased printing	**zōsatsu**
増設	increased construction	**zōsetsu**
増殖	increase, multiply, diffuse	**zōshoku**
増収	increased income	**zōshū**
増税	tax hike, tax increase	**zōzei**
肉増し	thickening, fattening	**nikumashi**
建て増し	extension of a building	**tatemashi**
割り増し	extra, premium	**warimashi**
焼き増し	extra printing	**yakimashi**

殖ncrease, 784	複ultiply, 830
加articipate, 201	拡nlarge, 205
携articipate, 151	多umerous, 187

憎nimosity, 837

694-C

A 僧uddhist-monk once said: 増ncrease of 憎atred consumes
   the hater instead...

心 ⇔ 忄 ⇔ 小 (feelings)

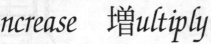

憎atred   憎nimosity

niku(mu), niku(rashii), niku(shimi), ZŌ
hatred, animosity, antagonism, belligerence, enmity, hostility, aversion

FLIP: 7.0.a. Right (flat)

憎しみ	hate, hatred, enmity	**nikushimi**
憎らしい	hateful, despiseful	**nikurashii**
憎憎しい	hateful, despiseful	**nikunikushii**
憎み合う	mutual hatred	**nikumiau**
憎まれ口	verbal abuse, foul mouth	**nikumareguchi**
憎まれ役	villain, bad guy	**nikumareyaku**
憎まれっ子	despised child	**nikumarekko**
生憎	"unfortunately, unluckily..."	**ainiku**
愛憎	love & hate	**aizō, ainiku**
憎気	ill-feeling, hatred, grudge	**nikuge**
憎悪	hatred, abhorrence, loathing	**zōo**
憎悪心	hatred, abhorrence, loathing	**zōoshin**
心憎い	detestable, deplorable	**kokoronikui**
小憎らしい	hatred, provocative	**konikurashii**
面憎い	provoking, inciteful, instigating	**tsuranikui**

憤nrage, 848	侮espise, 711
嫌espise, 805	鬼evil, 935
卑espise, 936	魔evil, 332

僧uddhist monk, 836

695-A

層ayers of 贈ifts to send by airlift...

尸 (corpse)

層tratum   層ayer

SŌ
stratum, layer

FLIP: 8.0.a. Inner (flat)
FLIP: 4.0.a. Bottom (flat)

地層 *stratum* **chisō**
中層 *middle stratum* **chūsō**
断層 *dislocation, fault* **dansō**
⇒活断層 *active faultline* **katsudansō**
⇒世代の断層 *generation gap* **sedai no dansō**
表層 *outer layer* **hyōsō**
一層 *all the more, even further* **issō**
一層目 *first layer* **issōme**
上層 *upper-level* **jōsō**
階層 *level, stratum* **kaisō**
階層化 *social stratification* **kaisōka**
各層 *every class, all sectors* **kakusō**
下層 *lower classes* **kasō**
鉱層 *ore bed deposits* **kōsō**
高層 *high-rise, towering structure* **kōsō**
深層 *depths, abyss* **shinsō**
層状 *layer, stratum* **sōjō**
層卒 *sudden, hurried* **sōsotsu**
層雲 *stratum clouds* **sōun**

炭層 *coal bed deposits* **tansō**
油層 *oil stratum, petroleum deposits* **yusō**
知識層 *educated class* **chishikisō**
沖積層 *alluvium* **chūsekisō**
泥土層 *dirt bed* **deidosō**
電離層 *ionosphere* **denrisō**
高木層 *tree layer* **kōbokusō**
洪積層 *diluvium* **kōsekisō**
乱層雲 *nimbostratus* **ransōun**
成層圏 *stratosphere* **seisōken**
社会層 *social classes* **shakaisō**
超高層ビル *skyscraper* **chōkōsō biru**

級*evel, 189*	段*evel, 555*	位*tatus, 235*
等*rade, 251*	階*evel, 129*	

膚*kin, 69*

695-B

層ayers of 贈ifts to send by airlift...

貝 (shell, old money)

贈onation   贈ift

oku(ru), ZŌ, SŌ
donation, gift

FLIP: 5.0.a Left & Right

遺贈 *property disposition upon death* **izō**
受贈 *receiving a gift* **juzō**
受贈者 *gift recipient* **juzōsha**
恵贈 *receiving a gift* **keizō**
寄贈 *present, gift* **kizō**
寄贈品 *gift, donation, present* **kizōhin**
寄贈者 *donor, presenter* **kizōsha**
贈り物 *present, gift* **okurimono**
贈り名 *posthumous title, ~rank* **okurina**
追贈 *conferment, award* **tsuizō**
贈号 *posthumous name* **zōgō**
贈本 *gift book, complimentary book* **zōhon**
贈位 *posthumous rank conferment* **zōi**
贈呈 *presentation, offering* **zōtei**
贈呈本 *complimentary book* **zōteibon**
贈呈品 *present, gift* **zōteihin**
贈呈者 *presenter, donor* **zōteisha**
贈呈式 *presentation ceremony* **zōteishiki**
贈答 *exchange-of-gifts* **zōtō**

贈答品 *present, gift* **zōtōhin**
贈賄 *bribery, payoff* **zōwai**
贈賄罪 *bribery, payoff* **zōwaizai**
贈賄事件 *bribery case* **zōwai jiken**
贈与 *donation, presentation* **zōyo**
贈与者 *giver, donor, contributor* **zōyosha**
贈与税 *gift tax, donation tax* **zōyozei**
贈与物 *gift, present* **zōyobutsu**
贈収賄 *bribery, payoff, grease money* **zōshūwai**

施*estow, 649*	献*onation, 414*
賜*estow, 150*	呈*onation, 618*
催*ponsor, 416*	賄*urnish, 806*

憎*nimosity, 837*

696-A

Magic 鏡irror at the 境oundary in East Timor...

鏡*irror*   鏡*ptical*

金 (metal)

FLIP: 5.0.b. Left & Right

kagami, KYŌ

mirror, optical, reflecting glass

銅鏡	*bronze mirror*	**dōkyō**
円鏡	*round mirror*	**enkyō**
破鏡	*broken mirror*	**hakyō**
胃鏡	*gastroscope*	**ikyō**
検鏡	*microscopic examination*	**kenkyō**
鏡台	*dressing table; vanity*	**kyōdai**
鏡高	*mirror height*	**kyōkō**
鏡面	*mirror surface*	**kyōmen**
眼鏡	*eyeglasses, spectacles*	**megane, gankyō**
⇒老眼鏡	*old person eyeglasses*	**rōgankyō**
⇒双眼鏡	*binoculars, field glasses*	**sōgankyō**
⇒天眼鏡	*magnifying glass*	**tengankyō**
⇒検眼鏡	*ophthalmoscope*	**kengankyō**
⇒虫眼鏡	*magnifying glass*	**mushimegane**
眼鏡屋	*optical shop, optometrist*	**meganeya**
水鏡	*mirror-like water surface*	**mizukagami**
神鏡	*sacred mirror*	**shinkyō**
手鏡	*hand mirror*	**tekagami**
望遠鏡	*telescope, field glasses*	**bōenkyō**

鼻眼鏡	*pince-nez*	**hanamegane**
反射鏡	*reflexive mirror*	**hanshakyō**
色眼鏡	*coloured eye glasses*	**iromegane**
拡大鏡	*magnifying glass*	**kakudaikyō**
顕微鏡	*microscope*	**kenbikyō**
万華鏡	*kaleidoscope*	**mangekyō**
内視鏡	*endoscope*	**naishikyō**
凹面鏡	*concave mirror*	**ōmenkyō**
立体鏡	*stereoscope*	**rittaikyō**
潜望鏡	*periscope*	**senbōkyō**
凸面鏡	*convex mirror*	**totsumenkyō**

鑑*irror*, 857	射*hoot*, 504	容*ppearance*, 492
映*eflect*, 217	象*mage*, 530	姿*ppearance*, 609

境*oundary*, 839

696-B

Magic 鏡irror at the 境oundary in East Timor...

❶境*oundary*   ❷境*ituation*

土 (ground, soil)

FLIP: 5.0.b. Left & Right

sakai, KYŌ, KEI

boundary, borderline; situation

❶	越境	*trespassing, illegal entry*	**ekkyō**
	辺境	*frontier, borderland*	**henkyō**
	国境	*national border, territorial boundary*	**kokkyō**
	境域	*boundary, border*	**kyōiki**
	境界	*boundary, border*	**kyōkai**
	魔境	*demon-infested place*	**makyō**
	見境	*distinction, discernment*	**misakai**
	村境	*village boundary*	**murazakai**
	老境	*old age, senility*	**rōkyō**
	境目	*border, borderline, boundary line*	**sakaime**
	仙境	*fairyland, enchanted land*	**senkyō**
	心境	*frame of mind, mental state*	**shinkyō**
	潮境	*intersecting point*	**shiosakai**
	幽境	*fantasy land*	**yūkyō**
	新境地	*new area, fresh grounds*	**shinkyōchi**
	桃源境	*Shangri-la, paradise*	**tōgenkyō**
❷	画境	*painting mood*	**gakyō**
	逆境	*adversity, bad times*	**gyakkyō**
	悲境	*adverse situation*	**hikyō**

秘境	*unexplored regions*	**hikyō**
順境	*prosperity, the good times*	**junkyō**
佳境	*climax, highlight*	**kakyō**
環境	*environment, surroundings*	**kankyō**
境内	*Shintō grounds*	**keidai**
苦境	*difficulties, adversity, dilemma*	**kukyō**
境地	*stage, state, ground, path*	**kyōchi**
境涯	*circumstances, environment*	**kyōgai**
境遇	*circumstances, environment*	**kyōgū**
進境	*progress, improvement*	**shinkyō**
生死の境	*verge of life & death*	**seishi no sakai**

限*oundary*, 771		最*aximum*, 423	
涯*imit*, 890		囲*nclose*, 361	
限*imit*, 771		郭*nclose*, 398	

鏡*irror*, 839

697-A

隠idden 穏ranquillity in the islands of Tahiti...

β ⇔ 阜 (village=left)

隠idden   隠onceal

kaku(reru) kaku(su), IN
hidden, conceal, confidential, covert, secret

Facing: 3.0. ☞☜ Across
Facing: 4.0. ☜☞ Apart

隠微 hidden, abstruse **inbi**
隠元 green beans **ingen**
隠語 secret language **ingo**
隠見 appearing & disappearing **inken**
隠居 retirement from active life **inkyo**
隠忍 patience, endurance, diligence **innin**
隠士 reclusive person, hermit **inshi**
隠退 seclusion, secluded life **intai**
隠匿 concealment, keeping secret **intoku**
⇒犯罪隠匿 wrongful imprisonment **hanzai intoku**
隠然 concealed, hidden, latent **inzen**
隠密 private, secret **onmitsu**
神隠 hidden deity, hidden blessing **shin'in**
隠れ家 hideout, safehouse **kakurega**
隠れ蓑 cover, shield **kakuremino**
隠れん坊 hide-&-seek game **kakurenbō**
隠し女 mistress, paramour **kakushi onna**
隠しカメラ hidden-, security camera **kakushi kamera**
隠しマイク hidden microphone **kakushi maiku**

隠し芸 parlour trick, stunt **kakushigei**
隠し子 illegitimate child **kakushigo**
隠し釘 covered nail **kakushikugi**
隠し財産 hidden wealth **kakushi zaisan**
隠し場所 hide-out, hidden place **kakushibasho**
隠し撮り sneak shot **kakushidori**
隠し通す prevent from leaking out **kakushitoosu**
隠密 secret, hidden, covert **onmitsu**
目隠し blindfold, blinkers, blind, screen **mekakushi**
角隠し Shintō brides head dress **tsunokakushi**
内隠し inner pocket, secret pocket **uchikakushi**
包み隠す conceal, keep secret **tsutsumikakusu**

匿onceal, 277	覆onceal, 602	秘ecret, 219
忍onceal, 535	秘idden, 219	密ecret, 220

穏alm, 840

697-B

隠idden 穏ranquillity in the islands of Tahiti...

禾 (tree branch) 穏

穏alm   穏ranquillity

oda(yaka), ON
calm, tranquillity, mild

Facing: 3.0. ☞☜ Across
Facing: 4.0. ☜☞ Apart

穏やか calm, quiet, mild **odayaka**
安穏 peace & quiet **an'on**
不穏 disquieting, unsettling **fuon**
不穏当 improper **fuontō**
不穏分子 disturbing element **fuon bunshi**
平穏 calmness, quietness, serenity **heion**
穏便 gentle, amicable **onbin**
穏健 moderate, mild **onken**
穏健派 moderates, middle ground **onkenha**
穏当 appropriate, proper **ontō**
穏和 moderate, mild **onwa**
静穏 calmness, serenity **seion**

康ranquillity, 881	黙uiet, 846
静uiet, 230	幽uiet, 897
寧uiet, 967	康olace, 881

隠onceal, 840

698-A
緑*reen Peace laments* 録*ecord on* 緑*nvironment...*

糸 (thread, continuity)

緑*reen*　　緑*nvironment*

midori, RYOKU, ROKU
green, ecology, Environment

Facing: 3.0. ☞ ☜ Across

浅緑	*pale green* **asamidori**
深緑	*dark green* **fukamidori**, **shinryoku**
黄緑	*yellow green* **kimidori**
緑色	*green* **midoriiro**
緑青	*copper rust, ~green* **rokushō**
緑化	*reforestation, tree planting* **ryokuka**
緑化運動	*tree-planting, reforestation* **ryokuka undō**
緑便	*green stool* **ryokuben**
緑茶	*Japanese green tea* **ryokucha**
緑地	*green land, tract of land* **ryokuchi**
緑土	*green area* **ryokudo**
緑風	*early summer wind* **ryokufū**
緑玉	*emerald* **ryokugyoku**
緑肥	*green manure* **ryokuhi**
緑陰	*tree shade* **ryokuin**
緑樹	*greenery* **ryokuju**
緑門	*arch of green field* **ryokumon**
緑林	*horse-riding bandits* **ryokurin**
緑酒	*green wine (sweet)* **ryokushu**

緑藻	*green algae* **ryokusō**
緑豆	*green beans* **ryokutō**
緑野	*green field* **ryokuya**
緑葉	*green leaves* **ryokuyō**
青緑	*blue green* **seiryoku**, **aomidori**
新緑	*fresh green leaves* **shinryoku**
薄緑	*pale green* **usumidori**
葉緑素	*chlorophyll* **yōryokuso**
暗緑色	*dark green* **anryokushoku**
緑柱石	*beryl* **ryokuchūseki**
緑内障	*glaucoma* **ryokunaishō**

環*nvirons, 165*	菜*egetable, 915*
地*and, 688*	植*egetation, 783*
陸*and, 140*	農*arming, 446*

線*ine, 531*

698-B
緑*reen Peace laments* 録*ecord on* 緑*nvironment...*

金 (metal)

録*ecord*　　録*egistry*

ROKU
record, registry, archive, documentation, journal, transcript

FLIP: 6.0.a. Left (flat)
Facing: 1.2. ☜ West (V)

付録	*appendix, reference* **furoku**
語録	*analects, proverbs* **goroku**
秘録	*secret record* **hiroku**
実録	*factual record* **jitsuroku**
記録	*record, chronicle* **kiroku**
⇒判決記録	*court records* **hanketsu kiroku**
⇒最高記録	*a best record* **saikō kiroku**
⇒世界記録	*a world record* **sekai kiroku**
漫録	*random commentary* **manroku**
目録	*catalogue, listing* **mokuroku**
日録	*daily journal, logbook* **nichiroku**
録画	*videotaping, video recording* **rokuga**
録音	*audio recording* **rokuon**
録音機	*tape recorder* **rokuonki**
採録	*record, listing* **sairoku**
抄録	*extract, abstract* **shōroku**
集録	*compilation, collection, anthology* **shūroku**
収録	*collect & record* **shūroku**
登録	*registration, signing up* **tōroku**

追録	*addendum, postscript* **tsuiroku**
雑録	*miscellaneous records* **zatsuroku**
議事録	*minutes, proceedings record* **gijiroku**
芳名録	*list of names, logbook* **hōmeiroku**
住所録	*address book, directory* **jūshoroku**
会議録	*minutes, minute journal* **kaigiroku**
回顧録	*reminiscences, memoirs* **kaikoroku**
講義録	*transcript of lectures* **kōgiroku**
紳士録	*"who's who..."* **shinshiroku**
速記録	*shorthand-, stenograph notes* **sokkiroku**
随想録	*essays, memoirs* **zuisōroku**

記*ecord, 728*	歴*istory, 595*
簿*ecord, 64*	暦*alendar, 595*
紀*arration, 727*	書*ritings, 116*

鉄*ig iron, 155*

699-A

鳴owling 鶏hickens, when dawn thickens...

鳴*owling*   鳴*hirping*

鳥 (birds)

na(ku), na(ru), na(rasu), MEI
howling, chirping, shriek, twitter

FLIP: 6.0.a. Left (flat)
Facing: 2.2. East ☞ (V)

爆鳴 *blasting, detonation, demolition* **bakumei**
悲鳴 *scream, shriek* **himei**
鶏鳴 *crowing of a rooster* **keimei**
共鳴 *resonance, reverberation* **kyōmei**
鳴動 *rumbling, deep sound* **meidō**
鳴禽 *songbird* **meikin**
鳴鐘 *time bell* **meishō**
鳴子 *hand clapper* **naruko**
鳴戸 *whirlpool, maelstrom* **naruto**
雷鳴 *thunderous-, roaring applause* **raimei**
遠鳴 *sound of a distant thunder* **tōnari**
怒鳴る *thunderous shout, yelling* **donaru**
地鳴り *ground rumblings* **jinari**
烏鳴き *cry of the crow* **karasunaki**
耳鳴り *ringing in the ears* **miminari**
鳴き声 *song, cry, note, chirp* **nakigoe**
鳴り物 *sound-, musical instrument* **narimono**
奏鳴曲 *sonata* **sōmeikyoku**

高鳴る *loud ringing, roar* **takanaru**
海鳴り *roar of the seas* **uminari**
山鳴り *rumbling of a mountain* **yamanari**
家鳴り *house rumbling (train passing)* **yanari**
鳴り響く *resounding, reverberating* **narihibiku**
鳴り渡る *resound, ring, echo* **nariwataru**
吹き鳴らす *whistle blowing* **fukinarasu**
踏み鳴らす *stamp on* **fuminarasu**
掻き鳴らす *strumming, thrumming* **kakinarasu**
打ち鳴らす *clap, ring, jingle, hum* **uchinarasu**
鳴かず飛ばず *inactive, dormant* **nakazu tobazu**

声*oice*, 428	涙*rying*, 541
泣*rying*, 235	叫*cream*, 693

鶏*hicken*, 842

699-B

鳴owling 鶏hickens, when dawn thickens...

鶏*hicken*

鳥 (birds)

niwatori, tori, KEI
chicken

FLIP: 6.2. Left Bottom
Facing: 2.2. East ☞ (V)

花鶏 *brambling of a chicken* **hananiwatori**
牝鶏 *hen* **hinkei**
鶏群 *flock of chickens* **keigun**
鶏冠 *cockscomb* **keikan**
鶏鳴 *roosters crowing, cockcrow* **keimei**
鶏卵 *chicken egg* **keiran**
鶏舎 *chicken den, poultry house* **keisha**
鶏頭 *cockscomb* **keitō**
鶤鶏 *black songbird* **konkei**
水鶏 *mud hen* **kuina**
雌鶏 *hen, female chicken* **mendori**
雄鶏 *rooster, cook* **ondori**
軍鶏 *cockfighting rooster* **shamo**
震鶏 *roosters crowing at dawn* **shinkei**
闘鶏 *cockfighting* **tōkei**
闘鶏場 *cockfighting arena* **tōkeijō**
鶏肉 *chicken meat* **toriniku**, **keiniku**
鶏冠 *comb, crest* **tosaka**
若鶏 *young chicken* **wakadori**

養鶏 *poultry raising, ~breeding* **yōkei**
養鶏業 *poultry industry* **yōkeigyō**
養鶏場 *poultry farm* **yōkeijō**
養鶏家 *poultry farmer, ~breeder* **yōkeika**
一番鳥 *first crowing* **ichibandori**
鶏小屋 *henhouse, poultry house* **niwatorigoya**

鳥*irds*, 125	畜*aising*, 528
焼*oasting*, 817	糧*ood supply*, 451

鳴*owling*, 842

700-A

Their defences 徹ierced, troops 撤ithdraw in tears...

イ (stroll)

徹ierce-thru　徹enetrate

TETSU

pierce-thru, penetrate, go-thru

Facing: 3.0. ☞☜ Across
FLIP: 7.1. Right (Sort Of)

澄徹　clear, transparent **chōtetsu**
一徹　stubborn, obstinate, hard-headed **ittetsu**
貫徹　accomplishment, attainment **kantetsu**
冷徹　cold-hearted, impersonal, indifferent **reitetsu**
徹宵　all night long **tesshō**
徹夜　staying up all night **tetsuya**
徹底　exhaustiveness, thoroughness **tettei**
徹底的　thorough, exhaustive **tetteiteki**
透徹　penetration, infiltration **tōtetsu**
不徹底　half-hearted, non-committal, indecisive **futettei**
徹頭徹尾　thorough, from start to end **tettō tetsubi**

突hrust, 576
刺ierce, 875
挿nsert, 126

撤ithdraw, 843

700-B

Their defences 徹ierced, troops 撤ithdraw in tears...

手⇔扌 (hand, manual)

撤ithdraw　撤bandon

TETSU

withdraw, abandon, back off, discontinue, disengage, evacuate, pull-out, retreat

Facing: 3.0. ☞☜ Across
FLIP: 7.1. Right (Sort Of)

撤回　retraction, withdrawal **tekkai**
撤去　removal, abolition, dismantlement **tekkyo**
撤廃　abolition, termination **teppai**
撤兵　troop withdrawal **teppei**
撤収　dismantling, discarding **tesshū**
撤退　withdrawal, evacuation **tettai**

退ithdraw, 770　　去eave-out, 360
却ithdraw, 387　　出epart, 173
罷ithdraw, 322　　廃bolish, 368

徹ierce-thru, 843

701-A

Be of good 徳irtue, 聴isten to your curfew...

彳 (stroll)

徳irtue   徳ighteous

TOKU
virtue, righteous, goodness

FLIP: 7.2.a. Right Top (flat)

悪徳 *immoral, crooked, corrupt* **akutoku**
美徳 *virtue, morality* **bitoku**
道徳 *morality, virtue* **dōtoku**
不徳 *immortality, eternity* **futoku**
背徳 *immorality, corruption* **haitoku**
背徳行為 *immoral behaviour* **haitoku kōi**
人徳 *innate virtues, inborn traits* **jintoku**
高徳 *eminent virtues* **kōtoku**
功徳 *pious act, charity* **kudoku**
才徳 *able & virtuous* **saitoku**
神徳 *divine virtues* **shintoku**
淑徳 *feminine virtue* **shukutoku**
徳行 *virtuous deeds* **tokkō**
徳利 *sake bottle* **tokkuri**
徳望 *renowned virtues* **tokubō**
徳分 *winnings, victories* **tokubun**
徳川 *Tokugawa Shogun* **tokugawa**
徳義 *morals, morality, virtues* **tokugi**
徳育 *moral education, ~upbringing* **tokuiku**

徳目 *virtues, morals* **tokumoku**
徳政 *benevolent government* **tokusei**
徳性 *virtuosity, morality, good deed* **tokusei**
徳沢 *grace, blessing, favour* **tokutaku**
徳用 *economical, cost-effective* **tokuyō**
徳用品 *cost-efficient goods* **tokuyōhin**
余徳 *good-, high reputation* **yotoku**
公徳心 *community-, public spirit* **kōtokushin**
性道徳 *sexual morals* **seidōtoku**
聖徳太子 *Prince Shotoku* **shōtoku taishi**

仁*irtue, 457*	義*ighteous, 341*
倫*thics, 787*	善*ighteous, 450*
儒*onfucius, 548*	孔*onfucius, 684*

聴*isten, 844*

701-B

Be of good 徳irtue, 聴isten to your curfew...

耳 (ears)

聴isten   聴udio

ki(ku), CHŌ
listen, hearing, audio, harken

FLIP: 7.2.a. Right Top (flat)

傍聴 *hearing, listening* **bōchō**
傍聴券 *entrance-, admission ticket* **bōchōken**
傍聴人 *audience, listener* **bōchōnin**
傍聴席 *public galleries* **bōchōseki**
聴覚 *sense of hearing* **chōkaku**
聴講 *attendance, audience* **chōkō**
聴講生 *auditor, books inspector* **chōkōsei**
聴音 *hearing, listening* **chōon**
聴力 *hearing ability* **chōryoku**
聴視 *viewers & listeners* **chōshi**
聴取 *listening, hearing* **chōshu**
聴衆 *audience, listener* **chōshū**
幻聴 *hearing hallucination* **genchō**
拝聴 *listening earnestly* **haichō**
傾聴 *listening intently* **keichō**
謹聴 *listening intently* **kinchō**
難聴 *hearing difficulties* **nanchō**
来聴 *attend a lecture* **raichō**
清聴 *"your kind attention..."* **seichō**

試聴 *audition, trial listening* **shichō**
視聴 *one's attention, look & listen* **shichō**
盗聴 *wire-tapping, bugging* **tōchō**
聴聞会 *public hearing* **chōmonkai**
聴神経 *hearing nerves* **chōshinkei**
聴診器 *stethoscope* **chōshinki**
聴取者 *listener* **chōshusha**
可聴性 *audibility* **kachōsei**
公聴会 *public hearing* **kōchōkai**
視聴覚 *watching & listening* **shichōkaku**
盗聴器 *wiretap device* **tōchōki**

聞*isten, 282*	解*nderstand, 400*
耳*ars, 228*	声*oice, 428*
分*nderstand, 518*	音*ound, 314*

徳*irtue, 844*

702-A
慢*rrogant* & 慢*luggish officialdom at* 漫*andom...*

心⇔忄⇔小 (feelings)

慢*rrogant*　　慢*luggish*

MAN
arrogant, sluggish

FLIP: 7.0.b2. Right (stem)

暴慢 *arrogant, overbearing, haughty* **bōman**
我慢 *patience, tolerance* **gaman**
⇒痩せ我慢 *pride for the sake of pride* **yasegaman**
傲慢 *arrogant, self-conceited* **gōman**
傲慢無礼 *arrogant & insolent* **gōman burei**
自慢 *pride, self-esteem* **jiman**
⇒力自慢 *boasting one's strength* **chikara jiman**
⇒声自慢 *proud of one's voice skills* **koejiman**
⇒腕自慢 *proud of one's skills* **udejiman**
⇒お国自慢 *proud of one's nation* **okunijiman**
自慢話 *bragging, big talk* **jimanbanashi**
自慢高慢 *high pride* **jiman kōman**
緩慢 *slow, dull, slack, inactive* **kanman**
高慢 *pride, conceit* **kōman**
驕慢 *arrogance, haughtiness* **kyōman**
慢性 *chronic condition* **mansei**
慢性病 *chronic disease* **manseibyō**
慢性化 *chronic condition* **manseika**

慢心 *pride, self-conceit* **manshin**
怠慢 *negligent, remiss, default* **taiman**

忘*orget, 34*	失*ailure, 19*
妄*houghtless, 34*	敗*ailure, 137*
疎*eglect, 955*	

漫*andom, 845*

702-B
慢*rrogant* & 慢*luggish officialdom at* 漫*andom...*

水⇔氵 (water)

漫*andom*　　漫*omical*

MAN
random, rambling, comical

FLIP: 7.0.b2. Right (stem)

放漫 *indiscretion, laxity* **hōman**
冗漫 *diffused, verbose* **jōman**
漫罵 *revile, deride, belittle* **manba**
漫文 *random notes, scribble* **manbun**
漫談 *rambling monologue* **mandan**
漫談家 *humourist* **mandanka**
漫読 *browse, skim thru* **mandoku**
漫画 *comics, caricature, cartoons* **manga**
漫画本 *comic book* **mangabon**
漫画家 *cartoonist, caricaturist, comic artist* **mangaka**
漫画映画 *film-, movie cartoon* **manga eiga**
漫楽 *comedy music* **mangaku**
漫漫 *vast, enormous* **manman**
漫筆 *random notes, scribble* **manpitsu**
漫歩 *stroll, pleasant walk* **manpo**
漫評 *rambling criticism* **manpyō**
漫録 *random comments* **manroku**
漫遊 *leisure tour, pleasure trip* **manyū**
漫遊記 *travel notes* **manyūki**

漫才 *comedy* **manzai**
漫才師 *stage comedian* **manzaishi**
浪漫 *romanticism* **roman**
浪漫的 *romanticism* **roman teki**
浪漫派 *romanticists* **romanha**
浪漫主義 *romanticism* **roman shugi**
散漫 *desultory, vagrant* **sanman**
漫然と *rambling away, desultory* **manzento**
漫ろ雨 *sudden rain shower* **sozoroame**
漫ろ言 *rambling talk* **sozorogoto**
天真爛漫 *naïve & innocent* **tenshin ranman**

散*catter, 337*	紛*ixture, 778*
敷*catter, 170*	雑*iverse, 776*
混*ixture, 38*	諸*iverse, 794*

慢*egligence, 845*

703-A

獣*east* so 黙*ilent, turned out violent...*

獣*east*   　　　獣*onster*

犬 ⇔ 犭 (dog; beast)

FLIP: 6.0.a. Left (flat)

kemono, kedamono, JŪ
beast, monster, brute, leviathan

珍獣	rare animal	**chinjū**
鳥獣	birds & beasts	**chōjū**
百獣	all animals	**hyakujū**
獣疫	cattle disease	**jūeki**
獣皮	animal skin	**jūhi**
獣医	veterinarian	**jūi**
獣姦	bestiality, animalistic behaviour	**jūkan**
獣行	brutality, bestiality, barbarity	**jūkō**
獣毛	animal hair	**jūmō**
獣肉	animal meat	**jūniku**
獣類	animals & beasts	**jūrui**
獣性	brutality, bestiality, barbarity	**jūsei**
獣脂	animal fat	**jūshi**
獣心	beast-hearted, bestial	**jūshin**
獣的	bestial, animalistic	**jūteki**
獣欲	carnal desires, lust	**jūyoku**
怪獣	monster, beast	**kaijū**
怪獣映画	monster film	**kaijū eiga**
海獣	sea animals	**kaijū**

獣道	animal trail, animal footprints	**kemonomichi**
禽獣	birds & beasts	**kinjū**
猛獣	beast of prey, wild animal	**mōjū**
猛獣狩り	big game hunting	**mōjūgari**
猛獣使い	wild animal tamer	**mōjūzukai**
霊獣	sacred beast	**reijū**
野獣	wild beast	**yajū**
野獣狩り	wild beast hunting	**yajūgari**
一角獣	unicorn	**ikkakujū**
肉食獣	beast of prey, wild animal	**nikushokujū**

厳	*evere, 449*	慌	*urried, 507*
烈	*evere, 585*	蛮	*avage, 627*
激	*ierce, 170*	怖	*cary, 209*
猛	*ierce, 657*	恐	*cary, 906*

黙*uiet, 846*

703-B

獣*east* so 黙*ilent, turned out violent...*

黙*ilence*   　　　黙*uiet*

黒 (black, charred)

FLIP: 6.1. Left Top

dama(ru), MOKU
silence, quiet, hush-hush

黙り屋	non-talkative person, taciturn	**damariya**
黙りこくる	remain silent	**damarikokuru**
黙り込む	sink into silence, fall dumb	**damarikomu**
押し黙る	keeping silent	**oshidamaru**
暗黙	tacit consent, acquiescence	**anmoku**
沈黙	falling into silence	**chinmoku**
寡黙	reticent, taciturn, silent, quiet	**kamoku**
黙契	tacit agreement	**mokkei**
黙考	meditation, contemplation	**mokkō**
⇒沈思黙考	deep meditation	**chinshi mokkō**
黙許	tacit consent, acquiescence	**mokkyo**
黙諾	tacit consent, acquiescence	**mokudaku**
黙読	silent reading	**mokudoku**
黙劇	pantomime, impersonation play	**mokugeki**
黙秘	silence, quietness, hush	**mokuhi**
黙秘権	right to remain silent	**mokuhiken**
黙過	tacit approval, look the other way	**mokuka**
黙黙	in silence, quietly	**mokumoku**
黙然	silent, tacit	**mokunen**

黙認	tacit approval, look the other way	**mokunin**
黙礼	bow, salute	**mokurei**
黙殺	ignoring another's presence	**mokusatsu**
黙視	watching in silence	**mokushi**
黙示	falling into silence	**mokushi, mokuji**
黙思	silent contemplation	**mokushi**
黙止	remaining silent	**mokushi**
黙想	meditation, contemplation	**mokusō**
黙祷	silent prayer, minute of silence	**mokutō**
黙約	tacit approval, acquiescence	**mokuyaku**

静	*uiet, 230*	穏	*ranquillity 840*
寧	*uiet, 967*	康	*ranquillity, 881*
幽	*uiet, 897*	康	*olace, 881*

獣*east, 846*

704-A

壊estroyed encyclopaedia left only 懐ostalgia...

土 (ground, soil)

壊estroy   壊reak-down

kowa(reru), kowa(su), KAI
destroy, break-down, tear down

FLIP: 7.2.a. Right Top (flat)

壊れ物 *fragile, breakable* **kowaremono**
打ち壊し *smash; ruin, upset (plans)* **buchikowashi**
壊死 *necrosis, gangrene* **eshi**
壊疽 *gangrene, necrosis* **eso**
破壊 *destruction, demolition* **hakai**
⇒偶像破壊 *iconoclasm* **gūzō hakai**
⇒環境破壊 *environmental destruction* **kankyō hakai**
破壊的 *destructive, ruinous* **hakaiteki**
半壊 *partial destruction* **hankai**
崩壊 *collapse, breaking down* **hōkai**
自壊 *disintegrate, self-destruction* **jikai**
壊廃 *ruin, decay, rot* **kaihai**
壊滅 *destruction, annihilation* **kaimetsu**
壊滅的 *fatal, crushing, destructive* **kaimetsuteki**
壊乱 *corruption, debasement* **kairan**
壊走 *routed out* **kaisō**
決壊 *collapse, break, washout* **kekkai**
朽壊 *rot & crumble* **kyūkai**
倒壊 *collapse, fall apart* **tōkai**

全壊 *complete destruction, annihilation* **zenkai**
壊血病 *scurvy* **kaiketsubyō**
叩き壊す *split apart, wreck* **tatakikowasu**
取り壊す *pull down* **torikowasu**

破estroy, 715	落ollapse, 826
陥ollapse, 893	折reak, 471
崩ollapse, 912	裂plit-up, 585

懐ostalgia, 847

704-B

壊estroyed encyclopaedia left only 懐ostalgia...

心⇔忄⇔小 (feelings)

懐ostalgia   懐entimental

natsu(kashii), natsu(kashimu), natsu(ku), natsu(keru); futokoro, KAI
nostalgia, sentimental, long for, reminiscence

FLIP: 7.2.a. Right Top (flat)

懐刀 *one's right hand; dagger* **futokoro katana**
懐銭 *pocket money* **futokorozeni**
雅懐 *aesthetic yearning* **gakai**
抱懐 *cherish, harbour* **hōkai**
本懐 *life ambition* **honkai**
述懐 *reminiscence, recollection* **jukkai**
懐中 *pocket, mini, micro* **kaichū**
懐疑 *scepticism, doubt* **kaigi**
懐柔 *conciliation, appeasement* **kaijū**
懐柔策 *conciliatory-, appeasement policy* **kaijūsaku**
懐剣 *dagger, blade* **kaiken**
懐古 *retrospection, reminiscence* **kaiko**
懐郷 *homesickness, longing* **kaikyō**
懐旧 *reminiscence, recollection* **kaikyū**
懐旧談 *nostalgic talks* **kaikyūdan**
懐妊 *pregnancy, conceiving a child* **kainin**
懐炉 *body warmer* **kairo**
懐石 *tea lunch* **kaiseki**
懐紙 *Japanese paper* **kaishi**

懐胎 *pregnancy, conceiving a child* **kaitai**
感懐 *impressions, thoughts* **kankai**
襟懐 *inner heart, real intention* **kinkai**
胸懐 *impressions, thoughts* **kyōkai**
所懐 *impressions, thoughts* **shokai**
素懐 *long-cherished desire* **sokai**
追懐 *recollection, reminiscences* **tsuikai**
内懐 *inner heart, real intention* **uchibutokoro**
山懐 *deep in the mountains* **yamafutokoro**
人懐こい *social, amiable, friendly* **hitonatsukoi**
手懐ける *win over; tame* **tenazukeru**

憶emory, 339
懇ntimacy, 164
親ntimate, 669

壊reak-down, 847

705-A

墳*ncient tombs* 憤*nraged,* 噴*pew-out plague...*

墳*ncient tomb* 墳*umulus*

土 (ground, soil)

FUN
ancient tomb, tumulus

墳墓 *grave, tomb* **funbo**
墳墓の地 *one's ancestral home* **funbonochi**
円墳 *burial mound* **enpun**
⇒前方後円墳 *ancient Japanese tomb*
　　zenpōkōenfun
古墳 *ancient tomb, tumulus* **kofun**

FLIP: 7.0.b2. Right (stem)

葬*urial, 513*	昔*lden-times, 281*
墓*ravesite, 602*	史*istory, 85*
碑*ombstone, 937*	歴*istory, 595*
陵*ausoleum, 140*	

憤*nrage, 848*

705-B

墳*ncient tombs* 憤*nraged,* 噴*pew-out plague...*

憤*nrage* 憤*utrage*

心 ⇔ 忄 ⇔ 小 (feelings)

ikido'o(ru), ikido'o(ri), FUN
enrage, outrage, infuriate, flare-up, incense, indignant, ruckus

憤り *indignation, resentment, fury* **ikidoori**
憤慨 *indignation, resentment, rage* **fungai**
憤激 *indignation, rage, fury* **fungeki**
憤懣 *anger, indignation* **funman**
憤怒 *anger, indignation* **fundo, funnu**
憤死 *death by indignation* **funshi**
憤然 *anger, indignation* **funzen**
激憤 *indignation, rage, fury* **gekifun**
義憤 *indignation, resentment, fury* **gifun**
発憤 *getting aroused, ~stimulated* **happun**
悲憤 *indignation, resentment, fury* **hifun**
公憤 *righteous indignation* **kōfun**
私憤 *personal grudge, bad blood* **shifun**
痛憤 *fierce indignation* **tsūfun**
鬱憤 *resentment, rage, rancour* **uppun**
余憤 *bottled-up anger, suppressed rage* **yofun**

FLIP: 7.0.b2. Right (stem)

憎*atred, 837*	卑*espise, 936*
嫌*espise, 805*	侮*espise, 711*

墳*ncient tomb, 848*

705-C

墳*ncient tombs* 憤*nraged,* 噴*pew-out plague...*

口 (mouth)

噴*pew-out* 噴*omit*

fu(ku), FUN
spew-out, vomit, puke, spout

FLIP: 5.0.b. Left & Right

噴き出る *spout, spurt, gush* **fukideru**
噴煙 *smoke emission* **fun'en**
噴火 *eruption, explosion* **funka**
噴火口 *volcano crater* **funkakō**
噴火山 *spewing volcano* **funkazan**
噴気 *gas emission* **funki**
噴門 *cardia* **funmon**
噴飯 *utterly ridiculous* **funpan**
噴流 *jet stream* **funryū**
噴泉 *water fountain, ~spring* **funsen**
噴射 *jet water* **funsha**
⇒逆噴射 *backfiring* **gyakufunsha**
噴射推進 *jet propulsion* **funsha suishin**
噴出 *spouting, gushing, spurting* **funshutsu**
噴水 *water fountain* **funsui**
噴霧器 *spray, vaporizer* **funmuki**

吐*omit, 703*	否*ejection, 300*
斥*ejection, 424*	除*xclude, 501*
排*ejection, 795*	断*ejection, 958*

憤*nrage, 848*

706-A

曜*eekday of happy* 躍*umping, after dish* 濯*ashing...*

日 (sunlight, daytime)

曜*eekday* 曜*eekly*

YŌ
weekday, weekly, day-of-the-week

FLIP: 6.0.a. Left (flat)
Facing: 3.0. ☞☜ Across

曜日 *day of the week* **yōbi**
何曜日 *what day of the week* **nanyōbi**
月曜日 *Monday* **getsuyōbi**
火曜日 *Tuesday* **kayōbi**
水曜日 *Wednesday* **suiyōbi**
木曜日 *Thursday* **mokuyōbi**
金曜日 *Friday* **kinyōbi**
土曜日 *Saturday* **doyōbi**
日曜日 *Sunday* **nichiyōbi**
黒曜石 *obsidian* **kokuyōseki**
毎月曜日 *every Monday* **maigetsuyōbi**
聖金曜日 *Good Friday* **seikinyōbi**

日*ay, 14*	週*eekly, 279*
月*onth, 22*	昼*aytime, 575*
暁*aybreak, 818*	年*ear, 27*

躍*umping, 850*

706-B

躍eekday of happy 躍umping, after dish 濯ashing...

足 (feet, legs)

躍umping　躍opping

odo(ru), YAKU

jumping, hopping, leaping

Facing: 3.0. ☞☜ Across
Facing: 4.0. ☜☞ Apart

躍り出る jump **odorideru**
躍り込む rush, leap on **odorikomu**
躍り越す jumping over **odorikosu**
躍り上がる jump for joy **odoriagaru**
躍り懸かる spring upon, jump over **odorikakaru**
暗躍 engaged in secret schemes **anyaku**
跳躍 jump, leaping **chōyaku**
跳躍板 springboard **chōyakuban**
跳躍台 springboard **chōyakudai**
跳躍運動 jumping exercise **chōyaku undō**
飛躍 leap, jump **hiyaku**
飛躍的 "by leaps & bounds..." **hiyakuteki**
一躍 great success at one stroke **ichiyaku**
雀躍 jumping with joy **jakuyaku**
活躍 activity, action, project **katsuyaku**
躍起 eager, hot, bent **yakki**
躍動 throbbing pulse **yakudō**
躍動感 sense of full energy **yakudōkan**
躍動的 energetic, vigorous, spirited **yakudōteki**

躍如 vivid-, graphic description **yakujo**
躍如たる vivid, lifelike, graphic **yakujotaru**
躍進 progress, strides, advance **yakushin**
勇躍 high spirits, zestful, cheerful **yūyaku**
小躍り jumping with joy **koodori**
跳ね躍る jump, leaping **haneodoru**

踊ancing, 671	脚egs, 387
足egs, 481	動ovement, 422

曜eekday, 849

706-C

曜eekday of happy 躍umping, after dish 濯ashing...

水⇔氵 (water)

濯inse-out　濯ashing

susugu, TAKU

rinse-out, washing, laundry, clean with water

Facing: 3.0. ☞☜ Across
Facing: 4.0. ☜☞ Apart

洗濯 laundry, washing **sentaku**
洗濯ばさみ clothespin, clothespeg **sentaku basami**
洗濯板 washboard **sentakuita**
洗濯物 laundry clothes **sentakumono**
洗濯機 laundry machine **sentakuki**
洗濯屋 laundromat; laundry clerk **sentakuya**

洗ashing, 478	清leansing, 793
掃leaning, 785	

躍opping, 850

707-A

繰pinning to 操perate, need to concentrate...

糸 (thread, continuity)

繰*pinning*　繰*ircling*

ku(ru)
spinning, circling, twisting, reel, shift onward

FLIP: 7.0.b1. Right (stem)

繰り言 *"same old story..."* **kurigoto**
繰り戸 *sliding door* **kurido**
繰り綿 *cotton gin* **kuriwata**
繰越金 *running balance (money)* **kurikoshikin**
繰り上げ *advance, moving up* **kuriage**
繰り出す *turn out continually* **kuridasu**
繰り返し *repetition, recurrence* **kurikaeshi**
繰り込む *add, transfer, carry* **kurikomu**
繰り越し *transfer, move location* **kurikoshi**
繰り回す *roll-over (loan)* **kurimawasu**
繰り戻す *put back* **kurimodosu**
繰り取る *reel off* **kuritoru**
繰り広げる *unfold, develop, unravel* **kurihirogeru**
繰り入れる *add, transfer, carry* **kuriireru**
繰り延べる *postpone, delay, put off* **kurinoberu**
繰り下げる *postpone, put off, move back* **kurisageru**
繰り寄せる *draw into* **kuriyoseru**
繰り合わせる *manage, supervise* **kuriawaseru**
船繰り *ship schedule* **funaguri**

臍繰り *hidden savings (belly button)* **hesokuri**
臍繰り金 *hidden savings* **hesokurigane**
順繰り *order, turn* **junguri**
金繰り *money raising* **kaneguri**
勘繰り *suspicion, doubts, apprehension* **kanguri**
手繰る *draw in, pull in* **taguru**
爪繰る *finger, pinpoint* **tsumaguru**
遣り繰り *"getting by with..."* **yarikuri**
差し繰る *manage skilfully* **sashikuru**
資金繰り *fund-raising* **shikinguri**

回*otate, 458*	再*epeat, 225*
旋*irculate, 651*	渦*entrifugal, 798*

曜*eekday, 849*

707-B

繰pinning to 操perate, need to concentrate...

手⇔扌 (hand, manual)

操*perate*　操*anipulate*

ayatsu(ru), misao, SŌ
operate, manipulate, steering

FLIP: 7.0.b1. Right (stem)

情操 *sentiment, feeling* **jōsō**
情操教育 *cultivation of sentiments* **jōsō kyōiku**
節操 *integrity, fidelity, honesty* **sessō**
志操 *principle, fundamentals* **shisō**
操舵 *steering, navigating* **sōda**
操舵手 *helmsman* **sōdashu**
操業 *operation, control* **sōgyō**
操縦 *operation, control* **sōjū**
操縦桿 *joystick* **sōjūkan**
操縦席 *airplane cockpit* **sōjūseki**
操縦士 *airplane pilot* **sōjūshi**
操行 *behaviour, conduct, demeanour* **sōkō**
操練 *military drill* **sōren**
操作 *operation, manipulation* **sōsa**
⇒遠隔操作 *remote control* **enkaku sōsa**
操車 *operation, control, running* **sōsha**
操車場 *switchyard, operation yard* **sōshajō**
操守 *fidelity, consistency, constancy* **sōshu**
操短 *operations-downsizing* **sōtan**

操典 *operations manual* **sōten**
体操 *gymnastics, callisthenics* **taisō**
⇒ラジオ体操 *radio callisthenics* **rajio taisō**
⇒柔軟体操 *callisthenics* **jūnan taisō**
貞操 *chastity, virtue* **teisō**
貞操帯 *chastity belt* **teisōtai**
徳操 *morals, ;virtue, chastity* **tokusō**
新体操 *rhythmic callisthenics* **shintaisō**
操り人形 *puppet, marionette* **ayatsuri ningyō**

管*ontrol, 917*	宰*upervise 377*
轄*ontrol, 968*	営*anagement, 580*
導*uidance, 312*	

燥*rying-up, 852*

708-A
藻*ater-plants,* 燥*rying-up so fragrant...*

⺾ (grass)

藻*ater plants*　　藻*lgae*

mo, SŌ
water plants, aquatic plants, algae

FLIP: 7.3.b. Right Bottom (stem)

甘藻 *eelgrass, tape grass* **amamo**
文藻 *literary talent, writing skills* **bunsō**
光藻 *luminous algae* **hikarimo**
海藻 *saltwater plant, seaweeds* **kaisō**
松藻 *hornwort* **matsumo**
藻草 *waterplants* **mogusa**
藻屑 *seaweeds* **mokuzu**
藻塩 *salt from seaweeds* **moshio**
尾藻 *gulfweeds* **omo**
詩操 *prose & poetry* **shisō**
藻類 *waterplants* **sōrui**
⇒紅藻類 *red algae* **benisōrui**
⇒緑藻類 *green algae* **ryokusōrui**
玉藻 *seaweed* **tamamo**
藻菌類 *algal fungi* **mokinrui**
殺藻剤 *algaecide* **sassōzai**
藻塩草 *seaweed used in salt-making* **moshiokusa**

植*lant, 783*　　苗*aplings, 270*
畑*lantation, 482*　　栽*aplings, 803*
稲*ice plant, 893*　　芽*prout, 57*

操*anipulate, 851*

708-B
藻*ater-plants,* 燥*rying-up so fragrant...*

火⇔灬 (fire)

燥*rying*　　燥*esiccate*

SŌ
drying, desiccate

FLIP: 7.0.b1. Right (stem)

乾燥 *dryness, desiccation* **kansō**
⇒無味乾燥 *insipid, dry-like-dust* **mumi kansō**
乾燥器 *dryer, desiccator* **kansōki**
乾燥室 *drying room* **kansōshitsu**
乾燥季 *dry season* **kansōki**
乾燥剤 *desiccant, desiccating agent* **kansōzai**
枯燥 *dry up, parch* **kosō**
焦燥 *impatience, fretfulness, whining* **shōsō**
高燥地 *dry highland* **kōsōchi**
乾燥野菜 *dried vegetables* **kansō yasai**

乾*rying, 661*
干*rying-up, 74*

操*anipulate, 851*

709-A

Farmer to 譲oncede, his 壌ertile cows breed...

土 (ground, soil)

壌*ertile soil*　壌*rable soil*

JŌ
fertile soil, arable soil

FLIP: 7.2.a. Right Top (flat)

土壌 *earth, soil* **dojō**
⇒酸性土壌 *acid soil* **sansei dojō**
土壌流出 *soil erosion, desolation* **dojō ryūshutsu**
土壌汚染 *soil pollution* **dojō osen**
平壌 *Pyongyang, Korea* **pyonyan**
天壌 *heaven & earth* **tenjō**
天壌無窮 *eternal as heaven & earth* **tenjō mukyū**
雲壌 *great difference (clouds & earth)* **unjō**

肥*ertilizer, 717*	植*lant, 783*
農*arming, 446*	田*ice field, 482*
野*ield, 873*	豊*bundance, 965*
畑*lantation, 482*	種*eedling, 430*

嬢*aughter, 854*

709-B

Farmer to 譲oncede, his 壌ertile cows breed...

言 (speaking)

譲*oncede*　譲*ssign rights*

yuzu(ru), JŌ
concede, assign rights, transfer

FLIP: 7.2.a. Right Top (flat)

譲り状 *deed of assignment* **yuzurijō**
譲り合い *give-and-take, concessions* **yuzuriai**
譲り受ける *inherit, succeed, continue* **yuzuriukeru**
分譲 *parcel sale of lands* **bunjō**
分譲地 *parcel sale of house & lot* **bunjōchi**
分譲中 *"subdivision lots for sale..."* **bunjōchū**
互譲 *mutual concessions* **gojō**
移譲 *transfer of rights (new ownership)* **ijō**
委譲 *transfer of rights (new ownership)* **ijō**
辞譲 *one's decline benefiting another* **jijō**
譲歩 *concession, conciliation* **jōho**
譲位 *abdication, relinquishment* **jōi**
譲渡 *transfer, assignment* **jōto**
⇒営業譲渡 *transfer of business ownership*
　eigyō jōto
⇒権利譲渡 *transfer of rights* **kenri jōto**
⇒利権譲渡 *transfer of rights* **riken jōto**
⇒詐欺譲渡 *fraudulent transfer* **sagi jōto**
譲渡人 *transferor, assignor* **jōtonin**

譲渡証書 *deed of transfer* **jōto shōsho**
譲渡抵当 *mortgage, collateral* **jōto teitō**
譲与 *transfer, concession* **jōyo**
割譲 *cession, ceding* **katsujō**
謙譲 *modesty, humility* **kenjō**
退譲 *humility, modesty* **taijō**
禅譲 *abdication to a virtuous person* **zenjō**
親譲り *inheritance from one's parents* **oyayuzuri**

移*ransfer, 188*
屈*ield, 212*
伏*ield, 702*

壌*ertile soil, 853*

710-A

醸*rewer's* 嬢*aughter prefers tonic water...*

西 (liquor)

醸*rewery*　醸*istillery*

kamo(su), JŌ
brewery, distillery

FLIP: 6.0.a. Left (flat)
FLIP: 7.2.a. Right Top (flat)

醸し出す *cause, bring about* **kamoshidasu**
吟醸 *sake brewing* **ginjō**
醸母 *yeast, leaven* **jōbo**
醸成 *brewing* **jōsei**
醸造 *brewing, distilling* **jōzō**
醸造学 *science of brewing* **jōzōgaku**
醸造業 *distillery-, brewing industry* **jōzōgyō**
醸造家 *distiller, brewer* **jōzōka**
醸造所 *brewery, distillery* **jōzōjo, jōzōsho**
醸造酒 *distilled alcohol* **jōzōshu**

酒*lcohol, 789*	宴*anquet, 610*
酔*runk, 760*	麦*arley, 606*
酵*east, 669*	

嬢*aughter, 854*

710-B

醸*rewer's* 嬢*aughter prefers tonic water...*

女 (woman)

嬢*aughter*　嬢*oung girl*

JŌ
daughter, young girl

FLIP: 7.2.a. Right Top (flat)
Facing: 2.2. East ☞ (V)

愛嬢 *favourite daughter* **aijō**
令嬢 *daughter, young lady* **reijō**
老嬢 *spinster, old maid* **rōjō**
案内嬢 *usherette, usher girl* **annaijō**
交換嬢 *telephone operator (archaic)* **kōkanjō**
お嬢様 *your daughter (honorific)* **ojōsama**
お嬢さん *your daughter (honorific)* **ojōsan**

娘*aughter, 254*
嫁*aughter-in-law, 824*
妹*ounger sister, 114*

壌*ertile soil, 853*

711-A

職*areer in* 織*nitting cottage, a skilled* 識*nowledge...*

耳 (ears)

職*mploy*　職*areer*

SHOKU
employ, career, working

FLIP: 8.0.a. Inner (flat)

復職	re-instatement, job recall **fukushoku**
激職	extremely busy at work **gekishoku**
軍職	military service, ~profession **gunshoku**
本職	principal job, main occupation **honshoku**
奉職	government service **hōshoku**
辞職	resignation, quitting one's work **jishoku**
殉職	death on the job **junshoku**
兼職	holding two posts **kenshoku**
公職	government job **kōshoku**
求職	seeking a job, job hunting **kyūshoku**
免職	job dismissal, firing **menshoku**
無職	jobless, unemployed **mushoku**
内職	second job, sideline, moonlighting **naishoku**
汚職	corruption, scandal, disgrace **oshoku**
離職	losing one's job, work separation **rishoku**
職権	authority, official power **shokken**
職場	worksite, workplace **shokuba**
職業	occupation, profession **shokugyō**
職員	staff member, employee **shokuin**

職歴	work experience, job history **shokureki**
職掌	duty, work **shokushō**
職種	type of job, work category **shokushu**
就職	job hunting, looking for a job **shūshoku**
僧職	monk hood, monasticism **sōshoku**
停職	job suspension **teishoku**
定職	regular job, full-time work **teishoku**
適職	suitable job, proper job **tekishoku**
天職	vocation, mission **tenshoku**
転職	switching to another job **tenshoku**
要職	important post **yōshoku**

雇*mploy*, 343	仕*ervice*, 9	働*abour*, 422
就*mploy*, 719	務*ervice*, 454	
勤*ervice*, 962	労*abour*, 351	

識*wareness*, 856

711-B

職*areer in* 織*nitting cottage, a skilled* 識*nowledge...*

糸 (thread, continuity)

織*nitting*　織*titching*

o(ru), SHOKU, SHIKI
knitting, stitching, weaving

FLIP: 8.0.a. Inner (flat)

綾織	twill weaving **ayaori**
紡織	spinning & weaving, textile **bōshoku**
羽織	half-length Japanese overcoat **haori**
交織	assorted fabrics **kōshoku**
織り姫	Star Vega **orihime**
織り方	weaving style **orikata**
織り子	weaver **oriko**
織り目	fabric texture **orime**
織り出す	weave **oridasu**
織物	textile fabrics, cloth **orimono**
織元	textile manufacturer **orimoto**
製織	weaving, textile manufacture **seishoku**
染織	dyeing & weaving **senshoku**
織機	weaving machine, loom **shokki**
織工	textile industry **shokkō**
織女	lady weaver **shokujo**
織女星	Star Vega **shokujosei**
組織	organization, establishment **soshiki**
⇒筋肉組織	muscular tissue **kinniku soshiki**

節織り	coarse silk fabric **fushiori**
太織り	coarse silk fabric **futoori**
平織り	plain fabric **hiraori**
糸織り	silk cloth fabric **itoori**
手織り	hand-woven **teori**
毛織物	woollen-, worsted fabric **keorimono**
絹織物	silk fabrics **kinuorimono**
綿織物	cotton fabrics **men'orimono**
織り込む	interweave, incorporate **orikomu**
織り交ぜる	include, interweave **orimazeru**
織り合わせる	interweave **oriawaseru**

縫*ewing*, 779	裁*lothes*, 802
繰*pinning*, 851	服*lothes*, 734
紡*pinning*, 735	編*nitting*, 42
布*loth*, 208	糸*hread*, 375

職*mploy*, 855

711-C

職areer in 織nitting cottage, a skilled 識nowledge...

言 (speaking)

識nowledge   識iscriminate

SHIKI
knowledge, discriminate

FLIP: 8.0.a. Inner (flat)
FLIP: 6.0.a. Left (flat)

美音識 *esthetical knowledge* **biishiki**
知識 *knowledge, intelligence* **chishiki**
智識 *knowledge, intelligence* **chishiki**
学識 *studious, scholarly* **gakushiki**
眼識 *insight, notion, cognition* **ganshiki**
博識 *extensive-, profound knowledge* **hakushiki**
標識 *sign, mark, beacon* **hyōshiki**
意識 *consciousness, awareness* **ishiki**
⇒無意識 *unconscious, lethargic* **muishiki**
⇒自意識 *self-consciousness, awareness* **jiishiki**
⇒階級意識 *class consciousness* **kaikyū ishiki**
⇒基礎知識 *basic knowledge* **kiso chishiki**
⇒競争意識 *sense of rivalry* **kyōsō ishiki**
⇒潜在意識 *sub-consciousness* **senzai ishiki**
常識 *common knowledge* **jōshiki**
鑑識 *judgement, identification* **kanshiki**
見識 *insight, discernment* **kenshiki**
面識 *acquaintance, casual friendship* **menshiki**
認識 *recognition, awareness* **ninshiki**

認識論 *epistemology, metaphysics* **ninshikiron**
良識 *good sense* **ryōshiki**
先識 *prior knowledge* **senshiki**
識別 *distinction, clarification* **shikibetsu**
識域 *threshold of consciousness* **shikiiki**
識字 *literacy* **shikiji**
識見 *knowledge, judgement* **shikiken**
識者 *knowledgeable persons* **shikisha**
相識 *mutual acquaintance* **sōshiki**
有識 *intellectual, schooled, learned* **yūshiki**
鑑識眼 *critical-, discerning eye* **kanshi kigan**

知*nowledge, 103*	想*dea, 524*
存*nowledge, 634*	念*dea, 182*
意*dea, 340*	思*hinking, 596*

職*mploy, 855*

712-A

濫xcessive 鑑attern of 艦arships needs 鑑ppraisal for reversal...

水⇔氵 (water)

濫xcessive   濫verdone

mida(rigamashii), RAN
excessive, overdone, superfluous, too much

FLIP: 4.0.a. Bottom (flat)

濫りがましい *disorderly, indecent* **midarigamashii**
氾濫 *overflowing, flooding* **hanran**
濫伐 *excessive tree cutting* **ranbatsu**
濫読 *random reading* **randoku**
濫獲 *overfishing, overhunting* **rankaku**
濫入 *gatecrashing, trespassing* **rannyū**
濫発 *overprinting of money* **ranpatsu**
濫費 *wasteful spending, squandering* **ranpi**
濫立 *great disorder, big mess* **ranritsu**
濫作 *overproduction of literary works* **ransaku**
濫設 *build too many (schools)* **ransetsu**
濫觴 *origin, genesis* **ranshō**
濫出 *publish in great quantity* **ranshutsu**
濫用 *abuse, taking advantage* **ranyō**
濫造 *shoddy manufacturing* **ranzō**

過*xcessive, 798*	極*xtreme, 947*
越*vertake, 663*	甚*xtreme, 293*
窮*xtreme, 876*	越*xceed, 663*

濫*atch-over, 592*

712-B

濫xcessive 鑑attern of 艦arships needs 鑑ppraisal for reversal...

舟 (vessel)

艦arship   艦attleship

KAN
warship, battleship, destroyer ship

FLIP: 7.3.a. Right Bottom (flat)

母艦 *flagship, mother ship* **bokan**
着艦 *landing on aircraft carrier* **chakkan**
軍艦 *warship, battleship* **gunkan**
廃艦 *decommissioned warship* **haikan**
発艦 *taking off from aircraft carrier* **hakkan**
砲艦 *gunboat, battleship* **hōkan**
砲艦外交 *gunboat diplomacy* **hōkan gaikō**
乗艦 *boarding a naval vessel* **jōkan**
艦尾 *warships stern* **kanbi**
艦長 *navy captain, ship captain* **kanchō**
艦上 *on-board a warship* **kanjō**
艦橋 *warships bridge* **kankyō**
艦砲 *naval artillery* **kanpō**
艦列 *naval armada, convoy fleet* **kanretsu**
艦載 *ships load* **kansai**
艦載機 *aircraft carrier plane* **kansaiki**
艦船 *ships & battleships* **kansen**
艦首 *bow of a warship* **kanshu**
艦種 *warship class* **kanshu**

艦隊 *naval fleet, armada* **kantai**
艦体 *warship hull* **kantai**
艦艇 *naval vessel* **kantei**
旗艦 *flagship* **kikan**
巨艦 *colossal warship* **kyokan**
僚艦 *consort ship, escort vessel* **ryōkan**
戦艦 *battleship, warship* **senkan**
敵艦 *enemy ship* **tekikan**
造艦 *naval construction* **zōkan**
護衛艦 *convoy vessel* **goeikan**
観艦式 *naval review* **kankanshiki**
潜水艦 *submarine* **sensuikan**

戦*ighting, 517*	隻*[ships], 50*	船*hip, 757*
闘*ombat, 946*	舟*hip, 90*	舶*hip, 742*
丸*[ships], 73*	航*avigation, 748*	帆*ailing, 641*

濫xcessive, *856*

712-C

濫xcessive 鑑attern of 艦arships needs 鑑ppraisal for reversal...

金 (metal)

❶ 鑑attern   ❷ 鑑ppraise

kanga(miru), kagami, KAN
pattern; appraise

FLIP: 7.3.a. Right Bottom (flat)
FLIP: 6.0.a. Left (flat)

❶ 武鑑 *book of pomp & pageantry* **bukan**
姫鑑 *young model* **himekagami**
宝鑑 *thesaurus* **hōkan**
印鑑 *official seal* **inkan**
印鑑証明 *certificate of seal* **inkan shōmei**
鑑札 *license, permit* **kansatsu**
鑑札料 *license fee* **kansatsuryō**
亀鑑 *pattern, paragon* **kikan**
名鑑 *directory, namelist* **meikan**
門鑑 *gatepass* **monkan**
年鑑 *yearbook* **nenkan**
⇒統計年鑑 *statistical yearbook* **tōkei nenkan**
図鑑 *illustrated-, picture book* **zukan**

鑑賞 *appreciation, satisfaction* **kanshō**
⇒映画鑑賞 *movie appreciation* **eiga kanshō**
鑑賞力 *ability to appreciate* **kanshōryoku**
鑑定 *appraisal, expert opinion* **kantei**
⇒筆跡鑑定 *handwriting analysis* **hisseki kantei**
鑑定家 *appraiser, connoisseur* **kanteika**
鑑定人 *appraiser, connoisseur* **kanteinin**
無鑑査 *unevaluated, unrated* **mukansa**
無鑑札 *without license* **mukansatsu**
賞鑑 *appreciate, admire* **shōkan**

❷ 鑑別 *discrimination, judgement* **kanbetsu**
鑑査 *evaluation, appraisal, assessment* **kansa**
鑑識 *judgement, identification* **kanshiki**
鑑識眼 *discerning eye* **kanshikigan**
鑑識家 *judge, connoisseur* **kanshikika**

鏡*irror, 839*	審*nspect, 339*
映*eflect, 217*	査*nspect, 624*
象*mage, 530*	検*nspect, 939*
調*nspect, 280*	閲*nspect, 942*

艦attleship, *857*

713-A

三*hree blind men in* 一*ne town climbing* 上*p &* 下*own...*

一 (one, single)

三*hree*

mi(tsu), mi, SAN
three

FLIP: 1.0.a. Whole (flat)

三日 *third day of the month* **mikka**
三百 *three hundred* **sanbyaku**
三弦 *three-stringed samisen* **sangen**
三国 *three countries* **sangoku**
三回 *thrice, three times* **sankai**
三階 *third floor* **sankai**
三角 *triangle* **sankaku**
三景 *top three famous sceneries* **sankei**
三脚 *tripod* **sankyaku**
三面 *page 3 (newspaper)* **sanmen**
三面記事 *newspaper city section* **sanmen kiji**
三文 *cheap, inexpensive* **sanmon**
三人 *three persons, a trio* **sannin**
三流 *third-rated, third class* **sanryū**
三世 *third-generation overseas Japanese* **sansei**
三思 *thinking thoroughly* **sanshi**
三食 *three meals daily* **sanshoku**
第三次 *tertiary, three-tier system* **daisanji**
第三者 *third person, external-, neutral party* **daisansha**

三十路 *one's thirtyish, 30~39 years old* **misoji**
三揃い *three-piece suit, formal attire* **mitsuzoroi**
胸三寸 *"do as you please..."* **munesanzun**
三原色 *red, blue & yellow colours* **sangenshoku**
三次元 *three-dimensional, 3D* **sanjigen**
三連勝 *three consecutive wins* **sanrenshō**
三周忌 *second death anniversary* **sanshūki**
三等賞 *third prize, bronze prize* **santōshō**
万歳三唱 *banzai, 3 cheers hurray!* **banzai sanshō**
第三世界 *Third World nations* **daisan sekai**
二転三転 *incredible, untrustworthy* **niten santen**
三分の二 *two-thirds* **sanbun no ni**
三条天皇 *Emperor Sanjō (1011-1016)* **sanjō tennō**

丙*hird, 212*

二*wo, 457*

713-B

三*hree blind men in* 一*ne town climbing* 上*p &* 下*own...*

一 (one, single)

一*ne*

hito(tsu), hito, ICHI, ITSU
one

FLIP: 1.0.a. Whole (flat)

一息 *breathing, inhalation* **hitoiki**
一言 *short remarks, comments* **hitokoto**
第一 *the first (in a series)* **daiichi**
一番 *the most~, the best~, number one* **ichiban**
一部 *one part of a whole, a component* **ichibu**
一同 *everyone, all members* **ichidō**
一月 *January* **ichigatsu**
一ヶ月 *one month* **ikkagetsu**
一時 *temporary, in the meantime* **ichiji, ittoki**
一応 *"as of now, tentatively..."* **ichiō**
一流 *first class, second-to-none* **ichiryū**
一夜 *one evening* **ichiya**
一家 *whole family* **ikka**
一括 *lumped amount, bulk; in one time* **ikkatsu**
一見 *obvious, a view* **ikken**
一杯 *one drink, a toast* **ippai**
一般 *general; regular* **ippan**
一筆 *few written lines* **ippitsu**
一方 *one side, on the otherhand* **ippō**

一票 *one vote, your vote* **ippyō**
一切 *entire, whole* **issai**
一説 *one version* **issetsu**
一瞬 *instant, moment* **isshun**
万一 *"in the event of, in case..."* **man'ichi**
一コマ *one academic subject* **hitokoma**
一要素 *a factor, a cause* **ichiyōso**
一途に *with all energy, ~strength* **ichizu(ni), itto(ni)**
一緒に *together, altogether* **issho(ni)**
一等賞 *first place, top prize* **ittōshō**
一意専心 *single-minded, mind-set* **ichii senshin**
一生懸命 *with utmost effort, for life* **isshō kenmei**

十*en, 344* 万*en thousand, 465*
百*undred, 14* 億*undred-million, 340*
千*housand, 74* 零*ero, 874*

二*econd, 457*

713-C

三*hree blind men in* 一*ne town climbing* 上*p &* 下*own...*

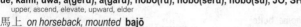

一 (one, single)

上*pper*   上*scend*

ue, kami, uwa, a(geru), a(garu), nobo(ru), nobo(seru), nobo(su), JŌ, SHŌ
upper, ascend, elevate, upward, elder

Facing: 2.0. East ☞ (W)
FLIP: 2.0.a. Sort Of (flat)

馬上 *on horseback, mounted* **bajō**
頂上 *overhead, peak, summit* **chōjō**
極上 *the very best, the finest* **gokujō**
上下 *up & down* **jōge**
上品 *good stuff, quality goods* **jōhin**
上院 *legislature upper chamber* **jōin**
上記 *"as mentioned above..."* **jōki**
上告 *court appeal* **jōkoku**
上京 *going to tokyo* **jōkyō**
上納 *tax payment* **jōnō**
上昇 *rise, ascend, going up* **jōshō**
上等 *high-quality, high grade* **jōtō**
上手 *skilled, expert, adept* **jōzu**
海上 *maritime, sea-faring* **kaijō**
向上 *improve, advance onself* **kōjō**
屋上 *rooftop, penthouse* **okujō**
陸上 *on land* **rikujō**
路上 *road* **rojō**
史上 *based on history* **shijō**

年上 *older than oneself* **toshiue**
頭上 *overhead* **zujō**
便宜上 *for convenience sake* **bengijō**
法律上 *based on the law* **hōritsujō**
上っ面 *appearance, surface* **uwattsura**
上げ下げ *fluctuation, up & down* **agesage**
売り上げ *sales volume* **uriage**
安上がり *economical, cheaper* **yasuagari**
申し上げる *say politely* **mōshiageru**
成り上がり *upstart* **nariagari**
思い上がる *flatter oneself* **omoiagaru**
作り上げる *complete, finish* **tsukuriageru**

高*igh*, 435	良*ood*, 253	天*eaven*, 83
立*tand up*, 234	空*ky*, 394	昇*scend*, 299

土*round*, 8

713-D

三*hree blind men in* 一*ne town climbing* 上*p &* 下*own...*

一 (one, single)

下*ower*   下*escend*

**shita, moto, shimo, sa(geru), o(rosu), kuda(su), sa(garu), o(riru), kuda(ru),
kuda(saru), KA, GE**
lower, descend, down, younger

Facing: 2.0. East ☞ (W)

足下 *foot, step* **ashimoto**
部下 *subordinate, underling, orderly* **buka**
下宿 *board, lodging* **geshuku**
陛下 *Your-, His-, Her Imperial Majesty* **heika**
下手①*clumsy, unskilled, shoddy* **heta**
下手②*lower part of the stage* **shimote**
左下 *bottom left* **hidarishita**
時下 *recently, lately* **jika**
下位 *low rank, lower rank* **kai**
下院 *lower chamber (legislature)* **kain**
下級 *lower class, the masses* **kakyū**
下線 *underline* **kasen**
川下 *riverbed* **kawashimo**
風下 *leeward* **kazashimo**
南下 *go south* **nanka**
落下 *descent, fall* **rakka**
下々 *common people, masses* **shimojimo**
下関市 *Shimonoseki City, Yamaguchi Pref.* **shimonoseki**

下腹 *lower abdomen* **shitabara**
下着 *underwear, undergarments* **shitagi**
年下 *younger than oneself* **toshishita**
地下鉄 *subway train* **chikatetsu**
氷点下 *fluctuation, up & down* **hyōtenka**
下り坂 *downhill* **kudarizaka**
見下す①*despise, detest, scorn* **mikudasu**
見下す②*look from an higher level* **miorosu**
下回る *lower movement* **shitamawaru**
下っ端 *underling, petty official* **shitappa**
下がり目 *slanted eyes* **sagarime**
切り下げる *reduce, cut* **kirisageru**
取り下げる *withdraw, call off, stop* **torisageru**

低*ow*, 700	堕*all-down*, 807	衰*ecline*, 374
陥*all-down*, 893	落*all-down*, 826	倒*verthrow*, 496

不*[negative]*, 300

714-A

邸*esidence* 底*ottom cool in autumn...*

邸*esidence*　　邸*illa*

ß ⇔ 阜 (village-right)

yashiki, TEI
residence, villa, stately residence

別邸 *summer house, vacation home* **bettei**
豪邸 *palatial residence, mansion* **gōtei**
藩邸 *Daimyo residence* **hantei**
本邸 *main residence* **hontei**
自邸 *one's residence* **jitei**
官邸 *official residence* **kantei**
⇒首相官邸 *premier's residence* **shushō kantei**
公邸 *official residence* **kōtei**
私邸 *private residence* **shitei**
邸内 *within the residence* **teinai**
邸宅 *mansion, residence* **teitaku**
御用邸 *imperial villa* **goyōtei**

Facing: 2.2. East ☞ (V)

家*ouse, 909*	宅*esidence, 82*
居*esidence, 384*	丁*lock-of-houses, 173*
住*esidence, 750*	軒*[houses], 710*

氏*urname, 489*

714-B

邸*esidence* 底*ottom cool in autumn...*

底*ottom*　　底*epths*

广 (rooftop)

soko, TEI
bottom, depths, abyss

払底 *shortage, scarcity, insufficiency* **futtei**
平底 *flat bottom* **hirazoko**
海底 *sea bed, ocean floor* **kaitei**
川底 *river floor, riverbed* **kawazoko**
基底 *basis, foundation* **kitei**
根底 *root, basis, foundation* **kontei**
靴底 *shoe soles* **kutsuzoko**
奥底 *bottom, depth* **okusoko, okuzoko**
心底 *true-, real intention* **shintei, shinsoko**
底意 *inner thoughts, bosom of one's heart* **sokoi**
底力 *one's real ability* **sokojikara**
底波 *groundswell, critical mass* **sokonami**
底無し *bottomless, pitiless* **sokonashi**
底値 *bottom price, rock bottom* **sokone**
底荷 *empty cargo, ballast* **sokoni**
底線 *base line* **sokosen**
谷底 *ravine bottom* **tanisoko**
底角 *angle* **teikaku**
底辺 *base* **teihen**

Facing: 2.1. East ☞ (H)

底本 *manuscript, original text* **teihon**
底面 *bottom, depth* **teimen**
底流 *undercurrent* **teiryū**
底止 *reaching the bottom, bottoming out* **teishi**
徹底 *thoroughness, exhaustiveness* **tettei**
徹底的 *thorough, exhaustive* **tetteiteki**
到底 *utterly, at all, absolutely* **tōtei**
底上げ *lifting to the surface* **sokoage**
上げ底 *false bottom* **agezoko**
尾底骨 *coccyx* **biteikotsu**
底冷え *"chilled to the bone..."* **sokobie**

深*epth, 788*	海*cean, 241*
床*loor, 633*	洋*cean, 247*

氏*urname, 489*

715-A
Fabulous 冠rown of 冗edundant clowns...

⌐ (cover)

冠*rown*

kanmuri, KAN
crown

Facing: 3.0. ☞☜ Across

栄冠 *crown; honour* **eikan**
宝冠 *crown* **hōkan**
弱冠 *young but accomplished* **jakkan**
花冠 *flower corona* **kakan**
冠者 *young fellow* **kanja**
冠状 *coronary, heart organ* **kanjō**
冠状動脈 *coronary artery* **kanjō dōmyaku**
冠詞 *word article* **kanshi**
冠水 *flood, water inundation* **kansui**
冠絶 *unsurpassed, unrivalled* **kanzetsu**
桂冠 *laurel wreath* **keikan**
金冠 *tooth gold crown* **kinkan**
光冠 *corona* **kōkan**
根冠 *root cap* **konkan**
極冠 *polar cap* **kyokukan**
無冠 *crownless, without a crown* **mukan**
王冠 *crown, bottle cap* **ōkan**
歯冠 *tooth crown* **shikan**
帝冠 *imperial crown* **teikan**

鶏冠 *comb, crest* **tosaka**
月桂冠 *crown of laurels* **gekkeikan**
冠動脈 *coronary artery* **kandōmyaku**
三重冠 *tiara* **sanjūkan**
戴冠式 *coronation, enthronement* **taikanshiki**
定冠詞 *definitive article* **teikanshi**
冠婚葬祭 *ceremonial occasions* **kankon sōsai**

玉*ewel, 11*	王*onarch, 12*
貴*recious, 913*	妃*rincess, 728*
重*eavy, 430*	姫*rincess, 542*

冗*edundant, 861*

715-B
Fabulous 冠rown of 冗edundant clowns...

冗*edundant*

JŌ
redundant, superfluous

⌐ (cover)

FLIP: 1.0.b. Whole (stem)

冗文 *redundant phrase* **jōbun**
冗長 *wordy, verbose, lengthy* **jōchō**
冗談 *joke, jest* **jōdan**
冗談口 *jocular, jestive, jockative* **jōdanguchi**
冗語 *redundant, repetitive phrase* **jōgo**
冗費 *squandering, wasteful spending* **jōhi**
冗員 *overstaffing, overhiring* **jōin**
冗官 *redundant staffing* **jōkan**
冗句 *redundant phrase* **jōku**
冗漫 *wordy, verbose, highfalutin* **jōman**
冗舌 *garrulity, loquacious* **jōzetsu**

再*epeat, 225*
又*gain, 177*
二*econd, 457*

机*esk, 747*

716-A

A warden's 恩*indness to all,* 囚*ause of* 囚*risoner* 困*rouble...*

心 ⇔ 忄 ⇔ 小 (feelings)

恩*indness* 恩*ratitude*

ON

kindness, gratitude, indebtedness, moral debt

FLIP: 3.0.a. Top (flat)

忘恩	*ingratitude, ungratefulness*	**bōon**
大恩	*great gratitude*	**daion**
報恩	*repaying a gratitude*	**hōon**
感恩	*gratitude*	**kan'on**
国恩	*gratitude to the nation*	**kokuon**
厚恩	*great kindness*	**kōon**
皇恩	*imperial favour*	**kōon**
旧恩	*gratitude from old favours*	**kyūon**
恩愛	*affection, love*	**on'ai**
恩寵	*grace, favour*	**onchō**
恩顔	*gentle face*	**ongan**
恩義	*obligation, kindness, favour*	**ongi**
恩威	*stern but kind*	**on'i**
恩人	*benefactor, patron, mentor*	**onjin**
恩情	*affection, compassion*	**onjō**
恩恵	*blessing, favour*	**onkei**
恩顧	*favour, patronage*	**onko**
恩給	*pension money*	**onkyū**
恩命	*gracious command*	**onmei**

恩赦	*amnesty, pardon*	**onsha**
恩師	*mentor, ex-teacher*	**onshi**
恩賜	*gift from the emperor*	**onshi**
恩賞	*award, prize*	**onshō**
恩沢	*favours, benefit*	**ontaku**
恩典	*special favour, ~request*	**onten**
恩徳	*favour, mercy*	**ontoku**
聖恩	*imperial favour*	**seion**
謝恩	*appreciation, gratitude*	**shaon**
恩返し	*repaying kindness*	**ongaeshi**
恩知らず	*ungrateful, ingratitude*	**onshirazu**

謝*ratitude, 876*	義*ighteous, 341*
得*dvantage, 940*	善*ighteous, 450*
利*dvantage, 686*	仁*ighteous, 457*

思*hink, 596*

716-B

A warden's 恩*indness to all,* 囚*ause of* 囚*risoner* 困*rouble...*

□ (enclosure)

囚*ause* 囚*actor*

yo(ru), IN

cause, factor, precipitate, trigger

FLIP: 1.0.a. Whole (flat)

悪因	*roots of evil*	**akuin**
病因	*cause of illness*	**byōin**
遠因	*distant factor, remote cause*	**en'in**
外因	*external factor*	**gaiin**
原因	*root cause, factor*	**gen'in**
敗因	*cause of defeat*	**haiin**
一因	*one of the causes*	**ichiin**
因果	*cause & effect*	**inga**
因業	*heartless, cold-hearted*	**ingō**
因循	*vacillating, wavering*	**injun**
因縁	*fate, relation, karma*	**innen**
因子	*factor, cause*	**inshi**
因襲	*convention, customs*	**inshū**
因習	*norm, custom, convention*	**inshū**
因数	*prime factor number*	**insū**
因由	*cause, factor*	**inyu**
禍因	*roots of evil*	**kain**
起因	*origin, source*	**kiin**
近因	*immediate cause*	**kin'in**

内因	*internal cause*	**naiin**
成因	*origin, cause*	**seiin**
死因	*cause of death*	**shiin**
真因	*real cause, true factor*	**shin'in**
心因	*psychogenic*	**shin'in**
勝因	*winning factor, cause of victory*	**shōin**
主因	*main-, primary cause*	**shuin**
素因	*main-, primary cause*	**soin**
訴因	*cause of an action, charge*	**soin**
要因	*main-, primary factor*	**yōin**
誘因	*bait, enticement*	**yūin**

兆*ymptoms, 214*	響*ffect, 452*
徴*ymptoms, 62*	果*esult, 287*
根*oot, 772*	理*eason, 872*

囚*rison, 863*

716-C

A warden's 恩indness to all, 囚ause of 囚risoner 困rouble...

□ (enclosure)

囚risoner 囚onvict

SHŪ
prisoner, convict, detainee, inmate

FLIP: 1.0.a. Whole (flat)

男囚 *male convict* **danshū, otokoshū**
獄囚 *convict, felon* **gokushū**
女囚 *female convict* **joshū**
虜囚 *prisoner-of-war, captive soldier* **ryoshū**
囚役 *prison labour, ~work* **shūeki**
囚衣 *prison clothes* **shūi**
囚人 *prisoner, convict* **shūjin**
囚徒 *convict, felon* **shūto**
幽囚 *detention, imprisonment* **yūshū**
脱獄囚 *escaped convict* **datsugokushū**
既決囚 *convict, felon* **kiketsushū**
未決囚 *unconvicted prisoner, detainee* **miketsushū**
死刑囚 *deathrow convict* **shikeishū**

獄*rison, 639*	罰*unishment, 759*
刑*unishment, 536*	罪*riminal, 289*
懲*unishment, 63*	犯*riminal, 640*

四*our, 17*

716-D

A warden's 恩indness to all, 囚ause of 囚risoner 困rouble...

□ (enclosure)

困rouble 困roblematic

koma(ru), KON
trouble, problematic, adversity, dilemma, predicament, quandary

FLIP: 1.0.a. Whole (flat)

貧困 *poverty, penury, destitution* **hinkon**
困苦 *hardships, adversities* **konku**
困却 *embarrassment, predicament* **konkyaku**
困窮 *distress, hardships, poverty* **konkyū**
困窮者 *needy & destitute* **konkyūsha**
困難 *difficult, troublesome* **konnan**
困憊 *exhaustion, weariness* **konpai**
困惑 *perplexity, puzzling, baffling* **konwaku**
困り者 *nuisance, bothersome* **komarimono**
困り切る *be baffled, be at a loss* **komarikiru**
困り果てる *completely at a loss* **komarihateru**

苦*nguish, 477*	挑*hallenge, 214*
悩*nguish, 48*	難*ifficulty, 927*

囚*ause, 862*

717-A

会eeting in 陰hadows, 陰idden John Does...

 *会ssembly*   *会eeting*

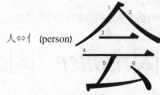

人⇔イ (person)

a(u), KAI, E
assembly, meeting, session

FLIP: 3.0.a. Top (flat)
Facing: 2.0. East ☞ (W)

学会 academic conference **gakkai**
議会 deliberative body, national assembly **gikai**
閉会 closing of a meeting **heikai**
会談 talks, conference **kaidan**
会議 meeting, conference **kaigi**
会合 meeting, conference **kaigō**
会員 member, membership **kaiin**
会場 meeting place **kaijō**
開会 opening of a meeting **kaikai**
会館 assembly hall **kaikan**
会計 payment, finance **kaikei**
会見 interview **kaiken**
会期 session, period **kaiki**
会社 company, corporation **kaisha**
会心 satisfaction, congeniality **kaishin**
会話 conversation, dialogue **kaiwa**
協会 association, society **kyōkai**
面会 interview visit **menkai**
流会 "meeting cancelled..." **ryūkai**

再会 reunion, get-together **saikai**
社会 society, public at large **shakai**
商会 company, business firm **shōkai**
集会 meeting, assembly **shūkai**
総会 general meeting, plenary session **sōkai**
大会 festival, large gathering **taikai**
停会 adjournment, suspension **teikai**
都会 urban city **tokai**
夜会 soiree, evening party **yakai**
出会い meeting, encounter **deai**
立ち会い presence, observation **tachiai**

組 roup, 138	遇 ncounter, 591
団 roup, 345	遭 ncounter, 326
談 onverse, 308	集 ather, 50

今 OW, 182

717-B

会eeting in 陰hadows, 陰idden John Does...

❶陰hadow   **❷陰idden**

阝⇔阜 (village=left)

kage, kage(ru), IN
shadow, shade; hidden, covert, secret, confidential

Facing: 3.0. ☞☜ Across

❶ 木陰 tree shade, under the tree **kokage**
陰影 shadow, shade **in'ei**
物陰 shade, shadow **monokage**
森陰 forest shade **morikage**
緑陰 tree shade, under the tree **ryokuin**
山陰 mountain shade **san'in, yamakage**
島陰 island shadows **shimakage**
太陰 moon **taiin**
夜陰 night darkness **yain**
日陰者 outcast, mysterious person **hikagemono**
陰電気 negative electric charge **indenki**
陰干し drying under a shade **kageboshi**
御陰で "thanks to, because of..." **okage(de)**
❷ 陰イオン ion, negative ion **in'ion**
陰謀 plot, conspiracy, intrigue **inbō**
陰部 female genital, vagina **inbu**
陰画 negative (film) **inga**
陰核 clitoris **inkaku**
陰茎 male genital, penis **inkei**

陰険 treacherous, cunning **inken**
陰気 gloomy **inki**
陰極 cathode, negative pole **inkyoku**
陰毛 genital hair, pubic hair **inmō**
陰惨 ghastly, horrible, ghoulish **insan**
陰性 negativity **insei**
陰晴 fine & cloudy weather **insei**
陰湿 damp & shady, dirty **inshitsu**
陰徳 secret deeds, hidden virtue **intoku**
陰口 backbiting, backtalking **kageguchi**
陰膳 meal set for the deceased **kagezen**

影 hadow, 546	隠 onceal, 840
秘 idden, 219	匿 onceal, 277
秘 ecret, 219	忍 onceal, 535
密 ecret, 220	覆 onceal, 602

険 teep, 938

718-A

諮nquire how rice should be 炊ooked from a Chinese book...

言 (speaking)

諮*nquire*　諮*onfer*

haka(ru), SHI
inquire, confer, question, consult

諮議 *consulting, conferring* **shigi**
諮問 *inquiry, consulting* **shimon**
諮問機関 *consultative body* **shimon kikan**

FLIP: 6.0.a. Left (flat)
FLIP: 7.3.a. Right Bottom (flat)

問uestion, 283	聞nquire, 282
伺nquire, 101	応esponse, 469
尋nquire, 868	答esponse, 232

諾onsent, 277

718-B

諮nquire how rice should be 炊ooked from a Chinese book...

火⇔灬 (fire)

炊*ooking*　炊*ooking rice*

ta(ku), da(ki), SUI
cooking, cooking rice

炊き出し *serving hot meal* **takidashi**
自炊 *cooking one's meal* **jisui**
炊婦 *lady kitchen helper* **suifu**
炊夫 *male kitchen helper* **suifu**
炊具 *cooking utensils, kitchenware* **suigu**
炊事 *cuisine, cooking, culinary work* **suiji**
炊事場 *kitchen, cooking place* **suijiba**
炊事婦 *lady cook* **suijifu**
炊事係 *chef, cook* **suijigakari**
炊事道具 *cooking utensils, kitchenware* **suiji dōgu**
炊爨 *cooking* **suisan**
雑炊 *porridge of rice & vegetables* **zōsui**
飯炊き *rice cooking* **meshitaki**
水炊き *cook by boiling* **mizutaki**
煮炊き *cooking, food preparation* **nitaki**
炊飯器 *rice cooker, ~steamer* **suihanki**
追い炊き *boil a little more* **oidaki**

Facing: 3.0. ☞☜ Across

米ice, 77	飯ooked rice, 256
食uisine, 255	煮oiling, 278
糧oodstuff, 451	沸oiling, 538

次ext, 460

719-A

別pecial 号igns & 号umbers for 別eparated members...

刀⇔刂 (blade, cutting)

別eparate 別part

waka(reru), BETSU
separate, apart, take-apart, break-off, detached

Facing: 3.0. ☞☜ Across

別館 annex-, adjacent building **bekkan**
別件 another matter, another crime **bekken**
別記 "as written in the attached..." **bekki**
別個 each, every, all **bekko**
別項 another chapter **bekkō**
別居 living apart, not living together **bekkyo**
別冊 separate volume **bessatsu**
別席 separate seating **besseki**
別紙 attached sheet, annexed form **besshi**
別荘 vacation home, summer residence **bessō**
別々 separately, individually **betsubetsu**
別便 by separate mail **betsubin**
別辞 farewell speech **betsuji**
別巻 supplement **bekkan**
別口 another-, separate-, special item **betsukuchi**
別離 separation, parting **betsuri**
分別 separate, segregate **bunbetsu**
決別 distinguishing, discerning **ketsubetsu**
個別 separate, private **kobetsu**

戸別 door-to-door, house-to-house **kobetsu**
告別 funeral farewell, last respects **kokubetsu**
区別 distinction, discerning **kubetsu**
類別 classification, sorting out **ruibetsu**
差別 discrimination, prejudice, bigotry **sabetsu**
種別 classification, kind **shubetsu**
別勘定 separate bill; extra charge **betsukanjō**
別れ話 divorce-, separation talks **wakare banashi**
死に別れ die, pass away **shi(ni) wakare**
別品 pretty woman (colloquial) **beppin**
特別 special, distinct, peculiar, unique **tokubetsu**

離eparate, 775	違isparity, 796
特pecial, 250	差ifference, 589
殊pecialty, 234	異ifferent, 239

刷rinting, 760

719-B

別pecial 号igns & 号umbers for 別eparated members...

口 (mouth)

号umber 号ign

GŌ
number, sign, symbol, marking, designation

FLIP: 3.0.a. Top (flat)

暗号 code, cipher, encryption **angō**
番号 number, numeral **bangō**
調号 key signature **chōgō**
怒号 roil, howling **dogō**
符号 sign, symbol **fugō**
負号 minus, negative sign, in-the-red **fugō**
雅号 pen name, pseudonym **gagō**
元号 name of an imperial year **gengō**
号外 extra issue, special edition **gōgai**
号砲 signal firing **gōhō**
号機 production **gōki**
号吸 calling loud **gōkyō**
号泣 crying bitterly, moaning **gōkyū**
号令 command, order **gōrei**
号線 Route #, road **gōsen**
号数 number of periodicals **gōsū**
一号 number one, first **ichigō**
次号 next issue, the next number **jigō**
記号 signal, symbol, mark, code **kigō**

⇒発音記号 phonetic symbol **hatsuon kigō**
呼号 "claiming to be as..." **kogō**
毎号 every issue **maigō**
年号 name of an imperial year **nengō**
略号 code, sign **ryakugō**
正号 positive sign, in-the-black **seigō**
信号 traffic lights, symbol **shingō**
称号 title, degree, rank **shōgō**
等号 equal mark **tōgō**
博士号 doctoral degree, Ph.D. **hakasegō**
先月号 last month issue **sengetsugō**
創刊号 publication first issue **sōkangō**

数umber, 156	順equence, 959
番umber, 338	第[order], 102

足oot, 481

720-A
Pot-bellied 胴orso of an 興ntertaining virtuoso...

肉⇔月 (flesh, body part)

胴orso　　胴runk

DŌ
torso, trunk, corpus, body

FLIP: 7.0.b2. Right (stem)

胴金 *metal clasp* **dōgane**
胴着 *undergarment, underwear* **dōgi**
胴衣 *jacket, vest* **dōi**
⇒救命胴衣 *life jacket, life vest* **kyūmei dōi**
胴元 *gambling bookie* **dōmoto**
胴長 *long body torso* **dōnaga**
胴中 *body torso* **dōnaka**
胴乱 *collecting botanical case* **dōran**
胴体 *body, trunk, torso, fuselage* **dōtai**
胴体着陸 *belly-landing* **dōtai chakuriku**
胴欲 *greed, avarice* **dōyoku**
胴慾 *greed, avarice* **dōyoku**
風穴 *air ventilation* **kazaana**
双胴 *twin-fuselage plane* **sōdō**
寸胴 *cylindrical* **zundō**
胴上げ *tossing shoulder-high* **dōage**
胴震い *shivering, trembling, shaking* **dōburui**
胴締め *waist belt* **dōjime**
胴間声 *thick-, stentorian voice* **dōmagoe**

胴巻き *waist belt pocket* **dōmaki**
胴まり *girth, belly, waist* **dōmari**
胴回り *girth of body torso* **dōmawari**
胴忘れ *mental lapse, forgetting* **dōwasure**

身ody, 504	背ack, 372
体ody, 347	肩houlder, 678

洞avern, 246

720-B
Pot-bellied 胴orso of an 興ntertaining virtuoso...

臼 (mortar)

興ntertainment　　興musement

oko(ru), oko(su), KŌ, KYŌ
entertainment, amusement, merriment, recreation

FLIP: 1.0.b. Whole (stem)

勃興 *sudden rise, upsurge* **bokkō**
中興 *restoration, revival* **chūkō**
復興 *reconstruction, recovery* **fukkō**
不興 *displeasure, discontentment* **fukyō**
一興 *amusement, recreation* **ikkyō**
感興 *interest, excitement* **kankyō**
興亡 *rise & fall, fate* **kōbō**
興奮 *excitement, agitation* **kōfun**
興奮剤 *stimulant* **kōfunzai**
興行 *performance, show* **kōgyō**
興業 *amusement, entertainment* **kōgyō**
興廃 *rise & fall, destiny, fate* **kōhai**
興隆 *prosperity, good times* **kōryū**
興味 *interest, liking* **kyōmi**
興味深い *deeply-interested* **kyōmibukai**
興味津々 *interesting, absorbing* **kyōmishinshin**
興趣 *interest* **kyōshu**
興醒め *kill joy, spoiling fun* **kyōzame**
再興 *revival, restoration* **saikō**

詩興 *poetic inspiration, ~sentiments* **shikyō**
新興 *newly-emerging, budding* **shinkō**
振興 *progress, advance* **shinkō**
酒興 *conviviality, merrymaking* **shukyō**
即興 *improvisation, impromptu* **sokkyō**
余興 *entertainment, dine & wine* **yokyō**
遊興 *pleasure-seeking* **yūkyō**
座興 *amusement, entertainment* **zakyō**
興行師 *entertainer, artist* **kōgyōshi**
興行主 *entertainment promoter* **kōgyōshu**
興信所 *detective agency* **kōshinjo**

曲elody, 476	悦leasant, 942	愉leasure, 922
喫njoy, 900	快leasant, 699	宴anquet, 610
享njoy, 398	歓leasure, 667	劇heatre, 759
遊njoy, 650	娯leasure, 453	俳cting, 795

同like, 245

721-A

尋*nquiry so* 急*rgent on* 当*his detergent..!*

尋*nquire*　尋*uestion*

寸 (measurement)

tazu(neru), JIN
inquire, question, query

Facing: 1.1. West (H)

尋ね物 *something to ask about; ~search for* **tazunemono**
尋常 *ordinary, average, mediocre* **jinjō**
尋問 *questioning, interrogation* **jinmon**
⇒証人尋問 *testimony* **shōnin jinmon**
⇒反対尋問 *cross examination* **hantai jinmon**
⇒誘導尋問 *leading question* **yūdō jinmon**
尋ね人 *missing-, vanished person* **tazunebito**
尋常一様 *ordinary, average, mediocre* **jinjō ichiyō**
千尋の谷 *abysmal valley* **senjin no tani**

伺*nquire, 101*	審*nspection, 339*
諮*nquire, 865*	調*nspection, 280*
聞*nquire, 282*	検*nspection, 939*
討*nvestigate, 691*	査*nspection, 624*
察*nspection, 328*	閲*nspection, 942*

詩*oetry, 250*

721-B

尋*nquiry so* 急*rgent on* 当*his detergent..!*

急*rgent*　急*udden*

心 ⇔ 忄 ⇔ 小 (feelings)

iso(gu), KYŪ
urgent, sudden, emergency

Facing: 3.0. Across
Facing: 4.0. Apart

準急 *local express* **junkyū**
火急 *urgency, emergency* **kakyū**
危急 *emergency, crisis* **kikyū**
緊急 *urgent, emergency* **kinkyū**
急募 *urgent recruitment, "now hiring..."* **kyūbo**
急激 *rapid, sudden, drastic* **kyūgeki**
急減 *rapid decrease* **kyūgen**
急派 *rescue mission, search party* **kyūha**
急迫 *urgency, imminence* **kyūhaku**
急患 *medical-, emergency patient* **kyūkan**
急行 *express, scurrying* **kyūkō**
救急 *emergency, crisis* **kyūkyū**
救急車 *ambulance, hospital van* **kyūkyūsha**
急務 *urgent business* **kyūmu**
急難 *sudden disaster* **kyūnan**
急落 *sudden decrease* **kyūraku**
急死 *sudden death* **kyūshi**
急信 *urgent message* **kyūshin**
急転 *sudden change* **kyūten**

急追 *hot pursuit, wanted* **kyūtsui**
急用 *urgent job* **kyūyō**
急増 *sudden increase* **kyūzō**
応急 *emergency, makeshift* **ōkyū**
至急 *as soon as possible* **shikyū**
早急 *immediate, urgent* **sōkyū, sakkyū**
特急 *express train* **tokkyū**
急降下 *nose dive, rapid fall* **kyūkōka**
売り急ぐ *rush sale, fire sale* **uriisogu**
急き込む *lose one's head, be flurried* **sekikomu**
息急き切る *panting, gasping* **ikisekikiru**

迅*uick, 95*	瞬*link, 921*
速*uick, 502*	秒*econds, 727*
早*arly, 373*	驚*urprise, 330*

争*onflict, 231*

721-C

尋*nquiry so* 急*rgent on* 当*his detergent..!*

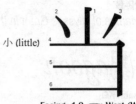

°当*his*　°当*it*

小 (little)

a(teru), a(taru), TŌ
this; hit

Facing: 1.0. 🖙 West (W)

❶ 当番 *on-duty (job rotation)* **tōban**
当駅 *this train station* **tōeki**
当該 *the abovementioned* **tōgai**
当時 *that time, that same moment* **tōji**
当日 *that day, that time* **tōjitsu**
当選 *prize winning* **tōsen**
当然 *natural, expected* **tōzen**
弁当 *Japanese meal-in-a-box* **bentō**
不当 *improper, unsuitable* **futō**
芸当 *performance, show, stunt* **geitō**
配当 *stock dividend, ~yields* **haitō**
⇒株式配当 *dividend payment* **kabushiki haitō**
本当 *real, true, genuine* **hontō**
順当 *proper, fit* **juntō**
充当 *appropriate, earmark, reserve* **jūtō**
勘当 *family disowning* **kandō**
見当 *make a guess, estimate* **kentō**
日当 *per diem, daily allowance* **nittō**
正当 *appropriate, just, right* **seitō**

相当 *proper, appropriate, equal to* **sōtō**
担当 *take charge* **tantō**
手当 *stipend; medical attention* **teate**
⇒夜勤手当 *night shift stipend* **yakin teate**
抵当 *mortgage, collateral* **teitō**
心当たり *knowledge, clue, hint* **kokoroatari**
割り当て *quota, allocation* **wariate**
❷当たり *hit, "bingo!"; per* **atari**
当たり前 *natural, expected* **atarimae**
当てもなく *aimless, no direction* **atemonaku**
探り当てる *locate, pry out* **saguriateru**

正*orrect, 30*	義*ighteous, 341*
是*orrect, 313*	善*ighteous, 450*

肖*esemble, 265*

722-A

印*tamps of Ulysses Grant in the* 潟*agoon of* 虐*yrants...*

卩 (joint; stamp)

印*eal*　　印*tamp*

shirushi, IN
seal, stamp, imprint

Facing: 2.2. East 🖙 (V)

拇印 *thumbmark, thumbprint* **boin**
調印 *signing, signature* **chōin**
封印 *stamped seal* **fūin**
極印 *stamp, hallmark, brand* **gokuin**
旗印 *motto, slogan, battlecry* **hatajirushi**
印字 *printing, letter press* **inji**
印鑑 *seal, stamp* **inkan**
印刻 *engraving, carving* **inkoku**
印刷 *printing, press work* **insatsu**
印紙 *revenue stamp* **inshi**
印章 *seal, stamp* **inshō**
印象 *impression, ideal* **inshō**
印税 *book-, author's royalties* **inzei**
実印 *registered-, official seal* **jitsuin**
影印 *facsimile copy* **kagejirushi**
検印 *"examined, inspected..." (seal)* **ken'in**
消印 *postmark, post-dated* **keshiin**
公印 *official seal* **kōin**
刻印 *carved seal* **kokuin**

丸印 *circle* **marujirushi**
目印 *mark, sign* **mejirushi**
日印 *Japan-India* **nichiin**
奥印 *seal of approval, imprimatur* **okuin**
烙印 *brand seal, trademark* **rakuin**
社印 *company seal* **shain**
矢印 *arrow, pointer* **yajirushi**
合い印 *mark, sign, symbol* **aijirushi**
偽造印 *fake seal, phoney stamp* **gizōin**
認め印 *private seal* **mitomein**
割り印 *tally impression, ~seal* **wariin**

署*ignature, 614*	承*pproval, 117*
銘*ignature, 425*	賛*pproval, 334*
可*pproval, 15*	諾*pproval, 277*

犯*riminal, 640*

722-B

印*tamps of Ulysses Grant in the* 潟*agoon of* 虐*yrants...*

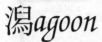

潟*agoon*   潟*nlet-water*

水⇔氵 (water)

kata, KO
lagoon, inlet-water, bay

干潟 *tideland* **higata**
潟湖 *lagoon* **sekiko**
難波潟 *Ōsaka Bay (former name)* **naniwagata**
新潟県 *Niigata Prefecture* **niigata-ken**

Facing: 3.0. ☞☜ Across

湖*ake, 801*	浦*eashore, 813*
江*ay, 176*	浜*eashore, 490*
湾*ay, 909*	涯*eashore, 890*
沖*ffshore, 695*	岸*eashore, 30*

濁*uddy, 924*

722-C

印*tamps of Ulysses Grant in the* 潟*agoon of* 虐*yrants...*

虐*yranny*   虐*ruelty*

虍 (tiger)

shi'ita(geru), GYAKU
tyranny, cruelty, ruthless, savagery, atrocity, brutality, inhuman

暴虐 *cruelty, tyranny* **bōgyaku**
虐殺 *slaughter, massacre* **gyakusatsu**
虐殺者 *slaughterer, murderer* **gyakusatsusha**
虐政 *tyrannical government* **gyakusei**
虐使 *overuse-, overwork someone* **gyakushi**
虐待 *ill-treatment, abuse, cruelty* **gyakutai**
自虐 *masochism, sadism* **jigyaku**
残虐 *cruel, brutal, ruthless* **zangyaku**
残虐行為 *cruel act, atrocity, barbarity*
        zangyaku kōi
悪逆無道 *heinous, treacherous, inhuman*
        akugyaku mudō

Facing: 2.1. East ☞ (H)

酷*ruelty, 266*	猛*ierce, 657*
拷*orture, 392*	烈*ierce, 585*
妄*houghtless, 34*	罪*riminal, 289*
激*ierce, 170*	犯*riminal, 640*

虚*utile, 436*

723-A

来ome & 味aste wasabi paste...

木 (wooden)

来oming　来rrive

FLIP: 1.0.b. Whole (stem)

ku(ru), kita(ru), kita(su), RAI
coming, arrive

伝来	generation-to-generation	**denrai**
元来	originally, by nature, essentially	**ganrai**
従来	so far, up to now, contemporary	**jūrai**
去来	recurrence, relapse	**kyorai**
往来	traffic, comings & goings	**ōrai**
来援	come to assist	**raien**
来月	next month	**raigetsu**
来場	coming to visit	**raijō**
来観	coming to see an exhibit	**raikan**
来客	visitor, caller, guest	**raikyaku**
来日	visit Japan	**rainichi**
来世	life after death, after life	**raise**
来週	next week	**raishū**
来春	next, coming spring	**raishun**
神来	spiritual inspiration	**shinrai**
招来	invitation, leading	**shōrai**
将来	future	**shōrai**
襲来	attack, raid, strike	**shūrai**
天来	heaven-sent, divine	**tenrai**

渡来	coming from a foreign country	**torai**
到来	incoming, advent	**tōrai**
由来	origin, source	**yurai**
出来事	incident, happening, affair	**dekigoto**
舶来品	foreign-, imported goods	**hakuraihin**
近未来	near-, immediate future	**kinmirai**
再来月	month after the next	**saraigetsu**
新来の人	newcomer, new face	**shinrai no hito**
遊びに来る	visit casually	**asobi(ni)kuru**
来合わせる	by chance	**kiawaseru**
生来の怠け者	born lazy, lazybones	
	seirai no namakemono	

到rrive, 496	着rrive, 589
帰eturn, 784	戻eturn, 541

平lat, 488

723-B

来ome & 味aste wasabi paste...

口 (mouth)

❶味aste　❷味ppreciate

FLIP: 5.0.b. Left & Right

aji, aji(wau), MI
taste; appreciate

❶	味見	food tasting, food sampling	**ajimi**
	甘味	sweetness	**amami, kanmi**
	珍味	delicacy, specialty	**chinmi**
	毒味	poison food tasting	**dokumi**
	玩味	food tasting, relishing	**ganmi**
	吟味	examination, test	**ginmi**
	意味	meaning, intent	**imi**
	嫌味	cutting remarks, irony	**iyami**
	滋味	deliciousness, tastiness	**jimi**
	辛味	hot taste, pungent, spicy	**karami**
	味覚	taste, palate	**mikaku**
	味噌	miso, bean paste	**miso**
	妙味	charm	**myōmi**
	中味	content	**nakami**
	酸味	sourness, acidity	**sanmi**
	渋味	astringency, refinement	**shibumi**
	新味	freshness	**shinmi**
	薬味	spice, flavour	**yakumi**
❷	興味	interest, liking	**kyōmi**

興味深い	deeply-interested	**kyōmibukai**
味読	joy of reading, voracious reading	**midoku**
味方	supporter, friend, ally	**mikata**
賞味	appreciation, relish	**shōmi**
趣味	hobby, liking, past time	**shumi**
臭味	stinky, bad odour	**shūmi**
凄味	gruesome, chilling, grisly	**sugomi**
味気ない	insipid, dull, boring	**ajikenai**
味の素	MSG, monosodium glutamate	**ajinomoto**
味付け	seasoning, flavouring	**ajitsuke**
敵味方	enemy view	**tekimikata**

貴recious, 913	価alue, 35
宝reasure, 92	値alue, 783
財reasury, 186	残eave-behind, 767

呼alling, 701

724-A

理ogic in 裏everse, 理eason perversed...

王⇔玉 (jewel)

理ogic　　理eason

kotowari, RI
logic, reason, rationale, dialectic

FLIP: 5.0.a. Left & Right

代理	proxy, delegate, representative	**dairi**
学理	academic theory	**gakuri**
条理	logic, reason	**jōri**
情理	logic & emotions	**jōri**
管理	management, control, supervision	**kanri**
無理	impossible, unreasonable	**muri**
理知	intellect, wisdom	**richi**
理学	science	**rigaku**
理科	science, natural science	**rika**
理解	understanding, comprehension	**rikai**
理屈	reason, theory, argument	**rikutsu**
倫理	ethics, morals, morality	**rinri**
理性	rationality, reasonability	**risei**
理想	ideal, exemplar, model	**risō**
理由	reason, cause	**riyū**
⇒存在理由	rational, raison d'etre	**sonzai riyū**
論理	logic, reason	**ronri**
料理	cooking, cuisine	**ryōri**

生理	physiology; menstruation period	**seiri**
心理	mental state, psychology	**shinri**
修理	repairs, fixing, servicing	**shūri**
哲理	philosophy principles	**tetsuri**
有理	rational function	**yūri**
合理化	rationalization, streamlining	**gōrika**
計理士	accountant	**keirishi**
熱処理	heat treatment	**netsushori**
理化学	physics & chemistry	**rikagaku**
生理日	menstruation period	**seiribi**
整理整頓	neat & tidy	**seiri seiton**
総理大臣	Japanese prime minister	**sōri daijin**

故eason, 960	哲isdom, 53	解nderstand, 400
由eason, 540	賢isdom, 598	分nderstand, 518

埋ury, 319

724-B

理ogic in 裏everse, 理eason perversed...

衣⇔ネ (clothing)

裏everse　　裏osterior

ura, RI
reverse, posterior, rear, back

FLIP: 3.0.a. Top (flat)

表裏	front & rear, duplicity	**omoteura, hyōri**
場裏	arena, battleground	**jōri**
庫裏	Buddhist temple kitchen	**kuri**
胸裏	bosom of one's heart	**kyōri**
脳裏	brain, mind	**nōri**
裏面	rear, reverse, opposite	**uramen, rimen**
裏話	inside story	**urabanashi**
裏蓋	rear lid	**urabuta**
裏金	blood money, dirty money	**uragane**
裏側	back side	**uragawa**
裏声	falsetto	**uragoe**
裏口	back door, back alley, secret door	**uraguchi**
裏腹	opposite of one's words, duplicity	**urahara**
裏地	lining cloth	**uraji**
裏町	back street district	**uramachi**
裏窓	rear window	**uramado**
裏目	undesired results, "the catch..."	**urame**
裏道	back alley	**uramichi**
裏門	rear gate	**uramon**

裏庭	backyard	**uraniwa**
裏作	secondary crop	**urasaku**
裏手	back, rear, reverse, opposite	**urate**
裏屋	slum house, back street house	**uraya**
裏山	mountain behind	**urayama**
舞台裏	back stage	**butaiura**
裏通り	back side, ~street, ~alley	**uradoori**
裏書き	endorsement, written at the back	**uragaki**
裏切り	betrayal, duplicity	**uragiri**
裏漉し	mashing, straining	**uragoshi**
裏街道	back road, side road	**urakaidō**

後osterior, 897		秘idden, 219
背osterior, 372		匿onceal, 277
陰idden, 864		忍onceal, 535
隠idden, 840		覆onceal, 602

震remble, 61

725-A

Contour of 野ields & 野lains by 序rder of rains...

野ields   野lains

里 (hometown)

no, YA
fields, plains

FLIP: 6.0.a. Left (flat)

平野	plain fields, open meadows	**heiya**
広野	wide field, open meadows	**kōya**
野火	field-, prairie fire	**nobi**
野原	field, plain, the greens	**nohara**
野宿	sleeping outdoors, camping out	**nojuku**
野道	rice field path	**nomichi**
野天	open air, field	**noten**
粗野	crude, coarse	**soya**
野営	outdoor camping, encampment	**yaei**
野猿	wild monkey	**yaen**
野外	outdoors	**yagai**
野合	illicit affair	**yagō**
野牛	wild ox, buffalo	**yagyū**
野砲	field artillery	**yahō**
野次	jeering, heckling, booing, hooting	**yaji**
⇒野次馬	nosy person	**yajiuma**
野獣	wild beast	**yajū**
野犬	stray-, homeless dog	**yaken**
野球	baseball	**yakyū**

野郎	fool, idiot, imbecile	**yarō**
野菜	vegetables, veggies	**yasai**
野性	wild nature	**yasei**
野戦	field battle	**yasen**
野心	ambition, dream	**yashin**
野手	baseball fielder	**yashu**
野党	opposition party	**yatō**
荒れ野	wilderness, wild life	**areno**
草野球	amateur baseball, minor league	
		kusayakyū
野育ち	uncultured upbringing	**nosodachi**
野蛮人	barbarian, savage person	**yabanjin**

| 原lains, 431 | 外utside, 188 |
| 平lains, 488 | 郊utskirts, 645 |

里ometown, 321

725-B

Contour of 野ields & 野lains by 序rder of rains...

序rder   序equence

广 (rooftop) 序

JO
order, sequence

Facing: 3.0. ☞ ☜ Across

秩序	order, discipline, system	**chitsujo**
自序	author's foreword	**jijo**
次序	order, sequence	**jijo**
序盤	early stage, initial phase	**joban**
序盤戦	start of a campaign	**jobansen**
序文	preface, foreword, prologue	**jobun**
序言	preface, foreword, prologue	**jogen**
序次	order, sequence	**joji**
序曲	overture, prologue	**jokyoku**
序幕	opening scene, prelude	**jomaku**
序列	order, rank, sequence	**joretsu**
序論	thesis abstract, preface, prologue	**joron**
序説	introduction, preface	**josetsu**
序詞	foreword, preface, introduction	**joshi**
序章	foreword, preface, introduction	**joshō**
序奏	overture, prologue	**josō**
序数	ordinal number, ordinal	**josū**
順序	turn, order, sequence	**junjo**
機序	biology mechanism	**kijo**

公序	public order, peace & order	**kōjo**
後序	postscript, epilogue	**kōjo**
序の口	preface, foreword; easy	**jonokuchi**
序開き	opening, start, beginning	**jobiraki**
無秩序	breakdown of order & discipline	
		muchitsujo
新秩序	new society, new order	**shinchitsujo**
長幼の序	"senior citizens priority..."	
		chōyō no jo

順equence, 959	旧efore, 464
翌ollowing, 237	先efore, 478
随ollowing, 807	後fter, 897
前efore, 118	

府overnment, 429

726-A

In any 領erritory, no guts 零ero glory...

頁 (large shell, page)

領*erritory*   領*omain*

RYŌ
territory, domain

FLIP: 7.0.b2. Right (stem)

英領 *British territory* **eiryō**
仏領 *French territory* **futsuryō**
本領 *main specialty, expertise* **honryō**
受領 *receipt, acceptance* **juryō**
綱領 *principles, political platform* **kōryō**
横領 *embezzlement, absconding* **ōryō**
領分 *one's turf, domain* **ryōbun**
領地 *domain, territory* **ryōchi**
領土 *territory, possession* **ryōdo**
領土権 *territorial rights* **ryōdoken**
領域 *territory, domain, sphere* **ryōiki**
領事 *consul* **ryōji**
領事館 *consulate-general* **ryōjikan**
領海 *territorial seas* **ryōkai**
領空 *territorial airspace* **ryōkū**
領内 *domain, territory* **ryōnai**
領主 *feudal lord* **ryōshu**
領収 *receiving, being in receipt* **ryōshū**
領袖 *leader, chief* **ryōshū**

領会 *consent, approval* **ryōkai**
領水 *territorial waters* **ryōsui**
領有 *possession, ownership* **ryōyū**
宰領 *supervision, guidance* **sairyō**
占領 *occupation, possession* **senryō**
首領 *chief, boss, head* **shuryō**
総領 *eldest child* **sōryō**
頭領 *chief, boss, head* **tōryō**
要領 *the point, the gist* **yōryō**
属領 *territory, dependency* **zokuryō**
領収証 *official receipt* **ryōshūshō**

統*overn, 885*	管*ontrol, 917*
府*overnment, 429*	導*uidance, 312*
轄*ontrol, 968*	旨*nstruct, 242*

頒*istribution, 835*

726-B

In any 領erritory, no guts 零ero glory...

雨 (weather)

零

零*ero*

REI
zero

FLIP: 3.0.b. Top (stem)

零度 *freezing point* **reido**
零敗 *lose without a score* **reihai**
零位 *zero point* **reii**
零時 *twelve midnight, twelve noon* **reiji**
⇒午後零時 *twelve noon* **gogoreiji**
⇒午前零時 *twelve midnight* **gozen reiji**
零下 *temperature below zero* **reika**
零落 *ruin, downfall, decline* **reiraku**
零露 *dripping dew* **reiro**
零細 *frivolous, petty, trifle, flimsy* **reisai**
零才 *less than a year old* **reisai**
零点 *zero, love score* **reiten**
零敗 *shutout, defeat with a zero score* **zerohai**
零歳 *below 12 months baby* **zerosai**
零戦 *Kamikaze plane* **zerosen**
お零れ *remainder, leftover* **okobore**
零細農 *poor peasant* **reisainō**
零余子 *propagule* **reiyoshi**, **mukago**
落ち零れ *"fallen & left behind..."* **ochikobore**

零細企業 *small business* **reisai kigyō**
取り零す *unexpected defeat, upset* **torikobosu**

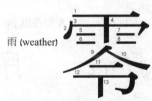

一*ne, 858*	万*en thousand, 465*
百*undred, 14*	億*undred-million, 340*
千*housand, 74*	無*othing, 49*

霧*oggy, 518*

727-A

Sound 策olicies 刺ierce for many years...

策*olicy* 　　策*easure*

竹 (bamboo)

SAKU
　policy, measure, scheme

FLIP: 4.0.b. Bottom (stem)

万策 *every means, all measures* **bansaku**
凡策 *mediocre plan* **bonsaku**
秘策 *secret measures* **hisaku**
方策 *policy, measures* **hōsaku**
一策 *plan, idea* **issaku**
⇒窮余の一策 *last resort* **kyūyo no issaku**
画策 *scheme, plan, machination* **kakusaku**
姦策 *sinister plot, machination* **kansaku**
献策 *suggestion, implication* **kensaku**
金策 *raising money* **kinsaku**
奇策 *clever scheme, skilful planning* **kisaku**
国策 *national policy* **kokusaku**
無策 *unplanned, haphazard, random* **musaku**
妙策 *clever scheme* **myōsaku**
策謀 *stratagem, tactics* **sakubō**
策動 *scheme, machination* **sakudō**
策動家 *schemer, wirepuller, manipulator* **sakudōka**
策略 *stratagem, trick, artifice* **sakuryaku**
策戦 *combat missions, ~operations* **sakusen**

策士 *strategist, tactician* **sakushi**
策定 *decision, judgement* **sakutei**
政策 *policy, measures* **seisaku**
施策 *policy, measures* **shisaku**
失策 *blunder, fiasco, bungling, boo-boo* **shissaku**
小策 *frivolous-, trivial-, petty measure* **shōsaku**
対策 *counter measure, remedy* **taisaku**
⇒災害対策 *calamity precaution* **saigai taisaku**
得策 *wise plan, clever scheme* **tokusaku**
懐柔策 *concession, conciliatory measure*
　　kaijūsaku
善後策 *remedial measure* **zengosaku**

略*ummary, 825*	従*omply, 551*
応*omply, 469*	措*onduct, 282*

策*[order], 102*

727-B

Sound 策olicies 刺ierce for many years...

刺*ierce* 　　刺*tabbing*

刀⇔刂 (blade, cutting)

sa(su), sa(saru), SHI
　pierce, stabbing, thrust, knifing, lunging, penetrate

FLIP: 6.0.b. Left (stem)

刺刺しい *harsh, stinging* **togetogeshii**
風刺 *satire, caricature, lampoon* **fūshi**
風刺画 *caricature sketch* **fūshiga**
針刺し *pin cushion* **harisashi**
刺青 *tattoo-marking* **irezumi**
名刺 *name card, business card* **meishi**
刺し網 *barbeque grill* **sashiami**
刺し子 *quilted coat (Karate)* **sashiko**
刺し身 *fresh raw fish cuisine* **sashimi**
刺し殺す *death by stabbing* **sashikorosu**
刺身包丁 *sashimi knife* **sashimi bōchō**
刺激 *stimulus, stimulant* **shigeki**
刺激物 *stimulant, tonic substance* **shigekibutsu**
刺激的 *provocative, inciteful* **shigekiteki**
刺激剤 *stimulant, energizer* **shigekizai**
刺客 *assassin, gun-for-hire* **shikaku**
刺殺 *death by stabbing* **shisatsu**
刺傷 *knife-, stab wound* **shishō**
刺し傷 *knife-, stab wound* **sashikizu**

刺繍 *embroidery, weaving* **shishū**
刺繍台 *embroidery frame* **shishūdai**
刺繍糸 *embroidery thread* **shishūito**
刺繍枠 *embroidery frame* **shishūwaku**
有刺 *thorny* **yūshi**
有刺鉄線 *barbed wire* **yūshi tessen**
突き刺す *stick, pierce* **tsukisasu**
突き刺さる *stick, be stuck* **tsukisasaru**

徹*ierce-thru, 843*
挿*nsert, 126*
突*hrust, 576*

制*ystem, 534*

728-A

窮xtreme 謝pologies for being rude with no 謝ratitude...

穴 (hole, cave)

窮*xtreme* 窮*ltra*

kiwa(maru), kiwa(meru), KYŪ
extreme, utmost, ultra

FLIP: 3.0.b. Top (stem)

貧窮 *indigence, poverty, destitution* **hinkyū**	
困窮 *distress, poverty, flat broke* **konkyū**	
窮乏 *indigence, poverty, destitution* **kyūbō**	
窮地 *difficult situation, predicament* **kyūchi**	
窮迫 *needy circumstances* **kyūhaku**	
窮状 *distress, trouble* **kyūjō**	
窮屈 *poor, cramped* **kyūkutsu**	
窮極 *extreme, ultimate* **kyūkyoku**	
窮民 *poor & needy* **kyūmin**	
窮地 *predicament, difficulties* **kyūchi**	
窮鳥 *cornered bird* **kyūchō**	
窮理 *fact-finding, truth-seeking* **kyūri**	
窮死 *dying in poverty* **kyūshi**	
窮鼠 *cornered rat* **kyūso**	
窮追 *driven into a corner* **kyūtsui**	
窮余 *desperate, despondent* **kyūyo**	
窮余の策 *desperate attempt* **kyūyo no saku**	
無窮 *infinite, eternity, perpetual* **mukyū**	
窮措大 *impoverished student* **kyūsodai**	

極*xtreme, 947*	最*aximum, 423*
甚*xtreme, 293*	限*imit, 771*
端*ndpoint, 974*	涯*imit, 890*

謝*ratitude, 876*

728-B

窮xtreme 謝pologies for being rude with no 謝ratitude...

言 (speaking)

❶謝*ratitude* ❷謝*pology*

ayama(ru), SHA
gratitude, moral debt, thank you, indebtedness; apology, atonement

FLIP: 6.0.a. Left (flat)
Facing: 1.2. 🔁 West (V)

❶月謝 *monthly tuition (not in universities)* **gessha**
⇒無月謝 *free lessons* **mugessha**
拝謝 *gratitude, appreciation* **haisha**
薄謝 *reward, token of gratitude* **hakusha**
報謝 *reward, remunerate* **hōsha**
慰謝 *consolation* **isha**
慰謝料 *consolation money* **isharyō**
感謝 *gratitude, appreciation* **kansha**
感謝状 *letter of gratitude* **kanshajō**
感謝祭 *thanksgiving festival* **kanshasai**
謝電 *thank you telegram* **shaden**
謝儀 *expression of gratitude* **shagi**
謝意 *gratitude, appreciation* **shai**
謝金 *cash gift of gratitude* **shakin**
謝恩 *gratitude, appreciation* **shaon**
謝恩会 *graduation party* **shaonkai**
謝礼 *reward, fee* **sharei**
謝絶 *refusal, denial* **shazetsu**
深謝 *deep appreciation* **shinsha**

代謝 *metabolism* **taisha**
⇒新陳代謝 *metabolism* **shinchin taisha**
多謝 *profound gratitude* **tasha**
謝肉祭 *carnival* **shanikusai**

❷陳謝 *apology, atonement* **chinsha**
謝辞 *thanks, apology* **shaji**
謝状 *letter of apology* **shajō**
謝罪 *apology, atonement* **shazai**
平謝り *apologizing profusely* **hiraayamari**

恩*ratitude, 862*	惜*egret, 281*
慨*egret, 316*	義*ighteous, 341*
憾*egret, 46*	善*ighteous, 450*

射*hoot, 504*

729-A

荷 *reight on the* 河 *iver,* 歌 *inging boatmen to deliver...*

荷 *argo*　　荷 *reight*

ni, KA
cargo, freight, loads

艹 (grass)

FLIP: 8.0.a. Inner (flat)
FLIP: 3.0.b. Top (stem)

荒荷 *bulk freight, extra trouble* **arani**
着荷 *cargo arrival, goods delivery* **chakka, chakuni**
電荷 *electric charge* **denka**
負荷 *load, cargo, freight* **fuka**
船荷 *cargo, freight* **funani**
初荷 *first shipment of the year* **hatsuni**
荷電 *electric charge* **kaden**
荷重 *load, cargo, freight* **kajū, niomo**
空荷 *empty cargo* **karani**
荷担 *participation, assistance* **katan**
倉荷 *freight-, cargo warehouse* **kurani**
荷札 *tag, label* **nifuda**
荷車 *cart, wagon* **niguruma**
荷物 *baggage, luggage, suitcase* **nimotsu**
荷縄 *cargo packing rope* **ninawa**
荷主 *consignor, goods owner* **ninushi**
荷役 *cargo loading & unloading* **niyaku**
入荷 *cargo delivery, ~arrival* **nyūka**
集荷 *cargo retrieval, ~claim* **shūka**

出荷 *cargo forwarding, shipment* **shukka**
装荷 *cargo loading* **sōka**
底荷 *empty cargo, in ballast* **sokoni**
在荷 *available stock, ~in store* **zaika**
小荷物 *small baggage, package* **konimotsu**
荷揚げ *cargo landing, unloading, arrival* **niage**
荷扱い *cargo handling, ~processing* **niatsukai**
荷馬車 *wagon, cart* **nibasha**
荷造り *packing, packaging* **nizukuri**
手荷物 *carry-on baggage (airline)* **tenimotsu**
積み荷 *cargo, freight, load* **tsumini**

貨 *reight, 191*	物 *hings, 647*
搭 *reight, 146*	品 *roducts, 901*

何 *omething, 101*

729-B

荷 *reight on the* 河 *iver,* 歌 *inging boatmen to deliver...*

河 *iver*

kawa, KA
river

水 ⇔ 氵 (water)

FLIP: 8.0.a. Inner (flat)

河豚 *balloon fish* **fugu**
銀河 *Milky Way, Galaxy* **ginga**
氷河 *glacier, ice field* **hyōga**
氷河時代 *glacial age, ice age* **hyōga jidai**
河馬 *hippopotamus, hippo* **kaba**
河岸 *river bank, river edge* **kagan, kashi**
河畔 *river side, river bank* **kahan**
河鹿 *river frog* **kajika**
河口 *mouth of a river* **kakō**
河峡 *river canyon, gorge* **kakyō**
河童 *river goblin, good swimmer* **kappa**
河流 *river stream, ~flow, ~current* **karyū**
河川 *river* **kasen**
河川敷 *river flood plain* **kasenshiki**
河心 *middle of a river* **kashin**
河神 *god of rivers* **kashin**
河床 *river bed* **kashō, kawadoko**
河水 *river water* **kasui**
河原 *river bank, river beach* **kawara**

河底 *river bed* **kawazoko**
決河 *river breaking thru* **kekka**
黄河 *yellow river* **kōga**
山河 *mountains & rivers* **sanga**
大河 *large river* **taiga**
渡河 *crossing a river* **toka**
運河 *canal (Panama Canal)* **unga**
天の河 *milky way* **amanogawa**
河岸端 *riverside* **kashibata**
魚河岸 *coastal fish market* **uogashi**
白河夜船 *fast asleep* **shirakawa yofune**

海 *cean, 241*	湖 *ake, 801*
洋 *cean, 247*	泳 *wimming, 729*
川 *iver, 76*	漁 *ishing, 48*

何 *omething, 101*

729-C

荷 *reight on the* 河 *iver,* 歌 *inging boatmen to deliver...*

❶歌*inging* ❷歌*oem*

欠 (lacking)

uta, uta(u), KA
singing; poem

Facing: 1.2. ⬅ West (V)

❶ 牧歌 *pastoral song* **bokka**
演歌 *Japanese ballad, ~sentimental song* **enka**
舟歌 *boatman's song* **funauta**
雅歌 *song, singing* **gaka**
軍歌 *war song, battle song* **gunka**
鼻歌 *humming* **hanauta**
歌劇 *opera, operetta* **kageki**
歌曲 *song, singing* **kakyoku**
歌詞 *song lyrics* **kashi**
歌唱 *singing* **kashō**
歌手 *singer, vocalist* **kashu**
歌集 *anthology of songs, ~poetry* **kashū**
校歌 *high school hymn* **kōka**
国歌 *national anthem* **kokka**
狂歌 *comic-, satirical poem* **kyōka**
作歌 *song writing, poem composition* **sakka**
讃歌 *song of praise* **sanka**
聖歌 *sacred song, hymn, carol* **seika**
選歌 *selected poem-, ~song* **senka**

歌声 *singing voice, vocals* **utagoe**
童歌 *children's song, nursery rhyme* **warabeuta**
祝い歌 *song of congratulation* **iwaiuta**
歌舞伎 *Kabuki show, ~performance* **kabuki**
替え歌 *parody, satire, lampoon* **kaeuta**
歌謡曲 *popular song, pop song* **kayōkyoku**
賛美歌 *hymn* **sanbika**
❷ 歌壇 *world of Tanka poetry* **kadan**
歌道 *art of Tanka poetry* **kadō**
歌人 *poet, poetess* **kajin**
詩歌 *poetry* **shiika**

曲 *elody, 476*	声 *oice, 428*
奏 *usic play, 579*	詠 *oetry, 729*
譜 *usical note, 455*	詩 *oetry, 250*

敬 *espect, 329*

730-A

示 *hown in all* 宗 *eligions,* 崇 *espect & devotion...*

示*isplay* 示*howing*

示⇔ネ (display, show)

shime(su), JI, SHI
display, showing, present, exhibit

FLIP: 1.0.b. Whole (stem)

暗示 *hint, suggestion, inference* **anji**
表示 *indication, showing, display* **hyōji**
示談 *out-of-court settlement* **jidan**
示威 *show-of-force, demonstration* **jii**
示威運動 *demonstration, protest rally* **jii undō**
示達 *instructions, directions* **jitatsu**
啓示 *revelation, apocalypse* **keiji**
掲示 *notice, bulletin* **keiji**
掲示板 *bulletin board* **keijiban**
顕示 *revelation, manifestation* **kenji**
誇示 *ostentation, showing-off* **koji**
公示 *public notification, ~notice* **kōji**
告示 *bulletin, notice* **kokuji**
訓示 *instructions, directions* **kunji**
教示 *instruction, teachings* **kyōji**
明示 *clear expression* **meiji**
黙示 *revelation, implication* **mokushi**
黙示録 *revelations, apocalypse* **mokushiroku**
内示 *internal notification, in-house notice* **naiji**

例示 *illustration, exemplification* **reiji**
指示 *instruction, indication* **shiji**
示教 *guidance, instruction* **shikyō**
示し合う *informing each other* **shimeshiau**
示唆 *suggestion, hint, inference* **shisa**
提示 *presentation, showing* **teiji**
呈示 *presentation, bringing up* **teiji**
展示 *exhibition, display, showing* **tenji**
展示会 *exhibition, exposition* **tenjikai**
予示 *makings of, foresigns of* **yoji**
図示 *illustration, sketching, drawing* **zushi**

範 *xample, 584*	載 *ublish, 802*	告 *nnounce, 266*
掲 *ublish, 810*	公 *ublic, 180*	宣 *nnounce, 899*

未 *ot yet, 12*

730-B

示*hown in all* 宗*eligions,* 崇*espect & devotion...*

宗*eligion* 宗*aith*

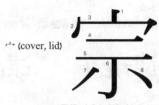

宀 (cover, lid)

FLIP: 1.0.b. Whole (stem)

mune, SHŪ, SŌ
religion, faith

邪宗 *heretical sect* **jashū**
改宗 *religious conversion* **kaishū**
改宗者 *religious convert* **kaishūsha**
真宗 *Shin Buddhist sect* **shinshū**
詩宗 *master poet* **shisō**
宗派 *sect, denomination* **shūha**
宗教 *religion, faith* **shūkyō**
宗教学 *theology, canon law* **shūkyōgaku**
宗教心 *religiosity, ~piousness* **shūkyōshin**
宗教改革 *Protestant Reformation* **shūkyō kaikaku**
宗門 *sect, denomination* **shūmon**
宗旨 *religion, sect, denomination* **shūshi**
宗旨変え *religious conversion* **shūshikae**
宗祖 *sect founder* **shūso**
宗徒 *sect follower, disciple* **shūto**
宗風 *customs, style* **shūfū**
宗法 *rules of a religion* **shūhō**
宗国 *native country* **shūkoku**
宗教劇 *religious drama* **shūkyōgeki**

宗教裁判 *Holy Inquisition* **shūkyō saiban**
宗制 *religious institutions* **shūsei**
宗家 *family head; school master* **sōke**
宗匠 *school master, head teacher* **sōshō**
宗主 *suzerainty* **sōshu**
宗族 *one's relatives* **sōzoku**
太宗 *imperial ancestors* **taisō**
禅宗 *Zen Buddhist sect* **zenshū**
浄土宗 *Jōdo Buddhist sect* **jōdoshū**
天台宗 *Tendai Buddhist sect* **tendaishū**
賢宗天皇 *Emperor Kenzō (485-487)*
    kenzō tennō

信*aith,* 252	神*ivine,* 712	拝*rayer,* 636
聖*acred,* 617	祈*rayer,* 184	堂*ltar,* 94

示*isplay,* 878

730-C

示*hown in all* 宗*eligions,* 崇*espect & devotion...*

崇*espect* 崇*evere*

山 (mountain)

FLIP: 1.0.b. Whole (stem)

SŪ
respect, revere, courtesy, homage

尊崇 *reverence, adoration* **sonsū**
崇拝 *worship, adoration* **sūhai**
⇒偶像崇拝 *idol worship, idolatry* **gūzō sūhai**
⇒祖先崇拝 *ancestral worship* **sosen sūhai**
崇拝者 *admirer, supporter, backer* **sūhaisha**
崇敬 *reverence, adoration* **sūkei**
崇高 *noble, lofty, sublime* **sūkō**
崇光天皇 *Emperor Sūkō (1349-1351)*
    sūkō tennō
崇神天皇 *Emperor Sūjin (97-30 BC)*
    sūjin tennō
崇峻天皇 *Emperor Sūshun (587-592)*
    sūshun tennō
崇徳天皇 *Emperor Sūtoku (1123-1141)*
    sūtoku tennō

恭*espect,* 620	礼*espect,* 685	
仰*espect,* 706	申*peak humble,* 89	
謹*espect,* 962	御*[honorific],* 380	
敬*espect,* 329	様*[honorific],* 944	
尚*espect,* 99	謙*umility,* 805	

宗*eligion,* 879

731-A

逮rrested for hidden wealth, 隷ervants in good 康ealth...

辶 (transport)

逮rrest 逮apture

TAI

arrest, capture, apprehend, accost

逮捕 arrest, capture, police custody **taiho**
⇒別件逮捕 arrest for another crime **bekken taiho**
逮捕状 warrant of arrest, arrest warrant **taihojō**
逮捕命令 arrest order, arrest warrant **taiho meirei**
逮夜 funeral eve **taiya**

FLIP: 7.1. Right (Sort Of)
Facing: 1.1. ☜ West (H)

拘rrest, 16	囚risoner, 863
捕atch, 812	威uthority, 520

建uilding, 390

731-B

逮rrested for hidden wealth, 隷ervants in good 康ealth...

隶 (slave, servant)

隷ervant 隷nderling

REI

servant, underling, subservient, submissive, docile

奴隷 slave, slavery **dorei**
奴隷解放 slave emancipation **dorei kaihō**
奴隷制度 slavery system **dorei seido**
隷従 subservience, blind obedience **reijū**
隷下 subordinates, followers **reika**
隷書 ancient square writing of Kanji **reisho**
隷属 subordination, subservience **reizoku**
隷属国 subject nation, colony **reizokukoku**

FLIP: 6.0.b. Left (stem)

僕asculine-servant, 157	務ervice, 454
勤ervice, 962	働abour, 422
仕ervice, 9	労abour, 351

逮rrest, 880

731-C

逮*rrested for hidden wealth,* 隸*ervants in good* 康*ealth...*

康*ealthy*   康*obust*

广 (rooftop)

KŌ

healthy, robust, sturdy

Facing: 3.0. ☞☜ Across

健康 *health, healthy* **kenkō**
健康美 *beauty of health* **kenkōbi**
健康体 *healthy body* **kenkōtai**
健康的 *healthy, robust, stout* **kenkōteki**
健康児 *healthy child* **kenkōji**
健康保健 *health maintenance* **kenkō hoken**
健康保険 *health insurance* **kenkō hoken**
健康状態 *health condition* **kenkō jōtai**
健康診断 *physical check-up* **kenkō shindan**
健康食品 *health foods, nutritious diet* **kenkō shokuhin**
康寧 *peace & tranquillity* **kōnei**
小康 *state of remission* **shōkō**
安康天皇 *Emperor Ankō (453-456)* **ankō tennō**
康安時代 *Kōan Era (1361-1362)* **kōan jidai**
康永時代 *Kōei Era (1342-1345)* **kōei jidai**
康元時代 *Kōgen Era (1256-1257)* **kōgen jidai**
康平時代 *Kōhei Era (1058-1065)* **kōhei jidai**
康保時代 *Kōhō Era (964-968)* **kōhō jidai**

康治時代 *Kōji Era (1142-1143)* **kōji jidai**
康正時代 *Kōshō Era (1455-1457)* **kōshō jidai**
康和時代 *Kōwa Era (1099-1104)* **kōwa jidai**

力*trength, 351*	強*trong, 894*	医*edicine, 19*
勢*igour, 153*	丈*obust, 463*	剤*edicine, 961*
精*igour, 792*	剛*trong, 975*	若*oung, 276*

唐*athay, 439*

732-A

徐*lowly going,* 塗*ainting* 途*n-going...*

徐*lowly*   徐*radual*

彳 (stroll)

JO

slowly, gradual

FLIP: 7.0.b1. Right (stem)

徐行 *"slow down, go slow..."* **jokō**
最徐行 *"drive extremely slow..."* **saijokō**
緩徐 *gentle & quiet* **kanjo**
徐歩 *slow walk* **joho**
徐徐に *gradually, little by little* **jojo(ni)**

鈍*luggish, 199*	迅*peedy, 95*
遅*ardy, 944*	速*peedy, 502*
疾*peedy, 681*	時*ime, 653*

除*xclude, 501*

732-B

徐*lowly going,* 塗*ainting* 途*n-going...*

塗*aint*　　塗*oating*

土 (ground, soil)

nu(ru), TO
paint, coating, apply on surface

塗れる *be painted, ~coated* **nureru**
糊塗 *glossing over, patching up* **koto**
塗布 *paint application, coating* **tofu**
塗工 *house-, building painter* **tokō**
塗抹 *paint over* **tomatsu**
塗料 *paints, coatings* **toryō**
⇒蛍光塗料 *luminous paint* **keikō toryō**
⇒油性塗料 *oil paints, paint materials* **yusei toryō**
塗擦 *smearing & rubbing* **tosatsu**
塗装 *coating-, paint* **tosō**
塗装工 *house-, building painter* **tosōkō**
塗装材 *coating-, paint materials* **tosōzai**
塗炭 *misery, distress, tragedy* **totan**
塗油 *anointing* **toyu**
粗塗り *rough painting* **aranuri**
血塗れ *bloodstains* **chimamire**
目塗り *plaster sealing* **menuri**
丹塗り *red-painted* **ninuri**
塗り箸 *lacquered chopsticks* **nuribashi**

FLIP: 4.0.a. Bottom (flat)
FLIP: 7.2.b. Right Top (stem)

塗り盆 *lacquered tray* **nuribon**
塗り絵 *colouring lines* **nurie**
塗り薬 *ointment, liniment* **nurigusuri**
塗り物 *lacquer ware* **nurimono**
塗り椀 *lacquered bowl* **nuriwan**
塗り潰す *paint over, re-painting* **nuritsubusu**
塗り立て *"wet paint..."* **nuritate**
塗り立てる *thick makeup* **nuritateru**
下塗り *undercoating* **shitanuri**
漆塗り *lacquered, Japanned* **urushinuri**
上塗り *final coating paint finishing* **uwanuri**

画*ainting, 35*	描*rawing, 271*
絵*rawing, 143*	彩*olour, 914*
図*rawing, 47*	色*olour, 403*

途*urrently, 882*

732-C

徐*lowly going,* 塗*ainting* 途*n-going...*

途*n-going*　　途*urrently*

辶 (transport)

TO
on-going, currently, on-the-way, progressing

別途 *special, different, extra* **betto**
長途 *long journey* **chōto**
半途 *halfway; unfinished* **hanto**
費途 *expense item* **hito**
方途 *ways, means* **hōto**
一途 *wholeheartedly* **ichizu**
官途 *"in the civil service..."* **kanto**
帰途 *on the way home* **kito**
冥途 *realms of the dead* **meido**
目途 *aim, goal, end, object* **mokuto**
征途 *military expedition; journey* **seito**
先途 *final destination* **sendo**
使途 *expenditure, purpose* **shito**
壮途 *ambitious undertaking* **sōto**
途中 *on the way, in the middle of* **tochū**
途中経過 *present condition* **tochū keika**
途次 *on the way, enroute* **toji**
途端 *moment* **totan**
途絶 *ceasing, termination* **tozetsu**

FLIP: 7.2.b. Right Top (stem)

用途 *use, application* **yōto**
雄途 *daring, courageous* **yūto**
前途 *prospect, future* **zento**
途絶える *come to stop* **todaeru**
途切れる *break off, interrupt* **togireru**
中途半端 *half-finished, incomplete* **chūto hanpa**
三途の川 *river styx* **sanzuno kawa**
途轍もない *exorbitant, excessive* **totetsumonai**
途方もない *absurd, exorbitant* **tohōmonai**
発展途上国 *developing nations* **hatten tojōkoku**
途方に暮れる *at a loss, baffled* **tohō(ni) kureru**

今*ow, 182*	歩*rogress, 272*
現*resent, 814*	展*rogress, 522*
進*rogress, 51*	中*iddle, 85*

余*urplus, 501*　　塗*aint, 882*

733-A

In 産hildbirth, life is 産roduced the 牲ictim of pain cannot refuse...

生 (life, birth)

❶産roduce ❷産hildbirth

u(mu), u(mareru), ubu, SAN
produce; childbirth, give birth

FLIP: 3.0.a. Top (flat)

❶ 畜産 *livestock raising, animal breeding* **chikusan**
治産 *property management* **chisan**
減産 *reduced production* **gensan**
破産 *bankrupt, insolvent* **hasan**
遺産 *legacy, inheritance, estate* **isan**
授産 *employment generating* **jusan**
国産 *locally-made, home-produced* **kokusan**
日産 *daily output, ~production* **nissan**
量産 *mass production* **ryōsan**
産馬 *horsebreeding* **sanba**
産業 *industry* **sangyō**
産業革命 *industrial revolution* **sangyō kakumei**
産院 *maternity hospital* **san'in**
産出 *production, output, yield* **sanshutsu**
資産 *property, fortune, assets* **shisan**
倒産 *bankrupt, insolvent* **tōsan**
財産 *property, estate, fortune* **zaisan**
副産物 *by-product, derivative* **fukusanbutsu**
農産物 *farm produce* **nōsanbutsu**

お土産 *gift from a visitor* **omiyage**
産み落とす *lay, breed, bear, spawn* **umiotosu**
❷ 難産 *difficult childbirth* **nanzan**
産科 *obstetrics* **sanka**
産痛 *childbirth pains* **santsū**
出産 *childbirth, baby delivery* **shussan**
産着 *newborn baby clothes* **ubugi**
産声 *infant's first cry* **ubugoe**
産湯 *infant's first bath* **ubuyu**
助産婦 *midwife* **josanpu**
産児制限 *birth control* **sanji seigen**

作roduce, 724	誕hildbirth, 515
造roduce, 267	命ife, 362
品roducts, 901	子hildren, 456

意hought, 340

733-B

In 産hildbirth, life is 産roduced the 牲ictim of pain cannot refuse...

牛⇔牛 (cattle)

牲ictim   牲acrifice

SEI
victim, sacrifice, martyr, prey, pawn

犠牲 *sacrifice, victim* **gisei**
犠牲者 *victim, casualty, fatality* **giseisha**
犠牲的 *sacrificial, martyrdom* **giseiteki**

FLIP: 7.1. Right (Sort Of)
Facing: 1.2. ☜ West (V)

犠acrifice, 342	逝eath, 54
殉artyr, 494	亡eath, 72
死eath, 513	栄lory, 580

特pecial, 250

734-A

充upply of 銃irearms won't 統ontrol 育pbringing in trouble...

儿 (human legs)

充llocate　　充upply

a(teru), JŪ
allocate, supply, dispense

補充 *replenishment, supplement* **hojū**
補充兵 *reserve troops* **hojūhei**
補充隊 *reserve troops* **hojūtai**
充分 *full, sufficient, enough* **jūbun**
⇒不充分 *insufficient, lacking, not enough* **fujūbun**
充電 *electric re-charging* **jūden**
充電器 *battery re-charger* **jūdenki**
充員 *reserve troops* **jūin**
充溢 *overflowing with energy* **jūitsu**
充実 *fulfilment, accomplishment* **jūjitsu**
充血 *blood congestion, ~clogging* **jūketsu**
⇒脳充血 *brain clogging* **nōjūketsu**
充満 *filled up, fully-satisfied* **jūman**
充足 *sufficiency, adequacy* **jūsoku**
充塞 *be clogged, be disabled* **jūsoku**
充填 *filling up, replenishment* **jūten**
充当 *appropriation, allotment* **jūtō**
充用 *appropriation, allotment, earmarking* **jūyō**

Facing: 2.0. East ☞ (W)

拡充 *expansion, enlargement* **kakujū**
填充 *fill up, plug* **tenjū**

給upply, 143	備urnish, 409
納upply, 296	賄urnish, 806
与upply, 349	配istribution, 754
満aturate, 567	頒istribution, 835

流urrent, 781

734-B

充upply of 銃irearms won't 統ontrol 育pbringing in trouble...

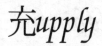

金 (metal)

銃irearm　　銃ifle

JŪ
firearm, rifle, pistol, handgun

銃尾 *gun breech* **jūbi**
銃弾 *bullet shot, gunfire* **jūdan**
銃眼 *gunport* **jūgan**
銃撃 *gunshot, gunfire* **jūgeki**
銃後 *homefront* **jūgo**
銃砲 *guns, firearms* **jūhō**
銃砲店 *gun store* **jūhōten**
銃火 *gunfire, gunshot* **jūka**
銃架 *arms rack, rifle stand* **jūka**
銃刑 *death by firing squad* **jūkei**
銃剣 *bayonet* **jūken**
銃器 *small arms, light weapons* **jūki**
銃口 *gun muzzle* **jūkō**
銃殺 *death by firing squad* **jūsatsu**
銃声 *gunfire explosion* **jūsei**
銃士 *musketeer* **jūshi**
銃身 *gun barrel* **jūshin**
銃床 *gun stock, gun armoury* **jūshō**
銃傷 *gunshot wound* **jūshō**

FLIP: 6.0.a. Left (flat)

銃創 *bullet wound* **jūsō**
銃座 *gun support* **jūza**
拳銃 *pistol, handgun* **kenjū**
機銃 *machine gun* **kijū**
騎銃 *carbine rifle* **kijū**
猟銃 *hunting gun, shotgun* **ryōjū**
小銃 *small firearms* **shōjū**
短銃 *pistol, handgun* **tanjū**
機関銃 *mechanized gun* **kikanjū**
空気銃 *airgun* **kūkijū**

武arrior, 100	衛rotect, 796
戦ighting, 517	護rotect, 828
闘ombat, 946	防rotect, 736

銃ig iron, 155

734-C

充upply of 銃irearms won't 統ontrol 育pbringing in trouble...

糸 (thread, continuity)

統ntegrate　　統ontrol

su(beru), TŌ
integrate, control, unite

Facing: 2.2. East ☞ (V)

伝統 tradition, custom, common practice **dentō**
系統 system; lineage, ancestry **keitō**
⇒神経系統 nervous system **shinkei keitō**
系統的 systematic, methodical **keitōteki**
血統 blood lineage **kettō**
正統 legitimacy, lawfulness **seitō**
総帥 supreme commander **sōsui**
総統 Fuehrer **sōtō**
統治 rule, reign, control **tōchi**
⇒委任統治 mandate, fiat **inin tōchi**
統語 syntax, order of words **tōgo**
統合 integration, combining **tōgō**
統御 rule, reign, control **tōgyo**
統一 unification, standardization **tōitsu**
⇒不統一 lacking unity **futōitsu**
統一スト unified strike, general strike **tōitsu suto**
統覚 control of one's consciousness **tōkaku**
統括 generalization **tōkatsu**
統轄 supervision, control **tōkatsu**

統計 statistics **tōkei**
統制 control, regulation **tōsei**
⇒無統制 lacking control **mutōsei**
⇒価格統制 price control **kakaku tōsei**
⇒物価統制 price control **bukka tōsei**
統率 command, leadership **tōsotsu**
統帥 high command **tōsui**
沖積統 alluvial series **chūsekitō**
大元帥 fleet admiral, general of the army
　　daigensui
大統領 the President **daitōryō**

令ommand, 362	将eneral, 521
帥ommander, 483	導uidance, 312
督ommander, 911	旨nstruct, 242

統ontinue, 260

734-D

充upply of 銃irearms won't 統ontrol 育pbringing in trouble...

肉⇔月 (flesh, body part)

育pbringing　　育reeding

soda(tsu), soda(teru), IKU
upbringing, breeding, raising

FLIP: 4.0.b. Bottom (stem)
Facing: 2.1. ☞ East (H)

愛育 raising in love **aiiku**
撫育 care, looking after, tending **buiku**
知育 intellectual, intelligentsia **chiiku**
発育 growth, development **hatsuiku**
肥育 fattening, growing stout **hiiku**
哺育 nursing, suckling **hoiku**
保育 child care **hoiku**
保育園 nursery, kindergarten **hoikuen**
保育所 day nursery **hoikujo**
育英 elite children education **ikuei**
育児 child care **ikuji**
育毛 hair restoration **ikumō**
育成 rearing, training, upbringing **ikusei**
育種 farm breeding, plant breeding **ikushu**
薫育 moral influence **kun'iku**
訓育 discipline **kun'iku**
成育 child raising, growth to adulthood **seiiku**
生育 growth, development **seiiku**
飼育 breeding, raising, rearing **shiiku**

飼育場 animal farm **shiikujō**
体育 physical education **taiiku**
徳育 moral education, teaching of virtues **tokuiku**
養育 upbringing, rearing, raising **yōiku**
子育て child care **kosodate**
野育ち unschooled upbringing, ill-bred **nosodachi**
性教育 sex education **seikyōiku**
早教育 childhood education **sōkyōiku**
山育ち mountain-bred **yamasodachi**
義務教育 compulsory education **gimu kyōiku**
田舎育ち countryside-bred, rural child
　　inakasodachi

教ducate, 385	子hildren, 456
児hildren, 464	童hildren, 564
稚hildren, 776	訓eachings, 959

盲lind, 623

735-A

瓶ottles 併ombined near the 塀ence behind...

併ombine 併ogether

人⇔亻 (person)

併

FLIP: 7.0.b2. Right (stem)

awa(seru), HEI
combine, together, integrate, merge, amalgam, converge

合併 *merger, coalition, combining* **gappei**
⇒吸収合併 *takeover, acquisition* **kyūshū gappei**
併置 *juxtaposition, placing next to* **heichi**
併読 *reading books alternately* **heidoku**
併呑 *merger, annexation* **heidon**
併願 *multiple applications (universities)* **heigan**
併合 *annexation, amalgamation* **heigō**
併発 *coincidence, by chance* **heihatsu**
併記 *putting down, setting forth* **heiki**
併殺 *double play (baseball)* **heisatsu**
併設 *annex building construction* **heisetsu**
併用 *combination, merger* **heiyō**
併有 *two things simultaneously* **heiyū**
併存 *co-existence, "live & let live..."* **heizon**
兼併 *joining together, uniting* **kenpei**
併出 *align side by side* **heishutsu**
併行 *going together* **heikō**
併起 *simultaneous occurrence* **heiki**
併称 *joint classification* **heishō**

合*ogether, 232*	随*ccompany, 807*
共*ogether, 302*	伴*ccompany, 949*
添*ccompany, 620*	

供*ook-after, 303*

735-B

瓶ottles 併ombined near the 塀ence behind...

瓶ottle 瓶ettle

瓦 (tile)

瓶

FLIP: 6.0.b. Left (stem)

kame, BIN
bottle, kettle, vase, container, jug, thermos

ビール瓶 *beer bottle* **biirubin**
茶瓶 *teapot* **chabin**
茶瓶頭 *bald-headed* **chabin atama**
土瓶 *earthen ware* **dobin**
花瓶 *flower vase* **kabin**
角瓶 *rectangular bottle* **kakubin**
小瓶 *small bottle* **kobin**
薬瓶 *medicine bottle* **kusuribin**
水瓶 *water jug* **mizugame**
尿瓶 *urine jar* **shibin**
鉄瓶 *iron kettle* **tetsubin**
釣瓶 *well bucket* **tsurube**
釣瓶打ち *rapid firing* **tsurubeuchi**
空き瓶 *empty bottle* **akibin**
瓶打ち *rapid firing* **bin'uchi**
瓶詰め *bottling* **binzume**
牛乳瓶 *milk-, dairy bottle* **gyūnyūbin**
火炎瓶 *Molotov cocktail* **kaenbin**
魔法瓶 *thermos, vacuum bottle* **mahōbin**

乳*airy, 970*	医*edicine, 19*
酒*lcohol, 789*	剤*edicine, 961*
栓*ork, 25*	箱*ox, 616*

併*ombine, 886*

735-C

瓶ottles 併ombined near the 塀ence behind...

土 (ground, soil)

塀ence   塀all

HEI
fence, wall, hedge

土塀　earthen fence **dobei**
石塀　stone fence **ishibei**
板塀　board fence **itabei**
外塀　outer wall **sotobei**
船板塀　fence made of old ship woods **funaitabei**
練り塀　tile & mud wall **neribei**
煉瓦塀　brick wall **rengabei**

FLIP: 7.3.b. Right Bottom (stem)

垣ence, 740	囲nclose, 361
壁all, 66	周icinity, 280
環urround, 165	辺icinity, 93

掘igging. 211

736-A

茎tems' 径iameter of a cactus, quite 怪uspicious...

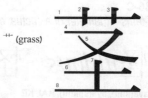

艹 (grass)

茎tem

kuki, KEI
stem

歯茎　gums **haguki**
包茎　phimosis **hōkei**
一茎　plant stem **ikkei**
陰茎　penis, male genital **inkei**
塊茎　tuber **kaikei**
茎葉　stem & leaf **keiyō**
根茎　rhizome, root stalk **konkei**
球茎　corn, bulb **kyūkei**
水茎　water stem **mizuguki**
水茎の跡　calligraphy, brush writing **mizuguki no ato**
芋茎　Taro stem **zuiki**
地下茎　subterranean stem, rhizome **chikakei**

FLIP: 1.0.a. Whole (flat)

根oot, 772
幹ree trunk, 662
枝ree-branch, 704

径iameter. 888

736-B

茎tems' 径iameter of a cactus, quite 怪uspicious...

❶径iameter ❷径ath

彳 (stroll)

KEI
diameter; path, course, passage

FLIP: 7.0.a. Right (flat)

❶長径 major axis **chōkei**
直径 diameter, circle width **chokkei**
直情径行 straightforward, direct path **chokujō keikō**
外径 outer diameter **gaikei**
半径 radius **hankei**
口径 caliber **kōkei**
大口径 large calibre **daikōkei**
内径 inner diameter **naikei**

❷径行 straight thru, go right ahead **keikō**
径路 process, route **keiro**
径庭 vast difference, great gap **keitei**
山経 mountain trail **sankei**
捷径 short cut **shōkei**
小径 path, lane **shōkei**
短径 minor axis **tankei**

路oad, 405	測easurement, 291
道ath, 312	寸easurement, 345
岐orked-road, 704	幅easurement, 640
畔ice-field path, 484	計easurement, 692

怪ubious, 888

736-C

茎tems' 径iameter of a cactus, quite 怪uspicious...

怪ubious 怪uspicious

心⇔忄⇔小 (feelings)

FLIP: 7.0.a. Right (flat)

aya(shii), aya(shimu), KAI, KE
dubious, suspicious, questionable, doubtful

怪し気 dubious, suspicious **ayashige**
怪聞 strange rumour **kaibun**
怪文書 spurious-, dubious document **kaibunsho**
怪物 monster **kaibutsu**
怪談 ghost story, horror story **kaidan**
怪童 monster child **kaidō**
怪異 mysterious, bizarre, eerie **kaii**
怪事 mystery, wonder **kaiji**
怪事件 mystery case **kaijiken**
怪人 mysterious person **kaijin**
怪獣 monster, beast **kaijū**
怪火 fire of unknown origin **kaika**
怪漢 suspicious person **kaikan**
怪傑 supernatural person **kaiketsu**
怪奇 mysterious, weird, eerie **kaiki**
⇒複雑怪奇 complex & inscrutable **fukuzatsu kaiki**
怪奇物語 mystery tale, ~story **kaiki monogatari**
怪光 mysterious light **kaikō**
怪力 marvellous strength **kairiki**

怪説 mysterious-, strange rumour **kaisetsu**
怪死 mysterious death **kaishi**
怪盗 phantom thief **kaitō**
怪我 injury, wound, bruises **kega**
怪訝 dubious, perplexed **kegen**
奇怪 mysterious, bizarre, eerie **kikai**
物の怪 supernatural being **mononoke**
醜怪 ugly & bizarre **shūkai**
妖怪 ghoulish-, ghastly apparition **yōkai**

奇trange, 269	幻antasy, 88
魂oul, 936	玄ystery, 358
霊oul, 444	

径iameter, 888

737-A

虞*hreat of one's* 誤*istake will never make...*

虞*hreat*　　虞*nxiety*

osore, GU
threat, anxiety, annoyance

危虞 *danger, fear, anxiety* **kigu**
優虞 *fear, anxiety* **yūgu**
雨の虞 *rain possibility* **ame no osore**
虞美人草 *poppy field* **gubijinsō**
失敗の虞れ *fear of failure* **shippai no osore**

虍 (tiger)

Facing: 2.1. East ☞ (H)
FLIP: 8.0.a. Inner (flat)

煩*nxiety, 832*	慨*egret, 316*
苦*nguish, 477*	憾*egret, 46*
悩*nguish, 48*	惜*egret, 281*
悔*egret, 712*	驚*care, 330*

虜*kin, 69*

737-B

虞*hreat of one's* 誤*istake will never make...*

誤*istake*　　誤*rror*

ayama(ru), GO
mistake, error, fallacy, fault, gaffe, blunder, erratum

言 (speaking)

FLIP: 6.0.a. Left (flat)
FLIP: 7.2.a. Right Top (flat)

誤聞 *misheard, misinformed* **gobun**
誤伝 *misinformation, misreporting* **goden**
誤読 *misreading, miscomprehension* **godoku**
誤配 *"delivered to the wrong address..."* **gohai**
誤判 *mistrial, erroneous verdict* **gohan**
誤報 *false reporting, misinformation* **gohō**
誤字 *misprint, typo* **goji**
誤解 *misunderstanding, miscomprehension* **gokai**
誤記 *writing error* **goki**
誤認 *misconception, misunderstanding* **gonin**
誤差 *margin of error* **gosa**
誤算 *miscalculation, miscomputation* **gosan**
誤射 *accidental firing, "friendly fire..."* **gosha**
誤写 *erroneous copying* **gosha**
誤信 *erroneous belief, misbelief* **goshin**
誤診 *erroneous diagnosis, misdiagnosis* **goshin**
誤審 *wrong judgement, erroneous decision* **goshin**
誤称 *misnomer* **goshō**
誤植 *misprint, typo* **goshoku**

誤答 *wrong answer* **gotō**
誤訳 *wrong translation* **goyaku**
誤用 *misuse* **goyō**
過誤 *error, mistake* **kago**
錯誤 *error, mistake* **sakugo**
誤動作 *faulty operation (manual)* **godōsa**
誤投下 *accidental bombing* **gotōka**
見誤り *oversight, fail to see* **miayamari**
正誤表 *list of errata* **seigohyō**
言い誤り *misspeak, say it wrong* **iiayamari**

失*issing, 19*	革*eform, 39*
失*ailure, 19*	改*eform, 725*
敗*ailure, 137*	矯*eformatory, 163*
謝*pology, 876*	整*djust, 31*

呉*[Wu dynasty], 453*

738-A
No 涯uter-limits of 佳eauty in the 封eudal scenery...

封eudal   封iefdom

寸 (measurement)

FŪ, HŌ
feudal, fiefdom

FLIP: 6.O.a. Left (flat)

封じる *seal, enclose, blockade* **fūjiru**
封じ目 *seal on an envelope* **fūjime**
封じ込める *confine, contain* **fūjikomeru**
封緘 *seal, closing* **fūkan**
封入 *enclose, seal in* **fūnyū**
封蝋 *sealing wax* **fūrō**
封鎖 *blockade, off limits* **fūsa**
封殺 *forcing out (baseball)* **fūsatsu**
封書 *sealed letter* **fūsho**
封筒 *envelope* **fūtō**
厳封 *tight sealing (documents)* **genpū**
封地 *fief, hacienda* **hōchi**
封土 *fief, hacienda* **hōdo**
一封 *sealed letter; an enclosure* **ippū**
開封 *unsealed letter* **kaifū**
完封 *shut out, excluded* **kanpū**
密封 *seal up* **mippū**
虫封じ *healing incantations* **mushifūji**
帯封 *half-wrappings (mailed subscriptions)* **obifū**

別封 *attached letter* **beppū**
同封 *enclosure, attachment* **dōfū**
封印 *seal, sealing* **fūin**
封切り *first-run, newly-released* **fūkiri**
金一封 *cash gift* **kin'ippū**
封建的 *feudalistic* **hōkenteki**
封建時代 *feudal period* **hōken jidai**
封建制度 *feudal system* **hōken seido**
封建主義 *feudalism* **hōken shugi**

藩 *eudal clan, 337*   昔 *lden-times, 281*
殿 *ordship, 522*   去 *y-gones, 360*

掛 *xpense, 107*

738-B
No 涯uter-limits of 佳eauty in the 封eudal scenery...

涯uter limits

水⇔氵 (water)

GAI
outer limits

FLIP: 8.O.a. Inner (flat)

境涯 *circumstances, environment* **kyōgai**
際涯 *limits, ends, bottomline* **saigai**
生涯 *one's lifetime, lifelong* **shōgai**
天涯 *very distant land, remotest area* **tengai**
天涯孤独 *completely isolated, ~alone* **tengai kodoku**
全生涯 *one's entire life* **zenshōgai**
一生涯 *lifelong, lifetime* **isshōgai**
新生涯 *new life, new career* **shinshōgai**

岸 *eashore, 30*   海 *cean, 241*
浦 *eashore, 813*   洋 *cean, 247*
浜 *eashore, 490*   島 *sland, 125*

佳 *eauty, 891*

738-C

No 涯uter-limits of 佳eauty in the 封eudal scenery...

佳*eauty*　佳*xcellence*

人⇔亻 (person)

yoshi, KA
　beauty, excellence, fine

FLIP: 7.0.a. Right (flat)

佳言 beautiful words **kagen**
佳品 high-quality goods **kahin**
佳人 pretty woman **kajin**
佳日 lucky day **kajitsu**
佳景 beautiful scenery **kakei**
佳客 valued client **kakkyaku**
佳句 beautiful passage **kaku**
佳境 climax, highlight **kakyō**
佳味 delicious food **kami**
佳麗 beauty, pretty **karei**
佳良 good, excellent **karyō**
佳作 fine work, good work **kasaku**
⇒選外佳作 honorable mention **sengai kasaku**
佳節 happy occasion, opportune time **kasetsu**
佳辰 happy occasion, opportune time **kashin**
絶佳 superb **zekka**

美*eautiful, 124*	雅*raceful, 58*
麗*eautiful, 68*	淑*raceful, 510*
韻*raceful, 315*	

侍*amurai, 249*

739-A

浴*hower* of 俗*orldly* 欲*esire* often inspire...

浴*hower*　浴*athing*

水⇔氵 (water)

a(biru), a(biseru), YOKU
　shower, bathing

FLIP: 7.0.a. Right (flat)

塩浴 bathing in salt water **enyoku**
混浴 mixed gender hot springs **konyoku**
沐浴 bathe, wash oneself **mokuyoku**
入浴 hot bathing **nyūyoku**
温浴 hot bath **onyoku**
浴後 after bathing **yokugo**
浴場 bathroom, bathhouse **yokujō**
⇒海水浴場 swimming beach **kaisui yokujō**
浴客 bather, hot springs client **yokukyaku**
浴室 bathroom **yokushitsu**
浴槽 bathtub, bath tank **yokusō**
浴用 "use for bathing..." **yokuyō**
浴用石鹸 toilet soap, bath soap **yokuyō sekken**
浴衣 summer kimono **yukata**
座浴 bathing seated **zayoku**
湯浴み bath **yuami**
電気浴 electric current (hotbath) **denkiyoku**
日光浴 sunbathing **nikkōyoku**
海水浴 ocean swimming **kaisuiyoku**

冷水浴 cold bath, ice bath **reisuiyoku**
森林浴 energizing moments in the forest
　shinrinyoku

雨*aining, 417*	洗*ashing, 478*
注*utpour, 750*	濯*ashing, 850*
流*lowing, 781*	射*plash, 504*
波*urrent, 32*	

俗*aiety, 892*

739-B

浴*hower of* 俗*orldly* 欲*esire often inspire...*

人⇔亻 (person)

俗*orldly*　俗*aity*

ZOKU
worldly, laity, mundane, secular

FLIP: 7.0.a. Right (flat)

俗っぽい *vulgar, common, worldly* **zokuppoi**	俗耳 *easy to understand* **zokuji**
凡俗 *vulgarity, gross, blaséé* **bonzoku**	俗人 *layman, worldly man* **zokujin**
脱俗 *out-of-the-world, unworldliness* **datsuzoku**	俗情 *worldliness, materialism* **zokujō**
風俗 *manners & customs* **fūzoku**	俗化 *vulgarisation* **zokka**
還俗 *returning to secular life* **genzoku**	俗名 *secular name* **zokumyō**
反俗 *anti-convention, non-conformity* **hanzoku**	俗吏 *petty officer* **zokuri**
平俗 *common & vulgar* **heizoku**	俗論 *vulgar opinion; popular view* **zokuron**
民俗 *folk customs* **minzoku**	俗説 *common saying, popular view* **zokusetsu**
良俗 *standards of decency* **ryōzoku**	俗称 *popular name, nickname* **zokushō**
世俗 *worldly things, materialism* **sezoku**	俗謡 *popular folk song* **zokuyō**
習俗 *manners & customs* **shūzoku**	俗世 *the world, daily life* **zokuse**
低俗 *vulgarity, gross, blaséé* **teizoku**	俗世間 *the world, daily life* **zokuseken**
通俗 *popular, common* **tsūzoku**	
俗界 *earthly-, secular life* **zokkai**	
俗悪 *vulgarity, gross, blaséé* **zokuaku**	
俗文 *colloquial language* **zokubun**	
俗物 *vulgar person* **zokubutsu**	
俗語 *slang expression, colloquial* **zokugo**	
俗事 *worldly affairs, daily routine* **zokuji**	

界*orld, 365*	公*ublic, 180*
世*orld, 411*	慣*ustomary, 532*
衆*opulace, 766*	

浴*ffluence, 758*　浴*hower, 891*

739-C

浴*hower of* 俗*orldly* 欲*esire often inspire...*

欠 (lacking)

欲*esire*　欲*ppetite*

hos(suru), ho(shii), YOKU
desire, appetite, liking, penchant

FLIP: 6.0.a. Left (flat)

愛欲 *lust, sexual desire* **aiyoku**	大欲 *avarice, covetousness* **taiyoku**
物欲 *materialistic, worldly desires* **butsuyoku**	欲求 *desire, wants, craving* **yokkyū**
胴欲 *avarice, covetousness* **dōyoku**	欲望 *desire, ambition, greed* **yokubō**
貪欲 *greedy, avaricious, ravenous* **donyoku**	欲深 *avarice, covetousness* **yokubuka**
我欲 *egoism, narcissism* **gayoku**	⇒欲深い *greedy, avaricious* **yokubukai**
強欲 *greed, avarice* **gōyoku**	欲情 *sexual desire, lust* **yokujō**
淫欲 *lust, sexual desire* **inyoku**	欲目 *partiality, bias, one-sided* **yokume**
意欲 *will to do, zest for life* **iyoku**	欲念 *desire, passion* **yokunen**
邪欲 *lewd, lust* **jayoku**	欲得 *altruistic, unselfish* **yokutoku**
獣欲 *animalistic desire* **jūyoku**	欲張り *avaricious, covetous* **yokubari**
禁欲 *abstinence, chastity* **kinyoku**	知識欲 *intellectual thirst* **chishikiyoku**
無欲 *free from avarice* **muyoku**	
肉欲 *lust, sexual desire* **nikuyoku**	
利欲 *avarice, covetousness* **riyoku**	
性欲 *sexual appetite* **seiyoku**	
制欲 *control of one's desires* **seiyoku**	
色欲 *lust, sexual desire* **shikiyoku**	
私欲 *personal-, self-interest* **shiyoku**	
食欲 *food appetite, craving to eat* **shokuyoku**	

希*esire, 208*	好*reference, 637*
望*esire, 618*	志*ntention, 426*

俗*aiety, 892*

740-A

稲ice-plants may 陥all when no rain at all...

禾 (tree branch)

稲ice plant

ine, ina, TŌ
rice plant

FLIP: 7.3.a. Right Bottom (flat)

晩稲 *late-growing rice* **bantō**
稲光 *lightning, thunderbolt* **inabikari**
稲田 *rice paddy* **inada**
稲車 *rice cart* **inaguruma**
稲穂 *ear of riceplants* **inaho**
稲荷 *god of harvest* **inari**
稲荷寿司 *rice-stuffed fried tofu* **inarizushi**
稲作 *rice growing, rice crop* **inasaku**
稲作地帯 *rice-producing area* **inasaku chitai**
稲妻 *flash of lightning* **inazuma**
陸稲 *upland rice plant* **okabo, rikutō**
陸稲 *dry-land rice* **rikutō**
水稲 *wet rice paddy* **suitō**
早稲 *early crops, early growing* **wase**
稲刈り *rice harvest cutting* **inekari**
稲扱き *rice threshing (machine)* **inekoki**

米*ice, 77*	飯*ooked rice, 256*
田*ice field, 482*	種*eedling, 430*
畔*ice-field path, 484*	

稲*ice plant, 893*

740-B

稲ice-plants may 陥all when no rain at all...

阝 ⟷ 阜 (village=left)

陥all-down   陥ollapse

ochii(ru), otoshii(reru), KAN
fall-down, collapse, downfall, founder

FLIP: 7.3.a. Right Bottom (flat)

陥没 *cave-in, depression, implosion* **kanbotsu**
陥入 *caving-in, subsiding* **kannyū**
陥落 *fall, surrender* **kanraku**
陥穽 *pitfall, trap, plot* **kansei**
欠陥 *defect, shortcomings* **kekkan**
欠陥商品 *defective-, inferior goods* **kekkan shōhin**
失陥 *surrender, capitulation* **shikkan**

崩*ollapse, 912*	壊*estroy, 847*
落*ollapse, 826*	破*estroy, 715*
降*escend, 133*	倒*opple down, 496*
堕*all-down, 807*	転*opple down, 661*

稲*ice plant, 893*

741-A

強trong 風inds in tornado 風tyle seen from a mile...

弓 (archery bow)

強*trong*　　　強*ortitude*

tsuyo(i), tsuyo(maru), tsuyo(meru), shi(iru), KYŌ, GŌ
strong, fortitude, potent, powerful, strengthen, reinforce, augment

Facing: 1.2. ☜ West (V)

勉強 *study, lesson* **benkyō**
強奪 *seizure, commandeering* **gōdatsu**
強引 *overbearing, high-handed* **gōin**
強情 *obstinacy, hard-headed* **gōjō**
強姦 *rape, forcible sex* **gōkan**
強盗 *robbery, burglary, break-in* **gōtō**
補強 *reinforcement, strengthen, beef-up* **hokyō**
強面 *frightening, tough-, mean-looking* **kowaomote**
強圧 *strong pressure* **kyōatsu**
強弁 *unreasonable argument* **kyōben**
強豪 *strong, powerful* **kyōgō**
強迫 *compel, compulsion, coercion* **kyōhaku**
強化 *strengthening, beefing up* **kyōka**
強権 *strong power; police power* **kyōken**
強行 *force oneself* **kyōkō**
強国 *Great Powers, conquering nations* **kyōkoku**
強制 *compel, coerce, force* **kyōsei**
強震 *violent earthquake* **kyōshin**
強運 *extreme-, sheer luck* **kyōun**

列強 *great powers, conquering nations* **rekkyō**
精強 *pure strength* **seikyō**
強火 *high flame, high fire* **tsuyobi**
強気 *boldness, aggressiveness* **tsuyoki**
増強 *reinforcement, build-up* **zōkyō**
力強い *strong & powerful* **chikarazuyoi**
心強い *reassuring, dependable* **kokorozuyoi**
根強い *deep-rooted, strong, firm* **nezuyoi**
粘り強い *tenacious, persevering* **nebarizuyoi**
忍耐強い *persevering, unyielding* **nintaizuyoi**
心抱強い *strong-hearted* **shinbōzuyoi**

剛*trong, 975*	固*ard, 491*	秀*xcellence, 383*
丈*obust, 463*	凝*arden, 57*	優*xcellence, 556*
緊*ard, 599*	硬*ardness, 402*	最*aximum, 423*

周*ap, 280*

741-B

強trong 風inds in tornado 風tyle seen from a mile...

風 (wind, breeze)

❶風*ind*　　❷風*tyle*

kaze, kaza, FŪ, FU
wind, fluttering, gale, gusting; style, form, manner

FLIP: 2.0.b. Sort Of (stem)

❶秋風 *autumn wind* **akikaze**
暴風 *windstorm* **bōfū**
風圧 *wind pressure* **fūatsu**
風害 *wind damage* **fūgai**
風化 *fade away, fade out in recollection* **fūka**
風白 *god of the winds* **fūhaku**
風雨 *storm, wind & rain* **fūu**
春風 *spring breeze* **harukaze, shunfū**
順風 *favourable wind* **junpū**
神風 *suicide pilots, divine wind* **kamikaze**
寒風 *cold-, icy wind* **kanpū**
風穴 *air hole, air ventilation* **kazaana**
風見 *wind vane* **kazami**
風下 *leeward* **kazashimo**
波風 *storm, wind & rain* **namikaze**
潮風 *ocean-, sea breeze* **shiokaze**
台風 *typhoon, storm* **taifū**
風雲児 *lucky adventurer* **fūunji**
鼻風邪 *cold in the nose, ~head* **hanakaze**

❷季節風 *seasonal wind, monsoon* **kisetsufū**
夏風邪 *summer cold* **natsukaze**
風月 *beauty of nature* **fūgetsu**
風格 *dignified appearance* **fūkaku**
風景 *scenery, landscape* **fūkei**
風紀 *public morals, discipline* **fūki**
風光 *natural beauty* **fūkō**
風呂 *hot bath* **furo**
風説 *rumour, hearsay* **fūsetsu**
風俗 *local customs & manners* **fūzoku**
和風 *Japanese style* **wafū**
日本風 *Japanese-style* **nihonfū**

吹*lowing, 642*	式*tyle, 418*
息*reathe, 586*	的*tyle, 696*

虫*osquito, 369*

742-A

Flower 香*ragrance,* 誘*empts a romance...*

香*ragrance*   香*cent*

香 (fragrance)

kao(ri), ka, KŌ, KYŌ
fragrance, scent, sweet smell, aroma

FLIP: 2.0.a. Sort Of (flat)

香り *scent, fragrance, aroma* **kaori**
調香 *perfume blending* **chōkō**
芳香 *fragrance, perfume* **hōkō**
芳香剤 *aromatic, fragrant, sweet smell* **hōkōzai**
香港 *Hong Kong, China* **honkon**
色香 *scent & colour* **iroka**
香蒲 *cattail, reed mace* **kaorigama**
香木 *fragrant tree* **kōboku**
香典 *funeral monetary gift* **kōden**
香道 *art of incense smelling* **kōdō**
香華 *flowers & incense* **kōge**
香気 *fragrance, scent, aroma* **kōki**
香炉 *incense burner* **kōro**
香料 *aromatic, fragrant* **kōryō**
香草 *fragrant herbs* **kōsō**
香水 *perfume, scent* **kōsui**
香油 *oil perfume, balm* **kōyu**
薫香 *incense, joss stick* **kunkō**
香車 *Shōji piece* **kyōsha**

抹香 *incense powder* **makkō**
線香 *incense stick* **senkō**
新香 *pickled vegetables* **shinko**
焼香 *incense lighting for the dead* **shōkō**
残香 *lingering scent* **zankō**
安息香 *benzoic* **ansokukō**
香辛料 *spices & seasonings* **kōshinryō**
残り香 *lingering scent* **nokoriga**
御新香 *pickled vegetable* **oshinko**
竜涎香 *ambergris* **ryūzenkō**
移り香 *lingering scent* **utsuriga**

臭*mell, 586*		花*lower, 191*	
薫*ragrance, 934*		華*lower, 40*	
芳*ragrance, 533*		咲*lossom, 707*	

秀*xcellence, 383*

742-B

Flower 香*ragrance,* 誘*empts a romance...*

誘*emptation*   誘*nticement*

言 (speaking)

saso(u), YŪ
temptation, enticement, inducement, inveigle

FLIP: 6.0.a. Left (flat)
Facing: 1.1. ☜ West (H)

誘い球 *lure pitch (baseball)* **sasoidama**
誘い水 *priming, loading* **sasoimizu**
誘い出す *invite out, lure away* **sasoidasu**
誘い入れる *entice, lure into* **sasoiireru**
誘き出す *lure out, lead to come out* **obikidasu**
誘き寄せる *lure, decoy, entice* **obikiyoseru**
勧誘 *invitation, solicitation* **kanyū**
勧誘員 *canvasser, sales catcher* **kanyūin**
誘爆 *induced explosion* **yūbaku**
誘致 *invitation, appealing* **yūchi**
誘電 *dielectric* **yūden**
誘導 *guidance, leading* **yūdō**
誘導尋問 *leading question* **yūdō jinmon**
誘導ミサイル *guided missile* **yūdō misairu**
誘導体 *derivative* **yūdōtai**
誘発 *setting off, triggering* **yūhatsu**
誘因 *immediate cause* **yūin**
誘引 *invitation, solicitation* **yūin**
誘拐 *abduction, kidnapping* **yūkai**

誘起 *giving rise, precipitation* **yūki**
誘殺 *seduce & kill* **yūsatsu**
誘発 *give rise to, precipitate* **yūhatsu**
誘惑 *temptation, seduction* **yūwaku**
誘蛾灯 *light trap, luring lamp* **yūgatō**

惑*emptation, 139*		偏*ncline, 43*	
釣*llure, 697*		傾*ncline, 833*	
幻*antasy, 88*			

謀*onspiracy, 293*

743-A

逆pposite 塑atterns used for Christmas lanterns...

辶 (transport)

逆pposite 逆everse

saka, saka(rau), GYAKU
opposite, reverse, contrary

FLIP: 7.1. Right (Sort Of)
Facing: 1.1. 🚩 West (H)

悪逆 atrocity, cruelty, heinous **akugyaku**
逆鱗 provoking, infuriating, upsetting **gekirin**
逆光 backlights **gyakkō**
逆行 reverse movement **gyakkō**
逆境 adverse circumstances, handicap **gyakkyō**
逆風 unlucky wind, bad luck **gyakufū**
逆上 going mad, ~despondent **gyakujō**
逆流 opposing current **gyakuryū**
逆算 counting backward **gyakusan**
逆説 paradox, irony; opposite opinion **gyakusetsu**
逆進 regression, retrogression **gyakushin**
逆襲 counter-attack, ~offensive, retort **gyakushū**
逆数 reciprocal number **gyakusū**
逆転 reverse, opposite **gyakuten**
逆徒 traitor, rebel, renegade, quisling **gyakuto**
逆用 abuse, take advantage **gyakuyō**
逆賊 traitor, rebel, renegade, quisling **gyakuzoku**
反逆 treason, rebellion, revolt **hangyaku**
逆子 baby delivered feet first **sakago**

逆波 choppy waters **sakanami**
逆手 foul trick, below the belt **sakate**
逆夢 opposite of one's dream **sakayume**
逆巻く rage, surge, roll **sakamaku**
逆比例 inverse proportion **gyakuhirei**
逆効果 counter-result, opposite effect **gyakukōka**
逆戻り reversal, retrogression **gyakumodori**
反逆者 traitor, renegade, quisling **hangyakusha**
可逆的 reversible, dual **kagyakuteki**
真っ逆 "quite the contrary..." **massaka**
真っ逆様 up-side down descent **massakasama**

| 裏everse, 872 | 抗pposition, 749 |
| 反ppose, 537 | 対gainst, 691 |

送ending, 708

743-B

逆pposite 塑atterns used for Christmas lanterns...

土 (ground, soil)

塑attern 塑odel

SO
pattern, model, moulding, template

FLIP: 4.0.a. Bottom (flat)
FLIP: 6.1. Left Top

彫塑 carving, modelling **chōso**
塑性 plasticity **sosei**
⇒可塑性 plastic elasticity **kasosei**
塑像 plastic figure **sozō**
塑造 moulding, modelling **sozō**
塑弾性 plastic elasticity **sodansei**

例xample, 357	型attern, 536
範xample, 584	柄attern, 213
鑑attern, 857	模attern, 827

逆pposite, 896

744-A

Look 後fter your 後ack for 幽loom may hack...

❶後*fter*　　❷後*osterior*

彳 (stroll)

nochi, ushi(ro), ushiro, ato, oku(reru), GO, KŌ
after, later; posterior, rear, back

Facing: 4.0. ✒ ☞ Apart

❶ 後口 *after taste* **atokuchi**
直後 *immediately after* **chokugo**
午後 *afternoon, p.m.* **gogo**
後輩 *one's junior colleague* **kōhai**
後半 *second half, second term* **kōhan**
後半生 *later half of life, one's fortyish* **kōhansei**
今後 *from now on, after this* **kongo**
後任 *successor, replacement* **kōnin**
後世 *after one's death* **kōsei**
後送 *send later* **kōsō**
後続 *succession, inheritance* **kōzoku**
後程 *afterwards, later* **nochihodo**
老後 *old age, remaining years* **rōgo**
最後 *finale, endgame* **saigo**
戦後 *post-war years (1945~47)* **sengo**
予後 *convalescence, recovery* **yogo**
後払い *payment on delivery, cod* **atobarai**
後書き *postscript, p.s.* **atogaki**
後回し *postponement, deferment* **atomawashi**

善後策 *remedial measure, stopgap* **zengosaku**
事後承諾 *ex-post facto approval* **jigo shōdaku**
❷背後 *back, rear* **haigo**
後衛 *back player* **kōei**
後進 *backing up; with hands tied up* **kōshin**
後戻り *turning back, recurrence* **atomodori**
後押し *support, assistance, help* **atooshi**
後援会 *support group, fan club* **kōenkai**
後継者 *successor, replacement* **kōkeisha**
後れ毛 *unkempt-, stray hair* **okurege**
後ろ前 *inside-out, worn in reverse* **ushiromae**
後ろ姿 *backside appearance* **ushirosugata**
後ろ向き *backside; "passively..."* **ushiromuki**

遅*ardy, 944*	次*ext, 460*

彼*[third person], 224*

744-B

Look 後fter your 後ack for 幽loom may hack...

幺 (short thread)

幽*loomy*　　幽*uiet*

YŪ
gloomy, quiet, dismal, melancholy

Facing: 2.2. East ☞ (V)

幽暗 *gloom, darkness* **yūan**
幽遠 *quiet & distant* **yūen**
幽玄 *mystery, profundity* **yūgen**
幽閉 *house arrest, lenient confinement* **yūhei**
幽寂 *quiet & secluded* **yūjaku**
幽界 *spiritual world* **yūkai**
幽閑 *quiet, leisure* **yūkan**
幽鬼 *dead spirits* **yūki**
幽谷 *deep ravine* **yūkoku**
⇒深山幽谷 *deep mountains & valleys*
　　shinzan yūkoku
幽居 *secluded life* **yūkyo**
幽境 *hidden-, secluded location* **yūkyō**
幽冥 *this & the other world* **yūmei**
幽明 *light & darkness* **yūmei**
幽門 *pylorus* **yūmon**
幽門部 *pyloric region* **yūmonbu**
幽霊 *ghost, apparition* **yūrei**
幽霊話 *ghost story* **yūrei banashi**

幽霊船 *phantom ship* **yūreisen**
幽霊会社 *dummy company* **yūrei gaisha**
幽霊屋敷 *haunted house* **yūrei yashiki**
幽棲 *secluded life* **yūsei**
幽愁 *gloom, melancholy* **yūshū**
幽囚 *confinement, imprisonment* **yūshū**
幽邃 *quiet & secluded* **yūsui**

静*uiet, 230*	穏*ranquillity, 840*
寧*uiet, 967*	康*ranquillity, 881*
黙*uiet, 846*	悠*olace, 898*

逃*scape, 216*

745-A

修ultivate a balance of 悠eisure from a 悠istance...

人⇔亻 (person)

❶修ultivate　　**❷修epair**

osa(meru), osa(maru), SHŪ, SHU
cultivate; repair

Facing: 3.0. ☞☜ Across

❶ 独修　*self-study* **dokushū**
監修　*editorial supervision* **kanshū**
研修　*training, drilling* **kenshū**
履修　*completion, finish* **rishū**
修行　*training, ascetic practices* **shugyō**
修業　*course completion* **shūgyō**
⇒花嫁修業　*housewife training* **hanayome shugyō**
修辞　*figurative speaking* **shūji**
修辞法　*rhetorics, oratory* **shūjihō**
修好　*friendly relations, amity* **shūkō**
修了　*course completion* **shūryō**
修正　*modification, correction* **shūsei**
⇒軌道修正　*course collection* **kidō shūsei**
修史　*history compilation* **shūshi**
修士　*master of arts, ~of science* **shūshi**
修身　*moral training, ~upbringing* **shūshin**
修飾　*ornamentation, modification* **shūshoku**
修得　*gaining skills, acquiring expertise* **shūtoku**
修養　*disciplined, well-mannered* **shūyō**

速修　*intensive studying, ~course* **sokushū**
修道院　*abbey, monastery, convent* **shūdōin**
必修科目　*compulsory subject* **hisshū kamoku**
修学旅行　*school excursion* **shūgaku ryokō**
❷ 補修　*repair, mending, servicing* **hoshū**
改修　*improvement, reform* **kaishū**
修築　*repairs, renovation, servicing* **shūchiku**
修復　*restoration, rehabilitation* **shūfuku**
修理　*repair, mending, servicing* **shūri**
修整　*retouch, touch-up* **shūsei**
修繕　*repair, mending, servicing* **shūzen**

教ducate, 385	勉fforts, 527	博xpertise, 514
習earning, 238	徒isciple, 497	巧xpertise, 738
考hinking, 392	師eacher, 483	博xpertise, 514

参emple-visit, 396

745-B

修ultivate a balance of 悠eisure from a 悠istance...

心⇔忄⇔小 (feelings)

❶悠eisure　　**❷悠istant**

YŪ
leisure, solace, serenity, calm, tranquillity; distant, remoteness, far-away

Facing: 3.0. ☞☜ Across

❶ 悠長　*leisurely, easy-going* **yūchō**
悠揚　*composed, calm, serene* **yūyō**
悠悠　*composed, calm, serene* **yūyū**
悠然　*calmly, leisurely, serenely* **yūzen**

❷ 悠遠　*remoteness, far distance* **yūen**
悠久　*eternal, everlasting, perpetual* **yūkyū**

遠istant, 916	泰alm, 612
疎istant, 955	穏alm, 840
距istance, 207	

修aster, 898

746-A

宣*nnouncement at the* 壇*odium after the symposium...*

土 (ground, soil)

壇*odium*　　壇*latform*

DAN, TAN
podium, platform, lectern

FLIP: 5.0.a Left & Right

文壇 *literary circles* **bundan**
仏壇 *Buddhist family altar* **butsudan**
壇上 *on stage* **danjō**
壇場 *stage, platform, rostrum* **danjō**
檀家 *temple congregationists* **danka**
演壇 *mounting a platform* **endan**
画壇 *artists circles* **gadan**
楽壇 *musical circles* **gakudan**
劇壇 *theatrical circles* **gekidan**
俳壇 *Haiku circles* **haidan**
雛壇 *tiered stand for dolls* **hinadan**
花壇 *bed of flowers, bed of roses* **kadan**
歌壇 *world of Tanka poets* **kadan**
戒壇 *temple ordination platform* **kaidan**
降壇 *leaving the rostrum* **kōdan**
講壇 *rostrum, podium* **kōdan**
教壇 *teaching platform* **kyōdan**
論壇 *platform; world of critiques* **rondan**
祭壇 *altar, tabernacle* **saidan**

聖壇 *altar; pulpit* **seidan**
詩壇 *poetic circles* **shidan**
登壇 *taking the rostrum, going onstage* **tōdan**
独演場 *unrivalled, unchallenged* **dokudanjō**
土壇場 *place of execution; critical time* **dotanba**
説教壇 *pulpit* **sekkyōdan**

神*ivine, 712*	拝*rayer, 636*
聖*acred, 617*	堂*ltar, 94*
祈*rayer, 184*	

宣*nnouncement, 899*

746-B

宣*nnouncement at the* 壇*odium after the symposium...*

宀 (cover, lid)

宣*nnounce*　　宣*roclaim*

SEN
announce, proclaim, broadcast, declare

FLIP: 1.0.a. Whole (flat)

宣撫 *placating, pacifying* **senbu**
宣伝 *advertisement, publicity* **senden**
⇒ 逆宣伝 *negative advertisement* **gyakusenden**
宣伝戦 *public relations battle* **sendensen**
宣伝屋 *publicist, public relations firm* **sendenya**
宣下 *imperial edict* **senge**
宣言 *declaration, proclamation* **sengen**
宣旨 *imperial command* **senji**
宣告 *sentencing, judgement, verdict* **senkoku**
宣告書 *written sentence* **senkokusho**
宣教 *missionary work, evangelism* **senkyō**
宣教師 *missionary* **senkyōshi**
宣明 *proclamation, declaration* **senmei**
宣命 *imperial edict* **senmei**
宣布 *proclamation, declaration* **senpu**
宣誓 *oath, swearing* **sensei**
宣誓式 *oath-taking* **senseishiki**
宣誓書 *written oath* **senseisho**

宣誓供述書 *affidavit, sworn statement, deposition*
　　sensei kyōjutsusho
宣戦 *declaration of war* **sensen**
宣戦布告 *declaration of war, war proclamation*
　　sensen fukoku
宣揚 *enhancement, augmentation* **senyō**
託宣 *oracle* **takusen**
宣伝ビラ *handbill, flier* **senden bira**
宣伝映画 *advertisement-, commercial film*
　　senden eiga
宣伝業者 *advertising executive, publicist*
　　senden gyōsha

告*eport, 266*	掲*ublish, 810*
報*eport, 733*	載*ublish, 802*
公*ublic, 180*	表*xpression, 378*

垣*ence, 740*

747-A

契ledge of chastity to 喫njoy one's 潔urity...

大 (grand)

契ledge   契romise

chigi(ru), KEI

pledge, promise, commitment, agreement, deal, understanding, covenant

契合 *coincide, agree* **keigō**
契印 *seal impression* **keiin**
契機 *opportunity, chance* **keiki**
契約 *contract, written agreement* **keiyaku**
⇒先契約 *pre-contract* **sakikeiyaku**
⇒賃貸契約 *lease contract* **chintai keiyaku**
⇒諾成契約 *consensual contract* **dakusei keiyaku**
⇒雇用契約 *employment contract* **koyō keiyaku**
⇒略式契約 *simple contract* **ryakushiki keiyaku**
⇒相互契約 *mutual contract* **sōgo keiyaku**
⇒双務契約 *bilateral contract* **sōmu keiyaku**
⇒短期契約 *short-term contract* **tanki keiyaku**
契約金 *contract money* **keiyakukin**
契約者 *contracting parties* **keiyakusha**
契約違反 *breach of contract* **keiyaku ihan**
契約期間 *life of a contract* **keiyaku kikan**
黙契 *tacit agreement, gentlemen's talk* **mokkei**
準契約 *quasi-contract* **junkeiyaku**
契約書 *written contract, contract text* **keiyakusho**

FLIP: 4.0.b. Bottom (stem)
FLIP: 6.1. Left Top

二世の契り *marital vows* **nise no chigiri**

約*romise, 697*	嘱*ntrust, 441*
誓*ledge, 53*	託*ntrust, 82*
信*aith, 252*	任*ntrust, 709*
委*ntrust, 583*	預*ntrust, 569*

喫*njoy, 900*

747-B

契ledge of chastity to 喫njoy one's 潔urity...

口 (mouth)

喫njoy   喫ngest

KITSU

enjoy, ingest

喫緊 *urgent, pressing* **kikkin**
喫茶 *tea drinking* **kissa**
喫茶店 *coffee shop, tea room* **kissaten**
喫水 *sea gauge, draft* **kissui**
喫水線 *water level* **kissuisen**
喫煙 *smoking* **kitsuen**
喫煙車 *smoking car* **kitsuensha**
喫煙者 *cigarette-, tobacco smoker* **kitsuensha**
喫煙室 *smoking room* **kitsuenshitsu**
満喫 *full satisfaction* **mankitsu**
喫禁事 *urgent matter, pressing concern* **kikkinji**

FLIP: 4.0.b. Bottom (stem)
FLIP: 8.0.a. Inner (flat)

楽*leasure, 447*	愉*leasure, 922*
歓*leasure, 667*	興*ntertainment, 867*
娯*leasure, 453*	宴*anquet, 610*

契*romise, 900*

747-C

契*ledge of chastity to* 喫*njoy one's* 潔*urity...*

水 ⇔ 氵 (water)

潔*urity*   潔*oncise*

isagiyo(i), KETSU
purity, concise, immaculate

潔しと *accept with grace* **isagiyoshi**
不潔 *uncleanliness, dirty* **fuketsu**
純潔 *purity, chastity* **junketsu**
簡潔 *concise, brief* **kanketsu**
潔白 *purity, innocence* **keppaku**
潔癖 *fastidious, cleanliness* **keppeki**
潔斎 *purify by fasting* **kessai**
高潔 *nobility, aristocracy* **kōketsu**
廉潔 *integrity, probity* **renketsu**
清潔 *clean, neat, tidy* **seiketsu**
貞潔 *virtuous, chastise* **teiketsu**

FLIP: 8.0.a. Inner (flat)
Facing: 3.0. Across

純*urity, 199*	簡*imple, 285*
浄*urity, 230*	単*imple, 517*
粋*urity, 762*	素*imple, 578*

喫*njoy, 900*

748-A

Quality 品*roducts &* 器*evices,* 臨*ttend to clients the highest...*

口 (mouth)

口
品

品*roducts*   品*oods*

shina, HIN
products, goods, inventory, article, wares, commodity

FLIP: 1.0.a. Whole (flat)

返品 *returned goods* **henpin**
品位 *character, dignity* **hin'i**
品行 *behaviour, attitude, demeanor* **hinkō**
品性 *character, personality* **hinsei**
品詞 *figurative speech* **hinshi**
品質 *quality, nature* **hinshitsu**
品種 *kind, variety, breed* **hinshu**
上品 *refined, elegant, graceful* **jōhin**
検品 *goods inspection, quality control* **kenpin**
納品 *delivery, shipment* **nōhin**
作品 *piece of work* **sakuhin**
製品 *manufactured goods* **seihin**
品形 *merchandise appearance* **shinakatachi**
品数 *inventory, number of merchandise* **shinakazu**
品薄 *stock shortage, running low on stock* **shinausu**
商品 *merchandise, items for sale* **shōhin**
賞品 *prize in kind* **shōhin**
食品 *foodstuff, perishables* **shokuhin**
薬品 *drug, medicine, pharmaceuticals* **yakuhin**

洋品 *clothes, accessories, ornaments* **yōhin**
用品 *wares, goods, merchandise* **yōhin**
美術品 *work of art* **bijutsuhin**
不良品 *defective goods* **furyōhin**
必需品 *necessity, necessary* **hitsujuhin**
課税品 *taxable-, dutiable goods* **kazeihin**
免税品 *duty-free goods* **menzeihin**
支給品 *inventory, stock supplies* **shikyūhin**
品揃え *stock of goods, inventory* **shinazoroe**
特価品 *bargain, discounted price* **tokkahin**
在庫品 *goods in stock* **zaikohin**

作*roduce, 724*	造*roduce, 267*	販*elling, 137*
産*roduce, 883*	物*hings, 647*	売*elling, 259*

品*rystal, 131*

748-B

Quality 品roducts & 器evices, 臨ttend to clients the highest...

口 (mouth)

器evice   器nstrument

utsuwa, KI

device, instrument, equipment, apparatus, gadget, gizmo

FLIP: 1.0.a. Whole (flat)

便器 *toilet stool, urinal* **benki**
武器 *weapon, arms, ammunition* **buki**
鈍器 *blunt weapon* **donki**
楽器 *musical instrument* **gakki**
磁器 *porcelain, china, ceramics* **jiki**
花器 *flower base* **kaki**
計器 *measuring device* **keiki**
器物 *container, utensil* **kibutsu**
器楽 *instrumental music* **kigaku**
器具 *utensil, implement, instrument* **kigu**
⇒避妊器具 *contraceptive device* **hinin kigu**
器械 *instrument, apparatus* **kikai**
器量 *ability, features, looks* **kiryō**
器用 *clever, skilful, cunning, shrewd* **kiyō**
器材 *equipment parts* **kizai**
性器 *sex organ, genitals* **seiki**
陶器 *pottery, ceramics* **tōki**
容器 *container, vessel* **yōki**
臓器 *internal organs* **zōki**

蓄音器 *phonograph, gramophone* **chikuonki**
聴診器 *stethoscope* **chōshinki**
充電器 *battery re-charger* **jūdenki**
核兵器 *nuclear weapons, ~arms* **kakuheiki**
拡声器 *loudspeaker* **kakuseiki**
検温器 *thermometer* **ken'onki**
蒸し器 *steamer* **mushiki**
消音器 *silencer, muffler* **shōonki**
炊飯器 *rice cooker* **suihanki**
抵抗器 *resistor* **teikōki**
盗聴器 *wiretap device* **tōchōki**

具*mplements, 487*		械*echanics, 493*
匠*rtisan, 106*		機*echanics, 547*
工*rtisan, 176*		

品*oodies, 901*

748-C

Quality 品roducts & 器evices, 臨ttend to clients the highest...

臣 (minister)

臨ttend to   臨ook-after

nozo(mu), RIN

attend to, look-after, caring

FLIP: 7.3.a. Right Bottom (flat)

降臨 *imperial descent on earth* **kōrin**
君臨 *reigning, ruling* **kunrin**
来臨 *imperial attendance* **rairin**
臨地 *on-site, on-the-spot* **rinchi**
臨月 *last month of pregnancy* **ringetsu**
臨時 *temporary, provisional* **rinji**
臨時費 *emergency expenses* **rinjihi**
臨時国会 *Diet special session* **rinji kokkai**
臨時政府 *provisional government* **rinji seifu**
臨場 *attendance, presence* **rinjō**
臨終 *hour of death, dying moments* **rinjū**
臨海 *facing the sea, ocean view* **rinkai**
臨界 *clinical* **rinkai**
臨界点 *critical point* **rinkaiten**
臨界実験 *clinical experiment* **rinkai jikken**
臨検 *on-the-spot inspection, field tour* **rinken**
臨機 *expedient, contingent, provisional* **rinki**
臨機応変 *adapting to circumstances* **rinki ōhen**
臨港 *facing the harbour* **rinkō**

臨港線 *harbour railroad* **rinkōsen**
臨休 *extended holidays* **rinkyū**
臨席 *attendance, presence* **rinseki**
臨戦 *going to the battlefield* **rinsen**
臨写 *copying* **rinsha**
臨書 *writing from a copy* **rinsho**
臨床 *clinical* **rinshō**
臨床医 *clinical doctor* **rinshōi**
臨在 *attendance, presence* **rinzai**
再臨 *second coming of christ* **sairin**
登臨 *ascend the throne; climb a height* **tōrin**

供*ook-after, 303*		護*rotect, 828*
看*ook after, 623*		防*rotect, 736*
衛*rotect, 796*		覧*bserve, 592*

品*roducts, 901*

749-A

奥nsiders' 迷onfusion at 菊hrysanthemum's evolution...

大 (grand)

奥nside   奥nterior

oku, Ō

inside, interior, internal, far end

FLIP: 1.0.b. Whole (stem)

奥さん	*Madame, Mrs., Your wife (honorific)* **okusan**		奥の院	*inner sanctuary* **okunoin**
奥まる	*secluded, far back* **okumaru**		奥の間	*inner room* **okunoma**
秘奥	*secrets, mysteries* **hiō**		奥深い	*profound, deep* **okubukai**
胸奥	*depths of one's heart* **kyōō**		奥御殿	*inner palace* **okugoten**
内奥	*depths, recesses* **naiō**		奥向き	*personal business* **okumuki**
奥義	*secrets* **ōgi**		奥床し	*refined, cultured, dignified* **okuyukashi**
奥歯	*tooth molar* **okuba**		奥行き	*depths, bottom* **okuyuki**
奥地	*hinterland, interior, depths* **okuchi**		奥座敷	*inner room* **okuzashiki**
奥方	*lady-of-the-house, one's wife* **okugata**		奥付け	*colophon* **okuzuke**
奥義	*secrets, mysteries* **okugi**			
奥印	*seal of approval* **okuin**			
奥庭	*inner backyard* **okuniwa**			
奥様	*Madame, Mrs., Your wife (honorific)* **okusama**			
奥底	*bottom, depth* **okusoko**			
奥山	*mountain depths* **okuyama**			
大奥	*inner palace* **ōoku**			
深奥	*depth, bottom* **shin'ō**			
心奥	*bosom of one's heart* **shin'oku**			
山奥	*mountain depths* **yamaoku**			

内 *nside*, 297		辺 *urroundings*, 93	
囲 *nclose*, 361		環 *urroundings*, 165	
郭 *nclose*, 398		外 *utside*, 188	

歯 *eeth*, 553

749-B

奥nsiders' 迷onfusion at 菊hrysanthemum's evolution...

艹 (grass)

菊hrysanthemum

KIKU

chrysanthemum

FLIP: 8.0.b. Inner (stem)

雛菊	*daisy* **hinagiku**
観菊	*chrysanthemum viewing* **kangiku**
黄菊	*yellow chrysanthemum* **kigiku**
菊花	*chrysanthemum* **kikka**
菊判	*octavo* **kikuban**
菊芋	*artichoke* **kikuimo**
菊見	*chrysanthemum viewing* **kikumi**
菊月	*September, ninth lunar month* **kikutsuki**
菊炭	*chrysanthemum charcoal* **kikuzumi**
夏菊	*early chrysanthemum* **natsugiku**
野菊	*wild chrysanthemum* **nogiku**
白菊	*white chrysanthemum* **shiragiku**
春菊	*chrysanthemum garlands* **shungiku**
菊の花	*chrysanthemum* **kiku no hana**
菊人形	*chrysanthemum dolls* **kikuningyō**
菊作り	*chrysanthemum growing* **kikuzukuri**
菊細工	*chrysanthemum products* **kikuzaiku**
菊の節句	*chrysanthemum festival* **kiku no sekku**

花 *lower*, 191		華 *lossom*, 40	
華 *lower*, 40		花 *lossom*, 191	
紋 *rest*, 558		咲 *lossom*, 707	

奥 *nside*, 903

749-C

奥nsiders' 迷onfusion at 菊hrysanthemum's evolution...

辶 (transport)

迷onfusion   迷uzzling

mayo(u), MEI
confusion, puzzling, perplex, bewilder, confound, baffle

FLIP: 3.0.b. Top (stem)

頑迷 bigotry, intolerance **ganmei**
混迷 confusion, chaos, disarray **konmei**
昏迷 bewilderment, enchantment **konmei**
迷子 lost child **maigo**
迷鳥 straggler, stray bird **meichō**
迷宮 maze, labyrinth, snarl **meikyū**
迷宮入り remaining unsolved **meikyūiri**
迷妄 illusion, delusion **meimō**
迷夢 illusion, delusion **meimu**
迷路 maze, labyrinth, snarl **meiro**
迷論 absurd reasoning, fallacy **meiron**
迷彩 camouflage, disquiet **meisai**
迷信 superstition, false belief **meishin**
迷信深い deeply-superstitious **meishinbukai**
迷走 straying, wandering **meisō**
迷想 illusion, fallacy **meisō**
迷答 stupid answer, absurd reply **meitō**
迷惑 troublesome, annoying **meiwaku**
⇒有り難迷惑 unwelcome favour **arigata meiwaku**

低迷 floundering, failing **teimei**
血迷う run amok **chimayō**
気迷い hesitation, wavering **kimayoi**
踏み迷う lose one's way **fumimayō**
立ち迷う float along, drift **tachimayō**

乱onfusion, 686	争onflict, 231
慌anic, 507	困roblematic, 863
狂razy, 639	難roblematic, 927

逃scape, 216

750-A

害njury to the 憲onstitution, not the solution...

宀 (cover, lid)

害njury   害amage

GAI
injury, damage, hurting, harm

FLIP: 1.0.a. Whole (flat)

妨害 disturbance, hindrance, obstacle **bōgai**
風害 wind damage **fūgai**
害悪 evil-, harmful influence **gaiaku**
害虫 harmful insect, vermin **gaichū**
害毒 evil, poison, harm **gaidoku**
害意 malice, harmful intent **gaii**
迫害 persecution, oppression **hakugai**
弊害 ill effect, evil, abuse **heigai**
被害 damage, harm, injury **higai**
被害者 victim, sufferer, injured party **higaisha**
実害 actual harm, ~damage **jitsugai**
干害 drought calamity **kangai**
危害 harm, injury, impairment **kigai**
公害 public harm **kōgai**
⇒騒音公害 noise pollution **sōon kōgai**
無害 unharmed, unscathed **mugai**
冷害 cold weather damage **reigai**
利害 pros & cons, merits & demerits **rigai**
災害 catastrophe, disaster, calamity **saigai**

殺害 murder, killing **satsugai**
雪害 snow damage **setsugai**
侵害 infringement, encroachment **shingai**
傷害 injury, damage, impairment **shōgai**
障害 difficulty, obstacle, hindrance **shōgai**
阻害 obstruction, impediment, hurdle **sogai**
霜害 frost damage **sōgai**
損害 damage, injury, loss **songai**
要害 stronghold, strategic point **yōgai**
有害 harmful, injurious **yūgai**
加害者 crime offender, offending party **kagaisha**

傷njury, 933	損njury, 410
障njury, 325	痛njury, 60

割ivide, 968

750-B

害njury to the 憲onstitution, not the solution...

心 ⇔ 忄 ⇔ 小 (feelings)

憲onstitution　憲harter

KEN
constitution, charter,basic law

FLIP: 3.0.a. Top (flat)

朝憲 constitution **chōken**
護憲 defending the constitution **goken**
合憲 constitutional **gōken**
合憲性 constitutional **gōkensei**
違憲 unconstitutional, constitutional violation **iken**
改憲 constitutional revision **kaiken**
官憲 government authorities **kanken**
憲兵 military police **kenpei**
憲兵隊 Japanese WWII secret police **kenpeitai**
憲法 constitution, basic law **kenpō**
憲法違反 unconstitutional **kenpō ihan**
憲法改正 constitutional revision **kenpō kaisei**
憲政 constitutional government **kensei**
憲章 charter, covenant **kenshō**
⇒大憲章 Magna Carta **daikenshō**
⇒国連憲章 United Nations Charter **kokuren kenshō**
立憲 constitutional, adopting a constitution **rikken**
制憲 framing a constitution **seiken**

法aw, 360	政olitics, 725
廷ourt-of-law, 26	則egulation, 290
規ule, 814	律egulation, 731
典ules, 476	国ation, 92

害amage, 904

751-A

粛ilent officers to 粛urge 庸ediocres...

聿 (writing brush)

❶粛ilence　❷粛urging

SHUKU
silence, quiet, hush-hush; purging

FLIP: 4.0.b. Bottom (stem)

❶ 厳粛 solemnity, gravity **genshuku**
自粛 self-control, self-discipline **jishuku**
静粛 "keep quiet, observe silence..." **seishuku**
深粛 strict enforcement **shinshuku**
粛粛 quietly, silently **shukushuku**
粛然と quietly, solemnly **shukuzento**

❷ 粛学 school purging, ~expulsion **shukugaku**
粛正 clean up, mop up **shukusei**
⇒綱紀粛正 discipline for the higher-ups
　　kōki shukusei
粛清 political purge, expulsion of rivals **shukusei**
粛正 cleaning up, purge, enforcing **shukusei**
粛党 party purging, ~cleansing **shukutō**

静uiet, 230	幽uiet, 897
寧uiet, 967	穏ranquillity, 840
黙uiet, 846	康ranquillity, 881

庸ediocre, 906

751-B

粛*ilent officers to* 粛*urge* 庸*ediocres...*

庸*ediocre* 庸*rdinary*

广 (rooftop)

YŌ
mediocre, ordinary

FLIP: 4.0.b. Bottom (stem)

凡庸 *mediocre-, inferior person* **bonyō**
中庸 *moderation, sobriety, temperance* **chūyō**
雇庸 *employment, hiring, recruitment* **koyō**
登庸 *appointment, promotion* **tōyō**
庸愚 *mediocre & stupid* **yōgu**
庸医 *quack doctor, mediocre physician* **yōi**
庸君 *foolish leader* **yōkun**
庸烈 *weakling, mediocre* **yōretsu**
庸才 *mediocre-, inferior skills* **yōsai**

般*egular, 323*	凡*ommon, 78*
常*egular, 94*	平*lain, 488*
普*ommon, 455*	劣*nferior, 572*

粛*ilence, 905*

752-A

恐*cared* 築*rchitect hiding in Czech...*

恐*cary* 恐*errifying*

心 ⇔ 忄 ⇔ ⺗ (feelings)

oso(reru), oso(roshii), kowa(i), KYŌ
scary, terrifying, horror, intimidate, menace, horrendous, shocking, spooky, terror, unnerving

Facing: 2.1. East ☞ (H)
FLIP: 6.1. Left Top

恐れ *fear, occurrence (negative)* **osore**
恐らく *likely, perhaps, possibly* **osoraku**
恐ろしい *frightening, terrifying, fearsome* **osoroshii**
恐れ入る *be embarrassed, ~ashamed* **osoreiru**
恐れ戦く *cower, tremble with fear* **osoreononoku**
恐れ多い *gracious, august, grand* **osoreooi**
空恐ろしい *vague fears* **soraosoroshii**
末恐ろしい *terrible, horrible, frightening* **sueosoroshii**
恐れながら *"most respectfully..."* **osorenagara**
恐恐 *scary, frightening* **kowagowa**
恐怖 *fear, terror, horror* **kyōfu**
恐怖症 *fear, phobia* **kyōfushō**
⇒閉所恐怖症 *claustrophobia* **heisho kyōfushō**
⇒高所恐怖症 *acrophobia, fear of heights*
　　kōsho kyōfushō
恐慌 *panic, hysteria, pandemonium* **kyōkō**
恐竜 *dinosaur, reptile monster* **kyōryū**
恐縮 *gratitude, shame* **kyōshuku**
大恐慌 *great panic, pandemonium* **daikyōkō**

恐妻家 *henpecked husband* **kyōsaika**
恐水病 *hydrophobia* **kyōsuibyō**
恐喝 *threat, intimidation, menace* **kyōkatsu**
恐喝罪 *extortion, blackmail* **kyōkatsuzai**
恐悦がる *self-congratulation* **kyōetsugaru**
恐怖心 *fear, fright, scare* **kyōfushin**
恐怖症 *morbid fear, phobia* **kyōfushō**
恐怖政治 *reign of terror* **kyōfu seiji**
物恐ろしい *horrible, terrible, frightening*
　　mono osoroshii

脅*hreaten, 577*	虞*hreat, 889*
威*hreat, 520*	驚*care, 330*
嚇*hreat, 261*	誘*emptation, 895*

築*rchitect, 907*

752-B

恐cared 築rchitect hiding in Czech...

竹 (bamboo)

築rchitect   築onstruct

kizu(ku), CHIKU
architect, construct, design

FLIP: 4.0.b. Bottom (stem)

築き上げる *build-up, construct* **kizukiageru**
築港 *harbour construction* **chikkō**
築城 *castle construction* **chikujō**
築堤 *embankment* **chikutei**
築造 *construction, building* **chikuzō**
移築 *reconstruction in a new location* **ichiku**
改築 *reconstruction, rebuilding* **kaichiku**
建築 *architecture, building design* **kenchiku**
⇒仮建築 *temporary construction (pre-fab)*
    kari kenchiku
⇒防火建築 *fireproof building* **bōka kenchiku**
⇒木造建築 *wooden building, ~construction*
    mokuzō kenchiku
⇒耐火建築 *fireproof building* **taika kenchiku**
建築物 *building, structure, construction*
    kenchikubutsu
建築学 *architecture science* **kenchikugaku**
建築費 *architectural fee* **kenchikuhi**

建築術 *architectural skills* **kenchikujutsu**
建築家 *architect* **kenchikuka**
建築者 *builder* **kenchikusha**
建築士 *builder* **kenchikushi**
構築 *building, structure, construction* **kōchiku**
新築 *newly-built construction* **shinchiku**
修築 *renovation, repair* **shūchiku**
築地 *reclaimed land* **tsukiji**
築山 *artificial hill* **tsukiyama**
増築 *annex construction* **zōchiku**

建onstruct, 390	匠rtisan, 106
創reativity, 399	工rtisan, 176
芸rts, 619	

恐enace, 906

753-A

琴ither music 班quad playing a ballad...

王⇔玉 (jewel)

琴ither

koto, KIN
zither

FLIP: 3.0.a. Top (flat)

弾琴 *playing a zither* **dankin**
風琴 *accordion, organ* **fūkin**
琴曲 *Japanese zither music* **kinkyoku**
琴線 *heart-moving, touching* **kinsen**
琴柱 *zither bridge* **kotoji**
琴爪 *plectrum* **kotozume**
木琴 *xylophone* **mokkin**
木琴奏者 *xylophonist* **mokkin sōsha**
竪琴 *harp* **tategoto**
提琴 *violin* **teikin**
提琴家 *violinist* **teikinka**
鉄琴 *musical chimes* **tekkin**
和琴 *Japanese harp* **wagon**
洋琴 *piano* **yōkin**
一弦琴 *one-stringed instrument* **ichigenkin**

曲elody, 476	弦usical string, 358
奏usic play, 579	歌inging, 878
譜usical note, 455	楽leasure, 447

班quad, 908

753-B

琴*ither music* 班*quad playing a ballad...*

班*quad*　　　班*eam*

HAN
squad, team

王⇔玉 (jewel)

FLIP: 7.0.a. Right (flat)
FLIP: 6.0.a. Left (flat)

隊*quad, 543*	員*ember, 410*
組*roup, 138*	協*ooperate, 577*
団*roup, 345*	

非*[negative].288*

班長　*squad leader*　**hanchō**
班田　*ancient farm allotment*　**handen**
班員　*squad member*　**han'in**
班次　*precedence, rank*　**hanji**
班点　*spot, speckle, dot*　**hanten**
首班　*chief, head*　**shuhan**
衛生班　*hygiene squad*　**eiseihan**
企画班　*project team*　**kikakuhan**
救護班　*relief squad, ~party*　**kyūgohan**
作業班　*work group, labourer team*　**sagyōhan**
写真班　*photographer-, camera crew*　**shashinhan**
取材班　*media coverage crew*　**shuzaihan**
特捜班　*investigation unit*　**tokusōhan**

754-A

弱*eak waves at the* 湾*ay near Bombay...*

弱*eakling*　　弱*nferior*

yowa(i), yowa(ru), yowa(maru), yowa(meru), JAKU
weakling, inferior, frail, shoddy

弓 (archery bow)

Facing: 1.2. ☜ West (V)

微弱　*faint, feeble, weak*　**bijaku**
病弱　*sickly, weak, invalid*　**byōjaku**
薄弱　*weak, feeble*　**hakujaku**
貧弱　*poor, meagre, impoverished*　**hinjaku**
胃弱　*indigestion, dyspepsia*　**ijaku**
弱冠　*early age, young age*　**jakkan**
弱年　*young person, youth*　**jakunen**
弱者　*weakling, faint-hearted*　**jakusha**
弱視　*poor eyesight*　**jakushi**
弱震　*minor earthquake*　**jakushin**
弱体　*weak body, weakling*　**jakutai**
弱体化　*weakening, deterioration*　**jakutaika**
弱点　*weakness, shortcoming*　**jakuten**
気弱　*timid, weak*　**kiyowa**
腰弱　*weak back*　**koshiyowa**
虚弱　*weak, delicate*　**kyojaku**
軟弱　*weak, soft, feeble*　**nanjaku**
軟弱外交　*weak-kneed diplomacy*　**nanjaku gaikō**
衰弱　*weakness, debility*　**suijaku**

⇒神経衰弱　*nervous breakdown*　**shinkei suijaku**
幼弱　*young & weak*　**yōjaku**
弱火　*low heat, low fire*　**yowabi**
弱気　*timidity, docility, meekness*　**yowaki**
弱味　*weak points*　**yowami**
弱虫　*coward, weakling, sissy*　**yowamushi**
弱音　*whining*　**yowane**
弱小国　*minor-, lesser power*　**jakushōkoku**
弱肉強食　*"survival of the fittest..."*
　　jakuniku kyōshoku
奥さんに弱い　*henpecked husband*
　　okusan(ni)yowai

劣*nferior, 572*	軟*oft, 659*
柔*oft, 568*	庸*ediocre, 906*

弓*rchery.348*

754-B

弱*eak waves in the* 湾*ay near Bombay...*

ulf　　*ay*

水 ⇔ 氵 (water)

FLIP: 7.2.b. Right Top (stem)
Facing: 1.2. ☞ West (V)

WAN
gulf, bay, anchorage

海湾 *gulf, bay* **kaiwan**
港湾 *harbour, port* **kōwan**
港湾施設 *harbour facilities* **kōwan shisetsu**
峡湾 *fiord, inlet, gulf* **kyōwan**
台湾 *Taiwan (Formosa), Republic of China* **taiwan**
湾岸 *Persian Gulf* **wangan**
湾岸戦争 *Gulf War (1991)* **wangan sensō**
湾口 *bay entrance, mouth of a bay* **wankō**
湾曲 *curving, bend* **wankyoku**
湾内 *within the bay* **wannai**
湾入 *inlet, gulf, bight* **wannyū**
湾流 *gulf stream* **wanryū**
湾頭 *shore of a bay* **wantō**
真珠湾 *Pearl Harbor, Hawaii* **shinjuwan**
東京湾 *Tōkyō Bay* **tōkyōwan**

江*ay, 176*	湖*agoon, 801*
海*cean, 241*	潟*agoon, 870*
洋*cean, 247*	島*sland, 125*

港*arbour, 512*

755-A

豪*ustralian* 家*amily* 家*xpert built a* 家*ouse for* 豚*igs*
　　that's 豪*plendid..!*

❶家*amily*　　家*ouse*　　❷家*xpert*

宀 (cover, lid)

FLIP: 3.0.b. Top (stem)
Facing: 1.1. ☞ West (H)

ie, ya, uchi, KA, KE
family, house, shelter; expert, specialist

❶ 家出 *running away from home, stowaway* **iede**
家発 *time leaving one's house* **iehatsu**
家元 *head of school, school master* **iemoto**
実家 *parent's house* **jikka**
家具 *furniture* **kagu**
家業 *family business* **kagyō**
家事 *domestic work, chores, errands* **kaji**
家計 *household finance* **kakei**
家内 *one's wife, household* **kanai**
家屋 *house, building* **kaoku**
家庭 *home, family* **katei**
家運 *family fortunes, ~wealth* **kaun**
家財 *household effects* **kazai**
家族 *family, household* **kazoku**
国家 *state, nation* **kokka**
民家 *private house* **minka**
家主 *landlord, house owner* **yanushi**
家系図 *family tree, family lineage* **kakeizu**
貸し家 *house-for-rent* **kashiya**

❷ 画家 *painter, artist* **gaka**
農家 *farmers* **nōka**
作家 *writer, novelist* **sakka**
史家 *historian, history scholar* **shika**
勉強家 *diligent student* **benkyōka**
美術家 *artist* **bijutsuka**
演出家 *director, producer* **enshutsuka**
実業家 *businessman, ~woman* **jitsugyōka**
旅行家 *seasoned traveller, tourist* **ryokōka**
政治家 *politician, statesman* **seijika**
専門家 *expert, specialist* **senmonka**

族*amily, 649*	子*hild, 456*	修*aster, 898*
父*ather, 467*	師*xpert, 483*	巧*killful, 738*
母*other, 90*	博*xpertise, 514*	術*kills, 110*

塚*ound, 825*

755-B

豪ustralian 家amily 家xpert built a 家ouse for 豚igs
that's 豪plendid..!

豕 (pig)

豚*ig*　　　　豚*ork*

Facing: 1.2. ☜ West (V)

buta, TON
pig, pork

豚箱	police cell, ~jail	**butabako**
豚草	ragweed	**butagusa**
豚汁	pork miso soup	**butajiru**
豚肉	pork, pig meat	**butaniku**
河豚	balloon-, blowfish	**fugu**
海豚	dolphin, porpoise	**iruka**
子豚	piglet, young pig	**kobuta**
雌豚	sow	**mebuta**
酢豚	sweet-&-sour pork	**subuta**
豚児	"my son..." (humble)	**tonji**
豚舎	pigsty, pigpen, pig house	**tonsha**
豚脂	lard, pork fat, pork oil	**tonshi**
土豚	aardvark, ground hog	**tsuchibuta**
養豚	pig raising, piggery	**yōton**
養豚場	piggery farm	**yōtonjō**
養豚者	piggery farmer	**yōtonsha**
豚カツ	deep-fried pork cutlet	**tonkatsu**
豚小屋	pigsty, pigpen, pig house	**butagoya**
焼き豚	roasted pork, pork barbeque	**yakibuta**

丸焼き豚 roasted whole pig **maruyakibuta**
豚骨ラーメン bone marrow rāmen
　　tonkotsu rāmen

飼 aising, 835	養 aising, 253
畜 aising, 528	肉 eat, 297

 隊 quad, 543

755-C

豪ustralian 家amily 家xpert built a 家ouse for 豚igs
that's 豪plendid..!

豕 (pig)

❶豪*plendour*　　❷豪*ustralia*

FLIP: 3.0.a. Top (flat)

era(i), GŌ
splendour, grandeur, grandiose, magnificent; Australia

❶文豪	literary genius, prolific writer	**bungō**
富豪	very wealthy	**fugō**
豪打	tremendous blast	**gōda**
豪語	big talk, boast	**gōgo**
豪放	broad-minded, eclectic	**gōhō**
豪華	gorgeous, magnificent	**gōka**
豪家	rich & famous family	**gōka**
豪快	heroic, hearty, tremendous	**gōkai**
豪傑	heroic, daring	**gōketsu**
豪気	stout-hearted	**gōki**
豪句	highly-articulate	**gōku**
豪農	wealthy farmer	**gōnō**
豪勢	luxurious, sumptuous, extravagant	**gōsei**
豪雪	heavy snowfall	**gōsetsu**
豪雪地帯	areas of heavy snowfall	**gōsetsu chitai**
豪奢	luxurious, sumptuous	**gōsha**
豪士	samurai farmer	**gōshi**
豪商	wealthy merchant	**gōshō**
豪壮	magnificent, gorgeous	**gōsō**

豪胆	bold, daring, fearless	**gōtan**
豪邸	palatial residence, mansion	**gōtei**
豪雨	heavy rain, downpour	**gōu**
豪遊	spree, frolic	**gōyū**
豪族	powerful & wealthy family	**gōzoku**
剣豪	master swordsman	**kengō**
古豪	experienced, veteran	**kogō**
強豪	invincible team	**kyōgō**
酒豪	heavy drinker, alcoholic	**shugō**
❷豪州	Australia	**gōshū**
日豪	Japan-Australia	**nichigō**

貴 recious, 913	傑 xcellence, 921
特 pecial, 250	秀 xcellence, 383
殊 pecialty, 234	優 xcellence, 556
超 xceed, 664	裕 uxury, 758

 高 igh, 435

756-A

寂onely 督ommander married a Hollander...

宀 (cover, lid)

寂onely   寂esolate

sabi(shii), sabi(reru), sabi, JAKU, SEKI
lonely, lonesome, desolate

FLIP: 7.3.b. Right Bottom (stem)
FLIP: 3.0.b. Top (stem)

寂しい *lonely, deserted* **sabishii**
⇒心寂しい *lonesome, desolated* **kokorosabishii**
円寂 *Nirvana, death of Buddha* **enjaku**
寂滅 *Nirvana, death, annihilation* **jakumetsu**
閑寂 *quiet, tranquillity, serenity* **kanjaku**
入寂 *death of a saint; entering Nirvana* **nyūjaku**
静寂 *stillness, silence, quiet* **seijaku**
寂寞 *loneliness, desolation, reclusion*
　　　sekibaku, jakumaku
寂寥 *lonely, desolate, reclusive* **sekiryō**
寂然 *lonely, desolate, reclusive* **sekizen**
幽寂 *quiet, tranquillity, serenity* **yūjaku**
侘と寂 *simplicity & quiet (Japanese ambiance)*
　　　wabi to sabi
寂光浄土 *Buddhist paradise* **jakkō jōdo**

寡*lone, 161*	唯*olitary, 642*
孤*lone, 148*	寂*onely, 911*
独*lone, 369*	

督*ommander, 911*

756-B

寂onely 督ommander married a Hollander...

目 (eyesight, visual)

督ommander   督upervisor

TOKU
commander, supervisor, director

FLIP: 4.0.a. Bottom (flat)

監督 *coach, director* **kantoku**
⇒大監督 *Archbishop of the Anglican Church*
　　　daikantoku
⇒美術監督 *art director* **bijutsu kantoku**
⇒舞台監督 *stage director* **butai kantoku**
⇒映画監督 *movie-, film director* **eiga kantoku**
⇒試験監督 *test proctoring* **shiken kantoku**
監督下 *"under the supervision of..."* **kantokuka**
監督官 *supervisor* **kantokukan**
家督 *head of the family* **katoku**
家督の権 *birthright, inheritance* **katoku no ken**
家督相続 *succession of family head* **katoku sōzoku**
総督 *governor-general* **sōtoku**
提督 *fleet admiral, ~commander* **teitoku**
督励 *encouragement, stimulating* **tokurei**
督戦 *exhorting to fight to the finish* **tokusen**
督戦隊 *supervising troops* **tokusentai**
督促 *pressing, demand, urging* **tokusoku**
督促状 *letter of demand* **tokusokujō**

都督 *governor-general, viceroy* **totoku**
督学官 *school inspector* **tokugakukan**

令*ommand, 362*	領*overn, 874*
帥*ommander, 483*	統*overn, 885*
導*uidance, 312*	指*inger, 242*

寂*onely, 911*

757-A

Cheap 棚abinets soon 崩ollapse like scraps...

棚*abinet*   棚*urniture*

木 (wooden) 棚

FLIP: 7.1. Right (Sort Of)

tana, dana, HŌ
cabinet, furniture

網棚 *rack, shelf* **amidana**
茶棚 *tea stuff cabinet* **chadana**
藤棚 *wisteria trellis* **fujidana**
本棚 *book shelf* **hondana**
岩棚 *ledge* **iwadana**
神棚 *Shintō family altar* **kamidana**
陸棚 *continental shelf* **rikudana**
炉棚 *mantelshelf* **rodana**
書棚 *book-, paper shelf* **shodana**
棚板 *shelf, tray* **tanaita**
戸棚 *closet, cupboard* **todana**
葡萄棚 *grapevine trellis* **budōdana**
違い棚 *staggered shelf* **chigaidana**
陳列棚 *showcase* **chinretsudana**
棚浚え *clearance* **tanazarae**
袋戸棚 *small cupboard on the wall* **fukurotodana**
飾り棚 *display shelf* **kazaridana**
食器棚 *cupboard, sideboard* **shokkidana**
大陸棚 *continental shelf* **tairikudana**

棚上げ *putting on the shelf* **tanaage**
棚引く *hang, lie, linger, trail* **tanabiku**
棚牡丹 *godsend, windfall* **tanabota**
棚卸し *inventory of goods* **tanaoroshi**
釣り棚 *hanging shelf* **tsuridana**

卓*able, 499*	座*eating, 109*
机*esk, 747*	席*eating, 91*

机*esk, 747*

757-B

Cheap 棚abinets soon 崩ollapse like scraps...

崩*ollapse*   崩*rumble*

山 (mountain) 崩

FLIP: 3.0.a. Top (flat)

kuzu(reru), kuzu(su), HŌ
collapse, crumble, downfall, founder, cave-in

崩御 *emperor's death* **hōgyo**
崩壊 *collapse, decay, crumbling* **hōkai**
崩潰 *collapse, decay, crumbling* **hōkai**
崩落 *collapse, caving in* **hōraku**
雪崩 *avalanche, snowslide* **nadare**
崖崩れ *landslide, mud slide* **gakekuzure**
型崩れ *lose body shape, deformation* **katakuzure**
着崩れ *becoming untidy* **kikuzure**
崩し字 *cursive writing* **kuzushiji**
崩し書き *wavy calligraphy* **kuzushigaki**
値崩れ *sudden fall in prices* **nekuzure**
総崩れ *total defeat* **sōkuzure**
山崩れ *landslide, mud slide* **yamakuzure**
土砂崩れ *washout, landslide* **dosha kuzure**
俳優崩れ *has-been actor, ~actress* **haiyū kuzure**
掘り崩す *demolish, tear down* **horikuzusu**
切り崩し *cutting thru, level a hill* **kirikuzushi**
崩れ去る *collapse, crumble* **kuzuresaru**
持ち崩す *self-inflicted ruin* **mochikuzusu**

済し崩し *little-by-little, one-by-one*
nashikuzushi
取り崩し *demolish, tear down* **torikuzushi**
突き崩し *striking thru* **tsukikuzushi**
打ち崩し *being knocked out* **uchikuzushi**
崩れ落ちる *collapse, crumble* **kuzure ochiru**
泣き崩れる *burst into tears, cry-out loud*
nakikuzureru

落*ollapse, 826*	堕*all-down, 807*	失*ailure, 19*
陥*ollapse, 893*	壊*estroy, 847*	負*ailure, 19*
降*escend, 133*	破*estroy, 715*	敗*ailure, 137*

棚*abinet, 912*

758-A

遣ispatch of 貴recious minds, 遣eaving nations in a bind...

辶 (transport)

遣ispatch 遣eployment

tsuka(wasu), tsuka(u), KEN
dispatch, deployment

FLIP: 3.0.a. Top (flat)

遣わす *send, give* **tsukawasu**
分遣 *detachment* **bunken**
派遣 *dispatch, deployment* **haken**
派遣軍 *deployed troops* **hakengun**
遣米 *dispatch to the US* **kenbei**
遣外 *overseas deployment* **kengai**
先遣 *advance deployment* **senken**
蛇遣い *snake charmer* **hebizukai**
息遣い *breathing, respiration, inhalation* **ikizukai**
金遣い *lavishness, ostentation* **kanezukai**
気遣う *feeling anxious* **kizukau**
心遣い *thoughtfulness, consideration* **kokoro zukai**
小遣い *pocket money* **kozukai**
見遣る *cast a glance* **miyaru**
遣い物 *present, gift* **tsukaimono**
指遣い *fingering, pinpointing* **yubizukai**
遣り場 *"where to turn..."* **yariba**
遣り方 *ways & means* **yarikata**
遣り水 *stream built thru a garden* **yarimizu**

遣り手 *doer, action-taker* **yarite**
遣り手婆 *brothel madam* **yaritebabaa**
遣り取り *give & take* **yaritori**
遣り繰り *makeshift, getting by* **yarikuri**
遣り返す *try again; retort, refute* **yarikaesu**
遣り過ぎ *overdoing, going too far* **yarisugi**
遣りっ放し *leave as is; negligent* **yarippanashi**
遣瀬ない *dreary, disconsolate* **yarusenai**
言葉遣い *wording, expression* **kotobazukai**
無駄遣い *waste, squander* **mudazukai**
思い遣り *thoughtfulness, consideration* **omoiyari**

送ispatch, 708	送ending, 708
搬ransport, 323	届eliver, 631
輸hipment, 660	運eliver, 295

追rive away, 108

758-B

遣ispatch of 貴recious minds, 遣eaving nations in a bind...

貝 (shell, old money)

貴recious 貴aluable

tatto(i), tōto(i), tatto(bu), tōto(bu), KI
precious, valuable, costly, noble, esteemed, *my lord, your honour*

FLIP: 1.0.b. Whole (stem)

貴方 *you (second person)* **anata**
兄貴 *one's elder brother* **aniki**
珍貴 *rare, precious, valuable* **chinki**
富貴 *noble & wealthy* **fūki**
貴重 *precious, valuable* **kichō**
貴重品 *precious articles, valuables* **kichōhin**
貴台 *you* **kidai**
貴殿 *you (honorific)* **kiden**
貴人 *nobleman, dignitary* **kijin**
貴女 *lady, you (feminine)* **kijo, anata**
貴下 *you (honorific)* **kika**
貴兄 *you (masculine)* **kikei**
貴顕 *distinguished, renowned* **kiken**
貴公 *you* **kikō**
貴公子 *young noble* **kikōshi**
貴命 *your orders (honorific)* **kimei**
貴覧 *look, observe* **kiran**
貴様 *you, sir, madam* **kisama**
貴札 *your letter* **kisatsu**

貴社 *your company (honorific)* **kisha**
貴信 *your letter (honorific)* **kishin**
貴族 *noble, aristocrat* **kizoku**
貴族的 *aristocratic* **kizokuteki**
高貴 *high & noble* **kōki**
騰貴 *sudden rise, upsurge* **tōki**
⇒物価騰貴 *price increases of goods* **bukka tōki**
貴婦人 *high-status woman* **kifujin**
貴賓席 *royal box* **kihinseki**
貴金属 *precious metals* **kikinzoku**
伯父貴 *uncle* **ojiki**

高igh, 435	珍are, 720	宝reasure, 92
上pper, 859	要ssential, 419	価alue, 35
最aximum, 423	尊steem, 544	値alue, 783

貫arry out, 532

758-C

遺*ispatch of* 貴*recious minds,* 遺*eaving nations in a bind...*

辶 (transport)

遺*equeath*   遺*eave-behind*

noko(su), I, YUI
bequeath, leave-behind, bequest

FLIP: 3.0.a. Top (flat)

補遺 *supplement, appendix* **hoi**
遺愛 *cherished by the deceased* **iai**
遺物 *relic, remains* **ibutsu**
遺伝 *hereditary, genetic* **iden**
遺詠 *farewell poem of the dead* **iei**
遺影 *funeral portrait* **iei**
遺風 *old traditions & customs* **ifū**
遺骸 *dead body, corpse, cadaver* **igai**
遺業 *unfinished work* **igyō**
遺品 *articles left by the dead* **ihin**
遺児 *orphan, parentless child* **iji**
遺憾 *regrettable, deplorable, lamentable* **ikan**
遺棄 *abandonment, withdrawal* **iki**
遺稿 *unpublished works of the dead* **ikō**
遺恨 *grudge, animosity, bad blood* **ikon**
遺骨 *bone & ashes* **ikotsu**
遺尿 *bedwetting, urinating in one's sleep* **i'nyō**
遺漏 *omission, leaving out* **irō**
遺作 *posthumous works* **isaku**

遺産 *legacy, inheritance* **isan**
⇒文化遺産 *cultural heritage* **bunka isan**
遺精 *uncontrolled ejaculation* **isei**
遺志 *dying wish, last wish* **ishi**
遺失 *loss, missing, unfound* **ishitsu**
遺書 *one's last letter, last writings* **isho**
遺体 *dead body, corpse* **itai**
遺贈 *property disposition upon death* **izō**
遺族 *bereaved family* **izoku**
遺言 *last will, dying wish* **yuigon**
後遺症 *sequel, after-effects* **kōishō**

置*eave-behind, 420*	死*eath, 513*
去*eave-out, 360*	逝*eath, 54*
残*emain, 767*	亡*eath, 72*

貴*recious, 913*

759-A

彩*olourful* 菜*egetables,* 採*dopted in variables...*

彡 (hair ornament)

彩*olour*   彩*ainting*

irodo(ru), SAI
colour, painting, beautiful colouring

FLIP: 6.2. Left Bottom

異彩 *conspicuousness, striking, marked* **isai**
光彩 *lustre, brilliance, sharpness* **kōsai**
虹彩 *eye iris* **kōsai**
迷彩 *camouflage* **meisai**
彩度 *chroma* **saido**
彩画 *coloured picture* **saiga**
彩管 *paintbrush* **saikan**
彩色 *colouring, painting* **saishiki**
彩層 *chromo sphere* **saisō**
彩雲 *clouds aglow* **saiun**
精彩 *colourfulness* **seisai**
生彩 *"colours-of-life..."* **seisai**
色彩 *colour, hue* **shikisai**
水彩 *water colouring* **suisai**
水彩絵の具 *water colouring tools* **suisai enogu**
単彩 *monochrome* **tansai**
淡彩 *weak-, light colouring* **tansai**
多彩 *multi-colour, colourful* **tasai**
油彩 *oil painting* **yusai**

極彩色 *heavy-, thick colouring* **gokusaishiki**

色*olour, 403*	明*right, 22*
描*rawing, 271*	英*rilliance, 217*
昭*right, 529*	著*tark, 279*

採*dopt, 915*

759-B

彩olourful 菜egetables, 採dopted in variables...

⁺⁺ (grass)

菜egetable   菜lant

na, SAI
vegetable, plant

FLIP: 4.0.b. Bottom (stem)

油菜 *rapeseed flower* **aburana**
青菜 *veggies, greens* **aona**
白菜 *celery cabbage* **hakusai**
根菜 *root crop* **konsai**
水菜 *potherb mustard* **mizuna**
菜種 *rapeseed* **natane**
菜種油 *rapeseed oil* **natane abura**
菜種梅雨 *early rainy season* **natane tsuyu**
菜漬 *vegetable pickles* **nazuke**
菜箸 *long chopsticks* **saibashi**
菜園 *vegetable garden* **saien**
菜食 *vegetable meal, vegetarian* **saishoku**
山菜 *wild vegetables* **sansai**
惣菜 *side dish* **sōzai**
総菜 *daily dishes, staple diet* **sōzai**
杉菜 *field horsetail* **sugina**
高菜 *mustard leaf* **takana**
若菜 *young greens* **wakana**
野菜 *vegetables, greens, mustard* **yasai**

⇒乾燥野菜 *dried vegetable* **kansō yasai**
⇒清浄野菜 *organic vegetables* **seijō yasai**
野菜サラダ *vegetable salad* **yasai sarada**
野菜スープ *vegetable soup* **yasai suupu**
嫁菜 *starwort* **yomena**
洋菜 *Western vegetables* **yōna**
前菜 *appetizer, hors d'oeuvre* **zensai**
青梗菜 *Chinese cabbage* **chingensai**
小松菜 *small cabbage* **komatsuna**
菜の花 *rapeseed flowers* **nanohana**
菜っ葉 *greens, vegetables* **nappa**

植*egetation, 783*	鮮*resh, 679*
緑*reen, 841*	生*aw, 474*

杉*edar-tree, 721*

759-C

彩olourful 菜egetables, 採dopted in variables...

手⇔扌 (hand, manual)

採dopt   採ather

irodo(ru), to(ru), SAI
adopt, gather

FLIP: 7.3.b. Right Bottom (stem)

伐採 *lumbering, logging* **bassai**
採伐 *timbering, logging* **saibatsu**
採譜 *copying a tune* **saifu**
採否 *adoption-or-rejection* **saihi**
採決 *vote, roll call, division* **saiketsu**
採血 *blood collecting* **saiketsu**
採光 *lighting, illumination* **saikō**
採鉱 *working in the mine* **saikō**
採掘 *mining, digging* **saikutsu**
採掘権 *mining concessions, ~rights* **saikutsuken**
採卵 *egg raising* **sairan**
採録 *recording, taping* **sairoku**
採算 *profit, earnings, yields* **saisan**
採石 *quarrying (marble)* **saiseki**
採石場 *quarry site* **saisekijō**
採取 *gathering, picking* **saishu**
採種 *seeds collecting* **saishu**
採集 *collecting, gathering* **saishū**
⇒昆虫採集 *insect collecting* **konchū saishū**

⇒植物採集 *plant collecting*
　　　shokubutsu saishū
採寸 *taking body measurement* **saisun**
採択 *adoption, selection, choosing* **saitaku**
採炭 *coal mining* **saitan**
採点 *marking, grading, grades* **saiten**
採用 *adoption, recruitment* **saiyō**
採油 *oil drilling, ~exploration* **saiyu**
採油権 *oil concession, drilling rights* **saiyuken**
仮採用 *temporary hire, temp* **karisaiyō**
採算割れ *below cost* **saisanware**
採り残す *leave behind* **torinokosu**

抱*mploy, 503*	頂*eceive, 134*	雇*ecruit, 343*
受*eceive, 539*	用*vail of, 409*	就*ecruit, 719*

彩*olour, 914*

760-A

遠*istant* 園*arden, in fact a* 猿*onkey's den...*

遠*istant*　　遠*ar away*

辶 (transport)

tō(i), EN, ON
distant, far away, remoteness

FLIP: 3.0.a. Top (flat)

永遠 *eternity, perpetuity, forever* **eien**
遠泳 *long-distance swim* **en'ei**
遠因 *remote factor, indirect cause* **en'in**
遠海 *deep sea* **enkai**
遠隔 *distance, remoteness* **enkaku**
遠景 *distant view* **enkei**
遠近 *far or near, distance* **enkin**
遠来 *visit from afar* **enrai**
遠雷 *distant thunder* **enrai**
遠路 *long way, distant, far* **enro**
遠慮 *reserve manner, prudence* **enryo**
遠慮深い *deep reservation, diffident* **enryobukai**
遠視 *far-sightedness* **enshi**
遠足 *field trip, excursion* **ensoku**
敬遠 *distancing, aloofness, indifference* **keien**
久遠 *eternity, perpetuity, forever* **kuon**
深遠 *deep, profound* **shin'en**
遠浅 *shoal away from the shore* **tooasa**
遠出 *going far away* **toode**

遠縁 *distant relationship* **tooen**
遠目 *sharp eyes* **toome**
遠耳 *hearing difficulties* **toomimi**
望遠鏡 *telescope, binoculars* **bōenkyō**
無遠慮 *lack of manners, ~restraints* **buenryo**
縁遠い *far removed; not close relationship* **endooi**
遠距離 *long distance* **enkyori**
遠心力 *centrifugal force* **enshinryoku**
遠巻き *encircle from a distance* **toomaki**
遠回り *roundabout way, detour* **toomawari**
遠乗り *long-distance drive, ~ride* **toonori**

疎*istant,* 955	距*istance,* 207
悠*istant,* 898	近*earby,* 184

違*ifference,* 796

760-B

遠*istant* 園*arden, in fact a* 猿*onkey's den...*

園*arden*

囗 (enclosure)

sono, EN
garden

FLIP: 8.0.a. Inner (flat)

梅園 *plum orchard* **baien**
茶園 *tea garden, ~plantation* **chaen**
田園 *countryside, rural* **den'en**
園長 *kindergarten headteacher* **enchō**
園芸 *gardening, horticulture* **engei**
園児 *kindergarten child, kindergrader* **enji**
園丁 *garden keeper* **entei**
園亭 *gazebo, arbour* **entei**
学園 *university town; educational institute* **gakuen**
祇園 *red-light district in Kyōto City* **gion**
花園 *flower garden* **hanazono**
閉園 *"park closed..."* **heien**
開園 *park opening* **kaien**
公園 *public park* **kōen**
農園 *farm, plantation* **nōen**
楽園 *paradise* **rakuen**
霊園 *cemetery, memorial park* **reien**
菜園 *vegetable garden* **saien**
荘園 *manor, mansion, estate* **shōen, sōen**

桑園 *mulberry orchard* **sōen**
卒園 *kindergarten graduation* **sotsuen**
庭園 *garden, botanical yard* **teien**
薬園 *herbal garden* **yakuen**
造園 *landscaping, land design* **zōen**
園遊会 *garden-, lawn party* **enyūkai**
保育園 *nursery, kindergarten* **hoikuen**
果樹園 *orchard, fruit plantation* **kajuen**
竹の園 *bamboo garden* **take no sono**
幼稚園 *kindergarten school* **yōchien**
遊園地 *amusement-, recreation park* **yūenchi**

庭*arden,* 27	草*rass,* 373
芝*awn,* 84	

遠*istant,* 916

760-C

遠istant 園arden, in fact a 猿onkey's den...

猿onkey   猿pe

saru, EN
monkey, ape

犬⇔犭 (dog; beast)

FLIP: 7.2.a. Right Top (flat)

猿戸	simple gate	**sarudo**
猿楽	medieval farce	**sarugaku**
猿轡	gag, injunction, prohibition	**sarugutsuwa**
猿股	underpants, shorts	**sarumata**
猿緬	monkey look-a-like face	**sarumen**
猿似	resemblance by chance	**saruni**
猿賢い	cunning	**sarugashikoi**
猿引き	monkey trainer	**saruhiki**
猿知恵	shallow cunning	**sarujie**
猿真似	awkward imitation	**sarumane**
猿回し	monkey showman	**sarumawashi**
猿芝居	monkey show	**sarushibai**
猿人	ape man, pithecanthropus	**enjin**
犬猿	mortal enemies (dog & monkey)	**ken'en**
三猿	"see-, hear- & speak no evil..."	**san'en**
野猿	wild monkey	**yaen**
山猿	mountain monkey	**yamazaru**
指猿	"aye-aye.."	**yubisaru**
人類猿	anthropoid ape	**jinruien**

虚仮猿	idiot monkey	**kokezaru**
日本猿	Japanese monkey	**nihonzaru**
尾長猿	guenon, ape with long tails	**onagazaru**
類人猿	anthropoid ape	**ruijin'en**
手長猿	ape with long arms	**tenagazaru**
意馬心猿	uncontrolled passions	**ibashin'en**

申onkey, 89	擬mitate, 56
飼aising, 835	倣mitate, 486
輿ntertainment, 867	

遠istant, 916

761-A

Cremation 管ipes 管ontrol 棺offins in a 館ublic-hall...

❶管ontrol ❷管ipe

kuda, KAN
control, administer; pipe, tube

竹 (bamboo)

Facing: 2.1. East ☞ (H)

❶
只管	anything but, nothing but	**hitasura**
保管	storage, custody, charge	**hokan**
移管	transfer of control-, jurisdiction	**ikan**
管長	chief abbot, head priest	**kanchō**
管轄	under the jurisdiction of, agency of	**kankatsu**
管見	narrow view	**kanken**
管理	management, supervision	**kanri**
管理人	manager, executor, caretaker	**kanrinin**
管制	control, administration	**kansei**
⇒為替管理	exchange control	**kawase kanri**
雷管	detonator, ignition device	**raikan**
専管	exclusive jurisdiction, ~administration	**senkan**
所管	jurisdiction, control	**shokan**
管財人	administrator, receivership (bank)	**kanzainin**

❷
土管	earthen pipe	**dokan**
導管	duct, pipe	**dōkan**
配管	pipe, plumbing	**haikan**
本管	main pipe	**honkan**

血管	blood vessel, ~vein, ~artery	**kekkan**
毛管	capillary	**mōkan**
木管	wooden pipe	**mokkan**
卵管	fallopian tube	**rankan**
涙管	lachrymal duct	**ruikan**
水管	water pipe, ~duct	**suikan**
鉄管	steel-, iron pipe	**tekkan**
管楽器	wind musical instrument	**kangakki**
管弦楽	orchestra music	**kangengaku**
給水管	water pipe, duct	**kyūsuikan**
試験管	test tube	**shikenkan**
真空管	vacuum tube	**shinkūkan**

轄ontrol, 968	導uidance, 312	宰upervise, 377
操perate, 851	筒ipe, 51	監upervise, 592

官ublic official, 105

761-B
Cremation 管*ipes* 管*ontrol* 棺*offins in a* 館*ublic-hall...*

木 (wooden)

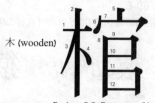

棺*offin* 棺*asket*

hitsugi, KAN
coffin, casket

Facing: 2.2. East ☞ (V)

棺桶 *coffin, casket* **kan'oke**
寝棺 *coffin, casket* **nekan, negan**
納棺 *putting corpse in a coffin* **nōkan**
入棺 *putting corpse in a coffin* **nyūkan**
石棺 *stone coffin* **sekikan, sekkan**
出棺 *taking coffin out for funeral march* **shukkan**
陶棺 *earthen coffin* **tōkan**

死*eath, 513*	墓*ravesite, 602*
逝*eath, 54*	碑*ombstone, 937*
亡*eath, 72*	陵*ausoleum, 140*
葬*urial, 513*	埋*ury, 319*

官*ublic official, 105*

761-C
Cremation 管*ipes* 管*ontrol* 棺*offins in a* 館*ublic-hall...*

食 (food)

館*ublic-hall* 館*arge hall*

yakata, KAN
large-hall, public hall

Facing: 2.2. East ☞ (V)

別館 *annex-, adjacent building* **bekkan**
分館 *annex-, adjacent building* **bunkan**
学館 *academy, hall* **gakkan**
閉館 *"library, hall closed..."* **heikan**
本館 *main building, mail hall* **honkan**
開館 *"library, hall open..."* **kaikan**
会館 *hall, assembly hall* **kaikan**
館長 *chief librarian, curator* **kanchō**
館外 *outside the library, ~hall* **kangai**
館内 *inside the library, ~hall* **kannai**
公館 *diplomatic missions* **kōkan**
休館 *"library, hall closed..."* **kyūkan**
入館 *entering a hall, library* **nyūkan**
旅館 *Japanese inn, hotel* **ryokan**
新館 *newly-built building* **shinkan**
商館 *trading house* **shōkan**
洋館 *Western-style building* **yōkan**
美術館 *museum, art gallery* **bijutsukan**
牧師館 *parsonage, vicarage* **bokushikan**

映画館 *theatre, cinema, playhouse* **eigakan**
迎賓館 *guest house* **geihinkan**
博物館 *museum, exhibit hall* **hakubutsukan**
絵画館 *picture gallery* **kaigakan**
公民館 *community centre* **kōminkan**
隣保館 *neighbourhood evacuation centre* **rinpokan**
領事館 *consulate* **ryōjikan**
水族館 *aquarium* **suizokukan**
体育館 *gymnasium* **taiikukan**
大使館 *embassy* **taishikan**
図書館 *library* **toshokan**

会*ssembly, 864*	衆*ultitude, 766*
集*ather, 50*	建*onstruct, 390*
建*uilding, 390*	築*onstruct, 907*

棺*asket, 918*

762-A

準*emi ghostly belief*, 焦*ocus on the* 礁*oral reef...*

火 ⇔ 灬 (fire)

Facing: 2.0. East ☞ (W)

焦*ocus*　　焦*corch*

ko(gasu), ko(geru), ko(gareru), ase(ru), ji(rasu) SHŌ
focus, scorch, impatient

焦り *impatience, fretfulness* **aseri**
焦らす *keep in suspense, fret* **jirasu**
焦れったい *annoying, irritating, impatient* **jirettai**
焦げる *be scorched, ~burned* **kogeru**
焦がれる *yearn, long for* **kogareru**
焦がれ死に *dying for love* **kogareji(ni)**
焦げ茶 *dark brown tea* **kogecha**
焦げ茶色 *dark brown* **kogechairo**
焦げ臭い *burnt-, charred odour* **kogekusai**
焦げ付く *be frozen, ~burned* **kogetsuku**
焦土 *scorched land* **shōdo**
焦熱 *scorching heat* **shōnetsu**
焦熱地獄 *hell, inferno* **shōnetsu jigoku**
焦慮 *worrying, fretting, whining* **shōryo**
焦心 *impatience, fretfulness* **shōshin**
焦燥 *impatience, fretfulness* **shōsō**
焦点 *focus, focal point, locus* **shōten**
焦点距離 *focal distance* **shōten kyori**
黒焦げ *charred black* **kurokoge**

焦電気 *pyroelectric* **shōdenki**
麦焦がし *dried barley flour* **mugikogashi**
焦眉の急 *urgency, pressing matter*
　　shōbi no kyū
焼け焦げ *scorched, burnt* **yakekoge**
恋焦がれる *love desperation, ~obsession*
　　koikogareru
待ち焦がれる *"cannot stand waiting for..."*
　　machikogareru
思い焦がれる *thinking of* **omoikogareru**

趣*nterest, 663*	核*uclear, 973*
目*oint, 462*	中*iddle, 85*
央*entral, 218*	注*utpour, 750*

集*ollect, 50*

762-B

準*emi ghostly belief*, 焦*ocus on the* 礁*oral reef...*

水 ⇔ 氵 (water)

FLIP: 4.0.b. Bottom (stem)
Facing: 2.1. East ☞ (H)

❶準*emi-*　　❷準*evel*

JUN
semi-, sub-, quasi-; level, ranking

❶準星 *quasar* **junsei**
準会員 *associate member* **junkaiin**
準契約 *quasi-contract* **junkeiyaku**
準決勝 *semi-final winning* **junkesshō**
準社員 *junior staff member* **junshain**

❷平準 *level, equal* **heijun**
標準 *standard* **hyōjun**
標準語 *standard language (accent)* **hyōjungo**
標準時 *standard time* **hyōjunji**
標準化 *standardization* **hyōjunka**
標準的 *standard* **hyōjunteki**
準備 *preparation, readying* **junbi**
準備金 *reserve funds* **junbikin**
準備室 *preparation room* **junbishitsu**
準縄 *rule, standard* **junjō**
準拠 *conformity, compliance* **junkyo**
準急 *local express train* **junkyū**
準則 *rule observance* **junsoku**

準用 *rule application* **junyō**
規準 *standard, datum* **kijun**
基準 *standard, datum* **kijun**
⇒環境基準 *environmental standards*
　　kankyō kijun
基準価格 *standard price* **kijun kakaku**
照準 *gun sight, aiming a gun* **shōjun**
水準 *standard, level* **suijun**
⇒物価水準 *price level* **bukka suijun**
⇒文化水準 *cultural level* **bunka suijun**
⇒生活水準 *standard of living, lifestyle*
　　seikatsu suijun

等*rade, 251*	級*evel, 189*	階*evel, 129*
格*tatus, 498*	段*tep, 555*	半*ne-half, 484*

推*ecommend, 777*

762-C

準*emi ghostly belief,* 焦*ocus on the* 礁*oral reef...*

礁*oral reef*

石 (stone)

Facing: 2.2. East ☞ (V)

SHŌ
coral reef

暗礁	*reef; deadlock, stalemate*	**anshō**
岩礁	*shore reef*	**ganshō**
漁礁	*fish-inhabited reef*	**gyoshō**
堡礁	*barrier reef*	**hoshō**
環礁	*atoll, reef*	**kanshō**
離礁	*raising a sunken ship*	**rishō**
礁湖	*lagoon*	**shōko**
座礁	*running aground (shallow waters)*	**zashō**
珊瑚礁	*coral reef*	**sangoshō**

浸*mmerse, 770*	沈*inking, 719*
潰*mmerse, 823*	潜*ubmerge, 335*
没*inking, 744*	埋*ury, 319*

焦*ocus, 919*

763-A

隣*eighbours* 瞬*link at Sara's* 傑*xcellent mink...*

隣*eighbour*

阝 ⇔ 阜 (village=left)

FLIP: 7.2.b. Right Top (stem)

tonari, tona(ru), RIN
neighbour

比隣	*vicinity, surroundings, neighbourhood*	**hirin**
近隣	*one's neighbourhood*	**kinrin**
又隣	*next-next door neighbour*	**matadonari**
隣人	*neighbour, neighbourhood*	**rinjin**
隣人愛	*neighbourly bond*	**rinjin'ai**
隣家	*next door house*	**rinka**
隣県	*neighbouring prefectures*	**rinken**
隣国	*neighbouring nation*	**rinkoku**
隣邦	*neighbouring nation*	**rinpō**
隣席	*next seat*	**rinseki**
隣接	*adjoining-, adjacent, neighbouring*	**rinsetsu**
隣接地	*adjacent land*	**rinsetsuchi**
隣接家屋	*adjacent house*	**rinsetsu kaoku**
隣室	*next room*	**rinshitsu**
隣村	*neighbouring village*	**rinson**
両隣	*both neighbours (left & right-side)*	**ryōdonari**
先隣	*next-next door neighbour*	**sakidonari**
四隣	*the whole neighbourhood*	**shirin**
隣組	*community association*	**tonarigumi**

隣村	*neighbouring village*	**tonarimura**
横隣	*next door neighbour*	**yokodonari**
隣保館	*resettlement house*	**rinpokan**
隣り合う	*become neighbours*	**tonariau**
隣同士	*fellow neighbours*	**tonaridōshi**
隣近所	*neighbourhood, neighbours*	**tonarikinjo**

近*earby, 184*	懇*ntimacy, 164*
周*icinity, 280*	款*oodwill, 42*
辺*icinity, 93*	歓*ordial, 667*
親*ntimacy, 669*	迎*ordial, 705*

障*njury, 325*

763-B

隣eighbours 瞬link at Sara's 傑xcellent mink...

目 (eyesight, visual)

瞬link   瞬oment

matata(ku), SHUN
blink, moment, flash, instant

FLIP: 6.0.a. Left (flat)

一瞬 blink of an eye, split seconds **isshun**
瞬き blink, wink **mabataki**
瞬時 moment, flash **shunji**
瞬間 moment, flash **shunkan**
瞬刻 instant, moment **shunkoku**

秒econds, 727	速peedy, 502
分inute, 518	迅peedy, 95
時ime, 653	驚care, 330

隣eighbour, 920

763-C

隣eighbours 瞬link at Sara's 傑xcellent mink...

人⇔イ (person)

傑xcellence   傑rominence

KETSU
excellence, prominence, outstanding

FLIP: 4.0.b. Bottom (stem)

英傑 heroic person **eiketsu**
豪傑 hero, bold man **gōketsu**
人傑 great person **jinketsu**
女傑 heroine, amazon **joketsu**
怪傑 extraordinary person **kaiketsu**
傑作 masterpiece work **kessaku**
傑出 excellence, prominence **kesshutsu**
傑物 great person **ketsubutsu**
傑人 outstanding person **ketsujin**
傑然 determined, decisive **ketsuzen**
俊傑 outstanding person **shunketsu**

妙uperb, 726	優xcellence, 556
秀uperb, 383	雅raceful, 58
秀xcellence, 383	韻raceful, 315

瞬link, 921

764-A

諭dmonished for drinking 愉leasures, 癒ecuperating from
　　　heart seizure...

言 (speaking)

諭dmonish　　諭aution

sato(su), YU

admonish, caution, counsel, enjoin

FLIP: 6.0.a. Left (flat)
FLIP: 7.2.a. Right Top (flat)

諭す　advise, persuade, convince **satosu**
教え諭す　give guidance, supervise **oshiesatosu**
勅諭　imperial mandate **chokuyu**
風諭　hint, implying, suggesting **fūyu**
告諭　counsel, admonition **kokuyu**
訓諭　admonition, warning **kunyu**
教諭　teacher (primary & high school) **kyōyu**
説教　sermon, scolding, admonition **sekkyō**
説諭　suggestion to a subordinate **setsuyu**
諭告　counsel, admonition **yukoku**
諭旨　official suggestion **yushi**
諭示　counsel, admonition **yushi**
諭旨免職　officially-hinted resignation **yushi menshoku**
諭達　official instruction **yutatsu**

戒dmonish, 493	威uthority, 520
警arning, 330	権uthority, 804
導uidance, 312	薦dvice, 68

傑xcellence, 921

764-B

諭dmonished for drinking 愉leasures, 癒ecuperating from
　　　heart seizure...

心⇔忄⇔小 (feelings)

愉leasure　　愉oyful

YU

pleasure, joyful, delight

FLIP: 7.2.a. Right Top (flat)

愉悦　joy, pleasure **yuetsu**
愉快　enjoyable, pleasant **yukai**
⇒不愉快　unpleasant, vexing **fuyukai**
愉楽　pleasure, joy **yuraku**
愉色　cheerful disposition, joyful look **yushoku**

悦leasant, 942	歓leasure, 667
快leasant, 699	喫leasure, 900
楽leasure, 447	娯leasure, 453

諭dmonish, 922

764-C

諭dmonished for drinking 愉leasures, 癒ecuperating from heart seizure...

癒ecuperate　癒ealing

iya(su), YU
recuperate, healing, convalesce, getting well

治癒 *healing, cure, recovery* **chiyu**
平癒 *health recovery, recuperation* **heiyu**
快癒 *complete recovery* **kaiyu**
癒着 *adhesion, sticking* **yuchaku**
癒合 *agglutination, conglutination* **yugō**
全癒 *complete recovery* **zenyu**
治癒力 *healing power* **chiyuryoku**
腹癒せ *revenge, getting even* **haraise**

疒 (sickness)

Facing: 2.2. East ☞ (V)

薬*rugs, 447*	患*ickness, 475*
剤*rugs, 961*	症*ickness, 788*
治*ecuperate, 210*	病*ickness, 213*
療*ecuperate, 67*	医*edicine, 19*

愉*leasure, 922*

765-A

触ouch a tortoise, hear a 濁urky 騒oise...

触ouch　触ontact

sawa(ru), fu(reru), SHOKU
touch, contact, feeling

筆触 *touch of the pen* **hisshoku**
感触 *touch, feel* **kanshoku**
接触 *touch, feel* **sesshoku**
接触点 *point of contact, ~intersection* **sesshokuten**
触覚 *sense-of-touch* **shokkaku**
触角 *feelers* **shokkaku**
触感 *sense-of-touch* **shokkan**
触官 *tactile organ* **shokkan**
触媒 *catalyst, reactant, enzyme* **shokubai**
触知 *perceive by touching* **shokuchi**
触発 *touching off, setting off* **shokuhatsu**
蝕目 *seeing, eyesight* **shokumoku**
蝕接 *touch, feel* **shokusetsu**
触診 *palpitation check-up* **shokushin**
触手 *feeler; tentacle* **shokushu**
抵触 *conflict, dispute; contrary to law* **teishoku**
肌触り *touch, feel* **hadazawari**
顔触れ *line-up, cast* **kaobure**
口触り *taste* **kuchizawari**

角 (horns)

触

Facing: 1.2. ☜ West (V)

前触れ *prior notice* **maebure**
耳触り *annoying-, irritating noise* **mimizawari**
先触れ *previous announcement* **sakibure**
舌触り *taste, food texture* **shitazawari**
手触り *feel, touch* **tezawari**
触れ合い *inter-mingling, interfacing* **fureai**
触れ踏み *public announcement* **furebumi**
触れ太鼓 *drum-beating in sumo* **furedaiko**
触れ込み *reputation, name-value* **furekomi**
触れ回る *rumour-mongering* **furemawaru**
言い触れ *reveal, divulge* **iifure**

結*onnect, 227*	膚*kin, 69*
絡*onnect, 826*	皮*kin, 224*
接*ontact, 587*	肌*kin, 747*

解*nderstand, 400*

765-B

触*ouch a tortoise, hear a* 濁*urky* 騒*oise...*

水 ⇔ 氵 (water)

濁*uddy*　　濁*urbid*

nigo(ru), nigo(su), DAKU
muddy, turbid, marshy

FLIP: 7.2.b. Right Top (stem)

濁り江 *muddy inlet/ creek* **nigorie**
濁り水 *muddy water* **nigorimizu**
濁り酒 *crude sake, unrefined sake* **nigorizake**
濁った頭 *vague head* **nigotta atama**
濁度 *turbidity, muddiness* **dakudo**
濁音 *voiced consonant* **dakuon**
濁流 *muddy stream, turbid current* **dakuryū**
濁声 *thick voice, hoarse voice* **dakusei**
濁世 *"this corrupt world..."* **dakusei**
濁酒 *unrefined sake* **dakushu**
濁点 *consonant symbol* **dakuten**
白濁 *urine nebula* **hakudaku**
懸濁 *suspension, hanging* **kendaku**
混濁 *murky, turbid, muddy* **kondaku**
乳濁 *murky, turbid, muddy* **nyūdaku**
汚濁 *pollution, contamination, corruption* **odaku**
⇒水質汚濁 *water pollution* **suishitsu odaku**
連濁 *compound voiced sound* **rendaku**
清濁 *purity & impurity* **seidaku**

油濁 *oil spill, oil leakage* **yudaku**
鼻濁音 *nasal sound* **bidakuon**
半濁音 *semi-voiced sound* **handakuon**
半濁点 *symbols attached to Katakana*
　　handakuten

泥*lay, 302*	沢*wamp, 753*
汚*irty, 737*	土*oil, 8*
沼*wamp, 356*	土*round, 8*

漫*andom, 845*

765-C

触*ouch a tortoise, hear a* 濁*urky* 騒*oise...*

馬 (horse)

騒*oise*　　騒*isturbance*

sawa(gu), SŌ
noise, disturbance, clamour

FLIP: 7.2.b. Right Top (stem)

騒ぎ *noise, uproar, fuss, clamour* **sawagi**
騒がしい *noisy, loud, rowdy, wilding* **sawagashii**
騒ぎ立て *raising a fuss* **sawagitate**
物騒 *dangerous, deranged* **bussō**
喧騒 *clamour, din* **kensō**
狂騒 *frenzy, madness, uproar* **kyōsō**
潮騒 *roar of the ocean, noisy tide* **shiosai**
騒動 *riot, looting, anarchy* **sōdō**
⇒米騒動 *rice riot, rice looting* **kome sōdō**
⇒御家騒動 *family dispute* **oiesōdō**
騒人 *literary person* **sōjin**
騒擾 *disturbance, disorder* **sōjō**
騒音 *noise, sound* **sōon**
騒音公害 *noise pollution* **sōon kōgai**
騒乱 *disorder, trouble, riot* **sōran**
騒然 *uproar, loud noise* **sōzen**
空騒ぎ *raising a fuss* **karasawagi**
心騒ぎ *distress, anxiety* **kokorosawagi**
胸騒ぎ *premonition, intuition, foreboding* **munasawagi**

大騒ぎ *uproar, loud noise* **oosawagi**
騒擾罪 *rioting, anarchy* **sōjōzai**
人騒がせ *false alarm* **hitosawagase**
騒騒しい *noisy, loud sound* **sōzōshii**
底抜け騒ぎ *rowdy merrymaking, hooliganism*
　　sokonuke sawagi

声*oice, 428*	聞*isten, 282*
争*onflict, 231*	耳*ars, 228*
聴*isten, 844*	音*ound, 314*

験*xperience, 673*

766-A

膨*ulging corpus, like a* 鼓*rum in the* 樹*ush...*

肉⇔月 (flesh, body part)

膨*ulge*   膨*welling*

fuku(reru), fuku(ramu), BŌ
bulge, swelling, bloated, expand

膨張 *swelling, expansion* **bōchō**
膨脹 *swelling, expansion* **bōchō**
膨大 *enormous, vast, huge* **bōdai**
膨隆 *swelling, expansion* **bōryū**
青膨れ *dropsical swelling* **aobukure**
膨張率 *rate of expansion* **bōchōritsu**
水膨れ *water blister* **mizubukure**
線膨張 *linear expansion* **senbōchō**
下膨れ *round face* **shimobukure**
膨らます *swell, inflate, bulge* **fukuramasu**
膨らし粉 *baking powder* **fukurashiko**
膨れっ面 *sullen look* **fukurettsura**
着膨れる *bundling, lumping together* **kibukureru**

FLIP: 8.0.a. Inner (flat)

脹*welling, 274*	巨*iant, 206*
大*arge, 7*	超*xceed, 664*
広*arge, 205*	余*xtra, 501*
拡*nlarge, 205*	剰*xtra, 511*

膨*hisel, 721*

766-B

膨*ulging corpus, like a* 鼓*rum in the* 樹*ush...*

鼓 (drum)

鼓*rum*

tsuzumi, KO
drum

FLIP: 5.0.b. Left & Right

腹鼓 *drumming one's belly* **haratsuzumi**
旗鼓 *colours & drums* **kiko**
鼓舞 *encouragement, inspiration* **kobu**
鼓動 *heartbeat, pulsation, palpitation* **kodō**
鼓腹 *drumming one's belly* **kofuku**
鼓膜 *eardrum* **komaku**
鼓吹 *advocate, propagandist* **kosui**
鼓笛 *drums & flutes* **koteki**
鼓笛隊 *drum & pipe band* **kotekitai**
舌鼓 *smacking one's lips* **shitatsuzumi**
鉦鼓 *drums & bells* **shōko**
太鼓 *drum* **taiko**
⇒陣太鼓 *"drums of war..."* **jindaiko**
⇒大太鼓 *bass drum* **oodaiko**
⇒触れ太鼓 *drum beating in sumo wrestling* **furedaiko**
太鼓判 *large seal* **taikoban**
太鼓腹 *potbelly, beer-belly* **taikobara**
太鼓持ち *flatterer, jester* **taikomochi**
鼓手 *drummer* **tsuzumite, koshu**

拍*empo, 743*
音*ound, 314*
曲*elody, 476*

殻*usk, 41*

766-C

膨*ulging corpus, like a* 鼓*rums in the* 樹*ush...*

木 (wooden)

樹*ushes*   樹*hrubbery*

JU

bushes, shrubbery, thicket, standing trees

FLIP: 8.0.a. Inner (flat)

一樹 *lone tree* **ichiju**	老樹 *old trees* **rōju**
一樹の陰 *pre-destined* **ichiju no kage**	緑樹 *green tree* **ryokuju**
樹液 *rubber tree sapping* **jueki**	植樹 *planting trees, reforestation* **shokuju**
樹皮 *tree bark* **juhi**	植樹祭 *Arbour Day* **shokujusai**
樹氷 *frozen-, ice-covered trees* **juhyō**	大樹 *large trees* **taiju**
樹陰 *tree shade* **juin**	幼樹 *young trees* **yōju**
樹上 *top of a tree* **jujō**	街路樹 *roadside trees* **gairoju**
樹海 *sea of trees* **jukai**	月桂樹 *laurel* **gekkeiju**
樹幹 *tree trunk* **jukan**	果樹園 *orchard, fruit farm* **kajuen**
樹間 *"in the trees..."* **jukan**	広葉樹 *broadleaf trees* **kōyōju**
樹木 *trees* **jumoku**	針葉樹 *conifer, needle-leaf tree* **shinyōju**
樹齢 *tree age* **jurei**	
樹林 *trees, woods* **jurin**	
樹立 *establishment, foundation* **juritsu**	
樹脂 *plastic, resins* **jushi**	
樹脂加工 *plastics manufacture* **jushi kakō**	
樹身 *tree trunk* **jushin**	
果樹 *fruit-bearing tree* **kaju**	
花樹 *flower-bearing trees* **kaju**	

野*lains, 873*	芝*awn, 84*
植*lant, 783*	森*orest, 526*
草*rass, 373*	林*oods, 526*

鼓*rum, 925*

767-A

With 漢*anjiHybrid no more* 難*ifficulties or grief, what a* 嘆*igh of relief...*

水⇔氵 (water)

漢*anji*   漢*hinese character*

KAN

Kanji, Chinese character

FLIP: 7.0.b2. Right (stem)

悪漢 *rascal, villain, evil-doer, bad guy* **akkan**	漢詩 *Chinese poetry* **kanshi**
暴漢 *tough, rowdy, ruffian* **bōkan**	好漢 *fine fellow* **kōkan**
暴漢 *hoodlum, gangster* **bōkan**	巨漢 *giant person* **kyokan**
痴漢 *pervert, molester* **chikan**	凶漢 *professional killer, gun-for-hire* **kyōkan**
怪漢 *suspicious-looking person* **kaikan**	無頼漢 *villain, hooligan, outlaw* **buraikan**
漢文 *Chinese literature, ~writing* **kanbun**	卑劣漢 *sneak, deceptive, cunning* **hiretsukan**
漢朝 *Han dynasty* **kanchō**	漢数字 *Chinese numerals* **kansūji**
漢土 *China* **kando**	門外漢 *outsider, layman* **mongaikan**
漢学 *study of Kanji characters* **kangaku**	熱血漢 *hot-blooded, mercurial* **nekketsukan**
漢語 *Chinese word* **kango**	冷血漢 *cold-hearted person* **reiketsukan**
漢字 *Kanji, Chinese characters* **kanji**	和魂漢才 *Japanese spirit and Chinese learning* **wakon kansai**
⇒常用漢字 *Kanji common usage (1,945)* **jōyō kanji**	漢和辞典 *Japanese Kanji dictionary* **kanwa jiten**
漢字ハイブリッド *Vee David's Kanji concept* **kanji haiburiddo**	
漢方 *Chinese herbal medicine* **kanpō**	
漢方医 *herb doctor, Chinese herbal doctor* **kanpōi**	
漢方薬 *Chinese medicine* **kanpōyaku**	
漢籍 *Chinese classics* **kanseki**	

字*etter, 346*	書*ritings, 116*
文*iteracy, 558*	読*eading, 260*

膜*embrane, 827*

767-B

With 漢anjiHybrid no more 難ifficulties or grief, what a 嘆igh of relief...

佳 (long-tailed birds)

難*ifficulty*   難*ardship*

muzuka(shii), kata(i), NAN
difficulty, hardship, exacerbate, aggravation, messy, problematic

FLIP: 6.0.b. Left (stem)

避難 *refuge, shelter, evacuation* **hinan**
百難 *countless obstacles* **hyakunan**
殉難 *martyrdom, self-sacrifice* **junnan**
海難 *ocean disaster* **kainan**
家難 *family tragedy* **kanan**
険難 *steep difficulties* **kennan**
困難 *difficulties, hardships, risks* **konnan**
苦難 *adversities, difficulties* **kunan**
救難 *rescue, save life, emergency assistance* **kyūnan**
難物 *difficult, problematic, inconsiderate* **nanbutsu**
難題 *unreasonable demand* **nandai**
難儀 *difficulty, trouble, hardship* **nangi**
難事 *difficulty, hard task* **nanji**
難渋 *difficulty, trouble, hardship* **nanjū**
難解 *difficult, problematic, unhelpful* **nankai**
難関 *difficulty, deadlock, impasse, stand-off* **nankan**
難航 *rough flight, difficult voyage* **nankō**
難局 *difficult situation, grave crisis* **nankyoku**
難民 *refugee, asylee, evacuee* **nanmin**

難問 *difficult problem* **nanmon**
難破 *shipwreck, cast away* **nanpa**
難所 *dangerous place, perilous path* **nansho**
難色 *disapproval, difficulty, obstacle* **nanshoku**
難点 *weakness, difficult point* **nanten**
難産 *hard child birth, difficult delivery* **nanzan**
災難 *misfortune, calamity, disaster* **sainan**
遭難 *shipwreck, disaster, accident* **sōnan**
盗難 *theft, robbery, burglary* **tōnan**
度し難い *hopeless, desperation* **doshigatai**
有り難がる *grateful, thankful* **arigatagaru**

苦*nguish, 477*　挑*hallenge, 214*　因*ause, 862*
悩*nguish, 48*　困*rouble, 863*　辛*ardship, 377*

漢*anji, 926*

767-C

With 漢anjiHybrid no more 難ifficulties or grief, what a 嘆igh of relief...

口 (mouth)

嘆

嘆*igh [relief]*   嘆*igh [despair]*

nage(ku); nage(kawashii), TAN
sigh of relief, sigh of despair

FLIP: 5.0.b. Left & Right

長嘆 *long sight-of-relief* **chōtan**
詠嘆 *admiration, praise, extolling* **eitan**
慨嘆 *deploring, lamentation* **gaitan**
悲嘆 *grief, sorrow, lamentation* **hitan**
感嘆 *admiration, praise, extolling* **kantan**
驚嘆 *admiration, wonder* **kyōtan**
嘆き *grief, sorrow* **nageki**
賛嘆 *admiration, praise, extolling* **santan**
三嘆 *admiration, extolling, praise* **santan**
讃嘆 *admiration, praise, extolling* **santan**
嗟嘆 *lamenting, deplore; admiration, praise* **satan**
傷嘆 *crying in pain, painful whining* **shōtan**
嘆美 *admiration, extolling, praise* **tanbi**
嘆願 *appeal, petition, suit* **tangan**
嘆願書 *written petition* **tangansho**
嘆声 *sight-of-relief, ~admiration* **tansei**
嘆賞 *high praise, extolling, accolade* **tanshō**
嘆息 *sigh-of-relief; lamenting* **tansoku**
痛嘆 *bitter lamentation, groaning, fuming* **tsūtan**

愁嘆場 *scene of disaster* **shūtanba**

感*eelings, 45*
気*eelings, 98*
情*eelings, 793*

漢*xpanse, 828*

768-A
In a 暫*hile, arriving* 漸*radual at the Nile...*

日 (sunlight, daytime)

暫*hile*　　暫*nterim*

shibara(ku), ZAN
while, interim, stop-gap, provisional, temporary, tentative, transient

暫時 *for a short time, in a while* **zanji**
暫留 *short stay* **zanryū**
暫定 *temporary arrangements* **zantei**
暫定案 *provisional plan, tentative bill* **zanteian**
暫定的 *interim, provisional, stop-gap* **zanteiteki**

FLIP: 4.0.a. Bottom (flat)
FLIP: 6.1. Left Top

間*etween, 286*	時*ime, 653*
隔*nterval, 963*	仮*emporary, 732*
遮*nterrupt, 371*	今*resently, 182*

監*atch-over, 592*

768-B
In a 暫*hile, arriving* 漸*radual at the Nile...*

水⇔氵 (water)

漸*radual*　漸*teady*

yōya(ku), ZEN
gradual, steady

西漸 *westward advance* **seizen**
東漸 *advancing eastwards* **tōzen**
漸減 *steady-, gradual decrease* **zengen**
漸次 *steadily, gradually* **zenji**
漸時 *gradually* **zenji**
漸加 *gradual increase* **zenka**
漸降 *gradual decline* **zenkō**
漸滅 *gradual destruction* **zenmetsu**
漸落 *gradual decrease* **zenraku**
漸進 *steady-, gradual progress* **zenshin**
漸進主義 *moderation, temperance* **zenshin shugi**
漸増 *steady-, gradual increase* **zenzō**
漸近線 *asymptote* **zenkinsen**

FLIP: 8.0.b. Inner (stem)

遅*radual, 304*	遅*ardy, 944*
徐*lowly, 881*	鈍*luggish, 199*

暫*nterim, 928*

769-A
Light 紫urple, a 雌emale colour...

糸 (thread, continuity)

紫*urple*

murasaki, SHI
purple

赤紫 *reddish purple* **akamurasaki**
藤紫 *dark lilac* **fujimurasaki**
濃紫 *deep purple* **komurasaki**
紫色 *purple colour* **murasakiiro**
紫電 *flashes of lightning* **shiden**
紫煙 *tobacco-, blue smoke* **shien**
紫紺 *bluish purple* **shikon**
紫苑 *aster* **shion**
紫蘭 *bletilla* **shiran**
紫蘇 *beefsteak plant* **shiso**
紫檀 *rosewood* **shitan**
紫雲 *purple clouds* **shiun**
薄紫 *light purple* **usumurasaki**
若紫 *light purple* **wakamurasaki**
紫陽花 *hydrangea* **ajisai**
暗紫色 *dark purple* **anshishoku**
紫水晶 *amethyst* **murasakizuishō**
濃紫色 *heavy purple* **nōshishoku**
紫外線 *ultraviolet rays* **shigaisen**

Facing: 2.1. East ☞ (H)

紫斑病 *purpura* **shihanbyō**
淡紫色 *light purple* **tanshishoku**

赤*ed colour, 261*	色*olour, 403*
丹*ed colour, 78*	彩*olour, 914*
紅*carlet, 175*	染*olouring, 607*
朱*carlet, 233*	緑*reen, 841*

雌*emale-animal, 929*

769-B
Light 紫urple, a 雌emale colour...

隹 (long-tailed birds)

雌*emale-animal/plant*

mesu, me, SHI
female-animal, female plant

雌蜂 *queen bee* **mebachi**
雌花 *feminine flower* **mebana**
雌豚 *sow, female hog* **mebuta**
雌滝 *waterfalls smaller side* **medaki**
雌熊 *female bear* **meguma**
雌鶏 *hen* **mendori**
雌鳥 *hen* **mendori**
雌蘂 *pistil* **meshibe, shizui**
雌犬 *bitch (derogatory); female dog* **mesuinu**
雌猫 *female cat* **mesuneko**
雌馬 *female horse* **meuma**
雌牛 *female cattle* **meushi**
雌伏 *biding one's time* **shifuku**
雌性 *female* **shisei**
雌雄 *animal gender* **shiyū**
雌螺子 *female screw* **meneji**

Facing: 2.2. East ☞ (V)

女*emale, 350*
匹*[animal], 17*

雄*ourage, 775*

770-A

Glamour 欄ulletin, 潤mbellished for teens...

木 (wooden)

欄ulletin 欄olumn

RAN
bulletin, column, discourse

上欄	*previous column* **jōran**
高欄	*banister, handrail* **kōran**
空欄	*blank column* **kūran**
欄外	*margin* **rangai**
欄人	*Dutch person* **ranjin**
欄干	*railing, rail, balustrade* **rankan**
欄間	*transom, fanlight* **ranma**
備考欄	*reference column, bibliography* **bikōran**
文芸欄	*literary column* **bungeiran**
解答欄	*correct answers column* **kaitōran**
家庭欄	*family column* **kateiran**
経済欄	*finance column* **keizairan**
広告欄	*classified advertisement* **kōkokuran**
死亡欄	*obituary column, death notices* **shibōran**
書評欄	*book review column* **shōhyōran**
相談欄	*advice column* **sōdanran**
摘要欄	*explanatory notes column* **tekiyōran**
投稿欄	*contributor's column* **tōkōran**

FLIP: 7.0.b1. Right (stem)

投書欄	*contributor's column* **tōshoran**
通信欄	*personal column* **tsūshinran**
運動欄	*sports column* **undōran**

報*eport, 733*	載*ublish, 802*
告*nnounce, 266*	刊*ublication, 687*
宣*nnounce, 899*	読*eading, 260*
掲*ublish, 810*	公*ublic, 180*

潤*mbellish, 930*

770-B

Glamour 欄ulletin, 潤mbellished for teens...

水⇔氵 (water)

❶潤oisten ❷潤mbellish

uruo(su), uruo(u), uru(mu), JUN
moisten, humidity; embellish

FLIP: 7.0.a. Right (flat)

❶
潤滑	*lubrication, greasing* **junkatsu**
潤滑油	*lubricating oil* **junkatsuyu**
浸潤	*permeation, infiltration* **shinjun**
⇒肺浸潤	*lung infection* **haishinjun**
湿潤	*wet, damp, moist* **shitsujun**

❷
潤色	*literary embellishment* **junshoku**
潤飾	*embellishments* **junshoku**
豊潤	*abundance, plenty* **hōjun**
潤筆	*painting & writing* **junpitsu**
潤筆料	*writing-, painting fee* **junpitsuryō**
潤沢	*abundance, plentiful, bountiful* **juntaku**
利潤	*profit, gain* **rijun**

粧*dorn, 656*	態*ppearance, 322*
飾*ecorate, 664*	容*ppearance, 492*
形*hape, 951*	液*iquid, 508*
姿*ppearance, 609*	泌*eakage, 219*

欄*ulletin, 930*

771-A

湿*oisture* 顕*pparent in summer tents...*

水 ⇔ 氵 (water)

湿*oisture*　湿*umidity*

shime(ru), shime(su), SHITSU
moisture, humidity, damp

FLIP: 7.0.a. Right (flat)

湿っぽい	*damp, humid, wet, moist* **shimeppoi**		低湿	*low humidity* **teishitsu**
防湿	*moisture-proofing* **bōshitsu**		湿気る	*get stale* **shikeru**
陰湿	*damp & shady* **inshitsu**		乾湿計	*humidity meter* **kanshitsukei**
除湿	*dehumidification* **joshitsu**		加湿器	*humidifier* **kashitsuki**
除湿器	*dehumidifier* **joshitsuki**		温湿布	*hot compress* **onshippu**
乾湿	*dryness & moisture* **kanshitsu**		冷湿布	*cold compress* **reishippu**
寒湿	*cold & moisture* **kanshitsu**		湿り声	*tearful voice* **shimerigoe**
高湿	*high humidity* **kōshitsu**		湿り気	*dampness, moisture* **shimerike**
湿地	*swamp, marsh, bog* **shicchi**		湿電池	*wet battery cell* **shitsudenchi**
湿気	*humidity, moisture* **shikke**		湿式法	*wet process, ~treatment* **shitsushikihō**
湿布	*compress, poultice* **shippu**		耐湿性	*moisture resistance* **taishitsusei**
湿性	*wet (pleurisy)* **shissei**			
湿疹	*eczema* **shisshin**			
湿板	*wet plate (photography)* **shitsuban**			
湿田	*undrained paddy* **shitsuden**			
湿度	*humidity, moisture, dampness* **shitsudo**			
湿度計	*hygrometer* **shitsudokei**			
湿潤	*damp, moist, humid* **shitsujun**			
多湿	*high humidity* **tashitsu**			

潤*oisten, 930*	汽*team, 98*	
沼*wamp, 356*	蒸*team, 117*	
沢*wamp, 753*	粘*ticky, 223*	

泥*lending, 38*

771-B

湿*oisture* 顕*pparent in summer tents...*

頁 (large shell, page)

顕*bvious*　顕*pparent*

KEN
obvious, apparent, conspicuous, explicit, manifest

FLIP: 5.0.b. Left & Right

隠顕	*"now you see, now you do not..."* **inken**
顕著	*remarkable, stark, striking* **kencho**
顕現	*revelation, manifestation* **kengen**
顕示	*revelation, manifestation* **kenji**
顕官	*high official* **kenkan**
顕彰	*praise, exalting, extolling* **kenshō**
顕正	*spreading the truth* **kenshō**
顕職	*prominent-, lofty post* **kenshoku**
顕揚	*praise, extol* **kenyō**
顕要	*prominent, important* **kenyō**
顕在	*tangible, clear & present* **kenzai**
顕然	*manifest, evident, obvious* **kenzen**
貴顕	*eminent person* **kiken**
露顕	*discovery, revelation* **roken**
顕微鏡	*microscope* **kenbikyō**
顕宗天皇	*Emperor Kenzō (485-487)* **kenzō tennō**

明*lear, 22*	英*rilliance, 217*
朗*lear, 800*	澄*ake clear, 437*
昭*right, 529*	著*tark, 279*

題*ubject, 834*

772-A

湯ot-water under the 陽un 易imply causes 傷njury to some...

水⇔氵 (water)

湯ot-water　　湯ot-bath

yu, TŌ
hot-water, hot-bath

FLIP: 7.2.a. Right Top (flat)

湯ぶね *bathtub, bath* **yubune**
湯たんぽ *hot-water bottle* **yutanpo**
腰湯 *hip-size bathing* **koshiyu**
給湯 *hot water supply* **kyūtō**
熱湯 *boiling water* **nettō**
入湯 *hot bath, hot springs* **nyūtō**
重湯 *thin rice gruel* **omoyu**
白湯 *plain hot water* **sayu**
銭湯 *public bathhouse* **sentō**
湯治 *hot springs therapy* **tōji**
湯治場 *spa, hot springs* **tōjiba**
湯治客 *hot-springs client* **tōjikyaku**
産湯 *baby's first bath* **ubuyu**
薬湯 *medicinal-, herbal bathing* **yakutō**
湯葉 *dried tofu* **yuba**
湯殿 *bathroom* **yudono**
湯気 *steam, vapour* **yuge**
湯屋 *pubic bath* **yuya**
茶の湯 *tea ceremony* **chanoyu**

煮え湯 *boiling water* **nieyu**
差し湯 *adding hot water* **sashiyu**
埋め湯 *hot water cooled by adding water* **umeyu**
湯引く *parboil* **yubiku**
湯豆腐 *boiled bean curd* **yudōfu**
湯通し *put in hot water* **yudōshi**
湯加減 *temperature of the bath water* **yukagen**
湯飲み *teacup, cup* **yunomi**
湯冷め *chill after bathing* **yuzame**
湯沸かし *boiling material* **yuwakashi**
湯冷まし *chilled boiled water* **yuzamashi**

煮 *oiling, 278*		温 *ot temperature, 622*
沸 *oiling, 538*		暑 *ot weather, 615*

772-B

湯ot-water under the 陽un 易imply causes 傷njury to some...

阝⇔阜 (village=left)

❶陽un　　❷陽ositive

YŌ
Sun; positive

FLIP: 7.2.a. Right Top (flat)

❶陽炎 *heat haze* **kagerō, yōen**
洛陽 *sunset* **rakuyō**
斜陽 *setting sun* **shayō**
斜陽族 *waning upper-class* **shayōzoku**
斜陽産業 *declining industries* **shayō sangyō**
太陽 *the sun* **taiyō**
太陽系 *solar system* **taiyōkei**
陽光 *sunlight, sunshine* **yōkō**
陽暦 *solar calendar* **yōreki**
残陽 *setting sun* **zanyō**
紫陽花 *hydrangea* **ajisai**
陽当たり *sunlight exposure* **hiatari**

❷陽イオン *positive ion* **yōion**
艶陽 *balmy late spring* **enyō**
陰陽 *ying & yang (positive & negative)* **inyō**
陽物 *male genital, penis* **yōbutsu**
陽電気 *positive electricity* **yōdenki**
陽画 *positive picture* **yōga**

陽報 *reward for hidden philanthrophy* **yōhō**
陽気 *weather, cheerful* **yōki**
陽極 *anode, positive pole* **yōkyoku**
陽性 *cheerful, extrovert, lively* **yōsei**
陽性反応 *positive reaction* **yōsei hannō**
陽子 *proton* **yōshi**
陽春 *springtime* **yōshun**
陽転 *changing to positive charge* **yōten**

日 *un, 14*	
肯 *ffirmative, 616*	

772-C

湯ot-water under the 陽un 易mply causes 傷njury to some...

日 (sunlight, daytime)

易imple   易asy

yasa(shii), EKI, I
simple, easy, basic, exchange

FLIP: 3.0.a. Top (flat)

安易 *easy-going, leisure* **an'i**
便易 *easy & convenient* **ben'i**
貿易 *trade* **bōeki**
⇒密貿易 *smuggling* **mitsubōeki**
貿易黒字 *trade surplus* **bōeki kuroji**
貿易収支 *balance of trade* **bōeki shūshi**
貿易不均衡 *trade imbalance* **bōeki fukinkō**
易断 *fortune telling* **ekidan**
易者 *fortune teller* **ekisha**
不易 *immutable, irreducible* **fueki**
平易 *plainness & simplicity* **heii**
辟易 *shrink from, withdraw* **hekieki**
改易 *attainder* **kaieki**
簡易 *plain, simplified* **kan'i**
簡易裁判所 *summary court* **kan'i saibansho**
軽易 *light & simple* **keii**
交易 *trade, trading* **kōeki**
難易 *ease-or-difficulty* **nan'i**
易易 *simple & easy* **yasuyasu, ii**

容易 *ease, easy, simple* **yōi**
見易い *easy to see, visible* **miyasui**
燃え易い *flammable* **moeyasui**
生易しい *simple & easy* **namayasashii**
飲み易い *easy to drink* **nomiyasui**
食べ易い *easy to eat* **tabeyasui**
使い易い *easy to use* **tsukaiyasui**
割れ易い *breakable, fragile* **wareyasui**
読み易い *easy to read, ~understand* **yomiyasui**
曲げ易い *easy to bend, flexible* **mageyasui**
分かり易い *easy to understand* **wakariyasui**

簡imple, 285	便onvenience, 480
素imple, 578	宜onvenience, 500
朴imple, 707	素lement, 578

鳥irds, 125

772-D

湯ot-water under the 陽un 易mply causes 傷njury to some...

人⇔亻 (person)

傷njury   傷ruise

kizu, ita(mu), ita(meru), SHŌ
injury, bruise, hurting, laceration, lesion, wound, harm

FLIP: 8.0.a. Inner (flat)

哀傷 *grief, sorrow, heartbreak* **aishō**
爆傷 *explosion injury, blast wound* **bakushō**
中傷 *slander, libel, defamation* **chūshō**
古傷 *old wound, past misdeed* **furukizu**
負傷 *injury, hurt, wound, harm* **fushō**
外傷 *external injury, bruise* **gaishō**
重傷 *deep-, severe wound* **jūshō**
感傷 *sentiments* **kanshō**
傷跡 *scar, bruise* **kizuato**
傷口 *wound, bruise* **kizuguchi**
傷薬 *ointment* **kizugusuri**
傷手 *heavy blow, hard blow* **kizute**
公傷 *injury in the line of duty* **kōshō**
生傷 *fresh wound* **namakizu**
裂傷 *lacerating-, bleeding wound* **resshō**
殺傷 *bloodshed, bloodletting* **sasshō**
戦傷 *war wounds* **senshō**
傷害 *injury, disability, handicapped* **shōgai**
傷心 *grief, sorrow, heartbreak* **shōshin**

愁傷 *painful grief, deep sorrows* **shūshō**
損傷 *damage, injury* **sonshō**
手傷 *injury, wound* **tekizu**
凍傷 *frostbite, chilblain* **tōshō**
火傷 *burns, burn wounds* **yakedo**
致命傷 *fatal-, mortal wound* **chimeishō**
噛み傷 *bitten wound* **kamikizu**
傷病兵 *invalid soldiers* **shōbyōhei**
擦り傷 *scratch* **surikizu**
突き傷 *knife-, stabbing wound* **tsukikizu**
打ち傷 *bruise, wounds* **uchikizu**

害njury, 904	損njury, 410
障njury, 325	痛njury, 60

偽raud, 509

773-A

薫*ragrant* 勲*xploits don't* 衝*ollide in Detroit...*

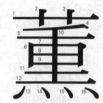

-艹- (grass)

薫*ragrance* 薫*almy*

kao(ru), KUN

fragrance, balmy, scent, sweet smell

FLIP: 2.0.b. Sort Of (stem)

薫り *smell sweet, fragrant* **kaori**
薫煙 *fragrant smoke* **kun'en**
薫育 *personal sway, moral influence* **kun'iku**
薫化 *influence of virtues* **kunka**
薫香 *incense, fragrance* **kunkō**
薫風 *balmy breeze* **kunpū**
薫製 *smoke food-processing* **kunsei**
薫製品 *smoked food* **kunseihin**
薫染 *good influence* **kunsen**
薫陶 *education, discipline* **kuntō**
余薫 *lingering fragrance* **yokun**

鼻*ose, 169*	芳*ragrance, 533*
臭*mell, 586*	花*lower, 191*
香*ragrance, 895*	華*lower, 40*

薦*ecommend, 68*

773-B

薫*ragrant* 勲*xploits don't* 衝*ollide in Detroit...*

力 (strength, force)

勲*xploits* 勲*eritorious*

isao, KUN

exploits, meritorious, feat

Facing: 4.0. 👈 👉 Apart

武勲 *distinguished military service* **bukun**
元勲 *elderly statesman, grand old man* **genkun**
偉勲 *brilliant exploits, outstanding feats* **ikun**
位勲 *rank & order merit* **ikun**
叙勲 *decoration, order, medal* **jokun**
功勲 *meritorious service* **kōkun**
勲位 *Order of Merit* **kun'i**
大勲位 *Grand Order of Chrysanthemum* **daikun'i**
勲記 *decoration, diploma* **kunki**
勲功 *great achievement* **kunkō**
勲労 *meritorious deed* **kunrō**
勲爵 *order of merit* **kunshaku**
勲章 *decoration, order, medal* **kunshō**
⇒文化勲章 *cultural medal* **bunka kunshō**
勲等 *order of merit* **kuntō**
殊勲 *distinguished service* **shukun**
帯勲 *wearing one's medals* **taikun**
有勲者 *award-, medal recipient* **yūkunsha**

偉*minent, 797*	誉*onour, 252*
彰*itation, 325*	栄*lory, 580*
遂*chieve, 479*	壮*agnificent, 367*
成*chieve, 244*	偉*agnificent, 797*

勲*ovement, 422*

773-C

薫*ragrant* 勲*xploits don't* 衝*ollide in Detroit...*

衝*ollision*   衝*rash*

行 (going)

FLIP: 8.0.a. Inner (flat)

SHŌ
collision, crash, smash up

緩衝 *buffer, cushion, bumper* **kanshō**
緩衝液 *buffer solution* **kanshōeki**
緩衝器 *shock absorber, bumper* **kanshōki**
緩衝国 *buffer nation* **kanshōkoku**
緩衝地帯 *buffer-, neutral zone* **kanshō chitai**
折衝 *negotiation, discussion* **sesshō**
衝動 *impulse, urge* **shōdō**
衝動的 *impulsive, spur-of-the-moment* **shōdōteki**
衝動買い *impulse buying* **shōdōgai**
衝撃 *shock, impact* **shōgeki**
衝撃波 *shock wave* **shōgekiha**
衝撃音 *impact noise* **shōgekion**
衝撃的 *shocking, revulsion* **shōgekiteki**
衝心 *heart failure* **shōshin**
衝天 *high spirits, zestful, animated* **shōten**
⇒意気衝天 *high spirits, zestful* **ikishōten**
衝突 *collision, conflict* **shōtotsu**
⇒正面衝突 *head-to-head crash* **shōmen shōtotsu**

⇒玉突き衝突 *multiple collision* **tamatsuki shōtotsu**
衝立 *screen* **tsuitate**
要衝 *important-, strategic point* **yōshō**
息衝く *breathe, inhale* **ikizuku**
雲衝く *towering* **kumotsuku**

害*njury,* 904	痛*njury,* 60
傷*njury,* 933	壊*estroy,* 847
障*njury,* 325	破*estroy,* 715
損*njury,* 410	爆*xplosion,* 561

衡*alance,* 110

774-A

鬼*evils* 卑*espise* 魂*pirits that are nice...*

鬼*evil*   鬼*emon*

鬼 (spirits)

Facing: 2.2. East ☞ (V)

oni, KI
devil, demon, Satan

鬼ごっこ *blind man's bluff game* **onigokko**
悪鬼 *devil, demon* **akki**
餓鬼 *mischievous child, brat* **gaki**
邪気 *devil, demon* **jaki**
剣鬼 *sword-bearing devil* **kenki**
鬼畜 *savage, brutal* **kichiku**
鬼女 *devil woman, witch* **kijo**
鬼気 *ghastly, ghostly, ghoulish* **kiki**
鬼気迫る *ghastly, bloodcurdling* **kikisemaru**
鬼面 *devil's face* **kimen**
鬼門 *ominous direction* **kimon**
鬼才 *genius, intelligent* **kisai**
鬼籍 *died, joining the dead* **kiseki**
鬼神 *evil gods, devils* **kishin, onigami**
鬼歯 *protruding teeth* **oniba**
鬼婆 *hag, witch* **onibaba**
鬼火 *will-o-the-wisp, jack-o-lantern* **onibi**
鬼瓦 *ridgepole endtile* **onigawara**
鬼子 *child born with teeth* **onigo**

鬼課長 *abusive-, cruel boss* **onikachō**
鬼女 *devil woman* **onionna**
債鬼 *loan shark, cruel lender* **saiki**
吸血鬼 *blood-sucker* **kyūketsuki**
鬼刑事 *crack detective* **onikeiji**
鬼武者 *daredevil warrior* **onimusha**
鬼百合 *tiger lily* **oniyuri**
殺人鬼 *murderous fiend* **satsujinki**
天の邪鬼 *pervert, molester* **ama no jaku**
神出鬼没 *elusive, appearing & disappearing*
　　shinshutsu kibotsu
疑心暗鬼 *suspicion & fear* **gishin anki**

悪*vil,* 389	魔*evil,* 332	懲*unishment,* 63
凶*vil,* 80	罪*riminal,* 289	刑*unishment,* 536
邪*vil,* 58	犯*riminal,* 640	罰*unishment,* 759

卑*espise,* 936

774-B

鬼*evils* 卑*espise* 魂*pirits that are nice...*

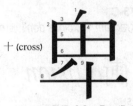

卑*espise*　　卑*ean*

十 (cross)

FLIP: 3.0.a. Top (flat)
FLIP: 2.0.b. Sort Of (stem)

iya(shimeru), iya(shimu), iya(shii), HI
despise, mean, detest

卑しん坊 *greedly, avaricious, glutton* **iyashinbō**
卑し笑い *mean smirk, macabre smile* **iyashiiwarai**
卑しい根性 *mean spirit* **iyashii konjō**
卑しい身形 *shabby looks* **iyashii minari**
下卑 *vulgar, gross* **gebi**
卑下 *humility, modesty* **hige**
卑語 *vulgarism, foul mouth* **higo**
卑見 *"in my humble opinion..."* **hiken**
卑近 *familiar, intimate* **hikin**
卑屈 *obsequious, base, servile* **hikutsu**
卑怯 *mean, cowardly* **hikyō**
卑怯者 *coward, sissy* **hikyōmono**
卑劣 *mean, dirty, sneak* **hiretsu**
卑劣漢 *sneak, mean fellow* **hiretsukan**
卑陋 *despicable, gross, vulgar* **hirō**
卑賤 *low position, low status* **hisen**
卑湿 *low & damp* **hishitsu**
卑小 *frivolous, petty, flimsy* **hishō**
卑称 *declining fame* **hishō**

卑猥 *indecent, obscene* **hiwai**
卑属 *direct descendant* **hizoku**
卑俗 *vulgarity, gross, lewd* **hizoku**
尊卑 *upper & lower classes* **sonpi**
野卑 *crude, coarse, vulgar* **yahi**
卑金属 *base metals* **hikinzoku**
男尊女卑 *masculine priority* **danson jōhi**
女尊男卑 *feminine priority* **joson danpi**
官尊民卑 *government-above-the-people priority*
　　kanson minpi

憎*nimosity, 837*	憤*nrage, 848*
嫌*espise, 805*	鬼*evil, 935*
侮*espise, 711*	魔*evil, 332*

鬼*evil, 935*

774-C

鬼*evils* 卑*espise* 魂*pirits that are nice...*

魂*pirit*　　魂*oul*

鬼 (spirits)

FLIP: 7.2.a. Right Top (flat)
Facing: 2.2. East ☞ (V)

tamashii, KON
spirit, soul, ghost, supernatural

亡魂 *departed soul* **bōkon**
鎮魂 *repose of souls* **chinkon**
鎮魂曲 *requiem, funeral song* **chinkonkyoku**
鎮魂祭 *services for the dead* **chinkonsai**
英魂 *departed spirit* **eikon**
人魂 *spirit of the dead, dead spirits* **hitodama**
入魂 *placing one's heart & soul* **jikkon, nyūkon**
魂魄 *soul, spirit, ghost* **konpaku**
魂胆 *ulterior design, ~scheme* **kontan**
霊魂 *soul, spirit, ghost* **reikon**
霊魂不滅 *soul immortality* **reikon fumetsu**
精魂 *heart & soul* **seikon**
詩魂 *poetic spirit* **shikon**
心魂 *heart & soul* **shinkon**
商魂 *shrewd merchant* **shōkon**
招魂 *calling dead spirits* **shōkon**
闘魂 *fighting spirit* **tōkon**
面魂 *fierce look, mean-looking* **tsuradamashii**
忠魂碑 *monument to the dead* **chūkonhi**

肝っ魂 *pluck, courage, gal* **kimottama**
負け魂 *never give-up spirit* **maketamashii**
負け死魂 *never-say-die spirit* **makejidamashii**
魂消る *be baffled, be astonished* **tamageru**
魂迎え *welcoming ancestral spirits* **tamamukae**
魂送り *sending off a dead spirit* **tamaokuri**
大和魂 *Japanese fighting spirit* **yamato damashii**

霊*oul, 444*	天*eaven, 83*
死*eath, 513*	聖*ivine, 617*
逝*eath, 54*	神*ivine, 712*
亡*eath, 72*	久*ternal, 379*

塊*ump, 937*

775-A
Forgotten 碑ombstones, 塊umps of the Unknown...

石 (stone)

碑*ombstone*　碑*ravesite*

ishibumi, HI
tombstone, gravesite, cemetery, crypt, sepulchre

FLIP: 7.2.a. Right Top (flat)
Facing: 3.0. ☞☜ Across

墓碑	gravestone, tombstone **bohi**
墓碑銘	tombstone epitaph **bohimei**
碑文	epitaph, inscription **hibun**
碑銘	epitaph, inscription **himei**
碑石	stone monument, tombstone **hiseki**
歌碑	song-inscribed monument **kahi**
建碑	erection of a stone monument **kenpi**
口碑	oral tradition, ~history **kōhi**
句碑	Haiku-inscribed monument **kuhi**
石碑	stone monument, tombstone **sekihi**
詩碑	poem-inscribed monument **shihi**
忠魂碑	war memorial monument **chūkonhi**
慰霊碑	cenotaph, memorial tower **ireihi**
記念碑	memorial, monument **kinenhi**

墓*ravesite, 602*	逝*eath, 54*
陵*ausoleum, 140*	亡*eath, 72*
葬*urial, 513*	埋*ury, 319*
死*eath, 513*	憶*emory, 339*

魂*pirit, 936*

775-B
Forgotten 碑ombstones, 塊umps of the Unknown...

土 (ground, soil)

塊*ump*　塊*luster*

katamari, KAI
lump, cluster, bump

FLIP: 7.2.a. Right Top (flat)
Facing: 2.2. East ☞ (V)

地塊	block, landmass **chikai**
鋳塊	ingot **chūkai**
団塊	lump, mass, clod **dankai**
鉛塊	lead ingot **enkai**
銀塊	silver nuggets **ginkai**
凝塊	a clot **gyōkai**
氷塊	ice blocks **hyōkai**
一塊	lump **ikkai**
塊土	clod, lump of earth **kaido**
塊状	monstrous, enormous **kaijō**
塊茎	tuber **kaikei**
塊根	tuberous root **kaikon**
塊鉱	lump ore **kaikō**
血塊	blood clot **kekkai**
金塊	gold bullion, ~nugget **kinkai**
肉塊	lump of flesh **nikkai**
山塊	isolated mountains **sankai**
石塊	block of stone **sekkai**
集塊	mass, cluster **shūkai**

大塊	large chunk **taikai**
土塊	clod, lump of earth **tsuchikure, dokai**
一塊り	lump **hitokatamari**
欲の塊	lump of greed **yoku no katamari**

房*luster, 676*	凝*arden, 57*
緊*ard, 599*	硬*ardness, 402*
固*ard, 491*	凸*rotrude, 23*

魂*pirit, 936*

776-A

険*teep* 倹*rugality to the core, a* 剣*word* 検*nspector...*

β ⇔ 阜 (village=left)

険*teep* 険*ugged*

kewa(shii), KEN
  steep, rugged, danger

FLIP: 7.0.b2. Right (stem)

冒険 *adventure, risk* **bōken**
冒険家 *adventurer* **bōkenka**
冒険心 *spirit of adventure* **bōkenshin**
保険 *insurance* **hoken**
⇒生命保険 *life insurance* **seimei hoken**
⇒失業保険 *unemployment insurance*
   shitsugyō hoken
保険料 *insurance premium* **hokenryō**
陰険 *dirty, cunning, deceptive; dark person* **inken**
邪険 *cool-hearted* **jaken**
険悪 *bad mood* **ken'aku**
険難 *steep, rugged* **kennan**
険路 *steep pass* **kenro**
険峻 *steep* **kenshun**
険阻 *steep, rugged* **kenso**
険相 *uncanny-, sinister look* **kensō**
危害 *harm, injury* **kigai**
危険 *danger, risk, hazard, peril* **kiken**
危険性 *danger, risk, hazard, peril* **kikensei**

探険 *adventure, expedition* **tanken**
天険 *natural stronghold* **tenken**

著*tark, 279*	底*epth, 860*
危*anger, 354*	奥*nterior, 903*
敢*aring, 449*	深*eep, 788*
挑*hallenge, 214*	暗*ark, 315*

除*xclude, 501*

776-B

険*teep* 倹*rugality to the core, a* 剣*word* 検*nspector...*

人 ⇔ 亻 (person)

倹*odest* 倹*rugal*

KEN
  modesty, frugal, austere, demureness, diffidence, reticence

FLIP: 7.0.b2. Right (stem)

倹吝 *miser, stinginess* **kenrin**
倹素 *thrift, frugality, simple lifestyle* **kenso**
倹約 *thrift, frugality, saving money* **kenyaku**
倹約家 *thrifty, frugal, miser, niggard* **kenyakuka**
勤倹 *diligence, frugality, conserving* **kinken**
恭倹 *modest & respectful* **kyōken**
節倹 *frugality, thrift, economizing* **sekken**

慎*odest, 831*
謙*odesty, 805*
申*peak humble, 89*

剣*word, 939*

776-C

険*teep* 倹*rugality to the core, a* 剣*word* 検*nspector...*

刀⇔刂 (blade, cutting)

剣*word*　剣*lade*

tsurugi, KEN
sword, blade

FLIP: 6.0.b. Left (stem)

抜剣	*drawn sword*	**bakken**
木剣	*wooden sword*	**bokken**
撃剣	*fencing*	**gekken**
銃剣	*bayonet*	**jūken**
懐剣	*dagger*	**kaiken**
剣舞	*sword dance*	**kenbu**
剣球	*cup & ball game*	**kendama**
剣道	*Japanese fencing*	**kendō**
剣劇	*sword play*	**kengeki**
剣豪	*master swordsman*	**kengō**
剣術	*fencing, swordsmanship*	**kenjutsu**
剣客	*swordsman*	**kenkyaku**
剣幕	*threatening look*	**kenmaku**
剣呑	*dangerous, hazardous, perilous*	**kennon**
剣法	*art of fencing*	**kenpō**
剣士	*swordsman*	**kenshi**
剣突	*scolding, censure*	**kentsuku**
剣山	*Ikebana needle plate*	**kenzan**
霊剣	*magical sword*	**reiken**

真剣	*serious, determined*	**shinken**
手裏剣	*throwing a knife*	**shuriken**
帯剣	*sabre, sword*	**taiken**
短剣	*dagger, short sword*	**tanken**
刀剣	*sabre, sword*	**tōken**

刃*word, 75*	矛*alberd, 568*
刀*lade, 353*	盾*hield, 407*
武*arrior, 100*	侍*wordsman, 249*
戦*ighting, 517*	闘*ombat, 946*

倹*rugal, 938*

776-D

険*teep* 倹*rugality to the core, a* 剣*word* 検*nspector...*

木 (wooden)

検*nspection*　検*heck*

KEN
inspection, check, examine

FLIP: 7.0.b2. Right (stem)

巡検	*inspection rounds*	**junken**
検案	*autopsy, dissection*	**ken'an**
検便	*stool examination*	**kenben**
検分	*examine, inspect, check*	**kenbun**
検疫	*quarantine inspection*	**ken'eki**
検閲	*censorship, inspection*	**ken'etsu**
検眼	*eye examination, optic test*	**kengan**
検印	*seal of approval, imprimatur*	**ken'in**
検事	*public prosecutor*	**kenji**
検挙	*arrest, apprehend, roundup*	**kenkyo**
検挙者	*detainee, arrested person*	**kenkyosha**
検認	*probate, inspector*	**kennin**
検温	*temperature reading*	**ken'on**
検温器	*thermometer*	**ken'onki**
検査	*inspection, examination*	**kensa**
⇒血液検査	*blood test*	**ketsueki kensa**
検索	*search, reference*	**kensaku**
検察	*criminal investigation*	**kensatsu**
検車	*motor inspection*	**kensha**

検死	*autopsy, post-mortem*	**kenshi**
検視	*investigate a crime scene*	**kenshi**
検診	*medical examination*	**kenshin**
検証	*verification, confirmation*	**kenshō**
検束	*arrest, custody, confinement*	**kensoku**
検体	*specimen, sample*	**kentai**
検討	*re-examination, review*	**kentō**
車検	*vehicle-safety inspection*	**shaken**
送検	*bring to trial, take to court*	**sōken**
探検	*exploration, expedition*	**tanken**
点検	*inspection, checking*	**tenken**

察*nspection, 328*	査*nspection, 624*
審*nspection, 339*	閲*nspection, 942*
調*nspection, 280*	確*onfirm, 804*

険*teep, 938*

777-A

得dvantage to 待ait, fish to bait...

イ (stroll)

待*aiting*   待*n hold*

ma(tsu), TAI
waiting, on hold

FLIP: 7.2.a. Right Top (flat)

虐待	ill-treatment, cruelty, barbarity **gyakutai**
歓待	hospitality, welcome, warmth **kantai**
期待	expectation, hopeful **kitai**
応対	receiving visitors, waiting for guests **ōtai**
接待	client entertainment, wine & dine **settai**
招待	invite, entreat **shōtai**
待望	look forward to **taibō**
待遇	treatment, reception **taigū**
待避	allow to pass, forgo, let go **taihi**
待機	standing by, watch & wait **taiki**
待命	awaiting orders **taimei**
優待	warm welcome, cordial reception **yūtai**
心待ち	anticipation, expectation **kokoromachi**
辻待ち	"waiting to be hired..." (rickshaw) **tsujimachi**
人待ち顔	expecting looks **hitomachigao**
招待状	invitation letter, invitation card **shōtaijō**
待ち針	marking pin **machibari**
待ち明かす	wait until dawn **machiakasu**
待ち合わせ	waiting to meet **machiawase**

待ちぼうけ	waiting in vain **machibōke**
待ち伏せ	ambush, suddenly appear **machibuse**
待ち遠しい	look forward to **machidooshii**
待ち時間	waiting time **machijikan**
待ち構える	anticipate **machikamaeru**
待ち兼ねる	eagerly wait for **machikaneru**
待ち焦がれる	long for, yearn for **machikogareru**
待ち望む	look forward to **machinozomu**
待ち受ける	wait **machiukeru**
待ち侘びる	getting tired waiting **machiwabiru**
キャンセル待ち	"on the waiting list..." **kyanseru machi**

止 *top*, 192	留 *taying*, 128
停 *top*, 393	滞 *taying*, 557

持*olding*, 249

777-B

得dvantage to 待ait, fish to bait...

イ (stroll)

得*dvantage*   得*cquire*

e(ru), u(ru), TOKU
advantage, acquire, benefit, gains, profit, plus

FLIP: 7.2.a. Right Top (flat)

得体	strange, suspicious-looking **etai**
得手	forte, specialty, expertise **ete**
一得	an advantage, a plus factor **ittoku**
獲得	acquisition, obtaining, procurement **kakutoku**
獲得物	purchase, acquisition **kakutokubutsu**
感得	realizing, comprehending, recognizing **kantoku**
既得	vested, acquired **kitoku**
納得	consent, assent, approval **nattoku**
利得	profit, gain, process **ritoku**
両得	double gain **ryōtoku**
説得	persuasion, convincing **settoku**
所得	income, salary, earning **shotoku**
習得	learning, master **shūtoku**
拾得	finding lost items **shūtoku**
損得	profit & loss, interest **sontoku**
得意	one's forte, one's strength **tokui**
得意顔	triumphant look, winning smile **tokuigao**
得意先	customer, client **tokuisaki**
得策	best way, wise way **tokusaku**

得心	satisfaction, convincing **tokushin**
得失	pros & cons, merits & demerits **tokushitsu**
得点	score, scoring **tokuten**
得票	number of votes **tokūhyō**
得票数	number of votes polled **tokūhyōsū**
役得	perquisite **yakutoku**
欲得	altruistic designs, charitable deeds **yokutoku**
余得	extra benefit, additional gain **yotoku**
有り得る	"could be, possible..." **arieru**
勝ち得る	win, gain, earn **kachieru**
買い得	bargain, good buy **kaidoku**

益 *rofit*, 622	便 *onvenience*, 480
獲 *cquire*, 829	昇 *scend*, 299
進 *dvance*, 51	登 *scend*, 437
宜 *onvenience*, 500	富 *ortune*, 333

復*ecovery*, 442

778-A

Some 脱emove revenue before a 税ax 閲eview...

肉⇔月 (flesh, body part)

脱*emove*　　脱*trip-off*　　脱

nu(gu), nu(gasu), DATSU
remove, strip-off, take off, escape from

FLIP: 7.0.b2. Right (stem)

脱サラ *employee-turned-entrepreneur* **datsusara**
超脱 *transcendence* **chōdatsu**
脱腸 *hernia* **dacchō**
脱会 *withdrawal, resignation* **dakkai**
脱稿 *manuscript completion* **dakkō**
脱穀 *threshing out* **dakkoku**
脱却 *breakaway, separation* **dakkyaku**
脱臼 *dislocation* **dakkyū**
脱法 *law evasion* **dappō**
脱線 *derailment; deviation, dislocation* **dassen**
脱脂 *fat removal* **dasshi**
脱色 *decolourisation, bleaching* **dasshoku**
脱臭 *deodorization* **dasshū**
脱疽 *gangrene, necrosis* **dasso**
脱走 *escape, flight, flee* **dassō**
脱水 *dehydration* **dassui**
脱帽 *taking off one's hat* **datsubō**
脱営 *desertion, abandonment* **datsuei**
脱獄 *jailbreak, prison escape* **datsugoku**

脱衣 *undressing, stripping* **datsui**
脱毛 *balding, loss of hair* **datsumō**
脱力 *physical exhaustion* **datsuryoku**
脱税 *tax evasion, tax cheats* **datsuzei**
脱俗 *rising from worldly desires* **datsuzoku**
脱党 *quitting one's political party* **dattō**
逸脱 *deviation, breakaway* **itsudatsu**
離脱 *breakaway, separation* **ridatsu**
肌脱ぎ *striping to the waist, half-naked* **hadanugi**
肩脱ぎ *baring of shoulders* **katanugi**
虚脱感 *despondency, desperation* **kyodatsukan**

外*emove, 188*	廃*bolish, 368*
絶*radicate, 403*	抹*ross-out, 13*
消*elete, 265*	捨*hrow-away, 388*

税*axes, 941*

778-B

Some 脱emove revenue before a 税ax 閲eview...

禾 (tree branch)

税*ax*　　税*ariff*　　税*evy*　　税

ZEI
tax, tariff, levy

FLIP: 7.0.b2. Right (stem)

地税 *land tax* **chizei**
徴税 *tax collection* **chōzei**
脱税 *tax evasion, tax cheats* **datsuzei**
減税 *tax cut, tax decrease* **genzei**
印税 *book-, author's royalties* **inzei**
課税 *taxation, levy* **kazei**
血税 *taxpayer's money, public money* **ketsuzei**
酷税 *heavy-, excessive taxation* **kokuzei**
免税 *tax exemption* **menzei**
無税 *tax-free, tax-exemption* **muzei**
納税 *tax payment, ~settlement* **nōzei**
租税 *tax imposition, taxation* **sozei**
郵税 *postal fees, mailing charges* **yūzei**
有税 *taxable, dutiable* **yūzei**
税額 *tax amount, due tax* **zeigaku**
税源 *tax source, ~revenue* **zeigen**
税関 *customs office* **zeikan**
税金 *tax, duty, levy* **zeikin**
税目 *tax items* **zeimoku**

税率 *tax rate, tariff rate* **zeiritsu**
税制 *taxation, tax system* **zeisei**
増税 *tax increase, take hike* **zōzei**
印紙税 *duty stamp* **inshizei**
事業税 *business tax* **jigyōzei**
戻し税 *tax refund* **modoshizei**
輸出税 *export duties* **yushutsuzei**
財産税 *property tax, estate tax* **zaisanzei**
税込み *tax-included in the price* **zeikomi**
税務署 *national tax agency* **zeimusho**
税理士 *licensed tax accountant* **zeirishi**

賦*evy, 160*	財*reasury, 186*
金*oney, 25*	官*ublic official, 105*
庁*ubic office, 633*	納*ayment, 296*

程*egree, 144*

778-C

Some 脱emove revenue before a 税ax 閲eview...

門 (gate, entrance)

閲eview   閲nspection

ETSU
review, inspection, check, auditing, scrutiny, inquest, probe

FLIP: 1.0.b. Whole (stem)

閲兵 *troop inspection, parade review* **eppei**
閲読 *reading, perusal, going thru* **etsudoku**
閲覧 *reading, perusal, going thru* **etsuran**
閲覧室 *reading room* **etsuranshitsu**
閲歴 *one's career, personal history* **etsureki**
巡閲 *inspection tour* **jun'etsu**
観閲 *parade inspection* **kan'etsu**
検閲 *censorship, inspection* **ken'etsu**
検閲官 *public inspector, ~censor* **ken'etsukan**
校閲 *revision, editing* **kōetsu**
内閲 *internal-, private inspection* **naietsu**
査閲 *inspection, examination* **saetsu**

察nspection, 328	検nspection, 939
審nspection, 339	査nspection, 624
調nspection, 280	確onfirm, 804

問uestion, 283

779-A

Too 悦leasant 説xplanations carry 鋭harp implications...

心⇔忄⇔ 小 (feelings)

悦leasant   悦oyful

ETSU
pleasant, joyful, delight, heartening

FLIP: 7.0.b2. Right (stem)

悦服 *voluntary submission* **eppuku**
悦楽 *pleasure, delight, gaiety* **etsuraku**
法悦 *religious exultation* **hōetsu**
喜悦 *joy, delight* **kietsu**
恐悦 *joy, delight* **kyōetsu**
満悦 *contentment & pleasure* **man'etsu**
愉悦 *joy, pleasure* **yuetsu**
悦に入る *be pleased with* **etsu(ni)iru**

楽leasure, 447	愉leasure, 922
快leasant, 699	喫njoy, 900
歓leasure, 667	享njoy, 398
娯leasure, 453	遊njoy, 650

税axes, 941

779-B

Too 悦*leasant* 説*xplanations carry* 鋭*harp implications...*

説*xplain*   説*heory*

言 (speaking)

to(ku), SETSU, ZEI
explanation, theory, description

FLIP: 5.0.b. Left & Right

珍説 *strange-, odd explanation* **chinsetsu**
伝説 *legend, folklore* **densetsu**
演説 *speech, lecture, oration* **enzetsu**
概説 *summary, outline* **gaisetsu**
学説 *theory, postulate, doctrine* **gakusetsu**
言説 *remarks, statement* **gensetsu**
愚説 *silly opinion* **gusetsu**
変説 *change-of-heart* **hensetsu**
邪説 *heretical doctrine* **jasetsu**
序説 *introduction, preface, foreword* **josetsu**
解説 *emphasizing, stressing* **kaisetsu**
仮説 *hypothesis, premise* **kasetsu**
虚説 *baseless opinion* **kyosetsu**
憶説 *conjecture, inference* **okusetsu**
論説 *editorial, comment* **ronsetsu**
略説 *outline, framework, plan* **ryakusetsu**
流説 *popular theory* **ryūsetsu**
説教 *sermon, preaching, scolding* **sekkyō**
説明 *explanation, exposition, clarification* **setsumei**

説問 *question, problem* **setsumon**
説話 *narration, old tale, legend* **setsuwa**
説得 *persuasion, convincing* **settoku**
社説 *newspaper editorial* **shasetsu**
新説 *new theory, ~doctrine* **shinsetsu**
諸説 *various views* **shosetsu**
小説 *novel, short story* **shōsetsu**
詳説 *detailed explanation* **shōsetsu**
総説 *general remarks* **sōsetsu**
遊説 *election-, campaign speech* **yūzei**
俗説 *common saying, popular belief* **zokusetsu**

釈*xplanation, 752*   記*ecord, 728*
叙*arrate, 648*   録*ecord, 841*
紀*arration, 727*   解*omprehend, 400*

税*axes, 941*

779-C

Too 悦*leasant* 説*xplanations carry* 鋭*harp implications...*

鋭*harp*   鋭*lunt*

金 (metal)

surudo(i), EI
sharp, blunt, razor-like

FLIP: 5.0.b. Left & Right

鋭敏 *sharp, keen* **eibin**
鋭兵 *picked troop, elite soldiers* **eihei**
鋭鋒 *brunt, butt of* **eihō**
鋭意 *wholehearted, zeal, zest* **eii**
鋭角 *acute angle* **eikaku**
鋭気 *vigour, energy, spirit* **eiki**
鋭利 *sharp, keen* **eiri**
気鋭 *energetic, spirited, lively* **kiei**
精鋭 *chosen, pick* **seiei**
先鋭 *sharp, radical* **sen'ei**
尖鋭 *acute; radical* **sen'ei**
鮮鋭 *clear, sharp* **sen'ei**
新鋭 *newly-selected* **shin'ei**
新鋭部隊 *newly-selected troops* **shin'ei butai**
尖鋭化 *radicalisation* **sen'eika**
尖鋭分子 *radical elements* **sen'ei bunshi**

削*harpen, 118*   侍*wordsman, 249*
鈍*luggish, 199*   切*utting, 352*
刃*word, 75*   刈*utting, 687*
剣*word, 939*

税*axes, 941*

780-A

様anner of 911 遅elay, 詳etails must convey...

木 (wooden)

❶様anner ❷様[honorific]

sama, YŌ
manner, mode, style; [honorific]

FLIP: 5.0.b. Left & Right

❶一様 *uniform, equal, same* **ichiyō**
今様 *up-to-date, current* **imayō**
異様 *queer, strange, odd* **iyō**
各様 *diverse, so many ways* **kakuyō**
唐様 *Chinese-style* **karayō**
文様 *pattern* **monyō**
模様 *design, pattern, model* **moyō**
⇒唐草模様 *arabesque design* **karakusa moyō**
⇒染め模様 *dyeing pattern* **somemoyō**
⇒渦巻模様 *scrollwork* **uzumaki moyō**
両様 *both ways* **ryōyō**
様々 *various, diverse* **samazama**
多様 *various, diverse* **tayō**
横様 *sideward, wayward* **yokozama**
様式 *style, form; situation* **yōshiki**
様相 *aspect, phase, condition* **yōsō**
様子 *state, behaviour, attitude* **yōsu**
様態 *aspect, phase, condition* **yōtai**
同様に *similarly, conversely* **dōyō(ni)**

雨模様 *signs of rain* **amemoyō**
言い様 *way of saying* **iiyō**
真っ逆様 *up-side down, ~fall* **massakasama**
❷人様 *other persons* **hitosama**
皆様 *"to everyone present..."* **minasama**
宮様 *prince, princess* **miyasama**
何様 *"what, what are you?..."* **nanisama**
奥様 *another man's wife* **okusama**
王様 *king, sovereign ruler* **ōsama**
外様 *outsider, outside person* **tozama**
様付け *calling one with "sama"...* **samatsuke**

御[honorific], 380	容ppearance, 492
姿ppearance, 609	御[honorific], 380
態ppearance, 322	的tyle, 696

楼ower, 127

780-B

様anner of 911 遅elay, 詳etails must convey...

辶 (transport)

遅elay 遅ardy

oso(i), oku(reru), oku(rasu), CHI
delay, tardy, lateness, retard

FLIP: 8.0.b. Inner (stem)
Facing: 4.0. ▱▱ Apart

遅め *"a little late, a little slow..."* **osome**
遅くとも *"at the latest..."* **osokutomo**
遅らせる *late, delay, defer, put off* **okuraseru**
遅着 *late arrival* **chichaku**
遅遅 *slow, lagging* **chichi**
遅鈍 *slow-witted, dullard* **chidon**
遅延 *delay, putting off, postponement* **chien**
遅配 *delayed delivery, late shipment* **chihai**
遅発 *starting late, late start* **chihatsu**
遅筆 *slow writing* **chihitsu**
遅日 *long days in spring* **chijitsu**
遅刻 *tardy, be late* **chikoku**
遅脈 *slow pulse* **chimyaku**
遅参 *coming late* **chisan**
遅速 *speed, slow-or-fast* **chisoku**
遅滞 *delay, arrears* **chitai**
巧遅 *slow & elaborate* **kōchi**
遅番 *late shift, night shift* **osoban**
遅霜 *late spring* **osojimo**

遅効性 *slow acting* **chikōsei**
出遅れ *off to a late start, belated* **deokure**
気遅れ *timidity, diffidence, pathetic* **kiokure**
遅蒔き *late sowing* **osomaki**
遅咲き *late-bloomer* **osozaki**
手遅れ *too late* **teokure**
月遅れ *a month late; back issues (monthly)* **tsukiokure**
遅生まれ *born after April 1 (fiscal yr.)* **osoumare**
申し遅れる *be late in saying* **mōshiokureru**
乗り遅れる *miss one's ride (train)* **noriokureru**
遅かれ早かれ *sooner-or-later, in due time* **osokare hayakare**

猶elay, 790	疾peedy, 681	速peedy, 502
徐lowly, 881	迅peedy, 95	時ime, 653

羊heep, 247

780-C

様*anner of 911* 遅*elay,* 詳*etails must convey...*

言 (speaking)

詳*etails*   詳*articulars*

kuwa(shii), SHŌ
details, particulars, specifics

FLIP: 5.0.b. Left & Right

詳しい *detailed, familiar* **kuwashii**
不詳 *unidentified, x- factor* **fushō**
各論 *item-by-item discussion* **kakuron**
未詳 *unknown, x- factor* **mishō**
詳報 *detailed report* **shōhō**
詳述 *detailed explanation, ~elaboration* **shōjutsu**
詳解 *detailed explanation, ~elaboration* **shōkai**
詳密 *details, minute* **shōmitsu**
詳論 *detailed discussion* **shōron**
詳細 *details, particulars* **shōsai**
詳察 *careful observation* **shōsatsu**
詳説 *detailed explanation, ~elaboration* **shōsetsu**
詳伝 *detailed biography* **shōden**
詳言 *detailed explanation, ~elaboration* **shōgen**
詳記 *full account, detailed journal* **shōki**
詳録 *detailed record* **shōroku**
詳論 *detailed argument* **shōron**
詳略 *detailed, particulars* **shōryaku**

細*etails, 138*   寡*ittle, 161*
微*light, 62*   幾*ew, 547*

詩*oetry, 250*

781-A

閣*abinet* 閥*liques in* 闘*ombat for power in Rabat...*

門 (gate, entrance)

❶閣*abinet*   ❷閣*ower*

KAKU
Cabinet; tower, tall building

FLIP: 2.0.b. Sort Of (stem)

❶仏閣 *Buddhist temple* **bukkaku**
銀閣 *lofty-, silver building* **ginkaku**
閣下 *Your-, His-, Her excellency* **kakka**
閣外 *outside the cabinet* **kakugai**
閣議 *cabinet session* **kakugi**
閣員 *cabinet ministers, ~members* **kakuin**
閣内 *within the cabinet* **kakunai**
閣令 *ministerial order* **kakurei**
閣僚 *cabinet minister* **kakuryō**
内閣 *the cabinet* **naikaku**
⇒超然内閣 *non-partisan cabinet* **chōzen naikaku**
⇒連立内閣 *coalition cabinet* **renritsu naikaku**
内閣改造 *cabinet reorganization* **naikaku kaizō**
入閣 *cabinet appointment* **nyūkaku**
組閣 *formation of a cabinet* **sokaku**
倒閣 *overthrowing a cabinet* **tōkaku**

❷天守閣 *castle tower* **tenshukaku**
金閣 *golden pavilion* **kinkaku**

高閣 *tall building, ~structure* **kōkaku**
楼閣 *lofty building* **rōkaku**
台閣 *tall building, ~structure* **taikaku**

相*inister, 524*   吏*fficial, 463*
省*inistry, 572*   塔*ower, 146*
府*overnment, 429*   楼*ower, 127*
役*fficial, 746*   高*levated, 435*

閲*nspection, 942*

781-B

閣*abinet* 閥*liques in* 闘*ombat for power in Rabat...*

閥*lique*　　閥*action*

門 (gate, entrance)

BATSU
clique, faction, sect, splinter

FLIP: 3.0.b. Top (stem)

閥族 *clan, clique, faction* **batsuzoku**
学閥 *academic elite, intelligentsia* **gakubatsu**
軍閥 *military clique, army clan* **gunbatsu**
派閥 *clan, clique, faction* **habatsu**
藩閥 *clanship, clan favouritism* **hanbatsu**
閨閥 *nepotism, dynasty* **keibatsu**
門閥 *birth lineage* **monbatsu**
党閥 *party clique, faction* **tōbatsu**
財閥 *financial empire* **zaibatsu**
郷土閥 *village clan* **kyōdobatsu**
薩摩閥 *Satsuma clan* **satsumabatsu**

盟*lliance, 21*	隊*quad, 543*
連*lliance, 305*	班*quad, 908*
組*roup, 138*	員*ember, 410*
団*roup, 345*	忠*oyalty, 475*

闘*ombat, 946*

781-C

閣*abinet* 閥*liques in* 闘*ombat for power in Rabat...*

闘*ombat*　　闘*kirmish*

門 (gate, entrance)

tataka(u), TŌ
combat, skirmish, encounter, blitzkrieg, warfare

FLIP: 3.0.b. Top (stem)

暗闘 *secret struggle, infighting* **antō**
奮闘 *struggle, wrestle, grapple* **funtō**
激闘 *fierce struggle* **gekitō**
格闘 *fight, grapple* **kakutō**
敢闘 *fighting courageously* **kantō**
拳闘 *boxing, fist fight* **kentō**
健闘 *putting up a good fight* **kentō**
決闘 *duel* **kettō**
苦闘 *hard struggle* **kutō**
共闘 *joint struggle* **kyōtō**
乱闘 *melee, free-for-all rumble, scuffle* **rantō**
力闘 *putting up a good fight* **rikitō**
戦闘 *combat, skirmish, encounter* **sentō**
戦闘機 *fighter jet, warplane* **sentōki**
死闘 *life & death struggle* **shitō**
私闘 *personal grudge, bad blood* **shitō**
春闘 *spring labour bargaining* **shuntō**
争闘 *struggle, fighting* **sōtō**
闘病 *battle with illness* **tōbyō**

闘技 *competition, contest* **tōgi**
闘魚 *fighting fish* **tōgyo**
闘牛 *bullfight* **tōgyū**
闘牛士 *bullfighter, matador* **tōgyūshi**
闘鶏 *cockfighting* **tōkei**
闘犬 *dogfight* **tōken**
闘魂 *fighting spirit* **tōkon**
闘士 *fighter, champion* **tōshi**
闘志 *fighting spirit* **tōshi**
闘将 *brave leader* **tōshō**
闘争 *fight, strife* **tōsō**

戦*ighting, 517*	伐*ttack, 96*
銃*irearm, 884*	撃*ttack, 613*
武*arrior, 100*	襲*ttack, 630*
争*onflict, 231*	攻*ttack, 635*

閥*action, 946*

782-A

極xtreme 誇oast creates woes...

極xtreme 極olar

木 (wooden)

Facing: 2.2. East ☞ (V)
FLIP: 7.3.b. Right Bottom (stem)

kiwa(meru), kiwa(maru), KYOKU, GOKU
extreme, polar, ultra, utmost, ultimate

分極	polarization **bunkyoku**
極悪	heinous evil **gokuaku**
極微	microscopic **gokubi, kyokubi**
極道	profligate, wicked **gokudō**
極意	secret, mysteries **gokui**
極印	stamp, hallmark, brand **gokuin**
極上	the very best, the finest **gokujō**
極楽	paradise **gokuraku**
極暑	intense heat, scorching heat **gokusho**
北極	North Pole, arctic **hokkyoku**
陰極	cathode, negative pole **inkyoku**
磁極	magnetic pole **jikyoku**
寒極	coldest spot on earth **kankyoku**
極刑	capital punishment, death penalty **kyokkei**
極光	aurora **kyokkō**
極右	extreme rightist **kyokuu**
極大	extremely great **kyokudai**
極言	speaking frankly, straight talk **kyokugen**
極限	limit, bounds, extremity **kyokugen**

極豪	grossly rich (dickson poon) **kyokugō**
極量	maximum dosage **kyokuryō**
極力	one's all strength **kyokuryoku**
極小	minimum **kyokushō**
極端	extreme, utmost **kyokutan**
究極	ultimate, final **kyūkyoku**
南極	South Pole **nankyoku**
対極	counter situation, ~pole **taikyoku**
多極	multifarious, all-around **takyoku**
積極的	optimistically, positively **sekkyokuteki**

窮xtreme, 876	最aximum, 423
甚xtreme, 293	過xcessive, 798
端ndpoint, 974	濫xcessive, 856

誇oastful, 947

782-B

極xtreme 誇oast creates woes...

誇oastful 誇ride

言 (speaking)

FLIP: 7.2.b. Right Top (stem)
FLIP: 6.0.a. Left (flat)

hoko(ru), hiko(ri), KO
boastful, pride, bragging

誇り	pride, honour **hokori**
誇り顔	triumphant look **hokorigao**
誇りに思う	proud, think highly of **hokori(ni) omō**
勝ち誇る	triumphant, victorious **kachihokoru**
誇張	exaggeration, overstatement **kochō**
誇張法	hyperbole **kochōhō**
誇張的	exaggerated, overstated **kochōteki**
誇大	exaggeration, overstated **kodai**
誇大妄想	megalomania, illusion of grandeur **kodai mōsō**
誇示	ostentation, display, show-off **koji**
誇称	exaggeration, overstatement **koshō**
誇色	boastful looks **koshoku**
咲き誇る	bloom magnificently **sakihokoru**

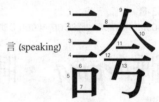

誉onour, 252	示isplay, 878
栄lory, 580	粧ecorate, 656
名ame, 425	飾ecorate, 664

誌hronicle, 426

783-A

郵ostal workers 睡sleep, when parcels missed the ship...

郵ostal office　郵ail service

β ⟷ 阜 (village-right)

YŪ

postal office, mail service, courier

Facing: 4.0. 👓 Apart

郵便 *mail, post* **yūbin**
⇒普通郵便 *regular mail, ~post* **futsū yūbin**
⇒速達郵便 *express delivery mail* **sokutatsu yūbin**
郵便ポスト *one's mailbox* **yūbin posuto**
郵便受け *mailbox, letter box* **yūbin'uke**
郵便物 *postage, mail* **yūbinbutsu**
郵便局 *post office, mail station* **yūbinkyoku**
郵券 *postal stamp* **yūken**
郵政 *postage, mailing* **yūsei**
郵船 *mail streamer, ~ship* **yūsen**
郵送 *mailing, shipping out* **yūsō**
郵送料 *postage, mailing cost* **yūsōryō**
郵袋 *postal bag* **yūtai**
郵税 *postage, postal charges* **yūzei**
郵便葉書 *postal-, post card* **yūbin hagaki**
郵便為替 *postal money order* **yūbin kawase**
郵便私書箱 *PO Box* **yūbin shishobako**

届eliver, 631	逓onvey, 304
送ending, 708	書ritings, 116
伝onvey, 619	読eading, 260

郭nclose, 398

783-B

郵ostal workers 睡sleep, when parcels missed the ship...

睡leeping　睡rowsing

目 (eyesight, visual)

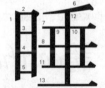

SUI

sleeping, drowsing, snoozing

FLIP: 6.0.a. Left (flat)
FLIP: 7.1. Right (Sort Of)

一睡 *catnap, siesta* **issui**
熟睡 *deep-, sound sleep* **jukusui**
仮睡 *catnap, siesta, afternoon sleep* **kasui**
昏睡 *comatose; deep trance* **konsui**
昏睡状態 *comatose, vegetative state* **konsui jōtai**
麻睡 *anaesthesia* **masui**
睡魔 *drowsiness, sleepiness* **suima**
睡眠 *sleep, sleeping* **suimin**
睡眠量 *amount of sleep* **suiminryō**
睡眠薬 *sleeping pill, ~aid* **suiminyaku**
睡眠剤 *sleeping pill, ~aid* **suiminzai**
睡眠不足 *lack of sleep* **suimin busoku**
睡眠時間 *sleeping hours* **suimin jikan**
睡蓮 *water lily* **suiren**
睡余 *after waking up* **suiyo**

寝leeping, 769	夢ream, 167
眠leeping, 495	覚wake, 307
泊leep-over, 742	起waken, 754

乗ide on, 511

784-A

Not to 伴ccompany 判udgements with money...

伴*ccompany*   伴*ttend on*

人⇔亻 (person)

tomona(u), HAN, BAN
accompany, attend on, together

FLIP: 7.0.b1. Right (stem)

伴食 *titular, nominal* **banshoku**
伴食大臣 *titular head, figurehead* **banshoku daijin**
伴奏 *musical accompaniment* **bansō**
伴走 *escort, companion* **bansō**
伴僧 *monk assistant* **bansō**
同伴 *going together, accompanying* **dōhan**
同伴者 *escort, companion* **dōhansha**
伴侶 *partner, companion, colleague* **hanryo**
接伴 *guest reception, entertainment* **seppan**
随伴 *accompanying, going together* **zuihan**
随伴者 *minder, attendant* **zuihansha**
相伴う *accompany, escort, usher* **aitomonau**
お相伴 *participation, co-operation* **oshōban**

随*ccompany, 807*	共*ogether, 302*
添*ccompany, 620*	合*ogether, 232*

半*ne-half, 484*

784-B

Not to 伴ccompany 判udgements with money...

❶判*udgement*   ❷判*aper size*

刀⇔刂 (blade, cutting)

HAN, BAN
judgement, ruling, decision, sentencing, verdict; paper size

FLIP: 6.0.b. Left (stem)

❶ 談判 *negotiations, bargaining* **danpan**
判別 *distinction, discernment* **hanbetsu**
判断 *judgement, decision, verdict* **handan**
判断力 *judgement ability, decisiveness* **handanryoku**
判読 *deciphering, making out* **handoku**
判事 *judge, justice, magistrate* **hanji**
判決 *judgement, verdict* **hanketsu**
⇒原判決 *original verdict* **genhanketsu**
判子 *official-, personal seal* **hanko**
判明 *clear decision, distinction* **hanmei**
判例 *judicial precedent* **hanrei**
判定 *decision, verdict* **hantei**
判然 *clear, distinct, evident* **hanzen**
批判 *criticism, lambasting* **hihan**
批判的 *critical, derogatory* **hihanteki**
評判 *reputed, noted, well-known* **hyōban**
印判 *seal, stamp* **inban**
血判 *blood compact, seal of blood* **keppan**
公判 *public trial, open court* **kōhan**

盲判 *rubberstamp, seal without approval*
    mekuraban
連判 *joint signature* **renpan**
論判 *argument, discussion* **ronpan**
裁判 *court, judgement* **saiban**
⇒弾劾裁判 *impeachment court* **dangai saiban**
裁判長 *presiding judge, magistrate* **saibanchō**
裁判権 *jurisdiction, jurisprudence* **saibanken**
裁判所 *court of law* **saibansho**
⇒最高裁判所 *supreme court* **saikō saibansho**
審判 *judge, umpire, referee, arbiter* **shinpan**
請け判 *surety seal* **ukehan**
❷A4判 *letter-size paper* "A"-yon ban

決*udgement, 699*	選*hoice, 303*
裁*udgement, 802*	択*hoice, 753*
定*efinite, 550*	枚*[sheets], 724*

伴*ccompany, 949*

785-A

Either 倍ultiply or 剖ivide, stock markets ride...

倍*ultiply* 倍*oubling*

人 ⇔ イ (person)

BAI
multiply, doubling

FLIP: 7.0.a. Right (flat)

倍大 *double size* **baidai**
倍額 *double amount* **baigaku**
倍加 *doubling, multiplication* **baika**
倍旧 *even more, further* **baikyū**
倍率 *magnification, doubling* **bairitsu**
倍数 *multiple* **baisū**
倍増 *doubling, multiplication* **baizō**
百倍 *a hundred times* **hyakubai**
一倍 *same number; double* **ichibai**
二倍 *two times, doubling* **nibai**
三倍 *thrice, three times* **sanbai**
数倍 *several times* **sūbai**
人一倍 *first among equals; more than one person*
      hito ichibai
公倍数 *common multiple* **kōbaisū**

度*egree, 91*	増*ncrease, 837*	多*lenty, 187*
殖*ncrease, 784*	拡*nlarge, 205*	複*eproduce, 830*

培*ultivate, 698*

785-B

Either 倍ultiply or 剖ivide, stock markets ride...

剖*ivide* 剖*issect*

刀 ⇔ リ (blade, cutting)

BŌ
divide, dissect, partition

FLIP: 6.0.a. Left (flat)

剖検 *autopsy, necropsy* **bōken**
解剖 *autopsy, dissection* **kaibō**
⇒生体解剖 *vivisection of alive body* **seitai kaibō**
⇒死体解剖 *autopsy of dead body* **shitai kaibō**
解剖学 *anatomy, study of human body* **kaibōgaku**

割*ivide, 968*
分*ivide, 518*
切*utting, 352*

培*ultivate, 698*

786-A

形hapes neatly 研olished look varnished...

彡 (hair ornament)

形hape   形orm

katachi, kata, KEI, GYŌ
shape, form, configuration, outlook

Facing: 1.2. 🖝 West (V)

台形 *trapezoid, trapezium* **daikei**
円形 *circle, circular shape* **enkei**
外形 *contours, outlines* **gaikei**
原形 *original form* **genkei**
語形 *word form* **gokei**
形相 *looks, expression, countenance* **gyōsō**
花形 *star, flower, lion* **hanagata**
変形 *deformation, contortion* **henkei**
雛形 *miniature, sample* **hinagata**
実形 *original size, actual size* **jikkei**
形状 *form, shape* **keijō**
形勢 *state-of-affairs, status quo* **keisei**
形成 *formation, fabrication* **keisei**
形跡 *remains, traces, relics* **keiseki**
形式 *form, formality, ceremony* **keishiki**
奇形 *deformation, distortion* **kikei**
固形 *solidity, hardness* **kokei**
球形 *spherical shape* **kyūkei**
無形 *formless, shapeless* **mukei**

人形 *doll, mannequin* **ningyō**
女形 *kabuki actor playing female* **onnagata**
整形 *orthopaedics, bone surgery* **seikei**
品形 *merchandise appearance* **shinakatachi**
隊形 *formation, squadron* **taikei**
定形 *standard form* **teikei**
筒形 *cylinder, slender tube* **tsutsugata**

姿 *ppearance, 609*	態 *ppearance, 322*
容 *ppearance, 492*	様 *anner, 944*
構 *osture, 714*	面 *urface, 36*

杉 *edar-tree, 721*

786-B

形hapes neatly 研olished look varnished...

石 (stone)

研olish   研esearch

to(gu), KEN
polish, refine, grind, research

FLIP: 7.1. Right (Sort Of)
Facing: 3.0. 🖝🖝 Across

研学 *study, research* **kengaku**
研究 *research, study* **kenkyū**
⇒地域研究 *area studies* **chiiki kenkyū**
研究費 *research money, ~grant* **kenkyūhi**
研究家 *researcher, scholar* **kenkyūka**
研究科 *graduate course, ~study* **kenkyūka**
研究心 *probing mind* **kenkyūshin**
研究室 *professor's-, research room* **kenkyūshitsu**
研究所 *research institute* **kenkyūsho**
研究開発 *research & development* **kenkyū kaihatsu**
研究論文 *thesis, treatise, dissertation* **kenkyū ronbun**
研磨 *research polishing* **kenma**
研米器 *rice polisher* **kenmaiki**
研削 *grinding, polishing* **kensaku**
研鑽 *study, research* **kensan**
研修 *training, instruction* **kenshū**
研修生 *trainee, instructee* **kenshūsei**
研修所 *training centre* **kenshūjo**
薬研 *chemist's-, pharmacist's mortar* **yakken**

磨研紙 *sandpaper* **makenshi**
研ぎ革 *polishing strop* **togikawa**
研ぎ物 *sharpening swords* **togimono**
研ぎ師 *sword polisher* **togishi**
研ぎ澄ます *sharpen well* **togisumasu**
粗研ぎ *rough polishing* **aratogi**

錬 *olish, 718*	了 *inish, 456*
終 *inish, 397*	締 *onclude, 432*
完 *omplete, 196*	究 *esearch, 575*

砕 *ulverize, 761*

787-A

欧*uropean tarots, Old World's* 枢*ivot...*

欠 (lacking)

欧*urope* 欧*estern*

ō

Europe, Western, Caucasian

中欧 *Central Europe* **chūō**
北欧 *Scandinavia* **hokuō**
北欧人 *Scandinavian* **hokuōjin**
北欧神話 *Norse mythology* **hokuō shinwa**
訪欧 *visit to Europe* **hōō**
南欧 *Southern Europe* **nan'ō**
欧亜 *Europe & Asia* **ōa**
欧米 *West, Europe & America* **ōbei**
欧米人 *Westerner, Caucasian* **ōbeijin**
欧文 *Roman languages* **ōbun**
欧風 *European-style* **ōfū**
欧化 *Europeanization* **ōka**
欧州 *Europe* **ōshū**
西欧 *Western Europe* **seiō**
西欧人 *European, Westerner* **seiōjin**
西欧化 *Westernisation, internationalisation* **seiōka**
西欧文明 *Western civilization* **seiō bunmei**
滞欧 *stay in Europe* **taiō**
渡欧 *visit to Europe* **toō**

FLIP: 7.1. Right (Sort Of)
Facing: 3.0. ☞☜ **Across**

東欧 *Eastern Europe* **tōō**
全欧 *entire Europe* **zen'ō**
印欧語 *Indo-European languages* **in'ōgo**
欧州同盟 *European Union* **ōshū dōmei**

米*merica, 77*	東*riental, 220*
西*estern, 18*	白*hite, 15*
亜*sia, 389*	

殴*unch, 745*

787-B

欧*uropean tarots, Old World's* 枢*ivot...*

木 (wooden)

枢*ivot*

sū

pivot

中枢 *centre, central* **chūsū**
⇒知覚中枢 *sensory core* **chikaku chūsū**
枢府 *privy council* **sūfu**
枢軸 *axis, pivot, centre* **sūjiku**
枢密 *state secrets* **sūmitsu**
枢要 *pressing matters, urgent business* **sūyō**
枢軸国 *Axis Powers (Nazi Germany, Japan, Italy)*
　　sūjikukoku
枢機 *state-of-affairs* **sūki**
枢機卿 *cardinal point; Catholic cardinal* **sūkikyō**
枢密院 *privy council* **sūmitsuin**

Facing: 2.2. East ☞ **(V)**
FLIP: 8.0.b. Inner (stem)

軸*xle, 659*	中*iddle, 85*
轄*edge, 968*	央*iddle, 218*

区*istrict, 80*

788-A

助ssistance from 祖ncestors made us victors...

力 (strength, force)

助ssist　助upport　助elp

tasu(keru), tasu(karu), JO
  assist, support, help, backing, back-up, aide

FLIP: 6.0.a. Left (flat)
Facing: 2.2. East ☞ (V)

援助　help, assistance, aid **enjo**
⇒経済援助　economic assistance **keizai enjo**
⇒対外援助　foreign aid, oda **taigai enjo**
扶助　help, support **fujo**
⇒相互扶助　mutual aid, ~assistance **sōgo fujo**
扶助料　allowance in aid **fujoryō**
互助　mutual aid, mutual help **gojo**
補助　assistance, support **hojo**
一助　aid, help, support **ichijo**
自助　self-help, self-supporting **jijo**
助長　promote, encourage, further **jochō**
助演　supporting role **joen**
助言　advice, counsel, suggestion **jogen**
助命　sparing a person's life **jomei**
助力　help, support, assistance **joryoku**
助祭　Catholic deacon **josai**
助成　aid, help, support **josei**
助詞　word particle **joshi**
助手　assistant, aide **joshu**

助役　deputy-, vice mayor **joyaku**
介助　aid, help, support **kaijo**
救助　rescue, relief, life-saving **kyūjo**
⇒災害救助　disaster assistance **saigai kyūjo**
飲助　drunkard, tipster, alcoholic **nomisuke**
賛助　support, patronage **sanjo**
助平　lewdness, lust, lecherous **sukebei**
天助　divine help, act-of-God **tenjo**
人助け　philantrophy, helping others **hitodasuke**
助教授　associate professor **jokyōju**
助産婦　midwife **josanpu**

援upport, 820	擁upport, 151
貢upport, 625	補upplement, 812
支upport, 201	協ooperate, 577

肌kin, 747

788-B

助ssistance from 祖ncestors made us victors...

示⇔ネ (display, show)

祖ncestor　祖orebear

SO
  ancestor, forebear, progenitor

FLIP: 7.0.a. Right (flat)

鼻祖　founder, originator **biso**
同祖　same ancestry **dōso**
遠祖　distant ancestors **enso**
父祖　ancestors, forebears, progenitors **fuso**
元祖　originator, founder **ganso**
開祖　founder, originator **kaiso**
高祖　sect founder **kōso**
皇祖　empire founder, first emperor **kōso**
教祖　sect founder **kyōso**
先祖　ancestors, forebears, progenitors **senzo**
始祖　dynasty founder, first emperor **shiso**
宗祖　sect founder **shūso**
祖母　grandmother **sobo**
祖廟　ancestral tomb **sobyō**
祖父　grandfather **sofu**
祖父母　grandparents **sofubo**
祖語　mother tongue, native language **sogo**
祖業　generation-old family business **sogyō**
祖述　extolling one's predecessor **sojutsu**

祖述者　advocate, exponent **sojutsusha**
祖国　homeland, motherland **sokoku**
祖先　ancestors, forebears, progenitors **sosen**
祖先崇拝　ancestral worship **sosen sūhai**
祖師　sect founder **soshi**
祖神　ancestral gods **soshin**
祖宗　forebears, ancestors **sosō**
太祖　dynasty founder, first emperor **taiso**
外祖父　maternal grandmother **gaisofu**
養祖母　foster grandmother **yōsobo**
養祖父　foster grandfather **yōsofu**

系osterity, 262	久ternal, 379
昔lden-times, 281	源ource, 431
永ternal, 10	縁inship, 675

視bservation, 815

789-A

辞uit 括undling forensics with 辞hetoric...

辛 (bitter)

❶辞*uitting* ❷辞*hetoric*

ya(meru), JI
quitting, job resignation; rhetoric, semantics

FLIP: 7.0.a. Right (flat)

❶ 辞表 *resignation letter* **jihyō**
辞意 *intention to resign* **jii**
辞去 *biding goodbye* **jikyo**
辞任 *resignation, leaving one's job* **jinin**
辞世 *death, demise, passing away* **jisei**
辞職 *resignation, leaving one's job* **jishoku**
辞退 *declination, refusal, turning down* **jitai**
送辞 *farewell speech* **sōji**
❷ 美辞 *flowery words, highfalutin* **biji**
弔辞 *words of condolence* **chōji**
言辞 *intemperate words* **genji**
返辞 *response, reply* **henji**
辞令 *official job appointment* **jirei**
辞林 *dictionary* **jirin**
辞書 *dictionary* **jisho**
辞色 *words & appearances* **jishoku**
辞典 *dictionary* **jiten**
⇒漢和辞典 *Japanese Kanji dictionary* **kanwa jiten**
献辞 *dedication, offering* **kenji**

訓辞 *exhortative-, inspirational speech* **kunji**
賛辞 *words of praise, eulogy* **sanji**
世辞 *compliment, praise, extolling* **seji**
接辞 *affix, attach* **setsuji**
謝辞 *speech of gratitude* **shaji**
式辞 *congratulatory speech* **shikiji**
修辞 *figurative speaking* **shūji**
修辞学 *rhetorics, oratory* **shūjigaku**
祝辞 *congratulatory speech* **shukuji**
答辞 *speech in reply, response* **tōji**
御辞儀 *bow, bowing* **ojigi**

止*top, 192*	句*hrase, 16*
停*top, 393*	弁*peech, 570*
棄*bandon, 608*	語*ord, 780*

乱*haos, 686*

789-B

辞uit 括undling forensics with 辞hetoric...

手⇔扌 (hand, manual)

括*undle* 括*ump together*

KATSU
bundle, lump together

FLIP: 7.1. Right (Sort Of)

概括 *summary, summing up* **gaikatsu**
包括 *inclusion, encirclement* **hōkatsu**
包括的 *comprehensive, thorough* **hōkatsuteki**
一括 *bundle, lump* **ikkatsu**
一括購入 *bulk purchase* **ikkatsu kōnyū**
括弧 *parenthesis* **kakko**
括れ *waist, hips* **kukure**
総括 *generalization, summarization* **sōkatsu**
総括質問 *summing-up interpellation*
　　sōkatsu shitsumon
統括 *generalization, summarization* **tōkatsu**
括約筋 *sphincter* **katsuyakukin**
丸括弧 *parenthesis* **marugakko**
締め括る *tie fast; manage; round out* **shimekukuru**

束*undle, 502*	擁*mbrace, 151*
略*ummary, 825*	捕*atch, 812*
抄*ummary, 726*	集*ather, 50*
握*rasp, 427*	

活*ctivity, 237*

790-A

勅*mperial-edics illuminate, not* 疎*lienate...*

勅*mperial-edict*

力 (strength, force)

CHOKU
imperial-edict

FLIP: 6.0.b. Left (stem)

勅許 *imperial sanction* **chokkyo**
勅題 *theme decided by the emperor* **chokudai**
勅願 *imperial prayer* **chokugan**
勅願寺 *temple built at imperial request* **chokuganji**
勅語 *imperial message, ~address* **chokugo**
勅命 *imperial decree, ~edict* **chokumei**
勅令 *imperial command* **chokurei**
勅裁 *imperial decision* **chokusai**
勅宣 *imperial decree* **chokusen**
勅選 *imperial nomination* **chokusen**
勅使 *imperial envoy, ~emissary* **chokushi**
勅旨 *imperial decree* **chokushi**
勅書 *imperial rescript* **chokusho**
勅答 *imperial response* **chokutō**
勅諭 *imperial mandate* **chokuyu**
違勅 *disobedience to an imperial decree* **ichoku**
回勅 *encyclical letter* **kaichoku**
密勅 *imperial secret edict* **micchoku**
神勅 *oracle* **shinchoku**

詔勅 *imperial proclamation, ~decree*
  shōchoku
勅撰集 *anthology at imperial request*
  chokusenshū

璽*mperial seal, 976*　皇*mperor, 113*
詔*mperial-edict, 817*　朕*mperial consent, 708*

頼*equest, 562*

790-B

勅*mperial-edics illuminate, not* 疎*lienate...*

疎*strange*　疎*lienate*

疋 (animal counter)

FLIP: 7.0.b1. Right (stem)

uto(mu), uto(i), maba(ra), SO
estrange, alienate, distant, lethargy, neglect

注疎 *detailed comments* **chūso**
過疎 *underpopulated, low population* **kaso**
空疎 *empty, non-substantial* **kūso**
親疎 *degree of intimacy* **shinso**
疎遠 *estrangement, alienation* **soen**
疎外 *alienation, neglect* **sogai**
疎外感 *sense of alienation* **sogaikan**
疎音 *long silence, not keeping in touch* **soin**
疎開 *evacuation, removal* **sokai**
疎隔 *estrangement, alienation* **sokaku**
疎密 *sparseness, luxuriant* **somitsu**
疎放 *rough, sloppy, crude* **sohō**
疎林 *sparsely-grown woods* **sorin**
疎漏 *carelessness, negligence* **sorō**
疎略 *coarse, crude* **soryaku**
疎水 *irrigation canal* **sosui**
疎水性 *hydrophobic* **sosuisei**
疎通 *understanding, comprehension* **sotsū**

距*istance, 207*
遠*istant, 916*
悠*istant, 898*

勅*mperial-edict, 955*

791-A

招nvited after a nap, a child 拐idnapped...

招nvite   招eckon

手⇔扌 (hand, manual)

mane(ku), SHŌ
invite, beckon

FLIP: 7.3.a. Right Bottom (flat)

招致 *invitation, summons* **shōchi**
招宴 *party invitation* **shōen**
招聘 *invitation* **shōhei**
招魂 *invoking dead spirits* **shōkon**
招客 *invitation; invited guest* **shōkyaku**
招来 *invitation, leading, engendering* **shōrai**
招請 *invitation* **shōsei**
招集 *summons, convocation, assembly* **shōshū**
招待 *invitation, entreaty* **shōtai**
招待状 *letter-of-invitation, invitation card* **shōtaijō**
招待券 *invitation ticket* **shōtaiken**
招待客 *invited guest* **shōtaikyaku**
招待席 *reserved seats for guests* **shōtaiseki**
手招き *beckoning* **temaneki**
招き猫 *porcelain cat* **manekineko**
差し招く *beckon to; take command of* **sashimaneku**

呼nvite, 701	篤ordial, 317
迎elcome, 705	客uest, 559
宴anquet, 610	賓uest, 161

拓lear-up, 363

791-B

招nvited after a nap, a child 拐idnapped...

拐idnap   拐bduct

手⇔扌 (hand, manual)

kadowaka(su), KAI
kidnap, abduct, abscond, snatching

FLIP: 7.2.a. Right Top (flat)

拐取 *abduction, kidnapping* **kaishu**
誘拐 *abduction, kidnapping* **yūkai**
誘拐犯人 *kidnap-for-ransom criminal* **yūkai hannin**
誘拐事件 *kidnapping crime* **yūkai jiken**
拐帯犯人 *absconder, con artist* **kaitai hannin**

虜aptive, 70	捕eize, 812
逮apture, 880	獄rison, 639
拘rrest, 16	囚risoner, 863
逮rrest, 880	犯riminal, 640

招nvite, 956

792-A
部art of the 陪ury believed another theory...

部section　部art

ß ⟷ 阜 (village-right)

FLIP: 6.0.a. Left (flat)

BU
section, part, component, segment, sector

部分 part, component **bubun**
部長 director, department chief **buchō**
部員 club member, staff member **buin**
部品 parts, components **buhin**
部下 subordinates, underlings **buka**
部会 sectional meeting **bukai**
部門 department, division **bumon**
部室 clubroom **bushitsu**
部署 post assignment **busho**
部数 circulation, number of copies **busū**
部隊 force, military unit, corps **butai**
部材 member, parts **buzai**
部族 tribe, primitive group **buzoku**
学部 college of~ **gakubu**
部屋 room, flat **heya**
部屋代 room rental fee **heyadai**
部屋割り room allotment **heyawari**
本部 headquarters **honbu**
一部 one part of a whole, a component **ichibu**

陰部 female genital, vagina **inbu**
述部 predicate **jutsubu**
患部 afflicted part of the body **kanbu**
幹部 executive, officer level **kanbu**
凹部 concavity **ōbu**
頭部 head, skull **tōbu**
全部 entire, whole, everything **zenbu**
部外者 outsider, outcast **bugaisha**
中央部 mid-section **chūōbu**
執行部 executive department **shikkōbu**
低音部 bass **teionbu**

分ivide, 518	全ntire, 24
割ivide, 968	各very, 498

郵ostal office, 948

792-B
部art of the 陪ury believed another theory...

陪ury-trial　陪ccompany

ß ⟷ 阜 (village-left)

FLIP: 7.0.a. Right (flat)

shitaga(u), BAI
jury trial, accompany a superior

陪侍 nobility retainer **baiji**
陪乗 riding with one's superior **baijō**
陪従 attending, accompanying **baijū**
陪観 watch with one's superior **baikan**
陪席 seated with one's superior **baiseki**
陪臣 vassal retainer **baishin**
陪食 dining with one's superior **baishoku**
陪審員 juror, jury panellist **baishin'in**
陪審員席 jury box, jury bench **baishin'inseki**
陪審裁判 trial by jury system **baishin saiban**
陪審制度 trial by jury system **baishin seido**

恭espect, 620	決ecide, 699
仰espect, 706	典ode, 476
敬espect, 329	法aw, 360

部ection, 957

793-A

Friends' 継ontinuing 断efusal, highly unusual...

糸 (thread, continuity)

継*ollow*　継*ontinuity*

tsu(gu), KEI
follow, continuity, succession

FLIP: 7.1. Right (Sort Of)
FLIP: 8.0.b. Inner (stem)

継ぎ端 *continuing topic for a conversation* **tsugihashi**
継ぎ目 *joint, crux, seam* **tsugime**
継ぎ手 *joint, coupling* **tsugite**
継ぎ歯 *post tooth crown* **tsugiba**
継ぎ合わせ *joint, crux, seam* **tsugiawase**
中継 *broadcast, relay* **chūkei**
継母 *stepmother, foster mother* **keibo, mamahaha**
継泳 *continuous swimming* **keiei**
継父 *stepfather, foster father* **keifu**
継受 *inheritance* **keiju**
継嗣 *heir, heiress, successor* **keishi**
継子 *stepchild, adopted child* **keishi**
継室 *second wife (after the first died)* **keishitsu**
継承 *succession, inheritance* **keishō**
継走 *relay race* **keisō**
継続 *continuation, renewal* **keizoku**
後継 *continuity, succession* **kōkei**
継親 *step parents, adoptive parents* **tsugioya**
跡継ぎ *successor, replacement* **atotsugi**

継電器 *electricity relay* **keidenki**
世継ぎ *heir, heiress* **yotsugi**
語り継ぐ *word-of-mouth* **kataritsugu**
言い継ぐ *pass on by word of mouth* **iitsugu**
引き継ぎ *succession, taking over* **hikitsugi**
受け継ぐ *inherit, succeed to* **uketsugu**
舞台中継 *stage relay* **butai chūkei**
衛星中継 *satellite broadcast* **eisei chūkei**
実況中継 *field broadcast* **jikkyō chūkei**
宇宙中継 *space broadcast* **uchū chūkei**
継体天皇 *Emperor Keitai (507-531)* **keitai tennō**

続*ollow*, 260	結*onnect*, 227
随*ollowing*, 807	絡*onnect*, 826
翌*ollowing*, 237	後*fter*, 897

綱*ord*, 159

793-B

Friends' 継ontinuing 断efusal, highly unusual...

斤 (axe)

断*efusal*　断*ut-off*

kotowa(ru), ta(tsu), DAN
refusal, cut off, rejection, resolve

FLIP: 8.0.b. Inner (stem)

中断 *discontinuance, termination* **chūdan**
断案 *conclusion, decision* **dan'an**
断言 *affirmation, declaration* **dangen**
断食 *fasting, food abstinence* **danjiki**
断交 *breaking-off relations* **dankō**
断行 *firm execution* **dankō**
断面 *profile, cross section* **danmen**
断念 *abandonment, relinquishment* **dannen**
断片 *fragment, shrapnel* **danpen**
断想 *random ideas, stray thoughts* **dansō**
断首 *beheading, decapitation* **danshu**
断水 *water supply interruption* **dansui**
断定 *decision, conclusion, resolution* **dantei**
断罪 *conviction, "guilty..."; decapitation* **danzai**
断然 *resoluteness, decisiveness* **danzen**
断絶 *severance, rupture, breaking off* **danzetsu**
判断 *judgement, verdict, decision* **handan**
縦断 *running thru, traversing* **jūdan**
決断 *decision, resolution, judgement* **ketsudan**

禁断 *prohibition, forbidden* **kindan**
盲断 *blind judgement, hasty conclusion* **mōdan**
無断 *without permission* **mudan**
裁断 *decision, judgement* **saidan**
遮断 *interception, cutting off* **shadan**
診断 *medical check-up, diagnosis* **shindan**
速断 *hasty-, impulsive decision* **sokudan**
寸断 *cutting into pieces* **sundan**
溶断 *fusion, merging* **yōdan**
油断 *carelessness, clumsiness* **yudan**
勇断 *firm-, resolute decision* **yūdan**

拒*efusal*, 207	斥*ejection*, 424
否*efusal*, 300	排*ejection*, 795

粋*urity*, 762

794-A

訓nstructions on word 順equence led to coherence...

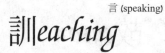

言 (speaking)

訓nstruction　訓eaching

KUN
instruction, teaching, guidance

FLIP: 6.0.a. Left (flat)
FLIP: 7.1. Right (Sort Of)

遺訓 dying instructions **ikun**
字訓 Japanese reading of Kanji **jikun**
回訓 government order to an envoy **kaikun**
家訓 family precepts **kakun**
校訓 school motto, university precepts **kōkun**
訓電 telegraphic instructions **kunden**
訓義 Kanji pronunciation & meaning **kungi**
訓育 discipline, education **kun'iku**
訓示 instructions, directions **kunji**
訓戒 admonition, lecture, warning **kunkai**
訓告 reprimand, censure **kunkoku**
訓令 instructions, orders **kunrei**
訓練 training, drill, exercise, practice **kunren**
⇒職業訓練 vocational training, job training
　　shokugyō kunren
訓練生 trainee, apprentice **kunrensei**
訓釈 explanation of old words **kunshaku**
訓点 punctuation marks **kunten**
訓話 moral lesson, moral story **kunwa**

教訓 lesson, instruction **kyōkun**
内訓 secret instructions **naikun**
難訓 Kanji reading difficulties **nankun**
音訓 Chinese Kanji reading **onkun**
請訓 request for instructions **seikun**
社訓 company motto, ~philosophy **shakun**
垂訓 teaching, instruction **suikun**
特訓 intensive, thorough training **tokkun**
訓読み Japanese Kanji pronunciation **kunyomi**
処世訓 instructions on worldly wisdom **shoseikun**

師eacher, 483	徒isciple, 497	教ducate, 385
授eaching, 539	練rill, 718	授ducate, 539
習earning, 238	学ducate, 346	

順equence, 959

794-B

訓nstructions on word 順equence led to coherence...

頁 (large shell, page)

順equence　順bedience

JUN
sequence, order, obedience, consecutive

FLIP: 7.0.b2. Right (stem)

着順 order of arrival **chakujun**
忠順 allegiance, loyalty **chūjun**
語順 word order **gojun**
筆順 Kanji writing strokes **hitsujun**
柔順 compliant, docile, meek, submissive **jūjun**
順番 turn, order, sequence **junban**
順調 favourable, satisfactory **junchō**
順延 postponement, deferment **jun'en**
順位 order, ranking **jun'i**
順次 one after another, serial, consecutive **junji**
順序 order, sequence **junjo**
順化 acclimation, adaptation, adjustment **junka**
順行 moving forward, advancing **junkō**
順境 prosperity, the good times **junkyō**
順応 adaptation, accommodation **junnō**
順法 law-abiding, law-observance **junpō**
順風 favourable wind, good omen **junpū**
順列 permutation, alteration **junretsu**
順路 route, path, passage **junro**

順良 good & obedient **junryō**
順守 law-abiding, law-observance **junshu**
順当 proper, fitting, suitable **juntō**
帰順 submission, surrender, capitulation **kijun**
恭順 compliant, meek, submissive **kyōjun**
道順 route, way, path, passage **michijun**
温順 compliant, meek, submissive **onjun**
席順 seating order, seating list **sekijun**
手順 arrangement, plan **tejun**
随順 compliant, meek, docile, submissive **zuijun**

番umber, 338	次ext, 460
号umber, 866	翌ext, 237
第[order], 102	随ollowing, 807
数umber, 156	

訓nstruction, 959

795-A

Unburied 故eceased 枯ithering with disease...

❶故eceased ❷故eason

攵 (action)

FLIP: 6.0.a. Left (flat)

yue, furu, KO
deceased, departed, dead; reason

❶ 縁故 *relation, relative* **enko**
故里 *hometown, birthplace* **furusato**
故郷 *hometown, birthplace* **furusato, kokyō**
反故 *scrap of paper* **hogo**
事故 *accident, incident, mishap* **jiko**
事故死 *accidental death* **jikoshi**
故買 *buying stolen goods* **kobai**
故知 *old ways of doing things* **kochi**
故意 *deliberateness, willed* **koi**
故事 *historical fact* **koji**
故事来歴 *origin & history* **koji raireki**
故人 *deceased, departed, dead* **kojin**
故実 *ancient way of life, ~practices* **kojitsu**
故国 *native land, ~country* **kokoku**
故旧 *old acquaintance* **kokyū**
故老 *wise elderly* **korō**
故殺 *manslaughter, murder* **kosatsu**
故紙 *waste paper* **koshi**
故障 *broken, out-of-service* **koshō**

⇒ 車両故障 *"car broken..."* **sharyō koshō**
故主 *one's former master* **koshu**
故山下文夫氏 *the late Dr Fumio Yamashita*
　　ko-Yamashita Fumio-shi
故山 *hometown, birthplace* **kozan**
世故 *public at large* **seko**
物故者 *departed, dead* **bukkosha**
無事故 *safe & sound, without accident* **mujiko**
❷ 故に *therefore, ergo* **yue(ni)**
何故 *why, reason* **naze, naniyue**
其れ故 *therefore, ergo* **soreyue**

枯*ecay, 960*	理*eason, 872*
昔*lden-times, 281*	訳*eason, 752*
由*eason, 540*	

教*ducate, 385*

795-B

Unburied 故eceased 枯ithering with disease...

枯ither　　枯ecay

木 (wooden)

FLIP: 7.0.a. Right (flat)

ka(reru), ka(rasu), KO
wither, decay, rotten

枯ればむ *begin to wither* **karebamu**
栄枯 *flourish & wither away* **eiko**
栄枯盛衰 *rise & fall, vicissitudes* **eiko seisui**
枯渇 *exhaustion, draining, drying up* **kokatsu**
枯死 *withering, decaying, dying* **koshi**
枯淡 *simple but refined* **kotan**
冬枯れ *winter decay* **fuyugare**
草枯れ *withering grass (autumn)* **kusagare**
水枯れ *drought* **mizugare**
夏枯れ *summer slump* **natsugare**
霜枯れ *wintry, frosty, bleak* **shimogare**
霜枯れ時 *winter time* **shimogaredoki**
枯れ枝 *dead tree branch* **kareeda**
枯れ葉 *dead-, withered leaves* **kareha**
枯れ木 *dead tree, withered tree* **kareki**
枯れ草 *dried grass, hay* **karekusa**
枯れ野 *desolate field* **kareno**
木枯らし *cold winter wind* **kogarashi**
枝枯れ病 *twig blight* **edagarebyō**

立ち枯れ *blight, spoil, ruin* **tachigare**
末枯れる *withering leaves (winter)* **uragareru**

朽*ecay, 738*	昔*lden-times, 281*
歳*ears old, 111*	翁*ld man, 238*
齢*ears old, 553*	婆*ld woman, 32*

故*eceased, 960*

796-A
Narcotic 剤rugs, 済ettled by thugs...

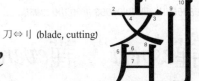

刀⇔刂 (blade, cutting)

剤rugs   剤edicine

ZAI

drugs, medicine, preparation

FLIP: 6.0.b. Left (stem)

調剤	*drug preparation* **chōzai**		除草剤	*herbicide, weed killer* **josōzai**
液剤	*fluid medicine* **ekizai**		覚醒剤	*drug stimulant, pep pill* **kakuseizai**
下剤	*laxative* **gezai**		乾燥剤	*desiccant, desiccating agent* **kansōzai**
配剤	*drug dispensation* **haizai**		興奮剤	*stimulant* **kōfunzai**
錠剤	*tablet, pill* **jōzai**		殺菌剤	*germicide, bactericide* **sakkinzai**
寒剤	*coolant, refrigerant* **kanzai**		酸化剤	*oxidizer* **sankazai**
滑剤	*lubricant, grease* **katsuzai**		整腸剤	*intestinal medicine* **seichōzai**
乳剤	*emulsion* **nyūzai**		整髪剤	*hairdressing solution* **seihatsuzai**
洗剤	*detergent, cleanser* **senzai**		刺激剤	*stimulant* **shigekizai**
粒剤	*powdered drug* **tsubuzai, ryuzai**		止血剤	*astringent* **shiketsuzai**
薬剤	*medicine, drug* **yakuzai**		消化剤	*digestive medicine* **shōkazai**
薬剤師	*pharmacist* **yakuzaishi**			
溶剤	*solvent* **yōzai**			
油剤	*ointment* **yuzai**			
安定剤	*tranquilliser, sedative* **anteizai**			
鎮静剤	*sedative, tranquilliser* **chinseizai**			
鎮痛剤	*anodyne, lenitive, analgesic* **chintsūzai**			
栄養剤	*nutrient, vitamin* **eiyōzai**			
漂白剤	*bleaching agent, ~powder* **hyōhakuzai**			

治*ecuperate*, 210	患*ickness*, 475	医*edicine*, 19
癒*ecuperate*, 923	症*ickness*, 788	健*ealthy*, 390
療*ecuperate*, 67	病*ickness*, 213	丈*obust*, 463

剣*word*, 939

796-B
Narcotic 剤rugs, 済ettled by thugs...

水⇔氵 (water)

済ettle   済onsummate

su(mu), su(masu), SAI

settle, consummate, relieve

FLIP: 7.0.b2. Right (stem)

済みません	*"sorry, pardon me..."* **sumimasen**		未決済	*outstanding accounts* **mikessai**
弁済	*repayment, payment* **bensai**		用済み	*business finished, affairs settled* **yōzumi**
返済	*repayment, refund* **hensai**		払い済み	*paid up, settled* **harai zumi**
皆済	*full payment, fully-paid* **kaisai**		検査済み	*"examined, passed..."* **kensa zumi**
完済	*full payment, fully-paid* **kansai**		気が済む	*be satisfied* **kigasumu**
経済	*economy, economics* **keizai**		済し崩し	*instalment payments* **nashikuzushi**
⇒計画経済	*economic planning* **keikaku keizai**		多士済々	*many able people* **tashi saisai**
決済	*payment, account settlement* **kessai**		登録済み	*registered* **tōroku zumi**
既済	*paid-up, fully-paid* **kisai**		約定済み	*committed; engaged* **yakujyō zumi**
共済	*co-operative, mutual aid* **kyōsai**		成り済ます	*pose, disguise as* **narisumasu**
救済	*relief, aid* **kyūsai**		受け取り済み	*"payment received..."*
救済策	*relief measures, remedy* **kyūsaisaku**			**uketori zumi**
未済	*unsettled, unpaid, outstanding* **misai**			
内済	*out-of-court settlement* **naisai**			
済度	*redemption, salvation* **saido**			
済民	*relieving people's suffering* **saimin**			
済生	*life saving* **saisei**			
済世	*social reform* **saisei**			
不経済	*poor economy* **fukeizai**			

終*inish*, 397	既*lready*, 316
了*inish*, 456	即*mmediate*, 421
完*omplete*, 196	納*ayment*, 296

剤*rugs*, 961

797-A
謹*espectful* 勤*mployees fired the least...*

謹*espect* 謹*evere*

言 (speaking)

FLIP: 5.0.a Left & Right

tsutsushi(mu), KIN
respect, revere, courtesy, homage

謹んで *"heartily, reverently..."* **tsutsushinde**
謹聴 *listening attentively, ~intently* **kinchō**
謹直 *conscientious, dutiful, responsible* **kinchoku**
謹厳 *sober, solemn, calm* **kingen**
謹言 *"yours sincerely..."* **kingen**
謹啓 *"Dear Sir, Dear Madame..."* **kinkei**
謹告 *"respectfully..."* **kinkoku**
謹製 *carefully-made* **kinsei**
謹撰 *"carefully chosen for you..."* **kinsen**
謹慎 *house confinement; penitence* **kinshin**
謹書 *respectfully written* **kinsho**
謹呈 *"compliments from the author..."* **kintei**
謹呈本 *complimentary book* **kinteihon**
謹話 *polite salutations* **kinwa**
細謹 *minor defect, ~flaw* **saikin**
不謹慎 *rash, imprudent* **fukinshin**
謹賀新年 *"Happy New Year!..."* **kinga shinnen**

申 *peak humble*, 89	尚 *espect*, 99
恭 *espect*, 620	崇 *espect*, 879
仰 *espect*, 706	礼 *espect*, 685
敬 *espect*, 329	徳 *irtue*, 844

護 *efence*, 828

797-B
謹*espectful* 勤*mployees fired the least...*

勤*mploy* 勤*ervice*

力 (strength, force)

FLIP: 6.0.a. Left (flat)

tsuto(meru), tsuto(maru), KIN
employ, service, serve

勤め口 *workplace, duty station* **tsutomeguchi**
勤め先 *office, workplace* **tsutomesaki**
忠勤 *work loyalty, company loyalty* **chūkin**
外勤 *outside duty* **gaikin**
勤行 *religious service* **gongyō**
常勤 *full-time staff, regular worker* **jōkin**
皆勤 *perfect work attendance* **kaikin**
皆勤賞 *perfect work attendance award* **kaikinshō**
欠勤 *work absence* **kekkin**
勤勉 *persevering, tenacious, diligent* **kinben**
勤倹 *frugality, thrift* **kinken**
勤務 *service, work, duty* **kinmu**
⇒超過勤務 *overtime work* **chōka kinmu**
勤務条件 *working conditions* **kinmu jōken**
勤務成績 *job performance record* **kinmu seiseki**
勤皇 *loyalty to the emperor* **kinnō**
勤労 *work, labour, service* **kinrō**
勤労意欲 *work vigour, eagerness to work* **kinrō iyoku**
勤続 *continuous-, long service* **kinzoku**

勤続年数 *length of service* **kinzoku nensū**
勤続手当 *long-service allowance* **kinzoku teate**
内勤 *indoor service* **naikin**
日勤 *daily work, daily grind* **nikkin**
精勤 *diligence, hardworking* **seikin**
精勤賞 *attendance award* **seikinshō**
出勤 *going to one's workplace* **shukkin**
転勤 *work re-assignment, job transfer* **tenkin**
通勤 *commuting to work* **tsūkin**
夜勤 *night duty, ~shift, ~work* **yakin**
在勤 *work, earn a living* **zaikin**

採 *mploy*, 915	雇 *mploy*, 343	仕 *ervice*, 9
抱 *mploy*, 503	就 *mploy*, 719	働 *abour*, 422
務 *mploy*, 454	職 *mploy*, 855	労 *abour*, 351

勘 *ntuition*, 294

798-A

Distance 隔ntervals 融issolve with click & portal...

隔nterval   隔istance

阝 ⇔ 阜 (village=left)

FLIP: 7.0.b2. Right (stem)

heda(teru), heda(taru), KAKU
interval, distance, apart, spacing

心隔て *secretive, reticent, tight-lipped* **kokorohedate**
分け隔て *distinction, discrimination* **wakehedate**
中隔 *septum* **chūkaku**
遠隔 *distance, gap* **enkaku**
遠隔地 *remote place* **enkakuchi**
遠隔操作 *remote control* **enkaku sōsa**
従隔 *mediastinum* **jūkaku**
隔晩 *taking turns on duty* **kakuban**
隔月 *every other month* **kakugetsu**
隔意 *reservation, alienation* **kakui**
隔日 *every other day* **kakujitsu**
隔膜 *diaphragm* **kakumaku**
隔年 *every other year* **kakunen**
隔離 *isolation, quarantine* **kakuri**
隔離病棟 *isolation ward* **kakuri byōtō**
隔世遺伝 *atavism, reversion* **kakusei iden**
隔室 *compartment* **kakushitsu**
隔週 *every other week* **kakushū**
隔壁 *partition, divider wall* **kakuheki**

隔絶 *isolation, separation* **kakuzetsu**
間隔 *interval, space* **kankaku**
懸隔 *gap, disparity* **kenkaku**
離隔 *isolation, insularity, segregation* **rikaku**
疎隔 *estrangement, alienation* **sokaku**
横隔膜 *diaphragm* **ōkakumaku**

差ifference, 589	悠istant, 898
違isparity, 796	遠istant, 916
間nterval, 286	疎istant, 955

融issolve, 963

798-B

Distance 隔ntervals 融issolve with click & portal...

融issolve   融elting

虫 (insect)

FLIP: 6.0.a. Left (flat)

YŪ
dissolve, melting, fusion

金融 *finance, banking* **kinyū**
金融界 *financial world* **kinyūkai**
金融機関 *financial institution* **kinyū kikan**
特融 *special financing* **tokuyū**
闇金 *loan shark, illegal lending* **yamikin**
熔融 *fuse, melt* **yōyū**
熔融点 *melting point* **yōyūten**
溶融 *meltdown* **yōyū**
融合 *fusion, merger, harmony* **yūgō**
融氷 *melting ice* **yūhyō**
融解 *fusion, melting, dissolution* **yūkai**
融解点 *melting point* **yūkaiten**
融解熱 *fusion heat* **yūkainetsu**
融熱 *melting heat* **yūnetsu**
融接 *fusion welding* **yūsetsu**
融資 *loan, financing* **yūshi**
融点 *melting point* **yūten**
融化 *softening, melting away* **yūka**
融雪 *thawing, melting snow* **yūsetsu**

融和 *harmony, reconciliation* **yūwa**
融通 *flexibility, accommodation* **yūzū**
融通性 *flexibility, leeway, leverage* **yūzūsei**
融通手形 *accommodation bill* **yūzūtegata**
雪融け *snow thawing, de-icing* **yukidoke**
核融合 *nuclear fusion* **kakuyūgō**

溶issolve, 758	解issolve, 400
混ixture, 38	液iquid, 508
紛ixture, 778	

隔nterval, 963

799-A

厚*hick writing of* 願*equests to the King...*

❶厚*hick* ❷厚*indness*

厂 (cliff)

atsu(i), KŌ
thick, broad, bulky; kindness

FLIP: 8.0.a. Inner (flat)

❶厚ぼったい *heavy, very thick* **atsubottai**
厚かましい *shameless, brazen* **atsukamashii**
厚手 *heavy, thick* **atsude**
厚紙 *cardboard* **atsugami**
厚着 *heavy clothing* **atsugi**
厚板 *thick board* **atsuita**
厚地 *thick cloth* **atsuji**
厚め *thick* **atsume**
厚み *thickness* **atsumi**
重厚 *profoundness, seriousness* **jūkō**
重厚長大 *large & heavy, bulky* **jūkō chōdai**
寛厚 *generous, largehearted* **kankō**
厚顔 *temerity, shameless, "thick face"* **kōgan**
厚遇 *warm welcome, cordial reception* **kōgū**
厚薄 *relative thickness* **kōhaku**
肉厚 *thickness (wall)* **nikuatsu**
濃厚 *thick, deep, strong, rich* **nōkō**
厚切り *sliced thick* **atsugiri**
厚化粧 *heavy makeup* **atsugeshō**

分厚い *bulky, hefty, thick* **buatsui**
❷厚意 *kind feelings, good-heartedness* **kōi**
厚情 *kind feelings, good-heartedness* **kōjō**
厚恩 *great kindness, magnanimous* **kōon**
厚生 *social welfare* **kōsei**
厚生年金 *pension money* **kōsei nenkin**
厚生施設 *welfare facilities* **kōsei shisetsu**
厚志 *"your kindness..."* **kōshi**
温厚 *mild, gentle, mild-mannered* **onkō**
深厚 *deep, heartfelt, sincere* **shinkō**
手厚い *cordial, hospitable; generous* **teatsui**

太*hick, 6*	広*arge, 205*	重*eavy, 430*
濃*hick, 446*	巨*iant, 206*	
拡*nlarge, 205*	超*xceed, 664*	

原*riginal, 431*

799-B

厚*hick writing of* 願*equests to the King...*

願*equest* 願*sk a favour*

頁 (large shell, page)

nega(u), GAN
request, ask a favour

FLIP: 7.0.b2. Right (stem)

哀願 *imploring, invoking* **aigan**
勅願 *imperial prayer* **chokugan**
代願 *proxy requesting* **daigan**
願望 *wish, desire* **ganbō**
願力 *will power, determination* **ganriki**
願書 *written application* **gansho**
悲願 *earnest wish* **higan**
依願 *at one's request* **igan**
結願 *expiry of a vow* **ketsugan**
祈願 *prayer, prayer wish* **kigan**
懇願 *entreaty, solicitation* **kongan**
満願 *vow fulfilment* **mangan**
念願 *desire, wish, request* **nengan**
熱願 *burning wish, ardent desire* **netsugan**
立願 *prayer, prayer wish* **ritsugan**
請願 *petition, appeal* **seigan**
誓願 *vow, commitment* **seigan**
切願 *entreaty, appeal, petition* **setsugan**
志願 *application, volunteering* **shigan**

志願者 *applicant, candidate, hopeful* **shigansha**
心願 *heartful desire* **shingan**
宿願 *long-cherished desire* **shukugan**
出願 *application, petition, request* **shutsugan**
訴願 *entreaty, appeal, petition* **sogan**
大願 *aspiration, dream* **taigan**
嘆願 *entreaty, appeal, petition* **tangan**
請願書 *written petition* **seigansho**
嘆願書 *written petition, request* **tangansho**
願い事 *wish, something to request* **negaigoto**
他力本願 *depending on others* **tariki hongan**

陳*etition, 132*	請*emand, 791*	望*esire, 618*
依*equest, 355*	頼*equest, 562*	
求*equest, 256*	希*esire, 208*	

顧*onsider, 343*

800-A

豊*bundant harvest, farmers'* 喜*-appiness...*

豆 (beans)

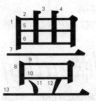

豊*bundance* 豊*lenty*

yuta(ka), HŌ
abundance, plenty, bountiful, opulence, plenitude, prosperous, largesse

FLIP: 1.0.a. Whole (flat)

豊艶 *beautiful body, voluptuous* **hōen**
豊富 *abundant, plentiful* **hōfu**
豊穣 *abundant harvest* **hōjō**
豊饒 *abundant harvest* **hōjō**
豊熟 *abundant harvest* **hōjuku**
豊潤 *abundance, richness* **hōjun**
豊胸 *large breast; to enlarge* **hōkyō**
豊凶 *rich-or-poor harvest* **hōkyō**
豊満 *plump, abundant* **hōman**
豊年 *good harvest year* **hōnen**
豊漁 *large fishing catch* **hōryō**
豊作 *rich harvest, bumper crop* **hōsaku**
豊水 *water supply abundance* **hōsui**
豊水期 *rainy season* **hōsuiki**
豊沃 *good harvest, fertile farm* **hōyoku**
実り豊か *fruitful, plenty, abundant* **minori yutaka**

多*lenty, 187*	繁*rosperity, 434*
富*ortune, 333*	隆*rosperity, 133*
裕*ffluence, 758*	盛*rosperity, 244*

農*griculture, 446*

800-B

豊*-bundant harvest, farmers'* 喜*-appiness...*

口 (mouth)

喜*appiness* 喜*oyful*

yoroko(bu), KI
happiness, joyful, heartening, felicity, rejoice

FLIP: 1.0.a. Whole (flat)

悲喜 *joy & sorrow* **hiki**
悲喜劇 *tragicomedy* **hikigeki**
歓喜 *joy, delight, ecstasy* **kanki**
喜悦 *joy, happiness, delight* **kietsu**
喜劇 *comedy play, satire* **kigeki**
喜劇的 *comic, satirical* **kigekiteki**
喜劇俳優 *comedy actor, comedian* **kigeki haiyū**
喜寿 *seventieth birthday* **kiju**
喜捨 *charity, donation* **kisha**
喜色 *joy, happiness* **kishoku**
喜憂 *joy & sorrow* **kiyū**
驚喜 *joy, happiness* **kyōki**
狂喜 *exultation, ecstasy* **kyōki**
喜歌劇 *operetta* **kikageki**
大喜び *great joy* **ooyorokobi**
喜び事 *happy incident* **yorokobigoto**
喜び勇む *high spirits, jolly* **yorokobi isamu**
一喜一憂 *laughter & tears* **ikki ichiyū**
喜怒哀楽 *feelings, emotions, passions* **kido airaku**

延喜時代 *Enji Era (901-923)* **enji jidai**
寛喜時代 *Kangi Era (1229-1231)* **kangi jidai**
天喜時代 *Tengi Era (1053-1058)* **tengi jidai**

幸*appiness, 268*	賀*elebration, 202*
祥*appiness, 248*	祝*elebration, 716*
慶*ejoice, 69*	

善*ighteous, 450*

801-A

Direct 嫡eirs of my 敵nemy, now after me..!

女 (woman)

嫡*eirling*　嫡*egitimate child*

CHAKU, TEKI
heirling, legitimate

FLIP: 7.0.a. Right (flat)

嫡男 *eldest son, heir apparent* **chakunan**	
嫡流 *succession in favour of eldest son* **chakuryū**	
嫡妻 *one's real wife* **chakusai**	
嫡子 *legitimate child* **chakushi**	
嫡嗣 *legitimate heir* **chakushi**	
嫡室 *legitimate wife* **chakushitsu**	
嫡出 *legitimate birth* **chakushutsu**	
⇒非嫡出 *illegitimate birth* **hichakushutsu**	
嫡出子 *legitimate child* **chakushutsushi**	
嫡孫 *eldest grandson* **chakuson**	
廃嫡 *disinheritance, disowning* **haichaku**	
正嫡 *legal wife; legitimate heir* **seichaku**	

嗣*uccessor, 836*	縁*inship, 675*
副*eputy, 332*	遺*eave-behind, 914*
次*ext, 460*	残*eave-behind, 767*
継*ontinuity, 958*	

嬢*aughter, 854*

801-B

Direct 嫡eirs of my 敵nemy, now after me..!

攵 (action)

敵*nemy*　敵*ival*

kataki, TEKI
enemy, rival, foe, opponent, competitor

FLIP: 6.0.b. Left (stem)

匹敵 *perfect match* **hitteki**	敵性 *hostility, animosity, acrimony* **tekisei**
敵役 *villain role* **katakiyaku**	敵視 *hostile-looking, menacing* **tekishi**
恋敵 *love rival* **koigataki**	敵失 *enemy error* **tekishitsu**
無敵 *unrivalled, overwhelming* **muteki**	敵襲 *enemy attack* **tekishū**
内敵 *enemy from within* **naiteki**	敵対 *hostile, belligerent, hot-blooded* **tekitai**
難敵 *formidable opponent* **nanteki**	敵前 *facing one's enemy* **tekizen**
怨敵 *sworn-, blood enemy* **onteki**	残敵 *remaining enemy* **zanteki**
利敵 *enemy advantage* **riteki**	敵討ち *revenge, getting back at* **katakiuchi**
論敵 *enemy argument* **ronteki**	目の敵 *threatening looks* **menokataki**
索敵 *enemy search* **sakuteki**	敵愾心 *hostility, animosity, acrimony* **tekigaishin**
小敵 *weak opponent* **shōteki**	敵味方 *friend & foe, opposite sides* **tekimikata**
宿敵 *old enemy, blood enemy* **shukuteki**	
敵地 *enemy territory* **tekichi**	
敵弾 *enemy fire* **tekidan**	
敵軍 *enemy soldiers* **tekigun**	
敵陣 *enemy line* **tekijin**	
敵状 *enemy strength & weakness* **tekijō**	
敵機 *enemy plane* **tekki**	
敵国 *enemy country* **tekikoku**	

戦*ighting, 517*	盟*lliance, 21*	勝*ictory, 406*
争*onflict, 231*	連*lliance, 305*	競*ompetition,*

商*ommerce, 135*

802-A

貯*tore-up savings net* 寧*ather-than be* 寧*ourteous &* 寧*uiet...*

貝 (shell, old money)

貯*torage*　　貯*avings*

CHO
storage, savings, deposits, lay up

FLIP: 6.0.b. Left (stem)

貯木　*stock lumber* **choboku**
貯蓄　*savings, reserve funds* **chochiku**
貯蓄心　*savings propensity* **chochikushin**
貯金　*savings, money deposits* **chokin**
⇒預貯金　*bank deposit, bank savings* **yochokin**
⇒定額貯金　*scheduled money for savings*
　　teigaku chokin
⇒定期貯金　*certificate-of-deposits (CDs), time deposit*
　　teiki chokin
貯金箱　*piggy bank, savings box* **chokinbako**
貯金通帳　*savings book, bankbook* **chokin tsūchō**
貯水池　*water reservoir* **chosuichi**
貯水量　*volume of stored water* **chosuiryō**
貯水槽　*water reservoir* **chosuisō**
貯水塔　*water tower tank* **chosuitō**
貯炭　*stored coal* **chotan**
貯炭所　*coal storehouse* **chotanjo**
貯蔵　*storage, preservation* **chozō**

貯蔵物　*stored goods, provision* **chozōbutsu**
貯蔵品　*stored goods, supplies* **chozōhin**
貯蔵庫　*storehouse, storage* **chozōko**
貯蔵米　*stored rice* **chozōmai**
貯蔵室　*storeroom, storage* **chozōshitsu**

庫*torage, 306*	給*upply, 143*
倉*torage, 399*	納*upply, 296*
蔵*torage, 565*	与*upply, 349*
予*dvance, 569*	充*upply, 884*

財*inance, 186*

802-B

貯*tore-up savings net* 寧*ather-than be* 寧*ourteous &* 寧*uiet...*

宀 (cover, lid)

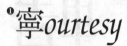寧*ourtesy*　　❷寧*ather than*

mushi(ro), NEI
courtesy, quiet; rather than

FLIP: 8.0.a. Inner (flat)
FLIP: 4.0.b. Bottom (stem)

❶安寧　*peace & order, well-being* **annei**
安寧秩序　*peace & order, social peace* **annei chitsujo**
康寧　*tranquillity, serenity, calm* **kōnei**
寧日　*tranquil-, serene day* **neijitsu**
丁寧　*courteous, polite, respectful* **teinei**
安寧時代　*Annei Era (549-511)* **annei jidai**
清寧時代　*Seinei Era (480-484)* **seinei jidai**

❷寧ろ　*"but rather, on the otherhand..."* **mushiro**

黙*uiet, 846*	康*ranquillity, 881*
幽*uiet, 897*	異*lse, 239*
穏*ranquillity, 840*	他*lse, 688*

漫*andom, 845*

803-A

割amaged steel 轄edge, 割ivided the bridge edge...

刀⇔刂 (blade, cutting)

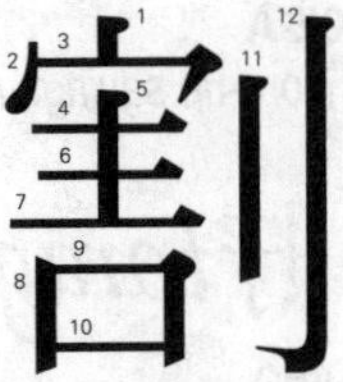

FLIP: 6.0.a. Left (flat)

割ivide 割artition

wa(ru), wa(reru), sa(ku), KATSU
divide, partition, discount, on sale

分割 *division, partition* **bunkatsu**
学割 *student discount* **gakuwari**
掘割 *canal, waterway* **horiwari**
一割 *ten percent* **ichiwari**
割拠 *holding one's ground* **kakkyo**
割烹 *Japanese-style cooking* **kappō**
割賦 *instalment, partial payment* **kappu**
割愛 *giving up reluctantly* **katsuai**
割譲 *ceding, cessation* **katsujō**
割礼 *circumcision* **katsurei**
正割 *secant* **seikatsu**
割引 *price discount* **waribiki**
割線 *secant* **warisen**
役割 *part, role, duty* **yakuwari**
日割り *daily rate* **hiwari**
水割り *mixing alcohol with water* **mizuwari**
割れ目 *crack, crevice, cranny* **wareme**
割り印 *tally impression, tally seal* **wariin**
割り勘 *Dutch treat, pay for oneself* **warikan**
割り前 *share, part, cut* **warimae**
割り算 *mathematical division* **warizan**
部屋割り *room allotment* **heyawari**
時間割り *schedule, timetable* **jikanwari**
均等割り *per capita rate* **kintōwari**
割り当て *assignment, allotment* **wariate**
割り出す *detect, find out, calculate* **waridasu**
割り振り *allotment, distribution* **warifuri**
割り切る *give a definite solution* **warikiru**
割り込み *interruption, obstruction* **warikomi**
割り増し *extra, premium, overtime pay* **warimashi**

分*ivide, 518*	違*isparity, 796*
剖*ivide, 950*	差*ifference, 589*
別*eparate, 866*	離*eparate, 775*

害*njury, 904*

803-B

割amaged steel 轄edge, 割ivided the bridge edge...

車 (vehicle, wheel)

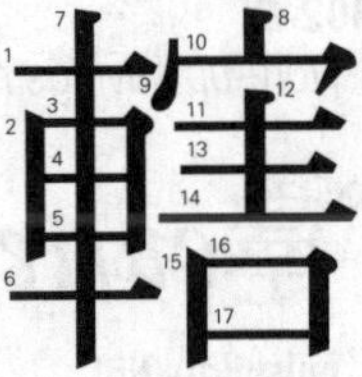

FLIP: 5.0.a. Left & Right

轄edge 轄urisdiction

KATSU
wedge, jurisdiction, control

分轄 *separate jurisdiction* **bunkatsu**
直轄 *direct control* **chokkatsu**
管轄 *jurisdiction, judicature* **kankatsu**
管轄違い *"no jurisdiction..."* **kankatsu chigai**
管轄官庁 *competent authorities* **kankatsu kanchō**
管轄区域 *territorial jurisdiction* **kankatsu kuiki**
車轄 *linchpin* **shakatsu**
所轄 *jurisdiction, judicature* **shokatsu**
所轄官庁 *competent authorities* **shokatsu kanchō**
総轄 *general supervision, control* **sōkatsu**
統轄 *supervision, control* **tōkatsu**
統轄者 *supervisor, in-charge* **tōkatsusha**

管*ontrol, 917*
軸*xle, 659*
枢*ivot, 952*

輪*ing, 786*

804-A
醜*gly* 魅*harm does no harm...*

醜*gly*　　　醜*ad-looking*

miniku(i), SHŪ
ugly, bad-looking

美醜 *looks, beauty or ugliness* **bishū**
醜男 *ugly man* **buotoko**
老醜 *senility ugliness* **rōshū**
醜悪 *ugly & mean* **shūaku**
醜聞 *scandalous news* **shūbun**
醜業 *shameful trade, prostitution* **shūgyō**
醜業婦 *prostitute, hooker* **shūgyōfu**
醜状 *shameful state-of-affairs* **shūjō**
醜女 *ugly woman* **shūjo, buonna**
醜怪 *ugly & bizarre* **shūkai**
醜行 *disgraceful behaviour* **shūkō**
醜交 *illicit intercourse* **shūkō**
醜類 *ugly types* **shūrui**
醜態 *shameful conduct* **shūtai**
醜と美 *beauty & ugliness* **shūtobi**
醜関係 *illicit relations* **shūkankei**

酉 (liquor)

FLIP: 6.0.a. Left (flat)

| 獣*onster, 846* | 魔*emon, 332* |
| 獣*east, 846* | 鬼*emon, 935* |

魂*pirit, 936*

804-B
醜*gly* 魅*harm does no harm...*

魅*harm*　　　魅*ppeal*

MI
charm, appeal, beauty, charisma, enchantment

魅せられる *be enchanted* **miserareru**
魑魅 *mountain devils* **chimi**
魔魅 *deceiving spirit* **mami**
魅入る *evil-possessed* **miiru**
魅了 *charm, fascination* **miryō**
魅力 *charm, appeal, attraction* **miryoku**
魅力的 *attractive, appealing, charming* **miryokuteki**
魅惑 *fascination, charm* **miwaku**
魅惑的 *fascinating, charming* **miwakuteki**

鬼 (spirits)

FLIP: 7.2.b. Right Top (stem)

美*eautiful, 124*	韻*raceful, 315*
麗*eautiful, 68*	雅*raceful, 58*
佳*eauty, 891*	淑*raceful, 510*

魂*pirit, 936*

805-A

乳*ilk bottle that* 浮*loats thrown from a boat...*

乙⇔乚 (fish hook)

 乳*ilk*　　　　乳*airy*

Facing: 4.0. ⬅️➡️ Apart

chichi, chi, NYŪ
milk, dairy

母乳	breast-feeding, mother's milk	**bonyū**
乳房	breast, nipple	**chibusa, nyūbō**
乳首	breast nipple	**chikubi**
粉乳	powdered-, dry milk	**funnyū**
牛乳	milk, dairy	**gyūnyū**
牛乳瓶	milk bottle, dairy bottle	**gyūnyūbin**
牛乳屋	milk shop, dairy	**gyūnyūya**
授乳	breast-feeding, lactation	**junyū**
乳棒	pestle	**nyūbō**
乳液	milky lotion, latex	**nyūeki**
乳癌	breast cancer	**nyūgan**
乳業	dairy industry	**nyūgyō**
乳牛	dairy cattle, milk cow	**nyūgyū**
乳児	suckling, baby	**nyūji**
乳化	emulsification, soluble	**nyūka**
乳面	nipple	**nyūmen**
乳酸	lactic acid	**nyūsan**
乳歯	milk tooth, baby tooth	**nyūshi**
乳質	milk grade, ~quality	**nyūshitsu**

乳頭	breast nipple	**nyūtō**
乳糖	milk sugar, lactose	**nyūtō**
離乳	weaning away	**rinyū**
搾乳	milking, lactating	**sakunyū**
搾乳器	milking device, milker	**sakunyūki**
豆乳	soybean milk	**tōnyū**
乳母	nurse, midwife	**uba**
乳母車	baby car, ~carriage	**ubaguruma**
乳臭い	milk smell; immature	**chichikusai**
乳製品	dairy produce	**nyūseihin**
乳幼児	infant, babies	**nyūyōji**
乳飲み子	breast-fed baby	**chinomigo**

酪*airy*, 670	畜*reeding*, 528	健*ealthy*, 390
飼*reeding*, 835	養*reeding*, 253	飲*rinking*, 255

浮*loat*, 970

805-B

乳*ilk bottle that* 浮*loats thrown from a boat...*

水⇔氵 (water)

 浮*loat*　　　浮*igh spirits*

Facing: 1.2. ⬅️ West (V)

u(kabu), u(kaberu), u(ku), u(kareru), FU
float, high spirits, buoyant, vibrant

浮沈	rise & fall, vicissitudes	**fuchin**
浮動	fluctuating, floating	**fudō**
浮言	wild rumour, fancy tale	**fugen**
浮薄	flippant, frivolous	**fuhaku**
浮上	rising to the surface	**fujō**
浮華	empty show	**fuka**
浮力	buoyancy	**furyoku**
浮流	drifting around, ~about	**furyū**
浮生	temporal life	**fusei**
浮説	unfounded story, rumour	**fusetsu**
浮腫	swelling, dropsy	**fushu**
浮腫み	swelling, dropsy	**mukumi**
浮氷	floating ice	**fuhyō**
浮標	buoy, float	**fuhyō**
浮遊	floating	**fuyū**
浮島	floating island	**ukishima**
浮気	flirting, illicit sex relations	**uwaki**
浮浪者	homeless, vagabond, wanderer	**furōsha**
浮き世	temporal world, transient life	**ukiyo**

浮き袋	life buoy, float	**ukibukuro**
浮き雲	floating cloud	**ukigumo**
浮き草	floating plants, duckweed	**ukikusa**
浮き沈み	ups & downs	**ukishizumi**
浮き立つ	be cheered up	**ukitatsu**
浮き浮き	cheerful, light-hearted, jestful	**ukiuki**
浮き出る	stand out, break out, protrude	**ukideru**
浮き上がる	rise, surface	**ukiagaru**
浮き足立つ	waver, falter, unsteady	**ukiashidatsu**
浮世絵	type of Japanese woodblock print	**ukiyoe**
浮かぬ顔	gloomy-, grave look	**ukanukao**
思い浮かぶ	float in one's mind	**omoiukabu**

浪*rifting*, 254		方*irection*, 533
波*urrent*, 32		義*ighteous*, 341
流*urrent*, 781		善*ighteous*, 450

乳*airy*, 970

806-A

Golden 卵ggs for free by the 柳illow-tree...

卵*gg*　　　　卵*vum*

tamago, RAN
egg, ovum

魚卵 *fish eggs, roe* **gyoran**
排卵 *ovulation* **hairan**
抱卵 *incubation* **hōran**
抱卵器 *incubator* **hōranki**
煎り卵 *scrambled egg* **iritamago**
寒卵 *winter egg* **kantamago**
鶏卵 *chicken egg* **keiran**
生卵 *raw egg* **namatamago**
卵殻 *egg shell* **rankaku, tamagogara**
卵管 *oviduct, fallopian tubes* **rankan**
卵形 *oval, egg shape* **rankei**
卵黄 *egg yolk* **ran'ō**
卵白 *albumen, egg whites* **ranpaku**
卵生 *oviparous* **ransei**
卵生動物 *oviparous animal* **ransei dōbutsu**
卵子 *ovum* **ranshi**
卵巣 *ovary* **ransō**
採卵 *egg farming, egg raising* **sairan**
産卵 *laying eggs* **sanran**

卩 (joint; stamp)

FLIP: 2.0.b. Sort Of (stem)

卵色 *yellowish egg-like colour* **tamagoiro**
卵酒 *eggnog, egg flip* **tamagozake**
孵卵器 *egg incubator* **furanki**
夢精卵 *unfertilised eggs* **museiran**
落し卵 *poached egg* **otoshi tamago**
卵とじ *egg* **tamagotoji**
卵焼き *fried egg, omelette* **tamagoyaki**
茹で卵 *boiled egg* **yudetamago**
輸卵管 *oviduct, fallopian tubes* **yurankan**

誕*hildbirth, 515*	娠*regnancy, 61*
産*hildbirth, 883*	妊*regnancy, 709*

命*estiny, 362*

806-B

Golden 卵ggs for free by the 柳illow-tree...

柳*illow-tree*

yanagi, RYŪ
willow-tree

青柳 *surf clam meat* **aoyagi**
箱柳 *Japanese aspen* **hakoyanagi**
蒲柳 *purple willow* **horyū**
蒲柳の質 *delicate state* **horyū no shitsu**
糸柳 *weeping willow* **itoyanagi**
花柳 *Geisha girl* **karyū**
花柳界 *red-light district* **karyūkai**
花柳界病 *venereal disease* **karyūkaibyō**
川柳 ① *purple willow* **kawayanagi**
川柳 ② *Japanese humour poem* **senryū**
猫柳 *pussy willow* **nekoyanagi**
柳眉 *pretty eyebrows* **ryūbi**
柳腰 *slim waist, slender body* **yanagigoshi**
雪柳 *kind of spirea* **yukiyanagi**
枝垂れ柳 *weeping willow* **shidareyanagi**

木 (wooden)

FLIP: 7.1. Right (Sort Of)

杉*edar-tree, 721*
齢*ge, 553*
巨*olossal, 206*

卵*gg, 971*

807-A

劾mpeached at a 刻oint-in-time, dictator turned 刻culptor...

力 (strength, force)

劾mpeach   劾xpose crimes

GAI

impeach, expose crimes

Facing: 2.2. East ☞ (V)

弾劾 *impeachment* **dangai**
弾劾演説 *impeachment speech* **dangai enzetsu**
弾劾裁判 *impeachment trial* **dangai saiban**
弾劾裁判所 *impeachment court* **dangai saibansho**
劾奏 *complaint to the emperor* **gaisō**

斥*ejection, 424*	打*trike, 636*
排*ejection, 795*	外*emove, 188*
断*ejection, 958*	脱*emove, 941*
否*ejection, 300*	倒*opple down, 496*

劾*ffect* 645

807-B

劾mpeached at a 刻oint-in-time, dictator turned 刻culptor...

刀⇔刂 (blade, cutting)

❶刻culpture ❷刻oint-in-time

kiza(mu), KOKU

sculpture, carve, engraving; point-in-time

Facing: 3.0. ☞➥ Across

❶刻み目 *notch, nick* **kizamime**
刻み込む *"engrave in memory..."* **kizamikomu**
彫刻 *sculpture, engraving* **chōkoku**
彫刻家 *sculptor, engraver* **chōkokuka**
打刻 *make record of* **dakoku**
復刻 *reproduction, reprinting* **fukkoku**
復刻本 *reprinted book* **fukkokubon**
腐刻 *etching, engraving* **fukoku**
翻刻 *reprint, reprinting* **honkoku**
刻印 *engraved seal* **kokuin**
刻字 *engraved letters* **kokuji**
切り刻む *mince, chop up* **kirikizamu**
❷遅刻 *late, tardy* **chikoku**
後刻 *later on, afterwards* **gokoku**
一刻 *moment* **ikkoku**
時刻 *time, hour* **jikoku**
⇒到着時刻 *arrival time* **tōchaku jikoku**
時刻表 *time schedule, ~chart* **jikokuhyō**
刻下 *present time* **kokka**

刻限 *appointed time, ~hour* **kokugen**
例刻 *the usual time* **reikoku**
漏刻 *water clock* **rōkoku**
先刻 *"a while ago, shortly before..."* **senkoku**
深刻 *serious, grave* **shinkoku**
瞬刻 *brief time, moment* **shunkoku**
即刻 *right away, immediately* **sokkoku**
数刻 *a few hours* **sūkoku**
寸刻 *brief time, moment* **sunkoku**
定刻 *fixed-, appointed time* **teikoku**
夕刻 *evening, night* **yūkoku**
刻一刻 *moment by moment* **kokuikkoku**

彫*hisel, 721*	芸*rts, 619*
像*tatue, 530*	巧*killful, 738*
工*rtisan, 176*	術*kills, 110*
匠*rtisan, 106*	象*mage, 530*

劾*mpeach, 972*

808-A

The 該[said] nations possess 核uclear weapons...

言 (speaking)

該*[the said]* 該*orresponding*

GAI
[the said], corresponding

該案 *proposal under discussion* **gaian**
該当 *application, corresponding* **gaitō**
該問題 *the concerned matter* **gaimondai**
該博知識 *intellectual thirst* **gaihaku chishiki**
当該人物 *concerned individuals* **tōgai jinbutsu**
当該官庁 *concerned authorities* **tōgai kanchō**

FLIP: 6.0.a. Left (flat)
Facing: 2.2. East ☞ (V)

述*ention, 95*
例*xample, 357*

核*uclear,973*

808-B

The 該[said] nations possess 核uclear weapons...

木 (wooden)

核*uclear* 核*ore*

KAKU
nuclear, core, kernel

核ミサイル *nuclear missile* **kakumisairu**
地核 *earth's core* **chikaku**
中核 *core, kernel, nucleus* **chūkaku**
反核 *anti-nuclear* **hankaku**
非核 *non-nuclear, conventional arms* **hikaku**
陰核 *clitoris* **inkaku**
痔核 *haemorrhoids* **jikaku**
核力 *nuclear energy* **kakuryoku**
核仁 *nucleus* **kakujin**
核膜 *nuclear membrane* **kakumaku**
核酸 *nucleic acid* **kakusan**
核心 *core, heart* **kakushin**
結核 *tuberculosis* **kekkaku**
結核菌 *tubercle bacillus* **kekkakukin**
熱核 *thermonuclear* **netsukaku**
原子核 *atomic nucleus* **genshikaku**
肺結核 *tuberculosis, lung disease* **haikekkaku**
核爆発 *nuclear explosion* **kakubakuhatsu**
核分裂 *nuclear fission* **kakubunretsu**

Facing: 2.2. East ☞ (V)
FLIP: 6.0.b. Left (stem)

核武装 *nuclear armament* **kakubusō**
核弾頭 *nuclear warhead* **kakudantō**
核反応 *nuclear reaction* **kakuhannō**
核兵器 *nuclear weapons* **kakuheiki**
核実験 *nuclear test* **kakujikken**
核燃料 *nuclear fuel, ~energy* **kakunenryō**
核戦争 *nuclear war* **kakusensō**
核融合 *nuclear fusion* **kakuyūgō**
核家族 *immediate family* **kakukazoku**
神経核 *neuron* **shinkeikaku**
核反応炉 *nuclear reactor* **kakuhan'ōro**

中*iddle, 85*   内*nside, 297*
央*entral, 218*   軸*xis, 659*
奥*nside, 903*

刻*culpture,972*

809-A

端xtreme 耐ndurance tests mind tolerance...

立 (standing)

端dge   端ndpoint

hashi, hata; ha, TAN
edge, endpoint, utmost

FLIP: 5.0.b. Left & Right

万端 *all, everything* **bantan**
船端 *sides of a boat* **funabata**
端株 *odd lot* **hakabu**
半端 *odd* **hanpa**
端面 *end face* **hashimen**
端数 *fraction, decimal* **hasū**
端役 *small part, extra* **hayaku**
片端 *one edge, one side* **katahashi**
末端 *end, tip, butt* **mattan**
目端 *quick witted* **mehashi**
右端 *right end* **migihashi**
炉端 *fireside, "by the fire..."* **robata**
戦端 *taking up arms* **sentan**
端倪 *inscrutable, mysterious* **tangei**
端末 *terminal, station, depot* **tanmatsu**
端正 *handsome, good-looking* **tansei**
端子 *terminal, station, depot* **tanshi**
端緒 *beginning, start* **tansho**
端的 *straightforward, frank* **tanteki**

端座 *sitting erect* **tanza**
多端 *many, varied* **tatan**
途端 *moment* **totan**
突端 *tip, point* **tottan**
端書き *preface, foreword* **hashigaki**
端折る *skip, cut short, leave out* **hashoru**
木っ端 *wood chips* **koppa**
下っ端 *underling, petty official* **shitappa**
端境期 *off-crop season* **hazakaiki**
初っ端な *from the beginning* **shoppana**
井戸端会議 *housewives' gossip (hang-out)*
   idobata kaigi

窮xtreme, 876	甚xtreme, 293	終inish, 397
極xtreme, 947	角ngle, 400	了inish, 456

需emand, 548

809-B

端xtreme 耐ndurance tests mind tolerance...

而 (rake)

耐ndure   耐ithstand

ta(eru), TAI
endure, withstand, resistant

FLIP: 6.0.b. Left (stem)
Facing: 3.0. ☞☜ Across

忍耐 *endurance, perseverance* **nintai**
忍耐力 *endurance-, perseverance ability* **nintairyoku**
忍耐強い *patience, persevere, steadfast* **nintaizuyoi**
耐え忍ぶ *bear, stand, put up with* **taeshinobu**
耐え切れる *endurable, bearable* **taekireru**
耐乏 *austerity, frugality, thrift* **taibō**
耐圧性 *pressure resistance* **taiatsusei**
耐風性 *wind resistance* **taifūsei**
耐火性 *fire resistance* **taikasei**
耐火材 *fireproof material* **taikazai**
耐火建築 *fireproof building* **taika kenchiku**
耐火構造 *fireproof construction* **taika kōzō**
耐火レンガ *firebrick* **taika renga**
耐久 *durability, endurance* **taikyū**
耐久力 *durability, persistence* **taikyūryoku**
耐久性 *durability, persistence* **taikyūsei**
耐久寿命 *long life, longevity* **taikyū jumyō**
耐性 *tolerance, resistance* **taisei**
耐用 *durability, long lasting* **taiyō**

耐用年数 *ever-lasting durability* **taiyō nensū**
耐寒性 *cold-, freezing endurance* **taikansei**
耐寒訓練 *winter training* **taikan kunren**
耐熱性 *heat-resistance* **tainetsusei**
耐酸性 *acid resistance* **taisansei**
耐雪性 *snow resistance* **taisetsusei**
耐震性 *earthquake-shock resistance* **taishinsei**
耐湿性 *moisture resistance* **taishitsusei**
耐食性 *corrosion resistance* **taishokusei**
耐水性 *water resistance* **taisuisei**

堪ndure, 294	寿ongevity, 440
励iligence, 465	永ong-lasting, 10
働abour, 422	久ong-lasting, 379
労abour, 351	

需emand, 548

810-A

鋼*teel gong must be solid* 剛*trong...*

鋼*teel*　　　鋼*etal*

hagane, KŌ
steel, metal, alloy

棒鋼　*steel bar* **bōkō**
鋳鋼　*steel casting* **chūkō**
鋼玉　*corundum, emery* **kōgyoku**
鋼板　*steel plate* **kōhan**
鋼管　*steel pipe* **kōkan**
鋼索　*wire rope, cable* **kōsaku**
鋼製　*steel manufacturing* **kōsei**
鋼線　*steel wire, iron wire* **kōsen**
鋼鉄　*steel, metal* **kōtetsu**
鋼鉄板　*steel plate* **kōtetsuban**
鋼鉄製　*made-of-steel* **kōtetsusei**
鋼鉄線　*steel wire, iron wire* **kōtetsusen**
鋼鉄車　*steel traincar* **kōtetsusha**
鋼材　*structural steel* **kōzai**
軟鋼　*mild steel* **nankō**
錬鋼　*wrought steel* **renkō**
製鋼　*steel manufacturing* **seikō**
製鋼所　*steel plant* **seikōjo**

金 (metal)

FLIP: 5.0.b. Left & Right

粗鋼　*crude steel* **sokō**
鍛鋼　*forged steel* **tankō**
鉄鋼　*steel, iron* **tekkō**
鉄鋼業　*steel industry* **tekkōgyō**
鉄鋼石　*iron ore* **tekkōseki**
特殊鋼　*special steel* **tokushukō**
圧延鋼　*rolled steel* **atsuenkō**
耐熱鋼　*heat-resistant steel* **tainetsukō**

銅*opper, 246*	鉛*ead, 757*
鉱*ineral-ore, 206*	鋳*asting, 440*
鉄*ron, 155*	

綱*ord, 159*

810-B

鋼*teel gong must be solid* 剛*trong...*

剛*trong*　　　剛*ough*

GŌ
strong, tough

剛直　*upright integrity* **gōchoku**
剛腹　*magnanimity, generosity; obstinacy* **gōbara**
剛愎　*magnanimity, generosity; obstinacy* **gōfuku**
剛健　*robust, sturdy, virile* **gōken**
剛毅　*resolute, firmness, determined* **gōki**
剛気　*brave, courageous* **gōki**
剛球　*fast ball (baseball)* **gōkyū**
剛毛　*bristle, seta* **gōmō**
剛力　*strong physical strength* **gōriki**
剛性　*stiffness, rigidity* **gōsei**
剛体　*stiff-, rigid body* **gōtai**
剛腕　*strong arm* **gōwan**
剛勇　*valour, bravery, courage* **gōyū**
金剛　*diamond* **kongō**
金剛石　*diamond stone* **kongōseki**
強剛　*strong, sturdy, robust* **kyōgō**
外柔内剛　*gentle-looking but tough* **gaijū naigō**

刀⇔刂 (blade, cutting)

FLIP: 6.0.b. Left (stem)

強*trong, 894*	固*ard, 491*
丈*obust, 463*	凝*arden, 57*
緊*ard, 599*	硬*ardness, 402*

綱*ord, 159*

811-A

璽mperial-seal coming soon, for the movie, " 繭ocoon..."

王⇔玉 (jewel)

璽mperial seal

JI
imperial seal

FLIP: 2.0.a. Sort Of (flat)

御璽 imperial seal **gyoji**
玉璽 imperial seal **gyokuji**
璽書 document bearing the imperial seal **jisho**
国璽 seal of the state **kokuji**
国璽尚書 lord chancellor **kokuji shōsho**

宮rince, 105	皇mperor, 113
詔mperial-edict, 817	后mpress, 87
勅mperial-edict, 955	朕mperial consent, 708

繭ocoon, 976

811-B

璽mperial-seal coming soon, for the movie, " 繭ocoon..."

糸 (thread,

繭ocoon

mayu, KEN
cocoon

FLIP: 3.0.b. Top (stem)
Facing: 2.2. East ☞ (V)

春繭 spring cocoon **harumayu**
繭価 cocoon price **kenka**
繭糸 cocoon silk thread **kenshi**
繭玉 festive cocoon **mayudama**
山繭 giant silkworm **yamamayu**

羅hin silk, 563
絹ilk, 158
蚕ilkworm, 628

璽mperial seal, 976

Important Kanji Characters with Multiple Meanings

I. Synonym Index

M

U

II. Stroke Index

1

了inish....456
一ne....858
乙econd group....5

2

又gain....177
刀lade....353
丁lock-of-houses....173
子hildren....456
十ross....344
八ight....4
入nter....2
九ine....73
人erson....2
七even....72
力trength....351
十en....344
二wo....457

3

勺[18 ml]....470
寸[3 cm]....345
弓rchery....348
孔onfucius....684
工raft....176
亡eath....72
下own....859
干rying-up....74
夕vening....187
才enius....185
土entleman....8
孔ole....684
大arge....7
久ong-lasting....379
山ountain....172
口outh....458
口pening....458
凡rdinary....78
及each....190
川iver....76
丈obust....463
丸ound....73
丸[ships]....73
己elf....5
小mall....459
土oil....8
与upply....349
刃word....75
万en thousand....465
千housand....74
三hree....858
上pper....859
女oman....350
才ears old....185

4

升[1.8 ltr]....298
斗[18 ltr]....195
匀[3.75 gm]....75
尺[30 cm]....574
斤[600 gm]....471
匹[animal]....17
欠bsence....460
予dvance....569
午fternoon....178
反gainst....537
化ecome....192
支ranch....201
仏uddha....683
牛attle....179
中hina....85
円ircle....24
収ollect....178
比ompare....466
切utting....352
刈utting....687
日ay....14
屯eployment....198
斗ipper....195
方irection....533
厄isaster....354
区istrict....80
分ivide....518
犬og....7
戸oor....428
凶vil....80
幻antasy....88
父ather....467
少ew....459
火ire....3
五ive....86
仏rance....683
友riendship....408
手and....370
心eart....469
天eaven....83
夫usband....83
内nside....297
込nward....93
日apan....14
夫ale labourer....83
介ediate....365
中iddle....85
王onarch....12
月onth....22
月oon....22
弔ourning....538
互utual....86
不[negative]....300
今ow....182
元rigin....195

片artial....359
方erson....533
比hilippines....466
乏overty....84
公ublic....180
引ulling....348
丹ed colour....78
冗edundant....861
介hellfish....365
六ix....3
毛kin hair....468
止top....192
日un....14
支upport....201
氏urname....489
太hick....6
木ree....461
双win....177
分nderstand....518
辺icinity....93
仁irtue....457
水ater....9
井ater well....361
文ritings....558
円en....24

5

必bsolutely....218
加ddition....201
司dminister....376
他nother....688
巡round....571
矢rrow....18
付ttach....382
冊[books]....20
本ook....461
加anada....201
央entral....218
幼hildhood....88
市ity....304
布loth....208
出ome-out....173
令ommand....362
凹oncave....23
写opy....349
正orrect....30
犯riminal....640
出epart....173
示isplay....878
字istrict....346
代poch....96
存xist....634
目ye....462
代ee....96
奴ellow....44
甲irst-group....89

平lat....488
旧ormerly....464
占ortune-telling....223
四our....17
且urther....500
巨iant....206
矛alberd....568
仙ermit....416
史istory....85
穴ole....4
氷ce....10
玉ewel....11
汁uice....344
存nowledge....634
札abel....685
広arge....205
末atter-part....13
去eave-out....360
左eft-side....310
字etter....346
生ife....474
好iking....637
永ong-lasting....10
本ain....461
市arket....304
功erits....635
失issing....19
札oney-bills....685
母other....90
北orthern....372
未ot yet....12
号umber....866
尼un....301
占ccupy....223
古ld....477
兄lder-brother....203
半ne-half....484
外utside....188
以[prefix]....472
払ayment....682
民eople....495
句hrase....16
詞hrase....376
皿late....21
台latform....209
目oint....462
可ossible....15
圧ressure....632
主rincipal....11
囚rison....863
玄rofound....358
厅ublic office....633
刊ublication....687
用urpose....409
生aw....474

12

13

III. Radical Index

IV. Readings Index: ON-KUN yo...

字istrict...... 346	匠rtisan...... 106	熟ipen...... 152	歌inging...... 878
耳ars...... 228	醸rewery...... 854	塾utorial school...... 152	夏ummer...... 606
除xclude...... 501	城astle...... 243	**JUN**	仮emporary...... 732
持olding...... 249	貞hastity...... 506	旬[10 day]...... 494	価alue...... 35
璽mperial seal...... 976	譲oncede...... 853	巡round...... 571	何hat...... 101
地and...... 688	状ondition...... 702	循irculation...... 407	渦hirlpool...... 798
字etter...... 346	情ondition...... 793	潤mbellish...... 930	**ka**
磁agnet...... 54	嬢aughter...... 854	準evel...... 919	日ay...... 14
次ext...... 460	定efinite...... 550	殉artyr...... 494	香ragrance...... 895
滋ourishment...... 55	情eelings...... 793	潤oisten...... 930	蚊osquito...... 654
磁orcelain...... 54	壌ertile soil...... 853	遵bedience...... 544	**kabe**
辞uitting...... 954	畳old-up...... 624	純urity...... 199	壁all...... 66
治ecuperate...... 210	場ocation...... 147	准atify...... 777	**kabu**
辞hetorics...... 954	常ormal...... 94	準emi-...... 919	株tocks...... 130
侍amurai...... 249	錠adlock...... 550	順equence...... 959	**kabuto**
自elf...... 462	盛rosperity...... 244	盾hield...... 407	甲irst-group...... 89
仕ervice...... 9	浄urity...... 230	**jun(zuru)**	**kado**
似imilar...... 472	静uiet...... 230	殉artyr...... 494	角orner...... 400
寺emple...... 248	冗edundant...... 861	**JUTSU**	門ate...... 286
十en...... 344	乗ideon...... 511	述ention...... 95	廉onest...... 525
時ime...... 653	丈obust...... 463	術echnique...... 110	**kadowaka(su)**
ji	縄ope...... 158	**KA**	拐idnap...... 956
路oad...... 405	蒸team...... 117	加ddition...... 201	**kaeri(miru)**
JIKI	剰urplus...... 511	寡lone...... 161	顧elf-reflect...... 343
直irect...... 420	錠ablet...... 550	佳eauty...... 891	省elf-reflect...... 572
食oods...... 255	畳atami...... 624	化ecome...... 192	**ka(eru)**
JIKU	上pper...... 859	禍alamity...... 799	変hange...... 581
軸xis...... 659	**JŌ**	菓andies...... 123	換eplace...... 819
JIN	従omply...... 551	加anada...... 201	替eplace...... 334
神ivine...... 712	十ross...... 344	荷argo...... 877	代eplace...... 96
陣ncampment...... 132	銃irearm...... 884	華hina...... 40	**kae(ru)**
尽xhaust...... 574	重eavy...... 430	嫁aughter-in-law...... 824	帰eturn...... 784
甚xtreme...... 293	汁uice...... 344	下own...... 859	返eturn...... 537
尋nquire...... 868	獣onster...... 846	過xcessive...... 798	**kae(su)**
人erson...... 2	重verlap...... 430	家xpert...... 909	帰eturn...... 784
臣etainer...... 542	拾ick-up...... 231	科aculty...... 194	返eturn...... 537
迅peedy...... 95	渋eluctance...... 613	家amily...... 909	**kae(tte)**
臣ubjects...... 542	住esidence...... 750	火ire...... 3	却ithdraw...... 387
刃word...... 75	柔oft...... 568	華lower...... 40	**kagami**
仁irtue...... 457	充upply...... 884	花lower...... 191	鏡irror...... 839
ji(rasu)	十en...... 344	暇ree time...... 653	**kaga(miru)**
焦ocus...... 405	縦ertical...... 551	貨reight...... 191	鑑ppraise...... 857
JITSU	**JOKU**	果ruit...... 287	**kaga(mu)**
日ay...... 14	辱umiliate...... 588	架anging...... 202	屈end...... 212
実ruth...... 121	**JU**	家ouse...... 909	**kagaya(ku)**
JO	樹ushes...... 926	課esson...... 287	輝parkling...... 296
助ssist...... 953	儒onfucius...... 548	寡ittle...... 161	**kage**
如qual...... 364	需emand...... 548	稼ake-a-living...... 824	陰idden...... 864
除xclude...... 501	就mploy...... 719	箇[objects]...... 52	影hadow...... 546
叙arrate...... 648	授rant...... 539	歌oem...... 878	陰hadow...... 864
序rder...... 873	寿ongevity...... 440	可ossible...... 15	**kage(ru)**
徐lowly...... 881	珠earl...... 233	箇[places]...... 52	陰idden...... 864
女oman...... 350	受eceive...... 539	果esult...... 287	陰hadow...... 864
JŌ	授eaching...... 539	河iver...... 877	**kagi(ru)**
成chieve...... 244	**JUKU**	課ection...... 287	限imit...... 771
条rticle...... 607	宿odging...... 448	靴hoes...... 40	**kaguwa(shii)**

V. Grade Level Index

VI. Japanese Language Proficiency Level Index

The following index is for the convenience of JLPT examinees. Kanji characters are classified from Fourth Level through First Level based on increasing difficulty. The First Level encompasses all Jōyō Kanji characters **except** for 19 Kanji characters listed on page 1090. The index was compiled based on published materials (see Bibliographical Reference) provided by the **Japan Foundation**. Kindly consult the Test Division of the Japan Foundation for details and updates.

===================

FIRST LEVEL
(Includes All Levels)

A

B

C

Excluded in the First-Level Japanese Language Proficiency Test

(Consult the JLPT Testing Centre)

VII. Kana Index

VIII. Flip-It Index

2.0.a. Sort Of ■
(Flat Base)

2.0.b. Sort Of ■
(Stem Base)

鳴owling 842
訟ndictment 181
諮nquire 865
唆nstigate 764
討nvestigate 691
鉄ron 155
訴awsuit 424
功erits 635
鉱ineral-ore 206
鋳intage 440
誤istake 889
謙odesty 805
獣onster 846
峠ountain trail 646
錠adlock 550
部art 957
割artition 968
鑑attern 857
舗ave 813
珠earl 233
許ermit 180
詞hrase 376
野lains 873
詩oetry 250
詠oetry 729
銘recepts 425
昨revious 722
護rotect 828
珍are 720
故eason 960
認ecognize 535
記ecord 728
録ecord 841
亭estaurant 393
酬eward 670
畝oof-ridge 379
喝colding 808
部ection 957
酌erve-wine 696
勤ervice 962
叫hout 693
銘ignature 425
銀ilver 773
誠incere 245
巧killful 738
眠leep 495
睡leeping 948
崎lope 270
鈍luggish 199
唯olitary 642
話peak 236
班quad 908
舗tore 813
的tyle 696
吸uction 190
略ummary 825

峰ummit 779
喚ummon 820
助upport 953
錠ablet 550
語alking 780
談alks 308
訓eachings 959
鍛emper 555
誘empt 895
時ime 653
訳ranslate 752
試rial 418
該[the said] 973
瞬winkle 921
醜gly 969
諸arious 794
詞erse 376
副ice 332
酢inegar 723
訪isit 737
暖armth 821
曜eekday 849
酔east 669

6.0.b. Left Whole ▣
(Stem Base)

対cross 691
粧dorn 656
対gainst 691
款rticle 42
戦attle 517
賜equeath 150
瓶ottle 886
就areer 719
執arry-out 268
彫hisel 721
彰itation 325
邦ountry 694
刈utting 687
斜iagonal 648
難ifficulty 927
献onation 414
剤rugs 961
乾rying 661
朝ynasty 662
効ffect 645
就mploy 719
耐ndure 974
敵nemy 966
戦ighting 517
財inance 186
靴ootwear 40
赦orgive 262
欺raudulent 658
新resh 668
款oodwill 42

執rasp 268
削rind 118
地round 688
勅mperial-edict 955
賦nstalment 160
親ntimate 669
邦apan 694
判udgement 949
耗essen 655
賦evy 160
料aterials 194
剤edicine 961
販erchandise 137
朝orning 662
塚ound 825
新ew 668
核uclear 973
判aper size 949
親arent 669
料ayment 194
刑enalty 536
期eriod 658
粘ersevere 223
刺ierce 875
銑ig iron 155
松ine-tree 181
賊iracy 160
粉owder 778
刊ublication 687
刑unishment 536
粋urity 762
静uiet 230
軌ailroad 660
帳egistry 641
則egulation 290
報eport 733
救escue 257
転oll over 661
帆ailing 641
散catter 337
販elling 137
隷ervant 880
影hadow 546
削harpen 118
輸hipment 660
靴hoes 40
軟oft 659
散pread-out 337
静tillness 230
貯torage 967
剛trong 975
郊uburbs 645
嗣uccessor 836
糖ugar 439
剣word 939
対owards 691

斜rajectory 648
財reasury 186

6.1. Left Top ▸

弊buse 171
整djust 31
起rise 754
撃ttack 613
襲ttack 630
裁lothes 802
照mbarass 529
郭nclose 398
熱eat 153
弊umble 171
想dea 524
趣nterest 663
暫nterim 928
勘ntuition 294
裁udgement 802
恐enace 906
幣oney 171
数umber 156
越vertake 663
塑attern 896
赴roceed-to-work 706
契romise 900
整ectify 31
熟ipen 152
栽aplings 803
離eparate 775
照hine 529
黙ilence 846
数pread-out 170
題ubject 834
超uper 664
題heme 834
熱hermal 153
題opic 834
塾utorial school 152
勢igour 153
勢itality 153
却ithdraw 387
FLIP: 6.2. Left Bottom ....
戒dmonish 493
到rrive 496
雑ssortment 776
髄one-marrow 806
致arry-out 381
鶏hicken 842
彩olour 914
郡ounty 258
創reativity 399
範xample 584
薪irewood 668
戯lirt 436
島sland 125

締ighten 432
鮮ivid 679
洋estern 247
鯨hale 679
抹ipe-out 13
妹ounger sister 114
禅en Buddhism 782

7.0.b2. Right Whole ▪
(Stem Base, Double)

積ccumulate 822
績chievement 822
額mount 559
填ncient tomb 848
供ttend to 303
焼arbeque 817
跳ounce 216
洞avern 246
祝elebration 716
穀ereal 41
挑hallenge 214
柄haracter 213
棋hess [Shōgi] 819
項lause 134
奴olleague 44
収ollect 178
併ombine 886
責ondemn 115
況ondition 716
情ondition 793
儒onfucius 548
顧onsider 343
済onsummate 961
続ontinue 260
綱ord 159
紋rest 558
債ebt 823
消elete 265
机esk 747
鍛iscipline 555
慎iscreet 831
頒istribution 835
溝itch 226
憤nrage 848
預ntrust 569
積stimate 822
倫thics 787
験xamine 673
役xecutive 746
漠xpanse 828
消xtinguish 265
滴xtract 799
顔ace 833
淡aint 309
扶amily-support 97
情eelings 793

奴ellow 44
洪looding 512
続ollow 260
挟orked 762
額rame 559
頻requent 272
倹rugal 938
般eneral 323
慣et used to 532
淑raceful 510
穀rain 41
慣abit 532
頭ead 832
漬mmerse 823
朕mperial consent 708
傾ncline 833
償ndemnity 554
痛njury 60
損njury 410
検nspection 939
院nstitution 196
隔nterval 963
漢anji 926
横ateral 197
跳eap 216
肢imbs 200
債oan 823
捜ook for 36
供ook-after 303
殿ordship 522
男asculine 597
僕asculine-servant 157
撲auling 157
膜embrane 827
嚇enace 261
併erge 886
慎odest 831
倹odest 938
蚊osquito 654
狭arrow 763
航avigation 748
慢egligence 845
漠bscure 828
役fficial 746
頻ften 272
抗pposition 749
憤utrage 848
殿alace 522
淡ale 309
柄attern 213
模attern 827
納ayment 296
桃each 215
演erformance 198
願etition 964
摘icking 800

漬ickling 823
悦leasant 942
摘luck 800
校roofreading 773
殴unch 745
清urify 793
漫andom 845
頂eceive 134
般egular 323
脱emove 941
願equest 964
抗esistance 749
焼oasting 817
綱ope 159
硝alt-peter 264
満atisfy 567
挟cissor 762
捜earch 36
順equence 959
済ettle 961
瀬hallows 562
横idewards 197
絹ilk 158
没inking 744
況ituation 716
肌kin 747
飢tarve 746
険teep 938
段tep 555
撲trike 157
脱trip-off 941
題ubject 834
頂ummit 134
納upply 296
取ake 229
稿anuscript 435
税ax 941
技echnique 200
鍛emper 555
領erritory 874
題heme 834
嚇hreat 261
投hrow 745
絞ighten 774
題opic 834
胴orso 867
搬ransport 323
滴rickle 799
渓alley 97
叔ounger aunt 510
叔ounger uncle 510

7.1. Right Whole ▪
(Sort Of...)

俳cting 795
許llow 180

独lone 369
悩nguish 48
逮rrest 880
敏stute 434
秋utumn 415
踏ased on 672
拠asis 473
伏end down 702
脳rain 47
橋ridge 163
建uilding 390
括undle 954
棚abinet 912
禍alamity 799
捕atch 812
吟hant 183
冷hilly 684
冷old 684
僚olleague 66
柱olumn 751
往ome & go 749
状ondition 702
絡onnect 826
建onstruct 390
継ontinuity continue 958
便onvenience 480
談onverse 308
株orporation 130
敢ourage 449
飾ecorate 664
嫌espise 805
任uty 709
訂diting 174
使nvoy 480
偵spionage 506
欧urope 952
夜vening 508
過xcessive 798
排xclude 795
爆xplosion 561
括asten 954
僚ellow 66
終inish 397
継ollow 958
擦riction 329
津arbour 731
硬ardness 402
駄orseload 674
謙umility 805
猟unting 657
倣mitate 486
廷mperial court 26
廉ncorruptible 525
挿nsert 126
訓nstruction 959
鉄ron 155

B. Non-Flippable

☜ 1.0. Facing West (Whole)

☜ 1.1. Facing West (Horizontal Split)

☜ 1.2. Facing West (Vertical Split)

3.0. Facing Across

☞ ☜

4.0. Facing Apart

☞

Answers to Kanji IQ Test (see p. 604)

1. b	51. c
2. b	52. a
3. a	53. b
4. c	54. c
5. b	55. a
6. a	56. c
7. c	57. a
8. a	58. c
9. b	59. c
10. d	60. b
11. a	61. c
12. b	62. c
13. c	63. a
14. a	64. c
15. a	65. c
16. b	66. b
17. c	67. c
18. b	68. a
19. a	69. c
20. c	70. b
21. d	71. c
22. a	72. d
23. b	73. c
24. c	74. d
25. a	75. c
26. b	76. c
27. c	77. c
28. b	78. d
29. a	79. c
30. c	80. a
31. c	81. b
32. a	82. c
33. b	83. a
34. c	84. c
35. d	85. c
36. a	86. b
37. b	87. a
38. c	88. c
39. b	89. c
40. c	90. a
41. d	91. c
42. a	92. b
43. b	93. c
44. c	94. b
45. a	95. c
46. b	96. a
47. b	97. a
48. c	98. c
49. a	99. b
50. c	100. c